Employment Tribunal Practice and Procedure

Employment Law Handbook

May 2014

IDS

D0231235

THOMSON REUTERS

Ref
EMPL LNH
Ids

Employment Tribunal Practice and Procedure

Employment Law Handbook

Previous edition 2006

Incomes Data Services
Finsbury Tower, 103-105 Bunhill Row, London EC1Y 8LZ
Tel: 0845 077 2911 Fax: 0845 310 5517
Email: ids.sales.support@thomsonreuters.com
Website: www.incomesdata.co.uk

ISBN 978 0 414 03000 8

IDS Employment Law Handbook, 'Employment Tribunal Practice and Procedure', is published by Thomson Reuters (Professional) UK Limited trading as Incomes Data Services Limited (Registered in England & Wales, Company No. 16790446). Registered Office: Aldgate House, 33 Aldgate High Street, London EC3N 1DL.

The information contained in this journal in not intended to be a substitute for specific legal advice and readers should obtain advice from a qualified adviser in relation to individual transactions or matters.

No natural forests were destroyed to make this product: only farmed timber was used and re-planted.

A CIP catalogue record for this book is available from the British Library.

Typeset by DC Graphic Design Ltd, Swanley Village, Kent BR8 7PA
Printed by St Austell Printing Co, 41 Truro Road, St Austell, Cornwall PL25 5JE

Contents

Abbreviations

Courts

ECJ	European Court of Justice
ECHR	European Court of Human Rights
PC	Privy Council
SC	Supreme Court
HL	House of Lords
CA	Court of Appeal
Ct Sess	Court of Session
NICA	Northern Ireland Court of Appeal
QBD	Queen's Bench Division
Div Ct	(Queen's Bench) Divisional Court
KBD	King's Bench Division
ChD	Chancery Division
NIRC	National Industrial Relations Court
EAT	Employment Appeal Tribunal
ET	Employment Tribunal

Case references

AC	Law Reports, Appeal Cases
All ER	All England Law Reports
Ch	Law Reports, Chancery Division
CMLR	Common Market Law Reports
COET	Employment Tribunal folio number
EAT	Employment Appeal Tribunal unreported case number
ECR	European Case Reports
ET	Employment Tribunal unreported case number
EWCA	Court of Appeal unreported case number
ICR	Industrial Cases Reports
IRLR	Industrial Relations Law Reports
ITR	Industrial Tribunal Reports
KB	Law Reports, King's Bench Division
QB	Law Reports, Queen's Bench Division
SCOET	Scottish Employment Tribunal folio number
SLT	Scots Law Times
TLR	Times Law Reports
UKSC	Supreme Court unreported case number
WLR	Weekly Law Reports

Legislation

DDA	Disability Discrimination Act 1995
EA	Employment Act 2002
EqA	Equality Act 2010
EqA 2006	Equality Act 2006
EqPA	Equal Pay Act 1970
ERA	Employment Rights Act 1996
ERRA	Enterprise and Regulatory Reform Act 2013
ETA	Employment Tribunals Act 1996
PIDA	Public Interest Disclosure Act 1998
RRA	Race Relations Act 1976
SDA	Sex Discrimination Act 1975
TULR(C)A	Trade Union and Labour Relations (Consolidation) Act 1992

Introduction

This Handbook is designed as a guide for those involved in cases before the employment tribunals in England, Wales and Scotland or before the Employment Appeal Tribunal (EAT). It aims to explain clearly and in detail how the employment tribunal system works and how tribunal decisions can be challenged, by way of either a 'reconsideration' or an appeal to the EAT.

Employment tribunal practice and procedure is governed primarily by rules of procedure contained in regulations made under powers conferred by the Employment Tribunals Act 1996. The current rules – the Employment Tribunals Rules of Procedure 2013 ('the Tribunal Rules') – are contained in Schedule 1 to the Employment Tribunals (Constitution and Rules of Procedure) Regulations 2013 SI 2013/1237 ('the Tribunal Regulations'), as amended by the Employment Tribunals (Constitution and Rules of Procedure) (Amendment) Regulations 2014 SI 2014/271, and replace the previous rules found in the Employment Tribunals (Constitution and Rules of Procedure) Regulations 2004 SI 2004/1861.

The new rules, which came into effect on 29 July 2013, introduced a number of important changes to employment tribunal practice and procedure which, taken together with the new early conciliation regime and the introduction of employment tribunal fees, represent a marked transformation in the employment law procedural landscape.

The Tribunal Rules

The Tribunal Rules were introduced following a fundamental review of employment tribunal procedure conducted by Mr Justice Underhill (now Lord Justice Underhill), the former President of the EAT. The review was commissioned by the Government, which took the view – shared by senior members of the judiciary – that the rules governing procedure in the employment tribunals had become unnecessarily complicated and inflexible and needed modernisation. The result is a more user-friendly and slimmed-down version of the 2004 Tribunal Rules: the new Tribunal Rules are shorter, more succinct and expressed in simpler language than their predecessors in order to help in particular those who do not have the benefit of legal representation. In addition, the Presidents of Employment Tribunals have been given the power to issue Presidential Guidance about matters of practice in the jurisdiction for which they are responsible (i.e. England and Wales, or Scotland). The Guidance is intended, on the one hand, to explain to parties what is expected of them at various procedural stages of a claim and, on the other, to avoid wide regional variations in the way in which employment judges deal with similar matters. At the time of writing, three sets of Presidential

Guidance have been issued for England and Wales ('Rule 21 Judgment', 'Seeking a Postponement of a Hearing' and 'General Case Management') and one set has been issued for Scotland ('Seeking the Postponement of a Hearing'). Further guidance is expected in due course.

Another key focus of the new Tribunal Rules is robust case management and tribunals have been given increased case management powers in order to deal with cases efficiently. An initial sift stage has been introduced which is aimed at ensuring that weak cases that should not proceed to a full hearing are halted at the earliest possible opportunity. Once the claim and response forms have been received, an employment judge will review a case on the papers and, if he or she decides that the claim or response has no reasonable prospect of success, he or she may strike it out. Other important changes aimed at improving effective case management include the amalgamation of case management discussions and pre-hearing reviews into one preliminary hearing; a more flexible regime allowing tribunals to make deposit orders against a party who wishes to continue to pursue a weak element of a claim or response; a lead case mechanism for dealing with multiple claims; a rule on limiting oral evidence and submissions leading to more efficient timetabling of cases; and a simplified procedure for withdrawing claims. The requirement for costs orders over £20,000 to be referred to the county court for assessment has also been removed.

Mandatory early conciliation

Alternative dispute resolution – e.g. Acas conciliation, judicial mediation or any other means of resolving a dispute through agreement – is encouraged under the Tribunal Rules. However, the Government believes that there is a case for intervening in workplace disputes even before they enter the tribunal system. Encouraged by the success of Acas's pre-claim conciliation service, it therefore decided to make early conciliation mandatory for most employment tribunal claims from 6 May 2014. From that date, any claim presented to an employment tribunal without a unique reference number, demonstrating that the claimant gave prior notification of his or her intention to bring a claim to Acas, will be automatically rejected by the tribunal. However, while it is mandatory to notify Acas of a potential tribunal claim, engaging in early conciliation with a prospective respondent is not. Pre-claim conciliation of a dispute is entirely voluntary and either party may decline an offer to conciliate. The Government nevertheless hopes that Acas intervention at this early stage, even if the offer of conciliation is not taken up, will reduce the number of claims subsequently lodged at a tribunal.

Fees in the tribunal and the EAT

As if these changes were not far-reaching enough, at the same time as ushering in the new Tribunal Rules, the Government decided to introduce fees in the employment tribunal and in the EAT for the first time. Since 29 July 2013, a claim cannot be presented to an employment tribunal without payment of a fee or an application for remission of that fee. The Tribunal Rules specifically state that a claim that is not accompanied by a fee or an application for fee remission will be rejected. Furthermore, if the claim is accepted and proceeds to a hearing, another fee becomes payable by the claimant. Fees have also been introduced for appeals to the EAT. The details of the fees regime are found in the Employment Tribunals and the Employment Appeal Tribunal Fees Order 2013 SI 2013/1893, as amended by the Courts and Tribunals Fee Remissions Order 2013 SI 2013/2302 and the Energy Act 2013 (Improvement and Prohibition Notices Appeals) Regulations 2014 SI 2014/468.

As discussed in Chapter 19 of this Handbook, the introduction of fees has come in for considerable criticism but legal challenges have so far proved unsuccessful. In February 2014 the High Court rejected a challenge by the trade union UNISON, which had applied for judicial review of the Ministry of Justice's decision to introduce employment tribunal and EAT fees on the basis that these charges would make it 'virtually impossible' for workers to exercise their employment rights. The High Court rejected the application as premature, holding that there was a lack of evidence proving that fees deter claimants on low incomes from bringing tribunal claims (and appeals) to the extent that they are effectively prevented from enforcing their EU-derived employment rights. The High Court preferred to adopt a 'wait and see' approach to allow any problems that might arise to be addressed by the Lord Chancellor. UNISON has indicated that it intends to appeal against the High Court's decision. A similar challenge to the fees regime is also currently under way in Scotland.

On 13 March 2014, the Ministry of Justice published quarterly employment tribunal statistics for the period from October to December 2013, which showed a sharp decline in the number of claims submitted to tribunals since the introduction of fees. The total number of claims received in that period was 9,801, which represented a 79 per cent drop compared to the same quarter in the previous year. While more figures are needed to assess the long-term impact of fee charging, what is abundantly clear is that the simultaneous introduction of tribunal fees and new Tribunal Rules placed the employment tribunal system under unprecedented administrative pressure. In February 2014 Judge David Latham, then President of Employment Tribunals in England and Wales, remarked in the Senior President of Tribunals' Annual Report for 2014 that these two major changes resulted in software problems and confusion among tribunal users. Similarly, his counterpart in Scotland, Judge Shona Simon, spoke of 'significant difficulties' in dealing with the changes. Nevertheless, after some teething problems, the tribunal system now seems to have adjusted to the new regime.

Scheme of the Handbook

The scheme of this Handbook is as follows:

- Chapter 1 describes the nature of the employment tribunal system and the administration and composition of tribunals

- Chapter 2 considers the jurisdiction of employment tribunals, in terms of both the types of claim that can be heard by tribunals and the limitations placed on their powers, such as territorial limitations and national security restrictions

- Chapter 3 examines the law relating to early conciliation, settlements, the Acas arbitration scheme and judicial mediation

- Chapter 4 explains how tribunal proceedings are started

- Chapter 5 deals with the issue of time limits for bringing tribunal claims and sets out the circumstances in which such time limits can be extended

- Chapter 6 covers the procedures for defending an employment tribunal claim

- Chapter 7 discusses the initial judicial sift stage of proceedings at which a case is reviewed by an employment judge on the papers after the claim and response forms have been received

- Chapter 8 explains the ways in which pleadings can be amended and how to add, substitute or remove parties

- Chapter 9 deals with a number of preliminary matters, including requests for additional information and disclosure and inspection of documents

- Chapter 10 covers the service of notices and documents

- Chapter 11 is concerned with employment tribunals' case management powers, covering preliminary hearings, case management orders, stay of proceedings and striking out

- Chapter 12 deals with the procedure adopted at the hearing itself

- Chapter 13 examines the various issues that may arise in respect of evidence being presented at the hearing

- Chapter 14 is concerned with employment tribunal judgments and the procedure for registering those judgments

- Chapter 15 explains the circumstances in which a tribunal judgment or decision or order may be 'reconsidered'

- Chapter 16 deals with the constitution and jurisdiction of the Employment Appeal Tribunal

- Chapter 17 is concerned with the procedures to be followed when instituting and defending an appeal from an employment tribunal decision, including the 'sift' process and interlocutory applications

- Chapter 18 deals with hearings before the EAT and considers the circumstances in which the EAT may admit new evidence or hear arguments on new points of law. It also covers EAT decisions and explains how those decisions may be challenged

- Chapter 19 explains the fee regime in the employment tribunals and the EAT, which was introduced in July 2013

- Chapter 20 considers the rules relating to costs in both employment tribunals and the EAT and the power to impose a financial penalty on employers found to have breached employment rights

- Chapter 21 sets out the procedures to be followed in seeking to enforce an employment tribunal decision in the civil courts.

Note that in this Handbook we often refer to tribunal 'decisions'. However, except where indicated otherwise, we do not use the word 'decision' in a technical sense (as it is not a defined term in the Tribunal Rules), but rather as a convenient umbrella term which encompasses tribunal 'judgments' (final determinations of proceedings), decisions and 'case management orders'. We use the defined terms 'judgments' and 'case management orders' where it is appropriate to do so.

Statutory references

All references in Chapters 1–14 and Chapters 18–20 of this Handbook to the 'Tribunal Rules' are, unless otherwise stated, to the Rules of Procedure contained in Schedule 1 to the Employment Tribunals (Constitution and Rules of Procedure) Regulations 2013 SI 2013/1237, as amended by the Employment Tribunals (Constitution and Rules of Procedure) (Amendment) Regulations 2014 SI 2014/271. Note that the Industrial Tribunals (Constitution and Rules of Procedure) Regulations (Northern Ireland) 2005 SI 2005/150, which govern industrial tribunals in Northern Ireland, are outside the scope of this Handbook.

All references to the 'EAT Rules' in Chapters 15–18 are, unless otherwise stated, to the Employment Appeal Tribunal Rules 1993 SI 1993/2854, as most recently amended by the Employment Appeal Tribunal (Amendment) Rules 2013 SI 2013/1693.

There are special complementary procedural rules relating to 'equal value' tribunal claims brought under the Equality Act 2010. These are found in Schedule 3 to the Employment Tribunals (Constitution and Rules of Procedure) Regulations 2013 and fall outside the scope of this Handbook. However, equal value claims are explained in depth in IDS Employment Law Handbook, 'Equal

Pay' (2011). There are also special procedural provisions applicable to 'national security proceedings', which are contained in Schedule 2 to the 2013 Regulations. These also fall outside the scope of this Handbook.

The law is stated as at 1 April 2014. This Handbook replaces IDS Employment Law Handbook, 'Employment Tribunal Practice and Procedure' (2006), which should now be discarded.

This publication aims to provide accurate, authoritative information and comment on the subjects it covers. It is offered to subscribers on the understanding that the publisher is not in business as a lawyer or consultant.

1 Employment tribunals

What are employment tribunals?

Tribunal administration

Judicial composition

Employment tribunals are independent judicial bodies that exist primarily to **1.1** determine disputes over employment rights between employers and employees. Although employment tribunals exercise a judicial function, the tribunal system is largely independent of the ordinary courts, and is intended to be less formal (although overarching ministerial responsibility for both systems lies with the Ministry of Justice). The range of claims employment tribunals can deal with, and the limitations on their jurisdiction, are considered in Chapter 2, 'Tribunals' jurisdiction'. This chapter explains the nature of the employment tribunal system (see 'What are employment tribunals?'), and the administration and composition of tribunals (see 'Tribunal administration' and 'Judicial composition'). While there are a number of different types of tribunal operating in the UK, dealing with a myriad of issues from parking fines to immigration rights, in this Handbook we are concerned only with employment tribunals.

What are employment tribunals?   1.2

Employment tribunals, previously called industrial tribunals, were created under the Industrial Training Act 1964 to hear appeals against training levy assessments imposed by industrial training boards. This remains one of the functions of employment tribunals today. However, their jurisdiction has since expanded beyond all recognition to embrace a large number of different types of claim arising from the numerous Acts of Parliament and statutory instruments (see Chapter 2, 'Tribunals' jurisdiction', under 'Types of claim heard by tribunals').

The employment tribunal system discussed in this Handbook applies within the jurisdictions of England, Wales and Scotland. A different system appertains to Northern Ireland, where employment claims are made to the Industrial Tribunals and the Fair Employment Tribunal. These tribunals fall outside the scope of this Handbook, although, as noted under 'Tribunals in the court hierarchy' below, decisions of the Supreme Court bind tribunals in Northern Ireland.

1

1.3 Tribunals in the court hierarchy

In the vast majority of employment cases, employment tribunals are the bottom rung of a system of courts designed to resolve disputes between employees, or groups of employees, and their employer or, in some cases, between trade unions and employers or union members. Nearly all disputes are heard 'at first instance', but there are some cases in which tribunals hear appeals from the decisions of other bodies – e.g. appeals against unlawful act notices issued by the Equality and Human Rights Commission under S.21 of the Equality Act 2006. See the Appendix to Chapter 2, 'Tribunals' jurisdiction', for a full list.

Most appeals from employment tribunals lie to the Employment Appeal Tribunal (EAT), which has the status of the High Court, although its jurisdiction is almost entirely appellate and rigidly defined by statute. The jurisdiction of the EAT is considered in detail in Chapter 16, 'The Employment Appeal Tribunal', under 'Jurisdiction of the EAT'.

1.4 Appeals from the EAT lie to the Court of Appeal in England and Wales and to the Court of Session (Inner House) in Scotland, but only on a question of law or on the ground that the judgment was one which no reasonable tribunal could have reached, and subject to leave to appeal being granted. The next stage in the appeal process, again only with leave, is to the Supreme Court, which assumed the judicial role previously undertaken by the House of Lords with effect from 1 October 2009. Appeals from the Queen's Bench Division of the High Court and the Court of Session (Outer House) may take the same routes.

The EAT is a 'superior court of record'. Its decisions are a binding authority on employment tribunals throughout Great Britain and create 'precedents' which should be followed (though only if they tally with the particular circumstances of the case under consideration).

1.5 A decision of a court at the level of the High Court, such as the EAT, is not technically binding on another court at the same level. However, the EAT will normally, for the sake of consistency, try to follow previous EAT decisions. The EAT cannot overrule its previous decisions – all it can do, in exceptional circumstances, is decline to follow them. This will leave two conflicting decisions and it will be open to an employment tribunal to choose which it prefers, a prime reason for the EAT's reluctance to depart from its earlier decisions.

Decisions of the Court of Appeal are binding on the EAT and employment tribunals in England and Wales, while decisions of the Inner House of the Court of Session are binding on the EAT and employment tribunals in Scotland. Lord Justice Underhill, when President of the EAT, expressed his regret in Commissioner of Police of the Metropolis v Shaw 2012 ICR 464, EAT, that in considering the manner in which aggravated damages should be awarded, tribunals in England and Wales were bound to follow the Court of Appeal-approved practice rather

2

than the Scottish approach, which he considered preferable. Decisions of the Court of Appeal are only persuasive in Scotland, as are decisions of the Court of Session in England and Wales. The Court of Appeal confirmed in Caulfield and ors v Marshalls Clay Products Ltd; Clarke v Frank Staddon Ltd 2004 ICR 1502, CA, that the EAT in England and Wales was not obliged to follow a decision of the Court of Session in another case. However, the Court of Appeal acknowledged that it was unsatisfactory that there was a contradictory decision which was binding in Scotland and therefore referred the cases to the European Court of Justice (ECJ) (see Robinson-Steel v RD Retail Services Ltd; Clarke v Frank Staddon Ltd; Caulfield and ors v Hanson Clay Products Ltd 2006 ICR 932, ECJ). Decisions of the Supreme Court – and, before October 2009, of the House of Lords – are binding on all other courts, including those in Northern Ireland.

Decisions of the higher courts of other Commonwealth states, and of the **1.6** Judicial Committee of the Privy Council – which is the supreme court of appeal for the Crown Dependencies, British Overseas Territories, and a number of Commonwealth member countries – are not binding on courts or tribunals within the UK. However, where domestic courts face novel points which have been examined elsewhere in the Commonwealth, they may well draw assistance from those decisions. For example, in JGE v English Province of Our Lady of Charity and anor 2012 IRLR 301, HC (QBD), the High Court drew assistance from a decision of the Supreme Court of Canada in concluding that a Roman Catholic diocese could be vicariously liable for a priest's actions. Decisions of the Judicial Committee of the Privy Council are particularly persuasive, as the judges are usually Justices of the Supreme Court.

Finally, a decision of one employment tribunal is in no way binding on another. It is no more than persuasive, even if the facts and circumstances of the two cases appear to be identical.

Employment tribunal rules
1.7
All employment tribunal proceedings are regulated by the Employment Tribunals Rules of Procedure ('the Tribunal Rules'), which are contained in Regulations made by the Secretary of State under the Employment Tribunals Act 1996 (ETA). The principal Regulations currently in force are the Employment Tribunals (Constitution and Rules of Procedure) Regulations 2013 SI 2013/1237 ('the Tribunal Regulations'). The Tribunal Rules are contained in Schedule 1 to the Tribunal Regulations, and apply to all proceedings.

However, the Tribunal Rules in Schedule 1 may be modified by Schedule 2 or 3 in relation to the proceedings to which those Schedules apply. Schedule 2 contains the Employment Tribunal (National Security) Rules of Procedure and applies to proceedings in relation to which a direction is given, or an order made, under rule 94 of the Tribunal Rules, which concerns national security – rule 1, Sch 2. Rule 94 and Schedule 2 are dealt with in Chapter 9, 'Responding

3

to opponent's case', under 'Disclosure and inspection of documents – privilege', and in Chapter 12, 'The hearing', under 'National Security'. Schedule 3 contains the Employment Tribunal (Equal Value) Rules of Procedure and applies to proceedings involving equal value claims – rule 1, Sch 3. These rules contained in Schedule 3 are considered in IDS Employment Law Handbook, 'Equal Pay' (2011), Chapter 7, 'Work of equal value', under 'Introduction – complexity of equal value procedure' and 'Equal value procedure'.

1.8 The current Tribunal Regulations and Rules came into force on 29 July 2013 and apply to all proceedings in England, Wales and Scotland after that date, irrespective of when they were commenced, subject to transitional provisions set out in Reg 15(2) and (3) – Reg 15(1).

1.9 **Transitional provisions.** Regulation 15(2) provides that rules 23–25, which apply to employers' contract claims (known as 'counterclaims' under previous versions of the Rules), do not apply where the respondent received a copy of the claim form before 29 July 2013. In those circumstances, rule 7 of the previous Tribunal Rules, contained in Schedule 1 to the Employment Tribunal (Constitution and Rules of Procedure) Regulations 2004 SI 2004/1861 ('the Tribunal Rules 2004'), continues to apply. For a detailed discussion of employers' contract claims, see Chapter 6, 'Defending a claim', under 'Employers' contract claims'.

Furthermore, the Tribunal Rules 2013 do not apply to appeals against a levy imposed under the Industrial Training Act 1982, an improvement or prohibition notice under the Health and Safety at Work etc Act 1974, or an unlawful act notice imposed by the Equality and Human Rights Commission under the Equality Act 2006, where the notice of appeal was presented to a tribunal before 29 July 2013. In those cases, Schedules 3–5 of the Tribunal Rules 2004 continue to apply – Reg 15(3).

1.10 **Practice Directions.** Since 2004, the Presidents of Employment Tribunals have had the power to make, vary or revoke Practice Directions about employment tribunal procedure in the area for which they are responsible (England and Wales, or Scotland), including Practice Directions about:

- the exercise by tribunals of powers under the Regulations and the Rules (in all three Schedules) – Reg 11(1)(a)

- the provision by employment judges of mediation in relation to disputed matters in a case (including permitting an employment judge to act as mediator in a case even though he or she has been selected to decide that case) – Reg 11(1)(b).

1.11 Practice Directions may be of universal relevance – for example, the 'Presidential Practice Direction – Presentation of claims' (29 July 2013) sets out the methods by which a completed claim form may be presented under rule 8 (see further Chapter 4, 'Starting tribunal proceedings', under 'Making a claim') – or can 'make different provision for different cases, different areas, or different types of proceedings' – Reg 11(2). A Practice Direction can, for example, direct that cases concerning a particular issue be stayed pending the outcome of a test case – see the first Practice Direction (Practice Direction 1, dated 8 November 2007), which ordered that age discrimination claims concerning the 'default retirement age' under Reg 30 of the Employment Equality (Age) Regulations 2006 SI 2006/1031 (since repealed and superseded by the Equality Act 2010) be stayed pending the decision of the European Court of Justice in Incorporated Trustees of the National Council on Ageing (Age Concern England) v Secretary of State for Business, Enterprise and Regulatory Reform 2009 ICR 1080, ECJ, which challenged the legality of that provision. Or, where a number of claims have been lodged in different regions against the same respondent, the President may direct that these be combined, in keeping with the overriding objective of saving expense (see 'Overriding objective' below). This was the case with Practice Direction 96 of 10 June 2013 in respect of claims involving unpaid holiday pay and wages brought against Paymaster Ltd and the Secretary of State for Business, Innovation and Skills (see Thompson and ors v Paymaster Ltd t/a Back Office and anor ET Case No.1301594/13).

In all cases, the President must publish any Practice Direction made, varied or revoked 'in an appropriate manner to bring it to the attention of the persons to whom it is addressed' – Reg 11(3). This usually involves a copy of the Direction being sent to all the parties and/or their representatives, to all regional employment judges, and to Acas; and a copy being published on the employment tribunals' pages of the Ministry of Justice website.

Presidential Guidance. Rule 7 provides that the Presidents of Employment Tribunals may issue guidance 'as to matters of practice and as to how the powers conferred by these Rules may be exercised'. This power was introduced by the 2013 Rules, which are intended to be simpler and more flexible than previous versions. According to Lord Justice Underhill (in his letter to the Government accompanying the draft Tribunal Rules, dated 29 June 2012), Presidential Guidance is intended to 'enable some questions which are essentially matters of good practice or of internal procedure to be addressed more flexibly and informally than if they had to be the subject of rules. But it is also intended to address two concerns expressed by some users – first, that parties (particularly, but not only, unrepresented parties) do not know what to expect, or what is expected of them, at various procedural stages; and, secondly, a perception (which may or may not be justified) that there are wide variations between how different judges, particularly at different centres, deal with the same kinds of hearing.'

Presidential Guidance differs from Practice Directions (see 'Practice Directions' above) in that, while tribunals are bound to follow Practice Directions, they are **1.12** merely required to 'have regard' to Presidential Guidance. Ultimately, as Underhill LJ notes in his letter, judges must have discretion to deal with the particular case before them. Given, however, that Presidential Guidance must be published 'in an appropriate manner to bring it to the attention of claimants, respondents and their advisers', it is likely that parties will expect tribunals to show good reason for departing from guidance in any given case.

To date, three sets of Presidential Guidance have been issued for England and Wales:

- Presidential Guidance – 'Rule 21 Judgment' (4 December 2013)
- Presidential Guidance – 'Seeking a Postponement of a Hearing' (4 December 2013)
- Presidential Guidance – 'General Case Management' (13 March 2014).

And one has been issued for Scotland:

- Presidential Guidance – 'Seeking the Postponement of a Hearing' (16 January 2014).

All are available on the Ministry of Justice website.

1.13 **Overriding objective.** The overriding objective of the Tribunal Regulations and Rules is to enable tribunals to deal with cases 'fairly and justly' – rule 2. Dealing with a case fairly and justly includes, so far as practicable:

- ensuring that the parties are on an equal footing
- dealing with cases in ways which are proportionate to the complexity and importance of the issues
- avoiding unnecessary formality and seeking flexibility in the proceedings
- avoiding delay, so far as compatible with proper consideration of the issues, and
- saving expense.

Rule 2 states that tribunals must seek to give effect to the overriding objective when interpreting the Tribunal Rules, or exercising any power given to them by the Rules. Furthermore, the parties and their representatives are themselves under a duty to assist the tribunal to further the overriding objective, and, in particular, to cooperate generally with each other and with the employment tribunal. The EAT commented in Fairbank v Care Management Group and another case EAT 0139/12 that the practice of drafting extremely lengthy claim forms, akin to witness statements, might not be an appropriate way of furthering the overriding objective and that a claim form which focuses on the issues and the claims made might be 'more helpful' (for further discussion of claim forms, see Chapter 4, 'Starting tribunal proceedings', under 'Completing the claim form').

While the avoidance of undue formality has long been a characteristic of **1.14** employment tribunal hearings, its articulation as an aspect of the overriding objective was first introduced in the Tribunal Rules 2013. Arguably, parties could potentially seek to rely on this aspect to, for example, bolster an application for a late adjournment or for lenience in relation to a failure to comply with orders of the tribunal. However, given the overarching requirement to deal with cases 'fairly and justly', it is unlikely that a party could successfully rely on this argument to justify his or her own unreasonable behaviour where this might prejudice the other party or cause delay or unreasonable expense.

The overriding objective is wide-ranging and can affect a tribunal's decision-making in a variety of circumstances. But applying the overriding objective is not always straightforward. In the following cases (decided under earlier versions of the Rules which required tribunals to ensure that cases were dealt with 'expeditiously and fairly'), the EAT reversed a tribunal's decision on the basis that it had not properly applied, or had not had sufficient regard to, the overriding objective:

- **Senyonjo v Trident Safeguards Ltd and anor** EAT 0316/04: a tribunal refused to allow the claimant to adduce supplemental evidence, presented at a late stage in proceedings, of incidents going back well beyond three months before the date of the alleged discrimination. Reversing the tribunal's decision, the EAT commented that the tribunal had been 'rightly concerned' with expedition, but that in the end 'justice has to be preferred to expedition'. The evidence was admissible and if an adjournment was necessary an issue could be raised as to costs

- **Mid-Devon District Council v Stevenson** EAT 0196/07: an employment judge refused the employer leave to obtain its own medical expert's report on the question of whether the claimant had a mental impairment such that she was disabled within the meaning of the Disability Discrimination Act 1995 (now repealed and superseded by the Equality Act 2010). The judge considered that it would not be in keeping with the overriding objective of dealing with matters 'expeditiously and fairly' to allow the employer to obtain a further report, as this would cause delay, and the employer had declined an opportunity to instruct a joint expert earlier in the proceedings. Reversing the employment judge's decision, the EAT observed that although she had had regard to the issue of delay, she had failed to take into account the 'principal aim' of the overriding objective that cases should be dealt with justly, which included that the parties should, so far as practicable, be on an equal footing. The claimant had amended her claim to include the issue of mental impairment only after the employer had declined to instruct a joint expert. The employer was not obliged to accept her expert's report and was entitled to take reasonable steps to challenge and dispute his conclusions.

7

1.15 Unlike in earlier versions of the Rules, the 'principal aim' of dealing with cases justly is emphasised in the Tribunal Rules 2013. Although expedition is still an important factor – as tribunals and parties are encouraged to deal with cases proportionately, avoid delay and unnecessary formality, and save expense – the overarching objective no longer refers to expedition, but to dealing with cases 'fairly and justly'.

1.16 Civil Procedure Rules

The Civil Procedure Rules 1998 SI 1998/3132 (CPR) govern the procedure applicable to civil cases in the High Court and county courts. They are not incorporated into the Tribunal Regulations or Rules, although reference is made to them in rules 31 and 78. Rule 31 of the Tribunal Rules provides that an employment tribunal may order any person in Great Britain to disclose documents or information to a party, or to allow a party to inspect 'such material as might be ordered by a county court or, in Scotland, by a sheriff'; and rule 78(1)(b) provides that costs may, among other options, be determined 'by way of detailed assessment carried out either by a county court in accordance with the [CPR] or by an employment judge applying the same principles'; or the equivalent in Scotland. (For a full examination of these rules, see Chapter 9, 'Responding to opponent's case', under 'Disclosure and inspection of documents – power of tribunals to order disclosure or inspection'; and Chapter 20, 'Costs and penalties', under 'Methods of assessment and applicable limits – detailed assessment of costs'.)

Apart from the two occasions highlighted above, the Tribunal Rules do not refer to civil court procedure. Nevertheless, until the Court of Appeal's decision in Neary v Governing Body of St Albans Girls' School and anor 2010 ICR 473, CA (discussed below), a line of EAT cases suggested not only that the principles which apply to the rules of civil procedure may inform the principles to be applied in the employment tribunals, but also that employment judges must actively consider all nine factors listed in rule 3.9 CPR – factors civil courts must consider on an application for relief from a sanction imposed in consequence of a failure to comply with a court order – when making an analogous discretionary decision. In Goldman Sachs Services Ltd v Montali 2002 ICR 1251, EAT, the EAT, noting that the overriding objective in the Tribunal Regulations 2001 was borrowed from the CPR, said that this was 'the clearest possible indication that when exercising any power under the Rules, as here, the employment tribunal will follow the same principles as those spelt out in the CPR'.

1.17 The EAT took this a stage further in Maresca v Motor Insurance Repair Research Centre 2005 ICR 197, EAT, where an employment judge struck out M's claim of unfair dismissal after he failed to comply with an order for disclosure. Two days later, having complied with the order, M applied for a review, but the employment judge refused the application on the basis that

8

M had provided no explanation for his failure to comply. M appealed against the refusal to review, arguing that the employment judge should have had regard to rule 3.9 CPR. The EAT allowed the appeal. It held that although rule 3.9 was not to be taken to be incorporated into the Tribunal Rules, employment tribunals did have to exercise their powers under those Rules in accordance with the same principles that apply under the CPR. In M's case, the employment judge had had regard to one of the factors listed in rule 3.9 – the absence of an explanation – but to none of the others. In the EAT's view, another important consideration was the fact that M did comply with the order, albeit belatedly, but still in time for the hearing date to be kept. The Appeal Tribunal concluded that the employment judge should have asked herself whether, taking all the factors listed in rule 3.9 CPR into account, M had a reasonable prospect of persuading the tribunal that he should be relieved from the finality of the striking-out order; and that in so far as the employment judge had failed to have regard to those factors, she had fallen into error.

Maresca was subsequently followed in a number of appellate decisions. For example, in British School of Motoring v Fowler EAT 0059/06 the EAT considered that the factors in rule 3.9 that were applicable to the civil courts applied 'equally to an application for relief from sanction in the employment tribunal', while in Royal Bank of Scotland v Soper EAT 0080/07 the EAT allowed an appeal against an employment judge's refusal of a review application on the ground that the employment judge had not directed himself as to the 'wider considerations required', meaning the factors in rule 3.9. And in McGuire v Centrewest London Buses Ltd EAT 0576/06, an appeal from an employment judge's refusal to grant a review of a strike-out order following a failure to comply with an order for disclosure, the EAT considered that although the employment judge had considered the rule 3.9 factors, this had been insufficiently explicit.

However, Maresca v Motor Insurance Repair Research Centre (above), and **1.18** the EAT decisions that followed it, were eventually overruled by the Court of Appeal in Neary v Governing Body of St Albans Girls' School and anor (above). In that case N had failed to comply with a case management order to provide further particulars of his discrimination claim. An employment tribunal ordered that the claim would be struck out without further order, unless the particulars were provided by 26 September 2007. The claimant failed to provide the particulars, but wrote to the tribunal on that date saying that he did not know which parts of the order he had to comply with. His claim was automatically struck out, but the employment judge treated N's letter as an application for a review of that decision – which he then considered, but refused. The EAT allowed N's appeal against the employment judge's refusal of the review application, holding, inter alia, that it was incumbent on an employment judge, before exercising his or her discretion to refuse an application for review of a sanction, to consider, consciously, all of the factors

9

listed in rule 3.9 CPR that are relevant or potentially relevant to the case. The EAT considered that the employment judge had failed to do this and remitted the case to another judge.

However, the Court of Appeal restored the employment judge's order on appeal. The Court inferred that when Parliament incorporated the overriding objective into employment tribunal practice, it deliberately did not incorporate rule 3.9 CPR, for the 'obvious' reason that it has always been Parliament's intention that employment tribunal proceedings should be as short, simple and informal as possible. While it might be the case that employment tribunals should apply the same general principles as are applied in the civil courts, this was not to say that they were obliged to follow the letter of the CPR in all respects. The Court noted that the list of factors in rule 3.9 may provide a 'helpful checklist', but might not cover everything relevant, and – contrary to the EAT's decision – an employment judge is not required explicitly to consider every one of the factors which is potentially relevant. While it would have been better if the judge had provided more extended reasons for his decision, it could not be shown that he had misapplied the law. Given that this was a case involving a deliberate and persistent failure to provide the particulars, the judge was entirely justified in taking the view that a review of the automatic strike-out had no reasonable prospect of success.

1.19 Mr Justice Underhill, then President of the EAT, welcomed the Court of Appeal's clarification in Thind v Salvesen Logistics Ltd EAT 0487/09, a case which involved a tribunal's refusal to review its decision to strike out a claim for non-compliance with an 'unless' order. He commented: 'The law in this area had become undesirably technical and involved. It had also, I might note in passing, caused considerable concern in Scotland, where the CPR has of course no application. The law as it now stands is much more straightforward. The tribunal must decide whether it is right, in the interests of justice and the overriding objective, to grant relief to the party in default notwithstanding the breach of the unless order. That involves a broad assessment of what is in the interests of justice, and the factors which may be material to that assessment will vary considerably according to the circumstances of the case and cannot be neatly categorised... No one factor is necessarily determinative of the course which the tribunal should take. Each case will depend on its own facts.'

That said, the EAT's jurisdiction with regard to giving relief from sanctions is different from that of the employment tribunals, and it may apply rule 3.9 CPR where it is helpful to do so – Roberts v Carlin EAT 0183/09 and Abusabib and anor v Taddese EAT 1819/10.

Note that the proper bases for reviewing employment tribunal decisions are considered in detail in Chapter 15, 'Reconsideration of tribunal judgments and decisions', under 'Grounds for reconsideration'.

Tribunal administration 1.20

Since the Tribunals, Courts and Enforcement Act 2007 received royal assent on 9 July 2007, tribunals in the UK, such as the employment tribunals and EAT in England and Wales and in Scotland, have been part of a unified tribunals structure. Since April 2011, this has been administered by HM Courts and Tribunals Service (HMCTS), an executive agency of the Ministry of Justice, which is also responsible for providing administration for the courts.

Senior President of Tribunals 1.21

The Senior President of Tribunals is the statutory leader of the tribunal judiciary in the UK, and is independent both of the Government and of the Chief Justices, who carry out similar functions in relation to the courts. The Senior President, currently the Right Honourable Lord Justice Sullivan, has particular statutory powers and functions in relation to the employment tribunals and the EAT throughout the UK:

- he or she is responsible for arranging the 'training, guidance and welfare' of employment tribunal panel members, and that of EAT judges and members – Ss.5A and 24A ETA

- he or she has power to take the oath of allegiance and judicial oath from the Presidents and tribunal panel members, and from those appointed to the EAT – Ss.5C and 24B(2)

- he or she has power to nominate a judge to act as a tribunal panel member – S.5D(2)(a)

- he or she has power to make Practice Directions in relation to employment tribunal procedure, and EAT procedure, with the approval of the Lord Chancellor – Ss.7A(A1) and (2B) and 29A(1)(a) and (3)

- he or she approves Practice Directions issued by the Presidents of the Employment Tribunals and of the EAT – Ss.7A(2C)(a) and 29A(4)(a) and (6)(a).

Presidents and regional employment judges 1.22

Presiding over the employment tribunal system in England and Wales is the President of the Employment Tribunals for England and Wales (currently Judge Brian Doyle), who must have the same qualifications as a tribunal employment judge (see 'Employment Judges' below) and who is appointed by the Lord Chancellor – Reg 5(1) and (2) Tribunal Regulations. There is a separate President in Scotland (currently Judge Shona Simon) who is appointed by the Lord President of the Court of Session – Reg 5(1).

11

One of the salaried employment judges in each region in England and Wales is nominated by the President and appointed by the Lord Chancellor to serve as regional employment judge – Reg 6(1), (2) and (5). In Scotland, there are no regional employment judges, but the Lord President appoints a salaried employment judge nominated by the President to the role of Vice President, to fulfil an identical function in relation to the whole of Scotland – Regs 6(3) and 7(2). The duties of a regional employment judge or Vice President are to enable the President to fulfil his or her responsibilities:

- to secure, so far as practicable, the 'speedy and efficient disposal of proceedings' – Reg 7(1)(a)

- to determine the allocation of proceedings between tribunals – Reg 7(1)(b), and

- to determine where and when tribunals shall sit – Reg 7(1)(c).

1.23 Each President has the power to make, vary and revoke Practice Directions about employment tribunal procedure in the area for which he or she is responsible – Reg 11(1), and to issue guidance on matters of practice and as to how the powers conferred by the Rules may be exercised – rule 7. See the section 'What are employment tribunals?' above, under 'Employment tribunal rules – Practice Directions' and 'Employment tribunal rules – Presidential Guidance'.

1.24 Employment tribunal offices
Claims are registered and hearings held at a number of employment tribunal offices throughout England and Wales (contact details for which are provided on the Ministry of Justice website). The tribunal Secretary bears administrative oversight for all employment tribunal offices in England and Wales and delegates his or her functions to an authorised person (previously known as a regional secretary) at each office. Scotland has four tribunal offices, and a separate Secretary.

1.25 Register of employment tribunal judgments
The public register of employment tribunal judgments in England and Wales is based in Bury St Edmunds, and the Scottish register is based in Glasgow. Before the Employment Tribunal (Constitution and Rules of Procedure) Regulations 2004 SI 2004/1861 came into force, this register contained details of all claims brought, including the names and addresses of claimants and respondents, regardless of whether the claim was ultimately determined by a tribunal, settled or withdrawn. To address potential abuses, since 1 October 2004 the register has been required to contain simply a copy of all judgments and written reasons issued by a tribunal which are required to be entered in the register – Reg 14(1) Tribunal Regulations 2013. Though most judgments bear the names of the parties, they do not contain their addresses. The Lord Chancellor is required to delete any entry in the register six years from the date of judgment – Reg 14(2).

A certified copy of a registered judgment is sufficient evidence of it, unless proved otherwise – Reg 14(3).

Companies which provide employment litigation advisory services used to use the information contained in the register for marketing purposes, in order to solicit clients. In January 2005 one such company, PBS Ltd, requested from the then Department for Trade and Industry (DTI) the names and addresses of all respondents to employment tribunal claims presented in England, Wales and Scotland since 1 October 2004. The request was made under the Freedom of Information Act 2000 (FOIA), which gives any individual or organisation the right to request information held by a public authority in England, Wales and Northern Ireland. (An almost identical Act covers Scotland.) However, the public authority may lawfully refuse to accede to any such request where the information is exempt or otherwise excluded from disclosure.

Following the DTI's refusal to accede to its request, PBS Ltd complained to the **1.26** Information Commissioner, whose Office is responsible for overseeing the operation and enforcement of the FOIA. Although the Information Commissioner upheld PBS Ltd's complaint (Decision Notice FS50080369), this was subsequently overturned by the Information Tribunal, which on 29 April 2009 confirmed that the Employment Tribunal Service (now part of HMCTS) was under no obligation to disclose the requested information (Information Tribunal Appeal Number EA/2008/0087). The information fell under S.32(1)(c) FOIA, which provides that information held by a public authority is exempt from disclosure if it is held only by virtue of being contained in a document created by a court or the court's administrative staff for the purpose of particular proceedings. Thus, while for administrative purposes names and addresses must be provided in the claim form and the response (see Chapter 4, 'Starting tribunal proceedings', under 'Completing the claim form', and Chapter 6, 'Defending a claim', under 'Completing the response'), HMCTS remains entitled to refuse to provide any such information to third parties under the FOIA.

Judicial composition   1.27

Employment tribunal hearings take place before three, one or, more rarely, two individuals who will hear and decide part or all of the proceedings brought before them. The tribunal will always be presided over by an employment judge who may, depending on the claim(s) involved, sit with up to two lay members, chosen from a panel of lay members.

Tribunal panels   1.28
There are three panels of members for the employment tribunals in England and Wales, and three for those in Scotland – Reg 8(1) Tribunal Regulations. The President or a regional employment judge (or, in Scotland, Vice President)

13

selects members from these panels to hear particular employment tribunal proceedings – Reg 9(1). The panels consist of:

- a panel of employment judges appointed by the Lord Chancellor (or, in Scotland, by the Lord President of the Court of Session) – Reg 8(2)(a)

- a panel of lay members appointed by the Lord Chancellor after consultation with organisations or associations representative of employees (such as trade unions) – Reg 8(2)(b)

- a panel of lay members appointed by the Lord Chancellor after consultation with organisations or associations representative of employers (such as industry bodies) – Reg 8(2)(c).

The qualifying criteria for employment judges, together with their functions and responsibilities, are discussed under 'Employment judges' below, while those of lay members are discussed under 'Lay members' below.

1.29 Panel members may resign from office by written notice to the person who appointed them (normally the Lord Chancellor), but may be reappointed – Reg 8(3). Panel members may be removed from membership of a panel only with the agreement of the Lord Chief Justice, or, if he or she exercises functions wholly or mainly in Scotland, with the agreement of the Lord President of the Court of Session – S.5B(3) ETA. (The Lord Chief Justice and the Lord President may nominate others from the judiciary to fulfil this aspect of their role – S.5B(5) and (6).)

A public hearing before a full tribunal will be before a presiding employment judge, drawn from the panel of employment judges, and usually (but not always) two lay members drawn one from each of the other two panels – S.4(1) ETA. (The circumstances in which an employment judge may sit alone – or with a single lay member – are discussed under 'Employment judge sitting alone' and 'Tribunals comprising an employment judge and one lay member' below.) Note that as an alternative to selecting an employment judge from the panel of employment judges, the President, Vice President or regional employment judge may select him or herself – Reg 9(2).

1.30 **Specialist panels.** Reg 8(4) gives the President power to establish additional specialist panels of employment judges and lay members, from which to select persons to deal with proceedings 'in which particular specialist knowledge would be beneficial'. Such specialist knowledge might, for example, be particularly advantageous in complex equal value cases.

1.31 Employment judges

'Employment judge' was substituted for the previous term 'chairman' by the Tribunals, Courts and Enforcement Act 2007. Like Presidents of employment tribunals, employment judges must be either:

- a barrister in England and Wales, solicitor of the Senior Court of England and Wales, or fellow of the Chartered Institute of Legal Executives of at least five years' standing and with five years' legal experience

- an advocate or solicitor admitted in Scotland of at least five years' standing, or

- a member of the Bar of Northern Ireland or solicitor of the Supreme Court of Northern Ireland of at least five years' standing – Regs 8(2)(a) and 5(2)(a)–(c).

All panel employment judges are appointed by the Lord Chancellor (in England and Wales) or the Lord President of the Court of Session (in Scotland) – Reg 8(2)(a). Appointments are either on a salaried (full-time or part-time) basis, or on a fee-paid basis, although an employment judge should expect to serve on a fee-paid basis first before being appointed to a salaried position. Fee-paid employment judges are selected through open competition and appointed for a five-year term, which may be renewed for successive five-year terms, and are required to sit for at least 30 days each calendar year. The statutory retirement age is 70, but may be extended annually until the age of 75 if the Senior President of Tribunals considers this desirable in the public interest – S.26(1), (5) and (6) Judicial Pensions and Retirement Act 1993.

Role and functions. After a claim has been made and a response accepted (see **1.32** Chapter 4, 'Starting tribunal proceedings', under 'Processing the claim form', and Chapter 6, 'Defending a claim', under 'Processing the response'), the employment judge is required to consider all of the documents in relation to the claim to confirm whether there are arguable complaints and defences within the tribunal's jurisdiction – rule 26. He or she may order a party to provide further information if necessary to confirm this. This initial consideration, and its potential outcomes, are considered in Chapter 7, 'Judicial sift'.

Assuming the claim proceeds, the employment judge must assimilate the information contained in the papers and identify the claims and issues before any hearing or case management discussion. An important aspect of his or her function is to consider what, if any, case management orders to impose, whether on his or her own initiative or in response to a party's application. Case management, which is conducted by an employment judge acting alone, is considered in Chapter 11, 'Case management'.

At the hearing itself, the employment judge's main functions include: **1.33**

- controlling the manner in which the case is conducted (which will include having regard to the overriding objective of dealing with cases fairly and justly – see the section 'What are employment tribunals?' above, under 'Employment tribunal rules – overriding objective')

- ensuring that all parties, including those who are unrepresented, are able to have their cases presented, and have them considered, as fully and fairly as possible, and that there is a 'level playing field'

- taking a note of the evidence and proceedings

- deciding issues of law and procedure which arise

- determining claims – with lay members, if applicable – by finding facts from the evidence presented, applying the relevant law to the facts found, and giving, where appropriate, a full oral decision

- assessing and making any awards and deciding the amount and manner of payment

- giving any directions necessary to give effect to the judgment

- promulgating judgments and written reasons after the hearing.

1.34 Although an employment judge may advise any lay members on the relevant law and its application to the facts of the case, it is important to remember that an employment judge is not, by virtue of his or her legal expertise, in a privileged position. The employment judge's voice is equal to, but no louder than, those of his or her lay colleagues. He or she can, therefore, be outvoted and his or her opinion, when this happens, forms the minority decision of the tribunal. However, in the rare circumstances in which a tribunal is composed of two persons, the employment judge has a second or casting vote – rule 49.

1.35 **Lay members**
As noted above (under 'Tribunal panels'), lay panel members are appointed by the Lord Chancellor after consultation with organisations of employees and employers, of which the CBI and TUC are the most prominent – Reg 8(2)(b) and (c). They are people with special knowledge and experience in commerce and industry and are expected to bring this practical expertise to bear in their judicial role. Although they are appointed to one of two panels, depending on whether their background is employer- or employee-oriented, they are not allowed to betray bias towards their respective sides of industry, since the tribunal as a whole comprises a 'judicial' body responsible for the discharge of impartial judicial functions. In East Berkshire Health Authority v Matadeen 1992 ICR 723, EAT, Mr Justice Wood had cause to consider the role of lay members in the work of the EAT and there is no doubt that his comments apply equally to employment tribunal lay members. He stated: '[The Appeal Tribunal] has industrial members sitting not as assessors but as full members of the court... Their function is not only to give advice to the judge on numerous matters and aspects of industrial relations, but to bring their experience and industrial judgement to the application of the law and to the decision to be reached.' However, the particular value of lay members as non-lawyers who have experience of workplace involvement on behalf of both

employees and employers is not only substantive, but is also important to the *perception* of the employment tribunal by the parties – Birmingham City Council v Barker and ors EAT 0447/09 (discussed further under 'Employment judge sitting alone' below).

The lay members are, within limits, entitled to draw upon their specialised knowledge when assisting the tribunal to reach a decision. In particular, their knowledge of local conditions is often properly relied upon when assessing – for compensation purposes – the length of time for which a dismissed employee is likely to remain unemployed. In Gill v Harold Andrews Sheepbridge Ltd 1974 ICR 294, NIRC, for instance, the NIRC refused to say that a tribunal had erred in relying on the knowledge of the lay members in accepting the employer's evidence as to the period within which an employee could reasonably have been expected to find new work.

The Gill case was one in which the tribunal members used their own experience **1.36** as a guide to whose evidence they preferred. As a general rule, however, a tribunal should not make presumptions based on the experience of the members unless, in doing so, the tribunal members first draw the parties' attention to what their actual experience is and, if necessary, how it differs from the evidence that has been presented – Hammington v Berker Sportcraft Ltd 1980 ICR 248, EAT. For example, in Potter and ors v North Cumbria Acute Hospitals NHS Trust 2009 IRLR 900, EAT, the EAT criticised a tribunal for taking into account the 'firm view' of a lay member with 'vast experience' of working within the NHS in deciding that Agenda for Change fundamentally changed previous terms and conditions, without setting out why the lay member formed her view. The tribunal was wrong to do so without the lay member making clear her view, and the reasons for it, during the course of the hearing, so that the parties could have an opportunity to deal with it.

That said, it appears to be within the remit of tribunal members for them to bring to bear 'ordinary practical knowledge and experience', as opposed to a specialist or recondite piece of knowledge, without needing to inform the parties of that everyday knowledge so they can expressly deal with it. In Barke v SEETEC Business Technology Centre Ltd EAT 0917/04 the EAT saw nothing wrong in tribunal members using their knowledge that it was possible to obtain insurance to cover a person's parking another's car on private property, in a dispute related to a disabled parking space, without informing the parties and allowing them to respond. And in McCafferty v Royal Mail Group Ltd EATS 0002/12 the EAT upheld a majority decision of an employment tribunal (in which the employment judge dissented) that a postman had been fairly dismissed. The EAT commented that the case was an example of the lay members of an employment tribunal drawing on their valuable 'common sense' and knowledge of what any employee could be expected to know, in deciding that the claimant would, as a matter of common

17

sense, know that it was not common practice for an employer to pay for its employees to travel to work, and that the employer had reasonable grounds for its belief that the claimant had sought to hide his use of the company taxi account from his managers.

1.37 **Selection of lay members.** A related question is whether lay members may be selected to sit on particular tribunals on the basis of their specialist experience or knowledge. This scenario is clearly envisaged by the Tribunal Regulations, given that the President has power to establish separate panels of tribunal members with specialist knowledge – see 'Tribunal panels – specialist panels' above. However, the President or regional employment judge (or Vice President) will need to take care where selecting a particular tribunal member from the normal panels on the basis of his or her relevant experience, as was shown in Halford v Sharples and ors 1992 ICR 146, EAT, a case involving an allegation of sex discrimination by a senior employee of a police authority. In Halford, it was argued that the deliberate selection of a lay member because of his relevant experience as an equal opportunities adviser in the employment of another police force was improper. In accepting that argument, the EAT ruled that it was, on the whole, undesirable to select the members of tribunals on the basis of any specialised knowledge they may have, especially since their decisions might be informed more by their own knowledge than by the facts and evidence relevant to the particular case. The fairly obvious point was also made in the Halford case that lay members should not act in cases in which they have a possible personal, professional or monetary interest, unless they declare that interest and the parties do not object. (Note that the case was affirmed by the Court of Appeal – 1992 ICR 583, CA – but subsequently overruled by the House of Lords in R v Chief Constable of West Midlands Police and anor, ex parte Wiley and anor 1995 1 AC 274, HL, for other reasons.) For the circumstances in which 'interest bias' may disqualify tribunal members from sitting, see Chapter 12, 'The hearing', under 'Bias'.

Although selection based on experience may be inappropriate unless there is very good reason for it, in discrimination cases it might seem sensible to include on the tribunal panel a member of the same sex as the claimant or, as the case may be, a member with some special knowledge of race relations or a special interest in disability matters. In practice, tribunals always try to do this, but there is no statutory compulsion requiring the composition of the tribunal to be adjusted in this way. This was confirmed by the EAT in Habib v Elkington and Co Ltd 1981 ICR 435, EAT, where it held that an employee alleging race discrimination could not insist on the appointment of a member with special knowledge of his own ethnic culture: so long as the lay members were selected from panels drawn one from either side of industry in compliance with Reg 8(2), the tribunal would be validly constituted.

Employment judge sitting alone

Section 4(1) ETA establishes the general rule that proceedings before an employment tribunal should be heard by a tribunal composed of the chairman/woman (i.e. the employment judge) and two lay members (or one lay member if the parties agree – see 'Tribunals comprising an employment judge and one lay member' below).

However, there are specified circumstances in which an employment judge will sit alone to deal with proceedings. These are where:

- the claim is of a type that falls within a list set out in S.4(3) (unless the employment judge decides that it should be heard by a full tribunal)

- the Tribunal Regulations allow proceedings to be determined without a hearing – S.4(6) and (6A)(a), or

- the Tribunal Regulations provide for preliminary hearings or issues to be heard by an employment judge alone – S.4(6) and (6A)(b) and (c).

Section 4(3) claims. Section 4(2) provides that, unless the employment judge **1.39** dealing with the matter decides otherwise (see 'Discretion to convene a full tribunal' below), the proceedings specified in S.4(3) must be heard by an employment judge sitting alone. Those proceedings involve the following:

- complaints under the Trade Union and Labour Relations (Consolidation) Act 1992 (TULR(C)A) in respect of deductions of union subscriptions (S.68A), political funds (S.87) or remuneration under protective awards (S.192); and applications under the TULR(C)A for interim relief (Ss.161, 165 or 166) – S.4(3)(a)

- complaints under S.126 of the Pension Schemes Act 1993 in respect of unpaid contributions – S.4(3)(b)

- references under the Employment Rights Act 1996 (ERA) in respect of written statements of employment particulars or itemised pay statements (S.11), redundancy payments (S.163) or employers' payments (S.170); complaints under the ERA in respect of unauthorised deductions from wages (S.23), guarantee payments (S.34), unfair dismissal (S.111), insolvency (S.188) or remuneration while suspended (S.70); and applications under the ERA for interim relief (Ss.128, 131 or 132) or for appointments in respect of proceedings on behalf of the estates of dead employees (S.206) – S.4(3)(c)

- complaints under the Transfer of Undertakings (Protection of Employment) Regulations 2006 SI 2006/246 (TUPE) regarding the failure of employers to pay compensation in respect of their previous failure to inform or consult (Reg 15(10)) – S.4(3)(ca)

- complaints under the National Minimum Wage Act 1998 (NMWA) in respect of record keeping (S.11) – S.4(3)(cc); or appeals under the NMWA in respect of underpayment notices (S.19C) – S.4(3)(cd)

- complaints under Reg 30 of the Working Time Regulations 1998 SI 1998/1833 relating to an amount due under Regs 14(2) or 16(1) – S.4(3)(ce)

- complaints under Reg 18 of the Merchant Shipping (Working Time: Inland Waterways) Regulations 2003 SI 2003/3049 relating to an amount due under Reg 11 – S.4(3)(cf)

- complaints under Reg 18 of the Civil Aviation (Working Time) Regulations 2004 SI 2004/756 relating to an amount due under Reg 4 – S.4(3)(cg)

- complaints under Reg 19 of the Fishing Vessels (Working Time: Sea-fishermen) Regulations 2004 SI 2004/1713 relating to an amount due under Reg 11 – S.4(3)(ch)

- breach of contract claims where the employment tribunal has jurisdiction by virtue of S.3 ETA – S.4(3)(d)

- proceedings in which the parties have given their written consent to the proceedings being heard by an employment judge alone (whether or not they have subsequently withdrawn that consent) – S.4(3)(e)

- proceedings in which the person (or, where more than one, each of the persons) against whom the proceedings are brought does not, or has ceased to, contest the case – S.4(3)(g).

1.40 One of the more controversial additions to the above list were unfair dismissal complaints under S.111 ERA, which were added by the Employment Tribunals Act 1996 (Tribunal Composition) Order 2012 SI 2012/988 with effect from 6 April 2012 under the power to amend contained in S.4(4) – see S.4(3)(c) ETA. The Government's rationale for moving away from a panel of three in unfair dismissal cases, which form a significant proportion of the employment tribunals' workload, was the better use of tribunal resources: it is easier to list cases where it is only necessary to ensure the availability of one person, and hearing times are generally shorter where a judge sits alone. The consultation stated that most unfair dismissal cases give rise to relatively straightforward questions, which are capable of being determined by a single judge, but that, like other jurisdictions falling under S.4(3), judges would be able to direct that some cases be heard by a panel of three. This might occur where, for example, the issues are complex, there is a lot of factual evidence to sift, or the parties express a desire for a tripartite panel.

However, the EAT in McCafferty v Royal Mail Group Ltd EATS 0002/12 (discussed under 'Lay members' above) expressed disquiet about the presumption that employment judges should sit alone to hear unfair dismissal claims. In that case, the EAT upheld a majority decision by an employment tribunal that a postman's dismissal was fair, even though the employment judge had dissented. Lady Smith, presiding, observed that the case was an example of the lay members of an employment tribunal reaching a different conclusion on the facts of the case – drawing in part on their valuable 'common sense' and knowledge of what any employee could be expected to know – from that of the employment judge. Had the claim been one to which the 2012 Order applied, she observed, 'it seems likely that it would have been heard and determined by an employment judge sitting alone, in which case the result would evidently have been rather different. Some may consider that to be a sobering thought'. She underlined the need to give careful consideration to any views expressed by parties as to whether such proceedings should in fact be heard by a full tribunal (see 'Discretion to convene a full tribunal' below).

It is clear from the fact that S.4(3)(e) permits a tribunal to hear a claim without **1.41** lay members where the parties have consented to such a course that there is scope, in theory, for employment judge-only tribunals to cover any type of claim. However, in the absence of such consent, the types of claim that may be determined by an employment judge sitting alone are confined to the specific matters listed in the rest of S.4(3) (except for the limited situations covered by S.4(6)). The most notable exclusion from the list in S.4(3) relates to claims under the Equality Act 2010 (EqA), although there are other, less obvious, exclusions. If an employment judge sits alone to hear a claim without the jurisdiction to do so, his or her decision will be invalid and the claim will have to be listed again before a full tribunal. In Weedon v Pinnacle Entertainment Ltd and another case EAT 0217/11 an employment judge sitting alone considered a group of claims under S.189 TULR(C)A for a protective award. He dismissed W and R's claims on the ground that they had been made out of time. However, the EAT upheld W and R's appeal, on the ground that claims under S.189 are not listed in S.4(3) and therefore the employment judge had had no jurisdiction to hear them by himself. As His Honour Judge Peter Clark pointed out, there is a clear distinction between claims brought under S.189 for a protective award and claims brought under S.192 TULR(C)A, which deals with complaints by employees who fall within the description of employees to which a protective award relates, but where the employer has failed to pay the individual employee remuneration under that award. Complaints under S.192 can be heard before a judge alone; claims under S.189 cannot. The EAT remitted the case to a full employment tribunal for rehearing.

Where an employment judge sitting alone considers a number of claims, some of which fall within S.4(3) and others of which do not, only those claims that fall outside the jurisdiction of a judge-alone tribunal will need to be remitted for a rehearing by a full tribunal. In Insaidoo v Metropolitan Resources North West Ltd EAT 0365/10 the EAT held that I's pay claim had been properly decided by a judge sitting alone. However the judge had had (at that time) no

21

jurisdiction to hear I's unfair dismissal claim, so the EAT remitted this point only for a full hearing. (Note that the presence of mixed claims is one of the factors an employment judge should take into account when deciding whether the case should be heard by a full tribunal in the first place – see 'Discretion to convene a full tribunal' below.)

1.42 *Discretion to convene a full tribunal.* It is important to note that, by virtue of S.4(5) ETA, although a case may fall within one of the categories of proceedings listed in S.4(3), this does not necessarily mean that it will be heard by an employment judge alone. S.4(5) provides that any of the proceedings listed in S.4(3) may be heard by the employment judge together with two lay members (or, if the parties consent, with one lay member) if the employment judge so decides having regard to the following:

- whether there is a likelihood of a dispute arising on the facts which makes it desirable for the proceedings to be heard by a full tribunal

- whether there is a likelihood of an issue of law arising which would make it desirable for the proceedings to be heard by an employment judge sitting alone

- any views of any of the parties as to whether the proceedings ought to be heard either by a full tribunal or by an employment judge sitting alone

- whether there are other proceedings which might be heard concurrently but which are not proceedings specified in S.4(3).

1.43 The question arises as to whether an employment judge sitting alone can validly deal with a S.4(3) case without first giving express consideration to the discretion in S.4(5) and providing reasons for why that discretion was, or was not, exercised. For a number of years there were conflicting judicial opinions at EAT level on this issue. However, the debate took a decisive turn when Mr Justice Lindsay, then President of the EAT, considered the matter in Morgan and anor v Brith Gof Cyf 2001 ICR 978, EAT. He stated that: 'It is no doubt desirable for an employment judge to reflect upon subsection (5), even if he is not invited to do so. And certainly, of course, if he is addressed on the subject or it is raised in the papers, well then he has to turn his mind to the issues described in subsection (5). Whenever there is real doubt on the question, it must always, in our view, be better for him to prefer a panel of three. But it is not, in our view, an error of law on an employment judge's part, when dealing with a case which is a subsection (3) case and the point is not being raised by anyone, not to turn his mind to subsection (5). Nor is it an error of law for him not to have expressed openly the considerations that he might tacitly have had in mind.' The Court of Appeal approved this reasoning in Alharazim v Novas Ouvertures 2006 EWCA Civ 726, CA, finding that the EAT was entitled to hold that there had been no error of law where an employment judge, who had not been asked to exercise his discretion to sit as a full tribunal in a case of unlawful deduction of wages in which he would normally expect to sit alone, had failed to apply his mind to the question of discretion. This was the case even though the notice of hearing had, incorrectly, stated that the case would be heard by a full tribunal, and even though there were some disputed matters of evidence. The employment judge was not expressly asked to apply his mind to S.4(5) until after he had delivered his decision, and thus he made no error of law in failing to consider whether to exercise his discretion.

Two subsequent EAT cases took a similar line, although in neither case, apparently, was the EAT referred to the Court of Appeal's unreported judgment in Alharazim. In Gladwell v Secretary of State for Trade and Industry 2007 ICR 264, EAT, Mr Justice Elias, then President of the EAT, stated that he could see nothing wrong in the standard practice of all cases falling within S.4(3) being listed before an employment judge sitting alone, provided the parties are given an opportunity of making representations as to why a full panel should be constituted. However, Elias J disagreed with Lindsay J's statement that the only circumstance in which an employment judge is obliged actively to consider exercising his or her discretion is if the parties raise the issue. He was of the opinion that there will be some cases – for instance, where there are litigants in person – where the employment judge should actively consider exercising the discretion even where the issue has not been drawn to his or her attention. But in almost all circumstances, the failure by the parties to object when given the opportunity, especially where they are legally represented, will make a perversity challenge impossible to sustain. Turning to the facts of the case, it was plainly one for which an employment judge alone was suited and there was nothing in the case which ought to have caused the employment judge even to have raised the issue. It might have been prudent to do so, but the failure to do so betrayed no error of law.

The EAT followed Gladwell in Sterling Developments (London) Ltd v Pagano **1.44** 2007 IRLR 471, EAT, holding, on very similar facts to Alharazim, that an employment judge's failure to give reasons for sitting alone or to canvas the views of the parties does not give rise to an error of law. The EAT considered that although it is usually prudent to do so, the employment judge is not required to seek the views of the parties at the hearing. It will not be an error of law if the employment judge fails to consider whether a full tribunal should be convened where neither party challenges the tribunal's composition.

The EAT went on to give the following guidance to tribunals:

• listing is a judicial function. If there is an administrative error in the notice of hearing suggesting that a full tribunal will be convened, that does not mean that there will be an error of law if the employment judge actually sits alone

- where a preliminary hearing is held, any judicial decision as to the composition of the tribunal for the future full hearing should be accompanied by an invitation to make submissions on the point. If they are made, brief reasons should be given for the eventual decision, and the composition of the tribunal will be reflected in a case management order

- if there is no preliminary hearing and the employment judge directs that the full hearing will be before an employment judge alone, the notice of hearing sent to the parties must expressly invite representations on the issue. The employment judge's decision upon considering any representations will be a judicial decision, with reasons. As such, it will be capable of being appealed

- where representations are not made or an appeal against the decision on composition is not pursued before the final hearing, or representations are not made as a preliminary point at the final hearing itself, it will not be possible to challenge the tribunal's composition after the event by way of appeal.

1.45 In Sterling, no challenge to the employment judge sitting alone was made at the hearing. If it had been, the chairman would have made a judicial decision on a preliminary point as to whether or not to continue, which would have been capable of being appealed. The judgment following the final hearing could not be appealed opportunistically on the ground of the tribunal's composition. In the EAT's view, a legitimate challenge would have failed in any event. The case was factually simple and entirely suitable for an employment judge sitting alone, which was the default position under S.4(2).

The upshot of the EAT's decision in this case, and of the Court of Appeal's decision in Alharazim v Novas Ouvertures (above), is that if a party wishes to challenge the composition of the tribunal, it must do so before the full hearing on liability takes place. Any reasoned judicial decision taken after representations on the point will be susceptible to appeal, but a judgment on the substantive issues in a case presided over by a lone employment judge whose jurisdiction has not been questioned will not be open to challenge on the basis that it was made by an incompetent tribunal. Following the ratio of Alharazim, this may be the case even where a tribunal has failed to invite representations from the parties as recommended in Sterling.

1.46 *Quality of reasoning.* Note that, where an employment judge sits alone, his or her quality of reasoning does not have to be any fuller than it would have been had he or she been chairing a three-member tribunal. In Disotto Food Ltd v Santos EAT 0623/12 an employment judge, sitting alone, found that the claimant had been unfairly dismissed and that he had not received a statement of changes in his particulars of employment, and awarded him compensation. The respondent appealed, arguing, among other things, that the judge should have made further findings and given greater explanation of his conclusions because he was sitting alone without the benefit of lay members. However, the EAT rejected this argument, stating that 'the quality of reasons which is essential is judged against a standard which is the same, whether the tribunal is composed of one, three, or, for that matter, any other permitted number'. In providing that judges should sit alone in unfair dismissal cases, Parliament had made no consequential provisions that the conduct of the case should differ in any other way.

Determinations without hearing. Section 4(6) and (6A)(a) ETA provides that **1.47** under the Tribunal Regulations, certain acts of an employment tribunal may be done by an employment judge sitting alone – including the determination of proceedings in accordance with regulations under S.7(3A), (3B) or (3C)(a). S.7(3A), in turn, states that the Tribunal Regulations may 'authorise the determination of proceedings without any hearing' in prescribed circumstances. This may only happen, however, where all the parties to the proceedings consent in writing, or where the respondent has either not presented a response (or the response is not accepted), or does not contest the case – S.7(3AA) and (3AB). S.7(3B) allows Tribunal Regulations to authorise the determination of proceedings without hearing anyone other than the claimant or his or her representative in circumstances where the respondent has done nothing to contest the case, or the claim form suggests that the claimant is seeking relief which the employment tribunal has no power to give. S.7(3C)(a) allows the Tribunal Regulations to authorise the determination of proceedings without hearing anyone other than the claimant and respondent, where the tribunal is on undisputed facts bound by case precedent to dismiss the claim or response.

Accordingly, rule 21 of the Tribunal Rules provides that an employment judge (sitting alone) may determine a claim (or, under rule 25, an employer's contract claim) without a hearing if it can properly be determined on the available material, in circumstances where no response is presented, a response has been rejected and no application to have it reconsidered is outstanding, or the respondent has ceased to contest it. Rule 60 provides that any such decisions shall be communicated in writing to the parties, identifying the employment judge who has made the decision. See Chapter 6, 'Defending a claim', under 'Rule 21: "default judgments"'. If the employment judge considers that he or she cannot properly determine the claim without a hearing, a hearing will be fixed before an employment judge alone – rule 21(2).

Preliminary issues and hearings. Apart from deciding cases at a final hearing **1.48** in accordance with S.4(3) ETA (or, under rule 21, without a hearing), there is a large number of other tasks that an employment judge can carry out alone under the Tribunal Regulations. These range from making case management orders or decisions, to reaching determinations on preliminary jurisdictional issues and conducting preliminary hearings (see S.4(6) and (6A)(b) and (c) ETA). For example, an employment judge has authority to sit alone:

25

- to consider whether a claim (or employer's contract claim), or part of it, should be rejected on the ground that the tribunal does not have jurisdiction to consider it, or that it is in a form which cannot sensibly be responded to or is otherwise an abuse of process – rules 12 and 23

- to consider a claimant's application for a reconsideration of a rule 12 rejection, or an employer's application for reconsideration of a rejection of its contract claim – rules 13 and 23

- to consider a respondent's application for reconsideration of a decision to reject the response – rule 19

- to determine an application for an extension of time for presenting a response, or a response to an employer's contract claim – rule 20

- to carry out an initial consideration of the claim form and response – rules 26, 27 and 28

- to consider an application for reconsideration of a tribunal's judgment – rule 72

- to conduct Stage 1 equal value hearings – rules 3 and 12(3) of Schedule 2 to the Tribunal Regulations (see IDS Employment Law Handbook, 'Equal Pay' (2011), Chapter 7, 'Work of equal value', under 'Stage 1 equal value hearing'.

1.49 *Preliminary hearings.* Preliminary hearings must be conducted by an employment judge sitting alone, unless the following circumstances apply:

- notice has been given to the parties that any preliminary issues are to be, or may be, decided at the hearing

- a party requests in writing that the hearing be conducted by a full tribunal, and

- if so, the employment judge decides that it would be 'desirable' for the hearing to be conducted by a full tribunal – rule 55.

It may be 'desirable' for a preliminary hearing to be conducted by a tribunal where it deals with the question of whether a party is entitled to bring proceedings. In Sutcliffe and anor v Big C's Marine Ltd and ors 1998 ICR 913, EAT, Mr Justice Morison noted that the wisdom and experience of lay members will often be of great assistance to employment judges in such cases. More specifically, Morison J endorsed what was said by Lord Johnston in Fleming v Secretary of State for Trade and Industry EATS 341/96 – that the particular question of whether an individual is an employee is essentially one for an industrial jury where the input of lay members is of crucial importance. Morison J added that the issue of whether it is just and equitable to extend time for bringing a discrimination complaint is also one where the lay members' contribution is crucial. However, given the wording of rule 55, it appears that an employment judge is obliged to sit alone, even if it would be desirable for a tribunal to hear a preliminary hearing, if neither party makes a written request for a full tribunal.

In Birmingham City Council v Barker and ors EAT 0447/09 the EAT considered **1.50** whether or not an employment judge had properly directed himself in determining that it was desirable for him to sit alone to conduct a preliminary hearing. The case involved a large group equal pay claim, and it was directed that a preliminary hearing should be held to decide whether the respondent had a 'material factor' defence to the claims against it. For some claimants, this would determine the question of liability. At a case management hearing, the employment judge considered rule 18 of the Tribunal Rules 2004 (the precursor to rule 55) and held that, although the express wish of the parties was that the issue should be heard by a full tribunal and there were numerous disputes of fact, there would also be complex issues of law to determine. Given that the facts were likely to be mainly matters of detail, 'such as are tried by judge alone in the civil courts every day without difficulty', and that the lay members' participation in deciding the legal issues would be limited, and that their involvement would inevitably slow down the hearing so as to add to the cost of the litigation, the judge took the view that it was better for him to sit alone.

However, the EAT held that the judge had misdirected himself. He had taken no account of the fact that while the hearing was only preliminary, it would in practice involve the final determination of an issue which would be dispositive either way of the claims of some of the claimants, and decisive of a key substantive issue in the case of other claimants. He had failed to consider the undesirability of claimants losing their entitlement to have their substantive case decided by a full tribunal because the issue came before the tribunal 'packaged' as a preliminary issue – an issue the EAT had raised in Sutcliffe and anor v Big C's Marine Ltd and ors (above). The EAT considered that the employment judge's approach seriously undervalued the role of lay members, which was 'not limited to input on specific issues of industrial relations practice and the like'. While a hearing with lay members would generally take somewhat longer than a hearing before a judge sitting alone, the difference was not likely to be so great as to make a disproportionate impact on the length of the hearing or the costs for the parties. To the extent that the involvement of lay members did involve additional time and therefore additional cost, that was the inevitable price to be paid for the advantages that lay members brought; and the EAT expressed concern about any suggestion that the cost to the public purse was a relevant factor where the criteria for the use of lay members was otherwise satisfied. Nevertheless, the EAT concluded that the employment judge's decision to hear the preliminary hearing alone should stand, even though it was legally flawed, as the effect of substituting a decision that it should be heard by a full tribunal would be to necessitate a substantial adjournment in a case with a history of adjournments; and the involvement of lay members in the preliminary

27

hearing, while desirable, could not be said to be indispensable in the interests of justice.

1.51 Note that rule 48 allows a tribunal to 'convert' a preliminary hearing into a final hearing, *provided the tribunal is properly constituted* for the purpose and is satisfied that neither party will be materially prejudiced by the change. If a tribunal anticipates that it may make such an order, this may influence its decision as to whether or not to sit as a full tribunal from the outset. For example, if an employment judge elects to sit alone to conduct a preliminary hearing in a discrimination case, he or she could not then order that the hearing should be treated as a final hearing under rule 48, as discrimination cases are not listed in S.4(3) as a type of claim that may be heard by an employment judge sitting alone. In an appropriate case, this fact may convince the judge to convene a full tribunal from the start.

Preliminary hearings are discussed in Chapter 11, 'Case management', under 'Preliminary hearings'.

1.52 Legal officers

Since August 1998, the ETA has contained a power enabling regulations to be made to allow certain specified acts that may be carried out by an employment judge acting alone to be done by 'a person appointed as a legal officer' – S.4(6B) ETA. The specified acts do *not* include determining proceedings (other than those in which the parties have agreed settlement terms, or which the claimant has withdrawn), or carrying out 'pre-hearing reviews' (now known as 'preliminary hearings' – see Chapter 11, 'Case management', under 'Preliminary hearings') – S.4(6C).

In April 2013, the Enterprise and Regulatory Reform Act 2013 extended the potential remit of 'legal officers' by inserting S.4(6D) into the ETA. This provides that legal officers 'may determine proceedings' or 'make a decision falling to be made in the course of such proceedings', if the proceedings are of a description specified in an order made by the Secretary of State and Lord Chancellor (S.4(6D)(a)) and all the parties consent in writing (S.4(6D)(b)). In other words, a legal officer could be given power to make certain quasi-judicial decisions, not just decisions on procedural or interlocutory matters.

1.53 The aim of S.4(6D) was to reduce the administrative burden on tribunals by expanding the range of people who are able to take certain types of decision. However, a number of questions arise from these provisions. What qualifications or training should legal officers be required to have? What proceedings should they be allowed to determine? Could their decisions be subject to review by employment tribunal judges, or would they be appealable only to the EAT? Perhaps because of these uncertainties, to date none of the provisions regarding legal officers have been implemented and the Government has, as yet, given no indication that it plans to implement them in the foreseeable future.

Tribunals comprising judge and one lay member   1.54

In circumstances where a tribunal must consist of an employment judge and lay members, it is possible for just one lay member to sit, but only where the parties have given their consent to such a course – S.4(1)(b) ETA. The most common situations giving rise to a two-person tribunal are where a lay member is unable to get to the tribunal at the outset of the hearing or where a lay member becomes indisposed or dies during the course of a hearing. Where a tribunal consists of two people, the employment judge has a second or casting vote – rule 49.

In any event, the hearing can only proceed if *both* parties give their consent to only one lay member sitting. A failure to obtain such consent will render any tribunal invalidly constituted, with the result that any judgment will be set aside – see, for example, Quenchers Ltd v McShane EAT 514/92. This will be the case even where one party fails to turn up to the hearing and relies, instead, upon written representations – see, for example, Yardley Plastics (Bandeath) Ltd v Heathcote EAT 84/90. However, if an employer has failed to enter a response and is therefore barred from taking an active part in the proceedings, it will not be regarded as a 'party' for the purposes of S.4(1)(b), with the consequence that its consent is not a precondition before the case can proceed to be heard in the absence of one of the lay members – Comber v Harmony Inns Ltd 1993 ICR 15, EAT. Nevertheless, as Mr Justice Wood advised in Comber, in circumstances where the employer has not entered a response, rather than proceed by way of a two-person tribunal on the basis of the claimant's consent it would be good practice for the hearing to be adjourned and reconvened before a full tribunal.

In Rabahallah v British Telecommunications plc 2005 ICR 440, EAT, the EAT   1.55 decided that when a lay member can no longer participate in tribunal proceedings, the parties are entitled to know whether the remaining lay member has been drawn from the panel of employers' or employees' representatives. As the claimant had been refused this information, there was a serious irregularity in the composition of the tribunal and the case was remitted to a different tribunal for rehearing. The EAT observed that it would be sensible for the form giving consent to a case commencing or continuing before a panel of two rather than three to be signed by the parties beforehand. It should also contain an express reference to the identity of the employment judge and lay member who will try or continue the case, with a statement of the panel from which that member is drawn.

Substitute members   1.56

The President, Vice President or regional employment judge may select from the appropriate panel a substitute for a member previously selected to hear any proceedings – Reg 9(3) Tribunal Regulations. As with two-person tribunals (see 'Tribunals comprising an employment judge and one lay member' above) the need for a substitute member tends to arise where a lay member is unable

29

to get to the tribunal at the outset of the hearing or where a lay member becomes indisposed or dies during the course of a hearing.

Such a situation arose in Monfort International plc v McKenzie EAT 0155/06. In that case, the EAT rejected an argument that in appointing a substitute when a lay member fell ill after the liability hearing but before the remedies hearing, the regional employment judge ought to have informed the parties of his intention and offered the option of a two-person tribunal. The regional employment judge has power under what is now Reg 9(3) to appoint a substitute member, provided he or she does so acting judicially, which was the case here. Although substituting a tribunal member before the issue of liability had been decided would be undesirable, given that the new member would not have heard all the evidence on the issue, in this case all that remained was 'doing the maths' at the remedies hearing.

1.57 As to obtaining the parties' consent, the EAT commented that the fact that the parties' consent is required under S.4(1)(b) for a two-person tribunal to sit – but that no such consent is required for a substitution to be made under what is now Reg 9(3) – is explained by the fact that Parliament decided that cases should normally be determined by a panel consisting of an employment judge and two members. A three-member tribunal was therefore to be preferred to an 'unbalanced' two-member tribunal. In any event, the employment judge in this case had, at the outset of the remedies hearing, given the parties an opportunity to object to the new composition, which neither had done.

1.58 National security proceedings
The President of the Employment Tribunals must select a special panel of employment judges and special panels of lay members, from the general panels, who may act in national security proceedings – Reg 10(1). Where proceedings become 'national security proceedings', the President, Vice President or regional employment judge must select members for the tribunal from these special panels (or may select him or herself to act as employment judge) – Reg 10(2). Cases become national security proceedings if a direction has been given or an order made in respect of them under rule 94 – Reg 3. National security proceedings are discussed in Chapter 12, 'The hearing', under 'National security'.

1.59 Claims against the Secretary of State – independence of tribunal
Article 6 of the European Convention on Human Rights, which was incorporated into UK law by the Human Rights Act 1998, gives individuals the right to a fair trial conducted by an 'independent and impartial' tribunal. In the past, concerns have been raised about whether an employment tribunal hearing a claim against the Secretary of State for Trade and Industry could be said to be impartial. One reason for these concerns was the fact that, at that time, lay members of tribunals were appointed by the Secretary of State and paid for by him or her out of funds made available from the Treasury. The remuneration, fees and

allowances for the lay members were determined by the Secretary of State, who could, with the consent of the Lord Chancellor, terminate their appointment on one month's notice. In response to the concerns, changes were made in 1999 to the procedures for the appointment and payment of lay members and the termination of lay members' contracts. In Scanfuture UK Ltd v Secretary of State for Trade and Industry 2001 ICR 1096, EAT, the EAT considered whether the revised procedures concerning lay members were sufficient to ensure compliance with Article 6. The EAT noted that, although lay members were still appointed by the Secretary of State, the process now involved an element of open competition. Furthermore, all appointments were made for a renewable three-year period rather than for the previous period of one year. Finally, the EAT observed that the system for removing lay members from office and for non-renewal of office was now subject to judicial involvement. The EAT concluded that, under the new procedures, there would be no reason for a lay member to think that he or she could benefit from favouring the Secretary of State in proceedings. Accordingly, the EAT found that there were now guarantees in place which meant that an informed observer could no longer have an objectively justifiable fear that a tribunal lacked independence or impartiality.

Note that appointments are now made by the Lord Chancellor and may be made for a renewable five-year term, while responsibility for the administration of the lay membership now lies with HMCTS, an executive agency of the Ministry of Justice – see 'Lay members' above.

2 Tribunals' jurisdiction

Types of claim heard by tribunals

Territorial limitations

Relitigation: res judicata and abuse of process

State and diplomatic immunity

Scope of remission by Employment Appeal Tribunal

References to European Court of Justice

Appendix – claims heard by employment tribunals

Employment tribunals, being 'creatures of statute', have a narrowly defined **2.1** jurisdiction which covers most of the employment rights established by modern employment legislation. This chapter considers the range of statutory claims employment tribunals have power to hear, and the circumstances in which they may hear claims under contract law (see 'Types of claim heard by tribunals' below). However, it should be borne in mind that, even where a tribunal is competent to hear a particular claim, it may be prevented from doing so for a number of reasons. Some of these are procedural in nature and are dealt with elsewhere in this Handbook. For example, a tribunal may be barred from hearing a claim if, before commencing proceedings, the claimant failed to contact Acas with a view to reaching an early settlement of the dispute (see Chapter 3, 'Conciliation, settlements and ADR', under 'Early conciliation') or the claim has been presented outside the time limit laid down by statute (see Chapter 5, 'Time limits'). Similarly, a failure by one of the parties to pay the required fee will affect entitlement to pursue (or defend) a claim – see Chapter 19, 'Fees'. Other factors that may determine whether or not a tribunal can hear a claim are dealt in other Handbooks in this series. For example, the rules that determine whether an individual has the necessary period of continuous employment to bring a particular claim is considered in IDS Employment Law Handbook, 'Continuity of Employment' (2012), while the law governing employment status (and therefore locus standi) is discussed in IDS Employment Law Handbook, 'Contracts of Employment' (2009), Chapter 1, 'Basic requirements', under 'Who is an employee?'.

In this chapter, we also deal with a number of legal matters that may impose limitations on the jurisdiction of employment tribunals in particular proceedings. These include territorial issues (discussed in the section 'Territorial limitations', under 'Jurisdiction', 'Applicable law' and 'Territorial reach'); the doctrine of res judicata (see 'Relitigation: res judicata and abuse of process'); state and

33

diplomatic immunity from legal process (see 'State and diplomatic immunity'); and the extent of the tribunals' power to hear cases that have been remitted from the EAT (see 'Scope of remission by Employment Appeal Tribunal'). Finally, we discuss the scope of employment tribunals' power to refer questions to the European Court of Justice ('References to European Court of Justice').

2.2 As questions of jurisdiction are fundamental to the right of a tribunal to consider the substantive merits of a particular case, they must be dealt with by the tribunal – usually at a preliminary hearing – whether or not the parties raise them and even if the parties are willing to waive them, as 'parties cannot by agreement or conduct confer upon a tribunal a jurisdiction which it does not otherwise have' – Watt (formerly Carter) and ors v Ahsan 2008 ICR 82, HL. (For detail of the preliminary hearing process, see Chapter 11, 'Case management', under 'Preliminary hearings'.) If a point of jurisdiction is not raised before a tribunal, it can and should be raised on review or on appeal. As the EAT said in British Midland Airways Ltd v Lewis 1978 ICR 782, EAT, when considering a jurisdictional issue that had not been raised at a tribunal hearing, 'this being a question as to jurisdiction, the [employment] tribunal should have taken the point themselves even if the parties did not; and they cannot merely by silence confer upon themselves a jurisdiction which they do not have'.

2.3 Types of claim heard by tribunals

Employment tribunals have jurisdiction to hear claims under a large number of statutory provisions by virtue of S.2 of the Employment Tribunals Act 1996 (ETA). They may also hear certain contractual claims under S.3 – see 'Contractual claims' below. It is important that claimants take care when completing the claim form to ensure that their complaint(s) fall within the jurisdiction of the tribunal. If the tribunal does not have competence to hear a claim, it will be rejected under rule 12 of the Employment Tribunals Rules of Procedure ('the Tribunal Rules'), which are contained in Schedule 1 to the Employment Tribunals (Constitution and Rules of Procedure) Regulations 2013 SI 2013/1237 ('the Tribunal Regulations') (see Chapter 4, 'Starting tribunal proceedings', under 'Completing the claim form').

2.4 Statutory claims

The types of statutory claim employment tribunals can hear are listed in the Appendix to this chapter and include claims relating to:

- dismissal

- redundancy rights and business transfers

- maternity, adoption, paternity and parental leave, and flexible working

34

- discrimination and equal pay
- trade unions and union members
- time off
- working time.

Contractual claims 2.5

The contractual jurisdiction of employment tribunals is governed by S.3 ETA, together with the Employment Tribunals Extension of Jurisdiction (England and Wales) Order 1994 SI 1994/1623 ('the Order') or, in Scotland, the Employment Tribunals Extension of Jurisdiction (Scotland) Order 1994 SI 1994/1624. Under S.3(2) ETA and Article 3 of the Order, for a tribunal to be able to hear a contractual claim brought by an employee, that claim must *arise or be outstanding on the termination of the employee's employment*; and must seek one of the following:

- damages for breach of a contract of employment or any other contract connected with employment
- the recovery of a sum due under such a contract
- the recovery of a sum in pursuance of any enactment relating to the terms or performance of such a contract.

There is no requirement that the contractual claim arise in circumstances which 2.6 also give rise to proceedings already or simultaneously before the tribunal. However, the claim must be one that a civil court in England or Wales would have jurisdiction to hear and determine – Article 3(a).

(Note that Article 3(a) also states that the claim must be one to which S.131(2) of the Employment Protection (Consolidation) Act 1978 applies. That Act was repealed in 1996 and Article 3(a) should now be read as if it referred to S.3(2) ETA – see, for example, Simpson v Merrick (formerly t/a WA Merrick and Co Solicitors) EAT 0490/09.)

Exclusions. Contractual claims in respect of the following matters are 2.7 specifically excluded from the types of contractual claim that may be brought before an employment tribunal:

- the recovery of damages or a sum due in respect of personal injuries – S.3(3) and Article 3
- breach of a contractual term requiring the employer to provide living accommodation for the employee – Article 5(a)
- breach of a term imposing an obligation on the employer or employee in connection with the provision of living accommodation – Article 5(b)

35

- breach of a term relating to intellectual property (which may include copyright, rights in performances, moral rights, design rights, registered designs, patents and trade marks) – Article 5(c)

- breach of a term imposing an obligation of confidence – Article 5(d)

- breach of a covenant in restraint of trade – Article 5(e).

2.8 *Living accommodation.* The scope of Article 5(b) was considered in Qantas Cabin Crew (UK) Ltd v Alsopp and ors EAT 0318/13, where a group of employees who worked for an airline claimed that they were entitled to receive a living away from home allowance, comprising accommodation and food, on top of their basic salary. The EAT held that their claims should be struck out on the basis that they had no reasonable prospect of succeeding. One of the reasons for this was that the living away from home allowance fell within the exclusion in Article 5(b). The EAT noted that that provision was 'very wide', and certainly encompassed the term imposing an obligation on QCC (UK) Ltd to pay a living away from home allowance, in so far as it related to accommodation. However, any part of the allowance that related to food would not be covered by the exclusion.

2.9 *Obligation of confidence.* The EAT considered the ambit of Article 5(d) in Wright v Weed Control Ltd EAT 0492/07. W was managing director of WC Ltd until he was dismissed for gross misconduct. The alleged misconduct included paying VAT invoices by bad cheques which subsequently bounced and led to fines. W brought tribunal claims for unfair dismissal, wrongful dismissal and unlawful deductions from wages. In its response, WC Ltd included a counterclaim for damages for W's breach of the implied term of mutual trust and confidence. The tribunal upheld the counterclaim and awarded £18,159.79 against W, being the sum that WC Ltd lost in fines when the VAT was not paid promptly.

W appealed against the award of damages, arguing that breaches of the implied term of trust and confidence fell outside the employment tribunal's jurisdiction as defined by the Order, Article 5(d) of which provides that tribunals may not award damages in respect of 'a term imposing an obligation of confidence'. The EAT took the view that the scope of Article 5(d) was much narrower than that of the implied term of mutual trust and confidence, referring specifically to the duty of an employee with access to confidential information not to disclose that information to others or use it for his or her own purposes. Article 5(d) exists to prevent employment tribunals exercising powers in this specialist area, which is reserved to the Chancery Division of the High Court. By contrast, tribunals are likely to have a great deal of expertise when considering the implied term of mutual trust and confidence, and so should be able to award damages in respect of it. The EAT therefore dismissed W's appeal. It observed that to hold that the obligation of confidence encompassed the term of mutual trust and confidence would have the undesirable effect of depriving an employee of the right to claim damages for wrongful dismissal in the employment tribunal in a great many cases of constructive dismissal.

The implied term of trust and confidence is discussed in detail in IDS Employment Law Handbook, 'Contracts of Employment' (2009), Chapter 2, 'Contractual terms', under 'Principal implied terms – mutual trust and confidence'.

Arise or be outstanding on termination. In Sarker v South Tees Acute Hospitals **2.10** NHS Trust 1997 ICR 673, EAT, the EAT considered whether an employment tribunal had jurisdiction to hear a contractual claim relating to a contract that had been terminated before the employee in question had actually started work. In that case S was offered a job by the Trust in July, which she accepted. The parties subsequently agreed that S's 'start date' would be 1 October. However, in September the Trust withdrew the offer of employment and S brought a breach of contract claim before an employment tribunal. The tribunal held that it had no jurisdiction to hear S's claim, stating that S's employment with the Trust had never begun. In the view of the tribunal, S's claim could not be considered to be one that 'arises or is outstanding on the termination of the employee's employment' within the meaning of Article 3 of the Order.

On appeal, the EAT overturned the tribunal's decision. It stated that S had entered into a contract of employment with the Trust, the performance of which was not to start until a later date. The EAT noted that the term 'employee' is widely defined in the ERA as anyone who has entered into a contract of employment, without any requirement that the worker must actually have started performing the appropriate duties under the contract. The EAT stated that the relevant legislation seemed to support the proposition that 'employment' begins when a contract of employment is entered into, not when an employee starts work under that contract. Accordingly, the EAT held that the phrase 'the termination of the employee's employment' in Article 3 had to be construed by reference to the termination of the contract of employment, whether or not the employee has started work. Furthermore, the EAT stated that its conclusion was supported by the purpose behind the extension of contractual jurisdiction to employment tribunals, which was to avoid the situation where an employee is forced to use both a tribunal and a court of law in order to have all his or her claims determined. An employee whose contract of employment is terminated before starting work will be able to claim unfair dismissal if the termination is for an automatically unfair reason such as pregnancy or trade union duties. If an employee in that position did not also have the right to bring a breach of contract claim before the tribunal, the purpose of the Order would be defeated since the employee would have to use a different forum to pursue any contractual claims he or she had against the employer.

A different issue arose in Hendricks v Lewden Metal Products Ltd EAT 1181/95. **2.11** H was dismissed in 1994 and, within three months of her dismissal, brought a

37

contractual claim for unpaid sick pay in relation to absences in 1991 and 1992. The tribunal noted that H had not complained about LMP Ltd's breach under the Wages Act 1986 (now Part II of the Employment Rights Act 1996 (ERA)) at the time when the deductions had been made. It went on to rule that it could not be said that H's claim was outstanding on the termination of her employment in circumstances where the deduction had occurred a number of years before her dismissal and where H was precluded from making the claim under the Wages Act because she was out of time. The EAT upheld the tribunal's decision, stating that a claim could not be said to be 'outstanding' unless it had actually been raised by an employee during his or her employment. In this case, H had never complained about the deduction despite having ample opportunity to do so.

However, despite the EAT's decision in the Hendricks case, there is nothing in either the ETA or the Order which states that an employee has to have raised a matter with his or her employer during the currency of the employment in order for it to be classed as 'outstanding' when the employment ends. Furthermore, the right to claim breach of contract is independent of other statutory employment rights, so why should H have lost her right to claim breach of contract in the tribunal simply because she did not take action at the relevant time under the Wages Act? It is clear that, after H's dismissal, the breach of contract in question was 'live' in that H could still have brought a claim in the county court where the limitation period is six years from the date of the breach. Accordingly, there would appear to be no sound reason why H should have been prevented from bringing her claim in the tribunal. Such an argument becomes even stronger when considered in light of the EAT's judgment in Sarker v South Tees Acute Hospitals NHS Trust (above). As noted above, the EAT in that case emphasised that the purpose behind the extension of contractual jurisdiction to employment tribunals was to avoid the situation where an employee is forced to use both a tribunal and a court of law in order to have all his or her claims determined. Let us assume that the employee in the Hendricks case had wished to pursue a claim of unfair dismissal or discrimination upon the termination of her employment. Following the EAT's decision, she would have been able to pursue these claims in the tribunal, whereas she would have had to issue proceedings in the county court to recover her unpaid sick pay. Such an outcome would clearly have been contrary to the purposes of the Order. (Note that a different division of the EAT applied this reasoning when declining to follow the Hendricks decision – see Mitie Lindsay Ltd v Lynch EAT 0224/03.)

2.12 The EAT had to consider whether a claim was 'outstanding' on the termination of the employee's employment from another angle in Peninsula Business Services Ltd v Sweeney 2004 IRLR 49, EAT. S was employed as a sales executive and was entitled to commission on sales. Under the terms of the commission scheme, commission on a sale made by an executive became payable in the month after the customer had paid 25 per cent of the fee. The commission only became payable, however, if the executive was still in the company's employ at the end of that month. S resigned in July 2001 and brought a tribunal claim for around £21,000 commission on sales that had not generated a commission payment before the termination date. The employer argued that the employee's claim in respect of commission neither arose nor was outstanding at the date of the termination of his contract because the commission payments had not yet fallen due for payment at that point. The tribunal dismissed the employer's argument as to jurisdiction. It took a 'purposive view' of Article 3 which enabled a claim to be brought in the tribunal in respect of contingent claims existing as at the effective date of termination.

On appeal, the EAT held that the employment tribunal did not have jurisdiction to hear the employee's claim for the payment of commission on sales which he had achieved during his employment but which, under the terms of the contractual commission agreement he had signed, did not fall due for payment until after the date of the termination of his employment. A claim will only be 'outstanding' within the meaning of Article 3 if it is in the nature of a claim which, as at the date of termination, was immediately enforceable but remained unsatisfied. Moreover, the claim for commission did not 'arise' on the date of the employee's termination because at that stage he had only a prospective right to the payment of commission for which he could not sue until it had matured into an actual right. If a payment is only contingently due, it is not possible to claim payment until the contingency has happened. Before then, all that can be claimed is a declaration of entitlement to the payment if and when the contingency does happen, but a claim of that sort does not fall within Article 3.

Contract 'connected with employment'. As indicated above, the employment 2.13 tribunal has jurisdiction to hear contractual claims only where the claim relates to a breach of the employment contract, or another contract 'connected with employment'. In Ellrich v Sight Care Trading Ltd ET Case No.17507/95 a tribunal decided that it did not have jurisdiction to consider a claim brought by a managing director in respect of the repayment of a loan he had made to his employers. E had been involved in the creation of SCT Ltd and had loaned the company £25,000. The company's business plan stated that the loan would be repaid in accordance with the undertaking's financial resources but contained no firm commitment to repay at any particular time. On the termination of his employment, E brought a contractual claim before a tribunal to recover the loan. The tribunal decided that the loan agreement was not a 'contract connected with employment'. E's service agreement with the company made no mention of the loan and the business plan did not provide that the loan would be repaid if E's employment terminated. E argued that he was entitled to demand repayment of the loan at any time, even during the currency of his employment. In the tribunal's view, if this argument were right, it would be strong evidence that there was no link between the loan agreement and the contract of employment. If the company failed to repay the loan, the appropriate forum for complaint was the county court or High Court.

By contrast, the jurisdiction conferred on tribunals under S.3 ETA and the Order does extend to breaches of compromise agreements made contemporaneously with the termination of employment. In Rock-It Cargo Ltd v Green 1997 IRLR 581, EAT, G entered into a compromise agreement with RC Ltd under which she would finish work on a specified date and receive a specified sum of money. The compromise agreement included a confidentiality clause. RC Ltd later claimed that, after G's employment had terminated, she had breached that clause. Accordingly, it refused to pay G the majority of her termination package. G brought a contractual claim in the employment tribunal to recover the money. Before the tribunal, RC Ltd submitted that the compromise agreement was not a 'contract connected with employment' within the meaning of S.3 ETA and that, accordingly, the tribunal had no jurisdiction to hear the claim. The tribunal rejected RC Ltd's argument and RC Ltd appealed to the EAT. The EAT upheld the tribunal's decision. It held that the compromise agreement was an agreement as to the terms upon which G's employment was to end and, as such, was plainly a 'contract connected with employment'. As a result, G was entitled to have her claim heard in the employment tribunal.

2.14 It should be noted, however, that the compromise agreement in the Rock-It Cargo case was made contemporaneously with the end of the employee's employment. A claim relating to a breach of a compromise agreement where the agreement is made some time *after* termination of employment (for example, just prior to the commencement of the tribunal hearing on the substantive merits of an employee's claim) cannot be brought in the tribunal. This was confirmed in Miller Bros and FP Butler Ltd v Johnston 2002 ICR 744, EAT, where the EAT held that the tribunal's jurisdiction was limited to claims which are either outstanding on the date of termination of employment, or which arise – as a matter of timing, not causation – 'on termination'. Compromise agreements made after termination, if broken, are enforceable only in the ordinary civil courts.

2.15 **Employer's contract claims.** In limited circumstances, an employer can bring a contractual claim against an employee in the employment tribunal. The requirements that apply in respect of an employee making a contractual claim in a tribunal also apply to employers: in other words, the employer's contract claim must arise or be outstanding on the termination of the employee's employment and must relate to damages for breach of the contract of employment or other contract connected with employment, or a sum due under such a contract, or the recovery of a sum in pursuance of any enactment relating to the terms or performance of such a contract – Article 4 and S.3(2). In addition, the employee in question must already have brought tribunal proceedings by virtue of the Order against the employer and those proceedings must not have been settled or withdrawn – Article 4(d) and 8(a), and the employer's contract claim must arise out of a contract with that employee – Article 8(b). The exclusions to the type of contractual claim that may be brought, listed under 'Exclusions' above, also apply to employers. In effect, therefore, employers are restricted to bringing *counterclaims* in order to recover contractual damages or debts from employees, or to set off liability against sums owed.

If the employee's claim does not include a claim for breach of contract, but is purely in respect of statutory employment rights such as unfair dismissal or unlawful deductions from wages, then the employee's claim will not have been brought 'by virtue of' the Order within the meaning of Article 4(d) and the employment tribunal will have no jurisdiction to hear the employer's claim. In Hunter v Decorpart Ltd ET Case No.66809/94 H claimed unfair dismissal. In the section of his claim form which required him to set out the details of his complaint, he stated that his employer had failed to pay him his notice entitlement and that he had received only two days' holiday pay, but he did not make a claim for breach of contract. The employer denied unfair dismissal and brought a counterclaim for damages in respect of losses allegedly caused by H's negligent workmanship. The tribunal decided that it had no jurisdiction to hear the employer's claim. In order for an employer to bring a contract claim, it was not sufficient that the facts pleaded by the employee on the claim form would support a claim for breach of contract, if the proceedings themselves were not specifically based on the tribunal's contractual jurisdiction. The tribunal also noted that the employer's claim was framed in terms of the law of negligence, whereas a valid counterclaim must be a claim for damages for breach of contract or for a sum due under a contract.

Nevertheless, an employer's contract claim does not fall to be automatically **2.16** dismissed simply because the tribunal does not have jurisdiction to hear the employee's contractual claim – Patel v RCMS Ltd 1999 IRLR 161, EAT. So long as the employer's counterclaim is valid in the sense that it satisfies the criteria for such claims set out in the Order and is made within the time limit specified in that Order (see 'Time limits' below), then the employer is entitled to proceed with that claim even if the employee's own claim is dismissed by the tribunal for want of jurisdiction. In Simpson v Merrick (formerly t/a WA Merrick and Co Solicitors) EAT 0490/09, for example, S, who worked as a solicitor's clerk for M, was declared bankrupt on 5 June 2007. On 1 April 2008, following the termination of her employment, she brought proceedings against M in the employment tribunal and M counterclaimed in respect of a number of sums he claimed S owed him. An employment judge struck out S's claims of holiday pay, redundancy pay and notice pay on the basis that, as an undischarged bankrupt, she had no standing to bring those claims without the official receiver assigning it to her. However, her unfair dismissal claim was unaffected. S sought to strike out M's counterclaims but the EAT held that in so far as the counterclaims related to incidents arising after S was declared bankrupt, they were not provable debts in the bankruptcy and could therefore stand. Following Patel, the EAT reasoned that an employer will normally have no means of knowing whether or not a claim is a nullity, so the employer should be allowed to treat the claims as being validly made for the purpose of deciding whether or not it should counterclaim in the tribunal. All that Article 4 requires is that the employee bring a claim, apparently complying with the limitations imposed by Article 3 and S.3(2). (Note the EAT's observation that the employment judge had been somewhat harsh to strike out S's claims, as it is settled practice to stay claims that are brought without the permission of the trustee in bankruptcy or administrator until such permission, or that of the court, is made – see Unite the Union and ors v Sayers Confectioners Ltd (in administration) EAT 0513/08.)

The procedural rules relating to employers' contract claims are set out in rules 23–25 of the Tribunal Rules, and are discussed in Chapter 6, 'Defending a claim', under 'Employer's contract claim'.

2.17 **Time limits.** Article 7 of the Order provides that an *employee's* contractual claim must be made:

- within the period of three months beginning with the effective date of termination of the contract giving rise to the claim – Article 7(a), or

- where there is no effective date of termination, within the period of three months beginning with the last day upon which the employee worked in the employment which has terminated – Article 7(b), or

- where the tribunal is satisfied that it was not reasonably practicable for the complaint to be presented within the applicable time limit, within such further period as the tribunal considers reasonable – Article 7(c). (This formula is similar to that applicable to the majority of claims under the ERA and is discussed in Chapter 5, 'Time limits', under '"Not reasonably practicable"' and 'Extending the time limit'.)

(Note that Article 7(ba) refers to an extension of time under Reg 15 of the Employment Act 2002 (Dispute Resolution) Regulations 2004 SI 2004/752. However, these Regulations were repealed on 6 April 2009.)

2.18 In Capek v Lincolnshire County Council 2000 ICR 878, CA, the Court of Appeal confirmed that an employment tribunal does not have jurisdiction to hear a claim for breach of contract if it is presented *before* the effective date of termination of the employee's contract of employment. By virtue of Article 7(a), a tribunal only has jurisdiction if the claim is presented within a period of three months *beginning* with the effective date of termination, even if the claim relates to matters arising before termination which are still outstanding at the date of termination. The Court found that the Order clearly indicated that the

42

tribunal's jurisdiction is confined to those cases where the complaint is presented within the period between two fixed points in time: the start date, which is the effective date of termination, and the end date, which is the end of the period of three months beginning with the effective date of termination.

In reaching its decision, the Court also thought it significant that the employment tribunals' jurisdiction to consider contract claims only exists in those cases where the employee's employment has been terminated. Tribunals do not have jurisdiction to consider complaints for breach of contract where those breaches are alleged to have been committed during the currency of the contract of employment and no termination has occurred. In its view, this suggested that it was not contemplated that an employee should be entitled to invoke the jurisdiction of the tribunal in breach of contract claims before the end of his or her employment.

An *employer* who wishes to bring a counterclaim under Article 4 must do so **2.19** within the period of six weeks beginning with the day, or if more than one, the last of the days, on which the employer received from the tribunal a copy of the claim form in respect of the employee's contract claim – Article 8(c)(i). As with employees' claims, where the tribunal is satisfied that it was not reasonably practicable for the counterclaim to be presented within the specified period, it can extend the time limit by such further period as it considers reasonable – Article 8(c)(ii).

It is worth observing that although these time limits appear to be much shorter than those that apply to claims for breach of contract in the civil courts – where the limitation period is six years – they start running from different points in time. In the tribunal, the three-month limit starts running from the effective date of termination, whereas in the courts, the six-year limit starts running from the date of breach. It is thus conceivable that an employee whose employment has been terminated within the previous three months could seek to bring a claim in an employment tribunal in respect of a breach of contract that occurred *more* than six years previously, while he or she was still employed. Although there is no appellate authority on the matter, it appears that this is impermissible and that the six-year time limit that applies in the civil courts also applies to contract claims brought in the employment tribunal under the Order. In Taylor v Central Manchester University Hospitals NHS Foundation Trust ET Case No.2405066/12 the tribunal decided that, in enacting the Order, Parliament intended only to give employees an alternative jurisdiction in which to bring their contract claims, not to extend employees' rights. The Order gives employees the right to bring a contract claim in the tribunal only to the extent that the claim could otherwise have been brought in a civil court. According to the tribunal, this means that any restrictions and limitations on bringing such a claim in the civil court – such as the six-year limit set out in S.5 of the Limitation Act 1980 – should also apply in the tribunal.

43

2.20 *Mediation in cross-border disputes.* Note that Article 8A contains detailed provisions allowing for the time limits on both employees' and employers' contract claims to be extended to allow for mediation to take place in relation to certain cross-border disputes under the EU Directive on certain aspects of mediation in civil and commercial matters (No.2008/52/EC).

2.21 **Limit on payments.** The maximum amount that a tribunal can award in respect of proceedings for breach of contract is £25,000 – Article 10. This is an aggregate upper limit, so that if several claims are made relating to the same contract of employment, the total amount recoverable from the employment tribunal will still be £25,000. Unlike other statutory limits, the limit on contract claims in tribunals is not subject to annual up-rating and has stayed at the same level since 1994. There is, by contrast, no maximum limit on compensation in the High Court or county courts, so where the value of a claim potentially exceeds £25,000, it should be brought in the High Court or county courts rather than the employment tribunal. The employee cannot split the cause of action into two separate causes of action: one for damages up to £25,000 to be pursued in the tribunal, and another for the balance to be pursued in the High Court – Fraser v HLMAD Ltd 2006 ICR 1395, CA (a case discussed under 'Relitigation: res judicata and abuse of process – merger of causes of action' below).

2.22 **Choice of court or tribunal.** Many breach of contract claims fall within the jurisdiction of both the employment tribunals and the civil courts. The Order does not affect the jurisdiction of these courts to hear contractual claims which also fall within the jurisdiction of the employment tribunals – S.3(4) ETA. However, once a court or tribunal makes a determination on an issue, that determination is binding on all other courts and tribunals. Thus, if an employee loses his or her claim in the tribunal, it is not open to him or her to bring a claim on the same facts in the county court or High Court. Equally, if an employee recovers compensation in the tribunal, he or she cannot obtain further compensation in respect of the same claim or issue in the courts. This principle is discussed in full under 'Relitigation: res judicata and abuse of process' below. So the decision as to whether to proceed in the High Court or county court or in an employment tribunal is largely determined by the value of the claim. Employees should refrain from bringing wrongful dismissal claims in the tribunal unless they are certain they do not want to claim more than £25,000. If they do, the claim should be brought by way of proceedings in the High Court – Fraser v HLMAD Ltd (above).

However, other factors may also affect an employee's choice as to where to bring a claim. The employment tribunal is generally quicker and may be cheaper, and the parties are less likely to have to pay costs if unsuccessful. Employees can also have other related complaints, such as unfair dismissal, dealt with at the same time (meaning that the parties will not have to become involved in the complex issue of whether the tribunal proceedings should be stayed pending the outcome of the contractual claim in the civil courts). On the other hand, the applicable time limits may preclude a tribunal claim (see 'Time limits' above); and a claim may only be brought in an employment tribunal if the employment has ended, whereas this restriction does not apply to claims in the civil courts.

Impact of Human Rights Act and EU law   2.23

It is clear from the above that tribunals have jurisdiction to determine a broad range of statutory and contractual claims, subject to any limits to their jurisdiction that may apply (see the remaining sections of this chapter). However, it is important to bear in mind that in certain cases tribunals' powers to *interpret and apply* domestic legislation may be subject to, and in some cases significantly affected by, the influence of international legal considerations; in particular, the European Convention on Human Rights, EU Directives, and general principles of EU law and the rights as set out in the European Charter of Fundamental Rights.

Human rights. The European Convention on Human Rights (ECHR) is 2.24
incorporated into UK law by the Human Rights Act 1998 (HRA). S.3 HRA places a statutory duty on employment tribunals and courts to interpret and give effect to domestic legislation in a way which is compatible with Convention rights, so far as it is possible to do so. This does not allow claimants to enforce their Convention rights directly against their employers; rather, where their Convention rights are engaged in a claim under domestic legislation, S.3 requires tribunals if possible to interpret that legislation, whether it is primary or subordinate, in a way which is compatible with those rights. The Convention rights most commonly invoked in employment cases relate to Article 6, the right to a fair trial; Article 8, the right to respect for private and family life; and Article 11, freedom of assembly and association.

The relationship between domestic and Convention rights was considered by the Court of Appeal in Turner v East Midlands Trains Ltd 2013 ICR 525, CA, where the Court had to decide whether the test for determining the fairness of a dismissal under S.98(4) ERA was compatible with Article 8(1) of the ECHR (right to respect for 'private life', which, according to the European Court of Human Rights (ECtHR) in Niemietz v Germany 1193 16 EHRR 97, ECtHR, can include activities of a professional or business nature). T claimed unfair dismissal, arguing that her dismissal breached her rights under Article 8, and that the S.3 HRA duty required the tribunal to modify the 'range of reasonable responses' test under S.98(4) to do justice to what she considered were the stricter procedural safeguards required by Article 8. However, the tribunal held that Article 8 was not engaged and dismissed her claim. When the case reached the Court of Appeal, T conceded that, by the standards of domestic unfair dismissal law, the tribunal's conclusion that EMT Ltd's investigation was adequate, and thus fair, could not be impugned. However, she submitted that the consequences of her dismissal were such as to engage her rights under Article 8.

45

2.25 Lord Justice Elias, giving the leading judgment in the Court of Appeal, considered that Article 8 was potentially engaged in this case, given the adverse effect of the dismissal on T's reputation. However, he considered that S.98(4) ERA, as interpreted by case law, was compatible with Article 8, as there was no 'material distinction' between the procedural safeguards afforded by the two. Elias LJ – like Lord Justice Mummery LJ in X v Y 2004 ICR 1634, CA – found it difficult to see how a procedure which could be considered objectively fair if adopted by a reasonable employer could nonetheless properly be described as unfair within the meaning of Article 8. Although, where Article 8 interests were engaged, matters bearing on the employee's culpability had to be investigated with a full appreciation of the potentially adverse consequences to the employee, the range of reasonable responses test allowed for a heightened standard to be adopted where those consequences were particularly grave. The test accordingly provided a sufficiently robust, flexible and objective analysis of all aspects of the decision to dismiss to ensure compliance with Article 8. That conclusion, in Elias LJ's view, was reinforced by the fact that in Sanchez v Spain 2011 IRLR 934, ECtHR, the ECtHR recognised that employers generally have a broad discretion in determining the appropriate sanction to impose on an employee. Given the ECtHR's 'light touch' when reviewing human rights in the context of the employment relationship, Elias LJ proffered the view that the domestic test may, indeed, protect human rights even more effectively.

In some cases, however, courts and tribunals may find it necessary to read words into UK legislation in order to apply it in a way that is compatible with the ECHR. In Ghaidan v Godin-Mendoza 2004 2 AC 557, HL, the House of Lords held that whether it is possible to read a statute consistently with Convention rights depends not on the number of words that must be read into the statute by implication, but on whether the amendments would be consistent with the fundamental features of the legislation. If the insertion of one word would contradict the key principles and scope of the legislation, it would not be a permissible amendment, whereas the implication of dozens of words will be permissible if it is consistent with those principles and scope.

2.26 As the House of Lords observed in Ghaidan, the obligation in S.3 HRA to read UK law in a way which is compatible with the ECHR does not allow the courts or tribunals to change the substance of a provision completely. In Benkharbouche v Embassy of the Republic of Sudan and another case 2013 IRLR 918, EAT (discussed under 'State and diplomatic immunity – human rights and fundamental rights' below), for example, the EAT held that, although the absolute immunity conferred on two embassies by the State Immunity Act 1978 (SIA) in respect of the employment of two members of non-diplomatic staff was contrary to their right to a fair trial under Article 6, the SIA could not be interpreted to allow the claims to proceed. Parliament had intended to confer immunity subject to specific exceptions, and to amend some of these exceptions would affect the overall balance struck by the legislature. Changing Parliament's clear list of those to whom immunity applies would cross the line between interpretation and legislation.

However, neither the EAT nor an employment tribunal has the power to make a declaration of incompatibility under S.4 HRA. Thus, if a tribunal indicates that it has been unable to interpret domestic legislation in a way which is compatible with a particular Convention right, the claimant must pursue an appeal to the Court of Appeal or Supreme Court in order to seek such a declaration. It is then up to Parliament to consider whether and how to amend the incompatible legislation.

EU Directives. EU legislation that is 'directly effective' can be enforced by **2.27** individuals in national courts and tribunals. For a particular provision to have direct effect, it must be clear and precise, unconditional and unqualified, and not subject to the need for further implementing measures by Member States. Where the articles of EU Treaties have direct effect, they are 'horizontally' (as well as 'vertically') directly effective, meaning that they may be relied upon against private bodies and individuals, including private sector employers. For example, Article 157 of the Treaty on the Functioning of the European Union (TFEU), which sets out the principle of equal pay for equal work as between men and women, is horizontally directly effective and can be relied on directly in tribunal proceedings where the circumstances of an equal pay claim are not covered by the Equality Act 2010 (EqA).

Directives made under EU Treaties, however, are usually only 'vertically' directly effective, meaning that they can be relied upon by individuals in proceedings against a Member State, or an emanation of the state, but not against another individual or private company – Marshall v Southampton and South West Hampshire Area Health Authority (Teaching) 1986 ICR 335, ECJ. (Note, though, that this general principle is subject to qualification – see 'Fundamental rights and principles' below.) EU Directives do, however, have *indirect* effect on domestic law. This means that the courts and tribunals of Member States should 'as far as possible' interpret domestic legislation in order to give effect to the state's obligations under EU Directives – see Marlcasing SA v La Comercial Internacional de Alimentacion SA 1992 1 CMLR 305, ECJ. Tribunals hearing cases based on legislation that implements EU Directives – such as claims involving transfers of undertakings, working time, discrimination, equal pay or collective redundancies – should therefore be alert to the need to interpret such legislation so as to give effect to the underlying Directive, as interpreted by the European Court of Justice (ECJ).

For example, in Bleuse v MBT Transport Ltd and anor 2008 ICR 488, EAT, **2.28** (discussed in the section 'Territorial rights' below, under 'Territorial reach – EU-derived rights'), the EAT had to consider the territorial scope of the Working Time Regulations 1998 SI 1998/1833 ('the Working Time Regulations'). Mr Justice Elias, then President of the EAT, took the view that, disregarding any

47

questions of rights under European law, there would be no reason to hold that the territorial reach of rights under the Working Time Regulations was any different to that of rights under the ERA, and that the claimant would therefore be unable to bring a claim under the Regulations because of the circumstances of his employment. However, Elias P considered it highly relevant that the Working Time Regulations exist to give effect to the rights contained in the EU Working Time Directive (No.2003/88), and emphasised that domestic courts must, if at all possible, construe the Regulations so as to give effect to those rights in cases where English law is the proper law of the contract, or where English mandatory rules apply under the Rome I Regulation (see 'Territorial rights – applicable law' below). He held that statutory provisions should be construed so as to ensure that directly effective EU rights can be enforced by the English courts. Otherwise, the European principle of effectiveness would not be satisfied in that there would be no effective remedy for a breach of the EU right.

Sometimes the courts will consider it necessary to add words to legislation in an effort to give effect to EU law. In EBR Attridge Law LLP (formerly Attridge Law) v Coleman 2010 ICR 242, EAT, for example, the EAT determined that it was appropriate to insert whole subsections into the Disability Discrimination Act 1995 (DDA) (since repealed and superseded by the EqA) in order to give effect to the ECJ's decision in the same case (Coleman v Attridge Law and anor 2008 ICR 1128, ECJ), which held that the protection against disability discrimination in the EU Equal Treatment Framework Directive (No.2000/78) is not limited to people who themselves have a disability, but may be 'associative'. Relying on Ghaidan v Godin-Mendoza (above) (where the House of Lords accepted that the obligation under S.3 HRA is the same in substance as the obligation of courts and tribunals to 'as far as possible' interpret UK legislation in a way that gives effect to obligations under EU law), the EAT concluded that it would be consistent with the principle that underpinned the DDA – the elimination of discrimination on the ground of disability – to read the relevant statutory provisions so that both disabled and non-disabled people were protected.

2.29 It is clear from the decision in Attridge that it will be rare for a tribunal or court – faced with an ECJ decision which indicates that, on a literal interpretation, UK law does not give full effect to an EU Directive – to find that it is not possible to interpret the domestic legislation consistently with the Directive. This is because the underlying principles of the legislation are bound to include the implementation of the Directive, and the Directive in turn will expound general principles, which its measures are intended to promote.

That said, there are still limits to courts' and tribunals' powers in this regard, as highlighted by the EAT's decision in Ross v Eddie Stobart Ltd EAT 0085/10. In that case, R had claimed, among other things, automatically unfair dismissal for having refused to comply with instructions that he asserted were in breach of the Road Transport (Working Time) Regulations 2005 SI 2005/639. He put his claim on the basis of S.101A ERA, which renders dismissals automatically unfair where the reason for the dismissal relates to rights under the working time legislation. S.101A(2) lists the legislation to which the section applies but does not include the Road Transport Regulations. The EAT expressed its surprise at this omission, but held that no interpretative technique would allow it to add the Regulations to the list, when Parliament had clearly chosen not to do so.

Where the EU law at issue is not clear cut, a tribunal may seek clarification **2.30** from the ECJ by requesting a preliminary ruling under Article 267 TFEU. This power of referral, which is discussed further under 'References to the European Court of Justice' below, is available where the tribunal considers that a ruling is 'necessary' to enable it to give judgment. In Lyttle and ors v Bluebird UK Bidco 2 Ltd (Belfast IT Case No.555/12), for example, an industrial tribunal in Northern Ireland has asked the ECJ for guidance on when an employer's duty to carry out collective redundancies consultation is triggered where employees working in different stores were made redundant. The relevant legislation in Northern Ireland – the Employment Rights (Northern Ireland) Order 1996 SI 1996/1919 – essentially mirrors S.188 TULR(C)A, which restricts the number of redundancy dismissals required to trigger the obligation to consult to those proposed 'at one establishment'. The industrial tribunal has asked the ECJ to clarify the meaning of the term 'establishment' in Article 1(1)(a)(ii) of the EU Collective Redundancies Directive (No.98/59), and whether the obligation to consult arises when the overall number of proposed redundancy dismissals is at least 20 across *all* of an employer's establishments or whether there must be at least 20 at *each* establishment.

Note that a similar question arose in USDAW v Ethel Austin Ltd (in administration) and another case 2013 ICR 1300, EAT. However, in that case, rather than refer the question to the ECJ, the EAT concluded that, by restricting the number of redundancy dismissals required to trigger the obligation to consult to those proposed 'at one establishment', S.188 TULR(C)A was incompatible with the Directive, and that the words 'at one establishment' should therefore be deleted to give effect to the Directive's intention that the obligation to collectively consult arises regardless of whether the employees work at the same or separate establishments. Permission to appeal has been granted in this case, although the appeal may well be stayed pending the outcome of the Belfast Industrial Tribunal's reference to the ECJ in Lyttle.

Fundamental rights and principles. As we discussed under 'EU Directives' **2.31** above, the case of Marshall v Southampton and South West Hampshire Area Health Authority (Teaching) (above) established that EU Directives are usually only 'vertically' directly effective, meaning that they can be relied upon by individuals in proceedings against a Member State, or an emanation of the

49

state, but not against another individual or private company. However, a more recent line of ECJ decisions has held that certain principles, such as the prohibitions on discrimination, do not simply emanate from the relevant EU Directive, but are 'general principles of community law' to which the Directive gives expression – see Mangold v Helm 2006 IRLR 143, ECJ, and X v Mid Sussex Citizens Advice Bureau and anor 2011 ICR 460, CA. Consequently, in Kücükdeveci v Swedex GmbH 2010 IRLR 346, ECJ, the ECJ held that where a provision of national law is incompatible with a general and fundamental principle of EU law, and cannot be interpreted in accordance with that principle, the national court 'must decline to apply that provision' without being compelled to make a reference to the ECJ before doing so. The result of this decision is that general principles of EU law have horizontal direct effect (i.e. they apply in disputes between private individuals).

However, Advocate General Mazák has interjected a note of caution, warning against allowing a general principle of EU law 'a degree of emancipation' such that it can be invoked independently of the implementing legislation – see the Advocate General's opinion in Palacios de la Villa v Cortefiel Servicios SA 2009 ICR 1111, ECJ. In his view, such an approach would compromise legal certainty and call into question the distribution of competence between the EU and Member States. It is easy to imagine conceptual problems involved in applying general principles of EU law outside the specific framework of the relevant Directives. For example, if age discrimination is a fundamental principle of EU law, is it also a fundamental principle that direct age discrimination can be objectively justified? Would a fundamental prohibition on disability discrimination encompass the duty to make reasonable adjustments?

2.32 The language of 'general and fundamental principles' resonates with that of the EU Charter of Fundamental Rights, which contains 54 Articles said to be the 'core values' of the EU, many of which are potentially relevant in an employment context. The Charter was agreed between Member States in 2000 but it was not until the Treaty of Lisbon came into force in December 2009 that it was put on a legal basis. Even then, its potential to affect the decisions of UK employment tribunals was not fully realised until the EAT's decision in Benkharbouche v Embassy of the Republic of Sudan and another case (above). In that case the claimants, B and J, argued that, although the State Immunity Act 1978 (SIA) apparently barred them from asserting their employment rights by conferring absolute immunity upon their employers, it was necessary to read down or disapply the relevant provisions in order to give effect to their rights under Article 47 of the EU Charter, which guarantees the right to an effective remedy and a fair trial. The employment judge hearing B's claim was of the view that the right to an effective remedy and fair trial in Article 47 could not offer a means of enforcing rights above and beyond that provided for in respect of Convention rights by the HRA. In the proceedings brought by J, the employment

50

judge accepted that Article 47 was part of national law and directly effective, but held that it was not for the tribunal to consider what she regarded as a free-standing complaint under EU law.

Both claimants appealed to the EAT, where the cases were conjoined. They argued that, to the extent that the claims engaged their rights under EU law – i.e. claims related to discrimination, harassment and working time – the direct effect of the right to an effective remedy and a fair trial in Article 47 required the EAT to disapply the provisions which conferred immunity on their employers. The EAT noted that previous cases such as Bleuse v MBT Transport Ltd 2008 ICR 488, EAT (see 'EU Directives' above and 'Territorial limitations – territorial reach' below), had held that legislation can only be disapplied where the claim is made against an emanation of the state, which, for the purpose of tribunal proceedings, would be the UK. If that were still the case, the state immunity would continue to apply in the instant cases. However, the EAT noted that the understanding of the principle of effectiveness in EU law had advanced since the adoption of the Lisbon Treaty in 2009, a consequence of which was the declaration by the Supreme Court in Rugby Football Union v Consolidated Information Services Ltd (formerly Viagogo Ltd) 2013 1 CMLR 56, SC, that the Charter now has direct effect in national law, 'binding Member States when they are implementing EU law'. The EAT accepted that the ECJ's decision in Kücükdeveci v Swedex GmbH (above), supported by the more recent decision of the ECJ in Aklagaren v Fransson 2013 2 CMLR 46, ECJ, made it clear that a national court should set aside any provision of national law that conflicts with a Charter right.

Consequently, the EAT concluded that the direct effect of Article 47 of the EU **2.33** Charter required it to disapply the employers' immunity under the SIA, in so far as it applied to B's and J's claims of discrimination, harassment and breach of the Working Time Regulations, because these were matters falling within the material scope of EU law. However, the claims of unfair dismissal and non-payment of wages fell outside the scope of EU law and so remained barred by the provisions of the SIA.

The EAT's conclusion in Benkharbouche as to the legal effect of the EU Charter may seem surprising, given the wording of the 'opt-out' secured by the UK and Polish governments during the negotiations on the Lisbon Treaty. Article 1 of a protocol on the application of the Charter to Poland and to the UK states that the Charter does not extend the ability of the ECJ, or any court or tribunal in Poland or the UK, to find that the laws, regulations or administrative provisions, practices or action of Poland or of the UK are inconsistent with the fundamental rights, freedoms and principles that it reaffirms. The ostensible effect of this protocol is that, while the Charter may guide both domestic courts and the ECJ in their interpretation of EU law, it is unable to override existing domestic law. However, in the immigration case of NS v Secretary of State for the Home

Department and another case 2012 2 CMLR 9, ECJ, the ECJ held that Article 1 'does not intend to exempt the Republic of Poland or the United Kingdom from the obligations to comply with the provisions of the Charter or to prevent a court of one of those Member States from ensuring compliance with those provisions'. In light of this, Mr Justice Mostyn in R (on the application of AB) v Secretary of State for the Home Department 2013 EWHC 3453, HC (Admin), another immigration case, observed: 'The Human Rights Act 1998 incorporated into our domestic law large parts, but by no means all, of the European Convention on Human Rights. Some parts were deliberately missed out by Parliament. The Charter of Fundamental Rights of the European Union contains, I believe, all of those missing parts and a great deal more. Notwithstanding the endeavours of our political representatives at Lisbon [to obtain an 'opt-out'] it would seem that the much wider Charter of Rights is now part of our domestic law. Moreover, that much wider Charter of Rights would remain part of our domestic law even if the Human Rights Act were repealed.' He proceeded to hold that the claimant was entitled to rely on the right to protection of personal data contained in Article 8 of the Charter, which has no equivalent in the Convention.

2.34 Although Mostyn J's observation might seem to imply that the Charter creates free-standing rights in domestic law, there is an important limitation on its application: following the EAT's conclusion in Benkharbouche v Embassy of the Republic of Sudan and another case (above), not to mention the Supreme Court's declaration in Rugby Football Union v Consolidated Information Services Ltd (formerly Viagogo Ltd) (above) cited in that case, it seems clear that the Charter is only of effect when a court or tribunal is acting within the material scope of EU Law.

Given the significance of the issues at stake, the EAT in Benkharbouche granted permission to appeal, and we await the Court of Appeal's judgment with interest. It is pertinent to note in this regard that, in a statement to the House of Commons on the status of the EU Charter in the UK, Chris Grayling, Secretary of State for Justice, announced that: '[Mostyn J's] view was that the [ECJ] had, in the case of [NS v Secretary of State for the Home Department and another case (above)], held that the charter could create new rights that apply in the UK. It is important to be very clear to the House: we do not agree with that analysis of the NS case. We intend to find another case – we cannot do it with this one as the Home Office was successful and we cannot appeal a case we have won – at the earliest opportunity to clarify beyond doubt the legal effects of the charter and to put the record straight' (Hansard (HC), 19 November 2013, col 1087). For further discussion on this issue, see the House of Commons Standard Note on the 'Effects of the EU Charter of Rights in the UK' (SN/IA/6765), dated 26 November 2013.

Territorial limitations

2.35

As the working economy has become generally more globalised, increasing numbers of workers work wholly or partly abroad, are employed by non-UK based employers, or work under an employment contract governed by foreign law. As a consequence, the question of whether a tribunal in England and Wales or Scotland is seised with jurisdiction to hear a particular claim, and how far, territorially speaking, UK statutory employment rights extend, have become increasingly important.

As Mr Justice Langstaff, President of the EAT, emphasised in Simpson v Intralinks Ltd 2012 ICR 1343, EAT, a distinction must be made between three matters:

- the place (forum) where a case is determined

- the applicable law relating to a contract or tort, and

- the territorial scope of a domestic statute.

He went on: 'It is axiomatic that the fact that a UK statute purports to apply 2.36 with worldwide effect does not have the consequence that the parties trying their dispute in a foreign jurisdiction must determine it in accordance with the English statute. Nor, depending upon the wording of the statute itself, does it necessarily follow that if the dispute is to be determined in the UK, it will be determined in accordance with the statute as applicable law, rather than a different system of law which the parties have agreed should be applicable.'

In the following sections we consider first what rules of international jurisdiction apply to determine whether employment tribunals in England and Wales or Scotland are the appropriate forum to hear claims under employment contracts that have an international dimension ('International jurisdiction'). Secondly, we look at the rules that determine which country's domestic law is the applicable law to resolve a dispute with an international dimension ('Applicable law'). Finally, we discuss the territorial scope of various UK statutory employment rights ('Territorial reach').

International jurisdiction
2.37

Employment tribunals are entitled to exercise their jurisdiction only over those who are defined as being within certain territorial boundaries. Broadly speaking, the rules determining whether a state's courts and tribunals have jurisdictional capability to hear a claim – i.e. are the correct forum – differ depending on whether the defendant (or respondent) is domiciled in Europe. Where a defendant is domiciled in the European Union, European legislation applies to determine issues of jurisdiction (see 'Brussels I Regulation' below). If European

53

legislation does not apply, the position is determined according to traditional rules of international law (see 'Traditional rules' below).

Where, under international law, an employment claim is capable of being heard by courts or tribunals within the UK, it is then necessary to determine whether, under the Tribunal Rules, the claim should be presented to an employment tribunal in England and Wales, or to an employment tribunal in Scotland (see 'Jurisdiction of employment tribunals in England and Wales and in Scotland' below).

2.38 **Brussels I Regulation.** Where the defendant (or respondent) to a claim is domiciled in any EU Member State (except Denmark), the Brussels Regulation on jurisdiction and the recognition and enforcement of judgments in civil and commercial matters (Council Regulation No.44/2001) applies to determine where the claim may be heard, i.e. the forum. However, it does not determine what law is applicable. As Mr Justice Elias, then President of the EAT, put it in Bleuse v MBT Transport Ltd 2008 ICR 488, EAT, 'the Brussels Regulation is concerned with which courts should hear a claim; it does not affect the content of the substantive law applicable to the claim itself'. (Note that although the Brussels Regulation is not directly applicable to Denmark, it has effectively been extended to Denmark by a separate agreement between the EU and Denmark that took effect on 1 July 2007.)

The Brussels Regulation, known as the 'Brussels I Regulation' (Brussels II covers family law), is given force of law in the UK by the Civil Jurisdiction and Judgments Act 1982. Its underlying principle is that persons domiciled in a Member State are to be sued in the courts of that Member State, regardless of their nationality – Article 2. However, under Article 3, this rule may be displaced by special rules relating to specific types of contract, and special rules relating to individual contracts of employment are set out in Articles 18–21. The purpose of these rules is to ensure that the employee, who is generally considered to be the weaker party and thus needing a greater degree of protection, has the option of bringing proceedings in his or her own forum. Where a dispute arises over a contract of employment, jurisdiction is determined by Articles 18–21 alone, together with Articles 4 and 5(5) – GlaxoSmithKline and anor v Rouard 2008 ICR 1375, ECJ.

2.39 The effect of Articles 18–21 is that where an employer is domiciled in a Member State, the employee may sue it either:

- in the courts of the Member State where the employer is domiciled – Article 19(1)

- in the courts of the place where the employee habitually works or worked – Article 19(2)(a)

- if the employee does not or did not habitually carry out his or her work in any one country, in the courts of the place where the business which engaged the employee is or was situated – Article 19(2)(b), or

- if the dispute arises out of the operation of a branch, agency or other establishment of the employer, in the place where that branch, agency or other establishment is located – Articles 5(5) and 18(1). An employer who is not domiciled in a Member State but has a branch, agency or other establishment in one of the Member States, is deemed to be domiciled in that Member State in disputes arising out of the operations of that branch, agency or establishment – Article 18(2).

However, an *employer* may only bring proceedings against an employee in the **2.40** courts of the place where the employee is domiciled, with the proviso that counterclaims may be brought in the court in which the original claim is pending – Article 20. So if the employer wishes to bring an employer's contract claim, it may do so in whichever court the employee has lodged the initial proceedings, even if that is not the place where the employee is domiciled – Article 20(2). Employers' counterclaims are discussed in Chapter 6, 'Defending a claim', under 'Employers' contract claim'.

Where an employer is not domiciled in a Member State, the Brussels I Regulation does not apply and the UK's jurisdiction to hear a claim against such an employer is determined by ordinary principles of private international law – Article 4(1) (see 'Traditional rules' below); see also Powell v OMV Exploration and Production Ltd EAT 0131/13. Where the defendant is domiciled in Iceland, Norway or Switzerland, the 2001 Lugano Convention applies, which is similar to the Brussels I Regulation.

Domicile. Article 60(1) provides that a company is domiciled at the place where **2.41** it has its:

- statutory seat (see below)

- central administration, or

- principal place of business.

Thus, if the employer is registered as a UK company, an employee may bring a claim against it in the UK even if the employment is otherwise wholly based overseas. (This provision should not be confused with the effect of Article 18(2), which provides that where an employer is *not* domiciled in a Member State but has a branch, agency or other establishment in one of the Member States, it is deemed to be domiciled in that Member State in disputes arising out of the operations of that branch, agency or establishment.)

A company may be domiciled in up to three different places at once. If, for **2.42** example, an employer has its statutory seat in one Member State and its principal place of business in another, an employee has a choice as to where to bring a claim.

Note that the principal place of business may change over time. In Ministry of Defence and Support of the Armed Forces for the Islamic Republic of Iran v Faz Aviation Ltd (formerly known as FN Aviation Ltd) and anor 2007 EWHC 1042 (Comm), QBD, the defendant, FA Ltd, was a company incorporated in Cyprus. MODSAF argued that FA Ltd's place of central administration or principal place of business was in England, and that it could therefore be sued in England, but the High Court held that it had ceased to have any real business to administer or operate some time before proceedings commenced. Concluding that it had no jurisdiction to hear the claim, the High Court observed that a company could cease to have any principal place of business, or that place could change as the business of the company changed.

2.43 The 'statutory seat' of a company or legal person or association of legal persons is:

- its registered office

- if there is no registered office, its place of incorporation, or

- if there is no place of incorporation, the place under the law of which it was formed – Article 60(2).

The EAT considered the question of domicile in Powell v OMV Exploration and Production Ltd EAT 0131/13. P worked primarily in Dubai under a contract with OMV, which was registered in the Isle of Man (not an EU Member State). The contract provided that the Manx courts would have sole jurisdiction and that Manx law would apply. OMV had no place of business in the UK, and its administration was based in Austria. The EAT upheld an employment tribunal's finding that OMV was domiciled in Austria, where it had its central administration and place of business. Accordingly, under the Brussels I Regulation it had to be sued in Austria.

2.44 *Habitually worked.* Where an employee worked in a number of different countries, the place where he or she habitually worked means the place where he or she performed the essential part of his or her duties vis-à-vis the employer, which is in principle the place where he or she worked the longest on the employer's business over the course of the employment – Weber v Universal Ogden Services 2002 ICR 979, ECJ (a case decided in relation to Article 5(1) of the Brussels Convention on Jurisdiction and the Enforcement of Judgments in Civil and Commercial Matters 1968, which preceded the Brussels I Regulation). In Powell v OMV Exploration and Production Ltd (above) the EAT held that in considering the scope of the word 'habitually' in this context, it is appropriate to rely on case law based on Article 6(2)(a) of the Rome Convention, which is, according to the EAT, 'in terms which are so similar linguistically as almost to be indistinguishable from the provisions in the Brussels I Regulation'. Following Koelzsch v Grand Duchy of Luxembourg 2012 ICR 112, ECJ, which concerned the habitual place of work of a heavy goods vehicle driver for the purpose of establishing the applicable law of the contract under the Rome Convention, the EAT concluded that an employee cannot 'habitually work' in more than one country, and if he or she carries out activities in more than one, his or her habitual place of work is, per Koelzsch, that in which or from which, in the light of all the factors which characterise that activity, the employee performs the greater part of his or her obligations towards his or her employer (see further 'Applicable law' below.)

Branch, agency or other establishment. Note that an embassy will be regarded **2.45** as a 'branch' or other 'establishment' of the state – Mahamdia v People's Democratic Republic of Algeria 2013 ICR 1, ECJ. In that case, the ECJ held that an embassy of a foreign state was a 'branch, agency or establishment' of that state, and therefore the People's Democratic Republic of Algeria could be treated as domiciled in Germany for the purposes of a claim by an employee of the Algerian embassy in Berlin.

Exclusive jurisdiction agreements. Generally speaking, parties to a contract **2.46** may 'contract out' of the provisions of the Brussels I Regulation by conferring jurisdiction on a particular state or states, in accordance with the terms of Article 23 (which provides that such jurisdiction, once conferred, is exclusive unless the parties specify otherwise). However, the special provisions on employment contracts (Articles 18–21) may only be excluded in extremely limited circumstances. Article 21 provides that an 'agreement on jurisdiction' in an employment dispute will only be valid if it is either:

- entered into after the dispute has arisen, or
- allows the employee to bring proceedings in courts other than those indicated in Articles 18–21 (i.e. it is not an exclusive jurisdiction clause but expands the range of options open to the employee).

This renders exclusive jurisdiction clauses fairly useless in an employment context where the Brussels I Regulation applies, although they continue to be incorporated into many service agreements. In Mahamdia v People's Democratic Republic of Algeria (above) the ECJ held that a clause in an employment contract which purported to confer exclusive jurisdiction on the Algerian courts did not comply with Article 21 and thus could not be relied upon by the employer. And in Simpson v Intralinks Ltd 2012 ICR 1343, EAT, the EAT held that an exclusive jurisdiction clause in favour of the German courts was invalid because it was included in an employment contract that was entered into before the dispute between S and her employer arose. The EAT concluded that the jurisdiction clause was no bar to S bringing her claims in an employment tribunal in the UK, even though Germany was the place in which she habitually carried out her work. As Article 19 clearly provides that an employer may be sued either in the Member State in which it is based or in that in which the employee carries or carried out his or her work, it was S's choice where to bring her claim and it was not up to the courts to state a preference about the appropriate forum.

2.47 Traditional rules. As Article 4(1) of the Brussels I Regulation indicates, where the employer is not domiciled in a Member State (and the dispute does not arise out of the operations of a branch, agency or other establishment in one of the Member States for the purpose of Article 18(2)), then the Brussels I Regulation does not apply, and the question of whether the UK courts or tribunals have jurisdiction to hear the claim is determined according to ordinary principles of private international law. A detailed examination of private international law is beyond the scope of this Handbook but, broadly speaking, an employer will fall within the jurisdiction of the courts of England and Wales if the proceedings are served on it while it is physically within the jurisdiction or if it is served outside the jurisdiction with the permission of the court. However, proceedings may nevertheless be stayed, or jurisdiction declined, if, for example, there is another more appropriate forum, or there is a valid jurisdiction or arbitration clause in existence. Alternatively, an employer not domiciled in an EU Member State may be sued in England and Wales if it submits to the jurisdiction (by, for example, submitting a response).

In Wright v Deccan Chargers Sporting Ventures Ltd and anor 2011 EWHC 1307, QBD, the High Court held that a contractual claim against an employer based in India could proceed in England as the most appropriate forum in which to bring the claim. The employment agreement at the centre of the dispute had been governed by English law. While this choice of law was significant, it was by no means determinative. The conclusion that England was the most appropriate forum was based on a number of factors, including that the employer had agreed that the claimant would be based in London and that an office would be set up there to support his work; and that the legal issues in the case were complex, requiring a high level of expertise in English law.

2.48 Jurisdiction of employment tribunals in England and Wales and in Scotland. The jurisdiction of tribunals in England and Wales to determine a claim presented to them is limited by rule 8(2) of the Tribunal Rules to cases where:

- the respondent, or one of the respondents, 'resides or carries on business' in England and Wales – rule 8(2)(a)

- one or more of the acts or omissions complained of took place in England and Wales – rule 8(2)(b)

- the claim relates to a contract under which the work is or has been performed partly in England and Wales – rule 8(2)(c) or

- the tribunal has jurisdiction to determine the claim by virtue of a connection with Great Britain, which is at least partly a connection with England and Wales – rule 8(2)(d).

Corresponding provisions exist in respect of territorial jurisdiction over cases brought in Scotland – rule 8(3).

The purpose of rule 8 is to indicate whether tribunals in the UK have jurisdiction **2.49** to hear particular proceedings, and whether these should be dealt with in England and Wales or in Scotland. This is a different issue to that of the territorial scope of an employment right (see 'Territorial reach' below), and a tribunal which confuses them will be in error. In D Curran and Sons Ltd v Beswinski EAT 0476/09 the EAT heard an appeal by a transport company based in Northern Ireland against an English employment tribunal's decision that it had jurisdiction to hear various claims brought by an employee lorry driver. The tribunal had found that the driver worked almost exclusively in England, where he also lived. The EAT allowed the appeal, as the tribunal had failed to express sufficient reasons for its decision, simply saying that in concluding it had jurisdiction under Reg 19 of the Employment Tribunal (Constitution and Rules of Procedure) Regulations 2004 SI 2004/1861 (the Tribunal Regulations 2004) (the precursor to rule 8) it had had regard to Lawson v Serco Ltd and two other cases 2006 ICR 250, HL; Bleuse v MBT Transport Ltd and anor 2008 ICR 488, EAT, and Todd v British Midland Airways 1978 ICR 959, CA. These cases (all considered under 'Territorial reach' below) were concerned not with the question of where the employer did business, but with where the employee worked or was based for the purpose of considering the territorial reach of particular statutory claims – a 'closely analogous, but not identical, issue'.

Interestingly, the EAT has been prepared to hold that in a case where an employee enjoys certain UK statutory employment rights (as a result of the application of the rules on territorial reach – see 'Territorial reach' below), the Tribunal Rules must be broadly interpreted in order to allow him or her to enforce those rights in England and Wales, even if, on a straightforward reading of the Rules, the tribunal could not hear the claim. In Pervez v Macquarie Bank Ltd (London Branch) and anor 2011 ICR 266, EAT, P worked and lived in Hong Kong and his contract of employment was expressly governed by Hong Kong law. In September 2008 he was seconded to London to work for an associated company of his employer. In September 2009 he was dismissed and brought unfair dismissal and discrimination claims in an English employment tribunal. The tribunal found that P enjoyed the right not to be unfairly dismissed under the ERA – applying the 'substantial connection with Great Britain' test set out by the House of Lords in Lawson v Serco Ltd and other cases (above) (see 'Territorial reach' below). It also found that he had the right not to be discriminated against under the Race Relations Act 1976 and the Employment

Equality (Religion or Belief) Regulations 2003 SI 2003/1660 (both now repealed and incorporated into the EqA), which expressly applied to persons employed 'at an establishment in Great Britain'. P therefore came within the grasp of the legislation upon which his claims were based. Nevertheless, it went on to hold that it had no jurisdiction to hear any claims against P's employer because it was not 'carrying on business in England' for the purpose of Reg 19(1)(a) of the Tribunal Regulations 2004 (the precursor to rule 8 of the Tribunal Rules 2013). The EAT overturned this decision, although it had to adopt a 'strained' construction of Reg 19(1)(a) in order to do so. In the view of Mr Justice Underhill, then President of the EAT, Parliament could not have intended to confer rights on individuals and then deprive them of a forum in which those rights could be enforced. As a result, it was necessary to adopt a broad interpretation and hold that the secondment amounted to the carrying on of business for the purpose of the Tribunal Regulations 2004.

2.50 Such a strained interpretation would be unnecessary under rule 8 of the 2013 Rules – which Lord Justice Underhill was responsible for drafting – since the situation would clearly fall under both rule 8(2)(b) and rule 8(2)(c). However, the reference in rule 8(2)(d) to the tribunal having jurisdiction to determine the claim 'by virtue of a connection with Great Britain' seems to be referring to the test for territorial reach of rights under the ERA and other UK employment legislation (discussed under 'Territorial reach – unfair dismissal and other ERA rights' below). This implies that where a tribunal in England and Wales lacks jurisdiction under any of the other heads of rule 8(2), but the rights on which the claimant depends apply to him or her by virtue of a 'sufficiently strong connection with Great Britain', the tribunal will nonetheless have jurisdiction to hear the claims so long as that connection is, at least partly, a connection with England and Wales – rule 8(2)(d).

While the above argument seems somewhat circular, it achieves the same aim as Pervez – that of avoiding a situation where rights are conferred on individuals who are then deprived of a forum in which those rights can be enforced. However, it is certainly arguable that another division of the EAT might have taken a different approach. In Simpson v Intralinks Ltd 2012 ICR 1343, EAT, Mr Justice Langstaff (President of the EAT) expressed a preference for keeping apart the three issues of jurisdiction, applicable law and territorial reach, taking the view that while the claimant in that case was covered by the territorial reach of the Equal Pay Act 1970 and the Sex Discrimination Act 1975 (both now repealed and incorporated into the EqA), 'the scope of UK legislative provision cannot, in my view, dictate whether the Brussels Regulation is applicable or not'.

2.51 Note that old Reg 19(1)(b)–(d) of the Tribunal Regulations 2004 (and the equivalent provisions relating to jurisdiction in Scotland) were not carried forward into the Tribunal Rules 2013. These provided, among other things, that a tribunal had jurisdiction where, had the remedy been by way of action in the county court, the cause of action would have arisen wholly or partly in England, Wales or Scotland. They were presumably not deemed to be necessary in light of the redrafted criteria outlined above.

'Residence' and 'carrying on business'. A company 'resides' in England and **2.52** Wales (or Scotland) if it is incorporated in England and Wales (or Scotland) or if its central management and control are exercised there. A company will therefore be taken to 'reside' in England or Wales (or Scotland) if its registered office is within the territorial limits – Odeco (UK) Inc v Peacham 1979 ICR 823, EAT. This gives the company sufficient presence within the jurisdiction to be able to receive service of the claim form.

A company incorporated outside Great Britain but which establishes a place of business here is required by S.691 of the Companies Act 1985 to register with the registrar of companies. This involves, among other things, making a return showing the name and address of at least one person resident in Great Britain who is authorised to accept service of process and notices on behalf of the company. Where a company was incorporated in the US, but two of its directors, who held a majority shareholding in the company, lived in England, its central management and control were sufficiently exercised in the UK to amount to 'residence' – Jackson v Ghost Ltd and anor 2003 IRLR 824, EAT.

The question of whether a company 'carries on business' within the territorial jurisdiction is one of fact for tribunals to decide. This usually causes little difficulty in practice.

Acts or omissions complained of took place in England or Wales (or Scotland). **2.53** In most cases, the place in which an act or omission to act 'took place' will be uncontroversial, but in some the position may be slightly less clear. For example, in an unfair dismissal case, the act of which an employee complains is that he or she has been dismissed. So, if the act of dismissal takes place within England or Wales, a tribunal has territorial jurisdiction even where the respondent company has no registered office here because it has failed to comply with the registration requirements of the Companies Act – see, for example, Knulty and anor v Eloc Electro-Optiek and Communicatie BV 1979 ICR 827, ET.

However, where an employee is dismissed by a company that does not reside or carry on business in Great Britain and the letter of dismissal is sent to the employee from abroad, the 'act' may be deemed to have taken place outside the territorial limits – see, for example, Tweddell v Irish Shipping Ltd ET Case No.33517/78.

Performed partly in England and Wales (or Scotland). Note that the contract **2.54** only needs to be performed 'partly' in England and Wales (or Scotland). Under the Tribunal Regulations 2004, Reg 19(2)(b) applied a test of 'place of execution or performance' in relation to Scotland (although a different test was applicable to England and Wales). This wording was considered by the Court of Session in Prescription Pricing Authority v Ferguson 2005 IRLR 464, Ct Sess (Inner House). F was employed as a medical director. His contract of employment, which provided that his 'normal place of work was at Bridge House, Newcastle', had been executed in England. Although he commuted to and from his family home in Edinburgh every weekend, the only work he did in Scotland was the occasional lecture or conference speech. The Court of Session held that the occasional performance of contractual duties in Scotland was not sufficient to confer jurisdiction. The wording of the regulation indicated that the place of performance of the contract should be wholly, or at least substantially, in Scotland. This was clearly not the position in F's case. It is probable, however, that the Court might have reached a different conclusion under rule 8(3)(c) of the Tribunal Rules 2013, which mirrors rule 8(2)(c) and requires the claim to relate to a contract 'under which the work is or has been performed partly in Scotland'. Even occasional performance of contractual duties may well satisfy this test. The sticking point in such cases is likely to be whether or not occasional work carried out in the jurisdiction is truly 'contractual' in nature.

2.55 *Transfer of proceedings.* For details of the circumstances in which proceedings commenced in one territory may be transferred to the other under Reg 99, see Chapter 11, 'Case management', under 'Miscellaneous matters – transfer of proceedings'.

2.56 Applicable law

The question of which country's domestic law is the applicable law to resolve an employment dispute is governed by international conventions. Within the EU, the basic rule, set out in Articles 3(1) and 8(1) of the EU Regulation on the law applicable to contractual obligations (No.593/2008) – known as the 'Rome I Regulation' – is that an employment contract is governed by the law chosen by the parties. This choice may be made expressly, in a 'choice of law' clause, or be 'clearly demonstrated by the terms of the contract or the circumstances of the case' – Article 3(1). The Regulation, which covers all EU Member States except Denmark, applies to contracts concluded on or after 17 December 2009. (The 1980 Rome Convention applies to contracts concluded before that date – see 'Position in respect of contracts concluded before 17 December 2009' below.)

Where the parties have not made a choice, Article 8(2)–(4) applies to determine the applicable law of the contract. This provides that the contract shall be governed by the law of the country:

• in which, or from which, the employee habitually carries out his or her work in performance of the contract (even if he or she is temporarily employed in another country) – Article 8(2)

- in which the place of business through which he or she was engaged is situated (assuming the applicable law cannot be determined in accordance with Article 8(2)) – Article 8(3), or

- with which the contract is 'more closely connected' than either of the countries identified under Article 8(2) or (3) above, if such a closer connection appears from the circumstances as a whole – Article 8(4).

The recitals to the Rome I Regulation give some assistance as to what is meant **2.57** by 'temporarily employed' in Article 8(2). Recital 36 states that work carried out in another country should be regarded as temporary 'if the employee is expected to resume working in the country of origin after carrying out his tasks abroad. The conclusion of a new contract of employment with the original employer or an employer belonging to the same group of companies as the original employer should not preclude the employee from being regarded as carrying out his work in another country temporarily.'

Even if the parties have agreed a choice of law, Article 8(1) provides that the employee may not be deprived of the protection of provisions that cannot be derogated from by agreement under the law that would have been applicable under Article 8(2)–(4) in the absence of a choice of law. In the UK, 'provisions that cannot be derogated from by agreement' would constitute most statutory employment rights, apart from, for example, the right not to work in excess of a 48-hour week under Reg 4(1) of the Working Time Regulations 1998 SI 1998/1833. In other words, if an employment contract states that French law is to apply to it, but the employee habitually carries out his or her work in England, he or she will be able to rely on non-derogable rights of English law, such as unfair dismissal, in addition to rights under French law.

Position in respect of contracts concluded before 17 December 2009. The **2.58** 1980 Rome Convention on the Law Applicable to Contractual Obligations, implemented into UK law by the Contracts (Applicable Law) Act 1990, applies to contracts concluded before 17 December 2009. Its provisions are substantially the same as those of the Rome I Regulation. Under the Rome Convention, Article 3 sets out the basic rule that an employment contract is governed by the law chosen by the parties. Where the parties have not made a choice, the contract is governed by the law of the country with which it is 'most closely connected' – Article 4. In an employment context, the country with which the contract is most closely connected is:

- the country where the employee habitually carries out his or her work in performance of the contract (even if he or she is temporarily employed in another country) – Article 6(2)(a)

- if the employee does not habitually carry out his or her work in one country, the country in which the place of business through which he or she was engaged is situated – Article 6(2)(b), or

- another country, if it appears from the circumstances as a whole that the contract is more closely connected with it than either of the two above – Article 6(2).

Even if the parties have agreed a choice of law, Article 6(2) provides that their choice cannot deprive the employee of the protection afforded by the 'mandatory rules' of the country in which the employee 'habitually carries out his work', unless the contract is more closely connected with another country. Article 3(3) explains that mandatory rules are those laws of a country which 'cannot be derogated from by contract'.

2.59 **'Habitually works'.** If an employee works peripatetically, there may be difficulty in establishing in which country he or she 'habitually works' – if indeed he or she habitually works anywhere. This issue arose in Koelzsch v Grand Duchy of Luxembourg, 2012 ICR 112, ECJ, a case to which the Rome Convention applied. K, who was based in Germany, was employed as a lorry driver to transport flowers and plants from Denmark to other European countries, in particular Germany. He was also a works council representative. His employer, G, was a Luxembourg subsidiary of a Danish company. G's lorries were registered in Luxembourg and its drivers, including K, were covered by Luxembourg's social security law. K's employment contract, which had been signed in Luxembourg, contained a choice of law clause in favour of Luxembourg and conferred exclusive jurisdiction on the Luxembourg courts. K was dismissed but the German courts declined jurisdiction to hear his claim, and the Luxembourg courts, while they accepted jurisdiction, declined to apply a German law which protected works council representatives from dismissal. K subsequently brought a claim against the state of Luxembourg on the basis that, in finding Luxembourg law to be the applicable law of the contract, its courts had breached the Rome Convention. The Luxembourg Court of Appeal was unsure whether an employee who works in several countries but returns systematically to a particular one (in this case Germany) must be regarded as habitually carrying out his or her work in that country under Article 6(2)(a), with the result that its mandatory rules would apply. The Court therefore referred the issue to the ECJ for a preliminary ruling.

The ECJ noted that the Rome Convention's explanatory report made it clear that Article 6 was intended to provide 'more adequate protection' for employees, as they are regarded as the weaker party from a socio-economic perspective. It followed that Article 6 must be understood as guaranteeing the applicability of the law of the country in which the employee carries out his or her working activities – rather than that of the country in which the employer is established – since it is there that the employee performs his or her economic and social duties, and it is the business and political environment there that affects his or her employment activities. This meant that the employment protection rules of that country must, so far as possible, be guaranteed.

64

Therefore, in the ECJ's view, the phrase 'the country in which the employee **2.60** habitually carries out his work' under Article 6(2)(a) (now Article 8(2) of the Rome I Regulation) must be given a broad interpretation. The mandatory rules of the country in which the place of business is situated ought only to apply, under Article 6(2)(b) (or Article 8(3) of the Rome I Regulation), where it is not possible to determine the country in which the work is habitually carried out. With this in mind, the Court considered that Article 6(2)(a) could apply in a situation, such as the one in this case, where the employee carries out his or her activities in more than one country, provided it is possible to determine the country with which the work has a significant connection.

The European Court was fortified in this analysis by ECJ decisions on the 1968 Brussels Convention, which preceded the Brussels I Regulation (discussed under 'International jurisdiction – Brussels I Regulation' above). These held that, for the purpose of determining jurisdiction, where work is carried out in more than one country, the 'country in which the work is habitually carried out' must be given a broad interpretation and be understood as referring to the place in which, or from which, the employee carries out his or her working activities (or, in the absence of a centre of activities, to the place where he or she carries out the majority of those activities). Such cases also held that it is necessary to take due account of the need to guarantee the employee's adequate protection. In other words, where an employee carries out his or her activities in more than one country, the country in which he or she habitually works is that in which, or from which, the employee performs the greater part of his or her obligations, having regard to all the factors that characterise those activities. In this particular instance, the referring court would need to determine the country or countries in which K's work tools were situated and from which K carried out his transport tasks, received instructions and organised his work. The court would also need to determine where the transport activities were principally carried out, where the goods were unloaded, and the country to which K returned after his tasks were completed.

Thus it is possible for peripatetic employees who work in several countries to **2.61** habitually work in one of those countries and therefore be protected by that country's non-derogable employment laws. The ECJ stated that its conclusion was consistent with the Rome I Regulation. Furthermore, the wording of Article 8(2) of the Rome I Regulation makes it clear that even if an employee does not habitually carry out his or her work *in* one country, the law of the country *from which* he or she works will be applicable. So, for example, in the case of an airline pilot who is based in Great Britain, the UK's mandatory employment laws are likely to apply despite any contrary 'choice of law'.

It is generally considered more favourable to employees if they can rely upon the law of the country in which they habitually work or are based – hence the broad interpretation given to Article 6(2)(a) of the Rome Convention by the

ECJ in Koelzsch. The ECJ did not specifically address what would happen if, in fact, the employment law of the country in which the place of business is situated is more favourable to the employee. However, the wording of Article 8(3) indicates that the place in which the business which engaged the employee is situated only becomes relevant if Article 8(2) cannot determine the applicable law (in other words, where there is no habitual place of work) – see also Voogsgeerd v Navimer SA C-384/10. Given the broad interpretation given to Article 8(2) by the ECJ, there are likely to be few cases where Article 8(3) will apply instead.

2.62 **Country of closer connection.** However, even if there is a habitual place of work (or there is not and Article 8(3) ostensibly applies), the law of another country may nonetheless apply if the contract is 'more closely connected' with that country – Article 8(4). This may work to the employee's advantage, but not necessarily. In Schlecker (t/a Firma Anton Schlecker) v Boedeker 2013 ICR 1274, ECJ, the ECJ considered the equivalent provision in Article 6 of the Rome Convention. B worked for S, a German company, in the Netherlands. Her employment contract did not specify a choice of law. When B's position ceased to exist, she brought proceedings against S in the Netherlands, where the laws were more favourable to her. The lower courts held that her employment contract was governed by Dutch law under Article 6(2)(a) of the Rome Convention, because she had habitually worked in the Netherlands, and S appealed to the Dutch Supreme Court, arguing that the contract had a closer association with Germany. The Supreme Court referred the case to the ECJ for a preliminary ruling, having found that although S had habitually worked without interruption for a long period in the Netherlands, all the other relevant 'connecting factors' suggested a closer connection with Germany: S was a German company; B was paid in German marks (prior to the introduction of the euro); B's pension was arranged with a German provider; B lived in Germany and paid German social security contributions; the employment contract referred to the mandatory provisions of German law; and S reimbursed B's travel costs from Germany to the Netherlands.

The ECJ held that even where an employee habitually and for a long and unbroken period had carried out his or her work in one country – and even if the law of that country were favourable to the employee – a national court might still find that the laws of another country are the applicable law if, looking at all the circumstances of the employment relationship, it is more closely associated with that other country. Although Article 6 was intended to protect employees, this did not automatically mean that the law of the country most favourable to the employee should be applied. It is for a national court to determine which factor or factors are most significant in determining the country to which the contract is most closely connected, but particular account should be taken of the country in which the employee pays taxes on the income from employment, and the country in which he or she is covered by a social security scheme and pension, sickness insurance and invalidity schemes. If a contract is more closely connected with a state other than that in which the work is habitually carried out, the law of the state where the work is carried out must be disregarded in favour of the law of that other state.

Overriding mandatory provisions of the law of the forum. The applicable 2.63 law governing an employment contract is a separate issue to that of forum – i.e. the country in which a dispute arising under the applicable law may be adjudicated – and the two should not be confused. However, where the applicable law of a contract is the law of one country, and the appropriate forum for adjudicating a claim under that contract is another, 'nothing in [the Rome I] Regulation shall restrict the application of the overriding mandatory provisions of the law of the forum' – Article 9(2). In other words, an employment tribunal hearing a case to which the law of another country applies should apply any 'overriding mandatory provisions' of UK law *in addition to* the foreign law that is generally applicable. The EAT made this clear in Simpson v Intralinks Ltd 2012 ICR 1343, EAT, a case under the Rome Convention. S lived and predominantly worked in Germany, though I Ltd was registered in the UK. Her contract provided that any disputes would be governed and construed exclusively in accordance with German law, and that the place of jurisdiction was Frankfurt. S brought claims in an employment tribunal in the UK, relying on the Sex Discrimination Act 1975 (SDA) and Equal Pay Act 1970 (EqPA) (both now repealed and superseded by the EqA). An employment judge decided that the employment tribunal did not have jurisdiction to hear S's claims as the parties had chosen German law as the proper law of the contract and, as S also habitually worked in Germany, there were no additional mandatory rules to apply within the meaning of Article 6(2)(a) of the Rome Convention. By virtue of the jurisdiction clause, and the fact that S was based in and worked in Frankfurt, he concluded that the Frankfurt courts or tribunals had exclusive jurisdiction.

The EAT disagreed. Article 19 of the Brussels I Regulation (to which the employment judge had not been referred) permitted the claims to be brought in the UK, as this was where I Ltd was domiciled; and the jurisdiction agreement had no effect as it did not comply with Article 21 (see 'International jurisdiction – Brussels I Regulation' above). The employment judge was correct to decide that the applicable law of the contract was German law, applying Article 6(2) of the Rome Convention. However, given that the forum was the UK, and that it had to apply the law of another Member State, the tribunal had to take into account the effect of Article 7(2) of the Rome Convention (the precursor to Article 9(2) of the Rome I Regulation). This provided that 'nothing in the Convention shall restrict the application of the rules of the law of the forum in a situation where they are mandatory irrespective of the law otherwise applicable to the contract'.

67

2.64 The EAT considered that the tribunal applying German law had to ask whether, under the mandatory rules of UK law, it should give effect to those mandatory rules ('mandatory rules' in this context meaning rules that must be applied whatever the law applicable to the contract). In the EAT's view, the provisions of the EqPA and the SDA were mandatory provisions by definition, because the law provided that they could not be derogated from by agreement. Thus, notwithstanding that the applicable law was generally German, the employment tribunal could also apply the SDA and EqPA (and was not precluded from doing so by considerations of territorial reach – see 'Territorial reach' below). In remitting the case to the tribunal, the EAT observed that the claims might not be easy to determine in some respects. In particular, whether there was a contract of employment within the meaning of the SDA and EqPA might depend on German law, rather than English common law.

Mr Justice Langstaff (President of the EAT), who gave the EAT's judgment in this case, acknowledged that it might seem 'counterintuitive' that an employee should be able to bring an employment claim in the UK even though the law governing the employment relationship is foreign. However, in his view, this was a consequence 'tending to justice' of the policy of seeking to protect employees, who are generally in a weaker position than employers when negotiating their contracts of employment, by widening their choice of where to litigate.

2.65 Note that there was potential for some confusion under the Rome Convention (which still applies to contracts concluded before 17 December 2009) between the 'mandatory rules' referred to in Article 6, which means the mandatory rules of the law that would have been applicable under Article 6(2) had the parties not made a choice of law agreement, and the 'mandatory rules' referred to in Article 7, which are relevant not only to individual employment contracts but generally, and apply where the situation has a close connection with a country other than the country whose law applies to the contract. This confusion has been substantially ironed out in the Rome I Regulation. Article 8 (which is equivalent to Article 6 of the Convention) does not use the term 'mandatory rules' at all, instead adopting the phrase 'provisions that cannot be derogated from by agreement'. Article 9 (which is equivalent to Article 7 of the Convention) refers to 'overriding mandatory provisions', defined as those which it is crucial to respect in order to safeguard a country's public interests 'to such an extent that they are applicable to any situation falling within their scope' irrespective of the applicable law of the contract. Recital 37 clarifies that the concept of 'overriding mandatory provisions' should be distinguished from the expression 'provisions which cannot be derogated from by agreement' and should be construed more restrictively.

2.66 **Territorial reach**
UK legislation is, as the House of Lords put it in Lawson v Serco Ltd and two other cases 2006 ICR 250, HL, 'prima facie territorial. The United Kingdom

rarely purports to legislate for the whole world.' This means that territorial boundaries apply to employment rights: if an employee, or his or her employment, falls outside those boundaries, he or she will be unable to enforce them. Hence, we tend to speak in terms of the jurisdictional limitations on employment tribunals to hear and determine claims, although strictly speaking it is the employment right itself which is limited.

The precise extent of the applicable territorial boundaries can be difficult to determine and varies depending on the legislation applicable to the claim. Some pieces of legislation, such as the National Minimum Wage Act 1998, expressly state the territorial application of the rights they contain. Many, however, including the ERA and EqA, do not, leaving it up to the courts to determine what limits apply. The position is further complicated by the application of EU law: if a particular right derives from EU law, its territorial reach may be affected (see 'Rights deriving from EU law' below).

The question of whether, on given facts, a case falls within the territorial scope **2.67** of an employment right is a question of law; but it is also one of degree – Ravat v Halliburton Manufacturing and Services Ltd 2012 ICR 389, SC. As such, the tribunal's role as primary fact-finder will be crucial.

Extent of legislation. It is worth clarifying here that the territorial scope of an **2.68** employment right should be distinguished from the extent of the piece of legislation in which it is contained. As Lady Smith observed in Transocean International Resources Ltd and ors v Russell and ors EATS 0074/05, the 'extent' of a piece of legislation concerns the geographical area or legal system or systems throughout which it must be recognised as law. For example, S.244(1) ERA says that the Act 'extends' to England, Wales and Scotland – in other words, to Great Britain. But, as Lord Hoffmann pointed out in Lawson v Serco Ltd and two other cases (above), that means only that it forms part of the law of Great Britain and does not form part of the law of any other territory (like Northern Ireland or the Channel Islands) for which Parliament could have legislated. To take a further example, Reg 1(3) of the Transfer of Undertakings (Protection of Employment) Regulations 2006 SI 2006/246 states that the Regulations 'extend' to Northern Ireland – in other words, that the Regulations form part of the law of the whole of the UK. However, the persons and matters that such legislation affects – in other words, its 'application' – may well be wider than its geographical extent.

Unfair dismissal and other ERA rights. Section 196 ERA used to exclude **2.69** employees who ordinarily worked outside Great Britain from the right to claim unfair dismissal and from other protections contained in that Act, such as the right to a redundancy payment. However, it was repealed by the Employment Relations Act 1999 and was not replaced with alternative wording, leaving the ERA silent with regard to its territorial scope. This left the tribunals and the appeal courts to struggle with the question of whether, and if so to what extent, ERA rights apply to employees working outside Great Britain.

From case law, a general formula has emerged for determining the circumstances in which an employee who works wholly or partly outside Great Britain can claim unfair dismissal under S.94(1) ERA or, by extension, other rights under the ERA (see 'Extension of connection principle to other rights' below). The basic rule is that the ERA only applies to employment in Great Britain. However, in exceptional circumstances it may cover working abroad. As summarised by the Court of Appeal in Bates van Winkelhof v Clyde and Co LLP and anor 2013 ICR 883, CA:

- where an employee works partly in Great Britain and partly abroad, the question is whether the connection with Great Britain and British employment law is sufficiently strong to enable it to be said that Parliament would have regarded it as appropriate for the employment tribunal to deal with the claim – Ravat v Halliburton Manufacturing and Services Ltd 2012 ICR 389, SC

- where an employee works and lives wholly abroad, a more restrictive, comparative exercise is appropriate: whether his or her employment relationship has much stronger connections both with Great Britain and with British employment law than with any other system of law – Duncombe v Secretary of State for Children, Schools and Families (No.2) 2011 ICR 1312, SC.

2.70 To understand this formula, it is helpful to trace how it has developed since the repeal of S.196 in 1999.

A number of conflicting decisions followed the repeal of S.196 before the issue finally came before the House of Lords in Lawson v Serco Ltd and two other cases (above). Their Lordships heard three conjoined appeals that raised issues as to the circumstances in which employees working overseas have the right to bring claims of unfair dismissal under the ERA. In Lawson v Serco Ltd, L, who was of British nationality and domiciled in England, worked as a security supervisor for S Ltd, a company registered in the UK and based in England. The job required L to carry out all his work on Ascension Island in the South Atlantic, where the company was contracted to provide security services to the Royal Air Force. In the second case, Botham v Ministry of Defence, B was a British national employed by the MoD in Germany. He was considered part of the 'civil component' of the British Forces in Germany, he paid UK tax on his earnings, and his contract of employment was expressly stated to be governed by the law of England and Wales. Furthermore, his statement of employment particulars described him as 'UK-based'. In the third case, Crofts and ors v Veta Ltd and ors, C was employed as a pilot by V Ltd, a wholly-owned subsidiary of CPA Ltd. Both V Ltd and CPA Ltd were registered in Hong Kong. C's contract was governed by Hong Kong law and his flight instructions were issued from Hong Kong. However, his 'permanent home base' – where his flight cycle would start and end – was Heathrow Airport. Each of these employees brought unfair dismissal claims in a UK employment tribunal, and all three cases made their way to the House of Lords on the question of jurisdiction.

Lord Hoffmann, who delivered the leading judgment in the case, emphasised **2.71** that it would be 'a mistake to try to formulate an ancillary rule of territorial scope, in the sense of a verbal formula such as S.196 used to provide'. Nevertheless, his Lordship accepted that Parliament must have intended, as a general principle, for the unfair dismissal rules to apply to 'the employee who was working in Great Britain'. He divided employees into three categories for the purpose of establishing whether a UK employment tribunal has territorial jurisdiction to hear a claim of unfair dismissal under S.94(1):

- in the standard case, the question will depend on whether the employee was working in Great Britain at the time of dismissal, rather than upon what was contemplated when the contract was entered into. Though they are not determinative of that question, the terms of the contract and any prior contractual relationship between the parties may be of relevance in determining whether the employee was actually working in Great Britain or on a casual visit

- in the case of peripatetic employees, who owing to the nature of their work do not perform services in one territory, the employee's base – the place at which he or she started and ended assignments (Heathrow airport in the case of the pilots in Crofts and ors v Veta Ltd and ors) – should be treated as his or her place of employment. The question then is whether the base was in Great Britain at the time of dismissal. Determining where an employee's base is requires more than just looking at the terms of the contract – it is necessary to look at the conduct of the parties and the way they had been operating the contract in practice

- 'expatriate' employees working and based abroad may in exceptional circumstances be entitled to claim unfair dismissal. Lord Hoffmann gave two examples of circumstances where such an employee would enjoy unfair dismissal protection. The first was of an employee posted abroad by a British employer for the purposes of a business carried on in Great Britain – for example, a foreign correspondent on the staff of a British newspaper. The second was of an expatriate employee of a British employer 'who is operating within what amounts for practical purposes to an extraterritorial British enclave in a foreign country'. His Lordship accepted that there may be other qualifying situations, but stated that in order to come within the scope of S.94(1) employees would need to show 'equally strong connections with Great Britain and British employment law'.

2.72 Immediately following the decision in Lawson, courts and tribunals tended to assume that every case had to be fitted into one or other of the three broad categories of employee outlined by their Lordships. For example, the EAT in YKK Europe Ltd v Heneghan 2010 ICR 611, EAT, held that a tribunal had erred in failing to identify which of the three categories set out in Lawson applied to the case before it. However, subsequent decisions by the Supreme Court questioned this assumption and refined Lord Hoffmann's guidance on how tribunals should approach questions of territorial reach. In Ministry of Defence v Wallis and anor 2011 ICR 617, CA, the claimants were two British employees who commenced employment with the MoD at NATO's overseas headquarters, in the British section of International Schools, after their husbands were posted there to serve in the British armed forces. Despite the fact that they were employed wholly outside Great Britain, the Court of Appeal held that the necessarily 'strong connection' with Britain was provided by the fact that the employees were engaged on terms and conditions reserved for dependants of the British military or civilian component posted to serve abroad. Their contracts were governed by English law and their terms and conditions were essentially English, and they paid national insurance contributions. The Court approved the employment judge's finding that their employment had 'such clear, firm, sound connections with Britain or England that it is appropriate that each claimant should have the protection of English unfair dismissal law'. The Supreme Court subsequently approved that decision in Duncombe v Secretary of State for Children, Schools and Families (No.2) 2011 ICR 1312, SC, which involved a similar set of circumstances. The claimants had been employed as teachers in European Schools abroad by the Department for Children, Schools and Families under a series of fixed-term contracts. Lady Hale, giving the judgment of the Court, summarised Lawson v Serco Ltd and two other cases (above) to the effect that, to be covered by the ERA, the employment must have much stronger connections both with Great Britain and with British employment law than with any other system of law. In the Supreme Court's view, that was established in the case before it.

Lady Hale set out several factors that indicated sufficiently strong connections with British employment law. First, the claimants' employer was not just based in Britain but was the Government of the UK, the closest connection with Great Britain that any employer can have. Secondly, the claimants' contracts were governed by English law, which must be relevant to the parties' expectation as to the protection that employees will enjoy. Although the law of unfair dismissal does not form part of the contractual terms of employment, it was devised by Parliament in order to fill a well-known gap in the common law. Thirdly, the claimants were employed in international enclaves that had no particular connection with the country in which they were situated and which were governed by international agreements between the participating states. The claimants were there because of commitments entered into by the British

Government. Fourthly, it would be anomalous if a teacher who happened to be employed by the British Government to work in the European School in England were to enjoy different protection from the teachers who happened to be employed to work in the same sort of school in other countries. In conclusion, Lady Hale noted that this was a 'very special combination of factors' and that to admit the case as another example of the principle laid down in Lawson would scarcely extend those exceptional cases very far or offend against the sovereignty and equality of nations.

The territorial scope of unfair dismissal law came before the Supreme Court **2.73** once more in Ravat v Halliburton Manufacturing and Services Ltd 2012 ICR 389, SC, a case involving circumstances that could not easily be fitted into any of the three categories identified in Lawson v Serco Ltd and two other cases (above). There the Court – Lord Hope giving the only reasoned opinion – upheld the decision of a Scottish employment tribunal that a British citizen, living in England, who was employed by a Scottish-registered company and, at the time of his dismissal, was working for its German subsidiary in Libya on a month-on, month-off basis, could bring a claim of unfair dismissal. Noting that the tribunal, EAT and Court of Session had all come to varying conclusions about which of the Lawson categories the claimant fell into, Lord Hope reiterated the comments of Lady Hale in Duncombe v Secretary of State for Children, Schools and Families (No.2) (above) that Lawson did not set out a hard and fast rule, and it would be an error of law for a tribunal to attempt to 'torture' factual circumstances to make them fit one of the Lawson categories. Those categories were but examples of a general principle: that the right to claim unfair dismissal will only exceptionally cover employees working and based abroad and, for it to apply, the employment must have stronger connections with Great Britain and British employment law than with any other legal system. Lord Hope observed that this was the critical issue: although the general rule was that the place of employment is decisive, it is not an absolute rule. Ordinarily, such a connection derives from the work being done in Great Britain (Lord Hoffmann's 'standard' cases), but Parliament, in repealing the old S.196 ERA, had disavowed an absolute rule, which led to the conclusion that there must be exceptions – cases where the work is done outside Great Britain but the connection is still sufficiently strong. Two such exceptions were the peripatetic and expatriate categories identified in Lawson. The reason why an exception can be made in such cases is that the connection between Great Britain and the employment relationship is *sufficiently strong for it to be presumed that Parliament must have intended S.94(1) to apply to that employment.* Lord Hope reasoned that, in order for an expatriate employee to fall within S.94(1), it will be necessary to show that he or she is exceptional, as there would ordinarily be a greater connection to the country where the employee lives and works. However, a 'commuter' type employee – i.e. one who lives in Great Britain but travels overseas for working assignments – faces

73

a less onerous burden in establishing the necessary connection to Great Britain. On the facts of R's case, there was ample material from which the tribunal could conclude that his employment was most closely connected with Great Britain. The documentation he was given indicated that it was the employer's intention that the relationship should be governed by British employment law. This was borne out in practice, as matters relating to the termination of his employment were handled by the employer's human resources department in Aberdeen. This all fitted into a pattern of employment under British law.

2.74 A similar employment pattern (of working some of the time in one country and much of the time in another) was considered by the EAT in Powell v OMV Exploration and Production Ltd EAT 0131/13. P brought claims under the ERA in an employment tribunal and the question of territorial scope arose as P worked for an Isle of Man-registered company in Dubai (although he also worked for a few days a year while at home in England when he was 'resting'). The EAT started from the assumption that the ERA does not apply to work outside the UK unless, following Ravat v Halliburton Manufacturing and Services Ltd (above), there was a 'sufficiently strong' connection with Great Britain and British employment law to enable it to be said that Parliament would have regarded it as appropriate for the tribunal to deal with the claim. P argued that he was domiciled in the UK and was recruited and had his required medical examination here; that his employer was incorporated in the Isle of Man, which was a British crown dependency; that he had supervisory responsibilities for two UK-based personnel and paid tax and national insurance to the UK tax authorities (among others); and that he spent some time working within the UK. However, the EAT declined to interfere with the employment judge's decision that the relevant connection was insufficiently strong. There was ample material to justify his conclusion: the employer was not British (a highly material, albeit not conclusive, factor), and the work was performed abroad by agreement, and largely so in practice. The EAT considered that it was also relevant that the parties had made non-UK choices of law and jurisdiction.

2.75 *Place of employment in Great Britain.* As noted above, the House of Lords in Lawson v Serco Ltd and two other cases (above) and the Supreme Court in Ravat v Halliburton Manufacturing and Services Ltd (above) ruled that whether an employee is entitled to bring an unfair dismissal claim will *generally* depend on whether he or she was working in Great Britain at the time of dismissal, though exceptions may be made where an employee works abroad. In considering whether an employee was really working in Great Britain or was merely on a casual visit, the terms of the contract of employment and the history of the contractual relationship may be relevant, but they are not determinative.

In Bleuse v MBT Transport Ltd and anor 2008 ICR 488, EAT, B, a German national, was employed by a company registered in England, but lived in Germany and worked solely in mainland Europe. He failed in his unfair dismissal claim because, as the EAT held, although he worked for a company based in the UK, he did not operate out of the UK and had virtually no connection with it. It made no difference that his contract provided that it was to be governed by and construed in accordance with English law, as S.204 ERA makes it plain that the law of the contract of employment is 'immaterial'. The only issue was whether, as a matter of fact, the employee was based in the UK, and neither the terms of the contract nor its applicable law determined that question. (Note, though, that the EAT did allow B's claim under the Working Time Regulations 1998 SI 1998/1833 – see 'EU-derived rights' below.)

By contrast, in Vizzard v Last Mile Communications Ltd ET Case No.1700249/08 **2.76** a tribunal found that it did have jurisdiction to hear an employee's unfair dismissal claim on the basis that he was working in Britain at the time of dismissal. V had worked for many years in France. When he joined LMC Ltd, his contract acknowledged that his residence was in Paris and the applicable law covering his contract was both English and French, whichever was more beneficial to him. LMC Ltd's principal place of business was Exeter and it also had a small London office. V continued to live in France, but travelled regularly to Exeter and London. He and other employees based in France were paid by LMC Ltd's wholly-owned French subsidiary (which had no trading income) to ensure that local social security payments were made. The tribunal found that LMC Ltd was a UK company whose business was predominantly in the UK. V's residence outside the jurisdiction was agreed by the parties and specifically taken into account in his employment, during which, including at the time of dismissal, he worked exclusively in the main part of the business in the UK.

The implication of Lawson v Serco Ltd and two other cases (above) is that if an employee is 'merely on a casual visit' to Great Britain at the time of dismissal, then he or she will not be regarded as working here for the purposes of establishing the right to claim under the ERA. What the decision leaves unclear is at what point on the sliding scale between being 'on a casual visit' and 'really working in Great Britain' is the employee to be regarded as being employed here. For example, what is the situation where an employee is on an extended business trip, or working on a temporary secondment to Great Britain? It is unlikely that someone on an extended trip would be able to bring a claim under the ERA, whereas someone on a secondment might possibly have a better chance. In such cases, it would be appropriate to ask the crucial question expounded by the Supreme Court in Ravat v Halliburton Manufacturing and Services Ltd 2012 ICR 389, SC: is the connection of the employment relationship with Great Britain sufficiently strong for it to be said that Parliament would have regarded it as appropriate for the employment tribunal to deal with the claim? In answering this question, a tribunal will need to consider the broader circumstances: for example, the reasons the employee was in Great Britain, the length of the trip, and the place where the contract was being operated from at the time of dismissal.

2.77 The focus on where an employee is working at the time of dismissal also raises the question of in what circumstances, if any, a tribunal will be able to hear a claim brought by an employee who normally works in Great Britain but is dismissed while working on an overseas secondment or while on an extended business trip. However, given the general principle set out by the Supreme Court in Ravat v Halliburton Manufacturing and Services Ltd (above), it seems inevitable that an employee who normally works in Great Britain but who is dismissed while temporarily abroad would be able to establish a connection with Great Britain 'sufficiently strong to enable it to be said that Parliament would have regarded it as appropriate for the employment tribunal to deal with the claim'.

2.78 *Peripatetic employees.* In respect of peripatetic employees, the House of Lords in Lawson v Serco Ltd and two other cases (above) agreed with the commonsense approach adopted by the Court of Appeal in Todd v British Midland Airways 1978 ICR 959, CA. Peripatetic employees – such as airline pilots, international management consultants and salespeople – do not perform their services in one territory, owing to the nature of their work. Lord Hoffmann held that in such cases, the employee's base – the place at which he or she started and ended assignments – should be treated as his or her place of employment. Determining where an employee's base is requires more than just looking at the terms of the contract – it is necessary to look at the conduct of the parties and the way they operated the contract in practice. Applying this principle to the case of Crofts and ors v Veta Ltd and ors (one of the cases heard as part of the Lawson appeal), his Lordship held that there were no grounds for overturning the tribunal's decision that the claimant – a peripatetic airline pilot whose 'permanent home base' (where his flight cycle would begin and end) was at Heathrow – was entitled to bring a claim of unfair dismissal under S.94(1). This was despite the fact that Veta Ltd was registered in Hong Kong, his contract was covered by Hong Kong law, and his flight instructions were issued from Hong Kong.

Two cases in which the appeal courts considered whether peripatetic employees were able to claim unfair dismissal (albeit decided before the Supreme Court's rulings in Duncombe v Secretary of State for Children, Schools and Families (No.2) (above) and Ravat v Halliburton Manufacturing and Services Ltd (above)):

- **Anderson v Stena Drilling Pte Ltd** EAT 0080/04: a Scottish employee worked for a Singapore-registered subsidiary of a Swedish company on an oil rig in Far Eastern waters. From 1999 onwards, A lived in Thailand, although he was domiciled in Scotland. The EAT found that A was a peripatetic worker, but held that he could not establish that his base was Great Britain and thus was not eligible to pursue an unfair dismissal claim. The involvement of Scottish-based companies in the operation of the rig and

A's contract of employment did not have the effect of making Scotland his base. In the absence of further supporting evidence, the fact that an employer received instructions from elsewhere or had a relationship with companies in another country would not be determinative of an employee's base. The EAT could discern no link between A and Scotland other than that he was domiciled there. It distinguished A's situation from that in Crofts and ors v Veta Ltd, where the pilots began and ended their tours of duty in London, reported to London to be 'positioned' and had the centre of their operations in London. However minimal the work carried out by the pilots in Great Britain appeared to be, it was a 'regular, established and significant feature of their work pattern'. In contrast, A could not point to any work he had performed in Great Britain. In addition, there was evidence that SD Ltd was actively involved in A's employment and much more than the 'postbox' that A had portrayed

- **Diggins v Condor Marine Crewing Services Ltd** 2010 ICR 213, CA: CMCS Ltd – a Guernsey-based company – employed D as chief officer on a ship which, although registered in the Bahamas, operated between the Channel Islands and Portsmouth. D was required to stay on board throughout his fortnightly rosters, but otherwise his home was in Lowestoft. In April 2007 he was dismissed and his subsequent unfair dismissal claim was rejected by the employment tribunal for lack of jurisdiction. As the vessel was registered outside Great Britain, D did not meet the conditions set down in S.199(7) ERA, which governs the right of mariners to claim unfair dismissal. The EAT allowed D's appeal against this decision, holding that the tribunal did have jurisdiction as D was a 'peripatetic employee' based in Great Britain. CMCS Ltd appealed to the Court of Appeal. The Court pointed out that S.199(7) only applies to those who are employed on ships registered under S.8 of the Merchant Shipping Act 1995. However, if S.199(7) does not apply, a tribunal may still have jurisdiction under the principles in Lawson. It went on to find that D was based in Great Britain. CMCS Ltd may have been based in Guernsey but D 'had no real connection with that place and he had even less so with the Bahamas, where the ship was registered'. It supported the EAT's conclusion that his tours of duty started and finished in Portsmouth.

Absent employees. In Lawson v Serco Ltd and two other cases (above) the **2.79** House of Lords emphasised that in 'standard' cases it is the claimant's working location – or, in the case of peripatetic employees, his or her base – at the time of dismissal that determines whether his or her unfair dismissal claim may be heard. This raises the question of how the employee's location should be determined when he or she is absent from work, say on sick leave, at the time he or she is dismissed. In these cases, a broader factual inquiry is required to decide what the true position was when the employee was dismissed.

In Hunt v United Airlines Inc 2008 ICR 934, EAT, the claimant was a peripatetic flight attendant who had been based in Paris for five years. She was due to transfer to London Heathrow but went on long-term sick leave before the transfer and remained in Paris until her dismissal nearly two years later. The question arose as to whether she was based in Paris or London, where she would have been transferred but for her sickness absence. H brought an unfair dismissal claim in an employment tribunal, arguing unsuccessfully that she was a peripatetic employee whose base, at the time she was dismissed, was London. The EAT recognised that it would be too narrow a test simply to look at where H was working at the date of her dismissal, but this did not lead to a conclusion that a tribunal should ask itself what would have been the position had she not been off sick. The application of a 'but for' test would have led to the conclusion that she was based in London. Rather, following Lawson, a tribunal should consider the circumstances which indicated how the contract was being operated at the time of the dismissal. The tribunal had concluded that H's transfer to London had not taken effect and her ill-health absence was being managed by her employer from the US. Accordingly, its decision that it did not have jurisdiction to hear the claim was upheld.

2.80 In YKK Europe Ltd v Heneghan 2010 ICR 611, EAT, a tribunal accepted jurisdiction under S.94(1) ERA in the case of a claimant who had a 'global remit' but was absent from work on garden leave in the UK at the date of dismissal. The EAT held that the tribunal had erred in two respects. First, it had failed to identify which of the three categories identified in Lawson applied to the employee (a decision that would not now stand following the Supreme Court's ruling in Duncombe v Secretary of State for Children, Schools and Families (No.2) (above) that there is no need to fit cases into the Lawson categories – see above). Furthermore, the EAT considered that when examining how the employment contract was being operated at the date of dismissal, the tribunal had adopted too narrow a test. In this regard, the EAT held that if an employee was not working at the date of dismissal, a broad factual inquiry would be required. The tribunal appeared to have considered a snapshot of what was happening immediately before the time of dismissal, when the emphasis was on a negotiated termination of the relationship, rather than looking more broadly at the facts. The questions to be asked might include: why was the employee absent from work; how long was the period of absence; where was the employee ordinarily working, or based, and for how long, before the absence began; where would the employee have been working at the time of dismissal if he or she had not been absent; was there an active employment relationship between the date of absence and the date of dismissal; from where was the contract being operated at the time of the dismissal; and would the tribunal have had territorial jurisdiction at the date on which the claimant became absent?

One result of these two decisions is that different divisions of the EAT have divergent views as to the relevance of the 'but for' test. In the Hunt case, the

EAT rejected the argument that, where an employee was absent at the date of her dismissal, the tribunal should determine where she would have been based but for her absence. Following YKK Europe Ltd, on the other hand, it appears that the 'but for' test, while not decisive, is one of the factual circumstances that a tribunal may take into account in determining how the contract was being operated at the time of dismissal.

Employees based and working abroad. The leading authority on whether an **2.81** employee who works and is based abroad – Lord Hoffmann's so-called 'expatriate employee' – is within the territorial reach of S.94(1) ERA is the Supreme Court's 2011 ruling in Duncombe v Secretary of State for Children, Schools and Families (No.2) (above). However, earlier decisions can nonetheless provide helpful examples of how the courts and the EAT have approached such situations, so long as they are considered in the light of the Supreme Court's guidance. In Lawson v Serco Ltd and two other cases (above) itself, Lord Hoffmann held that the circumstances would have to be unusual for an employee who works and is based abroad to come within the scope of S.94(1) ERA. He considered it 'very unlikely' that someone working abroad would be covered unless he or she was working for an employer based in Great Britain – but noted that that by itself would not be enough. Many companies based in Great Britain or the UK also carry on business in other countries and employment in those businesses will not attract jurisdiction. Nor should the fact that the employee also happens to be British, or even that he or she was recruited in Britain, be in itself sufficient to distinguish the case from the general rule that the place of employment is decisive.

Lord Hoffmann gave the following example to demonstrate how someone posted abroad to work for the purpose of a business conducted in the UK might, or might not, be able to claim unfair dismissal under the ERA:

• an employee selling advertising space in San Francisco for a UK newspaper as part of the business conducted in London would attract the protection of the ERA. By contrast, an employee working for a business that the paper or an associated company conducts in the US – for example, selling advertising space in the American edition of the paper – would not be protected.

On the facts of one of the cases before him, Botham v Ministry of Defence, his **2.82** Lordship held that the claimant, who was working on a military base in Germany, was operating within what amounted to a British enclave in a foreign country. He was a British national employed by the MoD and considered to be part of the 'civil component' of the British Forces in Germany; he paid UK tax on his earnings, his contract was stated to be governed by the law of England and Wales; and his statement of employment particulars described him as 'UK-based'. His claim of unfair dismissal was allowed to proceed. The same was true of the claimant in Lawson v Serco Ltd, who was employed at the RAF base on Ascension Island. L was a British national and domiciled in England, and

79

worked for S Ltd, a company registered in the UK and based in England. Although L's case was less clear in that he was in the employ of a private firm to provide security on the base, his Lordship considered that it would be unrealistic to regard him as having taken up employment in a foreign community. There was no local community on Ascension Island and the base was in practice a British outpost in the South Atlantic. Although there was a local system of law, the connection between the employment relationship and the UK was overwhelmingly stronger.

2.83 It is important to note, however, Lord Hoffmann's emphasis on the fact that it is only in exceptional circumstances that expatriate employees will be entitled to claim unfair dismissal. In neither of the following cases were the claimants successful:

- **Dolphin Drilling Personnel Pte Ltd v Winks and anor** EAT 0049/08: W, a British citizen, was employed by DDP Ltd, a Singapore company, to work as a storeman on an oil rig, first in the Gulf of Mexico and then off the coast of Nigeria. The rig was registered in Singapore but managed and operated by DD Ltd, a UK company registered in Aberdeen. Following a disciplinary process conducted in Aberdeen W was dismissed, and he brought an unfair dismissal complaint before an employment tribunal. The tribunal decided that it had jurisdiction to hear W's claim on the basis that there was a substantial connection between Great Britain and his employment, but the EAT overturned this decision. The EAT considered that the tribunal had erred in holding that the test for the existence of jurisdiction was whether the employment had a 'substantial connection' with Great Britain. As a rule, the place of employment determines the territorial scope of the right to claim unfair dismissal, and only in exceptional circumstances would a tribunal have jurisdiction where an employee works wholly abroad. W, who worked wholly abroad for a foreign employer, could not establish that a British employment tribunal had jurisdiction to hear his claim

- **Williams v University of Nottingham** 2007 IRLR 660, EAT: W was employed by the University of Nottingham (UN) from 1 September 2003 for a fixed three-year term as a senior lecturer. He was specifically recruited to work in Malaysia for a joint venture company, University of Nottingham in Malaysia (UNM), through which UN ran locally approved degree programmes. Although UN had only a minority shareholding in UNM, that organisation was described in publicity material as an integral part of UN, and as UN's Malaysian campus. It was a condition of W's contract with UN that he would be seconded to Malaysia – although his work there was to last for just two years of his three-year contract, due to work permit issues. His salary was paid by UN, but indirectly by UNM, which reimbursed UN in respect of it. W only ever worked in Malaysia, although some of his research work was in conjunction with colleagues in Nottingham. Following UN's termination of W's secondment in October 2005, he was obliged to return to UN in November but did not do so and resigned in December 2005. W brought claims of unfair constructive dismissal and disability discrimination against UN in an employment tribunal in England. The EAT upheld the tribunal's decision that W's unfair dismissal claim could not proceed. The tribunal had correctly concluded that M's work was for the purpose of the separate and distinct business of UNM and was not for UN's purposes, notwithstanding the fact that there were certain necessary and consequential benefits accruing to UN from the work performed by M in Malaysia.

The EAT in Dhunna v Creditsights Ltd 2013 ICR 909, EAT – a case which **2.84** post-dated Duncombe v Secretary of State for Children, Schools and Families (No.2) (above) and Ravat v Halliburton Manufacturing and Services Ltd (above) – reviewed all the leading authorities and extracted a number of general principles. In that case D worked for C Ltd – a UK subsidiary of C Inc based in New York – which had a global client base. In 2009, C Inc took the decision to open a Dubai office and, although D did not move there until it opened in October of that year, he started his new role in January, transferring his British and European clients to another employee at C Ltd and focusing exclusively on sales to clients in the Middle East, Asia and Africa. He also started receiving remuneration from C Ltd in US dollars (instead of having US dollars converted into sterling). However, from a legal standpoint, the Dubai office was designated a branch of C Ltd. Consequently, any sales made in Dubai were handled in London in terms of invoicing and the remittance of payments. As for reporting, D was line-managed by M, who worked in New Delhi for a subsidiary of C Inc. Eventually, a decision was made to close the Dubai office and D was dismissed. As well as bringing an unfair dismissal complaint against C Ltd in the employment tribunal, D also claimed that his former employer had breached his right under S.10 of the Employment Relations Act 1999 (ERelA) to be accompanied, and had failed to give him holiday pay in contravention of the Working Time Regulations 1998 SI 1998/1833 (this part of the claim is discussed below under 'EU-derived rights'). Before the case could proceed to a substantive hearing, it fell to an employment judge to determine whether the tribunal had territorial jurisdiction to entertain D's claims.

In denying jurisdiction to hear the ERA and ERelA complaints, the judge rejected D's primary argument that he fell within the second of the two expatriate employee categories envisaged by Lord Hoffmann in Lawson, i.e. that he was working in Dubai for the purpose of maintaining and developing a business carried on by C Ltd in Great Britain. In the judge's view, the Dubai office was not a representative office of C Ltd and D was not working as a representative of C Ltd in Dubai. Instead, he was part of the Asian business of C Inc. Furthermore, the judge rejected D's alternative submission that, if he did not fall within Lord Hoffmann's second category of expatriate employee, then he had 'equally strong connections' with Great Britain and British employment

81

law sufficient to establish jurisdiction. The reality was that D had moved from the UK and had severed his links with it. He was only on C Ltd's payroll and receiving administrative support from C Ltd as a matter of convenience.

2.85 D appealed to the EAT, arguing that the employment judge had considered jurisdiction in terms of Lawson alone, which was wrong following the judgments in Duncombe v Secretary of State for Children, Schools and Families (No.2) (above) and Ravat v Halliburton Manufacturing and Services Ltd (above). D argued that it is no longer appropriate to try to fit the circumstances of a particular case into one of the examples given by Lord Hoffmann in Lawson, and that the current approach is to determine whether the employee had stronger connections with Great Britain and British employment law than with any other system of law.

Mrs Justice Slade, sitting alone in the EAT, set out a number of general principles. She emphasised that the question of whether a case falls within the territorial scope of S.94(1) should be treated as one of law, while the question of whether the connection between the circumstances of the employment and Great Britain and British employment law is sufficiently strong is one of fact and degree on which the decision of the primary fact-finder is entitled to considerable respect. She accepted that at the time of the employment judge's decision in this case the leading authority was Lawson but argued that, since then, the issue had been considered by the Supreme Court in Duncombe and Ravat, as well as by the Court of Appeal in Bates van Winkelhof v Clyde and Co LLP and anor 2013 ICR 883, CA. She held that while the fundamental issue remained unchanged, the approach to the exceptions to the general rule that the right to claim unfair dismissal only exceptionally covers employees who were working abroad had been developed.

2.86 After reviewing Duncombe, Ravat and Bates van Winkelhof, Slade J distilled the following principles to be applied when considering whether an employee who works and/or lives abroad falls within the territorial scope of S.94(1) ERA:

- the overarching question is whether Parliament intended that S.94(1) ERA should apply to a person in the claimant's circumstances

- the general rule is that the place of employment is decisive, but where the employment has much stronger connections with Great Britain and British employment law than with any other system of law, the claimant will fall within the scope of S.94(1) if the connection is sufficiently strong

- a comparative exercise is appropriate where the claimant is employed wholly abroad. The comparison is between Great Britain and the jurisdiction in which the claimant works

- the country in which the claimant lives is relevant. If he or she lives as well as works abroad, an especially strong connection with Great Britain and

British employment law is required before an exception can be made for him or her

• when the claimant lives and/or works for at least part of the time in Great Britain, a comparison of connections between Great Britain and the country in which he or she works is not required. All that is required is a sufficiently strong connection to enable it to be said that Parliament would have regarded it as appropriate for a tribunal to deal with the claimant's unfair dismissal claim.

Elaborating, Slade J explained that, in cases in which an employee is employed wholly abroad and lives abroad, it may not be sufficient to establish in a comparative exercise that his or her employment has much stronger links with Great Britain and with British employment law than with that of the jurisdiction where he or she works. It must still be shown that those links are sufficiently strong that Parliament can be thought to have regarded it as appropriate for the tribunal to deal with the claim. This may be relevant where a claimant who works and lives abroad has stronger links with Great Britain and British employment law than with the country in which he or she works but also has links with a third country. Although another comparative exercise may not be required, ties with a third country may diminish the employee's ties with Great Britain and British employment law so that they are insufficiently strong to support the inference that Parliament must have intended S.94(1) to apply.

2.87 Applying the above principles to D's case, Slade J noted that the employment judge had given some consideration to the strength of D's connections with Great Britain and British employment law. However, the focus of his decision was on whether the operation in Dubai was a representative office of C Ltd. The judge did not compare these connections with the strength of the connections that D had with Dubai, a comparison now required by the authorities subsequent to Lawson. Slade J considered whether – had the employment judge approached the jurisdiction issue in accordance with these authorities – he would have come to the same conclusion, and decided that it could not be said with the degree of confidence required to uphold the employment judge's decision that the outcome with regard to S.94 ERA and S.10 ERelA would have been the same had the correct approach been followed. Further findings of fact might be necessary and a different emphasis might need to be given to the relevant facts. Slade J remitted the case to a fresh tribunal to consider the jurisdiction issue anew.

This case demonstrates that the approach to determining the issue of jurisdiction for unfair dismissal claims vis-à-vis expatriate employees has developed significantly since the landmark decision in Lawson v Serco Ltd and two other cases (above). However, it is important to remember, as Slade J pointed out, that the fundamental principles applicable to this issue – as set down by Lord Hoffmann in Lawson – remain unchanged. It is very unlikely for someone who

83

is both living and working abroad to come within the scope of unfair dismissal protection. Such a claimant would have to prove that his or her employment had a much stronger connection both with Great Britain and with British employment law than with any other system of law, which is no small hurdle.

2.88 Even if the facts of a case seem to be on all fours with those of another case, all cases should be considered by applying the principles set down in the leading authorities and not by extrapolation from the facts of decided cases. The wrong approach was taken by the EAT in Rogers v Deputy Commander (as Trustee of the Garrison Amenities Fund) and anor EAT 0455/12, where R, the wife of a serving soldier, was employed to manage a children's play area at a Navy, Army and Air Force Institutes complex in Germany. However, R was herself a German national; was engaged to work wholly in Germany under a contract made in Germany for an employer based in Germany, on a site which was open to the public; and she was paid in euros. Given these facts, together with the fact that she had been offered the chance to have British citizenship but had rejected it, the EAT considered that an employment judge was entitled to decide that R could not bring an unfair dismissal claim in the UK, even though she argued that her circumstances were similar to that of the (successful) claimant in Ministry of Defence v Wallis and anor 2011 ICR 617, CA. The EAT warned against relying on examples of previous decisions, when what mattered was principle. Following the Supreme Court's decisions in Duncombe v Secretary of State for Children, Schools and Families (No.2) (above) and Ravat v Halliburton Manufacturing and Services Ltd (above), it was clear that cases in which work done outside the UK gave rise to the right to claim unfair dismissal within the UK would be exceptional. There must not only be a stronger connection, but a *much* stronger connection, both with Great Britain and British employment law, than with any other system of law, to enable it to be said that it would be appropriate for the employee to have a claim for unfair dismissal in Great Britain. The situation of the employees in Wallis was different in important respects from that of R: although they were also married to serving officers in mainland Europe, they were recruited and employed by the Ministry of Defence; the terms of their contracts were governed by English law; the posts they occupied were ones for which they were specifically eligible as dependants of serving members of the armed forces; they were part of the civilian component of NATO; and they appeared to be British citizens.

2.89 **Extension of connection principle to other rights.** Note that while Lord Hoffmann in Lawson v Serco Ltd and two other cases 2006 ICR 250, HL, considered that there was no reason why all the various rights contained in the ERA should have the same territorial scope as the right to claim unfair dismissal, in practice this is the assumption that tends to be made. In Bleuse v MBT Transport Ltd and anor 2008 ICR 488, EAT, for example (a case also considered below under 'EU-derived rights'), the EAT held that there was no reason why a different test should apply to a claim of unlawful deduction from wages.

What is more, the courts (not to mention Parliament) have tended to assume that where any other piece of employment law legislation is silent as to its territorial scope, then the case law on the territorial reach of unfair dismissal is applicable. For example, according to the Explanatory Notes to the EqA, the decision to remove any express provision on territorial scope follows the precedent of the ERA and 'leaves it to tribunals to determine whether the law applies, depending for example on the connection between the employment relationship and Great Britain' (para 15). The Court of Appeal in Bates van Winkelhof v Clyde and Co LLP and anor (above) assumed that the case law relevant to the ERA also applied to a claim under the EqA – but indicated that it would have been prepared to hear an argument that the territorial reach of discrimination and whistleblowing claims was wider than that applicable to unfair dismissal, because of the public interest element: see 'Discrimination' below. There is clearly no hard-and-fast rule and a party would be at liberty to argue that a different principle on territorial reach might be appropriate in particular cases (see, for example, our suggestion under 'Transfer of undertakings' below that the connection principle might be modified in relation to TUPE to refer to the UK as opposed to Great Britain).

EU-derived rights. Following the House of Lords' decision in Lawson v Serco **2.90** Ltd and two other cases 2006 ICR 250, HL, it was widely assumed that the territorial reach of *any* claims silent as to their scope could generally be determined by reference to the House of Lords' guidance concerning the unfair dismissal claims under the ERA. For example, in Ashbourne v Department for Education and Skills and ors and another case EAT 0123/07 the EAT held that the Lawson principles should be followed in determining whether an employee working abroad was able to claim under the Fixed-term Employees (Prevention of Less Favourable Treatment) Regulations 2002 SI 2002/2034. The claimants in those cases worked exclusively abroad and did not fall within any of Lord Hoffmann's examples of overseas employees who, exceptionally, could claim. The EAT specifically rejected an argument that regulations, such as the Fixed-term Employees Regulations, that implement an EU Directive must be construed differently to unfair dismissal legislation, as the right to claim unfair dismissal is a purely 'domestic' employment right (in other words, the UK Parliament created the right independently of European influence). The point is crucial, as many other UK employment rights are also derived from European legislation – for example, those contained in the EqA, the Transfer of Undertakings (Protection of Employment) Regulations 2006 SI 2006/246, and the Working Time Regulations.

However, shortly after Ashbourne was decided, another division of the EAT had to consider the territorial scope of the Working Time Regulations (and the right to claim unfair dismissal) in Bleuse v MBT Transport Ltd and anor 2008 ICR 488, EAT. In that case Mr Justice Elias, then President of the EAT, took the view that, disregarding any questions of rights under European law, there would be no reason to hold that the territorial reach of rights under the Regulations was any different to that of rights under the ERA. However, he considered it highly relevant that the Regulations exist to give effect to the rights contained in the EU Working Time Directive (No.2003/88), and emphasised that domestic courts must, if at all possible, construe the Regulations so as to give effect to those rights in cases where English law is the proper law of the contract, or where English mandatory rules apply under the Rome I Regulation (see 'Applicable law' above). He held that statutory provisions should be construed so as to ensure that directly effective EU rights can be enforced by the English courts. Otherwise, the European principle of effectiveness would not be satisfied in that there would be no effective remedy for a breach of the EU right.

2.91 The Bleuse case was considered by the Court of Appeal in Secretary of State for Children, Schools and Families v Fletcher and another case 2010 ICR 815, CA (also known as Duncombe v Secretary of State for Children, Schools and Families). In that case D was employed by what was then the Department for Education and Skills to work under a succession of fixed-term contracts in a European School in Germany. D's contract stated that it 'shall be governed by English law and the English courts shall have exclusive jurisdiction in all matters regarding it'. Teaching posts in European Schools were subject to a maximum of nine years' duration by virtue of regulations governing the schools (the Nine Year Rule). D brought tribunal proceedings arising out of the expiry of his last contract, claiming wrongful dismissal and unfair dismissal. It was accepted that these claims could only get off the ground if Reg 8 of the Fixed-term Employees Regulations applied to convert his succession of fixed-term contracts into a permanent one. The claims were dismissed by the tribunal at a pre-hearing review on the basis that they relied on Reg 8, from whose scope D was excluded according to the territorial jurisdiction test set out in Lawson. Therefore, his claims had no reasonable prospect of success.

D's appeal against the ruling on unfair dismissal failed at the EAT. However, he successfully challenged the wrongful dismissal aspect of the tribunal's decision on the basis of a new point of appeal; namely, that Bleuse was authority for the proposition that limitations on territorial scope have to be modified where necessary to give effect to a claimant's directly effective rights under EU law. D argued that, assuming the Fixed-term Work Directive (No.99/70) is directly enforceable, no distinction could be drawn between his case and that of Bleuse. Thus he should, by analogy, be entitled to rely on the Fixed-term Employees Regulations. The EAT allowed D's appeal and declared that the tribunal had jurisdiction, in hearing the wrongful dismissal claim, to apply the relevant provisions of the Regulations to determine the question of whether the employer could justify employing D under fixed-term contracts.

D appealed against the unfair dismissal part of the EAT's judgment and the **2.92** Secretary of State appealed against the EAT's decision on wrongful dismissal. Dealing first with the wrongful dismissal claim, the Court of Appeal agreed with the Secretary of State that D would not be able to satisfy the Lawson test if it applied to the Regulations. However, the Court accepted D's 'simple' and 'beguiling' argument that he still had a cause of action for wrongful dismissal based on the fact that the parties had chosen English law as the law of the contract. The Fixed-term Employees Regulations apply to all fixed-term employment contracts governed by English law regardless of where those contracts are performed – there is no territorial limitation in the Regulations themselves. On that basis, the Court decided, the Lawson principles became irrelevant. The result was that D's fixed-term contract was converted into a permanent one. Furthermore, the availability of a remedy for breach of a contract, whether or not modified by the operation of the Regulations, was founded in common law and was not dependent upon the ERA. D's claim for wrongful dismissal could therefore proceed and the Secretary of State's appeal was dismissed.

As to the unfair dismissal claim, the Court acknowledged that different considerations applied. Whereas the choice of English law as the law of the contract meant that D's contract claim could be brought in the tribunal, a claim of unfair dismissal had to be brought under the ERA and so was subject to domestic territorial limitations. The Court agreed with the Secretary of State that, on a straight application of Lawson, D would not be able to establish the right to bring an employment claim in Great Britain. However, the Court went on to endorse Bleuse, holding, moreover, that in accordance with the EU principle of effectiveness it should be applied to permit an unfair dismissal claim to be made where that was necessary for the effective vindication of a right derived from EU law – in this case, the Fixed-term Employees Regulations. To that extent, the implied territorial limitation on the right not to be unfairly dismissed, as identified in Lawson, should be modified. The Court noted that D's EU-derived right to a permanent contract would be denied if he could be dismissed on the basis that he was employed on a fixed-term contract that had expired, as in such a situation he would have no remedy for unfair dismissal. The Court therefore allowed his appeal and directed that his unfair dismissal claim should be allowed to proceed.

This principle was also applied by the Court of Appeal in the sex discrimination **2.93** case of Ministry of Defence v Wallis 2011 ICR 617, CA. However, Fletcher subsequently came before the Supreme Court. In Duncombe v Secretary of State for Children, Schools and Families (No.2) 2011 ICR 1312, SC, the Supreme Court disagreed with the Court of Appeal's conclusion that, on a straight application of Lawson, D would not have the right to claim unfair dismissal, as D had established a sufficiently strong connection with Great Britain to satisfy the test set out by the House of Lords (see 'Unfair dismissal

87

and other ERA rights' above). In its first decision, however, the Supreme Court briefly touched on the question of whether the Lawson test should be modified so as to give a remedy for directly effective EU rights, in a decision limited to the claimants' rights under the Fixed-term Employees Regulations – Secretary of State for Children, Schools and Families v Fletcher and another case 2011 ICR 495, SC. The Court held that the claimants' employment as teachers at European Schools on fixed-term contracts for a period of up to nine years was objectively justified under the Regulations. Accordingly, it did not need to consider whether the Regulations applied to D and other teachers working at European Schools overseas, though the majority of the Court expressed the obiter view that they did. Nevertheless, had it been necessary to answer that question, Lady Hale took the view that a reference to the ECJ would probably have been required, given that the scope of protection offered by the Directive is a question of EU law to which there should be a uniform answer across the Member States. Lady Hale also noted that while there was no need to reach a decision on whether the principle in Bleuse applied, she considered that if the protection of EU law applies to workers wherever they work within the EU, that protection should not depend on enforcing a directly effective right against the state, but extend to private as well as public employment.

If Bleuse v MBT Transport Ltd and anor (above) is correct, UK legislation that implements directly effective rights derived from an EU directive must be construed so as to give effect to those rights – even if this means displacing normal domestic rules about territorial scope. The question then arises: what is the territorial ambit of EU employment rights? Would an employee working exclusively outside the EU be able to rely on directly effective EU-derived rights if the UK tribunal had jurisdiction over his or her claim (see 'International jurisdiction' above)?

2.94 In Ministry of Defence v Wallis (above) Lord Justice Elias touched on this matter. Having stated that 'once a claimant is seeking to enforce a directly effective EU right, it matters not which national law is applicable to the right in question, provided at least that it is the law of a Member State... once the British court is properly seised of the issue, it would be obliged to give effect to the directly effective right one way or another, irrespective of which body of national rules applies,' he recognised that 'the situation becomes more complex if either the domestic law of non-EU countries may be involved, or if reliance is placed on EU rights which do not have direct effect. In the former situation, it may be necessary to determine the geographical reach of the Directive itself to determine whether it extends to workers employed outside the EU: see, by analogy, Ingmar GB Ltd v Eaton Leonard Technologies Inc 2001 1 CMLR 9, ECJ. In the latter situation, there may be an issue whether the relevant applicable law determined by the choice of law rules can be read consistently with EU rights in accordance with the Marleasing principle (see Marleasing SA v La Comercial Internacional de Alimentacion SA 1992 1 CMLR 305, ECJ). If it cannot, then no substantive enforceable rights would be afforded to the claimant by the applicable law.' In Dhunna v Creditsights Ltd 2013 ICR 909, EAT, the EAT was not prepared to uphold an employment judge's decision to extend the Bleuse principle to an employee working in Dubai, noting that the judge identified no provision in the Working Time Directive which stated that it applied to employees working outside the EU, nor any provision of EU law which would lead to the Directive having that effect. Similarly, in Hasan v Shell International Shipping Services (PTE) Ltd and ors EAT 0242/13 the EAT declined to apply the Bleuse principle to events that took place outside the EU and upheld a tribunal's decision that it did not have jurisdiction to hear the discrimination claims of a sailor relating to his service aboard a non-UK flagged vessel in international waters.

Discrimination. Unlike previous discrimination legislation, the EqA is silent as 2.95 to its territorial scope. Previous statutes applied to employment 'at an establishment in Great Britain', and provided protection to those who worked 'wholly or partly' in Great Britain as well as those who worked wholly outside Great Britain but fulfilled specific criteria. (The latter was subject to some exceptions such as colour – a complaint of race discrimination on the ground of colour would only be heard if the claimant did his or her work wholly or partly in Great Britain.) Those criteria, in short, were that the employee worked for a business which had an establishment in Great Britain, the employee's work was for the purposes of the business carried on at that establishment, and he or she was resident in Great Britain either when he or she applied for the job or at any time during the course of the employment.

According to the Explanatory Notes to the EqA, the decision to make no express provision as to territorial scope in the Act follows the precedent of the ERA and leaves it to employment tribunals to determine whether the Act applies. This means that when determining whether they have jurisdiction to hear a claim brought under the EqA, tribunals will generally be obliged to follow the approach set out by the House of Lords in Lawson v Serco Ltd and two other cases 2006 ICR 250, HL, as interpreted by the Supreme Court in Duncombe v Secretary of State for Children, Schools and Families (No.2) 2011 ICR 1312, SC, and Ravat v Halliburton Manufacturing and Services Ltd 2012 ICR 389, SC. The Equality and Human Rights Commission's Code of Practice on Employment advises that where an employee works partly or wholly outside Great Britain, in considering whether a 'sufficiently close' link exists a tribunal may consider such matters as where the employee lives and works, where the employer is established, what laws govern the employment relationship in other respects, where tax is paid, and 'other matters it considers appropriate' (para 10.71).

The Court of Appeal in Bates van Winkelhof v Clyde and Co LLP and anor 2.96 2013 ICR 883, CA, assumed that the case law relevant to the ERA also applied

89

to claims under the EqA. In that case a junior equity partner, BvW, brought various claims against the limited liability partnership for which she worked, including claims of discrimination under S.45(2) EqA. The Court held that she could pursue her discrimination claims despite spending most of her time working on secondment in Tanzania, as she had a sufficiently strong connection with Great Britain and British employment law. The employment judge had found that BvW worked at least partly in Great Britain; the LLP agreement was governed by English law; BvW was a member of the LLP, which resulted in her agreeing budgets with her partners in London; she visited London, for work, on a regular basis; she was mainly paid from London; all her time-recording was done on C and Co's system; all invoices were generated from Great Britain; she was provided with administrative support from London; she appeared on the Law Society website as a member of C and Co; and C and Co's press releases detailed her as being its member. The Court of Appeal rejected the need for a comparative exercise to be made between the jurisdictional systems of Great Britain and Tanzania. All that was required was that the tribunal should satisfy itself, following Ravat, that the connection was 'sufficiently strong to enable it to be said that Parliament would have regarded it as appropriate for the tribunal to deal with the claim'.

In coming to its conclusion, the Court acknowledged that, as Lord Hoffmann himself pointed out in Lawson, it does not necessarily follow that all the rights under the ERA should have the same territorial scope, although 'uniformity of application is desirable in the interests of simplicity'. With respect to alleged unlawful discrimination, while the Court saw 'some attraction' in the argument that, if anything, it would be in the public interest for the territorial scope of discrimination claims to be wider than that for unfair dismissal, it considered that it would be 'difficult to identify in practical terms what looser test could be adopted, unless perhaps the principle adopted was that it would suffice for the employer to be in Great Britain irrespective of where the employee works, and that might be a step too far'. The Court left this as 'an argument for another day'.

2.97 The territorial reach of the ERA, and thus the EqA, is arguably narrower than that of previous discrimination legislation, since it potentially excludes those recruited in Britain for a British business but who work outside Great Britain, unless their circumstances constitute a connection with Great Britain that is sufficiently strong to enable it to be said that Parliament would have regarded it as appropriate for the employment tribunal to deal with the claim. Consequently, some employees who were previously covered by discrimination law may be excluded from the protection of the EqA. If this is the case, the most likely solution for claimants will be to seek to apply the principle established by the EAT in Bleuse v MBT Transport Ltd and anor (above) and followed by the Court of Appeal in Ministry of Defence v Wallis (above). As explained above, the Bleuse principle is that the Lawson guidance ought to be modified in its application to UK law where necessary to give effect to directly effective rights derived from EU law. Since most discrimination laws are so derived, it is arguable that a wider test will apply to claims brought under the EqA. Furthermore, ECJ decisions such as Mangold v Helm 2006 IRLR 143, ECJ, and Kücükdeveci v Swedex GmbH und Co KG 2010 IRLR 346, ECJ, suggest that the principle of non-discrimination is a general and fundamental principle of EU law, which can be relied on against private individuals as well as against the state. So, the wider test is likely to apply to workers in the private sector as well as their public sector counterparts. In Bates van Winkelhof v Clyde and Co LLP and anor (above) the claimant indeed sought to argue that the employment tribunal had jurisdiction to hear her EU-derived claims by analogy with Bleuse. However, as the Court had heard little argument on what it described as this 'difficult point' and as it was not necessary for it to deal with the matter in view of its conclusion on the principal argument, it declined to address the issue.

It is also important to bear in mind that different considerations apply to discrimination and unfair dismissal claims so case law on the territorial scope of the previous discrimination legislation may well continue to be relevant in some respects, even though the old legislation has now been replaced by the EqA. For example, whereas dismissal occurs at a point in time, discrimination frequently takes place over a long period. For the House of Lords in Lawson, a crucial question in determining whether a tribunal had territorial jurisdiction over a claimant's unfair dismissal claim was where the employee was working at the time of dismissal. Tribunals may have difficulty applying this principle in the context of a discrimination claim based on treatment, such as a campaign of discrimination, allegedly inflicted on an employee over a period of time, covering work in the UK (or Great Britain) and abroad.

2.98 In Tradition Securities and Futures SA v X and anor 2009 ICR 88, EAT, the EAT held that an employment tribunal did not have jurisdiction to hear sex discrimination claims relating to a period during which the claimant worked wholly in France for a French company prior to transferring to its London office. The EAT rejected the argument that the acts occurring in France and London could be treated as part of a continuing act, holding that an employment tribunal cannot acquire jurisdiction retrospectively for a complaint about an alleged act that was not unlawful under domestic legislation at the time it was done. However, evidence of acts alleged to have occurred during that period could be admitted as background material.

2.99 **Equal pay.** Like discrimination claims, equal pay complaints were previously subject to an express territorial jurisdiction. S.1(1) of the Equal Pay Act 1970 (EqPA) (now repealed and replaced by the EqA) restricted the operation of the equality clause to the contracts of those 'employed at an establishment in Great Britain'. However, that restriction was not carried through into the EqA. Para 56 of the statutory Code of Practice on Equal Pay, published by the Equality and Human Rights Commission, notes that although no geographical location is specified, 'in most cases the woman and her male comparator will be based in Great Britain'. While that is undoubtedly true, the EqA does not require this to be so.

Equal pay law is in a slightly different position to discrimination law, being an entirely contractual issue, and so the key question is whether the contract in question is covered by domestic contract law. How this is determined is dealt with under 'Applicable law' above. Certainly, where the parties have chosen the law of England and Wales to govern the contract of employment, an employee will be able to bring an equal pay claim in an employment tribunal in England, assuming the English courts have jurisdiction, i.e. are the appropriate forum (see 'International jurisdiction' above). But an employee working abroad may be able to claim equal pay in certain circumstances even if English law is not the governing law of the contact: see Simpson v Intralinks Ltd 2012 ICR 1343, EAT, discussed under 'Applicable law – overriding mandatory provisions of the law of the forum', for an example of a case in which an employee was able to claim equal pay in an employment tribunal despite the fact that English law was not the governing law of the contract.

2.100 **National minimum wage.** Unlike the ERA and EqA, some domestic legislation expressly sets out the territorial scope of the rights it contains. The rights contained in the National Minimum Wage Act 1998 (NMWA) are an example. S.1 provides that persons who, under their contracts, are working, or ordinarily work, in the UK qualify for the national minimum wage (NMW). Although courts are obliged to examine the wording of legislation in context, it is fair to assume that the case law dealing with the concept of 'ordinarily working', which arose in the context of unfair dismissal law before S.196 ERA was repealed, will be relevant to the question of whether someone ordinarily works in the UK for the purposes of the NMW (although it should be noted that the NMW legislation applies to 'workers', a wider category of individuals than the 'employees' to whom the ERA applies).

The Court of Appeal in Carver v Saudi Arabian Airlines 1999 ICR 991, CA, confirmed that, for the purposes of the ERA, the place where an employee 'ordinarily works' was to be decided by the terms of the employee's contract of employment, having regard to the whole period contemplated by the contract at the date it was made. Thus, in that case C could not claim unfair dismissal even though she was working in London at the time of dismissal as the original contract had envisaged she would be based in Jeddah. Where the contract of employment was inconclusive as to where an employee ordinarily worked, the matter was to be determined according to where the employee's base was, going by 'the conduct of the parties and the way they have been operating the contract' – Todd v British Midland Airways Ltd 1978 ICR 959, CA.

Since the NMWA does not derive from EU law, the 'Bleuse principle' (see EU-derived rights' above) does not apply – although similar legislation may exist in other EU countries. In Bullen v Club Cantabrica Coach and Air Holidays Ltd and anor ET Case No.3303362/09 a tribunal held that it did not have jurisdiction to hear an employee's claims for unpaid commission and minimum wage, where he worked wholly in France despite having been recruited in the UK.

Trade union rights. The Trade Union and Labour Relations (Consolidation) **2.101** Act 1992 (TULR(C)A) expressly sets out the territorial scope of many of the rights it contains. S.285 TULR(C)A provides that rights in relation to trade union membership and activities under Ss.137, 138, 145A, 145B, 146, and 168–170 'do not apply to employment where under his contract of employment an employee works, or in the case of a prospective employee would ordinarily work, outside Great Britain'. As this formula is identical to that which used to apply under the ERA, it may be assumed that case law arising from S.196 ERA prior to its repeal will be relevant to the question of whether someone ordinarily works outside Great Britain for the purpose of claiming rights under the TULR(C)A, such as the right not to be subjected to detriment on grounds relating to union membership and activities under S.146 – see futher 'National minimum wage' above.

However, it should be noted that the statutory provisions on trade union recognition contained in Schedule 1A to the TULR(C)A have no explicit territorial restriction, so their implied territorial scope is guided by the principles governing the right to claim unfair dismissal under the ERA – see 'Unfair dismissal and other ERA rights' above. In Netjets Management Ltd v Central Arbitration Committee and anor 2012 IRLR 986, QBD, the High Court held that there were no territorial restrictions on a union's application to be recognised for collective bargaining in respect of pilots employed by a private aircraft operator, even though the business was managed from Portugal and a large majority of pilots lived or operated from a 'gateway' airport outside the UK. In determining whether the connection between the employment and Great Britain and British employment law was 'sufficiently strong', it was relevant that the employer was registered in Great Britain, that the pilots' contracts were governed by English law and subject to the English courts' jurisdiction, and that the pilots paid UK national insurance contributions. (Applications for recognition are heard by the Central Arbitration Committee, not employment tribunals.)

Transfer of undertakings. The Transfer of Undertakings (Protection of **2.102** Employment) Regulations 2006 SI 2006/246 (TUPE) contain no territorial restrictions, with the result that considerations similar to those applicable to claims under the ERA are likely to apply to TUPE claims (see 'Unfair dismissal and other ERA rights' above) – with the proviso that references to 'employment in Great Britain' should be read as references to 'employment in the United Kingdom', given that TUPE extends to the whole of the UK, not just Great Britain – see 'Extent of legislation' above. Moreover, as TUPE is derived from EU-law, the Bleuse principle (see Bleuse v MBT Transport Ltd and anor (above)) may apply so as to modify the approach laid down in Lawson v Serco Ltd and two other cases 2006 ICR 250, HL, where necessary (see 'EU-derived rights' above).

Note that the questions of what amounts to a relevant transfer for the purposes of TUPE and whether an employee who is ordinarily working outside the UK is 'assigned' to the undertaking being transferred also have territorial dimensions. However, these are distinct issues – see IDS Employment Law Handbook, 'Transfer of Undertakings' (2011), Chapter 1, 'Identifying a relevant transfer', under 'Standard transfers – entity situated in the United Kingdom immediately prior to transfer', and Chapter 2, 'Who transfers?', under 'Who is an employee for TUPE purposes? – employees employed abroad'.

2.103 **Working time.** The Working Time Regulations do not set out the territorial reach of the rights they contain. The EAT in Dhunna v Creditsights Ltd 2013 ICR 909, EAT, held that Reg 1(2) – which provides that the Regulations 'extend' to Great Britain only – contains an express territorial limitation, but, with respect, this is an incorrect reading. Lady Smith in Transocean International Resources Ltd and ors v Russell and ors EATS 0074/05 made it clear that Reg 1(2), while it states that the Regulations extend to Great Britain and thus form part of the law of England, Wales and Scotland, does not determine the application of the Regulations. The EAT in Bleuse v MBT Transport Ltd and anor 2008 ICR 488, EAT, made the same point in relation to a claim for holiday pay – see 'Extent of legislation' above.

Thus, disregarding any question of rights under European law, there seems to be no reason why the reach of rights in the Working Time Regulations should be any different to those in the ERA – see Bleuse. However, the EAT in Bleuse was prepared to hold that the Regulations, and other legislation giving force of law to EU rights, should be construed so as to ensure that directly effective EU rights can be enforced by the English courts, even if this means widening their territorial scope (see 'EU-derived rights' above).

It should also be noted that if a British worker is posted to another Member State, he or she will, in any event, be covered by the legislation implementing the EU Working Time Directive (No.93/104) in that Member State.

2.104 **Contractual claims.** As discussed under 'Types of claim heard by tribunals – contractual claims' above, the contractual jurisdiction of employment tribunals is governed by S.3 ETA together with the Employment Tribunals Extension of Jurisdiction (England and Wales) Order 1994 SI 1994/1623 ('the Order') (or, as relevant, the Employment Tribunals Extension of Jurisdiction (Scotland) Order 1994 SI 1994/1624). Under S.3(2) ETA and Article 3 of the Order, for an employment tribunal to be able to hear a contractual claim brought by an employee, that claim must be one that a court in England and Wales would have jurisdiction to hear and determine. To ascertain this, regard must be had to the rules of international jurisdiction – see 'International jurisdiction' above. (The question of which law applies to a contract of employment is discussed under 'Applicable law'.)

Relitigation: res judicata and abuse of process 2.105

Where an issue has already come before a court or tribunal and has been decided, or an issue could have been brought before a court or tribunal in previous proceedings but was not, a party who seeks to reopen or raise such an issue in subsequent proceedings before a different court or tribunal may be barred, or 'estopped', from doing so if his or her opponent successfully pleads the defence of 'res judicata'. Our discussion in this section will centre on the doctrine of res judicata as it is applied in England and Wales. It should be noted that the approach taken in Scotland is slightly different. A discussion about the applicability of the doctrine in employment tribunals in Scotland can be found in British Airways plc v Boyce 2001 IRLR 157, Ct Sess (Inner House).

The Court of Appeal in Divine-Bortey v Brent London Borough Council 1998 ICR 886, CA, identified three categories of estoppel falling within the doctrine of res judicata (though, strictly speaking, the term 'res judicata' as a rule of law covers only the first two of these). These are:

- cause of action estoppel – which prevents a party pursuing a cause of action that has been dealt with in earlier proceedings involving the same parties (see 'Cause of action estoppel' below)

- issue estoppel – which prevents a party reopening an issue that has been decided in earlier proceedings involving the same parties (see 'Issue estoppel' below), and

- 'the rule in Henderson v Henderson' (arising from Henderson v Henderson 1843 3 Hare 100, PC) – which, as reformulated by the House of Lords in Johnson v Gore Wood and Co 2002 2 AC 1, HL, essentially provides that if a party fails to raise an issue in proceedings that he or she could and should have raised, he or she may be estopped from raising that issue in the future if to do so would amount to an abuse of legal process. This doctrine – which is a wider form of issue estoppel – is a procedural rule based on the need to prevent proceedings amounting to an 'abuse of process' and is discussed under 'Abuse of process' below.

What is a decision? 2.106
Before turning to examine each form of estoppel it should be noted that in order for the doctrine of res judicata to apply to a determination of a tribunal,

95

that determination should be a judicial decision (as opposed to merely an administrative act). A 'decision' was defined in the 2001 version of the Tribunal Regulations as a declaration, an order (including an order striking out any claim form or response but not including an interlocutory order), a recommendation, an award or a determination concerning entitlement to bring proceedings. However, the 2004 Tribunal Regulations removed this definition and rule 1(3)(b) of the Tribunal Rules 2013 now uses the term 'judgment' for a decision that finally determines a claim, or part of a claim, as regards liability, remedy or costs; any issue that is capable of disposing of a claim even if it does not necessarily do so (for example, an issue whether a claim should be struck out or a jurisdictional issue); or a financial penalty under S.12A ETA. For the purpose of examining the case law on the application of the doctrine of res judicata and abuse of process, we will continue to use the generic term 'decision'.

Pre-2004, it was explicit in the Tribunal Rules that an interlocutory (i.e. interim) order was not a 'decision'. In Air Canada and anor v Basra 2000 IRLR 683, EAT, a tribunal, before dismissing B's claim for race discrimination, refused B leave to amend her claim form to bring claims of both sex and race victimisation. Subsequently, B brought her victimisation claims before a second tribunal. In the course of an appeal over whether the victimisation claims were estopped, the EAT held that the first tribunal's decision to refuse leave to amend was simply an interlocutory order and, accordingly, was not a decision. Therefore there was no cause of action estoppel in respect of the victimisation claims that the tribunal had refused to hear, and both the sex and race victimisation claims could proceed. It is possible, however, that the EAT might have come to a different conclusion had the Tribunal Rules 2013 applied to the case. A refusal to allow a claimant leave to amend his or her claim form to add certain claims could arguably amount to a jurisdictional issue capable of finally disposing of a claim. If so, this would fall squarely within rule 1(3)(b)(ii), thereby amounting to a 'judgment'.

2.107 In Crown Estate Commissioners v Dorset County Council 1990 1 All ER 19, ChD, the High Court held that there was no reason, subject to certain safeguards, why the decision of an inferior tribunal, with limited jurisdiction and a strictly limited function, should not be capable of creating estoppel in proceedings before a superior court. This issue most commonly arises with regard to the effect of decisions by tribunals in unfair dismissal cases on related actions for wrongful dismissal in the High Court. An example:

- **Green and anor v Hampshire County Council** 1979 ICR 861, ChD: following protracted unfair dismissal litigation involving appeals to the National Industrial Relations Court (NIRC) and remissions for rehearing, a tribunal finally concluded that G and his wife had not been unfairly dismissed for misconduct from their respective jobs as superintendent and matron of a young persons' home. Their further appeal to the NIRC was dismissed and leave to appeal refused, whereupon they commenced proceedings in the High Court seeking a declaration that their dismissals were illegal, ultra vires and void. The Council applied to have the statement of claim struck out on the ground that the issues raised in it were res judicata. Mr Justice Fox held that the decision of the tribunal on the substantive claim of unfair dismissal was fully reasoned and constituted a judicial decision by a judicial tribunal for the purposes of the doctrine of res judicata. As such it gave rise to an estoppel, binding on the parties, that the plaintiffs had been dismissed fairly. The statement of claim was therefore struck out.

It is important to bear in mind that the rules on estoppel apply only to *judicial* decisions. In Christou and anor v London Borough of Haringey 2013 ICR 1007, CA, the Court of Appeal rejected the claimants' attempt to argue that their employer was precluded from reopening disciplinary proceedings against them on the basis of res judicata and/or abuse of process. The employer's exercise of disciplinary power, the Court concluded, was conferred by reason of the hierarchical nature of the employment relationship and disciplinary proceedings did not function as an adjudication between employer and employee but to enable the employer to inform itself whether the employee had acted inappropriately or in breach of contract. The fact that disciplinary procedures might be contractual or provide safeguards typically found in adjudicative bodies did not alter this basic function. Nevertheless, the Court acknowledged that some domestic tribunals set up by contractual agreement can constitute judicial bodies, provided they operate independently of the parties such that it is appropriate to describe their function as an adjudication between them. In R (Coke-Wallis) v Institute of Chartered Accountants in England and Wales 2011 ICR 224, SC, for example, the Supreme Court held that the doctrine of res judicata did apply to a disciplinary committee of the Institute of Chartered Accountants.

Withdrawal. The dismissal of a claim upon withdrawal by the claimant **2.108** constitutes a 'decision' for the purposes of the res judicata doctrines. In Barber v Staffordshire County Council 1996 ICR 379, CA, B withdrew a claim for a redundancy payment because she believed that she lacked the necessary qualifying service. The tribunal declared that 'the unanimous decision of the tribunal is that this application is dismissed on withdrawal by the applicant'. However, following a House of Lords' decision that the relevant qualifying period was unlawful, B brought a fresh claim for a redundancy payment before a second tribunal. That tribunal ruled that B's claim could proceed but the Council successfully appealed to the EAT, which held that B was estopped from bringing her second claim. B appealed to the Court of Appeal, which agreed with the EAT. Lord Justice Neill, giving the judgment of the Court, stated that the principles of cause of action estoppel are not restricted to cases where a tribunal has given a reasoned decision on the issues of fact and law in previous litigation: rather, those principles will apply where a tribunal has made any judicial decision in the exercise of its powers under the Tribunal Regulations and what is now the ETA. The Court of Appeal held that the declaration of the first tribunal that the claim be dismissed upon the withdrawal of the claimant was such a judicial decision, as it was within the tribunal's discretion. It was not a mere administrative act. This meant that B could not proceed with her claim to the second tribunal.

Until the Tribunal Regulations 2013 were brought into force on 29 July 2013, settled or withdrawn claims were not, as a matter of course, formally dismissed by the employment tribunal. Rather, tribunals tended to advise the parties that the case would be removed from the hearing lists and that the tribunal had closed its file (although under rule 25(4) of the Tribunal Rules 2004 the respondent could, within 28 days, apply to the tribunal for the claim to be formally dismissed). The question therefore arose as to whether a withdrawal, per se, constituted a 'decision', such that a claim, once withdrawn, could not be relitigated even if it had not been formally dismissed. In Khan v Heywood and Middleton Primary Care Trust 2007 ICR 24, CA, the Court of Appeal addressed this in the context of old rule 25(4). K withdrew a claim against his employer after receiving legal advice. He changed legal advisers and sought to set aside the withdrawal of his claim, while the respondent applied to have the withdrawn claim dismissed. Both the employment tribunal and the EAT held that there was no power under rule 25 for a tribunal to revive a withdrawn claim. Endorsing this view, the Court of Appeal nonetheless confirmed that a withdrawal of a claim, in and of itself, did not create an issue or cause of action estoppel, since it did not involve a judicial act. A fresh claim based on the same cause of action would not be barred by a withdrawal (though it might be by the expiration of the relevant time limits) – Ellis and anor v Yansen EAT 0132/06. However, where a respondent successfully applied to have the claim dismissed under rule 25(4), this would involve the necessary judicial act and the claimant would be estopped from bringing further claims on the same facts.

2.109 Now, under rule 52 of the Tribunal Rules 2013, the position has been clarified. Under this rule, the tribunal will automatically issue a judgment dismissing a claim (or part) that has been withdrawn *unless*:

- the claimant expresses, at the time of withdrawal, a wish to reserve the right to bring a further claim against the respondent raising the same, or substantially the same, complaint and the tribunal is satisfied that there would be legitimate reason for doing so – rule 52(a), or

- the tribunal believes that to issue such a judgment would not be in the interests of justice – rule 52(b).

Rule 52, which clearly acknowledges that the withdrawal of a claim, in and of itself, does not constitute a decision such that the claim cannot be brought again, was presumably intended to rectify a problem highlighted by British

Association for Shooting and Conservation v Cokayne 2008 ICR 185, EAT. In that case, C was persuaded to withdraw his claim for constructive dismissal when his employer wrote to him saying, among other things, that since he had not completed the grievance procedure it would seek to reduce any award the tribunal might make. The employer then successfully applied to have the claim dismissed under rule 25 of the Tribunal Rules 2004. When the employee issued a new claim, which he had always maintained he would do, the employer argued that he was 'estopped' from doing so. Although the tribunal rejected that argument and was prepared to hear the claim, the EAT allowed the employer's appeal against that decision: estoppel prevented the employee litigating the same cause of action twice. (However, the EAT noted that the employee might still ask the tribunal to reconsider the decision to dismiss the original claim under what is now rule 70, and that tribunals are obliged to consider the justice of doing so.)

In Cokayne C had argued that, as he had made his intention to relodge his **2.110** claim clear in his e-mail to the tribunal withdrawing his claim, there should be no estoppel following the Court of Appeal's decision in Ako v Rothschild Asset Management Ltd 2002 ICR 899, CA. In that case A brought claims against RAM, but then became aware that her employment might have transferred to a second company, MB. She withdrew her claim and a few days later presented a second complaint, substantially the same, against both RAM and MB, thinking that this was the proper course of action for naming MB as a second respondent. However, the tribunal dismissed her withdrawn claim in a consent order before the second claim was presented. When the issue of cause of action estoppel came before the Court of Appeal, it held that a tribunal could have regard to the factual circumstances surrounding a consent order to determine the extent of the consent and the extent of estoppel arising from it. However, the EAT in Cokayne distinguished Ako, noting that it addressed a problem that existed before the introduction of the Tribunal Rules 2004, whereby a claimant could not withdraw a claim without it being dismissed by the tribunal (and was thus unable to avoid an estoppel situation occurring where, as in Cokayne, withdrawal was made to allow for a grievance to be heard). Since 2004 there has been a distinction between withdrawal and dismissal of a claim, so the same problem does not arise. The EAT, following the Court of Appeal's judgment in Fraser v HLMAD Ltd 2006 ICR 1395, CA (see 'Merger of causes of action' below), held that the existence of a dismissal in previous proceedings means that those proceedings cannot be brought again because of estoppel. Issues as to the merits of whether the claimant always intended to bring those proceedings again are irrelevant.

Rule 52 significantly reduces the risk of injustice such as occurred in Cokayne, without diluting the law on estoppel (as, arguably, the Court of Appeal did in Ako), in that it concentrates the minds of the parties and the tribunal, at the moment of withdrawal, as to the reason for it and whether dismissal is or is

99

not an appropriate response. Note that rule 52(a) requires a claimant to reserve his or her right to bring a further claim *at the time of withdrawal*. The implication is that if the claimant neglects to do this at the time, he or she will be unable to do so later and the tribunal will automatically dismiss the claim (although note that the rule sets out no time frame within which dismissal must occur). However, assuming dismissal has not yet taken place, a claimant in such circumstances could seek to rely on rule 52(b), arguing that although he or she did not expressly reserve the right to relitigate at the time of withdrawal, it would be in the interests of justice for the tribunal not to dismiss the claim. Although, following Khan v Heywood and Middleton Primary Care Trust (above), the tribunal would not be empowered to revive the withdrawn claim, the claimant might be able to bring a fresh claim based on the same issues or cause of action, assuming that this would not amount to an abuse of process.

2.111 It is worth observing that a claimant's expression of wish under rule 52(a) will not automatically be granted. Not only must the claimant express the wish to reserve the right to bring a further claim against the respondent raising the same, or substantially the same, complaint, but the tribunal must also be satisfied that there would be *legitimate reason* for doing so. Presumably the tribunal would not be so satisfied if to bring a further claim would be likely to amount to abuse of process.

See Chapter 4, 'Starting tribunal proceedings', under 'Withdrawals', for further discussion of rule 52.

2.112 **Want of juridiction.** In Nayif v High Commission of Brunei Darussalam 2013 EWHC 3938, QBD, the High Court held that issue estoppel prevented an employee bringing High Court claims of negligence and breach of the Management of Health and Safety at Work Regulations 1999 SI 1999/3242 after an employment tribunal had rejected his race discrimination claim, based on much the same facts, because it was out of time. The Court accepted that where a claim that fell totally outside the employment tribunal's jurisdiction, such as a claim for personal injury arising out of an employer's negligence, was brought in the tribunal, the fact that the tribunal would issue an order dismissing that claim would not prevent it being pursued in the civil courts. However, in this case, N's race discrimination claim was one that the tribunal could consider but it had been brought outside the primary time limit. The employment judge had reached a reasoned decision that the claim was out of time and that it would not be just and equitable to extend time. This was a far more substantive decision than a dismissal on withdrawal and it would be 'very strange indeed' if, after the employment tribunal had heard evidence on the merits and had refused to extend time and had dismissed the claim, issue estoppel did not apply because of the classification of the decision as jurisdictional.

Cause of action estoppel   2.113

Cause of action estoppel prevents a party pursuing a cause of action that has been dealt with in earlier proceedings involving the same parties. Where two sets of proceedings are brought in relation to similar circumstances, the issue generally will be whether they both rely on the same cause of action, or whether they are sufficiently different such that cause of action estoppel does not apply. This was one of the issues before the EAT in British Association for Shooting and Conservation v Cokayne (above) – see 'What is a decision? – withdrawal' above. At a preliminary hearing a tribunal had found that C's second claim differed significantly from his first, principally because it included complaints about the grievance process. However, the EAT held that estoppel had arisen: both of C's claims were for constructive dismissal concerning the same resignation letter with the same termination date. The tribunal had erred in law in deciding that, because C's two causes of action were not 'identical', no estoppel could exist: in all material respects, both claims were the same. The tribunal's point that employees who allowed employers time to conduct grievance hearings should not lose their right to claim if such hearings were unsatisfactory had no bearing on the test of whether estoppel existed; namely, whether two claims were fundamentally the same.

An interesting attempt to circumvent the principle of cause of action estoppel was considered by the EAT in Agbenowossi-Koffi v Donvand Ltd t/a Gullivers Travel Associates EAT 0337/12. A-K brought a claim of racial harassment based on a single incident. It was out of time and at a preliminary hearing an employment judge declined to extend time to admit it. She also refused an application to amend the claim to add two further complaints which, if they had been accepted, might have allowed A-K to plead a continuing act of discrimination. This would have brought the first claim 'back in time', as the time limit would have started running from the end of the continuing act rather than from the isolated incident. A-K then presented a new claim form, repeating the original incident alongside the two further complaints. However, an employment judge held that the claim was estopped and the EAT agreed. The decision that there was no jurisdiction to hear A-K's claim in respect of the first incident was binding between the parties, as an issue necessary to the presentation of that claim had been finally determined, and the absence of any consideration of the claim's merits did not affect this. Estoppel could not be avoided by the repetition of the original claim in the second claim form coupled with the argument that, had the original incident been presented on the basis that it was part of a continuing act, it would (or might) not have been held to have been out of time. The claim as originally presented in the first proceedings had not been put forward in that way and the attempt to do so by amendment had been rejected. (See 'Abuse of process' below for further comment on this case.)

One of the circumstances in which a cause of action estoppel might arise is   2.114
where the claimant fails in his or her claim on the basis of one legal approach

101

and then seeks to relitigate the matter on the basis of another. In Blaik v Post Office 1994 IRLR 280, EAT, B had first alleged that his dismissal for persistent non-compliance with an instruction to wear a tie at work was contrary to the Sex Discrimination Act 1975 because a female employee would not have been dismissed for refusing to do what he had refused to do. However, B's complaint was rejected by a tribunal. Subsequently, he sought to complain of the same matter but this time under the provisions of the EU Equal Treatment Directive (No.76/207) (now No.2006/54). The second tribunal held that B had no right to apply for a decision under that Directive in view of the fact that his earlier complaint on the same matter had been considered under provisions of UK legislation that fully implemented the Directive. The EAT upheld the second tribunal's decision on appeal, with Mr Justice Mummery stating that: 'If there is a sufficient remedy given by the domestic law, it is unnecessary, and indeed impermissible, to explore the same complaint under the equivalent provisions in the Directive. It is only if there is a disparity between the two that it becomes necessary to consider whether the provisions in EEC law are directly enforceable by the complainant in his proceedings against the respondent.'

2.115 Issue estoppel

This form of estoppel prevents a party reopening an issue that has been decided in earlier proceedings involving the same parties. It does not mean that one tribunal, upon hearing evidence, can never disagree with another tribunal's finding of fact. The test which is used to establish whether a party is estopped from raising an issue is more complicated than that. The nature of the required inquiry was described by Lord Justice Diplock in Thoday v Thoday 1964 P 181, CA. Essentially, where a tribunal has made a finding of fact 'the existence of which is a condition the fulfilment of which is necessary to the cause of action' which the tribunal was considering, the parties will be estopped from calling that finding of fact into question in subsequent proceedings. Where, on the other hand, a tribunal has made a finding of fact 'the existence of which is not of itself a condition the fulfilment of which is necessary to the cause of action... but which is only relevant to proving the fulfilment of such a condition', there will be no issue estoppel. Or, to put it another way: 'Issue estoppel may arise where a particular issue forming a *necessary ingredient* in a cause of action has been litigated and decided and in subsequent proceedings between the same parties involving a different cause of action to which the same issue is relevant, one of the parties seeks to reopen that issue' – Lord Keith in Arnold v National Westminster Bank plc 1991 2 AC 93, HL (our stress).

Given that issue estoppel arises only in relation to a tribunal's necessary findings of fact or determinations, it will not arise in relation to findings that were in excess of the tribunal's jurisdiction. The Court of Appeal made this clear in Foster v Bon Groundwork Ltd 2012 ICR 1027, CA, in which F, a 78-year-old carpenter for BG Ltd, was laid off without pay in April 2009. He objected to the lay-off and also requested a written copy of his terms and conditions of employment. F was subsequently informed by a letter dated 21 May that he would be dismissed by reason of retirement on 31 July. On 10 June F submitted a claim form, seeking a redundancy payment. The form expressly stated that F was still in employment. That claim was heard in August, by which time F had been dismissed. The employment judge found that F was not entitled to a redundancy payment. He rejected the lay-off-based redundancy claim because F had not served on the employer a notice of intention to claim a redundancy payment in accordance with S.148 ERA. He then held that there was no dismissal-related redundancy, holding that 'the claimant was dismissed not by reason of redundancy but by reason of retirement and no other reason'.

Following the rejection of his first claim, F launched a second set of tribunal **2.116** proceedings. He brought various claims, including that his dismissal was 'automatically' unfair under S.103A ERA because he had made a protected disclosure (his complaints about the lay-off), and under S.104 because he had asserted a statutory right (again arising from those complaints). An employment judge determined that these claims of automatically unfair dismissal both required the claimant to show that the reason for dismissal was something other than retirement – which, she reasoned, was not possible given the finding of the first tribunal. On appeal, the EAT overturned the employment judge's decision, noting that although the doctrine of issue estoppel will bar a claimant from raising in fresh proceedings an issue that has already been adjudicated on, it is a prerequisite that the court or tribunal actually had jurisdiction to adjudicate on the issue in question. On this basis, it held that issue estoppel did not apply to F's unfair dismissal claims because the claim form in respect of the first tribunal case did not raise the issue of dismissal, but sought a redundancy payment due to lay-off. The finding that the dismissal was by reason of retirement was not a necessary ingredient of that claim. BG Ltd appealed to the Court of Appeal, where it argued that, since employment judges are encouraged to act informally and to assist litigants in person, it was plainly desirable in the instant case for all relevant claims to be heard together, and as such the EAT should not have interfered with the first tribunal's finding, particularly as it was not that case which was on appeal, but the strike-out order by the second tribunal.

Lord Justice Elias, who gave the leading judgment, held that the claim that the dismissal was by reason of redundancy was never properly before the first tribunal, and there was no basis for thinking that it was. The claimant's ET1 clearly referred to lay-off, and other documentation was wholly inconsistent with the employment tribunal judge's assumption that F was pursuing a dismissal-related redundancy claim. There had been no formal amendment to the claim and F had not been asked whether he also wanted the tribunal to deal with his dismissal. According to Elias LJ, 'it was the judge who thought it appropriate to determine this aspect of the case without expressly raising the issue with the parties at all. I do not think that a litigant in person should be

103

prejudiced by a ruling made in that context.' Since the dismissal issue had not been properly before the first tribunal, there was no question of F being estopped from raising it in the second claim. Elias LJ further considered that, if he was wrong and the issue of dismissal-related redundancy was properly before the first tribunal, it only needed to find that F was not dismissed for redundancy. A positive finding that the dismissal was for retirement was unnecessary. While the ruling would have meant that F could not assert that he had been dismissed for redundancy, he would not have been prevented from basing a dismissal claim on a different reason.

2.117 The Foster case demonstrates that tribunals should be cautious of dealing with matters not pleaded in a claimant's ET1. Although tribunals do have an obligation to assist unrepresented claimants, that obligation does not extend to supplanting the provisions on jurisdiction.

Some cases in which the doctrine of issue estoppel was found to apply, and which demonstrate the potential breadth of its application:

- **Lennon v Birmingham City Council** 2001 IRLR 826, CA: L brought a sex discrimination complaint alleging that she had been subjected to harassment and bullying, which had resulted in a stress-related illness. The complaint was withdrawn before the hearing and the tribunal made an order in the following terms: 'The application is dismissed on withdrawal by the applicant.' L then brought an action in the ordinary courts for breach of contract or negligence, which was struck out on the ground of issue estoppel. The Court of Appeal dismissed L's appeal, holding that her common law action repeated the same allegations and was based on the same facts as the tribunal proceedings. The decision of the tribunal, although not a decision on the merits, could and did found an issue estoppel

- **Deman v Association of University Teachers and ors** EAT 142/03: D brought a series of complaints against the Association and various of its officers alleging, inter alia, racial discrimination and victimisation. One of the tribunals was invited to consider, as relevant to complaints of specific acts of discrimination up to 14 November 1999, certain matters that had occurred after that date. In particular D wished the tribunal to take into account 'for background purposes' whether he had been wrongly denied 'legal aid' assistance by the Association. The tribunal acceded to that application and went on to consider various factual matters and developments in relation to the legal aid application that had arisen between January 2000 and March 2001. It found that D had been refused legal aid but that the refusal had been due to his own failure to provide reasonably required information. D then brought another claim before a different tribunal raising complaints of discrimination and victimisation, which included matters occurring between November 1999 and June 2001. The Association successfully applied to have the claim struck out on the basis that the matters contained in it had been determined by the first tribunal. D appealed but the EAT held that the second tribunal had been correct to order the strike-out on the basis of issue estoppel. Although the disputes of fact arising between the parties concerning matters in 2000 and 2001 would not themselves have been determinative of the substantive issues before the first tribunal, they informed its determination. Those findings were binding on any subsequent tribunal and, in so far as any subsequent complaint sought to reopen the findings in relation to that material, it would be prevented from doing so by operation of the principle of issue estoppel

• **Soteriou v Ultrachem Ltd and ors** 2004 IRLR 870, QBD: in August 1987 U Ltd engaged S's services as an accountant. In 1988 S registered for VAT and thereafter invoiced U Ltd using the name AGS Services. In November of that year the Contributions Agency commenced an investigation into S's employment status but on the basis of information provided by him the DSS accepted that he was self-employed. In January 2000 the engagement was terminated and S made an application to the employment tribunal claiming unfair dismissal. The tribunal held that S had been self-employed until 1996 but that some time during that year his status changed and he became an employee. However, it concluded that he had knowingly committed a fraud in relation to the employment contract and therefore could not rely on that contract to claim unfair dismissal. On appeal, the EAT agreed that S could not claim unfair dismissal because his contract of employment was tainted by illegality and was therefore unenforceable. S then commenced proceedings in the High Court for wrongful dismissal but the claim was struck out by the Master on the ground that he was bound by the tribunal's findings that the contract of employment was unenforceable due to illegality and that this operated as an issue estoppel. Judge Altman, sitting as a Judge of the High Court, agreed.

By contrast, in the following cases subsequent proceedings were not estopped **2.118** on the basis of issue estoppel:

• **Friend v Civil Aviation Authority and ors** 2001 IRLR 819, CA: F was unfairly dismissed on procedural grounds after he objected to the CAA's safety procedures, but he was found to have contributed 100 per cent to his dismissal. He then brought a claim for breach of contract and various employment-related torts which he alleged had led to his dismissal. The claim was struck out on the ground of issue estoppel by the High Court on the basis that the tribunal had found that the cause of dismissal was entirely F's own conduct. The Court of Appeal allowed F's appeal, holding that the issue before the High Court was not the same as the one that had been decided in the earlier tribunal proceedings. A decision under S.123(6) ERA that a claimant's conduct contributed to his or her dismissal, and that

105

it would be just and equitable to reduce the amount of the compensatory award by 100 per cent, could not be regarded as a decision that any loss resulting from the claimant's dismissal was not caused by anything done by the employer

- **UNISON v Kelly and ors** 2012 IRLR 442, EAT (appealed to the Court of Appeal on different issues in UNISON v Kelly and ors 2012 IRLR 951, CA): four union members were disciplined by UNISON for producing a leaflet which alleged that the union had breached its own rules. They brought an employment tribunal claim against UNISON under the Employment Equality (Religion or Belief) Regulations 2003 SI 2003/1660 (now repealed and superseded by the EqA), alleging that UNISON had pursued disciplinary proceedings against them on the ground of their Marxist/Trotskyite beliefs. This claim was unsuccessful. Subsequently, after they were banned from holding office, they brought further proceedings alleging that they had been unjustifiably disciplined contrary to Ss.64 and 65 TULR(C)A. In the course of these proceedings, UNISON submitted that a finding of fact by the first tribunal – that the disciplinary proceedings had been brought because of complaints by some people who considered the leaflet racially offensive – created an issue estoppel which determined an issue under S.65(5) that was relevant to the question of justification. However, the EAT held that the two employment tribunal decisions were dealing with different time periods and different decisions by the union. The issue before the first tribunal was whether the decision to hold the investigation was made on the ground of the respondents' political beliefs, whereas the issue before the second tribunal was whether the respondents were banned from holding office because they had asserted a breach of union rules. The EAT agreed with the second tribunal's self-direction that while it was estopped from deciding and reaching any different conclusions on the issues that had been determined by the previous tribunal, it was not bound by every finding of fact that that tribunal had made. Accordingly, the EAT held that issue estoppel did not apply.

2.119 Parties should be cautious when making admissions or concessions in tribunal proceedings as they may be unable to retract these in subsequent proceedings. In Storrie v Consignia plc EAT 0217/02 S claimed that she had been constructively dismissed on 22 January 2001. The tribunal found against her, but agreed that the effective date of termination of employment was indeed 22 January. Subsequently S presented a fresh claim in which she cited 28 February 2001 as the effective date of termination – a date which the documentation clearly supported. Assuming the date of termination was 28 February, her second claim was submitted in time. If it was 22 January, it was not. The second tribunal accepted the first tribunal's finding that the date of termination was 22 January and dismissed S's claim. On appeal, the EAT held that even though it was strongly arguable in the light of the documents that S's admission in the first hearing (that she was constructively dismissed on 22 January) was incorrect, it was bound to follow the principle of res judicata. The first tribunal was not obliged to argue S's case for her; and the second tribunal committed no error of law in not adjudicating again a matter that had already been decided. The EAT quoted with approval the Court of Appeal's statement in Khan v Golechha International Ltd 1980 1 WLR 1482, CA, that the law treated an issue as laid at rest 'not only if it is embodied in the terms of the judgment, or implicit in the judgment because it is embodied in the spoken decision, but also if it is embodied in an admission made in the face of the court'. This case is particularly interesting because the first tribunal's finding as to the date of termination was not, in the circumstances of the case, strictly crucial to its decision. However, it was because of its indication that it would consider the exercise of its discretion to allow a claim out of time that it made a decision about the effective date of termination and S launched the second proceedings.

Abuse of process
2.120

As discussed under 'Relitigation: res judicata and abuse of process' above, the case of Henderson v Henderson 1843 3 Hare 100, PC, gave rise to a wider form of issue estoppel known as the rule in Henderson v Henderson, or Henderson abuse of process. Essentially, this procedural rule provides that if a party fails to raise an issue in proceedings that he or she could and should have raised, he or she may be prevented from raising that issue in the future if to do so would amount to an abuse of legal process. The primary difference between Henderson abuse of process and the estoppels discussed above is that to deny a party the opportunity of litigating for the first time a question that has not previously been adjudicated is prima facie a denial of his or her right of access to the court under common law, guaranteed by Article 6 of the European Convention on Human Rights. As a result, the Henderson rule should be invoked only where there is a need 'to protect the process of the court from abuse and the defendant from oppression' – per Lord Millett in Johnson v Gore Wood and Co 2002 2 AC 1, HL. There is no presumption that successive actions should not be brought.

The modern understanding of the rule in Henderson v Henderson was explained by Lord Bingham in Johnson in a key passage which is worth quoting at length:

'Henderson v Henderson abuse of process, as now understood, although separate and distinct from cause of action estoppel and issue estoppel, has much in common with them. The underlying public interest is the same: that there should be finality in litigation and that a party should not be twice vexed in the same matter. This public interest is reinforced by the current emphasis on efficiency and economy in the conduct of litigation, in the interests of the parties and the public as a whole. The bringing of a claim or the raising of a defence in later proceedings may, without more, amount to abuse if the court is satisfied (the onus being on the party alleging abuse) that the claim or defence should have been raised in the

107

earlier proceedings if it was to be raised at all. I would not accept that it is necessary, before abuse may be found, to identify any additional element such as a collateral attack on a previous decision or some dishonesty, but where those elements are present the later proceedings will be much more obviously abusive, and there will rarely be a finding of abuse unless the later proceeding involves what the court regards as unjust harassment of a party. It is, however, wrong to hold that because a matter could have been raised in earlier proceedings it should have been, so as to render the raising of it in later proceedings necessarily abusive. That is to adopt too dogmatic an approach to what should in my opinion be *a broad, merits-based judgment* which takes account of the public and private interests involved and also takes account of all the facts of the case, focusing attention on *the crucial question whether, in all the circumstances, a party is misusing or abusing the process of the court by seeking to raise before it the issue which could have been raised before*. As one cannot comprehensively list all possible forms of abuse, so one cannot formulate any hard and fast rule to determine whether, on given facts, abuse is to be found or not. Thus while I would accept that lack of funds would not ordinarily excuse a failure to raise in earlier proceedings an issue which could and should have been raised then, I would not regard it as necessarily irrelevant, particularly if it appears that the lack of funds has been caused by the party against whom it is sought to claim. While the result may often be the same, it is in my view preferable to ask whether in all the circumstances a party's conduct is an abuse than to ask whether the conduct is an abuse and then, if it is, to ask whether the abuse is excused or justified by special circumstances' (our stresses).

2.121 In summary, tribunals considering the application of the rule in Henderson v Henderson should adopt a 'broad, merits-based' approach, taking into account all the circumstances. A simple finding that a party should have raised a matter in earlier proceedings is insufficient: the crucial question is whether, taking into account all the circumstances, the party is abusing the process of the court by seeking to raise a matter that it should have raised before.

The EAT applied Lord Bingham's analysis in Parker v Northumbrian Water Ltd 2011 ICR 1172, EAT. In that case, P brought a claim for unpaid wages. Following a case management discussion, the claim was amended to a claim for a declaration of the terms and conditions of P's employment under S.11 ERA. Following his subsequent dismissal, P brought more claims, including one of unlawful deductions from wages, and another of detriment for making a protected disclosure. An employment judge decided that the rule in Henderson v Henderson applied to prevent P from bringing these claims, as he could have raised them earlier. However, on appeal, the EAT held that the employment judge had applied Henderson abuse of process in 'far too rigid a way' and had not followed Lord Bingham's approach of a merits-based analysis. The

108

employment judge had excluded the claims because the matters could have been raised earlier but were not, but had not considered why any claim *should* have been raised at an earlier time as opposed to the fact that it could have been. In the EAT's judgement, the case illustrated the dangers of starting from the premise that, if the claims could have been advanced at an earlier time, then it would be an abuse of process to allow them to be pursued, unless 'special circumstances' could be established. In the EAT's judgement, a broad, merits-based approach to determining whether it would be abusive or oppressive to let P air the matters in second proceedings should take account of, inter alia, the fact that case management had resulted in P's case taking a certain form; that P's agreement to that case management decision did not place the primary responsibility for it upon him; and once the claim was reformulated as a claim for a declaration of terms, it was unrealistic to protest that complaints about deductions were not put forward at that time.

In the course of its judgment, the EAT advised that employment tribunals **2.122** should consider the Henderson abuse of process point from the perspective identified by Lord Bingham in Johnson v Gore Wood and Co (above), and not from that put forward by the Court of Appeal in Divine-Bortey v Brent London Borough Council 1998 ICR 886, CA. In that case, D-B was dismissed on the ground of redundancy and brought a claim of unfair dismissal against the Borough. During the hearing of his complaint, one of the Borough's witnesses referred to the claimant's 'African accent' as one of the reasons for his not being selected for an alternative post. The tribunal dismissed D-B's unfair dismissal claim and he subsequently brought a claim of race discrimination against the Borough. A second tribunal held that it had no jurisdiction to hear the race discrimination claim, and the Court of Appeal subsequently confirmed that, on hearing the evidence that his accent had been one of the reasons for his dismissal, D-B should have grafted his race discrimination claim onto the existing unfair dismissal proceedings, seeking an adjournment for the purpose if necessary. It considered that the fact that the initial proceedings occurred in a tribunal, where parties are encouraged not to be legally represented, could not constitute a special circumstance under which the rule in Henderson v Henderson should not apply.

The 'special circumstance' exception derives from Sir James Wigram VC's judgment in Henderson v Henderson where he stated that the rule will apply 'except in special circumstances', which might include such matters as where a claimant has made a genuine mistake of fact as to who is the appropriate respondent to his or her claim – see Bezant v Tertiary Enterprises (formerly Wadhurst Park Ltd) (in liquidation) EAT 0348/04. However, following Lord Bingham's analysis in Johnson v Gore Wood and Co (above), as interpreted by the EAT in Parker v Northumbrian Water Ltd (above) (an interpretation the EAT agreed with in Deer v University of Oxford EAT 0532/12), it is doubtful that this approach to Henderson abuse of process cases remains relevant in

109

employment cases. In so far as the Court of Appeal's 'special circumstances' approach in Divine-Bortey is inconsistent with the House of Lords' merits-based approach in Johnson, the latter must prevail.

2.123 Although an appellate court should not lightly interfere with an employment tribunal's application of these principles, the tribunal's decision on an issue of abuse of process is not a matter of discretion as there is a right or wrong answer – see Foster v Bon Groundwork Ltd 2012 ICR 1027, CA, and Aldi Stores Ltd v WSP Group plc 2008 1 WLR 748, CA.

Lord Bingham's broad, merits-based approach to considering Henderson abuse of process was adopted by the EAT in the following cases:

* **Owolabi v Bondcare Ltd and ors** EAT 0624/12: O was suspended from his work in a nursing home for alleged misconduct. While suspended, he brought a claim in an employment tribunal alleging race discrimination by his colleagues. At a preliminary hearing, the tribunal ordered O to provide further particulars of his claim, including whether he contended that any disciplinary action taken against him was taken on racial grounds, but he supplied no particulars in response to that requirement. Some 14 months after the determination of that claim, O brought a second claim which included a claim of victimisation relating to the fact that he had been suspended and that he had remained suspended for so long. An employment judge struck out this claim as being an abuse of process under the rule in Henderson v Henderson, and the EAT upheld this decision. Given that O could have raised the question of his suspension at the hearing of his first claim – by which time his suspension had been in place for around 16 months – the question arose as to whether he should have done so. O could provide no good reason for not raising the issue earlier, and particularly given the fact that he had not responded to a specific request to provide further particulars as to whether he was complaining about any disciplinary steps taken, the employment judge had not erred in striking out the claim

* **Fox and ors v Bassetlaw District Council** EAT 0274/12: the claimants brought a grievance against the Council complaining that they were not receiving equal pay with male Council officers working within two departments, including pest control. After the Council rejected this grievance, the claimants brought equal pay claims in an employment tribunal, in which they compared themselves to four male comparators, none of whom were pest control officers. Subsequently, the claimants withdrew their claims and brought new equal pay proceedings comparing themselves with pest control officers. An employment judge considered that the second proceedings amounted to an abuse of process, and the EAT found that he had been entitled to do so. The claimants had been advised by their union when raising their initial grievance. Taking account of all the facts of the case,

they clearly could have pursued their second set of claims in the original proceedings, and should have done so: their late change to the basis of the equal value claims prejudiced the Council

- **Deer v University of Oxford** EAT 0532/12: D, a research fellow, brought a sex discrimination claim against the University in 2007, which was settled. In 2009 she brought a claim in the employment tribunal against a professor and the University, claiming that the professor's refusal to provide her with a reference in connection with her application for a fellowship amounted to victimisation for which the University was vicariously liable. This was dismissed on the basis that the professor did not know of her protected act in bringing the sex discrimination claim. A few months later she sought to pursue an alternative claim on the basis that, contrary to her primary case, the professor was the innocent conduit of acts of victimisation by others in not providing the reference. The EAT agreed with an employment judge that the second claim amounted to a 'plain abuse of process'. If D knew that she wanted to bring the alternative claim, she wholly failed to make it clear to the University or to the tribunal during a lengthy case management process

- **Thomas Cook Airline Services Ltd v Wolstenholme (as personal representative of Mr D Wolstenholme)** EAT 0353/12: DW was employed by TCAS Ltd as a pilot. On 8 July 2009 he was arrested for drink driving, after which he failed to report for work. He was invited to a disciplinary hearing, which he did not attend, and TCAS Ltd stopped his salary. Some days later, DW purchased a one-way ticket to Amsterdam, and subsequently fell from a bridge there, sustaining serious injuries from which he never recovered. He remained in a coma until his death on 28 May 2010. In October 2010 his trade union instructed solicitors to bring proceedings for unfair and wrongful dismissal and arrears of pay, on the basis that he had been dismissed on 22 July 2009. These proceedings were stayed pending rights of representation being granted to W, DW's wife. In November 2011, the solicitors withdrew these proceedings and, in September 2012, issued a claim in the High Court on the basis that his employment did not end until his death, and claiming substantial damages for contractual sick pay and a death-in-service payment. TCAS Ltd applied for the tribunal proceedings to be dismissed under rule 25(4) of the Tribunal Rules 2004 (see 'What is a decision? – withdrawal' above), but an employment judge rejected the application, and the EAT confirmed that he had permissibly concluded that in so far as the High Court proceedings sought to resurrect a claim of breach of contract between the parties, they did not amount to an abuse of process. Although the factual matrix was common to both sets of proceedings, the High Court claim proceeded on a wholly different basis and arose out of developments following the institution of the original tribunal proceedings

- **Foster v Bon Groundwork Ltd** 2012 ICR 1027, CA (also discussed under 'Issue estoppel' above): F was laid off without pay in April 2009 and submitted a claim for a redundancy payment based on lay-off. The claim was heard in August, by which time F had been dismissed. The employment judge found that F was not entitled to a redundancy payment based on lay-off, and also held that 'the claimant was dismissed not by reason of redundancy but by reason of retirement and no other reason'. F then launched a second set of tribunal proceedings making various claims, including ordinary unfair dismissal and automatic unfair dismissal for failure to comply with the statutory retirement procedure then in force. An employment judge determined that these claims, though not estopped by the judgment of the first tribunal, should be struck out as an abuse of process on the basis that they could and should have been pleaded before the first tribunal. The EAT overturned this decision, noting that Henderson abuse of process is not established simply because the second set of claims could have been heard with the first. Rather, it is necessary to show that bringing the later claims was abusive having regard to the public and private interests involved and all the circumstances. However, when the case reached the Court of Appeal, Lord Justice Elias considered that the finding of abuse of process was linked to the erroneous assumption that a claim arising out of the dismissal was properly before the first tribunal. In the absence of that premise, the abuse of process finding simply fell away. In any event, Elias LJ considered, it would not have been an abuse of process to bring the claims. There would be a real injustice to F if, for example, he could not contend that he was unfairly dismissed due to a failure to follow the statutory retirement procedure

- **Agbenowossi-Koffi v Donvand Ltd t/a Gullivers Travel Associates** EAT 0337/12 (also discussed above under 'Cause of action estoppel'): A-K brought a claim of racial harassment based on a single incident. It was out of time and at a preliminary hearing an employment judge declined to extend time to admit it. She also refused an application to amend the claim to add two further complaints which, if they had been accepted, might have allowed A-K to plead a continuing act of discrimination. This would have brought the first claim 'back in time', as the time limit would have started running from the end of the continuing act rather than from the isolated incident. A-K then presented a new claim form, repeating the original incident alongside the two further complaints. However, an employment judge held that the claim was estopped, and that, because the claim in respect of the subsequent acts had only been put forward in an attempt to serve the claim in respect of the first act (by enabling A-K to argue a continuing act of discrimination), those further complaints should be struck out as an abuse of process. The EAT agreed, holding that the employment judge had taken into account permissible factors in reaching her conclusion as to abuse of process. She had found that A-K's first claim was drafted, by solicitors, in terms which acknowledged that the claim was well out of time; that if A-K genuinely believed that she had good claims in respect of the two subsequent acts of discrimination, she would have relied on them from the start, given that they would have enabled her to avoid the consequences of the lateness of the presentation of the first claim; that the two additional acts were only put forward as a tactical measure in order to seek to save the original claim, and that they were being pursued in the second claim form in order to seek to resurrect the first claim, which had already been dismissed.

Merger of causes of action   2.124

In Fraser v HLMAD Ltd 2006 ICR 1395, CA, the employee brought proceedings for unfair dismissal and wrongful dismissal in the employment tribunal. However, in his ET1 he expressly reserved the right to bring a claim in the High Court 'in so far as my claim for damages for wrongful dismissal exceeds the tribunal's jurisdiction of £25,000'. Before the determination of his claims in the tribunal, F brought a wrongful dismissal claim in the High Court in order to recover his damages in excess of £25,000. He did not, however, withdraw the tribunal claim and the tribunal went on to find that he had been unfairly and wrongfully dismissed. Although it assessed his damages for breach of contract at just over £80,000, in view of the statutory cap on damages for breach of contract brought in tribunals, it awarded the maximum of £25,000.

The employer successfully applied to have the High Court claim struck out on the ground that it was 'res judicata'. F appealed to the Court of Appeal, where the employer relied upon the principle of merger of causes of action. Under that principle, following a determination by a competent court – in this case, the employment tribunal – the cause of action is merged into the judgment and ceases to exist. In the Court's view, F's wrongful dismissal claim had clearly merged into the judgment of the tribunal in respect of his wrongful dismissal and was therefore extinguished. F's express statement in his ET1 form reserving the right to bring High Court proceedings for damages in excess of the £25,000 limit had not prevented the merger from taking place. Nor was it possible to split the cause of action for wrongful dismissal into two separate causes of action: one for damages up to £25,000 and another for the balance. As a result, F no longer had any cause of action that he could pursue in the High Court.

The Court advised that claimants and their legal advisers should not, therefore,   2.125
bring wrongful dismissal claims in the tribunal unless they are certain they want to limit compensation to £25,000. If they wish to recover more, a wrongful dismissal claim should only be made to the High Court. It was further recommended that the Employment Tribunals Service (now HMCTS) review its literature to make it clear that a wrongful dismissal claim should not be brought in an employment tribunal where a claimant expects to be awarded more than £25,000.

113

For further discussion of the various factors involved in deciding the appropriate forum for a contractual claim, see the section 'Types of claim heard by tribunals' above, under 'Contractual claims – choice of court or tribunal'.

2.126 State and diplomatic immunity

Under the provisions of international law, immunity from legal process can be conferred on the actions of states within the territory of other states and on the personnel responsible for operating the official 'establishments' of a state such as embassies, missions and consulates. The principal UK legislation enacting the international treaties on state immunity is the State Immunity Act 1978 (SIA). Its provisions, together with statutory provisions relevant to other kinds of immunity such as diplomatic and consular immunity, are discussed below. It is essential, however, to read the scheme of the SIA in conjunction with recent decisions of the European Court of Human Rights and of the EAT which apply the European Convention on Human Rights and the EU Charter of Fundamental Rights in a way that, potentially, significantly restricts the application of state immunity in employment cases. These decisions are discussed under 'Human rights and fundamental rights' below. First, however, we consider the basic statutory position.

Note that as the embassies of foreign states are located in London, the London Central Employment Tribunal has particular expertise in dealing with matters of state and related immunities. This may inform a case management decision as to where a claim in which such immunity is invoked should be heard – Faleye and anor v UK Mission Enterprise Ltd and ors EAT 0359/10.

2.127 State immunity

Section 1 SIA establishes the general rule that foreign states are immune from the jurisdiction of all courts and tribunals within the UK. But this rule is much qualified and the exceptions to it (together with the exceptions to those exceptions) make the law relating to state immunity complex. The following is an outline only of the general principles affecting an employee's ability to bring claims where the employee is employed by a foreign state.

The relevant definition of 'state' is found in S.14(1) and includes the government of a state or any department of that government so that, as a general rule, any emanation, arm or alter ego of a state will be immune from legal proceedings unless that immunity is waived. However, 'state' does not include a 'separate entity' that is distinct from the executive organs of the government of the state and capable of suing and being sued *unless*: (a) the legal proceedings relate to anything done by it in the exercise of sovereign authority, and (b) the circumstances are such that a state would have been immune – S.14(2).

114

Clearly, the question of whether or not a particular institution, organisation or **2.128** body constitutes a 'department' or organ of a state will turn on the facts of the case in question. However, it is possible to extract certain general pointers from the Court of Appeal's judgment in Trendtex Trading Corporation Ltd v Central Bank of Nigeria 1977 1 All ER 881, CA. These are:

- the general test requires the totality of the evidence to be looked at including, in particular, the constitution, functions and activities of the body claiming immunity and the extent to which the body's central government retains control over it, in order to determine whether there is any satisfactory basis on which to conclude that the body is so related to the government of the state in question as to form part of that government

- the certificate of an ambassador stating whether or not an organisation is a department of government is of substantial weight but is not decisive of the issue

- the fact that a state exempts a particular organisation from prosecution or from being sued under its own domestic law is no more than a guide when determining whether that immunity extends beyond the state's own territorial boundaries

- the burden of proving the right to claim immunity rests four-square on the body claiming it

- the presence or absence of an express provision in the domestic statute or enactment establishing the body or institution in question will be a pointer towards whether the government intended that body or institution to be a department or organ of it. An express declaration in the statute is not a condition that has to be satisfied before an English court can ascribe sovereign status to a body claiming it. But its absence is an important factor to be taken into account, and in any event the body alleging that it is a department of government must satisfy the court that the intention to make it such can necessarily be inferred from any constituting Act or amendments to it.

A 'separate entity' as defined by S.14(2) can claim immunity only in respect of acts by it that are of a sovereign nature. In Lubega v Coffee Marketing Board of Uganda ET Case No.34020/81 a tribunal had to decide whether dismissing an employee was, in the circumstances of the case, a 'sovereign act'. L had been dismissed by the Board on the ground that, by having access to confidential and sensitive information, she had become a threat to national security when her husband joined a political group allegedly committed to opposing the existing government in Uganda. The Board contended that it was immune from the tribunal proceedings because it was a 'separate entity' whose actions, in dismissing L, had been of a sovereign or governmental nature taken for the preservation of the security of the state. The tribunal found that there was scant

115

evidence that L's husband was involved in activities prejudicial to the safety of the state of Uganda or that L had access to information which, if passed on to her husband, would have assisted him were he involved in the pursuit of such activities. Therefore, the Board had entirely failed to satisfy the tribunal that the dismissal of L was a governmental or sovereign act such as to entitle it to claim immunity.

2.129 Section 1(2) provides that a court or tribunal must give effect to the immunity of a state even if the state does not appear before it. In other words, the court must consider the issue of state immunity of its own motion, even if the state does not raise it in the proceedings. In Mauritius Tourism Promotion Authority v Wong Min EAT 0185/08 WM made various claims to an employment tribunal. The Authority resisted the claim on its merits, but did not raise the question of state immunity. Nevertheless, a tribunal considered that the issue arose, and at a preliminary hearing which the Authority did not attend and for which it submitted no evidence, decided that there was no state immunity on the basis of S.4(3) (discussed under 'Exceptions' below). The Mauritius High Commission wrote to the tribunal stating that the Authority was part of the High Commission and therefore entitled to immunity. The tribunal wrote to the Authority informing it that it was treating this as an application for review (now called 'reconsideration'), but that if the Authority was not represented at the review hearing, the tribunal would affirm its judgment. Despite phone calls being made to the High Commission on the day of the hearing, no representative of the Authority attended. Satisfied that every opportunity had been given for the Authority to attend, the tribunal dismissed the application for review, as there was no basis for questioning the original ruling that immunity was not applicable. The Authority did not appeal and at a full merits hearing, which the Authority did not attend, the tribunal found in favour of WM in relation to all of her claims. Two weeks later, the Authority sought to raise the issue of state immunity and claimed that it had not received notice of the hearing. The tribunal treated this as an application for review of its original decisions as to immunity, but the application was made well out of time and the tribunal considered that it was not just and equitable for time to be extended. The Authority appealed, arguing that the tribunal was obliged to permit it to argue the issue of state immunity, but the EAT upheld the tribunal's decision. It acknowledged that 'considerable leeway' is given to states to submit evidence in support of a claim for state immunity; the court is under a duty, when an issue of state immunity arises, to consider the position carefully and make appropriate enquiries, and the state must be allowed to appear and submit evidence and argument with respect to any disputed issues of fact, even if time needs to be extended to allow this. However, in this case the tribunal raised the matter of state immunity of its own motion, even after the Authority had purported to put in a response on the merits, and it notified the Authority of its initial decision and gave it every opportunity to counter WM's evidence. The

EAT considered that 'there must come a point when the court is taken to have done enough' – the Authority had been informed unambiguously that it needed to adduce evidence and it chose to do nothing. It was not the case that the Authority was under some misapprehension as to what steps it could properly take consistent with it raising the issue of state immunity (as in the Gamal-Eldin case, discussed under 'Exceptions' below). In any event, even if there was initially some misunderstanding, this could not have continued in the light of the unambiguous letter sent by the tribunal to the Authority explaining precisely what it had to do if it wished to challenge the tribunal's jurisdiction. The appeal therefore failed. The tribunal was entitled to refuse the application to review the decisions relating to state immunity. It was a lawful exercise of discretion which made proper allowance for the much more generous treatment afforded to foreign states when procedural discretions touching upon the right of a state to claim state immunity are exercised.

Section 2 allows for the waiver of state immunity. This is discussed below under 'Waiver of state or diplomatic immunity'.

Exceptions. As mentioned above, S.1 sets out the general rule that a 'state', as **2.130** defined, is ordinarily immune from proceedings against it. But Ss.4 and 5 provide important exceptions to the general rule concerning the liability of a state in circumstances that may arise out of an employment relationship to which it is a party.

Employment contracts. By virtue of S.4(1), a state will not in general be immune **2.131** in proceedings relating to a contract of employment between the state and an individual where either (a) the contract was made in the UK, or (b) the work under the contract was to be wholly or partly performed in the UK. Proceedings 'relating to a contract of employment' include claims in respect of any statutory duties owed by the state as employer – S.4(6).

But there are exceptions to the general denial in S.4(1) of immunity in respect of employment contracts. These are set out in S.4(2) and provide that, subject to yet further qualifications noted below, a state *will* be immune if one of the following circumstances applies:

- at the time when the proceedings were instituted, the claimant was a national of the state concerned – S.4(2)(a)

- at the time when the contract was made, the claimant was neither a UK national nor habitually resident here – S.4(2)(b), or

- the parties to the contract have agreed in writing to bestow immunity on the employing state – S.4(2)(c).

If, however, the work performed under the contract is for 'an office, agency or **2.132** establishment maintained by the state in the United Kingdom for commercial purposes', the immunity which would otherwise be provided by S.4(2)(a) or (b)

117

does not apply, *unless* the individual was habitually resident in the employing state at the time when the contract was made – S.4(3). In Mauritius Tourism Promotion Authority v Wong Min (above) the claimant was a national of Mauritius, meaning that prima facie her employer would have had immunity by virtue of the exclusion in S.4(2)(a). However, because the employer was a commercial organisation, this exclusion was removed by S.4(3), meaning that it did not enjoy state immunity.

As for the state immunity provided by S.4(2)(c), this can never form the basis of immunity in respect of employment tribunal proceedings because, by virtue of S.4(4), any written agreement by the parties to bestow immunity is void where the substantive law entitles a claimant to bring proceedings only before a UK court or tribunal. Since UK statutory employment rights can only be enforced in UK tribunals S.4(4) would always apply to prevent S.4(2)(c) conferring immunity.

2.133 Section 4(2) was relied upon successfully by the respondent employer in Arab Republic of Egypt v Gamal-Eldin and anor 1996 ICR 13, EAT. In that case the two claimants were dismissed from their jobs as drivers for a medical office forming part of the Embassy of the Arab Republic of Egypt in London. In the event, the EAT held that they were 'members of the staff of the mission' with the consequence that S.16(1) applied to exclude the provisions of S.4(1) and confer upon the Arab Republic of Egypt immunity in respect of the unfair dismissal proceedings – see below. However, the EAT then went on to hold that even if the claimants were not 'members of a mission', the Arab Republic of Egypt was nonetheless entitled to immunity from suit on the ground that the purposes of the medical office for which the claimants worked were not 'commercial purposes' within the meaning of S.4(3). Instead, the purposes of the office came within the sphere of governmental or sovereign activity as shown by the fact that the medical office was used by the Egyptian Government to provide guidance, advice and expert care to patients referred by that Government for medical treatment in the UK and the fact that the office acted throughout as a representative of the Arab Republic of Egypt and its embassy. This meant that S.4(3) did not apply to exclude the immunity conferred by S.4(2) in respect of proceedings relating to a contract of employment brought against a state by an individual who is a national of that state.

As mentioned in the Gamal-Eldin case, another exception to the general denial of immunity in S.4(1) is set out in S.16(1). This provides that S.4 does not apply to proceedings concerning the employment of *members of a mission* within the meaning of the Vienna Convention on Diplomatic Relations 1961 or *members of a consular post* within the meaning of the Vienna Convention on Consular Relations 1963. One of the categories of persons defined as comprising 'members of a mission' are those employed in the 'administrative and technical service' of an embassy, which can include relatively minor staff. In Ahmed v

Government of the Kingdom of Saudi Arabia 1996 ICR 25, CA, the Court of Appeal held that a British national who worked as a secretary in the Saudi Arabian Embassy was 'a member of a mission' within the meaning of Article 1 of the 1961 Convention as she was to be regarded as being a member of the embassy's staff employed in the administrative and technical service of the embassy. This meant that S.16(1) applied to confer immunity on Saudi Arabia in respect of the employee's claim for unfair dismissal.

One outcome of S.4 is that, unless the employee is covered by S.16, a state **2.134** cannot claim immunity where the employee is a *UK national* even if he or she was habitually resident in the employing state and the contract of employment was made there. A UK national is defined as a British citizen, a British overseas territories citizen, a British National (Overseas) citizen, a British Overseas citizen, a British subject under the British Nationality Act 1981 or a British protected person under that Act – S.4(5) SIA. So, for example, where unfair dismissal proceedings were commenced by a Jamaican passport holder who was employed by the US at an air base within the UK, the state was not able to claim immunity notwithstanding that the employment contract was made in the US and the employee was habitually resident there. Under the law in force at that time, the claimant was regarded as a national of the UK and its colonies – Tai v USA ET Case No.3151/86.

In Campbell v USA ET Case No. 21433/79, on the other hand, the US was able to rely on the fact that the claimant was one of its own nationals to claim immunity. There C was a US national and had been habitually resident in the UK for many years. He was employed to work at a bowling centre run by a US Army depot used by soldiers and members of the public alike. When he was dismissed and brought tribunal proceedings, the respondent state claimed immunity on the basis that C was a US national. C, however, contended that his employment fell within the qualification set out in S.4(3) since the bowling centre was an 'agency... maintained by the [US] in the UK for commercial purposes'. The tribunal held that the bowling centre was maintained by the respondent state principally for the welfare of its soldiers and their families rather than for commercial purposes. The centre was not expected to make a profit, S.4(3) did not apply, the US Government was immune, and the tribunal had no jurisdiction to entertain C's substantive complaint.

Note that S.4 only applies to proceedings in respect of contracts of employment **2.135** entered into after the date on which it came into force (i.e. 22 November 1978) – S.23(3). In the rare event that the Act does not apply, the common law rules of state immunity do. These allow a state to enjoy immunity only in respect of 'public acts' done by it under its sovereign powers. Acts of a 'private law' character are not covered by common law immunity – I Congreso del Partido 1981 2 All ER 1064, HL.

119

2.136 *Death, personal injury and loss of or damage to property.* A further exception to state immunity applies under S.5 SIA. This provides that a foreign state is *not* immune where proceedings are in respect of (a) death or personal injury, or (b) damage to or loss of tangible property, in either case caused by an act or omission in the UK – S.5 SIA. Unlike S.4, S.5 is not subject to the qualification of S.16 or of any other provision: a foreign state enjoys no immunity in respect of these matters. In an employment context, S.5 has been particularly relevant in discrimination claims, where the question may arise as to whether the detriment allegedly suffered by a claimant constitutes 'personal injury', such that the claimant may bring the claims against a foreign state.

In Military Affairs Office of the Embassy of the State of Kuwait v Caramba-Coker EAT 1054/02 C-C was summarily dismissed from his post as a shipping clerk at the Embassy of the State of Kuwait. He presented a claim to the employment tribunal complaining of wrongful dismissal and race discrimination. The employer did not file a response and it elected not to attend the hearing or make written representations to the tribunal. The tribunal upheld the employee's complaint and awarded him damages for wrongful dismissal and compensation of £4,000 for 'loss of employment and injury to feelings' in respect of his race discrimination claim. The employer appealed, claiming that the tribunal had no jurisdiction to hear C-C's complaint because the employer was immune under S.1(1) SIA. The employee contended that the employer's immunity had been removed in relation to the race discrimination claim, although not the wrongful dismissal claim, by S.5 SIA, as the employee's complaint of race discrimination amounted to 'proceedings in respect of... personal injury'. The EAT considered that if the only claim for non-pecuniary loss which the employee made in his complaint of race discrimination was for injury to feelings, that would not amount to a claim for compensation for personal injury. If, however, C-C was in fact claiming damages for personal injury, as opposed to injury to feelings, his claim *would* come within S.5. As the EAT did not know what the employee's evidence in the tribunal was or whether the tribunal wrongly applied the label 'injury to feelings' to that evidence, the question of whether C-C's complaint of race discrimination amounted to proceedings in respect of personal injury would be remitted to, if practicable, the same tribunal.

2.137 The Caramba-Coker case was followed in Federal Republic of Nigeria v Ogbanna 2012 ICR 32, EAT, where O brought claims of unfair dismissal and disability discrimination against the Nigerian High Commission. She alleged that her treatment by the High Commission had damaged both her physical and mental health by way of a recurrence of her sciatica and depression. The FRN claimed state immunity. A tribunal considered that O's unfair dismissal claim was excluded by state immunity under S.16(1)(a) because she was a member of a diplomatic mission. However, it allowed O's disability discrimination claim to proceed on the basis that a claim of ill health caused by discrimination constituted a claim for personal injury, following

120

Caramba-Coker, and thus fell within S.5. On appeal, the EAT affirmed the tribunal's decision, holding that the term 'personal injury' in S.5 should be given the meaning ordinarily attributed to it in domestic law, which, it is well established, is apt to cover psychiatric as well as physical injury.

Thus, where a member of a diplomatic mission or consular post wishes to bring a claim of discrimination in employment, the focus of the parties and the tribunal will immediately turn to the schedule of loss to determine whether the complaint involves allegations of personal injury, since economic loss or injury to feelings will not found valid claims. Tribunals hearing such claims will also have the unenviable task of determining where injury to feelings ends and personal injury begins. See IDS Employment Law Handbook, 'Discrimination at Work' (2012), Chapter 30, 'General exceptions', under 'State immunity – death and personal injury'.

Diplomatic immunity   2.138

The right to immunity recognised in international law in respect of personnel employed in diplomatic missions extends to tribunal proceedings. Unless waived, immunity from legal proceedings is conferred on 'diplomatic agents' (i.e. the head of a diplomatic mission and the diplomatic staff of the mission) under the Diplomatic Privileges Act 1964 (DPA). The principle behind this immunity is the need to protect the agent's special vulnerability so that he or she should not be impeded in carrying out his or her official functions. It is thus wider than state immunity, which is based on the concept of equality between sovereign states, such that the laws of one cannot hold sway over the other in the absence of agreement – Al-Malki and anor v Reyes and anor 2014 ICR 135, EAT.

Section 2(1) DPA gives statutory effect to the Vienna Convention on Diplomatic Relations 1961, Article 31 of which provides that: 'A diplomatic agent shall enjoy immunity from the criminal jurisdiction of the receiving state. He [or she] shall also enjoy immunity from its civil and administrative jurisdiction, except in the case of:

- a real action relating to private immovable property situated in the territory of the receiving state, unless he holds it on behalf of the sending state for the purposes of the mission

- an action relating to succession in which the diplomatic agent is involved as executor, administrator, heir or legatee as a private person and not on behalf of the sending state

- an action relating to any professional or commercial activity exercised by the diplomatic agent in the receiving state outside his official functions.'

A former diplomat will not necessarily have immunity in relation to claims by **2.139** employees carrying out domestic duties – Wokuri v Kassam 2012 ICR 1283, ChD. Once the diplomatic agent's duties have come to an end, he or she enjoys

121

residual immunity in respect of acts performed in the exercise of his or her 'functions as a member of a mission' – Article 39(2). Examples of such functions are listed in Article 3, and would include some matters ancillary to the central functions of the mission, such as employing staff to entertain nationals of both the sending and receiving states – Abusabib and anor v Taddese 2013 ICR 603, EAT. However, as the EAT held in that case, the employment of a domestic worker who performed no task outside the diplomat's home had such little connection with the 'functions of his mission' that it was unlikely to fall within that phrase. A personal assistant, on the other hand, whose job involved replying to correspondence, both official and personal, and managing the diplomat's diary and travel arrangements, would fall towards the other end of the spectrum, and thus be more likely to be covered.

By virtue of Article 37, the immunity afforded to diplomatic agents by Article 31 is extended to the following classes of persons:

• members of the family of the diplomatic agent forming part of his or her household provided they are not nationals of the receiving state

• members of the administrative and technical staff of the mission together with their families forming part of their respective households provided they are not nationals of, nor permanently resident in, the receiving state (but immunity from the civil and administrative jurisdiction of the receiving state extends only to acts which are performed by such persons in the course of their duties).

2.140 Although diplomatic agents and other members of a mission retain a residual immunity after their duties have ended under Article 39(2), this does not apply to family members. Thus, in Abusabib and anor v Taddese (above) the wife of a diplomat was not immune from claims of discrimination and harassment brought by a domestic worker arising out of the couple's alleged mistreatment of her while she was working for them in a previous posting at the Sudanese embassy in London (regardless of whether or not her husband enjoyed residual immunity under Article 39(2)).

Private servants of diplomatic agents are not entitled to immunity from the jurisdiction of the courts, although the receiving state must exercise its jurisdiction over such servants in a manner that does not interfere unduly with the performance of the functions of the mission.

2.141 As the principle behind diplomatic immunity is different from that behind state immunity (see 'State immunity' above), care needs to be taken not to confuse the two. In Al-Malki and anor v Reyes and anor 2014 ICR 135, EAT, two domestic workers brought claims against a diplomat and his wife, alleging that they had been denied their contractual or minimum wages and had been discriminated against on the ground of their race. The employment tribunal considered that their employment constituted a commercial activity exercised outside the diplomat's official functions, within the meaning of Article 31, and thus immunity did not apply. The employment judge reasoned that although the employment of domestic staff was not, on the face of it, commercial activity, to claim that immunity operated as a procedural bar represented a disproportionate interference with the claimants' right to access a court, contrary to Article 6 of the European Convention on Human Rights (see 'Human rights and fundamental rights' below). As S.3 of the Human Rights Act 1998 required domestic legislation to be interpreted in line with the Convention, 'commercial activity' was to be interpreted as including the employment of staff such as the claimants. However, on appeal, the EAT disagreed. In reaching her decision, the employment judge had relied on authority which concerned state rather than diplomatic immunity. That in turn had been heavily influenced by the 2004 United Nations Convention on Jurisdictional Immunities of States and their Property – which related to state but not diplomatic immunity.

As with state immunity, diplomatic immunity can be waived. This is discussed below under 'Waiver of state or diplomatic immunity'.

Note that S.16(1) SIA expressly states that none of the exclusions contained in Part 1 of the Act (i.e. Ss.1–17) will prejudice the availability of immunities conferred by the Diplomatic Privileges Act 1964.

Consulates   2.142
Under Articles 43 and 58 of the Vienna Convention on Consular Relations 1963 – scheduled to the Consular Relations Act 1968 – career and honorary consular officers and consular employees are, as a general rule, immune from the jurisdiction of the courts for acts performed in the exercise of consular functions.

However, immunity cannot be claimed in respect of civil actions arising out of a contract concluded by a consular officer or employee in which he or she did not contract expressly or impliedly as an agent of the sending state. This would mean, for example, that a consular officer or employee would not be immune from claims brought by his or her private servants.

As in all situations where immunity is claimable, provisions exist which allow 2.143
for its *waiver* so that the jurisdiction of the courts can be admitted. These provisions are discussed under 'Waiver of state or diplomatic immunity' below.

Note that S.16(1) SIA expressly states that none of the exclusions contained in Part 1 of the Act (i.e. Ss.1–17) will prejudice the availability of immunities conferred by the Consular Relations Act 1968.

Foreign vessels and aircraft   2.144
The jurisdiction of the British courts will generally be ousted in respect of proceedings relating to the contract of employment of any crew of any ship or

123

aircraft belonging to a foreign state which has concluded a convention recognised by an Order in Council made pursuant to S.4 of the Consular Relations Act 1968. In such cases, a court or tribunal will be entitled to proceed with the claim or action only where, having first been notified of the proceedings, an authorised consular officer of the state to which the ship or aircraft belongs has failed to object to those proceedings within the period of two weeks from the date of notification. It should be noted that an Order made pursuant to S.4 of the 1968 Act is not overridden by S.4 SIA (which restricts the availability of immunity in respect of proceedings relating to contracts of employment) since such Orders are the subject of separate bilateral treaties with the countries concerned.

2.145 International organisations
The International Organisations Act 1968 permits Orders in Council to be made which confer similar, though not equivalent, immunities and privileges to those conferred by the SIA, the Diplomatic Privileges Act 1964 and the Consular Relations Act 1968 on certain international organisations and persons connected with such organisations. In the main, Orders under this Act have related to specialised agencies of the United Nations and other international agencies. The extent of the immunities and privileges conferred is a matter for the UK Government.

As an international organisation, the Commonwealth Secretariat enjoys immunity from suit and legal process under the Commonwealth Secretariat Act 1966 – see Jananyagam v Commonwealth Secretariat EAT 0443/06.

2.146 Waiver of state or diplomatic immunity
All the various pieces of legislation conferring state and diplomatic immunity contain provisions allowing for the waiver of such immunity.

2.147 Waiver of state immunity. Section 2(2) SIA provides that: 'A state may submit [to the jurisdiction of the courts of the UK] after the dispute giving rise to the proceedings has arisen or by a prior written agreement; but a provision in any agreement that it is to be governed by the law of the United Kingdom is not to be regarded as a submission.'

Once given, a waiver is irreversible. In USA v Nolan 2011 IRLR 40, CA, the US army closed a base in Hampshire resulting in the loss of 200 jobs. A tribunal found that the US had failed to carry out collective consultation in good time under S.188(1) TULR(C)A and made a protective award. It dismissed a last-minute argument put forward by the US that, as a sovereign state, it enjoyed state immunity, on the basis that it had unequivocally submitted to the tribunal's jurisdiction having defended the liability proceedings on the merits. The Court of Appeal confirmed that the US was thereby estopped from claiming state immunity, even though it considered it self-evident why a sovereign state would not wish to consult about a possibly sensitive strategic decision to close a military base. The Court rejected the US's argument that a foreign sovereign state is impliedly exempt from the S.188 requirement to engage in collective consultation: there was no indication in the TULR(C)A that an exemption for foreign states existed and, in any event, this was not necessary since a sovereign state's interests are fully protected by its ability to claim sovereign immunity – an immunity it had, in this case, waived.

In Ahmed v Government of the Kingdom of Saudi Arabia 1996 ICR 25, CA **2.148** (discussed under 'State immunity – exceptions' above), A was employed as a secretary by the Defence Office of the Saudi Arabian Embassy in London. Initially she was not given a contract of employment. She then received a copy of a letter sent by a solicitor to the military attaché which expressed the view that embassy staff would have employment rights under what is now the ERA. At the top of the letter the military attaché scribbled a note to his assistant in Arabic, reading 'For your information. Do whatever you think fit.' Following the subsequent termination of A's employment, a question arose as to whether an employment tribunal had jurisdiction to entertain her claim of unfair dismissal. By a majority, the tribunal held that the letter amounted to a 'prior written agreement' for the purposes of S.2(2) SIA and that the Saudi Arabian Government had thus waived state immunity. However, on appeal, the EAT overturned the tribunal's decision, ruling that the letter did not constitute an agreement between A and the Embassy; it was merely a letter containing legal advice. Nor could the words in Arabic be construed as an agreement with another party. The Court of Appeal upheld the EAT's decision.

Under S.2(3) and (4) SIA, a state will be deemed to have submitted to the jurisdiction of the UK courts whenever someone with the necessary authority under S.2(7) institutes, intervenes or takes steps in any proceedings, other than for the purpose of claiming immunity or asserting an interest in property. In this regard, the service of a defence or response or the taking of any other steps to defend the case on its merits will normally be construed as a submission to the jurisdiction. However, a letter declaring an *intention* to defend threatened proceedings is unlikely to constitute a 'step' in proceedings. In de Barros v Federal Republic of Brazil and ors ET Case No.2200034/03, for example, the claimant worked as secretary to the Brazilian air attaché until her dismissal. Her solicitor wrote to her employer saying that her dismissal appeared to be unfair and in breach of the Disability Discrimination Act 1995 (now repealed and superseded by the Equality Act 2010), and that the firm was instructed to bring employment tribunal proceedings. The employer replied, denying that it had treated the claimant unfairly or in breach of the DDA and stating that it would defend any proceedings fully. The employment tribunal held that this letter did not have the effect of waiving the Brazilian state immunity. The employer did not 'intervene or take any step in the proceedings' within the meaning of S.2(3)(a) SIA, because the proceedings were not under way when the letter was written.

125

2.149 Two further cases where immunity was not waived:

- **London Branch of the Nigerian Universities Commission v Bastians**
1995 ICR 358, EAT: B presented a complaint of unfair dismissal against the
Universities Commission, which claimed to be a unit of the Nigerian High
Commission. The Foreign and Commonwealth Office (FCO) forwarded
copies of the claim form to the Nigerian Ministry of Foreign Affairs and
the Nigerian High Commission. The High Commission returned its copy of
the response form to the FCO uncompleted, together with a brief note 'for
transmission to the appropriate authority' stating that B had been dismissed
owing to incompetence and that his unfair dismissal claim was 'grossly
incorrect'. Following service of a notice of hearing, the High Commission
stated that it was seeking 'diplomatic immunity'. At a preliminary hearing,
the tribunal ruled that the note written by the High Commission had, in
effect, been a response and that the submission of it had constituted a 'step in
the proceedings' for the purposes of S.2(3) SIA, with the result that immunity
had been waived. The EAT, however, overturned the tribunal's decision. It
held that, although the note contained a statement of the reasons why the
claimant's employment was terminated, it did not in other important respects
comply with the characteristics of a response. Furthermore, since it formed
correspondence between the High Commission and the FCO, the note was
in the nature of a diplomatic communication between representatives of
two sovereign states in which the one explained to the other the conduct
about which complaint had been made. The fact that the note stated that
it was 'for transmission to the appropriate authority' did not change what
was essentially a diplomatic communication into a response. In forwarding
the note together with the blank response form to the employment tribunal,
the FCO could not be taken to have submitted a response on behalf of the
High Commission or to have taken any other steps in the proceedings on
the Commission's behalf. The EAT remitted the case to the tribunal for
determination of the question whether the High Commission was a body
entitled to state immunity under the SIA

- **Arab Republic of Egypt v Gamal-Eldin and anor** 1996 ICR 13, EAT: the
claimants, Egyptian nationals resident in London, were dismissed from
their posts as drivers at the medical office of the Egyptian Embassy. They
claimed unfair dismissal. The director of the medical office at the mission
where the claimants had been employed wrote two letters to the tribunal
regarding the unfair dismissal proceedings in which it was explained that the
claimants were Egyptian nationals and were, in the director's view, covered
exclusively by Egyptian law. A formal response was not served in respect of
either claimant and the Arab Republic of Egypt was not represented at the
preliminary hearing convened by the tribunal. Nevertheless, the tribunal
held that the director of the medical office had, on behalf of the relevant

state, submitted to the jurisdiction of the UK courts by writing the two letters to the tribunal, since these amounted to a response and their service on the tribunal thereby constituted intervention or taking steps in the proceedings for the purposes of S.2(3). The EAT overturned the tribunal's decision for two reasons: first, that the letters sent by the director of the medical office to the tribunal did not amount to responses since in neither letter was there any expression of intention to resist the claims; and secondly, that the director of the medical office who wrote the letters had no authority under S.2(7) SIA to submit the state to the jurisdiction of the UK courts. He did not occupy the position of the head of the diplomatic mission of Egypt in the UK, nor was he the person who had entered into the contracts of employment with the claimants. Accordingly, the employment tribunal had no jurisdiction to hear the complaints.

2.150 (Note that while these cases remain of interest and give some indication of how the courts approach the question of waiver, they are of limited legal relevance as employers wishing to enter a response must now use the mandatory response form (ET3) prescribed by the Secretary of State – see rules 16 and 17 of the Tribunal Rules and Chapter 6, 'Defending a claim', under 'Responding to a claim – the response form (ET3)'.)

There are two circumstances where immunity will not be lost even though the state has ostensibly taken a step in the proceedings. These are where the step was taken:

• in ignorance of facts entitling the state to immunity provided those facts could not reasonably have been ascertained and immunity is claimed as soon as reasonably practicable – S.2(5) SIA, or

• by someone who lacked the necessary authority under S.2(7) to submit to the jurisdiction of the UK courts. S.2(7) provides that the head of a state's diplomatic mission in the UK, or the person for the time being performing his or her functions, is deemed to have authority to submit on behalf of the state in respect of any proceedings (see Arab Republic of Egypt v Gamal-Eldin and anor (above)); and any person who has entered into a contract on behalf of and with the authority of a state is deemed to have authority to submit on behalf of the state in respect of proceedings arising out of that contract.

2.151 Both these 'defences' were raised by the Republic of Yemen in Aziz v Republic of Yemen 2005 ICR 1392, CA, where A was employed as an accounts assistant at the London Embassy of the Republic of Yemen until his dismissal. He brought a claim of unfair dismissal and the Republic submitted a response, stating that it intended to resist the claim. However, in the course of the tribunal hearing the Republic's counsel claimed state immunity under the SIA. The Republic accepted that by serving a response, it had taken a 'step in proceedings'

127

within the meaning of S.2(3)(b) SIA. However, it argued that the step had been taken by the Republic in ignorance of facts thereby entitling it to immunity under S.2(5). The tribunal rejected this claim and concluded that by entering a response the Republic had clearly waived its sovereign immunity.

On appeal, the Republic took a different approach. Rather than relying on S.2(5), it argued that it had not taken any step in proceedings at all, because any steps taken by its solicitors had not been properly authorised by the Republic in accordance with S.2(7). The EAT admitted evidence from the Yemeni Ambassador in London, who claimed that he did not authorise the taking of any step in the proceedings before the tribunal and did not authorise the waiver of immunity. Following Arab Republic of Egypt v Gamal-Eldin and anor (above), the EAT considered that it was appropriate to admit this new evidence on the basis that it is the duty of the EAT to correct a tribunal's failure to give effect to immunity where it did not have all the relevant evidence. Taking the Ambassador's evidence at face value, the EAT allowed the appeal.

2.152 A appealed to the Court of Appeal, arguing that the further evidence should not have been admitted by the EAT and that, if admitted, it should in the circumstances have been subjected to critical analysis and not merely accepted at face value. The Court of Appeal concluded that whether the Republic had taken a step in the proceedings and thereby submitted to the jurisdiction could only be decided upon a consideration of the evidence. Having considered the case law the court extrapolated the following principles:

- when state immunity is claimed in appellate proceedings, the court may consider evidence called to substantiate such a claim because, if substantiated, the court below had no jurisdiction to hear the case

- in a case where the other party claims that immunity has been waived, the court should scrutinise the available evidence

- whether the issue is as to the status of the entity claimed to be an emanation of the state or as to a claimed waiver of immunity, the evidence of the Ambassador, as representative of the state, is important but not necessarily conclusive evidence of the relevant matters.

2.153 The Court went on to consider how the deemed authority of the head of mission may be exercised. It decided that action taken by a member of the diplomatic mission (or solicitors instructed by the mission) must be taken with the authority of the head of mission or the person for the time being performing his or her functions. The head of mission has deemed authority to submit under S.2(7) and that includes authority to delegate. However, a solicitor acting without authority could not waive immunity. Nevertheless, authority could be conferred on solicitors either directly or indirectly by a member of the mission authorised by the head of mission to do so. The Court held that the EAT should have remitted the point as to whether immunity had been waived to the fact-finding tribunal. It had substantial material before it on which there was a real question as to whether there had been a waiver of immunity or not. The EAT should not have concluded that it was so obvious that immunity applied that it was unnecessary to enquire into the facts.

Waiver of diplomatic immunity. The relevant waiver provisions in respect of 2.154 diplomatic missions are contained in S.2(3) of the Diplomatic Privileges Act 1964 and Article 32 of the Vienna Convention on Diplomatic Relations 1961 and those in respect of consulates are contained in S.2(5) of the Consular Relations Act 1968 and Article 45 of the Vienna Convention on Consular Relations 1963. These provide that a waiver will be deemed to have been made by a state where the head of the diplomatic mission or consular post makes an express waiver.

Human rights and fundamental rights 2.155
It has been argued that the SIA is incompatible with Article 6 of the European Convention on Human Rights (ECHR) (incorporated into UK law by the Human Rights Act 1998 (HRA)), which provides that 'everyone is entitled to a fair and public hearing within a reasonable time by an independent and impartial tribunal'. In Fogarty v United Kingdom 2002 IRLR 148, ECtHR, the European Court of Human Rights rejected this argument, holding that 'measures taken... which reflect generally recognised rules of public international law on state immunity cannot in principle be regarded as imposing a disproportionate restriction on the right of access to court as embodied in Article 6(1). Just as the right of access to court is an inherent part of the fair trial guarantee in that Article, so some restrictions on access must likewise be regarded as inherent, an example being those limitations generally accepted by the community of nations as part of the doctrine of state immunity.'

However, subsequent to the decision in Fogarty, the 2004 Convention on Jurisdictional Immunities of States and their Property was adopted by the General Assembly of the United Nations. Article 11 of the Convention sets down the basic principle that, unless otherwise agreed between them, a state cannot invoke immunity before a court of another state which relates to a contract of employment between the state and an individual for work performed or to be performed in whole or in part in the territory of that other state. However, this principle does not apply if:

- the employee has been recruited to perform particular functions in the exercise of governmental authority
- the employee enjoys diplomatic immunity
- the proceedings relate to the recruitment, renewal of employment or reinstatement of an individual

129

- the proceedings relate to dismissal or termination of employment and would interfere with the employer state's security interests (as determined by the head of state, the head of Government or the state's minister for foreign affairs)

- the employee is a national of the employer state at the time when the proceedings are instituted (unless his or her permanent residence is in the state of the forum)

- the employer state and the employee have otherwise agreed in writing.

2.156 Relying on the 2004 Convention, the ECtHR has taken a different approach to that adopted in Fogarty in subsequent cases. In Cudak v Lithuania 2010 51 EHRR 15, ECtHR, C was hired as a secretary and switchboard operator by a Polish Embassy in Lithuania. She complained to a Lithuanian ombudsman that she had been sexually harassed by a colleague and fallen ill in consequence. When dismissed for absence, she brought an action for unfair dismissal. The Lithuanian courts declined jurisdiction on the basis of Polish state immunity, but the ECtHR upheld her complaint that there had been a breach of Article 6 ECHR. It held that the 2004 Convention applied to Lithuania and none of the exceptions set out in Article 11 of that Convention were relevant to C's case: C was a switchboard operator whose duties could not objectively have been related to the sovereign interests of the Polish government, and the acts of sexual harassment had been established by the ombudsman and could hardly be regarded as undermining Poland's security interests. The ECtHR took a similar approach in Sabeh el Leil v France 2011 IRLR 781, ECtHR, concluding that an accountant to the Kuwaiti Embassy in Paris could challenge the reasons for his dismissal in a French employment tribunal, as the provisions of the 2004 Convention applied to France and the claimant did not fall within any of the exceptions in Article 11.

The Cudak and Sabeh el Liel cases – together with Article 47 of the EU Charter of Fundamental Rights ('the EU Charter') – were relied on by the EAT in Benkharbouche v Embassy of the Republic of Sudan and another case 2013 IRLR 918, EAT, when holding that the immunity conferred on two embassies by the SIA in respect of two members of non-diplomatic staff was contrary to their right to a fair trial under Article 6 ECHR. B and J were Moroccan nationals, employed respectively as a member of the domestic staff at the Sudanese Embassy in London and as a cook at the Libyan Embassy. Following their dismissals, B and J separately attempted to bring employment tribunal claims, which the two Embassies resisted on the basis that both B – as a member of mission – and J – as a member of service staff – fell within the exclusions provided for in Ss.4(2) and 16 SIA. Both claimants argued that, although domestic law apparently barred them from asserting their employment rights, it was necessary to read down or disapply the relevant provisions in order to give effect to their rights under Article 6 ECHR and Article 47 of the EU Charter, which guarantees the right to an effective remedy and a fair trial.

Both claims failed at first instance and the claimants appealed to the EAT, **2.157** where the cases were conjoined. They argued, first, that the immunity conferred on the employers was contrary to Article 6 ECHR, with the result that the EAT should adopt an interpretation of the SIA that permitted a fair trial of the claimants' civil rights and obligations or, if such an interpretation proved impossible, the EAT should set aside the relevant provisions; and secondly, that to the extent that the claims engaged the claimants' rights under EU law – i.e. claims related to discrimination, harassment and working time – the direct effect of the right to an effective remedy and a fair trial in Article 47 of the EU Charter required the EAT to disapply the provisions which conferred immunity on the employers.

The EAT – Mr Justice Langstaff, President of the EAT, presiding – agreed with the view of the employment judge in J's case that the absolute immunity in respect of the employment of members of a diplomatic mission under S.16 SIA was incompatible with Article 6. The decisions in Cudak v Lithuania (above) and Sabeh el Leil v France (above) showed that the ECtHR recognised the recent and gradual erosion of absolute state immunity in favour of a judge-led assessment of whether such immunity should apply in a given case, and the growing extent to which employment contracts could not be barred by the assertion of absolute immunity. Accordingly, there was a breach of Article 6 in so far as S.16 SIA was applied. As for S.4(2)(b), the EAT had 'much greater hesitation' in accepting the argument that Article 6, read with the prohibition on discrimination on the basis of nationality in Article 14, was also breached by the immunity conferred in respect of individuals who were not habitually resident in the UK when the contract was made. However, he was prepared to assume for the purposes of argument that Article 6 was breached by the tribunals permitting the employers to assert state immunity.

Nevertheless, the EAT agreed with the tribunals that the SIA could not be **2.158** interpreted to allow the claims to proceed. Parliament had intended to confer immunity subject to specific exceptions, and to amend some of these exceptions would affect the overall balance struck by the legislature. As the House of Lords observed in Ghaidan v Godin-Mendoza 2004 2 AC 557, HL, the obligation in S.3(1) HRA to read UK law in a way that is compatible with the ECHR does not allow the courts to change the substance of a provision completely. Changing Parliament's clear list of those to whom immunity applies would cross the line between interpretation and legislation.

The EAT then considered whether, in so far as the claims related to EU law, the principle of effectiveness required the SIA to be disapplied where it conflicted with a fundamental right guaranteed by EU law, such as Article 47 of the EU Charter. It noted that previous cases such as Bleuse v MBT Transport Ltd 2008

131

ICR 488, EAT, had held that legislation can only be disapplied where the claim is made against an emanation of the state, which, for the purpose of tribunal proceedings, would be the UK. If that were still the case, the state immunity would continue to apply in the instant cases. However, the EAT noted that the understanding of the principle of effectiveness in EU law had advanced since the adoption of the Lisbon Treaty in 2009, a consequence of which was the declaration of the Supreme Court in Rugby Football Union v Consolidated Information Services Ltd (formerly Viagogo Ltd) 2013 1 CMLR 56, SC, that the EU Charter now has direct effect in national law, 'binding Member States when they are implementing EU law'. Furthermore, in Kücükdeveci v Swedex GmbH 2010 IRLR 346, ECJ, the ECJ held that where a national law is incompatible with a general and fundamental principle of EU law, and cannot be interpreted in accordance with that principle, the national court 'must decline to apply that provision' without being compelled to make a reference to the ECJ before doing so. The EAT accepted that the result of this decision is that general principles of EU law have horizontal direct effect (i.e. they apply in disputes between private individuals). That conclusion was further supported by the more recent decision of the ECJ in Aklagaren v Fransson 2013 2 CMLR 46, ECJ, in which it was made clear that a national court should set aside any provision of national law that conflicts with a Charter right.

2.159 Consequently, the EAT concluded that the direct effect of Article 47 of the EU Charter required it to disapply the immunity under Ss.4(2) and 16 SIA, in so far as it applied to B's and J's claims of discrimination, harassment and breach of the Working Time Regulations 1998 SI 1998/1833, because these were matters falling within the material scope of EU law. However, the claims of unfair dismissal and non-payment of wages fell outside the scope of EU law and so remained barred by the provisions of the SIA.

The EAT acknowledged and sympathised with the reluctance of the employment judges below to disapply provisions of national law that could not be disapplied if the claims were considered solely under the HRA. However, it was clear that the EAT was bound by the EU principles in the cited cases. The EAT also acknowledged that it may be seen as undesirable that 'the regime for paying respect to the ECHR, which carefully balances the roles of the courts and the legislature, does not operate where EU rights of a somewhat unspecific nature are concerned, because they are said to be general and fundamental principles of the Union'. Permission was granted to all the parties to appeal, as the law 'cannot necessarily be regarded as finally settled in this area'. On appeal, B and J would have the opportunity to seek a declaration of incompatibility between the SIA and the ECHR in respect of their domestic claims of unfair dismissal and the national minimum wage. If such a declaration were granted, it would be up to Parliament to amend the SIA, as necessary, to bring it into line with Article 6.

Thus, unless and until the EAT's decision in Benkharbouche is overruled, **2.160** workers based in embassies in the UK may be able to pursue employment claims in respect of EU-derived rights, even where the SIA appears to provide foreign states with immunity. However, it is important to note that this principle applies only to state immunity, not to diplomatic immunity, as the underlying rationales for the two kinds of immunity are distinct – see the discussion of the EAT's decision in Al-Malki and anor v Reyes and anor 2014 ICR 135, EAT, under 'Diplomatic missions' above.

Scope of remission by Employment Appeal Tribunal

2.161

Where a case is remitted to a tribunal for a rehearing, the tribunal's jurisdiction is limited to the scope of the remission. This was made clear by the Court of Appeal in Aparau v Iceland Frozen Foods plc 2000 ICR 341, CA. In that case A was issued with a new written contract containing a mobility clause that would permit IFF plc to move her to a different location at any time. A was asked to sign the contract and return a copy as confirmation of acceptance of the terms. She did not do so. A year later, A was instructed to transfer to another store. The transfer would have increased her journey time to and from work by 20 minutes each day. She refused to transfer and terminated her employment with immediate effect on the ground that IFF plc did not have the right to make her transfer without her consent. A then brought a claim for unfair constructive dismissal on the ground that IFF plc's attempts to force her to move amounted to a repudiatory breach of her contract of employment. The only issue before the employment tribunal was whether A had been constructively dismissed. IFF plc did not seek to argue that, in the event that the tribunal found that A had been dismissed, the dismissal was fair within the meaning of S.98(4) ERA.

The tribunal dismissed A's claim. It held that, since A had voiced no objection to the introduction of the new contract, she had accepted it and the mobility clause it contained. A appealed to the EAT, which held that the tribunal had misdirected itself in law in reaching this decision. It therefore remitted the matter to the tribunal for a rehearing of the issue of whether, having regard to the facts and the EAT's guidance as to the correct application of the law, A had agreed to the new terms. Following the EAT's decision, IFF plc wrote to the secretary of the employment tribunals stating that it was prepared to concede that A's contract did not contain an express mobility clause and that she had therefore been constructively dismissed. IFF plc also pointed out that the issue of whether the dismissal was fair, within the meaning of S.98(4), had not yet been considered. It requested permission to amend its response to include an argument that the dismissal was fair for 'some other substantial reason' within the meaning of S.98(4). The tribunal secretary replied to IFF plc informing it

133

that the request had been granted by the employment judge. By the time the matter came before the tribunal, A was fully aware of the issues that IFF plc intended to raise and made no objection to the tribunal considering those issues. The tribunal held that the dismissal had been fair and, accordingly, A's claim was dismissed.

2.162 A again appealed to the EAT, arguing that the tribunal had misdirected itself in its approach to the question of fairness. The EAT dismissed her appeal and A appealed to the Court of Appeal. It was only when the case came before the Court of Appeal that A sought permission to amend her notice of appeal and raise the issue of whether the question of the fairness of the dismissal fell outside the scope of the EAT's remission to the tribunal.

The Court of Appeal held that the employment tribunal had acted outside its jurisdiction in considering whether A's dismissal was fair within the meaning of S.98(4) ERA. The matter had been remitted by the EAT for the limited purpose of determining whether A had agreed to new terms of employment which made her subject to a mobility clause. The remission did not give the tribunal jurisdiction to reopen the case generally or hear any arguments from IFF plc in relation to fairness. The Court of Appeal commented that, by virtue of S.35(1)(b) ETA, the EAT has the power to remit a case to the tribunal for further consideration. This power is wide enough for remission to be for the purpose of a general reconsideration or for a more specific purpose. Although an order for remission revives the jurisdiction of the tribunal, the scope of that jurisdiction is derived from, and therefore limited to, that which is specified in the EAT's order. The parties cannot consent, tacitly or otherwise, to give a tribunal additional jurisdiction. Accordingly, the decision of the employment tribunal on the issue of fairness was a nullity. In view of IFF plc's concession that the contract did not contain an express mobility clause, it followed that A had been dismissed and that her dismissal was unfair.

2.163 An example of an unsuccessful challenge on the scope of a remission:

- **Redcar and Cleveland Borough Council v Scanlon** EAT 0088/08: the Council successfully appealed against a tribunal's decision that S had been victimised contrary to S.4 of the Sex Discrimination Act 1975 and unfairly dismissed for making a protected disclosure. The EAT held that the tribunal had failed to direct itself properly on the nature of the causal link that needed to be established between the dismissal/victimisation and the making of the protected disclosure; and that it had failed to focus on the conduct of M, the person who had taken the responsibility to dismiss. The EAT remitted the case for the tribunal to apply itself to these two issues on the basis of the facts found by it in the course of its initial hearing and, having done so, the tribunal came to the same conclusion as at first. The Council appealed to the EAT, arguing that the tribunal had exceeded its remit in that it had not limited itself to the findings of fact it had originally made, but had made findings of secondary fact against M. However, the EAT disagreed. One of the tribunal's tasks on remission was to consider M's conduct applying the correct test of causation in the light of the primary findings of fact already reached. This involved looking at M's role as established by those findings of fact and drawing inferences from those findings where this was necessary to determine what went through his mind. In seeking to explain why it reached the conclusion that M had dismissed S by reason of her protected disclosure, it was necessary for the tribunal to reveal the inferences which it saw fit to draw from the primary findings of fact already made. These inferences were rooted, entirely properly, in its primary findings of fact, and there was nothing to suggest that the tribunal had gone beyond the task it was asked to undertake by embarking upon a new fact-finding exercise. All of its conclusions were based upon ample primary findings of fact and it had not acted outside the authority the EAT had given it.

A tribunal may not widen the terms of remission even to take account of a **2.164** change in understanding of the applicable law. In Chief Constable of Avon and Somerset Constabulary v Dolan EAT 0295/09, for example, a tribunal found that an employer's threat to put D on half pay if he did not return to work constituted an act of unjustified disability-related discrimination under the Disability Discrimination Act 1995 (DDA) (now repealed and superseded by the EqA). The employer appealed and the EAT remitted the case to the tribunal to reconsider its reasoning in relation to its conclusion that the employer had failed to justify the threat. Shortly after the appeal, the House of Lords handed down judgment in the case of Mayor and Burgesses of the London Borough of Lewisham v Malcolm 2008 IRLR 700, HL, which changed the approach to be taken to the question of less favourable treatment under the DDA. At the remitted hearing, the employer argued that the tribunal should decide whether D had been less favourably treated for a reason related to his disability in the light of the Malcolm decision before it considered the remitted issue of justification, but the tribunal refused to do so. The EAT upheld the tribunal's decision, holding that it had not erred in law in considering that it only had power to determine the issues remitted to it. Employment tribunals are creatures of statute, with powers derived from statute, and apart from their limited powers to reconsider their judgments under rules 70–73 of the Tribunal Rules, they do not have any right to reopen proceedings once they have disposed of them. The principle of finality in litigation is important. While this disposed of the appeal, the EAT noted that it was also understandable that the tribunal considered that the question of less favourable treatment was one of mixed fact and law and that to deal with it would have necessitated recalling witnesses, and was thus another reason why it should restrict its inquiry to the issues remitted to it.

If a tribunal considers matters that fall outside the the scope of the remission but those matters had no material effect, nor could reasonably be considered to

135

have had any material effect, upon its ultimate conclusion, then its decision will nonetheless stand. This was the conclusion of the EAT in Gardner v Chief Constable of West Midlands Police EAT 0207/13, another case under the DDA. In that case, although the EAT considered that it might not have been strictly necessary for the tribunal to have identified the relevant PCP within the scope of its remission, there was, in fact, no issue about it. That being so, the tribunal would have made no material error of law if it did stray outside the scope of the remission in that respect (although the EAT made no finding as to whether it had in fact exceeded the scope of the remission).

2.165 References to European Court of Justice

Many of the most significant developments in UK employment law in recent years have been made as a result of the direct application of European law. For example, interpretations given by the European Court of Justice (ECJ) to Article 157 of the Treaty on the Functioning of the European Union (TFEU) (formerly Article 141 of the EC Treaty), which enshrines the right to equal pay for equal work, have required UK courts to revolutionise their interpretations of domestic equal pay legislation. ECJ decisions concerning provisions in the EU Equal Treatment Framework Directive (No.2006/54) and its precursors have had a comparable effect on UK legislation covering sex discrimination. The influence of European law on the development and interpretation of UK employment law is now well established and recourse to the ECJ has become a vital weapon in the armoury of employees who seek to show either that UK domestic law fails to implement in full provisions enshrined in European Treaties and Directives or that interpretations given by UK courts to domestic law fail to ensure compatibility with European law requirements. The question arises, therefore, whether – and to what extent – tribunals have the power to refer cases to the ECJ for a ruling on the interpretation and effect of relevant European provisions where these are ambiguous.

2.166 Power to refer

Article 267 TFEU (formerly Article 234 of the EC Treaty) provides that: 'The Court of Justice of the European Union shall have jurisdiction to give preliminary rulings concerning: (a) the interpretation of the Treaties; (b) the validity and interpretation of acts of the institutions, bodies, offices or agencies of the Union.' Thus, any question of the proper interpretation of provisions contained in the TFEU (and Directives made under it) can be ruled upon by the ECJ – and it should be noted that 'interpretation' includes the 'effect' of such provisions, so the question of the direct effect of any particular provision may also be referred. However, the ECJ does not have jurisdiction to rule on questions of fact or issues raised about national law, and nor can it consider the application of such law to a particular case. These limitations are important when

136

considering the circumstances in which a UK court or tribunal may make a reference to the ECJ.

The second paragraph of Article 267 permits a national court or tribunal to refer a question of interpretation where it considers that a decision on that question 'is necessary to enable it to give judgment'. But what does 'necessary' mean in this context? As a general rule, the ECJ will not look behind a reference to question whether it is necessary unless it is plain that European law is inapplicable. It should be borne in mind, however, that it is not the reference that must be shown to be necessary, but a ruling on the question referred. Hence the ECJ's decision must be capable of determining the outcome of the case: if the outcome would be inevitable whichever way the ECJ decided, then it could not be said that the ECJ's decision was necessary to enable the national court to give judgment. That said, it may sometimes be difficult to know whether the ruling of the ECJ will be conclusive of the outcome of a case in circumstances where crucial facts have yet to be established. In such cases, a reference would probably be validly made so long as the decision of the ECJ on the question referred is potentially decisive. But tribunals that are asked to make a reference before being fully aware of the facts of the case may well be reluctant to accede to the request because, until such facts are known, the extent to which a ruling by the ECJ is necessary will remain unclear.

An employment tribunal had to consider whether a reference to the ECJ was **2.167** necessary in Martinez v Harbour and General Works Ltd ET Case No.2401125/00. M's employment was governed by a collective agreement providing that his normal working hours were 39 per week. It was a condition of his employment that the employer could require him to work overtime at any time and that he could not unreasonably refuse to work overtime. In practice, he worked for 53.7 hours a week on average, including overtime, and had signed an agreement opting out of the 48-hour week. However, he was paid holiday pay on the basis of a 39-hour week. It was argued on his behalf that the Working Time Regulations 1998 SI 1998/1833 introduced a European dimension into domestic law and should be interpreted according to a principle of fairness in the context of an industry that worked more overtime than any other. M's holiday pay should therefore be calculated by reference to his actual average working hours. The tribunal dismissed his claim. There was nothing in the Working Time Directive (No.93/104 – now No.2003/88) to suggest that there had to be a minimum level of pay for holiday and, as Reg 16 of the Regulations correctly transposed into UK law the provisions of Article 7 of the Directive, there was nothing requiring a reference to the ECJ. M had normal working hours of 39 a week and he had been paid holiday pay in accordance with the Regulations.

The Martinez case should be compared with another tribunal case, Coleman v Attridge Law and anor ET Case No.2303745/05, in which an employment

137

tribunal did consider it necessary to make a reference to the ECJ. The claimant, who was not herself disabled but who cared for her disabled son, brought claims under the Disability Discrimination Act 1995 (DDA) (since repealed and superseded by the Equality Act 2010) on the basis that she had suffered discrimination by association with her son's disability. The employment tribunal had to determine whether the EC Equal Treatment Framework Directive (No.2006/54), with which the DDA had to comply, prohibited disability discrimination by association. If so, it had to consider further whether the Act was capable of being interpreted so as to provide for such protection. The tribunal found that the wording of the Directive – which refers to discrimination 'on the grounds of' disability – suggested that discrimination by association was covered. However, a literal reading of the relevant provisions of the DDA revealed that such discrimination was not covered by that Act, and that, since the matter had not been ruled on directly by the ECJ, it would be too bold a step to imply words into the Act to achieve compliance. The tribunal therefore decided to refer the matter to the ECJ for a preliminary ruling.

2.168 **Tribunal's discretion**
Article 267 states that a national court or tribunal 'may' refer an appropriate question to the ECJ (so long as it regards a ruling on that question as necessary). Thus a discretion is vested in the court or tribunal that extends not only to deciding whether to make a reference but also to what stage such a reference should be made. Although there are no specific provisions in the Tribunal Rules governing the circumstances in which a reference should be made, provisions do exist in respect of references made by the civil courts. Rule 68.2 of the Rules of the Supreme Court (contained in Schedule 1 to the Civil Procedure Rules 1998 SI 1998/3132) provides that a reference may be ordered by the court at any stage of the proceedings. There is no requirement that evidence must already have been heard and, if it is a party who is seeking to have a reference made, the application may be presented before or at the hearing. However, a reference cannot be made after the delivery of the court or tribunal's judgment or decision, even if this has yet to be formally recorded – SA Magnavision NV v General Optical Council (No.2) 1987 2 CMLR 262, QBD.

As already mentioned, in deciding whether and at what stage to make a reference, tribunals may well be influenced by doubts about the propriety of making a reference before all the relevant facts have been established. The general policy of employment tribunals appears to be that the decision to refer is best left to the EAT and the higher courts. By the time an appellate court is charged with the case, it will have the benefit of the full facts as found by the tribunal and so may be in a better position to determine the necessity or otherwise of a ruling by the ECJ. Tribunals should also bear in mind that a reference to the ECJ will inevitably involve considerable delay and expense.

138

Any order for a reference must be subject to the remedies normally available **2.169**
under national law – which means that a right of appeal must be extended if
such appeal would normally exist in respect of other orders by the court or
tribunal making the reference – see Rheinmühlen Düsseldorf v EVSt (No.1)
1974 1 CMLR 523, ECJ. In the context of tribunals, it would clearly be open
to a party to appeal to the EAT against a tribunal's order to make a reference
or against any refusal to make such an order. Leave to appeal in either case
would not be necessary since appeals to the EAT are not subject to leave.

Form and effect of a reference   2.170

Rule 100 of the Tribunal Rules provides that where a tribunal or employment
judge makes an order referring a question to the ECJ for a preliminary ruling,
the tribunal secretary must send a copy of the order to the registrar of the ECJ.
Normally, an order for a reference will contain the following:

- a brief summary of the facts of the case

- the order sought by the claimant

- an outline of the respondent's defence

- the main arguments of both parties on the point at issue in the reference

- the reasons of the court/tribunal for making the reference

- a clear statement of the relevant national law (if any)

- the question(s) to be decided.

In Coleman v Attridge Law (above) the parties were given time to draft and
agree between themselves the precise formulation of the reference, including the
question(s) to be put, which was then presented to the tribunal for consideration.

Since the ECJ can only rule on the interpretation and effect of EU law, the **2.171**
question posed in any reference should be abstractly worded. In other words,
the ECJ should not be asked to decide the application of a particular provision
of EU law to national law but rather be asked whether such a provision has a
particular meaning or should be interpreted in a particular way. Usually, in
giving judgment, the ECJ will give its interpretation of the provision and then
state that the application of that interpretation to particular facts is a matter for
the national court to decide.

Once the questions referred have been answered by the ECJ and the case
remitted, the proceedings resume in the national court or tribunal from the
point at which they left off. The effect of the reference will have been to stay
the proceedings pending determination of the questions referred to the ECJ.
Unless the decision of the court or tribunal is reached on grounds which have
nothing to do with the issues referred (in which case the reference was, strictly
speaking, unnecessary), the court or tribunal is bound by the ECJ's decision.

139

Once an issue is decided by the ECJ, its decision comprises a 'precedent' which binds all national courts in respect of the same matter of interpretation – unless, that is, the same issue is referred to the ECJ once again. This is possible since the ECJ is not bound by its own decisions and a national court may make a reference even where the same issue has arisen before and has been decided by the ECJ, in circumstances where there are grounds for believing that the earlier decision was wrong or that relevant policy considerations have altered.

Appendix – claims heard by employment tribunals

2.172

Below is a list of the major employment rights that can be enforced in the employment tribunals. A full list can be found at www.justice.gov.uk/tribunals/employment/claims/jurisdiction

Dismissal

2.173

Employment tribunals have jurisdiction to hear the following statutory claims relating to dismissal:

* written reasons for dismissal – Ss.92 and 93 Employment Rights Act 1996 (ERA) (see IDS Employment Law Handbook, 'Unfair Dismissal' (2010), Chapter 21, 'Written reasons for dismissal')

* unfair dismissal – S.94 ERA (see IDS Employment Law Handbook, 'Unfair Dismissal' (2010))

* unfair dismissal for a reason connected with jury service – S.98B ERA (see IDS Employment Law Handbook, 'Unfair Dismissal' (2010), Chapter 10, 'Automatically unfair dismissals', under 'Dismissal in connection with jury service')

* unfair dismissal in connection with the right to time off for dependants under S.57A ERA – S.99 ERA (see IDS Employment Law Handbook, 'Maternity and Parental Rights' (2012), Chapter 10, 'Time off for dependants')

* unfair dismissal for a reason relating to pregnancy, childbirth or family leave (i.e. maternity, adoption, parental or paternity leave) under Reg 20 of the Maternity and Parental Leave etc Regulations 1999 SI 1999/3312 or Reg 29 of the Paternity and Adoption Leave Regulations 2002 SI 2002/2788 – S.99 ERA (see IDS Employment Law Handbook, 'Maternity and Parental Rights' (2012), Chapter 12, 'Detriment and unfair dismissal', under 'Unfair dismissal')

* unfair dismissal for a health and safety reason – S.100 ERA (see IDS Employment Law Handbook, 'Unfair Dismissal' (2010), Chapter 11, 'Health and safety dismissals')

* unfair dismissal for refusing to work on a Sunday – S.101 ERA (see IDS Employment Law Handbook, 'Unfair Dismissal' (2010), Chapter 10, 'Automatically unfair dismissal', under 'Dismissal for refusing to work on Sunday')

* unfair dismissal in connection with the entitlement to paid annual leave and other rights under the Working Time Regulations 1998 SI 1998/1833; the Merchant Shipping (Working Time: Inland Waterways) Regulations

141

2003 SI 2003/3049; the Fishing Vessels (Working Time: Sea-fishermen) Regulations 2004 SI 2004/1713; or the Cross-border Railway Services (Working Time) Regulations 2008 SI 2008/1660 – S.101A ERA (see IDS Employment Law Handbook, 'Working Time' (2013))

- unfair dismissal for performing functions as an occupational pension scheme trustee – S.102 ERA (see IDS Employment Law Handbook, 'Unfair Dismissal' (2010), Chapter 10, 'Automatically unfair dismissal', under 'Dismissal in connection wtih occupational pensions')

- unfair dismissal for performing functions as an employee representative – S.103 ERA (see IDS Employment Law Handbook, 'Unfair Dismissal' (2010), Chapter 10, 'Automatically unfair dismissal', under 'Dismissal of employee representatives')

- unfair dismissal related to making a protected disclosure – S.103A ERA (see IDS Employment Law Handbook, 'Whistleblowing at Work' (2013), Chapter 6, 'Dismissal', under 'Unfair dismissal')

- unfair dismissal for asserting a statutory right – S.104 ERA (see IDS Employment Law Handbook, 'Unfair Dismissal' (2010), Chapter 12, 'Dismissal for asserting a statutory right')

- unfair dismissal related to the national minimum wage – S.104A ERA (see IDS Employment Law Handbook, 'Wages' (2011), Chapter 5, 'The national minimum wage')

- unfair dismissal for enforcing right to working tax credits – S.104B ERA (see IDS Employment Law Handbook, 'Unfair Dismissal' (2010), Chapter 10, 'Automatically unfair dismissal', under 'Dismissal in connection with tax credits')

- unfair dismissal in relation to a request for flexible working – S.104C ERA and Reg 16(3) Flexible Working (Procedural Requirements) Regulations 2002 SI 2002/3207 (see IDS Employment Law Handbook, 'Maternity and Parental Rights' (2012), Chapter 11, 'Flexible working')

- unfair dismissal because of any action taken to enforce the requirements imposed on the employer by the Pensions Act 2008 to make pension provision for the employee – S.104D ERA

- unfair dismissal in connection with the right to request study and training – S.104E ERA and Reg 18(3) Employee Study and Training (Procedural Requirements) Regulations 2010 SI 2010/155 (see IDS Employment Law Handbook, 'Unfair Dismissal' (2010), Chapter 10, 'Automatically unfair dismissal', under 'Dismissal relating to study and training')

- unfair dismissal for a reason relating to a trade union blacklist prohibited under the Employment Relations Act 1999 (Blacklists) Regulations 2010

SI 2010/493 – S.104F ERA (see IDS Employment Law Handbook, 'Trade Unions' (2013), Chapter 12, 'Unfair dismissal', under 'Trade union blacklists')

- unfair redundancy dismissal – S.105 ERA, S.153 of the Trade Union and Labour Relations (Consolidation) Act 1992 (TULR(C)A) (see IDS Employment Law Handbook, 'Redundancy' (2011), Chapter 8, 'Unfair redundancy')

- unfair dismissal because of a 'spent' conviction within the terms of the Rehabilitation of Offenders Act 1974 (see S.4(3)(b) of that Act), unless the employee falls into a category excluded from the provisions of that Act by a statutory order (see IDS Employment Law Handbook, 'Unfair Dismissal' (2010), Chapter 6, 'Conduct', under 'Criminal offences at work – previous convictions')

- unfair dismissal in connection with trade union membership, activities or use of union services – S.152 TULR(C)A (see IDS Employment Law Handbook, 'Trade Unions' (2013), Chapter 12, 'Unfair dismissal')

- unfair dismissal in connection with an application or campaign for trade union recognition or the securing of bargaining arrangements – para 161, Sch A1 TULR(C)A (see IDS Employment Law Handbook, 'Trade Unions' (2013), Chapter 6, 'Statutory recognition', under 'Detriment and dismissal')

- unfair dismissal for taking official industrial action in certain circumstances – S.238A TULR(C)A (see IDS Employment Law Handbook, 'Industrial Action' (2010), Chapter 8, 'Industrial action dismissals')

- unfair dismissal in connection with the right to be accompanied at disciplinary and grievance hearings – S.12(3) Employment Relations Act 1999 (see IDS Employment Law Supplement, 'Disciplinary and Grievance Procedures' (2009), Chapter 6, 'Right to be accompanied')

- unfair dismissal by reason of a business transfer, or a reason connected with it, which is not an economic, technical or organisational reason entailing changes in the workforce – Reg 7(1) Transfer of Undertakings (Protection of Employment) Regulations 2006 SI 2006/246 (TUPE) (see IDS Employment Law Handbook, 'Transfer of Undertakings' (2011), Chapter 4, 'Unfair dismissal')

- unfair dismissal relating to the performance of the functions of, or activities as, a member or representative (or candidate for election as a member or representative) of a European Works Council or in relation to a request made for time off in order to perform such functions/activities – Reg 28 Transnational Information and Consultation of Employees Regulations 1999 SI 1999/3323

143

- unfair dismissal in connection with the rights of part-time workers under the Part-time Workers (Prevention of Less Favourable Treatment) Regulations 2000 SI 2000/1551 – Reg 7

- unfair dismissal in connection with the rights of fixed-term employees under the Fixed-term Employees (Prevention of Less Favourable Treatment) Regulations 2002 SI 2002/2034 – Reg 6

- unfair dismissal in connection with the establishment of a European public limited liability company under the European Public Limited-Liability Company Regulations 2004 SI 2004/2326 – Reg 42

- unfair dismissal relating to the performance of functions or activities as an information and consultation representative or candidate under the Information and Consultation of Employees Regulations 2004 SI 2004/3426 – Reg 30 (see IDS Employment Law Supplement, 'Information and Consultation Regulations 2004' (2005))

- unfair dismissal in connection with the information and consultation rights of occupational or personal pension scheme members under the Occupational and Personal Pension Schemes (Consultation by Employers and Miscellaneous Amendment) Regulations 2006 SI 2006/349 – para 5, Sch 1 (see IDS Employment Law Handbook, 'Unfair Dismissal' (2010), Chapter 10, 'Automatically unfair dismissal', under 'Dismissal in connection with occupational pensions')

- unfair dismissal in connection with the information and consultation rights of employees of European cooperative societies under the European Cooperative Society (Involvement of Employees) Regulations 2006 SI 2006/2059 – Reg 31

- unfair dismissal in connection with the information, consultation and negotiation rights of employees involved in cross-border mergers under the Companies (Cross-Border Mergers) Regulations 2007 SI 2007/2974 – Regs 46 and 47

- unfair dismissal in connection with the information, consultation and negotiation rights of employees of European public limited liability companies under the European Public Limited-Liability Company (Employee Involvement) (Great Britain) Regulations 2009 SI 2009/2401 – Reg 29

- unfair dismissal of an agency worker who has the status of 'employee' for alleging a breach of (or asserting rights, bringing proceedings, giving evidence or doing anything under) the Agency Workers Regulations 2010 SI 2010/93 – Reg 17

- application for interim relief – S.128 ERA; S.161 TULR(C)A.

144

Redundancy rights/business transfers   2.174

In addition to claims for unfair dismissal (see 'Dismissal' above), employment tribunals have jurisdiction to hear the following statutory claims relating to redundancy rights and business transfers:

- right to a redundancy payment – Part XI ERA (see IDS Employment Law Handbook, 'Redundancy' (2011), Chapter 10, 'Enforcement', under 'Statutory redundancy payments')

- failure to properly consult with appropriate representatives over proposed redundancies under S.188 TULR(C)A or to make proper arrangements for the election of employee representatives under S.188A TULR(C)A – S.189 TULR(C)A (see IDS Employment Law Handbook, 'Redundancy' (2011), Chapter 12, 'Collective redundancies', under 'Complaints about breach of S.188')

- failure to comply with protective award made under S.189 TULR(C)A – S.192 TULR(C)A (see IDS Employment Law Handbook, 'Redundancy' (2011), Chapter 12, 'Collective redundancies', under 'Complaints about breach of S.188')

- failure by transferor to notify transferee of employee liability information – Reg 12 TUPE (see IDS Employment Law Handbook, 'Transfer of Undertakings' (2011), Chapter 8, 'Information and consultation', under 'Employee liability information')

- failure to inform and consult with appropriate representatives over a business transfer or to make proper arrangements for the election of employee representatives – Reg 15 TUPE (see IDS Employment Law Handbook, 'Transfer of Undertakings' (2011), Chapter 8, 'Information and consultation', under 'Informing and consulting representatives')

- failure to comply with a compensation order made under Reg 15 – Reg 15(10) TUPE (see IDS Employment Law Handbook, 'Transfer of Undertakings' (2011), Chapter 8, 'Information and consultation', under 'Informing and consulting representatives').

Maternity, adoption, paternity and parental leave, and   2.175
flexible working

In addition to claims for unfair dismissal (see 'Dismissal' above), discrimination and equal pay (see 'Discrimination' below) and time off (see 'Time off' below), employment tribunals have jurisdiction to hear the following statutory claims relating to maternity and parental rights:

- right to 26 weeks' ordinary maternity leave – S.71 ERA and Reg 7(1) of the Maternity and Parental Leave etc Regulations 1999 SI 1999/3312

145

(MPL Regulations) (see IDS Employment Law Handbook, 'Maternity and Parental Rights' (2012), Chapter 3, 'Maternity leave')

- right to 26 weeks' additional maternity leave – S.73 ERA and Reg 7(4) MPL Regulations (see IDS Employment Law Handbook, 'Maternity and Parental Rights' (2012), Chapter 3, 'Maternity leave')

- right to 26 weeks' ordinary adoption leave – S.75A ERA and Regs 15–19 Paternity and Adoption Leave Regulations 2002 SI 2002/2788 (PAL Regulations) (see IDS Employment Law Handbook, 'Maternity and Parental Rights' (2012), Chapter 6, 'Adoption leave and pay,' under 'Ordinary adoption leave')

- right to 26 weeks' additional adoption leave – S.75B ERA and Regs 20–21 PAL Regulations (see IDS Employment Law Handbook, 'Maternity and Parental Rights' (2012), Chapter 6, 'Adoption leave and pay', under 'Additional adoption leave')

- right to two weeks' ordinary paternity leave – Ss.80A–80E ERA and Regs 4–14 PAL Regulations (see IDS Employment Law Handbook, 'Maternity and Parental Rights' (2012), Chapter 7, 'Paternity leave and pay', under 'Ordinary paternity leave')

- right to 26 weeks' additional paternity leave – Ss.80AA and 80BB ERA and the Additional Paternity Leave Regulations 2010 SI 2010/1055 (APL Regulations) (see IDS Employment Law Handbook, 'Maternity and Parental Rights' (2012), Chapter 7, 'Paternity leave and pay', under 'Additional paternity leave')

- right to 13 weeks' unpaid parental leave (or 18 weeks for a disabled child) – S.80(1) ERA and Regs 13–16 MPL Regulations (see IDS Employment Law Handbook, 'Maternity and Parental Rights' (2012), Chapter 9, 'Parental leave', under 'Statutory framework and guidance')

- right to return to same job after ordinary maternity leave, ordinary adoption leave, ordinary or additional paternity leave, or a period of parental leave of four weeks or less – Reg 18(1) and (3) MPL Regulations, Regs 13 and 26(1) PAL Regulations and Reg 31 APL Regulations (see IDS Employment Law Handbook, 'Maternity and Parental Rights' (2012), Chapter 4, 'Returning to work after maternity leave', under 'Returning after ordinary maternity leave'; Chapter 6, 'Adoption leave and pay', under 'Returning to work after adoption leave'; Chapter 7, 'Paternity leave and pay', under 'Right to return after paternity leave'; and Chapter 9, 'Parental leave', under 'Key elements – returning to work after parental leave')

- right to return to same job or, if that is not practicable, to suitable alternative job after additional maternity leave, additional adoption leave, ordinary or additional paternity leave not falling within the above provisions, a period of parental leave of more than four weeks, or consecutive periods of statutory leave – Reg 18(2) MPL Regulations, Regs 13 and 26(2) PAL Regulations, and Reg 31 APL Regulations (see IDS Employment Law Handbook, 'Maternity and Parental Rights' (2012), Chapter 4, 'Returning to work after maternity leave', under 'Returning after additional maternity leave'; Chapter 6, 'Adoption leave and pay', under 'Returning to work after adoption leave'; Chapter 7, 'Paternity leave and pay', under 'Right to return after paternity leave'; and Chapter 9, 'Parental leave', under 'Key elements – returning to work after parental leave')

- right to be offered alternative work before maternity suspension under S.67 ERA – S.70 ERA (see IDS Employment Law Handbook, 'Maternity and Parental Rights' (2012), Chapter 2, 'Health and safety protection', under 'Suspension on maternity grounds' and 'Remedies')

- right to be paid during maternity suspension under S.68 ERA – S.70 ERA (see IDS Employment Law Handbook, 'Maternity and Parental Rights' (2012), Chapter 2, 'Health and safety protection', under 'Suspension on maternity grounds' and 'Remedies')

- right not to suffer detriment in relation to pregnancy, childbirth or maternity, maternity leave, adoption leave, paternity leave, parental leave, or dependant care leave – S.47C ERA (see IDS Employment Law Handbook, 'Maternity and Parental Rights' (2012), Chapter 12, 'Detriment and unfair dismissal', under 'Right not to suffer detriment')

- right of agency worker to receive remuneration under S.68C ERA where supply ended on maternity grounds, and to be offered suitable alternative work under S.68B – S.70A ERA (see IDS Employment Law Handbook, 'Maternity and Parental Rights' (2012), Chapter 2, 'Health and safety protection', under 'Suspension on maternity grounds – ending the supply of an agency worker on maternity grounds')

- right to request flexible working and to appeal against a refusal – S.80H ERA and Reg 6 Flexible Working (Procedural Requirements) Regulations 2002 SI 2002/3207 (see IDS Employment Law Handbook, 'Maternity and Parental Rights' (2012), Chapter 11, 'Flexible working', under 'Complaints to employment tribunals')

- right not to suffer detriment in relation to flexible working – S.47E ERA (see IDS Employment Law Handbook, 'Maternity and Parental Rights' (2012), Chapter 11, 'Flexible working', under 'Detriment and unfair dismissal rights').

Discrimination and equal pay
2.176

Employment tribunals have jurisdiction to hear the following statutory claims relating to anti-discrimination rights:

- direct discrimination because of a relevant protected characteristic – S.13 Equality Act 2010 (see IDS Employment Law Handbook, 'Discrimination at Work' (2012), Chapter 15, 'Direct discrimination')

- discrimination arising from a disability – S.15 EqA (see IDS Employment Law Handbook, 'Discrimination at Work' (2012), Chapter 20, 'Discrimination arising from disability')

- discrimination against a transsexual person because of absence from work relating to gender reassignment – S.16 EqA (see IDS Employment Law Handbook, 'Discrimination at Work' (2012), Chapter 22, 'Other forms of prohibited conduct', under 'Gender reassignment discrimination due to absence')

- discrimination on grounds of pregnancy or maternity – S.18 EqA (see IDS Employment Law Handbook, 'Discrimination at Work' (2012), Chapter 22, 'Other forms of prohibited conduct', under 'Pregnancy and maternity discrimination')

- indirect discrimination because of a relevant protected characteristic – S.19 EqA (see IDS Employment Law Handbook, 'Discrimination at Work' (2012), Chapter 16, 'Indirect discrimination: proving disadvantage', and Chapter 17, 'Indirect discrimination: objective justification')

- failure to comply with a duty to make reasonable adjustments – S.21 EqA (see IDS Employment Law Handbook, 'Discrimination at Work' (2012), Chapter 21, 'Failure to make reasonable adjustments')

- harassment related to a relevant protected characteristic – S.26 EqA (see IDS Employment Law Handbook, 'Discrimination at Work' (2012), Chapter 18, 'Harassment')

- victimisation – S.27 EqA (see IDS Employment Law Handbook, 'Discrimination at Work' (2012), Chapter 19, 'Victimisation')

- equal pay – Ss.120 and 127 EqA; Article 157 TFEU (see IDS Employment Law Handbook, 'Equal Pay' (2011), Chapter 9, 'Enforcement', under 'Jurisdiction of tribunals')

- instructing, causing and inducing discrimination – S.111 EqA (see IDS Employment Law Handbook, 'Discrimination at Work' (2012), Chapter 28, 'Liability of employers, employees and agents', under 'Instructing, causing and inducing discrimination')

- aiding discrimination – S.112 EqA (see IDS Employment Law Handbook, 'Discrimination at Work' (2012), Chapter 28, 'Liability of employers, employees and agents', under 'Aiding discrimination')

- applications for declarations of rights in relation to a 'non-discrimination rule' regarding an occupational pension scheme – S.120 (see IDS Employment

Law Handbook, 'Discrimination at Work' (2012), Chapter 34, 'Enforcing individual rights', under 'Jurisdiction of tribunals')

- a complaint that a term of a collective agreement is void, or a rule of an undertaking unenforceable – Ss.145 and 146 EqA (see IDS Employment Law Handbook, 'Discrimination at Work' (2012), Chapter 34, 'Enforcing individual rights', under 'Jurisdiction of tribunals').

Trade unions and union members

2.177

In addition to claims for unfair dismissal (see 'Dismissal' above), employment tribunals have jurisdiction to hear the following statutory claims relating to trade union rights:

- right not to suffer detriment in connection with being or seeking to be a union member, taking part in union activities or using union services, or for the purpose of compelling trade union membership – S.146(1) TULR(C)A (see IDS Employment Law Handbook, 'Trade Unions' (2013), Chapter 11, 'Detriment and unlawful inducements', under 'Detriment on trade union grounds')

- right not to suffer detriment because of failure to accept an inducement – S.146(2C) TULR(C)A (see IDS Employment Law Handbook, 'Trade Unions' (2013), Chapter 11, 'Detriment and unlawful inducements', under 'Detriment on trade union grounds')

- right not to suffer detriment for the purpose of enforcing a requirement that non-union members must make payments – S.146(3) TULR(C)A (see IDS Employment Law Handbook, 'Trade Unions' (2013), Chapter 11, 'Detriment and unlawful inducements', under 'Detriment on trade union grounds')

- unlawful exclusion/expulsion from union – S.174 TULR(C)A (see IDS Employment Law Handbook, 'Trade Unions' (2013), Chapter 3, 'Trade unions and their members', under 'Right to union membership')

- application for compensation after successful S.174 complaint – S.176 TULR(C)A (see IDS Employment Law Handbook, 'Trade Unions' (2013), Chapter 3, 'Trade unions and their members', under 'Right to union membership')

- unjustifiable discipline by union – S.66 TULR(C)A (see IDS Employment Law Handbook, 'Trade Unions' (2013), Chapter 3, 'Trade unions and their members', under 'Unjustifiable discipline')

- application for compensation after successful S.66 complaint – S.67 TULR(C)A (see IDS Employment Law Handbook, 'Trade Unions' (2013), Chapter 3, 'Trade unions and their members', under 'Unjustifiable discipline')

- unauthorised deduction of union subscriptions under S.68 – S.68A TULR(C)A (see IDS Employment Law Handbook, 'Wages' (2011), Chapter 9, 'Check-off')

- complaints by trade unions over employer's failure to comply with collective bargaining obligations regarding training under S.70B – S.70C TULR(C)A (see IDS Employment Law Handbook, 'Trade Unions' (2013), Chapter 8, 'Information and consultation rights', under 'Training')

- wrongful deductions of political fund contributions or refusal to deduct union dues – S.87 TULR(C)A (see IDS Employment Law Handbook, 'Trade Unions' (2013), Chapter 2, 'Political funds', under 'The political fund')

- refusal of employment on grounds related to union membership – S.137 TULR(C)A (see IDS Employment Law Handbook, 'Trade Unions' (2013), Chapter 10, 'Refusal of employment on union grounds', under 'Tribunal proceedings and remedies')

- refusal of services of employment agency on grounds related to union membership – S.138 TULR(C)A (see IDS Employment Law Handbook, 'Trade Unions' (2013), Chapter 10, 'Refusal of employment on union grounds', under 'Tribunal proceedings and remedies')

- inducements relating to trade union membership or activities or to collective bargaining – Ss.145A and 145B TULR(C)A (see IDS Employment Law Handbook, 'Trade Unions' (2013), Chapter 11, 'Detriment and unlawful inducements', under 'Unlawful inducements')

- detriment short of dismissal in regard to trade union recognition, bargaining arrangements and balloting – para 156(5), Sch A1 TULR(C)A (see IDS Employment Law Handbook, 'Trade Unions' (2013), Chapter 6, 'Statutory recognition', under 'Detriment and dismissal')

- detriment for a reason relating to a prohibited list – Reg 9 Employment Relations Act 1999 (Blacklists) Regulations 2010 SI 2010/493 (see IDS Employment Law Handbook, 'Trade Unions' (2013), Chapter 11, 'Detriment and unlawful inducements', under 'Trade union blacklists').

2.178 Time off
In addition to claims for unfair dismissal (see 'Dismissal' above), employment tribunals have jurisdiction to hear the following statutory claims relating to time off rights:

- right to unpaid time off for public duties under S.50 – S.51 ERA

- right to paid time off to look for work or make arrangements for training where notice of dismissal by reason of redundancy has been given under

Ss.52 and 53 ERA – S.54 ERA (see IDS Employment Law Handbook, 'Redundancy' (2011), Chapter 11, 'Time off during notice period')

- right to paid time off for antenatal care under Ss.55 and 56 ERA, or Ss.57ZA and ZB in respect of agency workers – Ss.57 and 57ZC ERA (see IDS Employment Law Handbook, 'Maternity and Parental Rights' (2012), Chapter 1, 'Time off for ante-natal care')

- right to unpaid time off to care for dependants under S.57A ERA – S.57B ERA (see IDS Employment Law Handbook, 'Maternity and Parental Rights' (2012), Chapter 10, 'Time off for dependants')

- right to paid time off for pension scheme trustees under Ss.58 and 59 ERA – S.60 ERA

- right to paid time off for employee representatives under Ss.61 and 62 ERA – S.63 ERA (see IDS Employment Law Handbook, 'Redundancy' (2011), Chapter 12, 'Collective redundancies', under '"Appropriate representatives"')

- right to paid time off for study or training under Ss.63A and 63B – S.63C ERA

- right to time off for members of a European Works Council or special negotiating body, and for information and consultation representatives and election candidates – Reg 27 Transnational Information and Consultation of Employees Regulations 1999 SI 1999/3323

- right to time off for negotiating representatives and information and consultation representatives – Reg 29 Information and Consultation of Employees Regulations 2004 SI 2004/3426 (see IDS Employment Law Supplement, 'Information and Consultation Regulations 2004' (2005))

- right to time off for members of a special negotiating body, etc – Reg 41 European Public Limited-Liability Company Regulations 2004 SI 2004/2326

- right to paid time off for union-appointed safety representatives to carry out their functions and related training – Reg 4(2) Safety Representatives and Safety Committees Regulations 1977 SI 1977/500 (see IDS Employment Law Handbook, 'Trade Unions' (2013), Chapter 7, 'Time off rights', under 'Safety representatives')

- right of union officials to paid time off for union duties and related training – Ss.168 and 169 TULR(C)A (see IDS Employment Law Handbook, 'Trade Unions' (2013), Chapter 7, 'Time off rights', under 'Union duties and training')

- right of trade union learning representatives to paid time off to carry out their activities or to undergo related training – S.168A TULR(C)A (see IDS Employment Law Handbook, 'Trade Unions' (2013), Chapter 7, 'Time off rights', under 'Union learning representatives')

- right of union members to unpaid time off for union activities – S.170 TULR(C)A (see IDS Employment Law Handbook. 'Trade Unions' (2013), Chapter 7, 'Time off rights', under 'Union activities').

2.179 Working time

In addition to claims for unfair dismissal (see 'Dismissal' above), employment tribunals have jurisdiction to hear the following statutory claims under the Working Time Regulations 1998 SI 1998/1833 ('the Working Time Regulations'):

- right to daily rest – Reg 10 (see IDS Employment Law Handbook, 'Working Time' (2013), Chapter 3, 'Rest periods and rest breaks', under 'Daily rest')

- right to weekly rest – Reg 11 (see IDS Employment Law Handbook, 'Working Time' (2013), Chapter 3, 'Rest periods and rest breaks', under 'Weekly rest')

- right to rest breaks – Reg 12 (see IDS Employment Law Handbook, 'Working Time' (2013), Chapter 3, 'Rest periods and rest breaks', under 'Rest breaks')

- right to compensatory rest in cases where the above regulations are modified or excluded – Reg 24 (see IDS Employment Law Handbook, 'Working Time' (2013), Chapter 3, 'Rest periods and rest breaks', under 'Compensatory rest')

- right to annual leave – Reg 13 Working Time Regulations; Reg 18 Merchant Shipping (Working Time: Inland Waterways) Regulations 2004 SI 2004/3049; Reg 19 Fishing Vessels (Working Time: Sea-fishermen) Regulations 2004 SI 2004/1713 (see IDS Employment Law Handbook, 'Working Time' (2013), Chapter 4, 'Annual leave', under 'Right to paid annual leave')

- right to payment in lieu of holiday on termination of employment – Reg 14(2) (see IDS Employment Law Handbook, 'Working Time' (2013), Chapter 4, 'Annual leave', under 'Holiday pay')

- right to pay during annual leave – Reg 16(1) (see IDS Employment Law Handbook, 'Working Time' (2013), Chapter 4, 'Annual leave', under 'Holiday pay')

- right not to suffer detriment in relation to working time – S.45A ERA (see IDS Employment Law Handbook, 'Working Time' (2013), Chapter 7, 'Enforcement and remedies', under 'Complaints to tribunals').

2.180 Miscellaneous

Employment tribunals have jurisdiction to hear the following miscellaneous claims:

- written particulars of employment and statement of changes, and itemised pay statements – Ss.1–12 ERA (see IDS Employment Law Handbook, 'Contracts of Employment' (2009), Chapter 3, ' under 'Required particulars'; and IDS Employment Law Handbook, 'Wages' (2011), Chapter 8, 'Other statutory provisions', under 'Itemised pay statements')

- unlawful deductions from wages – Part II ERA (see IDS Employment Law Handbook, 'Wages' (2011), Chapter 4, 'Protection of wages – 2', under 'Complaints to employment tribunals')

- guarantee payments – Ss.28–35 ERA (see IDS Employment Law Handbook, 'Wages' (2011), Chapter 6, 'Guarantee payments', under 'Complaints to tribunals')

- rights on insolvency of employer – Part XII ERA

- right to medical suspension pay under S.64 ERA – S.70 ERA (IDS Employment Law Handbook, 'Wages' (2011), Chapter 8, 'Other statutory provisions', under 'Medical suspension pay')

- right to be accompanied at a grievance or disciplinary hearing, or at a meeting to discuss a flexible working request or appeal – Ss.10–15 Employment Relations Act 1999 and Reg 14 Flexible Working (Procedural Requirements) Regulations 2002 SI 2002/3207 (see IDS Employment Law Handbook, 'Unfair Dismissal' (2010), Chapter 6, 'Conduct', under 'Disciplinary proceedings – right to be accompanied'; and IDS Employment Law Handbook, 'Maternity and Parental Rights' (2012), Chapter 11, 'Flexible working', under 'Right to be accompanied')

- unlawful infringement of human rights by public sector employer – Human Rights Act 1998

- access to records relating to national minimum wage – Ss.9–11 NMWA (see IDS Employment Law Handbook, 'Wages' (2011), Chapter 5, 'The national minimum wage', under 'Record keeping' and 'Enforcement')

- enforcement of national minimum wage by HMRC compliance officers – Ss.17–19H NMWA (see IDS Employment Law Handbook, 'Wages' (2011), Chapter 5, 'The national minimum wage', under 'Enforcement')

- right not to be treated less favourably because of part-time status – Reg 5 Part-time Workers Regulations 2000 SI 2000/1551

- right not to be treated less favourably because of fixed-term status, and right of fixed-term employees to be informed of permanent vacancies under Reg 3(6) – Reg 7 Fixed-term Employees (Prevention of Less Favourable Treatment) Regulations 2002 SI 2002/2034

- right not to suffer detriment in relation to: jury service – S.43M ERA; health and safety – S.44 ERA; Sunday working – S.45 ERA; working time – S.45A

ERA; performing functions as a pension trustee or as an employee representative – Ss.46 and 47 ERA; time off for study or training – S.47A ERA; protected disclosures – S.47B ERA; dependant care leave – S.47C ERA; tax credits – S.47D ERA; flexible working – S.47E ERA; study and training – S.47F ERA; employee shareholder status – S.47G ERA; part-time working – Reg 7 Part-time Workers Regulations 2000 SI 2000/1551; fixed-term employment – Reg 6(2) Fixed-term Employees Regulations 2002 SI 2002/2034; right to be accompanied at a grievance or disciplinary hearing – S.12 Employment Relations Act 1999; right to be accompanied at a meeting to discuss a flexible working request or appeal – Reg 16 Flexible Working (Procedural Requirements) Regulations SI 2002/3207; national minimum wage – S.23 NMWA; payment of tax credits by the employer – para 1, Sch 3 Tax Credits Act 1999; rights in relation to European Works Councils – Reg 32 Transnational Information and Consultation of Employees Regulations 1999 SI 1999/3323; rights of members of a special negotiating body – Reg 45 European Public Limited-Liability Company Regulations 2004 SI 2004/2326; or rights of information and consultation representatives and candidates – Reg 33 Information and Consultation of Employees Regulations 2004 SI 2004/3426

- failure to consult about a proposed contracting out of a pension scheme – Social Security Pensions Act 1975

- breach of contract claim by employee or employer – S.3 ETA

- unpaid contributions to occupational pension schemes – S.126(1) Pension Schemes Act 1993

- appeal against an enforcement, improvement or prohibition notice – S.24 Health and Safety at Work etc Act 1974; Reg 18 Control of Major Accident Hazards Regulations 1999 SI 1999/743; para 6, Sch 3 Working Time Regulations 1998 SI 1998/1833 (see IDS Employment Law Handbook, 'Working Time' (2013), Chapter 7, 'Enforcement and remedies', under 'Health and safety enforcement')

- appeal against national minimum wage notice of underpayment – S.19C NMWA (see IDS Employment Law Handbook, 'Wages' (2011), Chapter 5, 'The national minimum wage', under 'Enforcement – enforcement by the enforcement agency')

- appeal against the levy assessment of an Industrial Training Board – S.12(4) Industrial Training Act 1982

- appeal against an unlawful act notice issued by the Equality and Human Rights Commission – S.21 EqA 2006 (see IDS Employment Law Handbook, 'Discrimination at Work' (2012), Chapter 37, 'Equality and Human Rights Commission', under 'Enforcement').

154

3 Conciliation, settlements and ADR

A large majority of claims to employment tribunals are disposed of without a **3.1** hearing ever taking place. According to figures from Her Majesty's Courts and Tribunals Service, 61 per cent of the tribunal cases disposed of between 1 April 2012 and 31 March 2013 were settled by the parties or withdrawn by the claimant (Tribunal Statistics Quarterly, April to June 2013). The Coalition Government, which came into power in 2010, has introduced a number of legislative changes through the Enterprise and Regulatory Reform Act 2013, aimed at further increasing that number and encouraging parties to resolve their workplace disputes outside the tribunal system.

Early conciliation, which became compulsory on 6 May 2014, is likely to have the most tangible impact on the number of employment tribunal claims brought. It is now mandatory for any potential claimant to first contact the Advisory, Conciliation and Arbitration Service (Acas) and be offered conciliation before being allowed to submit an employment tribunal claim. Settlement agreements, which were previously known as 'compromise agreements', are also encouraged by a new provision (in force since 29 June 2013) which provides that any discussions between an employer and an employee with a view to ending the employment relationship on agreed terms are not normally admissible as evidence in an 'ordinary' (as opposed to 'automatically') unfair dismissal claim. Other recent law reforms are also likely to discourage parties from going down the tribunal route: since July 2013 the majority of claims submitted to an employment tribunal require the payment of a fee and, from 6 April 2014, an employer found to have breached employment rights may be ordered to pay a

155

financial penalty on top of the ordinary compensation already payable. The fees regime and the financial penalty are discussed in detail in Chapter 19, 'Fees', and Chapter 20, 'Costs and penalties', respectively.

3.2 If disputes do end up at tribunal, the tribunal has a greater role in encouraging alternative dispute resolution than before. The Employment Tribunal Rules of Procedure 2013 ('the Tribunal Rules'), which are contained in Schedule 1 to the Employment Tribunals (Constitution and Rules of Procedure) Regulations 2013 SI 2013/1237 and which replaced the previous 2004 version with effect from 29 July 2013, give employment tribunals a clear mandate to encourage and facilitate the use of alternative forms of dispute resolution at all appropriate stages of the tribunal process. Rule 3 of the Tribunal Rules, which follows on from the tribunal's overriding objective, expressly states that: '[A] tribunal shall wherever practicable and appropriate encourage the use by the parties of the services of Acas, judicial or other mediation, or other means of resolving their disputes by agreement.' Furthermore, rule 53(1)(e) provides that the tribunal may explore the possibility of settlement or alternative dispute resolution (including judicial mediation) at any preliminary hearing. In his letter accompanying the publication of the revised procedural rules, Lord Justice Underhill, who led the working group on them, acknowledged that encouraging parties to take advantage of the various alternative forms of dispute resolution is 'a matter of culture as much as of rules' but he considered that the culture was reinforced by the express reference to alternative dispute resolution in the Tribunal Rules.

3.3 **Chapter structure and terminology.** In this chapter we begin by looking at the new statutory provisions on early (i.e. pre-claim) conciliation and in particular the requirement that, before commencing employment tribunal proceedings, potential claimants contact Acas in order to be offered conciliation with a view to reaching a settlement of their dispute. We then turn to the position once tribunal proceedings have commenced, discussing in particular the statutory provisions preventing parties from agreeing to exclude or contract out of statutory employment protection rights as a condition of settlement. Next we look at the two principal exceptions to the prohibition against contracting out of rights that enable parties to reach a binding and conclusive settlement of their present and any future claims through the medium either of an Acas-conciliated agreement or a private 'settlement agreement' (formerly called a 'compromise agreement'). We then outline the grounds on which any agreement to settle a tribunal claim may be judged to be invalid and thus set aside. Following that, we examine two alternative means by which employment disputes can be resolved other than by employment tribunal proceedings – arbitration and judicial mediation. And finally we turn our attention to the extent to which any money payable pursuant to an agreement to settle is subject to taxation.

156

Note that any reference to 'contracting-out agreements' in this chapter is to the resolution of disputes through either Acas-conciliated agreements or settlement agreements.

Exclusionary evidence rules applicable to settlement negotiations. Certain **3.4** evidential rules that may apply to exclude details of settlement negotiations and the terms of any resulting agreement from being disclosed as evidence in employment tribunal proceedings are not discussed in this chapter but are instead dealt with in Chapter 13, 'Evidence'. Particularly relevant in this regard is the 'without prejudice' common law rule that generally precludes written or oral communications between the parties concerning efforts to settle litigation disputes from being adduced as evidence in the litigation; and the new statutory provision in S.111A ERA on pre-termination settlement negotiations, which precludes a tribunal from taking into account any offer or discussion of settlement made before the termination of employment when considering the evidence in ordinary unfair dismissal proceedings. Both these topics are discussed in detail in Chapter 13, under '"Without prejudice" negotiations' and 'Pre-termination negotiations' respectively.

Early conciliation   3.5

From 6 May 2014, anyone who is considering bringing a complaint to an employment tribunal must first contact Acas and be offered 'early conciliation' (EC) before being allowed to submit the claim to the tribunal. If the parties wish to take up the offer, Acas will attempt to resolve the dispute quickly and cost-effectively.

The details of the EC scheme are set out in Ss.18A and 18B of the Employment Tribunals Act 1996 (ETA), which were inserted by the Enterprise and Regulatory Reform Act 2013, and in the Early Conciliation Rules of Procedure ('the EC Rules'), which are contained in the Schedule to the Employment Tribunals (Early Conciliation: Exemptions and Rules of Procedure) Regulations 2014 SI 2014/254 ('the EC Regulations'). In essence, the EC scheme operates as follows:

* **Stage 1:** the potential claimant notifies Acas that he or she intends to bring an employment tribunal claim

* **Stage 2:** an Early Conciliation Support Officer makes reasonable attempts to contact the potential claimant and, if he or she agrees to EC, passes the case details on to the conciliator

* **Stage 3:** the conciliator, having obtained the prospective respondent's consent to EC, has a month to attempt to resolve the dispute between the parties. If a settlement is reached, Acas records the terms of the agreement between the parties

- **Stage 4**: if EC is refused or is unsuccessful, the prospective claimant is issued with an EC certificate confirming that Acas notification has been complied with.

3.6 If at any stage of the process the parties indicate that they do not want to participate in EC, the Acas officer in charge will proceed directly to stage 4 and issue the prospective claimant with an EC certificate. He or she will then be able to submit a claim to the tribunal.

It is important to emphasise that, while the EC scheme makes it mandatory to notify Acas that a tribunal claim may be brought, Acas's offer of EC is simply that: an *offer* to attempt to resolve the parties' differences at an early stage, which either party may accept or decline. In other words, there is no obligation on the parties to actually engage in EC through Acas. A potential claimant can send Acas the required notification of his or her claim and thereafter decline EC and, provided that Acas has issued him or her with a certificate confirming that notification was received (see 'Issuing the EC certificate' below), then proceed to lodge a claim with the tribunal. The tribunal will not have any regard to whether or not the protective claimant (or for that matter the prospective respondent) has declined EC when considering a subsequently brought claim. For some, EC may be perceived as little more than an administrative step – a gateway – that they are required to go through before they can take their complaint to an employment tribunal. For others, however, it may present a genuine opportunity to find an amicable solution to a workplace dispute and avoid the stress and anxiety of having to enforce their employment rights before a tribunal. It is also likely to be particularly appealing to those who wish to avoid the payment of tribunal fees.

3.7 Another important aspect of the EC process is the impact it has on the time limit for presenting an employment tribunal claim. Where applicable, the normal time limit is extended by up to one calendar month (and, if the parties are still actively engaging in a process of conciliation, by a further two weeks). These 'stop the clock' provisions, as they have come to be called, are discussed in detail under 'Impact of EC on time limits' below.

The one other general matter of note is that, while in the majority of cases the prospective claimant will submit a request for EC, it is entirely possible for the initial request for pre-claim conciliation to come from the prospective respondent. We discuss this option, and its implications, under 'Request for EC from prospective respondent' below.

3.8 Cases to which EC requirement applies

The duty to make an EC request to Acas before lodging a tribunal claim applies to most potential claimants. S.18A(1) ETA provides that before a prospective claimant can institute *relevant proceedings* relating to any matter he or she must first notify Acas about that matter. S.18(1A) further clarifies that the

158

obligation to notify Acas applies in respect of matters that could be the subject of relevant proceedings. 'Relevant proceedings' are those listed in S.18(1) and encompass the majority of claims in which individual employment rights are alleged to have been infringed – see the Appendix to this chapter.

That said, the list in S.18(1) is not exhaustive. There are two pieces of legislation which are not included in the list of 'relevant proceedings' but which nevertheless appear to be covered by the EC requirement. The first is the right to be accompanied at a disciplinary or grievance hearing, which is governed by Ss.10–13 of the Employment Relations Act 1999 (ERelA). This right is absent from the list of 'relevant proceedings' in S.18(1) ETA but S.14 ERelA appears to incorporate it by treating the relevant sections of the ERelA as provisions of Part V of the ERA for these purposes. It provides: 'Ss.10 to 13 of this Act shall be treated as provisions of Part V of the Employment Rights Act 1996 for the purposes of... S.18(1)(b) of the Employment Tribunals Act 1996.'

3.9 The second notable omission from the list of 'relevant proceedings' in S.18(1) ETA is the Transfer of Undertakings (Protection of Employment) Regulations 2006 SI 2006/246. While TUPE is not expressly included in the list, it appears that claims under Regs 12 (failure to notify employee liability information) and 16 (failure to inform or consult) are nevertheless covered. This seems to be the intention behind Regs 12(7) and 16(1), which specifically refer to EC. Reg 12(7), for example, provides that: 'Sections 18A to 18C of the [ETA] shall apply to the right conferred by this regulation and to proceedings under this regulation as it applies to the rights conferred by that Act and the employment tribunal proceedings mentioned in that Act.' When the Government first consulted on the EC requirement, it *did* include Reg 12 in the list of claims (set out in Annex C of the consultation document, 'Early conciliation: a consultation on proposals for implementation' (January 2013)) that it believed would not be appropriate for EC. However, when it published its response to the consultation, it noted that some of the respondents had suggested that most TUPE claims should be excluded from EC altogether. The Government replied that, having reviewed these claims again, it did not consider there to be 'a case for not including them in the list of jurisdictions appropriate for EC'. It therefore appears that claims under Regs 12 and 16 *are* subject to the EC requirement. Furthermore, the TUPE Regulations *have* been amended to include provisions for extending the time limit in circumstances where the parties engage in EC – see 'Impact of EC on time limits' below.

3.10 **Cases in respect of which EC is excluded.** During public consultation about its proposal for statutory early conciliation, BIS stated that, although it wants EC to be a requirement in most potential employment tribunal claims, it acknowledged that it is not appropriate in some circumstances. The first is where complying with the EC requirement is not practicable because there is a very short period in which to present a claim. For instance, where a claimant complains of unfair dismissal and, on the ET1, also makes an application for interim relief, he or she is not required to have complied with the EC requirement in relation to the underlying unfair dismissal claim. This situation is covered by the exemption under Reg 3(1)(d) of the EC Regulations – see 'Exemptions in cases to which EC would otherwise apply' below.

The second basis on which the Government thought it necessary to exclude EC entirely is where settlement would not be appropriate in view of the particular type of case. This applies to the following:

- an application by the Secretary of State to prohibit a person from running an employment agency (Ss.3A and 3C of the Employment Agencies Act 1973)

- an appeal against an improvement or prohibition notice (S.24 of the Health and Safety at Work etc Act 1974; para 6, Sch 3 to the Working Time Regulations 1998 SI 1998/1833; para 6(2), Sch 2 to the Road Transport (Working Time) Regulations 2005 SI 2005/639; and Reg 18 of the Control of Major Accident Hazards Regulations 1999 SI 1999/743)

- an appeal against the assessment of a training levy (S.12 of the Industrial Training Act 1982)

- the duty of the Secretary of State to pay unpaid contributions into a pension scheme (S.124 of the Pension Schemes Act 1993)

- a reference to the employment tribunal determining an employee's entitlement for payment out of the National Insurance Fund (S.170 ERA)

- an application to the Secretary of State for payment out of the National Insurance Fund where the employer is insolvent (S.182 ERA)

- an application for a declaration that a term of a collective agreement is void or unenforceable in so far as it constitutes, promotes or provides for treatment that is prohibited under the EqA (S.145 EqA)

- an appeal against a decision of the compensating authority (Reg 42 of the Colleges of Education (Compensation) Regulations 1975 SI 1975/1092); and

- an appeal against a notice from the Health and Safety Executive or local authority (Part 2, Sch 8 to the REACH Enforcement Regulations 2008 SI 2008/2852).

Employer contract claims (i.e. counterclaims) are also not within the scope of the EC requirement.

3.11 The jurisdictions listed above have all been omitted from the list of 'relevant proceedings' in S.18(1), with the consequence that the requirement for EC does not apply to them.

160

In its response to the public consultation, the Government specifically rejected the view that claimants should be relieved of the requirement to apply for EC in cases where they are intending to make claims for failures to comply with awards already made by a tribunal (e.g. awards for failure to inform and consult under the Transfer of Undertakings (Protection of Employment) Regulations 2006 SI 2006/246 (TUPE)). It reasoned that if Acas is able to persuade an employer to make the outstanding payment, this would avoid the need for a claim to be brought to the tribunal and so realise the objective of EC. Nor was it convinced by the arguments put forward in some responses to the consultation that whistleblowing (i.e. protected disclosures) should be excluded from the EC provisions. In so far as it was argued that there is a greater risk of the individual suffering yet further detriment than that already suffered as a result of making a protected disclosure, this was mitigated in the Government's view both by the prospective claimant's right to decline EC and by the protections that already existed under the statutory protected disclosure provisions.

Exemptions in cases to which EC would otherwise apply. Where the 3.12 prospective claimant intends to bring proceedings that are on the face of it subject to the requirement for EC, he or she may nevertheless institute proceedings without complying with S.18A(1) in certain circumstances. These are that the prospective claimant:

- wishes to institute proceedings on the same claim form as another person who has complied with the EC requirement in relation to the same dispute – Reg 3(1)(a) EC Regulations. (Note that in these circumstances, the special time limit rules extending the limitation period for the claim will apply (see under 'Impact of EC on time limits' below) – Reg 3(2))

- is bringing relevant proceedings on the same claim form as proceedings which are not relevant proceedings – Reg 3(1)(b)

- is able to show that the prospective respondent has contacted Acas in relation to a dispute, Acas has not received information from the prospective claimant under S.18A(1) ETA in relation to the dispute and the proceedings on the claim form relate to that dispute (see 'Request for EC from prospective respondent') – Reg 3(1)(c)

- is bringing a claim under Part X of the ERA (i.e. unfair dismissal) together with an application for interim relief under S.128 ERA or S.161 of the Trade Union and Labour Relations (Consolidation) Act 1992 – Reg 3(1)(d), or

- is instituting proceedings against the Security Service, the Secret Intelligence Service or the Government Communications Headquarters – Reg 3(1)(e).

Even if the prospective claimant falls within one of the above exemptions, it 3.13 remains open to him or her to contact Acas and ask it to conciliate on his or her

161

behalf – S.18B(2) ETA. Where such a request is made, Acas comes under a duty to endeavour to promote a settlement between the parties until such time that it concludes that no settlement is possible – S.18B(3) and (4)(a).

3.14 Stage 1: applying for early conciliation

Stage 1 of the EC process entails the prospective claimant sending 'prescribed information' in the 'prescribed manner' to Acas. As previously indicated, the mandatory obligations entailed in EC whenever it applies begin and end with compliance by a prospective claimant with this stage 1. Once undertaken, the claimant is under no further duty to actively engage in the EC process, although it is clearly the hope and expectation of Government in enacting the EC requirement that both prospective claimants and respondents will avail themselves of the opportunity that Acas conciliation offers to reach a settlement of their disputes without recourse to tribunal proceedings.

3.15 **Prescribed information in prescribed manner.** To satisfy the requirement for EC the prospective claimant must either:

- present a completed EC form to Acas – rule 1(a) EC Rules, or
- telephone Acas in respect of EC – rule 1(b).

Under the first option, the prospective claimant complies with the EC requirement by submitting the form online via the Acas website or by posting it to the Acas address provided on the form – rule 2(1). The EC form – prescribed under Reg 4(1)(a) EC Regulations by the Secretary of State – requires a prospective claimant to provide the following basic information: his or her name and address, together with the prospective respondent's name and address – rule 2(2). If there is more than one prospective respondent, a separate EC form must be presented in respect of each – rule 4. Acas can reject the form as incomplete and return it to the prospective claimant if any of this information is missing, or contact the prospective claimant to obtain the missing information – rule 2(3) and (4).

3.16 Given the basic level of information needed to complete the EC form, it is far from onerous to comply with S.18A(1). In particular, the form does not ask the prospective claimant to provide any details of the nature of the claim he or she is considering bringing. During public consultation about the EC proposals, the Government expressed concern that prospective claimants – particularly those without legal representation – might find it difficult to understand the full breadth and nature of their dispute(s) at the outset. For example, a prospective claimant intending to bring an unfair dismissal claim against a prospective respondent may only realise during or after EC that he or she could also potentially bring a claim for discrimination. If the legislation required all potential claims to be listed on the EC form prior to being included on an ET1 claim form, the prospective claimant would be prevented from presenting the discrimination claim until such time that he or she had first submitted the discrimination matter to EC. The Government took the view that such a requirement was unduly burdensome on prospective claimants. Nor did it consider it necessary for a prospective claimant to provide this level of detail of the potential claim on the EC form in order for the parties to engage in meaningful conciliation. In its view, it was for Acas to bring to light this information as part of its conversations with the prospective claimant. Accordingly, the right to bring tribunal claims is not restricted to matters of which Acas was made aware either on the EC form or in subsequent discussions between Acas and the parties. The EC form is therefore materially different from the ET1 claim form that is needed to formally start the tribunal process, which must set out sufficient details of the claim – see Chapter 4, 'Starting tribunal proceedings', under 'Completing the claim form'.

When the second option is used to comply with the EC requirement, the prospective claimant must call Acas, using the phone number provided on the form, and inform it of the name and address of the prospective claimant as well as the prospective respondent – rule 3(1). Again, if there is more than one prospective respondent, each respondent must be named – rule 4. Acas will then insert the information provided onto an EC form – rule 3(2).

3.17 Upon receiving the EC request, Acas will record the date the prospective claimant complied with the EC requirement. This date is important for two reasons: first, it signifies the date when the running of the limitation period is suspended in order to allow conciliation to take place (see 'Impact of EC on time limits' below) and, secondly, it marks the start of the statutory period during which Acas is under a duty to attempt conciliation. A copy of the accepted form is automatically sent to a conciliation officer – S.18A(2) ETA.

Although not specifically provided for in the EC Regulations or Rules, it is understood that the following actions will then be taken by Acas. The prospective claimant will be formally notified that the EC request has been received either through an electronic or written acknowledgement (depending on how the request was received), advising the prospective claimant that Acas will be in contact. In the majority of cases, Acas will contact the prospective claimant directly on the telephone number provided. However, where the prospective claimant is legally represented and included his or her representative's details on the EC form, Acas will contact the representative instead.

3.18 Where a prospective claimant says that he or she has complied with the obligation to contact Acas and submitted the EC form but Acas has no record of it, the prospective claimant will be unable to lodge a claim with the employment tribunal. However, he or she can make a second request for EC. If this results in the claim being presented out of time, it is open to the tribunal to accept the claim under its general power to extend the time limit where, depending on the type of claim brought, it considers that it was not reasonably

163

practicable to submit the claim within the relevant time limit and the claim was presented within a reasonable time thereafter or it considers it just and equitable to hear the out-of-time claim – see Chapter 5, 'Time limits', under 'Escape clauses'.

3.19 **Stage 2: initial contact by Acas**

Once Acas receives the EC request, the process of contacting the prospective claimant and gathering information about the dispute will be conducted by an Early Conciliation Support Officer (ECSO). If the prospective claimant agrees to EC, the ECSO will pass the details of the case to an Acas conciliator. It is then up to the conciliator to contact both parties, and if they agree to engage in EC, to attempt to find a resolution to the dispute. Where settlement is not reached, the EC procedure comes to an end by Acas issuing an EC certificate as evidence that S.18A(1) ETA has been complied with. A claim can only be presented to an employment tribunal with the certificate – S.18A(8).

The ECSO's initial call to the prospective claimant – to explain the EC process and find out if he or she is interested in participating in it – will generally be made by the end of the working day after the EC request is received by Acas. Where the ECSO is having difficulty establishing contact, there is no hard-and-fast rule as to how long he or she should keep trying. Rule 5(1) of the EC Rules states that the ECSO must make 'reasonable' attempts to contact the prospective claimant, which suggests that, while the ECSO is likely to make repeated attempts at contact, these will not continue indefinitely. During public consultation about the EC proposal, the Government acknowledged that there may come a point in time when the ECSO, having made several attempts at contact, can reasonably assume that the prospective claimant has no interest in taking up the EC offer. In its response to the consultation, Acas itself suggested that it should be left to the ECSO's personal judgement as to when exactly that point is reached and the Government has accepted this. Accordingly, the decision as to when to terminate the EC process is left to the ECSO's discretion at this stage. Where the ECSO is not able to make contact with the prospective claimant, he or she must conclude that settlement is not possible and issue an EC certificate – rules 5(3) and 7(1) EC Rules and S.18A(4)(a) ETA.

3.20 Where contact is made with the prospective claimant, the ECSO will verify the information provided on the EC form. Should it transpire that the employer is insolvent, the ECSO simply issues a certificate to the prospective claimant to allow him or her to proceed to tribunal straightaway. Otherwise, the ECSO will outline the conciliation process and check whether the prospective claimant requires any reasonable adjustments to accommodate a disability or needs an interpreter. The ECSO also establishes the most convenient time and method for any future contact with the prospective claimant. If the prospective claimant agrees to participate in EC, the relevant details are passed to a conciliator to enable the conciliation to be undertaken. If, however, the prospective claimant

164

declines to take up the offer of EC, the ECSO will issue an EC certificate forthwith – rule 7(1) and S.18A(4)(a).

Regulation 2 of the EC Regulations provides that a prospective claimant is a person who 'is *considering* presenting a claim form to an employment tribunal in relation to relevant proceedings' (our stress). It is important to emphasise that it is not the role of the ECSO to vet potential claims and weed out weak ones at the initial stage. However, the ECSO does inform the prospective claimant of the limitation period and the service requirement for claims and it may well be that, after receiving this information, the prospective claimant concludes that he or she is unlikely to be able to bring a claim and therefore does not want to participate in EC. In this situation, the ECSO is still required to issue an EC certificate to confirm that the individual has complied with the obligation to contact Acas. This is because the decision as to whether the individual has a valid claim is ultimately one for the tribunal to make and, in the event that the prospective claimant changes his or her mind and decides to present a claim, he or she will have to show that the obligation under S.18A(1) was complied with.

Contact by conciliator. Once the case has been passed to a conciliator, his or her first task will be to formally establish that the prospective claimant wants to enter into EC. The conciliator will therefore contact the prospective claimant, ideally within one working day of being passed the case, with a view to obtaining his or her express agreement to EC and asking permission to contact the prospective respondent. The respondent will not be approached unless the prospective claimant consents to this – rule 5(2) EC Rules. **3.21**

Where the prospective claimant confirms that he or she is still interested in EC and agrees to the employer being contacted, the conciliator approaches the prospective respondent to see if it will engage in discussions to resolve the dispute. Again, rule 5(2) provides that it is the conciliator's responsibility to make 'reasonable' attempts at contact and (as discussed above) it will be up to him or her to decide how many attempts are reasonable in the circumstances. If the conciliator is unable to reach the prospective respondent, he or she must conclude that settlement is not possible and issue an EC certificate to the prospective claimant – rules 5(3) and 7(1) and S.18A(4)(a) ETA. An EC certificate is also issued if, after having established contact, the prospective respondent declines the EC offer – rule 7(1) and S.18A(4)(a).

Stage 3: attempt to promote a settlement 3.22
Where the potential parties to a claim agree to participate in EC, the conciliator has up to *one calendar month* from the date the EC form was received by Acas, or from the date of the prospective claimant's telephone call to Acas, to facilitate a settlement – rule 6(1) EC Rules. That period may be extended by up to an additional *two weeks*, but only where the conciliator considers that there is a

165

reasonable prospect of achieving a settlement before the expiry of the extended period and the parties consent to the extension – rule 6(2) and (3). The statutory EC period can only be extended once in relation to any particular EC form – rule 6(3). (For further details of these 'stop the clock' provisions, see 'Impact of EC on time limits' below.)

If the conciliator concludes at any point during the statutory period (including any extension) that a settlement of the dispute (or of part of it) is not possible, or the period expires without a settlement having been reached, he or she will issue an EC certificate to the prospective claimant – rule 7 and S.18A(4) ETA. However, even if no settlement is reached, S.18A(5) gives the conciliation officer the power to continue to endeavour to promote a settlement after the expiry of the statutory period.

3.23 A specific provision in S.18A(9) ETA states that, in a case where the prospective claimant has ceased to be employed by his or her employer and is proposing to claim unfair dismissal, the conciliator may seek to promote reinstatement or re-engagement on terms that appear to be equitable or, in the event that the prospective claimant does not wish to be re-employed or where this is impracticable, may instead seek to promote agreement between the parties as to payment of compensation.

If the prospective claimant and respondent agree to settle, Acas will draw up an agreement recording that settlement (on a COT3 form). For full details of the binding nature of such agreements, see 'Acas-conciliated (COT3) agreements' below.

3.24 Stage 4: issuing the EC certificate
The EC certificate that is sent to the prospective claimant contains:

• the name and address of the prospective claimant

• the name and address of the prospective respondent

• the date of receipt of the EC form by Acas or the date of the telephone call to Acas

• the unique reference number given by Acas to the EC certificate, and

• the date of issue of the certificate, i.e. the date the certificate is sent by Acas, and a statement indicating the method by which the certificate is to be sent – rules 8 and 9(1) EC Rules.

The certificate will be posted to the prospective claimant unless an e-mail address has been provided – rule 9(2). And where Acas had contact with the prospective respondent during the EC period, a copy of the certificate will also be sent to the respondent – rule 9(1).

In multiple claims, a certificate is issued to the lead prospective claimant (i.e. the **3.25** individual who contacted Acas and complied with the EC requirement). Other prospective claimants who relied on the submission of the lead EC form can rely upon the certificate in relation to any claim which they have in common with the lead prospective claimant. If a prospective claimant has a claim that differs from the claim(s) to be brought by the lead prospective claimant, he or she is required to have presented a separate ET1 in relation to that matter and so is unable to rely upon the certificate obtained by the lead prospective claimant.

Importance of date of issue and reference number. The date the certificate is **3.26** issued by Acas and the means by which it is sent are important matters because together they inform the employment tribunal when the certificate will have been received (or deemed to have been received) by the prospective claimant, which in turn enables the tribunal to determine whether any claim that is subsequently made is presented within the relevant time limit. Normal time limits are adjusted to take into account the EC process whenever it applies – see 'Impact of EC on time limits' below. The date of receipt of the EC certificate depends on whether the certificate is sent by Acas in electronic form or in hard copy. If the certificate is sent by e-mail, which will be the case if the prospective claimant has provided an e-mail address, it is deemed to be received on the date it is sent – rule 9(3)(a) EC Rules. A hard-copy certificate is deemed to have been received by the prospective claimant on the day on which it would be delivered in the ordinary course of the post – rule 9(3)(b).

If the prospective claimant decides to present a tribunal claim after receiving the EC certificate, he or she must include the *unique reference number* given by Acas on any subsequent ET1 claim form to demonstrate compliance with the EC requirement. If the ET1 does not include the EC reference number, the tribunal will dismiss the claim – see Chapter 4, 'Starting tribunal proceedings', under 'Processing the claim form – rejection of claim'.

Request for EC from prospective respondent
3.27
There may be circumstances where the request for EC comes not from the prospective claimant but from the prospective respondent. For example, the employer may be aware that the employee is considering bringing a tribunal claim and pre-empts his or her EC request by contacting Acas first. Where this has happened, Acas is as much under a duty to conciliate as if the prospective claimant had begun the formal EC process – S.18B(3) ETA. However, there is no specified period of time within which EC must take place.

Although neither S.18B nor the EC Regulations and Rules explicitly say so, it is envisaged that respondents' requests for EC can be made by completing a respondents' request form or by speaking to Acas directly. The Government's response to the public consultation about the EC proposals explained that where EC is requested by the prospective respondent the case is immediately referred

167

to an Acas conciliator (and thus bypasses the ECSO). Where the prospective claimant declines the offer of EC or no settlement is reached, he or she is able to proceed directly to the tribunal. This is because he or she is exempt from complying with S.18A(1) as the EC request came from the prospective respondent – see 'Cases to which EC requirement applies – exemptions in cases to which EC would otherwise apply' above. However, the crucial difference to the EC process when triggered by the prospective respondent is that the clock will *not* stop for limitation purposes (see 'Impact of EC on time limits' below). It is therefore prudent for a prospective claimant who is inclined to accept such a request to put in his or her own EC request in order to suspend the limitation period, provided the 'stop-the-clock' provisions apply to his or her particular claim.

3.28   **Impact of EC on time limits**

In order to encourage parties to engage in EC with Acas, legislation has been amended to allow for the following extensions of the relevant time limit:

- when determining whether a time limit has been complied with, the period beginning the day after the EC request is received by Acas up to and including the day when the EC certificate is received or deemed to have been received by the prospective claimant is not counted. In other words, the clock will stop when Acas receives the EC request and start to run again the day after the prospective claimant receives the EC certificate

- if a time limit is due to expire during the period beginning with the day Acas receives the EC request and one month after the prospective claimant receives the EC certificate, the time limit expires instead at the end of that period. This effectively gives the prospective claimant one month from the date when he or she receives (or is deemed to receive) the EC certificate to present the claim. (For details about the date of receipt, see 'Issuing the EC certificate' above.)

3.29   With regard to the first basis on which an extension of the normal time limit can be granted, it needs to be remembered that, once Acas has received the EC request, it generally has up to a month to attempt to resolve the dispute between the parties. Furthermore, this period may be extended by an additional two weeks if Acas considers that there is a reasonable prospect of achieving a settlement. The time limit for bringing the relevant tribunal claim will therefore be 'stopped' at the point in time when Acas receives the EC request and will only 'resume' when the prospective claimant receives (or is deemed to receive) the EC certificate. It follows from this that the prospective claimant may have a full calendar month, or a full calendar month plus two weeks (if an extension has been granted), of additional time in which to lodge a tribunal claim if pre-claim conciliation ends without an agreement having been reached.

The second basis for the extension of normal time limits mentioned above is specifically aimed at prospective claimants who enter the EC process close to

168

the end of the limitation period. During public consultation on the early conciliation proposal, the Government acknowledged that prospective claimants might be reluctant to settle a claim close to the end of the EC period because they might not be guaranteed to receive payment of the settlement sum before the limitation period for making the claim runs out. For this reason, it added another extension of the time limit provision to ensure that claimants have at least one month from when they first receive the EC certificate to submit their claim.

The time limit provisions apply to almost all claims in respect of which a **3.30** conciliator has a duty to act – see 'Acas-conciliated (COT3) agreements – cases to which duty to conciliate applies' below and the Appendix to this chapter.

Also, as noted under 'Request for EC from prospective respondent' above, these provisions do not apply where the EC process is triggered by the prospective respondent. If the prospective claimant nevertheless wants to make use of them, he or she is required to put in his or her own EC request.

For a full list of claims to which the time limit adjustment provisions apply, **3.31** see Chapter 5, 'Time limits', under 'Extension of time limit under early conciliation rules'.

Note that where a claim is presented outside the extended time limit, it is up to the employment tribunal to decide whether to exercise its discretion and further extend the relevant limitation period and accept the claim. The rules on time limits are explained in detail in Chapter 5. The statutory formula that may allow for a further extension depending on the nature of the particular claim is discussed in that chapter under '"Not reasonably practicable"' and '"Just and equitable"'.

Prohibition against contracting out of statutory rights
3.32

A contracting-out agreement is an agreement that has the effect and purpose of contracting out of employment rights and obligations and of settling current and/or prospective litigation. In an employment context, such agreements – if they are to be regarded as legally binding on the parties – must take one of three forms, namely:

- an agreement between the parties the terms of which are set out in the body of a judgment of the employment tribunal or in a schedule or annex to a judgment

- an 'Acas-conciliated settlement' reduced into writing, usually on what is known as a COT3 form

169

- a 'settlement agreement' (formerly termed 'compromise agreement'), which is a private legal agreement that satisfies certain legal conditions (including that the employee or worker has received independent legal advice before signing the agreement).

The second and third of these types of agreement – and the statutory provisions that govern them – are separately discussed later in this chapter. The discussion in this section focuses on the advantages and disadvantages from the parties' point of view of 'contracting-out' agreements and examines the common law and statutory provisions that determine the extent to which such agreements can be enforced.

3.33 Advantages and disadvantages of contracting-out agreements

When entered into prior to a tribunal hearing, a contracting-out agreement is often advantageous to both sides. From the employer's point of view, the early settlement of a dispute usually means that a substantial saving in working hours will be made, legal costs will be minimised, disruptions caused by attendance of witnesses will be prevented and – especially in cases involving large public companies – the risk of adverse publicity will be avoided. Furthermore, employers can take the opportunity to include restrictive covenants – such as preventing the solicitation of clients or employees – in the contracting-out agreement. Advantages to the employee may also be significant. By agreeing to settle, the claimant obviously avoids the risk of losing his or her case. Of the cases disposed of in 2012/13, only 11 per cent were successful at an employment tribunal hearing. But even assuming that the claimant were to win, by accepting a settlement he or she avoids any potential award being reduced for failure to mitigate or on account of contributory conduct. Moreover, the claimant is likely to receive his or her compensation far sooner than would otherwise be the case and, in contrast to tribunal awards, settlements are not subject to the recoupment provisions of the Employment Protection (Recoupment of Jobseeker's Allowance and Income Support) Regulations 1996 SI 1996/2349 (see further IDS Employment Law Handbook, 'Unfair Dismissal' (2010), Chapter 20, 'Recoupment'). This means that a smaller sum agreed in a settlement may, in real terms, be more valuable than a larger one awarded by a tribunal, particularly taking into account that the claimant would have also had to have paid an issue and a hearing fee in order to take the claim to the tribunal.

Another advantage to an employee who agrees to settle is that he or she may be able to incorporate matters into the contracting-out agreement that lie outside the tribunal's jurisdiction. The parties may, for instance, agree that the employer will provide a reference, the exact wording of which should be fully discussed and agreed on as well as accurately recorded – Cox v Sun Alliance Life Ltd 2001 IRLR 448, CA. Beneficial pension arrangements can also form part of the settlement. And finally, of course, a claimant who enters into a contracting-out agreement avoids the trauma of a public hearing – a benefit which should not be underestimated.

There are also disadvantages to contracting-out agreements, however – **3.34** particularly for employees. An employer who settles a claim, even if it would probably have won a contested case before a tribunal, may still be a net-gainer through avoiding the costs of a tribunal hearing. An employee, on the other hand, may not be so lucky as it is entirely possible that he or she might accept an offer of settlement that falls far short of any compensatory award that the tribunal would have awarded in the event of a successful claim. Another disadvantage is the fact that, by agreeing to settle, the employee is deprived of an opportunity to air his or her grievance and of the chance of obtaining a public declaration in his or her favour. This may be of particular importance in certain cases – discrimination and protected disclosure (whistleblowing) cases, for example – where a point of principle is often at issue.

In so far as Acas-conciliated agreements and settlement agreements are concerned, one other disadvantage should also be considered. A settlement that is reached under the auspices of an Acas conciliator or which fulfils the conditions governing settlement agreements binds the parties legally, so that an employee cannot subsequently present a complaint to a tribunal about the same subject matter. This may be an important sacrifice from the employee's point of view and his or her decision, being irrevocable, needs to be weighed up carefully.

Should the parties decide to go down the contracting-out route, either through **3.35** Acas or through a valid settlement agreement, the tribunal should be informed of any agreement reached as soon as possible so as not to waste any more judicial time or incur further costs. In Yell Ltd v Garton 2004 EWCA Civ 87, CA, the Court of Appeal stated that those advising parties to litigation have a professional obligation to notify the court if there is a likelihood of settlement.

Effect of contracting-out agreements   3.36
The contents of contracting-out agreements can vary enormously, depending on the requirements of the parties, but almost all include some provision for the payment of a sum of money by the employer in exchange for an undertaking by the employee not to take any legal action in respect of his or her complaint(s). Such an agreement will not always be valid and effective, however. The extent to which an employer can enforce the employee's waiver of rights largely depends on whether or not it is being invoked as a bar to a common law action (e.g. wrongful dismissal) or to a statutory one (e.g. unfair dismissal).

Common law. A contracting-out agreement is, in effect, a contract made **3.37** between the parties providing for the payment of a sum of money in full and final settlement of all claims. In so far as it fulfils the common law requirements for a binding legal contract – i.e. that there has been a valid offer and acceptance,

171

mutual consideration and an intention by the parties to create legal relations – it will be effective to bar a subsequent claim in the form of a civil action by the employee for breach of the employment contract. This is subject to exceptions where the employee is induced to enter into the contract by misrepresentation, under duress or undue influence, or because of a mistake. These 'defences' are normally very difficult to prove, however – see 'Invalid agreements' below.

In the event of the employer failing to comply with the terms of the agreement, the employee has two options. He or she may either accept the employer's breach, bringing the contracting-out agreement to an end, and revive the original claim, or stand and sue on the terms of the agreement for the monies due under it.

3.38 **Statutory rights.** The position is quite different when an employee is claiming in respect of a statutory right conferred by employment protection legislation. The general rule here is that contracting-out agreements between the parties are not legally binding as such. Accordingly, if an ex-employee agrees to accept a cheque in full and final settlement of any claims he or she may have against the employer, there is nothing to stop him or her from banking the cheque and then bringing unfair dismissal proceedings. This is because provision is made in a number of employment statutes to the effect that employees cannot contract out of their statutory employment rights. The provision cited in most of the decided cases is S.203(1) of the Employment Rights Act 1996 (ERA), which renders void any provision in an agreement (whether a contract of employment or not) in so far as it purports to:

- exclude or limit the operation of any provision of the ERA, or

- preclude any person from bringing any proceedings under the ERA before an employment tribunal.

3.39 Similar provisions can be found in:

- S.144(1) of the Equality Act 2010 (EqA)

- S.288(1) of the Trade Union and Labour Relations (Consolidation) Act 1992 (TULR(C)A)

- S.49(1) of the National Minimum Wage Act 1998 (NMWA)

- Reg 35 of the Working Time Regulations 1998 SI 1998/1833 (but note that the Regulations themselves provide for agreements that have the effect of supplementing, or in some instances introducing derogations from, the strict application of the Regulations)

- Reg 41 of the Transnational Information and Consultation of Employees Regulations 1999 SI 1999/3323 ('the TICE Regulations')

- Reg 9 of the Part-time Workers (Prevention of Less Favourable Treatment) Regulations 2000 SI 2000/1551 ('the Part-time Workers Regulations')

- Reg 10 of the Fixed-term Employees (Prevention of Less Favourable Treatment) Regulations 2002 SI 2002/2034 ('the Fixed-term Employees Regulations')

- Reg 19 of the Merchant Shipping (Working Time: Inland Waterways) Regulations 2003 SI 2003/3049 ('the Merchant Shipping Regulations')

- Reg 20 of the Fishing Vessels (Working Time: Sea-fishermen) Regulations 2004 SI 2004/1713 ('the Fishing Vessels Regulations')

- Reg 40 of the Information and Consultation of Employees Regulations 2004 SI 2004/3426 ('the ICE Regulations')

- Reg 18 of the Transfer of Undertakings (Protection of Employment) Regulations 2006 SI 2006/246 (TUPE)

- para 12(1) of the Schedule to the Occupational and Personal Pension Schemes (Consultation by Employers and Miscellaneous Amendment) Regulations 2006 SI 2006/349 ('the OPPS Regulations')

- Reg 41 of the European Cooperative Society (Involvement of Employees) Regulations 2006 SI 2006/2059 ('the ECS Regulations')

- Reg 62 of the Companies (Cross-Border Mergers) Regulations 2007 SI 2007/2974

- Reg 18 of the Cross-border Railway Services (Working Time) Regulations 2008 SI 2008/1660

- Reg 39 of the European Public Limited-Liability Company (Employee Involvement) (Great Britain) Regulations 2009 SI 2009/2401 ('the EPLLC Regulations')

- Reg 15 of the Agency Workers Regulations 2010 SI 2010/93

- Reg 16 of the Employment Relations Act 1999 (Blacklists) Regulations 2010 SI 2010/493 ('the Blacklists Regulations').

Most of the decided cases in this regard have been brought under S.203(1) ERA. For the sake of simplicity, we shall concentrate on that section in this chapter, on the understanding that the same considerations apply to the other provisions noted above.

Scope of statutory prohibition on contracting out. The scope of S.203(1) is **3.40** very wide. In Naqvi v Stephens Jewellers Ltd 1978 ICR 631, EAT, the EAT held that the words 'bringing any proceedings' are not limited to the initiation of proceedings by the employee but also cover the continuation of proceedings after a claim has already been made. Thus a letter recording the parties'

173

agreement in the Naqvi case that the employee would withdraw a complaint he had already presented to a tribunal in return for an agreed job reference was held to be caught by S.203(1) and could not therefore be relied upon by the employer to prevent the employee from changing his mind and proceeding with his claim.

In Courage Take Home Trade Ltd v Keys 1986 ICR 874, EAT, an agreement to settle a claim was made after the employment tribunal had found in favour of the employee on the question of unfair dismissal but before any remedy had been determined. The EAT held that the agreement was void under S.203(1) because the section did not cease to have effect after liability (as opposed to remedy) had been determined. In other words, S.203(1) is broad enough to catch a contracting-out agreement made at any time before the tribunal reaches a final determination on the question of remedy.

3.41 The non-contracting-out provision was also infringed by the employer's internal dispute resolution procedures in the case of Clyde and Co LLP v Bates van Winkelhof 2012 ICR 928, QBD. There, W was a partner in CC LLP, a firm of solicitors operating as a limited liability partnership. Following her expulsion from the partnership, W brought claims of sex discrimination and unlawful detriment for whistleblowing before an employment tribunal. CC LLP sought a stay of the proceedings on the ground that, under clause 41 of the members' agreement, any dispute between the LLP and one its members had to be determined by arbitration. The High Court rejected the application, holding that the binding arbitration clause, which precluded W from continuing with her unlawful detriment claim, was clearly rendered void by S.203(1) ERA. Although the wording of S.144(1) EqA differed from that of S.203(1) ERA, the High Court held that the same prohibition applied in respect of her discrimination claim.

3.42 *Exceptions.* There are three major exceptions to the general rule that contracting-out agreements are not binding in respect of statutory claims. The first is where the contracting-out agreement is formally incorporated into a tribunal decision. Where an agreement has been incorporated into a tribunal decision dismissing the claim, the claimant will be prevented or 'estopped' from bringing another claim in respect of the same facts or issues. This is because the doctrine of 'res judicata' – which bars the reopening of a legal issue which has already been decided – is not restricted to cases where a tribunal has given a reasoned decision on the substantive issues in the case. For a more detailed discussion of the doctrine of res judicata, see Chapter 2, 'Tribunals' jurisdiction', under 'Relitigation: res judicata and abuse of process'.

The second major exception is where the agreement has been reached under the auspices of an Acas conciliator. S.203(2)(e) ERA provides that any agreement reached either before a complaint has been made to a tribunal or after proceedings have been commenced will be effective to block a claim if an Acas conciliator has taken action in accordance with his or her duties under Ss.18A–18C of the Employment Tribunals Act 1996 (ETA) in respect of that agreement. Similar provisions exist in S.144(4)(a) and (5) EqA; S.288(2) TULR(C)A; S.49(2) NMWA; Reg 35(2)(a) of the Working Time Regulations; Reg 41(2)(a) of the TICE Regulations; Reg 9 of the Part-time Workers Regulations; Reg 10 of the Fixed-term Employees Regulations; Reg 19(2)(a) of the Merchant Shipping Regulations; Reg 20(2)(a) of the Fishing Vessels Regulations; Reg 40(2) of the ICE Regulations; Reg 18 of TUPE; para 12(2) of the Schedule to the OPPS Regulations; Reg 41(2) of the ECS Regulations; Reg 62(2) of the Companies (Cross-Border Mergers) Regulations; Reg 18(2)(a) of the Cross-border Railway Services Regulations; Reg 39(2) of the EPLLC Regulations; Reg 15 of the Agency Workers Regulations; and Reg 16 of the Blacklists Regulations.

The third major exception to S.203(1) ERA is where the conditions governing **3.43** settlement agreements have been complied with – S.203(2)(f). This provision enables an employee or worker who has received advice from an independent adviser to enter into a legally binding settlement without the involvement of an Acas officer. Again, similar provisions are contained in S.144(4)(b) and (5) EqA; S.288(2A) TULR(C)A; S.49(3) NMWA; Reg 35(2)(b) of the Working Time Regulations; Reg 41(3)(a) of the TICE Regulations; Reg 9 of the Part-time Workers Regulations; Reg 10 of the Fixed-term Employees Regulations; Reg 19(2)(b) of the Merchant Shipping Regulations; Reg 20(2)(b) of the Fishing Vessels Regulations; Reg 40(3) of the ICE Regulations; Reg 18 of TUPE; para 12(3) of the Schedule to the OPPS Regulations; Reg 41(3) of the ECS Regulations; Reg 62(3) of the Companies (Cross-Border Mergers) Regulations; Reg 18(2)(b) of the Cross-border Railway Services Regulations and Reg 39(3) of the EPLLC Regulations.

Note also that S.203(5) ERA provides that an agreement under which the parties agree to submit a dispute to Acas arbitration is a valid contracting-out agreement. However, for the arbitration agreement to be valid it must have been drawn up following action by an Acas conciliation offer or by means of a valid settlement agreement. Similar provisions are found in S.144(6) EqA and S.288(6) TULR(C)A. The Acas Arbitration Scheme is discussed under 'Arbitration' below.

Effect on compensation. One last general point should be made about the **3.44** application of S.203(1) ERA. Even though that provision entitles an employee to bring tribunal proceedings despite an agreement not to do so, it does not stop the tribunal from taking any payment made to the employee under the contracting-out agreement into account when calculating compensation. In other words, the payment will be treated like any other ex gratia payment. For instance, in Courage Take Home Trade Ltd v Keys (above), the EAT ruled that the tribunal had been correct in holding that it was not just and equitable to make a compensatory award to an employee who had accepted an ex gratia

175

payment 'in full and final settlement of the claim before the tribunal'. However, the EAT did go on to say: 'There may be situations in which a respondent has unduly persuaded an employee to accept a figure by way of agreement, or brought pressure on him; it may be in that situation that an [employment] tribunal would rule that the employer could scarcely be heard to say that it was unjust or inequitable if he were called on to pay a further sum. That question must, in the end, depend on the particular facts of the case.'

A distinction should be made here between the compensatory award and the basic award. While an ex gratia payment will generally be offset against any compensatory award because it will directly reduce the employee's financial loss, it will not necessarily be treated as meeting the liability for a basic award. The leading case in this regard is Chelsea Football Club and Athletic Co Ltd v Heath 1981 ICR 323, EAT. H was unfairly dismissed and then given a cheque for £7,500 with a letter describing it as 'the ex gratia compensation that was agreed by the board, as a result of the termination of your employment'. The tribunal that heard H's unfair dismissal claim made no compensatory award because £7,500 exceeded the statutory maximum which it could have awarded H at that time and because H had rapidly found new employment and seemed to have suffered no loss. But it held that none of the statutory grounds for reducing a basic award were present so it felt constrained to make a full basic award of £1,920. The EAT, however, pointed out that the employer's argument was not that the basic award should be reduced but that it had already been paid in full because it should be treated as forming part of the £7,500 paid to H. The EAT said that whether or not a severance payment should be treated as extinguishing liability for a basic award was a 'matter of construction'. If an employer stated clearly that a severance payment was intended to meet any possible liability for a basic award, then a tribunal would not be required to make a basic award. But when the employer simply made a general payment – particularly one expressed as being 'ex gratia' – he or she would run the risk that a tribunal would find nothing relating to liability for a basic award. In H's case the use of the word 'compensation' seems to have tipped the scales and the EAT accepted that the 'ex gratia compensation' amounted to an offer to compensate H for such rights as he might have in respect of his dismissal. The EAT set aside the tribunal's award.

3.45 However, the opposite conclusion was reached in Pomphrey of Sittingbourne Ltd v Reed EAT 457/94. In that case the question arose as to whether a tribunal should have deducted 12 weeks' salary in lieu of notice, which the employer had paid to R on the termination of his employment, from R's basic award. At the tribunal and before the EAT the employer argued that because R had been off sick for a number of months by the time of his dismissal no salary was due to him under the terms of the contract and the payment should be offset against his basic award. Applying the approach in the Chelsea Football Club case, the EAT stated that ex gratia payments that are intended to cover an employer's liabilities in respect of a dismissal may be deducted from the award which they were intended to cover. However, in the instant case the employer had expressly stated that the sum was a payment in lieu of notice; it was not an ex gratia payment paid on account of the basic award. The employer could not later change its mind and have the payment appropriated to the basic award.

The message for employers is clear: any severance payment to a dismissed employee should be expressly referred to as covering any possible liability arising out of a complaint to a tribunal. Ideally, from an employer's perspective, any severance payment should be endorsed by an Acas conciliator (if Acas has been involved in promoting an agreement) or should satisfy the conditions for settlement agreements. This would prevent the employee pursuing an unfair dismissal claim at a later date and sidestep the issue of whether the payment could be interpreted as extinguishing a basic award.

Transfer of undertakings. The TUPE Regulations 2006 contain an express **3.46** provision restricting the capacity of any party to a transfer – transferor, transferee or employee – to contract out of the employment protection provisions contained within the Regulations. Reg 18 states that 'Section 203 of the [ERA] (restrictions on contracting out) shall apply in relation to these Regulations as if they were contained in that Act, save for that section shall not apply in so far as these Regulations provide for an agreement (whether a contract of employment or not) to exclude or limit the operation of these Regulations.' The provision effectively applies the same restrictions on contracting out as apply to substantive claims contained within the ERA (such as unfair dismissal and unlawful deductions from wages) unless the TUPE Regulations expressly provide for a right to contract out of, or limit the application of, specific provisions of the Regulations. The circumstances in which the TUPE Regulations expressly allow parties to contract out of the specific protections derived under them are mentioned under 'Acas-conciliated agreements' below. However, a full discussion of contracting-out agreements in the context of a TUPE transfer is contained in IDS Employment Law Handbook, 'Transfer of Undertakings' (2011), Chapter 10, 'Practical aspects of transfers', under 'Avoidance of TUPE provisions'.

Acas-conciliated (COT3) agreements   3.47

As noted under 'Prohibition against contracting out of statutory rights – effect of contracting-out agreements' above, one major exception to the general rule that contracting-out agreements are void in so far as they purport to exclude a claimant from bringing a complaint before an employment tribunal is where the agreement has been reached under the auspices of an Acas conciliator. The importance of Acas's role in conciliating tribunal claims, both actual and potential, cannot be overestimated: Acas-conciliated agreements accounted for 33 per cent of all tribunal cases disposed of in 2012/13 and

177

77 per cent of cases referred to it for early conciliation in that period did not result in an employment tribunal claim.

We have already seen that, as from April 2014, Acas has had an important role in offering 'early conciliation' to persons who are thinking of bringing claims to a tribunal – see 'Early conciliation' above. However, in addition to this, it has a highly significant role in helping settle claims once a tribunal claim has been lodged, and this capacity to conciliate post-claim can even extend to after a tribunal has determined a dispute and a party has lodged an appeal to the EAT. In this regard, rule 36 of the Employment Appeal Tribunal Rules 1993 SI 1993/2854 states that the EAT may, at any stage in the proceedings, refer the parties to conciliation if it thinks that there is a reasonable prospect that an agreement can be reached between the parties or that the appeal or a part of it can be disposed of by consensual means. The availability of Acas conciliation at any stage of the EAT process is reinforced in paras 12(5) and 26 of the EAT Practice Direction (July 2013).

3.48 **What is 'conciliation'?**
In its booklet 'Conciliation explained', Acas describes conciliation as a process whereby the conciliator tries to assist the parties in dispute to reach a voluntary resolution of a complaint, or potential complaint, without the need for a tribunal hearing. Conciliation is said to be impartial, confidential, voluntary, independent and free of charge.

Importantly, a conciliator's function does not extend to advising on the merits of the case. The best and most experienced conciliation officers know that there is a line beyond which they cannot go without being open to the criticism that they are stepping into the shoes of a partisan representative. The legitimate aim is to assist the parties to reach an informed decision about how best they should proceed. Advice on whether to proceed or not, assessment of the merits of a party's case, or anything which suggests a particular outcome (especially encouragement to withdraw or pressure to settle against the parties' wishes) are all actions beyond the proper scope of the conciliator's role. Similarly, the conciliator should not impose or even recommend a particular agreement. The terms of an agreement are the responsibility of the parties concerned.

In order to help parties decide whether or not conciliation is for them, Acas has produced a short video that explains how the conciliation process works. This can be accessed via the Acas website.

3.49 **Nature of statutory duty.** Conciliators have a statutory duty to attempt to conciliate settlements of disputes where complaints have been or could be made to an employment tribunal under most employment protection legislation. However, a conciliator cannot act as a representative for either party – the role of conciliator is to offer to assist both parties involved in a dispute to settle their differences without the need to go to an employment tribunal hearing. Thus a conciliator may, where he or she considers it necessary, legitimately provide the following services:

- explain the conciliation process

- explain the way tribunals operate, including what they will take into account in deciding a case

- explain the legal issues involved

- discuss the options available, including, where appropriate, arbitration

- help each side understand how the other side views the case, and explore how it might be resolved without a hearing

- relay any proposals for a settlement between the employer and the employee.

By being at hand during an early and vital stage in the evolution of an **3.50** employment dispute, Acas officers should be well placed to help prevent the parties from retreating into entrenched positions. Their aim in providing independent information and advice of the kind mentioned above is to gain the confidence of the parties, thus making the parties more disposed to settle their dispute amicably. The costs in terms of time, expense and anxiety that a tribunal hearing involves can therefore be avoided by conciliation. It is also possible to include a reference or an apology as part of an agreement, something which cannot be done by the tribunal. Another feature of Acas conciliation is confidentiality.

As Acas is under a continuing duty to offer conciliation from the date it is first notified that a tribunal claim could be brought right up to the date the claim is determined by the tribunal, it could potentially make repeated attempts to settle a dispute. However, it is likely to be a rare case where Acas's assistance is sought before as well as after the presentation of a tribunal claim.

Confidentiality and non-disclosure. Nothing communicated to an Acas **3.51** conciliator in the process of individual conciliation is admissible in evidence before a tribunal without the consent of the party concerned. Furthermore, S.251B TULR(C)A, which was inserted by the Enterprise and Regulatory Reform Act 2013 with effect from 25 April 2013, specifically prohibits Acas from releasing any information relating to a worker, a worker's employer or a trade union that it holds in connection with the provision of its services. This is subject to a number of exceptions, which are listed in S.251B(2) TULR(C)A. For example, Acas is not prohibited from disclosing information where the disclosure is made for the purpose of enabling or assisting an Acas conciliation officer to carry out his or her functions, the individuals to whom the information relates have given their consent to the disclosure, or the information is disclosed for the purpose of a criminal investigation. Cases examining the confidential nature of the conciliator's role are discussed under 'Confidentiality' below.

179

3.52 Cases to which duty to conciliate applies

There is statutory provision for Acas conciliation in most employment protection and discrimination cases. S.18(1) ETA lists the proceedings, referred to as 'relevant proceedings', in which Acas has a legal duty to conciliate. These are listed in the Appendix to this chapter. Claims against the Secretary of State on the insolvency of the employer (Part X ERA) are expressly excluded from the conciliator's remit. Note that the Secretary of State and the Lord Chancellor, acting jointly, have the power to add or remove any relevant proceedings from the list in S.18(1) – S.18(8).

Provided a conciliator has the power to act in a particular case, he or she may become involved:

- prior to a claim having been brought, as part of the early conciliation procedure (in force since 6 April 2014) – see 'Early conciliation' above, or

- once a claim has been presented, if he or she is requested to do so by both parties or, in the absence of such a request, if he or she considers that there is a reasonable prospect of success in reaching a settlement – see 'Conciliation after presentation of ET1' immediately below.

3.53 Conciliation after presentation of ET1

If a dispute is not settled through early conciliation and an employment tribunal claim is subsequently brought, Acas's conciliation services remain available to the parties right until the time that the claim is determined by the tribunal. Once the claim is under way, the tribunal will send a copy of the claim form and the response form to the conciliator – S.19(1)(a) ETA and rule 93(1)(a) Tribunal Rules. This ensures that conciliators are made aware of the existence of each claim. The parties to the claim are also informed that the services of an Acas conciliation officer are available to them – S.19(1)(b) and rule 93(1)(b).

Where a claim has been presented by the claimant, an Acas conciliator may become involved in one of two ways:

- he or she may be requested to do so by either party, or

- in the absence of such a request, if he or she considers that he or she could endeavour to promote a settlement with a reasonable prospect of success – S.18C(1).

3.54 A conciliator should ensure that he or she becomes involved in negotiations to settle in one of the two ways set out in S.18C(1) ETA. Otherwise, any agreement reached will be void and the claimant will be entitled to proceed with any tribunal claim. In Shopland v Capitol Security ET Case No.3200812/01 the respondent communicated a settlement offer of £300 to the claimant's solicitor. The solicitor took instructions and was told that he could settle for that amount. He called an Acas conciliator to communicate the acceptance of the offer to the

180

respondent. However, the respondent then informed the conciliator that the offer was withdrawn. The tribunal held that, as a result of the conciliator's communicating the acceptance of the offer (as agent) to the respondent, there was a binding contract between the parties before the respondent's withdrawal of the offer. However, the contract did not exclude the jurisdiction of the tribunal because the conciliator had not become involved as required by the ETA. In the absence of a conciliation request by both parties, the only way to become involved is for the conciliator to consider that he or she could act under the section with a reasonable prospect of success. The tribunal could find no evidence suggesting that the conciliator had actually considered that there was a reasonable prospect of success. Rather, he had become involved because the claimant's solicitor had asked him to.

Cases are normally allocated to conciliators on a geographical basis, each officer being broadly responsible for a particular area. Conciliators deal with a variety of claims, although discrimination cases are allocated to particular officers with special training in this subject. Ordinarily, the conciliator will take the initiative for contacting the parties to establish whether there is a reasonable prospect of helping them settle their differences. He or she should explain that the service is free, impartial and confidential, and that he or she does not act as a representative of either party or as a fact-finder for the tribunal. If it appears from the ET1 that, for example, the complainant lacks sufficient qualifying service or is otherwise excluded from the right to claim, the conciliator will explain the legal position to the complainant. He or she will also draw the parties' attention to the risk of costs being awarded should the tribunal find that either party has acted vexatiously, abusively, disruptively or otherwise unreasonably, or that the bringing or conducting of the proceedings by a party has been misconceived (see further Chapter 20, 'Costs and penalties').

3.55 If either side is obviously unwilling to contemplate a settlement, the conciliator may withdraw, while making it clear that Acas's services remain available if one or both sides change their minds. Otherwise the conciliator will carry out his or her statutory duties to try to promote a settlement, provided there is a 'reasonable prospect of success' in reaching such a settlement.

Where the claimant decides not to proceed with the claim, or to settle the claim, following Acas conciliation, he or she should notify the tribunal that the claim is being withdrawn. The procedure for withdrawing a tribunal claim is discussed in Chapter 4, 'Starting tribunal proceedings', under 'Withdrawals'.

The conciliator's duties

3.56 The conciliator's general duty whenever he or she takes action is to 'endeavour to promote a settlement' between those who would be, or already are, parties to relevant proceedings before an employment tribunal – Ss.18A(3), 18B(3) and 18C(1) ETA. With specific regard to unfair dismissal claims, Ss.18A(9), 18B(6) and 18C(2) go on to state that:

- the conciliator may seek to promote the reinstatement or re-engagement of the complainant on terms that appear to the conciliator to be equitable, or

- where re-employment is not practicable or not sought by the complainant, the conciliator may seek to promote agreement between the parties as to a sum by way of compensation to be paid by the employer. (Note that, for the purposes of S.18C(2) only, i.e. where an unfair dismissal claim has already been presented, the parties must also 'desire the conciliator to act' under this provision.)

It is worth emphasising that the conciliator's power to consider re-employment in these circumstances is discretionary only. This is in contrast to the position prior to April 2014, where the conciliator – at least where an unfair dismissal had already been presented – was under a duty to consider re-employment. However, it is not suggested that this change in the law will make much difference in practice, as conciliated agreements rarely provide for reinstatement or re-engagement. Rather, what is normally at issue are the terms for a financial settlement.

3.57 The conciliator is required by S.18(6) ETA to have regard, where appropriate, to the desirability of encouraging the use of other procedures available for the settlement of grievances. The conciliator should therefore consider whether a dismissed employee has exhausted the available internal appeal procedures. In practice, the employee will often have made use of the employer's internal dispute resolution procedures prior to bringing a tribunal claim (see IDS Employment Law Guide, 'Statutory Disciplinary and Grievance Procedures' (2009), for further details).

Note that the cases discussed below were decided under the law as it stood prior to April 2014. However, unless otherwise stated, it is not suggested that any of these cases would be decided differently under the law as it currently stands. References are to the current statutory provisions where appropriate.

3.58 **Meaning of 'taken action'.** Section 203(1) ERA, which as a general rule prevents employees from contracting out of their statutory rights (see 'Prohibition against contracting out of statutory rights – effect of contracting-out agreements' above), states that a contracting-out agreement *will* be effective where a conciliator has 'taken action' under any of Ss.18A–18C ETA – S.203(2)(e). The question of when a conciliator has 'taken action' was considered by the House of Lords in Moore v Duport Furniture Products Ltd and anor 1982 ICR 84, HL. M was suspended by D Ltd on suspicion of theft. The employer called in Acas but made it clear that it would not agree to reinstatement or re-engagement. The conciliator suggested a financial settlement and then withdrew before M arrived. When the conciliator returned to the scene M had resigned (under protest) and had agreed to waive his right to claim unfair dismissal in return for a payment of £300. The conciliator recorded the terms of the agreement on a COT3 form (the standard form on which settlements agreed following Acas conciliation are recorded) and took the parties through the form step by step, explaining its effect before they signed it. He did not speak to the employee separately, and nor did he explain his legal rights to him. M later changed his mind and presented a complaint of unfair dismissal.

It was argued before the House of Lords that the agreement was invalid on two grounds. The first objection was that when the conciliator intervened M had not made any claim of unfair dismissal or of entitlement to complain of unfair dismissal – i.e. that action had been taken against him that could form the basis of a complaint. Secondly, the conciliator had not 'taken action' in accordance with S.134 of the Employment Protection (Consolidation) Act 1978 (the precursor to Ss.18A–18C ETA) because he had not sought to promote anything, but had simply rubber-stamped an agreement that the parties had reached between themselves. It was argued that the conciliator was required actively to promote reinstatement or re-engagement or, where that proved impracticable, a financial settlement.

The House of Lords rejected both contentions. It said that a 'claim' that an **3.59** employee was entitled to complain of unfair dismissal includes 'an implied claim to be inferred from the overt acts or attitudes of the employee concerned in the particular circumstances of the case'. It was clear that M was resigning under protest – the employer had conceded that this was in effect a dismissal – and that he thought this was unfair. That was sufficient to trigger the intervention of the conciliator. On the second point their Lordships noted that a conciliator's paramount duty was to 'promote a settlement of the complaint without its being determined by an [employment] tribunal'. In their view this phrase must be given a 'liberal construction capable of covering whatever action by way of such promotion is applicable *in the circumstances of the particular case*' (our stress). In this case, that action consisted of recording the terms of the agreement, seeing that it was signed, and explaining the consequences of the agreement to the parties. This was sufficient to create a binding agreement although the conciliator took no part in reaching it. Furthermore, the conciliator was under no obligation to try actively to achieve the reinstatement or re-engagement of M in the circumstances of the case, since the employer had made it clear that it was adamantly opposed to re-employing him.

Despite only minimal involvement by an Acas conciliator, an agreement to settle was also held to be valid in Allma Construction Ltd v Bonner 2011 IRLR 204, EAT. There, B complained to an employment tribunal of unfair dismissal. Shortly before the hearing date, AC Ltd offered him £1,000 to settle the claim. B instructed his solicitor that the offer was acceptable and his solicitor informed

Acas that an offer had been received and that it was acceptable to B. Acas then called AC Ltd's solicitor and left a message for him that the offer had been accepted. When B subsequently changed his mind and requested more money, AC Ltd, taking the view that an agreement had already been reached, applied to the tribunal to dismiss the claim. The tribunal found that no agreement had been reached, partly because the parties had not agreed any other terms in addition to the amount of the settlement sum, and allowed B's claim to proceed to hearing. On appeal, the EAT overturned that decision. According to Lady Smith, sitting alone, the threshold for an Acas conciliator to have 'taken action' is very low and covers 'any action taken by an Acas officer in relation to the claim'. Lady Smith put it as follows: the conciliation officer 'does not require to broker the settlement nor does he require to record it. His statutory duty goes no further than that he is to endeavour to promote a settlement of the proceedings. How he does that will be a matter for him and will vary from case to case according to the particular circumstances. Whilst there is a practice of Acas being involved in the recording of settlements in standard paperwork (Forms COT3), that practice does not need to have been followed for the tribunal's jurisdiction to be ousted.' In this case, the fact that the Acas officer had communicated B's acceptance was sufficient to satisfy the statutory requirement that he had 'taken action' to promote settlement of the claim.

3.60 What these cases show is that a conciliator does not have to do very much in order to 'take action'. A conciliator's function is to help the parties to reach a voluntary settlement on their own terms. It is not the conciliator's job to advise on the merits of the case, to recommend any particular settlement, or even to ensure that any financial settlement reached is a fair one (although the ETA does require that any reinstatement or re-engagement should be on terms the conciliator considers equitable, so a complete failure by a conciliator to consider the fairness of such terms might invalidate a settlement).

Furthermore, a conciliator is certainly under no obligation to advise the parties on their legal rights, although he or she may do so if such a course of action appears necessary or desirable. But even in these circumstances any failure will not render the settlement ineffective. In Slack v Greenham (Plant Hire) Ltd and anor 1983 ICR 617, EAT, the employee argued that an agreement to settle his prospective complaint of unfair dismissal was void because the conciliator had omitted to advise him of the right to claim compensation for future loss of earnings in an unfair dismissal claim. The EAT upheld the tribunal's decision that it had no jurisdiction to entertain the employee's complaint. The conciliator was not 'obliged to go through the framework of the relevant legislation and to explain the employee's rights to him'. Once he had recorded the terms agreed between the parties he had 'taken action' giving rise to a binding agreement.

3.61 An Acas conciliator need not meet with the parties face to face in order to 'take action'. In Whittaker v British Mail Order Corporation Ltd 1973 IRLR

296, ET, the conciliator's only contact with the parties took place over the telephone and the COT3 form was mailed to them for their signatures. This was nonetheless held by the tribunal to be sufficient action to make the agreement binding.

However, although a conciliator need not have done very much in order to have 'taken action', he or she must have had some involvement, even if minimal, in the process. In the booklet 'Individual Employment Rights', Acas states that if a firm binding agreement between the parties has been reached before contact is made with the conciliator, it will not be possible for him or her to become involved. This is because the dispute has already been settled and there is therefore no room for conciliation. Thus, an Acas officer cannot simply rubber-stamp a settlement to which the parties to an employment dispute have already agreed. In Jones v Bedybuys Ltd ET Case No.19844/84, for instance, a conciliator took part in the initial negotiations but withdrew after they broke down. The parties later reached a separate agreement on their own. The tribunal held that the conciliator could not be said to have 'taken action' in relation to the final settlement and it was therefore ineffective to bar the employee's claim for unfair dismissal. This case can be contrasted with that of Moore v Duport Furniture Products Ltd (above), where the conciliator had been called in and had given some advice to the employer before the settlement was reached, and had taken such action as the House of Lords considered practicable in the circumstances on being presented with the terms of the settlement.

If the parties to a dispute reach an agreement without the involvement of Acas, **3.62** but express that agreement as being conditional on a conciliator taking action, Acas takes the view that the conciliator must ask whether it is accepted that the terms of the agreement might be changed as a result of conciliation action. The conciliator will be able to act only if that possibility exists.

In Hennessy v Craigmyle and Co Ltd and anor 1986 ICR 461, CA, Sir John Donaldson MR commented that where an issue arises under what is now S.18A(9) ETA (which governs conciliated agreements in unfair dismissal cases during the process of 'early conciliation' before any complaint has been presented – see 'Early conciliation – stage 3: attempt to promote a settlement' above) – it is not for the tribunal or court to consider whether the conciliator correctly interpreted his or her duties under that section, and that 'it is sufficient that he intended and purported to act under that section'. However, this view seems inconsistent with the cases discussed above, which were decided on the assumption that the ETA lays down certain preconditions, albeit very limited, for a valid agreement. S.203(2)(e) ERA expressly requires that for an agreement to be effective a conciliator must have taken action in accordance with Ss.18A–18C, which seems clearly to indicate that some objective assessment of compliance with these provisions is necessary.

185

3.63 **Parties 'desiring' conciliator to act to promote settlement.** Another issue raised in Hennessy v Craigmyle and Co Ltd (above) concerned the word 'desire' in what is now S.18C(2)(b) ETA, which deals with conciliation after an unfair dismissal claim has been submitted to the tribunal. The provision states that where re-employment is not practicable and the parties 'desire the conciliator to act' under this section, he or she should seek to promote a financial settlement. The employee argued that this meant that a conciliator would not be acting in accordance with his or her duties if he or she promoted a financial settlement in a situation where the employee wished to keep the job rather than obtain compensation. The Court, however, held that, in order for the settlement to be effective, it was sufficient that the employee desired the conciliator to act in accordance with S.18C as a whole. The employee need not specifically 'desire' compensation. A conciliated settlement would not therefore be rendered void solely on the basis of the kind of technicality that the employee was asserting.

The employee in Hennessy also argued that the conciliator in question had not carried out his duty under what is now S.18(6) ETA, which, as stated above, requires him to consider 'the desirability of encouraging the use of other procedures available for the settlement of grievances' – for example, an internal disciplinary procedure. The Court of Appeal disagreed. It was not, in its view, necessary for the conciliator to give any outward or visible sign of having regard to these matters, and it would be wholly unreasonable to infer from the absence of such signs that he had no such regard.

3.64 **Summary of principles governing action by conciliation officer.** The principles under which Acas conciliation officers must act were summarised by the EAT in Clarke and ors v Redcar and Cleveland Borough Council and another case 2006 ICR 897, EAT. In that case the claimants challenged the validity of a COT3 agreement, which settled their equal pay claim against the Council. They argued that the Acas conciliation officer who had assisted in the agreement had failed properly to observe her duties under the ETA, such that the contract was not made 'with the assistance of a conciliation officer' for the purposes of S.77 SDA (now S.144 EqA). An employment tribunal rejected the claimants' argument, whereupon they appealed to the EAT. The EAT noted that, despite finding against the claimants, the tribunal had made two criticisms of Acas's actions: first, Acas had not set up public meetings attended by its own officers to explain the terms on offer to the numerous claimants involved; and secondly, it had failed to recommend to recipients of the COT3 offer that they take legal advice if unsure of their rights. In the EAT's view, however, these criticisms simply highlighted best practice for an Acas officer. The fact that the conciliation officer in this case had fallen short of best practice did not mean that she had failed to meet the standards required by law. After reviewing the law on the role of conciliation officers, the EAT derived the following principles from a number of cases:

186

- Acas officers have no responsibility to see that the terms of an agreement are fair on the employee

- the expression 'promote a settlement' in what is now S.18C(1) ETA demands a liberal construction covering whatever action by way of such promotion is applicable in the circumstances of the particular case

- Acas officers must never advise as to the merits of the case

- it is not for the tribunal to consider whether an officer correctly interpreted his or her duties under Ss.18A–18C ETA – it is enough that the officer intended and purported to act under that section (see Hennessy v Craigmyle and Co Ltd and anor (above))

- if an officer were to act in bad faith or adopt unfair methods when promoting a settlement, the agreement might be set aside and might not operate as a bar to proceedings.

Applying these principles, the EAT rejected the claimants' assertion that the Acas officer should have given advice, evaluated the claims and ensured that the claimants understood the nature and extent of all their potential claims. Accordingly, the EAT concluded that the COT3 agreement was valid and rejected the claimants' appeal. **3.65**

Confidentiality **3.66**

Investigation into whether a conciliator has acted in accordance with his or her duties under Ss.18A–18C ETA will often be very difficult, if not impossible, to carry out because S.18(7) provides that anything communicated to a conciliator in connection with the performance of his or her functions is not admissible in evidence before an employment tribunal except with the consent of the 'communicator'. In Marshall v Alexander Sloan and Co Ltd 1980 ICR 394, ET, a tribunal considered that this 'privilege' (as lawyers call it) might possibly be waived by the conduct of the communicator – which in that case took the form of an allegation by the employee of undue influence on the part of the conciliator.

In Hughes-Maher and Co v Cowley and anor EAT 472/90 the EAT considered whether a tribunal had been allowed to hear evidence from the conciliator that an agreement had been reached between the parties. In the EAT's view, S.134(5) of the Employment Protection (Consolidation) Act 1978 (the precursor to S.18(7) ETA) made it clear that a tribunal should not receive any evidence from the conciliator in relation to his or her efforts to promote a settlement or to any negotiations between the parties prior to settlement, as this would undermine the parties' confidence in Acas's conciliatory role. However, evidence of the fact that a concluded agreement had been reached was entirely acceptable and thus admissible before the tribunal.

187

3.67 What is clear is that neither party can use the 'privilege' to conceal inconvenient evidence that would otherwise be admissible simply by communicating it to the conciliator. In M and W Grazebrook Ltd v Wallens 1973 ICR 256, NIRC, the employer sought to prevent the minutes of a management-union meeting held before the employee was dismissed and three internal memoranda, prepared after dismissal – all of which had been given to the conciliator to assist him in obtaining a settlement – from being put before the tribunal. The tribunal found that none of the documents were privileged and they were all therefore admissible at the hearing. On appeal, the NIRC refused to interfere, holding that:

- the admissibility of documentary evidence depends upon the general law relating to privilege and not upon the terms of S.146(6) of the Industrial Relations Act 1971 (a precursor to S.18(7))

- documentary evidence prepared solely for the purpose of communication to a conciliator and made with a view to the litigation in hand and the mode of its conduct is privileged, and

- the correct procedure for the tribunal to adopt was to order discovery of the minutes and memoranda as if they had never been sent to the conciliator. The tribunal should then consider whether the documents were privileged or not.

3.68 Thus, while oral statements to a conciliator are protected, documentary evidence remains admissible (so long as it is not privileged on other grounds), regardless of whether or not it has been communicated to a conciliator.

Note that in Freer v Glover and anor 2006 IRLR 521, QBD, the High Court found that statements made by a respondent's solicitor in a letter sent to an Acas conciliation officer were covered by the legal doctrine of absolute privilege, with the effect that they could not found the basis of a libel action. In the letter, the solicitor stated that this was not a case suitable for conciliation since the claimant's claims were not genuine, but were made in bad faith and were an abuse of process. The claimant brought a claim before the High Court contending that the solicitor's statements were defamatory. However, the High Court decided that they were covered by absolute privilege, which not only covered the sending of the letter to the conciliation officer concerned, but also extended to any of Acas's staff who happened to see the letter in the course of their employment. Without this form of protection, the solicitor would have been unable to inform Acas as to why the respondent did not want to attempt conciliation without, at the same time, opening herself up to a claim being made against her.

3.69 Contractual agreement required
If an agreement is reached by way of Acas conciliation, this will generally be recorded on a standard form known as a COT3. However, it is not necessary

that an Acas-conciliated agreement be in writing. This was established by the EAT in Gilbert v Kembridge Fibres Ltd 1984 ICR 188, EAT. In that case, G was dismissed and an Acas conciliator was called in. The employer agreed to settle on terms put forward by G. The conciliator then phoned the tribunal to tell it that the case had been settled. G received the COT3 form and signed it, but then had second thoughts, crossed out his signature and returned the papers to the conciliator. He proceeded with his unfair dismissal claim, but the tribunal found that there was an enforceable agreement to settle the claim despite the fact that the COT3 had not been signed by both parties. The EAT upheld the tribunal's decision. There had been an offer by the employer and an acceptance by G. This amounted to a legally binding contract and there was no need for the agreement to be reduced to writing.

The same conclusion was reached in Allma Construction Ltd v Bonner 2011 IRLR 204, EAT. There, B complained to an employment tribunal of unfair dismissal. Shortly before the hearing date, AC Ltd made an offer of £1,000 for him to settle the claim. B instructed his solicitor that the offer was acceptable and his solicitor informed Acas that an offer had been received and that it was acceptable to B. Acas then called AC Ltd's solicitor and left a message for him that the offer had been accepted. B subsequently changed his mind and informed AC Ltd that he would settle for £5,000. AC Ltd, taking the view that an agreement had already been reached, applied to the tribunal to dismiss the claim. The tribunal found that no agreement had been reached, partly because the parties had not agreed any other terms in addition to the amount of the settlement sum, and allowed B's claim to proceed to hearing.

Allowing the appeal, Lady Smith, sitting alone in the EAT in Scotland, held that **3.70** a valid agreement had been reached. In her view, a contract is concluded where one party makes an offer to another that is sufficiently definite to indicate an intention to be bound, covering the essentials of the contract in question, and which is then accepted. It does not matter that additional matters could be included in the contract at a later date by way of a further agreement. As to what the 'essentials' of the contract are, that will depend on the circumstances of each case. But where a contract to settle litigation is concerned, Lady Smith thought that 'the essentials' could amount to nothing more than a certain sum of money being paid by the defending party to the pursuing party as the price of bringing the litigation to an end. In the instant case, the tribunal had been wrong to treat the offer to settle as merely an invitation to negotiate. A settlement of B's claim had been validly concluded: the terms of the settlement were that AC Ltd would pay B the sum of £1,000 in full and final settlement of his claim. B's claim was therefore dismissed.

Although an agreement to settle a claim does not have to be in writing, Gilbert v Kembridge Fibres Ltd (above) established that the parties must have entered into a contractually binding agreement. As the following cases demonstrate, it is important that the technical requirements of contract law are satisfied:

- **Duru v Granada Retail Catering Ltd** EAT 281/00: D told a conciliator during a telephone call that he would accept an offer of £250 and that he would contact her on receipt of the draft COT3 agreement. A tribunal found that at the end of that telephone call there was a binding oral agreement and that, accordingly, D was barred from proceeding with his unfair dismissal complaint. The EAT overruled this decision, holding, among other things, that there had not been an offer in a contractual sense because it had not been clear when the employer told the conciliator to offer D £250 that it intended to be bound immediately the offer was 'accepted' by D. Indeed, the EAT took the view that the offer was made subject to the employer's seeing it set out in the COT3. The facts also supported the view that D had not accepted an offer to settle the claim because he also was expecting to see the offer set out in a draft COT3. The contractual principles of offer and acceptance had not been satisfied because there had never been a meeting of minds between the parties as to what exactly was being agreed

- **Rees v Thayers Ice Cream Ltd** ET Case No.1601854/01: the employer had, during conciliation to settle R's equal pay claim, written to Acas offering £1,934 in settlement. The conciliator replied that R was seeking a further payment for an additional one month and 20 days, which she wanted included in the calculation. The conciliator's letter concluded by asking whether the employer 'would be prepared to consider making a revised offer'. The employer then replied that it was prepared to offer the additional payment and ended its letter by stating 'if this is acceptable to [R] please supply me with a COT3 for signature'. In the event, no COT3 was drawn up and R presented her complaint to the tribunal. The employer argued that the conciliator's letter amounted to a counter-offer by R, which it then accepted in its subsequent letter. The tribunal disagreed. Looking at the wording of the employer's final letter, the employer had made a fresh offer, which had not been accepted by R. There was therefore no valid agreement and R could proceed with her complaint

- **Leak v Mansfield Inns Ltd** ET Case No.2601283/99: L began working as a kitchen assistant on 1 April 1999. She was paid nothing until 19 April, when she was told she would be paid £3.20 per hour for six months because she would be 'in training' for that period. L resigned and brought a claim for the national minimum wage. Her employer conceded her claim and agreed with L, through Acas, to pay the outstanding amount 'in full and final settlement of all claims arising from the claimant's contract of employment or its termination'. In June L brought a claim for unfair constructive dismissal, on the basis that the employer had committed a repudiatory breach of contract by refusing to pay her the national minimum wage. The tribunal held that her new claim could proceed. In purporting to settle L's employment claims, her employer had only agreed to pay L what it was legally obliged to pay her. That payment did not provide consideration for L's agreement to forbear from complaining of unfair dismissal, meaning that the agreement was not binding upon her.

Ostensible authority to settle

3.71

Where a party has appointed a representative and provided his or her details, either on an early conciliation application form or the ET1, Acas will deal with that representative. A party may be bound by an Acas-conciliated agreement entered into by his or her representative despite the fact that the representative does not have actual authority to make the agreement on behalf of the party in question. It is sufficient that the representative has *ostensible* authority to do so.

In Freeman v Sovereign Chicken Ltd 1991 ICR 853, EAT, the claimant sought to have a COT3 agreement, which had been signed on her behalf by a Citizens Advice Bureau adviser, set aside on the ground that it had been entered into without her authority. The employment tribunal accepted that there may well be cases where a CAB adviser's authority to settle proceedings has been specifically excluded or restricted by the client and that, in such cases, an adviser acting in excess of his or her authority may be liable to the client. If, however, a CAB adviser, having been named as a representative of a party, holds him or herself out as having authority to negotiate a settlement on behalf of the client, the other party is entitled to assume that the adviser does in fact have that authority, provided there is no notice to the contrary. In this case F's representative had ostensible authority that was binding on her as against the other party, whether or not the CAB adviser had in fact any explicit authority to enter into the agreement. The EAT upheld the tribunal's decision, adding that where a barrister, a solicitor, or even a CAB adviser or law centre is involved, the likelihood of disproving their ostensible authority to settle the proceedings is very slim. However, clients should, where possible, see and approve the wording of a proposed agreement. The client could indicate approval by initialling a letter or the COT3 form itself, or by signing a COT3 countersigned by his or her representative.

The Freeman case was distinguished in Gloystarne and Co Ltd v Martin 2001 **3.72** IRLR 15, EAT. In that case, M was dismissed from his employment for gross misconduct, and submitted an unfair dismissal claim on an ET1. He left blank the box headed 'if a representative is acting for you please give details'. A process of conciliation took place involving an Acas conciliator, the employer and J, who was the regional organiser from M's union. Two days before the hearing, J contacted the employment tribunal by telephone and fax notifying it that the case had been settled through Acas and that he was awaiting the COT3 form detailing the agreement. The conciliator also contacted the tribunal that

191

day to confirm that a COT3 was being prepared. The tribunal subsequently made an order that 'the conciliation officer having taken action... and terms of settlement having been reached between the parties, the originating application is hereby stayed'. In the event, it transpired that M had not, in fact, authorised J to settle the case and had not even discussed any monetary figures with him. J's instructions had been to report back to M with any proposals from the employer in order to give M the opportunity to consider whether he was prepared to settle. Upon discovering what had happened, M refused to sign the COT3 and instructed J to write to the tribunal asking to have the case relisted. The tribunal then held a hearing and found that M had not agreed to the terms and that J had known or ought reasonably to have known that he did not have any authority, express or implied, to settle the case without further recourse to M. The tribunal lifted the stay and relisted the case for a full hearing.

The employer appealed to the EAT. Relying on Freeman v Sovereign Chicken Ltd, it argued that it was entitled to rely on the ostensible authority of J, as M's representative in the proceedings, to bind M in any conciliated agreement. The EAT held, however, that ostensible authority to settle a claim only arises where the party to the tribunal proceedings him or herself holds out that a person is authorised to act on his or her behalf. It does not arise simply by virtue of a representative – e.g. counsel, a solicitor, a CAB adviser or some other adviser – holding out that he or she has authority to enter an agreement on the party's behalf. In the instant case, however much the union official advising the employee described himself to the employer as representing the employee, that, of itself, did not make the official the employee's agent in dealing with the employer, and nor did it authorise the official to bind the employee in those dealings. The EAT's earlier decision in Freeman could be distinguished from the facts of the instant case because, in the Freeman case, the representative had been named as such by the employee on his claim form, whereas in the instant case the employee had left the relevant part of the form blank. The tribunal had made no finding of fact to indicate that the employee had held out to the employer that the union official was his representative.

3.73 Scope of the agreement

Where the parties wish to reach an agreement that goes further than settling the matter which is the subject of the complaint – for example, one which purports to preclude all rights of further complaint to a tribunal – conciliators should ensure that the parties understand the full implications of the proposed agreement. Where that agreement is to extend not only to statutory rights but also to contractual rights, conciliators should give examples of the most common contractual rights that are the subject of dispute. Since the parties seeking such agreements frequently do not intend to include matters relating to pensions and industrial injuries, the conciliator should ascertain whether or not they do actually intend to cover such issues.

Discrimination claims. Where the parties concerned in a complaint under the **3.74** ERA wish also to include possible discrimination complaints under the EqA in the conciliated agreement, they should identify such complaints or potential complaints separately. This point is illustrated by the case of Livingstone v Hepworth Refractories Ltd 1992 ICR 287, EAT, in which the EAT held that 'a COT3 agreement under the 1978 Act [the precursor to the ERA] does not cover a claim under the [Sex Discrimination Act 1975] or the [Equal Pay Act 1970] unless expressly stated to do so'. This was because the wording of S.77(4) SDA made it clear that an agreement would only be effective under that section if it settled a complaint under the SDA or the EqPA. The same principle continues to apply by virtue of S.144(4) EqA. Accordingly, if no specific complaint or potential complaint under the EqA has been identified, the COT3 agreement will not be effective in this regard.

In the Livingstone case, it followed that the COT3 agreement, which had not mentioned the SDA, could not bar L's subsequent claim under that Act. Nor could the agreement bar a discrimination claim brought directly under European law – i.e. Article 141 of the Treaty on the Functioning of the European Union. The European Court of Justice stated in Emmott v Minister for Social Welfare and anor 1993 ICR 8, ECJ, that 'it is for the domestic legal system of each Member State to determine the procedural conditions governing actions at law intended to ensure the protection of the rights' so derived. It followed that as the COT3 agreement signed by L did not satisfy the provisions of the SDA, it could similarly present no bar to a tribunal hearing the claim under what is now Article 141.

Although not argued in Livingstone, it should be emphasised that conciliators, **3.75** in any case, have no power to conciliate in disputes in the absence of express statutory provision. As no powers have been conferred on them to act in claims brought directly under European law, it is unlikely that any COT3 agreement excluding such a claim would be binding upon the parties to it in any event.

'General release' clauses and the settlement of future claims. It is perfectly **3.76** possible for the terms of an Acas-conciliated agreement to purport to bar not only present claims but also future claims. In fact, it is theoretically possible that if an Acas-conciliated agreement clearly indicates that this was the intention of the parties, a claimant can effectively release claims or rights that he or she has not even contemplated.

In Bank of Credit and Commerce International SA v Ali and ors 2001 ICR 337, HL, the House of Lords considered the effect of a COT3 agreement purporting to be 'in full and final settlement of all claims whether under statute, common law or in equity of whatsoever nature that exist or may exist and, in particular, all or any claims, rights or applications of whatsoever nature that the claimant has or may have or has made or could make in or to the [employment] tribunal, except the claimant's rights under the respondent's pension scheme'.

3.77 Their Lordships held that this agreement did not prevent an employee proceeding with a claim for 'stigma damages' arising out of the employer's breach of the implied duty of trust and confidence, because neither party could have contemplated such a claim as the law stood at the time the agreement was signed. However, the majority of their Lordships allowed for the possibility that certain specific wording might defeat the assumption that a party did not intend an employee to surrender rights and claims of which he or she was unaware and could not have been aware. Although it is unclear what kind of specific wording their Lordships had in mind that might have defeated the 'stigma damages' claim, what is certain is that the precise wording of a general release given in an employment settlement is of paramount importance.

This point is supported by the case of Royal National Orthopaedic Hospital Trust v Howard 2002 IRLR 849, EAT. There, the EAT considered whether a COT3 barred a claim that arose from an employer's future act not contemplated by the parties at the time of the agreement. In that case H brought claims of sex discrimination, marital discrimination and constructive dismissal, each of which was settled after Acas conciliation. The COT3 stated that the employer's payment was made 'in full and final settlement of these proceedings and of all claims which the claimant has or may have against the respondent' under a number of listed statutory provisions, including the SDA (the relevant provisions of which are now contained in the EqA). Subsequently, the hospital prevented H from carrying out a day's work at the hospital in a private capacity. H complained of victimisation contrary to the SDA – a claim, argued the hospital, that was barred by the conciliated agreement. The EAT held that 'the law does not decline to allow parties to contract that all and any claims, whether known or not, shall be released'. The question is whether, looking objectively at the agreement, this was the *intention* of the parties, or whether some limitation has to be placed on the agreement's scope. If the parties wish to achieve the 'extravagant result' of contracting out of claims of which they have and can have no knowledge – whether those claims already exist or not – they must use language which is 'absolutely clear and leaves no room for doubt as to what it is they are contracting for'. The EAT concluded that the COT3's reference to claims which the claimant 'has or may have' could cover claims existing at the time of the agreement (whether or not they were known to the employee), but that it was not sufficient to cover possible future claims. Thus, H's victimisation claim could proceed.

3.78 In McLean v TLC Marketing plc EAT 0429–30/08 the EAT similarly held that clear language was needed in an Acas-conciliated agreement to preclude claims arising from events that took place after the date the agreement was entered into. In that case M had settled equal pay, sex discrimination and victimisation claims against TLC by way of a COT3 agreement, which was stated to be 'in full and final settlement of her employment tribunal claims against the respondents and of any other claim whatsoever arising out of or connected

194

with her employment... and its termination'. TLC failed, among other things, to pay the full amount due under the agreement and M successfully sued for the balance in the county court. She then brought a victimisation claim in the employment tribunal, alleging that she had suffered a detriment by TLC's failure to adhere to the terms of the agreement. The tribunal decided that it did not have jurisdiction to hear the claim by reason of the COT3 agreement. The EAT overturned the decision. In its view, it was clear from the Howard case that clear words are needed in a COT3 agreement to preclude a claimant from pursuing any claim arising from facts that had not yet arisen at the date of the agreement, but which may arise at any time thereafter. The language of the clause in the instant case did not lend itself to such a construction.

Claims outside Acas's remit. Where a complaint covers an issue for which **3.79** conciliation is not provided – for example, a claim under S.11 ERA in respect of a failure to provide written particulars of the terms of employment – a conciliator will decline to act. However, if the parties wish such a complaint to form part of a wider agreement, the conciliator should advise them to identify the particular issue in the wording of the agreement. This would not preclude a claim being made to a tribunal but would make it clear that the parties had intended to deal with the matter.

Note that parties cannot contract out of the continuity of employment provisions contained in the ERA. In Collison v British Broadcasting Corporation 1998 ICR 669, EAT, C worked for the BBC from May 1978 until September 1989, when his contract was terminated. He claimed unfair dismissal but the parties settled the claim and an agreement was drawn up by an Acas conciliator. C resumed employment with the BBC, but his employment was terminated again in August 1995. He claimed, among other things, unfair dismissal and redundancy, and contended that he had been continuously employed since 1978. The BBC, however, argued that the Acas agreement precluded C from making a claim in respect of continuous employment prior to his first termination in September 1989. A tribunal accepted the BBC's argument but was overturned on appeal by the EAT, which held that there was nothing in S.203(2)(e) ERA which allowed the continuity of employment provisions to be set aside.

Enforcing an agreement
3.80

Once a conciliated agreement has been reached, its terms are normally recorded on a COT3 form, which is signed by the parties. Acas will then inform the tribunal that an agreement has been reached. At this point, the tribunal might be persuaded to make a judgment by consent under rule 64 of the Tribunal Rules, incorporating the terms of the agreement. Rule 66 goes on to specify that any money due must be paid within 14 days of the date of the judgment unless the judgment, or any of the Rules, specifies a different date for payment or the tribunal has stayed (or in Scotland sisted) the proceedings.

195

The wording of S.203 ERA (and its equivalent in other statutes) seems to suggest that, once a conciliated agreement has been reached, all tribunal claims are barred and an employee's only remedy, in the event of the employer's failing to honour its side of the bargain, is either a claim for breach of contract or, if the agreement has been incorporated into a finalised judgment of the tribunal, a claim for the enforcement of a judgment debt in the county court or High Court. However, there seems to be some disagreement about whether this is in fact the case. In Johnson v Communications Associates Ltd ET Case No.29768/76, for instance, an employment tribunal suggested that where an employer defaults on an agreement the employee can either enforce the terms of the agreement in the county court or High Court in an action for breach of contract or accept the employer's breach, thereby bringing the agreement to an end and entitling the employee to revive the original claim. In Kelly v Moran Transport Ltd ET Case No.1276/87, on the other hand, the tribunal held that once an agreement has been reached it is binding in law on both parties and the employee's only remedy thereafter, in the event of non-compliance, is to enforce the agreement in the ordinary courts.

3.81 In both these cases the tribunal proceedings had been adjourned until the employer had complied with the terms of the agreement so no final decision or order had as yet been made. This seems to be where most of the uncertainty arises. Where the terms of the agreement have been incorporated into a tribunal decision, there seems to be a stronger case for arguing that that decision becomes like all other tribunal decisions which are only enforceable in the county court or High Court.

In the event of non-payment of the settlement sum, the Acas-conciliated agreement can be enforced through the civil courts. S.19A ETA, which came into force on 1 April 2009, provides that sums payable under Acas-conciliated agreements are enforceable in England and Wales as if they were sums payable under a county court order, and in Scotland through the sheriff court. However, in each case, the sum is not recoverable if the person by whom it is payable obtains a declaration in the relevant jurisdiction that the sum would not be recoverable from it under the general law of contract.

3.82 Since 2010, Acas-conciliated agreements can also be enforced through the Acas and Employment Tribunal Fast Track Scheme, which is run by the Registry Trust, a non-profit company which operates the Register of Judgments, Orders and Fines on behalf of the Ministry of Justice. Upon payment of a £60 fee, a High Court Enforcement Officer files a writ of fieri facias ('fi fa') with a court on behalf of the individual and then pursues the debt. Note, however, that conditional Acas-conciliated agreements, i.e. agreements that provide for the payment of a settlement sum and also require the individual to undertake certain actions, cannot be enforced via the Fast Track Scheme. For more information, see Chapter 21, 'Enforcement of tribunal awards', under 'Enforcement of Acas-conciliated agreements'.

Settlement agreements

Settlement agreements represent another exception to the general principle – set out in S.203(1) ERA and equivalent provisions in other statutes – that individuals cannot contract out of their statutory employment rights. Settlement agreements allow parties to settle an employment dispute for themselves – before or after employment tribunal proceedings have been instituted – without the need to negotiate a COT3 agreement through Acas. Like a COT3 agreement, a properly constituted settlement agreement will bar the employee from taking a claim any further.

The types of claim that can be the subject of a settlement agreement are broadly the same as those covered by Acas-conciliated agreements. Note, however, that there is *no* provision for settlement agreements – as opposed to Acas-conciliated agreements – in relation to the following types of claim:

- claims for failure to inform and consult with appropriate representatives about proposed collective redundancies under S.188 TULR(C)A

- claims for failure to notify employee liability information and failure to inform and consult employee representatives on a transfer of an undertaking under the Transfer of Undertakings (Protection of Employment) Regulations 2006 SI 2006/246

- claims under the Agency Workers Regulations 2010 SI 2010/93, and

- claims for breach of Regs 5, 6 and 9 of the Employment Relations Act 1999 (Blacklists) Regulations 2010 SI 2010/493.

Change in terminology

As mentioned at the beginning of this chapter, settlement agreements were known as 'compromise agreements' until 29 July 2013, when S.23 of the Enterprise and Regulatory Reform Act 2013 (ERRA) came into force. A 'compromise contract' under the EqA also became a 'settlement agreement' on that date. The change in terminology was made because the Government was of the opinion that settlement agreements more accurately described the content of these agreements and that it was a more widely understood term. However, the ERRA only effected the name change in primary legislation – e.g. in the ERA, the TULR(C)A, the NMWA and the EqA. Similar changes affecting the renaming of compromise agreements in secondary legislation were made on 30 August 2013 – see the Enterprise and Regulatory Reform Act 2013 (Consequential Amendments) (Employment) Order 2013 SI 2013/1956.

The name change has potentially created its own peculiar drafting issue, as one of the statutory requirements for a valid agreement is that it must contain a statement confirming that the statutory conditions regulating settlement

197

agreements under the ERA (or other relevant legislation depending on the principal claims beings settled) have been satisfied – see 'Statutory requirements – statement that conditions have been met' below. If the agreement uses the terms 'compromise agreement' or 'compromise contract' instead of 'settlement agreement' (as it would do if, for example, it attempts to settle claims under the antecedent discrimination legislation), this does not, strictly speaking, comply with the legislation. That said, it seems unlikely that a court or employment tribunal would take a restrictive view of this condition for effecting a valid settlement agreement and decide that it was unenforceable simply on account of the use of outdated nomenclature.

3.85 Statutory requirements

The relevant statutory provisions governing settlement agreements are S.203(2) (f) and (3)–(4) ERA; Ss.144(4)(b), (5) and 147 EqA; S.288(2A)–(2C), (4)–(5) TULR(C)A; S.49(3)–(11) NMWA; Reg 35(2)(b)–(7) of the Working Time Regulations; Reg 41(3)–(9) of the TICE Regulations; Reg 9 of the Part-time Workers Regulations; Reg 10 of the Fixed-term Employees Regulations; Reg 19(2)(b)–(7) of the Merchant Shipping Regulations; Reg 20(2)(b)–(8) of the Fishing Vessels Regulations; Reg 40(3)–(9) of the ICE Regulations; paras 12(3) and 13 of the Schedule to the OPPS Regulations; Reg 41(3)–(10) of the ECS Regulations; Reg 62(3)–(10) of the Companies (Cross-Border Mergers) Regulations; Reg 18(2)(b)–(8) of the Cross-border Railway Services Regulations and Reg 39(3)–(8) of the EPLLC Regulations.

In order to be legally binding, settlement agreements must:

- be in writing – S.203(3)(a) ERA

- relate to the particular proceedings – S.203(3)(b)

- only be made where the employee or worker has received advice from a relevant independent adviser as to the terms and effect of the proposed agreement and, in particular, its effect on his or her ability to pursue his or her rights before an employment tribunal. There must be in force, when the adviser gives the advice, a contract of insurance, or an indemnity provided for members of a professional body, covering the risk of a claim by the worker or employee in respect of loss arising in consequence of the advice – S.203(3)(c) and (d)

- identify the relevant independent adviser – S.203(3)(e), and

- state that the conditions regulating settlement agreements have been satisfied – S.203(3)(f).

3.86 Note that the statutory requirements for settling discrimination claims under the EqA deviate slightly from the well-established conditions set out in S.203(3) ERA and equivalent legislation. S.147(3)(f) EqA, contrary to the antecedent discrimination legislation, only requires a statement confirming that two specific conditions – the provision of independent advice and the contract of insurance that must be in place when that advice was given – have been satisfied. The EqA does not require the statement to confirm that all the conditions under the Act have been satisfied – see 'Statement that conditions have been met' below.

Relevant independent adviser. A person is a 'relevant independent adviser' for **3.87** the purposes of S.203(3)(e) ERA if he or she:

- is a qualified lawyer (i.e. in England and Wales, a person authorised to exercise a right of audience or to conduct litigation within the meaning of the Legal Services Act 2007; in Scotland, an advocate or a solicitor who holds a practising certificate – S.203(4)) – S.203(3A)(a)

- is an officer, official, employee or member of an independent trade union who has been certified in writing by the trade union as competent to give advice and as authorised to do so on behalf of the trade union – S.203(3A)(b)

- works at an advice centre (whether as an employee or a volunteer) and has been certified in writing by the centre as competent to give advice and as authorised to do so on behalf of the centre – S.203(3A)(c), or

- is a person of a description specified in an order made by the Secretary of State – S.203(3A)(d).

The Settlement Agreements (Description of Person) Order 2004 SI 2004/754 (as amended) extends the type of person who can give legal advice in relation to settlement agreements to Fellows of the Institute of Legal Executives employed by a solicitors' practice, although many such Fellows are in fact authorised to conduct litigation or have rights of audience and will count as qualified lawyers within the meaning of S.203(4).

Section 203(3B) ERA adds that a person is not a relevant independent adviser **3.88** in relation to the employee or worker if he or she is:

- employed by or is acting in the matter for the employer or an associated employer – S.203(3B)(a)

- a trade union or advice centre adviser and the trade union or advice centre is the employer or an associated employer – S.203(3B)(b)

- an advice centre adviser and the employee or worker makes a payment for the advice received – S.203(3B)(c), or

- a person specified in an order made by the Secretary of State under S.203(3A)(d) and any condition specified in the order in relation to the giving of advice by persons of that description is not satisfied – S.203(3B)(d).

199

The issue of whether solicitors – engaged and paid for by the employer to advise on proposed settlement agreements – were relevant independent advisers for contracting-out purposes arose for determination in McWilliam and ors v Glasgow City Council 2011 IRLR 568, EAT. In that case, the respondent Council, realising that it was at risk of multiple equal pay claims, met with representatives of the main trade unions and agreed to settle what it termed its 'apparent equal pay liability'. As the number of affected employees was estimated to exceed 10,000, the Council selected a panel of six law firms to act as independent advisers to the employees concerned. The Council and the panel solicitors agreed on the terms of a draft settlement agreement. The solicitors then decided that information obtained from the Council was not sufficiently detailed to enable them to advise individual employees on their own particular position and that their advice to individual employees would be limited to the terms and effect of the settlement agreement. The advice was subsequently provided to employees in group and individual sessions, following which many of them, including the six claimants, signed the settlement agreement on offer. The claimants then sought to bring equal pay claims in the employment tribunal but were prevented from doing so when the tribunal decided that their claims had been validly settled under the SDA (now the EqA).

3.89 On appeal to the EAT, the claimants contended that their claims should be allowed to proceed because the solicitors were not qualified to advise them as they were 'acting in the matter' for the Council within the meaning of S.77(4BA)(a) SDA (now S.147(5)(d) EqA). Lady Smith, sitting alone in the EAT, disagreed. Although the solicitors could not properly be said to have been acting for the employees until the individual meetings, they were all, prior to that, acting to protect the employees' interests as a group – by negotiating changes to the proposed settlement agreement that were favourable to the employees, not allowing the Council access to the group presentation, and ensuring the confidentiality of the individual meetings. Nor did the panel firms, which were paid a fixed fee, gain anything by persuading employees to sign the settlement agreements. While it was true that the scope of the advice the solicitors gave was dictated by the information provided by the Council, Lady Smith considered that that could be the case in any consultation on a settlement agreement. Moreover, the Council gave the impression that it was at pains to see to it that the employees were provided with advice that was truly independent of it by solicitors who were not in any sense acting for it. Accordingly, the solicitors were not barred from advising the employees by virtue of S.77(4BA)(a) SDA and the claimants had validly settled any potential equal pay claims against the Council.

3.90 *Discrimination claims.* Note that S.147(5)(a) EqA was amended on 6 April 2012 following concerns that, on a literal interpretation of the provision, a complainant's solicitor was excluded from the category of 'independent adviser'. This drafting error, and its rectification, is discussed in IDS Employment

Law Handbook, 'Discrimination at Work' (2012), Chapter 34, 'Enforcing individual rights', in the section 'Settling claims' under 'Settlement agreement – drafting error'.

Identifying the adviser. One of the statutory conditions in S.230(3)(e) ERA is **3.91** that the agreement must 'identify' the relevant independent adviser and it is generally best practice for the adviser's name, position and address to be inserted in the agreement. However, there is some uncertainty as to whether the adviser has to be identified in the body of the agreement in order for the agreement to be valid. In Lambert v Croydon College ET Case No.35472/96 an agreement failed to state the name of the legal adviser. Although it was clear who the adviser was from the surrounding correspondence, the employment tribunal found that, as the terms of the statute had to be applied strictly, the agreement failed to satisfy the requirements of S.203. By contrast, in Topping v ABP Meat Processors Ltd ET Case No.2900133/07, the tribunal took the view that the statutory conditions did not include a requirement as to how the adviser was to be identified or the extent of the information to be provided. It went on to find that the S.230(3)(e) requirement was satisfied by the adviser having signed the final page of the agreement. The signature was clear and was accompanied by a statement saying that it was signed by the adviser.

In Sankyo Pharma (UK) Ltd v Bartlett EAT 687/99 the EAT also cast doubt on whether the settlement agreement itself has to identify the adviser. In that case again there was no reference to the employee's adviser – a solicitor – in the body of the settlement agreement, although a covering letter with the agreement did identify the adviser. An employment tribunal found that the conditions regulating settlement agreements had not been complied with. In the course of allowing the appeal and remitting the case to a freshly constituted tribunal, the EAT commented that so far as it was aware, there was no EAT authority suggesting that a solicitor's signature must be on the document containing the settlement agreement or that the agreement itself must only be in one document.

In practice, many settlement agreements require the independent legal adviser **3.92** either to countersign the agreement or to write to the employer separately to confirm that the statutory conditions are fulfilled. This may give the employer peace of mind, but is not itself necessary for the agreement to comply with the statutory conditions. In Rule v Blanc Aero Industries UK Ltd ET Case No.1301574/03 R's solicitor signed a settlement agreement on R's behalf, but deleted a phrase stating that the solicitor certified that 'all conditions and regulations in respect of a [settlement] agreement of this kind have been satisfied'. R claimed that this deletion rendered the agreement invalid. The employment tribunal held that there was nothing in the requirements of S.203(3) requiring a settlement agreement to contain any certification from the independent adviser. The settlement agreement satisfied all the requirements of S.203(3), leaving the tribunal unable to hear R's claim of unfair dismissal.

201

3.93 **Role of the adviser.** Any settlement agreement signed by an employee who has not received independent advice will not be effective in barring any potential claims. In McKeown v Business Post Ltd ET Case No.1901495/99 M went on sick leave suffering from depression in January 1999. On 10 February the employer wrote asking for further details of his condition and raising the possibility of terminating his employment. While medical reports were being obtained the general manager visited M at home, discovered he was desperate for money, and discussed making a payment to him if he left employment. In May M signed a settlement agreement in return for a termination payment, which confirmed that he had received advice from an independent adviser. M had not received such advice and wrote 'not required' by the relevant provision. He subsequently claimed unfair dismissal and disability discrimination. The tribunal found that these claims were not barred by the agreement as he had not obtained independent legal advice.

The scope of the advice that will satisfy the statutory requirement was considered by the EAT in McWilliam and ors v Glasgow City Council (above). There, the Council engaged six law firms to advise thousands of its employees on agreements to settle potential equal pay claims. The solicitors had decided that, as the information obtained from the Council was not sufficiently detailed to enable them to advise individual employees on their own particular position, their advice to individual employees would be limited to the terms and effect of the settlement agreement – initially as part of a group session, and thereafter in individual meetings. At the group sessions, the solicitors gave PowerPoint presentations covering the basis of an equal pay claim, what was meant by a settlement agreement in general, the specific terms of the particular settlement agreements in question, what would be their effect if signed, and what would happen if the employees signed and then breached them. The group presentation also stressed that the solicitors could not advise employees as to whether what was on offer was a good deal for each of them personally, and that if employees were in any doubt, they should not sign the agreement and should seek advice on their own individual circumstances. At the individual meetings, the employees were again told that advice could not be given on whether they had a valid equal pay claim or what it might be worth, following which many of them, including the six claimants, signed the settlement agreement on offer.

3.94 The claimants subsequently sought to bring equal pay claims in the employment tribunal, but the tribunal concluded that their claims had been validly settled. Dismissing an appeal against that decision, the EAT specifically rejected the argument that S.77(4A)(c) SDA (now S.147(3)(c) EqA) – i.e. the requirement for the employees to have received advice – was not satisfied in this case because the claimants had not received proper advice in the context of a solicitor-client relationship. In the EAT's view, taking the information from the group presentations together with the advice given at the individual meetings, there was enough to satisfy the requirement. Nor did it matter that the information received at the PowerPoint presentations might have been given by 'unidentified' solicitors, different from those who held the individual meetings – the advice given to the group was clearly incorporated into the advice that was then given to employees individually. According to the EAT, the crux of the claimants' contention was that the solicitors had not told them individually whether the deal on offer was a good one for them personally. However, this is not required to effect a valid settlement agreement. Rather, the statutory requirement is that an employee must have received advice from a relevant independent adviser, but only as to the *terms and effect* of the proposed agreement. It does not require the independent adviser to offer a view on whether the deal is a good one or whether he or she thinks that the employee should accept it. Once all the communications to employees were taken into account, it was clear that the claimants had received advice on the terms and effect of the proposed agreement and that they were therefore prevented from proceeding with their equal pay claims.

Statement that conditions have been met. The clause stating that the relevant **3.95** statutory conditions governing settlement agreements have been satisfied is a crucial part of a settlement agreement, without which the employee will be at liberty to pursue the statutory claims that the agreement purported to settle. Care must be taken when drafting this clause as the case of Palihakkara v British Telecommunications plc EAT 0185–86/06 demonstrates. There, the settlement agreement between the claimant and employer provided that the conditions in S.203 ERA had been satisfied. However, there was no similar declaration that the conditions set out in either the Race Relations Act 1976 or the SDA (now both contained in the EqA) had been complied with. Notwithstanding the fact that, as a matter of substance, all the conditions regulating the agreement in both statutes had been satisfied, the EAT held that the race and sex discrimination claims could not be settled where the relevant declarations were missing.

As noted above, the EqA – which repealed and replaced the provisions of the RRA and the SDA with effect from 1 October 2010 – considerably 'slimmed down' the contents of the statement necessary to effect a valid settlement agreement. S.147(3)(f) EqA only requires the statement to confirm that the conditions in S.147(3)(c) and (d) – i.e. that independent advice was given while a contract of insurance in respect of that advice was in place – have been met. It is no longer necessary to include a declaration that the requirements of a valid settlement agreement have been fulfilled in respect of each allegation of discrimination, as all the protected characteristics are now covered by the same statute. Accordingly, if the case of Palihakkara was decided today, it is arguable that the result would have been rather different, in that the claimant's race and sex discrimination claims would have been validly settled.

203

3.96 Settlement negotiations

For many employers – particularly those faced with instituting disciplinary or capability proceedings that could well end in dismissal – settlement agreements represent a quick and effective way of resolving workplace issues and ensuring that any claims that the employee may have will not reach a tribunal. However, employers may be reluctant to enter into settlement negotiations for fear that, if they do not end in agreement, anything said during negotiations may be disclosed by the employee in subsequent legal proceedings.

3.97 Risks to employer if negotiations fail.

The potential risk associated with making a settlement offer to an employee is neatly illustrated by the case of Billington v Michael Hunter and Sons Ltd EAT 0578/03. There, B, a bathroom sales assistant, was called at short notice to a disciplinary meeting to discuss a number of serious written complaints from customers. She was subsequently given a written warning. A few weeks later an informal meeting was held to discuss new allegations of unsatisfactory performance. At that meeting B was told that if there were further customer complaints she 'would very likely be dismissed'. B's line manager suggested that she should think about her ability to do the job, and that 'should she decide that the job was beyond her capabilities', she could resign on 'favourable terms'. He added, however, that he hoped her performance would improve, making this unnecessary. B resigned and claimed that she had been unfairly constructively dismissed. An employment tribunal held that there had been no fundamental breach of the implied term of trust and confidence entitling B to claim constructive dismissal but, on appeal, the EAT decided that it had been wrong to do so. In the EAT's view, the employer's invitation to B to resign on favourable terms amounted to a 'vote of no confidence' that was calculated and likely to destroy or seriously damage its relationship with her. The EAT remitted the case to a fresh tribunal to decide whether or not the employer had conducted itself without reasonable and proper cause.

Clearly, not all settlement offers will amount to a fundamental breach of contract, as employers may have reasonable and proper cause for making them. Furthermore, there are two provisions which are potentially relevant in these circumstances and which may ensure that unsuccessful settlement negotiations will remain confidential between the employer and the employee. The first is the 'without prejudice' rule, which prevents written or oral statements made in a genuine attempt to settle an existing workplace dispute from being relied on in any subsequent legal proceedings. The without prejudice rule, and the circumstances in which it may apply, is discussed in detail in Chapter 13, 'Evidence', under 'Evidence of settlement negotiations – "without prejudice" negotiations'. The second is S.111A ERA, which provides that any offer made or discussions held with a view to an employment relationship being terminated on agreed terms is inadmissible in unfair dismissal proceedings. This provision, which came into force on 29 July 2013, is also discussed in Chapter 13, under 'Evidence of settlement negotiations – pre-termination negotiations'.

'Subject to contract'. Another point to bear in mind when conducting 3.98
settlement negotiations is that normal contractual principles apply. This means
that any proposed settlement offer should expressly be made 'subject to
contract' to enable the parties to continue to negotiate until all terms have been
finalised. This was the lesson learned by the employer in Newbury v Sun
Microsystems 2013 EWHC 2180, QBD. N issued proceedings against SM in
the High Court for unpaid commission in the sum of approximately US$2m,
and SM counterclaimed for recovery of an alleged overpayment. Previous
attempts at settlement had been unsuccessful and an eight-day trial was set to
commence on 12 June 2013. On 3 June SM's solicitors wrote to N's solicitors,
making a final settlement offer under which SM was willing to pay N, within
14 days of his acceptance, £601,464.98 inclusive of interest 'in full and final
settlement' of claim and counterclaim, plus a further £180,000 'in relation to'
his legal costs. The letter further provided that the settlement was to be 'recorded
in a suitably worded agreement' and was open until 5.30 pm. That same day,
at 5.21 pm, N's solicitors e-mailed a letter – marked 'without prejudice save as
to costs' – in response to SM's solicitors, accepting the terms of the offer and
went on to state that they would 'forward a draft agreement for your approval'.
When SM subsequently tried to insert new terms relating to other matters, N
applied for a declaration in the High Court that the proceedings between
himself and SM had been settled on the terms set out in correspondence between
the respective sets of solicitors on 3 June.

The High Court judge held that, viewed objectively, the correspondence showed
that there was an intention to create legal relations and that the parties had
agreed upon all the terms which they regarded as essential for the formation of
a legally binding contract. The fact that the offer was to be recorded in a
'suitably worded agreement' did not mean that a binding agreement had not
been reached. In the judge's view, the correspondence had to be seen against the
background that the parties were shortly to commence an eight-day trial, that
there had been previous attempts at settlement and that the offer on 3 June was
expressed to reflect SM's final position. Another reason that persuaded him
that the parties had concluded a legally binding contract on 3 June was that
SM's solicitors' initial offer was not expressed as being 'subject to contract'.
This indicated that the letter was an offer on terms capable of acceptance as it
stood; it was not intended to be subject to discussion and agreement on
additional or different terms. Furthermore, once an agreement was reached,
any conduct thereafter was irrelevant.

Accordingly, where the parties do not wish to be bound until all the terms of 3.99
the agreement have been finalised, they need to ensure that settlement
correspondence is expressed to be 'subject to contract'. Otherwise, they may be
presumed to have intended to conclude a binding contract even though a formal
document recording the terms agreed has not yet been executed. However,
were this to happen, it is worth remembering that it will only effectively settle

205

contractual claims. In order for the parties to settle any statutory claims that an employee may have, it is necessary that the conditions in S.203 ERA (or the equivalent in other statutes) have been complied with.

3.100 Common terms of settlement agreements

Apart from fulfilling the relevant statutory conditions, it is good practice for the agreement to regulate as far as possible all the major issues with regard to the employee's termination of employment or, where the working relationship is continuing, his or her continued employment. The non-statutory Acas Guide on Settlement Agreements ('the Acas Guide') gives some indication of common terms that should be included in the agreement and Annex 5 to the Guide contains a model settlement agreement that can be tailored to suit the parties' individual circumstances.

Obviously, apart from the payment that will be made in return for settling certain complaints, the parties to the agreement may want to add provisions with regard to share options and pension entitlements and the tax treatment of the settlement package. They may also wish to include non-financial elements, such as an apology or a reference. The employer may also want to add restrictive covenants, preventing former employees from competing with the employer for a period following termination.

We discuss some of the common terms of settlement agreements below.

3.101 Settlement package. The clause(s) setting out the settlement package will be of key importance to the employee and should ideally include details of payment arrangements and the date of payment. One of the chief difficulties for employers is deciding how much to offer. This is ultimately a commercial decision based on legal advice as to the risk that the employee's claim will be successful, coupled with the likely level of any ensuing award. The Acas Guide lists a number of factors to be considered when offering or negotiating a settlement amount. These include the employee's remuneration, notice period, untaken annual leave and length of employment as well as considerations such as the length of time it may take to resolve the problem if settlement is not reached, how difficult it would be to fill the employee's post, how long it might take the employee to find a new job and the reason for offering the settlement in the first place. Where the employee has already submitted a tribunal claim, he or she may also want to make sure that the recovery of the issue fee (and potentially the hearing fee, if the claim is settled shortly before the date of the tribunal hearing) will be part of the settlement package. Fees are discussed in detail in Chapter 19, 'Fees'.

In Gibb v Maidstone and Tunbridge Wells NHS Trust 2010 IRLR 786, CA, the employer took the unusual step of arguing that, in offering its senior executive an 'irrationally generous' payoff of £250,000 in return for signing a settlement agreement, it had stepped beyond a public body's boundaries of reasonableness and that the decision to enter into the agreement should be set aside. In that case the respondent Trust decided to terminate the employment of its Chief Executive, G, after outbreaks of a 'super bug' at several of its hospitals led to adverse publicity. It drew up a settlement agreement offering her £250,000, representing £75,427 in lieu of notice and a compensation payment of £174,573. Before the settlement was paid, however, the Trust received orders from the NHS Finance, Performance and Operations department instructing it to pay only the amount representing pay in lieu of notice. G responded by lodging a claim for the balance, which was rejected by the High Court. The High Court judge agreed with the Trust that the payment was 'irrationally generous' and thus ultra vires (i.e. beyond its legal authority to make). In its view, a reasonable assessment of the Trust's likely liabilities towards G would have produced a total figure of around £140,000, comprising notice pay plus the maximum award for unfair dismissal. G appealed.

The Court of Appeal allowed the appeal. Lord Justice Laws, giving the leading judgment, began by accepting the general proposition that a public body such as the Trust, in entering into a contractual obligation to make payments to an employee or ex-employee, is constrained by a general duty arising in public law not to enter into undertakings which may be described as 'irrationally generous'. That said, he considered that it would be a rare case where a public body would be allowed to escape commercial commitments on the ground that its decision was so unreasonable that no reasonable decision-maker could have arrived at it. Turning to the instant case, it was clear to Laws LJ that the High Court judge had adopted the wrong approach: instead of determining whether the Trust had acted outside the bounds of reasonableness, he had decided the case on the basis of what might have been 'financially prudent' for the Trust. Laws LJ did not share the judge's criticism of how the Trust had arrived at the final settlement figure. The judge had assumed that, absent a settlement agreement, the Trust would simply have admitted unfair dismissal and paid the statutory maximum compensation, thereby saving the cost of an employment tribunal claim. But the evidence indicated that the Trust might well have chosen to defend the claim. Nor could the Trust be criticised for taking into account the legal and management costs that might have been incurred in meeting a tribunal claim, G's long service and her likely difficulties in finding new employment. A reasonable employer is not limited to replicating the statutory maximum remedy – it is not irrational to display some generosity for the sake of good relations and mutual respect between employer and employee. Lord Justice Sedley concurred, adding that, in the circumstances, the compensation was not outlandish, given that the settlement would have spared the Trust public controversy, the 'near-certainty' of an adverse tribunal finding, a drain on management resources, and damage to staff morale. In Sedley LJ's view, only if the figures are 'inexplicable on their face' or 'palpably inflated in the light of the evidence' should the court examine their elements, **3.102**

207

and then not in order to remake the calculation but to see if it has indeed gone beyond the bounds of reasonableness. Accordingly, the Trust was bound by the terms of the settlement agreement.

3.103 **Job reference.** Although there is generally no legal obligation to provide a job reference, the employer and the employee will be well advised to have stipulated in the settlement agreement that a fair and accurate reference will be provided. In fact, to avoid potential litigation, the parties should attach to the settlement agreement the exact wording, as the Court of Appeal strongly recommended in Cox v Sun Alliance Life Ltd 2001 IRLR 448, CA. Employers should agree only to wording that they feel is fair and accurate so as to avoid potential liability in misrepresentation or negligence to those to whom the reference is later supplied. Employees should ensure that the agreement makes clear that no oral statements – at least, negative ones – contrary to the agreed reference will be made. The Acas Guide states that, where it is not possible to agree a full and comprehensive reference, the parties may agree that the employer will supply a short statement confirming that the employee was employed, the dates of the employment and his or her job title when it receives a request for a reference from a new or potential employer.

3.104 **Repayment clauses and warranties.** Repayment clauses and warranties are also commonly included in any settlement agreement. The employer may want the employee to warrant that he or she has no statutory claims other than those settled under the agreement and to include an undertaking that the claimant will not litigate, together with a provision requiring repayment of the settlement money if this is breached.

There is no guarantee that repayment clauses will be enforceable and careful drafting will be required to ensure that such a clause genuinely reflects the employer's loss. The issue will be whether the clause amounts to an unenforceable 'penalty' clause or an enforceable 'liquidated damages' clause. To be treated as the latter, the payment must be a genuine pre-estimate of the loss likely to flow from the breach – i.e. it must seek to compensate the wronged party for breach of the settlement agreement. By contrast, a penalty clause is the provision for the payment of a sum of money which is designed to secure performance of the agreement or, to put it another way, to deter breach of it. If a clause is found to be a penalty clause, the court will declare it void and ignore it.

3.105 An unenforceable penalty clause in a settlement agreement was found to exist in CMC Group plc and ors v Zhang 2006 EWCA Civ 408, CA. In that case the Court of Appeal held that a clause in a settlement agreement requiring the employee to repay the settlement sum in the event of 'any breach' was unenforceable because the sum due to be repaid – US$40,000 – was 'extravagant and unconscionable' compared with the potential loss arising from the breach. The clause amounted to an unenforceable penalty clause. This did not, however, affect the enforceability of the remainder of the agreement.

By contrast, in Imam-Sadeque v BlueBay Asset Management (Services) Ltd 2013 IRLR 344, QBD, a former employee was unable to persuade a court that a payment which became due on the breach of a settlement agreement was unenforceable as a penalty clause. In that case, I-S wanted to leave his employment, but this would have made him a 'bad leaver' under the terms of a bonus plan and lost him the benefit of unvested fund units and shares. When a reorganisation was announced, he reached an agreement with the company, as reflected in a settlement agreement, that he would stay and help with the transition and, provided he complied with his contractual obligations, he would then leave the company as a 'good leaver' and thus acquire his fund units at the vesting date. In the event, I-S breached express and implied contractual terms not to compete with the company and lost the benefit of the fund units. He subsequently sought to recover them by commencing proceedings in the High Court, arguing that their forfeiture for breach of the settlement agreement was unenforceable on the basis that it offended the penalty doctrine.

The High Court disagreed for two reasons. First, it held that nothing in the **3.106** settlement agreement caused him to lose the benefit of the fund units upon breach; rather, it made him a 'good leaver' for the purposes of the bonus plan, provided he complied with his contractual obligations. This he did not do, and he therefore reverted to being a 'bad leaver' under the terms of the bonus plan. It followed that the settlement agreement itself did not impose a penalty and it was not suggested by I-S that the terms of the bonus plan were unenforceable. Secondly, even if the forfeiture were to be treated as having occurred by reason of breach of the settlement agreement, the penalty doctrine had no application to his contingent future interests in the fund units, as they could not be treated as the equivalent of the payment of a sum of money. The penalty doctrine only applied to accrued rights and, given that it was an exception to the general rule that parties are free to negotiate contractual terms, the High Court was not prepared to extend its application beyond the currently understood limits. In any event, even if I-S had given up an accrued right to the fund units, and the penalty doctrine were applicable in principle, the Court said that it would not have regarded the provisions of the settlement agreement as penal: they contained rights and obligations that might operate to the advantage and disadvantage of either party, and to which each freely agreed, and it was entirely possible that the loss suffered by the company as a result of I-S's breach of the agreement exceeded the value of the fund units.

It is clear from the above cases that much depends on the exact wording of the repayment clause. As a general rule, clauses should be worded so that, where they provide for amounts to be repaid, they make a genuine attempt to reflect the employer's potential loss, rather than fixing a single sum as the penalty for any and all breaches of the agreement. Alternatively, employers may take the view that even though a 'penalty-type' clause may not be enforceable, it nevertheless operates as a sufficient deterrent to make its inclusion worthwhile.

209

3.107   It is commonplace for employers to require employees to warrant in a settlement agreement that they have not committed any repudiatory breaches of their contract of employment that would have entitled the employer to dismiss them without notice or payment in lieu of notice. In Collidge v Freeport plc 2008 IRLR 697, CA, the employee lost out on a settlement payment for making a false warranty. The High Court found that there was evidence of circumstances entitling F plc to dismiss C summarily – C had removed equipment from one of F plc's sites to a hotel he owned, with no intention of paying for it, and had used a driver employed by F plc to do work for him in company time. Each of these actions was sufficient to justify summary dismissal. In addition, C had misused his company credit card for personal expenses without reimbursing the company. Applying the terms of the settlement agreement, the judge concluded that, at the time C gave the warranty, there were numerous circumstances of which he was aware that constituted repudiatory breaches on his part and which would have entitled F plc to terminate his employment without notice. Given the conclusion that payment of the settlement money was conditional upon the accuracy of C's warranty, it followed that C was not entitled to the benefits provided by the agreement. On appeal, the Court of Appeal upheld this decision.

Similarly, in Stanley v Capital Law LLP EAT 0417/08 the EAT upheld an employment tribunal's decision that the employer was entitled to withhold payment of the settlement figure in circumstances where the employee had falsely warranted that he knew of no circumstances that would entitle the employer to summarily dismiss him. The employee had been under an obligation to inform the employer that he had failed to give a client clear advice on the limitation period for bringing an unfair dismissal claim and that a negligence claim might be brought against the firm.

3.108   **Confidentiality.** Employers are often anxious to ensure that settlement agreements contain a confidentiality clause, preventing the employee from disclosing details of the settlement or any other potentially damaging information. An explicit clause to this effect is necessary because the Court of Appeal has held that a general duty of confidentiality will not be implied in the absence of some express provision – see Brooks v Olyslager OMS (UK) Ltd 1998 IRLR 590, CA. The Brooks case concerned an employer who withheld a severance payment under a settlement agreement after discovering that the employee had told a potential investor about various financial difficulties the employer was having. The Court of Appeal concluded that there was no legal justification for withholding the money. The information the employer was seeking to protect did not amount to a 'trade secret' and therefore fell outside the scope of any implied duty of confidentiality.

In the public sector, disclosure of the terms of a settlement agreement may be sought by a member of the public under the Freedom of Information Act 2000.

However, as the case of Trago Mills (South Devon) Ltd v Information Commissioner and anor Case No.EA/2012/0028 shows, a public authority employee will usually have a reasonable expectation of privacy regarding any terms of a settlement agreement entered into, even in the absence of an express confidentiality clause. In that case, the Information Rights Tribunal held that a local authority was entitled to refuse a request under the Freedom of Information Act 2000 by a third party to disclose the terms of a settlement agreement it entered into with a senior employee. The evidence demonstrated that the employee's departure had not been influenced by any misconduct on his part. Although he was a senior decision-maker in a public-facing role, his reasonable expectation of privacy outweighed the authority's duty of accountability regarding the expenditure of public money. Accordingly, disclosure would have breached the first data protection principle set out in the Data Protection Act 1998 and the information was exempt from disclosure under the Freedom of Information Act 2000.

Scope of the settlement   3.109
Like a COT3 agreement, a properly constituted settlement agreement will bar the employee from taking a tribunal claim any further. However, unlike COT3 agreements, there is a requirement that settlement agreements 'relate to the particular proceedings' – S.203(3)(b) ERA (or the equivalent in other statutes). This does not mean that each claim or potential claim must be settled by a separate agreement. As with COT3 agreements, a single settlement agreement is capable of settling all the matters in dispute between the parties – Lunt v Merseyside TEC Ltd 1999 ICR 17, EAT.

'Particular proceedings'. In Hinton v University of East London 2005 ICR **3.110** 1260, CA, the Court of Appeal handed down a significant decision on what is required for an agreement to 'relate to the particular proceedings' for the purposes of S.203(3)(b). There, H, a lecturer, took voluntary redundancy. In June 2003 he signed a settlement agreement expressed to be 'in full and final settlement of all claims in all jurisdictions (whether arising under statute, common law or otherwise) which the employee has or may have against the University... arising out of or in connection with his employment with the University, the termination of his employment or otherwise'. There followed a lengthy list of possible claims to be settled (although H had not, in fact, raised most of them). The list did not include claims under S.47B ERA, which protects employees from being subjected to a detriment because they have made a protected disclosure. This was despite the fact that H had in the past complained to his employer that he had suffered such detriments.

In October 2003 H brought tribunal proceedings on the basis of these alleged detriments. The tribunal held that the settlement agreement did not prevent H from bringing the proceedings, because it did not specifically cover H's complaint. The EAT, however, allowed the employer's appeal. In its view,

211

H's S.47B allegations did not have to be particularised in the agreement to be settled. The list of claims expressly excluded by the agreement was not intended to be exhaustive, but was merely illustrative of the type of claims covered, and the claim under S.47B was settled by the general 'full and final settlement of all claims' wording. H appealed to the Court of Appeal.

3.111 Lord Justice Mummery, giving the leading judgment, was in no doubt that, *contractually*, the settlement agreement was wide enough to cover H's S.47B claim. The agreement made it plain that 'the intention of the parties was to settle all their differences, actual and potential, arising under statute and at common law'. This did not mean, however, that the agreement complied with the S.203 requirement that it relate to 'particular proceedings'.

Turning to S.203, Mummery LJ rejected the contention that, for a settlement agreement to relate to 'particular proceedings', tribunal proceedings must have been initiated before the agreement was signed. A settlement agreement can apply 'to the compromise of anticipated proceedings in relation to a claim or complaint raised between the parties prior to the compromise, though not the subject of any actual proceedings'. Mummery LJ stated that 'no sensible or useful purpose would be served by requiring an employee to go through the formal steps of issuing tribunal proceedings for the sole purpose of enabling a valid and binding [settlement] agreement to be made'. However, the policy behind S.203 was 'to protect claimants from the danger of signing away their rights without a proper understanding of what they are doing'. To achieve this, the requirement that an agreement 'relate to the particular proceedings' had to mean that the particular proceedings were clearly identified, either by a generic description such as 'unfair dismissal' or by reference to the section of the statute giving rise to the claim. It was not sufficient for a settlement agreement to use 'a rolled-up expression such as "all statutory rights"', nor even to identify the proceedings only by reference to the statute under which they arose. In H's case, although from a contractual point of view the wording of the agreement was wide enough to cover his potential S.47B claim, the agreement had not specifically referred to S.47B, and thus did not 'relate to the particular proceedings' within the meaning of S.203(3)(b). H could therefore proceed with his claim.

3.112 Having dealt with the statutory requirements, the Court in Hinton went on to make some general observations about good practice when drafting settlement agreements. Mummery LJ stated that if actual proceedings which have already been commenced are being settled, the agreement should include a brief factual and legal description of their particulars and the allegations on which they are based. In the case of any claim that is not already the subject of proceedings, good practice requires a brief description of the nature of the allegations and of the statute under which they are made or the common law basis of the alleged claim. Lady Justice Hale (as she then was) agreed, adding that employers should not use standard form agreements that refer to every conceivable employment right irrespective of whether it is relevant to the particular circumstances of the case.

This guidance has left advisers in a difficult position. On the one hand, it suggests that using an off-the-peg agreement without adapting it to address the particular circumstances of the case will be contrary to good practice and will be frowned upon. On the other hand, the temptation will surely be to err on the side of caution by including every conceivable claim in the agreement. After all, in the Hinton case it was a lack of inclusiveness in the employer's settlement agreement, which failed to refer to a claim under S.47B ERA, that was the cause of the agreement being ineffective.

Despite the Court of Appeal's guidance in Hinton v University of East London (above), a comprehensive list of employment protection claims without further particulars was found to be sufficient to settle claims in Topping v ABP Meat Processors Ltd ET Case No.2900133/07. In that case T brought claims for unfair dismissal and disability discrimination despite having signed a settlement agreement listing specific jurisdictions that included unfair dismissal and disability discrimination. She argued that the agreement was not effective to settle these claims because it did not – as suggested in Hinton – contain brief particulars of them. However, the employment tribunal disagreed, holding that the inclusion of such particulars was merely best practice and not a statutory requirement. In any event, the tribunal recognised that, where proceedings have not commenced and are not even contemplated at the time the settlement agreement is signed, giving particulars is not an easy thing to do. Accordingly, the claims had been validly settled. **3.113**

Even where the agreement is drafted in accordance with the guidance in Hinton, an employer still needs to pay attention to how the agreement is worded in order to ensure those claims are effectively compromised. In Hilton UK Hotels v McNaughton EATS 0059/04 M entered into a settlement agreement upon termination of her employment. The agreement was stated to be 'in full and final settlement of any and all present and future claims… which you have or may have' including all of the 'Statutory Claims'. The definition of 'Statutory Claims' amounted to a comprehensive list of employment protection legislation, which included the Equal Pay Act 1970 (EqPA) (since repealed and replaced by provisions in the EqA), but was qualified in two ways. First, it stated that these were claims 'that you believe you have against the Company'. Secondly, it stated that these were claims that 'you have raised with the Company but which the Company and its officers, employees and agents dispute'. There was no evidence that M had in fact raised any specific claims with H Ltd prior to signing the agreement. M then brought an equal pay claim against H Ltd on the ground that she had been excluded from its pension scheme while working part time. She maintained that she had not been aware of the possibility of bringing this claim when she signed the settlement agreement, but had only realised she could bring

213

it after reading a newspaper article. Relying on Hinton, the EAT considered that, in order to be validly settled, the equal pay claim had to at least be identified in the agreement by a generic description or by reference to the section of the statute giving rise to it. The EAT accepted that a reference in a settlement agreement to the EqPA as a whole was sufficient to identify the 'particular complaint' for the purposes of S.77(4A) of the Sex Discrimination Act 1975 (the statutory condition for settling equal pay claims, now contained in S.147(3)(b) EqA) as interpreted in the Hinton case. No reference to a particular section is required, since the Act contained only one section giving rise to an employment tribunal claim. However, in this case the reference to the equal pay claim was made subject to the qualification that such a claim was only excluded if, when signing the agreement, M believed that she had such a claim and had raised it with H Ltd. As she had no knowledge of this claim at the time of agreement between the parties, M had not waived her right to bring it.

3.114 The importance of careful drafting is also illustrated by Palihakkara v British Telecommunications plc EAT 0185–86/06. There, the EAT held that a settlement agreement entered into with P purporting to settle 'all claims past or future arising out of her *termination* of employment' (our stress) did not cover the race and sex discrimination claims that arose during the course of her employment. P's unfair dismissal claim and claim for a redundancy payment were therefore settled but her claims of race and sex discrimination were not, and she was accordingly free to bring proceedings in respect of those claims.

In McWilliam and ors v Glasgow City Council 2011 IRLR 568, EAT, the claimants argued that there must be a pre-existing tribunal claim or a prior grievance before either of these things could constitute 'a particular complaint' such as to be bindingly settled. The EAT gave this argument short shrift. In its view, it would be absurd to insist that the time, trouble and expense of presenting a claim to a tribunal had to be incurred before a valid settlement agreement could be entered into. The term 'complaint' is wide enough to include circumstances where there is nothing more than an expression of dissatisfaction about something. If Parliament had intended that an employee's complaint had to have reached the stage of being articulated in a claim that had been presented to a tribunal, it would have said so explicitly.

3.115 The EAT's decision in McWilliam also made it clear that the legislation does not require the complaint to have been articulated by the employee at some earlier stage before it can be effectively settled. What matters is that both parties know to which particular complaint the settlement agreement relates, i.e. which particular complaint cannot be litigated in the future. It does not matter whether there has been a history of communication or dialogue about the particular complaint or complaints. In any event, the claimants in the particular case had in fact complained of unequal pay before signing the settlement agreements, and so there was no doubt at that stage what claim was intended to be settled.

214

Settling 'future' claims. In Lunt v Merseyside TEC Ltd 1999 ICR 17, EAT, the **3.116**
EAT stated that Parliament did not intend to permit a blanket settlement
agreement settling claims which had never been raised. Accordingly, a settlement
agreement cannot exclude complaints that have not yet arisen – unlike a
negotiated settlement arising by way of Acas conciliation (see 'Acas-conciliated
(COT3) agreements' above), a settlement agreement cannot be used to sign
away all the employee's rights to bring employment tribunal claims. It would
seem, then, that settlement agreements will be valid only in so far as they settle
those complaints that have been raised – as a potential tribunal claim if not in
actual proceedings – by the date of the agreement.

However, in Hilton UK Hotels v McNaughton (above), a differently constituted
EAT stated that the Lunt case did not determine that a party cannot contractually
settle a future claim of which he or she has no knowledge. The EAT went on to
refer to Royal National Orthopaedic Hospital Trust v Howard 2002 IRLR
849, EAT, a case on the scope of Acas-conciliated agreements, which suggested
that future claims can be settled, but must be so 'in language which is absolutely
clear and leaves no room for doubt as to what it is [the parties] are contracting
for'. In principle, therefore, the EAT considered it entirely possible for parties
to settle future claims, provided they do so in language that leaves no room for
doubt that this is indeed their intention.

Contractual claims. Where a settlement agreement is found to be ineffective in **3.117**
barring an employee's statutory claims, it should nevertheless be remembered
that his or her contractual (as opposed to statutory) claims will have been
settled, provided there is a binding agreement between the parties. This point
was made by the EAT in Sutherland v Network Appliance Ltd and anor 2001
IRLR 12, EAT. In that case S entered into a settlement agreement expressed to
be 'in full and final settlement of any claims you might have against the company
arising out of your employment or its termination'. It was common ground that
the agreement did not fulfil the statutory requirements for settlement agreements
set out in S.203 ERA. However, the EAT held that the employment tribunal
had been correct to hold that the agreement was effective to prevent S from
pursuing claims for breach of contract, to which the S.203 restrictions on
contracting out of statutory rights did not apply.

Enforcing a settlement agreement
3.118
We have already discussed the question of whether an employee can bring or
resurrect an employment tribunal claim where the employer fails to honour its
side of a settlement bargain under 'Acas-conciliated (COT3) agreements –
enforcing an agreement' above. The extent to which this is possible is unclear.
What is certain, though, is that where the employer defaults, the employee has
a claim for breach of contract, or, if the terms of settlement have been
incorporated into a judgment of the tribunal, a claim for the enforcement of a
judgment debt in the county court or High Court.

215

Furthermore, an employment tribunal may be able to hear the employee's claim for breach of a settlement agreement under the contractual jurisdiction given to it by the Employment Tribunals Extension of Jurisdiction (England and Wales) Order 1994 SI 1994/1623. However, tribunals have jurisdiction in contractual matters only in respect of a claim that 'arises or is outstanding on the termination of the employee's employment'. On this basis, a tribunal was able to hear a claim for breach of a settlement agreement in Rock-It Cargo Ltd v Green 1997 IRLR 581, EAT, because the agreement in that case was concerned with the terms upon which the employee's employment was to be brought to an end. This ruling established that settlement agreements made on or before termination of the employment can be enforced in tribunals. Many settlement agreements, however, are made some time after termination, when a hearing of a claim by a tribunal is pending. In Miller Bros and FP Butler Ltd v Johnston 2002 ICR 744, EAT, for example, a settlement agreement was made some days after termination, and could not therefore fall within the tribunal's limited jurisdiction to entertain breach of contract claims.

3.119 Invalid agreements

There are a number of circumstances that may render a contracting-out agreement invalid and unenforceable. Some of these only affect Acas-conciliated agreements or settlement agreements. Others, which derive from the common law, apply to all contracting-out agreements (including settlement agreements).

3.120 Acas-conciliated agreements

In certain circumstances a settlement will not be enforced, notwithstanding the fact that a conciliator has taken action in accordance with his or her statutory duties, but these circumstances are limited. The House of Lords in Moore v Duport Furniture Products Ltd and anor 1982 ICR 84, HL, expressly rejected the employee's claim that the terms of a contracting-out agreement must be just and equitable in order to be enforceable. It also rejected the claim that it is the duty of a conciliator, in endeavouring to promote a settlement, to ensure that this is the case. The legislation does ask the conciliator to satisfy him or herself that the terms of any agreement to *reinstate or re-engage* an employee appear to be equitable. However, unlike previous versions of the relevant sections, Ss.18A(9) and 18C(2) ETA leave it to the conciliator's discretion to seek to promote the employee's re-employment whenever he or she intends to bring, or has already brought, a claim for unfair dismissal. Thus, there appears to be no legal basis for arguing that a conciliated agreement should be set aside on account of a conciliator's failure to consider the fairness of such terms.

Lack of *good faith* or the adoption of unfair methods by a conciliator in promoting a conciliated agreement can, however, be grounds for avoiding any such agreement according to the EAT in Slack v Greenham (Plant Hire) Ltd and

216

anor 1983 ICR 617, EAT. If the conciliator, for instance, deliberately misled a party to the settlement as to its effect or consequences, then a tribunal might accept that the agreement should be set aside. Ultimately, this would be a matter of proof – and such proof would have to be extremely cogent before a tribunal would conclude that a conciliator had acted in bad faith.

An Acas-conciliated agreement may also be invalid if it amounts to a *sham*. In **3.121** Trafford Carpets Ltd v Barker EAT 206/90 B thought that he had been dismissed by way of redundancy and so accepted from his employer a redundancy payment as well as three months' pay in lieu of notice. Later, in order to qualify for a Government Enterprise Allowance, he entered into an agreement with the company to reclassify the payment in lieu as part of his redundancy payment. The parties approached Acas and recorded the agreement formally on a COT3. B then discovered that another person had been appointed to his old job and he decided to bring a claim for unfair dismissal. The employment tribunal decided that no action had been taken by Acas in relation to any unfair dismissal claim – or, for that matter, in relation to any claim for pay in lieu of notice under what was then the Wages Act 1986 – and that it would hear B's complaint despite the agreement. The EAT upheld this decision on appeal because the COT3 agreement amounted to a sham or rewrite of the original agreement. The COT3 agreement was misleading in so far as it was intended to indicate to the relevant government department, or anyone else, that pay in lieu had not been paid. The EAT's view was that it was no part of the statutory machinery to protect settlements that lent validity to this sort of misleading transaction. The case was remitted to a tribunal for a hearing on the merits of the unfair dismissal claim.

Settlement agreements **3.122**
As stated under 'Settlement agreements' above, a settlement agreement will be invalid with regard to settling certain statutory claims if it fails to satisfy any of the stringent conditions set out in the relevant statutory provisions (for example, in S.203(3)–(4) ERA).

However, employees should be aware that the invalidity of a settlement agreement will not, of itself, permit the continuance of a tribunal claim. In Mayo-Deman v University of Greenwich and ors 2005 IRLR 845, EAT, M-D brought race and sex discrimination claims against the university, which were settled by way of settlement agreement shortly before the hearing. She did not attend the hearing, at which the tribunal, having been informed that a settlement had been reached between the parties, dismissed her claims. M-D appealed to the EAT. In her view, since the settlement agreement did not comply with S.77(4A) SDA or the equivalent S.72(4A) RRA (being the provisions to ensure the validity of a compromise agreement, now to be found in S.147(3) EqA), it was not binding on the parties. She submitted that the tribunal had erred in law in dismissing her claims without first having ascertained that a valid – i.e.

217

statute-compliant – agreement had been concluded. The EAT disagreed. There was nothing in law that required an employment tribunal to ensure that the terms agreed complied with the statutory provisions before it permits a claim to be dismissed. The tribunal, forming the correct view that the parties had agreed terms of settlement, had been entitled to dismiss the claim on that basis.

3.123 Common law doctrines

At common law an agreement is invalid if either party was induced to enter into it in reliance on a *misrepresentation*, owing to a *mistake* or because of *undue influence or duress* by the other side. These doctrines apply to all contracting-out agreements, whether conciliated or not. Some courts have doubted whether employment tribunals – as opposed to the civil courts – have the power to set aside contracting-out agreements on common law grounds. For example, in Byrnell v British Telecommunications plc EAT 0383/04 – a case in which the claimant sought to set aside a settlement agreement he had entered into with his former employer – the EAT took the view that the only jurisdiction of an employment tribunal in relation to the validity of a settlement agreement is to determine whether it complies with the statutory requirements in S.203 ERA. However, in Hennessy v Craigmyle and Co Ltd and anor 1986 ICR 461, CA, the Court of Appeal – hearing an appeal against the EAT's decision that a tribunal did have jurisdiction to determine whether a COT3 agreement should be set aside on the ground of economic duress – appeared to accept the proposition that tribunals do have such a power.

The issue of whether employment tribunals have jurisdiction to consider the validity of contracting-out agreements under common law principles, or whether such issues have to be determined in the county court, again arose for determination in Horizon Recruitment Ltd and anor v Vincent 2010 ICR 491, EAT. In that case, V entered into an agreement whereby she agreed to resign in return for a monetary settlement but the money remained unpaid following a change in ownership of the company. She applied to the employment tribunal to have the settlement agreement set aside on the basis that either or both companies must have known that they were not going to be able to comply with the payment provisions and had misled her into entering into the agreement. The EAT held that the tribunal did have jurisdiction to consider whether such an agreement was void for misrepresentation. In its view, there is nothing in the ERA precluding tribunals from ensuring that settlement agreements are valid outside the confines of the Act. In reaching this decision, it noted that the differently constituted EAT in Byrnell v British Telecommunications plc (above) had reached the opposite conclusion. However, the EAT in that case had not referred to the ruling in Hennessy, which lent powerful support to the approach taken by the tribunal in the instant case that it was entitled to consider whether a settlement agreement can and should be avoided before deciding if it constituted a valid agreement for the purposes of S.203 ERA.

Mistake. In O'Rourke v Airport Catering Services ET Case No.31930/83 both **3.124** parties mistakenly believed that the employee's pension was worth more than it actually was. In reliance on this, the employee agreed to settle but he managed to have the settlement set aside later when the truth was discovered. The tribunal accepted that the employee was induced to enter into the COT3 agreement on the assumption that he would receive a further £150 in respect of his pension contributions, whereas he actually received considerably less than that figure.

In another case, Bousie v Steelwall of Cardiff (Eng.) Ltd ET Case No.24092/87, the tribunal agreed to revoke an earlier decision to stay a claim made after the parties had reached a settlement. It did so because there had been no genuine agreement to settle the employee's claim – each party had intended a different form of settlement. The employer had treated the payment due under the settlement as an ex gratia payment and had therefore deducted tax and national insurance. The employee, on the other hand, considered the payment to represent a settlement of his claims to a basic and a compensatory award, neither of which would have been subject to tax or national insurance. The tribunal concluded from this that the parties did not agree the payment to be in full and final settlement of the claim.

Economic duress. As previously noted, the Court of Appeal in Hennessy v **3.125** Craigmyle and Co Ltd and anor (above) accepted the argument that the doctrine of economic duress could apply to avoid an Acas-conciliated agreement where the will of the employee was overborne to such an extent that his or her entering into a contract was not a voluntary act. However, the Court took the view that instances of economic pressure such as to render the actions of the employee involuntary would be very rare and held that, in the particular case, the choice between accepting a lump sum or drawing social security while pursuing an unfair dismissal claim did not amount to economic duress.

Economic duress was defined by the EAT in Sphikas and Son v Porter EAT 927/96 as 'a combination of pressure and the absence of practical choice'. In that case, P pressed ahead with an unlawful deduction of wages claim, despite an earlier settlement agreement purporting to settle it. He persuaded the tribunal that his employer had withheld payment from him prior to the settlement negotiations. The tribunal further accepted that the consequent 'economic inducement' to accept less than his full entitlement was sufficient to amount to duress, thereby invalidating the settlement agreement. The EAT considered this to be the wrong approach. Not all pressure will amount to duress, it said. It is inevitable that during the course of negotiations one side will seek to exploit the other's apparent weakness. However, in disputes between employer and employee the 'availability of a cheap and quick procedure to employees' – employment tribunals – 'is an important antidote to the inequality of bargaining power inherent in an employment relationship'. In the

219

EAT's view, tribunal proceedings had always provided P with a 'practical and effective' alternative to settling his claim. For that reason, there was no 'absence of practical choice' in his case and thus he was not entitled to rely on a plea of economic duress. The employer's appeal was therefore allowed.

3.126 An employment tribunal adopted a similarly hard line in an unfair dismissal case, Sanderson v Farnell Electronic Components plc ET Case No.12126/96. There, the employer threatened the employee that unless he entered into the settlement agreement it would stop him exercising share option rights worth around a quarter of a million pounds. This threat was not sufficient to amount to economic duress, in the tribunal's opinion. The employee still had a real alternative to signing the settlement agreement – namely, making his unfair dismissal claim and taking action to enforce his rights under the share option scheme.

Given the introduction of fees in the employment tribunal in July 2013, it remains to be seen whether employees will now be on stronger ground when arguing that the financial pressure on them to settle was such as to call into question the validity of a contracting-out agreement. With claimants obliged to pay an issue fee as well as a hearing fee before being able to enforce their individual rights, the assertion in Sphikas and Son v Porter (above) that tribunals represent a 'cheap and quick procedure' of enforcing individual rights no longer seems sustainable, which may mean that arguments of unequal bargaining power feature more frequently where individuals seek to set aside agreements or refuse to abide by them.

3.127 **Bad faith and misrepresentation.** An employment tribunal may also set aside a contracting-out agreement where it finds that an employer acted in bad faith, misrepresented the true position, or adopted unfair methods in concluding a contracting-out agreement. However, where a party alleges bad faith during the course of negotiations, such allegations have to be backed up by cogent evidence in order to persuade the tribunal to set aside the agreement on that basis. In Crystal Palace FC (2000) Ltd v Dowie 2007 IRLR 682, QBD, the High Court encountered no such difficulty: it held it proven on the facts that a football manager fraudulently misrepresented to his club chairman that he wanted to leave his job to move closer to his family, with the intention and effect of inducing the chairman to enter a settlement agreement releasing him from a contractual agreement to pay the club compensation. The manager in fact intended to join a neighbouring club. The High Court held that the manager's stated reason for leaving was a major factor influencing the club's decision to waive its right to compensation. In the circumstances, the appropriate remedy was financial relief, not the rescission of the settlement agreement.

Below are three more examples where tribunals were satisfied that settlement agreements were unenforceable for reasons relating to bad faith:

- **Seaman and anor v Serviceteam Ltd** ET Case Nos.2100013–14/01: S and D were made redundant in March and April 2000 respectively. They received enhanced redundancy payments in return for entering into settlement agreements that were concluded on 19 April 2000. In November 2000 D was told by a former colleague, whose services had been retained, that the colleague's brother had been on the panel that had selected people to be retained. Before the interviews, the colleague had been told by his brother what questions would be asked. Upon hearing this, a tribunal held that it had jurisdiction to set aside the settlement agreements. If allegations are made that cast doubt on the facts known to one of the parties at the time of an agreement, it would be unfair to allow the agreement to prevent that party seeking justice. In S and D's case, even if senior managers did not know of the possible corruption, it would be totally unacceptable for the tribunal to allow the employer to rely on the agreements

- **Morrison v Governing Body of Parkstone Grammar School** ET Case No.3105212/00: M was a head teacher. Her relationship with the chairman of governors deteriorated, and she began to tape-record her meetings with him without his knowledge. She obtained another post to start in the next school year and handed in her notice. When an unauthorised tape-recording was discovered, M was suspended and forced to leave the school. The chairman wrote a confidential letter to all governors giving details of the suspension and the reasons for it. He also sought to introduce disciplinary allegations against M. Subsequently, it came to the chairman's notice that his confidential letter was in the hands of the local press, but he did not inform the governors or M of this. Two days after M signed a settlement agreement, the press published full details of her suspension, as a result of which she was unable to take up her new post. She claimed unfair dismissal. The tribunal found that the chairman had, in bad faith, raised unjustified allegations during the course of negotiations, with the sole intention of putting pressure on M to sign away her legal rights, and had thereby breached the implied term of trust and confidence. The tribunal also held that the chairman's non-disclosure of the fact that the press had information relating to M's suspension invalidated the settlement agreement, as it destroyed its purpose. M was entitled to pursue her claim

- **Simpson v Focus Training and Assessment Ltd (in liquidation)** ET Case No.2402759/00: S was told that if she resigned and entered into a settlement agreement she would be paid a redundancy package. She did resign and her solicitor signed a settlement agreement. Some five weeks later the employer went into liquidation. The tribunal held that the settlement agreement was not binding as the employer had entered into it in bad faith. It had known of its financial position at the time and the tribunal concluded that the agreement was merely an attempt to put off paying S the money she was owed.

221

3.128 However, in Greenfield v Robinson EAT 811/95 the EAT reached a different conclusion. There, G claimed that she entered into a COT3 agreement after R told her that the employer's business was about to be declared bankrupt. In the event, a deal was found that saved the business. The EAT held that the tribunal was entitled to find that R only said that there was a *risk* of bankruptcy, and that G was not induced to settle on the basis of an actionable misrepresentation.

Similarly, in Rosner v Learning Skills Network (in liquidation) ET Case No.2204973/11 the employment tribunal decided that there was insufficient evidence to accede to the employee's request to find a settlement agreement void for misrepresentation. R signed a settlement agreement and left LSN's employment on 30 September 2011. The agreement provided for him to be paid £30,000 in four instalments: £5,000 by 4 October 2011, £5,000 by 1 November 2011, £10,000 on 15 November 2011 and £10,000 on 15 December 2011. R only received the first payment and administrators were appointed on 3 November 2011. Before the tribunal, R maintained that the settlement agreement was void for misrepresentation, LSN having represented that it would be able to make the instalment payments when it knew this was not the case. The tribunal disagreed. In its view, LSN knew that its financial situation was difficult but there was not enough evidence to find that it knew it could not make all the payments. Therefore, the settlement agreement was not void for misrepresentation.

3.129 **Lack of capacity**. In Oatley v EMI (UK) Ltd EAT 148/83 the EAT thought it at least arguable that lack of capacity as a result of a mental condition might be sufficient to render a contracting-out agreement void.

3.130 Arbitration

The Acas Arbitration Scheme was introduced on 21 May 2001 in England and Wales, and extended to Scotland in 2004. The scheme, which is voluntary – both parties must agree to refer the dispute to arbitration – is intended to provide a faster, non-legalistic, more cost-effective and informal alternative to employment tribunals for the resolution of

* unfair dismissal and,

* since April 2003, flexible working disputes (i.e. disputes arising out of an employee's application for a change in his or her terms and conditions of employment made under S.80F ERA).

The scheme is contained in the Schedules to the Acas Arbitration Scheme (Great Britain) Order 2004 SI 2004/753 – for unfair dismissal – and the Acas (Flexible Working) Arbitration Scheme (Great Britain) Order 2004 SI 2004/2333 – for flexible working. (Note that S.212A of the Trade Union and Labour Relations (Consolidation) Act 1992, which confers on Acas the power to prepare an arbitration scheme in the above specified disputes, was amended in April 2010 to include disputes arising out of applications in respect of the right to request study and training under Ss.63F–63I ERA. However, at the time of writing, no arbitration scheme had been drawn up in respect of such disputes.)

Although the scheme has a number of advantages as compared to the traditional forum of an employment tribunal, it also has disadvantages that may put off one or both sides. In fact, the scheme has not proved particularly popular. In the period from the scheme's inception on 21 May 2001 until 31 March 2009, Acas accepted a total of 61 cases for resolution. Since then, it has not produced any more uptake figures. **3.131**

Below, we look at some of the advantages and disadvantages of the scheme and briefly outline its most important aspects. A more detailed explanation of the scheme can be found in Acas's booklets, 'The Acas arbitration scheme for the resolution of unfair dismissal disputes (England and Wales)', 'The Acas arbitration scheme for the resolution of unfair dismissal disputes (Scotland)' and 'The Acas arbitration scheme for the resolution of flexible working disputes – a guide to the scheme' ('the Guides'), which are available from the Acas website.

Pros and cons of the scheme **3.132**
Some of the attractions of the scheme for both parties are as follows. Hearings are conducted in an informal manner and are held at a location convenient to the parties. It is also Acas's intention that hearings will not normally last more than half a day, with an arbitration hearing taking place, at the latest, within 28 days of the parties' notifying Acas of their agreement to go to arbitration. There is no cross-examination of witnesses by parties or representatives, no oaths or affirmations, no formal pleadings, and proceedings are confidential, so cases involving embarrassing evidence will not hit the headlines. Awards are also confidential.

The informality and confidentiality of the proceedings may well appeal to both parties. However, as noted above, the scheme has a very limited scope in that it is available as an alternative to a tribunal hearing only for cases of alleged unfair dismissal and flexible working requests. The scheme excludes from its scope other kinds of claim which are often related to or raised at the same time as these claims – for example, claims for unpaid wages or discrimination. Thus, where a claim eligible for resolution under the scheme has another claim linked to it, it is likely that many claimants will want all the issues dealt with at the same time in an employment tribunal rather than undergo the inconvenience and anxiety of two hearings.

Furthermore, the scheme is not suitable for cases which raise complex legal issues. Nor is it suitable for cases which raise questions of EU law – Acas 'strongly recommends' that these cases are dealt with by an employment **3.133**

223

tribunal. Examples of such cases are given in the Guides and include those where an employee is claiming that the reason for his or her dismissal or failure to consider a request for flexible working was sex discrimination, was connected with the transfer of an undertaking, or was related to exercising a right under the Working Time Regulations 1998 SI 1998/1833. However, where cases involving matters of EU law or the Human Rights Act 1998 (HRA) are referred under the scheme, the arbitrator has the power to appoint a legal adviser who will report to the arbitrator and the parties.

In addition to the above, arbitration is not suitable for cases where there is a jurisdictional dispute between the parties – for example, whether the employee had the necessary period of service to bring the claim or whether the employee brought the claim within the required time limit. These kinds of issue cannot be contested as part of arbitration proceedings and, when agreeing to go to arbitration, both parties waive their ability to have such issues considered and are accepting that no such jurisdictional issue is in dispute. It is likely that where there is a jurisdictional point, employers will simply not agree to arbitration because they will want to 'kill off' the claim before it gets past first base.

3.134 As regards unfair dismissal, many constructive dismissal cases are not appropriate for this forum unless the employer agrees that there has been a constructive dismissal or a tribunal has already found that there was a dismissal and the parties then decide to go to arbitration.

Also, it would not be appropriate for an employee to take a case to arbitration where he or she is claiming that the dismissal is automatically unfair. This is because the concept of automatically unfair dismissal does not apply in arbitration hearings – the arbitrator has to decide whether a dismissal was fair or unfair. Accordingly, it would be folly for an employee to lose the advantage conferred by the fact that a dismissal is deemed to be automatically unfair unless there are other good reasons to go to arbitration – for example, the employee is not confident that he or she can actually establish there was indeed a dismissal, and therefore wants to take advantage of the fact that arbitration proceedings operate on the assumption that there has been a dismissal.

3.135 Entry into the scheme
Once both parties have signed an agreement stating that they wish to go to arbitration under the scheme, the claim can no longer be heard by an employment tribunal. It is important, therefore, that all the parties involved are fully aware of the effect of referring their dispute to arbitration and know how the arbitration process works. To ensure that parties are fully informed, an agreement to go to arbitration can only be reached with the assistance of an Acas conciliator or through a settlement agreement following advice to the employee from a relevant independent adviser. The settlement agreement must

224

conform to the requirements contained in the ERA – see 'Settlement agreements' under 'Statutory requirements' above.

The agreement to go to arbitration must be in writing and must state that the parties have agreed to submit their dispute to arbitration in accordance with the Acas scheme. In doing so the parties are accepting all the provisions of the scheme, including the terms of reference, and that the arbitrator's decision is final and binding. They are also accepting the way in which the arbitration and the hearing itself, as explained in the relevant Guide, will be conducted. Suggested wording for inclusion in arbitration agreements is included in the Guides. Parties cannot in their agreements ask the arbitrator to do anything, or make any award, which is not covered by the scheme.

In agreeing to refer a dispute to arbitration under the scheme, both parties **3.136** agree to waive rights that they would otherwise have with regard to the claim. There is a special form (which is attached to the Guides) setting out the rights the parties are agreeing to waive – for example, the rights to have a public hearing and to cross-examine witnesses. Signing the waiver confirms that the parties understand and accept the arbitration process. This waiver must be signed by both parties and submitted to Acas along with an agreement to undertake arbitration. Again, this is an aspect of the scheme that might not appeal to one or both sides.

Acas must be notified within two weeks of the date on which the agreement to go to arbitration was concluded. The relevant date is the date the agreement was signed (or, if signed by different people on different dates, the date of the last signature), although to avoid delay parties should send their agreement as soon as possible. Acas will not provide a hearing under the scheme if it is notified after this period unless it was not reasonably practicable to notify Acas within the time limit.

Once the parties have agreed to go to arbitration, the employee is free to withdraw **3.137** from the arbitration process at any time by writing to either the Acas Arbitration Section or to the arbitrator (via the Acas Arbitration Section) if one has been appointed. An employee who withdraws from arbitration will not, however, be allowed to reopen the original claim to the employment tribunal, since this has been disposed of by the agreement to go to arbitration. Unlike the employee, an employer cannot unilaterally withdraw its agreement to go to arbitration.

It should also be noted that the parties may agree to settle the case and ask the arbitrator to make an award based on the terms of their settlement. However, the arbitrator will do this only if the settlement terms cover items that the arbitrator has the power to award under the scheme. Alternatively, the parties can settle the dispute on any terms they wish, in which case the employee should write to the Acas Arbitration Section or the arbitrator (via the Acas Arbitration Section) asking to have the case withdrawn.

225

3.138 Role of arbitrators

Arbitrators have two roles: to decide the claim in question and to determine remedies. When determining a claim, arbitrators will not apply strict legal tests (although they do apply EU law and the HRA). This means that an arbitrator dealing with an unfair dismissal claim will not apply the famed 'band (or range) of reasonable responses' test applicable in a tribunal, but will have regard to general principles of fairness and good conduct in employment relations – including, for example, the principles referred to in the Acas Code of Practice on Disciplinary and Grievance Procedures and the Acas Guide, 'Discipline and grievances at work'. Many employers may be put off arbitration for this reason because they often win unfair dismissal cases in employment tribunals on the basis that their decision to dismiss did not fall outside the range of responses open to an employer.

In relation to flexible working disputes, the arbitrator will decide whether to uphold the flexible working claim by having regard to the Flexible Working (Procedural Requirements) Regulations 2002 SI 2002/3207 and the Flexible Working (Eligibility, Complaints and Remedies) Regulations 2002 SI 2002/3236. He or she may also have regard to Acas's booklet, 'Flexible working and work-life balance'.

3.139 Arbitration hearing procedure

Both Guides set out a suggested standard arbitration hearing procedure, although they stress that procedures are flexible and an arbitrator may structure the procedure in any way that is appropriate in accordance with his or her general duty. A summary of the procedure:

- Stage 1: introduction – the arbitrator asks everyone present at the hearing to introduce themselves, then explains the way in which the hearing will be conducted and deals with any domestic arrangements applicable to the location such as fire instructions

- Stage 2: oral presentations – each party makes an opening statement covering the main points of his or her case and can comment on the other party's written submission. The employer usually makes a statement first

- Stage 3: discussion of the issues – the arbitrator questions the parties. The party to whom the question is directed may respond personally or call upon anyone accompanying him or her to respond. The arbitrator also seeks views on remedy if the dismissal is found to be unfair and asks for information that helps to calculate any award of compensation

- Stage 4: closing statements – the parties may make a final statement of the main points supporting their case. The arbitrator does not announce his or her decision at the hearing.

226

In unfair dismissal cases, an employee may apply for reinstatement, re-engagement **3.140** or compensation – the calculation of which is analogous to tribunal awards.

Where the arbitrator decides to uphold a flexible working claim, he or she may, after taking account of the employee's wishes, order reconsideration of the request for flexible working. The arbitrator can also award compensation of an amount it considers just and equitable, having regard to the parties' conduct, subject to a maximum of eight weeks' pay. The remedies and compensation which an arbitrator can award are the same as those in tribunal proceedings.

Limited right of appeal
3.141

An arbitrator's award is binding. There are very limited grounds for challenging an award. Challenges can only be made on the ground of 'substantive jurisdiction' or serious irregularity, and parties cannot appeal against an arbitrator's award on points of law except in cases where EU law or the Human Rights Act 1998 are relevant.

'Substantive jurisdiction' covers any issue as to the validity of the arbitration agreement and the application of the scheme to the dispute, the way in which the arbitrator was appointed, or the matters which have been submitted to arbitration in accordance with the arbitration agreement. Challenges should be made to the High Court or Central London County Court within 28 days of the date the award was despatched to the party by Acas.

Challenges in respect of the conduct of the arbitrator, the proceedings or the **3.142** award can only be made on the ground of serious irregularity which has caused or will cause substantial injustice to the party making the challenge. Such challenges concern the way in which the dispute was determined rather than the end result itself. Again, challenges should be made to the High Court or Central London County Court within 28 days of the date the award was despatched to the party by Acas.

Where a point of EU law or a matter under the HRA has been considered by the arbitrator, a party may appeal to the High Court or Central London County Court on a question of law arising out of an arbitrator's award. As with the challenges above, a time limit of 28 days applies.

Although the limited right to appeal means that there is a quicker finality of outcome for the parties, this very finality may well deter a lot of people from going to arbitration in the first place.

Judicial mediation
3.143

Another alternative means of resolving employment disputes is for disputing parties to be brought together for judicial mediation during the course of employment tribunal proceedings. The Employment Tribunals Service's judicial

227

mediation scheme – which began in June 2006 as a 12-month pilot in three employment tribunals (Newcastle, Birmingham and London Central) – has been available throughout England, Wales and Scotland since 2009. Details of the operation of the scheme in England and Wales can be found in the Presidential Guidance on 'General Case Management', published on 13 March 2014. The Law Society has also produced a practice note, which explains the benefits of the scheme for both claimants and respondents. However, it is important to stress that judicial mediation is not offered free of charge. Article 4(3) of the Employment Tribunals and the Employment Appeal Tribunal Fees Order 2013 SI 2013/1893 introduced a fee of £600 on 29 July 2013, which is payable by the respondent on the date specified in the notice accompanying the notification of listing for judicial mediation. It may well be the case that the fee will deter parties from considering judicial mediation altogether. This was the view taken by Lord Justice Underhill in his letter accompanying the publication of the Tribunal Rules where he took the opportunity to express the strong view that the proposal (as it then was) to charge a fee for judicial mediation was 'likely to be a powerful disincentive to its use'. The fees regime is discussed in Chapter 19, 'Fees'.

Cases suitable for judicial mediation are generally identified by the employment judge at a preliminary hearing - rule 53(1)(e). The parties are then informed of the availability of this type of dispute resolution at the hearing and their interest, or lack of it, is recorded. If the parties identify a willingness to participate in judicial mediation, the case is passed to the Regional Employment Judge, who determines whether the case is suitable. An important factor in assessing suitability is whether there is an ongoing employment relationship. If the case is selected for judicial mediation, the parties are informed and the dates for meetings under the scheme agreed. At the same time, any case management orders in respect of any hearings that have already been made are stayed. As with all mediation, the mediator remains neutral and helps the parties to reach their own settlement but does not make a decision about the case or give opinions.

3.144 Regulation 11(1)(b) of the Employment Tribunals (Constitution and Rules of Procedure) Regulations 2013 SI 2013/1237 provides that the President of Employment Tribunals may issue a practice direction and may permit a judge to act as mediator in a case even if he or she has been selected to decide matters in that case. However, the Presidential Guidance states that the employment judge who mediates will play no further role in the case should it proceed to a hearing.

3.145 ## Taxation of payments on settlement

Where the parties have reached a valid settlement, either with the help of Acas or by entering into a settlement agreement, the tax treatment of any payment to the employee needs to be considered. There is a widespread misconception that contracting-out payments made on the termination of employment are automatically subject to a tax exemption of £30,000. However, the tax position in relation to such payments is not always so clear cut.

The relevant employment taxation provisions are contained in the Income Tax (Earnings and Pensions) Act 2003 (ITEPA). As a general rule, earnings derived from employment are liable to income tax under S.6 of the Act. Taxable earnings are defined in S.62 and include an employee's salary, benefits in kind and any other emolument paid in return for services rendered by the employee by virtue of his or her employment.

Most payments received by employees on the ending of their employment will **3.146** be taxed as earnings under S.62 ITEPA. However, settlement payments are paid upon termination of the employee's contract of employment. As settlements are separate from the employment contract and deal only with the termination of employment (by, for example, retirement, redundancy, dismissal, death, resignation and so forth), payments and benefits made in respect of them generally fall within the scope of S.401 ITEPA, which applies to payments and benefits not chargeable to income tax under any other provision of the Act that are received in consideration or in consequence of the termination of employment. Subject to some minor exceptions, payments and benefits covered by S.401 are charged – under S.403 – as employment income, but only to the extent that they exceed £30,000.

Section 401 ITEPA has the effect of bringing almost any kind of payment or benefit that might be paid on an *ex gratia* (non-contractual) basis as compensation for loss of office or employment within its scope. So, for example, a payment under a settlement agreement or Acas-conciliated agreement made wholly in respect of a claim of unfair dismissal or sex or race discrimination will be chargeable to tax under S.401 (and subject to the £30,000 exemption). If the total sum of all those elements of a termination package that are taxable under S.401 exceeds £30,000, then the excess will be taxed at the employee's marginal rate of tax – i.e. as if it were the 'top slice' of the employee's income for that tax year. A termination payment chargeable to tax under S.401 is also subject to the PAYE Regulations. Accordingly, an employer must deduct tax from any sum given to the employee on termination of employment once any exemptions and relief have been taken into account.

Although S.401 will apply to the majority of settlement packages, there may be **3.147** parts of that package that will attract tax liability in the normal way. In Carter v Wadman 1946 28 TC 41, CA, for instance, it was held that part of a £2,000 settlement, which was alleged to be wholly compensation for loss of office, was chargeable to tax under what is now S.62 because it satisfied a right to remuneration in the employee's contract, which had been met by the provision that the agreement was 'in full and final settlement of all claims'. Accordingly, it is necessary to consider whether any contractual entitlements have crystallised in order to see whether there are any charges under sections other than S.401, such

229

as a contractual payment in lieu of notice. Similarly, a specific payment that the employee receives in consideration for agreeing to enter into new restrictive covenants curtailing future employment or business activities are also chargeable to tax under S.62. This is the effect of S.225 ITEPA, which treats any payment relating to restrictive covenants as earnings from the employment.

By contrast, statutory redundancy payments made under the ERA are specifically exempted from general earnings under S.62 by S.309. However, such payments fall within S.401 and are chargeable to tax under that section, subject to the £30,000 exemption. Similarly, a payment under a contractual redundancy scheme will usually be tax-free so long as it is less than £30,000. This is the result of the House of Lords' decision in Mairs v Haughey 1993 66 TC 273, HL, that such a payment is not taxable under S.19 ICTA (now S.62 ITEPA) as an emolument, since it is not paid for services rendered but rather as a means of compensating an employee for not being able to continue to earn a living from the former employment. However, in order to secure the tax advantages of S.401, all redundancy payments – statutory or contractual – must be made on account of genuine redundancy only.

3.148 Her Majesty's Customs and Revenue has also confirmed that the existence of a 'repayment clause' in a settlement agreement will not normally mean that payments made under the agreement are susceptible to tax. Such clauses require the employee to repay some or all of the agreed payment if he or she subsequently litigates in respect of the employment (see 'Settlement agreements – common terms of settlement agreements' above).

It is therefore good practice to break a settlement package down and indicate clearly what each part is intended to cover. This will ensure that each element is taxed appropriately. Most settlement agreements contain a tax indemnity clause in the employer's favour, so if any future tax liability arises, it will fall on the employee. Where the package is made up of some elements which are taxable as earnings under S.62 ITEPA and some which are intended to compensate for loss of employment under S.401, then the £30,000 threshold applies in respect of the S.401 elements only. For example, if an employer pays an employee a termination payment comprising £5,000 as a contractual payment in lieu of notice and a further £34,000 by way of ex gratia payment for loss of employment, the taxable sum would be £9,000, comprising the £5,000 payment in lieu, which is chargeable under S.62, and the balance of £4,000 – after the £30,000 exemption has been taken into account – on the compensation payment, which is taxable under S.401.

Note that the Office of Tax Simplification is currently looking at how the tax treatment of termination payments can be simplified.

Appendix – cases to which duty to conciliate applies

There is statutory provision for Acas conciliation in most employment protection and discrimination cases. S.18(1) ETA lists the proceedings, referred to as 'relevant proceedings', in which Acas has a legal duty to conciliate. These are:

- unfair dismissal for a range of reasons (Part X ERA)

- sex discrimination (S.120 EqA)

- equal pay (Ss.120 and 127 EqA)

- race discrimination (S.120 EqA)

- disability discrimination (S.120 EqA)

- sexual orientation discrimination (S.120 EqA)

- religion or belief discrimination (S.120 EqA)

- age discrimination (S.120 EqA)

- flexible working (Ss.47E and 80H ERA)

- parental leave (S.80(1) ERA)

- time off to care for dependants (S.57A ERA)

- written statement of employment particulars (Ss.1 and 4 ERA)

- itemised pay statements (S.8 ERA)

- guarantee payments (S.28 ERA)

- time off and remuneration for pension scheme trustees (Ss.58 and 59 ERA)

- time off and remuneration for employee representatives (Ss.61 and 62 ERA)

- time off and remuneration for young persons to study or train (Ss.47A, 63A and 63B ERA) (note that, since 28 June 2013, these provisions only apply in Wales and Scotland)

- remuneration while suspended on medical grounds (S.64 ERA)

- remuneration while suspended on maternity grounds (S.68 ERA)

- remuneration where supply of an agency worker to a hirer ended on maternity grounds (S.68C ERA)

- right to be offered alternative work while suspended on maternity grounds (S.67 ERA)

231

- right to be offered alternative work where supply of an agency worker to a hirer ended on maternity grounds (S.68B ERA)

- detriment in connection with jury service (S.43M ERA)

- detriment in health and safety cases (S.44 ERA)

- detriment in connection with Sunday shop working (S.45 ERA)

- detriment in connection with working time rights (S.45A ERA)

- right of pension trustees not to suffer detriment (S.46 ERA)

- right of employee representatives not to suffer detriment (S.47 ERA)

- detriment in connection with study leave or training (S.47A ERA) (Wales and Scotland only)

- detriment for making a protected disclosure (S.47B ERA)

- detriment for family and domestic leave reasons (S.47C ERA)

- detriment in connection with working tax credit (S.47D ERA)

- detriment in connection with flexible working (S.47E ERA)

- detriment for refusing offer to become employee shareholder (S.47G ERA)

- time off for public duties (S.50 ERA)

- time off and remuneration in the event of redundancy to look for work or arrange training (Ss.52 and 53 ERA)

- right to request study and training (Ss.47F and 63F(4)–(6) ERA) (note that the right currently only applies to employers with 250 or more employees)

- redundancy payments (S.135 ERA)

- compensation for loss of employment approved by the Treasury or the Minister for the Civil Service (S.177 ERA)

- time off and remuneration for ante-natal care (Ss.55–56 ERA)

- time off and remuneration for ante-natal care for agency workers (Ss.57ZA–ZB ERA)

- written statement of reasons for dismissal (S.92 ERA)

- unauthorised deductions from wages (Ss.13 and 18(1) ERA)

- unlawful payments to employer (Ss.15 and 21(1) ERA)

- unjustifiable discipline by a trade union (S.64 TULR(C)A)

- deduction of unauthorised union subscriptions (S.68 TULR(C)A)

- exemption from, or objection to, contributing to political fund (S.86 TULR(C)A)

- refusal of employment or service of employment agency on grounds related to union membership (Ss.137 and 138 TULR(C)A)

- inducements relating to union membership or activities and collective bargaining (Ss.145A and 145B TULR(C)A)

- detriment on grounds related to trade union membership or activities (S.146 TULR(C)A)

- time off for trade union duties and activities (Ss.168–170 TULR(C)A)

- right not to be excluded or expelled from a trade union (S.174 TULR(C)A)

- duty to consult employee representatives about proposed redundancies (S.188 TULR(C)A)

- duty to comply with requirements in relation to the election of employee representatives for the purposes of collective redundancy consultation (S.188A TULR(C)A)

- entitlement under protective awards (S.190 TULR(C)A)

- various rights in connection with union recognition and collective bargaining (S.70B and para 156, Sch A1 TULR(C)A)

- breach of contract rights (S.3 ETA)

- right to be accompanied at a grievance or disciplinary hearing (S.10 of the Employment Relations Act 1999)

- various rights in connection with the NMWA, including right not to suffer detriment (Ss.11, 19D(1)(a) and 24 NMWA)

- right not to suffer detriment in relation to automatic pension enrolment (S.55 of the Pensions Act 2008)

- failure to notify employee liability information on a transfer of an undertaking (Reg 12(7) TUPE)

- failure to inform and consult employee representatives on a transfer of an undertaking (Reg 16(1) TUPE)

- right to paid time off for representatives of employee safety (Reg 4(2) of the Safety Representatives and Safety Committees Regulations 1977 SI 1977/500 and Reg 7(1)(b) and (2) of and Schedule 1 to the Health and Safety (Consultation with Employees) Regulations 1996 SI 1996/1513)

- various rights set out in Reg 30 of the Working Time Regulations

- various rights set out in Regs 29 and 33 of the ICE Regulations

233

- various rights set out in Regs 27 and 32 of the TICE Regulations

- right to be accompanied at a meeting to discuss a flexible working application (Reg 14(2) and (4) of the Flexible Working (Procedural Requirements) Regulations 2002 SI 2002/3207)

- right not to suffer less favourable treatment or detriment in connection with rights contained in the Part-time Workers Regulations (Regs 5(1) and 7(2))

- various rights set out in the Fixed-term Employees Regulations, including right not to suffer less favourable treatment or detriment (Regs 3, 6(2) and 9)

- right to paid annual leave for persons employed or engaged on board a sea-going UK ship (Reg 12(1) and (2) of the Merchant Shipping (Hours of Work) Regulations 2002 SI 2002/2125)

- right to rest periods and paid annual leave for workers employed on ships operating services for passengers or goods (Reg 18 of the Merchant Shipping Regulations)

- right to rest periods and paid annual leave for workers employed on fishing vessels (Reg 19 of the Fishing Vessels Regulations)

- various rights set out in the Civil Aviation (Working Time) Regulations 2004 SI 2004/756, including rights to paid annual leave and free health assessments (Regs 4, 5(1), (4), 7(1) and 7(2)(b))

- right to time off and right not to suffer detriment for employee representatives in European Public Limited-Liability Companies (Regs 28 and 32 of the EPLLC Regulations)

- right to time off and right not to suffer detriment for employee representatives consulting on proposed changes to occupational and personal pension schemes (paras 4 and 8 of the Schedule to the OPPS Regulations)

- right to time off and right not to suffer detriment for employee representatives in European Cooperative Societies (Regs 30 and 34 of the ECS Regulations)

- right to time off and right not to suffer detriment for employees participating in cross-border company mergers (Regs 45 and 51 of the Companies (Cross-Border Mergers) Regulations)

- right to rest periods for workers assigned to cross-border train services (Reg 17 of the Cross-border Railway Services Regulations)

- right to written statement of particulars of office and to itemised statement of stipend for ecclesiastical office holders (Regs 3, 6 and 8 of the Ecclesiastical Officer (Terms of Service) Regulations 2009 SI 2009/2108)

- right not to be refused employment, the services of an employment agency or to suffer detriment for a reason that relates to a prohibited list (Regs 5, 6 and 9 of the Blacklists Regulations)

- rights of agency workers in relation to basic working and employment conditions, pay between assignments (if applicable), access to employment, collective facilities and amenities and the right not to suffer detriment (Regs 5, 10, 12, 13 and 17(2) of the Agency Workers Regulations)

- right to be accompanied at a meeting to discuss request in relation to study or training (Reg 16(2)–(3) and (5) of the Employee Study and Training (Procedural Requirements) Regulations 2010 SI 2010/155.

4 Starting tribunal proceedings

Preliminary considerations

Early conciliation

Making a claim

Completing the claim form

Processing the claim form

Withdrawals

Appendix – employment tribunal offices for personal presentation

Nearly all cases that reach a hearing at an employment tribunal are begun by a **4.1** claimant – usually an employee or ex-employee – submitting a claim form known as an ET1 to the employment tribunal. However, before a claimant reaches the stage of completing a claim form and sending it off, there are a number of important preliminary matters that he or she should consider. We deal with these first before looking at the claim form in detail.

Preliminary considerations
4.2

Obviously, the claimant has to consider the nature of his or her complaint – i.e. what statutory or contractual right, or rights, he or she is relying upon, and what infringement of that right, or those rights, might form the basis of a complaint to the tribunal (see Chapter 2, 'Tribunals' jurisdiction', under 'Types of claim heard by tribunals', and the Appendix to that chapter, for a list of the claims that tribunals may hear).

Potential claimants who are not (or not yet) in receipt of legal advice may find information to assist them in deciding whether or not they have a claim from any of a number of freely available sources: online on the 'Working, jobs and pensions' page at www.gov.uk or in person from a Jobcentre Plus office; on the 'Work' page at www.adviceguide.org.uk or in person at a Citizens Advice Bureau; from Acas, either using the helpline or the 'Advice and guidance' page of the website; from any trade union of which the potential claimant is a member; or, in relation to discrimination issues, from the Equality Advisory Support Service (EASS). (Note, however, that the EASS, while it can explain legal rights and remedies and help a claimant prepare and lodge a claim, cannot provide legal advice or representation.)

4.3 There are a number of matters the claimant or his or her representative must then consider before bringing a claim or claims, or engaging in pre-claim conciliation (see 'Early conciliation' below). Some of these, such as the appropriate time limit for bringing the claim(s) or length of qualifying service, will usually be readily ascertainable. Others, such as whether the claimant falls within the territorial reach of the claim, will not necessarily be so obvious, but the possibility of any issues arising should be considered at this stage so as to anticipate any arguments the respondent or tribunal may later raise that might have the effect of excluding the claimant from bringing his or her claim, or of reducing his or her bargaining power in pre-claim settlement negotiations.

4.4 **Qualifying service.** Some types of claim may only be brought where a claimant has been employed for a particular period of time. For example, to claim unfair dismissal, the claimant must have been employed for at least two years up to the effective date of termination; for a discrimination claim, on the other hand, no particular length of qualifying service is required. A full list of the periods of continuous employment relevant to particular statutory claims is set out in the Appendix to IDS Employment Law Handbook, 'Continuity of Employment' (2012), which also considers the rules governing how qualifying service is computed.

4.5 **Time limits.** A further preliminary consideration is the time limit applicable to the claim in question. The claimant or his or her representative needs to ascertain the date by which the claim form must be received by the employment tribunal in order for it to be validly submitted. Note that time limits may in certain cases be extended while any early (pre-claim) conciliation procedure is complied with – see Chapter 3, 'Conciliation, settlements and ADR', under 'Early conciliation – impact of EC on time limits', and also below, under 'Early conciliation'. Where such extensions do not apply, the claimant or his or her representative must allow extra time for any applicable early conciliation procedure to be pursued. Time limits are discussed in detail in Chapter 5, 'Time limits'.

4.6 **Fees.** Consideration must be given at an early stage to the level of fees that are applicable to the prospective claim, and whether the claimant can afford them (bearing in mind that a further fee becomes payable if the claim progresses to a final hearing), and, if not, what evidence he or she will need to provide in order to apply for remission of fees. The fee, or an application for remission, must be provided with the claim form, otherwise the claim will be rejected under rule 11 of the Tribunal Rules (set out in Schedule 1 to the Employment Tribunals (Constitution and Rules of Procedure) Regulations 2013 SI 2013/1237 (see 'Processing the claim form' below), and time will continue to run in relation to the time limit relevant to the claim. Fees and remission are discussed in detail in Chapter 19, 'Fees'.

4.7 **Employment status.** A potential claimant should consider whether his or her employment status is such that he or she is entitled to bring the claim. This differs depending on the nature of the claim. Most employment rights attach to 'employees', so if the claimant is self-employed, he or she will be unable to claim. However, other rights extend to a wider category of claimant: 'employee' for the purpose of discrimination claims under the Equality Act 2010 has a broader definition than that applicable to unfair dismissal, for example, under the Employment Rights Act 1996 (ERA); and some rights, such as those under the Part-time Workers (Prevention of Less Favourable Treatment) Regulations 2000 SI 2000/1551, attach to a wider category still of 'workers'. In addition, some categories of employee or worker are excluded from bringing certain claims. For example, certain rights under the ERA do not apply to mariners or police officers – Ss.199 and 200 ERA. Such exclusions, and the employment status relevant to particular statutory claims, are discussed in the IDS Employment Law Handbook dealing with the substantive law relating to different employment rights. As the rules differ relating to different claims, each should be considered separately.

Territorial issues. Where a claimant works or worked overseas, thought should **4.8** be given as to whether the employment tribunal has jurisdiction to hear his or her claims, and to whether the claimant falls within the territorial reach of the claim in question. These matters are discussed in Chapter 2, 'Tribunals' jurisdiction', under 'Territorial limitations – international jurisdiction' and 'Territorial limitations – territorial reach'.

Furthermore, some claimants may need to consider whether England and Wales or Scotland is the appropriate forum for their claim. In limited circumstances, the claimant may have a choice. For example, where there is more than one respondent, and at least one of them resides or carries on business in England and Wales, a claimant will be able to bring a claim in England and Wales even if he or she otherwise worked in Scotland, under rule 8(2)(a) of the Tribunal Rules; but he or she could alternatively bring the claim in Scotland under rule 8(3)(b) or (c), on the basis that an act or omission complained of took place in Scotland, or the claim relates to a contract under which the work has been performed in Scotland – see Chapter 2, 'Tribunals' jurisdiction', in the section 'Territorial limitations', under 'International jurisdiction – jurisdiction of employment tribunals in England and Wales and in Scotland'. However, care should be taken. As the guidance booklet 'Making a claim to an employment tribunal' (T420) issued by Her Majesty's Courts and Tribunals Service indicates, if the claimant submits a claim to the employment tribunal in England and Wales, but it turns out that that tribunal does not have jurisdiction over the claim, the claim will not be accepted, and the same is true for claims submitted to the employment tribunal in Scotland. If the claim is not accepted in one jurisdiction, time will continue to run for the purpose of the time limit for bringing the claim. See 'Making a claim – the claim form (ET1)' below, under 'Presenting the claim form', for further discussion of how to ensure presentation of claims in the appropriate jurisdiction.

239

4.9 Contractual claims: choice of forum. Although employment tribunals have jurisdiction to hear contractual claims, they may only award damages of up to £25,000. Thus, if the potential claimant is seeking damages in excess of this sum, he or she may wish to consider whether the civil courts would be a better forum for his or her claim. See Chapter 2, 'Tribunals' jurisdiction', in the section 'Types of claim heard by tribunals', under 'Contractual claims – choice of court or tribunal', for a discussion of this and other factors relevant to the decision of where to bring contractual claims.

4.10 Insolvency. If the potential claimant or respondent is insolvent, this is likely to affect how a claim is brought: see 'Leave to pursue claims where employer or claimant is insolvent' below.

4.11 Leave to pursue claims where employer or claimant is insolvent
Special statutory provisions applicable to the right of creditors to pursue legal redress against companies in insolvent administration or in the process of being wound up may affect the freedom of employees to bring tribunal proceedings.

4.12 Administration. Paragraph 43(6) of Schedule B1 to the Insolvency Act 1986 provides that where a company is in administration, 'no legal process (including legal proceedings, execution, distress and diligence) may be instituted or continued against the company or property of the company except... with the consent of the administrator, or... with the permission of the court'. An employment tribunal is regarded as a 'court' for these purposes, so that proceedings before a tribunal can only be commenced or continued by obtaining prior consent or leave. Failure to do so, however, will not render the claim a nullity. In those circumstances, the appropriate course for the tribunal is to stay the claim while the employee applies for the appropriate consent from the administrator and/or leave of the High Court – Carr v British International Helicopters Ltd (in administration) 1994 ICR 18, EAT.

In Unite the Union and ors v Sayers Confectioners Ltd (in administration) EAT 0513/08 the claimants requested the consent of the administrators of the respondent to their bringing proceedings. The administrators indicated that such consent was likely to be forthcoming, but as it had not been provided by early September 2008, and the statutory time limits were due to expire on 8 September, the claimants presented their claims in the employment tribunal before obtaining the administrators' consent. An employment judge refused to accept the claims on this basis, but the EAT overturned its decision. While acknowledging that it was not bound by the decision in Carr (above), the EAT considered that the reasoning in that case was convincing, especially in the light of evidence that it was normal practice for tribunals to accept such claims but to stay them pending a decision by the administrators. The only potential justification for a different approach being taken from that endorsed in Carr might be if there had been a material change in the Tribunal Rules to that effect.

Compulsory liquidation. A similar provision applies by virtue of S.130(2) of **4.13** the Insolvency Act 1986 to restrict the right of persons to commence actions against a company in compulsory liquidation. Such liquidation occurs by order of a court, as distinct from 'voluntary' liquidation, which occurs following a resolution of the company's members or creditors. S.130(2) provides that 'when a winding-up order has been made or a provisional liquidator has been appointed, no action or proceeding shall be proceeded with or commenced against the company or its property, except by leave of the court'. Although no cases have arisen on the issue of whether tribunal proceedings come within S.130(2), it is almost certain that employees would have to obtain the leave of the High Court before commencing or continuing tribunal proceedings against any company which is for the time being subject to a compulsory winding-up order.

Receivership and voluntary liquidation. The position is different in the case **4.14** of receivership and voluntary winding up. In general, the appointment of an administrative receiver or receiver/manager tends to have little effect on tribunal proceedings, since there is no rule requiring a claimant to obtain the consent of the receiver or court to initiate or continue proceedings against the company in respect of whom the receiver has been appointed. In the case of administrative receivership, the title of any tribunal proceedings will, however, be altered by the tribunal to include the words '(In Receivership)' after the respondent company's name. This reflects the fact that the administrative receiver is appointed to take control of all of the insolvent company's assets and, as such, becomes the agent of the company – see S.44 Insolvency Act 1986. The respondent will continue to be the company rather than the administrative receiver, unless he or she is regarded as having 'adopted' the contracts of employment of the company's employees, in which case the receiver becomes the employer and so should be joined to the proceedings as the respondent – Powdrill and anor v Watson and anor and other cases 1995 ICR 1100, HL.

In the case of a voluntary – as opposed to a compulsory – winding up or liquidation, the resolution to wind up is made by either the creditors or the members of the company, and, in either case, the appointment of a liquidator results in his or her replacing the directors with regard to authority over the company. Although a court has power to stay proceedings under its general power to issue directions under S.112 of the 1986 Act, unless this happens the appointment of a liquidator in a voluntary winding up will have little effect on tribunal proceedings, other than that the title of the proceedings will be altered to include the words '(In Voluntary Liquidation)' after the respondent company's name and the address for service will be changed to that of the liquidator.

Personal bankruptcy. Turning our attention from corporate insolvency to the **4.15** situation where it is the employee who is personally insolvent, under S.306 of the Insolvency Act 1986 the estate of a bankrupt vests in his or her trustee in

241

bankruptcy at the moment of the trustee's appointment. A bankrupt's estate is defined as including a 'thing in action' such as a right to bring or pursue legal proceedings – Ss.283(1) and 436. Where the right to bring legal proceedings vests in the trustee, the bankrupt will be precluded from pursuing it. This is the case where a claim is for property. Where, however, a claim is personal in nature, the bankrupt retains the right to pursue legal proceedings in connection with it. Personal claims are, in the words of Mr Justice Erle in Beckham v Drake 1849 2 HL Cas 579, HL, ones in which 'the damages are to be estimated by immediate reference to pain felt by the bankrupt in respect of his body, mind or character, and without reference to his rights of property'.

In Ord v Upton 2000 Ch 352, CA, it was held that a hybrid claim – i.e. one in which both monetary damages and personal relief are sought – vests in a trustee. However, in Grady v Prison Service 2003 ICR 753, CA, the Court of Appeal distinguished Ord v Upton and held that a bankrupt employee has standing to pursue a claim of unfair dismissal since a claim for reinstatement or re-engagement consequent on an unfair dismissal claim – and indeed, a significant element of the compensation which can be awarded in lieu of these – is not a 'thing in action' of the kind that forms part of a bankrupt's estate and therefore vests in the trustee in bankruptcy, but a cause of action that is personal to the employee. The principal basis for the distinction in Grady's case was that the substance of the claim was for personal relief, a point highlighted by the order in which the tribunal was required to consider the appropriate form of remedy. The remedies for unfair dismissal are reinstatement, re-engagement and compensation, and if the claimant seeks all three in the alternative the tribunal has to consider them in that order.

4.16   In Khan v Trident Safeguards Ltd and ors 2004 ICR 1591, CA, the Court of Appeal considered whether a bankrupt's claims of race discrimination and victimisation vested in the trustee in bankruptcy. Discrimination proceedings are of a different nature to unfair dismissal claims. In the words of Lady Justice Arden: 'The primary relief is a declaration as to the rights of the parties, and also an order for compensation, which may include but is not limited to compensation for injury to feelings.' A race discrimination claim is, accordingly, a hybrid claim which in principle vests in the trustee in bankruptcy. The crucial issue was whether the discrimination and victimisation appeal before the EAT could be amended so as to limit the relief claimed to that of a personal nature. This would prevent the claim being hybrid in nature and vesting in the trustee, thus allowing the bankrupt to pursue the appeal him or herself.

The Court of Appeal held by a majority that a bankrupt can limit his or her claim for relief to a declaration and compensation for injury to feelings, omitting any claim for damages for pecuniary loss and thereby changing the hybrid claim to a personal one. This principle is presumably not restricted to race discrimination cases and applies to all discrimination claims. Although the

242

issue in the Khan case was whether or not the claimant could pursue an appeal against the tribunal's decision that he had not been racially discriminated against, Lord Justice Wall LJ's judgment makes it clear that the same principles would have applied to the tribunal claim itself since an appeal is a continuation of a claim once it has failed at first instance.

Another interesting point about this case is that the claimant had submitted the **4.17** petition for bankruptcy himself after his claims were dismissed by the tribunal and he was ordered to pay the respondent's costs, which he could not do. Nevertheless, he wished to proceed to an appellate court. Other claimants may find themselves in similar circumstances and it is likely that tribunals will hear more claims in the future where bankrupt claimants wish to pursue court action in their own names in respect of personal relief.

Considering the merits

4.18

The next step is for the claimant and his or her advisers to consider the merits of the case: how likely is the claimant to succeed in his or her claim(s), and is it worth pursuing? This initial assessment may be difficult for a lay person to make alone, so it is advisable for a potential claimant to obtain advice. Information, advice and representation can be obtained from the following sources:

- a trade union (where the claimant is a member)

- a law centre or Citizens Advice Bureau (www.adviceguide.org.uk in England and Wales, or, in Scotland, www.cas.org.uk)

- a solicitor (a directory of solicitors, known as 'Find a Solicitor', is available from the Law Society of England and Wales)

- where the claimant wishes to apply for a redundancy payment, the Redundancy Payment helpline

- in respect of a national minimum wage claim, the Pay and Work Rights helpline

- Acas.

Information on representation and the forms of free legal advice that may be available to claimants in employment tribunals can be found in Chapter 12, 'The hearing'.

There are, in addition, some statutory means by which a potential claimant can **4.19** obtain important information to help him or her decide whether or not to present a complaint:

- in potential discrimination claims, the claimant can use the statutory questionnaire procedure under S.138 of the Equality Act 2010, asking the employer to give an initial response to allegations of discrimination. However, this statutory procedure is to be repealed from 6 April 2014.

243

Although a complainant will still be able to ask questions of the respondent and a court or tribunal will still be able to draw adverse inferences from a refusal to respond or from evasive answers, the repeal of its statutory foundation means that the questionnaire procedure is liable to be of lesser use in obtaining information to enable the claimant to decide whether or not to bring a claim in the first place – see IDS Employment Law Handbook, 'Discrimination at Work' (2012), Chapter 33, 'Proving discrimination', under 'Requesting information and disclosure of evidence', for details

- in potential claims of unfair dismissal, the claimant can request a written statement of the reasons for dismissal. An employer must reply within 14 days of the request and any such reply is admissible in evidence. Provided the employee has at least two years' continuous service (except in the case of dismissal during pregnancy or maternity or adoption leave, in respect of which no continuous service condition applies), the employer's failure to furnish such a statement can lead to an award of two weeks' pay and a declaration as to the reason for dismissal – Ss.92 and 93 ERA. See IDS Employment Law Handbook, 'Unfair Dismissal' (2010), Chapter 21, 'Written reasons for dismissal', under 'Preamble' and 'Entitlement', for more details

- the claimant can engage in early conciliation using the Acas conciliation service as a means of obtaining the initial response of the employer to his or her complaint, as well as ascertaining whether or not the claim can be resolved without recourse to litigation – S.18A Employment Tribunals Act 1996. In any event, before a claim may be brought, the assistance of Acas must usually be sought with a view to pre-claim conciliation – see 'Early conciliation' below. (However, note that when employers and employees are involved in a dispute, any written or oral communications between them that comprise genuine efforts to resolve the matter will not generally be admitted in evidence in tribunal or court proceedings under the 'without prejudice' rule – see Chapter 13, 'Evidence', under 'Evidence of settlement negotiations – "without prejudice" negotiations').

4.20 It is important to remember that at this stage a claimant is undertaking only a preliminary assessment of the grounds of his or her claim and the prospects of its success. His or her opinion may well alter if and when the claim proceeds. This is especially so once the employer has entered a response setting out the grounds (if any) on which the claim is to be resisted. It is, however, important to carry out an initial assessment of the merits because a manifestly weak claim is likely to be dismissed, and the claimant who brought it may then become liable to pay costs for bringing a claim 'vexatiously, abusively, disruptively or otherwise unreasonably' or for bringing a claim that had 'no reasonable prospect of success' under rule 76(1) of the Tribunal Rules – see Chapter 20, 'Costs and penalties', under 'Costs'.

By considering the initial matters outlined above, the claimant should reach a position from which he or she can decide whether or not to proceed. However, if the choice is made to go ahead, the claimant must, with certain exceptions, inform Acas of his or her complaint under the 'early conciliation' procedure before he or she may start the claim. This mandatory procedure is discussed under 'Early conciliation' below, and the process of starting the claim under 'Making a claim'.

Early conciliation
4.21

From 6 April 2014, a claimant will not normally be allowed to bring a claim in an employment tribunal unless he or she has informed Acas of the complaint, thereby giving Acas the opportunity to try to resolve the case by 'early conciliation' (EC). This process, including the extent of the obligations it imposes upon Acas conciliation officers, is discussed in detail in Chapter 3, 'Conciliation, settlements and ADR', under 'Early conciliation'. Here, we summarise precisely what this procedure requires of the claimant as a pre-condition of bringing a claim.

The EC scheme is set out in Ss.18A and 18B of the Employment Tribunals Act 1996 (ETA), and in the Early Conciliation Rules of Procedure ('the EC Rules') contained in the Schedule to the Employment Tribunals (Early Conciliation: Exemptions and Rules of Procedure) Regulations 2014 SI 2014/254 ('the EC Regulations'). Broadly, the procedure involves the following stages:

- the potential claimant informs Acas that he or she intends to bring a claim

- if the claimant agrees to EC, Acas instructs a conciliation officer

- the Acas conciliation officer has one month to attempt to resolve the dispute between the parties, which may be extended, if the parties agree, for up to two weeks

- if settlement is not reached, or if either party decides at any point not to continue to participate in conciliation, the Acas conciliation officer issues the claimant with an EC certificate

- the prospective claimant may then bring the claim.

Proceedings in respect of which EC applies
4.22

The statutory requirement on claimants to contact Acas before bringing a claim is contained in S.18A(1) ETA. This provides that before a prospective claimant may bring 'relevant proceedings', he or she must provide certain information about it to Acas. 'Relevant proceedings' are those set out in S.18(1) over which Acas has power to conciliate generally – see Chapter 3, 'Conciliation, settlements and ADR', under 'Acas conciliation (COT3) agreements – when the conciliator may act'. Although the list excludes certain limited types of claim, it encompasses

245

the overwhelming majority of claims in which individual employment rights are alleged to have been infringed – see Chapter 3, under 'Early conciliation – cases to which EC requirement applies'.

However, in certain cases a claimant may bring 'relevant proceedings' – i.e. proceedings that would normally be subject to statutory conciliation – without first complying with the S.18A(1) requirement to contact Acas. These exclusions, set out in S.18A(7) read with Reg 3 of the EC Regulations, include the following:

- cases where the requirement to contact Acas is complied with by another person instituting relevant proceedings relating to the same set of facts on the same claim form (i.e. multiple claims) – S.18A(7)(a) ETA/Reg 3(1)(a) EC Regulations

- cases where proceedings that are relevant proceedings are brought in the same claim form as proceedings that are not – S.18A(7)(b)/Reg 3(1)(b)

- cases where a potential respondent to the claim has already contacted Acas to request the services of a conciliation officer, under S.18B(1) – S.18A(7)(c)/ Reg 3(1)(c)

- claims of unfair dismissal accompanied by an application for interim relief under S.128 ERA or S.161 TULR(C)A – Reg 3(1)(d)

- proceedings against the Security Service, the Secret Intelligence Service or the Government Communications Headquarters – Reg 3(1)(e).

Although, in such cases, the claimant is not obliged to contact Acas before bringing a claim, he or she may request conciliation if desired – S.18B(2).

4.23 Prescribed information in a prescribed manner
Assuming the proposed claim is caught by S.18A(1) ETA, the claimant must send 'prescribed information' to Acas in a 'prescribed manner'. This is the only mandatory aspect of the procedure: the claimant is not obliged to engage in conciliation as a precondition for bringing a claim in the employment tribunal, although he or she may do so if he or she wishes.

There are two alternative prescribed manners for providing information to Acas. The prospective claimant must either:

- submit a completed EC form to Acas in accordance with rule 2 of the EC Rules – rule 1(a), or

- telephone Acas in accordance with rule 3 – rule 1(b).

4.24 Under rule 2, an EC form must either be submitted online via the Acas website or be sent by post to the Acas address given on the form – rule 2(1). The form requires contact details for the prospective claimant and respondent – rule 2(2). However, the claimant is not obliged to provide any further details, such as of the type of claim he or she is considering bringing. Where the prospective claimant contacts Acas by telephone in accordance with rule 3, he or she must give Acas the names and addresses of the prospective claimant and respondent – rule 3(1). Acas will then insert this information onto an EC form – rule 3(2).

Whichever means is chosen to provide information to Acas, the name of only one prospective respondent may be supplied, even if there are more than one – rule 4.

Following receipt of the EC form, Acas will contact the prospective claimant. **4.25** If the claimant does not receive an acknowledgment of receipt, he or she should contact Acas as a matter of urgency, since if Acas has no record of the EC form it will not issue an EC certificate, leaving the prospective claimant unable to lodge his or her claim.

Early conciliation certificate   4.26

If either party does not wish to engage in conciliation, or if settlement is not reached within the applicable timeframe, or if the Acas conciliation officer considers that it will not be possible to settle the claim, then the Acas conciliation officer will issue an EC certificate as evidence that S.18A(1) ETA has been complied with – S.18A(4) ETA/rule 7 EC Rules. This certificate is vital where the claimant wishes to proceed with his or her claim, as he or she may not start proceedings without it in any case to which the EC requirement applies – S.18A(8). In multiple claims, the certificate is issued to the lead prospective claimant (i.e. the individual who contacted Acas under S.18A(1)). Another prospective claimant may rely upon this certificate in relation to any claim he or she has in common with the lead prospective claimant, but if his or her claim(s) differ he or she will be required to present a separate ET1 claim form to institute proceedings, and will require a separate EC certificate.

The certificate shows, among other information, the date on which Acas received the EC form in accordance with rule 2 (or the date that the prospective claimant telephoned Acas in accordance with rule 3) and the date on which the certificate was issued, and the means by which the certificate was to be sent to the prospective claimant and respondent (by e-mail or post) – rule 8. The significance of this information is that the time limit in which the claim needs to be brought may in certain cases be adjusted to take into account the EC process, where it applies. If the certificate is delivered by e-mail (which, under rule 9(2), it must be in circumstances where the prospective claimant or respondent has provided an e-mail address to Acas), it is deemed to be received by the prospective claimant on the date of sending; if it is delivered by post, it is deemed to be received in the ordinary course of post (i.e. two days after posting) – rule 9(3). For further details, see the section 'Making a claim' below, under 'The claim form (ET1) – presenting the claim form'; Chapter 3,

'Conciliation, settlements and ADR', under 'Early conciliation – impact of EC on time limits'; and Chapter 10, 'Service of notices and documents'.

4.27 The certificate also bears a unique reference number – rule 8(d). This number must be marked on the claimant's claim form as it is being completed (see 'Completing the claim form' below) to avoid the claim being rejected under rule 10 of the Tribunal Rules.

Note that where EC is started by the prospective *respondent* under S.18B(1) ETA, the EC certificate will still be issued to the prospective claimant where conciliation is unsuccessful or the prospective claimant does not want to engage with it, and the certificate will still be required before relevant proceedings may be brought. However, the time limits will not be adjusted to allow for conciliation to take place in such circumstances.

4.28 Making a claim

A claimant institutes employment tribunal proceedings by presenting a completed claim form to the employment tribunal, in accordance with the Presidential Practice Direction on the presentation of claims made under Reg 11 of the Tribunal Regulations – rule 8(1) Tribunal Rules (see Chapter 1, 'Employment tribunals', in the section 'What are employment tribunals?', under 'Employment tribunal rules – Practice Directions').

The significance of this document should not be underestimated. In Zyntek v Wickman Machine Tool Manufacturing Co Ltd EAT 340/79 Mr Justice May said: 'The [claim form] is an important document... It is the document by which the whole process embodied in the modern employment legislation is set in train. It has, as it were, the same function as a writ or summons in an ordinary civil action; or an information or a complaint in criminal proceedings; it starts the whole procedure. It must, therefore, be treated with a certain amount of respect.'

4.29 In addition to the ET1, claimants who use the printed version of the claim form must also complete and send a 'Fees and Remissions' cover sheet that accompanies the ET1. This requires details to be provided about the nature of the claim, the number of claimants and whether the claimant is intending to apply for fee remission. These details are then used to assist tribunal staff to determine whether an issuing fee is payable. If the claimant is submitting the ET1 online, the same information as is contained on the cover sheet is incorporated into the online form.

4.30 The claim form (ET1)

A claim will not be validly instituted unless it is presented on a prescribed form, known as the ET1 – rule 8(1). It is not sufficient simply to present the claim in writing. If the claim is not on a prescribed form or does not contain certain prescribed information, the tribunal must reject it under rule 10 of the Tribunal Rules – see 'Rejection of claims' below.

A 'claim' is defined in rule 1 as 'any proceedings before an employment tribunal making a complaint' – which, in turn, can be anything referred to as a claim, complaint, reference, application or appeal in legislation conferring jurisdiction on the employment tribunal. However, it is *not* necessary to use a prescribed form where:

- proceedings are referred to the tribunal by a court – Reg 12(2)(a) Tribunal Regulations

- the tribunal will be exercising its appellate jurisdiction (e.g. appeals against levy assessments for industrial training boards, or appeals against health and safety improvement or prohibition notices) – Reg 12(2)(b); or

- the proceedings are brought by an employer in relation to statements of employment particulars under S.11 ERA – Reg 12(2)(c).

4.31 The prescribed claim form ET1 is available in paper format at the back of the HMCTS guidance booklet 'Making a claim to an employment tribunal' (T420), to be completed and sent by post or in person, or to download from the employment tribunals website, also to be completed and sent by post or in person. Alternatively, it may be completed using the online form submission service provided by HMCTS, accessible at www.employmenttribunals.service. gov.uk. The HMCTS guidance booklets are available at local tribunal offices or by phoning the employment tribunals public enquiry line, or to download from the employment tribunals service website. They may also be obtained through Jobcentre Plus offices, law centres, and Citizens Advice Bureaux. Note that the claimant may obtain practical information and assistance, including advice on completing the claim form, from the employment tribunals public enquiry line. However, the employment tribunal will not provide legal advice.

4.32 **Presenting the claim form.** Once the ET1 has been completed, it should be presented to the tribunal to set the legal process in motion. This must be done in accordance with the appropriate Presidential Practice Direction relating to the presentation of claims to an employment tribunal (for England and Wales or for Scotland) – rules 8(1) and 85(2). These Practice Directions prescribe the following alternative methods by which the completed claim form may be presented to an employment tribunal:

- online using the online form submission service provided by HMCTS (see 'Online presentation' below);

- by post to a central office (see 'Presentation by post' below); or

249

- in person to one of the employment tribunal offices listed in the Schedule to the relevant Practice Direction within the stated tribunal business hours (see 'Presentation in person' below).

(Note that fax and e-mail are no longer prescribed methods of presentation, as rule 85(2) states that a claim form may *only* be delivered in accordance with the Practice Directions made under Reg 11 of the Tribunal Regulations, which supplement rule 8. However, sending the ET3 (response form) as an attachment to an e-mail is apparently still acceptable – see Chapter 6, 'Defending a claim', under 'Responding to the claim – presentation of the response'.)

Whichever method is used, it is important to ensure that the claim is presented within the appropriate time limit (see Chapter 5, 'Time limits').

4.33 Rule 90 of the Tribunal Rules sets out the assumptions that apply to determine when the claim form (or any other document) will be taken to have been received by the tribunal. This is particularly important in that if a claim form is presented late, the tribunal may refuse to accept it (see Chapter 10, 'Service of notices and documents'). Unless the contrary is proved, therefore, a claim will be taken to have been received:

- if sent by post, on the day on which it would be delivered in the ordinary course of post – rule 90(a)
- if sent electronically, on the day of transmission – rule 90(b)
- if delivered in person, on the day of delivery – rule 90(c).

Below, we examine the different methods of service and the assumptions in rule 90 in detail, and consider what happens where the ET1 gets lost.

4.34 *'Unless the contrary is proved'.* In the vast majority of cases, these assumptions will apply to determine when submission is deemed to have taken place. However, rule 90 states that these assumptions are *subject to the contrary being proved*. In other words, if the employment tribunal proves that it did not receive the claim form in the ordinary course of post, or on the day of transmission or delivery, but at a later date, then the date on which it did receive the claim should apply. This reading would appear to defeat the purpose of a rule on deemed submission, as it potentially makes uncertain the date on which a claim form should be treated as presented. However, the provision needs to be read in conjunction with the Court of Appeal's decision in Consignia plc (formerly the Post Office) v Sealy 2002 ICR 1193, CA, in which the Court held that if a letter does not arrive at the time when it would be expected to arrive in the ordinary course of post, but is unexpectedly delayed, a tribunal may conclude that it was not reasonably practicable for the complaint to be presented within the prescribed period for the purpose of exercising its discretion to extend the time limit – see Chapter 5, 'Time limits', under '"Presenting" the claim – meaning of "presenting"'. However, the claimant or his or her representative must make efforts to ascertain whether the claim form has been received, if its receipt is not acknowledged.

The qualification to rule 90 may also be read in favour of the claimant. In other words, it appears to allow for a situation where a claimant posts the claim form, and the form is date-stamped as having been received by the tribunal the following day – i.e., one day *earlier* than the day on which it would have been delivered in the ordinary course of post, as interpreted in Consignia (see 'Presentation by post' below). In such circumstances, the effect of the qualification appears to be that the claim form should be treated as having been received on the day that it was date-stamped, not on the following day on which it would have been deemed to have been delivered under the 'ordinary course of post' rule.

Online presentation. The HMCTS guidance booklet 'Making a claim to an **4.35** employment tribunal' (T420) advises that 'submitting a claim online is the quickest way of sending a claim to the tribunal', and the additional information to the Practice Directions on the presentation of claims asserts 'the speediest and most efficient method of presenting a claim will normally be by using the online submission service. The online system will assist in calculating the fee which is due, will ensure that a claimant does remember to pay or apply for remission (since it will not allow the claim to be submitted otherwise) and will reach the fee processing centre very quickly. It also leaves no room for doubt about when the claim was presented since this is recorded electronically; that may be important if the claim is being presented close to the end of the limitation period.'

As previously mentioned, the electronic version of the claim form can be found at www.employmenttribunals.service.gov.uk. Once submitted, the claim form will automatically be routed to the office of the tribunal appropriate to hear the claim (see 'Presentation in person' below). As the location of this tribunal is determined by postcode, it is important to quote the correct postcode for the place where the claimant works, worked or applied to work, or where the incident complained of took place. If an incorrect postcode is quoted, this may mean that the claim is sent to the wrong office, which may cause a delay. The employment tribunal public enquiry line, or the Post Office's online postcode finder, can assist in finding postcodes.

Once the claim has been successfully submitted online, the claimant or his or **4.36** her representative will receive an automatic receipt to confirm this (assuming the claimant has opted to receive communications by e-mail). The HMCTS guidance booklet advises that 'if you do not receive a receipt notification, you should contact the employment tribunal office immediately'. As there may be as much as a 20-minute delay before receiving the confirmation e-mail, it is strongly advisable not to leave submitting the form too close to the deadline.

251

The receipt will contain a unique reference number confirming the date and time of submission.

Despite the potential advantages of online submission, it has its pitfalls. As the landing page for the online submission site warns, any information entered will be lost if longer than 20 minutes is spent on a single page without progressing. The purpose of this is to protect the safety of the claimant's data, but its effect is that the content will need to be fully drafted in advance of filling in the online form, so as to avoid losing data and having to start all over again, since the form – once saved – cannot be amended. Further potential disadvantages are that any additional pages attached to the submitted form are not included in the e-mail receipt, so the claimant has no record of the content of the additional pages received by the tribunal; any such attachment is required to be in rich text format (rtf); and the form will only recognise information submitted in the correct format, so building numbers have to be specified, and it may have difficulty recognising international postcodes and telephone numbers. (Note that, at the time of writing, HMCTS is working to improve the online forms and it is hoped that at least some of the problems encountered by users will soon be ironed out.)

4.37 Rule 90(b) indicates that an ET1 will be presented to the tribunal on the day on which it has been successfully submitted online. It is important to note that submission is 'successful' not when the 'submit' button is pressed, but when the e-mail confirming receipt is received – see, for example, Miller v Community Links Trust Ltd EAT 0486/07, in which a claim was submitted nine seconds late although the 'submit' button was pressed one second inside the time limit. Nevertheless, once that receipt is received, submission is successful regardless of whether the ET1 subsequently fails to reach the tribunal office which will hear the claim, or is received there at a later date (which may be outside the time limit). This was made clear in Tyne and Wear Autistic Society v Smith 2005 ICR 663, EAT, in which the EAT held that, where a claimant receives an automated message that the claim form has been submitted, there is a reasonable expectation that it will reach the tribunal directly and it is thus presented. This principle applied regardless of the fact that the claimant was instructed to contact the tribunal in order to find out whether the claim had been received or not. In that case S submitted his claim electronically on the last day of valid service but was later told by the tribunal that it had not been received there. S had received the standard automated message upon pressing the 'submit' button and the tribunal accepted that his ET1 reached the host of the ETS website from where it should have been forwarded to the tribunal. However, the host service had failed to forward it. The tribunal nevertheless held that S's claim had been 'presented' to an employment tribunal upon successfully reaching the host of the employment tribunals service site. On appeal, the EAT affirmed the tribunal's decision. In its view, an individual who successfully submits his or her claim in time should not be adversely affected by subsequent problems with the computer technology of the website host or the tribunal office, or by communication problems between the two.

Note that the web address for online submission is the same for England and Wales as for Scotland. However, this does not mean that online presentation is effective for both jurisdictions simultaneously. The ET1 will be automatically routed to the tribunal office closest to the claimant's place of work, if this has been stated in the claim form, or, if not, to the tribunal closest to the respondent's address, and the form will thus be presented within whichever jurisdiction this lies (see the section 'Completing the claim form', under 'Practical advice on completing the ET1 – Section 2 (respondent's details)').

In McFadyen and ors v PB Recovery Ltd and ors EATS 0072/08 the EAT held **4.38** that an online claim form was not submitted to a Scottish tribunal on the same date it was wrongly submitted to an English tribunal, which rejected the claim for lack of jurisdiction. M was an employee of PBR Ltd, which had its registered office in Bristol, though he worked at a site in Scotland. After he was made redundant his solicitor, C, submitted an ET1 claim form online, providing details of PBR Ltd's registered office in Bristol as the address of the respondent. He did not enter the location in Scotland at which M had actually worked as this was not stated to be a 'required field' and he did not know the address. The claim was forwarded to the Bristol tribunal to be processed. However, an employment judge there decided that the claim could not be accepted because the tribunal in England and Wales had no jurisdiction to hear it. C contacted the Glasgow tribunal, which 'retrieved' the claim form from the IT system, but unfortunately by then it was out of time, and the tribunal dismissed it. M appealed, arguing that the claim should be treated as having been presented on the date when it was received by the Tribunals Service's host server. However, in the EAT's view, the host server could be treated as an agent for employment tribunals, receiving claim forms and transferring them to the appropriate tribunal, identified on the basis of the address provided in section 2 – i.e. the place of work or, if none is provided, the respondent's address. The host server's task is completed once the claim has been forwarded to the tribunal closest to that address: it does not hold the forms for all tribunals in the UK generally. Nothing in the ET1 itself, the statutory provisions or the accompanying guidance could give a claimant the legitimate expectation that the host server would deliver the form anywhere other than the tribunal nearest to the relevant address provided, or that the claim form was also being held by the host server on behalf of all or any other tribunals. Furthermore, the EAT thought that recognition needed to be given to the fact that the jurisdictions of England and Wales on the one hand and Scotland on the other are separate, and that a claim presented in England cannot be regarded as having been presented in Scotland. With this in mind, the tribunal had been correct to find that the claim was presented to the host server, directed to the Bristol office where it was rejected for lack of jurisdiction, and thus treated as if it had not been presented on that

253

date at all. The later presentation in Glasgow was therefore out of time. The EAT noted that the rejection by Bristol was unfortunate since that tribunal did appear to have jurisdiction. However, that could have been addressed by means of a timely application for review or appeal, neither of which occurred. Accordingly, M's appeal was dismissed.

If England and Wales and Scotland both have dual jurisdiction over a claim, as appears to have been the case in McFadyen, and the claimant wishes to pursue the claim in the jurisdiction other than that to which the claim has been automatically routed, he or she would have to apply for a transfer under rule 99 of the Tribunal Rules (see Chapter 11, 'Case management', under 'Miscellaneous matters – transfer of proceedings'). The claim would then be treated as having been received in Scotland on the same day it was presented in England. However, such a transfer relies on a timely claim being presented in the first place. It may be preferable in such cases, assuming there is sufficient time, for the form to be submitted, by post or in person, directly to the relevant address for the jurisdiction within which the claimant wishes to pursue the claim.

4.39 *Presentation by post.* If postal submission is chosen, the claim form should be sent to the appropriate central office. In England and Wales, the address is:

Employment Tribunal Central Office (England and Wales)
PO Box 10218
Leicester LE1 8EG
In Scotland, the address is:
Employment Tribunals Central Office (Scotland)
PO Box 27105
Glasgow G2 9JR

All claims are initially processed in the appropriate central office. Once the claim has been accepted, it will be passed to the appropriate local tribunal office (see 'Presentation in person' below).

4.40 Where a claimant sends an ET1 claim form by post, presentation will occur on the day on which it would be delivered 'in the ordinary course of post', unless the contrary is proved – rule 90(a) Tribunal Rules. Following the Court of Appeal's decision in Consignia plc (formerly the Post Office) v Sealy 2002 ICR 1193, CA, service under the 'ordinary course of post' rule is deemed to have taken place on the second day after first-class posting, excluding Sundays, public holidays, Christmas Day and Good Friday. This means that service can take place on a Saturday. In Metcalfe v Cygnet Health Care Ltd EAT 0421/05, for instance, the last day of valid service of the claim form was Saturday but the ET1 was delayed in the post and did not arrive until the following Monday. The tribunal found as a fact that the claimant had posted the ET1 on Thursday and, applying the 'ordinary course of post' rule, that it had been validly served on Saturday, notwithstanding that it physically arrived at the tribunal two days

254

later. (Following the decision in Consignia, the tribunal might alternatively have extended time as a matter of discretion: see the fuller discussion of this case in Chapter 5, 'Time limits', under '"Presenting" the claim – meaning of "presenting"'.)

Two further examples of cases in which the 'ordinary course of post' rule was applied:

- **Smith v James Hall and Co (Southport) Ltd** ET Case No.2411204/07: S posted his claim form to the employment tribunal on Friday 21 December 2007, using first-class mail. The claim was not received by the tribunal office until Thursday 27 December, after the relevant statutory time limit had expired at midnight on 24 December. Under the 'ordinary course of post' rule the claim form would have been expected to have arrived at the tribunal office on Monday 24 December, even allowing for Christmas postal deliveries. However, unknown to S, the tribunal office was closed on 24 December and there was no postal delivery to it that day. The tribunal found that, since Christmas Eve was not one of the 'excluded days' identified in Consignia plc v Sealy, and in the ordinary course of events the claim form would have arrived in time, it did have jurisdiction to consider the claim

- **Kinne v British Bookshops and Stationers Ltd** ET Case No.1103076/09: K posted her claim form to the employment tribunal by first-class post on Monday 26 October 2009, but due to postal strikes it was not received until 2 November, which was after the last day for presentation, which was 29 October. The tribunal held that K had been entitled to rely on the claim being presented in time in the ordinary course of post. At the time at which she posted the claim form, it was reasonable for her to expect it to be delivered to the tribunal by 29 October; she could not have been aware then of the further strikes planned.

4.41 Needless to say, the claimant is best advised to request proof of posting so that he or she has evidence in case the ET1 subsequently goes missing. Recorded delivery is advisable. Where this form of postage is chosen, should the form arrive on a date on which the tribunal office is closed it will not actually be delivered if someone is required to sign for it. Nevertheless, for the purposes of rule 90(a), it is still reasonable to expect the form to be presented on the day on which it would have been delivered under the 'ordinary course of post' rule.

If the form actually arrives *one* day after posting, and is date-stamped by the tribunal to that effect, or the claimant has obtained proof of delivery, then this earlier date may be taken to be the date of submission under the qualification to rule 90 – see 'Presenting the claim form – "unless the contrary is proved"' above.

4.42 In any event, the tribunal office that will be dealing with the claim should send confirmation of receipt to the claimant or his or her representative within five

255

working days. The notes to the ET1 advise that 'if you have not heard from them within five working days, please contact that office directly'.

4.43 *Presentation in person.* Alternatively, a claim may be presented in person to one of the employment tribunal offices listed in the Schedule to the Practice Direction (see the Appendix to this chapter). It must be presented within tribunal office hours (which, for these purposes, are 9 am to 4 pm, Monday to Friday, not including public holidays or weekends, albeit for other purposes the offices remain open until 5 pm). It follows that, although for the purpose of presenting a claim online the claim form may be submitted at any time of day (see 'Online submission' above), and for the purpose of presenting the claim by post it may be submitted on a Saturday (see 'Presentation by post' above), the times at which presentation in person is possible are more restricted. It is no longer the case that a claim may be successfully presented by being slipped through the letterbox of the tribunal office before midnight on the last day of presentation – see Post Office v Moore 1981 ICR 623, EAT.

The claim form may be presented to any tribunal office, and will be treated as having been presented on that day, even if that tribunal is not the appropriate one to hear the claim. However, once it has been accepted, the claim form will usually be transferred to the tribunal office nearest to the claimant's (former) place of work, determined by postcode, or, if the claimant has never been employed by the employer, to the tribunal office nearest to the place where he or she applied to work or where the matter complained of took place. A list of postcodes and the tribunal offices to which they correspond is contained in the HMCTS guidance booklet 'Making a claim to an employment tribunal' (T420).

The HMCTS booklet notes that the employment tribunal offices to which a claim may be presented in person do not have cash-handling facilities, so payment of fees in those offices may only be made by cheque or postal order.

4.44 *Duplicate copies.* Where claimants have presented the completed ET1 using the ETS's online facility, it is unnecessary to send an additional copy by post (except in the case of a claim accompanied by an application for interim relief – see 'Interim relief applications' below). Indeed, the Ministry of Justice website requests that duplicate copies of electronic correspondence are not re-sent by post or fax, to help the tribunal administration work more effectively. It is, however, strongly advisable to telephone the tribunal office for confirmation that it has received the ET1.

4.45 **Interim relief applications**
Special considerations apply where a claimant is applying for interim relief. This is an emergency procedure designed to ensure that, where a claimant is complaining of unfair dismissal for certain inadmissible reasons, he or she is reinstated or re-engaged, or his or her contract continues, pending determination of his or her complaint. The procedure applies in respect of unfair dismissal for

256

a trade union-related reason specified in S.152 of the Trade Union and Labour Relations (Consolidation) Act 1992 (TULR(C)A), under S.161 TULR(C)A, and in respect of unfair dismissal for a variety of reasons set out in S.128 ERA, including for making a protected disclosure. The details of the procedure are set out in full in IDS Employment Law Handbook, 'Unfair Dismissal' (2011), Chapter 19, 'Additional awards and interim relief', under 'Interim relief – application procedure', and to a lesser extent in IDS Employment Law Handbook, 'Trade Unions' (2013), Chapter 12, 'Unfair dismissal', under 'Tribunal proceedings and remedies – interim relief', and IDS Employment Law Handbook, 'Whistleblowing' (2013), Chapter 7, 'Enforcement and remedies', under 'Interim relief'. The timeframe within which an application for interim relief must be made is extremely tight. The application, together with an ET1 claiming unfair dismissal, must be submitted by the end of seven days immediately following the effective date of termination, with no possibility of an extension – S.161(2) TULR(C)A.

As the HMCTS guidance booklet 'Making a claim to an employment tribunal' (T420) points out, the effect of this tight timescale for the purposes of submission is that, in the interests of speed, the claim form should ideally be submitted online. However, the online submission form does not allow for PDF attachments, so the application for interim relief – and, in the case of claims for dismissal because of actual or proposed union membership or participation in union activities, a certificate from the authorised union official – cannot be submitted in this way. The HMCTS booklet advises that in such circumstances, the claimant should:

- submit the claim online

- send a copy of the claim form, the certificate (if relevant), and the application for interim relief by e-mail to the relevant tribunal office that will hear the claim; and

- clearly state in the body of the claim form submitted online that this has been done (see 'Completing the claim form – practical advice on completing the ET1' below).

Multiple claimants   4.46
Two or more claimants may make their claims on the same claim form if their claims are based on the same set of facts – rule 9 Tribunal Rules. This rule would be applicable, for example, in respect of a large-scale redundancy situation, where many different claimants might wish to apply for the same relief arising out of common facts and circumstances. If claims are wrongly included on the same claim form (in other words, they are not based on the same set of facts), this is treated as an 'irregularity' falling within rule 6. Under this rule the error will not, of itself, render the proceedings void. Rather, the tribunal 'may take such action as it considers just', such as waiving a requirement or awarding costs.

257

It is also true that while multiple claimants may use a single form if their claims do arise out of the same set of facts, they must nonetheless present 'their claims' in the ET1. According to the EAT in Hamilton and ors v NHS Grampian EATS 0067/10, this means that it must be clear from the form what each claimant alleges to have happened in his or her own case and what remedy each of them is seeking. If they do not do so, then they cannot be said to be presenting 'their claims' within the meaning of what is now rule 9.

See 'Completing the claim form – practical advice on completing the ET1' below for further guidance on how to submit a claim in respect of multiple claimants.

4.47 **Lead cases.** Note that claims made by multiple claimants that give rise to common or related issues of *law* cannot be made on the same claim form within the terms of rule 9 if they are not based on the same set of *facts*. However, where a tribunal considers that two or more claims give rise to 'common or related issues of fact *or law*' (our stress), rule 36(1) sets out a procedure under which the tribunal or the President may make an order specifying one or more of the claims as a lead case and staying (or in Scotland sisting) the others, thereby removing the need for additional hearings. If the tribunal makes a decision in the lead claim on the common or related issues, it will send a copy to each of the parties – rule 36(2). This will be binding on the parties in the related claims, unless one (or more) of the related parties applies, within 28 days after the date on which the tribunal sent the copy of the decision to that party, for an order that it should not be so binding – rule 36(2) and (3). For further details, see Chapter 11, 'Case management', under 'Combined proceedings, lead cases and representative respondents – lead cases'.

4.48 Completing the claim form

A claim presented to an employment tribunal must contain all of the following information:

- each claimant's name – rule 10(b)(i) Tribunal Rules

- each claimant's address – rule 10(b)(ii)

- the name of each person against whom the claim is made (the respondent) – rule 10(b)(iii)

- each respondent's address – rule 10(b)(iv)

- an early conciliation (EC) number or confirmation that the claim does not institute any 'relevant proceedings' – i.e. proceedings that would normally be subject to statutory conciliation; or (b) that one of the EC exemptions set out in Reg 3 of the EC Regulations applies – rule 10(c) (see 'Early conciliation – proceedings in respect of which early conciliation applies' above).

It is essential that a claimant provide all of the required information, as failure to do so will result in the claim being rejected by the tribunal office – see the section 'Processing the claim form' below, under 'Rejection of claim – technical defects'.

Rule 10(c) is intended to ensure that claimants have contacted Acas with a view **4.49** to being offered the opportunity of conciliation of the workplace dispute before tribunal proceedings are commenced. Proof of having taken this step comes in the form of a certificate issued by Acas. If a prospective claimant decides to present a tribunal claim after receiving the EC certificate, he or she must include the unique reference number given by Acas on any subsequent ET1 claim form to demonstrate compliance with the EC requirement. If the ET1 does not include the EC reference number, the tribunal will dismiss the claim if it is one to which the EC requirement applies. For further details of the EC process, see 'Early conciliation' above.

Note that details of the claim are not required under rule 10. However, it is still important to indicate the type of claim that is being brought and provide sufficient details of the claim, as a failure to provide such details is likely to lead to the claim being rejected for other reasons – see the section 'Processing the claim form' below, under 'Rejection of claim – substantive defects'.

Care should be taken as mistakes in names and/or addresses could lead to **4.50** delays and procedural problems – see, for example, Chowles t/a Granary Pine v West EAT 0473/08, in which a mistake in the spelling of the respondent's name, coupled with two errors in the address, meant that the tribunal did not send a copy of the claim form to the respondent within the meaning of what is now rule 15, and a default judgment in the claimant's favour had to be set aside.

Practical advice on completing the ET1 **4.51**
The ET1 and the HMCTS guidance booklet 'Making a claim to an employment tribunal' (T420) contain helpful information on how to complete the claim form. Both inform claimants that all sections marked with an asterisk *must* be filled in (i.e. the name and address of the claimant and respondent(s), and the type and details of the claim). Claimants should write clearly or, if possible, type; online submission will prevent any possible problems of legibility. Always retain a copy of the ET1.

The ET1 may be quite a lengthy document in some cases, particularly in discrimination claims, which can be heavily fact-dependent. Employment judges have no power to limit the length of the ET1 – Fairbank v Care Management Group and another case EAT 0139/12. The appropriate way of dealing with such claims is by identifying the relevant issues by case management. However, it should be noted that if a form is unreasonably prolix, costs may be awarded against the claimant.

259

4.52 Claimants may find the following practical advice helpful in completing each section. (Note that this advice applies in large measure whether the claim is being submitted in paper format or online. However, the online version does not carry section numbers but rather progresses through each page of the form in an interactive way. A progress bar indicates how much of the form has been completed and certain text boxes appear only if a particular option is selected (e.g. the box to type in your e-mail address only appears if you select 'e-mail' as the preferred method of contact).)

4.53 **Section 1 (your details).** First name, surname and full address are mandatory details. You should also provide a contact number on which you can be reached during normal working hours. If you tick the box to indicate that you would prefer to be contacted by e-mail, remember to check your e-mails every day. HMCTS notes that although it will usually try to use e-mail if preferred, this will not always be possible as some documents need to be signed by an employment judge. There is space for only one claimant's details here: if more than one claimant is using the same form, see 'Multiple Claim form' below.

4.54 **Section 2 (respondent's details).** The name of the employer or person or organisation you are claiming against (the respondent), and its or his address, are mandatory details. Try to find out the correct name of the employer, including information such as whether it is a limited company or a plc, to avoid any delay in processing the claim. This may be identified from a letter communicating a job offer, a contract of employment or a pay slip. If the employer is a limited company, you can obtain its registered address from Companies House, though a business address may be equally acceptable. Where the employer is a partnership, at least one of the partners must be named in order to make the partnership liable. Where the employer is an unincorporated organisation, name all the members of the management committee as respondents. If you are unsure who the correct respondent is, name all possible respondents (the tribunal may later remove any party apparently wrongly included, under rule 34 of the Tribunal Rules – see Chapter 8, 'Amendments', under 'Amending the parties'). If you are claiming discrimination, or victimisation for having made a protected disclosure, you may be able to claim against more than one respondent – for instance, the employer and any person the employer is responsible for, such as a work colleague, who you allege to have committed an act, or acts, of discrimination against you. Similarly, if your claim is under the Transfer of Undertakings (Protection of Employment) Regulations 2006 SI 2006/246, you may wish to claim against both transferor and transferee, if you are unsure who is liable. There is space for two additional respondents at section 2: section 13 provides space for listing two more. If you work, worked or applied to work from home, or at a different address, you should say so in section 2.3 and that address will be treated as your workplace.

Note that in respect of complaints under S.146(1) of the Equality Act 2010 (concerning allegedly discriminatory terms in collective agreements), certain persons will automatically be regarded as respondents whether or not they are identified as such in the ET1. Those persons are the claimant's employer (or prospective employer) and every organisation of employers and workers – together with every association of or representative of such organisations – which, if the allegedly discriminatory term were to be varied voluntarily, would be likely, in the opinion of an employment judge, to negotiate the variation – rule 97. Such an organisation or association will not, however, be treated as a respondent if the employment judge, having made appropriate enquiries, is of the opinion that it is not reasonably practicable to identify the organisation or association.

Section 3 (multiple cases). If you are aware that your claim is one of a number 4.55 of claims against the same employer arising from the same, or similar, circumstances, you have the opportunity to add the other claimants' names here, to enable tribunal staff to process the claims efficiently, perhaps by linking the claims. If multiple claims are being submitted on the same form under the same representation (where relevant), the names and addresses of additional claimants should be entered at the section at the back of the ET1 form. Where the number of additional claimants exceeds 28, the HMCTS multiple claim bulk upload facility allows for details in another database to be exported into .csv format and attached to the ET1. Note that group claimants may be able to access the 'fee group' fees structure – see Chapter 19, 'Fees', under '"Fee group" claims'.

Section 4 (cases where the respondent was not your employer). If you are 4.56 or were *not* employed by any of the respondents named on the form, but are making a claim for some other reason connected to employment (for example, relating to a job application or against a trade union), you should state the type of claim you are making here. You do not need to provide further details in this section.

Section 5 (employment details). If your complaint is against your employer or 4.57 ex-employer, give the date when your employment started and, if applicable, the date when it ended (or, if you are in a period of notice, the date when it is due to end). Use day/month/year format. You also need to state briefly what job you do or did for your employer, or give your job title.

Section 6 (earnings and benefits). Enter here the basic hours you work/ 4.58 worked each week, but not including overtime even if you work/worked overtime regularly. The box for 'Pay before tax' at section 6.2 should include your basic pay before tax and any deductions, but not including overtime. 'Normal take-home pay' should be the pay you receive, including overtime, commissions and bonuses, but after tax, national insurance and other deductions have been made. These figures should be included on your payslip. Round the

261

amounts to the nearest pound, and tick the box to indicate whether this is for a week or a month. Section 6.5 asks for details of any other benefits you received from your employer, such as a company car or medical insurance. You should describe what kind of benefit you received and give an idea of how much it was worth.

4.59 **Section 7 (if your employment with the respondent has ended, what has happened since).** Tick the box to indicate whether or not you have got another job since leaving your employment. If you have not, go straight to section 8. If you have got another job state at box 7.2 when it started (or will start), and whether it is permanent or temporary. If it is temporary, state when it is due to end, if you have this information. At 7.3 you need to state how much you are now earning, or will earn, in your new job – indicate whether this is weekly, monthly or annually.

4.60 **Section 8 (type and details of claim).** This section is mandatory: you must tick the appropriate box or boxes to say what you are complaining about at section 8.1, and give the background and details of your complaints at section 8.2. You should include all the claims you are making: for example, your complaint may arise from a dismissal which you believe was unfair and also discriminatory on the ground of your race, in which case you need to tick three boxes: one for unfair dismissal, one for discrimination, and one for race. While additional claims may sometimes be added later, it is better to include all possibilities at this stage. In the details of your claim you need to set out the main facts supporting the claim(s) you are making, in chronological order. Wherever possible, you need to include the date(s) when the event(s) you are complaining about happened. Use the blank sheet at section 15 if you need additional space. You need to provide sufficient relevant detail to identify and explain the basis for all your complaints, but concisely: there will be an opportunity later to give a witness statement.

If you are claiming unfair dismissal, use the box to explain the background to the dismissal and any other information that might be helpful. If you disagree with the reason the respondent gave for dismissing you, say what you think the reason was. Describe the events which led up to your dismissal and describe how it took place, including dates, times, and the people involved. If you are claiming that the respondent's actions led you to resign (constructive dismissal), explain in detail the surrounding circumstances.

4.61 If you are claiming discrimination, describe the incidents which you believe amounted to discrimination, the dates of these incidents and the people who were involved. Explain in what way you believe you were discriminated against. If you are complaining about discrimination when you applied for a job, state what job you were applying for. If you are complaining about more than one type of discrimination, provide separate details of the act (or acts) of discrimination. Describe how you have been affected by the events you are

262

complaining about. If you are unable to give the dates of all the incidents you are complaining about, give at least the date of the last incident, or say if the discrimination is ongoing (this will enable the tribunal to determine whether or not your claim is in time – see Chapter 5, 'Time limits'). Note that if a claimant is relying on a series of continuing discriminatory acts (for which time only begins to run when the last act is completed), it is not vital that the claim be pleaded expressly on that basis, so long as that line of argument is sufficiently apparent from the ET1 to put the respondent on notice of it – Khetab v AGA Medical Ltd and ors EAT 0313/10. However, merely mentioning discrimination in relation to pay or benefits will not be enough to bring an equal pay claim unless there is some specific allegation of a failure to provide equal pay or a reference to facts from which such a failure could reasonably and objectively be discerned – Badra v Gardiner and Theobald LLP EAT 0191/10.

If you are claiming a redundancy payment, state whether you have asked your employer for payment, and, if so, the date on which you asked for payment (in day/month/year format). Say whether you have applied to the Redundancy Payments Office for payment, whether your claim has been rejected, and, if so, the date shown on the rejection letter.

If you are complaining about outstanding unpaid wages, holiday pay, payment **4.62** for a period of notice or some other payments (such as unpaid expenses, commission or a bonus), say how much you are claiming. Explain why you believe you are entitled to this payment, setting out full details such as the period the payment covers and the rate of pay. If you have specified an amount, say how you worked it out. If you are claiming more than one type of payment, give the amounts you are claiming for each type of payment and explain how you worked out each amount.

If you have any other complaints, you should include them here – for instance, a claim relating to part-time working or a claim that you have suffered a detriment as a result of having made a protected disclosure.

Section 9 (what do you want if your claim is successful). State what you are **4.63** seeking from the respondent if your claim is successful by ticking the appropriate box. This is particularly relevant in claims of unfair dismissal, where you can ask to be reinstated or re-engaged in addition to requesting compensation (see IDS Employment Law Handbook, 'Unfair Dismissal' (2010), Chapter 14, 'Remedies', under 'Reinstatement and re-engagement' and 'Compensation'). Additionally, in discrimination claims you may request the tribunal to issue a recommendation that the employer take steps to reduce the effect of discrimination on you and on any other person such as your colleagues at work, by, for example, allowing flexible working or making a reasonable adjustment (see IDS Employment Law Handbook, 'Discrimination at Work' (2012), Chapter 34, 'Enforcing individual rights', under 'Remedies – recommendations').

At 9.2, enter details of what compensation or remedy you are seeking. If you are claiming financial compensation, give details of how you calculated the amount. You might include information of your efforts to mitigate any loss. However, any figure you give will not restrict what you can claim, and you may revise the sum claimed later. If you are seeking any other remedy from the tribunal not identified at 9.1, state it in the box at 9.2: in particular, you should request the tribunal to order the employer to reimburse any fees you have paid in connection with the case, if you are successful (see Chapter 19, 'Fees', under 'Reimbursement').

4.64 **Section 10 (information to regulators in protected disclosure cases).** If your claim consists of, or includes, a claim that you are making a protected disclosure (i.e. whistleblowing) under the ERA, tick the box if you wish the tribunal to forward a copy of the claim form, or extracts from it, to the relevant regulator (see 'Processing the claim form – other persons who may be notified of proceedings' below, and IDS Employment Law Handbook, 'Whistleblowing at Work' (2013), Chapter 4, 'Method of disclosure', under 'Disclosure to prescribed persons').

4.65 **Section 11 (your representative).** Only claimants who have appointed a representative have to fill in this section. If you appoint a representative, the tribunal will contact only your representative and not you, so do not give the name of a representative unless he or she has agreed to act for you. Do not give the name of a person who has simply advised you on completing this form unless he or she is continuing to represent you. It is important to give the full name and address of the representative's organisation (if applicable) at 11.2 and 11.3, though if you are unsure of the name of the person who will be representing you, leave 11.1 blank.

4.66 **Section 12 (disability).** Indicate here if you have a disability, and, if you wish to do so, state what the disability is and give details of what help, if any, you may need from tribunal staff, including any help you may require if your claim progresses to a hearing. The HMCTS guidance booklet 'Making a claim to an employment tribunal' (T420) gives, as examples of the help HMCTS can provide, converting documents to Braille or larger print, providing information on disc, and paying for sign language interpreters.

4.67 **Section 13 (details of additional respondents).** If there are more than three respondents, list the additional ones here.

4.68 **Section 14 (fees).** Tick the appropriate boxes to confirm (a) that you have reread the form and checked that you have entered all the relevant information and (b) that you have enclosed either the appropriate fee or an application for remission of the fee. As the form indicates, if you fail to enclose the fee or a remission application, your claim will be rejected and returned to you, and time will continue to run for the purpose of the time limit applicable to your claim

264

until you have resubmitted it with the fee or remission application – see the section 'Processing the claim form' below, under 'Rejection of claim – no fee or remission application'.

Section 15 (additional information). This box should be used for providing **4.69** further details of claim. If additional space is needed, a Word or PDF document may also be attached if a paper version of the claim is being submitted or a document in rich text format (rtf) if the claim is being submitted online. If you are making an application for interim relief, you could inform the tribunal here if the application and any certificate have been sent separately by e-mail to the relevant tribunal office – see 'Making a claim – interim relief applications' above. You may also use this section if there is some other information that you wish to draw to the tribunal's attention, e.g. dates when you will be on holiday and the tribunal will be unable to reach you.

Multiple Claim form. Use this section if two or more claims arising from the **4.70** same set of facts are being presented by different claimants on the same claim form. The names and addresses of the additional claimants should be inserted here.

Diversity Monitoring Questionnaire. This is optional and used for statistical **4.71** purposes only. If you do complete the questionnaire, any information provided is confidential.

Early conciliation. Note that, at the time of writing, the ET1 form has not yet **4.72** been amended to allow space for the claimant to insert his or her early conciliation (EC) reference number, or to confirm that the claim does not institute any 'relevant proceedings' – i.e. proceedings that would normally be subject to statutory conciliation – or that one of the EC exemptions applies. However, it is important to include this information to prevent the claim being automatically rejected by tribunal staff under rule 10 of the Tribunal Rules. See 'Early conciliation' above and 'Processing the claim form – rejection of claim' below.

Processing the claim form
4.73

When an ET1 is received by the tribunal office it will be date-stamped. It will then normally be coded as to the nature of the claim or claims. The Secretary of Employment Tribunals, or a tribunal officer acting under the Secretary's direction, will then decide whether the claim can be accepted or whether it should be rejected (see 'Rejection of claim' below). Once the claim has been accepted, at least in part, the respondent or respondents will be sent a copy of the claim form, a blank ET3 response form, and a notice explaining whether any part of the claim has been rejected, and how to present a response – rule 15 Tribunal Rules. For further details, see Chapter 6, 'Defending a claim', under 'Responding to claim'.

265

The claimant will also receive the HMCTS guidance booklet 'Your claim – what next' (T421), which sets out the tribunal's next steps and aims to answer the basic questions the claimant might have in connection with the claim. This is also available to download from the Ministry of Justice website.

4.74 Rejection of claim

A claim will be rejected in the following circumstances:

- the prescribed form ET1 has not been used – rule 10 Tribunal Rules (see 'Technical defects' below)

- the form does not contain the requisite minimum information – rule 10 (see 'Technical defects' below)

- the claim is not accompanied by a fee or remission application – rule 11 (see 'No fee or remission application' below)

- an employment judge considers that the tribunal does not have jurisdiction to hear the claim, as a whole or in part – rule 12 (see 'Substantive defects' below)

- an employment judge considers that the claim, or part of it, is in a form which cannot sensibly be responded to or is otherwise an abuse of process – rule 12 (see 'Substantive defects' below)

- an employment judge considers that the claim, or part of it, institutes 'relevant proceedings' – i.e. proceedings that would normally be subject to statutory conciliation – but the form contains neither an early conciliation (EC) number nor confirmation that one of the EC exemptions applies; or the form confirms that one of the EC exemptions applies but it does not – rule 12 (see 'Early conciliation' above, and 'Substantive defects' below)

- an employment judge considers that the claim, or part of it, institutes 'relevant proceedings', but the name of the claimant or respondent on the claim form is not the same as the name of the prospective claimant or respondent on the EC certificate to which the EC number relates (unless the judge considers that the claimant made a minor error in relation to a name or address and it would not be in the interests of justice to reject the claim) – rule 12 (see 'Early conciliation' above, and 'Substantive defects' below).

4.75 It should be noted that prior to the implementation of the Tribunal Rules 2004, tribunals took a flexible approach where the claim form was incomplete. For instance, a failure to provide the respondent's address would not ordinarily result in the claim being invalid. The tribunal would accept the claim and subsequently seek clarification or further and better particulars from the claimant. The 2004 Rules, however, changed that position, providing that a claim form that did not contain particular relevant required information would not be accepted by the tribunal. This stringent approach did not find unequivocal support among the judiciary. In Grimmer v KLM Cityhopper UK 2005 IRLR 596, EAT, His Honour Judge Prophet questioned whether, in cases where certain information is not provided on a claim form, it is essential that a tribunal be compelled to take the 'draconian step' of refusing the claim where 'there is no compelling reason why the merits of the complaint cannot be examined'. He pointed out that, in the future, questions may well arise as to whether such a strict policy might meet the tribunals' overriding objective of dealing with cases justly; whether it would have proper regard to the fact that claimants are often unrepresented; whether it might affect the expiry of time limits for bringing claims; and whether it might breach Article 6 of the European Convention on Human Rights.

In that case G made a flexible working request to her employer under S.80F ERA. When KLM refused, she submitted a claim to an employment tribunal, giving 'flexible working' as the type of claim, and, for the details, a statement which said that 'the company's business argument for refusing my application is based upon their assumption that, if they concede to my request, others would be requesting similar/same working arrangements'. The tribunal refused to admit G's claim on the ground that she had not provided 'details of the claim' as was then required by rule 1(4)(e) of the Tribunal Rules 2004. G appealed to the EAT, which considered that the Rules cannot 'cut down on an employment tribunal's jurisdiction to entertain a complaint which the primary legislation providing an employment right empowers it to determine'. What might be regarded as mandatory should not be taken to the point of denying a claimant access to the employment tribunal system. If there was a conflict, the Rules had to give way. With this in mind, the EAT concluded that the test for establishing whether 'details of the claim' have been provided is 'whether it can be discerned from the claim as presented that the claimant is complaining of an alleged breach of an employment right which falls within the jurisdiction of the employment tribunal'. If a tribunal chairman felt that a claim lacked sufficient particulars, the correct approach was to order further particulars rather than to refuse to admit the claim. The EAT noted that G had clearly indicated that she wished to pursue a complaint in respect of flexible working. Since this was an employment right provided for in primary legislation – namely S.80F ERA – she had provided sufficient information to satisfy rule 1(4)(e). It followed that neither the Secretary nor the employment judge had been entitled to conclude that it was appropriate to refuse G's claim on the basis that she had not provided the required information. Accordingly, the EAT allowed G's appeal.

4.76 However, the regime under the Tribunal Rules 2013 has changed substantially from that of the Tribunal Rules 2004, and it is doubtful whether the approach advocated in Grimmer still pertains. First, the minimum information required of the ET1 has been reduced to the absolute basics, as discussed under 'Technical defects' below. It is no longer the case that a form will be

267

automatically rejected for a failure to set out the details of the claim without any kind of judicial consideration. And secondly, the reconsideration procedure (described under 'Reconsideration of rejection' below) arguably meets many of HHJ Prophet's concerns. A rejection for a technical defect, such as a failure to supply an address, may be immediately challenged and the defect rectified, meeting the overriding objective of dealing with cases fairly and justly (see Chapter 1, 'Employment tribunals', in the section 'What are employment tribunals?', under 'Employment tribunal rules – overriding objective'). Admittedly, time limits may still be a problem but the unequivocal language of the rules requiring tribunals to reject claims for particular failings, coupled with the detailed rejection/reconsideration procedure, make it unlikely that tribunals will feel inclined to continue to adopt Grimmer's laissez-faire approach to technical failings.

4.77 **Technical defects.** As stated under 'Making a claim' above, nearly all employment tribunal claims must be commenced by using the prescribed ET1 form. Rule 10 of the Tribunal Rules specifies that a claim will be returned to the claimant with a notice of rejection if it

- is not made on a 'prescribed form' – rule 10(1)(a)

- does not contain the name and address of each claimant and respondent – rule 10(1)(b), or

- contains neither an EC number nor confirmation (a) that the claim does not institute any relevant proceedings, or (b) that one of the early conciliation exemptions applies – rule 10(1)(c).

Under the Tribunal Rules 2004, the EAT was prepared to allow some leeway to claimants who did not supply the minimum information: for example, in Hamling v Coxlease School Ltd 2007 ICR 108, EAT, the EAT held that a claimant had not breached those rules where she had failed to provide her address, as she had included the name, address and full contact details of her solicitors. The Tribunal Rules 2013, however, do not allow for such latitude: rule 10(1)(b) simply states that the tribunal 'shall reject' a claim that does not contain the names and addresses of all claimants and respondents. However, the reconsideration procedure under rule 13 allows for any injustices to be remedied – see 'Reconsideration of rejection' below; and if an error is made, such as a spelling mistake, it may be possible to correct this later – see Chapter 8, 'Amendments'.

4.78 The claimant's address may have to be the claimant's genuine residential address. In Zu Vert v Unisys European Services Ltd ET Case No.3318960/06 Z provided an address for herself of an office that was not where she lived, nor where she had a place of business, on the ground that she feared that if she revealed her residential address that might lead to harassment by the respondent (although she did provide details of her representative). After considering the position under the Civil Procedure Rules, the tribunal decided that the claim should be rejected, concluding that the words 'claimant's address' in what is now rule 10 of the Tribunal Rules 2013 should have their ordinary meaning as referring to the place where the claimant actually lives. As this is a first instance decision, it is not binding on other tribunals, so it remains to be seen what position may be taken generally on this point.

(Note that under the Tribunal Rules 2004 the equivalent rule also required the claim form to set out the 'details of the claim' – rule 1(4)(e) Tribunal Rules 2004. Although this requirement is absent from rule 10 of the Tribunal Rules 2013, a failure to set out sufficient details of the claim may lead to its rejection under rule 12 – see 'Substantive defects' below. The section of the ET1 requiring the claimant to set out the 'type and details of claim' is marked with an asterisk, indicating that completion of that section is mandatory.)

The notice of rejection must explain why the claim was rejected and set out how the claimant may apply for a reconsideration of the rejection (as to which see 'Reconsideration of rejection' below) – rule 10(2).

No fee or remission application. A claim will be rejected by the tribunal with **4.79** a notice of rejection explaining why if it is not 'accompanied by a tribunal fee or a remission application' – rule 11(1) and (4) Tribunal Rules. Like rejections of claims under rule 10, it is the tribunal staff who deal with rejections under rule 11. Only substantive defects under rule 12 require judicial involvement.

Where a claim is accompanied by a fee 'but the amount paid is lower than the amount payable for the presentation of that claim' – for example, because the claim has been incorrectly classified – the tribunal will send the claimant a notice specifying a date for payment of the additional amount due – rule 11(2). If the amount due is not paid by the date specified in the notice, the tribunal will reject the claim, or the part of the claim for which the fee has not been paid – rule 11(2). If the claimant's remission application is rejected, the tribunal will send the claimant a notice specifying a date by which the issue fee must be paid. If this is not paid by the deadline, the claim will be rejected at that point – rule 11(3).

For further information on the procedure relating to fees and remission applications, see Chapter 19, 'Fees'.

Substantive defects. A claim will also be rejected if it contains what are termed **4.80** by the heading to rule 12 'substantive defects'. Despite the wide heading, the prescribed circumstances in which a tribunal may reject a claim under that rule are, in fact, more narrowly drawn than the heading implies. The claim (or part of it) will ultimately be rejected if it is:

- one which the tribunal has no jurisdiction to consider – rule 12(1)(a)

269

- in a form that cannot sensibly be responded to or is otherwise an abuse of process – rule 12(1)(b)

- one which institutes 'relevant proceedings', but the form does not contain an EC number or confirmation that one of the EC exemptions applies; or the form confirms that one of the EC exemptions applies but it does not – rule 12(1)(c) and (d), or

- one which institutes 'relevant proceedings', but the name of the claimant or respondent on the claim form is not the same as the name of the prospective claimant or respondent on the EC certificate to which the EC number relates – rule 12(1)(e) and (f).

('Relevant proceedings' are defined in rule 1(1) as proceedings listed in S.18(1) ETA. In other words, proceedings over which Acas has power to conciliate and in respect of which claimants must seek conciliation before bringing an employment tribunal claim, unless an exception applies. See 'Early conciliation – proceedings in respect of which early conciliation applies' above.)

4.81 Unlike a rejection under rule 10 or rule 11 (see above), the matter must be decided by an employment judge: rule 12(1) provides that tribunal office staff must refer a claim form to an employment judge if they consider that the claim (or part of it) may fall within rule 12(1)(a)–(f). If the judge considers that the claim (or part) falls within rule 12(1)(a), (b), (c), or (d), he or she must reject it (or the relevant part of it) – rule 12(2). If the judge considers that the claim (or part) falls within rule 12(1)(e) or (f), he or she must reject it (or the relevant part of it), unless he or she 'considers that the claimant made a minor error in relation to a name or address and it would not be in the interests of justice to reject the claim' – rule 12(2A). The claim form will then be returned to the claimant, together with a 'notice of rejection' giving the judge's reasons for rejecting the claim and setting out how to apply for a reconsideration of the rejection (as to which, see 'Reconsideration of rejection' below).

The wording of rule 12(2A) (see above) is puzzling. It gives an employment judge discretion not to reject a claim form, in the interests of justice, if he or she considers that the claimant made a minor error in relation to a name *or address*. Yet neither rule 12(1)(e) nor rule 12(1)(f) empower an employment judge to reject a form if the claimant's or respondent's address on the claim form differs from those given on the EC certification to which the EC number relates. This is likely to be a drafting error.

4.82 There appears to be a potential crossover between rule 12(1)(c) and rule 10(1)(c) (see 'Technical defects' above). Rule 12(1)(c), read with rule 12(2), requires a tribunal to reject a claim form if an employment judge thinks that the claim (or part of it) is one which institutes relevant proceedings and is made on a claim form that contains neither an EC number nor confirmation that one of the EC exemptions applies. Rule 10(1)(c) requires a tribunal to reject a claim form outright (without any judicial intervention) if it contains neither an EC number, nor confirmation (a) that the claim does not institute any relevant proceedings, or (b) that one of the EC exemptions applies. Although not entirely clear, it seems probable that rule 12(1)(c) is directed at circumstances where the claim form confirms that the claim does not institute any relevant proceedings (which means that it may not be rejected under rule 10(1)(c)), but an employment judge considers that this confirmation is mistaken, as the claim does in fact institute relevant proceedings.

A claim should not be rejected under rule 12(1)(a) if there is simply some doubt as to whether the tribunal has jurisdiction. In Young v Hexion Speciality Chemicals UK Ltd EATS 0023/09 Y brought a claim for unfair dismissal. Although he gave his termination date, he did not give his start date, and an employment tribunal rejected his claim on the basis that it was unable to establish whether he had the required service to claim unfair dismissal. The EAT overturned this decision. Specification of the date of commencement of a claimant's employment was not an item of required information, and in any event, it could be inferred from the fact that Y was claiming unfair dismissal that he was offering to prove that he had completed the relevant qualifying period of employment. More importantly, the EAT considered that the tribunal should have asked itself not whether it could be sure that it had jurisdiction to consider the claim, but whether it was clear that it did not have jurisdiction to do so. Even if it observed that it *might* not have jurisdiction, this would not have required it to reject the claim.

As noted under 'Technical defects' above, the claim form cannot automatically **4.83** be rejected under rule 10 for a failure to set out the details of the claim. Clearly, however, a claimant who fails to set out any such details risks the claim being rejected under rule 12(1)(b) because it 'cannot sensibly be responded to'. It should, in any event, be noted that the 'Type and details of claim' section of the new ET1 is marked with an asterisk, indicating that completion of that section is mandatory. Nevertheless, while a claim lacking any detail is clearly a good example of a claim that 'cannot sensibly be responded to', it is not yet clear how much – and what type of – detail is required in order for it to be a claim that can sensibly be responded to. It is probable that the provision will catch vague claims that air a sense of animosity towards the employer without setting out anything that could be described as a legal claim. It is likely also to cover situations where a claimant has tried to cover him or herself by ticking many of the boxes, but without supporting all of those claims in the details. In Baker v Commissioner of Police of the Metropolis EAT 0201/09, a case decided under the Tribunal Rules 2004, the EAT upheld a tribunal's decision that a claim form did not include a complaint of disability discrimination; it was not sufficient for the claimant to tick the box indicating that he was bringing such a claim without giving further details. However, the EAT considered that the tribunal had erred in refusing to consider an application to amend the form to include a

271

disability discrimination claim. Under the Tribunal Rules 2013, however, it is possible that the purported disability discrimination claim would have been rejected under rule 12(1)(b) from the start.

Rule 12(1)(b) is likely, too, to cover details that are entirely illegible. In May v Greenwich London Borough Council EAT 0102/10, a case decided under the Tribunal Rules 2004, the EAT considered that where a claimant presents an illegible claim form (which, in its view, implied one that needed to be read with a magnifying glass), the tribunal should not refuse to accept it if that refusal would effectively preclude the claimant from presenting a more legible copy without having to apply for an extension of time. In the EAT's view, the correct course would be for the tribunal to require the claimant to provide a more readable copy within a defined period and, if necessary, to impose sanctions on a failure to do so. In any event, illegibility of part of the document would not justify a refusal to accept the entire claim, if sufficient details were legible. However, under the Tribunal Rules 2013, rule 12 quite clearly requires an employment judge to reject any claim, or any part of a claim, that he or she considers cannot sensibly be responded to. Thus, the correct approach now would presumably be for the judge to reject the claim or part that is illegible, under rule 12, and for the claimant to apply for a reconsideration of that rejection under rule 13 (see 'Reconsideration of rejection' below). Such a reconsideration would be likely to succeed if the illegibility could simply be remedied by typing out the form.

4.84 On the whole, however, apart from the type of wholesale failure to legibly set out the rudiments of the claimant's complaint as discussed above, employment tribunals can be expected to continue to assert fairly minimal expectations regarding the sufficient outlining of a case in the ET1. This will particularly be so where the claimant is unrepresented. So long as the rudiments of a legitimate claim can be ascertained from the particulars of claim, it is unlikely that the more prescriptive nature of the Tribunal Rules 2013 will be interpreted in a way that causes many claims which would previously have been regarded as sufficiently particularised to be rejected on the basis that the claim cannot sensibly be responded to.

4.85 Reconsideration of rejection

If a claim, or part of it, is rejected for a technical defect under rule 10 of the Tribunal Rules, or a 'substantive' defect under rule 12, a claimant may apply for a 'reconsideration' of the decision under rule 13. (Under the Tribunal Rules 2004 this was known as applying for a 'review'.) Note that it is arguably possible for claimants, in the alternative, to apply for a reconsideration of a judgment under rule 70. This is discussed in Chapter 15, 'Reconsideration of tribunal judgments and decisions', under 'Reconsideration of a tribunal judgment – reconsideration of decision to reject a claim, response or counterclaim'.

Under rule 13, a claimant can apply for a reconsideration on either of the following two grounds:

- that the decision to reject was wrong
- that the notified defect can be rectified – rule 13(1).

4.86 The application must meet the following procedural requirements, set out in rule 13(2):

- it must be in writing
- it must either explain why the decision is said to have been wrong, or rectify the defect
- it must be presented to the tribunal within 14 days of the date on which the notice of rejection was sent
- if the claimant wishes to request a hearing, this must be stated in the application.

A failure to request a hearing will result in the application being determined without one – rule 13(3). If there is a hearing, this will be attended only by the claimant. If, however, the employment judge decides on the papers that the claim should be accepted in full, a hearing will not go ahead (even if the claimant has requested one) – rule 13(3).

4.87 Where the judge decides that the original rejection was correct but that a defect has been corrected, the claim shall be treated as presented 'on the date that the defect was rectified' – rule 13(4). It is not clear from this wording whether the defect will be treated as rectified on the date that the application remedying the defect was sent, received or accepted by the judge. However, the effect is that the date on which the rectified claim is treated as presented will be some time later than the date on which it was originally presented, which may have implications for the claimant in terms of meeting the applicable statutory time limits for presenting tribunal claims.

Where there is sufficient time, the claimant may consider, as an alternative to following the 'reconsideration' process, simply correcting the defect and resubmitting the ET1. However, on a strict reading of the Employment Tribunals and the Employment Appeal Tribunal Fees Order 2013 SI 2013/1893, such a tactic would involve the claimant's incurring liability for a further fee. Under Article 4(1)(a) of the Fees Order, an issue fee is payable 'when a claim form is presented to an employment tribunal': there is no indication that a 'resubmitted' claim in such circumstances would be treated otherwise than as an entirely fresh claim. Unless a claimant's resources are infinite, this strategy is therefore unlikely to represent a viable alternative to following the procedure laid out in rule 13. For a full discussion of liability for fees upon issue of a claim, see Chapter 19, 'Fees', under 'Tribunal issue fee'.

273

4.88 **Rejection under rule 11.** It is important to note that a claimant cannot apply under rule 13(1) for a reconsideration of a decision to reject a claim under rule 11 – i.e. because it was not accompanied by a tribunal fee or remission application. Claimants will be expected to resubmit their claim form with the correct fee or a remission application. However, it may be that claimants (particularly, of course, those for whom time has run out to resubmit their claim) could apply for a reconsideration under rule 70. This provides that 'a tribunal may, either on its own initiative... or on the application of a party, reconsider any judgment where it is necessary in the interests of justice to do so'. The claimant would need to satisfy the tribunal that a decision to reject a claim under rule 11 falls within the definition of 'judgment' under rule 1(3)(b). While it is not immediately obvious that it does, the fact that it is not specifically excluded from the definition – unlike a decision under rule 13 (reconsideration of rejection under rules 10 or 12) or 19 (reconsideration of rejection of a response under rules 17 or 18) – may provide some hope to claimants in this regard. See Chapter 15, 'Reconsideration of tribunal judgments and decisions', for further discussion.

Otherwise, it seems that the only option for a claimant would be to appeal to the EAT against the tribunal's decision not to accept the claim, in which case an additional £400 issue fee and a £1,200 hearing fee would be payable.

4.89 ## Other persons who may be notified of proceedings
Assuming at least part of the claim has not been rejected, the employment tribunal will notify the respondent or, if there is more than one, the respondents. In addition to the parties, however, the tribunal is under a statutory duty to send copies of specified documents to the following 'interested persons' or deemed parties:

- in proceedings concerning any enactment providing for conciliation by Acas, copies of the claim form and response to a conciliation officer – rule 93 Tribunal Rules

- in proceedings which may involve payments out of the National Insurance Fund, the Secretary of State (who is treated as a party for the purposes of the Tribunal Rules and is thus entitled to be sent copies of the claim form, response form, and all other documents and notices) – rule 96

- where a devolution issues arises, the claim form and response to the Advocate General for Scotland and the Lord Advocate (in the case of a Scottish devolution issue), or to the Attorney General and the Counsel General to the Welsh Assembly Government (in the case of a Welsh devolution issue) – rule 98

- in proceedings under Ss.120, 127 or 146 of the Equality Act 2010, copies of all judgments and written reasons (except where issues of national security apply) to the Commission for Equality and Human Rights – rule 103.

274

Additionally, if a claim alleges that the claimant has made a protected disclosure under S.43A ERA – i.e. it contains a whistleblowing claim – the tribunal may, with the consent of the claimant, send a copy of any accepted claim to a regulator specified in Schedule 1 to the Public Interest Disclosure (Prescribed Persons) Order 1999 SI 1999/1549 – rule 14. This procedure is intended to allow the relevant regulator to investigate the underlying issue where appropriate and to take action if necessary.

The EAT has held that the above requirements do not affect the tribunal's **4.90** jurisdiction, which means that the parties can agree to waive them in the event of non-compliance by the tribunal. In other words, non-compliance will not of itself nullify the proceedings. In Sheringham Development Co Ltd v Browne 1977 ICR 20, EAT, the claimant applied for a redundancy payment (a type of claim with which Acas did not then get involved). At the hearing, the tribunal amended the proceedings to include a claim of unfair dismissal and the employer raised no objection. The tribunal found that the claimant had been unfairly dismissed and the employer appealed, arguing that the proceedings were a nullity because the requirement to notify Acas of the unfair dismissal complaint had not been complied with. The EAT held that the requirement did not affect the tribunal's jurisdiction and that, in any case, it was to be deemed waived by the employer when it consented to the amendment of the tribunal proceedings.

Withdrawals

4.91

A claimant may withdraw all or part of his or her claim at any time, either orally at a hearing, or otherwise in writing. The decision to withdraw may be made because the claimant has concluded that his or her claim is hopeless or, given the possibility of costs being awarded, that it is not worth the risk of pursuing. A withdrawal may also conceal an agreement or settlement between the parties. Once the claim has been settled or a decision made to withdraw it for other reasons, the claimant should inform the tribunal and other parties as soon as possible so as to minimise the risk of incurring unnecessary costs.

It is possible to withdraw a claim against one respondent while continuing it against another or others. However, if a claimant is withdrawing only part of his or her claim, or only to the extent that the claim is brought against a particular respondent, he or she will need to take great care so as not inadvertently to withdraw more of the claim than he or she had intended.

Where a claimant informs the tribunal that a claim (or part of it) is withdrawn, **4.92** the claim (or part) comes to an end, subject to any application that the respondent may make for a costs, preparation time or wasted costs order – rule 51 Tribunal Rules. Once withdrawn, the tribunal has no power to set aside the withdrawal so as to 'reactivate' the claim – Khan v Heywood and Middleton Primary Care Trust 2006 ICR 543, CA.

275

Under rule 52, the tribunal will automatically issue a judgment dismissing the claim (or part) that has been withdrawn, unless:

- the claimant expresses, at the time of withdrawal, a wish to reserve the right to bring a further claim against the respondent raising the same, or substantially the same, complaint and the tribunal is satisfied that there would be legitimate reason for the claimant to do so, or

- the tribunal believes that to issue such a judgment would not be in the interests of justice.

4.93 In most cases, therefore, the respondent will have no need to make an application in order for the claim to be dismissed. A dismissal of the claim or part of it will prevent the claimant from issuing another claim that is the same or substantially the same as that claim or part – see Chapter 2, 'Tribunals' jurisdiction', under 'Relitigation: res judicata and abuse of process – what is a decision?'.

However, there are uncertainties. The Tribunal Rules do not specify precisely when withdrawal takes effect. Nor is there any timeframe within which the tribunal must issue its judgment dismissing the claim. Furthermore, the rules do not explain the process where a claim is settled via Acas. Where there is a delay in the tribunal dismissing a claim following withdrawal, the respondent may be minded to apply for the claim to be dismissed.

4.94 If the claimant reserves the right to bring further proceedings (perhaps in a different forum such as the civil courts), and the tribunal accordingly does not dismiss the claim, he or she may then bring a fresh claim provided that there is still time to do so. A good illustration of the circumstances in which a claimant may seek to withdraw a claim in order to issue fresh proceedings is Verdin v Harrods Ltd 2006 ICR 396, EAT, a case decided under the Tribunal Rules 2004. In that case, the claimant brought breach of contract and other claims in the tribunal. Shortly after presenting her claim form, she sought to withdraw the breach of contract claim by means of an amendment so that she could pursue that claim in the High Court, where it would not be subject to a damages cap of £25,000. A tribunal chairman decided that the breach of contract claim could only be withdrawn if it were dismissed. As this would have the effect of preventing the claimant from bringing the claim in the High Court, the claimant appealed against the chairman's decision. The EAT held that the claimant's intention to bring the breach of contract claim in the High Court did not amount to an abuse of process, and concluded that the tribunal should have permitted the claimant to withdraw her breach of contract claim without dismissing it. In reaching this decision, the EAT confirmed that part (as opposed to the whole) of a claim may be dismissed following withdrawal. It is worth noting that even if the tribunal makes a decision under rule 52 not to dismiss the claim, the respondent may still apply to the tribunal for 'dismissal following withdrawal, although it will have to pay a fee of (currently) £60 to do so – see Chapter 19, 'Fees'.

However, depending on the circumstances, there may be a risk that the second claim might be struck out as an abuse of process, or that the respondent may apply for a wasted costs order against the claimant. In Mills v London Borough of Brent EAT 0545/11 the EAT upheld an employment tribunal's decision to strike out a claimant's third claim, where she had withdrawn two previous virtually identical claims on the same facts without any indication of being under duress to do so. Although the identity of the respondent was different – the first claims being brought against the school in which the claimant worked, and the third against the local education authority – the employment judge had been entitled to take into account the fact that there was a privity of interest between the school and the local education authority: the reality was that if there had been a judgment against the school, the local education authority would have paid any compensation. It was also held to be relevant that the claimant had withdrawn her claim on the third day of a four-day hearing after she had completed her evidence.

The extent to which a claimant who withdraws a claim – particularly at the last **4.95** minute – might be at risk of costs being awarded against him or her is discussed in Chapter 20, 'Costs and penalties', under 'Grounds for making orders against a party – conduct', and 'Factors relevant to tribunal's discretion – late withdrawals'. Any pending applications for costs, preparation time, or wasted costs will be unaffected by the withdrawal, unless the claimant has obtained the respondent's agreement not to pursue costs as part of a settlement.

4.96 Appendix – employment tribunal offices for personal presentation

Below is a list of employment tribunal offices in England and Wales to which a claim form may be presented in person. Note that there are slight discrepancies between the addresses for the Birmingham and East Anglia offices in this list, which is taken from the Practice Direction on the presentation of claims for England and Wales, and those in the list found in the HMCTS guidance booklet, 'Making a claim to an employment tribunal' (T420).

Tribunal office	Address	Telephone number
Birmingham	13th Floor, Centre City Tower, 7 Hill Street, Birmingham B5 4UU	0121 600 7780
East Anglia	Huntingdon Law Courts and Tribunals Centre, Walden Road, Huntingdon, Cambridgeshire PE29 3DW	01480 415600
East Midlands	3rd Floor, Byron House, 2A Maid Marian Way, Nottingham NG1 6HS	0115 947 5701
Leeds	4th Floor, City Exchange, 11 Albion Street, Leeds LS1 4ES	0113 245 9741
London Central	Victory House, 30–34 Kingsway, London WC2B 6EX	020 7273 8603
London East	2nd Floor, Anchorage House, 2 Clove Crescent, London E14 2BE	020 7538 6161
London North and West	3rd Floor, Radius House, 51 Clarendon Road, Watford, Hertfordshire WD17 1HP	01923 281 750
London South	Montague Court, 101 London Road, West Croydon CR0 2RF	020 8667 9131
Newcastle	Quayside House, 110 Quayside, Newcastle Upon Tyne NE1 3DX	0191 260 6900
North West	Alexandra House, 14–22 The Parsonage, Manchester M3 2JA	0161 833 6100
South West	First Floor, Crescent Centre, Bristol BS1 6EZ	0117 929 8261
Wales	Caradog House, 1–6 St Andrews Place, Cardiff CF10 3BE	029 2067 8100

Below is a list of employment tribunal offices in Scotland to which a claim form may be presented in person.

Tribunal office	Address	Telephone number
Aberdeen	Mezzanine Floor, Atholl House, 84–88 Guild Street, Aberdeen AB11 6LT	01224 593137
Dundee	Ground Floor, Block C, Caledonian House, Greenmarket, Dundee DD1 4QB	01382 221578
Edinburgh	54–56 Melville Street, Edinburgh EH3 7HF	0131 226 5584
Glasgow	Eagle Building, 215 Bothwell Street, Glasgow G2 7TS	0141 204 0730

5 Time limits

5.1 Employment tribunal proceedings must, in virtually all cases, be started within time limits set out in the various statutes and statutory instruments that confer the right to bring the proceedings. The time limits for all major employment law claims are listed in the Appendix to this chapter. Time limits go to the tribunal's jurisdiction. They are not simply procedural niceties that can be waived by the parties. This is because they are nearly always expressed in mandatory terms – for example, 'an employment tribunal shall not consider a complaint... unless it is presented to the tribunal before the end of the period of three months beginning with the effective date of termination'. If a claim is out of time and cannot be brought within a statutory formula, if there is one, allowing for an extension of time, then the tribunal must refuse to hear the case.

The jurisdictional nature of time limits was confirmed in Rogers v Bodfari (Transport) Ltd 1973 ICR 325, NIRC, where R complained of unfair dismissal. His complaint was out of time but the employer did not raise the point and the tribunal proceeded to hear the case and to decide that the dismissal was indeed unfair. At an adjourned hearing on compensation the employer raised the issue of the limitation period (then 28 days) for the first time and the tribunal reluctantly dismissed R's claim on the ground that it had had no jurisdiction to hear it in the first place. The NIRC upheld the tribunal's decision and Sir John Donaldson said that 'the time limit must be regarded and interpreted as a jurisdictional provision – which, of course, the parties cannot waive – and not as a limitation provision which they can waive or may be stopped from taking'. This decision was subsequently approved by the Court of Appeal in Dedman v British Building and Engineering Appliances 1974 ICR 53, CA.

281

5.2 The Court of Appeal reaffirmed the position in Radakovits v Abbey National plc 2010 IRLR 307, CA. There R brought an unfair dismissal claim, which he presented one day outside the time limit. A tribunal directed that the question of whether it had jurisdiction to hear R's claim should be determined at a pre-hearing review but, when AN plc conceded that the claim was brought in time, the tribunal vacated the hearing in May 2006. However, at the start of the substantive hearing of the claim in April 2008, a subsequent tribunal of its own motion took the question of jurisdiction as a preliminary issue and decided that, the claim having been presented outside the time limit, it did not have jurisdiction to hear it. R unsuccessfully challenged the decision before the EAT and then appealed further to the Court of Appeal.

Lord Justice Elias, giving the Court of Appeal's judgment, held that the tribunal had been entitled to reopen the question of jurisdiction at the substantive hearing of the claim in April 2008. The leading authorities in this area had clearly established that time limits in the context of unfair dismissal claims go to jurisdiction and that jurisdiction cannot be conferred on a tribunal by agreement or waiver. An employer's decision to abandon any opposition to jurisdiction – as AN plc had initially done in the instant case – will not therefore bind the tribunal. Accordingly, the question of jurisdiction must be taken by a tribunal if it considers the issue to be a live one. However, while tribunals have properly to guard against exercising a jurisdiction when the statutory conditions are not met, Elias LJ stressed that 'they are not bloodhounds who have to sniff out potential grounds on which jurisdiction can be refused'. In other words, a tribunal does not have to explore fully every case where a jurisdictional issue could potentially arise. If, on the face of it, it appears to the tribunal that it does have jurisdiction, it can properly act on that. With regard to R's claim, Elias LJ continued, the only circumstance in which the tribunal would have been precluded from reopening the issue of jurisdiction in April 2008 was if the tribunal in May 2006 had finally determined the issue and issued a declaration that the claim was in time. If that had happened, the issue could only have been reopened on an application for review or on appeal, but there was no suggestion of this in the instant case. The tribunal had therefore been entitled to consider the time limit issue and to find against R on this point. His claim was dismissed.

5.3 The only possible exception to the rule that cases must be brought within the applicable time limit is where there has been deliberate fraud on the part of an employer which has caused the employee to suffer a real injustice by missing the time limit – Grimes v Sutton London Borough Council 1973 ICR 240, NIRC. This would normally be held to justify an extension of the time limit if there is statutory provision for extension, but fraud might be invoked by an employee in cases where there is no such provision. It is probable that, in the case of fraud, time would not begin to run until the fraud was, or ought to have been, discovered by the claimant.

The time limits for presenting a complaint are crucial and both sides need to understand the ground rules, particularly as those limits are relatively short. While the time limits for claims in the civil courts are measured in years, those for claims in employment tribunals are much shorter – usually three or six months.

This chapter deals first with the time limits for commencing tribunal **5.4** proceedings, how the time period is calculated, and what 'presenting' a claim to a tribunal means. It then goes on to explain the circumstances in which there will be an extension of the normal time limit where the mandatory rules on early conciliation apply. Finally, the chapter considers the 'escape' clauses, which allow the limits to be extended on a discretionary basis in certain circumstances in some but not all types of tribunal claim.

Note that there are also time limits within which respondents must reply to complaints. These are dealt with in Chapter 6, 'Defending a claim', under 'Time limit for presenting response'.

Time limits for starting tribunal proceedings 5.5

Leaving aside the special cases of equal pay claims and claims under European law (see 'Equal pay claims' and 'European law' below), the statutory provisions governing time limits fall into three groups, depending on the formula, if any, allowing for an extension of time:

* *no extension* of time allowed

* *'not reasonably practicable'* formula using the following or similar wording: 'within such further period as the tribunal considers reasonable in a case where it is satisfied that it was not reasonably practicable for the complaint to be presented before the end of the period of (three) months' – see '"Not reasonably practicable" extension' below

* *'just and equitable'* formula using the following or similar wording: 'a tribunal may nevertheless consider any such complaint... which is out of time if, in all the circumstances of the case, it considers that it is just and equitable to do so' – see '"Just and equitable" extension' below.

Pre-claim conciliation. Note that the normal time limit for bringing certain **5.6** claims may be extended as a result of mandatory 'early conciliation'. The early conciliation scheme came into force on 6 April 2014 and allows for a suspension of the relevant time limit while Acas offers, and attempts to reach, a resolution of the dispute before the claim is presented to a tribunal. The special time limit rules that apply in these circumstances are discussed under 'Extension of time limit under early conciliation rules' below.

5.7 **European cross-border mediation.** In addition, since 20 May 2011, the time limit for bringing claims may be extended where the parties make use of cross-border mediation. For example, the time limit for bringing an unfair dismissal complaint may be extended where the parties are engaged in mediation to resolve a cross-border dispute and that mediation started before the time limit was due to expire – Ss.111(2A) and 207A(2) Employment Rights Act 1996 (ERA). If, in these circumstances, the normal time limit under S.111(2)(a) ERA would expire before the mediation ends or less than four weeks after it ends, the time limit will be extended to the end of four weeks after the mediation ceases – Ss.111(2A) and 207A(3). A cross-border dispute is one in which at least one of the parties is domiciled or habitually resident in a Member State of the European Union other than that of any other party – Article 2 EU Cross-border Mediation Directive (No.2008/52).

5.8 **Repeal of statutory dispute resolution procedures.** Until April 2009, the normal time limit for bringing certain tribunal claims was automatically extended by a period of three months to allow for compliance with the statutory dismissal, disciplinary and grievance procedures set out in the Employment Act 2002. The statutory dispute resolution procedures were repealed in their entirety on 6 April 2009.

5.9 **Premature claims**

The period of time during which the claim must be presented is usually expressed as beginning on a certain date. This means that if a claim is presented before the specified date it will be premature and the tribunal will have no jurisdiction to consider it. There are, however, certain circumstances in which a premature claim may nevertheless be 'saved'.

5.10 **Unfair dismissal claims.** In respect of unfair dismissal claims, the general rule is set down in S.111(2)(a) ERA, which provides that the time for presenting an unfair dismissal claim runs from the *effective date of termination* (EDT) (for further details of the EDT, see IDS Employment Law Handbook, 'Contracts of Employment' (2009), Chapter 11, 'Date of termination'). However, S.111(3) allows a tribunal to consider an unfair dismissal complaint presented *after* notice of dismissal has been given but *before* the EDT has been reached. 'Notice' in this context means not only the employer's notice of dismissal, but also notice given by an employee who claims that he or she has been constructively dismissed under S.95(1)(c) ERA – Presley v Llanelli Borough Council 1979 ICR 419, EAT. But S.111(3) applies only where dismissal is with notice. It therefore has no relevance in cases of summary dismissal or where employment comes to an end on the expiry of a limited-term contract. In Throsby v Imperial College of Science and Technology 1978 ICR 357, EAT, for example, T was warned a year in advance that his fixed-term contract would not be renewed and he promptly complained of unfair dismissal. The EAT held that the claim was premature and that proceedings could not be started until the contract had actually expired.

The application of S.111(3) may well depend on whether notice has actually been given. In Rai v Somerfield Stores Ltd 2004 ICR 656, EAT, for example, the EAT decided that an ultimatum given to an employee to return to work by a specified date or face the sack was not notice to terminate the contract for the purposes of S.111(3).

In Patel v Nagesan 1995 ICR 988, CA, the employer unsuccessfully sought to **5.11** avoid the operation of S.111(3) by summarily dismissing the employee during the currency of the notice period. The employer wrote to N on 11 October giving her ten weeks' notice of dismissal. N presented a complaint of unfair dismissal on 19 November, before the expiry of her notice, as S.111(3) entitled her to do. The following day the employer summarily dismissed her. The employer then argued that once N had been summarily dismissed, she lost any right to pursue the complaint she had already lodged under S.111(3). Since N was dismissed on 20 November without notice, S.111(2) applied, with the result that N was required to present her claim within three months of the effective date of termination of her contract, i.e. 20 November. Accordingly, the employer argued that N's claim presented on 19 November was premature and the tribunal had no jurisdiction to consider it. The Court of Appeal rejected this argument and held that N's claim of unfair dismissal presented during her notice period was not invalidated by the fact that she was subsequently summarily dismissed. S.111(3) stipulates that a complaint may be considered by a tribunal if it is presented after notice is given but before the EDT, and in order for that provision to apply, although the dismissal must be with notice, it is not necessary that the notice actually comes into effect.

Section 111(3) was similarly held to apply in Governing Body of Wishmorecross School v Balado 2011 ICR D31, EAT. In that case, the school found B guilty of misconduct and sent her a letter saying that she would be summarily dismissed, but that she could lodge an appeal against dismissal within ten working days. The letter went on to state that 'the decision to dismiss you will not be put into effect unless (a) you decide not to appeal against the decision or (b) any appeal is unsuccessful', and that in the meantime she would 'continue to be suspended on full pay'. B lodged an appeal but then presented an unfair dismissal claim before the appeal was decided. The question for the EAT was whether her claim was premature, having been presented before the date on which the school stated she would be 'summarily dismissed'. The EAT held that it was not. The school's letter amounted to a dismissal with notice, subject to her right to appeal, and B could therefore avail herself of S.111(3).

Redundancy payments. There is no statutory equivalent to S.111(3) ERA in **5.12** respect of redundancy payment claims. S.164 ERA simply states that an employee will not be entitled to a redundancy payment unless he or she makes

285

a claim (in one of four ways set out in S.164(1)) 'before the end of the period of six months beginning with the relevant date'. (The relevant date is normally the effective date of termination of employment – see IDS Employment Law Handbook, 'Redundancy' (2011), Chapter 6, 'Redundancy payments', under 'Statutory redundancy pay scheme – relevant date and calculation date'.) On a literal interpretation of this wording, there would seem to be nothing to prevent a claim being made before termination of employment because that would be well before the end of the period of six months beginning with the relevant date. However, the EAT has held that this is not so and that a claim will be premature if it is made during notice of dismissal for redundancy – see Watts v Rubery Owen Conveyancer Ltd 1977 ICR 429, EAT; which was followed in Pritchard-Rhodes Ltd v Boon and anor 1979 IRLR 19, EAT.

Although the Watts decision must be taken as binding on tribunals unless overruled, it is certainly open to question. This is because one of the four circumstances in which a claim for a redundancy payment can be made under S.164(1) is where the employee has presented a complaint of unfair dismissal under S.111. As noted above, S.111(3) specifically allows a tribunal to consider an unfair dismissal complaint presented after notice has been given but before the EDT. However, the Watts decision was recently endorsed by the EAT in Foster v Bon Groundwork Ltd 2011 ICR 1122, EAT, a case concerning issue estoppel. In the course of the proceedings, a question arose as to whether the principle that a claim for a redundancy payment can only be pursued after the expiry of the notice period remained good law. In the EAT's view, it clearly did. According to Mr Justice Silber, 'Parliament has not changed the law on this when it could have done so when introducing the provision for unfair dismissal.' Although the employer appealed to the Court of Appeal – see Foster v Bon Groundwork Ltd 2012 ICR 1027, CA – the case was decided on other grounds and the Court declined to express an opinion on whether Watts remains good law.

5.13 **Breach of contract claims.** In relation to claims for breach of contract, Article 7 of the Employment Tribunals Extension of Jurisdiction (England and Wales) Order 1994 SI 1994/1623 provides that a claim must be brought '(a) within the period of three months beginning with the effective date of termination of the contract giving rise to the claim, or (b) where there is no effective date of termination, within the period of three months beginning with the last day upon which the employee worked in the employment which has terminated', unless the tribunal is satisfied that it was not reasonably practicable for the claim to be brought within the time limit. In Capek v Lincolnshire County Council 2000 ICR 878, CA, the Court of Appeal held that employment tribunals have no jurisdiction to hear claims for breach of contract that are presented prior to the termination of an employee's contract, even if the claims relate to matters arising before termination which are still outstanding at the date of termination.

While the correctness of this principle is not in doubt, it is worth noting that this will not necessarily spell the end of an employee's complaint. In Whitmore v Commissioners of Inland Revenue EAT 0727/02, for example, the EAT applied the Capek decision and held that the tribunal had correctly declined jurisdiction in respect of W's breach of contract claim on the ground that the claim was premature. However, it went on to hold that the tribunal should have asked itself whether, in substance, W's claim was not only for breach of contract but also for unlawful deduction from wages under S.13 ERA. Had it properly directed itself on the matter, the tribunal would have found that W's case did contain an unlawful deduction from wages claim which it had jurisdiction to hear.

Discrimination claims. With regard to discrimination claims – other than equal pay claims (for which see 'Equal pay claims' below) – the Equality Act 2010 (EqA) provides that the relevant time limit for starting employment tribunal proceedings runs from 'the date of the act to which the complaint relates' – S.123(1)(a). This is a minor change from the provisions in the antecedent discrimination legislation that were in force until October 2010, under which time ran from the date 'when the act complained of was done' (see, for example, S.76(1) of the Sex Discrimination Act 1975). Case law has established that where the 'act complained of' (now 'the act to which the complaint relates') is a dismissal, the date from which the time limit runs is the date on which the dismissal takes effect and not the date when notice of termination is given – Lupetti v Wrens Old House Ltd 1984 ICR 348, EAT. **5.14**

European law **5.15**
Neither European law nor UK domestic law set down time limits for claims brought under Community law in respect of directly enforceable EU Directives, such as the recast EU Equal Treatment Framework Directive (No.2006/54), or directly enforceable provisions of the Treaty on the Functioning of the European Union (TFEU), such as Article 157 on equal pay. Generally speaking, the European Court of Justice (ECJ) has accepted the right of Member States to impose reasonable time limits on claims in respect of EU rights. In this context, the ECJ has formulated two main principles: first, that a national procedural rule in proceedings designed to protect rights under European law must not be less favourable to claimants than other national procedural rules governing similar domestic actions – the principle of 'equivalence'; and secondly, that any national procedural rule should not make it 'impossible in practice' or 'excessively difficult' for individuals to exercise those rights – the principle of 'effectiveness' (see, for example, Marshall v Southampton and South West Hampshire Health Authority (Teaching) (No.2) 1993 ICR 893, ECJ; and Vroege v NCIV Instituut voor Volkshuisvesting BV and anor and another case 1995 ICR 635, ECJ).

Difficulties have arisen in applying the principle of effectiveness where a Member State has failed to implement or comply with a measure of EU law. In

287

this situation, it is likely that individual citizens of that state will either remain ignorant of their rights under EU law or will be disinclined to try to enforce those rights in the national courts (assuming of course, that the measure in question can be relied upon directly by the individual concerned – i.e. is directly effective). If, when proceedings are eventually commenced, the state (where it is the respondent) is able to defeat the claim by reference to a procedural time limit, the state could be said to have benefited from its own default.

5.16 For a time it was thought that the ECJ's ruling in Emmott v Minister for Social Welfare and anor 1993 ICR 8, ECJ, had struck a major blow against Member States which failed to implement EU law. The decision appeared to establish the general principle that time should not start to run against an individual who is suing the state until the relevant EU measure has been properly implemented into national law. This raised the prospect of large numbers of retroactive – and sometimes very old – claims being brought against emanations of the state whenever individuals were found to have missed the opportunity to take proceedings earlier because of the state's failure to implement the measure in question.

However, both the ECJ and the UK courts appear to have resiled from the position taken in Emmott, and in some subsequent cases their primary objective seems to have been to confine that decision as far as possible to its own special facts. For example, the ECJ has ruled that the 'Emmott principle' does not apply to time-based limits on backdated benefits – Steenhorst-Neerings v Bestuur van de Bedrijfsvereniging voor Detailhandel, Ambachten en Huisvrouwen 1994 IRLR 244, ECJ; Johnson v Chief Adjudication Officer 1995 ICR 375, ECJ. And in BP Supergas Anonimos Etairia Geniki Emporiki Viomichaniki Kai Antiprossopeion v Greece 1995 All ER (EC) 684, ECJ, it appears to have stated that national courts are entitled to uphold reasonable national procedural time limits in respect of claims based upon EU law even where a Member State breaches its obligation to transpose the mandatory provisions of a Directive into national law. Furthermore, in Biggs v Somerset County Council 1996 ICR 364, CA, the Court of Appeal concluded that the Emmott principle does not apply where the EU right relied upon derives from a directly effective Article of an EU Treaty – in that case, what is now Article 157 TFEU – rather than from a Directive.

5.17 It is worth noting that, while the Emmott principle may no longer apply to postpone or disapply domestic time limits, the scope of the time limit applicable to domestic discrimination law (much of which is derived from European Law) is potentially very wide. Under the EqA, tribunals can extend the time limit if it is 'just and equitable' to do so, and this can include a consideration of the date from which the complainant could reasonably have become aware of his or her right to present a worthwhile claim. In British Coal Corporation v Keeble and ors 1997 IRLR 336, EAT, the EAT decided that claims based on the Sex

Discrimination Act 1975 (SDA) – since repealed and re-enacted in the EqA – arising out of a discriminatory redundancy scheme could be accepted even though the claimants were nearly two-and-a-half years out of time, because it was 'just and equitable' to do so. The facts were that when the claimants were dismissed in 1989 they did not think they had a legal claim, and it was only after the ECJ decision in Barber v Guardian Royal Exchange Assurance Group 1990 ICR 616, ECJ, in June 1990 that they realised that they did. The EAT found that Lord Justice Neill's statement in Biggs v Somerset County Council (above) that 'it would be contrary to the principle of legal certainty to allow past transactions to be reopened and limitation periods to be circumvented because the existing law at the relevant time had not been explained, or had not been fully understood' was meant only to apply to the time limit provisions governing unfair dismissal and the consideration of whether it was 'reasonably practicable' for the claimant to bring the claim in time. The statement was not intended to cover the broader 'just and equitable' test in the SDA (and, by extension, the other discrimination legislation). While it is right for the tribunal to bear in mind the need for legal certainty and finality in litigation, that was only one factor to take into account when considering what was just and equitable in all the circumstances – see further '"Just and equitable" extension' below.

Equal pay claims   5.18

There is no time limit for claims relating to the operation of the equality clause under the Equality Act 2010 (EqA) while the claimant remains employed by the employer. However, where the claimant is no longer employed, S.129(3) EqA – read with S.130 – provides that, in 'standard cases', he or she must bring the claim within *six months* of the ending of employment. Similarly, where the claimant has been employed under what is described as 'a stable working relationship', which in essence covers employment under a series of contracts where an ongoing relationship subsists between contracts, the claimant must bring a claim within six months of that relationship ending – Ss.129(3) and 130(3) (a 'stable work case')

While six months is the default time limit, the EqA makes provision for an extension of the time limit in the following circumstances:

• where there is deliberate concealment of facts by the employer relevant to the claim without knowledge of which the claimant could not reasonably have been expected to institute proceedings, the six-month period only begins to run from the date the claimant discovered (or should have discovered) the facts in question – Ss.129(3), 130(4) and (6) (a 'concealment case')

• where the claimant has an incapacity, the six-month period does not start to run until the claimant has ceased to have the incapacity – Ss.129(3) and 130(7) (an 'incapacity case')

289

- where there is both concealment of relevant facts by the employer and the claimant has an incapacity, then the six-month time period only runs from whichever is the later of the dates of the ending of the concealment or incapacity – S.129(3).

These time limit provisions are discussed at length in IDS Employment Law Handbook, 'Equal Pay' (2011), Chapter 9, 'Enforcement', under 'Time limits'.

5.19 **Transfer of undertakings.** The question of time limits for equal pay claims can become complicated when the undertaking within which the employee is employed is transferred under the Transfer of Undertakings (Protection of Employment) Regulations 2006 SI 2006/246. The various issues that arise in these circumstances are discussed in IDS Employment Tribunal Law Handbook, 'Equal Pay' (2011), Chapter 9, 'Enforcement', under 'Time limits – effect of TUPE'.

5.20 Calculating the time for presenting claim

There are certain basic rules for calculating the period of time allowed for presenting a claim to an employment tribunal. Claimants frequently get at least one of these wrong and end up presenting a claim one or two days after the time limit has expired. It is therefore essential to understand the rules:

- when a claim is to be presented within a period 'beginning' with a particular date – e.g. the time limit for unfair dismissal claims, which begins with the EDT – that date must be included in the calculation of the time allowed – Hammond v Haigh Castle and Co Ltd 1973 ICR 148, NIRC. So a period of three months beginning with 10 March ends on 9 June and not, as the unwary often think, on 10 June

- when a time limit is expressed as 'beginning' with a date, the word 'date' means a complete period of 24 hours and time starts to run at the very beginning of this period. This applies even if the employee is summarily dismissed in the late afternoon or evening – Dorber v London Brick Co Ltd 1974 ICR 270, NIRC. If, for example, an employee is summarily dismissed late in the evening of 10 March, time starts to run at the first minute on 10 March and runs out at midnight on 9 June. It was confirmed by the Court of Appeal in RJB Mining (UK) Ltd v National Union of Mineworkers 1995 IRLR 556, CA (a union balloting case), that midnight cannot belong to both days either side of it and so midnight on 9 June cannot also be taken as the first moment of 10 June. Rule 4(1) of the Employment Tribunal Rules of Procedure 2013 ('the Tribunal Rules'), contained in Schedule 1 to the Employment Tribunals (Constitution and Rules of Procedure) Regulations 2013 SI 2013/1237 ('the Tribunal Regulations'), confirms that the deadline for presenting a claim is midnight of the last day of the limitation period, stating that 'an act required by these Rules… to be done on or by a particular day may be done at any time before midnight on that day'

- when a claim is to be presented within a period 'following' a certain date, that date is excluded from the calculation. For example, an application for interim relief must be presented to a tribunal 'before the end of the period of seven days immediately following the effective date of termination' – S.161(2) Trade Union and Labour Relations (Consolidation) Act 1992 (TULR(C)A). This means that the seven days start to run on the day after termination, so that an employee whose employment ends on a Tuesday has until the following Tuesday to present his or her application

- 'month' means a calendar month. The rule is that, in calculating a period of a month or months, the period ends one day before the corresponding date in the appropriate subsequent month. If the month in which the period expires has no corresponding date, then the period expires on the last day of that month. Thus, a month beginning with 31 January ends on 28 February (or 29 February in a leap year).

In University of Cambridge v Murray 1993 ICR 460, EAT, M's EDT was 30 **5.21** April 1991. She presented a complaint to a tribunal on 30 July 1991. The EAT upheld the tribunal's finding that the complaint should have been presented on 29 July 1991 and, in doing so, reiterated a number of well-established principles governing the calculation of time limits for unfair dismissal claims. It began by noting that in regard to any statutory time limit two questions must be determined. First, how is the period to be computed, paying particular regard to the fact that the calendar months are of different lengths? Secondly, given a starting date, does the starting date count as part of the period or is it excluded? The EAT decided that, when computing the relevant period, the proper approach is to look at the corresponding date – i.e. the day with the same number as the EDT – in the relevant later month. Turning to the second question, the EAT noted that it is well established that where the relevant statute uses the term 'from' or 'after', then the starting date is not included in the relevant period. However, the expression in S.111(2) ERA, which governs time limits in unfair dismissal claims, is 'beginning with'. The starting date is therefore included in the period and it is necessary to count back one day to establish the final date on which a claim can be presented.

The EAT in Pruden v Cunard Ellerman Ltd 1993 IRLR 317, EAT, set out a 'simpler' approach to the calculation of time limits in unfair dismissal claims. It ruled that, because the EDT is included in the three-month period, the relevant date for calculating the period is the day before the EDT. Thus, if the EDT is day 31 of a month, then the relevant date is day 30 of that month; the claimant then counts forward three months. In 11 months out of the year there is no problem with this because, with the exception of February, there are at least 30 days in each calendar month. The only anomaly that arises with this

291

simple approach, according to the EAT, is if the EDT occurs on 30 November or 1 December of any one year, in which case the relevant date for calculating the three-month period will be 29 November and 30 November respectively. However, except during a leap year, there is no day 29 (and no day 30 in any event) in February, so in either situation, the calculator simply takes the last day in February.

5.22   The problem with the approach set out in Pruden is that it gives rise to a further anomaly where the EDT is the first day of a month immediately following a month in which there are fewer than 31 days. If, for example, the EDT is 1 May, then, according to the guidance given by the EAT in Pruden, the relevant date for the purposes of calculation will be 30 April – i.e. the day before the EDT – and the time limit will be three months later – i.e. 30 July. However, on the approach adopted in University of Cambridge v Murray (above), the EDT would be 31 July. For this reason the guidance set out in the Pruden case is to be treated with caution.

5.23   Effective date of termination

The EDT is the date on which time starts to run for a number of employment rights, in particular the right to complain of unfair dismissal. Disputes often arise over the EDT when a preliminary issue is raised at a tribunal as to whether a claim was in time, or an employee had enough continuous service to bring a claim. Complicating factors may be, for example, an ambiguous dismissal letter, a payment in lieu of notice, an error over the employee's notice entitlement or an internal appeal procedure which delay termination. These issues are covered in IDS Employment Law Handbook, 'Contracts of Employment' (2009), Chapter 11, 'Date of termination'. In the rest of this chapter we assume that the EDT or other date on which time starts to run is known and we concentrate on the other end of the limitation period – whether the claim was presented in time and the circumstances in which tribunals may extend the time limit.

5.24   'Presenting' the claim

Rule 8(1) of the Tribunal Rules states: 'A claim shall be started by presenting a completed claim form (using a prescribed form) in accordance with any practice direction made under Reg 11 [of the Tribunal Regulations] which supplements this rule.' The form that must be used in order to present the claim – the ET1 claim form – and the details that must be included are discussed in Chapter 4, 'Starting tribunal proceedings', under 'Completing the claim form'. The claim form must also be accompanied by the appropriate fee or a remission application – see Chapter 19, 'Fees'.

Methods of presenting the claim

5.25

On 29 July 2013, two Presidential Practice Directions were issued under Reg 11 of the Regulations: one in relation to the presentation of claims in England and Wales and another which applies to claims brought in Scotland. The Practice Directions state that a claim may be presented to an employment tribunal in one of three ways:

- *online* using the online form submission service (see 'Online presentation' below)

- *by post* to a central address (see 'Presentation by post' below)

- *in person* to a regional employment tribunal office (see 'Presentation in person' below).

Rule 85(2), which states that a claim form may *only* be delivered in accordance with the Practice Direction made under Reg 11, makes it clear that these are the only methods for presenting a claim to an employment tribunal. Accordingly, in a change from the Tribunal Rules 2004, fax and e-mail are no longer prescribed methods of presentation and cannot be used to submit a tribunal complaint.

Presentation by post. If the postal route is used, a completed ET1 claim form **5.26** must be sent by post to the appropriate central office – see Chapter 4, 'Starting tribunal proceedings', in the section 'Making a claim', under 'The claim form (ET1) – presenting the claim form'. Rule 90(a) provides that a claim sent by post will, unless the contrary is proved, be taken to have been received on the day on which it would be delivered in the ordinary course of post. The claimant is notified of the submission of the claim once the claim has been passed to the appropriate employment tribunal office, which will usually be determined by the claimant's place of work.

Presentation in person. It is also open to a claimant to take his or her claim **5.27** form to one of the employment tribunal offices listed in the Schedule to the relevant Practice Direction (see the Appendix to Chapter 4, 'Starting tribunal proceedings'). If the claim is accepted, the claim will then be sent to the appropriate tribunal office.

A claim delivered in person will, unless the contrary is proved, be taken to have been received on the day of delivery – rule 90(c).

Online presentation. The speediest and most efficient method of presenting a **5.28** claim will normally be through the online form submission service (accessible at www.employmenttribunals.service.gov.uk). If the claim is submitted electronically, the claim form will be automatically routed to the correct tribunal office. A claim sent electronically will, unless the contrary is proved, be taken to have been received on the day of transmission – rule 90(b). Nevertheless, claimants should contact the tribunal office if they do not receive an

293

acknowledgment of the receipt of their claim. The HMCTS guidance booklet, 'Making a claim to an employment tribunal' (T240), states that 'when a claim has been successfully submitted online you will receive a receipt to confirm this. If you do not receive a receipt notification, you should contact the employment tribunal office immediately.'

A claim submitted online is only presented to the employment tribunal to which it is directed and not to all employment tribunals generally. The consequences of submitting a claim to the wrong jurisdiction were considered in McFadyen and ors v PB Recovery Ltd and ors EATS 0072/08, where the EAT held that an online claim form was not presented to a Scottish tribunal on the same date it was wrongly submitted to an English tribunal, which rejected the claim for lack of jurisdiction. M was employed by PBR Ltd, which had its registered office in Bristol, though he worked at a site in Scotland. When M was made redundant, his solicitor, C, submitted an ET1 claim form online, providing details of PBR Ltd's registered office in Bristol as the address of the respondent. He did not enter the location in Scotland at which M had actually worked as this was not stated to be a 'required field' and he did not know the address. The claim was forwarded to the Bristol tribunal to be processed. However, an employment judge there decided that the claim could not be accepted because the tribunal in England and Wales had no jurisdiction to hear it. C contacted the Glasgow tribunal, which 'retrieved' the claim form from the IT system, but by then it was out of time, and the tribunal dismissed it. M appealed, arguing that the claim should be treated as having been presented on the date when it was received by the Tribunals Service's host server.

5.29   The EAT rejected the argument that the host server could be treated as an agent for all employment tribunals. The host server's task is completed once the claim has been forwarded to the tribunal closest to the address provided in section 2 – i.e. the place of work or, if none is provided, the respondent's address: it does not hold the forms for all tribunals in the UK generally. Nothing in the ET1 itself, the statutory provisions or the accompanying guidance could give a claimant the legitimate expectation that the host server would deliver the form anywhere other than the tribunal nearest to the relevant address provided, or that the claim form was also being held by the host server on behalf of all or any other tribunals. Furthermore, the EAT thought that recognition needed to be given to the fact that the jurisdictions of England and Wales on the one hand and Scotland on the other are separate, and that a claim presented in England cannot be regarded as having been presented in Scotland. With this in mind, the tribunal had been correct to find that the claim was presented to the host server, directed to the Bristol office where it was rejected for lack of jurisdiction, and thus treated as if it had not been presented on that date at all. The later presentation in Glasgow was therefore out of time. The EAT noted that the rejection by Bristol was unfortunate since that tribunal did appear to have jurisdiction. However, that could have been addressed by means of a timely application for review or appeal, neither of which occurred. Accordingly, M's appeal was dismissed.

If England and Wales and Scotland both have dual jurisdiction over a claim, as appears to have been the case in McFadyen, and the claimant wishes to pursue the claim in the jurisdiction other than that to which the claim has been automatically routed, he or she would have to apply for a transfer under rule 99 (see Chapter 11, 'Case management', under 'Miscellaneous issues – transfer of proceedings'). The claim would then be treated as having been received in Scotland on the same day it was presented in England. However, such a transfer relies on a timely claim being presented in the first place. It may be preferable in such cases, assuming there is sufficient time, for the form to be submitted, by post or in person, directly to the relevant address for the jurisdiction within which the claimant wishes to pursue the claim.

Meaning of 'presenting' 5.30

'Presenting' for the purposes of starting tribunal proceedings has a specific meaning in this context. In Hammond v Haigh Castle and Co Ltd 1973 ICR 148, NIRC, Sir John Donaldson said: 'In our judgment, a claim is presented to a tribunal when it is *received* by the tribunal, whether or not it is dealt with immediately upon receipt' (our stress). An illustration:

- **Post Office v Moore** 1981 ICR 623, EAT: M's solicitor put M's claim through the letterbox at the Employment Tribunal Office at 10 pm on the last day of the three-month period for presentation. The employer argued that the claim had not been presented until it had been handed to or received by a duly appointed officer of the tribunal, which did not happen until the day after it had been put through the letterbox, by which time the limitation period had expired. The EAT held that presentation of a complaint does not require the cooperation of a tribunal clerk or official. It only requires physical delivery at the tribunal offices. It followed that M's claim had been presented in time.

There is a particular problem when the limitation period expires on a non- 5.31 working day – e.g. a Saturday, Sunday or public holiday – when the tribunal offices are closed. The rule governing the issue of a writ to commence civil proceedings in the High Court is that if the limitation period runs out on a day when the court office is closed there is an automatic extension until the next day on which it is open – Pritam Kaur v S Russell and Sons Ltd 1973 1 All ER 617, CA. It might seem logical to apply the Pritam Kaur rule to claims to tribunals but the Court of Appeal has ruled otherwise:

- **Hetton Victory Club Ltd v Swainston** 1983 ICR 341, CA: the three-month period for S to claim unfair dismissal expired on a Sunday and he presented his claim at the employment tribunal office on the following Monday. He argued that the Pritam Kaur rule applied and that his claim

295

had been presented in time because the limitation period was automatically extended until the Monday. The EAT and the Court of Appeal, however, did not agree. The Court of Appeal held that 'presentation' requires physical delivery only and does not involve any further action on the part of the body to whom presentation is made. Although the office was closed on Sunday, there was a letterbox through which mail could have been put. It could not, therefore, be claimed that presentation at the office was impossible at the weekend, so that there was no need to extend the period for presentation until the Monday. The situation is different with the issue of a writ to start High Court proceedings, since this can only be completed when the writ is stamped in a court office: it follows that a writ cannot be issued when the court office is closed. S's claim had been presented out of time.

5.32 Two subsequent EAT decisions have gone some way towards mollifying the effect of this judgment, however:

- **Lang v Devon General Ltd** 1987 ICR 4, EAT: L was dismissed on 17 September, so that time expired on 16 December, which was a Sunday. Her claim was posted to the employment tribunal office on Friday 14 December. The office did have a letterbox but, by special agreement with the Post Office, post for delivery on Saturday when the office was closed was held over until it was open again on Monday. The EAT held that because of this special arrangement, the Post Office held the weekend mail as bailees for the tribunal. It followed that L's claim was deemed to have been presented on Saturday 15 December, when the Post Office received it as bailee or agent of the tribunal, and so it was in time

- **Ford v Stakis Hotels and Inns Ltd** 1987 ICR 943, EAT: F's claim was to be delivered to an employment tribunal office which had no letterbox and the limitation period ran out on a public holiday when the office was closed. F's solicitor delivered it by hand on the following day. The EAT held that since there was no proper means of presenting the claim on a day when the office was closed – and the EAT discounted the possibility of pushing it under the door – the time limit for presentation was automatically extended to the day after the holiday.

In the Ford case the EAT was, in effect, applying the Pritam Kaur rule to the special case in which an employment tribunal office has no letterbox: Mr Swainston (in Hetton Victory Club Ltd v Swainston (above), in which the Court of Appeal refused to apply the Pritam Kaur rule) had been unfortunate in that his local office did have a letterbox. (It should be noted that in the above cases the claimants were claiming that their claims were in time: they were not arguing for an extension of the time limit.)

5.33 In Consignia plc (formerly the Post Office) v Sealy 2002 ICR 1193, CA, the Court of Appeal sought to resolve the problems surrounding time limits and the presentation of claims. The facts, in brief, were that S was employed by Consignia (now known again as the Post Office) as a postman. His unfair dismissal claim should have been presented at the latest on 8 October, which was a Sunday. S posted his claim by first-class post on Friday 6 October. However, it was not received by the tribunal until Tuesday 10 October. When the case reached the Court of Appeal, Lord Justice Brook sought to lay down general guidance to help tribunal users and tribunals in determining whether a claim has been presented in time:

(1) A claim is 'presented' within the meaning of S.111(2) ERA when it arrives at an employment tribunal office.

(2) If a complainant or his or her agent proves that it was impossible to present a complaint in this way before the end of the time prescribed by S.111(2)(a) – for example, because the tribunal office was found to be locked at a weekend and did not have a letterbox – then it will be possible to argue that it was not reasonably practicable for the complaint to be presented within the prescribed period.

(3) If a complainant chooses to present a complaint by sending it by post, presentation will be assumed to have been effected, unless the contrary is proved, at the time the letter would be delivered in the ordinary course of post.

(4) If the letter is sent by first-class post, it is legitimate to conclude that in the ordinary course of post it will be delivered on the second day after it was posted (excluding Sundays, bank holidays, Christmas Day and Good Friday, being days when post is not normally delivered).

(5) If the letter does not arrive at the time when it would be expected to arrive in the ordinary course of post, but is unexpectedly delayed, a tribunal may conclude that it was not reasonably practicable for the complaint to be presented within the prescribed period.

(6) If a form is date-stamped on a Monday by a tribunal office so as to be outside a three-month period which ends on the Saturday or Sunday, it will be open to a tribunal to find as a fact that it was posted by first-class post not later than the Thursday and arrived on the Saturday; or, alternatively, to extend time as a matter of discretion if it is satisfied that the letter was posted by first-class post not later than the Thursday.

(7) This regime does not allow for any unusual subjective expectation, whether based on inside knowledge of the postal system or on lay experience of what happens in practice, to the effect that a letter posted by first-class post may arrive earlier than the second day (excluding Sundays, etc: see (4) above) after it is posted. The 'normal and expected' result of posting a letter

297

must be objectively, not subjectively, assessed and it is that the letter will arrive at its destination in the ordinary course of post.

5.34 The Consignia guidelines on postal delivery were revisited in Coldridge v HM Prison Service EAT 0728/04, where Mr Justice Burton, then President of the EAT, confirmed that they remained good law, and that they reflected the rule (now rule 90) on deemed delivery as set out in the Tribunal Rules. In reaching this decision, the EAT held that Anderton v Clywd County Council 2002 3 All ER 813, CA, in which the Court of Appeal concluded that the Civil Procedure Rules simply provide for deeming service two days after posting 'without reference to any question of ordinary course of post, posting days or business days', was not applicable to employment tribunals. In the Coldridge case the last day for presentation of the claim was Sunday 30 June. The claimant's solicitor posted the claim on Friday 28 June but it did not arrive at the tribunal office until Monday 1 July and was therefore one day out of time. In holding that the claim was out of time, the EAT pointed out that the position under Consignia accords with a claimant's 'reasonable expectation' of when a letter will arrive in the ordinary course of post. A party posting a letter on a Friday cannot reasonably expect that it will arrive on a Sunday because he or she knows that there is no post on a Sunday. The EAT concluded that when a claim form is posted first class it is deemed to be presented at the employment tribunal office two *posting* days later (i.e. excluding Sundays and bank holidays). The fact that Saturday is to be treated as a posting day for these purposes was confirmed in Metcalfe v Cygnet Health Care Ltd EAT 0421/05, where the EAT held that a tribunal can, if satisfied that a letter was posted by first-class post not later than the Thursday, find that it arrived on the Saturday by operation of the deemed posting rule.

The question of when a claim was 'presented' in the context of an online tribunal application was considered in Tyne and Wear Autistic Society v Smith 2005 ICR 663, EAT. S had submitted the online claim form with three days of the time limit remaining and received a confirmation message from the commercial web host which ran the system for the Employment Tribunals Service (ETS). He did not, however, receive a confirmation e-mail from the ETS and it transpired that the claim had never reached the ETS mailbox. He submitted a second claim two weeks later, which was received 16 days out of time. An employment tribunal found that, since the original claim had been received by the web host on the day it was submitted, the claim had been presented in time. On appeal, the EAT upheld this decision and stated that since the ETS held out online claims as a method of presenting claims to a tribunal, it had to follow that a claim was presented when successfully submitted to the ETS website. It did not matter whether the claim was forwarded to the ETS mailbox on a later date, or not at all.

That case can be contrasted with an earlier case, Mossman v Bray Management **5.35** Ltd EAT 0477/04, where a different division of the EAT held that an online claim form that does not arrive at an employment tribunal, for whatever reason, will not be regarded as having been 'presented'. However, in our view the Smith decision should be preferred. In Smith, the claimant's claim reached the commercial web host for the ETS website but, due to a technical glitch, not the ETS mailbox. But given that there was evidence (in the form of the web host's confirmation message) that the claimant had sent off his claim, it is arguable that there was a reasonable expectation that the claim would arrive at the intended tribunal office. Thus, in so far as the Mossman decision suggests that a claim will only be successfully presented electronically once it actually arrives at the tribunal, or the ETS website, it should be treated with caution.

That said, it is clear that simply pressing the 'submit' button is not sufficient to effect presentation. For example, in Miller v Community Links Trust Ltd EAT 0486/07 the EAT held that the tribunal was correct to decline jurisdiction where the claim was received nine seconds late although the 'submit' button was pressed one second inside the time limit.

Extension of time limit under early conciliation rules

5.36

Since 6 May 2014, anyone wishing to present a claim to an employment tribunal must first contact Acas and be offered early conciliation – see S.18A of the Employment Tribunals Act 1996. The early conciliation rules are discussed in detail in Chapter 3, 'Conciliation, settlements and ADR', under 'Early conciliation'. Suffice to say here that the prospective claimant starts the process by either sending an early conciliation form to Acas or telephoning Acas directly, and Acas will then contact the parties to see if the dispute can be resolved through early conciliation. Once Acas has received the claimant's request, it generally has up to a month to attempt to resolve the dispute, although this period can be extended by an additional two weeks if Acas considers that there is a reasonable prospect of achieving a settlement. If the parties do not want to take up the offer of conciliation, or conciliation ends without an agreement having been reached, Acas issues a certificate to the claimant as proof that he or she has contacted Acas about early conciliation. It is only once the claimant has received the certificate that he or she is allowed to present a tribunal claim.

In order to encourage parties to take up the offer of early conciliation – which is entirely voluntary – special provisions have been introduced, to allow for the following extensions of the relevant time limit:

- when determining whether a time limit has been complied with, the period beginning the day after the early conciliation request is received by Acas up

299

to and including the day when the early conciliation certificate is received or deemed to have been received by the prospective claimant is not counted. In other words, the clock will stop when Acas receives the request and start to run again the day after the prospective claimant receives the certificate

- if a time limit is due to expire during the period beginning with the day Acas receives the request and one month after the prospective claimant receives the certificate, the time limit expires instead at the end of that period. This effectively gives the prospective claimant one month from the date when he or she receives (or is deemed to receive) the certificate to present the claim.

5.37 Under the first head, the time limit for bringing the relevant tribunal claim will be 'stopped' at the point in time when Acas receives the early conciliation request and will only 'resume' when the prospective claimant receives (or is deemed to receive) the early conciliation certificate. It follows from this that the prospective claimant may have a full calendar month, or a full calendar month plus two weeks (if an extension has been granted), of additional time in which to lodge a tribunal claim if pre-claim conciliation ends without an agreement having been reached. At the very least, the time limit is extended by the amount of time it takes Acas to find out whether the parties wish to engage in early conciliation.

The second basis for the extension of normal time limits mentioned above is specifically aimed at prospective claimants who enter the early conciliation process close to the end of the limitation period. During public consultation on the early conciliation proposal, the Government acknowledged that prospective claimants might be reluctant to settle a claim close to the end of the conciliation period because they might not be guaranteed to receive payment of the settlement sum before the limitation period for making the claim runs out. For this reason, another extension of the time limit provision was added to ensure that claimants have at least one month from when they first receive the certificate to submit their claim.

5.38 The statutory claims in respect of which the new time limit provisions apply are listed in the Appendix to this chapter. The list is extensive and covers most employment protection rights..

5.39 Escape clauses

As mentioned in the introduction to this chapter, the statutory provisions governing time limits fall into three groups, depending on the formula, if any, allowing for an extension of time:

- no extension of time allowed
- 'not reasonably practicable' formula using the following or similar wording: 'within such further period as the tribunal considers reasonable in a case

where it is satisfied that it was not reasonably practicable for the complaint to be presented before the end of the period of (three) months'. This statutory formula is discussed under '"Not reasonably practicable" extension' and 'Presenting the claim within further reasonable period' below

- 'just and equitable' formula using the following or similar wording: 'a complaint... may not be brought after the end of... such other period as the employment tribunal thinks just and equitable'. This formula is discussed under '"Just and equitable" extension' below.

No extension of time allowed. For most tribunal claims, one or other of the **5.40** 'escape clauses' allowing for an extension of time at the tribunal's discretion applies (see the Appendix to this chapter). However, there are certain claims where no extension of the time limit is permitted – for example, claims for interim relief under the TULR(C)A. If such a claim is presented a day late, a tribunal will have no jurisdiction to hear it, whatever the reasons for the delay (subject to a possible exception for deliberate fraud on the part of the respondent). In addition, claimants claiming itemised pay statements have a financial incentive to get their applications in as quickly as possible, since any award that can be made by a tribunal is limited to the 13-week period preceding the date of the application – S.12(4) ERA. A claimant who has left his or her employment and who delays until the end of the three-month time limit before complaining that his or her former employer made unnotified deductions from pay will find that a tribunal has no power to make an award and will be left with a declaration as the only remedy.

'Not reasonably practicable' extension   5.41

This type of escape clause applies to many of the rights contained in the ERA, e.g. unfair dismissal and unlawful deductions from wages (but not redundancy and 'blacklisting' – see '"Just and equitable" extension' below) and to rights under the Working Time Regulations 1998 SI 1998/1833 – see the Appendix to this chapter for a list of all the main employment rights and the appropriate escape clause, if any. When a claimant tries to excuse late presentation of his or her ET1 claim form on the ground that it was not reasonably practicable to present the claim within the time limit, three general rules apply:

- S.111(2)(b) ERA should be given a 'liberal construction in favour of the employee' – Dedman v British Building and Engineering Appliances Ltd 1974 ICR 53, CA

- what is reasonably practicable is a question of fact and thus a matter for the tribunal to decide. An appeal will not be successful unless the tribunal has misdirected itself in law or has reached a conclusion that no reasonable tribunal could have reached. As Lord Justice Shaw put it in Wall's Meat Co

Ltd v Khan 1979 ICR 52, CA: 'The test is empirical and involves no legal concept. Practical common sense is the keynote and legalistic footnotes may have no better result than to introduce a lawyer's complications into what should be a layman's pristine province. These considerations prompt me to express the emphatic view that the proper forum to decide such questions is the [employment] tribunal, and that their decision should prevail unless it is plainly perverse or oppressive'

- the onus of proving that presentation in time was not reasonably practicable rests on the claimant. 'That imposes a duty upon him to show precisely why it was that he did not present his complaint' – Porter v Bandridge Ltd 1978 ICR 943, CA.

5.42 Even if a claimant satisfies a tribunal that presentation in time was not reasonably practicable, that does not automatically decide the issue in his or her favour. The tribunal must then go on to decide whether the claim was presented 'within such further period as the tribunal considers reasonable'. Thus, while it may not have been reasonably practicable to present a claim within the three-month time limit, if the claimant delays a further three months a tribunal is likely to find the additional delay unreasonable and decide that it has no jurisdiction to hear the claim (see further 'Presenting claim within further reasonable period' below).

5.43 **Meaning of 'reasonably practicable'.** Judicial attempts to establish a clear, general and useful definition of 'reasonably practicable' have not been particularly successful. This is probably because cases are so different and depend so much on their particular circumstances. However, in Palmer and anor v Southend-on-Sea Borough Council 1984 ICR 372, CA, the Court of Appeal conducted a general review of the authorities and concluded that 'reasonably practicable' does not mean reasonable, which would be too favourable to employees, and does not mean physically possible, which would be too favourable to employers, but means something like 'reasonably feasible'. Lady Smith in Asda Stores Ltd v Kauser EAT 0165/07 explained it in the following words: 'the relevant test is not simply a matter of looking at what was possible but to ask whether, on the facts of the case as found, it was reasonable to expect that which was possible to have been done'.

Multifarious reasons are adduced for late presentation and only the most common are considered below. Since the case law on the 'not reasonably practicable' escape clause relates almost entirely to unfair dismissal claims, we concentrate on these. However, the EAT made it clear in GMB v Hamm EAT 246/00 that the words 'not reasonably practicable' are to be given the same meaning whenever they appear in an equivalent context in comparable legislation, so similar considerations will apply to all other statutory employment claims using the same formula.

302

Ignorance of rights 5.44

A claimant's complete ignorance of his or her right to claim unfair dismissal may make it not reasonably practicable to present a claim in time, but the claimant's ignorance must itself be reasonable. As Lord Scarman commented in Dedman v British Building and Engineering Appliances Ltd 1974 ICR 53, CA, where a claimant pleads ignorance as to his or her rights, the tribunal must ask further questions: 'What were his opportunities for finding out that he had rights? Did he take them? If not, why not? Was he misled or deceived?' In Porter v Bandridge Ltd (above) the majority of the Court of Appeal, having referred to Lord Scarman's comments in Dedman, ruled that the correct test is not whether the claimant knew of his or her rights, but whether he or she *ought to have known* of them. The Court upheld a tribunal decision that P, who took 11 months to present an unfair dismissal claim, ought to have known of his rights earlier, even if in fact he did not. The EAT reached a similar conclusion in Avon County Council v Haywood-Hicks 1978 ICR 646, EAT, where H was about six weeks out of time in presenting an unfair dismissal claim. He said that he had no idea that he could bring a claim for constructive dismissal until he read a newspaper article, and that before then he had also been ignorant of the existence of employment tribunals. A tribunal found his ignorance extraordinary but held that it made it impracticable for him to claim in time. The EAT rejected the idea that 'ignorance however abysmal and however unreasonable is a universal excuse'. It said that this offended the notion of common sense, and that an intelligent and well-educated man – H was a polytechnic manager – ought to have investigated his rights within the time limit and claimed in time. Given that the unfair dismissal legislation has been in force since 1972, tribunals will rarely be sympathetic to the notion that claimants were wholly ignorant of their rights.

Exceptional cases will warrant an extension of time, however. In Theobald v Trustees of the Borough Market ET Case No.04938/84, for example, the employment tribunal found that the claimant's ignorance of his right to claim unfair dismissal was reasonable in the special circumstances of the case. T was mentally disabled and his sister looked after him. As soon as she was advised (out of time) that T might have a claim for unfair dismissal, she took him to a CAB and a claim was made promptly. The tribunal found that T's ignorance of his rights and his mental condition prevented him from being put on inquiry earlier, so that it was not reasonably practicable for him to have presented his claim in time.

Confusion as to rights. A claimant's confusion as to his or her rights may 5.45 excuse a late claim in certain circumstances. In Glenlake Computers Ltd v Hards EAT 434/99, for example, H's employer went into receivership on 19 May 1998. On 21 May 1998 his employer terminated H's employment, informing him that he might have claims against the Redundancy Payments Office and/or the Department of Trade and Industry (now the Department for

303

Business, Innovation and Skills). On the same day H submitted claims to both these bodies. Also on the same day, unknown to H, there was a sale of some parts of the employer's business to Glenlake. On 15 July 1998 H received a letter from the Redundancy Payments Office stating that his claims had been rejected as the business in which H had been employed had been transferred to a 'new employer'. The letter stated that the new employer was Glenlake and that Glenlake had taken on obligations in relation to the employees.

The tribunal found that the letter had confused H and had made no sense to him as he had no 'new employer'. The tribunal also found that the three-month time limit expired on 20 August 1998 but it was not until a former colleague sent H a letter on 7 September that he realised he had a claim enforceable in the tribunal against Glenlake. H finally presented a complaint on 22 September. The EAT upheld the tribunal's decision to allow H's claim to proceed. The tribunal was entitled to find that, arising out of his confusion and uncertainty after reading the letter from the Redundancy Payments Office, H was left with an understanding that any claim was subject to a time limit of three months from the date of that letter – i.e. three months from July 15. Read as a whole, the letter did not put H on inquiry as to his rights, and after that letter it remained not reasonably practicable for H to present his claim in time. The tribunal was also entitled to conclude that H had presented the complaint within a further reasonable period.

5.46 The EAT's decision in the Hards case should be contrasted with the Court of Appeal's decision in Biggs v Somerset County Council 1996 ICR 364, CA, which concerned employment rights under European law. B was a part-time teacher who was dismissed in 1976. At that time she worked for 14 hours per week and the legislation then in force specified that the right not to be unfairly dismissed was inapplicable to an employee who worked less than 21 hours per week. In March 1994 the House of Lords declared that this restriction on part-time employees claiming unfair dismissal was unlawful as it offended Article 141 of the EU Treaty (now Article 157 of the Treaty on the Functioning of the European Union), which provides for equal pay for work of equal value – see R v Secretary of State for Employment ex parte Equal Opportunities Commission and anor 1994 ICR 317, HL. B made a claim of unfair dismissal within three months of their Lordships' decision.

When B's case reached the Court of Appeal, the Court held that it was reasonably practicable for B to have brought her claim in time, i.e. within three months of her dismissal in 1976. The decision in the EOC case was merely declaratory of what the law has been ever since the European Communities Act 1972 established that European law should take precedence over UK law. In addition, in 1976 the ECJ decided in Defrenne v Sabena (No.2) 1976 ICR 547, ECJ, that Article 141 of the EU Treaty, upon which the EOC decision was based, was capable of being directly relied on by individual employees in national courts.

In the Court of Appeal's opinion, it was contrary to the principle of legal certainty to allow past transactions to be reopened and limitation periods to be circumvented because the law that existed at the time had not yet been explained or had not been fully understood.

Ignorance of the time limit. Where the claimant is generally aware of his or **5.47** her rights, ignorance of the time limit will rarely be acceptable as a reason for delay. This is because a claimant who is aware of his or her rights will generally be taken to have been put on inquiry as to the time limit. Indeed, in Trevelyans (Birmingham) Ltd v Norton 1991 ICR 488, EAT, Mr Justice Wood said that, when a claimant knows of his or her right to complain of unfair dismissal, he or she is under an obligation to seek information and advice about how to enforce that right. Failure to do so will usually lead the tribunal to reject the claim. Two examples:

- **Sodexo Health Care Services Ltd v Harmer** EATS 0079/08: H submitted an unfair dismissal claim 23 days late because she wrongly assumed that the time limit in respect of her claim would not start running until the end of the appeal process. The tribunal accepted jurisdiction, but the Scottish EAT overturned the decision on appeal. The crucial question for the tribunal was whether, in the circumstances, the employee was reasonably ignorant of the time limit. Given that she knew of the time limit and that she had failed to make proper inquiries about it, the only answer to the question whether she was reasonably ignorant of the start date of the time limit was no. The claim was accordingly dismissed

- **Reed in Partnership Ltd v Fraine** EAT 0520/10: F presented his unfair dismissal claim one day late, wrongly believing that the three-month time limit ran from the day after the EDT. The EAT overturned the employment judge's decision to accept F's late claim. F was not reasonably ignorant of the start date for the limitation period: he knew of his right to bring a claim, as well as the three-month time limit. Furthermore, he was not misled by the employer or any other agency or adviser, and he had made no enquiries through solicitors, the CAB or the Employment Tribunals website. F had simply proceeded on a false assumption for which he had no basis.

While it is generally difficult for a claimant who knows of the existence of the **5.48** right to claim to persuade an employment tribunal that he or she behaved reasonably in not making inquiries as to how, and within what period, to exercise the right, each case will depend on its own particular facts and any employment tribunal decision on the matter will be difficult to reverse on appeal. In Marks and Spencer plc v Williams-Ryan 2005 ICR 1293, CA, for example, the claimant believed that she had to exhaust the internal procedure before she could bring an unfair dismissal claim, and had had this confirmed by the CAB. Her employer had provided her with material about an unfair dismissal claim, but it had not mentioned the time limit. The tribunal allowed

305

her a time extension to enter her claim out of time. The Court of Appeal held that the employment tribunal had not erred in holding that it was not reasonably practicable for the claim to be presented within the three-month timescale. Lord Phillips (then Master of the Rolls) said: 'Were these conclusions on the part of the tribunal perverse? I have concluded that they were not. I think the findings were generous to the respondent, but they were not outside the ambit of conclusions that a tribunal could properly reach on all the facts before them.'

Special circumstances pertaining to the claimant also meant that ignorance of the time limit was reasonable in John Lewis Partnership v Charman EAT 0079/11. C, aged 20, was summarily dismissed from JLP on 13 March 2010. He thereafter lodged an internal appeal, which was rejected, and the letter confirming this was sent to him on 28 June. However, when the letter arrived C was on holiday in Denmark, and it was not until a friend visited him there in mid-July with his post that C learned of the appeal's outcome. He then promptly spoke to his father, who, after some online research into tribunal claims, submitted an ET1 on 21 July – almost six weeks after the deadline for unfair dismissal claims. An employment judge found that it was not reasonably practicable for C to present his claim in time and that he had submitted his claim within a reasonable period after the time limit's expiry. As well as being young and inexperienced, C had known nothing about employment tribunals or the right to claim unfair dismissal prior to his termination. Furthermore, after being dismissed, he consulted his parents and was thereafter dependent on their advice. Although C's father generally knew of the right to bring a tribunal claim for unfair dismissal, he was unaware of the time limits.

5.49 The EAT upheld the judge's decision. Following the Court of Appeal's ruling in Wall's Meat Co Ltd v Khan (above), the EAT stated that the starting point is that if an employee is reasonably ignorant of the relevant time limits it cannot be said to be reasonably practicable for him or her to comply with them. Because C was unquestionably ignorant of the time limits, the relevant question was whether that ignorance was reasonable. That, in turn, came down to a consideration of whether, immediately following his dismissal, C or his father should have made enquiries about how to process an employment tribunal claim. In the EAT's view, the judge's decision was plainly right, as it was obviously sensible for a party to await the outcome of an internal appeal before resorting to legal proceedings.

The Charman case was referred to in Webb v Carphone Warehouse ET Case No. 1402557/11, where W was dismissed for redundancy soon after his return from a four-month tour of duty in Afganistan. W, an army reservist, returned from Afganistan on 23 April and went back to work on 9 May. Within a few weeks of his return he was selected for redundancy and then offered alternative work, which he accepted on a trial basis but then resigned in July. At that time, he was suffering from stress and depression. He submitted a grievance about his redundancy but there was a considerable delay before it was dealt with. He attended a meeting on 26 October and was told he would get a decision within four weeks. He kept chasing the employer for a decision, and finally submitted his tribunal claim on 8 December when he had still not been given the outcome. The tribunal found that the claim could proceed. Bearing in mind the multiple difficulties W was facing following his period of service, his state of mind and the fact that he was awaiting the outcome of his grievance, he was reasonably ignorant of the time limit and it was therefore not reasonably practicable for him to bring his claim any earlier.

Misrepresentation by the employer. The employer's actions may be taken into **5.50** account by a tribunal considering the claimant's ignorance of the time limit. In Fisons plc and anor v Jeffries EAT 524/97, for example, the EAT found that it was not reasonably practicable for a complaint relating to a failure to consult under the Transfer of Undertakings (Protection of Employment) Regulations 2006 SI 2006/246 to be presented within three months. This was because the employer had sent a partial extract from an employment manual that made no reference to time limits to the claimant, an employee representative who was not an experienced trade union representative.

Similarly, in Andrews v Kings College Hospital NHS Foundation Trust EAT 0614/11 the EAT held that it was not reasonably practicable for an employee to present her claim within the applicable three-month time limit. A had been wrongly advised by P, the employer's head of pensions and payroll, that she had six months from the termination of her employment to lodge a breach of contract claim over her backdated pension entitlement. In refusing to extend time, the employment judge had wrongly focused on the question of whether the employer provided the wrong information in good faith, rather than whether the claimant was at fault for the delay. In the EAT's view, P was the person put forward by the employer as the appropriate person to approach in relation to A's pension entitlement and she was entitled to rely on what he had told her. Accordingly, A was not at fault for the failure to bring her breach of contract claim within the original three-month time limit, with the result that it was not reasonably practicable for her to have done so.

Ignorance of fact
5.51

Ignorance of a fact that is fundamental to the right to bring an unfair dismissal complaint may render it not reasonably practicable to present the complaint in time. Thus the discovery of new relevant facts can be grounds for an extension of time. The leading case in this area is Machine Tool Industry Research Association v Simpson 1988 ICR 558, CA. S was dismissed for redundancy, but she heard at the end of the limitation period that another employee had apparently been taken on to do her work (which the employer denied). This led her to think that she had not been redundant at all and she promptly presented an unfair dismissal claim – three days out of time. A tribunal held that it had not been reasonably practicable for her to bring a complaint within the time limit and accepted jurisdiction. The employer argued that the tribunal should have investigated the veracity of the fundamental fact relied on by S in making her claim before it accepted jurisdiction to hear the case, but appeals to the EAT and the Court of Appeal were unsuccessful. The Court of Appeal held that in a case like this the claimant must establish three things:

- that his or her ignorance of the fact(s) relied upon was reasonable

- that he or she had reasonably gained knowledge outside the time limit that he or she reasonably and genuinely believed to be crucial to the case and to amount to grounds for a claim

- that the acquisition of this knowledge was, in fact, crucial to the decision to bring the claim.

5.52   The Court added that it was not necessary for the tribunal at this stage to establish the truth of the new fact(s) relied on by the employee. The relevant question was whether the employee reasonably and genuinely believed in the truth of the fact(s) at the time he or she was considering whether or not to present a claim.

However, in Post Office v Sanhotra 2000 ICR 866, EAT, the EAT cautioned against a rigid application of the three-stage approach set out by the Court of Appeal in the Simpson case. The EAT stated that the three-stage approach should not be applied in substitution for the statutory wording of S.111 ERA and that it merely provides guidance as to the correct application of the statutory test.

5.53   In James W Cook and Co (Wivenhoe) Ltd (in liquidation) v Tipper and ors 1990 ICR 716, CA, eight shipyard employees were made redundant on 22 May 1986 but were led to believe that business would pick up in a few months and that they would get their jobs back. In fact, the shipyard closed down on 5 September 1986 and it was only then that the employees presented claims for unfair dismissal. A ninth employee was dismissed on 29 August 1986 but failed to present a claim until 13 January 1987, over six weeks late. A tribunal accepted that the nine employees had only fully realised in September that they had been misled and that their employer had no intention of keeping the shipyard going. It had not been reasonably practicable for them to complain of unfair dismissal until the closure of the business and the claims had all been made without undue delay once the true facts had emerged. This decision was upheld by the EAT and the employer appealed to the Court of Appeal, which upheld the tribunal's finding that it had not been reasonably practicable for the employees dismissed in May 1986 to bring their claims within the three-month time limit. However, it was reasonable for the claims to have been brought within two weeks of the closure of the yard, so that one of the eight employees dismissed in May, who had submitted a claim six weeks after the expiry of the statutory time limit and one month after the closure of the yard, was out of time. Moreover, the Court overturned the tribunal's finding that it had not been reasonably practicable for the claimant who had been dismissed in August 1986 to present his claim within the three-month time limit. The yard had closed down on 5 September and so it had been reasonably practicable for the claim to have been brought within the statutory period.

It is not enough for a claimant to say that he or she did not know the true facts at the time of the dismissal. The claimant must also show that his or her ignorance was reasonable and that he or she could not reasonably have been expected to find out what the true situation was during the limitation period. This latter point proved to be the stumbling-block in Borland v Independent Vegetable Processors Ltd, unreported 9.12.82, CA. B worked in a freezing plant and was made redundant along with all the other employees in the plant on 31 January 1980. The employer intended to dispose of the plant but, in the event, the freezing department where B worked started up again and on 1 April the business was sold to another company, which kept the freezing plant going. B knew of the right to claim unfair dismissal, but also knew that he had no grounds for claiming unfair dismissal as at the date of his dismissal. He said that he did not hear that the freezing plant was in full swing again until July and his claim was presented some weeks late on 18 July. He claimed that he had been misled or reasonably mistaken about the facts and that it was not reasonably practicable for him to claim before July, when he learned the true facts. The tribunal, the EAT and the Court of Appeal all rejected B's contentions. The Court of Appeal thought that the tribunal had been entitled to take the view that B's ignorance of the situation was unreasonable. The company was a large one, with 600–800 employees; B only lived three miles away and he had a car. It would have been reasonably practicable for him to have taken note of what was going on – e.g. by observing the transit of company vans. The tribunal's decision had been neither unreasonable nor perverse.

5.54 In cases where two or more crucial facts emerge at different times after the expiry of the time limit the tribunal should consider the various grounds for complaint separately and determine whether it was not reasonably practicable to present a complaint on each separate ground before the end of the three-month period – Marley (UK) Ltd and anor v Anderson 1996 ICR 728, CA.

The late discovery of a fact may entitle an employee to bring an unfair dismissal claim even if the employee already believed the dismissal to be unfair. This point is illustrated by Teva (UK) Ltd v Heslip EAT 0008/09, where H, a sales executive, was told that she was at risk of redundancy because the employer had decided that commercial sales in Cornwall – H's allocated territory – would cease. H did not apply for alternative employment because she was told that it was company policy that sales representatives could not live more than 20 minutes off territory and she was not willing to relocate. Her employment ended on 2 May 2008. On 13 August H received a telephone call from a former colleague, who informed her that a sales manager was working in Cornwall. H contacted solicitors on 19 August and presented an unfair dismissal claim on 29 August. H made a number of criticisms of the redundancy procedure, including that the consultation process had been a sham and that the selection criteria – in particular the '20-minute rule' – were unfair. Although the claim was presented outside the three-month time limit, the employment judge decided that it could proceed because, having only received the new information on 13 August, it was not reasonably practicable for H to have presented the claim before that date.

5.55 The EAT upheld the decision. It specifically rejected the employer's submission that the late claim could not be accepted on the ground that the information H received on 13 August did not lead her to believe that she had a new ground for claiming unfairness, but merely reinforced her existing belief that her dismissal was unfair. In the EAT's view, the fact that H always believed her dismissal to have been unfair was not decisive. The question is whether she already believed that she had a viable claim of unfair dismissal. The distinction between a belief that a dismissal is unfair on the one hand, and a belief that there is a viable claim for unfair dismissal on the other, is of particular significance in the case of a redundancy dismissal. It is very common for an employee who is made redundant to feel that he or she has been hard done by, but it does not necessarily follow that he or she will believe that there are reasonable grounds for mounting a claim of unfair dismissal. The belief in a viable claim may only arise as a result of the acquisition of some later information.

In the Heslip case, the EAT held that the newly acquired fact – i.e. that another employee was working in H's territory – was the catalyst that caused H to pursue the unfair dismissal claim. As the Court of Appeal had made clear in Marley (UK) Ltd and anor v Anderson (above), the new fact had to be applied to each head of complaint. However, given the nature of the new information, the EAT could see nothing wrong with the employment judge's approach of dealing with the matter in the round. In H's case, the new fact potentially gave substance to all her heads of claim. In other words, if the employer was prepared to allow an employee to work the Cornwall territory, then the whole basis on which it had consulted H was flawed. Likewise, the new fact undermined the employer's apparent decision to cease all commercial activities in Cornwall and its application of the '20-minute rule'. Therefore, the judge had not erred when he found that, although H was unhappy about how her employment ended, it was not reasonably practicable for her to have presented an unfair dismissal claim until she had acquired knowledge that another employee was actually doing her work in Cornwall.

5.56 Of course, ignorance of the true facts must actually be the cause of the delay. In Birmingham Optical Group plc v Johnson 1995 ICR 459, EAT, J worked as a sales representative until he was made redundant on 15 July 1993. J continued to sell articles for the employer on a commission basis after the termination of his employment but just over three months later the employer terminated the commission arrangement as well. J immediately claimed unfair dismissal and a tribunal held that it had not been reasonably practicable for J to claim within the three-month time limit. On appeal, the EAT overturned the tribunal's decision, holding that the commission arrangement was entered into primarily for commercial reasons and that the employer had not acted cynically to deceive J and prevent him from making a claim to a tribunal. Had the tribunal found that J was being manipulated by the employer, then the situation might have been different, said the EAT, but the tribunal had found that the arrangement was entered into in good faith. In these circumstances the EAT felt that it was merely inconvenient for J to take action within the three-month time limit as the damage done would be likely to exceed any benefit accruing. However, this did not make it not reasonably practicable to make a complaint. The EAT concluded that J's complaint was out of time.

Summary of legal principles. The EAT in Cambridge and Peterborough NHS **5.57** Foundation Trust v Crouchman 2009 ICR 1306, EAT, helpfully distilled the relevant principles governing the exercise of a tribunal's discretion under S.111(2)(b) ERA in circumstances where the claimant initially believes that he or she has no viable claim, but changes his or her mind when presented with new information after expiry of the primary time limit. In that case, a tribunal's decision to accept an unfair dismissal claim out of time was upheld where an appeal outcome letter, which had been received after the primary time limit, contained crucial new facts which genuinely and reasonably led the claimant to change his mind and believe that he had a viable claim. In reaching its conclusion, the EAT held that the core principles to be applied to this type of case were as follows:

- ignorance of a fact which is 'crucial' or 'fundamental' to a claim will, in principle, be a circumstance rendering it impracticable for a claimant to present that claim – Churchill v A Yeates and Sons Ltd 1983 ICR 380, EAT, approved by the Court of Appeal in Machine Tool Industry Research Association v Simpson 1988 ICR 558, CA, and Marley (UK) Ltd and anor v Anderson 1996 ICR 728, CA

- a fact will be 'crucial' or 'fundamental' if it is such that, when the claimant learns of it, his or her state of mind genuinely and reasonably changes from one where he or she does not believe that he or she has grounds for the claim to one where he or she believes that the claim is 'viable' – Machine Tool Industry Research Association v Simpson (above)

- ignorance of a fact will not render it 'not reasonably practicable' to present a claim unless, first, the ignorance is reasonable and, secondly, the change of belief in light of that new knowledge is also reasonable – Machine Tool Industry Research Association v Simpson (above)

- whether the 'belatedly learnt' crucial fact is true is not relevant. What matters is whether the information about the fact has genuinely and reasonably produced the change of belief – Machine Tool Industry Research Association v Simpson (above)

- the above tests must be applied to each head of claim upon which a complaint is founded. For example, if a redundant employee's out-of-time unfair dismissal claim alleged that, first, the employer had not proved redundancy as the reason for dismissal and, secondly, that in any event dismissal for that reason was unfair, then the above tests would need to be applied in respect of both allegations – Marley (UK) Ltd and anor v Anderson (above)

- in a case where it was reasonably practicable to bring a complaint under one head of complaint but not another, the latter can proceed (provided it is brought within a reasonable time once the relevant facts are known) but the former cannot.

5.58 The facts of the Crouchman case were as follows. C worked as a psychiatric nurse. In 2007, the Trust invoked its disciplinary procedure against him following complaints from a female patient, L, that C had acted inappropriately towards her. Five charges were levelled against C, including claims that he had made calls and sent text messages to L which were sexually explicit, and that he had tried to persuade her to have a personal relationship with him. At a subsequent disciplinary hearing, the Trust upheld all the allegations against C and he was summarily dismissed for gross misconduct on 21 February 2008. C challenged the decision to dismiss him and, a day before the three-month time limit for bringing an unfair dismissal claim expired, the appeal panel chairman made an oral statement upholding the Trust's decision to dismiss. He told C that the charges against him had been proved and that he would be notified of the details of this outcome. On 28 May, C received a letter recording the appeal panel's decision. Contrary to what he had understood, it transpired that the panel had not, in fact, endorsed all the charges that were found proven by the Trust. For example, although it agreed that he had texted and telephoned L – which alone constituted a breach of professional boundaries – it could find no clear evidence that those communications contained explicit sexual content. Furthermore, there was no evidence that C had visited L alone in breach of her request that she receive no lone male visitors. In total, four out of the five original charges were dismissed by the appeal panel and, as a result, C felt encouraged to make an unfair dismissal claim notwithstanding that the deadline for making such a claim had now passed. He presented a claim online that same day.

An employment judge found that the letter from the appeal panel 'transformed' C's opinion of whether he could succeed in a tribunal claim and exercised his discretion to extend the time limit. The Trust unsuccessfully appealed the judge's decision to the EAT. According to the EAT, the appeal outcome letter was a crucial or fundamental fact which genuinely and reasonably led C to believe that he now had a viable claim. Applying Marley (UK) Ltd and anor v Anderson (above), it identified C's three main heads of claim. The first was that, since the appeal panel had found him guilty of only one out of the five alleged charges, dismissal was not a reasonable sanction. In respect of this head, the EAT said that C could not have known that he had been found guilty on a single charge until he had received the appeal outcome letter, and that his change of belief based on this was reasonable. The second head was that, in respect of the single charge upheld by the appeal panel, deficiencies in the investigation rendered the finding of guilt on that charge unfair because it did not produce all of the relevant evidence. Here, the EAT said that it was less obvious why C's knowledge of his acquittal on four of the five charges should have transformed his view of the inadequacies of the investigation as those inadequacies were already known to him. However, the EAT accepted that the appeal panel's findings showed that they had accepted the inadequacies – to an extent – and that, as a result, C had a stronger belief that this head of claim would succeed at tribunal. Finally, C's last head of claim was that another employee had been found guilty of similar but more serious misconduct (in that he had conducted a sexual relationship with a patient), but had only received a final written warning. Again, the EAT accepted that the panel's findings would have made this head more 'arguable' in C's mind. Accordingly, the EAT rejected the Trust's appeal and held that C's unfair dismissal claim could proceed. The case was remitted for the same tribunal to hear on the merits.

Advisers at fault
5.59

Any substantial fault on the part of the claimant's adviser that has led to the late submission of his or her claim may be a relevant factor when determining whether it was reasonably practicable for the claimant to present the claim within the prescribed time limit. In the majority of cases, an adviser's incorrect advice about the time limits, or other fault leading to the late submission of a claim, will bind the claimant and a tribunal will be unlikely to find that it was not reasonably practicable to have presented the claim in time. However, much will depend on the circumstances and the type of adviser involved.

Below we examine the different categories of adviser, and the impact that their involvement may have on the 'reasonably practicable' test in S.111(2)(b) ERA. However, it should be noted that if a claimant is unable to proceed with a claim because of an adviser's negligence, he or she may nonetheless be able to bring a civil action against the adviser. But it will not be enough simply to show that the adviser has been negligent: the claimant will also need to show that he or she has suffered loss by being denied the opportunity of pursuing a claim – i.e.

that the claim would have had a reasonable chance of succeeding. In Siraj-Eldin v Campbell Middleton Burness and Dickson 1989 IRLR 208, Ct Sess (Inner House), the claimant sued his solicitors for negligence in not presenting his unfair dismissal complaint in time but lost because the Court held that on the facts it would not have been open to a reasonable tribunal to find the dismissal unfair.

5.60 **Solicitors.** If a claimant engages solicitors to act for him or her in presenting a claim, it will normally be presumed that it was reasonably practicable to present the claim in time and no extension will be granted. As Lord Denning MR put it in Dedman v British Building and Engineering Appliances Ltd 1974 ICR 53, CA: 'If a man engages skilled advisers to act for him – and they mistake the time limit and present [the claim] too late – he is out. His remedy is against them.' This rule is commonly referred to as the 'Dedman principle'.

In Wall's Meat Co Ltd v Khan 1979 ICR 52, CA, Lord Justice Brandon explained the Dedman principle in the following terms. In his view, ignorance or a mistaken belief will not be reasonable if it arises either from the fault of the complainant or from the fault of his solicitors or other professional advisers in not giving him such information *as they should reasonably in all the circumstances have given him.*

5.61 Solicitors do make mistakes. For example, in Armitage v Serck Services EAT 902/83 A's solicitor mistakenly thought that posting a claim was equivalent to presentation, while in Hill and anor v Chau EAT 761/86 the claimants' solicitor went still further astray by thinking that the time limit for an unfair dismissal claim was six months, rather than three months. In neither case was the claimant personally at fault but both claims were barred, so that the only remedy left to them was a claim against their solicitors for professional negligence. Indeed, in the Hill case the EAT encouraged this course.

If, by exercising reasonable diligence, the claim could have been presented in time, the tribunal is unlikely to exercise its discretion and extend the limitation period. In Agrico UK Ltd v Ireland EATS 0024/05 the Scottish EAT concluded that the employment tribunal had been wrong to find that it was not reasonably practicable for I to present her claim within the three-month period in circumstances where her solicitor had left the matter to the last minute, and then, having gone on holiday, instructed his secretary to complete and fax the claim to the tribunal office on the last day of the three-month period. The secretary fell ill but not, as the judge found, so ill as to prevent her from telephoning the office and instructing someone else to issue the claim. She failed to do so and faxed the claim when she returned to work the following day – i.e. one day after the deadline. The EAT said: 'Looking at the facts as a whole, it seems to us that it is impossible to say it was not reasonably practicable for [the claim] to be presented in time.'

314

Similarly, in El-Kholy v Rentokil Initial Facilities Services (UK) Ltd EAT **5.62**
0472/12 the EAT rejected any notion that the claimant's ignorance of the time
limit was reasonable where solicitors had advised him throughout the appeal
against his dismissal and, following its rejection, had advised him to instruct
specialist employment solicitors to submit his unfair dismissal claim. He duly
did, but by then the normal time limit had already expired. The EAT upheld the
tribunal's finding that, bearing in mind their professional status, the solicitors
initially acting for the claimant should have advised him (even if he had not
specifically asked) about the time limits for lodging the claim. And in Chambers
and ors v QCR Motors Ltd (in voluntary liquidation) and anor EAT 0545/09
– a case brought under the Transfer of Employment (Protection of Employment)
Regulations 2006 SI 2006/246 – the EAT held that it was reasonably practicable
to present claims before the expiry of the time limit because, as the tribunal had
correctly found, further inquiries would have put the claimants' solicitors on
notice that a transfer of the business (which had set time running) had already
occurred by the time they became involved.

A solicitor's failure to have a system in place to ensure that a claim is actually
received by the tribunal has also been ascribed to the claimant. In Capital Foods
Retail Ltd v Corrigan 1993 IRLR 430, EAT, C's solicitors posted her claim
form to the employment tribunal office but failed to check that it had been
received. On discovering that it had not, they resubmitted the claim some three
months out of time. Overruling the tribunal's decision that it was not reasonably
practicable for C to present the claim in time, the EAT held that the solicitors
were at fault for failing to have some system of checking to confirm that the
claim (and a consequent acknowledgment from the tribunal) had been received.
The claimant had not demonstrated that she or her advisers had taken all steps
reasonably necessary in the circumstances to ensure that the claim was
presented timeously.

The Corrigan case was followed in Camden and Islington Community Services **5.63**
NHS Trust v Kennedy 1996 IRLR 381, EAT, where the deadline for the
presentation of K's complaint was 27 December 1994. K's solicitor sent the
claim by first-class post on 19 December but did not receive an acknowledgment.
On 30 January he telephoned the employment tribunal office and was told that
the claim had not arrived. He resubmitted the claim out of time. The tribunal
decided that it was not reasonably practicable to present the claim in time. On
appeal, the EAT held that the tribunal had misapplied the Corrigan case. The
EAT said that the Corrigan case envisaged more than a system of checking, at
some unspecified date and perhaps well after the time when an acknowledgment
should have been expected, that the employment tribunal office had received
the claim. Solicitors must have a system in place which would alert them in
good time whether correspondence which should have been received at a given
date has or has not been received. K's claim was time-barred.

315

A different division of the EAT reached the same conclusion in Clark v H2O Water Services Ltd EAT 0149/12. In that case, the last day for the presentation of C's unfair dismissal claim was Friday 12 November 2010. C's solicitor posted the claim form to the tribunal on 5 November but, having realised on Saturday 13 November that no acknowledgment had been received from the tribunal, faxed another copy of the claim form to the tribunal on Monday 15 November. In fact, the earlier claim form had been lost in the post and the only claim form that arrived at the tribunal was the one sent on Monday 15 November. At a pre-hearing review, the tribunal decided that the claim was presented out of time and declined jurisdiction on the ground that it was reasonably practicable to have presented it in time. Before the EAT, C argued that this case should be distinguished from Capital Foods Retail Ltd v Corrigan (above) and that time should be extended because the claim form was sent shortly before the deadline. Accordingly, as an acknowledgment from the tribunal would have taken a few days, it was reasonable for his solicitor not to have checked if the claim form had been received. The EAT rejected this argument. In its view, a practising solicitor should diarise the date by which a claim is due. If the solicitor chooses to send the claim form by post, he or she should check that it has been received by the day of the deadline and, if he or she is posting the claim close to the deadline, a more careful check is needed. The appeal was accordingly dismissed.

5.64 *Scope of 'Dedman principle'.* The general rule derived from Dedman v British Building and Engineering Appliances Ltd 1974 ICR 53, CA, that a claimant who puts his or her case into the hands of a solicitor cannot plead ignorance if the solicitor gets it wrong is well established. However, the reach of that rule – i.e. the extent to which a solicitor's involvement will scupper a claimant's chances of having the time limit to present a claim extended – has been the subject of much judicial debate. The question that arises from Dedman is essentially whether a solicitor's involvement will *inevitably* lead a tribunal to reject a late claim on the basis that it was reasonably practicable to present it within the applicable time limit. Or, to put it another way, is it open for a tribunal to decide that, despite the solicitor's involvement, it was not reasonably practicable to submit a claim in time and accept jurisdiction?

In the Dedman case, Lord Denning appeared to categorically rule out the possibility that a claimant could claim to be in reasonable ignorance of the time limit if he or she had instructed solicitors, even if their advice turned out to be incorrect. However, subsequent decisions expressed doubt as to whether this is indeed the correct approach to the statutory test. In Riley v Tesco Stores Ltd and anor 1980 ICR 323, CA, Lord Justice Stephenson said that he would hesitate to say that in every case a claimant would be bound by the fault of the adviser as each case depends on its own facts and, in London International College Ltd v Sen 1993 IRLR 333, CA, Sir Thomas Bingham went further and questioned whether Dedman was really purporting to lay down a rule of law that a complainant loses for all time the right to rely on the escape clause if he or she consults solicitors who are prima facie liable for misleading advice (as opposed to advisers who are not, or may not be, liable for giving incorrect advice).

Despite these remarks, the Court of Appeal affirmed the Dedman principle in **5.65** Marks and Spencer plc v Williams-Ryan 2005 ICR 1293, CA. Conducting a thorough review of the relevant authorities, Lord Phillips (then Master of the Rolls) came to the conclusion that the comments in Riley and Sen were obiter and that Dedman remained good law. In his view, the correct proposition of law derived from Dedman is that where the employee has retained a solicitor to act for him or her and fails to meet the time limit because of the solicitor's negligence, the solicitor's fault will defeat any attempt to argue that it was not reasonably practicable to make a timely complaint to the tribunal.

The scope of the Dedman principle was revisited by the EAT in Northamptonshire County Council v Entwhistle 2010 IRLR 740, EAT, where Mr Justice Underhill, then President of the EAT, summarised the judicial treatment of – and ultimately confirmed – the principle. Nevertheless, he went on to note that, subject to the Dedman principle, the authorities – including Williams-Ryan (above) – also emphasised that the question of reasonable practicability is one of fact for the tribunal that falls to be decided on the particular circumstances of the case. It followed from this that there may be circumstances where a solicitor's failure to present a timeous complaint could, theoretically, result in a tribunal finding that it was not reasonably practicable for the claimant to present his or her claim in time. Underhill P therefore accepted that there could be exceptions to the Dedman principle, such as where the adviser's failure to give the correct advice was itself reasonable. He reasoned that this could happen, for example, where the employee and his or her solicitor had both been misled by the employer on some factual matter, such as the date of dismissal.

The facts of the Entwhistle case are as follows. E was summarily dismissed for **5.66** gross misconduct, a decision that was upheld following an internal appeal, and E had until 12 May 2009 to present a claim of unfair dismissal. However, the Council had written to him on 26 March 2009 confirming his dismissal and informing him – incorrectly – that the three-month time limit for bringing an unfair dismissal claim ran from the date of receipt of its decision to reject his appeal against dismissal. E's solicitor failed to spot this error in the Council's letter and wrongly believed that he had until 27 June to submit the claim. The claim was presented on 27 May – just over two weeks outside the time limit.

The employment judge noted that E's solicitor conceded that he could be considered negligent in not checking the Council's statement about the time limit. Nevertheless, the judge concluded that in all the circumstances it had not been reasonably practicable for E to submit the claim in time, and accepted the claim. The EAT overturned the decision on appeal. According to Underhill P, the judge had been correct to say that an adviser's fault will not necessarily

317

defeat an attempt to argue that it was not reasonably practicable to present a claim in time where there are exceptional circumstances. However, the judge had erred in finding that such exceptional circumstances existed in the instant case. The judge appeared to have based his decision to extend time on the fact that the Council had, in his words, created the very 'trap' into which E and his solicitor had fallen. However, E's solicitor had not acted reasonably because he should have checked the facts for himself instead of relying on the Council's letter. The burden of the Dedman principle, Underhill P explained, is that in a case where a claimant has consulted skilled advisers, the question of reasonable practicability is to be judged by what he could have done if he had been given such advice as he *should* reasonably in all the circumstances have been given. Once the judge had accepted that E's solicitor had been negligent in not checking the date the time limit expired, he was required to hold that it had been reasonably practicable for E to present the claim in time. Consequently, following Dedman, the judge did not have jurisdiction to hear E's late claim.

5.67 In reaching this decision, Underhill P distinguished London International College Ltd v Sen (above) – discussed under 'Employment tribunal and Acas staff' below – where the claimant had first consulted a solicitor but had then sought and received erroneous advice about the time limit from the employment tribunal. There, the misleading advice came later. In E's case, the misleading advice from the Council came first and should have been corrected by the solicitor. Furthermore, it was immaterial that the whole situation would not have arisen but for the Council's initial mistake. The test under S.111 ERA is not one of causation, but of whether it was reasonably practicable for the claimant, at the material time, to present his or her claim within the time limit. Accordingly, Underhill P allowed the appeal and dismissed E's claim.

Three more examples:

- **JO Sims Ltd v McKee** EAT 0518/05: M had been called to a meeting and presented with a settlement agreement by JOS Ltd in November 2004. He presented a claim of unfair and wrongful dismissal to a tribunal, whereupon JOS Ltd disputed the dismissal but agreed that M's employment ended on 19 November. At a pre-hearing review in April 2005, the employment tribunal ruled that M had in fact been dismissed on 24 December 2004 and dismissed the claims as premature. When, in May 2005, M filed a further claim citing the date of dismissal as 24 December, the tribunal accepted the claim on the ground that it would not have been reasonably practicable to bring the claim within the three-month time limit. Dismissing JOS Ltd's appeal and awarding costs to M, the EAT ruled that the tribunal had been entitled to find that M had been misled by JOS Ltd's response and that there was no substantial fault on the part of M or his solicitors in not filing the claim on time

- **T-Mobile (UK) Ltd v Singleton** EAT 0410/10: M had been summarily dismissed and he knew that the effective date of termination of his employment was 23 November 2009. However, he wrongly believed that the time limit for presenting an unfair dismissal claim ran from the date of the employer's letter confirming his dismissal, i.e. 26 November. He subsequently told the employer that he had to submit his claim no later than 25 February 2010 and the employer did nothing to correct his mistake. S then telephoned solicitors who, in a free consultation, advised him to await the outcome of the appeal against his dismissal before putting in a claim. S did so and, the appeal having been rejected, submitted his claim on 23 February 2010 – one day outside the time limit. The employment judge decided that S had just cause for not presenting his claim in time and extended the time limit, but the EAT overturned the decision on appeal. In its view, the critical point was that S had sought advice from solicitors about his dismissal and the time limit for bringing a claim and the advice they had given him was clearly negligent. The fact that the advice was given as part of a free consultation did not detract from this conclusion. Nor was this a case where the employer had misled the employee or misrepresented the true position. S had incorrectly calculated the time limit and the employer was not under a positive duty to check the limitation period and correct his error. Accordingly, it was reasonably practicable for S to have presented his claim in time

- **Remploy Ltd v Brain** EAT 0465/10: following her dismissal, B received informal advice from a solicitor whom she met in a café over a cup of coffee that she should follow the employer's internal appeal procedures before submitting a tribunal claim. After the time limit expired, but before the final stages of the internal procedures were completed, she was told about the limitation period for unfair dismissal claims by a former colleague. B then presented her claim, which was almost two-and-a-half months late. Despite the delay, the employment judge accepted jurisdiction on the basis that, it being 'highly unlikely' that B would have any remedy against the solicitor, it was not unreasonable for her to have acted on the informal advice. Thus, it was not reasonably practicable for her to have presented her claim in time and, once she had been made aware of the time limit for submitting a claim, she had acted promptly. On appeal, the EAT refused to interfere with the decision, which was essentially a matter of fact for the tribunal.

In Royal Bank of Scotland plc v Theobald EAT 0444/06 – a case concerning **5.68** incorrect CAB advice – Lady Smith suggested that the *nature of the relationship* between the claimant and his or her adviser may also be relevant in determining whether a late claim was precluded by S.111(2) ERA. She effectively drew a distinction between two different scenarios: the claimant instructing the adviser to present the claim on his or her behalf; and the claimant seeking one-off advice but retaining responsibility for presentation of the claim. In the first

319

scenario, it will be the adviser's fault that the claim has not been presented timeously and it will not usually be possible to suggest that it was reasonable for such an adviser to delay beyond a statutory time limit because the adviser should have known better. In the second scenario, the claimant is entitled to rely on advice misinforming him or her as to the right to present a claim. Although it may be possible to submit the claim in time, in these circumstances it is not reasonable to expect the claimant to do so.

However, these remarks were obiter and were subsequently doubted by Mr Justice Burton in Ashcroft v Haberdashers' Aske's Boys' School 2008 ICR 613, EAT. In Burton J's view, such a distinction – which was not founded on good authority – would be difficult to pursue in practice. In Remploy Ltd v Brain EAT 0465/10 His Honour Judge Birtles also found Lady Smith's suggestion unhelpful, noting that it was not necessary to make the factual distinctions suggested by her, which automatically led to a single conclusion. Rather, he thought it essential to go back to the wording of S.111 and to what was essentially a question of fact which was for the tribunal to decide after taking into account the circumstances of the particular case.

5.69 **Trade union representatives.** Trade union representatives also count as 'advisers' in this context and, if they are helping a claimant with his or her case, they are generally assumed to know the time limits and to appreciate the necessity of presenting claims in time. In Times Newspapers Ltd v O'Regan 1977 IRLR 101, EAT, the claimant knew of her rights and knew of the three-month time limit when she was dismissed. However, a union official advised her incorrectly that the three months did not start to run while negotiations were taking place about her possible reinstatement. Overruling the tribunal, the EAT held that the claimant was not entitled to the benefit of the escape clause because the union official's fault was attributable to her and she could not claim that it had not been reasonably practicable to claim in time.

Two further examples:

- **Alliance and Leicester plc v Kidd** EAT 0078/07: K's unfair dismissal claim was presented 19 days late. The tribunal found that the trade union official, who had represented her throughout the disciplinary process, wrongly believed that the time limit ran from the date the appeal against dismissal was determined, rather than from the effective date of termination of her employment. Nevertheless, it decided to accept the late claim on the ground that K was not personally to blame for the delay. The EAT overturned the decision, holding that the tribunal was bound by authority to find that K could not rely on the trade union official's negligent advice to excuse the late submission of her claim

- **London Borough of Islington v Brown** EAT 0155/08: B authorised her trade union to lodge an unfair dismissal claim on her behalf but, due to an internal misunderstanding as to which official should submit the claim, the union failed to do so. When B discovered this, she lodged the claim herself – almost 18 months after the expiry of the time limit. The EAT held that it was reasonably practicable to have presented the claim in time, as the action of the union officials had to be attributed to B herself.

Where a claimant relies on the advice of a trade union representative and, as a **5.70** result, his or her claim is time-barred, the claimant's remedy lies in a claim of negligence against the union, which owes a duty in tort to use ordinary skill and care in advising and/or acting for a member in an employment dispute – Friend v Institution of Professional Managers and Specialists 1999 IRLR 173, QBD. However, the High Court went on to say in that case that where the union engages solicitors to act on the member's behalf, the duty on the union ends and responsibility for any negligent advice falls on the solicitors.

Citizens Advice Bureau and other professional advisers. Incorrect advice **5.71** from an adviser employed by a Citizens Advice Bureau (CAB) has also been treated as the fault of the claimant him or herself. In Riley v Tesco Stores Ltd and anor 1980 ICR 323, CA, for example, R claimed to have presented her claim out of time because of erroneous advice from a CAB. A tribunal, upheld by the EAT, said that it had been reasonably practicable for her to have presented her claim in time because she had 'engaged skilled advisers'. The Court of Appeal held that there was evidence to support this finding, but thought that it was not really material whether or not the CAB advisers were 'skilled' and whether or not R had formally 'engaged' them. The key factor was that R had taken advice and this was relevant as part of the overall general circumstances (which were that R's claim was seven months out of time). A similar conclusion was reached in Hammond v Haigh Castle and Co Ltd 1973 ICR 148, NIRC, in relation to an employee's professional association, and in Croydon Health Authority v Jaufurally and anor 1986 ICR 4, EAT, in relation to the Free Representation Unit.

The position of advice given by employment consultants was considered in Ashcroft v Haberdashers' Aske's Boys' School 2008 ICR 613, EAT. There, the EAT held that the principle that negligence or delay by an adviser in presenting a tribunal claim is to be ascribed to the claimant applies to employment law consultants even though they are not qualified solicitors. Mr Justice Burton, sitting alone in the EAT, rejected the claimant's argument that since his adviser was an employment consultant and not a qualified solicitor, the present facts could be distinguished from those in Dedman v British Building and Engineering Appliances Ltd 1974 ICR 53, CA (see 'Solicitors' above). The Dedman line of authorities clearly establishes that the principle that an adviser's negligence or delay in presenting a claim is ascribed to the claimant applies equally where the adviser is not a solicitor. This principle has, for example, been held to apply to a representative of the CAB. Nowadays, according to Burton J, 'there is a

321

positive plethora of employment consultants who are not solicitors' but who are, or hold themselves out to be, skilled advisers in this field. A's adviser fell within this category, and should be treated as the equivalent of an employment law consultant. On the facts of the case, no extension of the time limit was granted where A's adviser had failed to issue proceedings in time.

5.72 **Employment tribunal and Acas staff.** The decision in Riley v Tesco Stores Ltd and anor 1980 ICR 323, CA, which concerned incorrect advice received from a CAB adviser, extended the category of persons whose fault may be attributed to the claimant. However, it does not follow that bad advice from any third party will automatically prevent a claimant from showing that it was not reasonably practicable to present a claim in time. For example, in Dixon Stores Group v Arnold EAT 772/93 A was told by an employment adviser at a Jobcentre not to apply for unfair dismissal until the outcome of an unemployment benefit appeal. As a result he presented his claim four months out of time. The tribunal held that it had not been reasonably practicable to present the claim in time. On appeal, the EAT noted that in Rybak v Jean Sorelle Ltd 1991 ICR 127, EAT, and London International College Ltd v Sen 1993 IRLR 333, CA (see below), claimants who had been wrongly advised by tribunal employees had successfully claimed that this made it not reasonably practicable for them to present their complaints within the time limit. The EAT rejected the employer's argument that it was necessary to distinguish between incorrect advice given by a tribunal employee and incorrect advice given by a civil servant at a Jobcentre. Nor did the EAT accept that the information given to A by the Jobcentre should have alerted A to the existence of a remedy at the tribunal and that A should have taken proper advice. In upholding the tribunal's decision, the EAT questioned the validity of any general legal principle to the effect that any particular individual's advice was conclusive in preventing a claimant from presenting an unfair dismissal complaint out of time.

As mentioned above, in Rybak v Jean Sorelle Ltd a tribunal employee mistakenly informed R that, because the final date for lodging a claim fell on a Saturday, the complaint need not be presented until the following Monday. The EAT ruled that this rendered it not reasonably practicable for R to present the claim in time. It drew a distinction between the type of case in which bad advice is given by an employee of the tribunal, and the type of case in which the claimant has been wrongly advised by a solicitor, union official, CAB adviser or other third party. Whereas solicitors and the like are individuals who are asked by an employee – whether for a fee or not – to advise on the prosecution of a claim against an employer, tribunal employees are servants of a body charged by Parliament with the task of resolving employment disputes between parties. The EAT concluded that it was open to a tribunal to find that it was not reasonably practicable for a claimant to bring a claim in time where a tribunal employee was responsible for giving erroneous advice.

Similarly, in London International College Ltd v Sen (above), S presented his **5.73** claim to the tribunal one day late after having received incorrect advice on the closing date from both a solicitor and an employee of the employment tribunal office. The tribunal allowed S's late claim on the basis of the Rybak decision and the EAT dismissed an appeal by the employer. The Court of Appeal rejected the employer's argument that advice from a solicitor of necessity rendered it reasonably practicable to bring a claim within the time limit, even where a member of tribunal staff had also been involved. The Court stated that each case should be decided on its facts and it did not accept that a complainant automatically lost his or her right to claim that it had not been reasonably practicable to present a claim in time once he or she had consulted a solicitor. If, as in the instant case, the advice was distrusted and the complainant sought and was offered confirmation of that advice by a member of the tribunal staff, the complainant's rights were preserved. The tribunal had correctly found that the substantial cause of the late claim was S's mistaken belief in the erroneous advice of the tribunal employee. It was, therefore, not reasonably practicable for him to present the claim in time.

Jurisdiction for an out-of-time complaint was also accepted in Drewery v Carphone Warehouse Ltd ET Case No.3203057/06, where the claimant had been in contact with Acas. Following his dismissal, D contacted his local Jobcentre and, when he expressed concern over his dismissal, was referred to Acas. He phoned Acas for advice and was informed that there was little point in pursuing a tribunal claim until after his internal appeal against dismissal was concluded. Nothing was said to D during the conversation to suggest that Acas was an independent body not empowered to give advice, and D was not told of the three-month time limit for making a claim. The appeal hearing was delayed due to errors on the employer's part and D presented his claim 12 days out of time. The tribunal found that it was not reasonably practicable for D to have presented the claim in time and accepted jurisdiction. While his ignorance of the time limit would not have excused his late claim, D had contacted the Jobcentre and Acas – the latter of which he considered to be an authoritative body – and relied on Acas's advice to await the outcome of his appeal. If such misleading advice had been given by an independent adviser, the claim would in all probability have been rejected, but with an organisation such as Acas it was to be expected that callers would be informed of the limits on its role, something which Acas failed to do on this occasion. The tribunal also took into account that the employer had significantly delayed the hearing of D's appeal. D's claim was accordingly allowed to proceed.

Claimant's illness
5.74
A debilitating illness may prevent a claimant from submitting a claim in time. However, this will usually only constitute a valid reason for extending the time limit if it is supported by medical evidence, particularly if the claimant in

323

question has taken legal advice and was aware of the time limit. In Midland Bank plc v Samuels EAT 672/92 S's unfair dismissal claim was presented almost a month late. Before the tribunal, S claimed that she had been suffering from illness and depression and that it had not been possible for her union to contact her about the claim because she had changed address and her mail had not been forwarded. The employer accepted these arguments and the tribunal granted an extension of time. On appeal, the EAT held that it was up to S to produce medical evidence as to the extent and effect of the illness and to keep in touch with her union representative. She could not rely on her failure to do so as an excuse for presenting her claim out of time. However, it would be a different matter if S had been unable to take the necessary steps as a result of her illness. The case was remitted for the tribunal to reconsider the evidence.

In Schultz v Esso Petroleum Co Ltd 1999 ICR 1202, CA, the Court of Appeal accepted that illness may justify the late submission of claims. In that case, the Court found that during the last six weeks of the three-month time limit S had been too depressed to instruct solicitors and, overruling the tribunal and the EAT, held that it was not reasonably practicable for S to have presented his claim in time. The Court emphasised that the test is one of practicability – what could be done – not whether it was reasonable not to do what could be done. In the Court's view, the tribunal had failed to have regard to all the surrounding circumstances, which included the fact that S had been trying to avoid litigation by pursuing an appeal against his dismissal. Although it was necessary to consider what could have been done during the whole of the limitation period, attention should be focused on the closing stages rather than the earlier ones. In this case S's disabling illness took place at the end of the period in question and it was not reasonably practicable for him to have made the claim in time.

5.75   Mere stress – as opposed to illness or incapacity – is unlikely to be sufficient. In Asda Stores Ltd v Kauser EAT 0165/07 K, a checkout operator, was summarily dismissed on 22 June 2006 after the employer suspected her of stealing from the tills. She was arrested by police and released on bail. On 30 July she was again interviewed and released on bail. On 19 September she returned to the police station where she was told that no charges would be brought against her. The three-month time limit for presenting an unfair dismissal claim ran out on 21 September. K presented her claim on 11 October. The tribunal found that it was not reasonably practicable for her to have presented the claim timeously because K thought that she could not present a claim until the police inquiries were complete and she was very stressed while those inquiries were ongoing. The EAT overturned the decision, holding that it was not sufficient that K was, as the tribunal had found, 'very stressed' and 'in some turmoil' during the period of the police inquiries. According to Lady Smith, something more than mere stress was needed to elide the statutory time limit. Nor did the fact that K was stressed explain why she could not obtain information about bringing a complaint while the police inquiries were ongoing. In any event, the stress she was under (and her erroneous belief that she had to await the conclusion of the police inquiries) became irrelevant once the possibility of prosecution was lifted on 19 September. As the Court of Appeal had made clear in Schultz, the tribunal should look at the closing stages of the limitation period. According to Lady Smith, had the tribunal done so, it would have found that it was reasonably practicable for K to have presented the claim on 19, 20 or 21 September.

Medical evidence showing that the claimant was struck down by illness at the relevant time will not necessarily be conclusive where that evidence is contradicted by the claimant's own actions during that time. In Chouafi v London United Busways Ltd 2006 EWCA Civ 689, CA, for example, C had been dismissed as a result of a medical condition – severe depression – on 21 January 2004. On 30 January, he was admitted to a psychiatric ward, where he remained until 9 March. In May 2004, C submitted claims of unfair dismissal and disability discrimination to an employment tribunal, accompanied by a letter from his doctor stating that the extent of C's mental disorder prevented him from lodging the claims on time. An employment tribunal declined to accept the claims out of time, in part due to the evidence that C had written coherent letters to third parties about his pension during the limitation period. The EAT declined to overturn the tribunal's decision and C appealed to the Court of Appeal, arguing that the tribunal had rejected uncontested medical evidence without good reason. Dismissing the appeal, the Court held that the tribunal had assessed the doctor's opinion in the light of all available evidence and had reached a permissible conclusion that it would have been reasonably practicable to lodge the claim within the time limit.

The opposite conclusion was reached in University Hospitals Bristol NHS **5.76** Foundation Trust v Williams EAT 0291/12 where the EAT refused to overturn a tribunal's decision to accept an out-of-time unfair dismissal claim. It specifically rejected the argument that the tribunal's decision that W's serious mental health problems made it not reasonably practicable for her to have put in a timeous complaint could not stand because she had been able to cope with domestic responsibilities. The tribunal had decided that an extension should be granted in this case because the fact that W was able to find new accommodation and a new school for her child – something that it considered to be essential tasks – did not mean that she was also able to cope with putting in an employment tribunal claim, and she had submitted the claim as soon as she was sufficiently stable to do so. The EAT could find nothing wrong in this decision and accordingly dismissed the Trust's appeal.

Three more examples of ill-health cases:

● **Mitchell v Inner London Probation Service** ET Case No.1100823/98: following a road accident in December 1995 M developed severe depression. He was dismissed on 19 May 1997 on the ground of ill health. After consulting solicitors in April 1998, he presented a complaint of unfair

325

dismissal on 15 May 1998. M argued that it had not been reasonably practicable to submit his claim in time as he had been too ill to deal with matters such as taking advice and instituting proceedings. The tribunal held that it was reasonably practicable for M to have submitted his claim in time. Following his dismissal, M had drafted a coherent letter of appeal and had discussed the matter with the union officer who represented him at the appeal. In addition, M had presented no medical evidence from either his GP or the community psychiatric nurse

- **Imperial Tobacco Ltd v Wright** EAT 0919/04: W was dismissed on 4 March 2004. After his dismissal, he 'descended into depths of drug-induced degradation'. Nearly two months after the expiration of the three-month time limit, he presented his claim for unfair dismissal. In his decision, the tribunal chairman said: 'I am satisfied on the evidence that I heard from Mr Wright, which, as I have said, in my judgment is entirely truthful, that between about 11 May and the middle of July, it was not reasonably practicable for him to commence these proceedings. He was simply in no fit state to do anything about it.' Therefore the claim was allowed out of time. The EAT rejected the appeal and agreed with the tribunal decision that the disabling effects of W's heroin abuse meant that it was not reasonably practicable for him to present the complaint within the three-month period

- **Abbey National plc v Riddick** EAT 0369/04: R suffered from a severe depressive disorder and failed to present his tribunal claim within the three-month time limit. His consultant wrote to the tribunal, stating that his condition had only recently improved to a level where he could initiate or take part in proceedings. The tribunal allowed his claim out of time and on appeal the EAT held that the tribunal had not erred in holding that it was not reasonably practicable for the claimant to present his claim in time and that he had presented it within a further reasonable period.

5.77 Claimant's disability

The fact that the claimant has a disability may be relevant to the question of reasonable practicability. For example, in Down v Emerson Electric Ltd ET Case No.1489/95 the tribunal held that it was not reasonably practicable for a profoundly deaf claimant to present his unfair dismissal claim within the three-month time limit. The tribunal took into account the fact that, as a deaf man whose wife was also profoundly deaf, the claimant faced great difficulties and was cut off from many sources of informal information. Similarly, in Pyle v Middlesbrough Council ET Case No.2503426/10 the tribunal allowed an out-of-time unfair dismissal claim to proceed because of the claimant's disability. In that case, P – who was profoundly deaf, epileptic and suffered from depression – relied on his parents, who had always assisted him, but felt such shame and guilt at his dismissal that he did not tell them until five months later. An ET1 was submitted within two weeks of his parents being informed. The tribunal found that, despite the fact that P had been represented by his trade union at the internal disciplinary hearings, time should not begin to run against him until he informed his parents of the loss of his job. Among other things, P's deafness made it extremely difficult for him to understand the relevant documentation and his epilepsy, which manifested itself in fits at night, affected his sleep pattern and thus, inevitably, his powers of concentration.

Internal proceedings pending

5.78

Employees who have been dismissed may feel that their chances at an internal appeal hearing will be prejudiced if they launch employment tribunal proceedings before the appeal takes place. However, there may be delays in organising the domestic appeal, or be several stages involved in the appeal procedure, which may mean that the three-month time limit will have expired before the internal appeal procedure has been completed. This gives rise to two questions:

- what is the effective date of termination (EDT) when there is an internal appeal procedure following a dismissal that may result in reinstatement? Is it the original date of dismissal or the date of termination of the appeal procedure?

- does the fact that dismissal was subject to a – possibly multi-stage – internal appeal procedure make it not reasonably practicable to present a claim to a tribunal before that procedure is completed?

The answer to the first question is that the existence of a contractual appeal procedure does not alter the EDT. If, for example, an employee is summarily dismissed and his or her domestic appeal succeeds, he or she will be reinstated with retrospective effect. If, however, the appeal fails – and these are the cases that come before employment tribunals – the dismissal takes effect from the original date of dismissal – J Sainsbury Ltd v Savage 1981 ICR 1, CA, expressly approved by the House of Lords in West Midlands Co-operative Society Ltd v Tipton 1986 ICR 192, HL. The only exception to this will be where there is an express or implied contractual provision to the contrary.

It follows that if there is a protracted appeal procedure, time is likely to run out **5.79** before the procedure has been completed. However, the EAT ruled in Bodha v Hampshire Area Health Authority 1982 ICR 200, EAT, that the existence of an impending internal appeal was not *in itself* sufficient to justify a finding that it was not reasonably practicable to present a complaint to a tribunal within the time limit and this view was expressly approved by the Court of Appeal in Palmer and anor v Southend-on-Sea Borough Council 1984 ICR 372, CA.

This can lead to some harsh results. For example, in London Underground Ltd v Noel 2000 ICR 109, CA, N was dismissed for assaulting a customer. Following various internal appeals, the employer made an offer of re-employment to

327

commence two days before N's time limit for claiming unfair dismissal expired. N accepted this offer but was unable to start work on the appointed day as she was ill. After the expiry of the time limit N failed a drugs test and the offer of re-employment was withdrawn. N immediately submitted a claim for unfair dismissal. The Court of Appeal held that the fact that the employer's offer of re-engagement had been withdrawn did not affect its ruling that it had been reasonably practicable for N to present a tribunal claim within three months of her dismissal.

5.80 There are situations, however, where the existence of an internal appeal can be a relevant factor for a tribunal to take into account when determining whether it was reasonably practicable for the employee to submit the claim within the time limit. An example:

- **Webb v Carphone Warehouse** ET Case No. 1402557/11: W was called up from the Reserve Forces and returned from a four-month tour of duty in Afghanistan on 23 April and went back to work on 9 May. Within a few weeks of his return he was selected for redundancy and then offered alternative work, which he accepted on a trial basis but then resigned in July. At that time, he was suffering from stress and depression. He submitted a grievance about his redundancy but there was a considerable delay before it was dealt with. He attended a meeting on 26 October and was told he would get a decision within four weeks. He kept chasing the employer for a decision, and finally submitted his tribunal claim on 8 December when he had still not been given the outcome. The tribunal found that the claim could proceed. Bearing in mind the multiple difficulties W was facing following his period of service, his state of mind and the fact that he was awaiting the outcome of his grievance, he was reasonably ignorant of the time limit and so in these circumstances it was not reasonably practicable for him to bring his claim any earlier. The tribunal accordingly granted an extension of the time limit and allowed the claim to proceed.

5.81 Similarly, in John Lewis Partnership v Charman EAT 0079/11 the EAT upheld an employment tribunal's decision to accept an out-of-time unfair dismissal claim where the claimant waited for the outcome of an internal appeal against his dismissal before deciding how to act. The deadline for C's unfair dismissal claim was 12 June 2010. He had appealed against his dismissal but the letter rejecting his appeal, which was sent to him on 28 June, arrived while he was on holiday. He did not learn of the outcome of the appeal until mid-July and, after consulting his father, submitted an ET1 on 21 July – almost six weeks after expiry of the time limit. The employment judge found C, who was 20, to be young and inexperienced, dependent on his parents' advice and, prior to his dismissal, ignorant of the right to claim unfair dismissal. Furthermore, the judge did believe it reasonable for a lay person to defer investigating the possibility of recourse to litigation until the appeal process was concluded.

Accordingly, he decided that it was not reasonably practicable for C to have presented the claim in time and extended the time limit.

Mr Justice Underhill, then President of the EAT, rejected the employer's appeal against the judge's decision. Underhill P considered whether C's ignorance of the time limit was reasonable. In his view, it was obviously sensible for a party to await the outcome of an internal appeal before resorting to legal proceedings. Furthermore, he held that the instant case could be distinguished from Bodha v Hampshire Area Health Authority (above) and Palmer and anor v Southend-on-Sea Borough Council (above), cases involving claimants with advisers who were, or should have been, aware of the relevant time limits, but delayed claiming nevertheless. In those cases the issue was whether the pursuit of an internal appeal in itself made it not reasonably practicable to present a claim to the employment tribunal, not whether it was reasonable for the claimant to be unaware of the time limits, which was the key question in the instant case. It followed from this that the rulings in Bodha and Palmer did not apply. Accordingly, he went on to hold that time should be extended in C's case because it was not reasonably practicable for C to present the claim before the end of the three-month time limit and it had been presented within a reasonable time thereafter.

Special circumstances that justified delaying an employment tribunal claim **5.82** while an appeal was ongoing were also found in Owen and anor v Crown House Engineering Ltd 1973 ICR 511, NIRC. In that case the employer expressly requested dismissed employees to 'hold their hands' pending negotiations over improved severance terms. The NIRC held that, since presenting the claims earlier would almost certainly have led to a breakdown in negotiations, it was not 'practicable' for the claims to be presented in time. In considering whether a course of action was practicable it was permissible to consider what its consequences would be. But note that this will apply only where the employer makes an express request for delay.

In another case where the time limit was extended – London Borough of Hackney v Allin EAT 158/93 – the Council had changed the terms of its appeals procedure so that an employee's contract was no longer stated as continuing throughout the appeals process. The Council misled A as to the situation and the EAT held that this was enough to mean that it had not been reasonably practicable for A to present his complaint in time.

Other proceedings pending   5.83

The fact that criminal proceedings are pending against an ex-employee and that these relate to the circumstances of his or her dismissal does not prevent that employee from presenting a claim for unfair dismissal. A claimant should not wait to see what happens at the criminal trial before deciding whether to make a claim. As Lord Denning MR put it in Wall's Meat Co Ltd v Khan 1979

329

ICR 52, CA: 'That is not an acceptable reason for saying that it was not "reasonably practicable" to present his claim within the three months.' The fact that criminal proceedings are pending make it likely that tribunal proceedings will be stayed until the criminal trial has concluded, but that is another matter – see Chapter 11, 'Case management', under 'Stay of proceedings – stay pending criminal proceedings'.

An employee charged with a criminal offence is likely to have legal representation – a factor that will make it difficult for him or her to rely on ignorance of his or her rights. In National Car Parks Ltd v Saroye EAT 729/82, for example, S made a late claim after his acquittal on criminal charges. A tribunal found that he had been genuinely ignorant of his right to complain of unfair dismissal and would have allowed the late claim. The EAT, however, pointed out that ignorance was not enough to make it not reasonably practicable to adhere to the time limit. The tribunal should have gone on to consider whether S's ignorance was reasonable, and in this regard the EAT thought it relevant that S had had union representation over his dismissal and the services of counsel and a solicitor for the criminal case. The case was remitted.

In Trevelyans (Birmingham) Ltd v Norton 1991 ICR 488, EAT, the Appeal Tribunal reiterated the general principle that simply deciding to await the outcome of criminal proceedings before issuing a tribunal claim is not an acceptable excuse for exceeding the time limit. It added that, when an employee is dismissed in connection with criminal charges, solicitors acting for that employee in the criminal proceedings will almost certainly know that a dismissal has taken place. They will then be under a duty to tell the employee that tribunal proceedings need to be started promptly.

5.84 What applies to criminal proceedings also applies to other proceedings – for example, proceedings before a tribunal determining entitlement to unemployment benefit. In House of Clydesdale Ltd v Foy 1976 IRLR 391, EAT, F thought that he had to wait for the benefit tribunal to adjudicate before he could complain of unfair dismissal. But the EAT noted that he had seen Department of Employment literature about unfair dismissal and had had union assistance: this was held sufficient to put him on inquiry about the time limit. A different result was reached in Wall's Meat Co Ltd v Khan (above) where K mistakenly thought that a national insurance tribunal was processing his unfair dismissal claim. A tribunal found that this mistaken belief made it not reasonably practicable to present the claim in time. The Court of Appeal held that the tribunal had been entitled to reach this conclusion as a matter of fact.

5.85 **Postal delays/losses**

Postal delays are a common cause of late claims. Tribunals may find that if a claim form was posted to the tribunal office in time to arrive within the relevant time limit in the ordinary course of post but arrived late because of a postal delay, then it was 'not reasonably practicable' to present it in time. This approach was approved by Lord Denning MR in Dedman v British Building and Engineering Appliances Ltd 1974 ICR 53, CA.

The leading case is Consignia plc (formerly the Post Office) v Sealy 2002 ICR 1193, CA, which sets out guidelines for the presentation of claims – see '"Presenting" the claim' above. When considering the application of the escape clause, the Court of Appeal stated that the case law established three general propositions:

- where a claimant has done something that, in the normal course of events, would have resulted in his or her claim being presented within the relevant time period, but owing to *some unforeseen circumstance* this did not happen, it will have been not reasonably practicable for the claimant to have presented the claim in time

- if the condition mentioned above is satisfied, it does not matter why the claimant waited until the last moment

- the question whether the condition has been satisfied is a question of fact to be determined by the tribunal on the evidence before it.

These propositions and the guidelines are applicable not only to claims sent by post but also to electronic transmission.

Addressing the claim incorrectly is likely to lead to postal delay and tribunals **5.86** may not be sympathetic. In Cummins v GL Drums Ltd ET Case No.31615/83 the time limit expired on 3 November and the claim was posted first class on 31 October. However, it was addressed incorrectly and arrived one day late. The correct postcode had been used but the tribunal rejected the argument that this should have ensured prompt delivery and ruled that it had been reasonably practicable to have presented the claim in time. In contrast, in Bartaby v Wiltshire County Council ET Case No.33300/84 a claim which was posted nine days inside the time limit was misaddressed, although it bore the correct postcode. It arrived five days late. The tribunal accepted jurisdiction: it thought that nine days was long enough for the Post Office to have affected delivery, and noted that the claim was posted comfortably within the time limit and that the correct postcode should have simplified matters for the Post Office.

These cases illustrate that claimants should always allow ample time for postal deliveries. If the deadline for presentation is close, it may be sensible for the claim to be presented online, or by hand – see '"Presenting" the claim' above and Chapter 4, 'Starting tribunal proceedings', under 'Making a claim – the claim form (ET1)'.

Where a claim gets lost in the post, slightly different considerations apply. In **5.87** Capital Foods Retail Ltd v Corrigan 1993 IRLR 430, EAT, the EAT held that

331

the tribunal had erred in accepting that there is a presumption that what is posted will be delivered. It concluded that the unexplained failure of a claim to reach the employment tribunal office will not excuse a late claim unless all reasonable steps have been taken, in the circumstances, to see that the claim was presented on time. On the facts of the instant case C's solicitors should have employed some system of checking that the tribunal's acknowledgment of C's claim had been received within a certain period. Since they failed to do this but simply relied on the assumption that the claim had been duly presented, C's complaint was out of time. But that case should be compared with Golub v University of Sussex, unreported 13.4.81, CA, where the Court of Appeal accepted that the fact that the claim was lost in the post made it not reasonably practicable to present it in time. However, a further delay of over two months defeated G's claim – see 'Presenting the claim within further reasonable period' below.

5.88 Technical problems

Where a claim is submitted via the online submission service, claimants should not automatically assume that the claim will be received by the tribunal. In Akhavan-Moosavi v Association of London Government EAT 0501/04 the claimant presented his claim electronically on 24 July, the final day of the three-month time limit. On pressing 'submit', he received a 'thank you' message informing him that an e-mail acknowledgement would be sent within one day and that he should contact the tribunal if it was not. He had not received the e-mail confirmation by 3.45 the next afternoon and, on ringing the tribunal office, found that it had no record of his claim. He therefore resubmitted his claim on 25 July, one day out of time. The employment tribunal rejected his claim on the ground that it was out of time and that it had been reasonably practicable for him to present the claim in time. It drew attention to the tribunal's guidance on electronic application, which stated, among other things, that there is no guarantee that claim forms will be received on the same day that they are submitted and advised that claimants with time-critical claims consider other methods of presentation. On appeal, the EAT noted that the tribunal had treated the issue of electronic applications on the basis of the principles applying to postal applications, and agreed that this was the correct approach. While an electronic application can usually, and reasonably, be expected to be received on the day it was sent, something more is required of claimants in these circumstances. However, given the ambiguous nature of the 'thank you' message, it could be read by an inexperienced claimant as acknowledging presentation of the claim. To require a claimant to call the tribunal office immediately after submitting the claim on time to check that it had been received would be too onerous a burden, even on the final day of the three-month period. The claim was therefore allowed to proceed.

In Sullivan v Project Services International Ltd ET Case No.2500572/10 S's employment was terminated on 21 August 2009. He took advice from a solicitor about an unfair dismissal claim, and was aware that the claim had to be submitted by midnight on 20 November. He had hoped to resolve the matter amicably by way of a settlement agreement but no agreement had been reached by 19 November and S completed an online claim form and pressed the 'submit' button. He did not get an error message but nor did he receive an acknowledgement that the claim had been received. A few days later, S went to the US and did not return to the UK until the middle of January. He phoned the employment tribunal office to find out what was happening to his claim, only to be told that no claim had been received. He wrote to the tribunal enclosing a copy of his ET1, which was received on 26 January 2010. The employment tribunal allowed S's late claim to proceed. The tribunal accepted his evidence that he had submitted the claim online and that he believed that he had done so in time. On his return to the UK, he had then enquired as to what was happening with his claim and, upon being told that it had not been received, had taken appropriate action. The tribunal therefore found that it was not reasonably practicable for the claim to have been presented in time, and that he had lodged it within a reasonable period thereafter.

Time running against minors   5.89

At common law there is a rule that time does not run against a minor, i.e. someone under the age of 18. However, this rule would seem to be inapplicable to cases involving statutory rights, such as the right not to be unfairly dismissed. In Beech v British Shoe Corporation Ltd ET Case No.13485/95, for example, a tribunal held that although the claimant was only 16 years old, the time limits contained in the ERA nevertheless applied.

Presenting claim within further reasonable period   5.90

In a case where the 'not reasonably practicable' formula applies, the question of tribunal jurisdiction is not settled by a finding that it was not reasonably practicable to present a claim within the prescribed time limit. The employment tribunal must then go on to decide whether the claim was presented 'within such further period as the tribunal considers reasonable'. In other words, the escape clause will only come to the claimant's aid if the tribunal decides that the period between the expiry of the time limit and the eventual presentation of the claim was reasonable in the circumstances. In University Hospitals Bristol NHS Foundation Trust v Williams EAT 0291/12 the EAT emphasised that this limb of S.111(2)(b) ERA does not require the tribunal to be satisfied that the claimant presented the claim as soon as reasonably practicable after the expiry of the time limit in order to allow the claim to proceed. Rather, it requires the tribunal

333

to apply the less stringent test of asking whether the claim was presented within a reasonable time after the time limit expired. That said, a tribunal is unlikely to accept a late claim where the claimant fails to act promptly once the obstacle that prevented the claim being made in time in the first place has been removed.

What amounts to a 'further reasonable period' for the purposes of S.111(2)(b) is essentially a matter of fact for the employment tribunal to decide on the particular circumstances of the case. There is no hard and fast rule about what period of delay is reasonable, and the extent of the delay is just one of the circumstances tribunals will need to consider. In Cullinane v Balfour Beatty Engineering Services Ltd and anor EAT 0537/10 Mr Justice Underhill, then President of the EAT, commented that the question of whether the period between expiry of the time limit and the eventual presentation of a claim is reasonable requires an objective consideration of the factors causing the delay and what period should reasonably be allowed in those circumstances for proceedings to be instituted. Crucially, this assessment must always be made against the general background of the primary time limit and the strong public interest in claims being brought promptly. In Nolan v Balfour Beatty Engineering Services EAT 0109/11 the EAT reiterated this last point, stating that tribunals, when considering whether to extend time under S.111(2)(b), should always bear in mind the general principle that litigation should be progressed efficiently and without delay. The EAT went on to hold that, when deciding what would have been a reasonable time within which to present a late claim, tribunals should have regard to all the particular circumstances of a case, including what the claimant did; what he or she knew, or reasonably ought to have known, about time limits; and why it was that the further delay occurred (see 'Relationship between "reasonably practicable" and "reasonable" tests' below).

5.91 The upshot is that when a claim is late, even if through no fault of the claimant or his or her advisers, the claimant must act quickly to minimise the delay as soon as he or she becomes aware of it. In Golub v University of Sussex, unreported 13.4.81, CA, the time for presenting G's unfair dismissal claim ran out on 30 March. A tribunal made a finding of fact that his solicitors had posted his claim on 10 March but that it was not received by the employment tribunal office, presumably through having been lost in the post. The tribunal concluded that it had not been reasonably practicable to present the claim in time. G, however, went abroad and did not telephone his solicitors to chase progress until 27 May. They then made enquiries and presented a fresh claim on 5 June. The tribunal thought that a two-month extension – i.e. to 31 May – might have been reasonable in the circumstances, but no more. Accordingly, the tribunal concluded that G's claim had not been presented within a reasonable further period after the original time limit expired. The Court of Appeal held that what further period was reasonable was a question of fact for the tribunal, which was entitled to reach the conclusion that there had been unreasonable delay in presenting G's claim.

Similarly, in Rumney v Kent County Council EAT 322/78 R was ill when the time limit expired and the EAT was prepared to accept that it might not have been reasonably practicable for him to present his claim in time. However, it pointed out that the reasonableness of further delay was a quite separate issue and held that an additional delay of three months was quite unreasonable. And in Moore v Messrs Thrings and Long EAT 422/93 the EAT emphasised that the question was essentially one of fact and that there was no error of law or perversity in the tribunal's decision that a further delay of four weeks was unreasonable.

The following two cases usefully illustrate how tribunals approach the question **5.92** of whether the claimant unreasonably delayed submitting the claim:

- **Royal Bank of Scotland plc v Theobald** EAT 0444/06: T was summarily dismissed by RBS plc for gross misconduct on 11 November 2005. On 19 November he consulted a CAB regarding a potential unfair dismissal claim and was erroneously advised that he had to use RBS plc's internal appeal procedure before presenting a tribunal complaint. He duly lodged an internal appeal, which was dismissed on 9 February 2006. Later that day, he downloaded a blank ET1 claim form from the Employment Tribunals Service's website but did not immediately complete it. The three-month time limit for his unfair dismissal claim expired at midnight on 10 February, but T did not present his claim until 23 February. The EAT held that, even taking into account the CAB's incorrect advice, T did not show that it was not reasonably practicable to have presented his claim in time – he still had time to present the claim within the time limit once he was told that his appeal had been rejected. In any event, the EAT considered a delay of 13 days between expiry of the time limit and the submission of the claim to be unreasonable. This was because T had downloaded the claim form and could have presented it electronically or in person; there was no indication that he had any difficulty filling in the form, which contained little detail; and he had not given a full and frank explanation as to why he had delayed in submitting the claim. T's claim was accordingly dismissed

- **Remploy Ltd v Brain** EAT 0465/10: the EAT upheld an employment tribunal's decision that a period of two-and-a-half months between expiry of the time limit and the eventual presentation of B's unfair dismissal claim was reasonable. In particular, it held that the tribunal had been entitled to have regard to the following factors in deciding to extend time: on discovering the actual time limit B had immediately contacted the employment tribunal office; there was no finding of fact that the office told B that she could submit the ET1 electronically and it was therefore reasonable for her to

335

wait for a pack to arrive in the post; on receiving the pack, it was reasonable of her to focus her energy on trying to save her job via the ongoing appeal process; and it was reasonable for her to take a further five days to prepare and submit the claim form to the tribunal.

5.93 In James W Cook and Co (Wivenhoe) Ltd (in liquidation) v Tipper and ors 1990 ICR 716, CA, the claimants were made redundant but were led to believe that they would be re-employed when business picked up. It was not until their workplace closed down that they realised that they had been misled, but by this time they had exceeded the three-month time limit for the presentation of their unfair dismissal claims. The Court of Appeal held that it had not been reasonably practicable to complain of unfair dismissal until the closure of the business, but that it was reasonable for the claims to have been brought within two weeks of the date of closure.

The tribunal in Marley (UK) Ltd and anor v Anderson 1994 ICR 295, EAT, assumed that the Tipper case established a principle that a delay of four weeks or more once the true facts were understood should be regarded as a longer than reasonable period. However, the EAT disagreed and said that the tribunal should look at the particular circumstances of the case and not focus on the extent of the delay to the exclusion of other factors. In this instance, the claimant's evidence referred to various matters relevant to the question of whether the claim had been presented within such further period as the tribunal considered reasonable, such as seeking legal advice, making an appointment with a solicitor and sending a letter before action. The case was remitted to the tribunal to consider, having regard to all the relevant facts, whether the claim had been presented within a reasonable further period.

5.94 An employment tribunal's failure to have regard to all pertinent factors is therefore likely to lead to its decision being overturned on appeal. This happened in Averns v Stagecoach in Warwickshire EAT 0065/08, where A's husband was dismissed in July 2006 and died in October 2006, some 11 days before the expiry of the three-month time limit for lodging an unfair dismissal claim. In early January 2007, A was advised that she could bring proceedings on behalf of her husband's estate and she presented an unfair dismissal claim on 21 January 2007. The employment tribunal was satisfied that it had not been reasonably practicable for the claim to be presented within the three-month time limit owing to the serious illness and subsequent death of A's husband. However, it felt that given A's and her husband's 'strong sense of injustice about the circumstances of dismissal from the outset', the unfair dismissal claim was not presented within a reasonable further period, meaning that the time limit could not be extended. The EAT overturned the tribunal's decision, holding that, in concluding that A had not acted promptly and reasonably, the tribunal had failed to fully address the important fact that she had not understood that she could make such claims on behalf of her husband's estate. The case was remitted to a different tribunal to reconsider whether the time extension should be granted.

An extension of time was granted in Locke v Tabfine Ltd t/a Hands Music Centre EAT 0517/10. There, the EAT took the view that a delay of five months beyond the three-month time limit was not unreasonable given that L was undergoing treatment for cancer and was in a very frail condition. In finding against L, the employment judge had incorrectly focused on what was practicable and not on what was reasonable for this claimant to do in the circumstances, and nor had the judge properly assessed the medical evidence.

5.95 The fault of the claimant's adviser in not submitting the claim earlier will also impact upon the question of reasonableness. For example, in Lezo v OCS Group UK Ltd EAT 0104/10 the EAT upheld the decision of an employment tribunal that waiting a further 11 days after the expiry of the time limit before submitting the claim was an unreasonable period. L was dismissed and a CAB referred him to his local law centre. The law centre agreed to take on his claim but was not able to see him straight away. The CAB notified the law centre that it considered the time limit would run out on 5 May 2009. L saw a law centre adviser on 27 April and the claim was presented on 6 May. The time limit actually ran out on 25 April, but the employment judge decided that it was not reasonably practicable for L to have presented it by then. However, he considered that the further period was not reasonable because, once she had checked the documentation, the adviser had become aware that the time limit had already expired. Thus, there was no explanation for only submitting the claim on 6 May.

These cases show that there are many factors that may be relevant to a tribunal's consideration of whether a claim was presented within such further period as was reasonable. What is more, the inquiry need not necessarily focus solely on the claimant. In Biggs v Somerset County Council 1996 ICR 364, CA, Lord Justice Neill made it clear that in considering the exercise of discretion to extend time, it was not just the claimant's difficulties that had to be considered but also the effect on the employer – an extension of time may be unreasonable if the employer were to face difficulties of substance in answering the claim. However, this will probably only be relevant in practice where there are substantial delays involved. In Whitbread plc v Rees EAT 1292/97 the EAT upheld a tribunal's decision that it was not reasonably practicable for the claimant to present her complaint within the three-month time limit because of ill health. It also upheld the tribunal's decision that the further delay of six-and-a-half months was reasonable. The EAT held that, in determining whether this further period was reasonable, the tribunal was entitled to take into account what prejudice would be caused to the employer by allowing the claim to proceed out of time. In

337

relation to this question the tribunal was right to take account of the fact that the claimant had made her complaints known to her employer at an early stage and that her employer was aware of her ill health.

5.96 Relationship between 'reasonably practicable' and 'reasonable' tests

The relationship between the first limb of S.111(2)(b) ERA – i.e. whether it was not reasonably practicable to present the claim within the time limit – and the second limb of that subsection – i.e. whether, after the end of the limitation period, the claim was presented within a further reasonable period – has been considered by the courts and tribunals on a number of occasions.

In Northumberland County Council and anor v Thompson EAT 0209/07 the question of how the tribunal should construe the words 'within such further period as the tribunal considers reasonable' in the second limb of S.111(2)(b) arose for determination. Mr Justice Silber began by noting that the tests of what is 'reasonably practicable' and what is 'reasonable' are different. For example, in Palmer and anor v Southend-on-Sea Borough Council 1984 ICR 372, CA, the Court of Appeal said that to construe the words 'reasonably practicable' as the equivalent of the word 'reasonable' was to take a view too favourable to the employee. Nevertheless, Silber J thought that, although the two tests are different, they both embrace, albeit in different ways, the concept of reasonableness. It followed from this that matters of crucial importance in determining the reasonableness aspect (rather than the practicability aspect) of the test of 'reasonable practicability' are also likely to be of substantial importance in ascertaining if a claimant has, after the end of the three-month period, launched proceedings 'within such period as the tribunal considers reasonable'. Thus, an employment tribunal considering the latter question should follow the approach on 'reasonable practicability' (while ignoring the practicability aspect) adopted in cases such as Marks and Spencer plc v Williams-Ryan 2005 ICR 1293, CA, and London International College Ltd v Sen 1993 IRLR 333, CA, and have regard to the state of mind of the employee and the extent to which he or she understood the position. In other words, it was necessary to consider what the employee knew or what he or she should have known about the right to bring a complaint and the time limit for making it. As the tribunal in the instant case had failed to have regard to these matters, the case was remitted for reconsideration.

The EAT followed this approach in Nolan v Balfour Beatty Engineering Services EAT 0109/11, where it held that tribunals determining whether a claim was submitted within a further reasonable time must consider all the circumstances of the particular case, including what the claimant did; what he or she knew, or reasonably ought to have known, about time limits; and why it was that the further delay occurred.

338

The correct application of S.111(2)(b) was also considered in Cullinane v **5.97** Balfour Beatty Engineering Services Ltd and anor EAT 0537/10. There, C, an electrician, believed that he had been denied various jobs over the years as a result of his name appearing on a 'blacklist', i.e. a database of workers in the construction industry who were perceived as troublemakers. C contacted the Information Commissioner's Office and, on 25 March, was sent a copy of the information on the database that related to him. On the basis of that information, he believed that he had been denied a job in 2000 with RM Ltd and a job with BBES Ltd in 2006 as a result of his name appearing on the blacklist. C contacted his trade union on 30 March and was given an appointment with a regional officer, P, on 29 April. On 30 April, P submitted a claim against RM Ltd on C's behalf but, in relation to a possible claim against BBES Ltd, P referred the matter to head office, which in turn instructed solicitors. The solicitors presented a claim against BBES Ltd on 14 May. The employment judge dismissed the claim against BBES Ltd. In his view, it was not reasonably practicable for C to have presented the claim within the prescribed time limit. However, C became aware of his potential claims when he received the information from the Information Commissioner's Office on 25 March and, while he had promptly sought advice from his trade union, the union had acted dilatorily in not giving him an appointment until 29 April and not issuing proceedings until 14 May. The delay of six-and-a-half weeks in submitting the claim was therefore unreasonable.

Mr Justice Underhill, then President of the EAT, allowed C's appeal against the employment judge's decision. In his view, P could not be criticised – as the judge had done – for presenting the claim against RM Ltd on 30 April but passing the case against BBES Ltd to his head office, which caused another 14 days' delay. The cases were factually different and it was reasonable for P to seek legal advice as to any potential claim C had against BBES Ltd. Given that this part of the decision could not stand, the appeal was allowed and the case remitted to a different tribunal to consider the matter afresh.

While this effectively disposed of the appeal, Underhill P nevertheless made **5.98** some general observations regarding the assessment of a 'reasonable' period for presentation of a late claim. C argued that, as there was a difference between the two tests in S.111(2)(b), the principle in Dedman v British Building and Engineering Appliances Ltd 1974 ICR 53, CA – that an employee is affixed with the conduct of his or her advisers – which applies to the 'reasonable practicability' test (see '"Not reasonably practicable" extension – advisers at fault' above) cannot also apply to the test of whether the claim was submitted within a further 'reasonable' period. Accordingly, he submitted that the judge had been wrong to treat any unreasonable delay by his union as unreasonable delay by himself. Underhill P rejected this submission. He accepted that there is a formal distinction between the two limbs in S.111(2)(b). At the second stage, the question is what period between the expiry of the time limit and the presentation of the claim is

339

reasonable, which is not the same as asking whether the claimant acted reasonably. However, he did not believe that this formal distinction made any real difference in practice. The test of what is 'reasonable' under the second limb of S.111(2)(b) requires an objective consideration of the factors causing the delay and what period should reasonably be allowed in the circumstances for proceedings to be instituted, having regard to the strong public interest in claims being brought promptly and within a primary limitation period of three months. If a period is, on that basis, objectively unreasonable, then the fact that the delay is caused by the claimant's advisers rather than him or herself makes no difference to that conclusion. According to Underhill P, this approach was correct in principle and had the added merit of not opening up an 'uncomfortable gap' between the two tests in S.111(2)(b).

5.99 'Just and equitable' extension

Complaints of unlawful discrimination must be presented to an employment tribunal before the end of the period of three months beginning with the date of the act complained of – S.123(1)(a) Equality Act 2010 (EqA). This time limit applies to all work-related discrimination complaints brought under Part 5 of the EqA (other than equal pay claims, as to which see 'Time limits for starting tribunal proceedings – equal pay claims' above), which covers discrimination because of sex, race, disability, religion or belief, sexual orientation, age, marriage and civil partnership and gender reassignment. There is, however, an escape clause which allows a court or tribunal to consider any such complaint which is out of time provided that it is presented within 'such other period as the employment tribunal thinks just and equitable' – S.123(1)(b) EqA.

Section 123 EqA essentially replicates the equivalent provisions in the anti-discrimination legislation in force until October 2010. Accordingly, the substantial body of case law concerning discrimination time limits that built up under antecedent discrimination legislation will continue to apply to the time limit provisions of the EqA.

5.100 Date of the act complained of

In order to establish whether a complaint of discrimination has been presented in time it is necessary to determine the date of the act complained of, as this sets the time limit running for the purposes of S.123 EqA. Where the act complained of is a *single* act of discrimination, this will not usually give rise to any problems. A dismissal, for example, is considered to be a single act and the relevant date is the date on which the employee's contract of employment is terminated. Where dismissal is with notice, the EAT has held that the act of discrimination takes place when the notice expires, not when it is given – Lupetti v Wrens Old House Ltd 1984 ICR 348, EAT. Rejection for promotion is also usually considered a single act. In this case, the date on which another person is

340

promoted in place of the complainant is the date on which the alleged discrimination is said to have taken place – Amies v Inner London Education Authority 1977 ICR 308, EAT.

The question of when the time limit starts to run is more difficult to determine where the complaint relates to a *continuing* act of discrimination, such as harassment, or to a *discriminatory omission* on the part of the employer, such as a failure to confer a benefit on the employee. S.123(3) EqA makes special provision relating to the date of the act complained of in these situations. It states that:

- conduct extending over a period is to be treated as done at the end of that period – S.123(3)(a)

- failure to do something is to be treated as done when the person in question decided on it – S.123(3)(b). In the absence of evidence to the contrary, a person is taken to decide on failure to do something either when the person does an act inconsistent with deciding to do something, or, if they do no inconsistent act, on the expiry of the period on which they might reasonably have been expected to do it – S.123(4).

Case law on when time starts to run in relation to continuing acts of **5.101** discrimination and discriminatory omissions is discussed in detail in IDS Employment Law Handbook, 'Discrimination at Work' (2012), Chapter 34, 'Enforcing individual rights', under 'Time limits – continuing acts of discrimination' and 'Time limits – discriminatory omissions'.

Extension of time in discrimination cases   **5.102**
Employment tribunals have a discretion to hear out-of-time discrimination claims where they consider it 'just and equitable' to do so – S.123(1)(b) EqA. By contrast, tribunals are only entitled to exercise their discretion to allow late claims to proceed in unfair dismissal cases under the ERA where it was not 'reasonably practicable' to present the claim in time (and then only if the claim was presented within a reasonable time thereafter) – see '"Not reasonably practicable" extension' above. The escape clause in S.123 EqA is therefore broader than that found in the ERA. An illustration:

- **Trusthouse Forte (UK) Ltd v Halstead** EAT 213/86: H presented a claim for unfair dismissal and race discrimination 11 days out of time. The tribunal had to apply the two different formulae to the same facts and decided to allow both claims to proceed out of time. On appeal, the EAT said that the tribunal had misdirected itself in allowing the unfair dismissal claim to proceed out of time. Rather than focusing on whether it had been reasonably practicable for H to have presented her claim in time, it had considered instead the reasonableness of her conduct. The complaint that she had not received very good advice was a fair one, but it did not make it

341

impracticable for her to present her complaint in time. On the discrimination claim, the EAT noted that the discretion given to tribunals to allow claims, if they thought it 'just and equitable' to do so, was a wide one, and in this case the EAT saw no reason to interfere with its application.

5.103 While employment tribunals have a wide discretion to allow an extension of time under the 'just and equitable' test in S.123, it does not necessarily follow that exercise of the discretion is a foregone conclusion in a discrimination case. Indeed, the Court of Appeal made it clear in Robertson v Bexley Community Centre t/a Leisure Link 2003 IRLR 434, CA, that when employment tribunals consider exercising the discretion under what is now S.123(1)(b) EqA, 'there is no presumption that they should do so unless they can justify failure to exercise the discretion. Quite the reverse, a tribunal cannot hear a complaint unless the applicant convinces it that it is just and equitable to extend time so the exercise of the discretion is the exception rather than the rule.' The onus is therefore on the claimant to convince the tribunal that it is just and equitable to extend the time limit. However, the Court of Appeal also stressed that the EAT should be very reluctant to overturn the exercise of an employment tribunal's discretion of what is 'just and equitable'. In order to succeed, it would have to be shown that the tribunal took into account facts which it ought not to have done, or that it took an approach to the issue which was very obviously wrong, or that the decision was so unreasonable that no tribunal properly directing itself could have reached it.

The same approach was adopted by the Court of Appeal in Chief Constable of Lincolnshire Police v Caston 2010 IRLR 327, CA. In that case, the employment judge accepted an out-of-time disability discrimination claim after taking into consideration the claimant's mental ill health. However, in the course of his judgment, the judge quoted with approval a comment from a textbook to the effect that tribunals and appellate courts had adopted 'a liberal approach' to extension of time. The Court of Appeal nevertheless upheld the judge's decision on appeal. In the Court's view, when considering whether a tribunal was entitled to find it just and equitable to extend time, the question that must be asked is whether there was material on which the tribunal could properly exercise its discretion. The essence of a judicial discretion is that two judges may exercise it differently without either being wrong. It was therefore irrelevant whether the judge in the instant case thought he was being 'liberal' or not in his exercise of discretion. The judge had found that the employee's mental ill health had caused her to mislead her solicitors as to when the claim needed to be lodged, and his conclusion that this constituted an exceptional circumstance making it just and equitable to extend time had been open to him on the evidence.

5.104 In determining whether to exercise their discretion to allow the late submission of a discrimination claim, the EAT in British Coal Corporation v Keeble and ors 1997 IRLR 336, EAT, suggested that tribunals would be assisted by considering the factors listed in S.33 of the Limitation Act 1980. That section deals with the exercise of discretion in civil courts in personal injury cases and requires the court to consider the prejudice which each party would suffer as a result of the decision reached, and to have regard to all the circumstances of the case, in particular, the length of, and reasons for, the delay; the extent to which the cogency of the evidence is likely to be affected by the delay; the extent to which the party sued has cooperated with any requests for information; the promptness with which the claimant acted once he or she knew of the facts giving rise to the cause of action; and the steps taken by the claimant to obtain appropriate advice once he or she knew of the possibility of taking action. In Lupetti v Wrens Old House Ltd 1984 ICR 348, EAT, the Appeal Tribunal added that tribunals may, if they consider it necessary, also consider the merits of the claim, but if they do so they should invite the parties to make submissions.

While the checklist in S.33 of the Limitation Act 1980 provides a useful guide for tribunals, it need not be adhered to slavishly. In Southwark London Borough Council v Afolabi 2003 ICR 800, CA, the Court of Appeal considered a case in which the claimant had brought a race discrimination claim nearly nine years after the expiry of the statutory time limit and the tribunal exercised its discretion to allow the claim as it was just and equitable to do so in all the circumstances. The Court of Appeal decided that the tribunal did not err in law by failing to consider the matters listed in S.33 when considering whether it was just and equitable to extend time, provided that it left no significant factor out of account in exercising its discretion. In other words, the checklist in S.33 should not be elevated into a legal requirement but should be used as a guide.

Some examples of how the discretion to extend time has been exercised: **5.105**

- **McRoberts v Adams** EAT 499/92: A's claim was presented to a tribunal in time but named the wrong respondent. By the time A discovered her mistake, the claim was time-barred. The EAT refused to interfere with the tribunal's decision to extend the time limit as there was clear evidence that A had made a genuine mistake as to the identity of her employer and there was no prejudice to the employer

- **Osajie v London Borough of Camden** EAT 317/96: O initially made an internal complaint of discrimination to her employer, which, in breach of its own equal opportunities policy, failed to provide a prompt response. As a result, O's subsequent tribunal claim was presented out of time. In overturning the tribunal's decision not to exercise its discretion, the EAT held that it was just and equitable to allow the claim to proceed. O had been perfectly entitled to seek information from her employer before deciding whether or not to pursue a discrimination claim

- **Barber v Bernard Matthews Foods Ltd** ET Case No.1501308/00: B, who suffered from carpal tunnel syndrome, was dismissed in September 1999

343

on capability grounds. However, his disability discrimination claim was not presented until July 2000. He had been to see a solicitor who had told him that he had three years in which to bring a personal injuries claim but failed to tell him that he had only three months in which to bring an employment tribunal claim. The tribunal held that his claim could proceed. It was reasonable for B not to have known about the three-month time limit before he went to see the solicitor and it was reasonable for him to have relied on what the solicitor said thereafter. Furthermore, the company would suffer no real prejudice, and if it did it was its own fault as notes should have been kept relating to the dismissal

- **Bahous v Pizza Express Restaurant Ltd** EAT 0029/11: the EAT overturned a tribunal's decision to reject B's out-of-time race discrimination claim for want of jurisdiction. The tribunal had erred by failing to consider the balance of prejudice between the parties when refusing to extend time. This factor was significant as the tribunal had found that the claim was made out on its merits, and B was the only one prejudiced by the delay in issuing proceedings. Furthermore, the tribunal had erred in visiting upon B his solicitor's failure to enter proceedings in time.

These cases highlight the fact that tribunals can take a wide range of matters into account when determining whether it is just and equitable on the facts to allow a claim to proceed out of time. We consider some of these matters below.

5.106 **Incorrect advice.** It is clear from the case law that an employment tribunal's discretion to extend time in discrimination cases is wider than the discretion available in unfair dismissal cases. Therefore, whereas incorrect advice by a solicitor or a wholly understandable misconception of the law is unlikely to save a late tribunal claim in an unfair dismissal case (see "Not reasonably practicable" extension – advisers at fault' above), the same is not necessarily true when the claim is one of discrimination – Hawkins v Ball and anor 1996 IRLR 258, EAT, and British Coal Corporation v Keeble and ors 1997 IRLR 336, EAT.

In Chohan v Derby Law Centre 2004 IRLR 685, EAT, for example, C was employed as an adviser on employment matters and as a trainee solicitor. She was dismissed and brought a claim for sex discrimination, but her claim was presented 18 days out of time. The employment tribunal decided that it would not be just and equitable to extend the time limit, as the delay was caused by the incorrect advice of her solicitors, and because C had legal experience. On appeal, the EAT reversed the tribunal decision and allowed the time limit to be extended. In respect of the incorrect legal advice, the EAT referred to a non-employment decision of the Court of Appeal in Steeds v Peverel Management Services Ltd 2001 EWCA Civ 419, CA, when holding that C should not be disadvantaged because of the fault of her advisers, for otherwise the defendant would be in receipt of a windfall. It also found that, following British Coal

Corporation v Keeble and ors (above), the tribunal should have considered all the circumstances and had erred in exercising its discretion without considering the checklist set out in the Limitation Act 1980. With regard to C's legal knowledge, the EAT said that the legal point concerning when the cause of action arose was a difficult one and C should not be blamed for getting it wrong.

In the subsequent case of Anderson v George S Hall Ltd EAT 0631/05 A's **5.107** claims for race and sex discrimination were presented 14 days out of time. The delay was due to the claimant's solicitor's mistaken belief that, as a formal grievance under the Employment Act 2002 (Dispute Resolution) Regulations 2004 SI 2004/752 (now repealed) had been lodged, time was automatically extended for three months. The tribunal refused to exercise its discretion to extend time, holding that the respondent had given a prompt reply to the grievance and, the solicitor's mistake aside, there was no reason why the claim could not have been lodged directly thereafter, and therefore in time. On appeal, the EAT ruled that the tribunal chairman had mistakenly taken the delay in action on the part of A's solicitor as a lack of promptness on the part of A, and had also failed to give proper reasons for his decision.

A similar approach has been taken where the delay was caused by the fault of an adviser who was not a qualified solicitor. In Wright v Wolverhampton City Council EAT 0117/08, for example, the EAT held that incorrect advice received by a trade union official before and after the claimant submitted out-of-time discrimination claims should not be ascribed to the claimant and that an extension of time should be granted. And in Benjamin-Cole v Great Ormond Street Hospital for Sick Children NHS Trust EAT 0356/09 the EAT decided that the tribunal had incorrectly laid the delay caused by the claimant's unqualified representative at the claimant's door. There, B had consulted I, a volunteer employment adviser at the Brighton and Hove Race Equality Project, about taking various complaints about her employer to an employment tribunal. I was aware of the time limit for B's victimisation claim but, due to a death in his family, he submitted the claim four hours and 16 minutes after the deadline. The employment tribunal refused to extend the time limit and rejected the claim, but the EAT overturned the decision on appeal. In the EAT's view, B had placed the matter into the hands of someone who was held out as a skilled representative in employment tribunal cases, even though not legally qualified, and the tribunal had incorrectly attributed his fault in not submitting the claim in time to her. The tribunal had also made findings, unsupported by the evidence, that B was herself to blame for the delay. As a result, the case was remitted to a different tribunal to consider the question afresh.

Of course, the bad advice must have actually been the reason for the delay. In **5.108** Hunwicks v Royal Mail Group plc EAT 0003/07 the claimant sought to excuse her late claim on the ground that her trade union representative incorrectly

345

advised her that she had to exhaust the employer's internal grievance procedure before bringing a tribunal claim. The EAT, upholding the tribunal's decision, rejected this argument. Mr Justice Underhill, then President of the EAT, noted that the authorities clearly established that where a claimant has missed a relevant time limit as a result of relying on bad advice from a skilled adviser, including a trade union, that is a relevant factor which the tribunal should consider in deciding whether it is just and equitable to extend time. Whether it is a decisive factor will depend on all the circumstances of the case. However, in the instant case the adviser's incorrect advice played no role in the tribunal's decision as to whether the claimant's out-of-time discrimination claim should be allowed to proceed. This was because the time limit had already expired before any question of her being misled by the union representative arose. Accordingly, the union representative's mistake had had no causative effect and her claim was dismissed.

5.109 **Ignorance of rights.** The fact that a claimant is unaware of his or her right to make a tribunal complaint is also much more likely to save an out-of-time discrimination claim than an out-of-time unfair dismissal claim. In Director of Public Prosecutions and anor v Marshall 1998 ICR 518, EAT, M, a transsexual, was offered a post with the Crown Prosecution Service when she was a man. The offer was withdrawn after she told her prospective employer that she would be taking up the job as a woman. However, M did not present a sex discrimination complaint until three years later, after learning of the European Court of Justice's decision in P v S and anor 1996 ICR 795, ECJ, that discrimination against transsexuals was contrary to EU law. In upholding the tribunal's decision that it was just and equitable to extend the time limit under what was then S.76(5) SDA, the EAT stated that the words 'just and equitable' 'could not be wider or more general... As a matter of statutory language, the discretion which is given by the Act to extend time is unfettered and may include a consideration of the date from which the complainant could reasonably have become aware of her right to present a worthwhile complaint.'

Although the discretion is wide, it seems that it will only apply where the claimant's ignorance is reasonable. In Perth and Kinross Council v Townsley EAT 0010/10, for example, T, a Scottish Gypsy traveller, sought to excuse the late presentation of her race discrimination claim by some 19 months on the ground that she had been ignorant of the existence of employment tribunals. The employment judge accepted this as the main reason for the lengthy delay in submitting the claim and extended the time limit. The EAT overturned the decision, holding that, while the judge had considered whether T's professed ignorance of her right to complain to an employment tribunal was genuine, he had failed to address the question of whether her ignorance was reasonable. According to the EAT, it was obvious that it is important when asking whether or not it is just and equitable to allow an extension of time in a case where the claimant was ignorant of the right to bring a complaint to consider whether it

346

was reasonable for him or her to have been ignorant, and to have remained so, throughout the period of the primary time limit. It followed from this that the need to consider not only whether the claimant was ignorant but also whether he or she was reasonably ignorant applied in the same way to the 'just and equitable' test as it applied to the 'not reasonably practicable' test (see '"Not reasonably practicable" extension – ignorance of rights' above). In the instant case, the evidence clearly showed that it could not be said that T was reasonably ignorant of the possibility of presenting a claim to a tribunal – for example, she knew of another traveller who had brought a claim in respect of a recruitment matter.

The EAT reached the same conclusion in University of Westminster v Bailey **5.110**
EAT 0345/09. There, B, a senior lecturer, brought a claim of sex discrimination against the university concerning the grade he had been given under a job evaluation scheme. B lodged a claim at the employment tribunal 22 months after he had been informed of the grading decision, which was 19 months out of time. By then, the records of the evaluation panel were unavailable. B argued that he had not understood that the Sex Discrimination Act 1975 (SDA) applied to men as well as women until he received advice from his union representative at the time of his grievance. The employment judge found that, although the university would be prejudiced by the unavailability of documentary evidence and the difficulty in identifying the decision-makers, it had not been unreasonable for B to hold back issuing a claim, as the law was difficult and he was a litigant in person unaware of legal rules. The judge therefore granted an extension of time. The EAT overturned the decision. In its view, B's misunderstanding of the elementary scope of the SDA was not a good reason for delay. He was a person who knew, or should have known, the importance of presenting a claim quickly. Furthermore, the unavailability of documentary evidence caused by the delay should have led to a decision in the employer's favour. The appeal was accordingly allowed and B's claim dismissed.

Ongoing internal procedure. The fact that a complainant has awaited the **5.111**
outcome of an internal grievance procedure before making a complaint is just one matter to be taken into account by a tribunal considering the late presentation of a discrimination claim. In Apelogun-Gabriels v Lambeth London Borough Council and anor 2002 ICR 713, CA, the claimant presented a race discrimination claim that was out of time due to the fact that he had been seeking redress through the employer's grievance procedure. The Court of Appeal dismissed his appeal but took the opportunity to clarify the case law in this area. It held that the correct approach to whether it is just and equitable to extend the time limit for presenting a discrimination complaint that is out of time because the claimant was using an internal procedure was laid down in Robinson v Post Office 2000 IRLR 804, EAT, rather than Aniagwu v London Borough of Hackney and anor 1999 IRLR 303, EAT. There is no general principle that it will be just and equitable to extend the time limit where the claimant was seeking redress

347

through the employer's grievance procedure before embarking on legal proceedings. The general principle is that a delay caused by a claimant awaiting completion of an internal procedure may justify the extension of the time limit, but it is only one factor to be considered in any particular case.

5.112 **Disability discrimination cases.** In Department of Constitutional Affairs v Jones 2008 IRLR 128, CA, the Court of Appeal highlighted the fact that in disability discrimination cases there is an additional factor to be taken into account when considering an application to extend the time limit – and that is the disability itself. In particular, in order to amount to a disability in law, the disability must last, or be expected to last, for at least 12 months, and this may involve the claimant having to predict whether he or she is likely to fall within the statutory definition of disability (for which, see IDS Employment Law Handbook, 'Discrimination at Work' (2012), Chapter 6, 'Disability', under 'Meaning of "disability"'). Further problems can arise with mental conditions. In Jones, the claimant was suffering from depression, but gave evidence that he was reluctant to acknowledge to himself that he had a mental illness amounting to a disability in law. The Court of Appeal refused to overturn the extension of time, although Lord Justice Pill stressed that he was not stating that there was 'any general principle that a person with mental health problems is entitled to delay as a matter of course in bringing a claim'.

Disabled claimants may also find it difficult to comply with the three-month time limit where the employer's inadvertent failure to make reasonable adjustments has set time running. In Kingston upon Hull City Council v Matuszowicz 2009 ICR 1170, CA, the Court of Appeal stressed that the power to extend time should be considered in situations 'where the employee does not realise that the start date has occurred, or... the employer's decision has not been communicated to him' or if 'the employer were to seek to lull the employee into a false sense of security by professing to continue to consider what adjustments it ought reasonably to make, at a time long after the moment has arrived... when the employee is entitled to make a claim and time has started to run'. Lord Justice Sedley noted that in deciding whether to enlarge time under S.123(1)(b) EqA employment tribunals 'can be expected to have sympathetic regard' to the difficulty created for some claimants. The duty to make reasonable adjustments is discussed in IDS Employment Law Handbook, 'Discrimination at Work' (2012), Chapter 21, 'Failure to make reasonable adjustments'.

5.113 **'Blacklisting' claims**
The 'just and equitable' formula also applies to 'blacklisting' dismissals under S.104F ERA. Where a complaint under that provision is presented out of time, the tribunal has a discretion to extend the time limit if, in all the circumstances of the case, it considers it 'just and equitable' to do so – S.111(5) ERA.

Redundancy payments   5.114

The time limit for claiming a statutory redundancy payment is subject to the 'just and equitable' formula for extension, but works in a slightly different way. S.164 ERA provides that an employee will lose his or her entitlement to a redundancy payment unless one of the following four events occurs before the end of a period of *six months* beginning with the relevant date (normally the effective date of termination of employment):

- the payment is agreed and paid – S.164(1)(a)

- the employee makes a written claim for the payment to the employer – S.164(1)(b)

- the question as to the employee's right to, or the amount of, the payment has been referred to an employment tribunal – S.164(1)(c). (A claim is 'referred to a tribunal' when it is physically received at the tribunal office, not when it is posted – Secretary of State for Employment v Banks and ors 1983 ICR 48, EAT), or

- the employee presents a claim of unfair dismissal to a tribunal under S.111 ERA – S.164(1)(d).

There is provision for extending the time limit beyond the initial six months,   5.115
but the following conditions must be satisfied:

- during the six months immediately following the first six months beginning with the relevant date, the employee must have taken one of the steps set out in S.164(1)(b)–(d) above, and

- it appears *just and equitable* to the tribunal that the employee should receive a redundancy payment having regard to the reason shown by the employee for his or her failure to take any of the specified steps earlier and to all the other relevant circumstances – S.164(2) and (3).

Cases on the exercise of a tribunal's discretion to extend the time limit into the second six-month period are in line with the general pattern of tribunal decisions on what is 'just and equitable' in relation to discrimination claims. These provisions are discussed in IDS Employment Law Handbook, 'Redundancy' (2011), Chapter 10, 'Enforcement', under 'Statutory redundancy payments – time limits'.

There is no discretion to extend the time limit for taking the necessary steps   5.116
beyond the second six-month period, so that a claim received one day after the end of the combined 12-month period will be out of time – Secretary of State for Employment v Banks and ors (above). However, there are some exceptions to this. The first exception applies where the parties are engaged in mediation to resolve a cross-border dispute and mediation started before the time limit was due to expire – Ss.164(4) and 207A(5). If, in these circumstances, the

349

normal time limit for bringing a tribunal claim under S.164(1)(c) or the extended time limit under S.164(2) would expire before the mediation ends or less than eight weeks after it ends, the time limit will be extended to the end of eight weeks after the mediation ends – Ss.164(4) and 207A(6). The second exception is where the employee dies. If the employee dies during the period of six months beginning with the relevant date, the period is extended to one year beginning with the relevant date – S.176(7)(a).

Note that special time limit rules apply where an employee's claim for a redundancy payment is based on a spell of lay-off or short-time working. These rules are explained in IDS Employment Law Handbook, 'Redundancy' (2011), Chapter 4, 'Lay-off and short-time'.

5.117 **Subsequent claims.** Section 164(1) states that an employee will not be entitled to a redundancy payment unless one of the specified events has taken place within the six-month period beginning with the relevant date. But if one of those specified events has occurred within the six-month period, there is no time limit for making a *subsequent* claim to a tribunal. Two examples:

- **Bentley Engineering Co Ltd v Crown and anor** 1976 ICR 225, QBD: M presented a redundancy pay claim to a tribunal nearly two years after his dismissal. But the employer had made a purported redundancy payment to him within six months of his dismissal. This satisfied one of the conditions in S.164(1), which meant that M was not time-barred from bringing his claim (which was that the employer had underestimated his continuous service and that the payment should have been larger than it was)

- **Allsop v Spalding Tools Ltd t/a Lodge Engineering** ET Case No.9551/86: A presented a redundancy pay claim to a tribunal some 22 months after his dismissal but died before the case came on for hearing. The tribunal appointed A's widow as his personal representative to pursue the claim. Evidence was produced that A had sent a written claim for a redundancy payment to his employer soon after his dismissal. This satisfied S.164(l), meaning there was no time limit for the subsequent tribunal claim, and A's widow was awarded a redundancy payment.

5.118 **Unfair dismissal claims.** Presenting an unfair dismissal claim to a tribunal is one of the specified events that must occur within six months of the relevant date if the employee is to be entitled to a redundancy payment – see S.164(1)(d). But the time limit for an unfair dismissal claim is three months, not six months (unless the tribunal decides that it was not reasonably practicable to present the complaint in time and that it was presented within a reasonable period thereafter – S.111 ERA). However, the EAT has held that an unfair dismissal complaint presented outside the three-month limit will still entitle the employee to a redundancy payment if it was presented within the six months specified in S.164(1) – Duffin v Secretary of State for Employment 1983 ICR 766, EAT. Mr

Justice Browne-Wilkinson thought that the normal limitation period of six months for redundancy payment claims should still apply where the claim has been mistakenly identified as an unfair dismissal claim, provided, of course, that the employee has actually been dismissed because of redundancy.

Contractual redundancy payment claims. It should be noted that the six- **5.119** month time limit under S.164 does not apply to claims for contractual redundancy payments, which are subject only to the general contractual limitation of six years (five years in Scotland) – Greenwich Health Authority v Skinner and anor 1989 ICR 220, EAT.

5.120 ## Appendix – employment law time chart

Below is a list of statutory employment protection rights, the periods of qualifying service (if any) that apply to those rights, and the time limits governing their enforcement.

5.121 ### Detriment

Statutory right/ complaint	Qualifying period	Time limit for complaint	Early conciliation (a)
Right not to suffer detriment in relation to jury service (S.43M ERA)	None	3 months starting with date of (last) act or failure to act* (b)	✓
Right not to suffer detriment in relation to health and safety (S.44 ERA)	None	3 months starting with date of (last) act or failure to act* (b)	✓
Right not to suffer detriment in relation to Sunday working (S.45 ERA)	None	3 months starting with date of (last) act or failure to act* (b)	✓
Right not to suffer detriment in relation to performing functions as a pension trustee (S.46 ERA)	None	3 months starting with date of (last) act or failure to act* (b)	✓
Right not to suffer detriment in relation to performing functions as an employee representative (collective redundancies and TUPE) (S.47 ERA)	None	3 months starting with date of (last) act or failure to act* (b)	✓
Right not to suffer detriment in relation to time off for study or training (S.47A ERA)	None	3 months starting with date of (last) act or failure to act* (b)	✓

352

Statutory right/ complaint	Qualifying period	Time limit for complaint	Early conciliation (a)
Right not to suffer detriment in relation to protected disclosures (S.47B ERA)	None	3 months starting with date of (last) act or failure to act* (b)	✓
Right not to suffer detriment in relation to tax credits (S.47D ERA)	None	3 months starting with date of (last) act or failure to act* (b)	✓
Right not to suffer detriment in relation to right to request study or training (S.47F ERA) (c)	None (d)	3 months starting with date of (last) act or failure to act* (b)	✓
Right not to suffer detriment for refusing to accept an offer to become an employee shareholder (S.47G ERA)	None	3 months starting with date of (last) act or failure to act* (b)	✓
Right not to suffer detriment in relation to European Works Councils (Reg 31 Transnational Information and Consultation of Employees Regulations 1999 SI 1999/3323)	None	3 months starting with date of (last) act or failure to act*	✓
Right not to suffer detriment in relation to information and consultation rights of employees (Reg 32 Information and Consultation of Employees Regulations 2004 SI 2004/3426)	None	3 months starting with date of (last) act or failure to act*	✓

Statutory right/ complaint	Qualifying period	Time limit for complaint	Early conciliation (a)
Right not to suffer detriment in relation to information and consultation rights of pension scheme members (para 7, Sch 1 Occupational and Personal Pension Schemes (Consultation by Employers and Miscellaneous Amendment) Regulations 2006 SI 2006/349)	None	3 months starting with date of (last) act or failure to act*	✓
Right not to suffer detriment in relation to information and consultation rights of employees of European cooperative societies (Reg 33 European Cooperative Society (Involvement of Employees) Regulations 2006 SI 2006/2059)	None	3 months starting with date of (last) act or failure to act*	✓
Right not to suffer detriment in relation to information, consultation and negotiation rights of employees involved in cross-border mergers (Regs 49 and 50 Companies (Cross-Border Mergers) Regulations 2007 SI 2007/2974)	None	3 months starting with date of (last) act or failure to act*	✓

Statutory right/ complaint	Qualifying period	Time limit for complaint	Early conciliation (a)
Right not to suffer detriment in relation to information, consultation and negotiation rights of employees of European public limited liability companies (Reg 31 European Public Limited-Liability Company (Employee Involvement) (Great Britain) Regulations 2009 SI 2009/2401)	None	3 months starting with date of (last) act or failure to act*	✓
Right not to suffer detriment in relation to automatic pension enrolment (S.55 Pensions Act 2008)	None	3 months starting with date of (last) act or failure to act*	✓
Right not to suffer detriment in relation to right to be accompanied at a grievance or disciplinary hearing (S.12(1) Employment Relations Act 1999)	None	3 months starting with date of (last) act or failure to act*	✓
Right not to suffer detriment in connection with right to be accompanied at meetings to discuss study or training (Reg 18(1) Employee Study and Training (Procedural Requirements) Regulations 2010 SI 2010/155) (c)	None (d)	3 months starting with date of (last) act or failure to act*	✓

355

Statutory right/ complaint	Qualifying period	Time limit for complaint	Early conciliation (a)
Right not to suffer detriment in relation to a trade union blacklist (Reg 9 Employment Relations Act 1999 (Blacklists) Regulations 2010 SI 2010/493)	None	3 months starting with date of (last) act or failure to act**	✓

5.122 Discrimination

Statutory right/ complaint	Qualifying period	Time limit for complaint	Early conciliation (a)
Discrimination claims made under the EqA in relation to the protected characteristics of: • age • disability • gender reassignment • marriage and civil partnership • pregnancy and maternity • race • religion or belief • sex • sexual orientation	None	3 months starting with date of act complained of** (e) (b)	✓
Equal pay/value claim under EU law (Article 157 Treaty on the Functioning of the European Union and Article 4 recast Equal Treatment Directive (No.2006/54))	None	3/6 months starting with termination of employment (f)	

Statutory right/ complaint	Qualifying period	Time limit for complaint	Early conciliation (a)
Equal pay claim (S.66 EqA)	None	6 months starting with termination of employment (b)	✓

Dismissal

5.123

Statutory right/ complaint	Qualifying period	Time limit for complaint	Early conciliation (a)
Written reasons for dismissal (S.92 ERA)	2 years – S.92(3) # (1 year for those who started work before 6 April 2012) (g)	3 months starting with EDT*	✓
Unfair dismissal (UD) under S.98 ERA for a reason related to: • capability or qualifications • conduct • redundancy • a duty or restriction imposed by or under an enactment • 'some other substantial reason'	2 years – S.108(1) ERA # (1 year for those who started work before 6 April 2012)	3 months starting with EDT* (b)	✓
UD for a reason connected with medical suspension (S.64(2) ERA)	1 month – S.108(2) ERA	3 months starting with EDT* (b)	✓
UD for reasons relating to jury service (S.98B ERA)	None – S.108(3)(aa) ERA	3 months starting with EDT*	✓

357

Statutory right/ complaint	Qualifying period	Time limit for complaint	Early conciliation (a)
UD for a reason connected with pregnancy, childbirth or maternity (S.99 ERA and Reg 20 MPL Regs)	None – S.108(3)(b) ERA	3 months starting with EDT*	✓
UD for a reason connected with maternity, adoption, paternity, parental or dependant care leave (S.99 ERA, Reg 20 MPL Regs, Reg 29 PAL Regs and Reg 34 APL Regs)	None – S.108(3)(b) ERA (h)	3 months starting with EDT*	✓
UD for a health and safety reason (S.100 ERA)	None – S.108(3)(c) ERA	3 months starting with EDT*	✓
UD of a shop or betting worker for refusing to work on a Sunday (S.101 ERA)	None – S.108(3)(d) ERA	3 months starting with EDT*	✓
UD for a reason connected with the Working Time Regulations 1998 SI 1998/1833 (S.101A ERA)	None – S.108(3)(dd) ERA	3 months starting with EDT*	✓
UD for performing functions as an occupational pension trustee (S.102 ERA)	None – S.108(3)(e) ERA	3 months starting with EDT*	✓
UD for performing functions as an employee representative (collective redundancies and TUPE) (S.103 ERA)	None – S.108(3)(f) ERA	3 months starting with EDT*	✓
UD related to making a protected disclosure (S.103A ERA)	None – S.108(3)(ff) ERA	3 months starting with EDT*	✓

Statutory right/ complaint	Qualifying period	Time limit for complaint	Early conciliation (a)
UD for asserting a statutory right (S.104 ERA)	None – S.108(3)(g) ERA	3 months starting with EDT*	✓
UD in connection with entitlement to the national minimum wage (S.104A ERA)	None – S.108(3)(gg) ERA	3 months starting with EDT*	✓
UD in connection with working tax credits (S.104B ERA)	None – S.108(3)(gh) ERA	3 months starting with EDT*	✓
UD in relation to the right to request flexible working (S.104C ERA)	None – S.108(3)(gi) ERA (d)	3 months starting with EDT*	✓
UD in connection with automatic pension enrolment under the Pensions Act 2008 (S.104D ERA)	None – S.108(3)(gj) ERA	3 months starting with EDT*	✓
UD in connection with the right to request study or training (S.104E ERA) (c)	None – S.108(3)(gk) ERA (d)	3 months starting with EDT*	✓
UD for a reason relating to a trade union blacklist (S.104F ERA)	None – S.108(3)(gl) ERA	3 months starting with EDT**	✓
UD for refusing to accept an offer to become an employee shareholder (S.104G ERA)	None – S.108(3) (gm) ERA	3 months starting with EDT*	✓
UD where reason for the dismissal is, or relates to, the employee's political opinions or affiliation (S.111(1) ERA)	None – S.108(4) ERA	3 months starting with EDT*	✓
UD for automatically unfair redundancy selection (S.105 ERA)	None – S.108(3)(h) ERA	3 months starting with EDT*	✓

359

Statutory right/ complaint	Qualifying period	Time limit for complaint	Early conciliation (a)
UD relating to the performance of functions or activities of a member or representative (or candidate for election as a member or representative) of a European Works Council (Reg 28 Transnational Information and Consultation of Employees Regulations 1999 SI 1999/3323)	None – S.108(3)(hh) ERA	3 months starting with EDT*	✓
UD in connection with the rights of part-time workers (Reg 7(1) Part-time Workers (Prevention of Less Favourable Treatment) Regulations 2000 SI 2000/1551)	None – S.108(3)(i) ERA	3 months starting with EDT*	✓
UD in connection with the rights of fixed-term employees (Reg 6(1) Fixed-term Employees (Prevention of Less Favourable Treatment) Regulations 2002 SI 2002/2034)	None – S.108(3)(j) ERA	3 months starting with EDT*	✓
UD relating to the performance of functions or activities of an information and consultation representative or candidate (Reg 30 Information and Consultation of Employees Regulations 2004 SI 2004/3426)	None – S.108(3)(l) ERA	3 months starting with EDT*	✓

Statutory right/ complaint	Qualifying period	Time limit for complaint	Early conciliation (a)
UD in connection with the information and consultation rights of pension scheme members (para 5, Sch 1 Occupational and Personal Pension Schemes (Consultation by Employers and Miscellaneous Amendment) Regulations 2006 SI 2006/349)	None – S.108(3)(m) ERA	3 months starting with EDT*	✓
UD in connection with the information and consultation rights of employees of European cooperative societies (Reg 31 European Cooperative Society (Involvement of Employees) Regulations 2006 SI 2006/2059)	None – S.108(3)(o) ERA	3 months starting with EDT*	✓
UD in connection with the information, consultation and negotiation rights of employees involved in cross-border mergers (Regs 46 and 47 Companies (Cross-Border Mergers) Regulations 2007 SI 2007/2974)	None – S.108(3)(p) ERA	3 months starting with EDT*	✓

Statutory right/ complaint	Qualifying period	Time limit for complaint	Early conciliation (a)
UD in connection with the information, consultation and negotiation rights of employees of European public limited liability companies (Reg 29 European Public Limited-Liability Company (Employee Involvement) (Great Britain) Regulations 2009 SI 2009/2401)	None – S.108(3)(q) ERA	3 months starting with EDT*	✓
UD in connection with rights of agency workers (Reg 17(1) Agency Workers Regulations 2010 SI 2010/93)	None – S.108(3)(r) ERA (i)	3 months starting with EDT*	✓
UD in connection with the right to be accompanied at disciplinary and grievance hearings (S.12(3) Employment Relations Act 1999)	None – S.12(4) Employment Relations Act 1999	3 months starting with EDT*	✓
UD in connection with the right to be accompanied at meetings to discuss flexible working (Reg 16(3) Flexible Working (Procedural Requirements) Regulations 2002 SI 2002/3207)	None – Reg 16(4) Flexible Working (Procedural Require-ments) Regulations 2002 SI 2002/3207 (d)	3 months starting with EDT*	✓

Statutory right/ complaint	Qualifying period	Time limit for complaint	Early conciliation (a)
UD in connection with right to be accompanied at meetings to discuss study or training (Reg 18(3) Employee Study and Training (Procedural Requirements) Regulations 2010 SI 2010/155) (c)	None – Reg 18(4) Employee Study and Training (Procedural Require-ments) Regulations 2010 SI 2010/155 (d)	3 months starting with EDT*	✓
UD for 'trade union' reasons (Ss.152 and 153 TULR(C)A)	None – S.154 TULR(C)A	3 months starting with EDT*	✓
UD for taking part in official industrial action (S.238A TULR(C)A)	None – S.239(1) ERA	6 months from complainant's date of dismissal* (j)	✓
UD in connection with trade union recognition under Schedule A1 to the TULR(C)A (paras 161 and 162, Sch A1 TULR(C)A)	None – para 164, Sch A1 TULR(C)A	3 months starting with EDT*	✓
UD by reason of a business transfer (Reg 7 TUPE)	2 years – S108(1) ERA # (1 year for those who started work before 6 April 2012)	3 months starting with EDT*	✓
UD because of a spent conviction (S.4(3)(b) Rehabilitation of Offenders Act 1974)	2 years – S.108(1) ERA # (1 year for those who started work before 6 April 2012)	3 months starting with EDT*	✓

363

Statutory right/ complaint	Qualifying period	Time limit for complaint	Early conciliation (a)
Interim relief pending complaint under Ss.100, 101A, 102, 103, 103A ERA or para 161, Sch A1 TULR(C)A (S.128 ERA)	None	7 days immediately following EDT***	✓

5.124 Maternity and parental rights

Statutory right/ complaint	Qualifying period	Time limit for complaint	Early conciliation (a)
Right to paid time off for ante-natal care (Ss.55 and 56 ERA)	None	3 months starting with date of appointment* (b)	✓
Right to be offered alternative work before maternity suspension (S.67 ERA)	None	3 months starting with first day of suspension* (b)	✓
Right to be paid during maternity suspension (S.68 ERA)	None	3 months starting with day in respect of which claim is made* (b)	✓
Right to statutory maternity leave (Ss.71 and 73 ERA)	None	N/A	
Right to statutory adoption leave (Ss.75A and 75B ERA)	26 weeks – Reg 15 PAL Regs (k)	N/A	
Right to statutory paternity leave (Ss.80A to 80BB ERA)	26 weeks – Regs 4 and 8 PAL Regs/ Regs 4 and 14 APL Regs (l)	N/A	

Statutory right/ complaint	Qualifying period	Time limit for complaint	Early conciliation (a)
Right to 13 weeks' unpaid parental leave (18 weeks for parents of disabled children) (Regs 13 and 14 MPL Regs)	1 year – Reg 13(1)(a) MPL Regs (m)	3 months from when employer refuses right*	
Right to unpaid time off to care for dependants (S.57A ERA)	None	3 months starting with date of refusal* (b)	✓
Right not to suffer detriment in relation to pregnancy, childbirth, maternity, maternity leave, adoption leave, paternity leave, parental leave, or time off for dependants (S.47C ERA)	None	3 months starting with date of (last) act or failure to act* (b)	✓
Right to request flexible working (S.80F ERA)	26 weeks – Reg 3(1)(a) Flexible Working (Eligibility, Complaints and Remedies) Regulations 2002 SI 2002/3207)	3 months starting with 'relevant date'* (b) (n)	✓
Right not to suffer detriment in relation to right to request flexible working (S.47E ERA)	None (d)	3 months starting with date of (last) act or failure to act* (b)	✓
Right to be accompanied at meetings to discuss flexible working (Reg 14 Flexible Working (Procedural Requirements) Regulations 2002 SI 2002/3207)	None (d)	3 months from date or threat of failure to comply*	✓

Statutory right/ complaint	Qualifying period	Time limit for complaint	Early conciliation (a)
Right not to suffer detriment in connection with the right to be accompanied at meetings to discuss flexible working (Reg 16(1) Flexible Working (Procedural Requirements) Regulations 2002 SI 2002/3207)	None (d)	3 months starting with date of (last) act or failure to act*	✓
Right to return to the same job or, if that is not practicable, to a suitable alternative job after additional maternity leave or a period of parental leave of more than 4 weeks (Reg 18(2) MPL Regs)	None	N/A	

5.125 Miscellaneous

Statutory right/ complaint	Qualifying period	Time limit for complaint	Early conciliation (a)
Written particulars of employment (Ss.1 and 4 ERA)	1 month – S.198 ERA	3 months starting with date on which employment ceased* (b)	
Right to written statement of particulars of office and to itemised statement of stipend for ecclesiastical office holders (Regs 3, 6 and 8 of the Ecclesiastical Offices (Terms of Service) Regulations 2009 SI 2009/2108	None	3 months starting with date the appointment ended*	✓

366

Statutory right/ complaint	Qualifying period	Time limit for complaint	Early conciliation (a)
Itemised pay statement (S.8 ERA)	None	3 months starting with date on which employment ceased* (b)	✓
Unlawful deduction from wages (Ss.13, 15, 18 and 20 ERA)	None	3 months from date of (last) deduction or (last) payment to employer* (b)	✓
Guarantee pay (S.28 ERA)	1 month – S.29(1) ERA	3 months starting with day for which payment claimed* (b)	✓
Medical suspension pay (S.64 ERA)	1 month – S.65(1) ERA	3 months starting with day in respect of which claim is made*	✓
Rights on insolvency of employer (S.182 ERA)	None (o)	3 months starting with date of communication of Secretary of State's decision*	
Right to be accompanied at a grievance or disciplinary hearing (S.10 Employment Relations Act 1999)	None	3 months from date or threat of failure to comply* (b)	✓
Unlawful infringement of human rights by public body (Human Rights Act 1998)	None	1 year from date of act complained of*****	

Statutory right/ complaint	Qualifying period	Time limit for complaint	Early conciliation (a)
Right to request study or training – S.63D ERA (c)	26 weeks – Reg 2 Employee Study and Training (Qualifying Period of Employment) Regulations 2010 SI 2010/800	3 months starting with 'relevant date'* (b) (p)	✓
Right to be accompanied at a meeting to discuss study or training (Reg 16 Employee Study and Training (Procedural Requirements) Regulations 2010 SI 2010/155) (c)	None (d)	3 months starting with date or threat of failure to comply*	✓
Right not to be refused employment or the services of an employment agency for a reason that relates to a trade union blacklist (Regs 5 and 6 Employment Relations Act 1999 (Blacklists) Regulations 2010 SI 2010/493)	None	3 months starting with date of conduct complained of**	✓
Breach of contract claim by employee	None	In the employment tribunal, 3 months starting with EDT or if no EDT the last day on which the employee worked* (b). In the county court or High Court, 6 years from breach of contract	✓

Statutory right/ complaint	Qualifying period	Time limit for complaint	Early conciliation (a)
Breach of contract claim by employer	None	In the employment tribunal, 6 weeks from receipt of employee's claim* (b). In the county court or High Court, 6 years from breach of contract	✓
Complaint that Secretary of State has not paid a sum in respect of the unpaid pensions contributions of an insolvent employer (S.126(2) Pensions Schemes Act 1993)	None	3 months starting with date on which the Secretary of State's decision was communicated to the person(s) presenting it*	

National minimum wage

5.126

Statutory right/ complaint	Qualifying period	Time limit for complaint	Early conciliation (a)
Failure to allow access to records relating to national minimum wage (Ss.9–11 National Minimum Wage Act 1998)	None	3 months after period of 14 days (longer if agreed) following receipt of production notice	✓
Right not to suffer detriment in relation to national minimum wage (S.23 National Minimum Wage Act 1998)	None	3 months starting with date of last act or failure to act*	✓

5.127 Part-time, fixed-term and agency workers

Statutory right/ complaint	Qualifying period	Time limit for complaint	Early conciliation (a)
Right not to be treated less favourably because of part-time status (Reg 5 Part-time Workers (Prevention of Less Favourable Treatment) Regulations 2000 SI 2000/1511)	None	3 months from date of less favourable treatment** (e)	✓
Right of part-time worker to receive written statement of reasons for less favourable treatment (Reg 6 Part-time Workers (Prevention of Less Favourable Treatment) Regulations 2000 SI 2000/1511)	None	N/A	
Right not to suffer detriment in relation to part-time working (Reg 7(2) Part-time Workers (Prevention of Less Favourable Treatment) Regulations 2000 SI 2000/1511)	None	3 months starting with date of last act or failure to act**	✓
Right not to be treated less favourably because of fixed-term status (Reg 3 Fixed-term Employees (Prevention of Less Favourable Treatment) Regulations 2002 SI 2002/2034)	None	3 months from date of less favourable treatment** (e)	✓

Statutory right/ complaint	Qualifying period	Time limit for complaint	Early conciliation (a)
Right of fixed-term employee to receive written statement of reasons for less favourable treatment (Reg 5 Fixed-term Employees (Prevention of Less Favourable Treatment) Regulations 2002 SI 2002/2034)	None	N/A	
Right not to suffer detriment in relation to fixed-time working (Reg 6(2) Fixed-term Employees (Prevention of Less Favourable Treatment) Regulations 2002 SI 2002/2034)	None	3 months starting with date of last act or failure to act**	✓
Right of fixed-term employee to be informed by employer of permanent vacancies (Reg 3(6) Fixed-term Employees (Prevention of Less Favourable Treatment) Regulations 2002 SI 2002/2034)	None	3 months from last date on which other individuals, whether or not employees of employer, were informed of vacancy** (e)	✓
Right of employee employed under successive fixed-term contracts to be regarded as a permanent employee (Reg 8 Fixed-term Employees (Prevention of Less Favourable Treatment) Regulations 2002 SI 2002/2034)	None	Dependent on circumstances	

Statutory right/ complaint	Qualifying period	Time limit for complaint	Early conciliation (a)
Right of employee employed under successive fixed-term contracts to receive written statement that he or she is a permanent employee (Reg 9 Fixed-term Employees (Prevention of Less Favourable Treatment) Regulations 2002 SI 2002/2034)	None	Dependent on circumstances	
Right to paid time off for ante-natal care for agency workers (Ss.57ZA and 57ZB ERA)	12 weeks – S.57ZD ERA	3 months starting with date of appointment*	✓
Right of agency workers to be offered alternative work where supply to hirer is ended on maternity grounds (S.68B ERA)	12 weeks – S.68D ERA	3 months starting with day on which supply of agency worker to hirer was ended on maternity grounds*	✓
Right of agency workers to be paid where supply to hirer is ended on maternity grounds (S.68C ERA)	12 weeks – S.68D ERA	3 months starting with day on which supply of agency worker to hirer was ended on maternity grounds*	✓
Right of agency worker to basic working and employment conditions (Reg 5 Agency Workers Regulations 2010 SI 2010/93)	None (i)	3 months from date of breach to which complaint relates**	✓

Statutory right/ complaint	Qualifying period	Time limit for complaint	Early conciliation (a)
Right of agency worker not to be treated less favourably in relation to collective facilities and amenities (Reg 12 Agency Workers Regulations 2010 SI 2010/93)	None	3 months from date of breach to which complaint relates**	✓
Right of agency worker to be informed of vacant posts (Reg 13 Agency Workers Regulations 2010 SI 2010/93)	None	3 months starting with (last) date on which other individuals were informed of vacancy **	✓
Right not to suffer detriment in connection with rights of agency workers (Reg 17(2) Agency Workers Regulations 2010 SI 2010/93)	None	3 months from date of breach to which complaint relates**	✓
Breach of terms or duties under permanent contracts providing pay between assignments (Reg 10 Agency Workers Regulations 2010 SI 2010/93)	None	3 months from date of breach to which complaint relates**	✓

5.128 Redundancy

Statutory right/ complaint	Qualifying period	Time limit for complaint	Early conciliation (a)
Statutory payment (Part XI ERA)	2 years – S.155 ERA	6 months starting with 'relevant date' (b) (q)	✓
Right to paid time off to look for work or arrange training where notice of dismissal by reason of redundancy has been given (Ss.52(1) and 53(1) ERA)	2 years – S.52(2) ERA	3 months starting with day time off should have been allowed* (b)	✓
Failure to pay remuneration under protective award (S.190 TULR(C)A)	None	3 months starting with last day in respect of which complaint is made*	✓
Consultation with appropriate representatives over proposed redundancies (S.188 TULR(C)A)	None	Either before dismissal or 3 months starting with date on which dismissal takes effect*	✓

5.129 Time off

Statutory right/ complaint	Qualifying period	Time limit for complaint	Early conciliation (a)
Right to unpaid time off for public duties (S.50 ERA)	None	3 months from date of failure to give time off* (b)	✓
Right to unpaid time off to care for dependants (S.57A ERA)	None	3 months starting with date when refusal occurred*	✓
Right to paid time off for pension scheme trustees (Ss.58 and 59 ERA)	None	3 months starting with date when failure occurred* (b)	✓

374 ————————————————————————

Statutory right/ complaint	Qualifying period	Time limit for complaint	Early conciliation (a)
Right to paid time off for employee representatives (collective redundancies and TUPE) (Ss.61 and 62 ERA)	None	3 months starting with day time off taken or on which time off should have been allowed* (b)	✓
Right to paid time off for young person for study or training (Ss.63A and 63B ERA)	None	3 months starting with day time off taken or on which time off should have been allowed* (b)	✓
Right to paid time off for representatives of employee safety and for candidates standing for election as such a representative (Health and Safety (Consultation with Employees) Regulations 1996 SI 1996/1513)	None	3 months starting with date when failure occurred*	✓
Right to paid time off for safety representatives (Safety Representatives and Safety Committees Regulations 1977 SI 1977/500)	None	3 months starting with date when failure occurred*	✓
Right to paid annual leave for persons employed or engaged on board a sea-going UK ship (Reg 12(1) and (2) of the Merchant Shipping (Hours of Work) Regulations 2002 SI 2002/2125)	None	3 months starting with day time off should have been permitted or payment should have been made*	✓

Statutory right/ complaint	Qualifying period	Time limit for complaint	Early conciliation (a)
Right to rest periods and paid annual leave for workers employed on ships operating services for passengers or goods (Regs 10(1), (3) and 11(1) of the Merchant Shipping (Working Time: Inland Waterways) Regulations 2003 SI 2003/3049)	None	3 months starting with day exercise of the right should have been permitted or payment should have been made*	✓
Right to rest periods and paid annual leave for workers employed on fishing vessels (Regs 7(1), (3), (4) and 11(1) of the Fishing Vessels (Working Time: Sea-fishermen) Regulations 2004 SI 2004/1713)	None	3 months starting with day exercise of the right should have been permitted or payment should have been made*	✓
Right to paid annual leave and free health assessments, among others (Regs 4, 5(1), (4), 7(1) and 7(2)(b) of Civil Aviation (Working Time) Regulations 2004 SI 2004/756)	None	3 months starting with day exercise of the right should have been permitted or payment should have been made*	
Right to rest periods for workers assigned to cross-border train services (Regs 3–7 of the Cross-border Railway Services (Working Time) Regulations 2008 SI 2008/1660)	None	3 months starting with date the appointment ended*	✓

Statutory right/ complaint	Qualifying period	Time limit for complaint	Early conciliation (a)
Right to paid time off for members of a European Works Council (Regs 25 and 26 Transnational Information and Consultation of Employees Regulations 1999 SI 1999/3323)	None	3 months starting with day time off taken or on which time off should have been allowed*	✓
Right to paid time off for information and consultation representatives (Regs 27 and 28 Information and Consultation of Employees Regulations 2004 SI 2004/3426)	None	3 months starting with day time off taken or on which time off should have been allowed*	✓
Right to paid time off in connection with the information and consultation rights of pension scheme members (paras 2 and 3, Sch 1 Occupational and Personal Pension Schemes (Consultation by Employers and Miscellaneous Amendment) Regulations 2006 SI 2006/349)	None	3 months starting with day time off taken or on which time off should have been allowed*	✓
Right to paid time off in connection with the information and consultation rights of employees of European cooperative societies (Regs 28 and 29 European Cooperative Society (Involvement of Employees) Regulations 2006 SI 2006/2059)	None	3 months starting with day time off taken or on which time off should have been allowed*	✓

377

Statutory right/ complaint	Qualifying period	Time limit for complaint	Early conciliation (a)
Right to paid time off in connection with the information, consultation and negotiation rights of employees involved in cross-border mergers (Regs 43 and 44 Companies (Cross-Border Mergers) Regulations 2007 SI 2007/2974)	None	3 months starting with day time off taken or on which time off should have been allowed*	✓
Right to paid time off in connection with the information, consultation and negotiation rights of employees of European public limited liability companies (Regs 26 and 27 European Public Limited-Liability Company (Employee Involvement) (Great Britain) Regulations 2009 SI 2009/2401)	None	3 months starting with day time off taken or on which time off should have been allowed*	✓
Right to time off to accompany a fellow worker at a grievance or disciplinary hearing (S.10(6) Employment Relations Act 1999)	None	3 months starting with date or threat of failure to comply*	✓

Trade unions and union members

Statutory right/ complaint	Qualifying period	Time limit for complaint	Early conciliation (a)
Interim relief pending S.152 complaint (S.161 TULR(C)A)	None	7 days immediately following EDT***	
Right not to suffer detriment in relation to trade union membership or activities (S.146 TULR(C)A)	None	3 months starting with date of (last) act or failure to act*	✓
Right not to suffer detriment in relation to trade union recognition or derecognition under Schedule A1 to the TULR(C)A	None	3 months starting with EDT*	✓
Unlawful exclusion/ expulsion from union (S.174 TULR(C)A)	None	6 months starting with date of exclusion/ expulsion*	✓
Application for compensation after successful S.174 complaint (S.176 TULR(C)A)	None	Not earlier than 4 weeks and not later than 6 months from date of employment tribunal's decision***	
Unjustifiable discipline by union (Ss.64–66 TULR(C)A)	None	3 months starting with date of union's decision****	✓
Application for compensation after successful S.66 complaint (S.67 TULR(C)A)	None	Not earlier than 4 weeks and not later than 6 months from date of employment tribunal's decision***	

Statutory right/ complaint	Qualifying period	Time limit for complaint	Early conciliation (a)
Unauthorised deduction of union subscriptions (S.68 TULR(C)A)	None	3 months starting with date of payment*	✓
Right to paid time off for union duties (Ss.168–169 TULR(C)A)	None	3 months starting with date when failure occurred*	✓
Right to unpaid time off for union activities (S.170 TULR(C)A)	None	3 months starting with date when failure occurred*	✓
Refusal of employment on grounds related to union membership (S.137 TULR(C)A)	None	3 months starting with date of conduct complained of*	✓
Refusal of services of employment agency on grounds related to union membership (S.138 TULR(C)A)	None	3 months starting with date of conduct complained of*	✓
Complaint by trade union over employer's failure to comply with collective bargaining obligations regarding training (S.70B TULR(C)A)	None	3 months starting with date of alleged failure*	✓
Complaint about either a wrongful deduction of contributions to a union political fund, or a refusal to deduct union dues (S.86 TULR(C)A)	None	3 months beginning with date of payment of emoluments*	✓
Complaint by worker about inducements relating to trade union membership or activities, or to collective bargaining (Ss.145A–145B TULR(C)A)	None	3 months beginning when offer, or last offer, was made*	✓

Transfer of undertakings

5.131

Statutory right/ complaint	Qualifying period	Time limit for complaint	Early conciliation (a)
Failure to consult with appropriate representatives over a business transfer (Reg 13 TUPE)	N/A	3 months starting with date of completion of transfer*	✓
Failure by transferor to notify transferee of employee information (Reg 12 TUPE)	N/A	3 months starting with date of relevant transfer*	✓
Failure to comply with a compensation order made under Reg 15 (Reg 15(10) TUPE)	N/A	3 months starting with date of tribunal's order*	✓

Working time

5.132

Statutory right/ complaint	Qualifying period	Time limit for complaint	Early conciliation (a)
Right to daily rest (Reg 10 WTR)	None	3 months from date when right should have been permitted * (b) (r)	✓
Right to weekly rest (Reg 11 WTR)	None	3 months from date when right should have been permitted (or, if rest period extended over more than one day, date when right should have been permitted to begin)* (b) (r)	✓
Right to rest breaks (Reg 12 WTR)	None	3 months from date when right should have been permitted* (b) (r)	✓

Statutory right/ complaint	Qualifying period	Time limit for complaint	Early conciliation (a)
Right to compensatory rest in case where the above regulations are modified or excluded (Reg 24 WTR)	None	3 months from date when right should have been permitted* (b) (r)	✓
Right to paid annual leave (Regs 13 and 16 WTR)	None	3 months from date when right should have been permitted (or, if leave extended over more than one day, date when right should have been permitted to begin)* (b) (r)	✓
Right to payment in lieu of holiday on termination of employment (Reg 14(2) WTR)	None	3 months from date payment should have been made* (b) (r)	✓
Right not to suffer detriment in relation to working time (S.45A ERA)	None	3 months starting with date of (last) act or failure to act* (b) (r)	✓

5.133 Notes

(a) Where the early conciliation rules apply and the claimant has complied with the requirement to notify Acas of his or her intention to bring a claim before an employment tribunal, the time limit is suspended during the conciliation period – i.e. from the day after Acas receives the claimant's notification until the day the claimant receives (or is deemed to receive) the certificate stating that early conciliation has been complied with. If the time limit for the relevant claim is due to expire in the period between Acas receiving the notification and one month after the end of the conciliation period, the time limit expires instead at the end of that period.

(b) Where the parties are engaged in mediation to resolve a cross-border dispute and the three-month time limit would expire before the mediation ends or less than four weeks (or two or eight weeks, depending on the type of claim) after it ends, the time limit expires instead at the end of four (or two

382

or eight) weeks after the mediation ends. However, the time limit will only be extended if the mediation has started before the end of the three-month time limit. A cross-border dispute is one in which at least one of the parties is domiciled or habitually resident in a Member State of the European Union other than that of any other party.

(c) This right does not currently apply to employees of 'small employers' (i.e. employers that employ fewer than 250 employees) – Schedule 3 to the Apprenticeships, Skills, Children and Learning Act 2009 (Commencement No. 2 and Transitional and Saving Provisions) Order 2010 SI 2010/303.

(d) While there is no qualifying period for the right as such, the right to request is only available to employees who have 26 weeks' continuous employment.

(e) However, an act may be treated as done at the end of a period if it is an act 'extending over' that period (S.123(3)(a) EqA) – see Barclays Bank plc v Kapur and ors 1991 ICR 208, HL.

(f) There are no expressly stated time limits governing actions under EU law. Time limits will generally be analogous to those under national law, i.e. three months under the recast Directive, and three or six months under Article 157 TFEU.

(g) Employees dismissed while they are pregnant or during maternity or adoption leave are entitled to such a statement without having to request it and regardless of their length of service – S.92(4) and (4A) ERA. This does not apply to paternity or parental leave, or to any other automatically unfair reasons for dismissal.

(h) While there is no qualifying period for the right as such, the employee may nonetheless need to show a period of continuous employment to be entitled to the leave in the first place; e.g. the right to parental leave is dependent on the employee having one year's continuous employment.

(i) No statutory minimum qualifying period, but the right to equal treatment is only available to agency workers who have at least 12 weeks' qualifying service.

(j) For these purposes, 'date of dismissal' means (a) where the employee's contract of employment was terminated by notice, the date on which the employer's notice was given, and (b) in any other case, the EDT – S.238(5) TULR(C)A.

(k) Ending with the week in which the employee was notified of having been matched with the child.

383

(l) Ending with the 15th week before the expected week of the child's birth or, in the case of adoption, ending with the week in which the child's adopter is notified of having been matched with the child.

(m) At the beginning of the 11th week before the expected week of childbirth.

(n) For these purposes, the 'relevant date' means (a) the date on which the employee is notified of the employer's decision on the appeal or (b) the date on which the breach was committed – S.80H(6) ERA.

(o) No statutory minimum qualifying period, but the rights in question – e.g. payment of statutory notice pay – in practice involve a period of qualifying employment.

(p) For these purposes, the 'relevant date' means (a) the date on which the employee is notified of the employer's decision on the appeal or (b) the date on which the breach was committed – S.63I(5)(a) and (6) ERA.

(q) If during those six months the employee gives a written notice to the employer claiming a redundancy payment or refers a redundancy pay claim to a tribunal or submits a claim for unfair dismissal to a tribunal. The time limit may be extended to one year if during the six months immediately following the first six-month period the employee makes a written claim for payment to the employer or refers a redundancy pay claim to a tribunal or presents an unfair dismissal claim to a tribunal and it appears to the tribunal to be just and equitable that the employee should receive a redundancy payment – S.164 ERA. It may also be extended to one year if the employee dies during the six months following the relevant date – S.176(7) ERA.

(r) In a case where Reg 38(2) applies (complaints by members of the armed forces), the time limit is extended from three months to six months (Reg 30(2)(a)).

\# One year in Northern Ireland – see the Employment Rights (Northern Ireland) Order 1996 SI 1996/1919

* Employment tribunal can extend time limit where it considers that it was 'not reasonably practicable' to present the complaint in time.

** Employment tribunal can extend time limit where it considers it 'just and equitable' to do so.

*** No extension of time allowed, except possibly where there has been deliberate fraud by the employer, causing the employee to suffer real injustice in missing the time limit – Grimes v Sutton London Borough Council 1973 ICR 240, NIRC.

**** Employment tribunal can extend time limit on 'not reasonably practicable' grounds, as above, or where delay was caused by reasonable attempts to pursue internal appeal, etc.

***** Under S.7(5) Human Rights Act 1998, the court or tribunal has the discretion to extend the time limit to such longer period as it considers equitable having regard to all the circumstances.

Abbreviations
5.134

APL Regs	Additional Paternity Leave Regulations 2010 SI 2010/1055
ASPP Regs	Additional Statutory Paternity Pay (General) Regulations 2010 SI 2010/1056
ERA	Employment Rights Act 1996
EqA	Equality Act 2010
MPL Regs	Maternity and Parental Leave etc Regulations 1999 SI 1999/3312
PAL Regs	Paternity and Adoption Leave Regulations 2002 SI 2002/2788
TULR(C)A	Trade Union and Labour Relations (Consolidation) Act 1992
TUPE	Transfer of Undertakings (Protection of Employment) Regulations 2006 SI 2006/246
WTR	Working Time Regulations 1998 SI 1998/1833

6 Defending a claim

Responding to a claim

Completing the response

The defence

Employer's contract claim

Processing the response

Rule 21: 'default judgments'

In Chapter 4, 'Starting tribunal proceedings', we explain how, in nearly all **6.1** cases, employment tribunal proceedings are initiated by a claimant submitting a claim form, known as an ET1, to the employment tribunal. Once the ET1 has been accepted, a copy will be sent to the respondent(s) who is (are) entitled to defend the claim by submitting a 'response' – which corresponds to filing a formal defence in civil court proceedings. To do so, the respondent must complete and return the response form (ET3) sent out by the employment tribunal for this purpose.

The response must be returned to the tribunal within 28 days of the date on which the respondent was sent a copy of the ET1 by the tribunal. Otherwise, the respondent may be precluded from participating in the further progress of the claim, and thus prevented from putting forward its version of events.

Responding to a claim   6.2

The steps taken by an employment tribunal once a claimant's claim has been presented are discussed in Chapter 4, 'Starting tribunal proceedings'. Briefly, in accordance with the Tribunal Rules of Procedure ('the Tribunal Rules') contained in Schedule 1 to the Employment Tribunals (Constitution and Rules of Procedure) Regulations 2013 SI 2013/1237 ('the Tribunal Regulations'), the claim will be accepted unless:

- the claimant has failed to:
  - use the prescribed form
  - supply the minimum information required
  - pay the tribunal issue fee (or present a remission application), or
- an employment judge considers that the claim (or part of it) is:
  - one which an employment tribunal has no jurisdiction to consider

387

   – in a form which cannot be sensibly responded to, or

   – otherwise an abuse of process (see rules 10, 11 and 12).

In any of the circumstances listed above, the claim (or part) will be rejected. Where the claim (or part) is rejected, the claimant may in certain circumstances be able to apply for a reconsideration of that rejection – rule 13 (see Chapter 15, 'Reconsideration of tribunal judgments and decisions'). Alternatively, he or she may appeal against the decision to the EAT (see Chapter 16, 'The Employment Appeal Tribunal').

6.3 Where the claim, or any part of it, is accepted, the employment tribunal will send a copy of the ET1 form to the respondent (or each of the respondents if there is more than one) with a notice providing information as to:

- whether any part of the claim has been rejected, and

- how to submit a response to the claim, the time limit for doing so and what will happen if a response is not received within the specified time limit – rule 15.

The tribunal will provide the respondent with a blank ET3 form and essential information such as the case reference number and the tribunal address for correspondence. In addition, the tribunal will provide the respondent with a copy of the guidance booklet, 'Responding to a claim to an employment tribunal' (T422/T423). (Note that there are two booklets with the same name – one aimed at those who already have a hearing date (T422) and one at those who do not (T423), which will be the most common scenario in practice.)

6.4 **Persons treated as respondents.** In most cases the persons identified as respondents on the claimant's ET1 will be the only respondents to the claim. However, in limited circumstances certain people will be treated, and added, as respondents. For instance, rule 97 of the Tribunal Rules provides that where a claim includes a complaint under S.146(1) of the Equality Act 2010 (in accordance with which a claimant can seek a declaration that a term of a collective agreement is void), certain persons will be regarded as persons against whom a remedy is claimed and shall be treated as respondents, whether or not they have been identified as such in the claim form. Those persons are the claimant's employer (or prospective employer) as well as every organisation of employers and organisation of workers, and every association of or representative of such organisations, which, if the terms of the agreement were to be varied voluntarily, would be likely, in the opinion of an employment judge, to negotiate the variation – rule 97(a) and (b). However, an organisation or association will not be treated as a respondent if the judge is of the opinion that it is not reasonably practicable to identify it.

Furthermore, in proceedings involving a payment out of the National Insurance Fund (because the respondent is insolvent) the Secretary of State is entitled to appear and be heard at any hearing and will be treated as a party for the purpose of the rules – rule 96. Similarly, S.3C(c) of the Employment Agencies Act 1973 provides that the Secretary of State will be made a party to proceedings in claims for the variation or revocation of an order prohibiting any person from carrying on any employment agency or business.

In relation to the transfer of an undertaking, Reg 15(5) of the Transfer of **6.5** Undertakings (Protection of Employment) Regulations 2006 SI 2006/246 ('Failure to inform or consult') provides for the transferee to be made a party to the proceedings where the transferor, following allegations that it has failed in its duty to inform and consult affected employees of the transferee's proposed measures, gives notice to the transferee of its intention to show that it was not reasonably practicable for it to perform the duty because the transferee had failed to provide the requisite information at the relevant time.

Notwithstanding these specific provisions, it also remains open to an employment tribunal to add any person as a party to proceedings (either on its own initiative or on the application of a party or a person wishing to become a party) by virtue of its power under rule 34 of the Tribunal Rules. It can exercise this power in circumstances where there are issues between that person and any of the existing parties falling within the jurisdiction of the tribunal which it is in the interests of justice to have determined in the proceedings. A tribunal also has a corresponding power to remove any party apparently wrongly included. The power to add, substitute and remove parties under rule 34, when read in conjunction with rule 29 (which provides an employment tribunal with a general power to make case management orders), applies 'at any time'. So, for example, a tribunal has the power to join another respondent to an existing claim even though the time limit for bringing a fresh claim against that respondent has expired – Drinkwater Sabey Ltd v Burnett and anor 1995 ICR 328, EAT. For more information about the joinder of parties see Chapter 11, 'Case management', under 'Addition, substitution and removal of parties'.

Although the Tribunal Rules provide for the addition of persons as **6.6** respondents in certain circumstances, they are silent on whether, and within what timeframe, these persons are required to file a response. Presumably, the tribunal will, upon joining them as respondents, give appropriate directions in this regard.

The response form (ET3) 6.7
When entering the response, it is important that the respondent only use the response form provided by the tribunal or, alternatively, obtained from the Employment Tribunals Service website. As with the claim form, a mandatory response form has been prescribed by the Secretary of State by virtue of Reg 12(1)(b) of the Tribunal Regulations for the purpose of responding to a tribunal claim. This form is known as an ET3 and must be used, subject to

389

some minor exceptions, when presenting a response to a claim – see rule 16(1). It is *not* necessary to use a prescribed form if the proceedings are:

- referred to an employment tribunal by a court

- proceedings in which the employment tribunal will be exercising its appellate jurisdiction, or

- proceedings brought by an employer under S.11 of the Employment Rights Act 1996 (for the employment tribunal to determine what particulars ought to have been included in a non-compliant written statement of employment particulars, a statement of changes, an itemised pay statement or a standing statement of fixed deductions, so as to comply with the requirements of the relevant section concerned) – Reg 12(2).

For all other proceedings, failure to use the ET3 form will result in automatic rejection of the response – rule 17(1)(a) (see 'Processing the response' below).

6.8 The ET3 form prescribed under Reg 12(1)(b) is largely the same as that prescribed under the old 2004 Regulations, requiring the respondent to set out much the same information as before. However, there are some differences and we discuss the changes as they arise.

The respondent can complete the blank ET3 sent by the employment tribunal. Alternatively, the form can be downloaded from the Employment Tribunals Service website and either be printed off and posted or faxed to the tribunal, or sent via e-mail. Another option is to complete and submit the form using the online facility provided by HMCTS, also accessible from the website. This facility does not have the advantage of allowing completion of the form in stages as the site does not currently enable a respondent to save the form and return to it at a later date. For practical tips on how to complete the ET3 response form, see 'Completing the response – practical advice on completing the ET3' below.

6.9 **Multiple respondents/claimants.** It is possible to use one ET3 form to submit the defences of more than one respondent where they are responding to a single claim and they all either resist the claim on the same grounds or do not resist the claim – rule 16(2).

Similarly, the response form can be used to respond to more than one claim if the claims are based on the same set of facts and the respondent either resists all of the claims on the same grounds or does not resist the claims – rule 16(3). This provision is no doubt intended to allow a respondent to submit one response form in defence to claims made by a number of claimants and will most commonly be used where a number of claimants have made their claims on one ET1 form in accordance with rule 9, which allows multiple claimants to make their claims on the same form if their claims are based on the same set of facts – see Chapter 4, 'Starting tribunal proceedings', under 'Making a claim – multiple claimants'.

Time limit for presenting response   6.10

Besides ensuring that the response is made on the correct form and contains all the required information (see 'Completing the response – requirement to supply minimum information' below), the respondent must make sure that the completed form is returned to the relevant employment tribunal office within the applicable time limit. Rule 16(1) of the Tribunal Rules stipulates that a respondent must present his or her response to the tribunal office within 28 days of the date on which the copy of the claim form was sent by the tribunal. This 28-day time limit applies to all proceedings except those that are commenced against a foreign state, in which case the time limit is extended to two months after the date on which the respondent state receives the copy claim form by virtue of S.12(2) of the State Immunity Act 1978.

Under the old rules, there was some confusion as to the date from which the 28-day time limit for presenting a response ran. Rule 4(1) of the Rules of Procedure contained in Schedule 1 to the Employment Tribunals (Constitution and Rules of Procedure) Regulations 2004 SI 2004/1861 ('the Tribunal Rules 2004') required a respondent to present his or her response to the tribunal office 'within 28 days of the date on which he was sent a copy of the claim'. In Bone v Fabcon Projects Ltd 2006 ICR 1421, EAT, an employment tribunal interpreted this to mean that the respondent had 28 days from *receipt* of the copy of the claim. However, on appeal the EAT held that it was impossible to ignore the specific wording of the rule which stated that time for submitting a response ran from the sending, not the receipt, of the claim form. The wording of rule 16(1) of the Tribunal Rules 2013 leaves no room for ambiguity. It provides that the response must be presented to the tribunal office 'within 28 days of the date that the copy of the claim form was sent by the tribunal'.

The date on which the copy of the claim form was sent by the employment   6.11
tribunal will usually be endorsed on the accompanying letter. For the purpose of calculating the time limit, that date itself is not included – rule 4(3). So, for example, if the copy of the claim form was sent on 1 October, the last day for presentation of the response is 29 October. In any event the last day of valid service is also recorded as a calendar date by the tribunal in the letter itself.

It is worth noting here that rule 4(2) of the Tribunal Rules 2013 has introduced a new provision not contained in previous versions of the rules. It states that if a time limit specified by the rules ends on a day other than a working day, the act is done in time if it is done on the next working day. For these purposes 'working day' means any day except a Saturday or Sunday, Christmas Day, Good Friday or a bank holiday under S.1 of the Banking and Financial Dealings

391

Act 1971. The time limit for presenting a response is a time limit specified by the rules. Therefore, if it expires on a weekend or bank holiday, the response will still be properly presented to the tribunal if it is presented on the next 'working day'.

The response must be presented to the tribunal before midnight on the day in question. If there is any dispute as to whether the response was presented in time, it will be for the respondent to prove compliance – rule 4(1).

6.12 **Consequences of submitting late response.** If a response is presented outside the 28-day time limit (or any extension of that limit granted within the original limit) it will be rejected by the tribunal. This is the case unless an application for an extension of time has already been made under rule 20 (see 'Procedure for applying for extension' below) or the response includes or is accompanied by such an application, in which case the response will not be rejected pending the outcome of that application – rule 18(1).

Where the response is rejected for being presented out of time, it will be returned to the respondent together with a notice of rejection explaining that the response has been presented late. The notice will explain how the respondent can apply for an extension of time and how to apply for a reconsideration of the rejection – rule 18(2). The procedure for applying for a reconsideration of the tribunal's rejection of the response is explained under 'Processing the response – reconsideration of rejection of response' below.

6.13 **Extension of time limit.** Under the 2001 Tribunal Rules a tribunal could, at its discretion, accept responses presented outside the time limit – provided the respondent offered a satisfactory explanation for the late submission, showed a meritorious defence, and the extension of the time limit for presenting the response did not unduly prejudice the claimant. Where a respondent had not entered a response in time, it could make an application under what was then rule 17 to extend the time limit. This rule specifically stated that the employment tribunal chairman (now an employment tribunal judge) was entitled to grant the application whether or not the time limit had expired. It was even possible to present an out-of-time response after a tribunal's decision had been announced and promulgated.

This provision allowing late responses was not replicated in the Tribunal Rules 2004. In fact, rule 4(4) of the 2004 Rules contained a restriction as to when an extension of time could be applied for. It provided that an application to extend the time limit for presenting a response had to be made to the tribunal office before the expiry of the 28-day time limit (unless the respondent was applying for a review of a default judgment). Furthermore, rule 10(2)(e) of the 2004 Rules, which related to a tribunal's case management powers and allowed the tribunal judge to extend any time limit 'whether or not expired', was subject to rule 4(4). Therefore, in practical terms a respondent, having been notified of the claim, was well advised to prepare the response without undue delay. And then, if additional time was needed to complete the response – for example, because of a delay in obtaining witness statements – it could apply for an extension of time without falling foul of rule 4(4).

The Tribunal Rules 2013 effectively turn back the clock and allow an application to be made even where the time limit has expired, thus reverting to the position that applied under the 2001 Rules.

Procedure for applying for extension. An application for an extension of time **6.14** for presenting a response must:

- be presented in writing and copied to the claimant, and

- set out the reasons why the extension is sought – rule 20(1).

If the time limit for presenting the response has already expired, the application must also be accompanied by a draft of the response which the respondent wishes to present or otherwise by an explanation of why that is not possible. If the respondent wishes to request a hearing, this must be done in the application. However, even if the respondent has requested a hearing, rule 20(3) states that an employment judge may determine the application without a hearing (though it does not state the basis upon which the judge can decide not to hold a hearing).

Unlike under the old 2004 Rules, a respondent is no longer required to include **6.15** in the application for an extension an explanation as to why it was unable to comply with the 28-day time limit. However, such an explanation will no doubt form part of the reasons why the extension is being sought, which should be set out in the application in accordance with the requirements of rule 20(1) (above).

Rule 92 provides that, with the exception of an application for a witness order, where a party sends a communication to the tribunal it must also send a copy to all other parties (unless the tribunal considers that it is in the interests of justice not to do so). Thus, a respondent applying for an extension of time must generally provide copies of the application to all other parties to the proceedings, including the claimant, at the same time as sending the application to the tribunal. The respondent must also inform the tribunal that this has been done. If, for example, the respondent's application is sent to the tribunal by e-mail, it will be sufficient to use the 'cc' address bar to comply both with its duty to send a copy to the other parties and its duty to inform the tribunal that this has been done.

Upon receiving a copy of the application, the claimant has seven days within **6.16** which to write to the tribunal to give reasons explaining why the application is opposed – rule 20(2).

393

If a respondent's application for an extension is refused, any prior rejection of the response will stand. If the extension is allowed, any judgment issued in accordance with rule 21 (see 'Rule 21: "default judgments"' below) will be set aside and the respondent's response will be accepted. The case will then be referred to an employment judge, who will carry out an initial consideration of the case (known as the judicial sift) to confirm whether there are arguable complaints and defences within the jurisdiction of the tribunal. For more information see Chapter 7, 'Judicial sift'.

6.17 *Grounds upon which extension may be granted.* Under the Tribunal Rules 2004 the chairman (now employment judge) could only extend time for submitting a response if he or she was satisfied that it was 'just and equitable to do so' – rule 4(4). However, the 'just and equitable' requirement has not been carried forward into the 2013 Rules. In fact, new rule 20 is silent as to the test a tribunal should apply when considering an application. Therefore it seems a tribunal has absolute discretion to extend the time limit for presenting a response. However, the overriding objective to deal with cases 'fairly and justly' (rule 2) is likely to carry significant weight in a tribunal's exercise of this discretion – and it is worth noting in this regard that the phrase 'fairly and justly' is not dissimilar to the old 'just and equitable' requirement; equitable meaning fair and impartial. It therefore stands to reason that the EAT's decision in Kwik Save Stores Ltd v Swain and ors 1997 ICR 49, EAT, which set out the correct test for determining what was 'just and equitable' under previous versions of the rules, remains relevant to the question of whether, having regard to the overriding objective, an application for an extension of time to submit a response under rule 20 should be granted. In that case the employer's responses in respect of three claimants' claims were entered between 14 and 26 days late. The employer applied for extensions of time, admitting that its failure to comply with the time limits had been due to an oversight. The tribunal judge found the employer's explanation to be unsatisfactory and refused to grant the extensions of time. The employer appealed to the EAT, arguing that the judge had exercised his discretion incorrectly. The EAT stated that 'the process of exercising a discretion involves taking into account all relevant factors, weighing and balancing them one against the other and reaching a conclusion which is objectively justified on the grounds of reason and justice'. In particular, the EAT held that, when exercising a discretion in respect of the time limit, a judge should always consider the following:

- the employer's explanation as to why an extension of time is required. In the EAT's opinion, the more serious the delay, the more important it is that the employer provide a satisfactory and honest explanation. A judge is entitled to form a view as to the merits of such an explanation

- the balance of prejudice. Would the employer, if its request for an extension of time were to be refused, suffer greater prejudice than the complainant would suffer if the extension of time were to be granted?

- the merits of the defence. If the employer's defence is shown to have some merit in it, justice will often favour the granting of an extension of time – otherwise the employer might be held liable for a wrong which it had not committed.

The EAT went on to note that an employment tribunal's discretion is wide and difficult to appeal against. An appeal should therefore only be brought where a judge has exercised his or her discretion contrary to well-established principles – for example, if he or she has failed to take all relevant factors into account. In the circumstances, however, the EAT allowed the employer's appeal. The employment judge had not taken into account the merits of the employer's defence or the prejudice that it would suffer as a result of his refusal to grant the extensions of time. The EAT remitted the question of whether the extensions of time should be granted to a different employment tribunal judge for reconsideration. **6.18**

Presentation of the response **6.19**
Once the ET3 has been completed, it should be presented to the tribunal office that notified the respondent of the claim. Under rule 85(1) service of the ET3 can be effected by:

- post
- direct delivery (including delivery by a courier or messenger service), or
- electronic communication (i.e. fax, e-mail or online).

The online form can be accessed at www.employmenttribunals.service.gov.uk/employment-tribunal-response. The printable version of the form, which can be presented by post, fax, e-mail or by direct delivery, can also be downloaded from this site.

If the response is submitted using the online system, it will be sent automatically to the tribunal office dealing with the case. Once it has been successfully submitted online, the respondent will receive an automatic receipt of the transaction (assuming he or she has entered an e-mail address for this purpose). However, despite the potential advantages of submitting the ET3 online, there are a few drawbacks. For example, the opening page of the form warns the respondent that any information entered will be lost if longer than 20 minutes is spent on a single page without progressing. This is designed to protect the safety of the respondent's data, but it may make it difficult for the respondent to complete the form online. To avoid the potential effects of the 20-minute time-out, a respondent might wish to draft all of its answers in advance using the printable version of the form before completing it online. Also, it is not possible to save a partially completed online response form in order to return and complete it at a later date. (Note that, at the time of writing, HMCTS is **6.20**

395

working to improve the online forms and it is hoped that at least some of the problems encountered by users will soon be ironed out.)

6.21 **Date of delivery.** As a general rule, a response is 'presented' when it is received at the tribunal office. In relation to the postal submission of an ET3, rule 90(a) states that a document sent by post is, unless the contrary is proved, taken to have been received on the day on which it would have been delivered in the ordinary course of post. The 'ordinary course of post' rule was affirmed by the Court of Appeal in Consignia plc (formerly the Post Office) v Sealy 2002 ICR 1193, CA, where it held that service of documents to an employment tribunal under the 'ordinary course of post' rule is deemed to have taken place on the second day after first-class posting, excluding Sundays, public holidays, Christmas Day and Good Friday. This means that service can take place on a Saturday, although the employment tribunal office is actually closed on Saturdays. The qualification to rule 90 allows for a situation where the respondent can prove that the response form was received the day after it was posted, i.e. one day earlier than it would otherwise be deemed to have been delivered in the ordinary course of post. In this situation the response form is treated as having been received on the day that it was actually delivered, not the day it would have been deemed to have been delivered.

Rule 90(b) provides that a document sent by electronic communication (i.e. fax, e-mail or online) will, unless the contrary is proved, be deemed to have been received on the day it is transmitted. As far as we are aware, there have been no reported cases dealing with the question of when a response is considered to have been 'presented' to the tribunal when submitted through these channels, but there have been cases looking at when an ET1 claim form is considered to have been 'presented' to the tribunal by electronic communication and these provide useful guidance. For example, in Initial Electronic Security Systems Ltd v Avdic 2005 ICR 1598, EAT, a case where an e-mailed ET1 never arrived at the tribunal office, the EAT held that the deemed postal rule also applies to e-mails on the basis that 'the reasonable expectation of the sender of an electronic mail communication is that it would arrive within a very short time thereafter'. This is likely to be between 30–60 minutes after transmission. As a result, in the instant case the claimant could reasonably have expected that her e-mail, sent eight hours before the expiry of the time limit, had arrived at the tribunal.

6.22 In Tyne and Wear Autistic Society v Smith 2005 ICR 663, EAT, the EAT held that, where a claimant using the online system receives an automated message that the claim form has been submitted, there is a reasonable expectation that it will reach the tribunal directly and it is thus presented. The application is presented when it successfully reaches the host of the online service and it does not matter if it is forwarded by the website host to the tribunal office computer on a later date, or date-stamped on a later date. On the same basis, once the response is successfully submitted to the host website, it will have been successfully presented even if there are subsequent problems with the computer of the website host or of the tribunal office, or in communications between the two.

Similarly, in Yellow Pages Sales Ltd v Davie 2012 ICR D11, EAT, the Scottish Appeal Tribunal held that where an ET1 had been faxed to an employment tribunal and the claimant had received automated confirmation that the fax had been received, the claim had been validly presented, notwithstanding that a technical failure resulted in there being no printout or record on the tribunal's machine.

Note that in the above cases service was time-critical: by the time it was **6.23** discovered that the completed ET1 form had not arrived at the tribunal office, the claim was out of time. To prevent problems of this nature arising, respondents should therefore always allow for unforeseen delays and avoid sending the response close to the date on which the time limit expires. In any event, proof of dispatch is a wise precaution and any fax transmission report and automated message received upon e-mailing or submitting the form online should be retained. However, it is not necessary (and is in fact inadvisable) to send another copy by post, although a follow-up telephone call to confirm satisfactory receipt before the expiry of the time limit is advisable.

Finally, if the ET3 is delivered to the relevant tribunal office in person, it will, unless the contrary is proved, be taken to have been received by the tribunal on the day of delivery – rule 90(c). Proof of hand delivery can be requested from the tribunal. Employment tribunal offices are open for delivery of documents in person from 9 am to 5 pm, Monday to Friday.

Completing the response

6.24

The first and most important thing that a respondent should do is carefully read the contents of the claim form. This, in particular, involves taking note of, and where necessary responding to, the following items completed by the claimant in the ET1:

- name/title of the respondent(s)
- the details of dates of employment, weekly working hours and pay
- the nature of the claim(s) made against the respondent(s) – as indicated and as inferred from the background and details of the claim the claimant has given, and
- the relief the claimant seeks if he or she is successful.

Examining these items in the claimant's ET1 will also help the respondent to decide whether to resist the claim. This, in turn, will give an indication of what should be included in the response. A respondent is not required to obtain legal

397

advice but if the claim raises complex legal issues (such as is often the case in discrimination, equal pay, TUPE and protected disclosure claims, for example) it may be advisable to consult a lawyer. Information and help is also available from Acas, the Citizens Advice Bureau or, if the respondent is a member, an employers' organisation such as the EEF. If the claimant has brought a discrimination claim, help is also available from the Equality and Human Rights Commission. In addition, the Employment Tribunals Service provides a public enquiry line and is able to answer any general queries, such as how the tribunal system works.

6.25 Requirement to supply minimum information

The provision of certain information on the response form is mandatory for all respondents (unless the claims made are those for which an ET3 is not compulsory: see 'Responding to a claim – the response form (ET3)' above). If a respondent does not provide the required information, the tribunal will not accept the response – rule 17(1)(b). The required information is:

- the respondent's full name – rule 17(1)(b)(i)

- the respondent's address – rule 17(1)(b)(ii), and

- whether the respondent wishes to resist any part of the claim – rule 17(1)(b)(iii).

6.26 **Effect of omitting required information.** Prior to the introduction of the 2004 Tribunal Rules, tribunals took a relaxed approach towards incomplete responses. If a response (or a claim, for that matter) was received at the tribunal office with insufficient information, the tribunal would accept it and, by way of subsequent directions, order further and better particulars. However, this practice has now ceased. Rule 4(1) of the 2004 Rules insisted that the response '*must* include all relevant required information' (our stress) and rule 17(1)(b) of the 2013 Rules stipulates that a tribunal '*shall reject* a response' (our stress) if it does not contain the minimum information required.

When the compulsory information requirements were introduced by the Tribunal Rules 2004 concerns were raised that the mandatory language could result in tribunals rejecting responses that contained only immaterial deficiencies, thereby preventing possibly meritorious respondents from being able to defend a claim. This issue was specifically addressed by Mr Justice Burton, then President of the EAT, in Richardson v U Mole Ltd 2005 ICR 1664, EAT. Recounting employment tribunal decisions he had seen where judges had rejected responses for immaterial omissions such as forgetting to include an address, he stressed that 'that is not an appropriate use of the Rules'. Instead, when deciding whether to accept a response containing an insignificant defect, the tribunal should have regard to the 'overriding objective', which required tribunals to deal with cases justly (now 'fairly and justly' – see rule 2).

The Richardson decision suggests that it will be appropriate for tribunals to **6.27** adopt a lenient approach towards adherence with the Rules in limited circumstances. Such circumstances existed in Crouch v Ant Marketing Ltd and ors EAT 0031/11, where the EAT upheld an employment tribunal decision that, even though only one of the two respondents was named in the relevant section of the ET3 form, the response had been validly presented on behalf of both respondents. This was clear from the fact that both respondents had been detailed in the separate grounds of resistance that had been lodged with the response form. The EAT held that the employment tribunal had therefore been right to refuse to issue a default judgment against the respondent whose details had not been included, and the claimant suffered no prejudice as a result of that decision.

However, unless special circumstances exist, a response that fails to include the minimum information required will be rejected by the tribunal – rule 17(1)(b). If a response is rejected on this ground the respondent may be able to apply for a reconsideration of the decision to reject on the basis that it was wrong or that the defect can be rectified – rule 19(1). This is discussed further under 'Processing the response – reconsideration of rejection of response' below.

Submitting a holding response. Under the Tribunal Rules 2004, as well as **6.28** providing the information listed above, it was also mandatory for a respondent to detail the grounds upon which it wished to resist the claim (if the claim was to be resisted). In the current ET3 form that must be used under the 2013 Rules the respondent is asked to detail the 'facts' upon which it relies to defend the claim. However, this is not a mandatory requirement under rule 17(1)(b). The Tribunal Rules 2013 require the respondent to confirm whether it wishes to resist any part of the claim (see rule 17(1)(b)(iii)) but say nothing about the tribunal having the power to reject a response because the respondent has failed to include the detailed facts upon which it relies. It therefore appears possible for a respondent to submit what is effectively a 'holding response' (giving its name and address and ticking the box to confirm that it intends to resist the claim), with the intention of providing the details of his or her response at a later date, without the risk of the response being immediately rejected by virtue of rule 17(1)(b).

Having said that, it is worth noting that on the printable version of the ET3 form it states 'you must complete all questions marked with an "*"'. Sections 2.1 and 2.3, which are marked with an asterisk, must be completed with the respondent's name and address respectively. Section 5.1, which is also marked with an asterisk, asks the respondent, 'Do you defend the claim?' and provides two tick boxes for the respondent to indicate either 'yes' or 'no'. It is therefore mandatory for the respondent to provide an answer to this question. The section in which the respondent is asked to set out the facts upon which he or she relies to defend the claim follows immediately after, but is not separately

399

numbered. It is therefore arguable that it is to be regarded as part of section 5.1 ('Do you defend the claim?'), which is marked with an asterisk and thus must be completed.

6.29 Even if a 'holding response' is accepted by the tribunal, an employment judge is required, as soon as possible thereafter, to carry out an initial consideration of the claim and response to confirm whether there are arguable complaints and defences within the jurisdiction of the tribunal (this is known as 'the judicial sift') – rule 26 (see further Chapter 7, 'Judicial sift'). For this purpose the employment judge can order a party to provide further information and a respondent who has submitted a 'holding response' will no doubt be ordered to provide further details before the judge can complete this process. If the respondent fails to provide this necessary information, the response will be at risk of being dismissed. Therefore, submitting a 'holding response' is unlikely to buy the respondent much extra time within which to provide the full details of its defence and to avoid any potential adverse consequences a respondent should, wherever possible, include all the details of its defence on, or annexed to, the ET3 form.

6.30 Practical advice on completing the ET3

The ET3 form and the guidance booklet that accompanies it, 'Responding to a claim to an employment tribunal' (T422/T423) ('the guidance booklet'), contain helpful information on how to complete the form. Users of the online form will note slight differences from the printable version. For example, unlike the printable version, the online form does not have numbered sections. Additionally, users of the online form are asked to complete the various sections of the response in a slightly different order to how they appear on the printable version.

Certain sections of the ET3 *must* be filled in. These are marked with an asterisk ('*') on the printable version of the form and as 'required' on the online form. On both versions of the form, the sections asking for the respondent's name and address, and whether or not he or she intends to defend the claim, are marked as mandatory. This is the minimum that must be provided in accordance with rule 17, otherwise the response will be automatically rejected (see 'Requirement to supply minimum information' above). However, when using the online version of the form certain additional sections must be completed in order for the respondent to complete and submit the form. For instance, on the page which asks for the respondent's details, the respondent must also state whether or not its organisation has more than one site in Great Britain – and, if so, how many people are employed at the place where the claimant worked – in order to proceed to the next page of the form. The section dealing with the claimant's dates of employment is also 'required' and must be completed in order to proceed to the next section of the form.

It is possible to use one ET3 form to submit the defences of more than one **6.31** respondent where they are responding to a single claim and they all either resist the claim on the same grounds or do not resist the claim – rule 16(2). However, neither the online nor the printable version of the form has a specific section where additional respondents' details can be added. The details of any additional respondents should therefore be set out in the box where the respondent is asked to outline its defence and it should be made clear that the ET3 form is being used to submit the defences of those additional respondents in accordance with rule 16(2).

It is also possible for a response form to include the response to more than one claim if the claims are based on the same set of facts and the respondent either resists all of the claims on the same grounds or does not resist the claims – rule 16(3). However, neither version of the ET3 form makes provision for a respondent to enter more than one case number or the details of more than one claimant. That said, if the claims are issued in accordance with the multiple claimant provisions of rule 9, which allows multiple claimants to make their claims on the same form if their claims are based on the same set of facts, it is likely that the tribunal will accept the claims under one case number. The respondent need then only enter that case number in the response form and can give details of all the claimants in the section of the form where the respondent is asked to set out the details of his or her defence.

Some practical tips for respondents completing an ET3:   **6.32**

- case number – there is a space at the top of the ET3 form to insert the case number. (This *must* be completed on the online version of the form.) The case number can be obtained from the tribunal correspondence enclosing the copy ET1 claim form. Completing this assists the tribunal to file the response with the correct proceedings

- claimant's name (section 1 on the printable version of the form) – the guidance booklet asks the respondent to confirm the full first name and family name of the claimant. This section is not mandatory

- respondent's details (section 2 on the printable version of the form) – the name and address (including the postcode) of the respondent individual, company or organisation is mandatory. The guidance booklet also asks the respondent to indicate whether he or she is a sole trader, or whether the business is a partnership, limited liability partnership, a plc, a limited company or otherwise, but a respondent does not have to provide this information. It is also advisable, although not mandatory, to confirm who will be the contact person in relation to the claim and who will receive the tribunal correspondence. This might, for instance, be a company manager or director, unless, of course, the respondent has appointed a legal representative – as to which, see below. If the respondent proposes to argue

401

that it has mistakenly been named as a respondent to the proceedings, this matter should be pleaded as part of the substantive response in the section where the respondent is asked to set out the details of the defence (see below). (We deal with the problem of where the wrong employer has been named in Chapter 8, 'Amendments')

- number of employees – the respondent is asked to state how many people are employed by the respondent organisation, whether it has more than one site in Great Britain, and, if so, how many people are employed at the site where the claimant works or worked. These sections are optional on the printable version of the form, but on the online version the respondent must state whether or not its organisation has more than one site in Great Britain – and, if so, how many people are employed at the place where the claimant works or worked. The guidance booklet states that the information provided here may be used anonymously for monitoring and research purposes

- employment details (section 3 on the printable version of the form) – here the respondent is asked to confirm, and if necessary correct, the employment details given by the claimant in the ET1. (This section must be completed on the online version.) This information may be important in determining whether the claimant has the necessary qualifying service for the complaint(s) he or she is making or, in an unfair dismissal case, whether he or she was actually dismissed

- earnings and benefits (section 4 on the printable version of the form) – the respondent should confirm whether the earnings and benefits details in the claim form are correct. If the claim is successful, this information will be used to assess compensation

- response (section 5 on the printable version of the form) – it is compulsory for the respondent to confirm whether or not the claim is resisted. If the respondent is only defending part of the claim, it should tick 'yes' and then outline which parts of the claim are resisted in the space provided

- facts of defence – if the respondent wishes to defend the claim, it is required to set out the facts upon which it relies. Every issue raised by the claimant should be addressed and information should be given in support of the defence. (Since this is undoubtedly the most important aspect of the ET3, we discuss the considerations relevant to completing this section in greater detail under 'The defence' below)

- employer's contract claim (section 6 on the printable version of the form) – an employer's contract claim (known as a counterclaim under previous versions of the rules) can only be made in limited circumstances, which are explained in the guidance booklet. (We discuss this in detail under 'Employer's contract claim' below.) If the respondent wishes to make an employer's contract claim he or she should tick the box to confirm this, and provide the details of the claim, including any important dates, in the space provided

- your representative (section 7 on the printable version of the form) – only respondents who have appointed a representative need to fill in this section. Where a representative's details are provided, the tribunal will correspond only with the appointed representative and not directly with the respondent

- disability (section 8 on the printable version of the form) – this section was not included in previous versions of the form. If the respondent has a disability or a particular need, that should be detailed here. If possible, the respondent should detail what the disability is and what help may be needed from tribunal staff. Tribunals can provide help including converting documents to Braille or larger print, providing information on compact disc and paying for sign language interpreters. A tribunal can also provide hearing-induction loops in the room where the hearing is held if needed. (Oddly, the online version of the form does not ask if the respondent has a disability at all – it only asks if the respondent's *representative* has a disability (if the respondent has confirmed that a representative has been appointed). Perhaps this is a typographical error as on the printable version of the form this section is clearly specific to the respondent's needs. Having said that, if the respondent's representative does in fact have a disability and/or if the respondent intends to call a witness who has a disability, it would be useful to inform the tribunal at this stage of the proceedings (any additional information in this regard can be included on the continuation sheet of the ET3 form) so that the tribunal can make any necessary arrangements.)

6.33 At the end of the printable version of the form the respondent is asked to tick a box to confirm that it has re-read the form and checked that all the relevant information has been entered before it is sent to the tribunal. The form must be sent to the tribunal office dealing with the claim. This can be done by post, fax, e-mail or in person (see 'Presentation of the response – responding to a claim' above). At the end of the online version a summary of the respondent's answers is provided, which can be checked before clicking 'Submit Form'. The form will automatically be sent to the relevant tribunal office. It is advisable to make and retain a copy of the completed ET3 for future reference.

The contact details for each tribunal office can be found at www.justice.gov.uk/tribunals/employment/venues. If the respondent is unclear about which office to contact he or she should call the employment tribunal national enquiry line.

6.34 Once the response has been received, the tribunal office dealing with the claim will send the respondent (or representative) a receipt. This should be received within five working days. If a receipt has not been received within five days, the respondent should contact the tribunal office directly to check that the ET3 has been received. It is the respondent's responsibility to ensure that the response is received at the relevant tribunal office before the time limit expires (see 'Responding to a claim – time limit for presenting response' above).

6.35 The defence

Where the respondent has ticked 'yes' indicating that it wishes to defend the claim, it is asked to 'set out the facts which you rely on to defend the claim'. This wording differs from that used in the ET3 response form that was prescribed under the Tribunal Rules 2004, which asked the respondent to set out the 'grounds' on which it resisted the claim. However, this change is unlikely to substantially affect the way in which the form is completed in practice, particularly where the response is being completed by a legal representative. A legal representative will be careful to set out not just the respondent's factual assertions but also the legal grounds upon which the respondent relies to resist the claim, including any jurisdictional issues with the claimant's claim. That said, the new wording does somewhat change the focus of what is being requested and may prove to be easier for unrepresented respondents to understand, particularly as such respondents may not be familiar with the legal grounds on which a claim should be defended. The respondent should be sure to reply to each and every allegation made by the claimant and set out its own version of events. Any legal or jurisdictional issues may then be identified, and if appropriate dealt with, at a preliminary hearing.

6.36 Jurisdictional grounds

Wherever possible, a respondent should be sure to raise any issues of jurisdiction in the ET3 response form. For example, in a complaint of ordinary unfair dismissal issues such as whether the claim was made in time, whether the claimant was an employee and whether he or she had worked for at least two years all go to the tribunal's jurisdiction and should, if appropriate, be pleaded.

Strictly speaking, a respondent can raise a jurisdictional point at any stage – even as late as at the hearing or on appeal. This is because it is not open to either the parties or the tribunal to agree to waive a jurisdictional bar to proceedings. However, a respondent who raises a question of jurisdiction for the first time at a late stage may take the claimant by surprise, in which case a postponement or adjournment of the hearing may become necessary and the respondent may be put at risk as to costs (see Chapter 20, 'Costs and penalties', under 'Grounds for making orders against a party – postponements and adjournments'). For this reason, it is proper and safer to raise any jurisdictional point in the ET3 and, if necessary, to apply for a preliminary hearing on the point in order to establish, as a preliminary issue, whether the claimant's case can proceed to a hearing on its full merits. There is another potential advantage to raising it at this stage – soon after the response form is accepted, an employment judge will carry out an initial consideration ('judicial sift') of the case in accordance with rules 26–28 to determine whether there are 'arguable complaints and defences *within the jurisdiction of the tribunal*' (our stress). If the employment judge considers that the tribunal has no jurisdiction to hear the claim(s), he or she will give notice that the claim(s) will stand as dismissed unless the claimant satisfies the judge otherwise. For more information, see Chapter 7, 'Judicial sift'.

Providing sufficient particulars of substantive defence 6.37

If the respondent proposes to resist the claim, it should clearly set out the facts upon which it intends to rely in the ET3, even if it believes that the claim falls outside the tribunal's jurisdiction. It is important to ensure that any facts given in the ET3 are consistent with facts or statements already set out in documents such as letters of dismissal, other correspondence to the claimant and replies to requests for written reasons for dismissal. Since all of these documents are admissible in evidence, any inconsistency between them and the information given in the response is likely to damage the credibility of the respondent's defence.

Submitting an alternative defence. A respondent that wishes to put forward 6.38 more than one argument to support its case should 'plead in the alternative'. For example, an employer facing a claim of unfair dismissal might plead that the employee in question was not dismissed or, in the alternative, if he or she was dismissed, that the dismissal was fair on the ground of (say) capability. In such circumstances, even if the tribunal finds against the employer on the first point, it will still rule in the employer's favour if it accepts the alternative argument (i.e. that the dismissal was fair). If, however, the employer simply denies that a dismissal has taken place and gives no reason for dismissal in the ET3, the tribunal is likely to find the dismissal unfair as a matter of course if it concludes that a dismissal did in fact take place. For example, in Derby City Council v Marshall 1979 ICR 731, EAT, the claimant claimed that she had been constructively dismissed. The respondent, in its ET3, denied dismissal. At the hearing, the tribunal held that there had been a constructive dismissal and, since the respondent had failed to plead in the alternative as to the reasons for the dismissal, found it to be unfair. On appeal, the EAT held that the tribunal had been right not to embark on an investigation into the reasons for the claimant's dismissal, since no reasons had been advanced by the respondent in its ET3.

As a general rule, however, tribunals will usually allow late amendments to the ET3 to enable respondents to plead the reasons for a dismissal where these were not originally included in the ET3. This is consistent with the overriding objective of dealing with cases fairly and justly. The powers of the tribunal to allow amendments are wide-ranging (see Chapter 8, 'Amendments') and the ET1 and ET3 will not necessarily be treated as sacrosanct for the purpose of

405

determining the scope of the issues which either party will be entitled to raise at the hearing. In more complex cases, however, the increased use of case management powers by tribunals will ensure that the parties have identified all the relevant issues in the proceedings well before the hearing, in which case an employment judge may issue case management orders stipulating that no ground in respect of the claim or defence that has not been identified in the pleadings will be permitted to be argued at the hearing without leave of the tribunal. Even in the absence of such a direction, respondents should make every effort to include all possible grounds of resistance in the ET3 from the outset, if for no other reason than to avoid unnecessary argument and potential costs orders.

6.39 Insufficient details in ET1 to defend claim

Historically, it was not uncommon for a claimant's ET1 to contain insufficient particulars, thereby preventing the respondent from effectively responding to the claim. However, claims presented on or after 1 October 2004 have to provide certain mandatory information in order to be accepted by the tribunal (see Chapter 4, 'Starting tribunal proceedings', under 'Completing the claim form'). A claim (or part) will be rejected if the claimant fails to include the necessary minimum information, use the prescribed form, or pay the claim fee (or submit a remission application), or an employment judge considers that the claim is one which a tribunal has no jurisdiction to consider, is in a form that cannot sensibly be responded to, or is otherwise an abuse of process (rules 10, 11 and 12 of the Tribunal Rules). Therefore, an ET1 that has been accepted should, by definition, contain sufficient detail to enable the respondent to prepare a response. However, if a respondent is of the opinion that the ET1 omits relevant information, it can apply to the tribunal for an order requesting 'additional information' in accordance with a tribunal's general power to manage proceedings in rule 29. Importantly, such an application should not be contemplated without first applying for an extension of time for submitting the response.

6.40 No defence to claimant's claim

Even where a respondent does not intend to resist a claim, an ET3 should be completed and returned to the tribunal. If a respondent concludes that there are no grounds upon which a claimant's claim can realistically be resisted, it merely has to indicate this in the relevant section of the ET3. Upon receipt of the ET3, the tribunal will accept the response and, unless the parties can reach an agreement for settlement, the claim will be dealt with in accordance with rule 21 – see 'Rule 21: "default judgments"' below.

6.41 Respondent in financial difficulties

If a respondent is in financial difficulties, he or she should explain this in the response form and tell the tribunal about any formal proceedings that are being taken in connection with its financial situation. If, for instance, insolvency

406

proceedings have been commenced, it may be necessary for the claimant to seek consent from the insolvency practitioner or leave from the High Court in order to pursue the claim. For more information, see Chapter 4, 'Starting tribunal proceedings', under 'Preliminary considerations – leave to pursue claims where employer or claimant is insolvent'.

Employer's contract claim   6.42

Employment tribunals have jurisdiction to hear a variety of breach of contract claims that are outstanding on the termination of a contract of employment. Where a claimant makes such a claim, the respondent can, in certain circumstances, bring an 'employer's contract claim' in response under rules 23–25 of the Tribunal Rules 2013, which is the equivalent to a 'counterclaim' under the 2004 Rules.

What claims can be brought?   6.43
Jurisdiction to hear employers' contract claims is conferred on employment tribunals by the Employment Tribunals Extension of Jurisdiction (England and Wales) Order 1994 SI 1994/1623 ('the Extension of Jurisdiction Order') (or, for Scotland, the Employment Tribunals Extension of Jurisdiction (Scotland) Order 1994 SI 1994/1624). Article 4 provides that an employer may bring proceedings before an employment tribunal for the recovery of damages or any other sum (other than a claim for damages, or for a sum due, in respect of personal injuries) as long as it arises or is outstanding on the termination of the employment of the employee against whom the claim is made and that employee has already brought proceedings under the Order in an employment tribunal against the employer. Certain exceptions to the type of contractual claim that can be dealt with by an employment tribunal are specified in the Order. These are claims alleging:

• breach of a contractual term imposing an obligation on the employee in connection with the provision of living accommodation

• breach of a contractual term relating to intellectual property

• breach of a contractual term imposing an obligation of confidence, and

• breach of a contractual term which is a covenant in restraint of trade – Articles 4(b) and 5.

The employer's contract claim must be presented at a time when the employee 6.44
has already presented his or her own contractual claim and that claim has not been settled or withdrawn – Article 8(a). Thus, if the employee's contract claim is dismissed, settled or withdrawn before the employer's contract claim is presented to the tribunal, the employer will not be able to pursue the claim in the tribunal. It may, however, be possible for the respondent to pursue the claim

407

through the civil courts. If the employee's claim is dismissed, settled or withdrawn *after* the employer's contract claim has been presented, the employer's claim can proceed to a hearing.

6.45 Making an employer's contract claim
There are some notable differences between the requirements for presenting an employer's contract claim under the current Tribunal Rules and the requirements for presenting a counterclaim under the old Rules. Most importantly, under the current Rules an employer's contract claim must be presented to the tribunal 'as part of the response, presented in accordance with rule 16' – rule 23 Tribunal Rules 2013. Rule 16 sets out, among other things, the requirement for a response to be presented on the prescribed ET3 form. Therefore, in order to be properly presented, an employer's contract claim must be made as part of the response on the ET3 form. In fact, the new prescribed ET3 form has a specific section that asks the respondent to indicate if it wishes to make an employer's contract claim by ticking the box provided and to include the background and details of any such claim, including (if possible) the amount claimed.

Under the old rules, a counterclaim did not have to be submitted as part of the response. Old rule 7(1) of the 2004 Rules provided that a respondent was required only to present the details of his or her counterclaim to the employment tribunal office 'in writing', giving its full name and address, the name and address of the claimant(s) against whom the counterclaim was being made and the details of the claim being pursued. That said, in practice, respondents commonly included the counterclaim in the 'other information' section of the old ET3 form.

6.46 Time limit. The Tribunal Rules 2013 appear to have introduced some confusion as to how long a respondent has to present an employer's contract claim. As mentioned above, rule 23 states that an employer's contract claim must be made as part of the response, 'presented in accordance with rule 16'. As well as setting out the requirement for a response to be presented on the prescribed ET3 form, rule 16 also provides that the response must be presented to the relevant tribunal office within *28 days* of the date that the copy claim form was sent to the respondent by the tribunal. Therefore, under the Rules, an employer's contract claim must be presented to the employment tribunal within the 28-day time limit that a respondent has to present its response. However, under the Extension of Jurisdiction Order (or the equivalent for Scotland) – which confers jurisdiction on an employment tribunal to hear an employer's contract claim – an employer has *six weeks* beginning with the day it received a copy of the claim form from the tribunal within which to present an employer's contract claim – Article 8(c)(i). Furthermore, where an employment tribunal is satisfied that it was not reasonably practicable for the claim to be presented within that period, it can extend time to allow the respondent to submit its claim within such further period as the tribunal considers reasonable – Article 8(c)(ii). (Note, in addition, that under the Extension of Jurisdiction Order, the six-week time limit begins with the day on which the employer 'received' a copy of the ET1 from the tribunal, while under the Tribunal Rules 2013 the 28-day time limit runs from the date that the copy ET1 was 'sent' by the tribunal.) The time limit issue did not arise under the 2004 Rules as the counterclaim did not have to be presented as part of the response and the Article 8 time limit therefore applied.

Article 8 remains in force and, indeed, is specifically referred to in the Tribunal Rules 2013: the interpretation provisions contained in rule 1 define an 'employer's contract claim' as 'a claim brought by an employer in accordance with articles 4 *and* 8 of the Employment Tribunals Extension of Jurisdiction (England and Wales) Order 1994 or articles 4 *and* 8 of the Employment Tribunals Extension of Jurisdiction (Scotland) Order 1994' (our stress). Therefore, unless and until Article 8 is repealed or the Tribunal Rules 2013 are amended, it would appear to be open to a respondent to argue that it has more than 28 days within which to submit an employer's contract claim. Such an argument might be relevant where, for example, the employer wishes to amend the ET3 to include an employer's contract claim outside the 28-day time limit for presentation of the ET3 but within the six-week time limit set out in the Order (or within such further period as the tribunal considers reasonable).

Employment tribunal fees. Although a respondent is not required to pay a fee **6.47** to submit a response to a claimant's statutory claims, a respondent is required to pay a fee (unless the respondent is an individual who qualifies for remission) of £160 to bring an employer's contract claim – Article 4(2) Employment Tribunals and the Employment Appeal Tribunal Fees Order 2013 SI 2013/1893. The fee does not need to be paid when the claim is presented to the tribunal. The guidance booklet, 'Responding to a claim to an employment tribunal' (T422/T423), states that the tribunal will write to the respondent after receipt of the claim and explain how to make the payment. If the respondent then fails to make the payment the contract claim will be dismissed.

The £160 fee payable in respect of an employer's contract claim is the same amount as the fee payable by a claimant bringing a breach of contract claim. The Government's decision to charge the respondent a fee in these circumstances was relatively uncontentious as, according to the Government's response to its consultation on the introduction of fees, the majority of business respondents seemed to recognise that to charge for an employee's contract claim but not a corresponding counterclaim would be unfair. The Government said at the time that it would also consider whether, if the breach of contract claim made by the employee is subsequently withdrawn, and the employer's contract claim proceeds to a hearing, it would be appropriate to seek a hearing fee from the respondent employer. However, this suggestion was not included in the fees Order.

For more information about the payment of fees, see Chapter 19, 'Fees'.

409

6.48 Processing an employer's contract claim

An employer's contract claim, or part of it, may be rejected on the same basis as a claimant's claim may be rejected under rule 12 – rule 23. Therefore, an employer's contract claim (or part thereof) may be rejected if it contains 'substantive defects'. That is:

- the claim, or part, is one which the tribunal has no jurisdiction to consider – rule 12(1)(a), or

- the claim is in a form which cannot sensibly be responded to, or is otherwise an abuse of the process – rule 12(1)(b).

The decision to reject the employer's contract claim can only be made by an employment judge. Rule 12(1) provides that tribunal office staff must refer the claim to an employment judge if they consider that the claim (or part of it) may fall within rule 12(1)(a) or (b). If the judge considers that the claim (or part) does indeed fall within one of these two categories, he or she must reject it (or the relevant part of it) – rule 12(2). The respondent will be sent a 'notice of rejection' giving the judge's reasons for rejecting the claim and setting out how to apply for a reconsideration of the rejection (see 'Reconsideration of rejection' below). For more information about the provisions of rule 12, see Chapter 4, 'Starting tribunal proceedings', in the section 'Processing the claim form', under 'Rejection of claim – substantive defects'.

6.49 Reconsideration of rejection

Rule 23 states that where an employer's contract claim is rejected for a 'substantive defect' under rule 12, rule 13 applies. Rule 13 sets out the basis upon which a claimant can challenge a decision to reject his or her claim by seeking a reconsideration. Therefore, by virtue of rule 23, a respondent can challenge a decision to reject its employer's contract claim by seeking a reconsideration of the rejection under rule 13. (Under the Tribunal Rules 2004 this was known as applying for a 'review').

It may be possible for a respondent to argue, in the alternative, that his or her application for a reconsideration should also be considered under rule 70. This is discussed in Chapter 15, 'Reconsideration of tribunal judgments and decisions'.

6.50 Under rule 13, an application for a reconsideration of a decision to reject a claim can be made on either of the following two grounds:

- that the decision to reject was wrong, or

- that the notified defect can be rectified – rule 13(1).

The application should be in writing and must be presented to the tribunal within 14 days of the date on which the notice of rejection was sent – rule

410

13(2). It must either explain why the decision is said to have been wrong or rectify the defect.

If a hearing is requested, this must be stated in the application – rule 13(2). If the claimant does not request a hearing, or an employment judge decides on the papers that the claim should be accepted in full, the application will be determined without a hearing (even if one has been requested) – rule 13(3). If there is a hearing, this will be attended only by the applying party.

Where the judge decides that the original rejection was correct but that the defect has been corrected, the claim shall be treated as presented 'on the date that the defect was rectified'– rule 13(4). It is not clear from this wording whether the defect will be treated as rectified on the date that the application remedying the defect was sent, received or accepted by the judge. However, the effect is that the date on which the rectified claim is treated as presented will be some time later than the date on which it was originally presented, which may have implications for the respondent in terms of meeting the applicable time limits – see 'Making an employer's contract claim – time limit' above. (If the 28-day time limit for presenting the response has not expired, it may be more straightforward for the respondent to simply correct the defect and resubmit the ET3, rather than make an application for a reconsideration under rule 13.) **6.51**

If the employer's contract claim is accepted, the tribunal will send a copy of it to all other parties, including the claimant, in accordance with rule 22. It will also send a copy to Acas – rule 93(1)(a).

Claimant's response to employer's contract claim **6.52**
In the same way that a respondent has the right to submit a defence to a claimant's claim, a claimant has the right to submit a defence to an employer's contract claim. When the tribunal sends a copy of a respondent's ET3 response form to the claimant it will include information for the claimant on how to submit a response to the claim, the time limit for doing so, and what will happen if a response is not received by the tribunal within that time limit – rule 24.

The claimant's response to his or her employer's contract claim must be presented to the tribunal within 28 days of the date on which the copy response was sent to him or her. (As with the time limit for an employer's response to an employee's claim, it is no doubt intended that the time limit for a claimant's response to an employer's contract claim will start to run from the date the copy ET3 is 'sent' by the tribunal, not the date that it is 'received' by the claimant – see 'Responding to a claim – time limit for presenting response' above.)

If the claimant fails to present a response within the time limit, rules 20 and 21 (which deal with applications for the extension of time for presenting a response **6.53** and the effect of non-presentation or rejection of a response, and with the situation where the case is not contested) apply – rule 25. The provisions of rule 20 are discussed in detail under 'Responding to a claim – time limit for presenting response' above. The provisions of rule 21 are discussed under 'Rule 21: "default judgments"' below.

6.54 Compensation capped at £25,000

While employment tribunals have jurisdiction to decide an employer's contract claim, there is a statutory limit of £25,000 on the amount of damages that they can award – Article 10 Extension of Jurisdiction Order. It is not possible to recover the statutory limit on damages in the employment tribunal and then seek to recover any excess damages over that amount for the same cause of action in the High Court – Fraser v HLMAD Ltd 2006 ICR 1395, CA. Thus, if the potential respondent is seeking damages in excess of this sum, he or she may wish to consider whether the civil courts would be a better forum for the claim.

6.55 Processing the response

Upon receipt of the respondent's ET3, the tribunal will consider whether the response should be accepted. Rules 17 and 18 of the Tribunal Rules 2013 set out the circumstances in which the response must be rejected.

An employment tribunal must reject a response if it is not made on the prescribed form – rule 17(1)(a). The only exception to this is where the claim falls within one of the exceptions listed in Reg 12(2) of the Rules – see 'Responding to a claim – the response form (ET3)' above. The response must also be rejected if it does not contain the minimum information required. As discussed under 'Completing the response – requirement to supply minimum information' above, as an absolute minimum the response must include:

- the respondent's full name – rule 17(1)(b)(i)

- the respondent's address – rule 17(1)(b)(ii), and

- whether the respondent wishes to resist any part of the claim – rule 17(1)(b)(iii).

6.56 Even if the respondent has used the prescribed ET3 form and included all the mandatory information, the response will still be rejected by the tribunal if it is received outside the 28-day time limit (or any extension of that time limit already granted) unless an application for an extension has already been made under rule 20 (see 'Procedure for applying for extension – time limit for presenting response' above) or the response includes or is accompanied by such an application (in which case the response shall not be rejected pending the outcome of the extension application) – rules 16 and 18(1).

412

If the response is rejected on any of these grounds, it will be returned to the respondent with a notice of rejection explaining why it has been rejected and the steps the respondent can take, including (if appropriate) how to apply for an extension of time, and how to apply for a reconsideration of the rejection – rule 17(2) and 18(2).

Unless the rejected response is subject to a reconsideration (or appeal), the claim will be dealt with in accordance with rule 21 – see 'Rule 21: "default judgments"' below. Similarly, if a reconsideration application or appeal is unsuccessful rule 21 will apply. **6.57**

Reconsideration of rejection of response **6.58**
A respondent whose response is rejected under rule 17 or 18 can apply for a reconsideration of the decision under rule 19. A reconsideration will only be granted where the decision to reject the response was wrong or, in the case of a rejection because the prescribed form was not used or the minimum information was not included (under rule 17), on the basis that the defect can be rectified – rule 19(1).

The respondent's application for a reconsideration must be presented in writing within 14 days of the date on which the notice of the rejection was sent by the tribunal. The application must explain why the decision is said to be wrong or rectify the defect, and the respondent must state whether he or she requests a hearing – rule 19(2). If the respondent does not request a hearing, or the employment judge decides – on considering the application – that the response should be accepted in full, the judge will determine the application without a hearing. Otherwise, the application will be considered at a hearing that will only be attended by the respondent – rule 19(3).

Unlike in the case of an application by a respondent for an extension of the time limit to present a response, a claimant does not have an express right to oppose a respondent's application for a reconsideration of a tribunal's rejection of the response. **6.59**

Rule 19(4) states that if the employment judge ultimately decides that the original decision to reject the response was correct, but that the defect has been rectified, the response will be treated as presented on the date that the defect was rectified. However, the judge may need to extend time in accordance with its power under rule 5 in order to ensure that the response can be accepted. Rule 5 gives tribunals a general power to extend or shorten any time limit specified in the rules (which includes the time limit for submitting a response) whether or not (in the case of an extension) the time limit has expired, either on its own initiative or on the application of a party. To this end, it may be prudent for a respondent making an application for a reconsideration to make a simultaneous application for an extension of time to present the response.

6.60 **Reconsideration under rule 70.** Rule 70 of the Tribunal Rules 2013 gives employment tribunals a general power to reconsider any 'judgment' where it is necessary in the interests of justice to do so. A 'judgment' is defined in rule 1(3)(b) as 'a decision, made at any stage of the proceedings… which finally determines –

(i) a claim, or part of a claim, as regards liability, remedy or costs (including preparation time and wasted costs); [or]

(ii) any issue which is capable of finally disposing of any claim, or part of a claim, even if it does not necessarily do so (for example, an issue whether a claim should be struck out or a jurisdictional issue)'.

The rejection of a response does not of itself finally determine the claim (or part of the claim) as regards liability, remedy or costs, or any issue which is capable of finally disposing of any claim (or part of a claim) as this can only occur when, following the rejection of the response, the tribunal proceeds to make an actual determination of the claim and, where appropriate, issues a judgment accordingly. Therefore, a respondent's only course of action may be to seek a reconsideration under rule 19.

6.61 However, if the respondent believes that a decision to reject the response does in fact fall within the definition of 'judgment', it may be open to it to apply for reconsideration of the decision under both rules 19 and 70 on an alternative basis. This could be beneficial where the respondent is unable to satisfy the test set out in rule 19 – i.e. that the original decision to reject was wrong or that the notified defect, such as failure to include minimum information or failure to use the prescribed form, can be rectified – but is nonetheless able to satisfy the more general 'interests of justice' test under rule 70.

For further discussion of the power to reconsider a decision not to accept a response under rule 70, see Chapter 15, 'Reconsideration of tribunal judgments and decisions', under 'Reconsideration of a tribunal judgment – reconsideration of decision to reject claim, response or counterclaim'.

6.62 **Appeal to EAT**
A respondent may be able to appeal to the EAT against the tribunal's rejection of the response. However, where, on a *procedural issue*, a reconsideration and an appeal are both options, a reconsideration should be generally be preferred as it is a speedier, less cumbersome and usually less expensive process.

Occasionally, a party may wish to appeal against a tribunal decision on a *point of law* while at the same time applying for a reconsideration. There is no legal reason why this cannot be done, provided the circumstances warrant it. In Blackpole Furniture Ltd v Sullivan and anor 1978 ICR 558, EAT, the EAT observed that if either the tribunal judge or one of the parties felt that it was, in the circumstances, undesirable for a review (now called a reconsideration) to take place while an appeal was pending, then the judge should contact the Registrar of the EAT to discuss the best course to take. The EAT made it clear that, even when a review was applied for, the time limit for lodging an appeal (as to which see Chapter 17, 'Processing an appeal', under 'Time limit for lodging an appeal') still ran from the date of the original decision.

Where response accepted 6.63

Where the response has been accepted, or the respondent has successfully applied for a reconsideration of a decision to reject the response, the employment tribunal will send a copy of it to all other parties, including the claimant – rule 22. Where the claim is one in respect of which Acas has a duty to attempt conciliation, the tribunal will also send a copy to Acas – rule 93(1)(a) (see Chapter 3, 'Conciliation, settlements and ADR', under 'Acas-conciliated (COT3) agreements').

The information given on the response form is put onto a computer database to help the Employment Tribunals Service monitor progress and produce statistics. The information is also passed to the Department for Business, Innovation and Skills to assist research into the use and effectiveness of employment tribunals. A warning that the information will be used in this way is included on the first page of the ET3 form.

Judicial sift. As soon as possible after the acceptance of the response, an 6.64 employment judge will carry out an initial consideration of the claim (also known as the 'judicial sift') where he or she will consider whether there are arguable complaints and defences within the jurisdiction of the tribunal. For more information see Chapter 7, 'Judicial sift'.

Rule 21: 'default judgments' 6.65

The Tribunal Rules 2004 introduced a system of default judgments allowing a tribunal judge, in certain circumstances and provided the relevant time limit for presenting a response had passed, to determine the substance of a claim without a hearing if he or she considered it appropriate to do so. The term 'default judgment' is not used in the Tribunal Rules 2013 but rule 21 makes similar – albeit less draconian – provision where the respondent has failed to present a response, the received response is rejected or the respondent has stated that no part of the claim is contested. In any of these situations an employment judge will decide whether, on the available material, a determination can properly be made of the claim. If a determination can be made, then a judgment will be issued accordingly. Such judgments are now known as 'rule 21 judgments', although it is likely that they will continue to be informally referred to as 'default judgments'.

Presidential Guidance issued on 4 December 2013 under rule 7 of the Tribunal Rules 2013, entitled 'Rule 21 judgment', sets out the procedure that will 'normally' apply. It states that unless there are exceptional circumstances no action is required by the parties for rule 21 to operate. If there are exceptional circumstances, then the party who believes them to exist must notify the employment tribunal in writing immediately. The Guidance gives no indication of what might amount to 'exceptional circumstances' in this regard.

6.66 The Guidance stresses that any documentation that will be considered in accordance with rule 21, including the claim form 'and any response form submitted', should provide sufficient detail for appropriate consideration to be made by the employment judge. This suggests that even where rule 21 has been engaged because the received response has been rejected, the information contained in the rejected response will still be considered by an employment judge when he or she seeks to make a determination of the claim. However, this would appear to negate the effect of rejecting the response in the first place. It surely only makes sense for the employment judge to consider the information contained in the response form if rule 21 is engaged because the respondent stated that no part of the claim is contested. In fact, this is confirmed in the section of the Presidential Guidance that confirms what action will be taken by an employment judge. It states that the employment judge will review all the material available, which will normally consist of the claim form and 'any response form that has been validly submitted'.

6.67 **Can a determination properly be made of the claim or part?**
Rule 21 applies where on the expiry of the time limit for presenting the response:

- no response has been presented (this includes failure by a claimant to submit a response to an employer's contract claim – rule 25)

- any response received has been rejected (and no application for a reconsideration is outstanding), or

- the respondent has stated that no part of the claim is contested.

Rule 21 is also brought into effect 'as if no response had been presented' where:

- the response is dismissed following an employment judge's initial consideration of the case – rule 28(5)

- the response is struck out in accordance with rule 37(1)(a)–(e) – rule 37(3)

- the response is dismissed for failure to comply with an unless order – rule 38(3), or

- the response is struck out for failure to comply with a deposit order – rule 39(4).

In any of the above circumstances, an employment judge will decide whether, on the available material, a determination can properly be made of the claim, or part of it.

Depending on the type of claim being pursued, it may not be possible for the **6.68** employment judge to determine the claim on the basis of the information available at the time. He or she therefore has the power to require any of the parties to provide further information for this purpose – rule 21(2). As mentioned above, the Presidential Guidance stresses that any documentation that will be considered in accordance with rule 21 should provide sufficient detail for appropriate consideration to be made by the employment judge.

Even then, it may not be possible for the employment judge to make a determination of the claim without a hearing. In Sadigh v Pannone and Partners ET Case No.2406500/04, for example, the tribunal decided against issuing a default judgment even though the employer's late presentation of the response to an employee's claims of unfair dismissal and disability discrimination led the judge to refuse to accept the response. The judge specifically addressed the question of why he had chosen not to issue a default judgment, explaining that 'it would not be appropriate to do so... because the nature of the claims made by the claimant... imposed a burden of proof on her'.

Where a determination can be made   6.69
Where the employment judge is of the view that a determination can properly be made of the claim (or part of it) he or she will issue a judgment accordingly.

Determination of liability/remedy. The judgment may either determine **6.70** liability only or both liability and remedy. If it determines liability only, the remedy will be decided at a subsequent hearing. However, although the judgment is in respect of liability only, rule 21(3) will prevent the respondent from taking part in the remedies hearing except to the extent permitted by the judge. The only way around this potential exclusion from the remedies hearing would be for the respondent to apply successfully for a reconsideration of the judgment and/or the decision not to accept the response – see 'Challenging a default judgment' below.

An employment judge must consider the extent to which a respondent should be permitted to participate in the remedies hearing. In American E-Z Self Storage Ltd v Prince EAT 0539/07 an employment tribunal erred when, after issuing a default judgment for liability against the respondent, it failed to consider the possibility of participation by the respondent in the remedies hearing. Therefore, the EAT set aside the remedies award and remitted the remedies hearing to a fresh employment tribunal.

Where the judgment determines both liability and remedy, the employment **6.71** judge will decide what compensation the claimant is entitled to on the basis of

417

the information before the tribunal. In practice, a judge will only make a judgment on remedy if he or she has a clear idea of the amount being claimed. Such certainty is only likely to exist in claims for unlawful deductions from wages or statutory redundancy payments.

6.72 **Entry of judgment on Register.** Once issued, the judgment is recorded in writing and signed by the employment judge. A copy of the judgment will then be sent to the parties and, if the proceedings were referred to the tribunal by a court, to that court. Subject to rules 50 ('Privacy and restrictions on disclosure') and 94 ('National security proceedings'), a copy of the judgment will also be placed on the Register, which contains copies of judgments or written decisions issued by tribunals. The detailed provisions of rule 50 and rule 94 are discussed in Chapter 11, 'Case management', under 'Privacy and restrictions on disclosure', and in Chapter 12, 'The hearing', under 'National security', respectively.

6.73 **Effect of prior settlement agreements or Acas-conciliated agreements.** Old rule 8(6) of the Tribunal Rules 2004 provided that a default judgment (as it was then called) had no effect where the parties had settled the case by means of a settlement agreement (previously known as a compromise agreement) or through Acas, either before or on the day on which the judgment was issued. Furthermore, old rule 33(5) stated that where a party had made an application for a review of a default judgment the judgment had to be revoked where, before the judgment was issued, the whole of the claim was satisfied or rule 8(6) applied. Thus, in these particular circumstances, the judge had no discretion but to allow the review and order revocation. While no such provisions exist under the Tribunal Rules 2013, common sense suggests that in such circumstances a tribunal will exercise its discretion and will, upon reconsideration, revoke a rule 21 judgment.

6.74 **Where a determination cannot be made**
If a determination cannot be made on the available material, including any additional material that may have been requested by the employment judge, a hearing will be fixed before an employment judge sitting alone for the purposes of seeking to properly determine the claim.

6.75 **Limited participation in hearings.** The respondent will receive notice of any hearings and decisions of the tribunal, but unless and until an extension of time is granted, the respondent will only be entitled to participate in any hearing to the extent permitted by the judge – rule 21(3). The fact that it is only the respondent's *participation at a hearing* which is subject to the judge's control means that the respondent is not precluded from making an application for the reconsideration of any judgment, from making an application for a particular case management order or from making an application for a preliminary hearing. It is also arguable that a respondent may be able to submit written skeleton arguments to the tribunal (copied to all other parties) in advance of the hearing for consideration at the hearing. Furthermore, the respondent may be called as a witness by the other party or parties.

This provision is less restrictive than old rule 9 of the Tribunal Rules 2004, under which a respondent who had failed to present a response or whose response had been rejected was automatically excluded from taking any part in the proceedings except to:

- make an application for a review of a default judgment

- make an application for a decision to be reviewed on the basis that it was wrongly made as a result of an administrative error, or because he or she did not receive notice of the proceedings leading to the decision

- be called as a witness, or

- be sent a copy of any default judgment or final hearing judgment.

The main difference is that old rule 9 was engaged automatically, while under new rule 21 the tribunal judge has discretion as to whether, and to what extent, the respondent can participate in the hearing.

Challenging a default judgment 6.76

The respondent, or the claimant, may apply to have a default judgment reconsidered in accordance with rule 70. The employment tribunal will only reconsider a judgment under rule 70 where it is considered necessary in the interests of justice to do so. Upon reconsideration, the tribunal may decide to confirm, vary or revoke the original decision. For a detailed discussion of the provisions dealing with the reconsideration of default judgments, see Chapter 15, 'Reconsideration of tribunal judgments and decisions', under 'Reconsideration of a tribunal judgment – reconsideration of a default judgment'.

Simultaneous appeal to the EAT. It is possible for a party to appeal against a 6.77 judgment to the EAT on a point of law while at the same time applying to the tribunal for a reconsideration. It is important to ensure that the strict time limit for submitting an appeal is observed, as an application for reconsideration will not affect the time limit for lodging an appeal to the EAT.

Note that the costs of a reconsideration are likely to be less than those of an appeal and this may influence a party to apply for a reconsideration instead of pursuing an appeal to the EAT.

7 Judicial sift

The Employment Tribunal Rules of Procedure 2013 ('the Tribunal Rules'), **7.1** which are contained in Schedule 1 to the Employment Tribunals (Constitution and Rules of Procedure) Regulations 2013 SI 2013/1237 ('the Tribunal Regulations'), introduced a judicial sift stage (called the 'initial consideration') at which every case is reviewed by an employment judge on the papers *after* the claim and response forms have been accepted. The claim or the response, or part of the claim or response, will be dismissed (i.e. struck out) if the judge is of the view that the tribunal has no jurisdiction to consider the claim (or part of it), or that the claim or response (or part of it) has no reasonable prospect of success.

This judicial sift applies to every case without exception. It is aimed at ensuring that weak cases that should not proceed to a full hearing are halted at the earliest possible opportunity. In its final impact assessment of the Tribunal Rules 2013 (completed in March 2013), the Government stated that it anticipated that the judicial sift would create a big saving for businesses. It estimated that around 270 whole claims or responses will be struck out each year at this point, with employers benefiting from reductions in the time they spend on the case and in costs for advice and representation by an estimated £95,000 per year.

The judicial sift mirrors the initial paper sift carried out in the EAT. However, **7.2** the EAT sift determines only whether the appeal raises an arguable question of law. The tribunal judge, by contrast, is required to make an assessment of the overall merits of the case on the papers alone, which will not always be a straightforward task. Many factual disputes can only be resolved by hearing oral evidence.

This chapter explains the requirement for an employment judge to carry out an initial consideration of the case, and the grounds and procedure for dismissing the claim or response, or part of the claim or response, at this stage of the proceedings.

421

7.3 Initial consideration of claim and response

Before the introduction of the new procedure, an employment judge would, upon presentation of the claim and response forms, review the papers with a view to making an order for the onward management of the case. This general practice, which was not a requirement under the old Rules, is now codified in the new Rules, with the addition of a new power allowing the employment judge to dispose of the case (or part thereof) at this stage on the papers alone where there is no arguable complaint or defence. Under the old Rules, a claim or response (or part thereof) could only be disposed of at a pre-hearing review.

New rule 26(1) provides that as soon as possible after the acceptance of the response, an employment judge will consider all of the documents held by the tribunal in relation to the claim to confirm whether the claim and response present arguable complaints and defences within the tribunal's jurisdiction. Under rule 27 the judge can dismiss all or part of the claim or response if he or she is of the view that the tribunal has no jurisdiction to consider the claim, or that the claim or response (or part of the claim or response) has no reasonable prospect of success (see 'Grounds for dismissal following initial consideration' below). However, before the claim or response (or part of the claim or response) is dismissed, the tribunal must send notice of its intention to dismiss the case to the parties to give the relevant party an opportunity to make representations as to why it should not be dismissed (see 'Notice to dismiss claim or response (or part)' and 'Sift hearing to consider representations' below).

7.4 If, on the other hand, having considered the papers, the employment judge is satisfied that the claim and response raise arguable complaints and defences, he or she must make a case management order (unless one has already been made) as to the future progression of the case – rule 26(2). The order may deal with the listing of a preliminary or final hearing, or may propose judicial mediation or other forms of dispute resolution (see 'Case management following sift' below).

There is no time period within which a judge must carry out an initial consideration of the papers – he or she is simply required to complete the process 'as soon as possible' after acceptance of the response. The time taken will vary depending on the tribunal's workload and the availability of judges. The parties will not know if the judge's initial consideration of the case has been completed until they receive either a notice of an intention to dismiss the claim or response (or part), or an order dealing with the ongoing management of the case.

7.5 In undertaking the judicial sift, the judge must consider 'all of the documents held by the tribunal', which, at the very least, will include the claim and response forms. But he or she may also order a party to provide further information for the purpose of the sift – rule 26(1). For example, in a case where the judge is not satisfied that the claimant has the requisite length of service to bring an ordinary unfair dismissal claim, he or she could order the respondent to provide a copy of the claimant's contract of employment and the dismissal letter in order to ascertain the claimant's period of employment. Even in the absence of any such order, the wide scope of this provision is likely to encourage the parties to send additional written submissions or documentary evidence to the tribunal voluntarily, particularly where, for instance, the claimant wishes to rebut contentions made in the response form. Neither the claim form nor the response form permit documents to be annexed to it for submission, but there is nothing prohibiting a party from sending documentary evidence to the tribunal under separate cover for consideration by the judge at the judicial sift stage. (Under rule 92, any correspondence sent to the tribunal should also be copied to all other parties.) To increase the likelihood of surviving the sift, the parties may also be inclined to submit longer and more comprehensive pleadings, including detail that would otherwise be disclosed in documentary evidence or contained in a witness statement.

Grounds for dismissal following initial consideration

7.6

Rules 27 and 28 set out the grounds on which a judge can dismiss all or part of the claim or response following his or her initial consideration of the papers: want of jurisdiction or no reasonable prospect of success. Where the judge intends to dismiss the claim or response (or part thereof), the tribunal must send a notice to the parties informing them of this and allowing them to make representations explaining why the claim or response (or part thereof) should not be dismissed. Such representations will be considered by an employment judge, who will either permit the claim or response (or relevant part) or fix a hearing to determine whether it should proceed.

For the purposes of a claim or response continuing past the judicial sift, the threshold is low. The likelihood of an employment judge being able to properly conclude on the papers alone that there is no reasonable prospect of the claim or response succeeding is slim, and not all issues of jurisdiction are easily resolved without further enquiry. As previously mentioned, the Government estimated that around 270 whole claims or responses would be struck out annually as a result of the initial sift. However, based on average figures, this equates to less than 0.2 per cent of all claims accepted by the tribunals each year. Thus, the vast majority of claims and responses are likely to survive the judicial sift – the few that do not are expected to be claims with clear-cut jurisdictional issues.

7.7 Grounds for dismissal of the claim (or part)

The claim, or part of it, can be dismissed at the judicial sift stage if the employment judge considers that the tribunal has no jurisdiction to consider it, or that it has no reasonable prospect of success – rule 27(1).

7.8 No jurisdiction.

The complaint raised must fall within the tribunal's jurisdiction. This means that the tribunal must have the statutory power to consider it and it must not be barred because, for example, the employee does not have the requisite period of continuous service to bring a claim, or because it was not presented within the statutory time limit or falls outside the territorial scope of the tribunal's jurisdiction. The extent of employment tribunals' jurisdiction is explained in detail in Chapter 2, 'Tribunals' jurisdiction'. Guidance on the HMCTS Employment Tribunals Service website provides a full list of claims employment tribunals can deal with. It also advises applicants who are unsure whether their claim can be heard by an employment tribunal to contact the public enquiry line or Acas for assistance.

The most common jurisdictional question is whether a claim has been presented within the time limit laid down by statute. If a claim is presented too early or too late the tribunal will have no jurisdiction to hear it. In the case of a complaint being presented out of time, a tribunal can only extend the time limit and allow the claim to proceed on certain specified grounds. Calculating the appropriate time limit may not always be an easy matter. In a complex discrimination case, for example, the statutory time limit may depend on whether the act complained of was a one-off event or whether it formed part of a continuing act of discrimination. In such cases, a tribunal may be unable to draw a conclusion as to whether the claim was presented in time on the papers alone and may need to allow the claim to proceed past the judicial sift stage, but list the case for a preliminary hearing in order to determine the issue of jurisdiction. Time limits are discussed in detail in Chapter 5, 'Time limits', while preliminary hearings are addressed in Chapter 11, 'Case management', under 'Preliminary hearings'.

7.9

It is worth noting that the issue of jurisdiction may have already been considered prior to the judicial sift stage. Rule 12(1)(a) allows the staff of the tribunal office to refer a claim form to an employment judge if they consider that the claim, or part of it, may be one which the tribunal has no jurisdiction to consider. This means that the tribunal staff must have in mind the question of whether a claim falls within the jurisdiction of the tribunal when they are processing the claim form, before it is seen by an employment judge. An employment judge will reject the claim, or part of it, if he or she agrees that the tribunal has no jurisdiction to hear it and the claim form will be returned to the claimant together with a notice of rejection containing information about how the claimant can apply for a reconsideration of the rejection – rule 12(2) and (3). In these circumstances, the claim form will not be copied to the respondent. This power is dealt with in Chapter 4, 'Starting tribunal proceedings', in the section 'Processing the claim form', under 'Rejection of claim – substantive defects'.

No reasonable prospect of success. The judicial sift may also be used to weed **7.10** out claims that have no reasonable prospect of success. The 'no reasonable prospect' test is a familiar concept. It applied under the old rules when a tribunal was considering whether to make a striking-out order at a pre-hearing review, and it continues to apply under the strike-out provisions in new rule 37 (see Chapter 11, 'Case management', under 'Striking out'). The case law concerned with the strike-out provisions will have a significant bearing on decisions made by tribunals at the judicial sift stage. For instance, it will not be enough to say that, on the balance of probabilities, the claim or response is unlikely to succeed. There must be 'no' reasonable prospect of success – Short v Birmingham City Council and ors EAT 0038/13.

Tribunal judges should be particularly cautious of dismissing complex and fact-sensitive cases – for example, discrimination or whistleblowing claims – on the ground of no reasonable prospects. In Anyanwu and anor v South Bank Students' Union and anor 2001 ICR 391, HL, the House of Lords highlighted the importance of not striking out discrimination claims except in the most obvious cases, because they are generally fact-sensitive and require full examination to make a proper determination. The Court of Appeal held that the same or a similar approach should generally inform whistleblowing cases, which have much in common with discrimination cases – Ezsias v North Glamorgan NHS Trust 2007 ICR 1126, CA. Such cases involve an investigation into why an employer took a particular step. The Court stressed that it will only be in an exceptional case that an application will be struck out as having no reasonable prospect of success when the central facts are in dispute.

This cautious approach to striking out – based on the view that it is unfair to **7.11** throw out a claim where there are crucial facts in dispute and there has been no opportunity for the evidence in relation to those facts to be considered – was also adopted by Lady Smith in Balls v Downham Market High School and College 2011 IRLR 217, EAT. She said that where strike-out is sought or contemplated on the ground that a claim has no reasonable prospect of success, the tribunal must first consider whether, on a careful consideration of all the available material, it can properly conclude that the claim has no reasonable prospect of success. The test is not whether the claim is likely to fail; nor is it a matter of asking whether it is possible that the claim will fail. It is not a test that can be satisfied by considering what is put forward by the respondent either in the ET3 or in submissions and deciding whether their written or oral assertions regarding disputed matters are likely to be established as facts. It is a high test. The tribunal should have regard not only to material specifically relied on by parties but to the employment tribunal file. There may be

425

correspondence or other documentation which contains material that is relevant to the issue of whether it can be concluded that the claim has no reasonable prospect of success.

7.12 Ground for dismissal of the response (or part)

The response, or part of it, can be dismissed only if the employment judge considers that it has no reasonable prospect of success – rule 28(1). A judge cannot strike out the response on the basis of jurisdictional issues at this stage of the proceedings. The same principles that apply to the dismissal of claims on the ground of no reasonable prospects – discussed under 'Grounds for dismissal of the claim (or part) – no reasonable prospect of success' above – will equally apply in relation to the dismissal of a response (or part). A holding, or vague 'coverall', response is not enough. If the response does not sufficiently particularise the basis upon which the claim is being defended, it could be at risk of being dismissed at this stage on the basis that it has no reasonable prospect of success.

7.13 Notice to dismiss claim or response (or part)

As well as detailing the grounds on which a claim or response (or part) can be dismissed at the judicial sift stage, rules 27 and 28 also set out the process to be adopted where, following his or her initial consideration of the papers, the judge is of the view that the tribunal has no jurisdiction to consider the claim (or part of it), or that the claim or response (or part) has no reasonable prospect of success.

7.14 Notice to dismiss the claim (or part)

If the employment judge considers that the claim (or part) does not fall within the tribunal's jurisdiction, or that it has no reasonable prospect of success, the tribunal will send a notice to the parties setting out the judge's view and the reasons for it and ordering that the claim, or the part in question, will be dismissed on a specific date unless, before that date, the claimant presents written representations explaining why the claim (or part) should not be dismissed – rule 27(1). If no such representations are received, the claim will be dismissed from the date specified without further order, though the tribunal will write to the parties to confirm what has occurred – rule 27(2). Note that the wording of rule 27(2) does not make explicit provision for the dismissal of part of a claim – stating only that 'the claim' will be dismissed. However, when read with the rest of rule 27 it is clear that the intention is that the relevant part of the claim identified in the notice under rule 27(1) will stand as dismissed from the date specified if written representations are not received before then.

In many cases, the receipt of a notice to dismiss from the tribunal will deter the claimant (particularly a litigant in person) from proceeding further. However, the problem may simply be a failure to properly articulate the complaint in the claim form and claimants would be well advised to take the opportunity to make written representations challenging the notice, focusing carefully on countering the reasons for dismissal given by the judge.

If the claimant makes representations within the specified time period they **7.15** will be considered by an employment judge (but not necessary the same judge as the one who carried out the initial consideration), who can either permit the claim (or relevant part) to proceed, or fix a hearing (a 'sift hearing') for the purpose of deciding whether it should be permitted to proceed – rule 27(3). The respondent may, but need not, attend and participate in the hearing. The sift hearing is discussed further under 'Sift hearing to consider representations' below.

Notice to dismiss the response (or part)   **7.16**
Rule 28 mirrors the notice requirements of rule 27 but in relation to the dismissal of a response. Where the tribunal judge considers that there is no reasonable prospect of the response (or part) succeeding, the tribunal will send the parties a notice setting out the judge's view with reasons, and stating that the response (or part) will be dismissed on a specific date unless, before that date, the respondent submits written representations explaining why the response (or part) should not be dismissed – rule 28(1)(a) and (b). However, in the case of a response, the notice from the tribunal must also specify the consequences of the dismissal of the response: that the case will proceed as if no response had been presented as set out in rule 21 – rule 28(1)(c) and (5). (Rule 21 is discussed in Chapter 6, 'Defending a claim', under 'Rule 21: "default judgments"'. Briefly, it states that, in the absence of a response, an employment judge will consider whether on the available material (including any further information the parties are required to provide), a determination can properly be made of the claim, or part thereof – rule 21(2). If a determination can be made, the judge will issue a judgment accordingly. If a determination cannot be made, a hearing will be fixed before an employment judge sitting alone. The respondent will be sent notice of any hearings and decisions of the tribunal but will only be entitled to participate in any hearing to the extent permitted by the judge – rule 21(3).)

If the respondent fails to submit representations by the date specified in the notice, the response will be dismissed from that date without further order, although the tribunal will write to the parties to confirm what has occurred – rule 28(2). The wording of rule 28(2) does not make explicit provision for the dismissal of a part of the response – stating only that 'the response' will be dismissed. However, when read with the rest of rule 28 it is again clear that the intention is that the relevant part of the response identified in the notice under rule 28(1) will stand as dismissed from the date specified if written representations are not received before then.

427

7.17 If representations are received, they will be considered by a judge (again, this need not be the same judge who carried out the initial consideration), who will either permit the response to stand or fix a sift hearing to decide whether it should be permitted to do so – rule 28(3). The claimant may, but need not, attend and participate in the hearing. For more information about the hearing, see 'Sift hearing to consider representations' below.

7.18 Sift hearing to consider representations

As explained above, the party to whom the notice to dismiss is addressed has the right to submit representations as to why the claim or response (or part) should not be dismissed. Where representations are made they will be considered by an employment judge, who will either permit the claim or response (or relevant part) to proceed, or fix a hearing (a 'sift hearing') to decide whether it should proceed – rules 27(3) and 28(3). After the party has made representations, the claim or response cannot be struck out without a sift hearing.

Where a sift hearing is held to consider representations from the claimant as to why the claim (or part) should not be dismissed, the respondent may, but need not, attend – rule 27(3). Similarly, where a hearing is held to consider representations from the respondent as to why the response (or part) should not be dismissed, the claimant may, but need not, attend – rule 28(3). However, rule 42 (found in the section of the rules entitled 'Rules common to all kinds of hearing') states that the tribunal will consider any written representations from a party, including a party who does not propose to attend the hearing, if they are delivered to the tribunal and to all other parties not less than seven days before the hearing. Therefore, where, for instance, a sift hearing will be held to consider representations from the claimant, the respondent can submit representations under rule 42 in support of why the claim (or part) should be dismissed at the sift stage. Such representations will be considered by the judge at the hearing as long as they are submitted to the tribunal and the other party at least seven days before the sift hearing is held.

7.19 There are no specific provisions governing the conduct of sift hearings, although under rule 46, which applies to all kinds of hearings, hearings may be conducted, in whole or in part, by use of electronic communication (including by telephone) where the tribunal considers that it would be just and equitable to do so. It is unclear what evidence, if any, can be presented. It is unlikely that the judge will be permitted to hear and draw conclusions on oral evidence, especially where the other party is not in attendance and therefore has no opportunity to cross-examine and challenge the individual giving evidence. As a result, where there are core factual disputes between the parties which cannot be solved without hearing evidence, the tribunal will be unable to exercise its power to dismiss.

Challenging dismissal orders   7.20

A tribunal judge's decision to dismiss the claim (or part) will constitute a 'judgment' as defined by rule 1(3)(b) – that is, 'a decision which finally determines a claim, or part of a claim, as regards liability, remedy or costs... [or] any issue which is capable of finally disposing of any claim, or part of a claim, even if it does not necessarily do so' – and, as such, may be open to 'reconsideration' under new rules 70–73. Reconsideration is discussed in detail in Chapter 15, 'Reconsideration of tribunal judgments and decisions'.

As mentioned under 'Notice to dismiss claim or response (or part)' above, where a response is dismissed, the effect is as if no response was presented. This situation is covered by rule 21, which provides that, in the absence of a response, an employment judge will consider whether on the available material a determination can properly be made of the claim, or part of it. If a determination can be made, the judge will issue a judgment accordingly. Where a determination cannot be made on the available material, a hearing will be fixed which will be conducted by an employment judge sitting alone. The respondent may challenge any judgment made in determination of the claim (including what is commonly referred to as a default judgment) by seeking a reconsideration under rules 70–73.

However, the decision to dismiss a response (or part), as opposed to a claim, **7.21** cannot itself be reconsidered. Only a 'judgment', as defined in rule 1(3)(b) (see above), can be reconsidered under rules 70–73. The dismissal of a response, or part of a response, does not of itself determine the claim or any issue that is capable of finally disposing of the claim – the claim, or any issue within the claim, is only determined finally when, following the dismissal of the response (or part), the tribunal issues a judgment dealing with the substance of the claim.

Note that a decision to dismiss a claim or response, or part of a claim or response, can be appealed to the EAT where there has been an error of law. Similarly, a default judgment can be appealed to the EAT on a point of law. See Chapter 16, 'The Employment Appeal Tribunal', under 'Grounds of appeal' for further details.

Tribunal and EAT fees. By virtue of Article 4(2), read with Schedule 1, of the **7.22** Employment Tribunals and the Employment Appeal Tribunal Fees Order 2013 SI 2013/1893, a fee of £100 (regardless of the type of claim concerned) is payable when making an application to an employment tribunal for reconsideration of a default judgment.

A fee of £400 is payable by an appellant following the receipt by the EAT of a notice of appeal – Article 13. A further fee of £1,200 is payable by an appellant following a direction by the EAT that the matter will proceed to an oral hearing at which the appeal is to be finally disposed of – Article 14. Fees are discussed in detail in Chapter 19, 'Fees'.

429

7.23 Case management following sift

If, after his or her initial consideration of the papers, the employment judge is satisfied that the claim and response raise arguable complaints and defences he or she must make a case management order (unless one has already been made) as to the future progress of the case – rule 26(2). Similarly, if, following a sift hearing, the claim or response (or any part) is permitted to proceed, the judge is required, under rules 27(4) and 28(4), to make a case management order. A tribunal has a wide general discretion to tailor orders to the case in hand. The order may, for example, deal with the listing of a preliminary or final hearing, or may propose judicial mediation or other forms of dispute resolution. Examples of types of case management orders a tribunal can make are discussed in Chapter 11, 'Case management', under 'Case management orders'.

Preliminary hearings can deal with all sorts of preliminary matters aimed at progressing the case – see Chapter 11, 'Case management', under 'Preliminary hearings'. For example, even if the employment judge is not satisfied that there is *no* reasonable prospect of the claim or response succeeding and therefore does not dismiss the case at the initial sift stage, he or she may be of the view that the claim or response (or part) is nonetheless weak. In these circumstances, the judge may order that a preliminary hearing be held in order to consider whether a deposit (of up to £1,000) should be paid as a condition of the claim or response (or a specific allegation or argument in the claim or response) continuing, on the basis that it has 'little reasonable prospect' of success. The 'little reasonable prospect of success' test is clearly not as rigorous as the 'no reasonable prospect' test and the tribunal therefore has greater leeway when considering whether or not to order a deposit – see Chapter 11, 'Case management', under 'Deposit orders'. Or the judge may consider that the claim involves a jurisdictional issue that requires more detailed deliberation and may schedule a preliminary hearing to consider the issue.

8 Amendments

General procedure

Amending the claim

Amending the response

Amending the parties

In an ideal world, the parties to any employment tribunal claim would be well- **8.1** prepared and their respective cases presented thoroughly from the start of their involvement in the claim. In practice, however, the claimant or respondent may at some point realise that the claim or response is lacking something: perhaps, for example, crucial details have been omitted; or the claimant has failed to appreciate that he or she had a particular ground of claim, or could claim against a particular party; or the respondent has made a concession that it subsequently wishes to withdraw. In such circumstances, the tribunal's leave will need to be obtained to make an amendment.

In contrast to the position under the Employment Tribunal Rules 2004 (contained in Schedule 1 to the Employment Tribunals (Constitution and Rules of Procedure) Regulations 2004 SI 2004/1861), there is no express power in the Employment Tribunal Rules 2013 (contained in Schedule 1 to the Employment Tribunal (Constitution and Rules of Procedure) Regulations 2013 SI 2013/1237) ('the Tribunal Regulations') for tribunals to give leave to the parties to amend a claim (ET1) or response (ET3). Nevertheless, tribunals retain the power to grant amendments under their broad power under rule 29 of the Tribunal Rules 2013 to make case management orders, combined with the general power under rule 41 to regulate their own procedure in the manner they consider fair, having regard to the principles contained in the overriding objective in rule 2. In addition, rule 34 clarifies that under the general power to make case management orders, tribunals have power to add, substitute or remove any party. The general power to make case management orders is discussed in Chapter 11, 'Case management', under 'Case management orders'. Here, we consider specifically the tribunal's powers to grant leave to amend the claim form and response, and to amend the parties to the claim.

Note that the claimant may be required to amend his or her claim before it is **8.2** even accepted by the tribunal. The claim will be rejected where it is not on the prescribed form or does not contain basic minimum information; or if an employment judge considers that the tribunal has no jurisdiction to hear it, or that it is in a form which cannot be sensibly responded to or is otherwise an abuse of process – rules 10 and 12. In such circumstances, the claimant may

---

431

apply for a reconsideration under rule 13, either by explaining why the decision to reject was wrong, or by rectifying the defect. This process is considered in detail in Chapter 4, 'Starting tribunal proceedings', under 'Processing the claim form – rejection of claim'. Likewise, the respondent may have to amend the response under rule 19 in order for the tribunal to accept it, if it does not comply with the requirements laid out in rule 17. This process is discussed in Chapter 6, 'Defending a claim', under 'Processing the response – reconsideration of rejection of response'.

Note, too, that the tribunal itself may wish to amend documents it has produced, such as an order or judgment. The correction of clerical mistakes by the tribunal is discussed in Chapter 15, 'Reconsideration of tribunal judgments and decisions', under 'Correcting mistakes'.

8.3 General procedure

The employment tribunal has a broad discretion to allow amendments at any stage of the proceedings, either on its own initiative or on application by a party – rule 29 Tribunal Rules. Such a discretion must be exercised in accordance with the overriding objective of dealing with cases fairly and justly in rule 2, which is discussed in detail in Chapter 1, 'Employment tribunals', in the section 'What are employment tribunals?' under 'Employment tribunal rules – overriding objective'.

We discuss the procedure by which a tribunal exercises its power to make case management orders in detail in Chapter 11, 'Case management', under 'Case management orders – tribunal's power to make case management orders', 'Case management orders – order on tribunal's own initiative' and 'Case management orders – application by party for order'. Suffice it to say here that the circumstances in which a tribunal may exercise the power to make amendments is very broad. An employment judge may think it appropriate to make an amendment on his or her own initiative after perusal of the case papers, especially where these disclose clerical or typing errors. In these circumstances, he or she can make an order for amendment with or without hearing the parties or giving them an opportunity to make written or oral representations; or he or she may decide to hold a preliminary hearing. Where a case management order is made without a hearing, it will be communicated in writing to the parties, identifying the employment judge who made the decision – rule 60. This is particularly important in the case of amendments to the claim form or response, or to the parties, as it is axiomatic that a party must know precisely what case it has to meet.

8.4 Alternatively, a party may apply for an amendment, either at a hearing or in writing to the tribunal – rule 30(1). The tribunal may deal with such an application in writing, before the hearing, or order that it be dealt with at a preliminary or final hearing – rule 30(3). Where a party applies in writing, that party is required to notify the other parties that any objections to the application should be sent to the tribunal as soon as possible – rule 30(2). If minded to grant an amendment at the hearing itself, a tribunal can do so subject to permitting the other party extra time (and, if necessary, an adjournment) in order to answer any new claim or ground of defence – see W Devis and Sons Ltd v Sexton EAT 558/79. An adjournment of a hearing is certainly likely to be granted where a claim is amended so as to involve a third party. The costs of such an adjournment are likely to be borne by the party whose amendment occasions the need for it.

In Selkent Bus Co Ltd v Moore 1996 ICR 836, EAT, the then President of the EAT, Mr Justice Mummery, gave some guidance as to how tribunals should approach applications for leave to amend, and in what circumstances it may be appropriate to hear representations and/or hold a hearing to decide the issue. He commented that although the tribunal is not required to seek or consider written or oral representations from each side before deciding whether to grant or refuse an application for leave to amend, the discretion to grant leave should be exercised 'in a manner which satisfies the requirements of relevance, reason, justice and fairness inherent in all judicial discretions'. Accordingly, in his view, an employment judge or tribunal may exercise the discretion on an application for leave to amend in a number of ways:

- it may be a proper exercise of discretion to refuse an application for leave to amend without seeking or considering representations from the other side. For example, it may be obvious on the face of the application and/or in the circumstances in which it is made that it is hopeless and should be refused

- if, however, the amendment sought is arguable and is one of substance which the tribunal considers could reasonably be opposed by the other side, the tribunal may then ask the other party whether they consent to the amendment or whether they oppose it and, if they oppose it, to state the grounds of opposition. In those cases the tribunal would make a decision on the question of amendment after hearing both sides

- in other cases, a tribunal may reasonably take the view that the proposed amendment is not sufficiently substantial or controversial to justify seeking representations from the other side and may order the amendment ex parte without doing so. If that course is adopted and the other side then objects, the tribunal should consider those objections and decide whether to affirm, rescind or vary the order which has been made.

In Edwards v London Borough of Sutton EAT 0111/12 the claimant applied to **8.5** amend her claim, but an employment judge simply refused the application and said that she should present a new claim to the tribunal. The claimant appealed. The EAT held that the employment judge had fallen into error in failing to see

433

that the claimant's proposed amendment was substantial and arguable. Although there might have been points that the respondent would have wanted to make, it was by no means clear that the proposed new claims were out of time or hopeless. The proper process, following the guidance in Selkent (above), would have been for the tribunal to have asked the respondent whether it consented to the amendment or opposed it, and, if it opposed it, to state the ground of opposition and then make a decision either taking into account the written submission only or arranging a hearing for the purpose and having a proper argument about whether the amendment should be allowed. The EAT remitted the matter to the tribunal to reconsider.

While there is no express provision limiting the number of times a party can apply for an amendment, a tribunal is entitled to refuse a repeated application where there has been no material change of circumstances and there is no other exceptional reason why the tribunal should allow the application to be renewed in the interests of justice. For example, in Okinedo v Northwest Guarding Ltd (debarred) and anor EAT 0510/07 the claimant brought a claim of racial discrimination, among other complaints, against his employer. When it appeared that the employer was likely to be dissolved, he applied for permission to amend to include a claim against the individual alleged to have discriminated against him. This application was refused. Four months later, he repeated the application on the basis that the dissolution had now occurred, but the employment judge refused it. On the claimant's appeal, the EAT upheld the employment judge's decision. There had been no material change of circumstances, and no other exceptional reason why the claimant should be allowed to renew his application in the interests of justice. The claimant had been offered an opportunity to appeal against the refusal of his first application for an amendment, or to issue fresh proceedings against the individual in question, but had pursued neither possibility.

8.6 The demands of justice require that where a tribunal accedes to a request to amend, all other parties are given an opportunity to 'reply' by making any necessary amendments to their own cases. Once an amendment has been allowed, the tribunal staff must note it on the ET1 or ET3, together with any consequential amendments made by the other parties in reply.

As decisions as to whether or not to allow a claimant to amend a claim are discretionary ones, it is only where it can be shown that the tribunal took account of an irrelevant factor, failed to take account of a relevant factor, or reached a decision that no reasonable tribunal would have reached in the circumstances of the case that it can be interfered with on appeal – Selkent Bus Company Ltd v Moore (above).

8.7 **Need to consider precise wording of proposed amendment**
It is vital that an application to amend sets out the terms of the proposed amendment, in the same degree of detail as would be expected had it formed

part of the original claim, and tribunals should ensure that the terms of any such proposed amendments are clearly recorded – see, for example, Scottish Opera Ltd v Winning EATS 0047/09. In Chief Constable of Essex Police v Kovacevic EAT 0126/13 the claimant applied on the opening day of the hearing for permission to amend his unfair dismissal claim form to include claims of direct and indirect race discrimination. The employment judge was not provided with the text of the proposed amendment, but, in the course of his written reasons, sought to identify, based on what the claimant had told him, what would be the subject matter of the application to amend. The judge apparently decided that he could entertain the application there and then, and ordered that there should be 'an extension of time for the claimant to bring his claims for race discrimination on the basis that it is just and equitable to do so'. His order did not record that he had given permission to amend the claim form, or in fact identify what the amendment was, though he directed the preparation of a schedule of particulars in support of the amended claim form.

The EAT allowed the employer's appeal, holding that it is fundamental that any application to amend a claim must be considered in the light of the actual proposed amendment. The employment judge did not have before him, reduced to writing or in any form, the terms of the amendment being proposed. It might be that in certain circumstances, such as where a very simple amendment is sought or a limited amendment asked for by a litigant in person, that an employment judge might be able to proceed without requiring the specifics of the amendment to be before him in writing. But this was a case in which the claimant was being represented by a professional representative, and the employment judge plainly could and should have required the representative to reduce the application to writing before considering it on its merits. In the EAT's view, the dangers of doing otherwise were obvious, and manifested in the case before it. One of the dangers of permitting an amendment without seeing its terms was that, having been given the green light to draft an amendment, a party might go beyond the terms which the judge was led to understand might be included in the amendment he or she was permitting. In this particular case, the schedule later drawn for the claimant in response to the judge's order set out a large number of allegations and incidents spanning a period of many years and involving many different individuals and occasions.

In Ladbrokes Racing Ltd v Traynor EATS 0067/06 (discussed under 'Does the   **8.8** tribunal have a duty to suggest amendments?' below) the EAT considered that a tribunal's decision to allow an amendment was 'fatally flawed' in that there had been no articulation of the detail of the amendment that was being proposed. It allowed leave to include an allegation that the claimant's dismissal was procedurally unfair, but left open the questions 'how, in what way and in what respects?' According to the EAT, those were questions to which the respondent was entitled to know the answers before any motion to amend was presented, debated and decided on. They were also questions to which the

435

tribunal needed to know the answers before it could pronounce any sensible order in respect of the amendment application which it decided it had before it.

A similar difficulty arose in Margarot Forrest Care Management v Kennedy EATS 0023/10 – a case which also involved the purported amendment of a claim form and which demonstrates the problems that may arise where an employment tribunal attempts to articulate the wording of a proposed amendment on behalf of the party applying for the amendment. The claimant in that case lodged an ET1 claiming wrongful dismissal. At the start of the hearing, the tribunal sought to identify the issues. Coming to the view that the complaint appeared to support an unfair dismissal claim, it asked the claimant's mother, who was representing her, to 'state the nature of the unfair dismissal complaint again orally so that that could be noted'. The claimant's mother said that the claimant 'was in a car accident, put a claim in on the respondents' vehicle insurance policy, [her director] called her in and said if she did not drop the claim it was her last day at work… She told him she was going to make a claim as the brakes had gone. He said "you give me no choice but to pay you off".' The tribunal advised the claimant's mother that she would have to make an application to amend 'if she wished the tribunal to deal with that as an issue' and, in response, she applied for leave to amend. Having asked the respondent if it had any objections, the tribunal adjourned to draft the wording of the amendment, and then allowed it in the terms it had drafted: namely, that this was a complaint of unfair dismissal pursuant to S.103A ERA that the claimant was dismissed for making a disclosure that a person had failed to comply with a legal obligation, or that someone's health and safety was being endangered.

8.9 On the respondent's appeal, the EAT accepted that it had been appropriate for the tribunal to draw the attention of the claimant's mother to the fact that her opening statement appeared to raise a new matter, that this could not form part of her case without amendment, and then to extract from her statement the basis of the complaint that she sought to add and invite the respondent to respond to this. However, the EAT concluded that the tribunal had fallen into error with regard to the procedure it had adopted after taking the steps mentioned above. Rather than consider whether or not to allow an amendment in the terms proposed by the claimant's mother, it had proceeded to draft an amendment in different terms and had not afforded the respondent the opportunity to make submissions on the wording it was proposing. The EAT was satisfied that the tribunal had no discretion to undertake this approach. Where amendments of claims are concerned, the discretion conferred on an employment tribunal is to grant leave to a claimant to allow the claimant to amend the ET1 *in the terms that he or she proposes*, if appropriate; it is not a discretion for the employment tribunal to give itself leave to amend the ET1 in whatever terms *it* thinks are best. The EAT accordingly revoked the tribunal's order and remitted the case to a fresh employment tribunal.

436

Is an amendment necessary and appropriate?

8.10

In some cases, a lack of detail may well require an amendment to be made to the existing claim or response. However, depending on the circumstances, there may simply be a need to provide additional information about the claim or response. Whether or not an amendment is required will depend essentially on whether the claim form or response sufficiently particularises the essential complaint or defence that the claimant or, as the case may be, respondent seeks to make. Such questions frequently arise on appeal in circumstances where an employment tribunal has at first instance refused an application to amend. (Requests for additional information are discussed in Chapter 9, 'Responding to opponent's case', under 'Obtaining additional information'.)

While tribunals generally interpret the ET1 flexibly when determining whether a particular claim can be gleaned from the facts pleaded fairly, their discretion to allow additional claims is not infinite. In Quarcoopome v Sock Shop Holdings Ltd 1995 IRLR 353, EAT, the EAT expressed the view that a claim of 'race discrimination' in an ET1 was sufficient to incorporate any claim for race discrimination – such as claims for direct, indirect and victimisation discrimination. However, subsequent authorities declined to follow this decision and it was overruled outright by the Court of Appeal in Ali v Office of National Statistics 2005 IRLR 201, CA. In that case, the claimant brought a race discrimination claim, which was particularised in his ET1 so as to indicate that he was bringing a direct race discrimination claim. Later on, he discovered that he might also have an arguable case of indirect race discrimination and sought to amend his ET1 to this effect. However, his argument, based on Quarcoopome, that the amendment was merely the addition of a claim already pleaded in the ET1 failed before the Court of Appeal. In the Court's view, Quarcoopome had incorrectly applied previous authorities on this issue. In the opinion of Lord Justice Maurice Kay, the EAT in Quarcoopome had taken an 'indulgent view of what is required of [a claimant] in setting out his claim in a discrimination case'. It was necessary for claimants to set out the specific acts complained of, as tribunals were only able to adjudicate on specific complaints. A general description of the complaint in the ET1 will therefore not suffice and, according to Lord Justice Waller, such a description 'cries out for particulars'. Moreover, an employer is entitled to know the claim it has to meet.

In Ali v Office of National Statistics (above) the Court of Appeal held that in 8.11 considering whether the ET1 contains a particular complaint that the claimant is seeking to raise, reference must be made to the claim form as a whole. Given this, the mere fact that a box is ticked indicating that a certain claim is being made may not be conclusive in determining whether it sets out the basis for such a complaint. This was demonstrated in Baker v Commissioner of Police of the Metropolis EAT 0201/09, in which the EAT upheld a tribunal's decision that a claim form did not include a complaint of disability discrimination. B, who suffered from learning difficulties and dyslexia, submitted a tribunal claim

437

form in which he ticked boxes marked 'disability' and 'race' to indicate what discrimination he was complaining about. When the claim was heard, the police force argued that the ET1 did not disclose a disability discrimination claim, there being no discernible complaint of such discrimination anywhere in the claim form apart from the ticked 'disability' box. The tribunal agreed, finding that nowhere in the claim form did B indicate that the alleged discrimination had anything to do with his learning difficulties or dyslexia; nor did he mention that any specific adjustments should have been made for him by reason of his disability. In contrast, his description of events recognisably raised a claim of race discrimination.

B appealed, contending that it was clear that the first ET1 included a claim under the Disability Discrimination Act 1995 (since repealed and superseded by the Equality Act 2010). Indeed, in its response to the first ET1, the police force had specifically denied disability discrimination. Furthermore, B had served a disability discrimination questionnaire on the police force less than a month after submitting the ET1, and allegations of disability discrimination had been substantiated in later ET1s and fully particularised at a later stage. The EAT cited Ali v Office of National Statistics (above), and also the comment of Mr Justice Neill in Burns International Security Services (UK) Ltd v Butt 1983 ICR 547, EAT, that it is inappropriate for a tribunal to adopt a technical approach when deciding whether an ET1 raises a particular claim. However, the EAT decided that, on the facts of this case, the tribunal did not err in law or come to a perverse conclusion in holding that, read as a whole, the first ET1 did not include a claim of disability discrimination. The fact that the police force in its response to the first ET1 denied discrimination under the DDA did not necessarily mean that such a claim had been made. Although a claimant could explain and elucidate a claim made in an ET1 by way of further particulars, the claim itself still had to be set out in the ET1. (Note, however, that the EAT went on to hold that the tribunal should have considered whether to allow an application to amend the form to include the disability discrimination claim – see 'Amending the claim – timing and manner of the application' below).

8.12 The question of whether the ET1 contains or does not contain a particular claim is 'a pure question of fact' – Redhead v London Borough of Hounslow EAT 0409/11. The Redhead case concerned a claimant's appeal from an employment judge's decision that her ET1 did not embrace claims of direct or indirect race discrimination, and therefore that if she wished to pursue such claims the ET1 would need to be amended to introduce them. The claimant argued that the claim form repeatedly referred to 'discrimination' and 'race discrimination'; and that it used the term 'discriminatory act'. However, the EAT considered that on a proper reading the references to 'discrimination' and 'race discrimination' simply rehearsed or described the background to the grievances that she was articulating to her employer, which, she claimed, were protected disclosures; and that the term 'discriminatory act' could and did embrace an act of racial discrimination by way of victimisation, which on an overall reading was what the claim form was complaining about. Even though the claimant had ticked the box marked 'race discrimination' the EAT considered that, as the Appeal Tribunal in Baker v Commissioner of Police of the Metropolis (above) had made clear, 'the ticking of a box is but one feature of construing whether as a whole an ET1 form does or does not contain a complaint of a particular type'. The EAT said that it had taken account of the tick in reviewing the employment judge's conclusion that overall the claim made no complaint of race discrimination, direct or indirect. It acknowledged that it may be unnecessary to refer to a specific section or subsection of a piece of legislation in the context of a claim form that already in plain language asserts a particular claim or gives sufficient particulars from which one can spell out such a claim. However, this claim form 'contained none of the usual language that one would expect to find' in a race discrimination claim, such as some sort of comparison with the treatment given to others. The form left the 'clear message' that the claimant's claim was confined to an allegation of multiple instances of victimisation and/or detriment for having made protected disclosures.

8.13 The following two cases reveal contrasting outcomes as to whether it was appropriate and necessary for the respective claimants to seek formal amendment of their ET1s:

- **Ennever v Metropolitan Police** EAT 0051/06: E brought a claim of discrimination on grounds of sex, race, religion and disability. At a case management discussion six months after her claim was launched, she sought leave to amend her claim form to include, inter alia, allegations of victimisation and that she had been subjected to a detriment because she had made a protected disclosure. The employment judge refused the amendments, and E appealed. The EAT held that leave to amend was not necessary in respect of the victimisation claim, since the paragraph of her ET1 in which she made a claim of discrimination could be read as including the complaint of victimisation, although additional information might be required. (However, in respect of the detriment claim, an amendment to the claim form was necessary as it amounted to a new claim that had not been previously particularised. Leave was granted, as the new claim was at least based on the facts that had already been alleged in the claim form)

- **Parekh v London Borough of Brent** EAT 0097/11: P made a claim of unfair dismissal and sex and disability discrimination. He wrote in his form, by way of explaining why he thought his dismissal was unfair: 'I was informed in June 2009 that I was on probation despite being employed by the school since August 2008... I took out a grievance in May 2009 which has yet to be investigated. I was dismissed on 02/09/09 and was given the right to appeal... The appeal was not upheld. My grievance has yet to be heard.

I was never informed that I was on probation and the school has been unable to provide any documents to prove that I was on probation.' Explaining which incidents he believed to amount to discrimination, he wrote: 'This relating to my grievances and whistle blowing statements that yet to be investigated' [sic]. He subsequently withdrew his discrimination claims, but sought to argue that his claim form enabled him to pursue a claim for automatic unfair dismissal for making a protected disclosure under S.103A of the Employment Rights Act 1996. However, the employment judge decided that 'despite the oblique reference to whistleblowing... it could not fairly be said that this claim now put forward... was covered by the existing claim', and the EAT, on appeal, agreed. Nothing in the ET1 spelled out, whether in layman's terms or by reference to the ingredients of the statutory provisions, that what was asserted was effectively a case of victimisation by dismissal by reason of the making of a protected disclosure. No reference was made to any particular disclosure, to whom disclosure was made or on what date disclosure was made.

See Chapter 4, 'Starting tribunal proceedings', for further guidance on the contents of claim forms.

8.14 Does the tribunal have a duty to suggest amendments?
Although it is the general practice of employment tribunals to give assistance to unrepresented claimants, there does not appear to be a duty on them to consider issues that have not been raised by the parties. In Gembah-Jah v Royal Lancaster Landmark Hotel Co Ltd EAT 536/99 the EAT stated that it was beyond the limits of the employment tribunal's responsibility to invite a claimant to pursue an unpleaded allegation.

On the other hand, in some circumstances a tribunal might be under a duty to inform a claimant that there is a need to amend his or her ET1 by way of adding a second respondent where it is clear that liability rests with that respondent. In Linbourne v Constable 1993 ICR 698, EAT, L named the manager of the hotel that had employed her as the respondent in a claim of unfair dismissal instead of proceeding against the hotel owners. The tribunal rejected the claim on the ground that L had brought her proceedings against the wrong party, although it found as a fact that the proper employer had dismissed unfairly, and refused to grant leave to amend the ET1 to substitute the correct employer. L appealed to the EAT, which overturned the tribunal's decision. It held that the failure of the tribunal at the conclusion of the hearing to tell the claimant's representative that a formal amendment was required in order to add the correct employer as respondent constituted a procedural irregularity in the original proceedings. There was no injustice in allowing the amendment given that the proper employer must have known that it had employed the claimant and the merits of the case had been investigated thoroughly.

In Ladbrokes Racing Ltd v Traynor EATS 0067/06 the EAT set out guidance **8.15**
for tribunals as to how to proceed where it appears that a claimant is pursuing
a line of cross-examination that is manifestly not foreshadowed in the ET1. In
that case, the claimant claimed that the decision to dismiss him was unreasonable,
but did not set out any case to the effect that there had been procedural
unfairness in the respondent's investigatory or dismissal procedures. During
cross-examination of the respondent's first witness, it became evident that the
claimant's representative was seeking to raise as an issue the fairness or
otherwise of the respondent's investigatory and disciplinary proceedings. The
respondent's representative objected. When the case reached the EAT, the EAT
observed that where a claimant is pursuing a line of cross-examination that
would be difficult to justify in the absence of an amendment to his or her ET1,
there is no difficulty with the tribunal enquiring of the claimant or his or her
representative whether he or she seeks to amend the ET1 in the light of the line
of evidence which he or she appears to be seeking to explore. If the claimant
does then wish to amend, the tribunal must enquire as to the precise terms of
that amendment, otherwise it cannot begin to consider the principles that apply
when considering an application to amend. It may be advisable – perhaps even
necessary – to allow the claimant a short adjournment to formulate the wording
of the proposed amendment. Only then can the respondent be expected to be
able to respond to it. Once the wording is known, the tribunal should allow
both parties to address it in respect of the application to amend before
considering its response. The tribunal may then retire to consider its decision,
for which it must give reasons.

Note that the EAT in the Ladbrokes Racing case envisaged that the claimant
supply precise terms of the amendment. To the extent that there is a duty upon
the tribunal to inform a party that the way in which his or her case is presented
would require an amendment, this does not extend to drafting the amendment
on his or her behalf. The dangers of such an approach are well exemplified in
Margarot Forrest Care Management v Kennedy EATS 0023/10, discussed
under 'General procedure – need to consider precise wording' above.

Amending the claim
8.16

Seeking to make minor amendments – such as a change in a party's address for
service – does not usually cause problems in employment tribunal proceedings
– see the discussion on 'Small mistakes' under 'Nature of proposed amendment'
below. But what happens if more substantial amendments are required?

In Chapman and ors v Goonvean and Rostowrack China Clay Co Ltd 1973
ICR 50, NIRC, Sir John Donaldson stressed that, in making use of their
discretionary power to amend, tribunals should seek to do justice between the
parties having regard to the circumstances of the case. Then, in Cocking v
Sandhurst (Stationers) Ltd and anor 1974 ICR 650, NIRC, he laid down a

441

general procedure for tribunals to follow when deciding whether to allow amendments to claim forms involving changing the basis of the claim or adding or substituting respondents. The key principle was that in exercising their discretion, tribunals must have regard to all the circumstances, in particular any injustice or hardship which would result from the amendment or a refusal to make it.

8.17 This test was approved in subsequent cases and was restated by the EAT in Selkent Bus Co Ltd v Moore 1996 ICR 836, EAT (whose approach was itself endorsed by the Court of Appeal in Ali v Office of National Statistics 2005 IRLR 201, CA). As we now discuss, it is foundational to the tribunal's discretion to amend.

8.18 Balance of hardship and injustice
In determining whether to grant an application to amend, an employment tribunal must always carry out a careful balancing exercise of all the relevant factors, having regard to the interests of justice and to the relative hardship that would be caused to the parties by granting or refusing the amendment – Selkent Bus Co Ltd v Moore (above). In Selkent, the then President of the EAT, Mr Justice Mummery, explained that relevant factors would include:

- *the nature of the amendment* – applications to amend range, on the one hand, from the correction of clerical and typing errors, the addition of factual details to existing allegations and the addition or substitution of other labels for facts already pleaded to, on the other hand, the making of entirely new factual allegations which change the basis of the existing claim. The tribunal has to decide whether the amendment sought is one of the minor matters or a substantial alteration pleading a new cause of action

- *the applicability of time limits* – if a new claim or cause of action is proposed to be added by way of amendment, it is essential for the tribunal to consider whether that claim/cause of action is out of time and, if so, whether the time limit should be extended

- *the timing and manner of the application* – an application should not be refused solely because there has been a delay in making it as amendments may be made at any stage of the proceedings. Delay in making the application is, however, a discretionary factor. It is relevant to consider why the application was not made earlier and why it is now being made: for example, the discovery of new facts or new information appearing from documents disclosed on discovery.

8.19 Each of the three factors outlined above are considered in more detail later below (under 'Nature of proposed amendment', 'Relevance of time limits' and 'Timing and manner of application for amendment'). Mummery P stressed that while he considered these factors to be 'certainly relevant' – a view endorsed by the

442

Presidential Guidance on 'General Case management' for England and Wales – this was not intended to be an exhaustive list. There may thus be additional factors to consider in any particular case – see 'Other relevant factors' below.

It is important to note that the balance of hardship and injustice test is a *balancing* exercise. Lady Smith noted in Trimble and anor v North Lanarkshire Council and anor EATS 0048/12 that it is inevitable that each party will point to there being a downside for them if the proposed amendment is allowed or not allowed. Thus, it will rarely be enough to look only at the downsides or 'prejudices' themselves. These need to be put in context, and that is why it is important to look at the whole surrounding circumstances. Moreover, it is important to ensure that amendments are not denied purely punitively or where no real prejudice will be done by their being granted – Sefton Metropolitan Borough Council and anor v Hincks and ors 2011 ICR 1357, EAT.

8.20 The EAT explained the nature of the balancing exercise required in Transport and General Workers' Union v Safeway Stores Ltd EAT 0092/07. In that case, a trade union brought claims on behalf of a large group of employees who had been made redundant for unfair and wrongful dismissal, breach of contract, and unlawful deduction from wages. Following a case management discussion, the union sought to amend the claim to add new claims of failure to comply with consultation requirements under S.188 of the Trade Union and Labour Relations (Consolidation) Act 1992 and Reg 10 of the Transfer of Undertakings (Protection of Employment) Regulations 1981 SI 1981/1794 (since repealed and replaced by SI 2006/246). The primary time limits for bringing these claims had expired. An employment judge found that the application to amend the claim amounted to 'a substantial alteration, pleading a new cause of action. It is more than an addition or substitution of another label for facts already pleaded'; and, on that basis, she concluded that the application must be dismissed.

In the EAT, however, Mr Justice Underhill (as he then was) considered that the employment judge's reasoning was deficient, in that there was no attempt to apply the Cocking test, and, specifically, no review of all the circumstances including the relative balance of injustice. Deciding the matter for himself, Underhill J took the view that the proposed amendment should be allowed, on the basis that there would be a greater injustice to the union – or, more accurately, to the employees in respect of whom it was recognised – if the amendment was refused, than there would be to the respondent if it was allowed. Although the claim for breach of the statutory consultation obligations was unquestionably a new claim, it was very closely related to the claim originally pleaded. Both claims depended centrally on the allegation of defective consultation, and almost all the facts material to the new claim would already have been in play in the old. Whether or not it was right to describe the new claim as a 'mere relabelling' was not decisive: the important point was that it depended on facts which were, substantially, already alleged. Underhill J also

443

considered it relevant that a claim by the union for breach of the statutory consultation obligations would reasonably have been anticipated by the respondent as the natural concomitant of any individual claims for unfair dismissal based on deficiencies in consultation. For the employees to be deprived of their claim through a lawyers' omission would seem peculiarly unjust. Even if any such employees might have a good claim in negligence, this was no reason for not taking the more straightforward course of permitting the amendment if it would otherwise be fair to do so. Finally, Underhill J noted that the application was made reasonably promptly, the respondent being put on notice of the intended claims within two or three months of the presentation of the ET1. The respondent could not in such circumstances point to any particular prejudice caused to it by the late amendment, over and above the inherent prejudice of being exposed to a claim which could not otherwise have been brought.

8.21 The respondent in the Safeway case sought to argue that the balance of hardship between the parties was essentially even because the hardship to the union of not being able to pursue its claim was evened out by the hardship to the respondent of being exposed to a claim to which it would otherwise have had a limitation defence. Underhill J pointed out that the problem with such an argument based solely on the potential value of the claim was that it would apply in every case of an amendment to introduce a new claim out of time, rendering the Cocking test 'largely empty'. In such cases it is therefore necessary to bring other factors into the equation, as Underhill J himself did in the Safeway case.

Two further examples in which the EAT overturned a refusal to allow an amendment, on the basis that the tribunal had failed properly to balance the prejudice between the parties:

- **Blackburn v Aldi Stores Ltd** 2013 ICR D37, EAT: B was employed by AS Ltd. He brought a grievance, which was partly upheld by H, the regional managing director. AS Ltd had a written grievance procedure, which provided that an employee wishing to appeal must notify the next level of management. B appealed against the decision in a letter to H, copying it to the group managing director. However, H dealt with the appeal himself during a brief meeting. The appeal was rejected and, a few days later, B resigned. He brought a claim of unfair constructive dismissal in the employment tribunal, relying on a breach of the implied term of trust and confidence in that he was effectively denied an appeal. At the tribunal hearing, B sought to amend his claim, having realised that the company's grievance procedure was, or at least could be, an express term of his contract of employment, and that AS Ltd's failure to follow it was a breach of an express contractual term. The tribunal refused B permission to amend, and went on to hold that there was no constructive dismissal. On appeal, however, the EAT held that the tribunal's reasons for refusing the amendment were flawed. Although the tribunal had referred to

444

the balance of prejudice, it had not properly applied it. It stated that AS Ltd was prejudiced 'in that the claim has been made at the last stage' but, as the EAT pointed out, lateness in making a claim is not necessarily prejudicial; it depends on whether there is any difficulty in meeting the claim and what it is, and the tribunal had said nothing on this subject. Even more important, in the EAT's view, was the tribunal's implication that B was not prejudiced because the tribunal would consider his allegation that he had been denied an appeal as part of the constructive dismissal claim. However, at the time at which it heard the application to amend the tribunal had not decided that it would consider this allegation as part of the constructive dismissal claim, and nor had it eventually gone on to do so

• **Thomas v Samurai Incentives and Promotions Ltd** EAT 0006/13: in her ET1 T, a litigant in person, ticked the boxes to indicate that she was bringing a money claim, but she did not tick to indicate that she was bringing a discrimination claim. In her particulars of complaint she referred to her request for an eye test voucher and childcare vouchers being ignored, stating that her employers had said, 'We made a mistake employing women at Samurai as it is too much hassle when they get pregnant,' and that on this basis she felt she had been discriminated against because she was a woman. Subsequently T obtained representation and her representative informed the tribunal that the claim included not only commission payments but also a claim that T was subjected to sex discrimination. She provided further particulars of the sex discrimination complaint. At a pre-hearing review an employment judge refused permission to amend the claim form to reflect the discrimination claim, considering that it was raising a new cause of action unconnected to the original claim. On appeal, the EAT considered that what was conspicuous by its absence from the judge's reasons was 'the critical exercise of looking at all the relevant circumstances and balancing the injustice and hardship of allowing the amendment against the injustice and hardship of refusing it'. The EAT was unable to infer that the judge had carried out that exercise, and referred the amendment issue to a different employment judge for determination.

8.22 Another case in which it was held to be 'unjust' to allow an amendment is Yendall v Commonwealth of Australia EAT 515/83. In that case the respondent state had agreed to waive state immunity in respect of Y's ET1, which detailed a claim of unfair dismissal. At the hearing, Y sought to amend her ET1 to add a claim of race discrimination. The EAT upheld the tribunal's decision that it would be unjust to allow the amendment. If the race discrimination claim had been raised at the outset, the respondent would not have waived its immunity.

Nature of proposed amendment
8.23 In the context of the discretion whether to allow a proposed amendment, the first key factor identified by Mummery P in Selkent Bus Company Ltd v Moore

445

1996 ICR 836, EAT, was the nature of the proposed amendment. He made it clear that this should be considered first, before any time limitation issues are brought into the equation, as it is only necessary to consider the question of time limits where the proposed amendment in effect seeks to adduce a new complaint, as distinct from 'relabelling' the existing claim (see 'Relevance of time limits' below). If it is a purely relabelling exercise then it does not matter whether the amendment is brought within the timeframe for that particular claim or not – Foxtons Ltd v Ruwiel EAT 0056/08.

Nevertheless, it is vital to appreciate that whichever 'type' of amendment is proposed, the core test is the same: the tribunal must review all of the circumstances, including the relative balance of injustice, in deciding whether or not to allow the amendment (i.e. the Cocking test, as restated in Selkent) – see Mr Justice Underhill's comments in Transport and General Workers' Union v Safeway Stores Ltd EAT 0092/07, as discussed under 'Balance of hardship and injustice' above. Tribunals conducting such a balancing exercise must therefore consider each case in its entirety.

8.24 In Selkent, Mummery P observed that 'applications to amend are of many different kinds, ranging, on the one hand, from the correction of clerical and typing errors, the addition of factual details to existing allegations and the addition or substitution of other labels for facts already pleaded to, on the other hand, the making of entirely new factual allegations which change the basis of the existing claim. The tribunal [has] to decide whether the amendment sought is one of the minor matters or is a substantial alteration pleading a new cause of action.'

8.25 **Small mistakes.** An example of an application to amend that fell at the former end of the spectrum was Beddoes and ors v Birmingham City Council and other cases EAT 0037/10, a group equal pay claim in which a number of claimants' claim forms had misdescribed the jobs that they were doing. For example, a large number of senior lunchtime supervisors had been described as 'lunchtime supervisors' (LTS), and nine care assistants had described themselves as 'health care assistants'. The claimants sought permission to amend their claim forms to correct the errors in question following an application by the employer to have their claims struck out. The employment tribunal granted permission to amend in all bar one of the LTS cases, but struck out the remaining claims, having refused the claimants permission to amend. The employer appealed and the claimants whose claims had been struck out also appealed.

The EAT observed that in the context of mass litigation it is inevitable that mistakes will occur in relation to job titles, particularly where there are so many titles and the distinctions between them are fine. It expressed the view that a tribunal should be very ready to allow the correction of such mistakes, subject to the question of any prejudice to the respondent or any specific jurisdictional points. An individual who by reason of such an error is prevented from pursuing her claim in circumstances where her colleagues' claims are proceeding will feel an acute and legitimate sense of injustice, whereas for the employer the fact that one claim out of thousands may or may not proceed is a matter of marginal significance. In the EAT's view, it made no real difference whether the effect of the amendment was to substitute a new cause of action; nor was it significant how the mistake arose; nor (unless there had been an abuse of process) whether it should have been picked up earlier.

Turning to the LTS cases, the EAT considered that the tribunal had allowed the **8.26** amendments because they did not seriously change the substance of the case and therefore would not cause the employer any real difficulty. In the EAT's view, the tribunal had clearly reached the right decision, despite various deficiencies in its reasoning. It therefore rejected the employer's appeal. The tribunal's decision to strike out one LTS claim was in all probability simply an error. If not, it was perverse on the basis that like cases must be treated alike. Either way, that decision had to be reversed. Moving on to the remaining cases where permission to amend had been refused, the tribunal had not identified any specific prejudice that would be caused by allowing the claimants to correct the errors in their claim forms and which justified treating them differently from the LTS claimants. Therefore, the difference in treatment had to be regarded as irrational. The EAT accordingly allowed the claimants' separate appeal.

New causes of action. The observations of Mummery P in the Selkent case **8.27** regarding the significance of the nature of the proposed amendment (see above) might be understood as an indication that the fact that an application introduces 'a new cause of action' would, of itself, weigh heavily against amendment. However, as the Court of Appeal in Abercrombie and ors v Aga Rangemaster Ltd 2013 IRLR 953, CA, stressed, it is clear from the relevant passage of Mummery P's judgment as a whole that he was not advocating so formalistic an approach. According to the Court, Mummery P's reference in Selkent to the 'substitution of other labels for facts already pleaded' is as an example of the kind of case where – other things being equal – amendment should readily be permitted, by contrast with 'the making of entirely new factual allegations which change the basis of the existing claim'.

Following the approach indicated by Abercrombie, tribunals should, when considering applications to amend that arguably raise new causes of action, focus 'not on questions of formal classification but on the extent to which the new pleading is likely to involve substantially different areas of enquiry than the old: *the greater the difference between the factual and legal issues raised by the new claim and by the old, the less likely it is that it will be permitted*' (our stress). Although many of the cases discussed below were concerned with whether or not particular circumstances did or did not amount to 'relabelling' – often because that question may determine whether or not time limits are a relevant consideration – it is important not to lose sight of the fact that tribunals

447

always retain a discretion in the matter of whether or not to grant leave to amend. Just because an amendment would require the other party and the tribunal to undertake new and substantially different lines of enquiry does not mean that the amendment should necessarily be refused, but it will clearly weigh in the balance against it, and may be conclusive depending on the other factors involved.

8.28 This was made evident in Cooper v Chief Constable of West Yorkshire Police and anor EAT 0035/06, where a claimant sought to amend her claim immediately before the start of the hearing to add a claim that the police force was vicariously liable for the acts of the Council for which the claimant worked, on the basis that the Council was the agent for the police force. The EAT upheld the employment tribunal's decision to refuse permission to amend on the basis that the application involved a substantial alteration in her case involving factual allegations not made clear in either the claim or her witness statement; the application was made at the last possible moment and no reason was given why it should not have been made earlier; the proposed amendment did not appear to further the overriding objective in determining the case between the parties; and the tribunal found the basis of the new claim difficult to conceive. The EAT noted that the claimant had decided only at the last moment to seek to amend in order to put the case against the police force on an entirely different basis.

Similarly, in Olayemi v Athena Medical Centre and ors EAT 0613/10 the EAT held that an employment judge had come to a conclusion well within the scope of his discretion in refusing to allow a (late) application to enlarge a claim of sex discrimination and unfair dismissal by adding a claim of automatically unfair dismissal by reason of making protected disclosures. The employment judge had considered to be relevant the lateness of the application in terms of the time that had passed since the claimant was dismissed and in the context of the proceedings; the impact on the scope of evidence that would arise by allowing the amendment; the fact that the cap on compensation would not be relevant, given the other claims before the tribunal; and that the prospects of the claimant succeeding with the amended claim did not appear good. On appeal to the EAT, the claimant criticised the employment judge's conclusion that the scope of evidence, in particular that pertaining to contentions around the 'protected' status of nearly 30 separate e-mails, would be considerably widened by the amendment. She argued that the materials essential to the protected disclosure claim were already substantively referred to in the materials before the tribunal. However, the EAT was satisfied that the judge was entitled to take into account the fact that there would be scope for argument as to whether what had occurred was a protected or qualifying disclosure and whether it had been made to the appropriate body to engage the statutory provisions. The EAT contrasted the situation in Olayemi with that in New Star Asset Management Holdings Ltd v Evershed 2010 EWCA Civ 870, CA (below), observing that whereas in the Evershed case the necessary additional material constituted one e-mail in relation to which there was no dispute as to whether it was sent or received, in Olayemi there were some 24 to 30 documents, not all of them sent to the respondent, and in relation to which there was a dispute about their receipt. Moreover, Evershed was a case in which the unfair dismissal claim itself raised the question of the state of mind of the employee, whereas no such consideration or concern arose in the underlying complaint made by the claimant in Olayemi.

In New Star Asset Management Holdings Ltd v Evershed (above) the Court of **8.29** Appeal upheld the decision of the EAT that a tribunal had erred in refusing to accede to a claimant's application to amend his original claim form, even though the amendment added a new cause of action. E sent an e-mail to the company's HR department, making a formal complaint of bullying against two senior members of staff. He was sent home and told not to return until further notice. He resigned and brought an unfair constructive dismissal claim, and later sought to amend it to introduce a whistleblowing claim. The judge dismissed E's application on the following grounds: the amendment raised a new cause of action which required wholly different evidence to that envisaged in the claim as pleaded; there was no causal link in the ET1 between the claim as pleaded and the new claim; E had failed to raise a prior grievance as then required by S.32 of the Employment Act 2002 in respect of the new claim; the amendment would prejudice the respondent; E had failed to give further reasons for his failure to include the new claim in his original ET1; if the amendment were refused, E still had an unfair constructive dismissal claim; and the time limit for making the protected disclosure claim had expired.

E appealed to the EAT, which overturned the judge's refusal and allowed the amendment, whereupon the respondent appealed to the Court of Appeal. Dismissing the appeal, the Court accepted that the employment judge's failure to articulate even briefly the basis for his conclusion that the new claim would require 'wholly different evidence' made it a difficult case to determine. However, a comparison of the allegations in the amendment showed that it raised no materially new factual allegations. Although not identical, the thrust of the complaints in both the original pleading and the amendment was essentially the same. The whistleblowing case made by the amendment would require the investigation of the various component ingredients of the case, but it would not require the adducing of 'wholly different evidence'. The Court therefore dismissed the respondent's appeal.

Relabelling the claim. Any mislabelling of the relief sought is not usually fatal **8.30** to a claim. Seeking to change the nature of the claim might sound like a drastic step, but where the effect of a proposed amendment is simply to put a different legal label on facts that are already pleaded, permission will normally be granted. For example, where a claimant in his or her ET1 claims a redundancy payment, he or she might, in reality, be attempting to claim that he or she was

449

unfairly dismissed. Provided the ET1 discloses facts from which such a claim can be discerned, tribunals tend to adopt a flexible approach and grant amendments that only change the nature of the relief sought.

The case of Abercrombie and ors v Aga Rangemaster Ltd 2013 IRLR 953, CA, is a classic example of 'mere relabelling', in the Court of Appeal's own assessment. The claimants sought to enforce their right under S.28 of the Employment Rights Act 1996 to receive guarantee payments (the entitlement to which is discussed in IDS Employment Law Handbook, 'Wages' (2011), Chapter 6, 'Guarantee payments', under 'Amount and entitlement'). Initially, they brought their complaint as a deductions from wages claim under S.23 ERA, but subsequently sought to amend the claim so as to base it on S.34, which allows complaints to be made to an employment tribunal that the employer has failed to pay the whole or part of a guarantee payment. The employment judge considered that the effect of the amendment, if admitted, would be to raise a new cause of action, but the Court of Appeal considered this 'very doubtful'. On either basis, the claim was a claim to enforce the right to a guarantee payment created by S.28. The conditions of liability were identical, and the only difference was in the statutory gateway chosen. Thus, not only the facts but the legal basis of the claim were identical. In the Court's view, this factor should have weighed very heavily in favour of permission to amend being granted. Only if there was a weighty reason – such as that the amendment would for some reason cause unfair prejudice to the other party – would the Court expect permission to amend to be refused in such circumstances.

8.31 More examples of cases which have been held to be instances of relabelling facts that had already been pleaded:

- **Golding v Southfields Community College** EAT 0395/06: the only complaint explicitly made in G's claim form was of unfair dismissal. However, in the form she explained that she had been asked by the head teacher of the school at which she worked to 'massage the figures' for pupil absences and that after she had made her objections to this known she had been bullied and intimidated. She was eventually dismissed, ostensibly for ill-health reasons. G subsequently applied for leave to amend her claim to include a claim of automatically unfair dismissal for making a protected disclosure. However, the tribunal refused leave on the basis that it was a substantive amendment to the original claim in respect of which time limits would have to be applied. G successfully appealed to the EAT. In its view, the claim form identified the essential basis of a claim that G had suffered dismissal by reason of a protected disclosure. Applying the principles established in Selkent Bus Company Ltd v Moore (above), it concluded that the application to amend merely involved the addition of factual details and another label for facts already pleaded. It did not, in the EAT's opinion, involve entirely new factual allegations changing the basis of the existing claim

- **Childs v Pegasus Engineers Ltd t/a Acorn Garage and MOT Centre** EAT 57/02: PE Ltd dismissed C for gross misconduct following allegations that he had maliciously made a complaint to the Vehicle Inspectorate that PE Ltd had been involved in illegal conduct. C brought a breach of contract claim. At the time he also wished to pursue an unfair dismissal claim but was informed that he needed 12 months' continuous service in order to do so. He was subsequently told that, as he was complaining that his employer had dismissed him for making a protected disclosure, he could bring a claim for automatically unfair dismissal for making a protected disclosure, to which the service requirement did not apply. C then sought to amend his ET1 to add the unfair dismissal claim. The tribunal dismissed the application but on appeal the EAT held that it had erred in not allowing the amendment. The facts that were the subject matter of the proposed amendment were the same as those that formed the subject matter of the initial ET1. This showed, if not explicitly then certainly implicitly, that C had been dismissed for making a complaint to the Vehicle Inspectorate

- **Street v Derbyshire Unemployed Workers' Centre** 2004 ICR 213, EAT (appealed to the Court of Appeal, but on separate grounds, at 2005 ICR 97, CA): S brought a claim under S.103A ERA, alleging that she had been unfairly dismissed as a result of having made a protected disclosure. On the first day of the tribunal hearing, S sought to amend her ET1 by adding a claim for 'ordinary' unfair dismissal under S.94 ERA. The tribunal ruled that the 'ordinary' unfair dismissal complaint constituted a new claim. As such, it had been made outside the relevant time limit and the tribunal ruled that no extension of time would be granted in respect of it. However, on appeal, the EAT reversed this decision. The tribunal had failed to realise that, within the ET1, there was the basis of a claim for 'ordinary' unfair dismissal that simply needed particularisation. The case was remitted for the tribunal to reconsider, applying the Selkent principles (see 'Amending the claim' above), whether the amendment should be granted

- **Barwick v Avon and Somerset Constabulary** EAT 0009/09: B, who was a police officer, brought a claim of unfair constructive dismissal, stating in his ET1: 'Since joining the service in 2001 the claimant has been a victim of several very serious incidents of racially motivated discrimination, harassment and bullying and now feels that he has no option other than to resign.' His claim was resisted on the ground that S.200 ERA prevents police officers from making claims for unfair dismissal, including constructive dismissal. However, a police officer could raise a claim for constructive dismissal in the context of a discrimination claim, so B applied to amend his claim to add a claim of discrimination on the ground of race. The employment judge concluded: 'I do not consider it is in the interests of justice to allow an entirely new cause of action to be incorporated into [the] existing claims' and struck out the claim entirely. On appeal, however, the EAT observed that

451

it was clear from the ET1 that B was saying that his constructive dismissal was a result of his having been a victim of incidents of racially motivated discrimination, harassment and bullying. On this basis, the amendment sought was essentially no more than relabelling.

8.32 The cases above illustrate the fine line between, on the one hand, raising a claim that is linked to the existing claim and, on the other, raising a new claim for the first time. They can be contrasted with the decision in Selkent Bus Co Ltd v Moore 1996 ICR 836, EAT, in which the claimant sought to introduce an automatically unfair dismissal claim (on the specific ground of his trade union activity) in addition to the 'ordinary' unfair dismissal claim pleaded in the ET1. The EAT refused the amendment, saying that the facts as originally pleaded could not, in themselves, support the new claim (and there would be a risk of hardship to the employer by way of increased costs if the claimant was allowed to proceed with his new claim). A distinguishing feature between Selkent and Street v Derbyshire Unemployed Workers' Centre (above), is that the EAT in Selkent thought that granting the proposed amendment would render it necessary to have new facts not previously pleaded put in evidence, and it was unfair to allow that to be done at the stage that had then been reached. This indicates that it may generally be easier to add an 'ordinary' unfair dismissal claim where a specific ground for the dismissal has already been asserted, as opposed to the reverse situation where the specific ground is sought to be added to the more general claim.

Clearly, however, it will not always be 'just' to allow an amendment, even where no new facts are alleged. As the EAT made clear in Selkent, the tribunal must always balance the injustice and hardship of allowing the amendment against the injustice and hardship of refusing it. In Lawson v Thomson EAT 324/93 the EAT upheld a tribunal's refusal to allow an amendment because the tribunal had properly considered the question of relative prejudice. What had particularly weighed with it was the claimant's failure to provide in advance of the hearing a clear statement of the terms of the proposed amendment despite several attempts to elicit this information by the tribunal office. As a result, witnesses whom the employer might have wished to call had dispersed. Therefore, the prejudice caused to the claimant in refusing the amendment was more than outweighed by the potential prejudice to the employer had the amendment been allowed.

8.33 It may be more difficult to ascertain whether a proposed amendment amounts to relabelling where the amendment seeks to introduce what appears to be an entirely new ground of complaint. In Housing Corporation v Bryant 1999 ICR 123, CA, the Court of Appeal addressed this question in a context where the claimant claimed unfair dismissal and sex discrimination but the latter claim was dismissed as it was out of time and the tribunal did not think it appropriate to extend time. The claimant then sought to amend her ET1 to include a complaint of victimisation. The employment tribunal refused, and the Court of Appeal subsequently upheld its decision. The Court ruled that, in order for the claimant to be able to allege that this was a mere relabelling exercise, it had to be shown that there was a proper factual substratum for the claim now being made. That in turn required there to be a causative link between the making of the allegation of sex discrimination and the dismissal. If there was no such causative link, this would be fatal to the issue of whether the ET1 made a claim in respect of victimisation. On this matter, Lord Justice Buxton remarked: 'It is not enough to say that the document reveals some grounds for a claim of victimisation, or indicates that there is a question to be asked as to the linkage between the alleged sex discrimination and the dismissal. That linkage must be demonstrated, at least in some way, in the document itself.' In the circumstances of the particular case, the claimant had not alleged in her initial ET1 that she had been dismissed for alleging sex discrimination, and so the proposed amendment did not merely constitute a relabelling.

The EAT followed this decision in Foxtons Ltd v Ruwiel EAT 0056/08. There, an employment judge allowed the amendment of an unfair dismissal claim to permit the addition of a sex discrimination claim. However, on appeal the EAT overturned this decision, remitting the matter to a fresh tribunal to reconsider. Mr Justice Elias, then President of the EAT, noted that, following Housing Corporation v Bryant, 'it is not enough even to make certain observations in the claim form which might indicate that certain forms of discrimination have taken place; in order for the exercise to be truly a relabelling one, the claim form must demonstrate the causal link between the unlawful act and the alleged reason for it'. In the case before him, the ET1 would have to identify not merely that there had been some discrimination but that the dismissal was by reason of sex discrimination. On the facts of the case, this could not be established. There was a one-sentence assertion of sex discrimination in a letter written by the claimants' lawyers to her employer before the claim form was filed, but neither that allegation nor any of the relevant facts necessary to sustain it were raised in the ET1 at all. The employment judge had therefore erred in failing to identify any information in the ET1 that established a causal link between the dismissal and the alleged reason of sex.

Relevance of time limits   8.34
The second factor identified by Mummery P in Selkent Bus Co Ltd v Moore 1996 ICR 836, EAT, as being relevant to the discretion whether or not to allow an amendment is that, if a new complaint is sought to be added, it is essential for the tribunal to consider whether that complaint is out of time and, if so, whether the time limit should be extended under the applicable statutory provisions. According to the Presidential Guidance on 'General Case Management' for England and Wales, an application for leave to amend when there is a time issue should be dealt with at a preliminary hearing as a

453

preliminary issue, allowing all parties to attend, to make representations and possibly even to give evidence.

The first point to note here is that this factor only applies where the proposed amendment raises what effectively is a brand new cause of action (whether or not it arises out of the same facts as the original claim) – see 'Nature of the proposed amendment' above for a discussion of how the proposed amendment may be categorised for these purposes. Where the amendment is simply changing the basis of, or 'relabelling', the existing claim, it raises no question of time limitation. For example:

- **London Borough of Hammersmith and Fulham v Jesuthasan** 1998 ICR 640, CA: J, who had been dismissed from Wormwood Scrubs Prison, brought a race discrimination claim. He did not initially claim unfair dismissal or a redundancy payment because, since he had only worked eight hours a week, the provisions of the Employment Protection (Consolidation) Act 1978 (which preceded the ERA) prevented him from doing so. However, some months after he had presented his claim, the House of Lords, in R v Secretary of State for Employment ex parte Equal Opportunities Commission and anor 1994 ICR 317, HL, held that the qualifying threshold for claiming unfair dismissal and a redundancy payment was indirectly discriminatory and thus unlawful. Shortly afterwards, J sought to add the unfair dismissal and redundancy claims to his ET1. The Court of Appeal upheld the tribunal's decision to allow him to do so. The proposed amendments did not allege any new facts, but simply attached new labels to facts pleaded in the ET1 that had been made by J within three months of his dismissal

- **Enterprise Liverpool Ltd v Jonas and ors** EAT 0112/09: EL Ltd completed 'relevant transfers' to three different companies under the Transfer of Undertakings (Protection of Employment) Regulations 2006 SI 2006/246 (TUPE). Groups of transferred employees lodged claims that EL Ltd had failed to observe its information and consultation obligations under Regs 13 and 14 of TUPE in respect of those transfers. The claimants were all members of Unite, the GMB or UCATT. When solicitors were instructed to act for the claimants after the claims had been presented, the solicitors realised that, as the unions were recognised by EL Ltd, Reg 15(1)(c) meant that the claims could only be brought by the unions. The solicitors accordingly applied to the tribunal for permission to change the names on the claim forms from the individual claimants to the relevant unions, which the tribunal granted. On appeal, EL Ltd submitted that the alteration amounted to substituting a wholly new claim not connected to the original claim at all, and that since the new claim would be out of time it should not have been admitted by way of amendment. The EAT dismissed the appeal, considering that the amendment did not amount to admitting a new claim out of time. Rather, it was simply altering the basis of an existing claim without raising a new head of complaint. Such an amendment was not affected by time limit considerations – the limitation provisions being intended to protect respondents from being faced with stale claims. Here, the original claim form was lodged in time, thus putting EL Ltd on notice of it. In the EAT's view, tribunals should take an 'overall view, following Selkent, when deciding whether to alter or add to that claim'. This was not the same as a brand new claim being launched out of time. The EAT went on to note that if it was wrong and the amendment was, in fact, substituting a new claim, it would nevertheless have upheld the tribunal's decision to allow the amendment having regard to the balance of injustice.

Where, in contrast to these cases, the claimant cannot show a causative link **8.35** between the grounds of complaint set out in the ET1 and the proposed amendment, the claimant will be regarded as raising an entirely new cause of action. In such circumstances, the tribunal must consider whether the new claim is in time, and, if it is out of time, whether time should be extended under whichever statutory test governs the time limits for the particular claim and the extension of those limits. The statutory tests for extending time limits are discussed in full in Chapter 5, 'Time limits'. Suffice it to say here that there are two different formulas, the application of which depends on the type of claim involved. They are:

- the 'just and equitable' formula, which applies to discrimination claims (see Chapter 5, 'Time limits', under '"Just and equitable" extension')

- the 'not reasonably practicable' formula, which applies to most other claims, including unfair dismissal and redundancy claims (see Chapter 5, 'Time limits', under '"Not reasonably practicable" extension').

Tribunals have a far wider discretion to extend time under the 'just and equitable' test than under the 'not reasonably practicable' test.

Amendment considered as at date of application. Note that the question of **8.36** amendment must be considered in the light of the circumstances existing *at the date when the application to amend was made* – Selkent Bus Co Ltd v Moore (above). Thus, the question of whether a new cause of action contained in an application to amend would, if it were an independent claim, be time barred, falls to be determined by reference to the date when the application to amend is made, not by reference to the date at which the original claim form was presented.

In Newsquest (Herald and Times) Ltd v Keeping EATS 0051/09 the claimant made an equal pay claim in respect of the role she carried out from 1 September 2008. She sought to amend her claim to introduce a fresh equal pay claim in respect of an earlier period in which she was employed in a different role. An employment judge allowed the amendment, but the EAT allowed the respondent's appeal. The employment judge had erroneously concluded that no time limit issue arose, in that she had compared the date at which the original claim was made to the date at which the time bar would have expired in respect of the fresh claim, when she should have looked back from the date at which the application to amend was made.

(Somewhat confusingly, where a claimant is applying for leave to add or substitute a respondent, the application relates back to the date of the original application – Cocking v Sandhurst (Stationers) Ltd and anor 1974 ICR 650, NIRC: see 'Amending the parties' below.)

8.37 **Importance of considering test for extension of time limits.** Note that it is essential for tribunals to consider the question of whether time falls to be extended under the appropriate test. In Rawson v Doncaster NHS Primary Care Trust EAT 0022/08 an employment judge refused a claimant leave to amend her claim of unfair dismissal and whistleblowing to add a new cause of action of disability discrimination outside the primary three-month limitation period. However, the employment judge did not consider the question of a just and equitable extension. On appeal, the EAT held that this was a wrong approach. The effect of an amendment is to backdate the new claim to the date on which the original claim form is presented. Once the amendment is granted, the respondent is thereafter prevented from raising the limitation defence. That is why consideration of the extension of time point is essential when deciding whether or not to grant permission to amend.

As previously explained, the question of whether a new cause of action contained in an application to amend would, if it were an independent claim, be time barred, falls to be determined by reference to the date when the application to amend is made, not by reference to the date at which the original claim form was presented. In Newsquest (Herald and Times) Ltd v Keeping (above) the claimant made an equal pay claim in respect of the role she carried out from 1 September 2008. She sought to amend her claim to introduce a fresh equal pay claim in respect of an earlier period in which she was employed in a different role. An employment judge allowed the amendment, but the EAT overturned that ruling. The employment judge had erroneously concluded that no time limit issue arose, in that she had compared the date at which the original claim was made to the date at which the time bar would have expired in respect of the fresh claim, whereas she should have looked back from the date at which the application to amend was made.

8.38 **Out of time claims – tribunals always retain discretion to allow amendment.** If the claim is in time, or if the tribunal considers that time should be extended, the tribunal may then move on to consider any other factors relevant to the issue of whether to exercise its discretion to allow the amendment. But if the claim is out of time, and the tribunal considers that time should not be extended under the appropriate test, what then? Is this fatal to the amendment?

Mummery P's observation in Selkent Bus Co Ltd v Moore (above) that if a new complaint or cause of action is proposed to be added by way of amendment it is 'essential' for the tribunal to consider the matter of time limits might, if taken out of context, be read as implying that if the fresh claim is out of time, and time does not fall to be extended under the applicable legislative test, then the application must necessarily be refused. But, as Mr Justice Underhill observed in Transport and General Workers' Union v Safeway Stores Ltd EAT 0092/07, this is not what Mummery P meant. According to Underhill J, the reason why it is, in Mummery P's words, 'essential' that a tribunal consider whether the fresh claim in question is in time is simply that it is 'a factor – albeit an important and potentially decisive one – in the exercise of the discretion'. In other words, the fact that the relevant time limit for presenting the 'new' claim has expired will not prevent the tribunal exercising its discretion to allow the amendment, although it will be an important factor on the side of the scales against allowing it.

The case authorities fundamentally support this position, albeit not entirely **8.39** with one voice. In Home Office v Bose 1979 ICR 481, EAT, an employment tribunal allowed B to amend an ET1 complaining of race discrimination to include a complaint of unfair dismissal. The EAT upheld the tribunal's decision despite the fact that the time limit for presenting the unfair dismissal claim had expired. The facts stated in the ET1 were sufficient to ground either complaint, and the amendment would neither prejudice the respondent nor cause it any injustice. Nevertheless, the EAT stated that it was not seeking to lay down any general principle in upholding the tribunal's decision.

However, in two subsequent cases the Court of Appeal was prepared to be a little more robust in making it clear that just because time limits have expired does not mean that amendments to allow in new claims or causes of action should be rejected. In British Newspaper Printing Corporation (North) Ltd v Kelly and ors 1989 IRLR 222, CA – a case that preceded the EAT's judgment in Selkent – a group of employees brought proceedings that appeared to constitute claims for redundancy payments. More than three months after their effective date of termination, they sought to amend their ET1s to plead alternative claims for unfair dismissal. The tribunal refused permission on the basis that the time limit for bringing fresh unfair dismissal claims had passed. However, the tribunal's decision was overturned by the EAT and its decision was subsequently upheld by the Court of Appeal. That Court pointed out that Parliament had not laid down any rules imposing time limits in respect of amending applications already presented to a tribunal and stated that the proper test was that laid down in Cocking v Sandhurst (Stationers) Ltd (above), which required an assessment of the relative hardships that would be caused to the parties depending on whether the amendment was or was not allowed.

This approach was subsequently endorsed in Ali v Office of National Statistics **8.40** 2005 IRLR 201, CA. Although the circumstances of that case were different,

457

the Court of Appeal acknowledged that there will be circumstances in which, 'although a new claim is technically being brought, it is so closely related to the claim already the subject of the [claim form], that justice requires the amendment to be allowed, *even though it is technically out of time*' (our stress).

The approach adopted in the above cases – which was described by Underhill J in Transport and General Workers' Union v Safeway Stores Ltd EAT 0092/07 as 'the orthodox position on the authorities' – was also applied in Lehman Brothers Ltd v Smith EAT 0486/05, in which the claimant – a city trader – made a number of complaints including unlawful deduction of wages and/or breach of contract in respect of the non-payment of his bonus. Following service of the respondent's response, he applied to amend the claim by adding identical complaints in respect of a previous year's bonus. The employment judge exercised his discretion to allow an application to amend a claim on the basis that the balance of hardship came down in favour of granting the amendment. The employer maintained that the judge had been wrong to take this into account in light of the fact that the amended claim was out of time. On appeal, the EAT concluded that, while the question of whether an application seeking to amend to add a new claim is made out of time is an important factor, it is not determinative. In the instant case the tribunal had been correct to take into account the balance of hardship and justice as between the parties. Not only was this the correct approach on the authorities, it also reflected the contrast between the Tribunal Rules 2004 and the more tightly drawn provisions of the Civil Procedure Rules 1998 SI 1998/3132. In the EAT's view, had Parliament intended to limit the tribunal's power to allow the addition of claims to those which would not have been time barred if they had been contained in the original claim form, the Tribunal Rules would have been drafted accordingly.

8.41 Set against these authorities is the case of Harvey v Port of Tilbury (London) Ltd 1999 ICR 1030, EAT. There, after having commenced an unfair dismissal claim and received the respondent's ET3, the claimant applied to the tribunal for leave to amend his ET1 to include a complaint of disability discrimination. The tribunal refused the amendment and that decision was confirmed by the EAT on appeal. The amendment, in the EAT's view, represented the addition of a new cause of action, and as the new claim had been made out of time, the key question was whether it would be just and equitable to allow the amendment. Since it was not, the application to amend had to be refused. For the EAT, the fact that the claim was out of time was not simply an important factor in the exercise of the tribunal's discretion, but was an absolute bar to the claim being added by way of amendment. It acknowledged that this conclusion appeared to be inconsistent with the decision of the Court of Appeal in British Newspaper Printing Corporation (North) Ltd v Kelly (above), but sought to distinguish that case on the basis that the statutory provisions relating to time limits for bringing an unfair dismissal claim were different from those for a disability discrimination complaint. In the later case Transport and General Workers' Union v Safeway Stores Ltd EAT 0092/07, Mr Justice Underhill expressed doubt that this was a legitimate basis for the EAT to have distinguished the Court of Appeal's approach in Kelly.

On balance, the weight of authority suggests that the fact that, had the amendment incorporating a new claim been a free-standing claim, it would have been out of time is not an absolute bar to allowing it. This view is endorsed by the Presidential Guidance on 'General Case Management' for England and Wales, which states that 'the fact that the relevant time limit for presenting the new claim has expired will not exclude the discretion to allow the amendment'. However, this does not mean that consideration of time limits is not a significant factor for the tribunal to weigh in the balance when considering how to exercise its discretion. It may well be that the greater the difference between the factual and legal issues raised by the amended claim in comparison to the original, the less likely the out-of-time amendment will be permitted. Even so, as Underhill J stressed in Transport and General Workers' Union v Safeway (above), this will still be 'a discretionary consideration and not a rule of law', which means that there may well be other circumstances that swing the balance back the other way.

Some other examples of how tribunals have factored time limits into the **8.42** balancing exercise:

- **Chaudhary v Secretary of State for Health** EAT 0512/04: C applied to amend his race discrimination claim to add two further comparators. In refusing the application the employment tribunal took into account a number of factors, including that the addition of the comparators would have the effect of introducing a new claim; that the amendment had been proposed very late; that the new claim was well out of time; and that the employer would be considerably prejudiced by the amendment. The EAT upheld the tribunal's decision not to allow the amendment and endorsed its approach

- **UCATT v Amicus and ors** 2009 ICR 852: UCATT sought to amend its claim to introduce a complaint that Glasgow City Council had failed in its duty to provide information in the context of a transfer of undertaking under Reg 13(2) TUPE. The employment tribunal exercised its discretion to refuse the application. After referring to the Selkent guidance, it noted that the request to amend was made well after the expiry of the three-month time limit for lodging a claim for a breach of Reg 13 and that there was nothing that made it not reasonably practicable for the claim to have been presented so as to include an allegation of failure to inform within the three-month time limit for bringing such a complaint. UCATT appealed to the EAT, arguing that the tribunal had misunderstood the time limit issue and treated it as determinative when it was not. In rejecting this, the EAT observed

459

that UCATT had put forward no reason to the tribunal for its application to be granted other than the lack of prejudice to the respondent (a point that was accepted by the tribunal). However, simply because allowing the amendment caused no prejudice to the respondent did not mean that refusal of the amendment inevitably caused prejudice to UCATT. The EAT concluded that, in this case, the tribunal had considered all the relevant factors, one of which was that UCATT was seeking to introduce a new and distinct claim well after the expiry of the relevant time limit. That time limit, had it been a new claim, could only have been extended if it had not been reasonably practicable to present the claim within three months of the date of transfer. However, it was reasonably practicable for UCATT to have done so, just as the other claimants in the case had done. Having considered all the relevant factors and having regard to the guidance in Selkent, it could not be said that the tribunal had fallen into error

- **Newsquest (Herald and Times) Ltd v Keeping** EATS 0051/09: an employment judge granted a claimant's application to amend her claim to introduce a fresh equal pay claim. In overturning this on appeal, the EAT held that, had the employment judge realised there was a time limitation issue, she should have then considered the guidance as to the importance of having regard to the time limits where allowing an amendment would enable the claimant in effect to evade a statutory bar. In that case, she should then have considered whether the claimant had provided an explanation for the lateness and the merit of that explanation. In this instance, no explanation was provided at all in the written application to amend. The EAT concluded that if the matter had been approached correctly the employment judge would inevitably have refused the application to amend. The onus was on the claimant to satisfy her that it was appropriate to allow the amendment. Since the new equal pay claim being sought to be introduced by way of amendment was significantly out of time with no explanation having been given as to why it was late, that onus had not been discharged.

8.43 **Just and equitable test.** As observed above, tribunals have a far wider discretion to grant an extension of time under the 'just and equitable' test than under the 'not reasonably practicable' test. Broadly speaking, the just and equitable test requires a consideration of all the circumstances of the case, including anything which the tribunal 'judges to be relevant' – Hutchison v Westward Television Ltd 1977 IRLR 69, EAT. Interestingly, the Court of Appeal has held that this test is, effectively, identical to the Cocking test reiterated by Mummery P in Selkent Bus Co Ltd v Moore 1996 ICR 836, EAT, which requires the tribunal, in exercising its discretion whether or not to allow an amendment, to take account of all the circumstances in the balance of injustice and hardship. In Ali v Office of National Statistics 2005 IRLR 201, CA, the Court of Appeal considered the appropriate test for allowing a claimant leave to amend his ET1 to advance a claim of indirect discrimination on the ground of race. It concluded that it was impossible to think that the result would be different if the 'just and equitable' test were adopted as opposed to the 'balance of injustice and hardship' test; and that it was difficult to conceive of circumstances where it would lead to a different result.

On this basis, the respondent in Mouteng v Select Services Partner Ltd EAT 0059/08 sought to argue that in a case where the 'just and equitable' test applies, it is unnecessary to apply both this test and the balance of injustice test. In Mouteng, the claimant sought to adduce significant changes to her unfair dismissal claim, effectively adding several claims of race and sex discrimination. An employment judge required her to file a fresh ET1, noting that all the arguments as to whether the amendment should be permitted would be heard by the tribunal when it considered whether it was just and equitable to extend time for lodging the fresh claim. The claimant appealed, and the EAT considered whether it made any practical difference for her discrimination claims to be considered in the context of an application to amend or on the basis that there was a fresh claim for which time would have to be extended. The respondent argued that in practice there was no reason at all why the just and equitable test could not, in the context of an amendment, achieve precisely the same result as the balance of injustice and hardship test (although it accepted that there might be circumstances where the balance of injustice and hardship might lead to a different result to the 'reasonably practicable' test applicable to claims of unfair dismissal, etc).

8.44 The EAT, however, considered that the employment judge was wrong to remove the case from the amendment context and place it under the rubric of extension of time. It might make no practical difference whichever test was adopted, as the ruling in Ali v Office of National Statistics (above) showed, but if, following Transport and General Workers' Union v Safeway Stores Ltd EAT 0092/07, out-of-time amendment applications must be treated as falling under the amendment rubric where the reasonably practicable formula is in issue, then it must in principle be the same where the just and equitable principle is the appropriate formula for extending time. As the Safeway case demonstrated, the relevant test changes in the context of an amendment: the tribunal always has a discretion to allow an amendment to permit a claim to be made out of time (including any legitimate extension). Treating the issue as one of amendment would be more likely to assist the tribunal to appreciate the potential range of relevant factors.

The EAT's conclusion in Mouteng is supported by that in Rawson v Doncaster NHS Primary Care Trust EAT 0022/08 (above), where the EAT observed that 'if it would be just and equitable to extend time that would be a strong, although... not necessarily determinative, factor in favour of granting permission. If it is not just and equitable to extend time that would be a powerful, but again not determinative factor, against'; and Chief Constable

461

of Essex Police v Kovacevic EAT 0126/13, in which the EAT found that an employment judge had erred in simply considering whether it would be just and equitable to extend time to allow a claim of race discrimination to be made out of time, without applying any further test. The judge was not simply dealing with a matter that was out of time but was dealing with an application to introduce into proceedings already under way a new cause of action by way of amendment. In such circumstances, it would be expected that he refer to the Selkent test and identify in his reasons those aspects going to injustice and prejudice if the application was allowed, and those going to injustice and prejudice if the application was not allowed.

8.45 A similar approach was adopted in Charles v Kuehne and Nagel Ltd EAT 0363/12. In that case, the President of the EAT, Mr Justice Langstaff, commented that while, in cases to which the 'just and equitable' test applies, the approach is likely to be very similar in determining whether to grant an amendment as it is to permit a claim to be raised out of time, 'it must always be remembered that the situation is not identical, the discretion is a wide one and there are no particular time limits that apply to the exercise of the discretion itself'.

8.46 **Equal pay claims.** It has been argued that different principles should apply to the amendment of equal pay claims on the basis that a strict six-month time limit applies to bringing such claims, with no provision for extension either on a just and equitable basis or because it was not reasonably practicable to bring the claims within the limit. In Walsall Metropolitan Borough Council and anor v Birch and ors EAT 0376/10 a group of 103 claimants brought a claim of arrears of equal pay against their former employer, the transferor in a TUPE transfer. Nearly a year later, they applied to amend their claim to join the TUPE transferee, but only after the expiry of the relevant time limit for the claim. The employment judge allowed the application, which had the effect of saving the claim as the transferee was the proper respondent for the claim. The respondents appealed, arguing that it was highly relevant that equal pay claims are subject to immutable time limits. However, the EAT, while it accepted that it is always an important consideration that the relevant limitation period has expired before the joinder of a new party, did not accept that equal pay claims were in a special category because they are subject to immutable time limits, whether as to the commencement of the claim or as to the period over which arrears may be claimed. The employment judge had taken into account that the limitation period had expired and accorded considerable weight to that matter. However, she also thought it important that the transferee already had to face similar claims brought by other employees.

8.47 **New claims in relation to matters arising after presentation of ET1.** It is even possible to bring a new claim by way of amendment in relation to matters that have only arisen after the presentation of the ET1. Previously, a claimant had to present a new ET1 in respect of the second claim and then apply to have both claims consolidated and heard together. In Okugade v Shaw Trust EAT 0172/05 the claimant wished to amend his ET1 in order to add complaints in respect of matters that had arisen after the presentation of the ET1. The tribunal held that it had no jurisdiction to deal with these matters. The EAT disagreed and allowed the appeal. The tribunal's approach had been 'too dogmatic' as it had viewed the matter in isolation without considering the broader issue of whether it was just and equitable to allow the matter to proceed. The case was remitted to the tribunal for reconsideration.

Similarly, in Prakash v Wolverhampton City Council EAT 0140/06 the EAT said that there was no reason in principle why a cause of action that has accrued after the presentation of the original claim form – and could therefore not have been included when the claim form was originally presented – should not be added by amendment if appropriate. There was nothing in the Tribunal Rules pertaining at the time that expressly prevented such an amendment being made, and that continues to be the case under the Tribunal Rules 2013.

Timing and manner of application for amendment 8.48

The third key factor identified by Mummery P in Selkent Bus Co Ltd v Moore 1996 ICR 836, EAT, governing the discretion to allow an amendment concerns the extent to which the applicant has delayed making the application to amend. Evidently, delay may count against the applicant. In Martin v Microgen Wealth Management Systems Ltd EAT 0505/06 the EAT stressed that the overriding objective requires, among other matters, that cases are dealt with expeditiously and in a way which saves expense: undue delay may well be inconsistent with these objectives. The EAT noted that while obviously later amendments would be permitted in an appropriate case, the later the application is made, the greater the risk of the balance of hardship being in favour of rejecting the amendment.

However, an application to amend should not be refused solely because there has been a delay in making it, as amendments may properly be made at any stage of the proceedings. According to the Presidential Guidance on 'General Case Management' for England and Wales, 'an application can be made at any time as can an amendment even after judgment has been promulgated... A party will need to show why the application was not made earlier and why it is being made at that time. An example which may justify a late application is the discovery of new facts or information from disclosure of documents.'

In Ahuja v Inghams 2002 ICR 1485, CA, Lord Justice Mummery observed that 8.49 employment tribunals should not be discouraged from exercising 'the powers they have to allow amendments to originating applications to deal, even at a comparatively late stage, with matters given in evidence at the hearing before them, but which are not features of the originating application. Such applications for late amendments may of course be contested... but the tribunal has a very

463

wide and flexible jurisdiction to do justice in the case... and they should not be discouraged in appropriate cases from allowing applicants to amend their applications, if the evidence comes out somewhat differently than was originally pleaded. If there is no injustice to the respondent in allowing such an amendment, then it would be appropriate for the employment tribunal to allow it rather than allow what might otherwise be a good claim to be defeated.'

So, for example, in Joao v Mesh Computers plc EAT 0529/08 the EAT held that a tribunal had paid insufficient regard to the fact that, even though the claimant applied to amend his claim to include an unfair dismissal complaint on the first day of the hearing, both the tribunal and the parties had been proceeding up to that point on the basis that the claim already included such a complaint. The case had been listed for hearing and prepared by both parties on the basis that a claim for unfair dismissal was before the tribunal; all the evidence necessary for determining such a claim was before them; and, in the EAT's view, no postponement would have been necessary. Thus, no prejudice would have been caused to the respondent by granting the application to amend.

8.50 In Ladbrokes Racing Ltd v Traynor EATS 0067/06 the EAT gave some guidance as to how a tribunal may take into account the timing and manner of the application in the balancing exercise. It will need to consider:

- why the application is made at the stage at which it is made and why it was not made earlier – Selkent Bus Co Ltd v Moore (above)

- whether, if the amendment is allowed, delay will ensue and whether there are likely to be additional costs because of the delay or because of the extent to which the hearing will be lengthened if the new issue is allowed to be raised, particularly if these are unlikely to be recovered by the party that incurs them; and

- whether delay may have put the other party in a position where evidence relevant to the new issue is no longer available or is rendered of lesser quality than it would have been earlier.

As previously indicated, the reason for any delay is a relevant factor. Consequently, tribunals will take into account a party's failure to explain the cause of any delay, especially if the application for amendment is made close to a hearing date. In Olayemi v Athena Medical Centre and ors EAT 0613/10 the EAT considered that an employment judge had given proper weight to this factor when refusing an application to amend. The application had been made very late in the procedural history, and at a stage significantly after the list of issues had been agreed and directions given for the hearing – a point that was significant for the evident reason that, according to the EAT, the whole function of seeking to agree lists of issues is to ensure that the cases that the parties wish to advance are those that the tribunal is prepared to receive by way of argument on each side. But it was also relevant that the cause of the delay was not explained in the initial application to amend.

There may, of course, be a very good reason why the application was not made **8.51** earlier: for example, because new facts have been discovered, or new information has appeared from documents disclosed on discovery. But does the tribunal need to assess the quality of the applicant's reason for delay?

In Glasgow City Council v Fox Cross Claimants and ors EATS 0004/13 the Council argued that not only must the reason why the application is made late be established, but the tribunal must consider the quality of that reason. However, the EAT disagreed. In that case, the tribunal had identified that the need for the amendment had arisen because the claimants had taken a 'strategic or, perhaps, tactical decision' to proceed on a particular basis. Although the tribunal had not expressed a view as to whether this reason for delay was 'good' or 'bad', the EAT considered that the absence of an evaluative judgment did not mean that the tribunal had improperly balanced the justice and injustice on both sides. Indeed, it observed that there may be good reason not to evaluate the quality of the reason for delay given that it is not correct to penalise the conduct of a party for having a bad reason for seeking an adjournment if, when considering the balance of justice, it would otherwise be permitted.

In the particular case, the EAT held that the tribunal had taken considerable **8.52** care to set out in detail its reasoning for and against granting the amendment and came to a conclusion that was not perverse. It had plainly had in mind the nature of the reason for seeking the amendment and for the matter having come to light so late in the day. The EAT considered that the tribunal must have had an opinion as to that reason, but this did not need to be expressed specifically. The main question it had to resolve was not whether the claimants' conduct was reprehensible but whether justice overall to both parties, balancing the hardship to each, required that the amendment as proposed be granted.

Some further examples of how tribunals have sought to weigh delay in the balance in considering applications to amend:

- **Cooper v Chief Constable of West Yorkshire Police and anor** EAT 0035/06: C worked for a Council on secondment from the police force. When it withdrew funding for her post she brought discrimination proceedings against the Council and against the police force for failing to support her adequately when the adverse funding decision was made. Immediately before the start of the hearing, C's advisers informed the police force of their intention to apply for permission to amend the claim to plead that the police force was vicariously liable for the acts of the Council. The employment tribunal refused the application and, on appeal, the majority of the EAT upheld that decision. C's advisers had decided only at the last moment to seek to amend and the effect of the proposed amendment was to put the case

465

against the police force on an entirely different basis to that on which it had previously been put. The first news that the tribunal had of the proposed amendment was when counsel for the police force told the tribunal that he had been informed of the proposed intention to seek an amendment. No explanation was offered as to why this new and different case was being advanced outside the limitation period, nor of any basis on which it would be just and equitable to allow it to be advanced so late. Furthermore, the majority of the EAT considered that it was obvious that the very belated amendment would have required further factual matters to be investigated in order to get the new case off the ground. In particular, the precise legal and practical nature of the partnership relationship between the Council and the police force and the details of the funding and its budgetary sources would have had to be looked into to see whether it could possibly be said that the police force was acting as principal and the Council as agent in the creation and maintenance of the post held by C as a contract worker with the Council. Against this background, the tribunal was perfectly entitled to take the view that the last-minute proposed amendment should not be allowed

- **Martin v Microgen Wealth Management Systems Ltd** EAT 0505/06: M was dismissed and claimed disability discrimination, among other things. At a pre-hearing review the respondent, who was then unrepresented, conceded that M was disabled for the purposes of the Disability Discrimination Act 1995. Four months later, and some ten days before the hearing, M sent a letter to the respondent setting out particulars of his claim in relation to the allegation that reasonable adjustments had not been made. He contended, for the first time, that the respondent should have given proper consideration to alternative employment as a reasonable adjustment, but gave no indication that he was intending to seek an amendment of his claim. On the morning of the first day of the hearing, M applied to amend his claim. The tribunal refused. It noted that it was acknowledged by both sides that the amendment was altering the basis of an existing claim rather than raising a new one. The tribunal also thought it relevant that M had been legally represented throughout; that the issues were clarified fully at the pre-hearing review; that the respondent's requests for further particulars of the reasonable adjustment claim prior to the hearing had been refused; and that the medical report M sought to rely on had been in the possession of M's solicitors for seven months. In the circumstances, the tribunal was not satisfied that there was any satisfactory explanation for the delay in making the amendment. The fact that it was prompted by a conference with counsel shortly before the letter was sent on 7 July was not a good explanation. The tribunal took into account the question of competing hardships, and concluded: 'It would not be appropriate at this late hour to allow the amendment... allowing an amendment with what, we judge, would be an inevitable need for an adjournment would not achieve the overriding objective.' M appealed, arguing that the tribunal had considered the delay in making the application to be determinative, rather than considering the balance of hardship. The EAT, however, considered that the tribunal had weighed up the factors fairly and carefully and reached a conclusion that it was fully entitled to reach in the circumstances. It had not focused on delay in itself, penalising M simply because of the lateness of the application. The key point was that the late application inevitably meant that there would have to be an adjournment

- **Anderson v Network Rail Infrastructure Ltd** EATS 0056/09: A submitted an ET1 claiming disability discrimination in April 2008 ('the original claim'). His solicitor wrote in December 2008 to say that he had resolved to proceed solely on the basis of the alleged disability-related discrimination said to have been involved when his job position was changed, and that he withdrew all other parts of his claim ('the amended claim'). At the start of the hearing nine months later, A's representative asked to make another amendment, broadening the claim to include a complaint that the employer had failed in its duty to make reasonable adjustments. A argued that the original claim was not dissimilar to a claim of failure to make reasonable adjustments, that the factual enquiry required would not be substantially different, and that the employer could have envisaged that A had intended to make such a claim. After balancing all the relevant factors, the employment tribunal concluded that it was not prepared to allow the amendment in view of fact that the claimant had been given an opportunity to clarify and specify exactly what his claims were, and that his advisers had done this in precise terms in the amended claim. No attempt was made from December 2008 until September 2009 to seek a further amendment to include a claim for breach of the duty to carry out reasonable adjustments. A appealed to the EAT, arguing, inter alia, that the tribunal had erred in assuming that the cogency of the evidence about the reasonable adjustments claim would have been affected by the passage of time. Dismissing A's appeal, the Appeal Tribunal held that the tribunal could not be criticised for regarding the restriction of the issues in the amended claim as being of considerable significance. As to the issue of the passage of time, the tribunal had not erred in taking into account the facts that some of the relevant witnesses were no longer in the respondents' employment; that memories may have dimmed in the time that had elapsed since the events complained of; that there was no reason to assume that witnesses would have been asked about these matters at the time of the original or amended claim; and that all this would be liable to involve the respondent in additional cost. In short, where A sought to amend his claim so as to introduce a claim for failure to make reasonable adjustments for the first time some 17 months after the presentation of his original claim and nine months after he had restricted his claim to a single issue that had nothing to do with a claim for reasonable adjustments, it was plainly open to the tribunal to refuse the amendment in circumstances where he would have been time barred if presenting the new claim as a fresh claim and where allowing the amendment was liable to cause some hardship to the employer.

8.53 In view of the balancing exercise that has to be conducted, it is perfectly possible that the correct outcome is to allow the proposed amendment even if there has been delay in making the application to amend. This is illustrated by the EAT's decision in Baker v Commissioner of Police of the Metropolis EAT 0201/09. In that case, B, a trainee police officer, submitted a tribunal claim against the police force. The tribunal held that it did not include a claim for disability discrimination and refused to hear B's application to amend the ET1 so as to incorporate such a claim because the application was made at a very late stage in the proceedings. B appealed, submitting that the police force would suffer no prejudice as a result of the amendment since it had in any event called evidence on disability discrimination during the tribunal hearing. He further argued that the reason the application was made so late in the proceedings was that the police force had itself only raised the argument that the ET1 did not include a disability discrimination claim in its closing submissions.

The EAT held that the tribunal had erred in treating the lateness of the application to amend as an insuperable reason for refusing to hear it, as opposed to simply constituting a relevant factor. The tribunal should also have considered whether the amendment was, in reality, merely an application to relabel acts of disability discrimination incidents already alluded to in the ET1; whether any such relabelled complaints would be out of time and, if so, whether it would be just and equitable to extend time; and, finally, the balance of injustice to the parties in granting or refusing the amendment. The EAT allowed the appeal on this point and remitted the case to determine B's application to amend the ET1. It directed that the application to amend should specify which provision of the DDA was alleged to have been breached by each act relied on, and how the relevant limitation periods affected the tribunal's jurisdiction to hear the complaints.

8.54 Other relevant factors
As already observed (see 'Amending the claim' above), the three factors set out in Selkent Bus Co Ltd v Moore 1996 ICR 836, EAT, are not intended to be exhaustive. There may thus be additional factors for the employment tribunal to consider when determining whether to grant leave to amend in any particular case.

8.55 **The merits of the claim.** It may, for example, be appropriate to consider whether the claim, as amended, has reasonable prospects of success. For example, in Cooper v Chief Constable of West Yorkshire Police and anor EAT 0035/06 (summarised under 'Timing and manner of application for amendment' above), one of the reasons the EAT gave for upholding the tribunal's decision to refuse an application to amend was that it would have required further factual matters to be investigated 'if this new and implausible case was to get off the ground'. Likewise, in Olayemi v Athena Medical Centre and ors EAT 0613/10 (also outlined above) one of the factors an employment judge took into consideration in refusing an application to add a claim of automatically unfair dismissal by reason of making protected disclosures to a sex discrimination and unfair dismissal claim was the fact that the prospects of the claimant succeeding with her amended claim 'do not appear good'. The claimant challenged this on appeal to the EAT, arguing that an employment judge dealing with an amendment of such a nature was not in a position to go into the prospects of success on a paper application to amend. However, the EAT observed that the context in which the employment judge had made his observation indicated that he meant that the amendment must be seen in the context of introducing a matter in respect of which there was already a considerable legal hurdle. He had observed that, to make out the claim based on protected disclosures, the claimant would have to show that a factor which had apparently been completely overlooked by her and her experienced representatives was 'now so clear that she can prove that this was not only influential in the respondent's decision for dismissal but that it was the "principal reason" for it'. He noted that the threshold was far higher under S.103A ERA than for her discrimination claim, where only sex had to be a significant factor in dismissal.

However, tribunals considering the prospects of success in the context of an application to amend should proceed with caution. Particularly in circumstances where the effect of the proposed amendment is to raise a new ground of complaint, it may not be clear from the pleadings what the merits of the new claim are. In Woodhouse v Hampshire Hospitals NHS Trust EAT 0132/12 the claimant, on the day before the hearing, requested an amendment to his claim of unfair dismissal, notice and holiday pay, to add five allegations of disability discrimination and a whistleblowing claim. The tribunal refused the application. Alongside other factors, it took into consideration that the claimant's witness statement contained no evidence of disability, and indeed contended that there had never been any health issues connected with his job performance. The tribunal concluded: 'In the absence of any evidence to support disability the tribunal is not satisfied the claimant has any realistic case to put forward.' The time delay was substantial and further substantial delay would be inevitable if the amendment were granted.

8.56 The claimant appealed, and the EAT observed that it was true that in the assessment of the balance of hardship and the balance of prejudice an examination of the merits may be a relevant consideration – in other words, there is no point in allowing an amendment to add an utterly hopeless case. But in the EAT's view, it should otherwise be assumed that the case is arguable.

469

No authority was provided to the EAT to say that there should be an examination on the merits; and, in the EAT's view, the tribunal had considered an irrelevant matter in examining the strength of the evidence that supported the new disability allegations. It was axiomatic that if the point is a new point, evidence on that point needs to be adduced. In this particular case, examining the material thus far adduced to support the claimant's constructive dismissal case would only take the tribunal so far in relation to the new claims sought to be introduced. Furthermore the tribunal had in any event not examined the claimant's witness statement sufficiently carefully. The tribunal was simply wrong to find that there was no evidence of disability and that on that basis there was no realistic prospect of success. As the tribunal had been quite substantially affected by its view of the merits, its decision could not stand.

8.57 **Validity of original claim.** It is worth observing that in Cocking v Sandhurst (Stationers) Ltd and anor 1974 ICR 650, NIRC, the NIRC advised that the first step employment tribunals should take, in considering a substantial amendment to a claim form, is to check whether the unamended ET1 complies with the requirements as to validity. If not, there is no power to amend and a new ET1 must be presented. This advice has little application in practice today, given that a claim will not be accepted by the tribunal in the first place if it is not on the prescribed form or does not contain the minimum information set out in rule 10 of the Tribunal Rules, or if an employment judge considers that the tribunal has no jurisdiction to consider it or that it is in a form which cannot sensibly be responded to or is otherwise an abuse of process, under rule 12 (see Chapter 4, 'Starting tribunal proceedings', under 'Processing the claim form – rejection of claim').

Nevertheless, in Abercrombie and ors v Aga Rangemaster Ltd 2013 IRLR 953, CA, an employment judge and the EAT accepted a respondent's submission, based on Cocking, that 'it is not permissible to amend an ET1 which the tribunal has no jurisdiction to accept in the first place' and that as the claimants had failed to comply with the statutory grievance procedure (since repealed) in respect of the claim in its unamended state, the tribunal had no jurisdiction to hear it and so the tribunal had no power to grant the application to amend. Although the statutory grievance procedures are no longer in force, it is possible to imagine other circumstances in which such an argument might be run. For example, to adopt the facts in Enterprise Liverpool Ltd v Jonas and ors EAT 0112/09, a claimant may bring a claim that a transferee on a TUPE transfer had failed to observe its information and consultation obligations under Regs 13 and 14 of the Transfer of Undertakings (Protection of Employment) Regulations 2006 SI 2006/246l; but if that claimant was a member of a recognised union, Reg 15 TUPE means that such a claim can only be brought by the union, and so the claimant would have had no standing to bring the original claim.

Following the reasoning of the respondent in the Abercrombie case, the tribunal would thus have no power to grant an application to amend.

However, the Court of Appeal in Abercrombie determined otherwise. Lord **8.58** Justice Underhill, giving the leading judgment, held that the fact that a claimant has commenced proceedings in respect of a claim which the tribunal decides in due course that it has no jurisdiction to determine is no bar to an amendment that would remove that difficulty. He agreed that if the claim were indeed a nullity from the start – in the full sense of that term – there would be no proceedings in being that could be the subject of an amendment. But that was not the case on the facts before him; and nor did he consider that the judgment of the NIRC in Cocking had any application to the issue. All Sir John Donaldson was saying there was that if the original application was fundamentally defective as regards the formal requirements, any new claim sought to be raised by amendment would be equally so.

Amending the response   8.59

As with the claim, the response (ET3) can be amended at any time with leave of the employment tribunal. The same general principles apply when determining whether to allow the amendment (see 'Amending the claim' above). In other words, in exercising their discretion, tribunals must have regard to all the circumstances, in particular any injustice or hardship which would result from the amendment or a refusal to make it – Cocking v Sandhurst (Stationers) Ltd and anor 1974 ICR 650, NIRC.

Changing the basis of the defence   8.60
Where a respondent seeks to make a substantial amendment, this almost invariably involves a proposed change to the grounds upon which he or she intends to resist the claimant's claim. The latitude which employment tribunals tend to show to parties means that respondents, on the whole, should face little difficulty in getting leave to amend, particularly at an early stage in the proceedings. However, amendments of substance sought at the hearing itself may be dealt with more severely. By that stage, it is not necessarily the case that the balance of fairness and convenience comes down in favour of allowing amendments.

However, just as tribunals will allow an ET1 to be amended at a late stage to add a new claim where the addition of that claim is essentially a change of label, they will usually grant a respondent leave to amend the ET3 at the hearing where the change is essentially one of nomenclature. This form of amendment often arises where, in order to hedge his or her bets, a respondent seeks to plead 'some other substantial reason' (SOSR) as an alternative reason for dismissal to redundancy (see Chapter 6, 'Defending a claim', under 'The defence'). Where the facts are fully established so that such a manoeuvre seeks

471

only to ensure that the appropriate label is given to the reason for dismissal, the Court of Appeal has endorsed the right of tribunals to allow late amendments – Nelson v BBC (No.1) 1977 ICR 649, CA. Two examples of such an amendment being allowed:

- **Gorman v London Computer Training Centre Ltd** 1978 ICR 394, EAT: the respondent pleaded in the response that G had been dismissed for redundancy. At the hearing, the employment tribunal concluded that G had been fairly dismissed on the ground of redundancy but it failed to set out its findings of fact or to state its reasoning in a clear form. On G's appeal, the EAT held that the case would have to be remitted. Furthermore, it held that, although the only reason given by the employer for G's dismissal was redundancy, and SOSR had not been expressly pleaded, in view of the informal character of pleadings before employment tribunals the respondent would be entitled to argue on the remission that even if G was not redundant he had nevertheless been fairly dismissed for SOSR. The tribunal would be confined, however, to considering only those matters that had been raised before in support of the respondent's claim that G had been dismissed by reason of redundancy

- **Hannan v TNT-IPEC (UK) Ltd** 1986 IRLR 165, EAT: following a business reorganisation, H was dismissed after refusing an offer of alternative employment. The respondent contended that the reason for dismissal was redundancy. However, the tribunal held that the real reason was SOSR and that the dismissal was nevertheless fair. H appealed on the basis that, since SOSR had neither been pleaded nor canvassed during the hearing, his case had been prejudiced in that he had had no notice of any alternative defence other than one based on redundancy. The EAT held that the tribunal was entitled to find the reason for dismissal to be SOSR notwithstanding that it had not been canvassed as an alternative to the reason given for dismissal, i.e. redundancy. However, it went on to make clear that a tribunal would not be entitled to find a dismissal fair on a ground not pleaded or argued where the difference in grounds goes to the facts and substance, or where there would or might have been some significant difference in the way the case was conducted by the claimant. Where, in contrast, the different grounds are really different labels and nothing more, the late introduction – even without pleading or argument – is not a ground for interference on appeal. In the instant case there was no basis for thinking that the employee's case would have been conducted differently or more thoroughly investigated, or that the cross-examination or evidence would have been significantly different.

8.61 Where an amendment would have wider repercussions, the balance of prejudice may swing the other way, making it more likely that a tribunal will refuse leave to amend. In cases where tribunals have refused leave, respondents have usually

472

been seeking to amend their defences so that they can plead further (and usually more realistic) grounds in the alternative. Some examples:

- **Kapur v Shields** 1976 ICR 26, QBD: the employer's pleaded defence was that S had asked to be dismissed as an aid to obtaining a council flat. During the hearing, the employer applied to amend his response in order to allege in the alternative that the dismissal was due to inefficiency and neglect of duty. The tribunal refused leave and the High Court upheld its decision. The discretion to allow or refuse amendments was a matter for the tribunal and, in the circumstances of the case, it was impossible to say that the tribunal had erred in exercising its discretion in the way it did

- **Ready Case Ltd v Jackson** 1981 IRLR 312, EAT: R Ltd denied in its response that J had been dismissed. At the hearing, its counsel attempted to amend the response so as to be able to argue alternatively that the dismissal was for SOSR. The tribunal refused leave to amend on the grounds that the request was made at a late stage and the company had received legal advice. The EAT held that the tribunal had not erred in refusing leave to amend during the hearing. The change sought would have involved an investigation by the tribunal into the reasons for dismissal and the whole question of fairness if, in the event, R Ltd's pleaded defence of 'no dismissal' failed. In turn, this would have necessitated further evidence and probably an adjournment to enable J to consider the new points raised. In these circumstances, the tribunal was justified in exercising its discretion to refuse to allow such a substantial amendment at so late a stage

- **Kammack 1988 Ltd v Ellison** EAT 844/93: the employer's original response stated that E had been dismissed. At the tribunal hearing, the employer applied to amend the response to allege that E had resigned. The tribunal refused the amendment, stating that to allow it would be contrary to the principles of natural justice requiring that each party is entitled to know in advance the case it will have to meet. Furthermore, the employer had been advised throughout by a professional firm and had had ample time before the hearing to seek the amendment. The EAT upheld the tribunal's decision, noting that the change requested by the employer was a substantial change which would have altered the burden of proof and the order in which the parties gave evidence

- **Chadwick v Bayer plc** EAT 1110/01: C brought claims for equal pay and sex discrimination in respect of non-payment of pension benefits. At the relevant time, C was employed by M, but, following a TUPE transfer, her new employer became B plc. B plc served its response, stating that it did not intend to resist C's claims and implying in subsequent letters that the only issue remaining was the amount of compensation that C would receive. However, on the day before the hearing, B plc sought to amend its response on the ground that it did not have legal representation when it completed

473

the response. It now wished to dispute liability on the basis that it could not be liable for the alleged non-payment of pension benefits, as liability for pension benefits does not transfer to the new employer under TUPE. The tribunal chairman allowed B plc to amend its response. Consequently, C made an application to have M added as the second respondent, which was granted, and she appealed to the EAT against the decision to allow B plc to amend its response. On appeal, the EAT overturned the tribunal's decision to grant leave to amend. Applying the principles derived from Selkent Bus Co Ltd v Moore 1996 ICR 836, EAT (see 'Amending the claim' above), it noted, first, that B plc not only intended to introduce a fundamental amendment to its response that represented a complete volte-face, but that the nature of the amendment meant that C ran the risk of losing her cause of action against both respondents through no fault of her own. Furthermore, there was a delay in making the amendment application. No adequate explanation was given for B plc's radical change of stance. The injustice and hardship involved in granting the amendment was very much greater than the injustice and hardship that would have been involved in refusing it.

8.62 Withdrawing a concession

From time to time a respondent may make a concession of fact or law in the course of proceedings that it subsequently wishes to withdraw in response to the unfolding of the claimant's case. As with any other amendment, the respondent may apply to the tribunal for leave to withdraw such a concession, and it will be a matter for the tribunal's discretion whether or not to grant such leave. While it is easier to achieve the withdrawal of a concession of law, there is no rule that a concession of fact cannot be withdrawn – Renfrewshire Council v Adamson EATS 0013/07.

There are conflicting decisions at EAT level as to the correct approach to adopt in considering whether to allow a respondent to withdraw a concession. In Centrica Storage Ltd and anor v Tennison EAT 0336/08, the EAT treated an application to withdraw a concession as akin to a standard application to amend the claim form or response, and thus considered that the proper approach was for the employment tribunal to apply the principles governing the discretion whether or not to grant leave to amend as outlined in Selkent Bus Co Ltd v Moore (above). Those principles have been discussed in detail under 'Amending the claim' above. In Centrica, a response filed in January 2008 to a claim for unfair dismissal and disability discrimination included an admission agreeing that the claimant was disabled. On 13 May 2008 the claimant's witness statements were filed, and, as a result, the respondent applied to the employment tribunal for leave to withdraw the admission on 16 May. It contended that the claimant had moved his position from that which had been always understood – that he was unable to perform offshore working – to one where he was contending that for some time he had been effectively symptom-free and completely able to perform offshore duties. The case was due to commence on 29 May 2008. At the hearing, having considered the Selkent principles, the tribunal refused the respondent's application, and the EAT upheld that decision on appeal. It ruled that the tribunal had properly found that, although the respondent's application had been made promptly following disclosure of the witness statements, there had not, in fact, been a change in the claimant's position and so the matter should have been raised at a much earlier stage.

By way of contrast, in Nowicka-Price v Chief Constable of Gwent Constabulary **8.63** EAT 0268/09 the EAT made no reference to the Selkent principles in considering the exercise of an employment judge's discretion to allow a response to be amended to withdraw most of the admissions the respondent had previously made. Instead, the EAT considered that as the Tribunal Rules 2004 (then in force) were silent on the question of withdrawal of admissions, it was appropriate to apply Part 14 of the Civil Procedure Rules 1998 SI 1998/3132, which governs admissions and withdrawal of admissions at various stages of civil court proceedings.

In the Nowicka-Price case, the employer stated in its ET3 that it did not intend to resist the claim and admitted that the claimant had 'received inappropriate treatment' that was the subject of current investigation. However, several months later, after discussions between the parties to resolve the matter had been unsuccessful, the employer applied to amend the response by withdrawing the admission. The tribunal allowed the application, after balancing the relative prejudice to the claimant and respondent of making such an amendment. It considered that the balance came down heavily in favour of the respondent, taking into account that as a public body, the respondent had an interest in defending its reputation, and that the value of the claim was substantial. On appeal, the EAT stated that 'on interim applications, there is no dispute that the approach of the employment tribunals should be assisted where the [Tribunal Rules] are silent, as they are on admissions, by [Rule 14 of the Civil Practice Rules (CPR)]. The Appeal Tribunal referred to the Practice Direction on Part 14 CPR. With regard to withdrawals, this states that in deciding whether to give permission for an admission to be withdrawn, the court will have regard to all the circumstances of the case, including:

- the grounds upon which the applicant seeks to withdraw the admission including whether or not new evidence has come to light which was not available at the time the admission was made

- the conduct of the parties, including any conduct which led the party making the admission to do so

- the prejudice that may be caused to any person if the admission is withdrawn

- the prejudice that may be caused to any person if the application is refused

475

- the stage in the proceedings at which the application to withdraw is made, in particular in relation to the date or period fixed for trial

- the prospects of success (if the admission is withdrawn) of the claim or part of the claim in relation to which the offer was made, and

- the interests of the administration of justice.

8.64 In Braybrook v Basildon and Thurrock University NHS Trust 2004 EWHC 3352, QB – a clinical negligence case – the judge set out the following principles to guide courts in exercising their discretion on withdrawing admissions, based on Practice Direction 14:

- the court will consider all the circumstances of the case and seek to give effect to the overriding objective

- among the matters to be considered will be: (a) the reasons and justification for the application which must be made in good faith; (b) the balance of prejudice to the parties; (c) whether any party is the author of any prejudice they may suffer; (d) the prospects of success of any issue arising from withdrawal; (e) the public interest, in avoiding where possible satellite litigation, disproportionate use of court resources and the impact of any strategic manoeuvring

- the nearer any application is to a final hearing the less chance it will have of succeeding, even if the party making the application can establish clear prejudice.

Considering these principles, the EAT in Nowicka-Price upheld the tribunal's decision. It held that the tribunal had weighed up the balance of prejudice. While, in its view, the financial value of the claim was an irrelevant consideration, it was relevant that the respondent would be prejudiced in not being given the opportunity to defend a discrimination claim, and that the application to amend was made well before any hearing of the merits.

8.65 Attractive as the reasoning in Nowicka-Price v Chief Constable of Gwent Constabulary (above) is, it is arguable that the EAT in that case places too much emphasis on the applicability of the CPR in employment tribunal cases. As discussed in Chapter 1, 'Employment tribunals', under 'What are employment tribunals? – Civil Procedure Rules', while tribunals may consider it appropriate to refer to the CPR, they are not bound by them. Rule 41 of the Tribunal Rules 2013 clearly states that 'the tribunal may regulate its own procedure and shall conduct the hearing in the manner it considers fair, having regard to the principles contained in the overriding objective' and seeking to avoid 'undue formality'. So long as a tribunal considering whether to allow a respondent to withdraw an admission properly exercises its discretion by balancing the relative prejudice this would cause to the parties in line with the principles set out in Selkent Bus Co Ltd v Moore (above), it is unlikely that its decision will be interfered with on appeal.

476

Amending the parties

8.66

It is sometimes necessary for one or more additional respondents to be joined to an extant claim – for instance, where the named respondent disputes that he is or was the employer; or where an issue arises as to whether the claimant's employment was transferred to a third party following a transfer of the former employer's undertaking; or where it is realised that a claimant's union, rather than the claimant, should have brought a particular claim – see Enterprise Liverpool Ltd v Jonas and ors EAT 0112/09.

Under rule 34 of the Tribunal Rules, employment tribunals have a wide discretion to add, substitute and/or remove parties to proceedings. A tribunal has the power, either on its own initiative or on the application of a party or any other person wishing to become a party, to add or substitute any person as a party. A tribunal also has a corresponding power to remove any party apparently wrongly included. The addition (or substitution) of parties can be exercised where it appears that there are 'issues between' the person to be joined (or substituted) and any of the existing parties falling within the jurisdiction of the tribunal which it is in the interests of justice to have determined. The potential range of circumstances in which there could be 'issues between' an existing party and a party to be joined to the proceedings that fall within the tribunal's jurisdiction are vast, and will include circumstances where a person might be liable for the remedy claimed or where a person otherwise has an interest in the outcome of the proceedings.

The power to add, substitute and remove parties under rule 34, when read in conjunction with rule 29, applies 'at any stage of the proceedings'. Therefore, a tribunal can, for example, join another respondent to an existing claim even after the time limit for bringing a fresh claim against that respondent has expired – Drinkwater Sabey Ltd v Burnett and anor 1995 ICR 328, EAT. **8.67**

The party joined by order of the tribunal can apply under rule 30 for the order to be varied or revoked under rule 29. The Presidential Guidance on 'General Case Management' for England and Wales states that such an application should be made 'promptly'.

A tribunal's power to join (or remove) a party is discussed further in Chapter 11, 'Case management', under 'Addition, substitution and removal of parties'.

Principles governing the tribunal's discretion to amend the parties. Exactly the same principles apply to an amendment to add, substitute or remove parties to a claim as to any other sort of amendment. In other words, the principles set out in Selkent Bus Company Ltd v Moore 1996 ICR 836, EAT, and discussed at length under 'Amending the claim' above, will apply. For example, in Enterprise Liverpool Ltd v Jonas and ors (above) EL Ltd completed 'relevant transfers' to three different companies under the Transfer of Undertakings **8.68**

477

(Protection of Employment) Regulations 2006 SI 2006/246 (TUPE). Groups of transferred employees lodged claims that EL Ltd had failed to observe its information and consultation obligations under Regs 13 and 14 of TUPE in respect of those transfers. The claimants were all members of Unite, the GMB or UCATT. When solicitors were instructed to act for the claimants after the claims had been presented, the solicitors realised that, as the unions were recognised by EL Ltd, Reg 15(1)(c) meant that the claims could only be brought by the unions. The solicitors accordingly applied to the tribunal for permission to change the names on the claim forms from the individual claimants to the relevant unions. At a pre-hearing review, an employment judge permitted the amendments. Following Transport and General Workers' Union v Safeway Stores Ltd EAT 0092/07, the judge applied the relative balance of hardship and injustice test. He concluded that this was a case of simple mistake by the unions, that the respondents were not caused prejudice, and that the claimants would be caused greater injustice if the application was refused. EL Ltd and one of the transferees appealed.

On appeal, EL Ltd argued that the EAT in Safeway had misconstrued the Selkent case. It submitted that the alteration amounted to substituting a wholly new claim not connected to the original claim at all. Since the new claim would be out of time, it should not be admitted by way of amendment. However, the EAT dismissed the appeal, rejecting EL Ltd's interpretation of Selkent. That case had emphasised the need to consider all the circumstances – including time limits – and balance the hardship and injustice caused by allowing the amendment against that caused by refusing it. It was not suggested that, even in a case where a new claim is substituted which would otherwise be out of time, this would be fatal to the application. The EAT pointed out that in Ali v Office of National Statistics 2005 IRLR 201, CA, Lord Justice Waller had thought that, where an amendment technically amounts to raising a new claim, if that 'new claim' is close to the original claim, justice requires the amendment to be allowed even though it is out of time. In any event, the EAT came to the view that the amendment sought in the instant case did not amount to admitting a new claim out of time. Rather, it was an amendment altering the basis of an existing claim without raising a new head of complaint. Such an amendment is not affected by time limit considerations. The EAT went on to note that if it was wrong about this, and the amendment was in fact substituting a new claim, it would have upheld the tribunal's decision on the balance of injustice.

8.69 By contrast, in Trimble and anor v North Lanarkshire Council and anor EATS 0048/12 an attempt to add a TUPE transferee as a new and additional respondent failed. The claimants had brought equal pay claims against their transferor employer but had later applied to add as respondent the company to whom their employment had transferred. Leave to amend was granted – in the absence of the transferee and without it having had the opportunity to make representations to the tribunal. Accordingly, a preliminary hearing was held at which the orders amending the claim and adding the transferee as second respondent were revoked. The claimants appealed. The EAT considered that the claimants had been unable to identify any relevant factor that the employment judge had failed to take into account, nor any irrelevant factor that she had taken into account. Applying the Selkent guidance, the judge had noted that the claimants' solicitors had provided no explanation for having failed to act on the information provided by their clients four years earlier that their employment had transferred. She had recognised that the claimants would be prejudiced by losing the chance to prosecute their claims, but that the transferee would also be prejudiced in that it would have to defend claims dating back five years prior to the transfer, which would inevitably be difficult as obtaining the relevant information and documents in such circumstances would not be straightforward. She gave more weight to this prejudice because of the failings of the claimants' solicitors. In the EAT's view, the issue of what to make of the competing factors in such a case is generally very much a matter for the employment tribunal, and there was nothing in the particular facts of this case to indicate otherwise.

The EAT also rejected the contention that the employment judge was not entitled to proceed on the basis that there would be inevitable difficulties for the transferee in responding to a claim that related to a period spanning five years prior to the date of transfer, where that date itself was some five years earlier, and the weighting the judge gave to the various factors could not be said to be perverse. The claimants had sought to argue that, by revoking the decision to amend, the rights that were meant to be protected on transfer would be lost, thus undermining the purpose of TUPE; but in rejecting this, the EAT observed that any delay was of the claimants' representatives' own making, and just because a European source for an asserted right can be identified, this does not mean that special weight has to be given to it in the kind of balancing exercise that a tribunal has to carry out when considering whether or not to allow the addition of a new respondent.

In Cocking v Sandhurst (Stationers) Ltd and anor 1974 ICR 650, NIRC, the **8.70** NIRC stated that a substitution or an addition of a respondent should only be allowed where a tribunal is satisfied that the mistake sought to be corrected was a genuine one and was not misleading or such as to cause reasonable doubt as to the identity of a party to the proceedings. This statement mirrored RSC Order 20, rule 5, which, at that time, laid down the requirements for the addition or substitution of a party in the High Court. However, the EAT in Drinkwater Sabey Ltd v Burnett and anor 1995 ICR 328, EAT, held that a tribunal's discretion to add a new respondent is not always limited in this way.

In the Drinkwater Sabey case B brought an unfair dismissal complaint against Kent County Council. However, the Council claimed that liability for B's dismissal had passed to DS Ltd under the Transfer of Undertakings (Protection

479

of Employment) Regulations 1981 SI 1981/1794 (now SI 2006/246). B then sought to join DS Ltd to the proceedings as second respondent and a tribunal granted him leave to amend his ET1. DS Ltd appealed to the EAT on the ground that the NIRC's decision in the Cocking case meant that, in circumstances where the time limit for presenting a fresh ET1 against a particular respondent has passed, a tribunal has jurisdiction to join that respondent to the proceedings only where the claimant has misnamed or misdescribed that respondent in his or her claim form. It accordingly contended that the tribunal did not have jurisdiction to add DS Ltd as second respondent where, owing to an error of law, B had mistakenly sued the wrong company altogether.

8.71 The EAT rejected DS Ltd's argument and upheld the decision of the tribunal. It accepted that where a misnomer has occurred it is important to ascertain whether it is a genuine misnomer or whether, in fact, it is an attempt to mislead or is not made in good faith. In these circumstances, the guidance laid down in the Cocking case will apply. However, the Cocking guidance is clearly not applicable where a claimant has mistakenly sued the wrong party – if it were applied in such circumstances, the guidance would preclude a tribunal from adding a new respondent even where it is clearly just for it to do so. The EAT held that such a preclusion would be contrary to the Tribunal Rules 2004 then in force, which stated that the addition or substitution of a respondent could take place at any time. The question of whether a new party should be joined to tribunal proceedings is a matter for the tribunal's discretion, which should be exercised in such a way as to arrive at a just result. (Note that under the Tribunal Rules 2013, while rule 34 does not explicitly state that parties may be added, substituted or removed at any time, rule 29 (which contains the general case management power of which rule 34 is a particular manifestation) states that the tribunal may make a case management order 'at any stage of the proceedings'.)

Following Drinkwater Sabey Ltd v Burnett and anor (above), where a claimant does not know the name of an individual he or she wishes to join as respondent, but makes his or her wishes clear and applies to do so as soon as the name becomes known, the application should be granted. In Parveen v International Dance Shoes Ltd and anor EAT 0447/10 the claimant resigned and brought proceedings against her employer claiming unfair constructive dismissal and discrimination on the grounds of her sex or pregnancy. In her ET1 she stated: 'Regarding the manager "Harry" referred to at section 5.2, I reserve the right to join him as a second respondent in these proceedings once his full name is disclosed by the first respondent.' The respondent referred to the manager's full name in the ET3. Accordingly, the claimant applied to the tribunal for permission to join him as a respondent, referring to the fact that she had expressed an intention in the ET1 to do so once she knew his name. An employment judge refused her application on the ground that any claim against an additional respondent would be out of time.

The claimant appealed, arguing that the judge's reason for refusing the **8.72** application was wrong, given the decision in the Drinkwater Sabey case that the fact that an application to join a further party was out of time was not an absolute bar but simply a matter to be taken into account as a matter of discretion. The EAT agreed, noting that this was in accordance with other decisions on the question of adding fresh causes of action, such as, for example, Transport and General Workers' Union v Safeway Stores Ltd EAT 0092/07 (discussed under 'Amending the claim – balance of hardship or injustice' and 'Amending the claim – time limits' above). The EAT could see no reason to refuse the application, given that the claimant's reasons for not naming the respondent in the original ET1 were understandable, and that she made her position plain from the start and then acted promptly as soon as she had the necessary information. No possible prejudice could have been done by the delay in formally joining the party concerned.

Technical mistakes. It is clear that tribunals will have little truck with **8.73** respondents who seek to exploit a purely technical mistake by the claimant in naming the wrong respondent on the ET1:

- **Oliphant and Sons (Storage and Distribution) Ltd v Gallacher** EAT 297/92: G accidentally misrepresented the name of his employer's company in his ET1. When it appeared to the company that it might succeed on this technicality, it ceased to take an active part in the proceedings, going so far as to not turn up to the hearing. In the event this ruse failed: at a review, the tribunal permitted an amendment to the ET1 in order to substitute the correct name of the employer. The EAT upheld the tribunal's decision, holding that it had exercised its discretion to amend reasonably

- **The Milestone School of English Ltd v Leakey** 1982 IRLR 3, EAT: a settlement was agreed between the parties in proceedings for unfair dismissal brought by L against the respondent. After the latter subsequently ceased trading, and at a time when the sum agreed in settlement remained unpaid, L sought to have the settlement set aside and to continue the proceedings against related companies trading as The Milestone School of English Ltd. The tribunal acceded to L's request and, on appeal, the EAT held that it had been right to do so. The EAT rejected the respondent's argument that L was debarred from proceeding against any other company because he had irrevocably elected to proceed against The Milestone School of English. L had wanted to make a claim against his 'employer' and, through no fault of his own, the identity of that employer was unclear. The EAT therefore ordered that the respondent to the restored proceedings should include the names of the related persons or companies who continued to trade.

Late applications. In Argyll and Clyde Health Board v Foulds and anor EATS **8.74** 0009/06 the EAT emphasised that where the application to include a new respondent can properly be regarded as a new complaint or cause of action the

481

tribunal is entitled to regard the lateness of the application as an important factor weighing against grant of the amendment. According to the EAT, if the application is being presented outside that time limit, the tribunal needs to look at the explanation given for that having occurred. It posed the following questions: Why was the respondent not included in the original claim? What was known by the claimant (and/or his or her solicitor) about his potential as a relevant respondent at that time? What should have been known? When did the claimant (and/or solicitor) realise that the respondent ought to be included? What steps were taken after that? What was the reason for any delay thereafter? Did the claimant (and/or solicitor) take prompt action once the need to seek to include the respondent was realised or not? If not, why not? Would there be injustice or hardship to the claimant if the application were refused? If so, of what nature? What would be its cause? Would there be injustice or hardship to the respondent in being brought in as a respondent at this stage?

8.75   If a tribunal, in refusing leave to add or substitute a respondent, bases its refusal solely on the ground that the time limit relevant to the claim against the new respondent has expired, it will have fallen into error. This is because an application for leave to substitute a fresh respondent relates back to the date of the original application – Cocking v Sandhurst (Stationers) Ltd and anor 1974 ICR 650, NIRC; and, of course, because the tribunal always retains a discretion to allow an amendment. Some examples:

- **Cocking v Sandhurst (Stationers) Ltd and anor** (above): C claimed unfair dismissal against S Ltd, which he believed to be his employer. (S Ltd was in fact a subsidiary of his real employer – which was the parent company.) At the hearing, C sought leave to amend his ET1 in order to join the parent company to the proceedings. However, since the amendment was sought after the time limit for presenting an unfair dismissal complaint against the parent company had expired, the tribunal refused leave. On appeal, the NIRC held that the protection that respondents gain from time limits depends not on when they first become parties but on when the ET1 is first presented. In this case, the ET1 naming the wrong respondent had been submitted within the time limit: the tribunal therefore had jurisdiction to amend the claim form. Applying the general principles which the NIRC then proceeded to set out (see 'Amending the claim' above), it held that, in the circumstances, the amendment should have been allowed

- **Gillick v BP Chemicals Ltd** 1993 IRLR 437, EAT: G presented an ET1 alleging unfair dismissal and sex discrimination against a company that had contracted out its services to BP Ltd. Over four months later, G sought to have BP Ltd joined as a second respondent. The tribunal held that G's complaints against BP Ltd were time barred. It decided that it was not appropriate to follow the Cocking case on the ground that that case only applied where the original and new respondents had a corporate relationship (for example, principal and subsidiary). On appeal, the EAT forcefully rejected the tribunal's qualification to the approach laid down in the Cocking case. There was no time limit applicable where it was proposed to add a respondent in circumstances in which the ET1 had been lodged timeously. The presence or absence of a connection between the respondents is relevant, if at all, only as a matter to be taken into account by the tribunal when exercising its discretion to allow the proposed amendment

- **Ryan v Bennington Training Services Ltd** EAT 0345/08: R brought an employment tribunal claim in May 2007 against a respondent named as Studyxpress. At a hearing in October a judgment was made that Studyxpress was not the employer, and that company was dismissed from the proceedings, with BTS Ltd being substituted as respondent. BTS Ltd applied to the tribunal, claiming that the claim against it was now out of time. An employment judge agreed that it was, assuming that the claim was effectively lodged against BTS Ltd on the date that the October judgment was promulgated. R successfully appealed to the EAT, which ruled that Cocking had made it 'crystal clear' that at a hearing before a tribunal an application for leave to substitute a fresh respondent relates back to the date of the original application. In the instant case, the legal effect of the substitution of BTS Ltd was to put it in the place of Studyxpress. The proceedings therefore related back to the date when the original claim form was submitted in May 2007; and there was no dispute that that claim form was in time

- **Walsall Metropolitan Borough Council and anor v Birch and ors** EAT 0376/10: an employment judge granted to a group of 103 claimants permission to amend their claims to join the TUPE transferee in circumstances where the TUPE transferor had originally been cited sole respondent. The application was made after the expiry of the time limit for claims brought following a TUPE transfer in respect of pre-transfer arrears of equal pay, as set out in Sodexo Ltd v Gutridge 2009 ICR 1486, CA. On appeal, the EAT held that the judge had made no error of law in applying the Selkent principles to the case. The authorities clearly established that an employment tribunal has discretion to allow an amendment which introduces a new claim out of time, and there was no rule of law that an amendment cannot be allowed because it would, if presented as a fresh claim, be time barred. The EAT observed that while it was always an important consideration that the relevant limitation period has expired before the joinder of a new party, it did not accept that equal pay claims were in a special category because they are subject to immutable time limits, whether as to the commencement of the claim or as to the period over which arrears may be claimed.

8.76 It is possible to substitute a new respondent (or to add another) very late in the proceedings – even after a decision on the merits has been reached. Rule 29 of the Tribunal Rules permits a tribunal to make a case management order 'at any

483

stage of the proceedings' and the following cases suggest that these words should not be limited in any way, in the context of the general power to add, substitute or remove parties under rule 34:

- **Watts v Seven Kings Motor Co Ltd and anor** 1983 ICR 135, EAT: in his ET1, W named S Ltd, which was a business conducted by R, as his employer. Neither S Ltd nor R entered a response and at the hearing the tribunal held that W had been unfairly dismissed. Afterwards, W discovered that S Ltd was in liquidation and that his real employer had been R trading as SKM Co Ltd. He applied for leave to amend the name of the respondent accordingly. The tribunal revoked the order of unfair dismissal against S Ltd but refused to substitute R because a complaint of unfair dismissal against him was out of time. The EAT, however, stated that, provided that R was afforded suitable safeguards (i.e. an opportunity to enter a response and apply for a review (now termed 'reconsideration')), the tribunal was wrong not to substitute him as the respondent in the proceedings and make him liable to pay the compensation ordered against S Ltd

- **Parry Bros (Builders) Co Ltd v Brown** EAT 714/84: B named B Group as his employer in the ET1. B Group did not enter a response and, after the tribunal found that he had been unfairly dismissed, B discovered that B Group did not exist. On a review, the tribunal ordered that P Ltd be substituted as the respondent. P Ltd appealed against the order. The EAT held that tribunals are entitled to give fresh consideration to a decision after it has been made and, if appropriate, allow an amendment to substitute a party. The EAT stressed that natural justice would require any substituted respondent to be given an opportunity to be heard. But on the facts of the case, P Ltd had been afforded that opportunity since it had been aware of B's claim all along.

8.77 What is clear from these cases is that where tribunals order a new respondent to be joined or substituted at a late stage, the new respondent must be given an opportunity to be heard. If a decision on liability has already been taken, then it will be appropriate to allow any application by the respondent for a reconsideration of that decision – see Gillick v BP Chemicals Ltd (above).

9 Responding to opponent's case

Obtaining additional information

Written answers

'Ask and respond' procedure in discrimination cases

Disclosure and inspection of documents

Production of documents by witnesses

Failure to comply with orders

In earlier chapters we deal with the issues involved in starting employment **9.1** tribunal proceedings and defending a claim. This involves each party 'pleading' their case using the prescribed forms: the ET1 for the claimant and the ET3 for the respondent. Each side will be sent a copy of their opponent's pleadings by the tribunal and, once this 'exchange' is complete, they will each stand informed of at least the outline of the other side's case. From this point on, the parties should attempt to gather as much additional information as possible about their opponent's case since this will place them in a position to bolster their own case in readiness for the hearing. In this chapter, we look at the ways in which the parties to an employment dispute can obtain information and documents from their opponents.

In the first instance, a party should always attempt to obtain the information he or she seeks directly from the other side. Where the opponent is uncooperative or provides an inadequate response, an application can then be made to the employment tribunal for an order requiring the other side to provide the relevant information. The Employment Tribunal Rules 2013 ('the Tribunal Rules'), contained in Schedule 1 to the Employment Tribunals (Constitution and Rules of Procedure) Regulations 2013 SI 2013/1237 ('the Tribunal Regulations'), give employment tribunals a wide discretion to manage proceedings and help progress a case. Rule 29 contains a general power that allows a tribunal, either on its own initiative or on the application of a party, to make a case management order. This power may be used to order the parties to provide each other with specified information. A tribunal's specific powers in relation to some (but not all) of the matters that may be the subject of a case management order are then set out in supplementary rules. These rules expressly deal with the disclosure of documents and information (rule 31) and the attendance of witnesses to give evidence (rule 32). Case management orders can be made at the judicial sift stage and at a preliminary hearing (an amalgamation of what used to be pre-hearing reviews and case management discussions under the Tribunal Rules 2004, contained in the Employment

---

485

Tribunals (Constitution and Rules of Procedure) Regulations 2004 SI 2004/1861) – see Chapter 7, 'Judicial sift', under 'Case management following sift', and Chapter 11, 'Case management', under 'Preliminary hearings' for more information.

9.2 A key objective of the review that led to the introduction of the Tribunal Rules 2013 was to simplify the rules governing procedure in the employment tribunal – in terms of both their length and their complexity. According to Mr Justice Underhill, who conducted the review, one of the ways in which this was achieved was by omitting rules that merely prescribed administrative practice. This is particularly evident when looking at the new case management powers on seeking information on an opponent's case. Rule 10(1) of the Tribunal Rules 2004 set out a tribunal's general power to make case management orders, but rule 10(2) then listed as examples specific case management orders that the tribunal could make in relation to the obtaining of information. These included orders for the provision of additional information, witness statements and other evidence, written answers and disclosure. The particular powers in respect of the provision of additional information and written answers have not been replicated in the new Rules. However, it is not suggested that these omissions will make any difference in practice. Rule 29 of the Tribunal Rules 2013 states that the specific powers do not restrict the tribunal's general power to make a case management order. Therefore, as was the case under the old rule 10(1), the tribunal has a general power to tailor orders to the case in hand and it is expected that tribunals will continue to make the same wide range of orders in relation to the conduct of proceedings as before. Case law decided under the previous rules therefore remains relevant.

Moreover, adopting a hands-on approach to case management is one way in which tribunals can further the 'overriding objective' of the Tribunal Rules, which is to enable tribunals to deal with cases 'fairly and justly' – see rule 2. Dealing with cases fairly and justly involves treating the parties equally, saving expense, acting in proportion to the complexity of the case and avoiding unnecessary formality and delay. By making and enforcing a wide range of case management orders, tribunals can limit the number of cases that are postponed at the last minute because one of the parties is taken by surprise by his or her opponent's arguments.

9.3 In this chapter, we begin by looking at the power to order the provision of additional information to clarify a claim or response, and the power to order a party to provide written answers to questions put to it by the tribunal. We also look at the new informal 'ask and respond' procedure in discrimination cases (which replaced the statutory questionnaire procedure from April 2014), under which complainants can request information that they think will help them prove their case. We then focus on the main source of obtaining information

486

about an opponent's case: orders for disclosure and inspection of documents. This leads to a discussion of when a document may be exempt from disclosure by virtue of being privileged or subject to the particular rules on the inadmissibility of evidence that apply in relation to 'without prejudice' communications and pre-termination negotiations. We then briefly consider the power to order witnesses to attend the tribunal to produce documents and information before looking at the sanctions for non-compliance with orders requesting information.

Obtaining additional information 9.4

All parties are required to give details of the grounds on which they are bringing or, as the case may be, resisting a claim – see Chapter 4, 'Starting tribunal proceedings', under 'Completing the claim form – practical advice on completing the ET1', and Chapter 6, 'Defending a claim', under 'The defence'. However, additional information about a claim or response may be necessary or desirable where an ET1 or ET3 fails to give sufficient details about the case or where the grounds stated are ambiguous as to the facts or the basis in law. Although, as mentioned in the introduction to this chapter, the Tribunal Rules 2013 no longer contain a specific power to order a party to provide additional information on their case, it is expected that tribunals will continue to make these orders under their general case management powers in rule 29.

The general purpose of asking for additional information from the other side at an early stage is to enable the parties to prepare adequately for the hearing by being informed in advance of sufficient details about the case they will have to meet. In White v University of Manchester 1976 ICR 419, EAT, Mr Justice Phillips explained the rationale behind (what were then called) 'further particulars' in the context of tribunal proceedings: 'We do not wish to say anything to encourage unnecessary legalism to creep into the proceedings of [employment] tribunals; but, while that should be avoided, it should not be avoided at the expense of falling into a different error, namely, that of doing injustice by a hearing taking place when the party who has to meet the allegations does not know in advance what those allegations are.'

Traditionally, the functions of additional information have been to: 9.5

- inform the other side of the nature of the case which he or she will be required to meet (as opposed to the way in which it is to be proved)

- prevent the other side from being taken by surprise

- enable the other side to prepare the necessary evidence

- limit the generality of the claim or defence

487

- define the relevant issues between the parties so as to determine the scope of disclosure.

Orders for additional information therefore serve a wider purpose than merely helping parties know what case they have to meet – they tell the parties, and the tribunal, what issues are involved in the case. One effect of an order being made is to 'formalise' the claim and response, with the consequence that the parties may find it more difficult to raise at the hearing any matters that they have not mentioned previously. A common phrase frequently used in applications for additional information is: 'to state with full particularity all facts and matters upon which the [claimant/respondent] will rely in saying that...'. If the tribunal orders additional information along these lines, a party may encounter difficulties if, at the hearing, he or she seeks to raise any issue that has not been particularised in response to the order.

9.6 Making an application for additional information
It is always advisable to try to obtain the necessary information directly from the other side first. This can be done by sending a letter to the opponent requesting the additional information to be provided on a voluntary basis. The letter should also state a deadline for complying with the request and make it clear that if, after that date, the information has not been received, an application will be made to the tribunal for an order without further notice. If an application is subsequently made to the tribunal for a formal order, it should be accompanied by a copy of the letter.

An order for additional information can be made at any stage in the proceedings on the application of a party or by the tribunal on its own initiative – rule 29. Where a party applies for an order, the application can be made either at a hearing or presented in writing to the tribunal – rule 30(1). If a written application is made, the party making the application must notify the other parties that any objections should be sent to the tribunal 'as soon as possible' – rule 30(2). This is a significant change from old rule 11(4), which allowed the other party only seven days to object to an application. Requiring objections to be submitted as soon as possible, with no end date, is ambiguous and there are likely to be inconsistencies in respect of how long tribunals wait for objections to be submitted before making a decision on the application. Rule 30(3) provides that the tribunal may deal with the application in writing or order that it will be dealt with at a preliminary hearing.

9.7 It is no longer necessary, as was required by rule 11(3) of the Tribunal Rules 2004, to state in an application how the order will assist the tribunal to deal with the proceedings efficiently and fairly. However, in light of the duty on the parties and their representatives to assist the tribunal to further the overriding objective of dealing with a case fairly and justly, it is good practice for the parties to follow a similar procedure to that which applied under the old rules when making an application. So, for example, parties claiming disclosure should show that the document(s) may contain information that will advance their own case or damage their opponent's case.

Time limit. When making the order, the tribunal may impose a deadline by **9.8** which the order must be complied with. Rule 4(5) provides that, where the tribunal imposes a time limit for doing any act, the last date for compliance must, wherever practicable, be expressed as a calendar date. Furthermore, an order of the tribunal for an act to be done on or by a particular day must be done before midnight on that day – rule 4(1). However, the time limit may be extended (or shortened) on the application of a party or on the tribunal's own initiative – rule 5.

Under rule 10(3) of the Tribunal Rules 2004, any order for additional information had to inform the parties of the potential consequences of non-compliance with the order. This is not an express requirement under the 2013 Rules but an order may provide that if it is not complied with by the date specified, the claim or response (or part of it) will be dismissed without further order – rule 38(1) (see 'Failure to comply with orders' below).

Format for delivering additional information. Where a party applies to the **9.9** tribunal for a formal order, neither that party nor, if a response is ordered, the other side, will be expected to comply with any standard form. It will suffice that any request or response identifies the passage in the ET1 or ET3 which requires elaboration. This should then be followed by, in the case of a request, a clear specification of the details required or, in the case of a response to the request, a clear exposition of the information necessary to answer the request.

Variation or revocation. Rule 29 provides that a tribunal can vary, suspend or **9.10** set aside an order where that is necessary in the interests of justice, and in particular where a party affected by the order did not have a reasonable opportunity to make representations before it was made. These powers are discussed further in Chapter 11, 'Case management', under 'Case management orders – varying, suspending or setting aside orders'.

When will additional information be ordered?   9.11
Notwithstanding the wide power conferred on tribunals by rule 29, orders for additional information are only likely to be made if they are necessary or appropriate. Essentially, an order will only be appropriate if one of the parties does not know sufficient details of the other side's case to enable proper preparation for the hearing.

The EAT's decision in Honeyrose Products Ltd v Joslin 1981 ICR 317, EAT, shows the extent to which a party is entitled to know the details of the case that he or she will have to meet. J claimed that he had been constructively and unfairly dismissed. He stated that there had been five specific breaches of

489

contract. H Ltd denied each allegation in its ET3. It also applied for an order for further particulars of each breach of contract alleged by J. The employment judge made an order for further particulars limited to requiring the dates and names of persons involved in the alleged breaches. H Ltd appealed against the judge's order on the ground that it was insufficient. The EAT agreed, holding that the judge's order was too narrow and that J should be required to give full details of the allegations made as well as particulars of any further breaches of contract to be relied on other than those specifically pleaded in his ET1.

9.12 In a nutshell, then, the tribunal should ask itself whether both parties are aware of the details of the case that they will have to meet. If it considers that one of the parties is not sufficiently aware, the tribunal should make an order for additional information. To determine the scope of the order, the tribunal should consider what is required to ensure that the case can be disposed of fairly and justly.

It is particularly important that the respondent is fully aware of the case being brought against it. In Nunez v Veritas Software Ltd EAT 0020/04, a disability discrimination claim, the employer sought further and better particulars of the nature of the claimant's disability, as well as details of the incidents upon which he relied to establish that he had suffered less favourable treatment. The claimant failed to comply with the tribunal's order on the basis that he himself needed further particulars of the employer's case in order to be in a position to provide the required further particulars. When dismissing an appeal from a judge's decision to strike out the claim for non-compliance, the EAT observed that a person bringing a claim must take the responsibility of formulating it and, if there is information relevant to that claim in the possession of the respondent, that further information must be disclosed as part of the process of discovery. In the instant case, the judge had not erred in any way in ruling that further information was not required for the employee to complete and supply the information specified.

9.13 Similarly, in Secretary of State for Work and Pensions (Jobcentre Plus) v Constable EAT 0156/10 the EAT held that additional information on the details of the claimant's claim was needed to help the employer prepare for the case it had to meet. C complained that he was unfairly dismissed for having made a protected disclosure. The employer sought further and better particulars of C's claim, arguing that it omitted vital information. In particular, the employer submitted that it needed to know the specific act of disclosure that C claimed to have made; when, how and to whom he had made the alleged disclosure; and how he alleged that that disclosure had led to his dismissal. The tribunal refused to grant the order but the EAT overturned the decision on appeal. In the EAT's view, the employer could not be expected to produce evidence from an array of witnesses, effectively charting C's entire employment history, in the hope that whatever he might say would be covered. This would be a time-consuming and costly exercise, which was not in line with the overriding objective. The employer was entitled to know the case against it and to know what witnesses to call. The EAT accordingly allowed the appeal and granted the order in the terms sought.

Evidence. It is clear that the main purpose of obtaining additional information **9.14** from the other side is to enable a party to know in sufficient detail the nature of the case that he or she will have to meet. In order to achieve this aim, it is likely that only details of the 'facts' to be relied on by the other side will be required. A party will not generally be ordered to provide details of the evidence he or she intends to adduce in an attempt to prove those facts.

However, the distinction between 'facts' and 'evidence' can be a difficult one to draw in practice. Essentially, evidence is the 'tool' by which material facts are proven. An example of this would be where a contractual relationship is alleged to exist as implied from a series of letters or conversations. The material fact is that a contractual relationship is alleged. An order for information would not be granted as to the precise detail of the evidence (i.e. the substance of letters and conversations) which will be relied on to prove that fact, although it would be reasonable for general details to be required about the source(s) from which it is claimed the implied contract derives.

One case (decided under the Tribunal Rules 1993) in which the EAT held that **9.15** a tribunal had gone beyond the scope of its powers in ordering further particulars is Nakatani v Japanese School Ltd EAT 391/97. The tribunal had ordered that N provide 'confirmation from the Home Office or the Japanese Embassy that on 31 May 1995 [he was] entitled to seek and obtain employment in the United Kingdom'. In setting aside the order, the EAT confirmed that particulars are for the purpose of identifying the issues, not for the production of the evidence. Clearly, the tribunal in that case was asking for evidence. JS Ltd would certainly have been entitled to know that N was claiming that he was allowed to work in the UK and, possibly, to know details of the grounds on which N was so claiming. However, it was not appropriate for the tribunal to require actual evidence to be produced at that stage of the proceedings.

It should be noted, however, that where the details requested are necessary to enable the party applying for additional information to prepare for the hearing, tribunals have long been inclined to order the other side to provide that information even where the incidental effect of the order will be the disclosure of some evidence.

Reason for dismissal. In most unfair dismissal cases claimants will not be **9.16** required to provide information of what they believe were the reasons for dismissal. In Springline Spares Ltd v Linacre EAT 575/88 the EAT held that, since the onus of proof as to the reason for a dismissal is on the employer, there is no justification for ordering an employee to provide information as to what

491

that reason for dismissal was. However, in Colonial Mutual Life Assurance Society Ltd v Clinch 1981 ICR 752, EAT, the EAT held that, where an employee states in his or her claim form what, in his or her view, was the reason for dismissal, the employer is entitled to further particulars of the employee's view in order to know the nature of the case it will have to meet. Accordingly, it seems that, where an employee makes a claim as to the reason for his or her dismissal of his or her own volition, a tribunal will be inclined to order the employee to provide additional information about that claim.

9.17 **'Relevant employees' in industrial action cases.** Information about the identity of a 'relevant employee' who was alleged to have taken part in industrial action but not to have been dismissed along with others participating in the same action was ordered in P and O European Ferries (Dover) Ltd v Byrne 1989 ICR 779, CA. There, B was among 1,025 P and O employees dismissed while on strike. In respect of his claim (which was the first to come before a tribunal), P and O contended that the tribunal had no jurisdiction to entertain the complaint under what is now S.238(2) of the Trade Union and Labour Relations (Consolidation) Act 1992 because all 'relevant employees' (i.e. those taking part in the strike) had been dismissed. B claimed otherwise, alleging that one relevant employee had not in fact been dismissed, meaning that the tribunal retained jurisdiction to hear his unfair dismissal claim. P and O sought an order for further particulars of B's allegation, including disclosure of the identity of the employee not dismissed. The application was refused on the ground that, if granted, it would enable the employer to identify and dismiss the employee before the claim of unfair dismissal had been decided, thereby depriving the tribunal of jurisdiction to hear not only B's claim but also the claims of the other 1,024 employees yet to be heard.

Although the EAT upheld the tribunal's decision, on further appeal the Court of Appeal ruled that both the tribunal and the EAT had wrongly refused to make the order for further particulars. While a party is not entitled to particulars solely for the purpose of ascertaining the names of an opponent's witnesses, a party is entitled to particulars to enable him or her to know the case which he or she has to meet even where one or more of the potential witnesses will be identified as a result. In the present case, it was necessary and proper that the information should be given, notwithstanding the fact that, by so doing, the employer would then be able to take action which, in the result, would frustrate the claims of the employees.

9.18 **Still further information**

There is no express provision limiting the number of times a party can apply for an order for additional information. Accordingly, if a party's response to an order for further information is inadequate or unsatisfactory, it is possible to apply for yet further additional information. This course of action is desirable where it is clear that a genuine, though in the event inadequate, effort to

492

respond to an order has been made. The ultimate sanction of striking out in such a situation (see 'Failure to comply with orders' below) is not likely to be appropriate so long as the defaulting party has been acting in good faith.

On the whole, however, tribunals are generally reluctant to allow the parties to become involved in a complicated and time-consuming process of acquiring still further information. In Delooze and ors v Davies Metcalfe Ltd EAT 550/81, for example, DM Ltd pleaded 'redundancy' as the reason for dismissal. The claimants accepted that a redundancy situation existed but claimed that the basis for their selection was unfair. Having sought and been granted an order for further particulars of DM Ltd's defence, the claimants sought a further order in respect of the particulars supplied which they said was confused and did not sufficiently disclose the procedure by which DM Ltd had made the selections for redundancy. The tribunal declined to make the further order and the claimants appealed. The EAT held that, although the first set of particulars was indeed vague, DM Ltd's grounds of resistance had become fully clear in the course of argument before it. Thus there was no longer any need to seek further information at that stage. If, at the tribunal hearing, DM Ltd purported to rely upon grounds which it had not disclosed, then the employees would be entitled to apply for an adjournment and to seek reimbursement of their costs caused by the delay.

If a party has made a bona fide attempt to provide all the relevant information **9.19** within his or her knowledge at the time when a request or order is made, but subsequently discovers other important information upon which he or she would wish to rely at the hearing, it will be in that party's interests to seek to add to the information already given or, if appropriate, to amend it. As already mentioned, the effect of granting orders for additional information is to formalise the pleadings to a significant degree: tribunals will rightly be disapproving of any party that has purported to comply with an order but then introduces into evidence new matters which should have been covered by any information already given.

Late provision of information   **9.20**
Where particulars requested in an order for additional information are only furnished by a party at a late stage in the proceedings, a tribunal should take care to ensure that the party in whose favour the order was made is not prejudiced by this and is given sufficient time in light of the new information to prepare for the hearing. In Inn Pro Training Ltd v Moore EAT 611/97 the respondent had on several occasions tried to obtain further information from the claimant about her claim and, in absence of a response, had sought an order for further particulars from the tribunal. By the time the particulars were furnished, the respondent was left with only one day to prepare for the hearing. Notwithstanding this, the tribunal refused an application for a postponement. On appeal, the EAT ruled that the interests of justice required that the hearing be postponed to give the employer a proper opportunity to prepare his case.

493

9.21 Written answers

As mentioned in the introduction to this chapter, rule 10(2)(f) of the Tribunal Rules 2004 empowered an employment tribunal to order the provision of written answers to any questions that were put by the tribunal. The Tribunal Rules 2013 no longer contain an express provision in this regard but the same type of order can now be made under the tribunal's general case management powers in rule 29.

As with all case management orders, a party applying for an order to provide written answers must comply with the requirements set out in rule 30 (see 'Obtaining additional information – making an application for additional information' above). Where the tribunal makes the order, it will normally specify a date by which the order must be complied with. The sanctions for non-compliance are considered under 'Failure to comply with orders' below.

9.22 While orders for obtaining additional information are made with a view to clarifying what the parties are actually claiming or alleging (see 'Obtaining additional information' above), orders to provide written answers provide a useful mechanism for identifying and narrowing the issues in contention, irrespective of what the parties have set out in their ET1 and ET3. In effect, such orders correspond to 'requests for information' under the Civil Procedure Rules 1998 SI 1998/3132 in civil litigation.

An order requiring the provision of written answers can be made against anyone and is not restricted to the parties to the proceedings. A tribunal can therefore ask questions of, for example, a particular employee of the respondent without having to consider whether he or she is strictly speaking a party. However, a case decided under the Tribunal Rules 2004 shows that there are some limitations as to the scope of the order that can be made. In Amey Services Ltd v Cardigan and ors and another case 2008 IRLR 279, EAT, an employment tribunal – hearing multiple equal pay claims – issued standard case management orders requiring production of documents and written answers to certain questions. The questions included, at 2(a): 'Is it the respondent's position that if there is found to be a difference in pay between the claimant and any of her male comparators that this difference is genuinely due to a material factor which is not the difference of sex?'; and at 2(b): 'If so, what is this difference and why would it justify any difference in pay which is found to exist?' The respondents objected to the questions and, on appeal, the EAT agreed. In the EAT's view, the tribunal had been over-zealous in its desire for information when it ordered the respondents to disclose their defence to the equal pay claims before the claimants had identified their comparators. The burden of proving the defence could only arise once the claimants had established a prima facie case. Accordingly, question 2(a) and (b) of the case management order was revoked.

'Ask and respond' procedure in discrimination cases

Direct evidence of discrimination is rare and any information that may substantiate, or dispel, someone's suspicions that they have been discriminated against will ordinarily be in the employer's possession. Therefore, generally speaking, an employee, or job applicant, who believes that he or she has suffered less favourable treatment because of a protected characteristic will need to obtain information from the employer prior to bringing any claim for discrimination under the Equality Act 2010 (EqA). This information will often be invaluable to an employee (or job applicant) when deciding whether to submit a claim (and pay an issue fee). But while the information is particularly useful at an early stage, it may also be helpful where a claim has already been presented and the claimant is collating information to support his or her case.

Until 6 April 2014 there was a formal 'question and answer' procedure for discrimination claims that allowed a person who thought that he or she might have been unlawfully discriminated against, harassed or victimised to question the employer about the allegations – see S.138 EqA (now repealed by S.66 of the Enterprise and Regulatory Reform Act 2013 (ERRA)). The questions were usually (but not necessarily) posed by using the statutory questionnaire prescribed for that purpose and, while responding to a questionnaire (whether or not on a prescribed form) was voluntary, the questions together with any replies supplied by the employer were admissible in evidence before an employment tribunal. Furthermore, the tribunal was entitled to draw an inference of discrimination from an employer's failure to answer the questions within eight weeks or from an evasive or equivocal answer.

Following a public consultation, and despite scant support for the move, the Government decided to repeal S.138 EqA with effect from 6 April 2014 in a bid to ease 'regulatory burdens' on employers. However, discrimination questionnaires are unlikely to disappear overnight as S.66(2) ERRA states that the statutory questionnaire procedure continues to apply 'for the purposes of proceedings that relate to a contravention occurring before [6 April 2014]'. S.138 EqA will therefore continue to operate where the allegedly discriminatory treatment took place before the cut-off date. For more information on the statutory questionnaire procedure, see IDS Employment Law Handbook, 'Discrimination at Work' (2012), Chapter 33, 'Proving discrimination', under 'Requesting information and disclosure of evidence – statutory questionnaires', and IDS Employment Law Handbook, 'Equal Pay' (2011), Chapter 9, 'Enforcement', under 'Statutory questionnaire procedure'.

Although the statutory questionnaire procedure has now been abolished, it is important to bear in mind that the basic mechanism for obtaining information

495

from an employer about alleged discriminatory treatment has not changed. The employee, or job applicant, is still entitled to write to the employer and ask questions in order to ascertain whether he or she was the victim of unlawful discrimination. And while the employer is not obliged to answer those questions, an employment tribunal may take the employer's failure to answer, or any evasive or equivocal answer, into account when determining whether or not there has been a breach of the EqA. As the mechanism for asking questions is no longer rooted in legislation, Acas has published non-statutory guidance, 'Asking and responding to questions of discrimination in the workplace' (January 2014) ('the Acas guidance'), to help explain the 'ask and respond' process and offer practical advice on how to use it. The guidance is discussed further below.

9.25 **Part-time, fixed-term and agency working.** While the 'ask and respond' procedure is specific to discrimination cases, it is worth noting that similar procedures exist in relation to part-time workers, fixed-term employees and agency workers. Reg 6 of the Part-time Workers (Prevention of Less Favourable Treatment) Regulations 2000 SI 2000/1551 and Reg 5 of the Fixed-term Employees (Prevention of Less Favourable Treatment) Regulations 2002 SI 2002/2034 allow workers to ask their employers to explain the reasons for the alleged less favourable treatment when compared to full-time or, as the case may be, permanent workers. The employer's written statement is admissible as evidence in tribunal proceedings and the tribunal is entitled to draw an adverse inference from a deliberate failure to provide a statement or from an evasive or equivocal statement. Reg 16 of the Agency Workers Regulations 2010 SI 2010/93 contains similar provisions in relation to agency workers.

9.26 **Drafting the information request**

The Acas guidance lists the basic information that anyone who suspects that they have been discriminated against – i.e. the 'questioner' – should include when they are requesting information from the person who is responsible for answering the questions – i.e. the 'responder'. In summary, the 'six step guidance for questioners' recommends that the information request should explain:

- who the questioner and responder are
- which protected characteristics under the EqA are affected
- what treatment is alleged to have occurred
- what type of discrimination is pleaded
- why the questioner thinks the treatment was discriminatory, and
- what additional questions the questioner wants answered.

We discuss each step below. A template form that can be used to draft and develop the questions for the responder is included in Annex 1 to the guidance.

Step 1: the questioner's and responder's details. The Acas guidance advises 9.27
that any request for information should start with the questioner setting out his
or her name and address, followed by the name and contact details of 'the
person or organisation and others who the questioner thinks may have
discriminated against [him or her]'. It would seem that 'others' in this context
could refer to, for example, the questioner's colleagues or any of the employer's
employees who he or she thinks played any part in the incident(s) complained of.

Step 2: the protected characteristics under the EqA. The EqA prohibits 9.28
discrimination on nine protected grounds: sex, race, disability, age, sexual
orientation, religion or belief, marriage and civil partnership, gender
reassignment and pregnancy and maternity. The questioner needs to identify all
the protected characteristics that are relevant to his or her complaint.

Step 3: a description of the alleged treatment. The information request should 9.29
contain a brief factual description of the treatment complained of, including
the date and time when, the place where, and number of instances on which the
treatment occurred. Anyone else involved in the incident(s) should also be
mentioned. The guidance recommends that the questioner conclude this part
by asking whether the responder agrees with his or her statement of what took
place and, if the responder does not agree, to give reasons.

Step 4: the type of discrimination. Next, the questioner should specify the 9.30
type of discrimination he or she has allegedly suffered. For example, the
questioner may complain of direct discrimination, harassment or a failure to
make reasonable adjustments. The guidance lists the types of discrimination
prohibited under the EqA, but it also notes that a questioner can obtain help in
identifying the type of discrimination by contacting the Citizens Advice Bureau
or the Equality Advisory Support Service, operated by the Equality and Human
Rights Commission.

Step 5: the reason for the questioner's belief that there was discrimination. 9.31
This is the section where the questioner sets out why he or she thinks that there
has been discrimination. The guidance states that the questioner should describe
in what context or capacity he or she experienced the alleged unfavourable
treatment being enquired about. The example explaining step 5 recommends
that a woman who believes that she was denied a promotion because of her sex
could include the following: that she believes that her treatment at the interview
was unlawful because she was asked questions around childcare which would
not have been asked of a man applying for the job; that she thinks she was
turned down for the promotion because her superior had apparent concerns
about her childcare arrangements; and that she was treated this way because
she is a woman.

Step 6: any additional questions. If the questioner wants to ask the responder 9.32
any additional questions that he or she believes to be relevant, then these should

497

be set out in the final section. The guidance notes that the questioner may ask for details of an employer's workplace policies on equality, discipline or grievance, or bullying and harassment. He or she may also ask for statistical information to show how others with the same protected characteristics are treated by the employer. So, returning to the example of the female employee who believes that she was refused promotion because of her sex, the guidance notes that she may ask to see the questions put by the interviewers to the other candidates for the job, whether the interviewers were trained in equality and recruitment and selection procedures, and for statistics to see how many other women compared to men were promoted to a supervisory role within the company.

9.33 Sending the information request

Once the six steps have been completed, the information request should be sent to the responder. The guidance states that this can be done in any form, including by letter, e-mail or questionnaire. This suggests that it remains acceptable for a questioner to continue to use the statutory questionnaire form previously prescribed for this purpose as a means of asking questions in cases of alleged discriminatory treatment.

The questions can be sent to the responder by post, e-mail or fax or delivered in person. The questioner should also inform the responder where to send the answers. For example, he or she may prefer any responses to be sent directly to their legal or trade union representative, in which case the representative's address should be given. Acas advises that, whichever method is chosen for delivery of the information request, the questioner should make it clear that the request will require action by the responder. Moreover, it recommends that, given the time limits for bringing a discrimination claim, the questioner should ask the responder to reply by a specified date. However, the responder is under no obligation to respond to the information request or, if it does respond, to do so within a certain timeframe.

9.34 Responding to the information request

As mentioned above, the responder is under no obligation to respond to the information request. However, the Acas guidance advises the responder to think through the implications before deciding not to answer any questions it has been sent. If a responder chooses not to respond, a claim may be lodged at the employment tribunal that could have been avoided. This is because the answers to the questions may demonstrate that any treatment meted out was not discriminatory or, even if it was, that the responder had justifiable grounds for the treatment. Furthermore, if the questioner's grievance does result in a tribunal claim, the responder may be ordered to provide the information in any event under the terms of a disclosure order. Moreover, the tribunal is likely to take into account the responder's failure to respond, or the way in which it responded, when determining the issue of whether the questioner was discriminated against. This point is discussed under 'Admissibility and drawing of adverse inferences' below.

If the responder decides to answer the questions, the Acas guidance sets out the key points that should be addressed in the response. It recommends a three-step approach to cover the main issues.

Step 1: agreement or disagreement with the questioner's description of the treatment? The responder needs to decide whether it agrees, agrees in part or disagrees with the questioner's statement of the treatment he or she is alleged to have suffered. Before setting out its views of what happened, the guidance recommends that the responder conduct some investigation into the incident(s) about which the complaint is made. 9.35

Step 2: does the responder consider the treatment was justified? As the EqA allows for a justification defence to some types of discrimination, the responder should state whether or not it considers that the alleged treatment was justified. For example, the responder may have a valid reason for requiring work on a Sunday even if the questioner considers this to be unlawful religious discrimination. 9.36

Step 3: responding to other questions. Finally, the responder should deal with any other questions that have been asked. If the responder thinks that some questions are not relevant or unclear, it should ask the questioner to clarify their purpose. If the responder decides not to answer a question, it should explain why. Similarly, if the responder believes that certain information, such as information relating to other employees, cannot be supplied because of data protection or confidentiality issues, it should say so. 9.37

Sending the answers to the information request
9.38
Once the answers have been compiled, the responder should send them to the address the questioner has provided. The answers can be sent by post, e-mail or fax or delivered in person. While there is no time limit for answering the questions, the Acas guidance states that it is important to respond within a reasonable period of time. If the responder cannot meet any deadline set by the questioner, it should contact him or her and agree an alternative date.

Equal pay claims
9.39
Additional considerations apply where the questioner is considering, or has already presented, an equal pay claim. In these circumstances, the questioner should identify any comparator he or she thinks is doing equal work and should include any pay-related questions in the information request. For example, he or she may ask for the comparator's job description or how pay is determined by the responder. On receiving the information request, the responder should assess whether the questioner is being paid less or employed on less favourable

499

terms and conditions than the comparator(s). In its response, the responder should either agree that there is gender pay discrimination and take steps to put this right, or challenge the selection of the comparator, or provide some material reason which would justify the difference in pay. For more information on the necessary elements for an equal pay claim, and the employer's defence, see IDS Employment Law Handbook, 'Equal Pay' (2011).

9.40 Admissibility and drawing of adverse inferences

Under the statutory questionnaire procedure, any questions asked, together with any answers provided, were admissible in evidence before an employment tribunal – see S.138(3) EqA. Crucially, S.138(4) went on to allow the tribunal to draw an inference of discrimination from a failure to answer questions within eight weeks or from an evasive or equivocal answer. These statutory provisions on admissibility and the drawing of adverse inferences were repealed on 6 April 2014 when the new informal 'ask and respond' procedure was introduced but it seems likely that tribunals will adopt the same approach as before. The Explanatory Notes to S.66 ERRA confirm that exchanges under the 'ask and respond' procedure will be admissible as evidence in employment tribunal proceedings. The Notes state: 'A potential complainant may still seek information from a potential respondent without the statutory procedure and a court or tribunal may consider any relevant questions and answers as part of the evidence in a case.' The Acas guidance also notes that, while the responder is under no obligation to answer any questions posed, a tribunal may look at whether and, if so, how the responder has answered the questions as 'a contributory factor in making [the] overall decision on the questioner's discrimination claim'. This suggests that the 'ask and respond' procedure will continue to represent a valuable source of information for a claimant seeking to establish a prima facie case of discrimination.

Furthermore, the drawing of adverse inferences is a matter for the tribunal's discretion. As the EAT made clear in D'Silva v NATFHE (now known as University and College Union) and ors 2008 IRLR 412, EAT, adverse inferences can only be drawn from a failure to provide information or an evasive or equivocal response to a statutory questionnaire in appropriate cases. The EAT observed that there was a tendency in discrimination cases for respondents' failures in answering a questionnaire, or in providing information or documents, to be relied on by claimants, and even sometimes tribunals, as automatically raising a presumption of discrimination. In its view, this was not the correct approach. In deciding whether it was appropriate to draw an inference, a tribunal should first consider whether, in the particular circumstances of a case, the failure in question is capable of constituting evidence supporting the inference that the respondent acted discriminatorily in the manner alleged. In other words, any alleged failure on the respondent's part, however reprehensible, is only of relevance if it potentially sheds light on the actual discrimination

500

complained of and thus, necessarily, on the 'mental processes' of the decision-maker. If it does, the tribunal must then consider the respondent's explanation for any alleged failure and whether, in light of that explanation, it is justified in drawing the inference.

Applying this approach to the facts of the case before it, the EAT went on to hold that a trade union's reasons for not recording acceptances and refusals under the legal assistance scheme along ethnic lines was held not to give rise to an inference of racial discrimination. There was no link between, on the one hand, the decision that led to the design of the union's computer systems which recorded and stored the information regarding the grant and refusal of legal assistance and, on the other, the actual decision regarding the provision of legal assistance to the claimant. Those two matters were wholly distinct. The union disclosed that it did not record acceptances or refusals under the legal assistance scheme according to members' ethnicity. This was because its computer systems did not permit this information to be recorded routinely, and the exercise of going through the files of every person who had applied for legal assistance and matching them with files that showed their ethnic origin would have been disproportionately burdensome. **9.41**

There is nothing to suggest that tribunals will depart from this approach now that S.138(4) EqA has been repealed. The case of Dattani v Chief Constable of West Mercia Police 2005 IRLR 327, EAT, corroborates this view. There, the EAT extended the principles that applied in the context of statutory questionnaires to questions raised by a claimant outside of the questionnaire procedure. It held that the provisions dealing with admissibility and the drawing of adverse inferences contained in (what was then) S.65 of the Race Relations Act 1976 (and, by extension, the equivalent provisions under the other discrimination strands) applied to questions posed by an aggrieved person whether in accordance with the statutory questionnaire procedure *or otherwise*. The policy informing these provisions is that an employer who is asked a direct question in writing by an aggrieved person and who fails to respond or does so evasively ought to be treated in the same way irrespective of whether the question has been asked under the statutory procedure. Accordingly, an employment tribunal was entitled to draw any inference it saw fit from incorrect or misleading information provided by an employer in a letter to the employee, in its notice of appearance or in further and better particulars.

Disclosure and inspection of documents **9.42**

In the process of preparing a case for hearing, it is very important to gather information about the documents on which an opponent intends to rely. Either party may apply for disclosure and/or inspection of any document in the other's possession that they think is relevant will help them prove their case. The Presidential Guidance on 'General Case Management' for England and Wales

501

explains that relevant documents may include documents which record events in the employment history such as a letter of appointment, statement of particulars or contract of employment; notes of a significant meeting such as a disciplinary interview; a resignation or dismissal letter; or even electronic and social media documents. The claimant may have documents to disclose which relate to looking for and finding alternative work.

9.43 'Disclosure' involves producing a list of documents as directed by the tribunal. 'Inspection' is the process by virtue of which the parties gain access to disclosed documents which are in their opponents' possession. Certain documents are exempt from disclosure and/or inspection, generally on the ground that they are either 'privileged' or subject to the 'without prejudice' rule – see 'Privilege', '"Without prejudice" communications' and 'Pre-termination negotiations' below.

9.44 **'Open disclosure'**
In practice, parties who make disclosure – either on a voluntary basis or under order – usually do so by sending copies of the requested documents and/or all documents upon which they will rely at the hearing to their opponents, thus rendering 'inspection' unnecessary. Tribunals encourage an 'open disclosure' policy and it is common practice for tribunals to order the parties to prepare an agreed bundle of documents upon which they intend to rely in advance of the hearing and to stipulate that disclosure be effected prior to this.

So, usually, both sides agree to exchange lists of all relevant documents in their power or possession and to provide copies of these documents or allow inspection and copying of such documents as are not 'privileged' or otherwise exempted from disclosure. The Presidential Guidance on 'General Case Management' for England and Wales points out that in most cases the respondent (usually the employer) has most or all of the relevant documents. This makes it sensible for the respondent to take the lead in disclosure. In a long or complex case, the formation of an 'agreed bundle' will certainly minimise the chances of either party being taken by surprise at the hearing – which could result in an adjournment and costly delay. It will also avoid duplication of documents and simplify matters by ensuring that the tribunal only has to refer to one set of documents throughout the hearing.

9.45 **Is there a duty to disclose where no order has been made?**
There is *no* general duty on a party to tribunal proceedings to allow disclosure or inspection of any of the documents in his or her possession. Only if the tribunal makes an order does a party come under a specific duty, although in practice such orders are commonly made as part of a tribunal's case management powers. A party should be aware, however, that if he or she discloses *some* documents voluntarily, there is a duty not to leave out others if to do so would mislead the other side as to the effect of those documents that have been disclosed. An example:

- **Birds Eye Walls Ltd v Harrison** 1985 ICR 278, EAT: H claimed unfair dismissal. BEW Ltd included the minutes of H's disciplinary interview in the list of documents which it exchanged with H's representatives. It failed, however, to disclose minutes of meetings of a working party set up to investigate suspected malpractices by employees, including H. One of those minutes apparently recorded that the decision to dismiss H had been taken before his disciplinary interview had occurred. It also recorded that one person present at the meeting at which H's dismissal was decided upon was later responsible for hearing a stage in H's internal appeal. The undisclosed documents also indicated other procedural lapses. Even in the absence of these minutes, an employment tribunal found H's dismissal unfair. BEW Ltd appealed to the EAT and during the appeal H's solicitor learned of the existence of the undisclosed minutes. Believing that they would assist him if the appeal were allowed and the case remitted for rehearing, H applied for an order for disclosure of the undisclosed documents. When the issue came before the EAT, it held that, in the absence of a formal order, there was no general duty of disclosure in tribunal proceedings. But where non-disclosure of a document might have the effect of misleading the other side concerning the true nature, purport or effect of any document which has been voluntarily disclosed, then full disclosure ought to be made. In this case, the EAT held that BEW Ltd had improperly withheld significant documents from H and by so doing had misled him about the effect of the minutes which it had chosen to disclose.

In the Birds Eye case the EAT went on to outline two general principles employment tribunals should bear in mind when considering the question of disclosure. These are that:

- the duty not to withhold from disclosure any document the suppression of which would render a disclosed document misleading is a 'high duty' that should be interpreted broadly and enforced strictly by tribunals

- a tribunal should ensure that a party does not suffer any avoidable disadvantage where that party can show at any stage of the proceedings that he or she has been at risk of having his or her claim/defence unfairly restricted by being denied the opportunity of becoming aware of a document in the possession of the other side material to the just prosecution of the party's case.

Power of tribunal to order disclosure or inspection   9.46
Rule 31 of the Tribunal Rules 2013 gives an employment tribunal the power to order 'any person in Great Britain to disclose documents or information to a party (by providing copies or otherwise) or to allow a party to inspect such material as might be ordered by a county court or, in Scotland, by a sheriff'. This wording is almost identical to that of rule 10(2)(d) of the Tribunal Rules

503

2004 and, as previously, links the power to order disclosure and inspection to the powers of a county court. It follows that a tribunal has the same powers to order disclosure as are conferred on a county court under Part 31 of the Civil Procedure Rules 1998 SI 1998/3132 (CPR). However, it has been observed that a Practice Direction that accompanies Part 31 (as opposed to Part 31 itself) is not necessarily binding on tribunals – see South Tyneside Council v Anderson and ors EAT 0002/05. There are currently two Practice Directions that supplement Part 31 of the CPR: Practice Direction 31A on 'Disclosure and Inspection', and Practice Direction 31B on 'Disclosure of Electronic Documents'.

An order for disclosure of documents and information can be made against any person in Great Britain. Rule 31 does not limit disclosure to the parties themselves. It is therefore open to a tribunal to require any third party to disclose documents and information in their possession to a party to the proceedings. Old rule 10(5) provided that an order could only be made against a person other than a party where the disclosure sought was necessary to dispose fairly of the claim or to save expense. This provision has not been carried over into the new Rules but rule 2 of the Tribunal Rules 2013 specifically requires tribunals to save expense as part of the overriding objective to deal with cases fairly and justly. Furthermore, rule 31.17 CPR provides that where a party applies for a disclosure order to be made against a third party, the court must be satisfied, among other things, that disclosure is necessary to dispose fairly of the claim or to save costs. The same approach as that which applied under the 2004 Rules is therefore likely to continue to apply under rule 31.

Note that the territorial scope of rule 31 is limited to Great Britain and a tribunal will not make a disclosure order where the party from whom documents are sought is not situated in Great Britain – Weatherford UK Ltd v Forbes EATS 0038/11. The tribunal does, however, have power under rule 33 to use the procedure laid down by the Council Regulation (EC) No.1206/2001 to request evidence from courts in other EU Member States. Such a request may relate to inspection of documents or other objects.

9.47 **Staged disclosure.** In South Tyneside Council v Anderson and ors (above) the EAT made it clear that it was not an appropriate exercise of its discretion for an employment tribunal to make an order for wide-ranging disclosure with a direction that the parties could subsequently invite the tribunal to restrict the scope of its order should the process throw up particular documents or classes of documents that in their view are 'privileged' or should not in any case be disclosed. The proper way of ordering disclosure was to order disclosure of material that at the time of the initial order appeared to be disclosable, then to permit a party seeking further disclosure to identify why, in the light of the documentation already disclosed, a further specific category of documentation should be ordered to be disclosed. This kind of step-by-step disclosure is envisaged by Practice Direction 31A that accompanies Part 31 of the CPR.

Powers of county court. The powers of the county court to order disclosure **9.48**
and inspection are set out in Part 31 of the CPR and are fleshed out by the
Practice Directions. Under these provisions, a court has the power to order
'standard disclosure' (or, if it so chooses, a limited form of standard disclosure)
and/or 'specific disclosure'.

Standard disclosure. Standard disclosure is governed by rule 31.6 CPR and **9.49**
requires a party to disclose: (a) the documents on which he or she relies, and (b)
the documents that adversely affect his or her own case, adversely affect another
party's case or support another party's case. When a court orders standard
disclosure, it will require the parties to make a reasonable search for documents
falling within (b) above – rule 31.7(1) CPR. In order to determine whether such
a search is reasonable, factors such as the number of documents involved, the
nature and complexity of the proceedings, the expense involved in retrieving
the documents and the significance of any document which is likely to be
located will be taken into account – rule 31.7(2) CPR.

Specific disclosure. Specific disclosure can be ordered in respect of any **9.50**
documents or class of documents of the court's choosing. Furthermore, the
court can order a party to carry out a search in respect of any documents or
class of documents and to disclose any documents located as a result of that
search. The court's powers in relation to ordering specific disclosure are set out
in rule 31.12 CPR.

Normally, the kind of order made by employment tribunals as part of their case
management functions equates to 'standard disclosure' in the county court.
However, in certain circumstances, or where a process of 'staged' disclosure is
used as described above, orders for specific disclosure may be appropriate.

General restrictions on what can be disclosed. There are some general **9.51**
restrictions on what must be disclosed. First, to be subject to disclosure, an item
must be a *document*. 'Document' is not defined in the Tribunal Rules but
according to rule 31.4 CPR it refers to 'anything in which information of any
description is recorded'. A document can therefore include information
recorded, held or stored by means other than paper. For example, the term
covers electronic recordings, such as e-mails, text messages and voicemail,
word-processed documents and databases, documents stored on portable
devices such as mobile phones, documents stored on servers and back-up
systems, and documents that have been deleted, as well as metadata and other
embedded data that is not normally visible on screen – see para 5(2) of Practice
Direction 31B. Tape-recordings are also covered – Grant v Southwestern and
County Properties Ltd 1974 2 All ER 465, ChD.

Secondly, a party is only obliged to disclose documents that are or have been
under his or her *control*. That covers documents that are or have been in his or

505

her possession or documents that he or she has had a right to take possession of, to inspect or to take copies of.

Thirdly, disclosure is limited to documents already *in existence*. An employment judge has no power to require a party to create evidence in, for example, the form of statistical information – Carrington v Helix Lighting Ltd 1990 ICR 125, EAT.

9.52 Applying for disclosure or inspection order

An order for disclosure or inspection may be made by a tribunal on its own initiative or on application by a party to the tribunal – rule 29. Applications for disclosure or inspection will not usually be acceded to unless and until the party has unsuccessfully sought disclosure from the other side on a voluntary basis. Therefore, before applying to the tribunal, a letter should be sent to the other side requesting copies of the specified documents and any other documents on which that party intends to rely at the hearing. Where appropriate, such a request can be incorporated into a letter requesting additional information in respect of the opponent's ET1 or ET3 (see 'Obtaining additional information' above). It is advisable to state that all reasonable photocopying charges will be reimbursed. Where it is likely that a large amount of copying will be involved, or where only small extracts from much larger documents will be needed, it may be preferable to request inspection of the documents at a convenient time and location with a view to taking only such copies as prove to be relevant.

As in the case of orders for additional information, attendance of witnesses and written answers, a party applying to the tribunal for an order for disclosure or inspection must comply with the requirements set out in rule 30 (see 'Obtaining additional information – making an application for additional information' above). Where the tribunal makes the order, it will normally specify a date by which the order must be complied with. The sanctions for non-compliance with the order are considered under 'Failure to comply with orders' below.

9.53 In granting an order, the tribunal can (and often does) set dates by which the terms of the order must be complied with – rule 4(5). As with all time limits under the Tribunal Rules, these can be extended (or shortened) at the tribunal's discretion – rule 5. Orders for disclosure and inspection are frequently accompanied by an 'unless' order stipulating that, unless the order is complied with by the deadline given, the claim or response will be automatically struck out without further consideration of the proceedings – see Chapter 11, 'Case management', under 'Unless orders'.

9.54 When will disclosure or inspection be ordered?

A tribunal's extensive powers to order disclosure and inspection will be exercised at the employment judge's discretion. However, in exercising that discretion, the judge must give effect to the overriding objective in rule 2 of the

Tribunal Rules, which is to enable cases to be dealt with 'fairly and justly'. This means that, when considering the issues of disclosure and inspection, a judge should bear in mind the need to treat the parties equally, to save expense, to act in proportion to the complexity of the case and to avoid unnecessary formality and delay. The judge is clearly required to conduct a balancing exercise when considering whether or not to make an order and in determining the scope of any such order. He or she must balance the importance of the disclosure and/or inspection in ensuring that the case will be disposed of fairly against the expense and inconvenience that such an order might lead to.

Even before the overriding objective was first introduced by the Tribunal Rules **9.55** 2001, tribunals generally adopted a sensible approach to the issues of disclosure and inspection, seeking to avoid excessive burdens for employers while simultaneously allowing claimants access to important information. Tribunals are therefore well versed in conducting the balancing act. The cases below are examples of how the issues of disclosure and inspection have been dealt with in the past and cast light upon the manner in which the issues are likely to be dealt with in the future:

- **British Telecommunications plc v Matthews** EAT 443/90: M claimed that she had been penalised by her employer on account of her trade union activities contrary to what is now S.146 of the Trade Union and Labour Relations (Consolidation) Act 1992. The basis of her claim was that she had been marked down in an assessment by an appraising officer, S, because she was a shop steward. The tribunal ordered disclosure/inspection of the appraisal forms of all staff in the same position as M at the relevant time. BT plc appealed against the order on the ground that it was too extensive. The EAT held that disclosure/inspection should only be ordered where it is necessary for disposing fairly of the case or for saving costs. The evidence revealed that the disclosure/inspection ordered by the tribunal would amount to over 70 forms, even though S appraised only seven other employees. Had the tribunal been aware of this at the time, it would probably not have made the order. Since the only relevance of the documents was to establish whether S had penalised M, it was appropriate to substitute a more restricted order that only the files of those other employees appraised by S should be disclosed. If, however, at any stage of the hearing the tribunal felt that further disclosure was needed, it should be free to order such disclosure as was required

- **Rolls-Royce Motor Cars Ltd v Mair and ors** EAT 794/92: RR Ltd decided to make redundancies across various different divisions of the company. 150 employees brought unfair dismissal claims arising from that decision. The tribunal, at a relatively early stage, ordered that RR Ltd should produce all documents relating to the assessment scores awarded in the selection process in respect of all of the 1,142 employees who were potentially eligible

507

for redundancy selection. RR Ltd appealed against the tribunal's order. In allowing the appeal, the EAT stated that the proper sequence when dealing with considerations of disclosure/inspection in circumstances where there are many claimants and several different issues is first to isolate the issues to which disclosure/inspection are relevant and then to make orders for disclosure/inspection appertaining to those issues, but only if such disclosure/inspection is necessary. Otherwise there was a danger of allowing an order to be used as a weapon on a broad front rather than as it should be; namely, confined to particular and relevant issues

• **South Tyneside Council v Anderson and ors** EAT 0002/05: the issue in this case was whether a job evaluation study was valid in the context of an equal pay claim. The tribunal granted the employee disclosure of two broad categories of documentation in respect of the study. However, on appeal, the EAT held that the order for disclosure went far beyond what was necessary for the purposes of the litigation. The correct approach was to order the disclosure of material that appeared relevant at that time, with permission to the parties to seek further disclosure at a later stage if necessary

• **GMB Union and ors v Hughes and ors** EAT 0528/08: the employer asserted that H was fairly dismissed by reason of capability – he had been sick for over a year and there was no possibility of him ever returning to work. H disputed this, brought a complaint of unfair dismissal, and requested information as to the treatment of other union officers who had been off sick for more than a year over the preceding three-year period and any instances of ill-health retirement among that class of officers. The tribunal granted the order and the EAT upheld the decision. In its view, the information was relevant to H's case and it was not unduly onerous on the employer to provide the information

• **Baraheni v Royal Berkshire NHS Foundation Trust** EAT 0137/11: B was refused an order for the disclosure of some 5,000 pages of documents in electronic form. The documents had already been disclosed in paper form but B argued that the order was necessary to prove her allegation that the employer had altered or faked the documents for the purpose of defending her claim. The EAT upheld the refusal of the order, holding that the order sought by B was time-consuming, expensive, unnecessary for the purpose of expert evidence and of little value. If B considered that there was a particular document that was faked or altered, and that inspection of the electronic material underlying that document would establish the falsity of the document, then she should have made an application in respect of that document only.

9.56 It is permissible for a party to seek disclosure of documents that post-dated the matter complained of. In Pinnock v Birmingham City Council and anor EAT 0185/13 P sought documents relating to the employer's investigation of a complaint she had made about eight fellow employees. The employment tribunal refused the application because her complaint had been made after she had been dismissed and had presented her unfair dismissal claim and therefore could not be relevant to her allegations. The EAT held that the tribunal's decision contained an error of law because documents were not necessarily irrelevant merely because they arose after the event; they could still support a party's case as to the events in question. In any event, it was evident that the complaint had been made prior to dismissal and related to events prior to dismissal and the tribunal's decision on this point was set aside.

The timing of the application may influence the tribunal's decision on whether or not to order disclosure. In Jones v Standard Life Employee Services Ltd EATS 0023/13 the EAT held that an employment judge had been entitled to take the lateness of the application – made only 12 days before the hearing – into account when refusing the order. The overriding objective made it clear that dealing with a case justly included, as far as practicable, ensuring that it was dealt with expeditiously. It did not help the expeditious and fair hearing of a case if applications were made late. Although urgent applications are sometimes necessary because of a sudden turn of events, this did not apply in the instant case. The judge had therefore been entitled to take into account the fact that the late application might adversely affect the hearing. In any event, the judge had correctly found that the employee had failed to demonstrate the relevance of the requested documents.

Disclosure in discrimination cases. Particular problems concerning disclosure 9.57 and inspection of documents can arise in the context of discrimination complaints. Broadly speaking, this is for two related reasons. The first revolves around the difficulties inherent in proving discrimination. Rarely will an employer openly and unequivocally discriminate against an employee, by either word or deed. More likely, the discrimination will take a disguised form, so much so that the employer might not be consciously aware of it.

The second reason relates to the sheer volume of documents often claimed to be relevant to the case. In seeking to make out a complaint that, say, a failure to promote was due to indirect race or sex discrimination, the claimant will usually expect the tribunal to draw inferences from the main facts. These facts often reveal themselves in documents and statistics relating to patterns of promotion and to the treatment of different groups by the same employer (e.g. men/women; black/white employees). Thus it becomes imperative for claimants to obtain the necessary 'ammunition' from which they can invite the tribunal to draw an inference that discrimination because of sex or race was responsible for their detrimental treatment.

In West Midlands Passenger Transport Executive v Singh 1988 ICR 614, CA, 9.58 the Court of Appeal held that, when considering the issues of disclosure and inspection, it is pertinent to bear in mind the special features of discrimination cases. Although the Singh case was one of race discrimination, the observations of the Court of Appeal are also relevant to other types of discrimination. The special features highlighted by the Court are that:

- the evidence sought to be adduced need not decisively prove that the respondent has acted on racial grounds: the question is whether it may tend to prove the case

- direct discrimination involves an individual being treated less favourably because he or she is a member of a particular group. Statistical evidence may show a discernible pattern in the treatment of that group. If that pattern demonstrates that members of that group regularly fail to gain promotion, and that they are under-represented in such jobs, it may give rise to an inference of discrimination against the group

- if a practice is being operated against a group then, in the absence of a satisfactory explanation, it is reasonable to infer that the claimant, as a member of that group, has been treated less favourably on the ground of race. Indeed, evidence of discriminatory treatment against the group may be more persuasive of discrimination in a particular case than previous treatment of the claimant, which might be solely due to personal factors

- evidence is regularly accepted from employers that they employ white and non-white employees and so have a policy of non-discrimination. If such evidence is accepted as having probative force, the converse is also true

- suitability of candidates can rarely be measured objectively. Subjective judgments are often made and a high rate of failure for members of a particular group may indicate a conscious or unconscious racial attitude involving stereotyped assumptions.

So, the kinds of document in respect of which a tribunal might order disclosure and inspection in, for example, sex discrimination cases include assessments of other candidates for a job or for promotion; the criteria used in past selection decisions; applications made at each stage of the selection procedure; documents showing the distribution by sex of rejected and accepted candidates; and documents showing the distribution by sex of employees for each job held by the workforce at the relevant company.

9.59 In Canadian Imperial Bank of Commerce v Beck 2009 IRLR 740, CA, B, a German, brought a race discrimination claim against CIBC, alleging that he would not have been made redundant if he had been Canadian or been hired in Canada. B sought disclosure of a large number of e-mails between senior employees, which was refused by the tribunal. The EAT allowed an appeal and the Court of Appeal upheld the decision. If there was a policy of differential treatment, as B alleged, this was likely to be revealed in communications between senior executives during the period when decisions about redundancies

510

were being taken. The documents sought were clearly necessary for the fair disposal of the proceedings, and the EAT had been right to make the order for disclosure.

In equal pay cases, disclosure can be ordered in favour of a claimant to assist in identifying an appropriate comparator. In Clwyd County Council v Leverton EAT 15/85, for example, the claimant sought disclosure of the pay and contractual details of certain male employees in order to identify and name a comparator for the purpose of her equal value claim. The EAT, although warning against using disclosure as a 'fishing' exercise designed to hunt around for grounds upon which a claim may be brought, held that a prima facie case had been made out so that disclosure along the lines requested was appropriate.

Disclosure in unfair redundancy cases. Claims of unfair dismissal arising in a **9.60** redundancy context often throw up particular issues concerning disclosure. These usually revolve around the disclosure of marking systems on which the selection for redundancy has been based.

In British Aerospace plc v Green and ors 1995 ICR 1006, CA, the Court of Appeal ruled that an employment judge erred in ordering the disclosure of the assessments of employees retained by the employer for the purpose of enabling the employees who had been selected for redundancy to decide which cases should be chosen as sample cases for hearing before a tribunal. In so holding, the Court emphasised that disclosure should only ever be ordered when it has been demonstrated that the material sought is relevant to the issues before the tribunal at any particular stage. In cases of alleged unfair selection for redundancy, it is only in the most exceptional circumstances that documents relating to those employees who have been retained by the employer (as opposed to those who have been dismissed for redundancy) will be relevant to any issue that the tribunal will be called upon to decide. A claimant who alleges that the selection process was unfairly applied in practice and who seeks an order for disclosure must specify the respect in which he or she claims that the process was unfairly applied with sufficient particularity to demonstrate the relevance of the material which is being sought. He or she is not entitled merely to say: 'The process was unfair: I do not know in what respect it was unfair. I want discovery in order to find out.'

In contrast to the British Aerospace case, the EAT in FDR Ltd v Holloway 1995 **9.61** IRLR 400, EAT, ruled that an employee was entitled to be given access to documents relating to the assessments of employees who had not been dismissed. In that case, the employee had alleged that his employer's selection criteria were unfairly applied, or not applied at all, in his case. He had been dismissed after more than four years' service while a comparable employee, who was retained, had only been employed for a matter of months. In respect of the employee's claim that this was a breach of an agreed procedure relating to redundancy

511

selection, the EAT held that the documents sought were clearly relevant to the issue of whether he had been unfairly dismissed.

The main difference between the two cases is that the allegations of unfairness in the Holloway case were specific and the claimant was able to point to a particular employee whom he claimed should have been selected for redundancy instead of him. It was also relevant that the claimant was asking for disclosure of the assessments of only seven other employees who had been retained, rather than 7,000 as was the position in the British Aerospace case. In Holloway, Mr Justice Mummery (then President of the EAT) declined to extend the reasoning of the Court of Appeal in the British Aerospace case into a general rule forbidding the discovery of assessment forms in cases where the fairness of a redundancy selection exercise is in question. (Note, however, that the Court of Session has doubted (obiter) the correctness of the Holloway decision as, in its view, it is irreconcilable with the Court of Appeal's decision in the British Aerospace case – King and ors v Eaton Ltd 1996 IRLR 199, Ct Sess (Inner House).

9.62 Continuing duty to disclose

Once an order for disclosure has been made, it imposes an obligation that remains continuous throughout the proceedings – Scott v Commissioners of Inland Revenue 2004 ICR 1410, CA. Therefore, if further documents come to light, or come into existence, during the course of the proceedings, they should be disclosed if they are relevant to any information already disclosed or fall within the terms of an order for disclosure. In the Scott case, having found that S had been unfairly and wrongfully dismissed and discriminated against on the grounds of sex and disability, a tribunal awarded him compensation, the future loss element of which was based on the fact that he would have had to retire from his employment at the age of 60 in any event. S appealed to the EAT against the amount of the compensatory award. However, before his appeal was heard, he discovered that his employer had changed its retirement policy to allow employees to work beyond the normal retirement age of 60 up to the age of 65. When the case reached the Court of Appeal, it took the view that the employer should have disclosed its new retirement policy as soon as it was introduced. The employment tribunal proceedings had not been determined at that date and it was plain that the prospective duration of S's employment would have been central to the calculation of his compensatory award. In particular, the Court pointed to the disclosure order made by the tribunal in January 2002, which it held to be an ongoing obligation.

It should be noted that rule 31.11 CPR – which, as we have seen, governs the scope of the tribunal's power to order disclosure or inspection of information and documents – explicitly provides that: '(1) Any duty of disclosure continues until the proceedings are concluded. (2) If documents to which that duty extends come to a party's notice at any time during the proceedings, he must immediately notify every other party.' This makes it clear that disclosure is a continuing obligation.

Privilege
9.63

Although employment tribunals are not bound by the rules of evidence applicable in other courts, the rules relating to privilege do apply. That is because they apply in respect of a county court's powers to order disclosure and inspection under Part 31 of the CPR and, as we have seen, tribunals have the same powers as the county court in this regard.

'Privilege' is a somewhat misleading term used by lawyers to denote that a document is protected from inspection in the interests of the administration of justice. Under the rules relating to privilege, a party can object to producing 'privileged' documents for inspection. Generally, there is no privilege from disclosure, only from inspection, although occasionally a privileged document will not be disclosed if such non-disclosure is in the public interest. Where a party claims privilege as the reason for not releasing a document, the tribunal has a duty to inspect the document itself in order to ascertain whether the grounds for non-release are valid – Science Research Council v Nassé 1979 ICR 921, HL.

A detailed examination of the complicated law relating to privilege is beyond **9.64** the scope of this Handbook. However, we deal briefly with the law relating to documents falling within the following categories:

- 'confidential' documents
- documents which should be withheld in the public interest
- documents protected by diplomatic privilege
- documents protected by legal professional privilege.

Confidential documents. Frequently, an employee will wish to see a document **9.65** that his or her employer regards as highly confidential. But confidentiality alone will not prevent an order for inspection. The House of Lords in Science Research Council v Nassé (above) made this clear, adding that confidentiality was nevertheless a consideration which an employment judge, in exercising his or her discretion whether or not to order inspection, could take on board. Their Lordships set out the following guidelines for employment tribunals:

- tribunals can have regard to the fact that documents are confidential and that to order inspection would involve a breach of confidence
- however, if inspection is necessary for the fair disposal of the proceedings, it must be ordered, notwithstanding confidentiality. Where a tribunal is impressed with the need to preserve confidentiality in a particular case, it

513

should consider carefully whether the necessary information has been or can be obtained by other means not involving a breach of confidence

- in order to reach a conclusion as to whether inspection is necessary notwithstanding confidentiality, tribunals should inspect the documents and consider whether justice can be done by special measures such as 'covering up' identifiably confidential features, substituting anonymous references for specific names or, rarely, hearing cases in private.

In National Probation Service (Teesside) v Devon EAT 0419/05 the EAT confirmed that the correct approach for a tribunal to take when dealing with the disclosure of a supposedly confidential document is to weigh up the conflicting interests of the parties and decide whether disclosure is necessary for a fair trial of the action.

9.66 In Plymouth City Council v White EAT 0333/13 the EAT helpfully set out a step-by-step approach for tribunals to follow when considering a disclosure application:

- the judge must first consider if the document sought is relevant. If it is not, then disclosure should not be ordered

- if the document is relevant, the judge must consider whether it is necessary for the fair trial of the case for it to be disclosed. Where there is objection, the judge should examine the document him or herself to determine whether, even if it is confidential, it should still be disclosed

- if the document is relevant and necessary and is to be disclosed, the judge should consider whether there is a more nuanced way of disclosing the material so as to respect confidentiality and the judge may then decide to order the document to be disclosed wholly or partially, usually by redaction (see 'Redaction' below)

- the disclosure judge, having read the disputed documents, should not conduct the full hearing unless the parties agree.

If an employment tribunal concludes that the relevant documents are disclosable, it should not restrict disclosure to itself but must disclose them to the other party or to his or her representative – Knight v Department of Social Security 2002 IRLR 249, EAT. In that case, K brought a disability discrimination claim after the respondent failed to invite him for an interview on the basis that he was unsuccessful in the preliminary written test. In order to assist in the preparation of his case, K requested disclosure of the original test papers and answers of other candidates. Although the tribunal accepted the relevance of those documents, it held that in view of their confidential nature they should be disclosed only to the tribunal itself to ascertain whether or not the test had been properly marked, and not to K or anybody representing him. On appeal, the EAT held that the tribunal had erred in failing to disclose the documents to K or his representative. It took the view that each party must have the right to see any relevant material which his or her opponent intends to place before the tribunal and which the tribunal is likely to take into account in arriving at its decision. In the instant case, all the documents requested by the claimant were relevant. There was therefore no justification for imposing any restriction on disclosure of those documents other than a specific order restricting or prohibiting their disclosure for any purpose other than use in the tribunal proceedings. In reaching its decision, the EAT also rejected the respondent's argument that the test questions were confidential in nature and if they were to enter the public domain a new test would have to be designed at a cost of around £150,000 to £200,000. While the EAT accepted that cost was a material factor, it held that, in the overall context of the case, it should not deprive the claimant of the particular disclosure sought.

Redaction. If necessary in order to preserve confidentiality, an employment **9.67** judge can order disclosure subject to anonymising the document and/or deleting passages that would or might reveal the identity of the author or source of a statement. This process is known as 'redaction'. In Asda Stores Ltd v Thompson and ors 2002 IRLR 245, EAT, the claimants were dismissed following allegations that they had used and supplied drugs at a staff party and a training event. Having lodged unfair dismissal claims, the claimants sought disclosure of the witness statements upon which AS Ltd had based its decision to dismiss. The employer, however, declined to provide this information on the ground that it had made a promise of confidentiality to the relevant witnesses. The employment tribunal agreed with the claimants that the disclosure of the witness statements was necessary for a fair disposal of their cases and went on to order that the statements be disclosed in their totality. On appeal, however, the EAT found that the tribunal had not given adequate weight to the question of confidentiality, particularly in light of the fact that the allegations concerned the use and supply of hard drugs. It went on to hold that it was not necessary for the claimants to know the identities of those employees who made the statements and that, in such circumstances, a tribunal should, where possible, order disclosure to be made 'with omissions' so as to protect the anonymity of the employees involved. Accordingly, the case was remitted to the tribunal to enable an appropriate process of redaction to be carried out.

On a subsequent appeal – Asda Stores Ltd v Thompson and ors (No.2) 2004 IRLR 598, EAT – a different division of the EAT explained how the witness statements should be redacted. AS Ltd had to send the original statements to the tribunal on the basis that they would not be disclosed to the claimants under any circumstances. At the same time, it would submit proposals for redaction, including grammatical rewriting where necessary, along with explanations for the proposed changes. Furthermore, AS Ltd should be given the chance to comment on the changes made by the tribunal before they were sent out to all parties. The EAT further directed that counsel for the claimants

515

be allowed to comment on the proposed changes in return for an undertaking neither to consult on the documents nor to disclose them to his clients or instructing solicitors.

9.68 Another case in which the EAT held that to order full disclosure would involve a breach of confidence was Fairmile Kindergarten v MacDonald EATS 0069/05. There, M had brought a claim for automatic unfair dismissal, alleging that she had been dismissed on account of her pregnancy. The employer, however, argued that its decision to dismiss her was based on a report which concerned allegations communicated to it by a set of parents that M had struck their child. At the parents' request, their names and the name of their child were not included in the report and M applied for an order disclosing their identities. The employment judge granted the order on the basis that it was necessary for the fair disposal of the case. On appeal, the EAT took the view that the disclosure order was not necessarily in the interests of justice and would involve forcing disclosure of the identity of a family who had provided information on the understanding that it could do so anonymously. While the promise of anonymity could not be determinative in a case in which the interests of justice required disclosure, the EAT noted that there are cases – such as the present – in which the interests of justice do not require disclosure. In such cases, the promise of confidentiality should not be overridden. The EAT accordingly allowed the appeal and struck out the tribunal's order.

9.69 *Medical reports.* Of all the different kinds of confidential document, medical or psychiatric reports often prove to be the most sensitive. Such reports may contain diagnoses or prognoses that are distressing to the patient or that may hinder recovery; or they may include statements made by the patient or relatives that could cause embarrassment or distress. However, in McIvor v Southern Health and Social Services Board 1978 2 All ER 625, HL, the House of Lords held that none of these reasons was sufficient for refusing inspection by a claimant in an appropriate case. The limits on confidentiality as a ground for non-inspection of medical reports are illustrated in the case below:

- **Department of Health and Social Security v Sloan (No.2)** EAT 342/81: medical experts on both sides were agreed that inspection of S's medical reports by S would be detrimental to her mental state. Nevertheless, S instructed her advisers that at the time of dismissal she had not been suffering from any psychiatric disorder. The employment tribunal decided that, since S had put her mental health in issue, the reports were relevant and should be disclosed and inspected. On the DHSS's appeal, the EAT held that in addressing the question of reasonableness of dismissal, the parties would have to refer to the medical reports. The tribunal's decision to order disclosure was therefore correct.

9.70 *Use of affidavits to support assertion of confidentiality.* Despite the desirability of informality in tribunal proceedings, the EAT has accepted the use of sworn affidavits to corroborate a 'defence' of confidentiality. In Demmel v YKK Fasteners (UK) Ltd EAT 188/87 the claimant was dismissed for misconduct on the basis of statements obtained from fellow employees under a pledge of confidentiality given by the employer. The claimant applied to inspect the statements and identities of the persons who made them but the employment tribunal refused the application and on appeal the EAT upheld that decision – although Mr Justice Wood added that the employer's assertion of confidentiality should be verified by a sworn affidavit. It is unlikely, however, that the EAT's purpose was to promote widespread resort to affidavits and it should perhaps have borne in mind that, as a general rule in civil litigation, privilege is not usually claimable solely on the ground that documents or information have been supplied in confidence by a third party – see Alfred Crompton Amusement Machines Ltd v Commissioners of Customs and Excise (No.2) 1973 2 All ER 1169, HL.

Public interest. A document may be privileged from disclosure and/or 9.71 inspection on the ground that this would be injurious to the public interest. What comprises the 'public interest' is not fixed at any given point in time but will change and develop as both social conditions and legislation alter. The public interest in non-disclosure/inspection must always be balanced against the public interest in the fair administration of justice – D v National Society for the Prevention of Cruelty to Children (NSPCC) 1977 1 All ER 589, HL. As already mentioned, there is no rule of public interest immunity which protects confidential documents from disclosure by reason of their confidential nature alone.

'Class' and 'contents' immunity. This head of privilege can be divided into 9.72 'class' immunity, covering an entire class of documents regardless of their contents, and 'contents' immunity, whereby only specified parts of the documents concerned are immune from disclosure. The Court of Appeal in Halford v Sharples and ors 1992 ICR 583, CA, stressed the importance of maintaining the distinction between various types of privilege. In a case of this kind, a tribunal should start by determining whether the document is covered by class public interest immunity and, if not, whether it falls under contents public interest immunity. If the documentation does not fall within either category, then confidentiality may be relevant and the principles set out in Science Research Council v Nassé 1979 ICR 921, HL, should be considered (see 'Confidential documents' above).

Greater justification is likely to be required of both 'class' and 'contents' claims in light of the House of Lords' decision in R (on the application of Wiley) v Chief Constable of West Midlands Police 1994 3 WLR 433, HL, where Lord Woolf held that statements made in connection with the statutory police complaints procedure and transcripts of evidence given at internal police disciplinary hearings should not enjoy 'class' immunity. It had previously been

517

thought that class immunity for these documents was justified because persons participating in the complaints process would be inhibited from making statements if they knew that they could be used in civil proceedings and because the requirement to scrutinise individual documents to see if a contents claim was justified would put an undue administrative burden on the police. These reasons, Lord Woolf concluded, were not enough. Recognition of a new class-based public interest immunity required clear and compelling evidence that it was necessary.

9.73 *Conflicting public interests.* Sometimes different public interests conflict. This occurred in Birds Eye Walls Ltd v Harrison 1985 ICR 278, EAT. One established rule of public policy is that a party who obtains possession of a document through inspection gives an implied undertaking to the court not to make use of or copy the document for any purpose outside of those proceedings. In the Birds Eye case, H had become aware of the existence of crucial documents only because they were disclosed in proceedings instituted by a colleague of his. The employer objected to H inspecting those documents on the ground that use of them would offend against the public policy rule. The EAT pointed out, however, that, as Lord Denning MR had made clear in Riddick v Thames Board Mills Ltd 1977 3 All ER 677, CA, the rule was not an immutable one. Where it conflicted with some other public principle (such as the public interest in the fair administration of justice), the court had to weigh up the competing interests involved. The balancing exercise in H's case involved weighing the rule of public policy concerning the protection of disclosed documents on the one hand against the public interest in discouraging the holding back of relevant documents on the other. In the EAT's view, the scales came down in favour of relaxing the rule protecting the documents.

9.74 *National security.* Protection from disclosure and inspection can be in the public interest where it is shown that there is an issue of national security involved. This rarely happens in the context of tribunal proceedings, but, just in case, S.202 of the Employment Rights Act 1996 provides that where, in certain specified proceedings, a Minister of the Crown is of the opinion that disclosure of information would be contrary to the interests of national security, such disclosure will be prohibited. The proceedings to which this section applies are those concerned with:

- written particulars of employment

- the right not to suffer detriment in relation to jury service, health and safety cases, working time cases and cases involving employee representatives or leave for family and domestic reasons

- time off for ante-natal care, dependants and employee representatives

- suspension on maternity grounds

- maternity rights

- in certain circumstances, written statements of reasons for dismissal

- unfair dismissal where the reason for dismissal is automatically unfair and relates to leave for family reasons, jury service, health and safety, rights of workforce and employee representatives, the assertion of a right to time off for dependants or redundancy selection for certain reasons.

Furthermore, in respect of all tribunal cases, rule 3 of Schedule 2 to the Tribunal **9.75** Rules 2013 provides that, in a case relevant to national security, a Minister (whether or not he or she is a party to the proceedings) may make an application to the tribunal objecting to an order for disclosure or inspection, or if such an order has already been made, requesting that it be varied or set aside. The tribunal will hear such an application in private.

Outside of these specific provisions, general common law rules govern the scope of public interest immunity on the ground of national security. In Balfour v Foreign and Commonwealth Office 1993 ICR 663, EAT – a case involving proceedings for unfair dismissal brought by a member of the diplomatic service – the question arose whether a tribunal could order inspection of documents relating to the security and intelligence services over which immunity had been asserted in the form of certificates issued by two Ministers of State. The EAT held that it would be incorrect to say that the chairman of an employment tribunal had no jurisdiction to order inspection of documents simply because a certificate of public interest immunity had been issued by a Minister. Even where the reasons stated by the Minister in the certificate were of a character which judicial experience was not competent to weigh, the chairman would still be required to balance the public interest in the proper administration of justice (which required full disclosure and inspection of relevant documents) against the public interest in protecting national security, although in such a case the argument against inspection would weigh decisively more. The crucial issue, however, is whether there is a factual link shown between the documents and the reasons set out in the certificate purporting to justify the assertion that inspection would prejudice security interests. The EAT's decision in this case was subsequently upheld by the Court of Appeal (Balfour v Foreign and Commonwealth Office 1994 ICR 277, CA).

In Coles and anor v Barracks (Secretary of State for the Home Department **9.76** intervening) 2007 ICR 60, CA, the Court of Appeal clarified the correct approach for tribunals to take when a party refuses to disclose relevant information due to a conflicting legal obligation relating to security. B, a black female officer, applied to join a task force dealing with gun crime in London's black communities. Following a security vetting procedure, she was told that her application was unsuccessful but was not informed of the reasons why. Believing, in the absence of an explanation, that she had been racially

519

discriminated against, she lodged a race discrimination complaint in an employment tribunal. In their response, the respondents claimed that they were prevented by law from revealing to B or to the tribunal not only the reason why B was not selected for the post but also the legal basis on which the prohibition on disclosure rested.

A case management hearing was held, at which the tribunal made an order providing that the case would be struck out unless the respondents supplied both the reason(s) for B's non-selection and the legal basis for their refusal to disclose such information. The respondents appealed to the EAT where, following a rare 'disclosure hearing' conducted pursuant to S.18(7) of the Regulation of Investigatory Powers Act 2000 (RIPA) in the absence of B, her counsel and solicitors, the EAT allowed the appeal. When the case reached the Court of Appeal, it accepted that the tribunal had been wrong to make an 'unless order' with which the respondents could not comply without breaking the law as they understood it to be. However, in remitting the case, the Court of Appeal made it clear – contrary to the ruling of the EAT – that B would not be prevented at the substantive hearing from making appropriate submissions as to the legal and evidential position in the event of the police refusing to answer questions put in cross examination or to produce documents relevant to her case. Those submissions might relate to the inferences to be drawn from the evidence, the burden of proof and the legal entitlement of the police to refuse to answer questions or disclose relevant documentation. Furthermore, to take account of the potential need for a 'disclosure hearing' to deal with any such arguments, the tribunal chairman should be a Circuit Judge, as envisaged by S.18 RIPA. Such a hearing – assuming it to be necessary – should, however, only take place once the tribunal had heard all the available evidence.

9.77 State and diplomatic immunity. As discussed in Chapter 2, 'Tribunals' jurisdiction', under 'State and diplomatic immunity', immunity from liability in respect of both civil and criminal proceedings can be asserted by states and certain personnel carrying out state functions. Even so, any immunity which would otherwise be claimable is frequently waived either deliberately or inadvertently by the state or diplomat in question. Where a case does proceed, embassy documents are protected by privilege which may be claimed notwithstanding any waiver of personal or state immunity by the respondent – Al-Fayed v Al-Tajir 1987 2 All ER 396, CA.

9.78 Legal professional privilege. Communications between a party and his or her lawyer are privileged from inspection provided they are confidential and written to or by the solicitor in his or her professional capacity for the purpose of obtaining legal advice or assistance for the client. This is known as 'legal advice privilege'. Confidential communications between a party and his or her legal adviser for the purpose of litigation are also protected under what is known as 'litigation privilege'.

The relevant test for determining whether legal advice privilege applies is to ask whether the communication was made confidentially for the purpose of legal advice, construing such purpose broadly – Balabel and anor v Air India 1988 2 All ER 246, CA. For example, the fact that a client is seeking 'backing' for a course of action that he or she already wishes to take does not put the communication outside the ambit of legal privilege – University of Southampton v Kelly EAT 0574/05.

The privilege extends to communications between a party's personnel **9.79** department and its in-house lawyers that were for the purpose of obtaining legal advice – University of Southampton v Kelly, and covers any notes made by an individual in meetings with solicitors – Burcher v Bradford Hospitals NHS Trust EAT 958/01. However, according to the EAT in Comfort v Department of Constitutional Affairs EAT 0137/05, notes of evidence taken by a solicitor at an employment tribunal hearing – excluding any comments or annotations – are not protected as such, even though the EAT acknowledged that it would not usually be appropriate to order disclosure of such notes. But in that particular case, an order for disclosure of part of the solicitor's notes had been appropriate so as to allow the other side to identify any previous inconsistent statements at the remitted hearing because the claimant did not have her own notes of the original evidence and the chairman's notes were not comprehensive.

In R (on the application of Prudential plc and anor) v Special Commissioner of Income Tax and anor 2013 2 All ER 247, SC, the Supreme Court confirmed that legal advice privilege applies only to advice given by qualified lawyers. It did not, therefore, on the facts of the case, extend to communications between a company and its accountants relating to legal advice on tax. But although this ground of privilege does not extend to any profession other than the legal profession, there is no distinction between solicitors in private practice and those employed by government departments or companies as in-house lawyers – Alfred Crompton Amusement Machines Ltd v Commissioners of Customs and Excise (No.2) 1973 2 All ER 1169, HL. In the same way, instructions and briefs to counsel and counsel's opinions are also protected.

Communications with an employment consultant who was also a solicitor and **9.80** who was contacted for that reason were held to be covered by legal advice privilege in Howes v Hinckley and Bosworth Borough Council EAT 0213/08. Communications with unqualified advisers or consultants would not be covered, however. In New Victoria Hospital v Ryan 1993 ICR 201, EAT, the employer argued that correspondence between himself and a firm of personnel consultants was protected from inspection. The EAT dismissed this argument. In its view, to extend legal privilege to unqualified advisers such as personnel consultants was both unnecessary and undesirable. Essentially, this means that a party to tribunal proceedings who has been advised by a trade union official, an advice worker or personnel or employment consultants (many of whom have specialist legal knowledge but are not legally qualified) cannot claim privilege in respect of any confidential legal communications from such an adviser. Accordingly, documents containing information revealing the strengths and weaknesses of a party's case may be inspected by the other side.

'Litigation privilege', on the other hand, does include communications with consultants so long as the information provided is for the sole purpose of litigation. In Scotthorne v Four Seasons Conservatories (UK) Ltd EAT 0178/10 the employer sought advice from employment consultants working for its insurer on how to proceed with a disciplinary process in the aftermath of a workplace altercation. According to the EAT, the employer was contemplating dismissal at that point and with it the possibility of litigation. As a result, the advice was protected by litigation privilege and did not fall to be disclosed to the claimant.

9.81 'Without prejudice' communications

Any communications between parties for the purpose of negotiating a settlement or resolving a dispute cannot generally be subject to an order for disclosure. This is known as the 'without prejudice' rule and it applies regardless of whether the words 'without prejudice' are used to describe the communications in question – Chocoladefabriken Lindt and Sprungli AG v Nestle Co Ltd 1978 RPC 287, ChD. In Independent Research Services Ltd v Catterall 1993 ICR 1, EAT, the EAT confirmed that the general principles for excluding 'without prejudice' correspondence apply to employment tribunal proceedings and explained the rationale behind the rule. Mr Justice Knox, giving the EAT's judgment, stated: 'The "without prejudice" privilege, if it is correctly so described, is one that is founded on a very clear public policy that it is desirable that parties should be free to try to settle their differences without the fear of everything that they say in the course of negotiations being used in evidence thereafter.' In that case, the employer had sought to admit into evidence a letter marked 'without prejudice' written to it by the employee offering to remain as an employee and relinquishing his directorship in return for a financial consideration. The tribunal refused to allow the letter to be put into evidence and the EAT upheld the decision on appeal.

Whether the 'without prejudice' rule applies depends on whether the parties are 'in dispute' with each other and whether they are making genuine efforts to find a resolution of that dispute. In Leclerc v BSI Products Services Ltd ET Case No.1201504/07, for example, an employment tribunal found that the rule was not engaged on the particular facts of the case. There, L raised an informal grievance about race discrimination, among other matters. She was dissatisfied with the outcome and went on to raise a formal grievance about race and sex discrimination. The grievance meeting was due to take place in January 2007 but, in December 2006, one of the company directors had a meeting with her to discuss complaints made against her by colleagues and her alleged team-working failures. There was then a further meeting before the grievance hearing took place, at which L and the director agreed exit terms. When L subsequently brought claims of victimisation and unfair constructive dismissal, among other things, the question arose whether the second meeting attracted the 'without prejudice' rule. The tribunal found that it did not. Even if L's raising of a grievance could be characterised as giving rise to a dispute, it related to her alleged discriminatory treatment and not the termination of her employment. The meeting could not, therefore, have been a genuine attempt to settle *that* dispute. The tribunal also took into account that there was no clear agreement between L and her employer that the meeting would be held on a 'without prejudice' basis.

9.82 Even if the 'without prejudice' rule applies, there may nevertheless be exceptional circumstances where the rule's protection is lost. In employment cases, it is commonly asserted that the rule should not serve as a cloak for 'unambiguous impropriety' and exclude evidence of alleged discrimination. However, the 'unambiguous impropriety' exception will only apply in cases of blatant discrimination – Woodward v Santander UK plc 2010 IRLR 834, EAT.

A full discussion of the scope of the 'without prejudice' rule, and its exceptions, can be found in Chapter 13, 'Evidence', under 'Evidence of settlement negotiations – "without prejudice" negotiations'.

Pre-termination negotiations
9.83 In addition to the 'without prejudice' rule, a new – albeit more limited – statutory restriction on disclosure has been introduced. S.111A of the Employment Rights Act 1996 (ERA), which came into force on 29 July 2013, renders evidence of pre-termination negotiations inadmissible in unfair dismissal proceedings, subject to certain criteria. In essence, the section provides that any settlement negotiations conducted between an employer and an employee with a view to ending the employment relationship on agreed terms cannot be relied upon in any subsequent unfair dismissal claim. While negotiations to end the employment relationship on mutually agreed terms may be initiated by either side, in practice it will usually be the employer who makes use of S.111A. The benefits to an employer are not difficult to fathom: it allows an offer to be made to an employee to terminate employment without fear that the employee will immediately resign in response and then rely on the offer to support a claim before an employment tribunal for unfair constructive dismissal.

However, there are some important limitations on the applicability of S.111A ERA. Confidentiality of pre-termination negotiations is only guaranteed where the employee is complaining of 'ordinary' unfair dismissal. This means that he or she will be able to rely on pre-termination negotiations as part of the evidence before an employment tribunal when alleging that the dismissal occurred for a reason that is automatically unfair, such as the employee's pregnancy or trade union membership. It also means that S.111A does not apply to any other type of claim, such as breach of contract or discrimination claims, even if brought together with an unfair dismissal claim. In these circumstances, settlement discussions may be inadmissible under S.111A in relation to the unfair dismissal claim but admissible in relation to the other claims (unless otherwise covered by the 'without prejudice' rule – see '"Without prejudice" communications' above). Furthermore, S.111A does not apply where there has been 'improper behaviour' on the part of the employer or the employee in relation to the settlement negotiations. Examples of what would amount to 'improper behaviour' in settlement negotiations include intimidation or harassment or undue pressure. Where a party has acted improperly, it is up to the tribunal to decide whether and, if so, to what extent the negotiations should be admissible in evidence.

The rule on inadmissibility of pre-termination negotiations pursuant to S.111A ERA is discussed in detail in Chapter 13, 'Evidence', under 'Evidence of settlement negotiations – pre-termination negotiations'.

9.84 Communications with a conciliation officer

Any communications between a party and an Acas conciliator are not subject to inspection unless the privilege is expressly waived by the person communicating with the conciliator – S.18(7) Employment Tribunals Act 1996. In M and W Grazebrook Ltd v Wallens 1973 ICR 256, NIRC, the National Industrial Relations Court held that the basis of this privilege is the public interest in achieving agreed settlements of disputes.

9.85 Production of documents by witnesses

An employment tribunal can, on its own initiative or on the application of a party, order 'any person in Great Britain to attend a hearing to give evidence, produce documents or produce information' – rule 32 Tribunal Rules 2013. This wording is almost identical to the power to order witnesses to attend under old rule 10(2)(c) of the Tribunal Rules 2004. Witness orders are a useful means of obtaining relevant documents held by third parties who are not prepared to produce the documents in question voluntarily.

The principles on which a tribunal will order production of documents by a witness are the same as those which apply generally to orders for disclosure or inspection. Witnesses can only be required to attend if they are in Great Britain. The powers of tribunals in respect of witness orders are discussed in detail in Chapter 11, 'Case management', under 'Disclosure and evidence – requirement to attend to give evidence (witness orders)'.

Failure to comply with orders

9.86

Under rule 6, non-compliance with a tribunal order does not of itself render the proceedings, or any step taken in the proceedings, void. However, the tribunal may take such action as it considers just, including:

- waiving or varying the requirement – rule 6(a)

- striking out the claim or the response in whole or in part – rule 6(b)

- barring or restricting a party's participation in the proceedings – rule 6(c)

- awarding costs – rule 6(d).

A tribunal can apply all or any of the sanctions set out in rule 6 but the most common sanctions for non-compliance with a case management order in relation to the disclosure of documents or information are strike-out and costs orders.

Costs and striking out

9.87

If a party subject to an order does not succeed in getting it varied or set aside, it is important that he or she complies with the terms of the order, since failure to do so can have dire consequences. As well as having a power to make a costs or preparation time order against parties who fail to comply, tribunals can strike out the whole or part of a defaulting party's claim or, as the case may be, response – rule 37. Moreover, it is becoming standard practice for tribunals, when issuing case management directions that contain orders for disclosure and inspection, to include an 'unless order' pursuant to rule 38. An unless order may specify that unless the order is complied with by a certain date, the claim or response (or part thereof) will be dismissed without further order. If a claim or response is dismissed on this basis, the tribunal must inform the parties in writing and the affected party has the right to apply to the tribunal in writing, within 14 days of the date on which the notice was sent, to have the order set aside on the basis that it is in the interests of justice to do so – rule 38(2). Unless any such application includes a request for a hearing, the tribunal can determine it on the basis of written representations only. Costs and strike-out orders are considered in Chapter 20, 'Costs and penalties', and Chapter 11, 'Case management', under 'Striking out', respectively. Unless orders are discussed in Chapter 11 under 'Unless orders'.

The way in which an employment judge deals with a party's failure to comply with an order is a matter largely left to his or her discretion and the EAT will only interfere if the judge makes an error of law or if his or her decision is perverse – see Chapter 16, 'The Employment Appeal Tribunal'. In Coueslant and anor v British Railways Board and anor EAT 244/95, for example, two women brought complaints of sex discrimination, stating in their ET1s that

525

they had been subjected to 'unwelcome comments and actions' by a male employee. The employment tribunal ordered them to provide further information on their complaints. However, the women's trade union representative wrote to the tribunal, pointing out that the claimants had already given details of their allegations to their employer during an internal investigation. The tribunal struck out the claims on the ground that the women had failed to comply with the order. On appeal, the EAT upheld the tribunal's decision. It stated that complaints of discrimination are taken very seriously and claimants must provide further information on their allegations when ordered to do so.

9.88 However, any decision to strike out must not be made arbitrarily and/or without full consideration of the representations of the parties. In PW Cleaning Services Ltd v Railton EAT 758/87 an employment judge ordered the respondent to provide further particulars in respect of the ET3 and set 21 September (one working week from the date of the order) as the deadline for compliance. The employer had still not provided the requested information by 23 September, so a further letter was sent to his solicitors requiring compliance by 2 October. The solicitors replied on 7 October pleading pressure of work as the excuse for late compliance. On 8 October, an employment judge (without holding a hearing on the matter) ordered that the employer's ET3 be struck out on the ground that its solicitors' explanation was unsatisfactory. The employer appealed. In dealing with the appeal, the EAT noted that the claimant had, in fact, never requested further particulars of the ET3 and that this had been done by the tribunal of its own volition. The Appeal Tribunal held that the tribunal's procedure had been 'oppressive' and that the judge, in making the striking-out order, had made up his mind to strike out and so had not exercised any proper discretion on the matter. The employer should have been given an opportunity to make oral representations and, in the light of these failings, the appeal was allowed and the matter remitted for rehearing by a different tribunal.

As a general rule, it will be an error of law for an employment tribunal to make an order for striking out for non-compliance with a disclosure order where, notwithstanding a party's non-compliance with an order, a fair trial of the issues would still be possible. This point was underlined by the EAT in National Grid Company plc v Virdee 1992 IRLR 555, EAT. There, NG plc, on the face of it, complied with an order for disclosure. However, in doing so, it denied the existence of a number of documents. During the course of the tribunal hearing it became clear that this denial had been erroneous. Following an adjournment, the tribunal made an order striking out part of NG plc's response. NG plc appealed. The EAT upheld the appeal, holding that the tribunal had erred in law. In reaching this decision, the EAT stated that the applicable test when deciding whether part of a response should be struck out is whether, owing to the failure to comply with an order, a fair trial of the issues is no longer possible. In its view, the tribunal's order for strike-out had been inappropriate in this case because a fair trial of all of the issues would have been possible notwithstanding NG plc's non-compliance with the disclosure order.

Similarly, in North Tyneside Primary Care Trust v Aynsley and ors 2009 ICR **9.89** 1333, EAT, the EAT revoked an order to strike out the Trust's response to equal pay proceedings. The tribunal had been wrong to maintain the strike-out, notwithstanding the employer's failure to provide the claimants with pay information by a specified date, since the employer had subsequently substantially remedied the breach and the case remained triable.

However, the EAT reached the opposite conclusion in Essombe v Nando's Chickenland Ltd EAT 0550/06. There, E complained of unfair dismissal (among other things). At the hearing, the tribunal ordered him to disclose the recording of the disciplinary hearing that he had made on his camcorder. E refused to comply with the order and the tribunal struck out his claim. The EAT upheld the strike-out decision on appeal. It considered it unlikely that E would have withheld the recording if it had advanced his case on the disputed evidence. His deliberate decision to disobey the disclosure order meant that the tribunal was prevented from having the best evidence on which to base its findings of fact and for the employer to establish its case. A fair hearing was no longer possible in these circumstances and the appeal was accordingly dismissed.

Note that it is possible for a tribunal to 'reconsider' striking-out orders, either **9.90** on the application of a party or on the tribunal's own initiative, where it is necessary in the interests of justice to do so. This power, which is governed by rules 70–73, is discussed in depth in Chapter 15, 'Reconsideration of judgments and decisions'.

Fine for non-compliance   9.91
In addition to the general civil sanctions for non-compliance discussed above, a party in default may be liable to a fine on conviction in the case of non-compliance with an order for:

- disclosure or inspection, or
- the attendance of a witness.

If a party fails, without reasonable excuse, to comply with one of the above orders, he or she is liable to a fine not exceeding level 3 on the standard scale (currently £1,000) on summary conviction in proceedings instituted by the tribunal – see S.7(4) of the Employment Tribunals Act 1996. Old rule 10(6) of the Tribunal Rules 2004 required that any order for disclosure, inspection, the attendance of a witness or the production of a document by a witness had to give notice of this potential liability. This is no longer a requirement under the 2013 Rules, although the sanction for non-compliance continues to apply.

10 Service of notice and documents

Delivery to the tribunal

Delivery to parties

Delivery to non-parties

Deemed service

Substituted service

Date of delivery

Copying documents to 'interested parties'

The provisions governing the service of notice and documents in employment **10.1** tribunal proceedings are set out in rules 85–93 of the Employment Tribunal Rules 2013 ('the Tribunal Rules'), contained in Schedule 1 to the Employment Tribunals (Constitution and Rules of Procedure) Regulations 2013 SI 2013/1237 ('the Tribunal Regulations'). Among other things, they set down conditions for the delivery of documents to the tribunal and other parties and specify the dates on which documents delivered by various methods (post, electronic communication, personal delivery) will be taken to have been received.

Delivery to the tribunal   **10.2**

Rule 85(1) of the Tribunal Rules, which applies to all documents *apart from the claim form* (see 'Presentation of claim form' below), provides that documents may be delivered to an employment tribunal by:

- post
- direct delivery to the appropriate tribunal office (including delivery by a courier or messenger service), or
- electronic communication.

'Electronic communication' is defined as 'a communication transmitted (whether from one person to another, from one device to another or from a person to a device or vice versa)... by means of an electronic communications network; or... by other means but while in an electronic form' – rule 1(1) (read with S.15(1) Electronic Communications Act 2000). This encompasses communications sent by fax and e-mail.

─── **529**

10.3 Following presentation of the claim, the tribunal will notify the parties of the address of the tribunal office dealing with the case (including any fax, e-mail or other electronic address) and all documents must be delivered to either the postal or the electronic address so notified – rule 85(3). The tribunal may from time to time notify the parties of any change of address, or that a particular form of communication should or should not be used, and documents must then be delivered in accordance with that notification – rule 85(3).

10.4 Sending copies of tribunal communications to other parties

Rule 92 requires that, with the exception of an application for a witness order, where a party sends a communication to the tribunal he or she must also send a copy to all other parties (unless the tribunal considers that it is in the interest of justice not to do so). The party must also inform the tribunal that this has been done. If an application is sent to the tribunal by e-mail, it will be sufficient to use the 'cc' address bar to comply with both the duty to send a copy to the other parties and the duty to inform the tribunal that this has been done.

10.5 Presentation of claim form

The prescribed methods of delivery set out in rule 85(1) do not apply to the claim form. Rule 85(2) makes it clear that a claim form may *only* be delivered in accordance with Presidential Practice Directions made under Reg 11 of the Tribunal Regulations. Two such Practice Directions have been issued: one in relation to the presentation of claims in England and Wales and the other in relation to the presentation of claims in Scotland. These stipulate that the claim form may be presented online, by post or in person. Accordingly, in a change from the Tribunal Rules 2004 (contained in the Employment Tribunals (Constitution and Rules of Procedure) Regulations 2002 SI 2004/1861) – and unlike the delivery of all other documents to the tribunal – fax and e-mail are no longer prescribed methods of presentation and cannot be used to submit a tribunal complaint. For further details, see Chapter 4, 'Starting tribunal proceedings', under 'Making a claim – the claim form (ET1)'.

10.6 Delivery to parties

Rule 86(1) states that documents may be delivered to a party (whether by the employment tribunal or by another party) by:

- post
- direct delivery to that party's address (including delivery by a courier or messenger service)
- electronic communication, or
- being handed over personally.

530

Documents may also be delivered to parties who are based abroad via any of the above methods. So far as the first three methods of delivery are concerned, rule 86(2) provides that the document must be delivered to the address given in the claim form or response (which will be the address of the party's representative, if one is named) or to a different address as notified in writing by the party in question. If a party has given both a postal address and one or more electronic addresses, any of them may be used unless the party has indicated in writing that a particular address should or should not be used – rule 86(3). Separate considerations apply when delivering a document by hand. These are discussed immediately below.

Hand delivery

10.7

The final method of delivery prescribed by rule 86(1) involves handing the documents over in person. The person to whom the documents should be given depends on whether the party being served is an individual or a corporate body, and whether that party is represented or unrepresented – see 'To whom should the documents be given?' below.

It does not appear to matter who delivers the documents; i.e. it seems that the deliverer can ask *any person* to hand the documents over.

To whom should the documents be given? Rule 86(1)(d) provides that documents can be handed directly to an *individual* party if he or she is:

10.8

* unrepresented, or

* represented but has not named an individual representative in the claim form (or response, as the case may be).

Where documents are being delivered to a *company*, personal delivery is not possible if the company is unrepresented or has failed to name an individual representative. Of course, companies will normally nominate an individual representative to whom documents should be given.

Where an individual representative has been named in the claim form or response, then the documents should be handed to that representative. In addition, documents may be handed over at a hearing to any person identified by the party as representing him or her at the hearing.

Service on a foreign state

10.9

Under S.12(1) of the State Immunity Act 1978, service of process (i.e. copies of the claim and details as to how to enter a response) on a foreign state must be transmitted through the Foreign and Commonwealth Office to the foreign ministry of the state concerned. Service will be deemed to be effected when the notice or document is received at that ministry. Under S.12(2), the time allowed to the respondent state for entering an appearance is two months after service is effected.

531

10.10 Delivery to non-parties

Documents addressed to non-parties should be sent to any address for service which they may have notified. Otherwise, the documents must be sent to:

- any known address or place of business in the UK
- if the party is a corporate body, its registered or principal office in the UK, or
- if permitted by the President of Employment Tribunals, an address outside the UK – rule 87.

The wording of this rule implies that documents for non-parties can only be delivered by post, and not by fax or e-mail.

Note that rule 87 does not apply to the 'special cases' listed in rule 88 – see '"Special cases"' immediately below.

10.11 'Special cases'

The addresses for service on the non-parties listed in rule 88 – 'special cases' – are set down in two Presidential Practice Directions: one for England and Wales, 'Address for serving documentation in special cases', issued on 18 December 2013, and an identical one for Scotland, issued on 17 December 2013. They cover:

- Redundancy Payments Service (UK)
- Secretary of State (Department for Business, Innovation and Skills)
- Attorney General's Office (England)
- Counsel General for Wales
- Advocate General for Scotland
- Lord Advocate (Scotland).

10.12 The Schedule to each Practice Direction sets out the respective addresses to which documents must be sent. Documents must be sent to these addresses and not by fax or e-mail.

Note that rule 88 only applies where the individuals/bodies listed above are *not* parties to the proceedings. If any of them are parties, the Practice Directions do not then apply and the provisions of rule 86 come into play – see 'Delivery to parties' above.

10.13 Deemed service

Rule 91 allows a tribunal to treat any document as having been delivered to a person, notwithstanding any non-compliance with rules 86–88, if it is satisfied that the document or its substance has in fact come to the attention of that person. There was no equivalent provision under the Tribunal Rules 2004.

Substituted service

10.14

The President or Vice-President of Employment Tribunals or a regional employment judge has power to order 'substituted service' in such manner as appears appropriate in the following circumstances:

- where no address for service (in accordance with the Tribunal Rules) is known, or

- where it appears that service at any such address is unlikely to come to the attention of the addressee – rule 89.

In practice, an order for substituted service will be made where service by the more orthodox means provided for elsewhere in the Rules proves to be ineffective (for example, because of deliberate evasion by the person to whom the notice is addressed). In this regard, rule 89 has a similar effect to that of rule 6.15 of the Civil Procedure Rules 1998 SI 1998/3132, which deals with alternative methods and alternative places of service in the civil courts.

Substituted service will normally take the form of service on an agent, solicitor **10.15** or banker known to be in communication with the elusive party, or service by advertisement in an appropriate newspaper or journal (but usually only where there is some reason for believing that the party will thereby be informed of the attempts to effect service).

Rule 61(4)(h) of the Tribunal Rules 2004 provided that if no address for service of documents was specified (or if a notice sent to such an address was returned), the document could be sent to any other known address or place of business in the UK. Although this is no longer spelled out in the Tribunal Rules 2013, it is open to the President, Vice-President or regional judge to direct that documents be sent to such an alternative address under rule 89.

Similarly, unlike the 2004 Rules, the Tribunal Rules 2013 no longer specifically **10.16** provide for service on a company at its registered or principal office in the UK or at such address outside the UK as the President, Vice President or regional employment judge may allow (see old rule 61(4)(h)(ii)). Again, however, it is open to the President, etc to direct that documents be served at a principal office in the UK or at an address abroad under rule 89.

Note that under Reg 7(1)(e) of the Overseas Companies Regulations 2009 SI 2009/1801 an overseas company that opens a UK establishment must deliver to the Registrar of Companies a return, which includes the name and address of every person resident in the UK authorised to accept service of documents on its behalf in respect of the establishment (or a statement that there is no such

533

person). This information will normally provide the appropriate address for service, but if the foreign company is in breach of its obligations under this provision then an obvious address for service would be at an established place of business in the UK or at the company's registered office in the country in which it principally operates or is incorporated.

10.17 Date of delivery

In the absence of any rules relating to deemed service in the Tribunal Rules 2001 (contained in the Employment Tribunals (Constitution and Rules of Procedure) Regulations 2001 SI 2001/1171), S.7 of the Interpretation Act 1978 was applied in order to establish when a document was deemed to have been served by post. However, rule 61(2) of the Tribunal Rules 2004 dealt specifically with deemed service by post, fax or other means of electronic communication, or personal service, and these provisions are now found in rule 90 of the Tribunal Rules 2013.

Rule 90 provides that where a document has been delivered in accordance with rule 85 or rule 86 (see 'Delivery to the tribunal' and 'Delivery to parties' respectively above), it shall, unless the contrary is proved, be taken to have been received by the addressee:

- if sent by post, on the day on which it would be delivered in the ordinary course of post (see 'Delivery by post' below)

- if sent by means of electronic communication, on the day of transmission (see 'Delivery by electronic communication' below)

- if delivered directly or personally, on the day of delivery (see 'Delivery in person' below).

(It is perhaps worth noting here that rule 90 applies to delivery of the claim form, as well as to all other documents, since this is regulated by rule 85(2) – see 'Delivery to the tribunal – presentation of claim form' above.)

10.18 Delivery by post

A document sent by post will be taken to have been received on the day on which it would have been delivered in the ordinary course of post, unless the contrary is proved – rule 90(a). The 'ordinary course of post' rule was affirmed by the Court of Appeal in Consignia plc (formerly the Post Office) v Sealy 2002 ICR 1193, CA, where it held that service of documents to an employment tribunal under the 'ordinary course of post' rule is deemed to have taken place on the second day after first-class posting, excluding Sundays, public holidays, Christmas Day and Good Friday. This means that service can take place on a Saturday, even though employment tribunal offices are actually closed on Saturdays. In Metcalfe v Cygnet Health Care Ltd EAT 0421/05, for instance, the last day of valid service of the claim form was Saturday but the ET1 was delayed in the post and did not arrive until the following Monday. The tribunal found as a fact that the claimant had posted the ET1 on Thursday and, applying the 'ordinary course of post' rule, that it had been validly served on Saturday, notwithstanding that it physically arrived at the tribunal two days later.

The qualification to rule 90 – 'unless the contrary is proved' – allows for a situation where the person sending the document is able to prove that it was received the day after it was posted, i.e. one day earlier than it would otherwise be deemed to have been delivered in the ordinary course of post. In this situation the document is treated as having been received on the day that it was actually delivered, not the day it would have been deemed to have been delivered. Conversely, if the person to whom the document was sent proves that he or she did not receive it in the ordinary course of post, or on the day of transmission or delivery, but on a later date, then it is treated as having been received on the day that it was actually received – see further 'Proving non-receipt' below.

Properly addressed, pre-paid and posted. By virtue of S.7 of the Interpretation **10.19** Act 1978, service is deemed to be effected 'by properly addressing, pre-paying and posting [the] letter'. While rule 90 does not explicitly state that the relevant document should be properly addressed, pre-paid and posted, it is generally thought that this is implied. In any event, S.7 is still likely to apply, for clearly there cannot be any deemed receipt if the document has not been properly addressed, pre-paid and posted.

When the 'properly addressing, pre-paying and posting' of a document is proved and it is not returned through the post undelivered to the addressee, there will be a prima facie assumption that it has been duly delivered – see A/S Cathrineholm v Norequipment Trading Ltd 1972 2 All ER 538, CA. Where, however, a document is properly addressed, pre-paid and posted but is returned through the Post Office undelivered, it will be treated as not having been duly served – R v Appeal Committee of County of London Quarter Sessions ex parte Rossi 1956 1 All ER 670, CA.

The words 'properly addressing' in S.7 do not mean that minor errors in the **10.20** address will entitle a party to claim that proper service has not been effected. In Genevieve Restaurants Ltd v Koura EAT 254/84, for example, the EAT upheld a tribunal's refusal to grant a review. The company had argued that the omission of the word 'Limited' from its title in all notices and correspondence sent out by the tribunal office meant that these had not been validly served upon it. The EAT rejected this argument.

Proving non-receipt. Where documents have been correctly posted, the burden **10.21** of proving that they have not been received lies on the party alleging non-receipt. Two examples:

- **Migwain Ltd (in liquidation) v TGWU** 1979 ICR 597, EAT: M Ltd failed to attend the hearing of a claim for a protective award. On a subsequent application for review, it contended that it had not received notice of the proceedings. The tribunal, after enquiry, established that a copy of the claim had been sent to M Ltd but that the company's name had been misspelt. Its address, in a minor respect, had also been misrepresented. It had, however, received subsequent notices. The tribunal held that the presumption of proper service of the copy of the claim had not been rebutted. On M Ltd's appeal, the EAT held (by a majority) that notices served on the company's registered address were deemed to have been received and that the tribunal was entitled, on the evidence, to conclude that the company had failed to prove the contrary

- **T and D Transport (Portsmouth) Ltd v Limburn** 1987 ICR 696, EAT: T and D Ltd failed to attend a tribunal hearing because it had not received notification of the date. The tribunal decided that L had been unfairly dismissed. T and D Ltd's application for a review of that decision was refused on the grounds that the notice of hearing had been posted and that, in the circumstances, the company had not displaced the presumption in S.7 of the Interpretation Act 1978 that the notice had been duly served by virtue of the act of posting. T and D Ltd appealed. The EAT upheld the tribunal's decision. It stated that the phrase 'the service is deemed to be effected by properly addressing, pre-paying and posting a letter' in S.7 indicated that the section was concerned with the receipt as well as the sending of the relevant document, and that the deeming provisions applied in respect of both events. The tribunal had correctly held that S.7 deemed the notice of hearing to have been received and the employer's appeal was dismissed.

10.22 **Recorded delivery.** Under the Tribunal Rules 2001 recorded delivery had to be used in certain circumstances. However, this requirement was removed by the Tribunal Rules 2004 and does not appear in the Tribunal Rules 2013. Nevertheless, recorded delivery remains a wise precaution and will provide the deliverer with evidence of posting if the documents subsequently go missing.

Where a document is sent by recorded delivery and is recorded as having been received, a denial of receipt will not (without more) have the effect of rebutting the presumption that it has been served. In order to do this, there must be evidence that (i) there was no acknowledgement of its having been received, or (ii), if there is evidence of receipt by someone, the receiver was not the person on whom the document was to be served and the receiver had not drawn it to the attention of the other – Lex Service plc v Johns, unreported 22.8.89, CA.

10.23 **Delivery by electronic communication**

Rule 90(b) provides that a document sent by electronic communication (i.e. fax, e-mail or online) will, unless the contrary is proved, be deemed to have been received on the day it is transmitted. There have been a number of cases dealing with the question of when an ET1 claim form is considered to have been 'presented' to the tribunal by electronic communication and these provide useful guidance. For example, in Initial Electronic Security Systems Ltd v Avdic 2005 ICR 1598, EAT, a case where an e-mailed ET1 never arrived at the tribunal office, the EAT held that the deemed postal rule also applied to e-mails on the basis that 'the reasonable expectation of the sender of an electronic mail communication is that it would arrive within a very short time thereafter'. This was likely to be between 30–60 minutes after transmission. As a result, the claimant in the case could reasonably have expected that her e-mail, sent eight hours before the expiry of the time limit, had arrived at the tribunal.

In Tyne and Wear Autistic Society v Smith 2005 ICR 663, EAT, the EAT held that, where a claimant using the online system receives an automated message that the claim form has been submitted, there is a reasonable expectation that it will reach the tribunal directly and has therefore been presented. The application is presented when it successfully reaches the host of the online service and it does not matter if it is forwarded by the website host to the tribunal office computer on a later date, or date-stamped on a later date. On the same basis, once the response is successfully submitted to the host website, it will have been successfully presented even if there are subsequent problems with the computer of the website host or of the tribunal office, or in communications between the two.

Similarly, in Yellow Pages Sales Ltd v Davie 2012 ICR D11, EAT, the Scottish **10.24** Appeal Tribunal held that where an ET1 had been faxed to an employment tribunal and the claimant had received automated confirmation that the fax had been received, the claim had been validly presented, notwithstanding that a technical failure resulted in there being no printout or record on the tribunal's machine.

Note that that fax and e-mail are no longer prescribed methods of presentation of the claim form – see 'Delivery to the tribunal – presentation of claim form' above.

Delivery in person
10.25
If a document is delivered in person, it will (unless the contrary is proved) be taken to have been received on the day of delivery – rule 90(c). Employment tribunal offices are open for delivery of documents in person from 9 am to 5 pm, Monday to Friday. Proof of hand-delivery can be requested from the tribunal.

Copying documents to 'interested parties'
10.26

The employment tribunal is under a statutory duty to send copies of specified documents to certain 'interested persons' or deemed parties as follows:

- in proceedings concerning any enactment providing for conciliation by Acas, copies of the claim form and response to a conciliation officer – rule 93

- in proceedings which may involve payments out of the National Insurance Fund, copies of the claim form, response, and all other documents and notices to the Secretary of State (who is treated as a party for the purposes of the Tribunal Rules) – rule 96

- where a devolution issue arises, copies of the claim form and response to the Advocate General for Scotland and the Lord Advocate (in the case of a Scottish devolution issue), or to the Attorney General and the Counsel General to the Welsh Assembly Government (in the case of a Welsh devolution issue) – rule 98

- in proceedings under S.120, S.127 or S.146 of the Equality Act 2010, copies of all judgments and written reasons (except where issues of national security apply) to the Commission for Equality and Human Rights – rule 103.

10.27 Additionally, if a claim alleges that the claimant has made a protected disclosure under S.43A ERA – i.e. it contains an allegation of whistleblowing – the tribunal may, with the consent of the claimant, send a copy to a regulator specified in Schedule 1 to the Public Interest Disclosure (Prescribed Persons) Order 1999 SI 1999/1549 – rule 14. This procedure is intended to allow the relevant regulator to investigate the underlying issue where appropriate and to take action if necessary.

The EAT has held that the above requirements do not affect the tribunal's jurisdiction and that the parties can agree to waive them in the event of non-compliance by the tribunal. In other words, non-compliance will not of itself nullify the proceedings. In Sheringham Development Co Ltd v Browne 1977 ICR 20, EAT, the claimant applied for a redundancy payment (a type of claim with which Acas did not then get involved). At the hearing, the tribunal amended the proceedings to include a claim of unfair dismissal and the employer raised no objection. The tribunal found that the claimant had been unfairly dismissed and the employer appealed, arguing that the proceedings were a nullity because the requirement to notify Acas of the unfair dismissal complaint had not been complied with. The EAT held that the requirement did not affect the tribunal's jurisdiction and that, in any case, it was to be deemed waived by the employer when it consented to the amendment of the tribunal proceedings.

11 Case management

It is in the interests of everyone concerned in a case – both the parties and the **11.1** tribunal – that issues be identified as early as possible. Traditionally, the approach to litigation was for the parties to prepare and present their respective cases with relatively little management of the proceedings by the courts. Nowadays, however, courts and tribunals take a more active and robust approach to case management. For employment tribunals, this approach was fortified by the introduction of the 'overriding objective' to deal with cases fairly and justly, which was first inserted into the rules of procedure issued in 2001. It was later carried into the Employment Tribunals (Constitution and Rules of Procedure) Regulations 2004 SI 2004/1861 ('the Tribunal Rules 2004') and is now contained in rule 2 of Schedule 1 to the Employment Tribunals (Constitution and Rules of Procedure) Regulations 2013 SI 2013/1237 ('the Tribunal Rules'). The overriding objective is discussed in more detail in Chapter 1, 'Employment tribunals', in the section 'What are employment tribunals?', under 'Employment tribunal rules – overriding objective'. But what is important to note here is that a tribunal must seek to give effect to the overriding objective in interpreting, or exercising any power given to it by, the rules, and that the parties (and their representatives) are required to assist the tribunal to further the overriding objective – rule 2 Tribunal Rules.

Case management enables the issues in a particular case to be identified at an early stage and for the parties to be fully prepared for the final hearing. It can deal with the listing of a preliminary or final hearing, and may pave the way for

539

judicial mediation or other form of dispute resolution. Stakeholder feedback on the 'Resolving Workplace Disputes' consultation in 2011 indicated that the rules in force at that time – the Tribunal Rules 2004 (as amended) – had become over-elaborate and could sometimes act as a barrier to effective and proportionate case management. In response, the Government asked Mr Justice Underhill (now Lord Justice Underhill), the then outgoing President of the EAT, to lead a thorough review of the rules, which he completed in July 2012.

11.2 The Underhill review focused on case management. He recommended the introduction of a new set of rules aimed at ensuring that tribunal cases are managed effectively, flexibly, proportionately and consistently in order to ensure a system that is fair to all parties. The review also addressed concerns from stakeholders that the employment tribunal system had become over-legalistic, particularly for parties who represented themselves, and made proposals aimed at simplifying the rules. Underhill J's recommendations included:

- the introduction of an initial judicial sift (on the papers alone) to be carried out by an employment judge

- clearer powers to strike out claims

- a more flexible regime allowing tribunals to make deposit orders against a party who wished to continue to pursue a weak element of a claim or response

- a lead case mechanism for dealing with multiple claims

- a simplified procedure for withdrawing claims

- a new procedure for preliminary hearings that combined separate pre-hearing reviews and case management discussions

- a clear rule on the provision of written reasons

- a rule on limiting oral evidence and submissions leading to more efficient timetabling of cases.

Mr Justice Underhill also recommended the publication of Presidential Guidance aimed at giving all parties a better idea of what to expect at a tribunal and what is expected of them, and to ensure that employment judges manage cases in a consistent manner. Rule 7 of the Tribunal Rules gives effect to this recommendation, enabling the Presidents of Employment Tribunals in England and Wales and in Scotland to publish guidance as to matters of practice and as to how the powers conferred by the Rules may be exercised. Pursuant to this power, Presidential Guidance for England and Wales on 'General Case Management' was published on 13 March 2014. This general Guidance does not supersede or alter previous Presidential Guidance on specific issues, such as the Guidance already issued on 'Seeking a postponement of a hearing', and while tribunals in England and Wales must have regard to it, they are not bound by it.

The Guidance starts by setting out the general rules for actions by the parties **11.3** and for actions by an employment judge. It then goes on to provide detailed examples of how the rules should be applied in relation to matters such as:

- disclosure of documents (see Chapter 9, 'Responding to opponent's case', 'Disclosure and inspection of documents'), and preparation of bundles (see Chapter 12, 'The hearing', under 'Listing – preparing for the hearing')

- witness statements (see Chapter 12, 'The hearing', under 'Presenting the evidence – statements of evidence')

- making amendments to the claim and response, including adding and removing parties (see Chapter 8, 'Amendments')

- costs (see Chapter 20, 'Costs and penalties')

- timetabling (see Chapter 12, 'The hearing', under 'Listing – length of hearing')

- concluding cases without a hearing, and

- judicial mediation (see Chapter 3, 'Conciliation, settlements and ADR' under 'Judicial mediation').

The Guidance also sets out an 'Agenda for case management at preliminary hearing' to aid employment judges dealing with preliminary issues.

The requirement for employment judges to carry out an initial sift of proceedings is considered in Chapter 7, 'Judicial sift', while Chapter 13, 'Evidence', deals with the power to limit oral evidence and submissions at hearings. The procedure relating to withdrawal of claims is considered in Chapter 4, 'Starting tribunal proceedings'. In this chapter we look at the large range of other preliminary matters with which tribunals commonly deal, and which form a key part of the redrafted rules. Where appropriate, we discuss the implications of the tribunal fees regime, which was introduced under the Employment Tribunals and the Employment Appeal Tribunal Fees Order 2013 SI 2013/1893. For a more detailed discussion of the fees regime see Chapter 19, 'Fees'.

Preliminary hearings

11.4

Under the Tribunal Rules 2004 there were two types of interim hearings – case management discussions (CMDs) and pre-hearing reviews (PHRs). CMDs were intended to deal with case management issues and matters of procedure and were held in private and conducted by a chairman sitting alone. They were introduced by the 2004 Rules and replaced the 'directions hearings' (sometimes referred to as 'case management conferences') that took place under the previous rules. If the parties were represented, the CMD would invariably be

541

listed to take place by telephone. The purpose of a CMD was to promote the efficient handling of a case.

In addition to dealing with the future progress of the claim, setting a timeframe for the case and identifying the issues to be dealt with at a substantive hearing, a CMD could also be used to address specific issues, such as disclosure. In potentially long or complex cases – for example, in a complicated discrimination or equal pay case – the tribunal would often fix a CMD as a matter of course.

11.5 Tribunals could also hold PHRs, at which they could exercise a range of powers, including the power to strike out a claim or response on a number of grounds. PHRs were aimed at discouraging weak cases on either side to minimise the waste of time and money involved in taking them through to a full hearing. PHRs could also be used to determine preliminary issues of fact or law; for instance, whether a dismissal had occurred, or whether the tribunal had the necessary jurisdiction to entertain the complaint. In certain cases, a judge was required to hold a separate CMD and PHR before the claim was considered at a full hearing.

Under the Tribunal Rules 2013 a distinction is no longer drawn between the separate functions of CMDs and PHRs. Both fall within the scope of 'preliminary hearings', which are governed by rules 53–56. The Government believed that the system of having separate CMDs and PHRs meant that, in certain circumstances, the parties incurred costs for the time and expense of preparing for each meeting and, in its view, combining these two procedures into one 'preliminary hearing', allowing for any case management issues to be considered alongside the detail of the case itself, would potentially lead to quicker disposal of cases and provide clear costs savings to all parties.

11.6 In practice, many tribunals already managed proceedings in this manner so as to avoid duplication of time and costs. For instance, in cases where a preliminary issue of fact or law needed to be determined at a PHR, tribunals often listed such matters for a combined PHR and CMD, with the case management issues to be addressed subject to the outcome of the preliminary issue. In fact, old rule 18(2)(b) provided that a tribunal could do anything at a PHR that could be done at a CMD.

11.7 **Agenda.** The Presidential Guidance on 'General Case Management' for England and Wales contains an 'Agenda for case management at preliminary hearing' to aid employment judges dealing with preliminary issues. The agenda, which is similar to the agenda tribunals used for a CMD, will be sent to the parties prior to a preliminary hearing. They should complete – and, if possible, agree – the agenda and return it to the tribunal in advance of the hearing.

11.8 **Tribunals' powers at preliminary hearings**. Rule 53(1) provides that at a preliminary hearing a tribunal may do one or more of the following:

- conduct a preliminary consideration of the claim and make a case management order (including an order relating to the conduct of the final hearing) – rule 53(1)(a)

- determine any preliminary issue – rule 53(1)(b)

- consider whether a claim or response, or any part, should be struck out under rule 37 – rule 53(1)(c)

- make a deposit order under rule 39 – rule 53(1)(d)

- explore the possibility of settlement or alternative dispute resolution (including judicial mediation) – rule 53(1)(e).

Each of these powers is discussed briefly below and, where appropriate, in more detail elsewhere in this chapter.

'Tribunal' can mean either a full tribunal or an employment judge sitting alone **11.9** (in accordance with the provisions of S.4(2) or (6) of the Employment Tribunals Act 1996 (ETA)) – rule 1(2). The circumstances in which either a full tribunal or an employment judge sitting alone will conduct a preliminary hearing are discussed below – see 'Constitution of tribunal for preliminary hearings'. For more information on the composition of tribunals, see Chapter 1, 'Employment tribunals', under 'Judicial composition'.

It should be noted that the powers in rule 53(1) are not the only powers available to a tribunal at a preliminary hearing. For instance, rule 50 allows tribunals to make orders 'at any stage of the proceedings' relating to privacy and restrictions on disclosure (see 'Privacy and restrictions on disclosure' below), while rule 64 provides tribunals with the power to make consent orders or judgments where the parties agree the terms of such an order or judgment, either in writing or orally at a hearing (including a preliminary hearing). Additionally, rule 95 states that an application for interim relief (or for its variation or revocation), under S.161 or S.165 of the Trade Union and Labour Relations (Consolidation) Act 1992 or under S.128 or S.131 of the Employment Rights Act 1996, will be addressed at a preliminary hearing. For a detailed consideration of the tribunal's power to order interim relief, see IDS Employment Law Handbook, 'Unfair Dismissal' (2010), Chapter 19, 'Additional awards and interim relief'.

Conversion from preliminary hearing to final hearing. Under rule 48 (one of **11.10** the 'rules common to all kinds of hearing'), a tribunal conducting a preliminary hearing may order that it should be treated as a final hearing. This is subject to two caveats. First, the tribunal must be properly constituted for the purpose of conducting a full hearing. So if the preliminary hearing is being conducted by an employment judge sitting alone but the claim is one that must be finally determined by a full tribunal composed of the employment judge and two lay members (or one lay member if the parties agree), then the tribunal will not be properly constituted for the purposes of a final hearing – see Chapter 1, 'Employment tribunals', under 'Judicial composition – employment judge sitting alone'. Secondly, the tribunal must be satisfied that neither party would be materially prejudiced by the change. A material prejudice would presumably arise where one of the parties is not legally represented at the preliminary hearing but intends to instruct solicitors for the final hearing or where one of the parties has not fully prepared all aspects of the case on the assumption that the preliminary hearing would only be dealing with one particular issue. Final hearings are dealt with in Chapter 12, 'The hearing'.

Note that while no fees are payable in respect of preliminary hearings, claimants are required to pay a final hearing fee (unless the claimant is entitled to fee remission). However, it is unclear how the requirement to pay a fee impacts on the application of rule 48 in those cases where the fee has not yet been paid by the date of the preliminary hearing. It may be that the claimant would have to commit to paying the fee (or seeking remission) after the hearing in order for the final hearing to go ahead. Some support for this approach comes from the only EAT decision on the impact of the fees regime to date – Dozie v Addison Lee plc 2013 ICR D38, EAT. There, D brought her appeals at short notice without paying the requisite issue fee and AL plc argued that they should therefore be struck out. The EAT acknowledged that changes to the Employment Appeal Tribunal Rules 1993 SI 1993/2854 meant that, where an appeal had been properly instituted (as in the instant case), it was liable to be struck out if an issue fee had not been paid or remission applied for. However, the EAT noted that a properly instituted appeal will remain extant until such a strike-out is effected and while, in the vast majority of cases, the EAT is unlikely to take action until the question of fees is resolved, in an urgent case such as this it was entitled to proceed and the appellant would be expected to pay the fee or apply for remission in due course. Whether or not tribunals adopt a similar tactic when converting a preliminary hearing to a final hearing under rule 48 remains to be seen. However, it should be noted that the fee in question in Dozie was an issue fee, not a final hearing fee, and that the EAT proceeded on the ground that the matter was urgent. The element of urgency is unlikely to arise in many tribunal cases.

11.11 Under rule 4(1)(b) of the Employment Tribunals and the Employment Appeal Tribunal Fees Order 2013 the obligation to pay a final hearing fee only arises 'on the date specified in a notice accompanying the notification of the listing of a final hearing of the claim'. It could therefore be argued that, as the claimant in a case where a preliminary hearing has been converted to a final hearing under rule 48 has not received a notice under rule 4, he or she is not required to pay a final hearing fee at all. However, this argument is unlikely to find favour with HMCTS. Tribunal fees are discussed in detail in Chapter 19, 'Fees'.

Preliminary consideration and case management orders 11.12

Rule 53(1)(a) grants tribunals an express power to use preliminary hearings to conduct a preliminary consideration of the claim and make a case management order, including an order relating to the conduct of the final hearing. In these circumstances, the preliminary hearing is, in effect, a CMD. The tribunal can use it as an opportunity to identify the relevant issues in the case to help focus the parties' minds in preparation for the final hearing. This is important, particularly in more complex cases, such as discrimination claims, whistleblowing or equal pay, where the pleadings are often long and detailed.

In Fairbank v Care Management Group and another case EAT 0139/12 the EAT held that the tribunal had erred by directing each of the claimants to reduce the length of their ET1 claim form to one side of A4 paper. This would have required the claimants to omit claims and other important material. The EAT said that the appropriate way to deal with lengthy claims is to identify the relevant issues at a CMD (now a preliminary hearing).

In Marks and Spencer plc v Martins 1998 ICR 1005, CA, Lord Justice 11.13 Mummery suggested that in most cases of race discrimination it would be good practice to hold a preliminary hearing, so as to ensure, as far as possible, that the parties and the tribunal identify the issues before the full hearing; and to consider making directions, such as agreement on the issues falling for determination at the full hearing and, if appropriate, the exchange of witness statements in advance of that hearing. It would also be important to obtain from the parties at that stage a reliable estimate of the likely length of the full hearing. If that course is taken, it should be possible for the regional office to allot a realistic slot in the list to ensure an uninterrupted hearing of the whole case, without damaging disruptions. Similar advice has been given in respect of protected disclosure ('whistleblowing') cases – see ALM Medical Services Ltd v Bladon 2002 ICR 1444, CA. While these cases were decided under previous versions of the rules, they illustrate the importance placed on encouraging more effective case management in the initial stages of proceedings so that delays and adjournments can be avoided at the substantive hearing.

A list of issues is a useful case management tool for tribunals to bring some semblance of order, structure and clarity to proceedings in which the requirements of formal pleadings are minimal. Although the tribunal will normally be assisted by a list of issues agreed between the parties, the responsibility to identify the issues remains with the tribunal – Land Rover v Short EAT 0496/10. Because the employment tribunal which hears the case is under a duty to ensure that the case is clearly and efficiently presented, it is 'not required slavishly to follow the list presented to it' where to do so would impair the discharge of its core duty to hear and determine the case in accordance with the law and the evidence – Price v Surrey County Council and anor EAT 0450/10. In Parekh v London Borough of Brent 2012 EWCA Civ 1630, CA,

545

the Court commented that case management decisions are not final decisions and they can therefore be revisited and reconsidered if, for example, there is a material change of circumstances. The fact that a tribunal has identified a list of relevant issues to be determined at the final hearing does not restrict the issues to be considered to those listed.

11.14 In many cases preliminary consideration of a claim will lead to the tribunal making case management orders. The scope of the tribunal's general power to make case management orders under rule 29 is addressed below – see 'Case management orders'.

11.15 **Determination of any preliminary issue**

A tribunal may hold a preliminary hearing to determine any preliminary issue – rule 53(1)(b). A 'preliminary issue' is defined in rule 53(3) as 'any substantive issue which *may* determine liability' (our stress). By contrast, the draft rules defined a preliminary issue as 'any substantive issue that will not necessarily determine liability'. The draft wording suggested that the substantive issue in question could not be determinative of liability. The amended wording implies that the substantive issue should have some bearing on liability but that in some cases the issue may not be determinative of the claim.

The following are examples of preliminary issues that could be determined at a preliminary hearing:

* an issue as to jurisdiction
* whether the claimant was an employee or worker so as to be entitled to the protection of employment legislation
* whether the claim was brought in time
* whether a dismissal had taken place
* whether a transfer amounted to a relevant transfer for the purposes of the Transfer of Undertakings (Protection of Employment) Regulations 2006 SI 2006/246
* whether the claimant had the necessary length of continuous service
* whether the claimant was disabled within the meaning of S.6(1) of the Equality Act 2010 (EqA) (but see SCA Packaging v Boyle 2009 ICR 1056, HL, below).

11.16 While in many cases the preliminary issue will concern questions of law, there will be some cases where the issue will be largely one of fact. This raises the question of whether the matter would be best dealt with at the final hearing before a full tribunal when all the evidence is available. Under the old rules, preliminary issues were often heard and adjudicated upon before the tribunal heard evidence on the substantive claim. This meant the hearing had two

546

separate parts: the evidence and decision relating to the point of jurisdiction, followed by the evidence and decision relevant to the substantive claim (assuming, of course, that the decision on jurisdiction had gone in favour of the claimant). An exception to this practice arose where the evidence which was germane to the preliminary issue substantially overlapped with that which was relevant to the main issue, in which case dividing the hearing into two parts was not appropriate – Munir and anor v Jang Publications Ltd 1989 ICR 1, CA. Nor was it appropriate to divide up the issues between preliminary and substantive points where the issue of jurisdiction could only be decided upon assumptions made about facts which could only be tested by the admission of evidence relating to the substantive claim – Turley v Allders Department Stores Ltd 1980 ICR 66, EAT.

In SCA Packaging v Boyle 2009 ICR 1056, HL, Lord Hope – quoting the EAT in CJ O'Shea Construction Ltd v Bassi 1998 ICR 1130, EAT – stated that a preliminary issue must be a 'succinct, knockout point which is capable of being decided after only a relatively short hearing. This is unlikely to be the case where a preliminary issue cannot be entirely divorced from the merits of the case, or the issue will require the consideration of a substantial body of evidence. In such a case it is preferable that there should be only one hearing to determine all the matters in dispute.' He disapproved of tribunals deciding whether a disability discrimination claimant was 'disabled' at a preliminary hearing and stated that it would rarely be appropriate to separate the question of hostile treatment and the question of 'disability' even if the parties are in favour of it.

11.17 It remains to be seen whether similar considerations will apply under the new rules when determining whether a matter should be dealt with as a preliminary issue. It should be noted in this regard that in Leeds City Council v Woodhouse and anor 2010 IRLR 625, CA, Lady Justice Smith expressed concern about the tribunal judge deciding the question of whether the claimant was a 'contract worker' under the Race Relations Act 1976 (now repealed and replaced by the EqA) as a preliminary issue, given that it was necessary for the tribunal to make extensive findings of fact. In her (obiter) view, in a case that is not clear and simple, it would be preferable for the status issue to be heard as part of the entire case by a full tribunal.

Note that in most cases the preliminary issue will relate to a particular evidential or legal burden that the *claimant* is required to prove. However, it could, for example, concern a question of whether the respondent has sufficient evidence to discharge a rebuttable presumption (e.g. the rebuttable presumption of continuity of employment found in S.210(5) of the Employment Rights Act 1996).

Consideration of whether claim/response should be struck out   11.18
Rule 53(1)(c) confirms that a tribunal has the power to consider the issue of strike-out at a preliminary hearing. Rule 37 sets out the grounds on which a

547

tribunal can strike out a claim or response (or part). In respect of claims, these grounds are broadly the same as those which existed under the old rules. However, the circumstances in which a response, or part, can be struck out have been widened. Now all the grounds apply to both claims and responses while previously some of the grounds were limited in their application to claims only.

The power for a tribunal to strike out a claim or response, or part, is discussed in more detail under 'Striking out' below.

11.19 Making of deposit orders
Under the Tribunal Rules 2004 a deposit order could only be made at a PHR – rule 20(1). This was because, when considering whether or not to make a deposit order, the employment judge could consider any oral or written representations or evidence. Such evidence had to be considered in public, unless exceptional circumstances applied, and case management discussions were held in private. Under new rule 53(1)(d), a deposit order can be made at a preliminary hearing, even if it is held in private. The provisions applicable to the making of a deposit order are contained in rule 39 and are discussed in more detail under 'Deposit orders' below.

11.20 Exploring possibility of settlement or ADR
The Tribunal Rules 2013 give tribunals a more formal role in promoting alternative forms of dispute resolution than previously existed under the old rules. Rule 3 states that wherever practicable and appropriate the tribunal should encourage the parties to use the services of Acas, judicial or other mediation, or other means of resolving their disputes by agreement.

Under rule 53(1)(e) a tribunal has an express power to explore the possibility of settlement or alternative dispute resolution at a preliminary hearing, although in keeping with rule 3, the parties should be prepared to consider it at all stages of the proceedings. In his review of the rules, Underhill J recognised that greater use of alternative dispute mechanisms is largely about creating a cultural shift in attitudes to dispute resolution, but that a standalone rule to this effect should help encourage such a shift.

For a detailed consideration of Acas-conciliation, settlement and alternative dispute resolution, see Chapter 3, 'Conciliation, settlements and ADR'.

11.21 Fixing of preliminary hearings
Rule 54 deals with the fixing of preliminary hearings. It provides that a preliminary hearing may be directed by the tribunal on its own initiative following its initial consideration under rule 26 (commonly referred to as the 'judicial sift' – see Chapter 7, 'Judicial sift') or at any time thereafter, or as

the result of an application by a party. No fees are payable in respect of preliminary hearings.

More than one preliminary hearing may be held in any particular case – rule 53(2). Thus, in appropriate circumstances different hearings may be held to determine different preliminary matters, and in some cases may in effect mirror the old distinction between CMDs and PHRs. However, tribunals will rarely hold a preliminary hearing simply to revisit a case management order that has already been made unless there has been some material change of circumstances – see 'Case management orders – varying, suspending or setting aside orders' below.

Under old rule 11 there were strict requirements that a party applying for a **11.22** CMD or PHR had to observe. For instance, unless it was not reasonably practicable to do so, the application had to be made not less than ten days before the date of the hearing at which it was to be considered (if any) – old rule 11(2). No formal requirements for applying for a preliminary hearing are contained in the 2013 Tribunal Rules. However, rule 2 ('Overriding objective') states that 'a tribunal shall seek to give effect to the overriding objective in interpreting, or exercising any power given to it by, these Rules. The parties and their representatives shall assist the tribunal to further the overriding objective.' Therefore, a party who applies for a preliminary hearing should, at the very least, state why the hearing is being requested, identify any orders sought, and explain how this will assist the tribunal by furthering the overriding objective.

Notice of a preliminary hearing. When the 2013 Rules were first drafted they **11.23** provided that the parties would be given 'reasonable notice' of the date of a preliminary hearing. However, concerns were raised about the need for the parties to have enough preparation time, particularly where substantive preliminary issues were at stake. The Government accordingly amended the provision so that a tribunal must give the parties reasonable notice of the date of the hearing *except* in the case of a hearing involving any preliminary issues, where the tribunal must give at least 14 days' notice and that notice must specify the preliminary issue(s) that are to be, or may be, decided – rule 54. If it becomes necessary to alter the nature of a preliminary hearing to consider a preliminary issue, the hearing will need to be postponed if there is not sufficient time to give 14 days' notice. However, it may be that the 14-day rule can be waived where the parties give their consent to less notice.

In its response to Lord Justice Underhill's review of the tribunal rules, the Government stated that an amendment had been made to the draft rules specifying that 14 days' notice would be required where the preliminary hearing was required to deal with any preliminary issues, 'including strike-out, deposit orders, or alternative ways of resolving the dispute'. However, this amendment was not in fact carried through into the enacted rules and no formal notice

549

period is required where the tribunal intends to consider strike-out, deposit orders or alternative dispute resolution, unless such consideration will involve the determination of any preliminary issue as defined in rule 53(3) (see 'Determination of any preliminary issue' above). It should be borne in mind, though, that what is considered 'reasonable notice' in these circumstances could be more (or less) than the 14 days required for a hearing to consider a preliminary issue.

11.24 **Conduct of preliminary hearing**
Responses to the Government's consultation on the proposal to combine CMDs and PHRs expressed concerns about how preliminary hearings would operate in practice. The basis of many of these concerns was that any potential cost savings would be negated if preliminary hearings were not conducted on the telephone as frequently as CMDs. Others felt that the change might increase costs, with parties more likely to instruct lawyers to represent them at the preliminary stages of a claim if substantive issues such as striking out a case, or deposit orders, were likely to be discussed. However, the Government was not persuaded that the combined preliminary hearings would lead to a rise in costs. It felt that the rule change would make little practical difference to the choices parties make, but would benefit all sides in more efficient use of both the tribunals' and the parties' time. It also said that it expected preliminary hearings to be conducted by telephone wherever possible. In reality, how a preliminary hearing will be conducted is dictated by the purpose for which the hearing is to be held.

11.25 **Constitution of tribunal for preliminary hearings.** Rule 55 states that preliminary hearings will ordinarily be conducted by an employment judge sitting alone. However, where notice has been given that any preliminary issues may be decided, a party may apply for the hearing to be conducted by a full tribunal and an employment judge will decide 'whether that would be desirable'. In contrast with the position under the draft rules, there is no specific period within which any such application should be made. Where the tribunal does consider it desirable for a full tribunal to conduct the hearing, the hearing panel will be made up of one tribunal judge and two lay members. The rules do not indicate when it might be desirable for a preliminary hearing to be conducted by a full tribunal but one example might be where the preliminary issue is largely one of fact, rather than law.

It is only the determination of a preliminary issue as defined by rule 53(3) that can be conducted by a full tribunal at a preliminary hearing. No provision is made for a full tribunal to conduct a preliminary hearing where the hearing will be used to determine whether a claim or response should be struck out, whether a deposit order should be made, to explore alternative dispute resolution, or to deal with issues of case management where these matters do not involve 'preliminary issues'.

Note that under rule 48 (one of the 'rules common to all kinds of hearing'), a **11.26** tribunal conducting a preliminary hearing may order that it should be treated as a final hearing, provided that the tribunal is properly constituted for the purpose of conducting a full hearing (and neither of the parties would be materially prejudiced by the change). So if the preliminary hearing is being conducted by an employment judge sitting alone but the claim is one that must be finally determined by a full tribunal composed of the employment judge and two lay members (or one lay member if the parties agree), the tribunal will not be properly constituted for the purposes of a final hearing – see Chapter 1, 'Employment tribunals', under 'Judicial composition – employment judge sitting alone'. If, however, the preliminary hearing was initially listed to determine a preliminary issue and a party successfully applied to have it heard by a full tribunal, then the tribunal would be able to treat it as a final hearing (if appropriate to do so). Final hearings are dealt with in Chapter 12, 'The hearing'.

Public or private? Under the old rules, a tribunal was prohibited from making **11.27** an order determining the civil rights or liabilities of a party at a CMD – old rule 17(2). The rationale behind this stemmed from Article 6 of the European Convention on Human Rights (ECHR), which requires such issues to be determined at a public hearing – and CMDs were held in private. The matter is now governed by new rule 56, which provides that where the hearing involves the determination of a preliminary issue or consideration of whether a claim or response, or any part, should be struck out, that part of the hearing must be held in public or, subject to rules 50 (privacy and restrictions on disclosure) and 94 (national security proceedings), the tribunal may direct that the entirety of the hearing be in public.

Rule 93(2) complements rule 56 by providing that, subject only to rules 50 and 94, a representative of Acas can attend any preliminary hearing. This is presumably to allow Acas to aid the tribunal in the exercise of its power under rule 53(1)(e) to consider settlement and alternative forms of dispute resolution at a preliminary hearing.

In person or by electronic communication? A tribunal may conduct a hearing **11.28** (including a preliminary hearing), or part of a hearing, using electronic communication (including by telephone) if it considers that it would be just and equitable to do so and provided that the parties (and, in the case of public hearings, members of the public) are able to hear what the tribunal hears and see any witnesses as seen by the tribunal. This power in contained in rule 46, which is one of the 'rules common to all kinds of hearing'.

Rule 46 reflects the position under rule 15 of the Tribunal Rules 2004, albeit more succinctly. However, unlike the old rule, rule 46 does not provide that when oral evidence is given, the tribunal and (where applicable) the public must be able to see and hear all parties to the communication. Instead, the

551

parties and any members of the public attending the hearing must be able to see and hear the parties only to the same extent as the tribunal can see and hear them. In other words, oral evidence can be provided by telephone, without a video link – not only in private hearings, but also, potentially, in public hearings – provided a speakerphone is used to enable the parties and members of the public to hear. However, such evidence, if accepted by the tribunal, could be open to challenge on the basis that the tribunal was not in a position to properly assess the witness's credibility without seeing him or her in person. In such circumstances, the tribunal should be prepared to fully justify its decision that allowing such evidence would be 'just and equitable' to both parties.

Clearly the Government's intention is that, wherever possible, preliminary hearings should be conducted in private, over the telephone, and by an employment judge sitting alone.

11.29 Case management orders

A case management order is 'any order or decision of any kind in relation to the conduct of proceedings, not including the determination of any issue which would be the subject of a judgment' – rule 1(3)(a). (A judgment is a decision made at any stage of the proceedings 'which finally determines a claim, or part of a claim, as regards liability, remedy or costs...; any issue which is capable of finally disposing of any claim, or part of a claim ... [or] the imposition of a penalty under S.12A ETA' – rule 1(3)(b).) The power to make case management orders – which is contained in rule 29 – is purely administrative, allowing tribunals to direct the parties as to how the proceedings should be conducted. A case management order may cover, for example, the listing of a preliminary or final hearing, or may give directions to the parties.

Under the old rules, tribunals commonly issued what were referred to as 'standard' case management orders. These provided for the mutual disclosure of evidence, the preparation of a hearing bundle and the simultaneous exchange of witness statements to take place a certain number of weeks before the final hearing date. The scope of the general power to make case management orders under rule 29 means that a tribunal is still take able to take this uniform approach to case management. Indeed, this may well be the approach taken in more straightforward cases, particularly when, following its initial consideration of the case, the tribunal is required to make a case management order – rule 26(2) (see 'Order on tribunal's own initiative – when a case management order must be made' below).

11.30 Tribunal's power to make case management orders
Under rule 29, the tribunal may at any stage of the proceedings, on its own initiative or on application by a party, make a case management order. Rules

31–40 list a number of specific powers the tribunal has to make orders in relation to:

- the disclosure of documents and information – rule 31

- the requirement to attend to give evidence – rule 32

- obtaining evidence from other EU Member States – rule 33

- the addition, substitution and removal of parties – rule 34

- permitting other persons to participate in proceedings – rule 35

- selecting a lead case – rule 36

- striking out all or part of a claim or response – rule 37

- unless orders – rule 38

- deposit orders – rule 39, and

- non-payment of fees – rule 40.

However, rule 29 states that these express powers do not restrict the tribunal's **11.31** general power to make orders. Therefore, as was the case under rule 10(1) of the 2004 Tribunal Rules (which empowered the tribunal chairman to make orders on any matter arising in connection with the proceedings as appeared to him or her to be 'appropriate'), the tribunal still has a wide general discretion to tailor orders to the case in hand. Furthermore, case law decided under previous incarnations of the rules suggests that the power of tribunals to make orders is extensive and this position remains unchanged under the new rules. In Charman v Palmers Scaffolding Ltd 1979 ICR 335, EAT, the EAT held that the tribunal's power to manage proceedings could even extend to directing a rehearing of the case before a differently constituted tribunal (although this power would be exercised rarely).

Any order made under the Tribunal Rules 2004 had to inform the parties of the potential consequences of non-compliance with the order – rule 10(3). This is not an express requirement under the Tribunal Rules 2013 but an order may provide that if it is not complied with by the date specified, the claim or response (or part of it) will be dismissed without further order – rule 38(1) (see 'Unless orders' below). Similarly, if a deposit order is made, the paying party must be notified of the potential consequences of the order – rule 39(3). Deposit orders are discussed in more detail under 'Deposit orders' below.

Order on tribunal's own initiative
11.32

An employment judge's power to make orders was greatly increased under the Tribunal Rules 2004, compared to previous versions of the rules. Under the 2004 Rules, a judge could decide to make an order on his or her own initiative with or without hearing the parties or giving them the opportunity to make written or oral representations. However, there were two exceptions to this. First, if the judge intended to make an order that different claims be heard together, notice had to be given to the parties concerned giving them a chance to make oral or written representations as to why such an order should not be made. Secondly, if the judge was considering making a restricted reporting order (other than what was known as a temporary order), the parties had to be given an opportunity to advance oral argument before such an order was made.

These two restrictions to a tribunal's power to make orders do not exist under the 2013 Rules. And, unlike old rule 12(2)(b), there is no longer any express requirement for the parties to be informed of their right to apply for an order to be varied, suspended or set aside where it is made without giving the parties the opportunity to make representations (although the right itself continues to exist – see rules 29 and 50(4)). However, rule 37(2) provides that a claim or response cannot be struck out unless the party in question has been given a reasonable opportunity to make representations, either in writing or, if requested by the party, at a hearing. Therefore, where a tribunal is considering strike-out, it must inform the relevant party before the order is made to allow that party to make representations.

11.33 When a case management order must be made. While orders can be made at any stage of the proceedings, the rules specifically provide that a case management order *must* be made (unless already made) where, after 'initial consideration' (see Chapter 7, 'Judicial sift'), the employment judge is of the view that:

- there are arguable complaints and defences within the tribunal's jurisdiction (rule 26), or

- where the judge has given notice under rule 27 or 28 that the tribunal has no jurisdiction to consider the claim or that the claim or response (or relevant part) has no reasonable prospect of success

but, following representations by the relevant party, he or she decides that the claim/response (or part) should be permitted to proceed – rules 27(4) and 28(4).

11.34 Application by party for order

An application by a party for a case management order may be made either at a hearing or in advance in writing to the tribunal – rule 30(1), although wherever possible it should be made in writing – see the Presidential Guidance on 'General Case Management' for England and Wales. The tribunal may deal with such an application in writing or order that it be dealt with at a preliminary or final hearing – rule 30(3). Where a party applies in writing, that party is required to notify the other parties that any objections to the application should be sent to the tribunal 'as soon as possible' – rule 30(2). This is a significant change from old rule 11(4), which allowed the other party only seven days to object to an application. Requiring objections to be submitted as soon as possible, with no deadline, is ambiguous and there are likely to be inconsistencies in respect of how long tribunals are prepared to wait for objections to be submitted before making a decision on the application.

Another significant change is that, under the old rules, only a legally represented party was required to notify the other parties of an application for a case management order and their right to object (with applications by unrepresented parties being copied to the other parties by the tribunal). The new rules require both represented and unrepresented parties to copy any applications to one another – see rule 30(2). This will save the tribunal administrative time and cost but it is likely that some unrepresented parties will inadvertently fail to comply and it remains to be seen how tribunals will view such a failure. New rule 6 allows a tribunal to take such action as it considers just in the case of non-compliance with the rules, including waiving or varying the relevant requirement.

11.35 (Note that witness order applications continue to be exempt from the requirement to be copied to the other parties. This was the position under old rule 11(4) and is restated in new rule 92. This is because in certain cases it may be inappropriate for a party to be aware that a witness order has been sought or granted.)

While there is no express provision limiting the number of times a party can apply for a case management order, a tribunal is entitled to refuse a repeated application where there has been no material change of circumstances and there is no other exceptional reason why the tribunal should allow the application to be renewed in the interests of justice – Okinedo v Northwest Guarding Ltd (debarred) and anor EAT 0510/07. This is also the case in respect of applications to amend or revoke orders – see 'Varying, suspending or setting aside orders' below.

11.36 In contrast to the position under the old rules, there is no requirement for an application to be submitted at least ten days before the hearing and there is no longer an express need for the party making the application to state how the order will assist the tribunal to deal with the proceedings efficiently and fairly. However, in accordance with the overriding objective in rule 2 – which is 'to enable employment tribunals to deal with cases fairly and justly' – a party who applies for an order should, at the very least, set out not only why it would be in the interests of justice to grant the order but also state how it will assist the tribunal by furthering the overriding objective. This is confirmed by the Presidential Guidance, which advises that the application 'should state the reason why it is made [and] why it is considered to be in accordance with the overriding objective' to make the order applied for.

555

11.37 Decision and reasons

Where a case management order is made without a hearing, it will be communicated in writing to the parties, identifying the employment judge who made the decision – rule 60. If the order is announced at a hearing, it will, by virtue of rule 65, take effect immediately (unless otherwise specified by the tribunal) and a written record will be provided to the parties as soon as practicable – rule 61(2).

Under rule 30(1) of the old rules, a tribunal had to give reasons – either oral or written – for any judgment. However, it was only obliged to give reasons for an order if a request for such reasons was made before or at the hearing at which the order was made. Unsurprisingly, this could lead to confusion when it came to challenging a decision on appeal. The EAT in Okoro and anor v Taylor Woodrow Construction Ltd and ors EAT 0318/10 acknowledged that it was best practice for an employment judge making an important procedural decision to keep a note of his or her decision and record the reasons for it. However, in the absence of a specific requirement, there was always the risk that this formality would be overlooked.

11.38
Under the new rules the process has changed. New rule 62(1) states that the 'tribunal shall give reasons for its decision on *any* disputed issue, whether substantial or procedural' (our stress). It goes on to provide that:

- in the case of a decision given in writing the reasons shall also be given in writing. In the case of a decision announced at a hearing the reasons may be given orally at the hearing or reserved to be given in writing later – rule 62(2)

- where reasons have been given orally, the employment judge shall announce that written reasons will not be provided unless they are asked for by any party at the hearing itself or by a written request presented by any party within 14 days of the sending of the written record of the decision. The written record of the decision shall repeat that information. If no such request is received, the tribunal shall provide written reasons only if requested to do so by the EAT or a court – rule 62(3)

- the reasons given for any decision shall be proportionate to the significance of the issue and for decisions other than judgments may be very short – rule 62(4).

Note that the requirement to give reasons for orders is very similar to the requirement to give reasons for judgments (both are governed by rule 62) – see further Chapter 14, 'Tribunal judgments', under 'Reasons for judgments'.

11.39 Time scale for compliance with orders

Unless otherwise directed by the tribunal, an order of the tribunal for an act to be done on or by a particular day must be done before midnight on that day –

rule 4(1). If the time specified by an order for doing any act ends on a day other than a working day, the act is done in time if it is done on the next working day. For these purposes, 'working day' means any day except a Saturday or Sunday, Christmas Day, Good Friday or a bank holiday under S.1 of the Banking and Financial Dealings Act 1971 – rule 4(2). This is new to the rules of procedure. Under the old rules, a time specified by an order ending on a day other than a working day had to be complied with before the end of the last working day prior to the specified date. For instance, an act required to be done by a specified date falling on a Saturday had to be done before the end of the preceding Friday. However, under the new rules the order will be taken to have been complied with if the act is done by the end of the following Monday. This is likely to cause confusion for litigants in person who may not be wholly familiar with the rules and who may accuse the other party of failing to comply with an order on the misunderstanding that the time limit has been breached.

If the order has to be complied with within a certain number of days of or from a particular event, the date of that event is not included in the calculation – rule 4(3). For instance, a case management order may require the claimant to provide the respondent with a schedule of loss within 14 days of the date of the preliminary hearing at which the order is made. If the preliminary hearing took place on 1 January, the claimant should ensure that he or she has complied with the order before midnight on 15 January. Similarly, where an order must be complied with not less than a certain number of days before or after an event, the date of the event shall not be included in the calculation – rule 4(4). For example, if a party is required to present written submissions to the tribunal not less than 7 days before the hearing and the hearing is fixed for 8 October, the submissions must be presented no later than 1 October. To avoid any confusion, rule 4(5) provides that wherever practicable the tribunal will express the last day for compliance with an order as a calendar date.

11.40 Sometimes the date for compliance with an order is specified by reference to the date when a document is sent to a person by the tribunal. In these circumstances, the date when the document was sent will be regarded as the date endorsed on the document as the date of sending or, if there is no such endorsement, the date shown on the letter accompanying the document – rule 4(6).

11.41 **Extension of interim time limits.** The only time limits that are governed expressly by statute are those relating to the presentation of complaints. Since such time limits go to jurisdiction, a tribunal can only extend them in accordance with statute (assuming that an extension is permitted at all). Statutory time limits are considered in detail in Chapter 5, 'Time limits'.

By contrast, the time for doing any act set by the Tribunal Rules 2013, or by any order of a tribunal made under the rules, can be extended at the tribunal's discretion – rule 5. This can be done on the application of a party or on the tribunal's own initiative, regardless of whether the time limit in question has

557

already expired. Under the Tribunal Rules 2004, this power was subject to the qualification that time could only be extended for certain specified purposes if the employment judge considered that it was 'just and equitable' or 'in the interests of justice' to do so. No such qualifications exist under new rule 5. The tribunal now has absolute discretion to extend or shorten any time limit specified in the rules and it is likely that the overriding objective will carry significant weight in the exercise of that discretion – see rule 2. No qualification exists even where the tribunal considers an application to extend the time for submitting the response form (see Chapter 6, 'Defending a claim', under 'Responding to a claim – time limit for presenting response').

11.42 Varying, suspending or setting aside orders

Under rule 29 the tribunal has the power to vary, suspend or set aside an earlier case management order where this is necessary in the interests of justice, and in particular where a party affected by the earlier order did not have a reasonable opportunity to make representations before it was made.

Case management orders are *not* capable of reconsideration under rule 70, which only applies to 'judgments'. A judgment is a decision (made at any stage of the proceedings) 'which finally determines a claim, or part of a claim, as regards liability, remedy or costs...; any issue which is capable of finally disposing of any claim, or part of a claim...; [or] the imposition of a penalty under S.12A ETA' – rule 1(3)(b). A case management order is defined in rule 1(3)(a) as 'an order or decision of any kind in relation to the conduct of proceedings, *not* including the determination of any issue which would be the subject of a judgment' (our stress). Note, though, that the test for reconsideration under rule 70 – that it is 'necessary in the interests of justice' – is the same as the test under rule 29.

11.43 Case management orders may, however, be appealed to the EAT. But appeals to the EAT are only permitted where there has been an error of law. As most interim orders are discretionary, successful appeals against interim orders are rare. In Ma v Merck Sharp and Dohme Ltd 2008 EWCA Civ 1426, CA, the Court of Appeal recognised that it should not be hypercritical or over-analytical in its treatment of employment tribunal decisions which, even if not technically discretionary case management decisions, are closely connected to the practical management of complex or intractable litigation. Unless the tribunal misapplied the law, appeals will only be granted where it has ignored relevant factors, taken account of irrelevant factors, or reached a decision that could be characterised as perverse or one that no reasonable tribunal could have reached – Carter v Credit Change Ltd 1979 ICR 908, CA.

There is no express limit on the number of times a tribunal can revisit one of its case management orders (either on its own initiative or on application by a party) under rule 29. However, in practice it would be extremely rare to revisit

558

an order unless there has been some material change of circumstance. It was stressed by the EAT in Goldman Sachs Services Ltd v Montali 2002 ICR 1251, EAT, that in exercising its power to vary or revoke interim orders under the Tribunal Rules 2001, a tribunal should follow the principles set out in the Civil Procedure Rules 1998 SI 1998/3132, and, in particular, should not vary or revoke orders in absence of a material change in circumstances after the order was first made. In Sodexho Ltd v Gibbons 2005 ICR 1647, EAT, the Appeal Tribunal confirmed that this principle applied equally to the power to vary or revoke orders under the 2004 Rules.

This principle is akin to the principle of issue estoppel under the Civil Procedure **11.44** Rules, the effect of which is to prevent an issue which has already been determined in the final judgment of a court from being relitigated between the same parties. But in an exceptional case an order can be revisited where a party wishes to argue a potentially significant point which could have been, but was not, advanced at an earlier hearing, even without any change in circumstance. The mere fact that the issue could have been raised earlier does not necessarily make it an abuse of process to do so at a later date – Hart v English Heritage (Historic Buildings and Monuments Commission for England) 2006 ICR 655, EAT. However this does not mean that a party can apply for an order to be revisited on the ground that the issue was not argued properly, or that the representative did not do it justice.

Sanctions for non-compliance with orders **11.45**
Under rule 6, non-compliance with the rules (except those relating to presentation of a claim or response) or with an order of the tribunal (except 'unless' orders and deposit orders) does not of itself render void the proceedings or any step taken in the proceedings. However, the tribunal may take such action as it considers just, including:

- waiving or varying the requirement – rule 6(a)
- striking out the claim or the response in whole or in part – rule 6(b)
- barring or restricting a party's participation in the proceedings – rule 6(c)
- awarding costs – rule 6(d).

A tribunal can apply all or any of the sanctions set out in rule 6. A tribunal could, for instance, strike out all or part of the claim or response and then proceed to award a costs or preparation time order. If, for example, a party has conducted the proceedings in such an unreasonable way as to have their case/ defence struck out, it is possible that a tribunal judge may feel that the other party should be reimbursed for the costs it has incurred. The power to award costs or make a preparation time order is fully considered in Chapter 20, 'Costs and penalties', while the power to strike out is considered under 'Striking out' below.

559

11.46 In addition to the general sanctions outlined above, a specific sanction applies where an individual, without reasonable cause, fails to comply with a witness order or an order for disclosure. In these circumstances, that person commits a criminal offence punishable on summary conviction with a fine not exceeding £1,000 – S.7(4) ETA. Under old rule 10(6), a tribunal was required to expressly warn the individual concerned of the potential criminal sanction. This requirement has not been carried over into the new rules but a prosecution is much more likely to be successful if the individual had prior warning that his or her failure to comply could amount to an offence.

Given the possibility of sanctions for non-compliance, the Presidential Guidance on 'General Case Management' for England and Wales advises that if a party is having difficulty in complying, he or she should discuss the matter with the other party and then apply to the tribunal to vary the order - see 'Varying, suspending or setting aside orders' above.

11.47 Disclosure and evidence

A tribunal's powers to order the disclosure of evidence and the attendance of witnesses are governed by rules 31–33. Rule 31 states that the tribunal may order 'any person in Great Britain to disclose documents or information to a party (by providing copies or otherwise) or to allow a party to inspect such material as might be ordered by a county court or, in Scotland, by a sheriff'. This is almost identical to the wording of old rule 10(2)(d).

Rule 33 inserts a new provision allowing for evidence (including witness evidence) to be obtained from other EU Member States. It provides that the tribunal may use the procedures for obtaining evidence prescribed in Council Regulation (EC) No.1206/2001 of 28 May 2001 on cooperation between the courts of the Member States in the taking of evidence in civil or commercial matters. (Note that the original version of the 2013 Rules contained a typographical error, as rule 33 referred to Council Regulation (EC) No.1026/2001 of 28 May 2001, which relates to suspending the issuing of import licences for certain sugar sector products qualifying as EC/OCT originating products. This mistake has now been rectified.)

These provisions are discussed in more detail in Chapter 9, 'Responding to opponent's case', under 'Disclosure and inspection of documents'.

11.48 Requirement to attend to give evidence (witness orders)

By virtue of rule 32, a tribunal can order 'any person in Great Britain to attend a hearing to give evidence, produce documents, or produce information'. An order requiring a person to attend a hearing to give evidence is commonly referred to as a witness order and can, in accordance with the wide remit of rule 32, be made in relation to a party to proceedings. A tribunal can also require such a witness to produce any relevant document in his or her possession (for the production of documents by witnesses, see Chapter 9, 'Responding to opponent's case', under 'Production of documents by witnesses').

Witness orders, which correspond to the power of subpoena in the ordinary courts, can be granted on application by one of the parties or on the tribunal's own initiative – rule 29. Such an order may be sought by one of the parties if a witness is believed to have relevant knowledge or information to give and the party seeking the order believes that he or she may not attend the hearing voluntarily. A witness order will also be useful, or even necessary, where a witness will not otherwise be released by his or her employer.

11.49 An application for a witness order may be made either at a hearing or in writing to the tribunal – rule 30(1). The applying party will need to inform the tribunal of the name and address of the witness, provide a brief summary of the evidence that it is anticipated the witness will give, and state why a witness order is necessary to secure attendance. As discussed under 'Case management orders – applying for orders' above, in contrast with the position under the old rules, there is no requirement for an application to be submitted at least ten days before the hearing and there is no longer an express requirement for the applicant to state how the order will assist the tribunal to deal with the proceedings efficiently and fairly. However, rule 2 requires the parties and their representatives to assist the tribunal to give effect to the overriding objective – to deal with cases fairly and justly – in interpreting or exercising any power under the rules. Thus, a party who applies for a witness order should set out not only why it would be in the interests of justice to grant the order but also state how it will assist the tribunal by furthering the overriding objective. An order must be applied for in good time before the hearing when the witness's attendance will be required so that the order can be served.

Witness order applications continue to be exempt from the requirement to be copied to the other parties. This was the position under old rule 11(4) and is restated in new rule 92. This is because in certain cases it may be inappropriate for a party to be aware that a witness order has been sought or granted.

11.50 The order will specify the time and place at which the person to whom it is adressed must be present. Failure to attend without reasonable excuse may result in him or her being liable to prosecution and a fine of up to level 3 on the standard scale (currently £1,000) if summarily convicted – S.7(4) ETA. It is worth noting that the requirement under old rule 10(6) for a tribunal to expressly warn the witness of this sanction has not been included in the new rules.

A person against whom a witness order has been made can apply to have the order varied or revoked. Such an application should be made as soon as possible after the order has been issued and, in any event, before the date on which the

561

witness is required to attend. Any such application must be properly considered by the tribunal if made within the prescribed period and it will be an error of law if a tribunal judge signals that a witness order will be maintained irrespective of the grounds upon which the person ordered to attend applies to have the order varied or set aside, or if the judge fails to give reasons for his or her decision to reject any such application – Siebe plc v Baker EAT 505/92.

11.51 When will witness order be granted?

The power to order attendance of witnesses is discretionary but, as always, tribunals must exercise their discretion judicially. This means that while the appellate courts will be reluctant to interfere with the tribunal's decision, in reaching that decision it will be expected to bear in mind that a party should be able to present the testimony of a witness whose evidence is relevant and also that witness orders, as a form of compulsion, should never be issued lightly. In Dada v Metal Box Co Ltd 1974 ICR 559, NIRC, Sir John Donaldson laid down two criteria to be applied by tribunals when exercising their discretion over applications for witness orders. An employment judge must be satisfied that:

• the intended witness can, prima facie, give evidence which is relevant to the issues in dispute, and

• it is necessary to issue an order to compel attendance.

11.52 In being satisfied that the evidence that a witness can give is likely to be of relevance, it is not necessary for the party applying for an order to disclose a full proof of evidence to the tribunal judge. The applicant should, however, indicate the subject matter of the intended witness's evidence and show the extent to which it is relevant. It is an error of law to refuse an order where the intended witness has relevant documents – Wilcox v HGS 1975 ICR 333, QBD. In that case the claimant was dismissed for failing to follow prescribed safety precautions. He claimed that his dismissal was unfair because the safety procedures were generally ignored throughout the company. He applied for a witness order to be made against an official of the regional Gas Board requiring him to produce documents concerning the respondent company's safety record. A chairman refused the application but the High Court, on appeal, overturned this decision. The evidence that the witness was required to produce was prima facie relevant since it related to the general disregard of safety in the respondent's work practices, and it was necessary to weigh this against the employee's failure to observe safety precautions. The witness order was accordingly granted.

However, as the Court of Appeal said in Noorani v Merseyside TEC Ltd 1999 IRLR 184, CA, it has never been the position that *any* evidence that might be relevant must be admitted: the decision as to whether it is 'sufficiently relevant' is ultimately a matter for the discretion of the tribunal and can only be appealed on the usual grounds for appealing an interim order (see 'Case management orders – varying, suspending or setting aside orders' above). In upholding a tribunal's refusal to grant a witness order, the Court of Appeal commented that if, during the course of the case, the judge decides that the original decision not to make a witness order was wrong, then it can always remedy the matter, adjourning if necessary.

In National Centre for Young People with Epilepsy v Boateng EAT 0440/10 the **11.53** EAT emphasised that the witness evidence must not only be prima facie relevant, but must also be admissible. In that case there was an issue as to whether the relevant evidence should be excluded on the ground of legal professional privilege. If so, a witness order in respect of the claimant's former solicitor ought not to be made. However, the EAT held that the claimant had prima facie waived her right to legal professional privilege in that she was reliant on her solicitor's alleged failure to act in her best interests and to advise her as to the means to avoid the effect of the compromise agreement. In those circumstances, it was manifestly unfair on the respondent not to have the opportunity to place the solicitor's evidence before the tribunal.

The second criterion identified in the Dada case is that a witness order must actually be *necessary*. This does not require the applicant to show that the intended witness blatantly refuses to turn up voluntarily. However, an applicant should always request attendance of the witness on a voluntary basis before applying for an order. If the witness refuses or equivocates, or simply does not reply – thereby leaving the party in doubt as to whether the witness will attend in the absence of an order – such an order will then be appropriate. An order may also be appropriate where, although the witness will attend voluntarily, it would be easier and less embarrassing for him or her to be subject to an order compelling attendance. This may be the case, for example, where the witness who is being called by the applicant is an employee of the respondent.

Hostile witnesses

11.54

Witnesses called by a party can be expected to give evidence which, on the whole, assists the case being put forward by that party. Obviously there are risks involved in calling reluctant witnesses. The party calling the witness cannot normally ask leading questions, dispute what the witness says or cross-examine him or her (see further Chapter 12, 'The hearing', under 'Presenting the evidence'), even where the witness wholly fails to live up to the expectation of the party who has called him or her or goes so far as to give testimony that supports the case of the opponent. It may also be difficult to establish in advance what evidence a reluctant witness is in a position to give.

In such circumstances, the witness may, at the tribunal judge's discretion, be regarded as 'hostile'. The principal advantage of regarding a witness as hostile is that it enables the party who called the witness to dispense with the rule against leading questions in examination-in-chief and to launch the kind of open attack possible only in cross-examination. If, however, it is clear at the

563

stage at which a witness order is applied for that the intended witness is likely to attend. In Pasha v DHSS EAT 556/80 P sought to call the compilers of an adverse departmental assessment made about him. One of the authors had been called by the respondent but P believed the other three should also give evidence. A tribunal chairman refused to grant witness orders on the ground that the witnesses would all be hostile and the only purpose of requiring them to be there was to enable P to cross-examine them. On appeal, the EAT confirmed that the grant of witness orders was a matter of discretion. In this case, P would be unable to cross-examine the witnesses since it would be he who called them. His case would probably be strengthened by not having the proposed witnesses there at all. The appeal was dismissed.

11.55 Privacy and restrictions on disclosure

To diminish the adverse effect on the parties of publicity in cases involving allegations of sexual misconduct, the Industrial Tribunals (Constitution and Rules of Procedure) Regulations 1993 SI 1993/2687 introduced a power for tribunals to restrict the reporting of such cases by way of a 'restricted reporting order' (RRO). This power was extended under the Industrial Tribunals (Constitution and Rules of Procedure) (Amendment) Regulations 1996 SI 1996/1757 to cover certain disability discrimination cases. The statutory basis for this power – which was carried into subsequent versions of the tribunal rules, including the Tribunal Rules 2004 – derives from Ss.11 and 12 ETA, which enable rules of procedure to include provision relating to the restriction of publicity in cases involving allegations of sexual misconduct (S.11) and disability discrimination cases where 'evidence of a personal nature' is likely to be heard (S.12).

The need for RROs primarily arises in the two circumstances addressed in Ss.11 and 12 ETA. However, case law has established that there are additional circumstances in which an employment tribunal or the EAT may need to make an RRO or anonymity order to protect rights derived from European law. In F v G 2012 ICR 246, EAT, for example, the EAT observed that the powers were insufficiently wide to cover all possible circumstances in which restrictions may be required in order to protect the rights of a party or another person under the European Convention on Human Rights (ECHR) and EU law. In that case, the EAT held that the employment tribunal had correctly issued an anonymity order permanently removing the names of the claimant, the respondent college which employed her and the college's students and staff from the employment tribunal's records. In approving the tribunal's decision, the EAT held that a tribunal can issue an anonymity order in accordance with its general case management powers where persons affected by the case would otherwise suffer an infringement of their right to a private and family life under Article 8 ECHR.

Similarly, in BG International Ltd v Flexman 2012 EWHC 1080, QBD, the **11.56** High Court granted an anonymity order in relation to three individuals who were otherwise unwilling to give evidence in relation to contempt of court proceedings between the parties. If the order was not granted, there was a risk that the contempt proceedings would be rendered nugatory. However, the court held that there was no justification for extending the order to protect the parties' identities. In so holding, the Court balanced the various competing interests which arose — including the Article 6 ECHR right to a fair trial for all parties; the Article 10 rights of freedom of expression, subject to the restrictions contained in Article 10(2); and, to an extent, the Article 8 rights of the three individuals concerned.

The Tribunal Rules 2013 reflect this case law by providing for a wider range of circumstances in which a tribunal can order anonymity or restrict the reporting of proceedings.

Power to make privacy and restricted disclosure orders   **11.57**

Rule 50 of the Tribunal Rules 2013 is much broader and more flexible than its predecessor in terms of the circumstances in which orders relating to privacy and restrictions on disclosure can now be made. Rule 50(1) provides that a tribunal may at any stage of the proceedings, on its own initiative or on application, make an order with a view to preventing or restricting the public disclosure of any aspect of those proceedings so far as it is considered necessary:

- in the interests of justice

- in order to protect the Convention rights of any person (for this purpose 'Convention rights' has the same meaning given to it in S.1 of the Human Rights Act 1998 – rule 50(6)); or

- in the circumstances identified in S.10A ETA (which permits tribunals to sit in private to hear evidence which could not lawfully be disclosed, is confidential, or would cause substantial injury to the undertaking in which a witness works).

This simplification of what was considered by many to be an overly prescriptive **11.58** provision is a welcome change. However, as might be expected, consultation on the new power elicited strong opposition from groups representing the media, which were concerned that the new approach would undermine the principle of open justice and was out of step with the prevailing degree of openness witnessed in other courts and tribunals. These responses considered that a more flexible privacy regime represented a move towards an augmentation in the number of closed hearings, with parties putting undue pressure on judges to restrict the reporting of tribunals for fear of damage to a business's reputation if cases were widely reported. However, in response, the Government pointed out that this rule simply brings the power into line with the ruling of the EAT

565

in F v G (above). The Government also noted that, just because the rule is now expressly stated, this does not mean it is intended to be operated any more frequently. It was important to bring the provisions on privacy in employment tribunals more into line with the requirements of the Human Rights Act 1998 (which incorporates the ECHR into domestic law) and EU jurisprudence. But, in recognising the concerns of the media around this amendment, the Government agreed that it should not become the normal practice of tribunals to hold proceedings in private.

11.59 Terms of privacy and restricted disclosure orders

Orders made under rule 50 'may include' the following:

- an order that a hearing that would otherwise be in public be conducted, or partly conducted, in private – rule 50(3)(a) (see further Chapter 12, 'The hearing', under 'Hearings in private')

- an order that the identities of specified parties, witnesses or other persons referred to in the proceedings should not be disclosed to the public, by the use of anonymisation or otherwise, whether in the course of any hearing or in its listing or in any documents entered on the Register or otherwise forming part of the public record – rule 50(3)(b)

- an order for measures preventing witnesses at a public hearing being identifiable by members of the public – rule 50(3)(c)

- an RRO within the terms of S.11 or S.12 ETA – rule 50(3)(d) (see further 'Restricted reporting orders' below).

As this list is not exhaustive, a tribunal has discretion to make other types of order, where appropriate. The language of rule 50(3)(d) appears to suggest that an RRO can only be made where the case involves allegations of sexual misconduct or is a disability discrimination claim involving evidence of a personal nature: the 'terms' in which Ss.11 and 12 of the ETA are drafted clearly limit the application of those sections to such cases. However, it may be that where the new rule mentions the 'terms' of S.11 or S.12 ETA it is in fact referring to the common definition of an RRO contained in Ss.11(6) and 12(7) ETA. This states that 'restricted reporting order' means an order '(a) made in exercise of a power conferred by regulations made by virtue of this section, and (b) prohibiting the publication in Great Britain of identifying matter in a written publication available to the public or its inclusion in a relevant programme for reception in Great Britain'. If it is simply this definition to which rule 50(3)(d) is referring, then an RRO can be made in any case falling within one of the three circumstances outlined in rule 50(1).

11.60 Under rule 49 of the Tribunal Rules 2004, there was a mandatory and automatic requirement on the employment judge or the Secretary of the employment tribunal to delete from the register of judgments or any public judgment, document or record of the proceedings any matter likely to identify persons making or affected by allegations of a sexual offence. This explicit requirement has not been replicated in the 2013 rules, but tribunals are vested with discretion under rule 50(3)(b) to delete such information from judgments, documents or records entered on the Register – by way of an anonymity order or otherwise – where it considers this to be necessary in the interests of justice, to protect the Convention rights of any person, or in any of the circumstances listed in S.10A ETA.

Procedure for making privacy and restricted disclosure orders 11.61
An order under rule 50 can be made at any stage in proceedings by a tribunal acting on its own initiative or on application (either in writing or orally at a hearing) – rule 50(1). Note that, unlike the Tribunal Rules 2004, this is not limited to applications by the parties. Thus, any person with an interest in the proceedings may make an application for a rule 50 order to be made. In X v Commissioner of Metropolitan Police 2003 ICR 1031, EAT, the EAT said that an application should be made at the earliest opportunity and ideally at the same time as the tribunal claim form is submitted.

The discretion to make an order should not be exercised automatically at the request of one party, or even both parties. In X v Z Ltd 1998 ICR 43, CA, the Court of Appeal stressed that a tribunal must still consider whether it is in the public interest that the press should be deprived of the right to communicate information to the public if it becomes available. This point has now been codified in the form of rule 50(2), which requires that, in considering whether to exercise the discretion to make an order, a tribunal 'shall give full weight to the principle of open justice and to the Convention right to freedom of expression'.

Under the Tribunal Rules 2004, an RRO could only be made at a hearing (a full 11.62 RRO could only be made at a PHR or substantive hearing while temporary orders could also be made at a CMD). The tribunal's power under rule 50 of the Tribunal Rules 2013 allows it to make an order at any stage of the proceedings. There is no requirement for an order to be made at a hearing. Likewise, under the old rules any person was allowed to apply to make representations before an RRO was made and, if the judge or tribunal considered that the person had a legitimate interest, then the representations would be heard. Now, under new rule 50(4), there is no specific right for anyone to make any representations before an order is made, although it would be within the tribunal's general power to allow this. A tribunal could, for instance, choose to make an order having only heard representations from one party (this used to be the case in respect of temporary RROs). However, once the order is in force, any person with a legitimate interest has a right to make representations in writing or at a hearing – see 'Revoking or discharging privacy and restricted disclosure orders' below.

567

11.63 **Revoking or discharging privacy and restricted disclosure orders**
The Tribunal Rules 2004 allowed any person to apply to the tribunal to make representations *before* a full RRO was made and, if the judge or tribunal considered that the person had a legitimate interest, then those representations would be heard. However, the rules were silent on whether there was any right to make representations once an RRO had been made. A tribunal could, however, exercise its general case management powers to allow an application for review. For instance, in Tradition Securities and Futures SA and ors v Times Newspapers Ltd and ors 2009 IRLR 354, EAT, the EAT held that the tribunal did not err by varying an RRO at a later stage of the proceedings to remove the two claimant employees who no longer wished to be named in the RRO.

Under the Tribunal Rules 2013, there is no specific right for anyone to make representations before any order under rule 50 is made, although it would be within the tribunal's general power to allow this. However, once an order is in force, any person with a legitimate interest has a right to make representations in writing or at a hearing. Rule 50(4) provides that any party or person 'with a legitimate interest', who did not have a reasonable opportunity to make representations before the order under rule 50 was made, may write to the tribunal applying for it to be revoked or discharged, either on the basis of written representations or, if requested, at a hearing. This provision therefore gives members of the press and other interested persons, not just the parties, an opportunity to challenge an order.

11.64 **Restricted reporting orders**
Under rule 50(3)(d), a tribunal can make an RRO within the terms of S.11 or S.12 ETA (see 'Terms of privacy and restricted reporting orders' above). Specific provisions apply to RROs under rule 50(5) that do not apply to other orders made under rule 50.

11.65 **Cases in which an RRO can be made.** RROs can only be made in two types of case: cases involving allegations of sexual misconduct and disability discrimination cases involving evidence of a personal nature.

11.66 *Allegations of sexual misconduct.* Section 11(2) ETA, when read with rule 50(3)(d), permits employment tribunals to make RROs in cases involving allegations of 'sexual misconduct'. This is defined in S.11(6) ETA and covers the commission of a sexual offence, sexual harassment or other adverse conduct related to sex. Conduct is related to sex whether the relationship with sex lies in the character of the conduct or in its having reference to the sex or sexual orientation of the person at whom the conduct is directed.

An RRO made under S.11 prohibits the publication in Great Britain of any matter (written or broadcast) likely to lead members of the public to identify an individual as a person affected by or making the allegations of sexual misconduct – S.11(6) ETA. Only the person making, and any other person 'affected by', the allegation of sexual misconduct can have their identities so protected – S.11(6) ETA. The phrase 'person affected' must be interpreted narrowly, having regard to the principle of freedom of the press, and the tribunal should not impose a 'blanket' ban on naming any of the parties or witnesses to a case simply because it involves sexual misconduct – see R v London (North) Industrial Tribunal ex parte Associated Newspapers Ltd 1998 ICR 1212, QBD, where the High Court quashed an RRO. The case involved a number of allegations, including two of sexual misconduct. The Court held that where allegations of sexual misconduct form only a limited part of a much lengthier catalogue of complaints, the tribunal should try to limit the scope of the order to those directly involved in the alleged sexual misconduct. These would normally include the alleged perpetrator and victim, and in an appropriate case a witness of any sexual incident where the disclosure of that witness's identity might be capable of preventing the proper conduct of the hearing. Other witnesses might be included if appropriate but the tribunal should always consider the extent to which this is justified.

11.67 *Disability cases involving 'evidence of a personal nature'.* Section 12(2) ETA, when read with rule 50(3)(d) of the Tribunal Rules 2013, gives employment tribunals the power to make RROs in disability discrimination cases where 'evidence of a personal nature' is likely to be heard. 'Evidence of a personal nature' is defined as 'any evidence of a medical, or other intimate nature, which might reasonably be assumed to be likely to cause significant embarrassment to the complainant if reported' – S.12(7). An RRO made under S.12 prohibits the publication in Great Britain, by means of print or broadcast or 'any other form', of any matter 'likely to lead members of the public to identify' the complainant or some other person named in the order – S.12(3) ETA.

11.68 **Procedural rules specific to RROs.** The making of RROs under rule 50 of the Tribunal Rules 2013 is simplified in a key respect compared to the making of such orders under the old rules. Under the Tribunal Rules 2004, RROs could be either full (remaining in force until both liability and remedy had been determined, unless revoked earlier), or temporary (where a party anticipated extensive media interest in the case and sought emergency protection from publicity). Under the 2013 Rules there is no such distinction. Instead, where a tribunal determines that it is appropriate to make an RRO within the terms of S.11 or S.12 ETA, it must:

- specify the person whose identity is protected; and may specify particular matters of which publication is prohibited as likely to lead to that person's identification – rule 50(5)(a)

- specify the duration of the order – rule 50(5)(b), and

569

- ensure that a notice of the fact that such an order has been made in relation to those proceedings is displayed on the notice board of the tribunal with any list of the proceedings taking place before the tribunal, and on the door of the room in which the proceedings affected by the order are taking place – rule 50(5)(c). (This is intended to ensure that journalists attending the hearing will understand the limits on what they are entitled to report.)

In addition, the tribunal may order that the RRO also applies to any other proceedings being heard as part of the same hearing – rule 50(5)(d).

11.69 **Scope of protection of RROs.** In Tradition Securities and Futures SA and ors v Times Newspapers Ltd and ors 2009 IRLR 354, EAT, the Court held that a restricted reporting order should be directed primarily at the protection of the complainant or affected person. However, a person who did not qualify for protection, but whose identification was likely to lead to the identification of somebody who did qualify, could also be included in the order. As a result, the tribunal had been entitled to specify particular types of identifying matter where it felt that this was conducive to the protection of the complainant.

There is no power to make an RRO to protect the reputation of a company or corporate body. The EAT decided in Leicester University v A 1999 ICR 701, EAT, that it was not Parliament's intention to protect the reputation of corporate respondents, even though that may lead to disparity between the parties as to the publicity that can be given to each of them. It refused to follow the EAT's earlier decision in M v Vincent 1998 ICR 73, EAT, where the Appeal Tribunal had held that the company should be included in the RRO on the basis that the word 'person' in S.11(6) ETA could include a body corporate. The EAT in Leicester concluded that, while the word 'person' in S.11(6) was capable of including a body corporate, on a proper construction of the words 'person affected by… the allegation' in that subsection, it was clear that they could only relate to an individual. The expression does not cover a body corporate or other respondent other than an individual respondent.

11.70 In R v London (North) Industrial Tribunal ex parte Associated Newspapers Ltd (above) the EAT similarly doubted whether a local authority could be protected by an RRO. However, as the Court pointed out in that case, an RRO prohibits not only the publication of the names of those persons listed in the order, but also anything likely to lead to their identification by members of the public (an 'identifying matter' under the Act). Depending on the facts of the case, it might therefore be unlawful to publish the name of the employer, and any other persons closely associated with the case, even if they are not listed in the order, because their names might constitute identifying matter in respect of the protected persons.

11.71 **Duration of RROs.** Under the old rules, a full RRO would remain in effect until liability and remedy had been determined in the case, unless revoked

570

earlier – old rule 50(8)(b). The Court of Session established in Davidson v Dallas McMillan 2010 IRLR 439, Ct Sess (Inner House), that this had the effect that, where a claim was withdrawn, the order remained in force in perpetuity. The Court said, 'It is one thing to lift the RRO and allow publication when the decision of the tribunal has been promulgated... since the decision will include the tribunal's assessment of all the evidence and its findings as to whether the allegations of sexual misconduct have been proved. It would be quite another thing to lift the RRO when the evidence has been part heard and the tribunal has expressed no view as to its credibility or reliability, so that the evidence alleging sexual misconduct could be reported without any of the evidence that might have been led in rebuttal.' The requirement under new rule 50(5)(b) that the tribunal must specify the duration of an RRO means that this is no longer an issue although, presumably, if the tribunal thought it appropriate for an order to remain in force forever, it could specify as much (any party with a legitimate interest would, however, be able to apply under rule 50(4) for the order to be discharged – see 'Revoking or discharging privacy and restricted disclosure orders' above).

Expiry of RROs. Once an RRO has expired, all details relating to a case may **11.72** be reported, including information withheld from the tribunal's records (this might happen where a party repeats something that forms part of their own knowledge). Note, however, the tribunal's more general power to make an order under rule 50(3)(b) to protect the identities of specified parties, witnesses or other persons referred to in the proceedings – see 'Terms of privacy and restricted disclosure orders' above.

Breach of RROs. Breach of an RRO made under rule 50(3)(d) constitutes a **11.73** criminal offence, triable in the magistrates' court and punishable by a fine not exceeding level 5 on the standard scale (currently £5,000). In the case of publication of identifying matter in a newspaper or periodical, criminal liability attaches to the proprietor, editor and publisher – Ss.11(2)(a) and 12(3)(a) ETA. With other publications, liability attaches to the person publishing the matter – Ss.11(2)(b) and 12(3)(b). In the case of identifying matter being included in a radio or television programme, liability attaches to any corporate body engaged in providing the service in which the programme is included, and any person having functions in relation to the programme corresponding to those of an editor of a newspaper – Ss.11(2), 12(3)(c) and 31(3). Ignorance and lack of suspicion that the publication or programme included identifying matter is a defence – Ss.11(3), 12(4) and 31(4).

The above provisions only apply in respect of breach of an RRO – they do not come into play where another type of order falling within rule 50(3) is breached. However, it is less likely that a breach of the other types of rule 50 order will occur, as they rely on steps that the tribunal will take when conducting the proceedings to anonymise individuals.

571

11.74 Addition, substitution and removal of parties

It is sometimes necessary for one or more additional respondents to be joined to an extant claim – for instance, where the named respondent disputes that it is or was the employer, or an issue arises as to whether the claimant's employment was transferred to a third party following a transfer of the former employer's undertaking.

The new rules provide tribunals with a wide discretion to add, substitute and/or remove parties to proceedings. Under rule 34 a tribunal has the power, either on its own initiative, or on the application of a party or any other person wishing to become a party, to add or substitute any person as a party. This power can be exercised where there are issues between that person and any of the existing parties falling within the jurisdiction of the tribunal which it is in the interests of justice to have determined in the proceedings. A tribunal also has a corresponding power to remove any party apparently wrongly included.

11.75 Under the old rules a tribunal could join as a respondent to the proceedings any person who it considered might be liable for the remedy claimed (rule 10(2)(k)); or join any person as a party to the proceedings who it considered had an interest in the outcome (rule 10(2)(r)). Now, the addition (or substitution) of parties can be exercised where it appears that there are 'issues between' the person to be joined (or substituted) and any of the existing parties falling within the jurisdiction of the tribunal which it is in the interests of justice to have determined. The potential range of circumstances in which there could be 'issues between' an existing party and a party to be joined to the proceedings that fall within the tribunal's jurisdiction are vast and will include circumstances where a person might be liable for the remedy claimed or where a person otherwise has an interest in the outcome of the proceedings.

The power to add, substitute and remove parties under rule 34, when read in conjunction with rule 29, applies 'at any stage of the proceedings'. Therefore, a tribunal can, for example, join another respondent to an existing claim even after the time limit for bringing a fresh claim against that respondent has expired – Drinkwater Sabey Ltd v Burnett and anor 1995 ICR 328, EAT.

11.76 The party joined by order of the tribunal can apply under rule 30 for the order to be varied or revoked under rule 29. The Presidential Guidance on 'General Case Management' for England and Wales states that such an application should be made 'promptly'.

A tribunal's power to join (or remove) a party is discussed further in Chapter 8, 'Amendments', under 'Amending the parties'.

Joinder in discrimination complaints 11.77

Under S.109(1) of the Equality Act 2010 (EqA) an employer is liable for acts of discrimination, harassment and victimisation carried out by its employees in the course of employment unless the employer can prove that it took all reasonably practicable steps to prevent the employee from doing the act in question. Similarly, under S.109(2) a principal is liable for the discriminatory acts committed by one of its agents acting under the principal's authority. Furthermore, where an employer or principal is liable for the discriminatory acts of employees or agents under S.109, the employees and agents may themselves be personally liable under S.110. In these circumstances, both the employer and employee or, as the case may be, the principal and agent, will be jointly liable for the unlawful act and the employee or agent or the employer or principal can be joined to the proceedings as a separate respondent in accordance with rule 34. This is frequently done in practice.

In addition, S.111 EqA makes it unlawful for a person to instruct, cause, or induce someone to discriminate, harass or victimise another person on any of the grounds covered by the Act, while by virtue of S.112, any person who knowingly aids any act of discrimination rendered unlawful by the Act is treated as having committed the discriminatory act him or herself. Both the person who aids, instructs, causes or induces and the person who is aided, instructed, caused or induced will be liable and can be joined to the proceedings in accordance with rule 34.

For a detailed consideration of discrimination law, see IDS Employment Law Handbook, 'Discrimination at Work' (2012).

Joinder of Secretary of State for Employment 11.78

Rule 96 concerns cases that may involve payments out of the National Insurance Fund. In these circumstances, the Secretary of State is to be treated for the purposes of the rules as if he or she were a party to the proceedings. Thus, he or she is entitled to notice of any application to vary or set aside an order made under rule 29; to make representations in writing and to advance oral argument at a preliminary or final hearing; to apply for a case management order under rule 30; to seek to have the proceedings transferred from England and Wales to Scotland; to receive copies of all documents and notices in connection with the proceedings; and to appear as if he or she were a party and be heard at any hearing.

When an employee is claiming *solely* from the National Insurance Fund because of the insolvency of the employer, he or she may name the Secretary of State as sole respondent without joining the employer – Jones v Secretary of State for Employment 1982 ICR 389, EAT.

573

11.79 Trade unions and shop-floor pressure

Special provisions for joinder apply in certain situations under the Trade Union and Labour Relations (Consolidation) Act 1992 (TULR(C)A). S.160 applies when an employee is dismissed for not belonging to a union and the dismissal is because of trade union or shop-floor pressure on the employer. Such dismissals will be automatically unfair under S.152 of that Act and a tribunal must disregard shop-floor pressure as a reason for dismissal – S.107(2) Employment Rights Act 1996. In such circumstances either the employer or the dismissed employee may request that a tribunal join the trade union or other person exercising pressure on the employer as an additional respondent to the unfair dismissal proceedings – S.160(1) TULR(C)A.

The timing of such a request is important. The tribunal must grant it if it is made before the hearing begins; it may refuse it if it is made later; and it must refuse the request if an award of compensation or an order for reinstatement or re-engagement has already been made – S.160(2). Note that on the wording of S.160(2) it is *mandatory* to grant a request for joinder of a union if it is made before a hearing. In Ashfield v (1) Crosville Motor Services Ltd (2) TGWU ET Case No.08059/85 the tribunal rejected an argument that the claimant should show a prima facie case before the union was involved. It pointed out that the union could apply for a pre-hearing assessment (now called a preliminary hearing – see above under 'Preliminary hearings'), at which the claimant could be required to pay a deposit before proceeding with a weak case (see 'Deposit orders' below).

11.80

Similar provisions to those in S.160 apply under S.150 TULR(C)A where the employee is complaining of being subject to any detriment under S.146. The provisions over timing are the same except that the tribunal must refuse a request for joinder if it has already made a declaration in the claimant's favour – S.150(2).

The practical importance of joinder is that the tribunal may order the union or other party joined to pay all or part of any compensation awarded – Ss.150(3) and 160(3). In Hood and ors v Cory King Towage and ors ET Case No.25947/84 the TGWU was joined as a respondent in successful unfair dismissal proceedings and was ordered to pay the full compensation bill.

11.81 Unincorporated associations

A tribunal's power to order joinder under rule 34 may need to be utilised where the claimant brings a claim against an unincorporated association (for example, a members' club or a charitable body not set up as a company under the Companies Act). In such cases, since the claimant will be regarded in law as being employed by the executive committee or governing body of the association and its members for the time being, these individuals will normally need to be joined as respondents – see further 'Combined proceedings and lead cases – representative respondents' below.

Other persons   11.82

Rule 35 introduces a new power for tribunals to permit any person to participate
in proceedings (though not necessarily as a party) in respect of any matter in
which that person has a legitimate interest. This power has a very wide remit
and can be utilised to allow participation by, for instance, an intervening party.

Combined proceedings, lead cases and representative respondents   11.83

The general power of tribunals to make case management orders under rule 29
can include the power to make an order for two or more different claims to be
considered together. This may involve different claims submitted by the same
claimant, or similar or related claims submitted by different claimants. In many
cases, such an order will be in the interests of all parties (as well as the tribunal)
as it can lead to a substantial saving in costs and time. There are no specific
criteria that must be satisfied in order for different claims to be considered
together, but an order combining claims made by different claimants is unlikely
to be made unless there is some common question of law or fact arising in some
or all of the claims or the relief claimed arises out of the same facts, or because
it is desirable for the claims to be heard together for some other reason.

Note that claims by multiple claimants that give rise to common or related
issues of law cannot be made on the same claim form. Only claims based on the
same set of facts can be presented to the tribunal on the same claim form –
rule 9. However, rule 36(1) allows a tribunal to select a lead case (or lead cases)
where it considers that two or more claims give rise to 'common or related
issues of fact or law'. The other related claims will be stayed and will be bound
by the decisions made in the lead case(s) on the related issue(s), unless the
related party successfully applies for the lead case decision to be disregarded in
his or her case.

Additionally, although there is no express provision to this effect, a tribunal   11.84
can exercise its discretion to order that where there are a number of respondents
with the same interest in defending a case, one respondent be appointed to
defend a case on behalf of all other related respondents – see further
'Representative respondents' below.

Consolidation of proceedings   11.85

The combining of proceedings is often referred to as 'consolidation', although
this does not bear the same meaning as it does in the High Court, whereby two
or more parties become one and have common representation. Consolidation
in an employment tribunal simply means that two or more cases are heard
together, usually because they will have much evidence in common. However,
the employment judge must bear in mind that he or she is hearing separate

575

claims and should consider whether exactly similar circumstances apply to each – Green v Southampton Corporation 1973 ICR 153, NIRC. In Krelle v Ransom and anor EAT 0568/05 the EAT was not satisfied that the tribunal had given proper consideration to the separate cases of the two claimants, albeit that their claims were being heard together, there were great similarities in the way in which they had presented their cases to the tribunal and their dismissals arose out of the same general background facts. The claims were remitted to a fresh tribunal for a rehearing.

In the majority of situations where an order for consolidation is made, the circumstances will involve *separate* claimants having made similar claims arising out of the same facts. Two common situations that often give rise to multiple claims are where large-scale redundancies occur or where groups of employees present equal pay claims. However, the consolidation procedure may also be appropriate where the *same* claimant has issued separate claims – for example, for unfair dismissal and discrimination – arising out of substantially the same set of facts.

11.86 An order that cases be considered together may be made by the tribunal on its own initiative or upon application by a party. Under the 2004 Rules, a notice had to be sent to all parties concerned giving them an opportunity to make oral or written representations as to why such an order should or should not be made – rule 10(7). This requirement is not replicated in the 2013 Rules. Therefore, a tribunal can order different claims to be heard together without seeking the parties' views as to whether this would be appropriate. However, tribunals have the power (either on their own initiative or on application) to vary, suspend or set aside an earlier case management order where that is necessary in the interests of justice, particularly where the affected party did not have a reasonable opportunity to make representations before the order was made – see 'Case management orders – varying, suspending or setting aside orders' above.

Claimants rarely object to the consolidation of their cases, but when this does happen it is usually because it is feared that one case may prejudice the other. Although this is a valid consideration to be taken on board by a tribunal, essentially the decision to consolidate is a matter of discretion, as the decisions below demonstrate:

- **Dietmann and anor v London Borough of Brent** 1987 IRLR 146, CA: D and W were both social workers dismissed in the light of the findings of a public inquiry into the death of a child under the care of the local authority. The tribunal decided to hear their unfair dismissal claims together. Both D and W argued that either or both of them would be prejudiced by a joint hearing because it would be possible for the employer to cross-examine either one of them and use her answers against the other. The EAT, by a majority, rejected an appeal against the chairman's order for consolidation.

On further appeal, the Court of Appeal held that the tribunal chairman had properly exercised his discretion under the Rules then in place in ordering the claims to be heard together. It might be to the claimants' advantage if neither was faced with the other and each could blame the other in her absence, but prevention of that unjust advantage was not a matter of 'prejudice'. Moreover, justice could be seen to be done if the tribunal considered not only individual responsibility but also any joint responsibility attaching to the two claimants. Justice would not be seen to be done if there were separate hearings at which each claimant was exonerated by the tribunal and the blame laid at the feet of the other

- **Gokce v Scottish Ambulance Service** EATS 0093/06: the EAT rejected G's assertion that the tribunal's decision for her case be heard with two others was unjust on the basis that the two other claimants were senior to her. The EAT held that it was 'obviously sensible' for all the cases to be heard together because they arose out of the same incident. All three had been involved, to a lesser or greater extent, in the deployment of an ambulance to collect a colleague from a nightclub for which each of them had been dismissed for gross misconduct. It was incumbent on the tribunal to consider the facts relating to each of the claimants separately, which it did.

In the following two cases, the EAT overturned the decision of a tribunal **11.87** refusing to order consolidation:

- **Courage Ltd v Welsh and ors** EAT 93/91: six beer delivery men who were dismissed on the ground of fraudulent conduct brought separate claims for unfair dismissal and the hearings were set down for a variety of dates. The employer applied for all the cases to be heard together but its application was refused. On appeal, the employer pointed out that 90 per cent of the relevant evidence applied to every one of the six claimants and that, if heard separately, each case would take five days whereas if heard together the single hearing would take ten days. The EAT accepted these points and ordered that the cases be consolidated

- **George Turton Platts and Co Ltd v Dilaurenzio and anor** EAT 524/92: the EAT allowed the employer's appeal against the decision of a tribunal that two claims by employees who had been dismissed for fighting should be heard separately. In the EAT's view, it was clearly in the interests of all the parties that the cases should be heard together and the tribunal's decision was plainly wrong. Furthermore, when refusing the employer's request for consolidation, the tribunal had erred in taking into account the fact that the trade union representative had wanted to represent both claimants separately because they intended to blame each other. The situation evidently entailed a conflict of interest, making it obvious that the trade union representative would not be able to represent both claimants.

577

11.88 **Tribunal fees.** Special rules apply in respect of the payment of fees in 'fee group' claims. However, these rules are not relevant to consolidated claims and the normal hearing fee is applicable (a single issue fee will already have been paid by the time the claims are consolidated). A 'fee group' is defined as 'the group of persons each of whom were named as claimants in the claim form at the time the claim was presented *and* are named as claimants in the notification of the listing of the final hearing' (our stress) – Article 2 Employment Tribunals and the Employment Appeal Tribunal Fees Order 2013 SI 2013/1893. This definition does not cover claimants who are joined to proceedings later on and such claimants will therefore be treated as single claimants for the purpose of the hearing fee – i.e. they cannot become part of the 'fee group' if they were not named in the original claim, regardless of whether they are named as claimants in the notice of hearing. For a more detailed discussion on the application of fees, see Chapter 19, 'Fees'.

11.89 Lead cases

Employment tribunals have had to deal with 'multiple' cases for many years. A large proportion of the cases brought in any one year are multiple cases brought by a number of individuals against the same employer on the same point of (undecided) law or fact, or cases brought against different employers which raise the same point of (undecided) law. But until the enactment of the Tribunal Rules 2013 there were no general rules on how such cases should be managed. There was, however, provision for 'lead claimants' to be identified in some equal pay claims – rule 3(f), Sch 6 Tribunal Rules 2004.

New rule 36(1) of the Tribunal Rules 2013 provides that where a tribunal considers that two or more claims raise 'common or related issues of fact or law', it can specify one or more of those claims as a lead case and stay (or in Scotland sist) the other related claim(s). This applies to all types of claims, not just equal pay. Subject to the right in rule 36(3) to apply for an order to disapply the tribunal's decision in the lead case (see 'Effect of decisions made in lead case(s)' below), the related claims will be bound by the decisions made in the lead case(s) on the related issue(s) – rule 36(2). If a lead case is withdrawn before the tribunal makes a decision in respect of the common or related issues, the tribunal is required to make an order as to whether another claim is to be specified as a lead case; and whether any order affecting the related cases should be set aside or varied – rule 36(4).

11.90 By deciding common or related questions of both fact and law, the tribunal can avoid unnecessary duplication of time and costs that would otherwise be incurred by having multiple hearings. Even in the absence of a specific provision relating to lead cases, most tribunals already dealt with multiple cases in this way in accordance with the general power to manage proceedings – see Bristol Channel Ship Repairers Ltd v O'Keefe and ors 1978 ICR 691, EAT. Lead cases – more commonly referred to as 'test cases' or 'representative action' – were used where there were a number of similar cases arising out of the same facts and all persons involved in the other cases agreed to be bound by the decision in the lead case(s).

Rule 36 is intended to give a clear legal structure to the handling of 'multiple' cases by formalising the lead case mechanism so that it is applied consistently. Significantly, it gives tribunals an explicit power to invoke the lead case mechanism without the parties' prior agreement. However, the parties may apply for any such order to be varied or revoked if they do not agree with the choice of lead case. The tribunal's power under rule 29 to vary or revoke any order can be exercised 'in particular where a party affected by the earlier order did not have a reasonable opportunity to make representations before it was made'.

An order selecting a lead case can also be made on application by one of the **11.91** parties. The provisions of rule 30 will apply in circumstances where a party wishes to apply for such an order – see 'Case management orders – application by party for order' above.

The power to consolidate proceedings can be exercised in conjunction with the power to select lead cases. In United Airlines v Bannigan and ors EAT 192/97 the EAT was critical of the tribunal's failure to join test cases that had been selected from a number of similar complaints presented against the same airline, in which subsequently conflicting conclusions had been drawn resulting in some claimants being successful and others not. It said that responsible employers and unions can be reasonably expected to foresee the need for one or more test cases and for them to be heard together, and so far as practical then to procure that such a course be adopted. It also said that costs sanctions might need to be developed to deter the exploitation of tactical advantages of cases being heard individually, which wastes valuable court time. The EAT's dissatisfaction at one or more of the test cases not being heard together was compounded when it discovered that there had been two separate hearings on the same point without comprehensive and reliable guidance emerging that could be used in other cases by flight attendants against the airline. The first test case was unreliable as the later test case reached the opposite conclusion and the later case was unreliable because the presentation of fact to the tribunal was one-sided and very likely incomplete.

Effect of decisions made in lead case(s). Where the lead case mechanism has **11.92** been invoked and the tribunal makes a decision in respect of the common or related issues, it shall send a copy of that decision to each party in each of the related cases and, subject to rule 36(3), that decision is binding on each of those parties – rule 36(2).

Rule 36(3) provides that, within 28 days after the date on which a tribunal sends a copy of a lead case decision to the parties, a party may apply in writing

579

for an order that the decision does not apply to, and is not binding on the parties to, a particular related case. However, the rules do not set out the procedure for considering any such application or the test that should be applied by the judge. During consultation on the 2013 Rules, the Government stated that it believed the finer practical details as to exactly how this rule should operate would be best addressed in Presidential Guidance. If no such guidance is forthcoming, it will be left to the tribunal's discretion and it is likely that the overriding objective in rule 2 will carry significant weight in such a decision.

11.93 **Tribunal fees.** Each individual claimant will have paid a single issue fee at the time of commencing his or her claim. However, potential issues arise as regards the liability to pay hearing fees where the lead case mechanism is invoked. Strictly speaking, a hearing fee is only payable by the claimant in the lead case, and there is no obligation for the tribunal to order that the related claimants share the cost of the hearing fee. There is therefore an advantage to a claimant whose case is stayed pending the outcome of a lead case as he or she could have his or her case decided without incurring a hearing fee. Tribunal fees are discussed in Chapter 19, 'Fees'.

11.94 Representative respondents

Where there are a number of respondents with the same interest in defending a claim, a tribunal can authorise one or more of them to defend the claim on behalf of them all. Such a power is particularly useful where, for instance, a discrimination complaint cites employees as well as the employer as co-respondents. In such circumstances, the tribunal could allow the employer to defend on behalf of itself and the named employees. It is equally relevant where the claimant wishes to sue an unincorporated association – for example, members' clubs and charitable bodies that do not have a separate legal identity. (Note that a person who works for an unincorporated association is employed not by the entire membership of the association but by the executive committee and its members for the time being, who should therefore be the respondents in any tribunal claim – Affleck and ors v Newcastle Mind and ors 1999 ICR 852, EAT.)

In the Affleck case the EAT said that in the case of an unincorporated association it would be desirable for one named individual to be sued in a representative capacity on behalf of the entire executive committee. If it then transpires that there are members of the committee who are not content to be thus represented, they may apply to be joined as individually named respondents pursuant to what is now rule 34 (see 'Addition, substitution and removal of parties' above).

11.95 In Nazir and anor v Asim 2010 ICR 1225, EAT, the EAT held that, in accordance with the decision in Affleck, it is good practice for a claimant to name a representative respondent who was a member of the management committee of an unincorporated association at the relevant time and state that he or she is being sued on his or her own behalf and on behalf of all other members of the executive committee at the relevant time. However, the Appeal Tribunal recognised that it is common for claimants to name an unincorporated association as a respondent. This, it held, is hardly surprising as they cannot be expected to know about the legal status of an unincorporated association, still less about the practice advocated in Affleck. Therefore, while in ordinary civil proceedings an unincorporated association can neither sue nor be sued in its own name, it is permissible for an employee to bring a claim in an employment tribunal against the management committee of an unincorporated association by using the name of the association. The association's name is used as the representative respondent on behalf of each member of the committee who would otherwise be named individually as respondents.

11.96 An express power to appoint a representative respondent was contained in the 2001 Tribunal Rules. However, this provision was not carried forward into the 2004 Rules and has not been replicated in the 2013 Rules either. Such an order can nevertheless be made under the tribunal's general power to make case management orders contained in rule 29 and in accordance with the overriding objective set out in rule 2. The parties may apply for an order appointing a representative respondent to be varied, suspended or set aside if they do not agree with the tribunal's choice of respondent – rule 29. The tribunal's power under rule 29 to vary, suspend or set aside any order can be exercised 'in particular where a party affected by the earlier order did not have a reasonable opportunity to make representations before it was made' – see 'Case management orders – varying, suspending or setting aside orders' above.

It is important to note that the decision to use a representative respondent is a decision that can only be made by a tribunal. It is not for a group of respondents to nominate one of them as a representative respondent. A response must therefore be presented to the tribunal on behalf of each of the respondents named on the claim form, whether they are presented on the same response form or separate forms. But a party can thereafter make an application under rule 30 for an order for a representative respondent to be selected – see further 'Case managements orders – application by party for order' above.

11.97 **Application-specific fees.** Under the rules governing the payment of employment tribunal fees, a respondent will be liable to pay an 'application-specific fee' if, for example, it makes an application seeking reconsideration of a default judgment. However, unlike a situation where several individual claimants' claims are consolidated but do not become a 'fee group' for the purposes of fees (see 'Consolidation of proceedings' above), only one application fee is payable where one of a number of respondents is appointed to act in a representative capacity on behalf of all of them. Tribunal fees are dealt with in Chapter 19, 'Fees'.

11.98 Stay of proceedings

A tribunal's general case management power under rule 29 allows it, either on its own initiative or on application by one of the parties, to stay (or in Scotland sist) the whole or part of any proceedings. This is a useful tool not only where it is appropriate for a lead case to be selected (see 'Combined proceedings, lead cases and representative respondents – lead cases' above), but also where there is an interim matter that must be determined before the case can proceed. For instance, where a claim is made against a company in administration without the consent of the administrators, the correct course of action for a tribunal is to accept the claim but stay the proceedings pending the issue of consent – Unite the Union and ors v Sayers Confectioners Ltd (in administration) EAT 0513/08.

Other common situations where it may be appropriate to stay proceedings are considered below. Although the case law referred to was decided under the Tribunal Rules 2004, which gave tribunals an express power to stay proceedings under rule 10(h), the principles established remain relevant under the 2013 Rules.

11.99 The power to stay proceedings is entirely dicretionary. In the leading case of Bastick v James Lane (Turf Accountants) Ltd 1979 ICR 778, EAT, B was dismissed for alleged dishonesty and also charged with theft and committed for trial at the Crown Court. He lodged an unfair dismissal complaint but applied for a postponement of the hearing on the ground that he would be prejudiced if it took place before the criminal trial. The tribunal chairman refused a postponement, saying that this would cause an unacceptable delay and that the issues for decision by the tribunal and the Crown Court were entirely different. The EAT refused to interfere with the decision: the chairman had neither taken into account irrelevant matters nor ignored a relevant matter, and the decision was not one that no reasonable chairman could have reached. His exercise of his discretion was neither wrong in law nor perverse.

Note that postponements and adjournments of hearings are discussed in Chapter 12, 'The hearing', under 'Postponements and adjournments'. However, the courts and tribunals tend to use the terms 'stay', 'postpone' and 'adjourn' interchangeably, as is clear from the many of the cases discussed below, and the distinction is no longer as relevant as it was under the 2004 Rules, which made separate provision for orders 'staying (in Scotland, sisting) the whole or part of any proceedings' (old rule 10(2)(h)) and orders 'postponing or adjourning any hearing' (old rule 10(2)(m)). The power to make either type of order is now subsumed into the tribunals' general power to make case management orders under new rule 29.

11.100 **Application procedure.** Presidential Guidance has been recently been issued on the procedure for applying for a postponement. There are two separate sets

582

of Guidance – one that applies in England and Wales, issued on 4 December 2013 (and which presumably took effect from that date), and a more detailed one that applies in Scotland, which is stated to have effect from 1 February 2014. Although Presidential Guidance is not binding on tribunals, they are required to have regard to it when considering applications.

Both sets of Guidance deal with applications for 'postponement' – or, to be pernickety, a stay (or sist) – where there are other proceedings pending. The procedural steps laid out in each are similar but not identical. In the case of an outstanding appeal to the EAT or other appellate court, the application should provide full details of the dates of the appeal and the matters being appealed. The Scottish Guidance adds that the application should also state why it is considered that the hearing cannot take place until the appeal is heard.

11.101 Where there are related civil or criminal court proceedings pending, details should be given as to when these proceedings were commenced, what they entail, and how it is said that they will affect the employment tribunal case or how the employment tribunal case will be said to affect those other proceedings. The Scottish Guidance asks for additional detail, including – in a criminal case – the name and address of the police officer or procurator fiscal dealing with the matter and, if possible, the case number; and – in a civil case – an explanation as to why it is said that the civil court proceedings should be progressed ahead of the employment tribunal proceedings.

For a more detailed examination of the two sets of Guidance, see Chapter 12, 'The hearing', in the section 'Postponements and adjournments', under 'Applying for a postponement or adjournment – Presidential Guidance on applying for a postponement'.

Stay pending determination of relevant legal issue by higher court **11.102**
The outcome of other proceedings may be relevant to a tribunal case when it is known that a higher court is due to determine a question of law that is also relevant to the outcome of the tribunal case. In these circumstances, the tribunal proceedings will usually be stayed until the determination has been made, at which point the tribunal proceedings can recommence with reliance on the higher court authority. In Pearson v British Airports Authority EAT 324/84 P claimed that she had been discriminated against on the ground of her sex by being made to retire at a lower age than a man. She asked for the hearing to be postponed pending a ruling of the European Court of Justice (ECJ) in an apparently indistinguishable case. The chairman refused a postponement but the EAT overruled him. It pointed out that P's case turned wholly on a question of law which could only be resolved by the ECJ and it held that the chairman had exercised his discretion wrongly.

In R v Secretary of State for Employment ex parte Seymour-Smith and anor (No.2) 2000 ICR 244, HL, the claimants brought judicial review proceedings claiming that the qualifying period of two years' continuous employment necessary at that time in order to bring an unfair dismissal claim constituted indirect sex discrimination and was therefore unlawful by virtue of the EU Equal Treatment Directive (No.76/207). The case proceeded slowly to the ECJ and was then remitted to the House of Lords, which ultimately rejected the employees' arguments on the basis that the requirement was objectively justified by social policy. In the meantime, however, a great many unfair dismissal claims brought by claimants with less than two years' service had been stayed pending the outcome of this litigation. As a result of the House of Lords' decision, these claims failed for want of jurisdiction. By the time the House of Lords ruled in the Seymour-Smith case, legislation had already been passed to reduce the qualifying period to one year. However, this did not affect the cases that had been stayed because it only applied to dismissals taking place after a certain date.

11.103 The EAT stayed a decision in Chief Constable of Strathclyde Police v Lavery EAT 0098/04, a case concerned with holiday pay during sickness absence, pending the House of Lords' judgment in Revenue and Customs Commissioners v Stringer 2009 ICR 985, HL. In that case, the Court of Appeal had rejected the claimants' contention that they were entitled to holiday pay while absent on long-term sick leave, but owing to the importance of this issue leave was granted to appeal to the House of Lords, which, following a reference to the ECJ, overturned the Court of Appeal's decision.

A similar situation arose in relation to R (Age UK) v Secretary of State for Business, Innovation and Skills (Equality and Human Rights Commission and anor intervening) 2010 ICR 260, QBD. Age Concern – now Age UK – asserted that the Government had exceeded the derogation afforded to it under Article 6(1) of the EU Equal Treatment Framework Directive (No.2000/78) by including in the Employment Equality (Age) Regulations 2006 SI 2006/1031 certain exemptions from the general prohibition on age discrimination. One of the complaints in what became known as the 'Heyday' case was that Reg 30, which set down a 'default retirement age' (DRA) of 65 – the age at which employees could lawfully be retired at that time – was not compatible with the Directive. Many tribunal cases were stayed pending the conclusion of this issue. In response to questions referred by the High Court, the European Court of Justice – in R (Incorporated Trustees of the National Council on Ageing (Age Concern England)) v Secretary of State for Business, Enterprise and Regulatory Reform 2009 ICR 1080, ECJ – held that the DRA came within the scope of the Directive and therefore fell to be justified by legitimate social policy objectives, such as those related to employment policy, the labour market or vocational training. However, it was for the national court to ascertain whether the legislation pursued such objectives and, if so, whether the means used were appropriate and necessary. The case returned to the High Court, which held that the DRA was lawful and that employers were entitled to retire staff at age 65. (Note that the DRA was abolished in 2011).

584

Note that a stay will not be granted simply because there is pending legislation **11.104**
which may affect the rights of the parties – Willow Wren Canal Carrying Co
Ltd v British Transport Commission 1956 1 All ER 567, ChD. A court or
tribunal must decide the case on the basis of statutory law as it is at the time
and not what it may become.

Stay pending other civil proceedings

11.105

Sometimes a claimant may wish to bring proceedings in both the employment
tribunal and the county court or, depending on the value of the claim, the High
Court. In particular, cases involving breach of contract will need to be brought
in the ordinary civil courts if the claimant is seeking contractual damages
exceeding the statutory limit available in the tribunal (currently £25,000 in a
contractual claim arising or outstanding on termination of employment). If a
claimant issues proceedings in both forums, either party may apply to have the
tribunal proceedings stayed pending the outcome of the civil action. It may also
be appropriate to stay proceedings in circumstances where both forums would
otherwise be required to determine the same point of fact or law. In Chorion
plc and ors v Lane, unreported 24.2.99, ChD, the High Court stated that where
the same questions must be determined, the courts should be wary of the
duplication of effort, costs and the waste of the tribunal's or court's time. And
in GFI Holdings Ltd v Camm EAT 0321/08 the EAT held that a tribunal should
have used its discretion to stay an unfair dismissal claim when the claimant was
also pursuing a claim in the High Court for unpaid bonus payments. Since the
bonuses were not payable if the claimant had been under notice of dismissal at
the time, both hearings would need to resolve at the first stage the issue of
whether or not there had been a dismissal. Consequently, the EAT found that
there was an overlap of the issues and the tribunal hearing should be stayed
until the High Court claim had been heard.

In Mindimaxnox LLP v Gover and anor EAT 0225/10 the EAT had to consider
which proceedings should take priority. It laid down a number of principles to
be applied in determining which proceedings should be dealt with first, giving
a clear indication that the High Court proceedings should generally take
precedence. It held that, as a general rule, an employment tribunal is entirely
capable of dealing with highly complex factual matters, but whether the
tribunal is the appropriate forum in which to decide them is essentially a
question of balance. Where there is a very substantial factual dispute, supported
by a voluminous number of documents, the proceedings are more appropriately
brought in the High Court. Similarly, complex legal matters will be susceptible
to detailed analysis in the High Court, which in turn will influence the decision-
making in the employment tribunal and are therefore better decided in the
High Court. In this case there was also a considerable overlap in that the factual
material was the same in both jurisdictions. On this ground alone, said the
EAT, it would have been appropriate to cede to the High Court. The central

585

issue before the High Court was the claimants' entitlement to, and the amount of, a bonus payment, which was of far higher value than the only real issue before the tribunal, i.e. the statutory tort of unfair dismissal. The EAT also noted that more issues could be determined in the High Court than in the tribunal, and that it was desirable to have the High Court proceedings first because the employment tribunal findings could be embarrassing for a judge in the High Court, who would find it difficult not to be bound by them. In the EAT's view, it was inconsistent with tribunals' overriding objective of dealing with cases justly to have duplicate proceedings in the tribunal and the High Court. The complex factual and legal issues involved and the high value of the High Court claim, among other things, meant that the High Court was the appropriate forum. The EAT therefore ordered the tribunal proceedings to be stayed pending the outcome of the High Court action.

11.106 The principles set out in Mindimaxnox only apply where the claimant has actually issued High Court proceedings – Halstead v Paymentshield Group Holdings Ltd 2012 IRLR 586, CA. H brought claims against PGH Ltd for unfair dismissal and holiday pay before an employment tribunal. H's solicitor then sent PGH Ltd a letter before action and draft particulars of claim indicating an intention to bring overlapping – and potentially inconsistent – action in the High Court for breach of contract, rescission, debt and interest. PGH Ltd applied for a stay of the tribunal proceedings pending the outcome of the High Court action. H did not contest the application and the stay was granted. However, H later applied to lift the stay on the basis that his financial circumstances had changed and he could only proceed with the High Court action if he first received compensation from the tribunal. He undertook not to pursue any High Court claim concurrently with the tribunal proceedings. PGH Ltd opposed H's application but the tribunal ordered the stay to be lifted because no High Court proceedings had been issued and, in the circumstances, it was not in accordance with the overriding objective for the stay to remain. A further application by PGH Ltd for a stay was refused. However, the EAT allowed an appeal against that decision. In its view, the principles set down in Mindimaxnox applied not only where a High Court claim had been lodged, but also where a letter before claim had been sent, and held that the tribunal had committed an error of law in failing to have regard to those principles. Exercising its discretion afresh, the EAT ordered a stay on the basis that there was a potential overlap of issues and the High Court was the more appropriate forum for H's claims. The Court of Appeal overturned the EAT's decision, holding that there was no need to stay employment tribunal proceedings when no proceedings had been commenced in the High Court. The Court considered that it would be wrong in principle to deprive H of a statutory remedy simply because he had evinced an intention to pursue a claim in the High Court. In so holding, the Court established that the principles identified by the EAT in

Mindimaxnox have force when there are concurrent proceedings but are not determinative in their absence.

In Dominic Faversham Group v McIntyre EAT 0290/11 the EAT accepted that the general trend of the cases is to give priority to High Court proceedings, but held that if this is not possible within an appropriate timescale an urgent hearing of the tribunal proceedings may be appropriate. On the facts it found that the tribunal had erred in law when it refused to stay M's disability discrimination claim on the ground that there was no overlap between that claim and High Court proceedings commenced by DFG. At the very least there was an overlap in relation to the question of remedy. Compensation for discrimination could not have been assessed without knowing whether M's employment was in any event liable to be terminated for fundamental breach. The tribunal had also failed to consider the potential disadvantages of separating the discrimination claim from M's unfair dismissal claim, which had been stayed. However, the EAT concluded that, given M's state of health, it might not be possible to give the High Court proceedings priority and it remitted the matter with a view to careful case management of both the High Court and the tribunal proceedings.

Stay pending other tribunal proceedings 11.107
Where a tribunal exercises its power to select a 'lead case' under rule 36, it will issue an order staying the related tribunal cases. The related proceedings will be stayed until a decision on the related issues of fact or law have been determined, which will be binding on those cases. A tribunal's power to select a lead case is discussed in more detail under 'Combined proceedings, lead cases and representative respondents – lead cases' above.

But even where the lead case mechanism does not apply, it may be appropriate to stay a tribunal case where the facts or legal principles are interlinked with one or more other tribunal cases. In South Ayrshire Council v Milligan 2003 IRLR 153, Ct Sess (Inner House), a tribunal was entitled to stay an equal pay claim brought by a male employee, the success of which was dependent upon the success of a claim brought by his named comparator, a female colleague. The tribunal had been entitled to take into account the prejudice that the male employee would suffer if his claim were heard before the outcome of his female colleague's claim was known.

Stay pending EAT proceedings 11.108
There is no automatic right to a stay of tribunal proceedings where an issue of law is appealed to the EAT. Clearly, questions of jurisdiction will need to be settled before a tribunal can proceed to a substantive hearing. But in other cases, whether or not a stay is granted is a matter for the tribunal's discretion and the EAT will be reluctant to interfere. For instance, a tribunal may be reluctant to stay proceedings where a remedies hearing is scheduled but the respondent has appealed against findings on liability. In Towry Law plc v

587

Crossfield EAT 833/93 the EAT, faced with this dilemma, balanced the pros and cons, weighing the potential waste of time and costs if a stay was not granted against the need for a reasonably swift assessment of quantum. It also took into account the fact that interest on compensation begins to accrue (except in the case of sex discrimination or equal pay) only once a tribunal's decision on compensation has been promulgated. In the end it concluded that the balance came down in favour of refusing to adjourn the compensation hearing, noting in passing that the problem raised by the case was compounded by the long delay in the hearing of appeals at the EAT.

It should be noted, however, that new rule 66, which states that a party must comply with a judgment for the payment of money within 14 days of the judgment, contemplates the possibility of a stay of remedy proceedings by providing that the 14-day time limit does not apply where the tribunal has stayed (or in Scotland sisted) the proceedings or judgment – rule 66(a). Rule 66 is discussed in Chapter 14, 'Tribunal judgments', under 'Promulgating judgments – when a judgment takes effect'.

In deciding whether to postpone a hearing pending an appeal to the EAT, a tribunal will need to consider whether a stay of proceedings would conflict with the overriding objective contained in rule 2 of the Tribunal Rules 2013 to deal with cases fairly and justly. In Somjee v United Kingdom 2002 IRLR 886, ECtHR, the European Court of Human Rights held that the delays of an employment tribunal and the EAT in resolving a claimant's race discrimination claim violated the right to a fair hearing contained in Article 6(1) of the European Convention on Human Rights. In reaching this decision, the Court pointed to several matters, including the tribunal's decision to stay a claimant's victimisation claim pending the EAT's decision on the appeal of her race discrimination claim.

11.109 **Stay pending criminal proceedings**
Where the claimant is subject to a criminal prosecution arising out of matters connected with his or her dismissal, a tribunal may be faced with an application to stay the case pending the outcome of the criminal trial. There is no overriding right, based on the privilege against self-incrimination (see Chapter 13, 'Evidence', under 'Admissibility of evidence – privilege against self-incrimination'), to have a civil action stayed pending the conclusion of criminal proceedings, and it is for the party seeking a stay to satisfy the court or tribunal that he or she will be prejudiced by continuance of the civil action – Guinness plc v Saunders and ors, unreported 17.10.88, CA.

In rare circumstances, the criminal proceedings may concern a prosecution against the employer. This happened in Cowman v Rowbotham Tankships Ltd ET Case No.8791/85. Following an explosion on a ship the claimant was dismissed and his claim of unfair dismissal set down for 22 October 1985. The employer was prosecuted for alleged breaches of the Health and Safety at Work etc Act 1974 and proceedings, in which the claimant was named as a witness for the prosecution, were to begin on 11 November 1985. The employer applied for a stay of the tribunal claim until the criminal proceedings were completed, fearing that if its counsel had to cross-examine the claimant in the tribunal proceedings it would lose the benefit of surprise when required to do the same in the criminal trial. The tribunal, however, refused an adjournment. It said that any possible prejudice to the employer in going ahead was far outweighed by prejudice to the claimant if the tribunal hearing were further delayed. Moreover, the issues in the two sets of proceedings were different and it was by no means certain that the respective lines of cross-examination would be the same.

Stay pending professional misconduct proceedings 11.110
In Parums v West Dorset General Hospital NHS Trust EAT 0288/04 the claimant, a consultant histopathologist, complained to an employment tribunal of constructive dismissal following allegations that she had tampered with a sample taken from a patient to conceal a prior misdiagnosis. Having been informed of the matter, the General Medical Council (GMC) decided to investigate her case and professional conduct proceedings were commenced. The claimant sought a stay of the tribunal proceedings pending the outcome of the GMC proceedings. However this application was refused by the tribunal chairman and the claimant appealed to the EAT.

The tribunal's decision was upheld by the EAT, which found that the issue in the GMC proceedings was not relevant to the issues of liability to be determined in the forthcoming tribunal hearing. Furthermore, the fact that the GMC proceedings were of greater concern to the employee was of marginal significance when balancing the interests of both of the parties to the proceedings. Taking these factors into account, the EAT concluded that the employer's desire to proceed and the interests of justice required a timely disposal of the tribunal proceedings.

Striking out 11.111

The Tribunal Rules 2004 gave tribunals a wider power than previously existed to strike out the whole or part of a claim or response on its own initiative or upon the application of either party on certain specified grounds – old rule 18(7). This power has been carried over into the 2013 Rules, but is now contained in a new standalone rule (rule 37) designed to give the power more prominence, so as to increase awareness of it and ensure more consistent use by tribunals.

Procedure for considering strike-out orders 11.112
A tribunal can exercise its power to strike out a claim or response (or part of a claim or response) 'at any stage of the proceedings' – rule 37(1). However, the

589

power must be exercised in accordance with reason, relevance, principle and justice – Williams v Real Care Agency Ltd 2012 ICR D27, EAT.

Rule 37(2) provides that a claim or response (or part) cannot be struck out unless the party in question has been given a reasonable opportunity to make representations. This means that a tribunal must give notice to the relevant party of its intention to strike out and invite that party to make representations. A party's representations can be made either in writing or, if requested by the party, at a hearing. If a hearing is requested, it can be either a preliminary or a full hearing at which the parties may make oral representations and present evidence to be considered. If no request for a hearing is made, a tribunal can exercise its power to strike out on the papers alone.

11.113   No notice is required where the ground for striking out is non-compliance with an order of the tribunal. In these circumstances, provided that the relevant party has been notified as part of the terms of the order that *unless* any requirement imposed by the order is complied with by a given date the claim or response will be struck out, the tribunal is empowered from the date of non-compliance to dismiss the claim or response (or part) without further order – rule 38(1). The notice requirements are discussed further under 'Notice requirements prior to striking out' below and 'unless orders' are considered under 'Unless orders' below.

11.114   **Applying for a strike-out order.** A party applying for strike-out of their opponent's case should state clearly upon what ground(s) the application is made and, in accordance with the requirements of rule 92, the application should be copied to the other party (and the tribunal should be informed that this has been done) so that the other party has a reasonable opportunity to make representations either in writing or, if requested, at a hearing. In practice, a party may apply for both an order for strike-out and a deposit order in the alternative on the basis that if the standard for issuing strike-out is not met the lesser test for issuing a deposit order is nonetheless satisfied. Deposit orders are considered under 'Deposit orders' below.

In Abertawe Bro Morgannwg University Health Board v Ferguson EAT 0044/13, the EAT remarked in the course of giving judgment that, in suitable cases, applications for strike-out may save time, expense and anxiety. However, in cases that are likely to be heavily fact-sensitive, such as those involving discrimination or public interest disclosures, the circumstances in which a claim will be struck out are likely to be rare.

11.115   **Grounds for striking out**
A claim or response (or part) can be struck out on the following grounds:

- that it is scandalous or vexatious or has no reasonable prospect of success – rule 37(1)(a)

- that the manner in which the proceedings have been conducted by or on behalf of the claimant or the respondent (as the case may be) has been scandalous, unreasonable or vexatious – rule 37(1)(b)

- for non-compliance with any of the tribunal rules or with an order of the tribunal – rule 37(1)(c)

- that it has not been actively pursued – rule 37(1)(d)

- that the tribunal considers that it is no longer possible to have a fair hearing in respect of the claim or response (or the part to be struck out) – rule 37(1)(e).

These grounds do not differ materially from the old grounds upon which a claim or defence could be struck out. The first two grounds for striking out are also similar to the grounds on which a tribunal may award costs under rule 76(1) and a tribunal may prefer to deal with an unmeritorious claim or unreasonable behaviour by awarding costs, rather than using the more extreme measure of striking out – for further information on costs see Chapter 20, 'Costs and penalties'.

Old rule 18(8) stated that a claim or response or any part of one could be **11.116** struck out *only* on the grounds specified in rule 18(7)(b)–(f) (now rule 37(1) (a)–(e)). This restriction is not repeated in the new rules but rule 37 appears to be exhaustive nonetheless. It does not, for instance, state that the power to strike out can be exercised on grounds 'including' those listed. Furthermore, striking out a claim or response remains a draconian measure and the Court of Appeal has held that the general powers of case management do not include any power to strike out cases in situations not otherwise specifically provided for by the rules – Care First Partnership Ltd v Roffey and ors 2001 ICR 87, CA.

The five grounds on which a claim or response can be struck out in accordance with rule 37(1)(a)–(e) are discussed in detail separately below.

Scandalous, vexatious or no reasonable prospect of success   **11.117**

Rule 37(1)(a) provides that all or any part of a claim or response may be struck out if it is 'scandalous or vexatious or has no reasonable prospect of success'. Note that under the old rules tribunals had the option of either 'striking out *or amending*' (our stress) all or part of any claim or response on the grounds that it was scandalous, or vexatious or had no reasonable prospect of success (old rule 18(7)(b)). Under new rule 37(1)(a) tribunals only have the option to strike out a claim or response on this ground, not to amend it.

Scandalous or vexatious. The word 'scandalous' in the context of rule 37(1)(a)   **11.118** means irrelevant and abusive of the other side. It is not to be given its colloquial meaning of signifying something that is 'shocking' – Bennett v Southwark London Borough Council 2002 ICR 881, CA. In Jones v Wallop Industries Ltd ET Case No.17182/81 J claimed that he had been unfairly selected for redundancy and, to back up his claim, alleged fraud, mismanagement, misrepresentation, criminal conspiracy, intimidation and 'other torts' against the employer. The tribunal found that J was 'hell-bent on causing the respondent company and a number of individuals as much inconvenience, distress, embarrassment and expense as possible' and ordered the whole claim to be struck out as being largely scandalous or vexatious.

A 'vexatious' claim or defence has been described as one that is not pursued with the expectation of success but to harass the other side or out of some improper motive – ET Marler Ltd v Robertson 1974 ICR 72, NIRC. The term is also used more widely to include anything that is an abuse of process. In Attorney General v Barker 2000 1 FLR 759, QBD (Civ Div), Lord Chief Justice Bingham described 'vexatious' as a 'familiar term in legal parlance'. He said that the hallmark of a vexatious proceeding is that it has 'little or no basis in law (or at least no discernible basis); that whatever the intention of the proceeding may be, its effect is to subject the defendant to inconvenience, harassment and expense out of all proportion to any gain likely to accrue to the claimant; and that it involves an abuse of the process of the court, meaning by that a use of the court process for a purpose or in a way which is significantly different from the ordinary and proper use of the court process'.

11.119 In Ashmore v British Coal Corporation 1990 ICR 485, CA, the Court of Appeal approved the striking out of a 'like work' claim for equal pay on the ground that it was 'vexatious' as it was bound to fail in the light of an earlier decision based on exactly the same facts against the same employer. The Court of Appeal said that the categories of conduct rendering a claim vexatious or an abuse of process were not closed but depended on all the relevant circumstances of the particular case: public policy and the interests of justice being very material considerations. Where, as in this case, 14 sample cases had been selected from 1,500 similar cases against the same employer to enable the tribunal fully to investigate and make findings on all the relevant evidence, then, unless there was fresh evidence which entirely changed the aspect of the case, relitigation of the same issues would defeat the purpose of sample selection and be contrary to the interests of justice and public policy.

However, the mere fact that one of the parties has previously been involved in litigation over substantially the same issues does not, without more, justify a tribunal striking out a further claim as an abuse of process. In Department of Education and Science v Taylor and ors 1992 IRLR 308, QBD, a tribunal ordered that the Department of Education's response defending an appeal against its refusal to pay compensation to employees under the Colleges of Education (Compensation) Regulations 1975 SI 1975/1092 should be struck out on the ground that exactly the same grounds for the defence had failed in other similar cases. On appeal, however, the High Court held that the tribunal had misdirected itself in holding that it was an abuse of the process of the tribunal for the Department to seek to defend claims on the same ground that had been rejected by another tribunal in claims brought by the respondent employees' colleagues. In so ruling, Mr Justice Auld warned against the ready use of the striking-out weapon as a means of preventing relitigation, pointing out that there is a general entitlement to relitigate the same issues between different parties unless abuse of process can be shown and that the onus of proving such abuse fell squarely on the party seeking to avoid the litigation.

The principle of 'res judicata' prevents parties relitigating a cause of action **11.120** where a court has already reached a decision related to that cause of action – see Chapter 2, 'Tribunals' jurisdiction', under 'Relitigation: res judicata and abuse of process'. In Foster v Bon Groundwork Ltd 2012 ICR 1027, CA, the Court of Appeal held that an employment tribunal had fallen into error when striking out claims of unfair dismissal on the grounds of res judicata and abuse of process due to a previous tribunal's findings. The first tribunal had exceeded its jurisdiction when considering the reason for the claimant's dismissal, since his claim was lodged before the dismissal and expressly stated that it was for a redundancy payment arising out of a lay-off. As a result, the doctrine of res judicata did not apply and the claimant's actions in bringing the second set of tribunal proceedings could not be characterised as an abuse of process.

One particular scenario that has given rise to conflicting EAT decisions is where a claimant withdraws a complaint but then presents a second complaint on the same grounds. In Mulvaney v London Transport Executive 1981 ICR 351, EAT, the EAT said that it was a wrong exercise of the tribunal's discretion to strike out a second claim as frivolous merely because it was a second claim. Since M's case was not on the face of it completely hopeless and he had a possible explanation for his earlier withdrawal, he should have been allowed to go ahead. However, in Acrow (Engineers) Ltd v Hathaway 1981 ICR 510, EAT, H's first claim was dismissed when he withdrew it after the tribunal had refused his request for a postponement. He then presented a second claim and also later applied for review of the first tribunal decision. The EAT held that the second claim was vexatious and should be struck out: H's proper course was to pursue the remedy of review (now called 'reconsideration' – see Chapter 15, 'Reconsideration of tribunal judgments and decisions').

In the Hathaway case H seems to have had a realistic explanation for his earlier **11.121** withdrawal and it does not appear that he was acting purely to harass the employer or with some improper motive – the accepted definition of 'vexatious'. If he had not in fact been acting vexatiously, the Mulvaney decision would seem to suggest that the relevant question to be considered was whether the application was 'frivolous' – or had no prospect of success – a point apparently not considered by the EAT in Hathaway.

In Telephone Information Services Ltd v Wilkinson 1991 IRLR 148, EAT, the tribunal refused to accede to the respondent's argument that, in pursuing his

593

claim when he had already been offered the maximum sum awardable to him as compensation, the claimant was being wholly vexatious and his claim should therefore be struck out. On appeal, the EAT upheld the tribunal's decision. It pointed out that the claim was for more than just compensation: the employee was seeking a finding that he had been unfairly dismissed. He had every right to maintain his claim to the tribunal for that purpose. If the respondent wished to concede the matter it could do so by expressly admitting liability but could not do so merely by conceding the monetary part of it. The EAT's reasoning was affirmed by the Court of Appeal in Gibb v Maidstone and Tunbridge Wells NHS Trust 2010 IRLR 786, CA.

11.122 **No reasonable prospect of success.** The power for tribunals to strike out a claim or response on the ground that it has 'no reasonable prospect of success' was first introduced in the Tribunal Rules 2004, replacing the term 'misconceived'. It requires a tribunal to form a view on the merits of a case and only where it is satisfied that the claim or response has *no* reasonable prospect of succeeding can it exercise its power to strike out.

In A v B and anor 2011 ICR D9, CA, an employment tribunal was wrong to strike out an employee's claims of sex discrimination and unfair dismissal on the basis that they had no reasonable prospect of success. In so holding, the Court of Appeal concluded that there was a 'more than fanciful' prospect that the employer would not be able to discharge the 'reverse' burden of proof to show that the employee's dismissal was not sex discriminatory. Accordingly, the EAT had been right to decide that the employer had not succeeded in demonstrating that claims had no reasonable prospect of success. Similarly, in Short v Birmingham City Council and ors EAT 0038/13 an employment judge had misdirected herself in law by considering whether 'on the balance of probabilities' the claimant was unlikely to succeed in her claims. Applying the approach taken in A v B, the EAT was satisfied that strike-out could not be justified in this case because it could not properly be said that the claims had no reasonable prospect of success.

11.123 Special considerations arise if a tribunal is asked to strike out a claim of discrimination on the ground that it has no reasonable prospect of success. In Anyanwu and anor v South Bank Students' Union and anor 2001 ICR 391, HL, the House of Lords highlighted the importance of not striking out discrimination claims except in the most obvious cases as they are generally fact-sensitive and require full examination to make a proper determination. With this guidance in mind, the Court of Appeal in Community Law Clinic Solicitors v Methuen 2012 EWCA Civ 571, CA, held that an employee's claim for age discrimination should not be struck out because the case required further examination of the facts so as to properly consider whether age discrimination could be inferred.

594

In Ezsias v North Glamorgan NHS Trust 2007 ICR 1126, CA, the Court of Appeal held that the same or a similar approach should generally inform whistleblowing cases, which have much in common with discrimination cases, in that they involve an investigation into why an employer took a particular step. The Court stressed that it will only be in an exceptional case that an application will be struck out as having no reasonable prospect of success when the central facts are in dispute. An example might be where the facts sought to be established by the claimant are totally and inexplicably inconsistent with the undisputed contemporaneous documentation. For instance, in Shestak v Royal College of Nursing and ors EAT 0270/08 the claimant appealed against the decision to strike out a multitude of claims arising out of the termination of her trainee nursing placement. Upholding the tribunal's decision, the EAT held that undisputed documentary evidence – in the form of e-mails which could not, taken at their highest, support the claimant's interpretation of events – justified a departure from the usual approach that discrimination claims should not be struck out at a preliminary stage.

Lady Smith expanded on the guidance given in Ezsias in Balls v Downham **11.124** Market High School and College 2011 IRLR 217, EAT, stating that where strike-out is sought or contemplated on the ground that the claim has no reasonable prospect of success, the tribunal must first consider whether, on a careful consideration of all the available material, it can properly conclude that the claim has no reasonable prospect of success. The test is not whether the claim is likely to fail; nor is it a matter of asking whether it is possible that the claim will fail. It is not a test that can be satisfied by considering what is put forward by the respondent either in the ET3 or in submissions and deciding whether their written or oral assertions regarding disputed matters are likely to be established as facts. It is a high test. The tribunal should have regard not only to material specifically relied on by parties but to the employment tribunal file. There may be correspondence or other documentation which contains material that is relevant to the issue of whether it can be concluded that the claim has no reasonable prospect of success or which assists in determining whether it is fair to strike out the claim. If there is relevant material on file and it is not referred to by the parties, the employment judge should draw their attention to it so that they have the opportunity to make submissions regarding it.

The cautious approach to striking out claims taken in Ezsias v North Glamorgan NHS Trust (above) and Balls v Downham Market High School and College (above) stems from the proposition that it is unfair to strike out a claim where there are crucial facts in dispute and there has been no opportunity for the evidence in relation to those facts to be considered. In Eastman v Tesco Stores Ltd EAT 0143/12 the EAT held that an employment judge was entitled to strike out a claim of unfair dismissal as having no reasonable prospect of success at a PHR, having heard evidence in order to resolve relevant factual disputes. The

595

judge had concluded that the claimant had completed a career break application form that was contained at the back of the career break booklet which made it clear that an employee was not guaranteed to return to his or her job after a career break. The judge also found that the claimant was not given an oral guarantee that she could definitely return to her old job at the end of her career break. The EAT held that the judge was entitled to resolve crucial core disputes as to facts at the PHR and so determine the prospects of the case on that factual basis. This case could therefore be distinguished from Ezsias and Balls, in which factual disputes remained unresolved at the PHR. The two relevant factual disputes were resolved against the claimant and, having so resolved them, the employment judge was entitled to conclude on that factual basis that the unfair dismissal claim had no reasonable prospect of success.

11.125 However, even where a case has no reasonable prospect of success, it does not necessarily follow that an order to strike out should be made – Lambrou v Cyprus Airways Ltd EAT 0417/05. In that case, a tribunal struck out a disability discrimination claim on the grounds that it was speculative and had no reasonable prospect of success. In its view, even if the claimant could establish that he was a disabled person – which seemed unlikely given that there appeared to be no medical evidence to support that contention – he appeared to be unable to establish a prima facie case that any less favourable treatment suffered by him was as a result of his disability. The EAT, however, disagreed with the tribunal's finding that the claim was purely speculative. In any event, it held that even when a ground for striking out the proceedings has been made out, a tribunal should consider alternatives to striking out. In this case, other remedies might have included the ordering of specific particulars and a medical report prepared by a single expert jointly instructed by both sides.

In Williams v Real Care Agency Ltd 2012 ICR D27, EAT, a tribunal struck out an unfair dismissal claim at the final hearing part-way through hearing the evidence on the basis that the claim had no reasonable prospect of success. This was because, among other things, the claimant had undermined her credibility by changing her account of various matters when giving evidence. On appeal the EAT held that the tribunal had erred, stating that only in very exceptional cases will it be appropriate for a tribunal to strike out a claim during the final hearing on the ground of evidential insubstantiality. Similarly, in Timbo v Greenwich Council for Racial Equality 2013 ICR D7, EAT, a tribunal erred by acceding to an employer's application, made part-way through the final hearing after the claimant had given evidence, to strike out the discrimination case on the ground that it had no reasonable prospect of success. There was a crucial core of disputed facts which could not be determined other than by evaluating all the evidence. The EAT held that it was inappropriate for the tribunal to dismiss the claims without hearing the employer's evidence and giving the claimant the opportunity to test that evidence in cross-examination.

Manner in which proceedings are conducted   11.126

Rule 37(1)(b) provides that a claim or response (or part) may be struck out if 'the manner in which the proceedings have been conducted by or on behalf of the claimant or the respondent... has been scandalous, unreasonable or vexatious'. The terms 'scandalous' and 'vexatious' in this context are used in much the same way as they are in rule 37(1)(a) – see 'Scandalous, vexatious or no reasonable prospect of success' above. A party may also find that his or her claim or defence is struck out on this ground if he or she has conducted the case in an 'unreasonable' manner. For a tribunal to strike out for unreasonable conduct, it has to be satisfied either that the conduct involved deliberate and persistent disregard of required procedural steps or has made a fair trial impossible; and in either case, the striking out must be a proportionate response – Blockbuster Entertainment Ltd v James 2006 IRLR 630, CA.

Conduct of party's representative. The power to strike out under rule 37(1)(b)   **11.127** expressly includes the manner in which proceedings have been conducted *on behalf of* the claimant or the respondent, making it clear that a representative's conduct can be considered. Useful guidance as to the scope of the power in this regard was given in Bennett v Southwark London Borough Council 2002 ICR 881, CA. There, a hearing in the context of a race and sex discrimination claim had been adjourned after ten days of evidence and was listed for a further eight days. On the first day back, the claimant was ill and her lay representative, H, a black man, asked for an adjournment. When this request was refused, he made remarks to the tribunal on more than one occasion to the effect that 'if I were a white barrister I would not be treated in this way'. The tribunal considered that it could not continue to hear the race discrimination claim once it had itself been accused of racism and it therefore discharged itself and remitted the case to a fresh tribunal. The second tribunal then struck out the claimant's discrimination claims on the ground that his repeated allegations of racial bias against the tribunal had been 'on any objective view quite scandalous'. B appealed and the EAT upheld the appeal, holding that the first tribunal should not have recused itself. However, the EAT nonetheless struck the case out on account of H's conduct. On further appeal, the Court of Appeal held that the tribunal and the EAT had erred in striking out the claimant's case on the ground of the legal representative's scandalous conduct. His conduct, though improper, was reversible and did not justify the striking out of the claim. In the circumstances, the tainting effect of the representative's remarks could and should have been dissolved with tact by the tribunal. In reaching that decision, the Court made a number of useful observations:

- it is not simply the representative's conduct that needs to be characterised as scandalous but the way in which he or she is conducting the proceedings on behalf of his or her client

597

- the tribunal must therefore consider: (a) the way in which the proceedings have been conducted, (b) how far that is attributable to the party the representative is acting for, and (c) the significance of the 'scandalous' conduct

- what is done in a party's name is presumptively, but not irrefutably, done on his or her behalf. When the sanction is the drastic one of striking out the whole of a party's case, there must be room for the party to disassociate him or herself from what his or her representative has done

- 'scandalous' in this context is not a synonym for 'shocking': rather it means either the misuse of legal process in order to vilify others, or the giving of gratuitous insult to the tribunal in the course of such process

- where the conduct of the proceedings is categorised as scandalous, a tribunal must go on to consider whether striking out is a proportionate response. (Note that in this particular case, the Court held, obiter, that even if the conduct of the proceedings could be categorised as scandalous, striking out was not a proportionate response. In its view, firm case management might well have provided a better solution).

11.128 By contrast, in Edmondson v BMI Healthcare and anor EAT 0654/01 the EAT upheld a tribunal's decision to strike out a claim on the basis that the conduct of the claimant's representative had been scandalous, frivolous and vexatious, and had made it impossible for a fair trial to continue. The claimant in this case was represented in her unfair dismissal and race discrimination claims by her friend, G. Prior to the hearing, G had sent abusive correspondence to the employer's representative, including a letter that was addressed to the 'racial abuse legal department'. At the hearing, he used abusive language, interfered with the claimant's evidence by completing sentences for her, disrupted her evidence by repeated loud sighing and puffing, and called the employer's solicitor a liar. Although G offered to apologize, he refused to retract that allegation. The solicitor subsequently applied for the claim to be struck out pursuant to what is now rule 37(1)(b). When invited to make representations as to why the claim should not be struck out, G stood by his allegation and invited the employer's solicitor to sue him for libel or slander.

In view of G's conduct, the tribunal released the claimant from her oath and adjourned to allow her to consider whether she wished him to continue representing her. Following the claimant's assertion that she did want G to continue as her representative, the tribunal struck out her claim on the ground that the conduct of the proceedings on her behalf had been scandalous, frivolous and vexatious. On appeal, the EAT held that the tribunal's approach had been entirely consistent with the guidelines set out in Bennett v Southwark London Borough Council (above). Furthermore, it agreed that G's conduct had made it impossible for a fair trial to continue and in such circumstances striking out was the necessary, proportionate and entirely appropriate response.

598

Is fair trial still possible? In considering whether a claim should be struck out **11.129** on the grounds of scandalous, unreasonable or vexatious conduct, a tribunal must take into account whether a fair trial is still possible – De Keyser Ltd v Wilson 2001 IRLR 324, EAT. In that case the EAT made it clear that certain conduct, such as the deliberate flouting of a tribunal order, can lead directly to the question of a striking-out order. However, in ordinary circumstances, neither a claim nor a defence can be struck out on the basis of a party's conduct unless a conclusion is reached that a fair trial is no longer possible.

Both the De Keyser case and Bennett v Southwark London Borough Council (above) were applied in Bolch v Chipman 2004 IRLR 140, EAT, a case in which the EAT overturned a tribunal's decision to strike out an employer's response on the ground that he had threatened the employee, who was claiming unfair dismissal, with physical violence. In doing so, the EAT set out the steps that a tribunal must ordinarily take when determining whether to make a strike-out order:

- before making a striking-out order under what is now rule 37(1)(b), an employment judge must find that a party or his or her representative has behaved scandalously, unreasonably or vexatiously when conducting the proceedings

- once such a finding has been made, he or she must consider, in accordance with De Keyser Ltd v Wilson (above), whether a fair trial is still possible, as, save in exceptional circumstances, a striking-out order is not regarded simply as a punishment. If a fair trial is still possible, the case should be permitted to proceed

- even if a fair trial is unachievable, the tribunal will need to consider the appropriate remedy in the circumstances. It may be appropriate to impose a lesser penalty, for example, by making a costs or preparation order against the party concerned rather than striking out his or her claim or response.

Applying this guidance to the facts of the case before it, the EAT held that while **11.130** the employer's conduct was clearly reprehensible, there was insufficient evidence on which the tribunal could conclude that his behaviour amounted to 'unreasonable conduct of the proceedings'. Moreover, the EAT was satisfied that the employer's behaviour would not prevent a fair trial. It therefore set aside the tribunal's decision to strike out his response.

A similar approach was taken by the EAT in Laing O'Rourke Group Services Ltd and ors v Woolf and anor EAT 0038/05. In that case, the tribunal struck out the employer's response on the ground that it had conducted the proceedings in a manner that was scandalous, unreasonable or vexatious. This occurred after the employer's representative had failed to attend a hearing in the mistaken belief that it would be adjourned by consent. When the matter was appealed, the EAT noted that although the employer's conduct could be described as

599

unreasonable, it was not wilful, deliberate or contumelious. 'Courts should not be so outraged by what they see as unreasonable conduct as to punish the party in default in circumstances where other sanctions can be deployed and where a fair trial is still possible.' In the EAT's view, the tribunal should also have considered whether striking out the claim was a proportionate sanction and whether an alternative, such as allowing the hearing to proceed without evidence from the employer, would have been more appropriate.

11.131 The Court of Appeal in Blockbuster Entertainment Ltd v James 2006 IRLR 630, CA, confirmed that it took something very unusual indeed to justify striking out on procedural grounds a claim that had arrived at the point of trial. In that case, J had – in breach of tribunal orders – failed to provide adequate further particulars of his claims and refused to allow the respondent to photocopy his disclosure documents. He had also attended on the first morning of the hearing with previously unseen documents and had made changes to a witness statement without notice to the employer. The employment tribunal concluded that the manner in which J had conducted the proceedings had been unreasonable. In its view, there had been wilful and persistent disobedience of the tribunal's orders and a real failure to cooperate with either the respondent or the tribunal. The tribunal was therefore satisfied that an order striking out J's claims was the only proportionate and fair course, given that a fair trial was no longer possible. The EAT overturned that decision and the employer appealed to the Court of Appeal.

While acknowledging that J had been 'difficult, querulous and uncooperative', the Court of Appeal noted that the courts and tribunals must be open to the difficult as well as to the compliant so long as they do not conduct their cases unreasonably. In considering whether a case has been conducted unreasonably, a tribunal should bear in mind that the time to deal with persistent or deliberate failures to comply with rules or orders is when they have reached the point of no return. The Court went on to suggest that it was undesirable for a strike-out application to be granted on the first day of a six-day hearing – even where the application is otherwise well-founded. If non-compliance is serious enough to warrant such an application, this ought to be clear before the trial begins. In any event, the Court took the view that it was not satisfactory for a tribunal to simply record that a strike-out is 'the proportionate and fair course to take'. Rather, it should have spelt out why a strike-out was the *only* proportionate and fair course to take.

11.132 The Court of Appeal's reasoning in the Blockbuster case was applied in Bayley v Whitbread Hotel Co Ltd t/a Marriott Worsley Park Hotel and anor EAT 0046/07. B, who was dyslexic, brought a claim of disability discrimination in which he was represented by his father. When it came to light during the hearing that the father had concealed sections of two expert reports on B's dyslexia which were unhelpful to his case, W plc applied to have the claim struck on the ground of unreasonable conduct. The tribunal determined that the father knew he was doing wrong in not disclosing the full reports and allowed the application. On appeal, the EAT expressed doubts over the tribunal's finding in relation to the father's dishonesty, noting that even in cases of deliberate deceit, the fundamental question for the tribunal was whether a fair trial was still possible. The tribunal's conclusions on this point were unsustainable. Nothing in the undisclosed sections of the reports would have influenced the tribunal's decision on the question of disability. Although there was material relevant to the issue of reasonable adjustments, W plc came into possession of this material prior to the full hearing. Accordingly, a fair trial remained possible and a strike-out was therefore too draconian a sanction.

However, in Force One Utilities Ltd v Hatfield 2009 IRLR 45, EAT, an employment tribunal was justified in striking out an employer's defence to a claim of unfair dismissal in circumstances where a witness had threatened the claimant. S, who was the executive director of a company associated with, and who had given evidence for, FOU Ltd, threatened the claimant with physical harm, telling him that he should be careful how he slept at night, and had blocked his attempt to leave the tribunal car park. Although the employer had decided not to call S to give further evidence and the claimant had indicated a willingness to continue with the case, the tribunal did not feel that he was free of the fear that S's conduct had caused him. Nor was it satisfied that the claimant could give reliable evidence if that evidence was to come into conflict with that of the employer. It concluded that a fair trial was no longer possible and struck out FOU Ltd's response in relation to both liability and remedy since the remedies hearing would be subject to the same considerations as the hearing on the merits itself. The EAT held that the conduct of S, who was directing matters on behalf of FOU Ltd, had made a fair trial of the issues impossible, and striking out the defence was a proportionate response to that conduct. It rejected the idea that tribunals should carry out a 'balancing act' in determining whether striking out is a proportionate response. Instead, the critical question is whether a fair trial remains possible. The EAT commented that where a tribunal has found intimidation of the kind displayed in the above case, it would be 'very exceptional' for that finding to be held to be perverse.

Reneging on agreement to settle. Where parties have negotiated a settlement **11.133** of a case but the 'agreement' is not legally enforceable, then it can be neither unreasonable nor vexatious for the claimant to renege on that purported agreement and continue with the case – Crown Prosecution Service v Bamieh EAT 309/99. In that case B brought several sex and race discrimination claims against her employer and eventually agreed to leave her employment on payment of a sum of money. The terms were set out in writing but the requirements for a valid compromise agreement (now known as 'settlement agreements') were not satisfied and the agreement therefore had no legal effect (see Chapter 3, 'Conciliation, settlements and ADR', under 'Settlement agreements'). When B sought to continue with her claims, the CPS applied to have them struck out on the basis that, even if the agreement were not strictly binding, B had behaved unreasonably and vexatiously in reneging on it. The tribunal refused to strike out B's claims and the EAT upheld that decision, commenting that to hold otherwise would be to subvert the plain intention of Parliament that settlement agreements, to be valid, must be made in a certain way so as to protect the rights and interests of the parties.

It should be noted that, at the time of the Bamieh decision, the striking-out rule that then applied in relation to the conduct of proceedings did not include 'unreasonableness' as a basis for striking out. However, new rule 37(1)(b) does include this ground and it is just possible that this might make a difference were similar facts to arise today, although the policy arguments that lay behind the EAT's reasoning remain cogent and would therefore carry considerable weight.

11.134 Non-compliance with tribunal rules or a tribunal order

A tribunal has the power to strike out the whole or part of the claim or response where the relevant party has failed to comply with any of the tribunal rules or with an order of the tribunal – rule 37(1)(c).

As explained under 'Notice requirements prior to striking out' below, before an order to strike out on the ground of non-compliance (or any other ground) can be made, the relevant party must be given a reasonable opportunity to make representations, either in writing or, if requested by the party, at a hearing (either a preliminary or final hearing), as to why such an order should not be made – rule 37(2). Rule 38(1) provides an exception to this where the order in respect of which there has been non-compliance states that if it is not complied with by the date specified, the claim or response (or part) will be dismissed without further order. Where this kind of 'unless order' has been made, a tribunal will issue a strike-out order for non-compliance without having to give the relevant party an opportunity to make representations under rule 37(2). Unlike strike-out orders under rule 37, a tribunal has no discretion in relation to orders under rule 38(1). Where an unless order is not complied with, the claim or response must be struck out as at the date of non-compliance. The only question for the tribunal is therefore whether or not there has been compliance in accordance with the order – Scottish Ambulance Service v Laing EATS 0038/12. In that case the tribunal had erred by finding that it was disproportionate to strike out the claim where an unless order had not been complied with. The EAT said that 'in such a case, the tribunal has already addressed the question of whether or not the deadly sword of strike-out should fall on the party against whom the order is sought and decided that unless a particular direction is complied with, it should'. 'Unless orders' are considered in more detail under 'Unless orders' below.

In deciding whether to strike out a party's case for non-compliance with an **11.135** order under rule 37(1)(c), a tribunal will have regard to the overriding objective set out in rule 2 of seeking to deal with cases fairly and justly. This requires a tribunal to consider all relevant factors, including the magnitude of the non-compliance; whether the default was the responsibility of the party or his or her representative; what disruption, unfairness or prejudice has been caused; whether a fair hearing would still be possible; and whether striking out or some lesser remedy would be an appropriate response to the disobedience – Weirs Valves and Controls (UK) Ltd v Armitage 2004 ICR 371, EAT. On the facts of that case, the EAT held that a tribunal had erred in striking out the whole of the employer's response for failure to comply with an order for simultaneous exchange of witness statements. The EAT took the view that a fair trial was still possible even though the employer had had the opportunity to tailor its witness statement in light of the witness statements served by the claimants by the due date. Had the tribunal carried out an investigation as to whether the claimant had suffered any prejudice as a result of the employer's default, it would have found that the employer had not taken any unfair advantage. The EAT went on to say that even if there had been some unfairness, the tribunal had the power under the rules to exclude all or part of a witness statement if it was proportionate to do so, having regard to the default and the overriding objective.

Whenever a tribunal is considering a strike-out on the ground of non-compliance with prior orders pursuant to rule 37(1)(c), it must consider whether a striking-out order is a proportionate response to the non-compliance. As we have seen, this same consideration applies to strike-out applications pursuant to rule 37(1)(b) on the ground that the manner in which the proceedings have been conducted has been scandalous, unreasonable or vexatious – see Blockbuster Entertainment Ltd v James 2006 IRLR 630, CA, under 'Manner in which proceedings are conducted' above. In Ridsdill and ors v D Smith and Nephew Medical and ors EAT 0704/05 the EAT held that the tribunal had erred by striking out the claimants' claims on the basis that they had failed to provide schedules of loss and had not exchanged witness statements. A proportionate response required the tribunal to consider whether there was a less drastic means of addressing the claimants' failures and achieving a fair trial for the parties. It was undoubtedly the case that an adjournment of the hearing, with appropriate unless orders and costs penalties, would have avoided the conclusion that a fair trial was impossible and would thereby have ensured fairness and justice as between the parties without debarring the claimants from a trial altogether. The tribunal had acknowledged, implicitly at least, that adjourning the hearing would have prevented it finding that a fair trial was no longer possible; and it was not in dispute that the tribunal had the power itself under the rules to order an adjournment. In observing that no request for an adjournment had been made, and then limiting its consideration to the question of whether a fair trial was possible on the dates fixed for hearing, the tribunal had erred.

603

11.136 In Hazelwood v Eagle EAT 0011/09 the EAT overturned a striking-out order made by a tribunal on the basis that the claimant had failed to provide a medical report and disability impact statement. There was no sign at all in the tribunal's terse reasoning that it had given any consideration to the guiding principles established in Weirs Valves and Controls (UK) Ltd v Armitage (above) and Blockbuster Entertainment Ltd v James (above). The claimant's representative had informed the tribunal that a consultant's report had been commissioned at substantial expense and was due at or close to the time when the striking-out order was made, and no hearing was imminent. Further, even though the claimant had failed to provide a disability impact statement, the tribunal's directions called for simultaneous service of the statement and the report for good reason, as it will often help in the preparation of the statement to know what the medical records and the medical report say. The EAT held that in these circumstances any tribunal should have refrained from immediate strike-out.

In North Tyneside Primary Care Trust v Aynsley and ors 2009 ICR 1333, EAT, the EAT revoked the striking out of the Trust's response to equal pay proceedings. The tribunal was wrong to maintain the strike-out, notwithstanding the employer's failure to provide the claimants with pay information by a specified date, since it had subsequently substantially remedied the breach and the case remained triable. Maintaining the strike-out – assuming eventual compliance with the order for disclosure – was therefore disproportionate.

11.137 **Claim or response has not been actively pursued**
Sometimes a case just 'goes to sleep': it may reach a certain point in the interim stage and then the momentum which the parties should provide to ensure that it reaches a hearing as soon as possible fizzles out. For example, a case might be adjourned pending settlement negotiations or other court proceedings, which then drag on interminably. Or the claimant might go abroad or simply disappear. In these circumstances, a tribunal can exercise its power under rule 37(1)(d), either on the application of a party or on its own initiative, to strike out the claim or response if it has not been actively pursued.

Rule 18(7)(d) of the Tribunal Rules 2004 provided that only a *claim* could be struck out if it had not been actively pursued – there was no scope for an order to be made striking out a response on this ground. But rule 37(1)(d) allows a tribunal to strike out either a claim or a response, or part of a claim or response, on this ground. But as with all striking-out orders (save for strike-out following an unless order), the tribunal must give the relevant party a reasonable opportunity to argue that the order should not be made before making an order under rule 37(1)(d) – rule 37(2).

11.138 The equivalent power under the 2001 Rules of Procedure referred to the striking out of a claim for 'want of prosecution', but the substance of the power has remained the same. As a result, the case law decided under the 2001 Rules

604

continues to be relevant to strike-outs under new rule 31(1)(d). In Evans and anor v Commissioner of Police of the Metropolis 1993 ICR 151, CA, the Court of Appeal held that an employment tribunal's power to strike out a claim for want of prosecution must be exercised in accordance with the principles that (prior to the introduction of the Civil Procedure Rules in 1998) governed the equivalent power in the High Court, as set out by the House of Lords in Birkett v James 1978 AC 297, HL. Accordingly, a tribunal can strike out a claim where:

- there has been delay that is intentional or contumelious (disrespectful or abusive to the court), or

- there has been inordinate and inexcusable delay, which gives rise to a substantial risk that a fair hearing is impossible, or which is likely to cause serious prejudice to the respondent.

The first category is likely to include cases where the claimant has failed to adhere to an order of the tribunal. As such, it overlaps substantially with the tribunal's power to strike out for non-compliance with tribunal rules or a tribunal order under rule 37(1)(c) – see 'Non-compliance with tribunal rules or a tribunal order' above. The second category requires not only that there has been a delay of an inordinate and inexcusable kind, but that the respondent can show that it will suffer some prejudice as a result. In O'Shea v Immediate Sound Services Ltd 1986 ICR 598, EAT, the EAT held that prejudice was inherent in the failure to prosecute a case in time and so it was not necessary for the tribunal to consider this factor separately. However, this was held to be erroneous by the Court of Appeal in Evans and anor v Commissioner of Police of the Metropolis (above) – although the Court considered that the decision in O'Shea was nonetheless correct on its facts. In any event, prejudice may not be difficult to show, as it will often be necessary 'to investigate the facts before memories have faded, not to allow hurt feelings to fester and to provide as summary a remedy as possible' – per Lord Justice Hoffmann in Evans.

11.139 Below are three examples of cases concerning strike-out in circumstances where the relevant claims had not been actively pursued. Although decided in relation to the power to dismiss a claim for want of prosecution under previous rules, they are still relevant to the power to strike out under rule 37(1)(d):

- **Credit Aid Ltd v Russell-Taylor** EAT 649/82: tribunal proceedings had been adjourned part-heard in September 1980 and there was a further adjournment while the parties negotiated unsuccessfully and related High Court proceedings got under way. In September 1982 the employer applied to have the claims struck out for want of prosecution but the tribunal chairman refused. The EAT upheld his refusal: the adjournment had been by consent and the claimant was not in default of any tribunal order; furthermore, there was no prejudice to the respondents because the evidence would have to be heard in the High Court anyway

605

- **Evans and anor v Commissioner of Police of the Metropolis** (above): the employee made sex discrimination and equal pay complaints in relation to the operation of the police pension scheme, which were first submitted to the tribunal in January 1984. At the time, it was thought that two cases in the European Court of Justice (ECJ) would have some bearing on the issues involved and the parties agreed to postpone the case sine die, i.e. indefinitely. However, when the ECJ gave judgment in the two cases, its decisions proved to be of no assistance. Despite this, no application was made by either party for the matters to be restored to the list for hearing by the tribunal. In 1990, a further case came before the ECJ which the claimant's representatives believed would decisively resolve the case in his favour. They therefore applied for the matter to be relisted. However, a tribunal chairman ordered the case to be struck out for want of prosecution on the ground of inexcusable delay, holding that the employer should not have to prepare for and meet a case which it must have thought was long since at an end. On appeal, the Court of Appeal ruled that the tribunal had not been entitled to hold, on the particular facts, that the respondent would be seriously prejudiced if the case went ahead. In a normal case, where facts are largely in issue, it might be important to ensure that legal proceedings are handled with expedition before feelings fester and memories fade. But here the issues were entirely legal ones (the facts not being in dispute), so it was not a case where, as a result of the delay, a fair hearing was impossible. According to Lord Justice Hoffmann, the 'corporate disappointment' of the employer in realising that the case was still alive was of itself quite inadequate as a ground of prejudice

- **O'Shea v Immediate Sound Services Ltd** (above): immediately before the hearing of O's unfair dismissal complaint, the tribunal granted his request for an adjournment pending negotiations with a view to settlement. The tribunal asked to be kept informed of any progress made. No reply was received and three months later the tribunal wrote asking to be advised of the current position but again received no reply. After a further three months the tribunal sent a notice to the claimant asking him to show cause why his claim should not be dismissed for want of prosecution. When no reply was received, the claim was struck out. At this point the claimant decided to appeal to the EAT, but was unsuccessful.

In both the Evans and O'Shea cases the EAT and the Court of Appeal observed that the more leisurely pace that is regarded as acceptable in the High Court (albeit perhaps less so now under the Civil Procedure Rules) is not acceptable in the tribunals.

11.140 More recently, in Rolls Royce plc v Riddle 2008 IRLR 873, EAT, an employment tribunal erred when it declined to strike out a claim after the claimant falsely informed it that he had been medically unfit to attend the hearing and failed to comply with its various directions. In so holding, the EAT noted that what is now rule 37(1)(d)) is not drafted in such a way as to oblige a tribunal to take account of any particular considerations. But, in accordance with the principles laid down in Birkett v James (above), as applied in the employment tribunal in Evans and anor v Commissioner of Police of the Metropolis (above), strike-out applications on this ground will generally fall into one of the two categories set out by the House of Lords:

- that the default is intentional and contumelious (showing disrespect or contempt for the tribunal and/or its procedures), or

- the conduct has resulted in inordinate and inexcusable delay such as to give rise to a substantial risk that a fair trial would not be possible or there would be serious prejudice to the other party.

Both categories recognise that a claimant's conduct may result in his or her losing the right to continue with a claim. Overall, the EAT felt that the claimant had shown considerable disrespect to the tribunal and its procedures, and to the respondent's interests. The EAT held that although striking out a claim on the basis of a claimant's failure to actively pursue it is a draconian measure, it is one that can be ordered where the claimant's default is intentional and shows disrespect for the tribunal and/or its procedures.

In Abegaze v Shrewsbury College of Arts and Technology 2010 IRLR 238, CA, **11.141** a tribunal had erred in concluding that, six years after it had upheld a race discrimination complaint, the claimant had failed to actively pursue the case such that a fair trial of the remedies hearing was no longer possible. Although the claimant had been uncooperative and this had prevented the remedies hearing taking place, a fair trial remained possible and an 'unless order' could encourage the claimant to cooperate. Furthermore, there was no basis for the employment judge's assertion that M (one of the respondent's key witnesses) would not have been able to give evidence after such a long time. While there were likely to be greater problems in recalling a specific conversation, it was by no means certain that M would be unable to do so, particularly since the conversation was conducted specifically with the present litigation in mind. M had not been asked whether he could provide such evidence. Instead, the judge had merely assumed that he could not. The judge had also been unnecessarily concerned about the risk of his sharing the view of the previous lay members (who had since retired) with the new lay members who would need to be appointed. However, a change in composition of the tribunal, while never ideal, does not go to the question of whether a fair trial is possible. Moreover, if the judge had had concerns over whether he could act properly, the correct approach would have been to recuse himself, rather than punish the claimant for his own lack of self-control. Finally, the judge had thought it impossible to disentangle to what extent the losses resulted from the unlawful act of discrimination perpetrated by the respondent and to what extent they were the result of other unsuccessful claims of discrimination against other employers. However, this would have been an issue even if the remedy hearing had gone ahead when it was listed in 2003 – nothing material had changed three years on. Accordingly, the Court upheld the appeal and overturned the strike-out order, directing that the case go to a fresh employment judge to make any appropriate case management orders and arrange a remedies hearing.

Abegaze was distinguished on the facts in Taylor v HP Enterprise Services UK Ltd EAT 1807/10. In Abegaze there had already been a full hearing on liability. The key witnesses had been heard, and only the issue of remedy remained. In Taylor, the claim was almost five years old and there was no prospect of it being ready for trial in the foreseeable future. There had been four preliminary hearings, and none had moved the case forward. The claims were insufficiently particularised with no proper disclosure, the claimant had not produced a witness statement, no documents had been agreed, the issues were not identified, and many of the witnesses had left the respondent's business some time ago. Most of the delay was caused by the claimant's failure to deal with the case. He had not obtained representation: he was suffering from depression, but he was not taking medication, preferring alternative treatments instead. The tribunal had made a very substantial number of interventions to try to get the case on the road, but to no avail. Accordingly, the EAT upheld the tribunal's decision to strike out the claim on the basis that it had not been actively pursued.

11.142 Even less action had been taken in Elliot v The Joseph Whitworth Centre Ltd EAT 0030/13. There the tribunal struck out the claimant's unfair dismissal complaint that had been inactive for almost two years because the Employment Tribunals Service had failed to process the claim and send it to the respondent. However, this failure had been compounded by the failure of the claimant's representative, the Community Trade Union, to chase it up. Applying the Court of Appeal's decision in Evans and anor v Commissioner of Police of the Metropolis (above), which confirmed that the criteria for striking out claims in the civil court also applied to employment tribunals, the EAT held that the judge could not be criticised for her approach to the case. The fact that JWC Ltd made a good attempt at a defence in its response did not detract from the problems it would face in putting live evidence before the tribunal to defend the unfair dismissal claim. Although the fact that people have left the organisation or gone abroad is not necessarily a reason as to why there cannot be a fair trial, fading memory is. Furthermore, what amounts to a delay, and how long it must be before it is inordinate, is a question of fact for a first-instance judge to decide. In the light of the Tribunals Service's response and the claimant's representative's acceptance that it sat on its hands, the judge was entitled to form the view that the delay was inexcusable and she had made a permissible decision on where the balance of prejudice lay. The EAT noted that in most strike-out cases there will be an equal and opposite balance of prejudice. If the application is granted, the claimant who has a strong case is prejudiced and the respondent receives a windfall because it can escape justice. On the other hand, if the application is refused, a respondent is prejudiced if a weak case is allowed to go ahead. The judge therefore rightly looked for something more to do with the case itself, such as memories fading, documents and witnesses going missing, the business becoming insolvent and a change of representation and all the cost that involved, in determining whether to exercise her discretion to strike out the claim. The appeal was dismissed.

Fair hearing no longer possible

11.143

Under rule 37(1)(e) a tribunal may strike out a claim or response (or part) where it considers that 'it is no longer possible to have a fair hearing'. This was a new ground introduced by the Tribunal Rules 2004 (rule 18(7)(f)) but it is not entirely clear what was being added given that, according to case law, the possibility of a fair hearing was (and remains) an important consideration under the other grounds for strike-out set out in rule 18(7) (now rule 37(1)). However, while this separate and specific ground is rarely used as the sole justification for the making of a striking-out order, there have been a few cases where it has been relied on.

Note that old rule 18(7)(f) provided that only a *claim* could be struck out where it was no longer possible to have a fair hearing. However, rule 37(1)(e) allows a tribunal to strike out both claims or responses on this ground.

In what was described as a 'truly extraordinary case' – Peixoto v British 11.144 Telecommunications plc EAT 0222/07 – the EAT held that an employment tribunal had not erred in striking out claims of unfair dismissal and disability discrimination made by a claimant suffering from chronic fatigue syndrome on the basis that it was no longer possible to have a fair hearing. The claimant had indicated that she would not be physically able to give oral evidence, the case could not be decided on the documents alone, and there was no prospect of the claimant being able to proceed at any time in the future, particularly given the nature of the medical evidence, which had persistently predicted a sufficient recovery that did not in fact materialise. In the absence of any prognosis for recovery, the tribunal was unable to establish any point in the foreseeable or even distant future when a trial could take place and concluded that a fair hearing was no longer possible. This conclusion was rooted in Article 6 of the European Convention on Human Rights, which lays down the right to a fair trial, including the right to have a trial within a reasonable time. The tribunal had considered less draconian measures, but was entitled to strike out the claims on the ground that a fair trial was impossible. Accordingly, the EAT could find no error of law in the tribunal's decision and the appeal was dismissed. In reaching its conclusion, the EAT commented that those who know most about whether a fair trial is possible in an employment tribunal are those specialist members and employment judges who are there day in and day out.

609

Similarly, in Riley v Crown Prosecution Service 2013 IRLR 966, CA, the EAT upheld an employment tribunal's order striking out claims of discrimination and whistleblowing brought by a claimant suffering from depression on the basis that a fair hearing was no longer possible. The employment judge had reached this conclusion having taken account of (1) the fact that there was no prognosis of when, if ever, the claimant would be in a position to be well enough to take part in the proceedings, and (2) the balance of prejudice to either party. The Court of Appeal found no error of law in this decision and dismissed the claimant's appeal against the order. There was an agreement between medical experts that, even after two years, the probability was that the claimant would not be well enough to participate in any hearing. In the Court's view it would be wrong to expect tribunals to adjourn heavy cases, which are fixed for a substantial amount of court time many months before they are due to start, merely in the hope that a claimant's medical condition will improve. It held that if doctors cannot give any realistic prognosis of sufficient improvement within a reasonable time and the case itself deals with matters that are already in the distant past, striking out must be an option available to a tribunal.

11.145 By contrast, in Osonnaya v South West Essex Primary Care Trust EAT 0629/11 the EAT held that an employment tribunal had erred in striking out a claim on its own motion on the basis that a fair hearing was no longer possible in circumstances where a preliminary hearing, initially listed for half a day, had still not been concluded 133 hearing days later. The tribunal sat on 32 of those days, but not even all of those were effective. The claimant was not at fault in any way for this. The principal reason was her serious illness (sarcoidosis) and its effects on the timetable. At a time when the claimant's case had closed and a central witness for the respondent was under cross-examination, with two other witnesses still to be called, the employment judge held that he could see no end to the case because of the claimant's ongoing ill health, and identified prejudice in the continuing cost to the respondent and the possible absence of a witness in Tanzania. The EAT held that to say that there was 'no end in sight' was an overstatement given the stage the case had reached. The judge had been right to focus on whether continuing would cause such unfairness and prejudice to the respondent that a fair trial was no longer possible, but this was not a case like Peixoto v British Telecommunications plc (above), in which no hearing of any evidence had ever begun. It was a case in which there had been progress; slow progress, but progress nonetheless. The judge could have asked for more detailed medical advice, but did not do so, and did not sufficiently consider the use of case management powers to ensure an expeditious hearing. Therefore, the EAT remitted the matter for the preliminary hearing to continue with strict case management.

11.146 Notice requirements prior to striking out

Before any striking-out order is made under rule 37(1), notice must be given to the relevant party, allowing him or her a reasonable opportunity to make representations as to why the order should not be made – rule 37(2). As has already been mentioned, rule 37(2) provides that such representations must be considered at a hearing if the party has so requested – see 'Procedure for considering strike-out orders' above. Otherwise such representations can be made in writing and the order for strike-out may be made in the absence of the parties. In Beacard Property Management and Construction Co Ltd v Day 1984 ICR 837, EAT, the EAT held that a failure to observe the rule requiring notice to be given prior to striking out will render any order to strike out invalid. Although this case was decided under an earlier version of the tribunal rules, it is thought that this remains the position under the current Tribunal Rules.

A tribunal is not required to give *written* notice to a party against whom a striking-out order may be made if that party is given the opportunity to make representations orally. But that opportunity must be reasonable. The case of Catton v Hudson Shribman and anor EAT 111/01 suggests that in order to be reasonable the opportunity must be adequate and genuine. There, the EAT held that a tribunal which struck out an employee's claims without giving him prior written notice could not rely on the fact that the claimant had been granted 25 minutes to consider his oral response to the strike-out application in circumstances where the application took him completely by surprise. Allowing the appeal, the EAT noted that it was not appropriate to rely on the opportunity given to the party to make oral representations in place of written notice where the grounds for the application to strike out concerned conduct occurring some time before the date on which the application was heard, or had occurred over a period of time. In those circumstances it is important to ensure that a party called upon to answer accusations about such conduct has proper notice of that application and is able properly to prepare to defend him or herself.

11.147 Note that, unlike the old rules, it is only the relevant party against whom the proposed order is to be made that has the right to request a hearing to make representations. However, in accordance with the rules common to all kinds of hearing, where a hearing is held, both parties can make representations on the issue to be considered – see rule 41.

11.148 **Failure to comply with an unless order.** Rule 38(1) provides that where there is a failure to comply with an unless order the claim or response, or part, will be dismissed without further order. The tribunal has no discretion – notice has been given in the order itself and if the order is not complied with then the claim or response is struck out as at the date of non-compliance without any further procedure. A tribunal is not required to give the relevant party any further opportunity to make representations before the strike-out order is made. This corresponds to old rule 19(1), which stated that before a strike-out order was made a tribunal was required to send notice to the party inviting him or her to give reasons why the order should not be made except in circumstances where an unless order had been made.

11.149 Challenging strike-out

Under rules 70–73, tribunals have the power to 'reconsider' certain judgments, either on their own initiative or upon application by a party, where it is necessary in the interests of justice to do so (see Chapter 15, 'Reconsideration of judments and decisions', for further details). This power is similar to the power to 'review' tribunal decisions and judgments that existed under old rules 33–36. On reconsideration, the original decision may be confirmed, varied or revoked, and if revoked it can be taken again – rule 70.

Only a 'judgment' can be reconsidered, which is defined in rule 1(3)(b) as a 'decision... which finally determines a claim, or part of a claim, as regards liability, remedy or costs...; any issue which is capable of finally disposing of any claim, or part of a claim ... [or] a financial penalty under S.12A ETA'.

11.150 Clearly, therefore, case management orders – defined in rule 1(3)(a) as being 'an order or decision of any kind in relation to the conduct of proceedings' – are not capable of reconsideration, although they may be varied, suspended or set aside under rule 29 (see 'Case management orders – varying, suspending or setting aside orders' above). The striking out of a claim on any of the grounds listed in rule 37(1), on the other hand, requires the determination of an issue which is capable of finally disposing of the claim. Accordingly, a decision to strike out constitutes a 'judgment' in accordance with rule 1(3)(b) and is capable of reconsideration under rules 70–73.

11.151 **Automatic strike-out of a claim.** Questions arose under the old rules as to whether the automatic strike-out of a claim on failure to comply with a deposit order or an unless order fell within the definition of 'judgment' in old rule 28(1)(a) – 'a final determination of the proceedings or of a particular issue in those proceedings'.

In Sodexho Ltd v Gibbons 2005 ICR 1647, EAT, an employee's claim was struck out when he failed to comply with an order requiring him to pay a deposit as a precondition for proceeding with his claim. The tribunal held that the decision to strike out was capable of review under rules 34–36 (now reconsideration under rules 70–73) because it amounted to a 'judgment' and proceeded to carry out a review. When the strike-out order was set aside, the employer appealed to the EAT, arguing, among other things, that the decision to strike out the claim did not fall within the definition of a 'judgment' because it had merely been an administrative act of the tribunal involving no consideration of the merits of the case. The EAT disagreed. It ruled that a decision to strike out a claim for failure to comply with a deposit order is a final judicial determination within the meaning of a 'judgment' because its effect, if upheld, is that the claim cannot be relitigated in a tribunal. A similar issue arose in Uyanwa-Odu and anor v Schools Offices Services Ltd and anor EAT 0294/05. There, the EAT considered whether the striking out of a claim following an 'unless order' was a decision capable of review. The EAT confirmed that an unless order is akin to a conditional judgment that becomes a final determination of proceedings if and when the party fails to comply with the order and is therefore open to review. In clarifying this, the EAT also explained that although the effect of an unless order is to strike out a claim automatically for non-compliance, the tribunal does not become functus officio (i.e. without power) at this point, but retains a role in hearing the review of the strike-out decision as well as the party's application to extend time for compliance with the underlying order (in this case, serving a list of documents and witness statements).

Although these cases were decided under the old rules of procedure, the **11.152** reasoning applies equally under the new rules in relation to the slightly amended definition of 'judgment' in rule 1(3)(b). In any event, rule 38(2) provides the claimant with the right to apply to the tribunal within 14 days of the date when its claim (or part of its claim) is struck out for failure to comply with an unless order to have the order set aside on the basis that it is in the interests of justice to do so.

Strike-out of a response. Where a response is struck out, the effect is as if no **11.153** response had been presented – rule 37(3). In these circumstances, in accordance with rule 21, an employment judge will decide whether, on the available material, a determination of the claim can properly be made. The striking-out of a response does not constitute a judgment as defined in rule 1(3)(b) and therefore cannot be reconsidered under rules 70–73. Rule 21 is discussed in more detail in Chapter 6, 'Defending a claim', under 'Rule 21: "default judgments"'.

The effect is the same where a response is automatically struck out following the issue of an unless order or a deposit order – rules 38(3) and 39(4). In North Tyneside Primary Care Trust v Aynsley and ors 2009 ICR 1333, EAT, the EAT held that the striking out of a response, as opposed to a claim, for non-compliance with an unless order is merely an order – namely, an 'automatic' strike-out order – not a judgment. The striking out of a response puts the respondent in the same position as if it had failed to present one, and is, therefore, liable to have a default judgment issued against it. The Court held that this type of automatic strike-out order can, however, be varied or revoked in accordance with a tribunal's general power to manage proceedings (now contained in rule 29). (Note that new rule 38(2) also provides the respondent with the right to apply to the tribunal within 14 days of the date when the response is struck out following a failure to comply with an unless order to have the order set aside on the basis that it is in the interests of justice to do so.)

A tribunal's strike-out decision can also be challenged on appeal to the EAT (assuming an error of law can be identified) – see Chapter 16, 'The Employment Appeal Tribunal', under 'Jurisdiction of the EAT'.

11.154 Unless orders

Rule 38(1) of the Tribunal Rules 2013 provides that an order of the tribunal may specify that unless it is complied with by a specified date the claim or response (or part of it) will be dismissed without further order. This power to make what is commonly referred to as an 'unless order' was introduced in the 2004 Rules and reflects a power that the courts have had in other civil litigation for some time. It gives tribunals sharper teeth when dealing with parties who fail to conduct their case in a reasonable manner.

Where an unless order is made and the relevant party fails to comply with the order the tribunal is not required to give that party any further opportunity to make representations, as would otherwise be required under the rule 37 strike-out provisions (see 'Striking out' above), before the automatic strike-out takes effect.

11.155 Automatic strike-out

Where there is non-compliance with an unless order in 'any material respect', a tribunal has no discretion as to whether or not the claim or response should be struck out. The claim or response (or part) is automatically struck out as at the date of non-compliance and there is no requirement for a further order addressed to the party against whom the unless order was made. Therefore, the party seeking to take advantage of the unless order need not make an application for strike-out on the basis of the failure to comply – Marcan Shipping (London) Ltd v Kefalas and anor 2007 EWCA Civ 463, CA.

In Scottish Ambulance Service v Laing EATS 0038/12 an employment tribunal erred in failing to appreciate that an unless order is a conditional judgment when it held that it was not proportionate to strike out the claimant's claim for failure to comply with an unless order. The EAT held that the tribunal had erred in several respects, possibly because of confusion between the principles that applied to strike-out under rule 18(7) (now rule 37) and to unless orders under rule 13(2) (now rule 38). Looking at matters in the round or in context, considering issues of fair notice, remembering that strike-out is a power that ought not to be readily exercised, considering proportionality and reaching a decision by means of the exercise of a discretion are all features that are relevant when considering whether or not to order strike-out under what is now rule 37. They are not, however, of any relevance when considering whether or not an unless order has been complied with. According to the EAT, 'in such a case, the tribunal has already addressed the question of whether or not the deadly sword of strike out should fall on the party against whom the order is sought and decided that unless a particular direction is complied with, it should'. It upheld the appeal and the claimant's claim, which had been the subject of the unless order, was dismissed.

Partial compliance with an unless order is not enough. Thus, once the **11.156** employment judge in Royal Bank of Scotland v Abraham EAT 0305/09 had determined that there was partial non-compliance with the unless order then, subject to an application for relief from the order or an appeal, automatic strike-out of the claimant's entire case, as provided for by the order, took immediate effect. The employment judge had erred by allowing part of the case to proceed on the basis that there had been partial compliance with the order.

But compliance need not be precise and exact. The phrase used by the Court of Appeal in Marcan Shipping (London) Ltd v Kefalas and anor (above) was non-compliance in 'any material respect'. In Johnson v Oldham Metropolitan Borough Council EAT 0095/13 Mr Justice Langstaff (President of the EAT) held that the test of 'substantial compliance' adopted by the employment judge was in accordance with the law but stated that 'material' is a better word than 'substantial' because it draws attention to the purpose for which compliance with the order is sought. In that case the claimant had failed to comply with an unless order requiring her to give sufficient particulars of her claim. Langstaff P held that in such cases what is relevant, i.e. material, is whether the particulars given enable the other party to know the case it has to meet or enable the tribunal to understand what is being asserted. He said that to use the word 'substantial' runs the risk of implying that a quantitative approach should be taken when in fact a tribunal must approach the question of whether there has been compliance qualitatively. He held that the employment judge had erred by treating the touchstone of 'substantial compliance' quantitatively rather than qualitatively.

An unless order does not have to be an all-or-nothing order. Where the **11.157** consequences of non-compliance with an unless order fall for consideration, all is likely to depend on the precise terms of the order. In the Johnson case Langstaff P suggested that judges making such an order could consider tailoring it to the case in hand by, for instance, providing that any allegation not sufficiently particularised might be struck out. 'Such an order would leave it open to a subsequent judge to conclude that there had been compliance in respect of some allegations, which would not therefore automatically be struck out, even though there had been non-compliance in respect of others which were.' Where the terms of the order are not tailored to the case in hand, its affect can be draconian. In Royal Bank of Scotland v Abraham (above), for example, there were three claims under consideration: sex discrimination, disability discrimination and unfair dismissal. A consequence of a failure to provide material in respect of the first two had the consequence that all three were struck out.

Given the automatic effect of an unless order, it is important that the relevant party is given clear unequivocal notice of the order – Chukwudebelu v Chubb Security Personnel Ltd 2008 EWCA Civ 327, CA. In that case Lord Justice Pill

615

emphasised that 'it is most important if a court is to make an unless order that the fact it is being made is clearly brought home to the parties'. It is also important that it records exactly what is going to happen if it is not complied with. This did not occur in Rogers v Department for Business, Industry and Skills EAT 0251/12, where the order stated that 'unless the claimant provides the following further and better particulars of his claims for unfair dismissal, race, sex and age discrimination on or before 2 November 2011 the whole or part of his claims will be struck out'. It was not sufficiently clear what the consequences of the unless order were: it did not say that the *claim* shall be struck out, it said *the whole or part of his claims* will be struck out. This, the EAT held, left things 'hopelessly ambiguous' as to what was to happen. Therefore, the employment judge had been wrong to conclude that any claim had automatically been struck out as a consequence of any failure to comply with the order.

11.158   When a claim or response is dismissed following a failure to comply with an unless order the tribunal must give written notice to the parties confirming what has occurred. Where a response is dismissed under rule 38, the effect is as if no response had been presented – rule 38(3). This has a significant impact upon the respondent's ability to challenge the strike-out of its response (see 'Setting aside unless orders' below).

11.159   **Setting aside unless orders**
Before the date for compliance with the unless order expires, the order can be revisited by a tribunal under rule 29, either on its own initiative or on application by a party. The tribunal can then issue a further order to vary, suspend or set aside the unless order where it is considered necessary in the interests of justice (see 'Case management orders – varying, suspending or setting aside orders' above). The granting of an unless order is also appealable to the EAT on a point of law.

Once dismissal for non-compliance has taken effect, the relevant party has the right to apply to the tribunal in writing, within 14 days of the date that notice of the dismissal was sent to the parties, to have the order set aside on the basis that it is in the interests of justice to do so – rule 38(2). In Thind v Salvesen Logistics Ltd EAT 0487/09 the EAT held that while it is important for tribunals to enforce compliance with unless orders, in certain circumstances the interests of justice would best be served by granting relief to the party in default. Factors to be considered include the reason for the default, the seriousness of the default, the prejudice to the other party and whether a fair trial remains possible. In that case T's claim for disability discrimination was struck out following an unless order that required him to provide an expert medical report and a witness statement by a specified date. T's solicitors had considerable difficulty in trying to obtain a report and had to make last-minute arrangements to obtain a report from a different consultant that was lodged on the last day

616

for compliance. But unfortunately, in concentrating on obtaining the expert report, they overlooked the requirement to serve a witness statement at the same time. The disability discrimination claim was therefore automatically struck out in accordance with the unless order. The EAT overturned the strike-out. It considered that, first, the default which triggered the operation of the unless order was a straightforward oversight and in no sense deliberate. Secondly, the non-supply of the witness statement was excusable up to and until the final period on the basis that it was clearly understood that T's own witness statement was to be supplied at the same time as the expert's statement, and the problems experienced with the expert were genuine. Thirdly, the error was that of T's solicitors rather than himself. (Though this point was by no means decisive, it was a relevant consideration.) Fourthly, T applied promptly for a review of the strike-out and included the missing statement with the application. And finally, the respondent was not seriously prejudiced by the default. There was ample time to prepare adequately for the final hearing. For all these reasons the EAT held that the interests of justice required that T be granted relief from the effect of the strike-out. However, it emphasised that all such cases turn on their own facts and it should not be assumed that relief will normally be granted from the effect of an unless order.

11.160 Unless an application under rule 38(2) includes a request for a hearing, the tribunal can determine it on the basis of written representations only. If an application includes a request for a hearing, the tribunal must hold a hearing to consider it.

Rule 38(3) provides that where a response is dismissed for non-compliance with an unless order, the effect is as if no response was presented, as set out in rule 21. In these circumstances, subject only to an application under rule 38(2) (see above), an employment judge will decide whether on the available material a determination can properly be made of the claim, or part of it. If a determination can be made, a judgment will be issued accordingly. Otherwise a hearing will be fixed before a judge alone – rule 21(2). The respondent will be sent notice of any hearings and decisions of the tribunal but, unless and until an extension of time is granted, shall only be entitled to participate in any hearing to the extent permitted by the judge – rule 21(3). Rule 21 is discussed in more detail in Chapter 6, 'Defending a claim', under 'Rule 21: "default judgments"'.

11.161 In Uyanwa-Odu and anor v Schools Offices Services Ltd and anor EAT 0294/05 the EAT held that an unless order is akin to a conditional judgment that becomes a final determination of proceedings if and when the party fails to comply with the order and is therefore open to review (now reconsideration under rules 70–73) – see further Chapter 15, 'Reconsideration of tribunal judgments and decisions'. However, in North Tyneside Primary Care Trust v Aynsley and ors 2009 ICR 1333, EAT, the EAT held that this only applies in

617

relation to the striking out of a *claim* following non-compliance with an unless order. It held that the striking out of a *response* for failure to comply with an unless order is not a judgment and therefore is not capable of being reviewed (reconsidered). (But note that, in any event, the power to set aside an unless order following strike-out under rule 38(2) and the power to reconsider a judgment under rules 70–73 are subject to the same test – the 'interests of justice' test.)

The striking out of a claim or a response, or part of a claim or response, following non-compliance with an unless order can be appealed to the EAT where an error of law can be identified. Note that any appeal to the EAT requires payment of a fee of £400 once the notice of appeal has been submitted and a fee of £1,200 when the matter proceeds to a final hearing. For more information about the payment of fees in the EAT see Chapter 19, 'Fees', under 'EAT fees'.

11.162 Deposit orders

Lord Justice Underhill's review of the tribunal rules of procedure in 2012 identified a need for an effective way of managing weaker cases, while still ensuring access to justice. As things stood under the Tribunal Rules 2004, where an employment judge regarded a party's contentions as having little reasonable prospect of success, he or she could make a deposit order requiring that party to submit a deposit of £1,000 to the tribunal as a condition of continuing. However, a deposit order could only be made as a condition of a *whole* claim or response proceeding. An employment judge could not order a deposit to be paid in respect of a particular aspect of a claim or response. For example, a claim might include multiple allegations, some of which were very weak and some of which appeared much stronger. However, the tribunal had no power to distinguish between the two and was required to take an all-or-nothing approach when deciding whether to make an order.

New rule 39(1) provides that where at a preliminary hearing a tribunal considers that any specific allegation or argument in a claim or response has little reasonable prospect of success, 'it may make an order requiring a party ("the paying party") to pay a deposit not exceeding £1,000 as a condition of continuing to advance that allegation or argument'. This new power allows for more targeted case management and is likely to discourage parties, particularly claimants, from pursuing weak elements of their case. There is no suggestion that £1,000 is an overall cap on the amount a party can be ordered to pay, regardless of the number of allegations or arguments that are considered to have little reasonable prospect of success. A deposit of up to £1,000 can be ordered in respect of 'any specific allegation or argument'. It would therefore appear that a party can be ordered to pay up to £1,000 for each individual aspect of a claim or response that has little reasonable prospect of succeeding.

Grounds for making a deposit order

11.163

The threshold for making such a deposit order remains the same as under the 2004 Rules. That is, the tribunal must be satisfied that there is 'little reasonable prospect' of the particular allegation or argument succeeding. This preserves the distinction between the criterion for making a deposit order and that for striking out a case under rule 37(1)(a) on the ground that the proceedings have '*no* reasonable prospect of success' (our stress) (see 'Striking out' above). Prior to the introduction of the 2004 Rules, the same test – based on whether a case had no reasonable prospect of success – applied to both deposit and striking-out orders. This caused difficulties, particularly in light of the EAT's conclusion in HM Prison v Dolby 2003 IRLR 694, EAT, that the phrase 'no reasonable prospect of success' could not have a different meaning under the two rules, raising the question as to why, if a case was considered to have no reasonable prospect of success for the purpose of the deposit provisions, it was not simply struck out instead.

The altered criterion now replicated in rule 39(1) of the Tribunal Rules 2013 allows a tribunal to use a deposit order as a less draconian alternative to strike-out where a claim or response (or part) is perceived to be weak but could not necessarily be described as having *no* reasonable prospect of success. In fact, it is commonplace for a party making an application for strike-out on the basis that the other party's case has no reasonable prospect of success to make an application for a deposit order to be made in the alternative if the 'little reasonable prospect' test is satisfied. The test of 'little prospect of success' is plainly not as rigorous as the test of 'no reasonable prospect'. It therefore follows that a tribunal has a greater leeway when considering whether or not to order a deposit. But it must still have a proper basis for doubting the likelihood of the party being able to establish the facts essential to the claim or response – Jansen Van Rensburg v Royal Borough of Kingston-upon-Thames and ors EAT 0096/07.

In Sharma v New College Nottingham EAT 0287/11 the EAT held that an employment tribunal had erred in concluding that the claimant's race discrimination claims had little reasonable prospect of success. This conclusion had been reached solely on the basis that the contemporaneous documentation was inconsistent with a claimant's account. However, there were underlying factual disputes. The claimant was asserting that, behind the documentation, there was verbal harassment, verbal threats and aggressive bullying behaviour towards him that constituted acts which, in the absence of an acceptable explanation, the tribunal could conclude were on the ground of his race. The EAT referred to the House of Lords' decision in Anyanwu and anor v South Bank Students' Union and anor 2001 ICR 391, HL, where Lord Hope said that 'discrimination issues... should, as a general rule, be decided only after hearing the evidence'. It held that it would be illogical to require an employment judge to have a different approach, depending on whether he or she is considering

11.164

619

striking out or making an order for a deposit as either order is, on any view, a serious, and potentially fatal, course of action. Accordingly, it upheld the claimant's appeal and quashed the deposit order.

The 'little reasonable prospect' threshold was satisfied in Spring v First Capital East Ltd EAT 0567/11. There, the EAT held that an employment judge had not erred in ordering a claimant to pay a deposit of £250 as a condition of being allowed to continue with his claims. Given that the company had correctly followed the statutory retirement procedure (then in force) when it dismissed him upon reaching 65, there was little reasonable prospect of him proving that his dismissal was for a reason other than retirement, or that it was age discriminatory. The EAT rejected the claimant's submission that the judge had erred by not following the approach that applies to striking out discrimination cases, promoted by the House of Lords in Anyanwu. It held that the judge had been entitled to have regard to the likelihood of the facts being established by the claimant when making the order. The judge had applied the correct test and, having balanced the contentions on the one side against the undisputed facts on the other, the judge was entitled to conclude on the evidence that the claimant had little prospect of proving his claims at a hearing.

11.165 Procedure for making a deposit order

Prior to the Tribunal Rules 2013, a deposit order could only be made at a PHR, which was usually held in public. Now deposit orders can only be made at preliminary hearings, which, in accordance with rules 55 and 56, can be heard in private and by an employment judge sitting alone. A preliminary hearing need only be conducted in public (wholly or in part) if the hearing will involve the determination of a preliminary issue or strike-out (rule 56) and need only be conducted by a full tribunal where a preliminary issue – that is, any substantive issue which may determine liability – is to be, or may be, determined and the tribunal agrees upon application by one of the parties that it would be desirable for the hearing to be conducted by a full tribunal (rule 55) – see 'Preliminary hearings' above.

As was the case under old rule 20(2), when considering whether to make a deposit order a tribunal is required under new rule 39(2) to make reasonable inquiries into the paying party's ability to pay the deposit and have regard to any such information when deciding the amount of the deposit. If a deposit order is made, the judge's reasons for making it must be provided to the parties. The paying party must also be notified about the potential consequences of the order – rule 39(3) (see 'Potential consequences of a deposit order' below). This is a change from the old Rules, under which a deposit order did not specifically need to warn the party that he or she risked having the claim struck out – Akanu-Otu v Secretary of State for Justice EAT 0295/13.

Under old rule 20(4)(a), the relevant party was required to pay the deposit **11.166** ordered within 21 days of the day on which notice of the order was sent. The new rules do not provide for a standard time limit for a deposit to be paid. Instead, the tribunal must specify a date by which the relevant party must pay the sum ordered – rule 39(4). In practice, tribunals may well adopt a similar 21-day time period. Alternatively, they may rely on rule 66, which provides that a party is required to comply with an order for the payment of an amount of money within 14 days of the date of the order. The paying party may seek to extend the time limit for paying the deposit by virtue of rule 5, which gives tribunals discretion to order an extension of any time limit specified in the Rules or in any decision.

For the purposes of making payment, a cheque is treated as payment from the moment it arrives at the tribunal. It is not necessary for the funds to clear within the payment period, although if the cheque is subsequently dishonoured then payment will not have been validly made – Kuttapan v London Borough of Croydon and ors 1999 IRLR 349, EAT.

Under the old rules, the judge (or, where relevant, a member of the tribunal) **11.167** who conducted a PHR at which a deposit order was considered was not permitted to sit on the panel forming the tribunal at the substantive hearing – rule 18(9) Tribunal Rules 2004. This was the case whether or not an order requiring the payment of a deposit was actually made. Such restrictions on the composition of the tribunal for the purposes of a final hearing were not replicated in the Tribunal Rules 2013.

Potential consequences of a deposit order   **11.168**
Where the relevant party fails to pay by the date specified, the allegation or argument to which the deposit order relates will be struck out – rule 39(4). A tribunal has no discretion about the matter: the strike-out occurs automatically upon the failure to pay. Where a response is struck out for failure to pay a deposit, the effect is as if no response was presented, as set out in rule 21. Under rule 21 an employment judge will decide whether, on the available material, a determination can properly be made of the claim, or part of it. Where a determination can be made, a judgment shall be issued accordingly. Otherwise, a hearing will be fixed before an employment judge sitting alone. The respondent will still receive notice of any hearings and decisions but will only be entitled to participate in any hearing to the extent permitted by the judge. Rule 21 is discussed in more detail in Chapter 6, 'Defending a claim', under 'Rule 21: "default judgments"'.

Potential cost implications. If, following the making of a deposit order, the **11.169** tribunal decides the specific allegation or argument against the paying party for substantially the reasons given in the order, the paying party will be treated as having acted unreasonably in pursuing that allegation or argument for the purpose of making a costs or preparation time order under rule 76, unless the contrary is shown – rule 39(5)(a). Furthermore, the deposit will be paid to the other party (or, if there is more than one other party, shared between those parties as the tribunal orders) – rule 39(5)(b). In order words, unless the paying party successfully shows that it did not act unreasonably in pursuing the specific allegation or argument that was ultimately unsuccessful, a costs or preparation time order can be made against it. If the paying party successfully shows that it did not act unreasonably, the deposit will be refunded.

Where a costs or preparation time order is made, the amount of the deposit will count towards the settlement of that order – rule 39(6). If the amount of the costs or preparation time order is less than the amount of the deposit, any excess will be refunded to the paying party. The issue of costs is discussed in detail in Chapter 20, 'Costs and penalties'.

11.170 Challenging deposit orders

There is no right to apply under rules 70–73 for reconsideration of a deposit order, or more specifically of the amount of the deposit ordered, since such an order is not a 'judgment' for the purposes of those rules. However, a tribunal can 'vary, suspend or set aside an earlier case management order' under rule 29 and this can be relied upon to set aside a deposit order made under rule 39 (see 'Case management orders – varying, suspending or setting aside orders' above). The party against whom an order has been made can apply in accordance with rule 30 to have the order varied, suspended or set aside and may apply for a further preliminary hearing to be held.

It may also be possible to appeal to the EAT against a tribunal's decision to make a deposit order, although it will be very rare for there to be any right of appeal to the EAT against the amount of the deposit since, as the EAT ruled in Orme v South Gloucestershire Council EAT 305/97, where the judge has exercised his or her judgment in accordance with the requirements of the rules and, in particular, enquired as to the relevant party's means before making the order for a deposit to be paid, no question of law is involved. Furthermore, the cost of pursuing an appeal will (in almost all cases) significantly outweigh the amount of the deposit ordered.

11.171 The strike-out of a claim, as opposed to a response, following a claimant's failure to comply with an order to pay a deposit is a 'judgment' for the purposes of the tribunal rules and can therefore be the subject of reconsideration under rules 70–73 – Sodexho Ltd v Gibbons 2005 ICR 1647, EAT (see further Chapter 15, 'Reconsideration of tribunal judgments and decisions'). On the other hand, the strike-out of a response following the respondent's failure to comply with an order to pay a deposit is not a 'judgment' for the purposes of the provisions on reconsideration – North Tyneside Primary Care Trust v Aynsley and ors 2009 ICR 1333, EAT. It is merely an order – namely, an 'automatic' strike-out order. But this type of order can be varied or revoked in accordance with a tribunal's general power to manage proceedings under rule 29 and a respondent can therefore make an application under rule 30 for such an outcome – see 'Case management orders – varying, suspending or setting aside orders' above). (Note that, despite the distinction drawn between an 'order' and a 'judgment' for the purpose of determining which provision applies, the test a tribunal is required to employ when considering whether to vary, suspend or set aside an order under rule 29 is in fact the same as the test it is required to use when reconsidering a judgment under rule 70 – the 'interests of justice' test.)

The automatic strike-out of a claim or a response, or part of a claim or response, under rule 39 can be appealed to the EAT where an error of law is identified. As mentioned above, to appeal any decision to the EAT, the appellant is required to pay an initial fee of £400 and a further fee of £1,200 when the appeal proceeds to an oral hearing – see Chapter 19, 'Fees', under 'EAT fees'.

Miscellaneous matters

11.172

In addition to general case management issues, there are a number of further miscellaneous preliminary matters a tribunal may need to consider. These include:

- directions in respect of minors and persons of unsound mind
- directions in the event of the death of a party
- directions for the transfer of proceedings
- contempt of court
- the power to inspect premises
- non-payment of fees.

Minors and persons of unsound mind

11.173

In ordinary civil proceedings special consideration is given to minors and to persons of unsound mind, and they can neither sue nor defend actions personally. No such restrictions are imposed in relation to tribunal proceedings, however. A claimant who is under 18 can present and prosecute any complaint he or she is qualified to bring and there is no necessity for him or her to be represented by an adult.

Similarly, there are no provisions in the rules relating to persons of unsound mind. Occasionally proceedings are brought by claimants who are clearly suffering from delusions, yet all a tribunal can do is try to give them a fair hearing, especially if they are unrepresented. A tribunal does not have the same powers as a civil court in these circumstances. In Johnson v Edwardian

International Hotels Ltd EAT 0588/07 J, a kitchen porter at the Radisson Sussex hotel in London, believed that his dismissal was procured by the Watch Tower Society of Great Britain – that is, by Jehovah's Witnesses. EIH Ltd submitted that J was evidently 'delusional', that he was plainly suffering from a mental illness of some kind, and that there were serious doubts about his capacity to bring and prosecute legal proceedings. Accordingly, it sought a stay of the proceedings pending a report by the Official Solicitor on J's mental capacity. The stay was granted and the tribunal made a request for the Official Solicitor to prepare a report. J appealed against the decision. After his appeal was lodged, the Official Solicitor declined to intervene on the basis that he had no role in employment tribunal proceedings. Before the EAT, EIH Ltd submitted that although the Official Solicitor was not prepared to provide a report at the invitation of the employment tribunal, a report could be obtained by the EAT by virtue of S.29(2) of the Employment Tribunals Act 1996, which gives the EAT the same powers, rights, privileges and authority (in England and Wales) as the High Court in relation to all matters incidental to its jurisdiction.

11.174 The EAT was very doubtful that it would be right for it to obtain a report on J's mental capacity from the Official Solicitor for use by the tribunal where the tribunal was not entitled to obtain such a report in its own right. But, even if it had such a power, the EAT was not prepared to exercise it. The EAT held that there were two 'cardinal points' a tribunal must bear in mind when dealing with a litigant it believes may not have capacity to conduct the case. First, the tribunal cannot appoint a litigation friend to conduct proceedings on behalf of the party in question, as is the case under the Civil Procedure Rules. The EAT could not accept that such an order can fall under the tribunal's general power to manage proceedings (now found in rule 29). Secondly, it noted that there is in the context of High Court proceedings a presumption that a party has capacity. It held that a similar presumption should apply in the employment tribunal. Those two considerations, taken together, suggested that 'tribunals should be very wary of embarking down the road of trying to investigate a party's mental capacity'. The EAT held that in cases of suspected mental incapacity an employment judge should use his or her general case management powers, including the power to strike out all or part of a claim on the ground that it has no reasonable prospect of success.

In limited circumstances a tribunal's own assessment of a litigant's mental capacity may be relevant to the management of a case. In Kotecha v Insurety plc (t/a Capital Health Care) and ors EAT 0537/09 a tribunal had not erred in refusing to grant an adjournment of K's claim on the basis that he was mentally unfit to conduct the hearing. K had presented the tribunal with a consultant psychiatrist's report which showed that K had a depressive illness and alcohol dependency. However, the report had been written almost six years earlier and had been significantly edited by K. In the absence of any further medical evidence the tribunal permitted the hearing to proceed. During the hearing, the tribunal was presented with a medical note which stated that K suffered from mental health problems and that as a result he would be unable to present his case at the tribunal. However, the medical note had been written by a medical practitioner following a ten-minute interview with K. The EAT held that the tribunal had been well able to judge that there was no issue over K's lack of mental capacity to act in the proceedings and there was no error in law in its decision to refuse his application for an adjournment.

Deceased parties

11.175

Section 206 of the Employment Rights Act 1996 (ERA) contains provisions covering the death of an employee or an employer. Proceedings relating to statutory employment rights may still be instituted, defended or continued on behalf of a deceased party's estate:

- in the case of a deceased employer, by a personal representative (i.e. one of the executors or administrators of the deceased's estate) – S.206(1) ERA

- in the case of a deceased employee, by a personal representative or, where there is no personal representative, by any appropriate person that the tribunal appoints – S.206(3) and (4) ERA.

In the latter case, the person appointed may be either a person authorised to act for him or her by the deceased employee before death or the deceased employee's widower, widow, surviving civil partner, child, father, mother, brother or sister – S.206(5). In Kidger Preston (deceased) v A Seymour and Son COET 1140/57 the tribunal appointed the deceased's widow to institute an unfair dismissal claim. In Boys (deceased) v Skim Milk Supplies Ltd ET Case No.3942/85 the deceased had submitted a claim naming a union district official as his representative. The official was appointed to continue the proceedings as having been authorised to act by the deceased employee.

Similar provisions covering the death of an employee/worker or an employer **11.176** are found in S.292 of the Trade Union and Labour Relations (Consolidation) Act 1992 (TULR(C)A). By virtue of S.292(2) and (3), where an employee or worker dies, proceedings relating to time off work for trade union duties and activities under Ss.168–173 or to the procedure for handling redundancies under Ss.188–198 may still be instituted, defended or continued by his or her personal representative or a person appointed by the tribunal on behalf of his or her estate. Under S.292(3), a person appointed by the tribunal will be selected from the same category of people listed in S.206(5) ERA. In the case of a deceased employer, such proceedings may still be defended by a personal representative of the deceased employer – S.292(2) TULR(C)A.

Section 206(6) ERA provides that where a tribunal appoints a person to act for the deceased employee, any award made by the tribunal must be in such terms and shall be enforceable in such manner as may be provided by regulations. For

625

this purpose, the Employment Tribunals Awards (Enforcement in Case of Death) Regulations 1976 SI 1976/663 provide that where a person has been appointed, or if an employee dies before the tribunal's award is made, any award shall be made in favour of the estate of the deceased employee – Reg 4. The appointed person may enforce the award on behalf of the estate of the deceased without the grant of letters of administration or probate of any will or, in Scotland, confirmation, and the receipt of that person is a sufficient discharge to the employer for any sum payable to the estate – Reg 5. Where no such person has been appointed, an award in favour of the estate or the deceased employee is enforceable on behalf of his or her estate by the person to whom a grant of letters of administration or probate or, in Scotland, confirmation has been made – Reg 6.

11.177 The provisions of S.206 ERA and S.292 TULR(C)A do not cover all employment tribunal cases: for example, the right to written particulars of employment and the right not to suffer deductions in wages are not included. More notably, all cases under the Equality Act 2010 (EqA) are omitted. However, it was held by the Court of Appeal in Lewisham and Guys Mental Health NHS Trust v Andrews (deceased) 2000 ICR 707, CA, which concerned a claim for race discrimination brought under the Race Relations Act 1976 (now repealed and replaced by the EqA), that a claim for compensation for discrimination is a 'cause of action' within the meaning of S.1(1) of the Law Reform (Miscellaneous Provisions) Act 1934 and is therefore capable of surviving for the benefit of the deceased complainant's estate (or, as the case may be, against the deceased respondent's estate). A 'cause of action' is defined as 'a factual situation the existence of which entitled one person to obtain from the court a remedy against another person' and for this purpose an employment tribunal is a court. The same would clearly apply to actions for breach of contract and, following this decision, there does not appear to be any reason in principle why any statutory employment claim cannot be brought by, or against, a deceased party's estate, unless the contrary intention appears from the statute.

The Andrews case was referred to in Fox v British Airways plc 2013 ICR 1257, CA. There, an employee died shortly after he was dismissed on the ground of ill-health. The issue was whether a claim could be made for the lump sum death-in-service payment of around £85,000 that would have been paid to his dependants had he still been in employment at the time of his death. The Court of Appeal upheld the EAT's decision that the payment could be claimed by the deceased's father on behalf of the estate as part of unfair dismissal and discrimination proceedings. The deceased's loss was his contractual entitlement to have a sum paid to others on his death. This was a valuable benefit and the EAT rejected the notion that he did not suffer its loss because he was not alive to enjoy it. Although in ordinary cases the appropriate measure of loss will be the cost of securing insurance to provide an equivalent benefit, in the unusual circumstances of the present case, where the employee died very soon after dismissal, the loss could not be less than the full value of the payout, being around £85,000.

Transfer of proceedings
11.178

It is sometimes necessary for proceedings to be transferred from one tribunal jurisdiction to another or between different tribunal regions or between the civil courts and a tribunal.

Transfer between tribunal jurisdictions. Rule 99 of the Tribunal Rules 2013 11.179
sets out the basis upon which proceedings can be transferred between Scotland and England or Wales. Rule 99(1) allows for the transfer of proceedings to Scotland from a tribunal in England or Wales. It states that where the President or regional employment judge of the Employment Tribunals (England and Wales) believes proceedings could have been started in Scotland (in accordance with rule 8(3), which sets out the requirements for presenting a claim in Scotland) and 'would more conveniently be determined there', he or she may, with the consent of the President of the Employment Tribunals in Scotland, order that the proceedings be transferred. Such an order can be made by either the President or the regional employment judge on his or her own initiative, or upon application by either of the parties. Rule 99(2) sets out equivalent provisions governing the transfer of proceedings from Scotland to England or Wales.

Transfer within the same tribunal territory. As for transfers between different 11.180
tribunal offices within the same territory, the fixing and transfer of venue is a matter entirely within the tribunal's discretion and the appellate courts will only interfere if that discretion is exercised in a way that no tribunal, properly directed, would have exercised it – Berrendero v Suffolk Area Health Authority EAT 365/81. The most common circumstances in which a transfer between different offices is appropriate is where all or many of the parties' witnesses live in an area different from that in which the employee worked. Occasionally, a tribunal will fix the hearing to take place in the region where the employer's head office is situated, which may be some considerable distance away from the site at which the claimant was or is actually employed. Again, in these circumstances, a transfer to a nearer venue may be appropriate. However, claimants have no absolute right to have their case heard in a particular region – Faleye and anor v UK Mission Enterprise Ltd and ors EAT 0359/10.

Transfer from a court to a tribunal. Rule 101 confirms that where proceedings 11.181
are transferred to a tribunal by a court, the Tribunal Rules of Procedure apply as if the proceedings had been presented by the claimant.

Contempt of court
11.182

Contempt of court is a serious matter as it is seen as an attack on the integrity of the court and is a threat to the administration of justice. Civil contempt

627

usually takes the form of non-compliance with a court order or an undertaking given to the court. In Aspect Capital Ltd v Christensen 2010 EWHC 744, ChD, the High Court sentenced a former employee to a three-month suspended prison sentence for contempt of court for deliberately disobeying a search and seizure order in relation to documents, data and electronic storage devices.

Unlike the High Court, an employment tribunal has no power to commit a person to prison for contempt of court – O'Keefe v Southampton City Council 1988 ICR 419, EAT. However, an order for committal for contempt in an inferior court can be made by the Queen's Bench Division of the High Court under rule 81.13 of the Civil Procedure Rules 1998 SI 1998/3132 and tribunals are regarded as 'inferior courts' since they discharge a judicial rather than administrative function and have many of the features of a court of law. For example, tribunals sit in public to decide cases which affect the rights of individuals and have powers to compel the attendance of witnesses, administer oaths, control the parties' pleadings by striking out and amendment, and order disclosure of documents – Peach Grey and Co v Sommers 1995 ICR 549, QBD.

11.183 The types of situation in which contempt may arise include where a person assaults or insults the tribunal judge, or does an act calculated to prejudice the due course of justice, such as interfering with a witness. For example:

- **Peach Grey and Co v Sommers** (above): S complained of unfair constructive dismissal against his employers, a firm of solicitors. The employer alleged that S had wrongfully taken money from clients. It transpired that a third party, at the instigation of S, had made implied threats and offered a bribe to one of the witnesses to persuade him to withdraw his evidence. On the employer's application to the High Court, S was found to be in contempt of court

- **Neckles v Yorkshire Rider Ltd t/a First Huddersfield** 2002 EWCA Civ 517, CA: N's refusal to admit how a transcript of a previous tribunal hearing had come into existence, despite being faced with substantial evidence to support the contention that the transcript had been produced from an electronic recording he had made without authority, constituted contempt.

11.184 Power to inspect premises

There is no specific provision entitling tribunal members to visit the employer's premises should they feel this to be relevant, although it is a practice that has been sanctioned in equal pay cases. In Dorothy Perkins Ltd v Dance and ors v 1977 IRLR 226, EAT, the EAT laid down some general guidelines as to how tribunals might approach the question of whether a complainant and her comparator are employed on 'like work'. Mr Justice Kilner Brown stated that the tribunal should first look at the contract of employment and any job description and examine their scope. The tribunal should also hear evidence and, once the evidence has reached a stage where the relevant issues are

628

formulated, the tribunal members can then visit the premises and observe the men and women at work. Before making such a visit, however, it is necessary for the members to have clearly in mind a preliminary identification of the comparator(s) so that they can see both the general nature of the work and the specific work of the claimant(s) and nominated comparator(s). The impression gained from any such visit may be used to determine the relevant issues but the tribunal should first give the parties an opportunity to make representations in respect of the views which the tribunal members have formed – Edward Gardiner and Sons Ltd v Cassidy EAT 826/77.

Non-payment of fees   11.185

Rule 40 deals with the non-payment of all fees (except issue fees, which are dealt with in rule 11). It provides that where a party has not paid a 'relevant tribunal fee', the tribunal will send the party a notice specifying a date for payment or presentation of a remission application, failing which that particular claim or application, etc will be dismissed. Tribunal fees are discussed in Chapter 19, 'Fees'.

12 The hearing

Employment tribunals have from their inception been encouraged to maintain **12.1** simplicity and informality in their proceedings, and since 1980 the tribunal rules have expressly required this. Rule 41 of the current rules, set out in Schedule 1 to the Employment Tribunals (Constitution and Rules of Procedure) Regulations 2013 SI 2013/1237 ('the Tribunal Rules'), states that the tribunal 'shall seek to avoid undue formality' and goes on to provide that the tribunal 'is not bound by any rule of law relating to the admissibility of evidence in proceedings before the courts'. The overriding objective in rule 2 also requires the tribunal to avoid unnecessary formality and seek flexibility in the proceedings.

While there is undoubtedly more informality in tribunals than in ordinary courts, proceedings in England and Wales tend nonetheless to follow the adversarial model upon which the English legal system is based. Each party takes responsibility for the conduct of his or her own case – calling witnesses, putting relevant documents into evidence, cross-examining the opponent's witnesses and making closing legal submissions – in much the same way as in any other court of law. However, rule 41 enables the tribunal or judge to

631

question the parties or any witnesses 'so far as appropriate in order to clarify the issues or elicit the evidence', explicitly recognising a more interventionist role for the employment tribunal or judge than would be appropriate in the civil jurisdiction. Notably, this is a power, not a duty – rule 41 states that the tribunal or judge *may* pose questions in this way. This is to be contrasted with rule 14(3) of the previous Tribunal Rules, contained in Schedule 1 to the Employment Tribunals (Constitution and Rules of Procedure) Regulations 2004 SI 2004/1861, which *required* the judge or the tribunal to 'make such enquiries of persons appearing before him or it and of witnesses as he or it considers appropriate and shall otherwise conduct the hearing in such manner as he or it considers most appropriate for the clarification of the issues and generally for the just handling of the proceedings'. Thus, while there used to be a duty on the tribunal to assist the parties in establishing the material facts and drawing out the relevant issues, now there is only a power to do so. Whether there are any practical implications flowing from this change in emphasis is considered under 'Assistance by the tribunal' below.

12.2 In this chapter we begin by looking at the formalities that precede the actual hearing of a claim, including the listing of the case and the means by which a claimant may arrange to be represented. We also review the issues that might arise in the period between receipt of notice of the hearing date and the hearing itself, such as those relating to case preparation and applying for postponement if required. We then go on to consider the rules and conventions that come into play as the proceedings unfold, including the public nature of the hearing, the procedure by which evidence is given and the role of the tribunal in assisting the presentation of the claim. (The kinds of evidence that may be admitted in an employment tribunal are considered separately in Chapter 13, 'Evidence'.) Finally, we look at the general requirements imposed by the rules of natural justice and the right to a fair hearing, and the particular class of cases of unfair proceedings that involve actual or apparent bias.

It is worth bearing in mind throughout the 'overriding objective' on tribunals. When interpreting or exercising any of its powers under the Tribunal Rules, a tribunal must seek to give effect to the overriding objective, set out in rule 2 of the Tribunal Rules, which is to enable tribunals to deal with cases 'fairly and justly'. This obligation is underpinned by the common law rules of natural justice, together with the right to a fair hearing contained in Article 6(1) of the European Convention on Human Rights. These principles are considered at the end of this chapter under 'Natural justice and the right to a fair hearing'.

12.3 Listing

The parties to a tribunal claim are entitled to minimum notice of a hearing date. For a preliminary hearing, the tribunal must give the parties 'reasonable notice' of the date of the hearing and, if the preliminary hearing involves any substantive issue that may determine liability (for example, an issue as to jurisdiction or whether an employee was dismissed), at least 14 days' notice is required – rule 54 Tribunal Rules. In the case of a final hearing, which is the hearing at which the tribunal determines the claim, or such parts of it as remain outstanding following the initial consideration (or 'sift') or any preliminary hearing, the tribunal must give at least 14 days' notice – rule 58.

The 2004 Rules stated explicitly that the 14-day minimum notice of a hearing was to be calculated by reference to the date the notice was posted, not the day it was received by the party – Reg 15(5) Employment Tribunals (Constitution and Rules of Procedure) Regulations 2004 SI 2004/1861. Accordingly, a notice placed in the post on 1 October would comply with the 14-day rule in respect of a hearing on 15 October, regardless of the date on which the notice was actually received. Under the Tribunal Rules 2013, the notice of hearing is no longer treated as a special case and so the general rules governing the date on which a notice is to be taken as sent or received will apply. These are set out in rule 4, subparagraph (4) of which provides: 'Where any act is required to be, or may be, done not less than a certain number of days before or after an event, the date of that event shall not be included in the calculation.' It goes on to give the example of a party wishing to make written representations at a hearing, who is obliged, under rule 42, to present them 'not less than seven days before the hearing'. If the hearing is fixed for 8 October, the representations must be presented no later than 1 October. Adapting and applying this rule to the giving of notice of a hearing, 1 October would be the date required for notice to be 'given' in respect of a hearing listed to take place on 15 October. However, if the 'giving' of notice is equated with delivery of notice to the party, then rule 90 applies. This provides, among other things, that where a document has been delivered to a party by post, it shall generally be taken to have been received by the addressee on the day on which it would be delivered in the ordinary course of post – i.e. in the case of first-class post, usually two days after posting. This suggests that, without a special saving provision, a notice of hearing on 15 October would ordinarily have to be sent on 29 September in order to comply with rule 58 or rule 54 (where applicable).

12.4 On receipt of the notice of hearing a party is well advised to contact the tribunal as soon as possible if the date fixed for the hearing is inconvenient. An application for postponement should be accompanied by an explanation of the reason for requiring it. As shall be seen later in this chapter, it is at the discretion of the judge whether a postponement should be granted – see 'Postponements and adjournments' below.

Pre-listing enquiry
12.5

In England and Wales, Employment Tribunal Offices may use a pre-listing enquiry system in which the parties are asked to inform the tribunal within, say, seven days of all the dates on which they will be able to attend in the month

633

in which it is proposed to list the case. This system also operates throughout the whole of Scotland. Having received their replies, the listing officer will select a mutually convenient date and list the case accordingly. The pre-listing letter carries a warning that if a party fails to reply within a specified time, a hearing date will be set and it will be difficult for the defaulting party to have the date changed if he or she is unavailable.

The pre-enquiry system received judicial approval in Hewson v The Travellers' Club EAT 338/85, where Mr Justice Peter Gibson (as he then was) recommended its adoption by all Employment Tribunal Offices. Indeed, failure to adopt the procedure has in some cases led to successful appeals. In HSBC Bank plc v Da Gama EAT 0532/08 the EAT, having allowed an appeal against a tribunal's refusal to postpone a hearing to accommodate the unavailability of two key witnesses, remitted the case with an instruction for the parties to notify the tribunal of their witnesses' unavailable dates, and for the tribunal to send out a pre-listing questionnaire for dates to avoid. The EAT noted in passing that, in fixing the original hearing, the tribunal had not investigated with the parties whether there were inconvenient dates. It commented that this was understandable in light of the fact that this was a short case (a two-day hearing) but that such a practice would help to avoid appeals of this nature. Similarly, in University of East Anglia v Amaikwu EAT 0361/12 the EAT allowed an appeal against a tribunal's decision not to grant a postponement where the tribunal had not asked for dates to avoid before listing. The EAT noted the claimant's solicitor's explanation that, at the Norwich tribunal, the general practice was for the tribunal to give dates for a hearing without seeking dates to avoid, on the understanding that a prompt response asking for another date based on witness availability would be dealt with sympathetically.

12.6   As is evident from these cases, the procedure for listing cases has not been consistent across all employment tribunals (at least in England and Wales), with some tribunals giving directions first and listing later, while others send out a hearing date and directions at the same time. In so far as this variation in practice remains, this might be a suitable matter for 'Presidential Guidance', which may be issued under rule 7 – see Chapter 1, 'Employment tribunals', under 'Presidential Guidance'. Indeed, the Employment Lawyers' Association, in its response to the consultation on the draft Tribunal Rules 2013, noted the variation in listing practice and called for specific judicial guidance on the subject.

12.7 Efficiency of listing

Where a party has a particular reason for wanting a hearing to take place as soon as possible (or for delaying a hearing), he or she should contact the tribunal and ask the listing officer to take notice of his or her request when setting the case down. This may be necessary where one of the parties or a witness is due to go abroad for a long time. Similarly, concurrent legal proceedings may be a reason for having a case held out of the list for hearing until such proceedings have been determined.

In 2011, following a successful pilot in Manchester, employment tribunals in England and Wales adopted a listing policy for 'standard track' cases – typically unfair dismissal – that was intended to improve efficiency of time allocation. Such claims would automatically be listed for a one-day hearing within 16 weeks of the acceptance of the claim. Parties would then be able to apply for postponement, if necessary, and any relisting would aim to be for a date within 26 weeks of the acceptance.

Although one-day listing for an unfair dismissal claim with several witnesses **12.8** may seem optimistic to the point of unreality, some tribunal users reported back that the tight timetable can be adhered to with good case management. Certain innovations in the 2013 Rules – such as the express powers for tribunals to take witness statements as read and to impose strictly enforced limits on the time for hearing oral evidence (see 'Presenting the evidence' below) – mean that tribunals are well equipped to make efficient use of limited time.

Tribunals in Scotland have commonly used the practice of 'overlisting' in order to maximise the use of hearing rooms. This involves listing up to three hearings per hearing room, in the expectation that at least some of the cases will settle before the day of the hearing comes round. Scottish tribunal users reported that this practice had led, unsurprisingly, to an increase in the number of cases being cancelled at the last minute. It might be thought that now that fees are payable for tribunal hearings (see Chapter 19, 'Fees'), tribunal users will feel even more aggrieved if their case does not proceed on the day for want of a hearing room, and so it remains to be seen if this practice can continue. In any event, overlisting may no longer be required if, following the introduction of the fees regime, the initial trend of declining tribunal applications continues.

'Floaters'   12.9
Normally, a case will be set down for a one-day hearing. Preliminary hearings rarely take that long and may be listed as 'floaters' or 'unallocated' cases – i.e. hearings that are not given a particular starting time but which will be heard by the first tribunal that becomes free on the date specified in the notice of hearing. Because some cases are settled on the morning of the hearing, a tribunal will usually become available relatively quickly. Occasionally, however, parties are kept waiting – even until after the lunch adjournment. Since parties will not usually be told until the morning of the hearing that their case is a 'floater', it is wise to check beforehand with the tribunal listing office if, for some reason, such an arrangement would greatly inconvenience a party or any witnesses.

In 2010, when it was suggested to the Scottish National Users Group, which convenes practitioners in employment tribunals in Scotland, that a practice of

635

floating cases should be adopted instead of 'overlisting' – i.e. assigning several cases to the same hearing room and time in the expectation that many will settle before the hearing date (see 'Efficiency of listing' above) – many of the group members resisted the move on the basis that it is likely to cause wasted time and expense for the parties. Given the variation in procedure and the potential for fee-paying parties to feel aggrieved by not having a hearing on the date and time specified, this might well be an appropriate matter for Presidential Guidance.

12.10 Length of hearing

Ensuring that an accurate assessment is made of the number of days that a case will occupy is a matter of convenience for all sides: once begun, a case that has to be adjourned part-heard might not be continued for weeks or even months after the first day's hearing. The same tribunal members have to be reconvened and, since the lay members are all part time, as are some employment judges, finding mutually convenient dates can prove difficult. Moreover, the continuation date has to suit the parties, their representatives and witnesses whose evidence has not yet been heard. Furthermore, a fragmented hearing of this nature is not only inconvenient but may also be detrimental to the interests of the parties' respective cases: evidence may be forgotten and recollections blurred as events recede into the past. The way to avoid this problem is to ensure that enough time is allocated to a case in the first place. It may also help for the tribunal and parties to agree a 'timetable' for the hearing, allocating a set amount of time to each part of the proceedings, e.g. presenting the evidence, cross-examination, etc. The 'timetabling' procedure is set out in the Presidential Guidance on 'General Case Management' for England and Wales.

Now that the Tribunal Rules contain provision for a preliminary consideration of the case (see Chapter 7, 'Judicial sift'), the employment judge has a specific opportunity to consider the needs of the case and direct its listing accordingly. Rule 26(2) provides that the judge, having considered the case and decided that it can proceed, may deal with the listing of a preliminary or final hearing. Given that the sift must take account of all the documents held by the tribunal, there is an incentive for parties to make it known at an early stage if their claim relies on extensive oral evidence from several witnesses, so that the sifting judge can take this into account.

12.11 Guidance as to the way relisting should be conducted in the event of a case having to be adjourned part-heard was given by the EAT in South Glamorgan Health Authority v Gould EAT 575/90. In that case Mr Justice Wood made the general observation that decisions on listing and adjournments are essentially matters of discretion and for the internal arrangements of the particular tribunals. In the specific matter of relisting a part-heard case, consideration will have to be given to the availability of the employment judge, each of the members, the advocates, witnesses and the parties themselves. It will be fruitful for all concerned to spend some time on the last day of the previous hearing discussing dates. Clearly, the listing officer will wish to have alternative dates upon which those affected are available. If agreement cannot be reached before the parties leave the tribunal premises, the delay is likely to be much longer.

Preparing for the hearing   12.12

Where parties are legally represented, the stages involved in the detailed preparation of a tribunal case for hearing do not greatly differ from those involved in litigation generally. But while these stages may be a matter of routine for solicitors, for inexperienced parties (or lay representatives) the preparatory tactics will not be second nature. Therefore, once the date of the hearing is known, both sides should attend to the following matters:

• inform all witnesses of the hearing date, the time the hearing will begin and its venue. If an important witness cannot make the date, apply immediately for a postponement giving the reasons for the application – see 'Postponements and adjournments' below

• interview all major witnesses as early as possible and take written statements of the evidence they will give. Provide them with a copy of this in advance of the hearing, along with copies of any documents to which they are likely to be referred at the hearing. Also prepare them for what they can expect to encounter at the hearing – i.e. employment judges, lay members, oaths, cross-examination, and the general pattern which the proceedings are likely to follow

• arrange relevant documents in appropriate order and either staple them together or, if the bundle is too thick, use a ring binder or lever arch file. Where there are many documents, these are best arranged in the order in which they will be referred to. Often this will be chronological, since the documents themselves will largely tell the story – e.g. where they consist of letters of appointment, the contract of employment, memos, letters expressing grievances, warnings and the notice of dismissal they will, in themselves, indicate the events which gave rise to the dispute. Where it is possible, allow the documents to 'shape' the order of the story told to the tribunal – using the testimony of the parties and witnesses simply to explain the necessary connections between one document and the next. Bundles should be paginated and ideally have a contents list at the front detailing in columns (i) the number of each document, (ii) a brief description of it, and (iii) its page number.

• agree a common bundle of documents if possible. In form ET4 (notice of hearing), parties and their representatives are expressly enjoined to do this as a device to save time and expense and avoid duplication, and instructions as to the preparation of the bundle are also now usually included in the standard case management orders issued by tribunals. Complying with

637

this will involve both parties' representatives merging into one bundle the documents upon which they will rely. Where the employer is represented and the claimant is not, the employer's solicitors usually take on responsibility for producing copies of the agreed bundle on the day, whether voluntarily or by order of the tribunal. Seven identical bundles will be needed in all if the tribunal sits with lay members (five if not): one for each of the parties, one for each tribunal member, one for the witness table and one for the public

- if there is a dispute over which documents should be included, disputed documents should be put in a separate section or folder – see the Presidential Guidance on General Case Management' for England and Wales

- try to anticipate the evidence of the opponent and his or her witnesses and prepare points to make in cross-examination

- prepare a list of any case authorities which may be cited at the hearing and send copies of this to the tribunal and the other side. Again, this is often the subject of standard case management orders.

12.13 In legally complex cases, the parties are also now frequently required as part of the case management orders issued by the tribunal to agree between them a 'statement of issues' and to forward a copy of this to the tribunal. A statement of this kind is used to delineate the legal issues arising in a case, enabling the parties and the tribunal to focus solely on the relevant issues that fall to be decided at any preliminary or substantive hearing.

12.14 Representation

Section 6(1) of the Employment Tribunals Act 1996 (ETA) states that a person may appear before an employment tribunal in person, or be represented by counsel, a solicitor, a representative of a trade union or an employers' association, or 'any other person whom he desires to represent him'.

When employment tribunals (then called industrial tribunals) were first set up in 1965, the aim was to make them easily accessible and informal forums at which unrepresented parties would feel sufficiently at ease to conduct their own cases without any prejudice being caused by lack of representation. However, as the complexity of the law with which tribunals have to deal has increased, the extent of legal representation has grown. The prevailing situation is that representation in some shape or form is now the norm rather than the exception.

12.15 The mere fact that a party is not legally represented will not in itself give grounds for a rehearing – Dalton v Burton's Gold Medal Biscuits Ltd 1974 IRLR 45, NIRC. However, the right to choose to be represented is absolute and anything done by a tribunal which diminishes or prejudices that right will be frowned upon by an appellate court. For example, in Smith v Alsecure Guards Ltd EAT 264/82 the claimant was dismissed from his job in Liverpool by a company whose head office was in Manchester. The case was listed for hearing in Manchester and the claimant's adviser applied for a transfer of the case to Liverpool. This was refused, notwithstanding that all the relevant witnesses lived in Liverpool and the adviser could not represent the claimant if the case were heard in Manchester. The chairman stated that there was no difficulty in the claimant conducting his own case as the tribunal proceedings are informal. The case was heard, with the claimant being unrepresented, and his claim of unfair dismissal was rejected. On appeal, the EAT held that the tribunal had ignored the claimant's right to be represented.

Later, in Bache v Essex County Council 2000 ICR 313, CA, a tribunal 'sacked' a lay representative whom it felt was causing enormous delay and clouding the issues, with the result that the claimant had to represent herself. The erstwhile representative was allowed to provide assistance to the claimant but was prevented from further examining any witnesses or making submissions. On appeal, the Court of Appeal held that the right to choice of representative was unqualified and that a tribunal's power to regulate the conduct of the hearing under what is now rule 41 of the Tribunal Rules 2013 does not empower it to order a party's chosen representative to stand down.

12.16 The EAT subsequently applied Bache in Dispatch Management Services (UK) Ltd v Douglas and ors 2002 IRLR 389, EAT. In that case, the claimants were senior employees of a London-based courier business. During the course of their employment, they had retained a firm of solicitors to act for the company in certain dealings with its US parent company. The claimants were summarily dismissed in February 2001 and they instructed the same firm of solicitors to act for them in their proceedings for unfair dismissal. The respondents sought an order to have the representatives dismissed from the proceedings and for the claimants to be required to obtain different representation, arguing that there was a clear conflict of interest. Having regard to the decision in Bache, the tribunal held that S.6(1) ETA gives a party to employment tribunal proceedings an unqualified statutory right to be represented by the person of his or her choice. This view was endorsed by the EAT on appeal; it held that the tribunal chairman had correctly followed the principle established by the Court of Appeal in Bache that, in accordance with S.6(1), an employment tribunal has no power to interfere with a party's choice of representation.

Presumably, the proper course of action for a tribunal chairman who is unhappy with a representative's conduct at a hearing is to give the party notice (whether orally or in writing) to show reasons why the claim or (as the case may be) response should not be struck out under rule 37(1)(b) of the Tribunal Rules on the ground that the conduct of the case has been 'scandalous, unreasonable or vexatious'. In Harmony Healthcare plc v Drewery EAT 866/00 the EAT upheld a tribunal's decision to strike out the employer's response because its representative's conduct had been scandalous: he had caused a commotion and

639

assaulted the claimant's representative in the waiting room while trying to secure the return of his client's witness statements. However, in Bennett v Southwark London Borough Council 2002 ICR 881, CA, the Court of Appeal made it clear that before making a striking-out order on account of a representative's behaviour, a tribunal must consider whether the way in which the representative is conducting the proceedings on behalf of his or her client is scandalous, vexatious or unreasonable – not simply whether his or her conduct could be characterised as such. Moreover, the tribunal must also consider whether a striking-out order is a proportionate response. The striking out of claims is dealt with in Chapter 11, 'Case management', under 'Striking out'.

12.17 In addition, the tribunal may penalise a representative's improper, unreasonable or negligent act or omission by making a wasted costs order against that representative, although only if that representative is acting for profit – rule 80. Wasted costs orders are considered in detail in Chapter 20, 'Costs and penalties', under 'Grounds for making orders against representatives'.

The right of representation extends to the right to be represented by the person of the party's own choosing or not to be represented at all. Where a party seeks to dispense with the services of a legal representative in the course of a tribunal hearing, it is not open to the tribunal to refuse to allow this – see D'Souza v Housing Corporation, *The Times*, 13 June 1985, CA.

12.18 However, the right to be represented by the person of the party's own choosing must be consistent with the principle that justice must be carried out as quickly as possible. In Preedy v HMO Giddy t/a Easterhill Furniture EAT 0287/03 the respondent sought costs after the claimant's unfair dismissal claim was dismissed by the tribunal. However, the tribunal agreed to a postponement of the application for costs on the ground that the claimant's mother was seriously ill. When further notice was issued seeking her available dates during May 2003, the claimant's husband – who was her representative – responded that he was unavailable between 28 April and July 2003 since he was a witness in a fraud case and expected to be called to give evidence. The tribunal chairman nonetheless decided that the case would be listed in May, stating that if the claimant wanted to be represented then she would have to choose someone who was available during this period. The claimant appealed to the EAT. While noting that the practice is usually to allow parties a representative of their choice, the EAT observed that this right had to be consistent with the principle that justice must be carried out as quickly as possible, especially as not only the claimant but also the respondent and the administrative resources of the tribunal are involved. Three months' notice of the hearing had been given and the hearing had already been postponed once. It followed that there was no error in the tribunal chairman's approach.

Informal restrictions may also apply to limit the choice of representative. In Singh v London Country Bus Services Ltd 1976 IRLR 176, EAT, for example, the EAT expressed the view that it is in general undesirable for a person who was a member of a company's internal appeal body which heard the claimant's domestic appeal to represent the employer before a tribunal. Nor is it advisable for lay members of tribunals to represent individual claimant or respondent companies in the region in which they sit. The same applies to solicitors or counsel who are instructed to act in cases at tribunals where they sit as part-time employment judges. It is also desirable wherever possible to avoid having as a representative someone who will also be giving evidence. Representation will always be most effective where some measure of independence is evident between the representative and the party being represented.

Legal aid and other assistance   12.19

Legal aid is not available for representation at employment tribunals in England and Wales. Claimants in Scotland may be eligible for assistance by way of representation, subject to a means test, if the claim is too complex for him or her to present to a minimum standard of effectiveness in person. The claim must be arguable and it must be reasonable in the circumstances to grant legal aid – see the Legal Aid (Scotland) Act 1986 and the Advice and Assistance (Assistance by Way of Representation) (Scotland) Regulations 2003 SI 2003/179.

Until April 2013, it was possible for claimants in England and Wales whose income and capital savings were below certain limits to qualify for limited legal advice and assistance in relation to employment tribunal proceedings. Reforms introduced on 1 April 2013 by the Legal Aid, Sentencing and Punishment of Offenders Act 2012 have scaled back even this limited provision of publicly funded legal assistance. Now, civil legal aid for advice and assistance remains available only in respect of discrimination claims brought under the Equality Act 2010 by claimants who meet the income and savings criteria. The advice and assistance available does not extend to advocacy (i.e. oral representation) in the employment tribunal. Legal aid for advocacy in a discrimination complaint is, however, available in the EAT and higher courts, subject to the means-testing criteria – see Schedule 1 to the Legal Aid, Sentencing and Punishment of Offenders Act 2012.

Note that a number of organisations offer free advice and may provide 12.20
representation. These include Citizens Advice Bureaux, Chambers of Commerce and employers' associations, trade unions and law centres. Furthermore, in relevant cases, the Equality and Human Rights Commission may offer help and advice – in particular, in equal pay claims, the Commission has a statutory discretion under S.28 of the Equality Act 2006 to grant assistance. Finally, representation might be offered by one of the organisations providing free legal advice, case preparation and tribunal advocacy services such as the Bar Pro Bono Unit and the Free Representation Unit (although these organisations generally only accept referrals through solicitors, law centres and advice agencies).

12.21 Representation under a contingency fee arrangement

It is possible to secure representation for a claim in the employment tribunal by way of a 'damages-based agreement' (DBA), which is a kind of 'contingency fee arrangement' or, more colloquially, 'no-win, no-fee agreement'. In short, under a DBA, a solicitor will agree to act in the claim and, if successful, will take a percentage of the compensation paid to the claimant. If the claimant fails, the solicitor usually gets nothing. The use of DBAs in the employment tribunal is regulated by S.58AA of the Courts and Legal Services Act 1990 and by the Damages-based Agreements Regulations 2013 SI 2013/609, which came into force on 1 April 2013. The main conditions are set out in S.58AA(4) of the 1990 Act and Regs 5–8 of the 2013 Regulations, and include that:

- the agreement must be in writing and must not be concluded until after the representative has provided prescribed information

- the prescribed information includes the circumstances in which the client may seek a review of the representative's costs and expenses and the procedure for doing so; the dispute resolution services provided by Acas; whether and how the claim may alternatively be funded through civil legal aid, legal expenses insurance, pro bono representation or trade union representation; and the point at which expenses become payable and a reasonable estimate of their likely amount

- the sum payable in the event of a successful claim (including VAT but not including expenses and disbursements) must not be more than 35 per cent of the sum ultimately recovered by the claimant

- the representative may not terminate the agreement unless the client has behaved unreasonably. In the event of termination, the representative may not charge more than the costs and expenses of work undertaken.

12.22 It is also possible to secure tribunal representation through a 'conditional fee arrangement'. Such arrangements, which are regulated by Ss.58 and 58A of the Courts and Legal Services Act 1990, differ from DBAs in that the representative usually charges no fee or a discounted fee if the claim is unsuccessful, and charges its standard rate plus a percentage mark-up if the claim succeeds.

12.23 Non-attendance

Where a party fails to appear at a hearing, either in person or through a representative, the employment tribunal may dismiss the claim or proceed with the hearing in the absence of that party – rule 47 Tribunal Rules. Before doing so, it shall consider any information which is available to it, after any enquiries that may be practicable, about the reasons for the party's absence. The previous incarnation of this rule – rule 27(5) of the Tribunal Rules 2004 – stated specifically that the tribunal could dismiss or dispose of the proceedings in the party's absence 'or may adjourn the hearing to a later date'. Rule 47 of the Tribunal Rules 2013 does not state, in terms, that the tribunal is entitled to adjourn in the party's absence. However, the tribunal has general powers under rules 29 and 41 to make case management orders and regulate its own proceedings, which would extend to adjourning the hearing if it considered it just to do so. Given that the tribunal is obliged under rule 47 to consider the reasons for the party's absence, it is implicit that the tribunal should be able to order an adjournment if it considers that the reason is good enough to warrant one.

If a party does not intend to attend the hearing but still wishes to pursue or respond to the claim, it may wish to submit written representations for consideration by the tribunal. Rule 42 provides that the tribunal is only obliged to consider written representations delivered to the tribunal and to all other parties not less than seven days before the hearing. Whereas rule 14(6) of the 2004 Rules permitted tribunals to consider written representations submitted other than in accordance with these conditions if the tribunal considered it appropriate, tribunals are not expressly granted a similar discretion under the current rules. However, the tribunal has a general power under rule 5 to extend or shorten any time limit, and so it would be able to consider late submissions if it considered it appropriate to do so.

12.24 The weight to be attached to written representations is a matter for the tribunal and in practice it is unlikely that they will be given much weight if there is a dispute as to the facts between the parties. This is because such representations cannot be challenged in cross-examination. But if the facts are not in dispute and only legal submissions remain, then it may be appropriate to rely on written representations in deciding a case. Furthermore, where there is a good reason for the absent party's non-attendance, a tribunal may properly prefer that party's written evidence to the oral evidence of the respondent – see the judgment of Lord Justice Pitchford in Duffy v George 2013 ICR 1229, CA, in a case where the reason for the claimant's non-attendance was that she feared being cross-examined by the man whom she had accused of sexual harassment. (This case is discussed in more detail under 'Presenting the evidence – cross-examination' below.)

Two examples of cases where it was inappropriate for a tribunal to rely on written representations to decide crucial issues of fact:

- **Tesco Stores Ltd v Patel** EAT 253/85: P was dismissed for taking rancid butter from the store. He contended that he had permission to do so but the employer wholly denied this. Although unfair dismissal was conceded on procedural grounds, the conflict over the question of permission became relevant when assessing the degree, if any, of P's contribution to his dismissal. The parties opted to rely on written representations pursuant to rule 14(5) of the 2004 Rules (now rule 42 of the Tribunal Rules 2013) and the tribunal decided that it could not justify a finding of contributory

643

fault on the basis of the written representations alone. On the employer's appeal, the EAT held that the tribunal had erred. It was open to it to say that written representations carried less weight than oral evidence, or to draw an inference that the absence of oral evidence revealed that one or other of the parties had something to hide. But it was not open to the tribunal to hold that, in the absence of any oral evidence, it was simply unable to make a finding of contributory fault. The burden of proof did not rest on either party and so it was impossible to resolve the direct conflict of fact between the parties on the basis of written representations alone. In the EAT's view, it was doubtful that the provision for written representations was ever intended to be a substitute for evidence where there is a direct dispute of fact. The tribunal ought to have drawn the parties' attention to this difficulty so that they could have a chance to deal with it

- **Harris v Spring** EAT 600/87: S presented an acrimonious claim of unfair dismissal against H, a solicitor in sole practice. The tribunal found unfair dismissal with a 75 per cent contribution on S's part. H had had S's telephone tapped and the tapes of his conversations had been admitted into evidence. S did not appear before the tribunal or the EAT, but submitted extensive written representations (including affidavits) which the tribunal apparently treated as evidence. On H's appeal against the finding of unfair dismissal, the EAT held: (i) that most of the written evidence was scandalous and irrelevant, and should therefore have been excluded; and (ii) that the tribunal was wrong to decide the issues of fact partly on the basis of written representations from one of the parties, since their versions of the facts were in direct conflict. The case would be remitted with a direction that an interlocutory hearing take place in order to 'lick the evidence into shape'.

12.25 On the other hand, where the dispute is one of pure law, written representations may be more effective. In Yarrow v Edwards Chartered Accountants EAT 0116/07 the issue concerned the correct approach to calculating holiday pay. Y claimed that he was owed over £700 in holiday pay. The employer, in its response, conceded that it owed Y holiday pay but asserted that it only amounted to £350. On receipt of that response, Y wrote to the tribunal challenging the employer's assertion, arguing that the employer had based its calculation on dividing annual salary by 365, instead of by the number of working days, and had used the wrong figure for his total salary. Y did not appear at the hearing and the tribunal dismissed his claim, apparently without taking into account his letter. The EAT allowed Y's appeal on the basis that the chairman had not taken into account written representations that had been validly presented. It also noted that one of the tribunal chairman's reasons for dismissing the claim was that the claimant was not present to adduce evidence or documents. However, the principal issue between the parties was not one of fact, but of law. The EAT was therefore able to resolve the question itself and substituted a judgment awarding Y the sum claimed.

644

Proceeding in a party's absence   12.26

It has long been good practice for a tribunal, before proceeding in a party's absence, to try to contact the absent party by telephone at his or her house, workplace or last known address, and this practice has received judicial approval – Southwark London Borough Council v Bartholomew 2004 ICR 358, EAT. Although a tribunal is not required to make telephone enquiries of an absent party in every case, it should at least consider doing so, and in the ordinary course it is best practice to make such enquiries unless there is a good reason not to, particularly where solicitors are on record or there is some doubt as to whether notice of the hearing has been received – Cooke v Glenrose Fish Co 2004 ICR 1188, EAT. The EAT went further in Quashie v Methodist Homes Housing Association 2012 ICR 1330, EAT, holding that the tribunal was in error in failing to make a call to enquire why a claimant had not made written submissions, having been directed to do so in an adjourned hearing. The EAT held that the situation was analogous to non-attendance, as considered in Bartholomew and Cooke, and that it was unsafe and perverse for the tribunal to assume that the claimant had decided not to file a submission instead of enquiring as to the reason for the lack of written representations.

Since the Tribunal Rules 2013 came into force, the practice has been given statutory support. Rule 47, which sets out the tribunal's options when faced with the non-attendance of a party, states that the tribunal may dismiss or continue with the proceedings only after taking into account any information in its possession about the reasons for the party's absence, 'after any enquiries that may be practicable'. Although this rule appeared in similar form in rule 27(5) and (6) of the Tribunal Rules 2004, the explicit requirement on the tribunal to make practicable enquiries is new. The cases cited above may still be useful as guides to tribunals on how to proceed in such circumstances. For example, in Cooke v Glenrose Fish Co (above), the EAT stated that the tribunal must enquire of the other party – particularly one that is represented – what news there is of the absent party and whether it is possible that the absent party was delayed or had forgotten about the matter but was, so far as could be understood, intending to come.

If contact is made with a colleague, relative or the party him or herself, then the   12.27
tribunal will normally allow the party, if he or she is already on the way or expresses an intention to attend, to arrive before proceeding. The tribunal may decide to occupy itself by taking a 'floater', or may simply wait until the absent party arrives. If, when contact is made, the party has a good explanation for not being able to attend, then the tribunal will usually adjourn the hearing to a future date. A party who cannot provide a good reason for not attending almost certainly risks having the case decided in his or her absence.

If contact is not made with a party who has failed to turn up, then the tribunal will have to decide whether to adjourn the hearing or to proceed in the party's

645

absence. If the tribunal decides to proceed in a party's absence it may, at its discretion, hear the oral evidence and witnesses of the party or parties who are in attendance. In Goomany v Degnan EAT 260/91 the respondent failed to appear at the scheduled unfair dismissal hearing and the tribunal, having made telephone enquiries, proceeded without him and found for the claimant. On appeal, the EAT held that the tribunal had not erred in exercising its discretion to proceed in this way. However, there is no duty on the tribunal to turn itself into an investigating forum and to take upon itself the responsibility of cross-examination or playing devil's advocate in place of the absent party. As Mr Justice May said in Mason v Hamer EAT 161/81: 'It is not... the duty of any [employment] tribunal to enter the arena and seek to act as the friend of one party or another in deciding the case put before [it]... We have in this country an adversarial system... and that applies in [employment] tribunals as it does in our courts.'

12.28 As for any written material that may be before the tribunal, this should be taken into account by the tribunal if it proceeds to dispose of the case, although rule 47 is not absolutely clear in this regard. Under rule 27(6) of the 2004 Rules, the tribunal had to consider 'any information in its possession which has been made available to it by the parties' before dismissing or disposing of the proceedings. This meant that the tribunal was obliged to take into account any written material that the absent party had already submitted, as the rule was clearly wide enough to require consideration of any arguments and written representations relating to the merits of the claim. Under current rule 47, the tribunal is required to consider 'any information which is available to it, after any enquiries that may be practicable, *about the reasons for the party's absence*' (our emphasis). This is, therefore, less wide-ranging, being expressly limited to consideration of the reasons for the party's absence rather than, for example, the merits of the claim or the complexity of the facts. However, rule 42 is clear that any written representations submitted at least seven days before the hearing must be taken into account, and this applies equally to representations submitted by a party who does not intend to appear.

The tribunal can decide to dismiss the claimant's claim in his or her absence or uphold the claim in the respondent's absence and make a costs or preparation time order against the absent party – see Chapter 20, 'Costs and penalties', under 'What orders can an employment tribunal make?'. The non-appearance of a party without prior explanation is a frequent ground upon which costs are awarded in tribunal proceedings.

12.29 Note that the absent party may be able to apply for a reconsideration of the tribunal's decision if the case is decided in its absence. Under the previous 'review' procedure provided for in the 2004 Rules, it was possible to apply for review of a decision on a number of grounds, one of which was that the decision was made in the absence of a party – rule 34(3)(c) 2004 Rules. The review procedure has been re-enacted as the 'reconsideration' procedure in rules 70–73 of the 2013 Rules but there is no longer a list of specific grounds on which reconsideration may be sought, comparable to that contained in old rule 34(3). Instead, a tribunal may reconsider any judgment if it is 'necessary in the interests of justice' to do so – rule 70. This general ground would certainly accommodate an application for reconsideration on the basis that there was a good reason for the party's absence, or the absence was beyond the party's control. Reconsideration is considered in detail in Chapter 15, 'Reconsideration of tribunal judgments and decisions'.

If the tribunal decides to proceed in a party's absence it should follow through on that decision. In Deman v Coates EAT 0468/05 one of the respondents, C, did not appear for the final four days of an adjourned hearing because of ill health. The tribunal carefully considered whether to adjourn the case further in her absence and decided against it. It went on to conclude that D's discrimination claim against C was well founded. The tribunal rejected a review of that decision – also in C's absence – but then dismissed the claim against C at the remedy hearing, which C did not attend either. Its reasoning was that it would not now be just and equitable to make any award against C as she was unlikely to have the opportunity, within a reasonable time, to argue her case on remedy. The EAT overturned that decision on appeal. It noted that it was the first case in its experience where a tribunal had found that the claimant should succeed on liability but then dismissed the claim at the remedies hearing. A liability hearing is much more factually complicated than a remedies hearing and it can be said that a party's ability to be present at a liability hearing is much more important than at a remedies hearing. The EAT accordingly decided to reinstate the claim against C and remit it to a fresh tribunal for consideration of compensation.

Postponements and adjournments 12.30

Whereas, under rule 10(2)(m) of the Tribunal Rules 2004, an employment judge or tribunal was specifically accorded the power to postpone or adjourn a hearing, there is no such express power in the Tribunal Rules 2013. This is because much of the detail of the old rules has been intentionally dropped in favour of more general powers – indeed, the list of 19 examples of the kinds of order that a tribunal or judge may make, which used to be in old rule 10(2), has not been maintained in the same form in the 2013 Rules. Instead, rule 29 states that 'the tribunal may at any stage of the proceedings, on its own initiative or on application, make a case management order', defined in rule 1(3)(a) as 'an order or decision of any kind in relation to the conduct of proceedings'. Rule 29 goes on to state that 'the particular powers identified in the following rules [i.e. rules 30–40] do not restrict that general power'. Accordingly, tribunals have a general power to make orders regulating the procedure of the case, which can undoubtedly include orders for postponement and adjournment.

647

The Presidential Guidance on seeking a postponement of a hearing, published under rule 7 of the 2013 Rules, confirms that this is the case.

Furthermore, although the power to postpone or adjourn is no longer expressly recognised in the rules, the impact of such an order on costs is still dealt with. Rule 76(2) gives tribunals specific power to make a costs award or a preparation time award if, among other things, 'a hearing has been postponed or adjourned on the application of a party'. In addition, rule 76(3) *requires* the tribunal to make a costs or preparation time award in relation to an adjournment or postponement caused by the respondent's failure, in unfair dismissal proceedings, to provide reasonable evidence relating to the feasibility of reinstatement or re-engagement, where such has been requested by the claimant. These powers, which were previously contained in rules 39, 40(1), 43 and 44(1) of the 2004 Rules, are discussed in detail in Chapter 20, 'Costs and penalties', under 'Grounds for making orders against a party – postponements and adjournments'.

12.31 Although the terms are sometimes used interchangeably by courts and tribunals, in this chapter we will take 'postponement' to mean the deferral of a hearing date before the hearing has started, and 'adjournment' to mean deferral of any further hearing once proceedings have begun. Although adjournments therefore only arise once the proceedings have started, not beforehand, we deal with them alongside postponements in this section for convenience. Another related term is a 'stay' of proceedings (known as a 'sist' in Scotland), which means the temporary suspension of the proceedings in their entirety. This usually occurs when the issues in dispute in the case are also being considered in another court in concurrent litigation or criminal proceedings. Stays are considered in Chapter 11, 'Case management', under 'Stay of proceedings'.

12.32 Applying for postponement or adjournment

An order for postponement or adjournment may be sought in the same way as any other kind of case management order. Rule 30 of the Tribunal Rules sets out the relevant conditions, which are simply that a party's application for an order may either be made at a hearing or be presented in writing to the tribunal (rule 30(1)); and that, if the party is applying in writing, he or she shall notify the other parties that any objections to the application should be sent to the tribunal as soon as possible (rule 30(2)). Although this rule does not expressly require notification of the application itself to be given to the other party, rule 92 is relevant in this context. It states that 'where a party sends a communication to the tribunal (except an application under rule 32) it shall send a copy to all other parties, and state that it has done so (by use of "cc" or otherwise)'. The tribunal may order a departure from this requirement where it considers it in the interests of justice to do so. Therefore, a combination of rules 30 and 92 requires that an application for postponement or adjournment, if it

648

is to be made in writing, be made to the tribunal and copied to the other party, along with notification to the other party of how to object.

It is important to note that the requirement to copy the application to the other side(s), and inform them of the means by which they may object, now applies to all parties, whether represented or not. Under the 2004 Rules, notification to the other parties only had to be given by the applicant (or his or her representative) if he or she was legally represented. Otherwise, the notification would be given by the Tribunal Secretary. There is no equivalent provision in the 2013 Rules and so the obligations set out by rules 30 and 92 fall on the applicant him or herself, even if acting in person.

There is no rule on the timing of an application for postponement or **12.33** adjournment. It used to be the case under rule 11(2) of the 2004 Rules that an application for any kind of case management order had to be made not less than ten days before the date of the hearing at which it was to be considered, unless it was not reasonably practicable to do so or the employment judge or tribunal considered it to be in the interests of justice to permit shorter notice. Under the 2013 Rules, only particular kinds of application – such as those for reconsideration – are subject to time limits for presentation, and there is no general rule on the timing of other kinds of application. Similarly, there is now no particular rule on the content of the application. Rule 11(2) and (3) of the 2004 Rules was prescriptive in this regard, requiring that any application for a case management order be made in writing, include the case number of the proceedings and the reason for the request, and contain an explanation of how the order sought would help the tribunal to deal with the proceedings efficiently and fairly. There is no equivalent provision in the 2013 Rules. However, the Presidential Guidance does state that this is still expected and indicates that an application will not ordinarily be considered if such information is not provided – see 'Presidential Guidance on applying for a postponement', below.

In the absence of specific rules on timing and content, general considerations of procedural fairness and common-sense case management apply. Although parties are not specifically required by the Tribunal Rules themselves to give any particular information, it is in their interests to set out the reasons why the postponement or adjournment ought to be granted, since the judge or tribunal is under no statutory duty to hold a hearing or make any enquiries before deciding the application. It is therefore in the parties' interests to make the case for the postponement or adjournment as strongly as possible in the application. Furthermore, the relevant Presidential Guidance states that the inclusion of such information is ordinarily required – see 'Presidential Guidance on applying for a postponement', below. As for timing, it is worth bearing in mind that, as noted above, tribunals are able to award costs in respect of a postponed or adjourned hearing under rule 76(2). The power is discretionary and tribunals can be expected to be more willing to exercise it where the

649

application has been made at the last minute without good excuse – see, for example, Jones v Standard Life Employee Services Ltd EATS 0034/13, where the EAT approved a tribunal's decision to award the costs of a Monday hearing when the claimant only put in his application for postponement at 16:55 on the previous Friday.

12.34 **Presidential Guidance on applying for a postponement.** As explained in Chapter 1, 'Employment tribunals', under 'Presidential Guidance', the Tribunal Rules 2013 allow the Presidents of the employment tribunals (one for England and Wales, one for Scotland) to issue Guidance on matters of practice – rule 7. Although the Guidance is not binding on tribunals, they are required to have regard to it. As such, the Guidance gives a reliable indication of how tribunals can be expected to deal with practical issues in a case.

Presidential Guidance has been issued on the procedure for applying for a postponement. There are two separate sets of Guidance – one that applies in England and Wales, issued on 4 December 2013 (and which presumably took effect from that date), and a more detailed one that applies in Scotland, which is stated to have effect from 1 February 2014. The procedural steps laid out in each set of Guidance are similar but not identical.

12.35 Both sets of Guidance indicate that an application should ordinarily be made in writing to the relevant employment tribunal office. The application should state the reason why it is being made and explain why the party making it considers that it would be in accordance with the overriding objective for the tribunal to grant the postponement. This replicates the position under the Tribunal Rules 2004 but, as noted above, was not included in the Tribunal Rules 2013. If the application is in writing, the applicant must notify all other parties that any objections should be sent to the tribunal as soon as possible. (Note that this aspect of the Guidance is actually a requirement of the Tribunal Rules 2013, set out at rule 30(2).) The applicant should provide all relevant documents.

The English and Welsh Guidance states that if *any* of these requirements are not complied with, the application will 'ordinarily' not be considered unless there are exceptional circumstances, in which case an explanation of the non-compliance and the exceptional circumstances should be given. The Scottish Guidance is not quite as draconian – stating that if an application has not been copied to the other side it will not be considered other than in exceptional circumstances. This implies that an application *will* be considered even if it does not include reasons and an explanation of how the postponement would be in accordance with the overriding objective. This more accurately reflects the position under the Tribunal Rules themselves since, as noted above, the Rules are no longer prescriptive about the content of an application and only the notification requirements are mandatory.

Both sets of Guidance state that a party wishing to apply for postponement **12.36** should, wherever possible, try to discuss the proposal with the other parties, although the Scottish Guidance suggests that this need only be done where the applicant is legally represented. Details of any such discussion should be provided to the tribunal, and the parties should indicate if there has been any agreement between them. Both sets of Guidance note that, where the hearing in question has been fixed by agreement with the parties, that fact will be taken into account by the employment judge considering the application.

As for the employment judge's duties in response to a postponement application, the English and Welsh Guidance states that, where the appropriate information has been supplied, the judge will deal with the application as soon as applicable. Both sets of Guidance state that if the information has not been supplied the employment judge may make further enquiries of the applicant, which will delay the consideration of the application. Once all the relevant information has been gathered, the judge will take account of all matters and information available in making the decision whether to grant the adjournment. Both sets of Guidance make clear that the decision is nonetheless at the discretion of the judge concerned.

Tribunal postponing or adjourning of its own motion   12.37
The availability under the Tribunal Rules of an order for postponement or adjournment is not simply a matter of administrative convenience. One of the objectives of the Rules as a whole is to enable tribunals and judges to protect the right to a fair trial. In this regard, parties to litigation are entitled to rely on the rules of natural justice and Article 6 of the European Convention on Human Rights. One aspect of these principles of fairness in litigation is that every party should be permitted to present his or her case fully and openly. The possibility of postponement or adjournment might, in some cases, be essential to enable a party to put his or her case fully, such as by preparing for an issue or evidence that has come out during the course of the hearing, or securing representation where a representative has become unavailable at the last minute. Not all obstacles in the parties' way can or should be overcome with a postponement or adjournment, of course, and it will be for the tribunal to decide in each case whether the delay would be fair to all parties. However, the right to a fair trial and the interests of justice may, in some cases, compel the tribunal or judge to consider postponing or adjourning even in the absence of any specific application by one of the parties.

As noted under 'Non-attendance – proceeding in a party's absence' above, where a party does not attend and is not represented at a hearing, the tribunal may dismiss the claim or proceed without the party, but must consider any information which is available to it, after any enquiries that may be practicable, about the reasons for the party's absence – rule 47. Although this rule appeared in similar form in rule 27(5) and (6) of the Tribunal Rules 2004, the requirement

651

on the tribunal to make any enquiries that are practicable is new. Although many tribunals would have done this anyway under the previous regime, there is now specific recognition of the onus on the tribunal to undertake some, albeit limited, investigation of why a party has not attended on the day of the hearing. If the tribunal discovers that the reason is a good one, then it must at least consider adjourning the proceedings.

12.38 Where the case for adjournment is sufficiently pressing, the tribunal might invite the relevant party to apply for such (if present). Alternatively, the tribunal might be required to infer an application for adjournment from the parties' conduct. In Hemming v British Waterways Board EAT 0102/13 the claimant did not turn up on the first day of an eight-day hearing. At around midday, the tribunal received an e-mail from the claimant's former husband informing it that she had been taken to Accident and Emergency. The tribunal directed the former husband to provide proof of the claimant's hospital admission by 2 pm that day. After he refused, pointing out that it was not practicable to do so in such a short space of time, the tribunal acceded to the respondent's application to have the claim struck out. It went on to award costs of £10,000 against the claimant in respect of the lost hearing time. On appeal, the EAT overturned all of these decisions. It held that the decision to strike out was made without proper notice to the claimant, rendering the decision a nullity. Although that determined the appeal, the EAT went on to state that, in any event, the tribunal erred in law in its response to being informed of the reasons for the claimant's non-attendance. The tribunal should have dealt with the former husband's e-mail as an application to adjourn the day's proceedings. Had it done so, the only proper course available to it would have been to grant the adjournment. It was wholly unreasonable of the tribunal to demand a medical report within the timescale given. The appropriate response would have been to adjourn to the morning of the next day, when a proper decision could be taken on whether to adjourn further or to strike out the claim.

As the Hemming case demonstrates, the possibility of adjournment is particularly important where the tribunal is considering striking out the claim. In Ridsdill and ors v D Smith and Nephew Medical and ors EAT 0704/05 the claimants had failed to comply with a number of case management orders and, at a pre-hearing review a week before the date set for the full hearing, the chairman struck out the claimants' claims on the basis that there could not be a fair hearing. The claimants appealed, arguing that the chairman had not taken the structured and proportionate approach advocated by the Court of Appeal in Blockbuster Entertainment Ltd v James 2006 IRLR 630, CA, and had narrowed the question of whether there could be a fair trial to whether there could be a fair trial on the dates already listed for full hearing. The EAT allowed the appeal. It agreed that the chairman had erred by restricting his consideration of whether a fair trial was possible to a 'fixed moment of fairness'.

He had failed to consider whether, in all the circumstances, a fair trial would still be possible if the proceedings were adjourned to another date and appropriate directions given for pre-trial preparation. The failure of either party to formally seek an adjournment did not bar the chairman from considering it as an option.

A tribunal might also be required to consider adjourning, or to invite a party to **12.39** apply for adjournment, where it is necessary to clarify the way in which the claim is being put. In Land Rover v Short EAT 0496/10 the EAT allowed an appeal against a tribunal's decision in a reasonable adjustments claim because the tribunal had not clarified whether one particular adjustment was part of the claim. The suggestion that the employer should have considered moving another employee out of his or her role, in order to accommodate the disabled employee in suitable alternative employment, came up during the claimant's evidence but was not specifically stated in the list of agreed issues before the tribunal. The EAT held that the tribunal was wrong to go ahead and determine the claim, including this point. It should first have made a clear ruling on whether the point was properly before it and, if not, whether the claim should be amended so as to include it. Failure to do so meant that the respondent was deprived of the opportunity to apply for an adjournment in order to call evidence and prepare for the issue.

Exercise of general discretion   **12.40**
The Tribunal Rules 2013 contain no general guidance on the factors that a tribunal or judge must consider when deciding whether to order a postponement or adjournment and so it is left to case law to fill the gap. The Court of Appeal established in Teinaz v London Borough of Wandsworth 2002 ICR 1471, CA – considering the Employment Tribunals (Constitution and Rules of Procedure) Regulations 1993 SI 1993/2687, which also contained no guidance on this point – that while the discretion is broad, it must be exercised judicially. As Mr Justice Langstaff, President of the EAT, put it in Pye v Queen Mary University of London EAT 0374/11, the discretion must be exercised 'with due regard to reason, relevance and fairness', and subject to the overriding objective. Under the current rule 2, the overriding objective includes 'avoiding delay' and 'saving expense'.

Some of the main grounds on which a postponement or adjournment may be sought are considered in the sections that follow. More generally, the interests of justice and the right to a fair trial, as set out in Article 6 of the European Convention on Human Rights (given effect in domestic law by the Human Rights Act 1998), will usually be the peg on which the applicant hangs his or her application, arguing that a postponement or adjournment is required to enable him or her to present his or her case as effectively as possible.

— 653

12.41 As will become apparent from the rest of this section, the kinds of factor that may be taken into account by tribunals in deciding whether to order a postponement or adjournment include:

- the degree of prejudice to the other side

- whether the parties had any say in the original listing date (e.g. by being asked for their dates to avoid)

- whether the case has previously been postponed or adjourned and the length of time the case has been waiting to be heard

- in the case of a party who is unable to attend though illness, the prospect of that party being well enough to attend within a reasonable time.

Furthermore, both the English and Welsh and the Scottish Presidential Guidance on seeking a postponement of a hearing indicate that, where the hearing sought to be postponed has been fixed after consultation with the parties, that matter will be taken into account by the employment judge hearing the postponement application. The Scottish Guidance notes that, where the postponement is sought because of the unavailability of a party, witness or representative, it will be relevant whether that unavailability was known when the parties discussed listing.

12.42 Grounds on which tribunal's decision might be appealed. Given that a decision whether to postpone or adjourn is one for the tribunal's discretion, and bearing in mind the respect to which tribunals' decisions on case management questions are usually entitled, it will not be easy to appeal successfully against a refusal or grant of a postponement or adjournment. The EAT has stressed that, in general, appeals against interim orders and directions are to be 'deplored' unless a clear case is made out showing the employment judge's decision to be misdirected in law or perverse in the result – R Mansell Ltd v Curry 1983 ICR 798, EAT. This is reflected in the Employment Appeal Tribunal Practice Direction 2013, which notes, at para 13.6.2, that 'employment judges and employment tribunals are themselves obliged to observe the overriding objective and are given wide powers and duties of case management... so appeals in respect of conduct of employment tribunals, which is in exercise of those powers and duties, are the less likely to succeed'.

Until recently, there had been some uncertainty over the proper approach for the EAT (and higher courts) to take when considering a tribunal's refusal or grant of a postponement or adjournment order. The Court of Appeal in Teinaz v London Borough of Wandsworth 2002 ICR 1471, CA, and Andreou v Lord Chancellor's Department 2002 IRLR 728, CA, apparently approached the cases before them on a 'Wednesbury unreasonableness' basis, looking only to intervene if the first instance decision was reached on the basis of an error of law or was perverse. (The approach derives from the judicial review case

654

Associated Provincial Picture Houses Ltd v Wednesbury Corporation 1948 1 KB 223, CA.) However, the Court of Appeal in both Terluk v Berezovsky 2010 EWCA Civ 1345, CA, and Osborn v Parole Board 2010 EWCA Civ 1409, CA, suggested that it was for the appellate court to decide for itself whether the first instance decision was the right one. Although neither case concerned employment tribunal proceedings, the EAT in O'Cathail v Transport for London 2012 ICR 561, EAT, took the view that there was nothing in those judgments that warranted confining the approach they endorsed to civil court jurisdiction. Accordingly, on this reading, it would be for the EAT to consider whether the tribunal's decision to grant or refuse an adjournment imperilled the fairness of the proceedings as a whole. The difference between the two approaches, in short, is that the Terluk approach allows the EAT to make its own discretionary decision on appeal, whereas the Teinaz approach prevents the EAT from intervening unless the tribunal's decision took account of irrelevant factors, failed to take account of relevant factors, or was perverse.

12.43 The correct approach was established when the Court of Appeal overturned the EAT's decision in O'Cathail – see O'Cathail v Transport for London 2013 ICR 614, CA. There, the Court held that Terluk v Berezovsky (above) could be distinguished from Teinaz v London Borough of Wandsworth (above) on the basis that Terluk was concerned with civil proceedings governed by the Civil Procedure Rules 1998 SI 1998/3132. Under the CPR, appeals are normally by way of review, and the decision of the lower court can be set aside if wrong or unjust by reason of a serious procedural or other irregularity in the proceedings. Appeals against employment tribunals' decisions, in contrast, are available on a point of law only. Accordingly, the Wednesbury approach is now established as the correct one for the EAT to follow and tribunal decisions will only be susceptible to challenge on appeal if there was 'an error of legal principle in the approach or perversity in the outcome', in the words of Lord Justice Mummery. In any event, as Mummery LJ noted, in the vast majority of cases the outcome will in practice be the same whichever approach is taken.

The O'Cathail case itself is a good illustration of the limited scope for appellate intervention in a case management decision. The claimant had already been granted an adjournment on medical grounds of the original hearing date for his various discrimination claims. The case was listed to be heard over five days. On the first day of the new hearing date, the claimant applied for a fresh adjournment on the ground that he was unfit to attend. The tribunal refused the application. He made further applications on the second and third days of hearing, producing a letter from his GP stating that he was suffering from a respiratory infection, which was being treated with antibiotics, and that he was unfit to attend. The tribunal refused the further applications and continued with the hearing in the claimant's absence. The tribunal decided that it was 'a very rare case' in which it was more unfair not to proceed than it would be to adjourn. However, it took into account that the proceedings were stale, having

655

been issued over 18 months previously; that there had been a previous adjournment; that two of the employer's witnesses had already become unavailable and a third was likely to become unavailable if the hearing were postponed; that the delays in determining the claim affected the determination of other pending claims and an internal appeal; that costs would be wasted if the matter were postponed; that the amount claimed was limited to a modest award for injury to feelings; that considerable tribunal resources had been dedicated to the claim; that the postponement would have an effect on other claims awaiting adjudication by the tribunal; and that many of the claims relied on documentary material rather than on oral evidence and could be fairly determined by the tribunal without the need for the claimant's evidence and submissions. The EAT allowed the claimant's appeal against the refusal but the Court of Appeal restored the tribunal's decision. Mummery LJ was impressed by the 'most anxious consideration' that the tribunal gave to taking the 'exceptional step of refusing an adjournment applied for on unchallenged medical grounds'.

12.44 Note that an appeal on the ground that the tribunal failed to take into account a relevant consideration does not have to show that the failure was the fault of the tribunal. In Abbey National plc v Bascetta EAT 0478/08 the EAT held that a judge's decision to refuse a postponement was made on the basis of an error of law that was no fault of his own. The error arose because the claimant (who opposed the postponement) failed to inform the judge of a relevant factor – namely, that she was at the same time seeking to delay the hearing of a substantive appeal in the EAT.

12.45 Tribunal's duty to give reasons

Under the Tribunal Rules 2004 there was no general requirement for a tribunal to record reasons for its case management decisions, including decisions whether to postpone or adjourn a hearing. Under rule 30 of those Rules the tribunal was only required to provide a party with reasons for a case management order if the party specifically requested them. Unsurprisingly, this could lead to confusion when it came to challenging a decision on appeal. The EAT in Okoro and anor v Taylor Woodrow Construction Ltd and ors EAT 0318/10 acknowledged that it was best practice for an employment judge making an important procedural decision to keep a note of his or her decision and record the reasons for it. However, in the absence of a specific requirement, there was always the risk that this formality would be overlooked.

The Tribunal Rules 2013 now extend the circumstances in which reasons must be given, and comprehensively explain the extent of the tribunal's obligations in this regard. Rule 62 provides, with regard to the giving of reasons for case management decisions, that:

- the tribunal shall give reasons for its decision on any disputed issue, whether substantive or procedural

- in the case of a decision given in writing the reasons shall also be given in writing. In the case of a decision announced at a hearing the reasons may be given orally at the hearing or reserved to be given in writing later

- where reasons have been given orally, the employment judge shall announce that written reasons will not be provided unless they are asked for by any party at the hearing itself or by a written request presented by any party within 14 days of the sending of the written record of the decision. The written record of the decision shall repeat that information. If no such request is received, the tribunal shall provide written reasons only if requested to do so by the EAT or a court

- the reasons given for any decision shall be proportionate to the significance of the issue and for decisions other than judgments may be very short.

12.46 In general, therefore, the parties will be entitled to reasons for an order postponing or adjourning a hearing. Note, though, that the duty to give reasons only relates to the tribunal's decisions on 'disputed' issues. Presumably, if the postponement or adjournment is ordered with both parties' agreement, reasons are not required. More significantly, if the decision is made in the absence of one of the parties, that party cannot be said to have disputed the proposal to postpone or adjourn and so reasons may not be required in this case either. This may make it difficult for an absent party to challenge a refusal to postpone or adjourn.

The requirement to give reasons for case management orders is dealt with more generally in Chapter 11, 'Case management', under 'Case management orders – decisions and reasons'.

Ill health of parties

12.47 The Court of Appeal suggested in Teinaz v London Borough of Wandsworth 2002 ICR 1471, CA, that the right to a fair trial under Article 6 of the European Convention on Human Rights (ECHR) will usually require a postponement when a litigant cannot attend a scheduled hearing through no fault of his or her own, however inconvenient this may be to the tribunal or the other parties. In that case, the employment tribunal refused an application to adjourn on the basis of ill health despite that application being accompanied by a medical certificate stating that the claimant should not attend the tribunal hearing due to severe stress. The tribunal doubted the accuracy of the doctor's letter and decided that the claimant had chosen to stay away from the hearing. Both the EAT and the Court of Appeal ruled that this was an incorrect exercise of the tribunal's discretion. Crucially, the Court of Appeal stated that 'although adjournment is a discretionary matter, some adjournments must be granted if not to do so amounts to a denial of justice'. The Court took the view that if a

657

medical practitioner has advised a litigant not to attend the hearing on the ground of ill health, then the person cannot reasonably be expected to attend.

The Court of Appeal went on to say, however, that a tribunal or court is entitled to be satisfied that the inability of the litigant to be present is genuine, and the onus is on the party making the application to prove the need for such adjournment. Where a tribunal is not satisfied with the initial medical evidence with which it has been provided, it has the discretion to give directions to enable such doubts to be resolved. For example, the party seeking to postpone could be ordered to provide further evidence promptly, or could be invited to grant the other party's representatives access to his or her doctor. However, a tribunal does not necessarily commit any error of law if such steps are not taken.

12.48 Further guidance on a tribunal's discretion to postpone or adjourn on the ground of ill health was given by the Court of Appeal in Andreou v Lord Chancellor's Department 2002 IRLR 728, CA, a case decided shortly after Teinaz. Here, the claimant requested a postponement on the basis of a medical certificate which stated that she was unfit to attend work. In view of the fact that she had been off work for the past two years, the tribunal was not satisfied that she would be in any better state in six months' time when the case would be relisted. It therefore adjourned proceedings for one week, with directions that a medical report be produced within three days, detailing the nature of and prognosis for the illness and the reasons why the claimant was unfit to attend the tribunal hearing. However, the claimant failed to provide adequate information about her inability to attend the hearing and, as a result, the tribunal struck out her claim on the ground that she had failed to comply with a direction.

The Court of Appeal considered that the circumstances of the instant case were different from those of Teinaz in a number of respects. In particular, it noted that in the instant case the tribunal had been provided with a medical certificate that did not address the question of whether the claimant was unfit to attend a hearing – something which, in the Court's view, was not an inevitable result of being signed off work. Unlike the approach taken by the tribunal in Teinaz, the tribunal here had also adopted the sensible option of giving the claimant a further limited opportunity of making good the deficiencies in the first report. The Court of Appeal went on to say that it was necessary for the tribunal to balance fairness to the claimant with fairness to the employer and anyone else named in the accusations of race discrimination, and, with this in mind, concluded that the tribunal's decision had not been perverse.

12.49 The Teinaz and Andreou decisions are now routinely cited in appeals against case management decisions relating to adjournment and postponement. However, the EAT in Iqbal v Metropolitan Police Service and anor EAT 0186/12 stated that, while the guidance in those cases has great value, it is not an error of law in itself for a tribunal to fail to refer to them in reasons. Furthermore, as Lord Justice Mummery spelled out in O'Cathail v Transport for London 2013

ICR 614, CA, there are two sides to a trial and the proceedings should be as fair as possible to both sides. The tribunal has to balance the adverse consequences of proceeding with the hearing in the absence of one party against the right of the other party to have a trial within a reasonable time and the public interest in the prompt and efficient adjudication of cases.

There is therefore no hard-and-fast rule that, if a party is unavoidably indisposed, an adjournment or postponement must necessarily follow. Although the Court of Appeal held in Teinaz v London Borough of Wandsworth (above) that this will usually be the case where a party has adequate medical evidence, it limited this general principle to cases where the party's presence is necessary for a fair trial of the issues. Even once the claimant's unfitness to attend a particular hearing has been established it does not automatically follow that the adjournment or postponement must be granted. In Riley v Crown Prosecution Service 2013 IRLR 966, CA, the Court of Appeal upheld a tribunal's decision to strike out claims of discrimination and whistleblowing victimisation, among other things, when the medical evidence indicated that, on the balance of probabilities, the claimant would not be fit enough to proceed for two years. The claims had been listed to be heard over 20 days and the earliest slot for such a lengthy hearing was seven months away. The judge rejected the claimant's contention that he should adjourn the case until then. Taking into account the fact that there was no prognosis of when, if ever, the claimant would be in a position to be well enough to take part in the proceedings, and the balance of prejudice to either party, a fair trial was not possible. The Court of Appeal considered that this analysis involved no error of law. Lord Justice Longmore observed that it would be wrong to expect tribunals to adjourn heavy cases, which are fixed for a substantial amount of tribunal time many months before they are due to start, merely in the hope that a claimant's medical condition will improve. If doctors cannot give any realistic prognosis of sufficient improvement within a reasonable time, and the case itself deals with matters that are already in the distant past, strike-out must be an option available to a tribunal.

Presidential Guidance on postponing for medical reasons. Both the English **12.50** and Welsh and the Scottish Presidential Guidance deal with the appropriate procedure when a party or witness is unable to attend a hearing for medical reasons. Both sets of Guidance state that all medical certificates and supporting medical evidence should be provided, in addition to an explanation of the nature of the health condition concerned. Where medical evidence is supplied it should include a statement from the medical practitioner that, in his or her opinion, the applicant is unfit to attend the hearing, the prognosis of the condition, and an indication of when that state of affairs may cease. The Scottish Guidance goes on to point out that a medical certificate to the effect that a person is not fit to attend a hearing is not conclusive evidence of that fact. It also states that where the illness develops so close to the start of the hearing that it is not possible to obtain the medical evidence before requesting a postponement, the request should be made at once with an undertaking to provide the necessary medical information within seven days.

12.51 **Assessment of medical evidence.** The cases noted above indicate that medical evidence will usually be highly persuasive in favour of postponing or adjourning a hearing on the ground of illness. Even if the evidence is less than clear as to the party's ability to participate or his or her prognosis for improvement, it will generally be best for a tribunal to resolve doubts over the conclusions to be drawn from medical evidence by seeking further comment from the relevant medical professional. Tribunals ought to be wary of going against the evidence or reading too much into it. In Pye v Queen Mary University of London EAT 0374/11 the employment tribunal assumed that the doctor was not very familiar with the claimant's case and, based on its own knowledge of the claimant's work history, it came to the conclusion that it was the litigation itself that was the prime cause of the claimant's illness. This conclusion was not stated in the medical evidence. Allowing an appeal against the tribunal's refusal to adjourn, the EAT held that the tribunal had came impermissibly close to resolving medical issues that it was not equipped to resolve without first taking the step of asking the claimant's doctor for further input. Although the tribunal did have proper grounds for being concerned that the medical report was not produced in light of all relevant background information, it should have at least considered exercising its discretion to order that further enquiries be made of the doctor, or even simply to allow the adjournment.

Similarly, in Beardshall v Rotherham Metropolitan Borough Council and ors EAT 0073/12 the EAT held that a tribunal had erred in assuming, without further enquiry, that the claimant might never be able to attend and that there was no reasonable prospect of the hearing taking place in the foreseeable future. Although the doctor who produced the medical evidence did not identify a time when the claimant would be fit to attend, he was not specifically asked to do so. The claimant had complied with the tribunal's order to provide evidence of his illness and his unfitness to attend and was not asked specifically to address this issue. The tribunal accordingly erred in proceeding on the basis that, as the claimant had not indicated when he would be able to attend, his application should be decided as if the medical evidence indicated that he never could.

12.52 There is also the question of the extent to which a tribunal is entitled to take into account its own impression of the party seeking the postponement or adjournment. Two examples:

- **Chang-Tave v Haydon School and anor** EAT 0153/10: the EAT held that the employment tribunal took into account irrelevant factors – namely the claimant's cogent letters and detailed and lucid witness statement – when refusing his application for an adjournment. These factors did not bear on the uncontradicted medical evidence that he had suffered from a major depressive disorder for about a year, the effect of which was such that his doctor had advised him not to attend lest his condition deteriorate. The evidence said nothing about his capability with regard to the matters that the tribunal relied on

- **Kotecha v Insurety plc (t/a Capital Health Care) and ors** EAT 0537/09: the EAT held that an employment tribunal was entitled to decide that the claimant was lucid and competent enough to present his claim, despite medical evidence warning against it. Unlike the situation in Teinaz v London Borough of Wandsworth (above), the claimant was not only able to be present at the hearing but also presented his application eloquently and, in the tribunal's opinion, had the mental capacity to act. Furthermore, in the EAT's view, the tribunal's conclusion on the claimant's state of health was much more relevant and cogent than the view of the doctor, who saw the claimant for only a short period and who did not know much about tribunal proceedings. The EAT also took into account that, on appeal, it should afford great deference to the tribunal's decision, and that, in the EAT lay members' experience, the members of the employment tribunal would be able to decide if a claimant could present his case properly and that should be a determinative factor. The tribunal had also found the claimant to be evasive and manipulative, and noted that the claimant had himself edited the medical report he submitted in support of his application, purportedly because it included personal information that he did not want made public.

12.53 Furthermore, an employment tribunal is entitled to draw a distinction between medical evidence showing that the claimant is unfit for work and medical evidence showing that he or she is unfit to attend a tribunal hearing. In Snowy's Ltd t/a Snowy's Autobody Repair Specialists v Cook EAT 0595/06 the EAT saw no error in a tribunal's decision to refuse to adjourn a hearing for the third time by reason of the absence of the respondent company's director, who was going to defend the claim. The director had put in a note from his GP that stated that he should refrain from work for two weeks. The EAT held that the tribunal was entitled not to accept this as a valid reason to put off, for what would then be the third time, the claimant's access to justice.

12.54 **Absence of medical evidence.** The EAT in Iqbal v Metropolitan Police Service and anor EAT 0186/12 addressed the situation where, in contrast to Teinaz v London Borough of Wandsworth (above), there is no direct evidence that the party requesting the adjournment or postponement is not fit to participate in the hearing. What duty is there on the tribunal to investigate the medical position before making a decision on adjournment? The Appeal Tribunal held that, in such a case, it is highly material to bring into account any information there is concerning the health of the person in question. If the person says that he or she is stressed but there is no significant history of depression or stress or treatment for it, the tribunal may more easily reach the

661

conclusion that fairness does not require any investigation of the medical position. If, however, there is a significant history of depression or stress requiring medical treatment, the tribunal will be more circumspect. A general practitioner with notes about the patient's prior consultations regarding his or her mental state may be well placed to give a view on the litigant's ability to cope. It will often be appropriate to apply the guidance in Teinaz by adjourning the case to enable the claimant to make an urgent appointment to see the medical practitioner who is treating him or her. The tribunal is entitled to ask the litigant to take a short letter drafted by the tribunal explaining the assistance that the tribunal can give to litigants in person and explaining what assistance and opinion it is that is required from the practitioner. The EAT recognised that time is limited and the medical practitioner's opinion will inevitably be a short one, but in such a case it may be of critical importance to the fairness of a decision that the tribunal makes.

In some circumstances, however, even if the tribunal concludes that the medical evidence is inadequate, there may be only one permissible conclusion from the available evidence. In Birdi v Dartford Visionplus Ltd and anor EAT 0289/12 the EAT allowed an appeal against a tribunal's refusal of an adjournment. The tribunal had refused the claimant's application for postponement, made two weeks before the start of a three-day hearing, on the basis that the medical evidence was inadequate. The evidence stated that the claimant was in the early stages of an assisted pregnancy and had previously suffered three miscarriages. On the first day of the hearing, the claimant did not attend and her representative informed the tribunal that, two days before, she had lost the embryo that had been implanted after a lengthy course of medication. The tribunal again refused to adjourn the hearing. On appeal, the EAT held that the tribunal had simply failed to do justice to the facts before it by the first day of the hearing. It did not require any medical expertise on the tribunal's part to realise that, in such circumstances, the claimant might well be very distraught and distressed and in no fit state to attend the hearing of her claim. If there was any doubt as to whether this was the case, any reasonable tribunal would have adjourned to enable her to obtain further medical evidence, so that it could be authoritatively ascertained whether she was in a fit state to present her claim.

12.55 Ill health of family or dependants
A party may be unavoidably prevented from attending a tribunal hearing through the ill health or care needs of a family member. Two examples:

- **Hibbert v Apple Europe Ltd** EAT 0134/11: the claimant was unable to attend at the hearing of his unfair dismissal claim because his ten-month-old daughter was ill and he had to take her to hospital. The tribunal proceeded in his absence, taking into account that there had already been five postponements in the case, that the claim was over two years old, that the respondent's witnesses were present, that the tribunal had the evidence of the bundle as well as the claimant's witness statement, and that the burden of proof was on the respondent, dismissal having been conceded. The EAT held that the tribunal should not have proceeded with the hearing. Applying the principles set out in Teinaz v London Borough of Wandsworth 2002 ICR 1471, CA, it ought to have taken into account that the claimant had a good reason for his absence, and weighed in the balance the impact on his right to a fair hearing

• **Kirkham v Outward Housing Ltd** EAT 1919/12: six days before the hearing, the claimant applied for a postponement and a transfer to a tribunal sitting closer to his home on the basis that his seriously ill partner required his constant assistance. He submitted a redacted medical report that appeared to relate to his partner, although the manner in which it had been redacted meant that this could not be definitively ascertained. An employment judge refused the application without taking that evidence into account. The EAT allowed the claimant's appeal against that decision. Bearing in mind that he was entitled to be afforded a reasonable opportunity to be heard, it was important that the judge consider the application properly with regard to the timing and venue of the hearing.

Late disclosure

12.56

The EAT has held that the right to a fair trial is also relevant where an adjournment is sought on the ground that a claimant is not equipped to present his case. In Eastwood v Winckworth Sherwood EAT 0174/05 the claimant sought an adjournment of a pre-hearing review (now called a 'preliminary hearing'), which had been convened to determine his employment status, after receiving inadequate and late disclosure from the respondent on this issue. The employment tribunal refused the application on the grounds that neither party had sought an order for disclosure and the parties had not notified the tribunal that there were difficulties between them as regards disclosure. In reaching this decision, the tribunal referred to the overriding objective then contained in Reg 3 of the Employment Tribunals (Constitution and Rules of Procedure) Regulations 2004 SI 2004/1861 (now rule 2 of the Tribunal Rules 2013), which requires tribunals and employment judges to deal with cases 'expeditiously and fairly' and with a view to 'saving expense'.

On appeal, the EAT considered whether the factors relied on by the tribunal were relevant and concluded that the tribunal should have considered: (i) the complexity of the issue(s) to be decided; (ii) that the respondent had initially agreed to the adjournment; (iii) that the parties had reached agreement as to the exchange of witness statements and other procedural steps which would have assisted the tribunal in dealing fairly with the case; (iv) that the respondent's late provision of a bundle of documents did not allow the claimant to prepare adequately for the pre-hearing review; and (v) that there had been no prior delay in the hearing of the case and it was not urgent. In addition, the EAT

663

found that the tribunal had been wrong to focus on whether adequate notice of the hearing had been given to the parties. The key issue was that there had been inadequate and late disclosure that had prevented the claimant from dealing with his claim properly. In these circumstances, the only way to prevent denial of justice would have been for the tribunal to grant the adjournment. Accordingly, the EAT overturned the tribunal's decision to dismiss the claim and remitted the matter to the tribunal.

12.57 In Jones v Corbin t/a Boo EAT 0504/10 the respondent failed to comply with case management orders and, on the day of the hearing, produced two witness statements and a bundle of documents. The employment tribunal refused to grant an adjournment to enable the claimant to consider the statements. On appeal, the EAT held that this was an error of law. It noted that there was a suggestion that the tribunal had set its mind to getting on with the hearing at the expense of any application that might be made. Whether that was so or not, the refusal placed an unfair burden on the claimant.

12.58 **Presidential Guidance on postponing because of late disclosure.** Both the English and Welsh and the Scottish Presidential Guidance set out the appropriate procedure when a postponement is sought on the basis of late disclosure of information or documents, or outright failure to disclose. The English and Welsh Guidance states that the applicant should give details of the documents or information concerned, how they are relevant to the issues in the case, the terms of any orders that have already been made by the tribunal or requests made by the parties for such information or documents, and the response of the other party concerned. The Scottish Guidance is broadly similar on this point, although it also requires, in the case of late disclosure, that the applicant set out why the hearing cannot proceed as a result of the lateness.

12.59 **Business inconvenience**
In Roeser v Commerzbank AG EAT 0552/05 the EAT held that the launch of the claimant's business was a sufficient reason for adjourning a complex unfair dismissal case. The claimant's representatives had made two applications to an employment tribunal for an adjournment of the hearing on the ground that the claimant was due to launch his own business during the week of the hearing. In doing so, they pointed out that the launch of the business was dependent on FSA approval, and that the claimant had only recently been informed that such approval was to be given. Rejecting both applications, the tribunal held that 'business inconvenience' was not a sufficient reason to postpone a lengthy hearing so late in the day. On appeal, however, the EAT decided that the claimant's predicament could not simply be described as 'business inconvenience'. In the absence of an adjournment, he would not be able to give his full attention to the running of his case without suffering or risking serious financial hardship and potential disaster for his new business. Having considered all the evidence, the EAT concluded that the claimant's reasons were genuine and it therefore

664

allowed the adjournment. In reaching that decision, the EAT stressed that, while employment tribunals are required to dispose of matters promptly, the need for promptness has to be measured against the importance of providing a fair trial to both parties.

Non-availability/incompetence of representation
12.60

The non-availability of a party's representative may justify an application for postponement. Clearly the interests of justice, as well as the provisions of Article 6 of the European Convention on Human Rights, entitle a party to be properly represented, although the reason for the representative's unavailability will be relevant to the exercise of an employment judge's discretion. For example, in Chandera v Royal Mail Group EAT 0709/05 the EAT held that an employment tribunal chairman had not erred in rejecting an application for postponement on the basis of a late change of representative and a failure by the previous solicitors to adequately prepare the claimant's case for trial. However, in Millington v KSC and Sons, *The Times*, 23 July 1986, CA, the Court of Appeal made it clear that an adjournment or postponement should not be refused solely because it is necessitated by the incompetence of a party's solicitor. In that case, the refusal meant that the evidence of two witnesses would not be heard. The Court of Appeal held that the evidence of at least one of the witnesses was of such importance that the interests of justice required the adjournment.

Two cases where the unavailability or fault of a representative was put in the balance as a reason for adjournment or postponement:

*   **Beswick Paper Ltd v Britton** EAT 0104/09: the employer's representative incorrectly noted the hearing date as 19 September, instead of 19 August, with the result that neither the employer nor its representative attended on the day of the hearing. The employment tribunal contacted the employer's office and discovered the mistake over the date but no one from the office attempted to contact the representative. The tribunal decided to proceed in the employer's absence and upheld the claims against it. On appeal, the EAT decided (by a majority) that the tribunal erred in not adjourning the hearing. In its view, where an explanation for the non-appearance has been given and no advice about requesting an adjournment is proffered, the tribunal is bound to consider the competing interests of the parties and whether an adjournment, on terms as to costs, ought to be ordered

*   **D'Silva v Manchester Metropolitan University** EAT 0336/09: the claimant appealed against the tribunal's refusal to grant an adjournment when he lost representation at the last minute. He also asserted that he was in poor health, although he did not provide medical evidence of this. The EAT held that there was no error of law in the tribunal's decision, taking into account the presence of the claimant and his witnesses, the fact that he was not

665

off work ill, and the absence of medical evidence. The EAT noted that the claimant was a man of conspicuous intellect, who was very familiar with the facts and issues in his case, and the tribunal was entitled to find that he was sufficiently well and able to represent himself.

12.61 Where an individual is represented by an organisation, the unavailability of the particular representative who has been dealing with the case might not of itself be decisive. This was the suggestion – albeit made very much by way of obiter observation – in Age of Elegance v Hammond EAT 0188/07. The tribunal had refused the employer's application for adjournment on the basis of the unavailability, through illness, of its key witness. In its decision, the tribunal adopted the claimant's reasons for opposing the application, one of which was that the claimant's representative, who was provided by Capita Insurance Services, was due to go on maternity leave in the near future and would be unavailable thereafter. The EAT dismissed the employer's appeal against the tribunal's decision. It noted that the employer's submission that a large company with Capita's resources ought to be able to provide alternative representation if need be was 'fairly arguable'. However, since the employer did not appear and was not represented on the appeal, the EAT did not reach a decision on this argument and was obliged to dismiss the appeal. Notably, the Scottish Presidential Guidance makes the point that a party applying for a postponement on the basis of a representative's unavailability should, if there is more than one qualified representative in the firm, explain why it is not possible for someone else in the firm to appear at the hearing.

In Council of the City of Newcastle Upon Tyne v Marsden 2010 ICR 743, EAT, the claimant was absent from a pre-hearing review (PHR) because his representative wrongly informed him that he need not attend. His representative did not tell the chairman conducting the PHR of his error and, in the absence of any explanation for the claimant's absence, the chairman proceeded to dismiss his disability discrimination claim. The claimant succeeded in having that decision reviewed and the employer appealed against the review decision. The EAT agreed that the original decision to dismiss the claim had been an error of law. The representative's lack of candour cost the claimant the chance to apply for an adjournment, which would very likely have been granted. This was an exceptional case where it would be unjust to the claimant to expect him to seek a remedy directly against his representative for the defective presentation of his case.

12.62 **Presidential Guidance on postponing because of representative's unavailability.** Both the English and Welsh and the Scottish Presidential Guidance set out the appropriate procedure when a party's representative has become unavailable, or a newly-appointed representative is unavailable. The English and Welsh Guidance states that the unavailability should be notified to the tribunal as soon as possible, together with details of the representative concerned, what attempts have been made to make alternative arrangements, and the reason for the unavailability. Any supporting documents should also be provided and, if a representative has withdrawn from acting, details should be given as to when this happened and whether alternative representation has been or is being sought. The Scottish Guidance is more exacting, requiring, among other things, an explanation of why it is considered that the representative's alternative commitment should take precedence.

Unavailability of witnesses   12.63

As soon as the parties are informed of the hearing date it is imperative that they make enquiries to determine whether the date is convenient for any witnesses they intend to call. Failure to do so might lead to a last-minute application for a postponement if it transpires that a crucial witness is, in fact, unavailable. In McCarthy Chrisanti Maffei Inc v Brann EAT 1019/93 the employer requested a postponement on the ground that a vital witness named in the claim would be unable to attend the hearing, which had been set down for two days, because she would be in South Africa. Although a tribunal chairman refused the application, on appeal the EAT held that the only reasonable course that could have been taken in these circumstances was to grant the postponement.

The pre-listing enquiry procedure, whereby the tribunal invites parties to submit unavailable dates before the case is listed for hearing, if used properly, goes some way towards preventing such problems arising (see 'Listing' above). In cases where a preliminary hearing is held to determine case management issues, parties or their representatives will be expected to come armed with any unavailable dates for themselves and their witnesses. Where a party has not complied with these requirements, he or she can expect little or no sympathy from an employment judge in respect of any future request for a postponement. In contrast, where the tribunal has not handled listing dates in this way, this will be a 'highly relevant factor' for the tribunal to take into account if an application for postponement arises because of witness unavailability – University of East Anglia v Amaikwu EAT 0361/12.

The 'interests of justice' in such a case include the interests of all parties   12.64
concerned to ensure that the system works speedily and efficiently. Indeed, the overriding objective in rule 2 of the Tribunal Rules now obliges the parties to assist the tribunal in dealing with cases 'expeditiously'. The principle is illustrated by the EAT case London Fire and Civil Defence Authority v Samuels EAT 450/00. There, the respondent's barrister turned up at the directions hearing (now known as a preliminary hearing) in February 2000 armed with the witnesses' unavailable dates up to the end of June. However, the solicitors had not enquired beyond that date. The tribunal set a hearing for one week in August but it very soon transpired that one of the respondent's key witnesses would be in Spain on holiday for 12 days from the first day of the hearing, although no travel bookings had yet been made. The tribunal refused to

postpone the hearing on the basis that: (a) the parties had already been warned to check availability; (b) no travel bookings had been made; and (c) the witness would be released as soon as his evidence had been given, thereby minimising any inconvenience. The tribunal pointed out that if the witness declined to attend, a witness order could be applied for. In sum, the interests of justice required the matter to be brought to a hearing on the dates listed. The EAT dismissed the respondent's appeal, holding that the tribunal had considered all the relevant factors and reached a decision that was not perverse. The EAT commented that the fact that the barrister's mistake was innocent did not advance the appeal and the fact that the claimant would suffer little or no prejudice as a result of an adjournment was not a conclusive factor, although it was relevant.

However, where the risk of injustice outweighs the need for an early hearing, an application for postponement may be granted. The issue in Rotherham Metropolitan Borough Council v Jones EAT 0726/04 was whether the employment tribunal had erred in refusing to adjourn a hearing dealing with race discrimination issues to take account of the unavailability of a key witness, who was hospitalised owing to a kidney condition. Taking into account the fact that the respondent had taken all reasonably practicable steps to obtain a substitute witness but had failed, the EAT observed that the tribunal should have granted an adjournment. The witness was important to the respondent's case and proceeding with the trial in his absence would be likely to result in injustice to that party.

12.65 As noted under 'Ill health of the parties' above, the Court of Appeal's decision in Teinaz v London Borough of Wandsworth 2002 ICR 1471, CA, establishes a presumption in favour of adjournment in cases where the claimant is unable to attend for medical reasons. It has been suggested that the same presumption may apply where a key witness is similarly unavailable. In Vision Information Services (UK) Ltd v Coutinho EAT 0466/06 the principal witness for the employer defending claims of race discrimination and unfair dismissal was seriously ill and unlikely to be able to attend for several months. The EAT held that there was no error of law in the tribunal's decision to refuse the employer's application for an adjournment and proceed in his absence. The EAT stated that, although this was not a case of a party being absent, as in Teinaz, the guidance given by Lord Justice Peter Gibson was broadly applicable to the situation where a key witness is unavoidably absent. However, the guidance is not an absolute rule and, although there is a strong presumption in favour of adjournment in the circumstances stated, the tribunal will still in each case have to decide what course it is right to take in the interests of justice to all parties. In the present case, the tribunal had been entitled to take into account that the witness was not the only possible source of evidence on key issues; that there had already been delay in the hearing of the case (although not through the employer's fault); and that there was no certainty from the medical evidence as to when, if ever, the witness would be well enough to give oral evidence.

Presidential Guidance on postponing because of unavailability. Both the **12.66** English and Welsh and the Scottish Presidential Guidance set out the appropriate procedure when a party or witness is unable to attend a hearing. Both sets of Guidance state that where parties and witnesses are not available this should be notified to the tribunal as soon as possible, together with the details of the witness or party concerned, what attempts have been made to make alternative arrangements, the reason for the unavailability, and – in the case of a witness – the relevance of his or her evidence. Any supporting documents should also be provided – the Scottish Guidance notes that this should include a travel document or hospital appointment confirmation, where relevant. The Scottish Guidance also states that where the hearing is due to last more than one day, the application should indicate whether a change in the normal order in which evidence is heard might deal with the problem.

Need to deal with new issue   **12.67**
As is explained under 'Natural justice and the right to a fair hearing – knowing the case that has to be met' below, an employment tribunal may, during the course of proceedings, raise an issue that has been overlooked by the parties in their case preparation or identify a different ground on which the same case may be argued. Similarly, a party may belatedly become aware of a point not taken in the claim or response and seek the tribunal's permission to amend accordingly. (The procedure in such cases is considered in Chapter 8, 'Amendments'.)

In any case where the tribunal allows a new point to be taken, either or both of the parties will often ask for an adjournment in order to be given an opportunity to deal with it. The adjournment is more likely to be granted in cases where new evidence is required to be able to deal with the point properly and less likely to be granted where the point is one that the party or parties should have considered in their case preparation. For example, in North Bristol NHS Trust v Harrold EAT 0548/11 the EAT held that the employment tribunal was entitled to consider a complaint of discrimination on the basis of a hypothetical comparator even though this issue was not listed during the case management discussion. It held that the legally represented employer was able to deal with the point and was not materially prejudiced by its introduction. The EAT also held that the tribunal was entitled to reject the employer's application for an adjournment. It took into account that the hypothetical comparator issue must have been so obvious to the employer and its legal advisers that it should not have required flagging up earlier. The tribunal's refusal to grant the adjournment was a result of the employer's decision not to call the most relevant witnesses on this point.

In Taskmaster Resources v Kanyimo EAT 0441/06 the EAT reviewed the legal **12.68** principles that apply when a tribunal seeks to raise a new point of its own

669

motion. It stated that the tribunal should deal only with the issues that are identified as live before it. If it is to deal with an issue not previously identified, it must give the parties a full opportunity to consider it and to make submissions upon both the admissibility of the issue and its substance. The Appeal Tribunal also considered that the tribunal is under a statutory duty to enquire into the matters before it, which may result in it raising a point that has not previously occurred to the parties or been raised at the preliminary stage (although the Scottish EAT in BAE Systems (Operations) Ltd v Paterson 2013 ICR D3, EAT, later doubted the existence of such a duty). In any event, the EAT in Kanyimo made it clear that an adjournment should be given if necessary and appropriate when a new point arises. The EAT in that case held that a tribunal had not been entitled to make a decision on direct discrimination in a case where only indirect discrimination had been agreed as an issue in case management. It was open to the tribunal to make the new point known to the parties – indeed, it would 'stultify' a tribunal if it did not have that power. However, the tribunal had proceeded to adjudicate on the issue without properly considering whether the unrepresented employer should be offered time to consider the point and take legal advice on it.

The increasingly common practice of many tribunals to require, as an explicit requirement in its case management order, the parties to formulate an agreed statement of issues is designed not only to ensure that hearing schedules are kept to but also to identify in a precise way *all* the legal issues that need to be resolved in the particular case. The hope and expectation behind this process is that the tribunal will not, either of its own motion or on application by one of the parties, be suddenly faced with the identification of an unexpected legal issue necessitating an adjournment to enable the matter to be addressed.

12.69 **Religious observance**
In Khan v Vignette Europe Ltd EAT 0134/09 the claimant, a Muslim, had been dismissed for gross misconduct because he had visited pornographic websites on a work computer during work time. He claimed unfair dismissal and, as part of the usual pre-listing procedure, the tribunal asked the parties to notify it of any unavailable dates. Neither side raised any problems and nor did either side object when the case was listed for the first five days in September. However, before the hearing began, K made two separate applications for postponement on various grounds, both of which were rejected. On the morning of the third day of the hearing he again applied for adjournment, this time relying on the fact that it was the week of Ramadan. The tribunal indicated its willingness to accommodate his need for prayer breaks during the day. However, the claimant wished to have the proceedings adjourned so that he would not have to consider sexually explicit material relating to the reason for his dismissal at a time when he required a period of mental and spiritual purity. The employment tribunal rejected the adjournment application. Among other things, it noted that the

claimant would have known at least a year in advance the date on which Ramadan would begin, to within a day or two, and that if had he raised the issue promptly in response to the pre-listing questionnaire his concerns would surely have been respected. The EAT endorsed that refusal on appeal. The tribunal had clearly given the matter the most anxious consideration and reached a balanced conclusion.

Hearings in private

12.70

In common with almost all other kinds of legal proceedings – both civil and criminal – final hearings are generally held in public and there are no restrictions as to who may attend – rule 59 Tribunal Rules. Moreover, details of the proceedings can be freely reported in the press (subject to any 'restricted reporting order' – see Chapter 11, 'Case management', under 'Privacy and restrictions on disclosure'). The need for cases to be heard in public flows from the common law principle that 'justice should not only be done but should manifestly and undoubtedly be seen to be done', and also from Article 6 of the European Convention on Human Rights as incorporated into UK law under the Human Rights Act 1998. The principle is so fundamental to the administration of justice that a decision taken illegally in private may, regardless of its merits, be overturned on appeal and remitted for a rehearing in public – Storer v British Gas plc 2000 ICR 603, CA.

The Court of Appeal in Storer had to consider the question of when a hearing could properly be said to be in public. In that case there had been inadequate courtrooms available to accommodate all that day's hearings and so the employment tribunal decided to use the Regional Chairman's office, which was behind a door marked 'Private', had a security-coded lock, and could only be accessed via a stairway marked 'Private. No admittance to public beyond this point'. The EAT held that as there was no suggestion that any member of the public had been prevented from attending the hearing, it could properly be described as having been held in public. The Court of Appeal disagreed and held that this was a clear case of a tribunal sitting in private: there was no chance of a member of the public 'dropping in' to see how tribunals were conducted and the fact that nobody attempted to do so did nothing to show that the hearing had been held in public.

The Storer decision was distinguished by the EAT in Redmond v Shortbros **12.71** (Plant) Ltd EAT 0542/04, where it held that the fact that a hearing was held in a locked room was not enough to render it in private. Although for security reasons entry and access for the public was only possible under supervision, there was a system in place whereby any member of the public who wished to attend could call the attention of a member of the tribunal staff by pressing a clearly advertised bell, and he or she would be given access to the hearing. It was therefore not possible to say that the hearing was not held in a place to

671

which the public had access, and so it did not infringe the rule that hearings must be held in public.

In exceptional circumstances, it is recognised that the hearing or some parts of it, or some of the material that would otherwise be disclosed in it, needs to be kept private. Such circumstances are provided for by rule 50 of the Tribunal Rules. Subparagraph (1) allows the tribunal to make an order with a view to preventing or restricting the public disclosure of any aspect of the proceedings so far as it considers necessary in the interests of justice, or in order to protect the Convention rights of any person, or in the circumstances identified in S.10A of the Employment Tribunals Act 1996. The circumstances identified in S.10A ETA are that the tribunal will hear evidence from any person which, in the opinion of the tribunal, is likely to consist of:

- information which that person could not disclose without contravening a prohibition imposed by a statutory enactment

- information communicated to that person in confidence or which has been obtained in consequence of the confidence placed in him or her by another person

- information the disclosure of which would cause substantial injury to that person's undertaking or any undertaking in which he or she works, other than by reason of its effect on negotiations for the purposes of collective bargaining as defined in S.178(2) of the Trade Union and Labour Relations (Consolidation) Act 1992.

The order may be made at any stage of the proceedings, on the tribunal's own initiative or on application from one of the parties.

12.72 This rule is substantially different to the provisions previously contained in rules 16, 49 and 50 of the Tribunal Rules 2004, in that the current rule 50 is less prescriptive and more general. The intention behind the reformulated provision was that the new regime would be more flexible, meaning that tribunals will be able to tailor any restrictions to make them proportionate to the needs of the particular case. The need for change in this area was highlighted by the EAT's decision under the 2004 Rules in F v G 2012 ICR 246, EAT, where it held that the rules did not specifically provide for anonymisation in a case where the claimant complained of sexual harassment in relation to a personal and sensitive matter involving her work as a care assistant for disabled students. Although the employment tribunal had a specific power to order that documents relating to a hearing involving sexual offences be anonymised, that rule did not cover the present facts. The EAT held that the tribunal could, in any event, make the required order under its general power under what was then rule 10 of the Tribunal Rules 2004 (now rule 29 of the Tribunal Rules 2013), in so far as necessary to protect the disabled students' rights to a private life, as protected by Article 8 of the European Convention on Human Rights.

Mr Justice Underhill, then President of the EAT, sat in the F v G case and it was he who reviewed the 2004 Rules and proposed the amended provisions that are now found in the 2013 Rules. Accordingly, rule 50 is drafted with the F v G concerns very much in mind. In his judgment in that case, Underhill P made it plain that he was balancing the requirements of open justice and the Convention rights of the disabled students. The need for a balancing act is now expressly recognised, with rule 50(2) stating that, in considering whether to make an order for privacy, reporting restrictions and/or anonymisation, 'the tribunal shall give full weight to the principle of open justice and to the Convention right to freedom of expression'. Furthermore, rule 50(4) provides that 'any party, or other person with a legitimate interest, who has not had a reasonable opportunity to make representations before an order under this rule is made may apply to the tribunal in writing for the order to be revoked or discharged, either on the basis of written representations or, if requested, at a hearing'. This means that, if there is press interest in the case and the media wishes to oppose (or argue for the lifting of) a privacy order on the basis of public interest, it may be able to do so under this rule.

Rule 50(3) lists the kinds of order that may be made. They are: **12.73**

- an order that a hearing that would otherwise be in public be conducted, in whole or in part, in private

- an order that the identities of specified parties, witnesses or other persons referred to in the proceedings should not be disclosed to the public, by the use of anonymisation or otherwise, whether in the course of any hearing or in its listing or in any documents entered on the Register or otherwise forming part of the public record

- an order for measures preventing witnesses at a public hearing being identifiable by members of the public

- a restricted reporting order within the terms of Ss.11 or 12 ETA. (Restricted reporting orders are considered separately in Chapter 11, 'Case management', under 'Privacy and restrictions on disclosure'.)

There is no particular requirement on the tribunal to give reasons for a privacy order. This is in contrast to the position under the 2004 Rules, rule 16(2) of which provided that, where a tribunal or judge decided to hold a hearing, or part of one, in private, it, he or she had to give reasons for doing so. In the absence of any equivalent provision in the 2013 Rules, reference must be made to the general requirement to give reasons for case management orders as set out in rule 62. (This rule is discussed in Chapter 11, 'Case management', under 'Case management orders – decisions and reasons'.) In short, the tribunal will be obliged to give reasons if the privacy order is disputed and, if it gives its decision in writing, it must also give reasons in writing. If it gives its decision orally, it may give reasons orally and will then only provide reasons in writing if asked to do so by one of the

673

parties, or by the EAT or another court. Furthermore, if the making of the order is not 'disputed', within the meaning of rule 62(1), there is no obligation to give reasons at all. This may present a problem where an individual or company who is not a party to the proceedings – such as a journalist or media organisation – wishes to challenge a privacy order on the ground of public interest. If the would-be challenger has no means of seeing the reasons, or if no reasons have been given, then it will be difficult to assess the prospects of a successful challenge.

12.74 A tribunal may also decide to sit in private for reasons of national security, and may be obliged to do so if a Minister so orders in relation to Crown employment proceedings – rule 94. This rule is considered in detail under 'National security' below.

12.75 Types of hearing held in private

The default requirement that hearings be in public applies to 'final hearings', by rule 59 of the Tribunal Rules. A 'final hearing' is defined by rule 57 as one 'at which the tribunal determines the claim or such parts as remain outstanding following the initial consideration (under rule 26) or any preliminary hearing'. Rule 57 goes on to note that there may be different final hearings for different issues – for example, liability, remedy or costs – such that all such hearings are required to be in public.

Under the Tribunal Rules 2004, there were several kinds of hearing: case management discussions (CMDs), full hearings, pre-hearing reviews (PHRs), reviews of default judgments and reviews of other decisions. The 2013 Rules do not make so many distinctions between types of hearing. The only significant distinction they draw is between 'preliminary hearings', which cover matters that used to be split between CMDs and PHRs, and 'final hearings'. Preliminary hearings are, by default, held in private – rule 56. Such hearings are dealt with separately in Chapter 11, 'Case management', under 'Preliminary hearings'.

12.76 It is not clear whether a hearing on reconsideration would count as a 'final hearing'. The equivalent under the 2004 Rules would have been a review hearing, which would have been held in public, and in the absence of any stated intention to change this approach it may be inferred that the new Rules maintain the status quo. In any event, a reconsideration hearing more comfortably fits within the definition of 'final hearing' than 'preliminary hearing' and so it should be safe to assume that a hearing on a reconsideration application should be held in public.

12.77 Stage at which decision on private hearing will be made

Although a party who desires a hearing in private may know well in advance that he or she wishes to make an application to that effect, a decision on whether to conduct the hearing in private will often only be made immediately before the hearing is due to begin. This means that the decision will usually fall to be decided by the full tribunal hearing the claim. A party does not have the right to insist that the question be decided at an interim stage so as to be given an opportunity to appeal if the decision goes against him or her – Milne and Lyall v Waldren 1980 ICR 138, EAT. In that case the employer applied for a direction that the claim should be heard in private (on the ground that information would be adduced which had been given in confidence by a third party) and requested that a decision on that issue be made prior to the date of the hearing. A tribunal chairman refused and directed that, in accordance with normal practice, the tribunal would consider the question of privacy immediately before the main hearing. On the employer's appeal, the EAT upheld the chairman's decision on the basis that the tribunal was acting within its powers to regulate its own procedure and that the chairman acting alone had power to make that direction on behalf of the tribunal.

That said, the decision in Waldren was made under the Industrial Tribunals (Labour Relations) Regulations 1974 SI 1974/1386, which contained no specific provision for preliminary hearings. Furthermore, as the EAT later pointed out in Chelsea Football Club plc v Smith EAT 0262/08, the 1974 rules required the decision whether to hold any part of a hearing in private to be made by the full tribunal that was due to hear the claim. Now that case management requirements and preliminary matters are discussed at a preliminary hearing under rule 53 of the 2013 Rules, and employment judges are clearly able to make any case management decision open to a full tribunal, it is more likely that a party can apply for a private hearing at the preliminary stage. Rule 53 does not specifically restrict the kinds of case management decision that may be taken at a preliminary hearing and, given that rule 50 allows for an order relating to privacy to be made 'at any stage of the proceedings', an order for a private hearing is apt to be made at a preliminary hearing. Indeed, there is a precedent for a private hearing to be ordered in a directions hearing (the predecessor to preliminary hearings) – see Magagnin v Chief Constable of West Yorkshire Police EAT 0653/04, a case decided under the 2001 Rules – and there is nothing in the 2013 Rules to suggest that a tribunal or judge sitting in a preliminary hearing cannot give a similar direction. A preliminary hearing may even be the best place for such decisions to be made given that, under rule 56, they are generally held in private. This means that arguments concerning potentially sensitive material that a party does not want to rehearse in open court can be heard in private before the decision is taken. Preliminary hearings are discussed in more detail in Chapter 11, 'Case management', under 'Preliminary hearings'.

12.78 In any event, although a decision on whether a hearing should be held in private can be made at the preliminary stage, the timing of the decision may ultimately be decided by other factors. For example, in Cahm v Ward and Goldstone Ltd 1979 ICR 574, EAT, an employment tribunal ordered that a claim of unfair dismissal be heard in private given that it might involve evidence that could damage the employer's business. It also acceded to the employer's application for a stay of proceedings pending the outcome of related High Court and Crown Court actions. On the employee's appeal, the EAT held that, although the tribunal might well have been entitled to direct a private hearing having regard to the nature of the evidence involved, its decision to do so at this stage was wrong. Since the High Court proceedings would be heard first, the High Court would have to decide whether or not the civil action would be held in public. The decision whether the same should apply to the tribunal hearing would best be considered once the adjourned hearing took place, at which time the tribunal would be able to benefit from any views on the matter given by the High Court in the earlier civil action.

It will often be difficult for a tribunal to know on the basis of preliminary submissions whether, in fact, the proceedings are such that some or all of the hearing should be conducted in private. In CSO Valuations AG v Taylor EAT 105/93 the EAT came up with some pragmatic advice for tribunals caught in this dilemma. In that case, the claimant had been dismissed by his employer for the theft of some diamonds. In accordance with normal procedure, the employer was expected to start the hearing by making representations. But in order to establish the reason for dismissal – namely, the theft of the diamonds – the employer would be obliged to reveal extensive security procedures. The tribunal, however, refused an application for the hearing to be conducted in private on the basis that the evidence would cause substantial injury to the employer's undertaking if disclosed in public, ruling that the employer could make applications for a private hearing to deal with specific aspects of the evidence as the hearing progressed. On appeal, the EAT accepted the employer's argument that it was difficult to know what contentions to advance when opening the case without knowing whether the tribunal would accede to an application for a private hearing. The EAT therefore suggested that the opening of the case should be heard in private. This would enable the tribunal to determine immediately whether the whole or some part of the hearing should be heard in private and would hopefully avoid successive applications by way of appeal to the EAT on various aspects of the evidence.

12.79 The concerns expressed by Mr Justice Underhill, then President of the EAT, in AB v Secretary of State for Defence 2010 ICR 54, EAT, as to the timing of an order made under the national security provisions may also be of some relevance here. Underhill P noted that the order for a private hearing, under what is now rule 94(2) of the Tribunal Rules 2013, appeared to have been made at a very early stage in proceedings, before the scope of the issues had emerged. The possibility of making the order had been raised at a case management discussion (CMD) under rule 17 of the 2004 Rules (the forerunner to what is now a preliminary hearing under the 2013 Rules), shortly after close of pleadings, and the decision itself had been made at a further CMD only a month later. While acknowledging that neither party had asked for the issue to be deferred and stressing that he was not criticising the employment judge, Underhill P stated that tribunals dealing with such applications in future may want to wait until such time as it is clear what matters may be canvassed in evidence. In his view, it would have been preferable to limit any national security directions to matters that were uncontroversial and/or had to be dealt with at that early stage, and to revisit the question of whether the substantive hearing should be in private at a further preliminary hearing once witness statements had been exchanged, when the extent of any sensitive evidence should have been capable of being established with some precision. Although this observation was concerned solely with the specific provision for private hearings in cases involving national security matters, it seems equally relevant to cases where there are other reasons for hearing some or all of the claim in private.

Circumstances in which a private hearing may be ordered   12.80
As would be expected, tribunals and employment judges are very reluctant to accede to any application for a hearing to be held in private and will only do so when they are given reasonable cause to believe that one of the grounds for ordering a private hearing set out in rule 50 of the Tribunal Rules exists. Two of the few examples we have come across where applications have been granted:

- **Neal v Christie Intruder Alarms Ltd** ET Case No.21467/76: the claimant was dismissed because of his bad workmanship in the installation of burglar alarms. On his claim of unfair dismissal on the ground of capability, the employer submitted that some of his evidence would disclose where such alarms had been fitted and, in some respects, the method of fitting them. The sensitivity of this information constituted a sufficient ground for ordering the hearing to be in private

- **Wilson v Crown Office** ET Case No.S/1498/76: W claimed that she had been unfairly dismissed from her job in the Procurator Fiscal's department in Dumfries. The respondent submitted at the beginning of the hearing that it would be necessary to lead evidence as to matters contained in Police Reports and Crown Precognitions (i.e. proofs of evidence) and that such information had been obtained in the course of investigation into suspected crimes. Also, such information was provided to the Crown, as prosecuting authority, on the basis that it was and remained confidential. Despite W's impassioned objections, the tribunal ruled that the hearing should be conducted in private.

In contrast, in Grant v MBI and Partners UK Ltd ET Case No.2201270/09, the   12.81
respondent applied for the hearing to be held in private on the ground that the evidence consisted of information that would cause substantial injury to its undertaking were it to be disclosed. It was in a difficult financial position and was concerned that if information about this got into the press, and so into the

hands of its bankers, its position would be made even more difficult. The employment tribunal refused the application. It held that the respondent had not considered alternatives to a private hearing, such as redacting the sensitive information where practicable, or asking the tribunal to read such information to itself rather than having it read aloud. Financial information might be determinative of the issues and ought to be heard in public.

12.82 National security

In addition to the general discretion afforded to tribunals under rule 50 of the Tribunal Rules to make orders for privacy in relation to hearings, documents and evidence, there are specific provisions for privacy in proceedings that potentially involve issues of national security. These are set out in rule 94, which substantially re-enacts rule 54 of the 2004 Rules. This includes a general duty on the tribunal, under rule 94(1), to ensure that in exercising its functions, information is not disclosed contrary to the interests of national security.

Under rule 94(1), if, in relation to Crown employment proceedings, a Minister considers it expedient in the interests of national security, the Minister may direct the tribunal to (a) conduct all or part of the proceedings in private; (b) exclude a person from all or part of the proceedings; and/or (c) take steps to conceal the identity of a witness in the proceedings. The term 'Crown employment proceedings' is defined in S.10(8) of the Employment Tribunals Act 1996 as proceedings relating to Crown employment or employment connected with the performance of functions on behalf of the Crown. This power for a Minister to direct the adoption of national security measures is therefore limited and cannot apply in all employment tribunal proceedings. However, there is also a more general power under rule 94(2). If a tribunal considers it expedient in the interests of national security in any proceedings (including Crown employment proceedings), it may do anything that it could be required to do under rule 94(1)(a)–(c), and/or may order a person not to disclose any document (or the contents of any document), where provided for the purposes of the proceedings, to any other person (save for any specified person). The tribunal's more extensive power under rule 94(2) may be exercised on the tribunal's own motion, or (under rule 94(4)) on application by a Minister. In considering whether to make an order under rule 94(2), the tribunal may consider material from a party, or from a Minister if that Minister is not already a party to the claim, without having to provide that material to any other person – rule 94(3). This material must be used solely for the purpose of deciding whether to issue the order, unless it is subsequently relied on in evidence by a party to the claim. Note that the Minister does not have to be a party to the proceedings to be able to make a direction under subsection (1) or an application under subsection (4) – rule 94(8).

12.83 Where directions or orders are made under rule 94(1) or (2), a modified version of the Tribunal Rules applies. These are known as the Employment Tribunals

(National Security) Rules of Procedure, and are set out in Schedule 2 to the Employment Tribunals (Constitution and Rules of Procedure) Regulations 2013 SI 2013/1237. Among other things, they provide for the tribunal to keep secret from any party the reasons for any decision made in national security proceedings. They also provide for a 'closed material procedure', under which a 'special advocate' is appointed by the Attorney General to represent a party who is excluded from proceedings on national security grounds. The detail of the Schedule 2 procedure is outside the scope of this Handbook.

The national security procedures are – unsurprisingly – rarely exercised and so there is little case law on their operation. The Supreme Court was told in Home Office v Tariq 2011 ICR 938, SC (discussed under 'Challenge to lawfulness of national security measures' below), that the ministerial power to direct that a tribunal adopt national security measures under rule 94(1) has never been invoked.

12.84 There have, however, been cases of employment tribunals exercising the power under what is now rule 94(2). In AB v Secretary of State for Defence 2010 ICR 54, EAT, Mr Justice Underhill, then President of the EAT, dismissed an appeal against a tribunal's decision to order a private hearing under what is now rule 94(2). The claimant, a member of the armed forces, sought to complain of discrimination by colleagues. The allegations covered periods while he was on operations overseas and also time when he was working back in the UK. The MoD requested a private hearing on the basis that the nature of the claimant's work overseas was highly sensitive, and that disclosure either of the nature of the work itself, or of the modus operandi of his unit, would be highly prejudicial to the effectiveness of that work, such that it might have to be abandoned altogether. Its case was therefore that disclosure would create a real risk to the lives of either the servicemen doing that work or of the others whose safety it was intended to promote. Underhill P was satisfied, on the basis of material submitted by the MoD which he considered in private, that the part of the claim dealing with the claimant's service overseas should be heard in private. However, he noted that it would have been different if the case involved alleged conduct of a kind that did not require reference to the details of the claimant's work. Furthermore, the part of the claim involving discrimination when the claimant returned to the UK ought to be dealt with in public, in so far as it was practicable to do so. Although he could not make a final decision on this point, since it would be a matter for the tribunal to decide on further evidence, Underhill P accepted that there is a public interest in exposing how complaints of discrimination in the armed forces are handled, even if the details of the particular incident cannot be addressed in a public hearing.

This ruling makes it clear that where the sensitive material relied on is really just the background to a claim it will not provide the basis for a hearing in private. Underhill P also went on to give guidance to tribunals considering

679

whether it is 'expedient' in the interests of national security to order restrictions on the publicity of the proceedings. He summarised the basic principle as being that cases involving national security are a free-standing category of exception, or potential exception, to the strong rule of open justice. Any such exception must be justified and, where national security grounds are put forward as justification, the court or tribunal must make an assessment of whether they suffice in the particular case. In principle, this assessment will involve a balancing act between national security interests on the one hand, and the principle of open justice and the rights of the individual on the other. In this respect, it will be easier to justify, for example, the anonymisation of witnesses or the redaction of documents than the conducting of an entire hearing in private. However, tribunals in these circumstances should not assume that their task is an ordinary application of the principle of proportionality. Where the interests of national security are engaged, the stakes are necessarily high: they will involve risks to the national interest generally, and, typically, direct risks to the lives of members of the armed forces, security services and others. The risk of such outcomes must, by its nature, weigh heavily against the principle of open justice, important though that is. Where it is not self-evident that an asserted risk is present or serious, the tribunal must be aware that the risks are of a kind which it is not well-placed to assess. This is not to say that the proportionality exercise is unnecessary or that it can only have one outcome whenever an application for national security measures is made – tribunals cannot and should not abdicate their responsibilities to make the necessary assessment whenever national security is invoked. But it does mean that it will be necessary for tribunals to approach any such application with a recognition of the weight which must necessarily be accorded to any real risk to the interests of national security and of the limits to the assessment of that risk which it may realistically be possible to carry out. Underhill P went on to note that in cases where the only danger is the risk of identifying certain individual witnesses (such as serving personnel), consideration would have to be given to whether the interests of national security, and of the vulnerable witnesses, could properly be protected by lesser steps such as their anonymisation, or by measures of the kind familiar in the criminal courts to protect vulnerable witnesses from being physically seen in court.

12.85 It is also worth noting Underhill P's concern that the rule 94(2) order appeared to have been made at a very early stage in proceedings, before the scope of the issues had emerged. The possibility of making the order had been raised at a case management discussion (replaced by 'preliminary hearings' under the 2013 Rules), shortly after close of pleadings, and the decision itself had been made at a further CMD only a month later. While acknowledging that neither party had asked for the issue to be deferred and stressing that he was not criticising the employment judge, Underhill P stated that tribunals dealing with such applications in future may want to wait until such time as it is clear what matters may be canvassed in evidence. In his view, it would have been preferable to limit any directions under what is now rule 94(2) to matters that were uncontroversial and/or had to be dealt with at that early stage, and to revisit the question of whether the substantive hearing should be in private at a further preliminary hearing once witness statements had been exchanged, when the extent of any sensitive evidence should have been capable of being established with some precision.

The AB case involved two types of claim, one that required a private hearing and one that could be heard in public (at least in Underhill P's provisional view). Where proceedings involve both sensitive and non-sensitive material the question may arise as to the order in which the claims should be heard. The EAT touched on this issue in Farooq v Commissioner of Police of the Metropolis EAT 0542/07, where a tribunal had ordered a closed material procedure for the hearing of a discrimination claim against the respondent police force. The EAT did not have to give a ruling on the substantial points sought to be argued, since they had already been decided in an earlier appeal to the EAT. However, it did accept that there were good reasons for the tribunal's decision to hear the closed evidence first, followed by the open evidence. The special advocate had argued that she would prefer to conduct the case the other way round, with the open evidence first, in order to learn as much as she could about the open material and to hear the witnesses cross-examined on it. She pointed out that this was the normal practice in the Special Immigration Appeals Commission (SIAC). The EAT noted that the tribunal does not need to follow the SIAC procedure, and that hearing the closed material first would enable the tribunal fully to understand the nature of the case on the closed side and thus better appreciate any arguments by the special advocate as to unjustness, unfairness, inconvenience or inappropriateness, which she could then put forward to an informed tribunal. She would also have the opportunity to raise points on the closed evidence that might have the effect of enlarging the scope of the open evidence to be heard later on. In the EAT's view, there would be no advantage to the special advocate or the claimant in taking the open evidence first, since its nature was already known, meaning that nothing would be learnt as a result of hearing the open evidence compared with the advantage of full disclosure to the tribunal and to the special advocate of the closed evidence.

Challenge to lawfulness of closed material procedure. In Home Office v **12.86** Tariq 2011 ICR 938, SC, an employment tribunal used its powers under rule 94(2) (on application by a Minister) to order a closed material procedure in the hearing of T's discrimination complaint. He had been dismissed from his employment as an immigration officer because of the Home Office's concerns that he had close associations with individuals suspected of involvement in planning terrorist attacks, which might render him vulnerable to attempts to exert pressure on him to abuse his position. The tribunal acceded to the Minister's application to adopt a closed material procedure, a decision that

681

gave rise to appeals that went as far as the Supreme Court. Two issues fell to be decided by the Justices – (i) whether the procedure breached T's right to an effective remedy in his discrimination claim and/or his right to a fair trial under Article 6 of the European Convention on Human Rights; and (ii) whether T was at least entitled to see the allegations forming the basis of the Home Office's case against him in sufficient detail to be able to challenge them effectively (a practice commonly referred to as 'gisting').

The Supreme Court decided unanimously that there had been no breach of T's discrimination or Convention rights; and by a majority (Lord Kerr dissenting) that there was no absolute requirement for 'gisting'. On the question of the lawfulness of the closed material procedure, the Court distinguished cases where national security measures had been successfully challenged in relation to criminal charges or potential restrictions of personal liberty, such as freezing orders. In the Court's view, an individual's civil right to a remedy for discrimination does not require such a high standard of protection. Furthermore, there were safeguards that ensured that T's rights would not go entirely unprotected. As Lord Hope pointed out, he would at least have a special advocate to represent him; his claim would be judicially determined by an independent and impartial tribunal, which could be expected to take full account of the fact that the details of the Home Office's case had to be kept closed; if inferences were to be drawn because of the quality or nature of the evidence for the Home Office, they would have to be drawn in T's favour; and, throughout the process, the need for the evidence to be kept closed would remain under review as required by what is now rule 94(2). As to 'gisting', the Court held that this was not an absolute requirement. However, it did take into account the fact that the Home Office had at least disclosed the general nature of its case against T.

12.87 Split hearings

It is sometimes necessary for a hearing to be split into two parts: the first part covering the substantive issues and the second covering remedies (when appropriate). A split hearing on remedies sometimes arises where the tribunal directs that the issues of fairness and remedy should be dealt with in separate sessions. More frequently, however, a split hearing arises where a decision in favour of the claimant is reached, but there is insufficient time to decide on compensation. This may occur where the computations are complex, as with valuation of pension rights; it may also apply when the employer wishes to argue that the claimant contributed to the dismissal or that factors that have come to light since the dismissal make it just and equitable to reduce or extinguish the compensation.

In Iggesund Converters Ltd v Lewis 1984 ICR 544, EAT, the EAT set out guidelines on the conduct of split tribunal hearings in cases where they have been directed by the employment tribunal:

- the tribunal should give some direction as to how the evidence on the two issues of fairness and remedy is to be dealt with

- such a direction may be that all evidence should be presented at the first hearing; conversely, it may be that evidence will be treated as divided into separate categories and dealt with piecemeal at the two hearings. What is important is that the parties should know where they stand at the outset

- the tribunal may be entitled to exercise its discretion to exclude evidence at the second hearing that could or should have been called at the first hearing.

In the Iggesund Converters case, as the EAT pointed out, the tribunal had **12.88** embarked on a split hearing without giving any directions as to evidence. The tribunal made a finding of unfair dismissal and the company wanted to argue the issue of contributory conduct: it had been left, however, in a state of uncertainty as to whether and when it would be allowed to produce evidence of such conduct.

This case was decided when the Industrial Tribunals (Rules of Procedure) Regulations 1980 SI 1980/884 were in force, which made no specific provision for case management discussions. Having been given rather a free hand by Parliament to determine how best to deal with claims involving several different issues, tribunals had developed their own standards of procedure and it was these practices that the EAT had in mind when giving the guidance noted above. Now that the rules provide explicitly for a judicial sift (rule 26) and the possibility of a preliminary hearing to determine questions of case management, among other things (rules 53–56), it is much less likely that a tribunal will proceed in such a case without making clear which evidence will be heard and which issues will be determined at which hearing. Nonetheless, the general principles set out in Iggesund Converters remain relevant.

Arriving at the tribunal   12.89

On arrival, each party should register at reception, give the names of representatives and intended witnesses and observers to the receptionist, and check who has already arrived from the other side. The parties (or their representatives) may wish to see each other before the hearing begins (see below). Each party should then go to his or her respective waiting room and await the clerk. When the clerk arrives he or she will want to know whether there are any 'bundles' of documents still to be given in, whether cases are likely to be cited and, if so, their citation references and, in the case of a claimant claiming unfair dismissal, the address of any Jobcentre or Social Security Office at which he or she signs on. At this stage, parties should ask the clerk about any procedural matters which need clarifying. (It may be a good idea to know whether the employment judge prefers to conduct proceedings in any particular way.)

12.90 Contact the other side before the hearing starts

While parties are waiting for their case to be called or for witnesses to turn up, they (or their representatives) should seize the chance to discover from the other side whether there is any prospect of a last-minute settlement. Very often the sight of the tribunal door concentrates the mind and the time, expense and acrimony involved in pressing ahead with the hearing may not seem worthwhile if satisfactory agreement can be reached. An approach should be made to the opponent and, if there is the possibility of a settlement, the clerk should be told so that he or she in turn may advise the tribunal – which will almost certainly grant the parties time enough to determine whether, and on what terms, the claim can be settled.

Even if a settlement is impossible, useful information can be gleaned from the other side, e.g. the names of witnesses and the case authorities to be cited (if not already known). Sometimes, where counsel has been instructed late, he or she may bring to bear on the case a practical realism which solicitors who have dealt with the case from the beginning may not have done. Certain contentions, though pleaded in the ET1 or ET3, may be dropped and the scope of the 'live' issues drastically narrowed before the hearing begins.

12.91 Witnesses

The parties are likely to have prepared and exchanged witness statements in advance of the hearing. If possible, witnesses should be given time to go over these before the hearing begins. Time should also be taken to help familiarise them with tribunal procedure. A witness who is put at ease in this way is likely to perform a good deal better when called. If a witness wishes to take the oath on (say) the Quran, the clerk should be told at this stage so that a copy can be made available in the hearing room.

12.92 Obligation to inform the tribunal

By virtue of rule 2 of the Tribunal Rules, the parties and their representatives are under an obligation to 'assist the employment tribunal to further the overriding objective' and, in particular, to 'co-operate generally with each other and with the tribunal'. This provision is similar to rule 1.3 of the Civil Procedure Rules 1998 SI 1998/3132 (CPR), which places parties to proceedings in the civil courts under a comparable duty, and which the Court of Appeal has held to impose a 'professional obligation' on those advising parties to litigation to notify the Court of the likelihood of judicial time being wasted in preparing for an appeal which has either been settled or is subject to negotiations which may well lead to settlement – Yell Ltd v Garton 2004 EWCA Civ 87, CA. That case arose out of an appeal from the EAT to the Court of Appeal for which a day and a half had been allocated, starting on a Monday morning. The parties were in serious settlement negotiations on the Friday before and, at 6 pm, reached an agreement that meant the appeal could be withdrawn. However, the Court was not informed of the withdrawal until 9 am on Monday morning. The Court of Appeal took the view that the list office should have been informed of the settlement negotiations on the Friday afternoon and that, even though agreement was only reached at the end of the working day, attempts should still have been made to contact the clerk to the senior presiding judge, or even one of the judges themselves, over the weekend.

The Court of Appeal in Garton expressed the hope that the judgment would receive wider publicity so that the profession was reminded of the obligation under the CPR. Given the similarity between the CPR and the Tribunal Rules 2013 in this respect, it is a case worth noting for those representatives who find themselves in a similar situation shortly before a tribunal hearing is due to begin. The overriding objective will clearly be frustrated if the tribunal is not informed as soon as it is known that a matter listed for hearing will not proceed – indeed, rule 2 specifically lists 'saving expense' as one of the principles included in the overriding objective.

When the case is called

12.93

The tribunal clerk will tell both parties when the tribunal is ready to proceed and they will be taken to the appropriate room in which the tribunal members may already be present. The respondent and his or her representatives will be asked to take the front table on the employment judge's right and the claimant should seat him or herself on the employment judge's left. Witnesses, observers (and in some cases the press) will seat themselves behind. It is rare in England and Wales for witnesses to be excluded from the tribunal room before giving evidence, and then only on application by one of the parties. Any child witnesses will probably be taken to the waiting room until they are called. In Scotland all witnesses remain in the waiting room until called.

If the tribunal members are not already present when the parties enter the tribunal room, the parties should stand up when they come in and seat themselves only when asked to do so by the employment judge. Thereafter, with the exceptions of witnesses affirming or being sworn, and when the tribunal rises to leave the room, all parties and their representatives are entitled to remain seated throughout the proceedings.

Starting the hearing

12.94

Being adversarial in nature, a tribunal hearing will usually be conducted along the lines of an ordinary trial, although in some respects more informally. It is customary to address the tribunal via the employment judge, who should be called either 'Sir' or 'Madam'. Should it be necessary to address either of the lay members directly, they may be similarly referred to as 'Sir' or 'Madam', or alternatively by name.

685

12.95 Preliminary matters

Preliminary matters involving questions of jurisdiction and case management issues are now far more commonly dealt with at a preliminary hearing than at the final hearing – see Chapter 11, 'Case management', under 'Preliminary hearings'. There may nonetheless be circumstances in which such matters have to be dealt with by the tribunal at the final hearing prior to any consideration of the substantive issues. If an adjournment is required, this is the first matter with which the tribunal should be asked to deal – see 'Postponements and adjournments' above. It is also right to raise any other preliminary matters still outstanding at this early stage – for example, where one party wishes the hearing to take place in private (see below), or where it is sought to exclude the witnesses from the tribunal room until they are called to give evidence.

Administrative issues may need to be dealt with on the day, including the question of the amount of time allotted to the hearing. In La Vertue v Ilex Energy Consultants Ltd EAT 0520/05 the full hearing had been listed for two days but, on the morning of the first day, it transpired that the chairman was double-booked for the second day. He proposed that the hearing could be dealt with in one day and there was no objection to this from either the respondent or the claimant, who was acting in person. However, after the claimant lost, she appealed, arguing that she had not had a fair hearing. Her main ground of complaint was that the tribunal had limited cross-examination of each witness to 30 minutes, which meant that she was prevented from asking certain questions of a particular witness, W. The EAT rejected that complaint. While the tribunal had indeed limited cross-examination in this way, it did not do so until after the claimant had finished cross-examining W. Thereafter, she had not in fact needed to take more than 30 minutes to cross-examine any of the other witnesses, and so she had no legitimate ground for complaint.

12.96 Applications for leave to amend the pleadings (the ET1 and ET3 together with any additional information) should also be made before the hearing proper begins. Straightforward, technical amendments are likely to be accepted by the tribunal and the other side. But if the amendment sought is substantial, a form of 'trial within a trial' may occur, in which the tribunal will listen first to the parties' respective submissions on the proposed amendment and then adjudicate on whether it should be allowed. Amendments are considered in Chapter 8, 'Amendments'. A similar procedure may also be adopted where a party, as a preliminary matter, draws the attention of the tribunal to the opponent's non-compliance with orders or practice directions; for example, over discovery or additional information. If the party who raises such a point applies to have the defaulting party's pleadings struck out either in whole or in part, then the tribunal will wish to hear the oral representations of both sides before it decides on what course of action to adopt.

Conversion from final hearing into preliminary hearing. It is possible for a **12.97** final hearing to be converted into a preliminary hearing under rule 48 of the Tribunal Rules, which provides that a tribunal conducting a preliminary hearing may order that it be treated as a final hearing, 'or vice versa'. The rule goes on to set out two conditions that must be satisfied before such conversion may be ordered. First, the tribunal must be 'properly constituted for the purpose'. Given that preliminary hearings must (subject to one limited exception) be heard by a judge alone, under rule 55, it will not usually be possible to convert proceedings being heard by a two- or three-person tribunal into a preliminary hearing. Although the lay members might step down in order to achieve the proper constitution, it is unclear whether the rule would be satisfied by this approach – rule 48 may be read as requiring the tribunal to be *already* properly constituted for the purpose of the converted hearing, excluding the possibility that it could make the order and then alter its constitution. The second condition is that the tribunal must be satisfied that neither party would be materially prejudiced by the change. This will be a matter for the tribunal's discretion but it is difficult to envisage a situation where parties who are prepared for a final hearing are in some way unprepared to deal with a preliminary matter. It may be that the matter only becomes apparent on the day, in which case a party – especially an unrepresented party – may struggle to deal with it at short notice. In that case, though, the proper course will usually be for the tribunal to adjourn rather than to press on with the substantive hearing.

One further complication is that, under rule 56, preliminary hearings must be conducted in private, unless they involve determination of a substantive issue or a strike-out. Final hearings, in contrast, are usually heard in public. Accordingly, if the tribunal wishes to convert a final hearing into a preliminary hearing for the purpose of determining anything other than a substantive issue or a strike-out, the tribunal may have to exclude members of the public from the hearing room.

It must be thought unlikely that such conversion will often occur in practice, **12.98** since it will rarely confer any advantage on the parties (or the tribunal). There is little to be gained in terms of the range of powers available to a tribunal at a preliminary hearing, as opposed to a final hearing. The tribunal has the power to make case management orders at any stage of the proceedings, including orders for adjournment and strike-out, and so if any such issues arise at the final hearing they can be dealt with by the tribunal as convened. The only power that a tribunal may exercise at a preliminary hearing and not at a final hearing is the power to make a deposit order under rule 39 – i.e. an order that a party submit a deposit of up to £1,000 as a condition of advancing an argument or allegation that the tribunal considers to have little reasonable prospect of success. It is conceivable that a tribunal conducting a final hearing could be so unimpressed by the development of a particular point that it considers it appropriate to make a deposit order before the case proceeds any further, in which case rule 48 will

687

allow it to do so without having to abandon the hearing. In such a case, the tribunal might convert into a preliminary hearing, make the order, then convert back into a final hearing and continue to hear the rest of the claim until the party makes the payment required under rule 39.

Preliminary hearings are dealt with in Chapter 11, 'Case management', under 'Preliminary hearings'.

12.99 Which side starts?

The party on whom the burden of proving his or her case lies will usually go first. In discrimination claims this will be the complainant. In unfair dismissal and redundancy cases, the first issue may be whether the employee was actually dismissed. When dismissal is denied, usually where the employee is alleging constructive dismissal, the claimant will be asked to begin. When dismissal is admitted, the employer will usually start by showing the reason for dismissal. However, in all cases, the procedure is a matter for the tribunal's discretion. So, for example, in Russell v Tube Lines Ltd ET Case No.3200944/08, which involved claims of discrimination and unfair dismissal, the employment tribunal, having heard submissions from both representatives, decided that the claimant should give evidence first. Furthermore, even where the formal burden lies on one side, the tribunal may decide to exercise its discretion and ask the other to open – see, for example, Hawker Siddeley Power Engineering Ltd v Rump 1979 IRLR 425, EAT, where the burden lay on the claimant but the employer was asked to give evidence first. (The burden of proof is discussed further in Chapter 13, 'Evidence', under 'Burden of proof and standard of proof'.)

In an unfair dismissal claim where dismissal is admitted, the order of the proceedings will normally take the following form: employer opens – employer's evidence – employee's evidence – employee's closing address – employer's closing address – tribunal's decision.

12.100 Opening statements

There is no absolute right to make an opening statement – it is a matter for tribunal discretion and practice will vary from one tribunal to another (and from case to case) as to whether this will be permitted. In England and Wales (but not in Scotland), tribunals commonly allow the party who is presenting evidence first to make an opening statement, especially if the issues are not clear from the papers or where the case looks to be a complex one in fact or in law. In a very complex case it may be helpful for both sides to submit a written skeleton argument.

A party who thinks that an opening statement will help the tribunal should ask permission to make one and should give reasons for the request. A tribunal is unlikely to object to a written statement prepared in advance being read out, in order to get the case off to a cogent and coherent start. The statement should:

- be brief – giving only the essence of the case and any relevant submissions that are to be made

- indicate the evidence proposed to be presented and who will give it

- refer to any questions of law which seem to arise – in outline only.

It is sometimes possible to anticipate the other side's arguments too, and to explain how it is proposed to counter these. It is inadvisable, however, to take too long over this, because most tribunals prefer this to emerge during proceedings. **12.101**

One of the main purposes of an opening statement is to outline the context within which the evidence will be given. Where the story is complex or convoluted, this will help make the evidence more understandable and identify the issues that arise from it and, in the case of a litigant in person or lay representative, the tribunal may spot an overlooked issue that could be raised by way of amendment. On the whole, however, tribunals prefer to proceed straight to the claimant's or respondent's evidence-in-chief and the employment judge may interrupt an opening statement if he or she feels that the party is in effect giving evidence. Also note that the statement will not form part of the recorded evidence of the tribunal – this is because it is not given on oath and has not been proved. All the facts and contentions it mentions must be proved by documentary evidence and the oral testimony of the party and his or her witnesses. One exception is where admissions of fact are made in a party's opening statement – in Brennan v C Lindley and Co Ltd 1974 IRLR 153, NIRC, the National Industrial Relations Court upheld a tribunal's decision to stop the proceedings when, during the employee's opening speech in which he sought to introduce his claim for unfair dismissal, he admitted that he had in fact resigned and not been dismissed at all. Such an admission is, needless to say, fairly unusual.

Presenting the evidence **12.102**

What follows is a bare outline of the way the average party or representative presents his or her case. At all times, the parties will be subject to the tribunal's overriding discretion to direct the way the proceedings are conducted. The tribunal's powers in this regard have been bolstered in the Tribunal Rules 2013, compared to their 2004 predecessor, in that rule 45 specifically states that the tribunal shall have power to 'impose limits on the time that a party may take in presenting evidence, questioning witnesses or making submissions, and may prevent the party from proceeding beyond any time so allotted'. In other words, the tribunal can deploy a 'guillotine' procedure to constrain the presentation of evidence within appropriate limits. When Mr Justice Underhill announced his

689

proposal for such a provision, following his review of the 2004 Rules, he noted that tribunals already had the power to prevent disproportionately lengthy questioning and submissions under their general discretion to manage proceedings, but that the introduction of an express rule should encourage its use. Accordingly, tribunals may now feel newly emboldened in forcing witnesses and parties to stick to time limits in presenting their evidence. The Presidential Guidance on 'General Case Management' for England and Wales notes that tribunals do not 'like' to deploy the guillotine but will do so if one side takes so long that the other side may be prevented from having a fair opportunity to put his or her case.

It is important for the parties or their representatives to take notes of the proceedings and the evidence given. Although the employment judge will take notes, there is no absolute right for a party to call for these notes when making any subsequent appeal – see Chapter 18, 'EAT hearings and decisions', under 'Evidence – evidence before the tribunal and employment judge's notes'.

12.103 Note that this section is concerned only with the giving of admissible evidence at the hearing. Whether evidence is in fact admissible is a question for the tribunal to decide. This is discussed in Chapter 13, 'Evidence', under 'Admissibility of evidence'.

12.104 **Right to call witnesses**
Whereas the Tribunal Rules 2004 specifically recognised the parties' right to call witnesses, the Tribunal Rules 2013 make no equivalent provision. Rule 27(1) of the 2004 Rules stated that, subject to the tribunal's general case management power, a party at the hearing was entitled to 'give evidence, to call witnesses, to question witnesses and to address the tribunal'. This is not expressly stated anywhere in the 2013 Rules. However, there is no doubt that these are still the basic rights of the parties to a hearing, since anything less would breach the rules of natural justice and the right to a fair trial.

Nor is there any doubt that these rights are qualified, since it has always been clear that an employment tribunal has power to restrict the number of witnesses that either party may call – see, for example, McBride v Standards Board for England EAT 0092/09. The tribunal is only required to admit evidence in so far as it is relevant and so it will not permit a party to call a witness who can add nothing to the proceedings, nor a proliferation of witnesses who all confirm essentially the same evidence. The question of whether any particular witness should be allowed to be called is really a question of admissibility – see Chapter 13, 'Evidence', under 'Admissibility of evidence – relevance'.

12.105 The McBride case also makes it clear that the tribunal or employment judge is able to decide which witnesses may be called at what is now called a preliminary hearing under rule 53 (previously a case management discussion under rule 17 of the 2004 Rules) – see Chapter 11, 'Case management', under 'Preliminary hearings'. The judge might also make this decision at the 'initial consideration' stage, under rule 26 – see Chapter 7, 'Judicial sift'.

Evidence on oath
12.106

By virtue of rule 43 of the Tribunal Rules, witnesses attending the hearing will be required to give evidence on oath or affirmation. A witness giving testimony on oath is required to 'swear by Almighty God' to tell the truth, the whole truth and nothing but the truth. In the case of a Christian, the oath will be taken while holding the New Testament in his or her raised hand. People of other religions may swear on whatever may be their appropriate Holy Book (if one is available at the tribunal). Where practicable, tribunals will usually allow customary religious ceremony to accompany this – for example, a Jewish person may swear on the Pentateuch with his or her head bowed and covered.

Under S.5 of the Oaths Act 1978, any person who objects, on religious or any other grounds, to being sworn may make a solemn affirmation, in which case he or she will 'solemnly, sincerely and truly declare and affirm' to tell the truth, the whole truth, etc. The effect of this will be the same as taking an oath – i.e. that a person who knowingly makes a false statement after having so affirmed may render him or herself liable to prosecution for perjury.

Where interpreters are required to translate the oral testimony of a party or **12.107** witness whose native language is not English or who is profoundly deaf, they will be asked to take the Interpreter's Oath or Affirmation, which involves undertaking to 'well and faithfully interpret all that is said to the best of my skill and understanding'. Having been sworn, the interpreter will then take the party or witness through the oath or affirmation in their native language and translate their statement back into English for the benefit of the tribunal. Where an interpreter's services are required, it is desirable that he or she be independent of the parties and properly qualified, since this will reassure the tribunal that the translation is both accurate and unbiased.

Evidence given by electronic communication
12.108

Provision for conducting proceedings by electronic communication has been part of tribunal procedure for some time. Rule 15 of the Tribunal Rules 2004 provided that a hearing could be conducted in whole or in part by use of electronic communications if the employment judge considered it just and equitable to do so. In practice, it was only case management discussions under old rule 17 (since subsumed into 'preliminary hearings' under rule 53 of the Tribunal Rules 2013) that were routinely conducted in this way, with the discussions taking place over the telephone. Full hearings have rarely, if ever, been conducted entirely via electronic communications. Such a procedure would have been difficult to achieve in practice given the requirement under old rule 15(2) that, when evidence was given via telecommunications in a public hearing, it had to be given in such a way that the public was able to 'see and

691

hear all parties to the communication'. In other words, evidence by telephone was not permissible; only live video evidence would suffice.

This rule has been relaxed under the Tribunal Rules 2013, meaning that there is now greater scope for the hearing, or parts of it, to be conducted with the use of telecommunications. Rule 46 states: 'A hearing may be conducted, in whole or in part, by use of electronic communication (including by telephone) provided that the tribunal considers that it would be just and equitable to do so and provided that the parties and members of the public attending the hearing are able to hear what the tribunal hears and see any witness as seen by the tribunal.' This is clearly less prescriptive than the previous rule as to how electronically communicated evidence must be given. Instead of requiring that the public be able to 'see and hear all parties to the communication', rule 46 requires that the public be able to see any witness 'as seen by the tribunal'. In other words, if the tribunal does not see the witness, the public do not need to either. Accordingly, evidence at a final hearing may now be given by telephone.

12.109 The question is whether a tribunal would ever consent to hearing evidence over the telephone. The main objection to such a course of action is that it may adversely affect the fairness of proceedings if the tribunal's ability to assess the credibility of the person giving evidence is diminished. It is well recognised – at least in adversarial proceedings – that a witness's credibility can only properly be assessed by a judge or jury if it has the benefit of seeing the witness give evidence. In the criminal case of R v D 2013 EqLR 1034, Crown Court, His Honour Judge Peter Murphy ruled that the defendant – a Muslim woman – was free to wear the niqaab face covering during the trial but not while giving evidence. He observed that, in the long experience of judges and counsel in adversarial proceedings, the ability to observe a witness's demeanour and deportment while giving evidence is essential to assessing accuracy and credibility. If the witness cannot be seen, he or she is effectively immunised from cross-examination, which is incompatible with an adversarial trial. These observations were made in a case where the inability to give evidence in plain view of the court arose from religious convictions, which compelled the court to examine the human rights implications. They were also clearly directed at adversarial trials and so may apply with less force in the more informal employment tribunal. Nonetheless, the case suggests that courts and tribunals should generally be reluctant to dispense with the need to see those giving evidence. If there are compelling reasons for the tribunal to hear evidence in a public hearing by telephone, the potential for adverse impact on the fairness of the proceedings will be lessened if the tribunal is able to proceed with the consent of both parties. The tribunal can also take into account any question of diminished credibility with regard to such evidence, if it sees fit, in the same way as it can accord less weight to written evidence than to oral evidence (see under 'Non-attendance' above.)

In any event, it is becoming easier to arrange for live evidence to be given via electronic means, either by video conferencing or through internet applications such as Skype and Facetime, and so the need for telephone evidence may not arise all that often. That said, these kinds of communication carry their own practical drawbacks. While tribunals commonly have video conferencing facilities available, not all witnesses will have access to the relevant equipment. And when it comes to communication over the internet, it is worth noting that tribunals do not generally have a network or wi-fi connection that is open to tribunal users and so a party wishing to arrange for evidence to be given with the use of an internet-based application may need to provide a laptop equipped with a mobile data card. Whichever method is chosen, early discussion with tribunal staff before the hearing date will be essential to ensuring that whatever preparations can be made are made in time.

Note that the tribunal also has power under rule 33 to use the procedure laid down by Council Regulation (EC) No.1206/2001 to request that a court in another EU Member State take evidence on its behalf. The procedure specifically provides for the evidence to be given via electronic communication. **12.110**

Statements of evidence
12.111
Evidence-in-chief is the evidence given by witnesses for the party who called them, usually involving questioning from the party or the party's representative (also termed 'examination-in-chief'). A party 'appearing in person' may find it difficult to give his or her own evidence-in-chief in an orderly way, so it is advisable to have prepared a written statement in advance and to make copies available for each tribunal member. The use of witness statements is more than a simple matter of convenience for the parties. The EAT in Senator Hotels Ltd v Ratkowski EAT 0318/12 commented that one of the major purposes of a witness statement is to enable the tribunal to concentrate on that which is important at the oral hearing. The statement therefore saves time at the hearing and assists focus. The EAT also pointed out that the statement, once exchanged, gives the other party advance warning of what is to be said at the hearing, enabling that party to prepare. It is now commonplace for tribunals to require the exchange of witness statements (including a statement of the claimant's evidence-in-chief) prior to the hearing as part of the standard case management order. Any witness statement that stands as evidence-in-chief will be made available for inspection during the course of the hearing to members of the public unless the tribunal decides otherwise or rule 50 (privacy and restrictions on disclosure) or rule 95 (national security) applies – rule 44.

There has been some inconsistency in practice as to whether witnesses in attendance at the hearing would be expected to read out their witness statements. Such was the usual course but tribunals were able to dispense with the requirement under their general case management powers. In Mehta v Child

693

Support Agency 2011 ICR D7, EAT, the EAT held that it was not unfair for a tribunal to require some of the employer's witnesses to read out their statements during a hearing but to take the unrepresented claimant's statement as read, in circumstances where the claimant had consented to this proposal and the tribunal had taken steps to ensure that she, as a litigant in person, had understood what it was proposing. It went on to note that it is not a requirement of fairness in every case that witness statements must be read aloud in full, or indeed at all. The EAT recognised that, in very many cases, doing so will achieve nothing and will be an unnecessary waste of time, especially where the statements in question are drafted by lawyers and consist of very detailed material.

12.112 This view has since been codified in the Tribunal Rules as a presumption that witness statements will be taken as read. The presumption was first given effect by the Employment Tribunals (Constitution and Rules of Procedure) (Amendment) Regulations 2012 SI 2012/468, which amended rule 27 of the Tribunal Rules 2004. The same presumption now appears at rule 43 of the Tribunal Rules 2013, which states that 'where a witness is called to give oral evidence, any witness statement of that person ordered by the tribunal shall stand as that witness's evidence-in-chief unless the tribunal orders otherwise'.

New rule 43 does not set out the circumstances in which the tribunal might see fit to depart from the default procedure. In this regard, the further comments of the EAT in Mehta may have some continued relevance. The EAT accepted that, in certain cases, there may be a good reason for a witness to read out his or her statement, particularly where it is the claimant's statement and he or she is unrepresented. Such reasons may include enabling the claimant to feel that he or she has had a say; to take a witness through a confused or inadequate witness statement and therefore obtain clarification and/or further information; to assist where the material is very technical; and to allow a witness the opportunity to 'settle him or herself' by first answering some neutral questions before being exposed to hostile cross-examination. The EAT went on to note that it does not have to be 'all or nothing'. There may be benefit in reading out only a part of a statement or for a witness to be 'walked through' his or her statement by counsel and only read out key points. Alternatively, a judge may choose to summarise an unrepresented party's statement to confirm that it has been understood properly. The EAT also noted that, when exercising their discretion, tribunals should try as far as possible to proceed with the agreement of the parties and, where one or both parties are unrepresented, should ensure that they understand what is being proposed. If it is necessary to make a direction about how witness statements should be handled, the tribunal should ensure that there is no perception of the parties being treated differently. This does not mean that all witnesses, or witnesses on different sides, should be treated in the same way – there may be good reasons for a difference in treatment – but if so, the reasons for the difference in treatment should be very fully explained to defuse any perception of unfairness.

Witnesses 12.113

Witnesses will normally be called in the order the party decides, and it has long been assumed that tribunals have no power to direct the order in which an party calls his or her witnesses – see, for example, Barnes and anor v BPC (Business Forms) Ltd 1975 ICR 390, EAT, and Aberdeen Steak Houses Group plc v Ibrahim 1988 ICR 550, EAT. However, the Court of Appeal in Yeboah v Crofton 2002 IRLR 634, CA, took a different view. Lord Justice Mummery referred to the tribunal's broad discretion under then rule 9(1) of the Employment Tribunals (Constitution and Rules of Procedure) Regulations 1993 SI 1993/2687 (now rule 41 of the Tribunal Rules 2013) to 'conduct the hearing in such manner as it considers most appropriate for the clarification of the issues before it and generally to the just handling of the proceedings'. He concluded that this meant that the claimant's submission that the tribunal had no discretion to determine the order in which witnesses are called was incorrect. There was accordingly no error of law in the tribunal's failure to conduct the proceedings in the way that the claimant wished, e.g. calling witnesses in the order he requested.

Once called, witnesses are directed to the witness table and sworn by the clerk to give their testimony orally. Since the party examining the witness is in control of this, the witness should not be left to ramble but rather should be encouraged to deal with the important points and be interrupted if he or she strays. All questions should be phrased simply and put one at a time. The party presenting the evidence should speak slowly so as to allow the employment judge to take his or her notes and should advise all witnesses to address their answers to the tribunal.

The first essential 'rule' in examining witnesses is to ask questions which are 12.114 relevant to the matter in issue. The second rule is for the party conducting examination-in-chief to avoid asking 'leading' questions of his or her own witnesses. A leading question is one that directly or indirectly suggests a particular answer, or that assumes the existence of a fact which has not yet been given in evidence and which is still in dispute. Examples of leading questions would be: 'What did you do after the claimant hit you?' if the witness has not yet given evidence that he or she was hit, and: 'Did you report him to the supervisor?' rather than 'What did you do next?'

Extracting testimony without recourse to leading questions can seem quite laborious to the inexperienced representative, but the purpose is to ensure that words are not put into the witness's mouth. Opponents (especially legally trained ones) may object to any leading; if this happens, the employment judge may require the question to be rephrased in a non-leading manner. That said, many employment judges use their discretion to permit leading questions and even welcome them where they are on non-contentious issues like the witness's identity, address and position with the employer. Even where matters are

695

disputed, an unrepresented party may be allowed some latitude. However, it is important to bear in mind that the tribunal's eyes and ears are directed to the witnesses themselves and they expect testimony to be given by them, not by the party whose witness it happens to be.

12.115 It is important that the party who opens the hearing should bring all relevant evidence before closing his or her case as it may be difficult to introduce, in cross-examination of the opponent's witness, a matter not already covered. In Aberdeen Steak Houses Group plc v Ibrahim (above) the EAT held that the employment tribunal was led into procedural error after the claimant sought to put to the respondent's witness in cross-examination the allegation that the witness had privately admitted to the claimant's wife that the claimant had been dismissed, a fact that was in dispute. The claimant had chosen, for tactical reasons, not to raise this with his wife when she gave her evidence. The claimant's wife was recalled and cross-examined about the matter but the tribunal then refused permission for the employer to recall the manager to respond to her evidence. The EAT held that this refusal was an error of law. It went on to observe that a tribunal should be astute to prevent the tactical presentation of evidence in a way which would not normally be permitted and which can cause embarrassment or prejudice to a party. Here, the witness's alleged confession was clearly relevant evidence and should have been called in chief.

12.116 **Introducing documents.** When questioning witnesses, a party may want to bring in documentary evidence – for example, a set of sales results or a report made about some matter in issue. The party or representative should not do this by saying, 'I've got these figures/this report to back this up' and then reading them out. Instead, the witness should be asked to turn to the relevant numbered page or document in the bundle and requested to read out or identify the document (sometimes it is best read out by the party or their representative). Meanwhile, the tribunal will have found it in the bundle and be studying it as it is being identified or read out. The witness should then be asked questions on the particular document with a view to explaining those parts which are being relied upon to support the party's case.

12.117 **Hostile witnesses.** Occasionally a witness who has agreed to give evidence for one party will change his or her story so that it is no longer favourable, or will become antagonistic during examination-in-chief. It is possible in such a situation to ask the employment judge for permission to treat the witness as 'hostile', enabling the party to cross-examine (see below) his or her own witness and use leading questions to try to elicit more favourable answers or discredit the adverse testimony. However, this is very rarely allowed in employment tribunals and parties will need very strong evidence that the witness is being deliberately obstructive or has changed his or her story before permission will be given. At the very least the tribunal will expect the party to show a prior witness statement from which the witness has departed in his or her oral evidence before the tribunal – see, for example, Kuttapan v London Borough of Croydon and ors EAT 39/00.

Cross-examination

12.118

When cross-examining the opponent's witnesses, the overall aim is always to discredit the opponent's case or boost the credence of one's own. Cross-examination is the right of any party whose opponent's witness has been called and sworn (see further under 'Natural justice and the right to a fair hearing – right to cross-examine and present evidence' below). The only exception to this is where the witness is called only in order to produce a document and, having done so, is not examined at all by the party calling him or her. Note that it is quite proper for the tribunal to limit the amount of time allocated to cross-examination in the interest of efficient time-management – see La Vertue v Ilex Energy Consultants Ltd EAT 0520/05.

Under cross-examination, the witness can be asked leading questions, and those questions do not have to be confined to the subjects and issues raised by the opponent in examination-in-chief. So, for example, questions can be put that are designed to interrogate a witness on matters of credibility about his or her own or other witnesses' testimony. The skill in cross-examination lies in asking incisive and succinct questions that have the effect of teasing out responses that disprove or, more commonly, cast doubt on the evidence adduced by the other side, or prove the case of the party cross-examining. Leading questions requiring short or one-word answers are often the most effective. Long rambling questions or, worse still, statements by the cross-examiner which allow the witness time to think (or time to lose the thread of the point being made) should be avoided.

An essential function of the party cross-examining is to put his or her own **12.119** version of any disputed facts to the opponent's witnesses and give them the opportunity to comment on it. A failure to challenge the witness on disputed facts in this way may prevent a party from bringing conflicting evidence, unless the tribunal recalls the witness for further cross-examination – see Chapter 13, 'Evidence', under 'Assessing the weight of evidence – parties' responsibilities in matters of evidence'.

Even if (as is likely) the witness sticks to his or her testimony, the tribunal will have been alerted to the disputed facts and to the ability of the party to call evidence which contradicts these facts. Thus: 'You say that you did not actually hit Mr Jones?' 'That's right, I didn't.' 'Well, he will be giving evidence to show that you did – medical evidence from a qualified doctor who saw him immediately afterwards.'

Introducing new matters in cross-examination. As noted in relation to **12.120** 'Statements of evidence' above, the matters on which a witness may be cross-examined may be limited by the evidence already presented. In Aberdeen Steak

697

Houses Group plc v Ibrahim 1988 ICR 550, EAT, the EAT warned that tribunals should be astute to prevent the tactical presentation of evidence. In that case, the claimant chose not to raise, during evidence-in-chief, an allegation that one of the employer's witnesses had privately admitted the fact of dismissal (which was disputed). He later sought to introduce this point when cross-examining the particular witness. The EAT disparaged this tactical approach, which led the tribunal into a procedural error requiring remission of the claim.

The EAT clarified in Jones v London Borough of Havering and anor EAT 1099/01 that the Ibrahim case does not lay down a principle that cross-examination is restricted to matters that the cross-examining party has already put forward as evidence-in-chief. There, it was a key part of J's case that her employer had not conducted a suitable mental health risk assessment in relation to the stress and anxiety she had claimed to suffer at work. She did not introduce any evidence as to what such an assessment should cover. When she sought to ask the employer questions in cross-examination, based on specialist material, relating to how such an assessment should be carried out, the tribunal prevented her from doing so, taking the view that she was thereby trying to introduce expert evidence that she should have disclosed earlier on. The EAT held that the tribunal's objection was unfounded. A tribunal should permit an opponent's witness to be cross-examined on any matter provided it is relevant. The claimant was not seeking to introduce unchallenged evidence, merely to ask questions from a document consisting of her own notes. It was open to the witness to agree with the questions (in which case they would quite permissibly become evidence), or to disagree with them (in which case they would not).

12.121 However, the EAT did accept in Contract Security Service v Adebayo EAT 0192/12 that a representative is not entitled, in cross-examination, to put a positive case that has not been pleaded or set out in his or her witness statements. It therefore saw no error of law in an employment judge admonishing the employer's representative during cross-examination of the claimant because there was no factual basis for his questions in any of the employer's witness statements.

12.122 **Cross-examination in sensitive cases.** It may be necessary for the tribunal to exercise its case management powers particularly carefully in cases where, for example, the claimant alleges harassment against a particular respondent who is acting in person. This was the situation that arose in Duffy v George 2013 ICR 1229, CA, where the claimant was a woman claiming sex discrimination and sexual harassment against her employer and a male colleague. She settled the discrimination claim against the employer, leaving only the harassment complaints against the colleague, who was unrepresented and intended to conduct the case himself. He had admitted making the comments on which the harassment claims were based but it was part of his defence that they were not unwanted, being merely 'banter' between them in which the claimant 'gave as good as she got'. The claimant refused to attend the hearing and sought an order from the tribunal excusing her from attending, stating that she was scared to face the respondent. The tribunal refused and heard the claim in her absence. It upheld the claim based on two incidents but declined to award any compensation for injury to feelings in the absence of any evidence from the claimant on this point.

When the matter reached the Court of Appeal it held that the tribunal had erred in proceeding in this way. It should have first held a pre-trial review for directions to consider the options for the conduct of a fair and just hearing in the light of the claimant's resolve not to give oral evidence. This would have involved exploring with the parties – either separately or together – whether the claimant was fearful of attending to be cross-examined and, if so, whether it could proceed with separate hearings at which each party would give evidence in the other's absence. Lord Justice Pitchford considered examples of how delicate cases are handled in other jurisdictions, such as criminal allegations of sexual offences, which may be relevant to employment tribunals exercising case management powers in similar circumstances. He considered that it was within the tribunal's wide case management power to prohibit cross-examination by the respondent personally of a claimant whose evidence was that she was sexually harassed by the respondent in the workplace. It was incumbent on the tribunal, assuming the claimant's fear was genuine, to consider how she could give oral evidence without being subjected to cross-examination and what status should be accorded to her written evidence if she persisted in refusing to attend. Other possibilities for consideration would have included the claimant answering questions from the tribunal rather than from the respondent in person, and the claimant giving evidence with the use of screens.

Questioning by tribunal
12.123

After cross-examination the tribunal members are likely to put their own questions to witnesses. These questions are very important to the conduct of the case, since they point to questions not asked or answered to their satisfaction and signal what work a party still has to do to establish his or her case or demolish the opponent's.

Often, the employment judge (and sometimes a lay member) will interrupt during the course of examination-in-chief and cross-examination in order to ask questions which occur to him or her at that particular point in time. This will be particularly so in the case of unrepresented parties and, if properly done, will do much to ensure that the crucial issues and questions are actually raised so that witnesses have an opportunity to consider them. However, where parties are represented, if the quality of the advocacy is adequate, then most judges will be less interventionist until the cross-examination stage is completed.

As to the extent to which tribunals are under a duty to assist parties and **12.124** ask questions or raise issues of their own motion, see 'Assistance by the tribunal' below.

699

12.125 Re-examination

When the tribunal has finished asking any questions which it may have, the party who first called the witness will be asked if he or she wants to question the witness further on matters disclosed by the tribunal's own queries or by the other side's cross-examination. The questions put to the witness in re-examination must be confined strictly to his or her statements made during cross-examination or in response to the tribunal's own questions, or to matters immediately arising out of those statements. No questions can be put (without the consent of the tribunal) which bear upon any matter which has not arisen directly out of the cross-examination or the tribunal's questions, since such matters should have been raised during examination-in-chief. Tribunals may be a little more flexible (but probably not by very much) if a witness is re-examined on matters raised in examination-in-chief but which were not touched upon at all during cross-examination. But note that leading questions are even less acceptable during re-examination and so questions should be direct and open-ended (i.e. they should not, in the way they are framed, suggest the answer required).

Following re-examination of a party's own witnesses, that party may apply for any of them to be released, and should do so if he or she is sure that they will not have to be recalled later to fill in any gaps in the evidence.

12.126 Challenging the opponent's or tribunal's handling of the case

If the other party repeatedly leads his or her witness on evidence which is in dispute, or cross-examines a party's witness in an irrelevant or deliberately harassing way, then the party may object by a polite intervention, pointing out to the tribunal why this should not be allowed to go on. The employment judge or lay members may get there first, of course, but if they do not, or if they overrule an objection, the party should try not to let this affect the conduct of the case.

The party may him or herself be interrupted when presenting his or her case and have to explain why a particular line of enquiry is being pursued. It is up to the employment judge whether to allow this to happen and his or her decision on the matter should be accepted with good grace. But where an opponent's or the judge's interruptions are groundless, it may be necessary for the person presenting the case to stick to his or her guns and to insist quietly but firmly upon pursuing the original line of enquiry.

12.127 Where the employment judge is being hostile or unjustly impatient or biased, it is sensible to apply for the particular difficulty to be 'noted on the record'. The tribunal may even be requested to stand down if the party affected has lost confidence in its impartiality or ability to handle the case justly. Where the tribunal refuses to do this, and there is a risk that the rules of natural justice may have been flouted, there may be grounds for appeal to the EAT – see 'Natural justice and the right to a fair hearing' below.

700

Assistance by the tribunal

There is a long-established practice whereby tribunal judges give assistance to unrepresented parties (be they claimant or respondent) in the formulation and presentation of the case before them. This arises out of the wide discretion given to an employment judge or tribunal as to the conduct of a case and his, her or its ability to question parties and witnesses. This quasi-inquisitorial role existed in the 2004 Rules (and in previous versions) but it has apparently been downgraded in the 2013 re-enactment. The relevant provision under the 2004 Rules was rule 14(3), which stated that the judge or tribunal '*shall* make such enquiries of persons appearing before him or it and of witnesses as he or it considers appropriate for the clarification of the issues and generally for the just handling of the proceedings' (our stress). Now, rule 41 of the 2013 Rules states, among other things, that the tribunal '*may* itself question the parties or any witnesses so far as appropriate in order to clarify the issues or elicit the evidence' (our stress).

None of the consultation documents on the draft 2013 Rules mentioned any intention to change the tribunal's role in this respect. It is more likely that the reformulated rule is merely intended to reflect the established understanding of the extent of the tribunal's role in this regard. For example, while the Court of Appeal in Mensah v East Hertfordshire NHS Trust 1998 IRLR 531, CA, strongly encouraged tribunals to be as helpful as possible to litigants in formulating and presenting their case, it nonetheless confirmed a long line of EAT decisions holding that it is the responsibility of the parties themselves to present the case and put the relevant evidence before the tribunal. Furthermore, in McNicol v Balfour Beatty Rail Maintenance Ltd 2002 ICR 1498, CA, the Court of Appeal rejected the suggestion that tribunals should adopt an inquisitorial and more proactive role in disability discrimination cases. Lord Justice Mummery reaffirmed the tribunal's role as being to adjudicate on disputes as presented to it by the parties. His Lordship acknowledged that, in disability discrimination claims, there will be difficult borderline cases but stressed that it is not the tribunal's duty 'to obtain evidence or to ensure that adequate medical evidence is obtained by the parties'.

Just as there is no specific duty on the tribunal to assist in the presentation of **12.129** the claim, so there is no particular duty for it to look out for the interests of a party in making decisions about the general handling and prosecution of the claim. In Drysdale v Department of Transport EAT 0171/12 the claimant, RD, was represented by his wife, MD, who was not legally qualified, in his claim of automatically unfair dismissal for having made a protected disclosure. The case had been set down for two days. At the end of the second day, when MD was at the point of re-examining RD, there were still three witnesses for the respondent waiting to be called. MD was frustrated that the hearing would not be finished that day and, when the judge proposed to adjourn to a date four months away, MD responded that in that case she wished to withdraw the claim. The judge asked her to confirm that this was what she wanted, which MD did. The respondent then immediately applied for the claim to be dismissed and the tribunal acceded to that application. RD appealed against the dismissal, arguing, among other things, that the tribunal should have intervened to ensure that MD was acting with his authority. The EAT rejected that argument. MD clearly did have authority and there can be no general duty upon the tribunal to enquire as to whether a litigant agrees with the course taken by his or her duly-appointed representative. Furthermore, while a tribunal is entitled to make such enquiries as appear fit to it to check that a self-representing litigant or lay representative means what he or she says, and is not acting hastily or in anger, the extent of such an enquiry is very much a matter for the tribunal. Here, the judge checked whether MD wanted to withdraw, she said that she did, and RD did not demur.

12.130 **Issues not raised by the parties**

In Mensah v East Hertfordshire NHS Trust 1998 IRLR 531, CA, the claimant had raised two allegations of discrimination in her claim form, but only one of the allegations was mentioned at the tribunal hearing. Her claim was rejected and she appealed, arguing that the tribunal had failed to give sufficient weight to her claim in respect of the other allegation. The Court stated that it would be good practice for tribunals to clarify the precise matters raised in the ET1 which are to be pursued, and confirm that any others are to be dropped, but that it was a matter for the judgement of the individual tribunal whether to investigate of its own motion a complaint which the claimant did not appear to be pursuing.

However, there have been some cases in which the EAT has held that a particular principle is so well established that a tribunal may be expected to consider it as a matter of course, whether or not it has been specifically raised by the parties. In Tidman v Aveling Marshall Ltd 1977 ICR 506, EAT, for example, the EAT held that when assessing compensation for unfair dismissal, a tribunal is obliged to consider the following five heads of claim: (1) immediate loss of wages; (2) manner of dismissal; (3) future loss of wages; (4) loss of statutory protection; (5) loss of pension rights. It is the duty of the tribunal to enquire into those categories of claim even if not specifically put forward by the employee (contrary to the position in the civil courts). And under the heading 'future loss of wages' the tribunal should consider, as a matter of course, whether there is any scope for a Polkey reduction in a case of procedurally unfair dismissal based on the possibility that a fair dismissal could have occurred if a fair procedure had been followed – Wallington and anor v S and B Car Hire Kent Ltd and anor EAT 0240/03. However, once the issues have been raised, the obligation is on the employee to prove his or her loss.

Similarly, in Langston v Cranfield University 1998 IRLR 172, EAT, the EAT **12.131** held that in a case where an employee claimed he had been unfairly dismissed for redundancy, the tribunal could not restrict itself to considering the fairness of the selection – it was obliged to ask whether there had been adequate consultation and whether the employer had made reasonable attempts to look for alternative employment. Even though the employee had not specifically addressed these issues in his submissions, they were 'implicit' in the claim of unfair dismissal by reason of redundancy.

Tribunals must, however, exercise caution. Before taking into account a matter not raised by the parties, the tribunal must give the parties the opportunity to make representations on that issue, otherwise it could be said that there has not been a fair hearing – see Haxey Engineering Ltd v Turner EAT 268/78, discussed in detail under 'Natural justice and the right to a fair hearing – knowing the case which has to be met' below. For example, in Birmingham City Council v Laws EAT 0360/06 a tribunal hearing a claim of disability discrimination erred when it raised the possibility of a reasonable adjustments claim during closing submissions and decided the case on that basis. The tribunal should also refrain from too interventionist a role. In Margarot Forrest Care Management v Kennedy EATS 0023/10 the claimant was dismissed after less than a year's continuous service (which was then the minimum service required to be able to claim unfair dismissal). She sought to bring a claim of wrongful dismissal, complaining in her ET1 of breach of contract and failure to comply with 'health and safety regulations'. At the start of the full hearing, the tribunal sought to identify the issues. Taking account of the claimant's opening statement, the terms of a witness order she had sought and a grievance she had raised with her employer, the tribunal considered that the circumstances of dismissal potentially gave rise to a claim of automatically unfair dismissal for having made a protected disclosure under S.103A of the Employment Rights Act 1996. The tribunal asked the respondent if it objected to the amendment (which it did), adjourned for 20 minutes and returned with an amendment it had drafted itself, on the basis of which it proposed to proceed. The EAT allowed the respondent's appeal against the tribunal's decision to proceed in this way. A new account of the circumstances of the claimant's dismissal appeared very late in the day, at the final hearing. That lateness called for an explanation of how and why it had not until then formed part of the claim. Furthermore, the tribunal was wrong to think that it had discretion to step in and draft the amendment itself. The tribunal may grant leave to a claimant to amend the ET1 in the terms that he or she proposes, if appropriate, but it may not amend the ET1 in whatever terms it thinks best.

Issues going to jurisdiction
12.132
There are some issues in an employment claim that, even if not raised by the parties themselves, ought to be raised by the tribunal because they affect the tribunal's jurisdiction to hear the claim. One such issue is whether the claim

703

was presented in time. The Court of Appeal confirmed in Dedman v British Building and Engineering Appliances Ltd 1974 ICR 53, CA, that a tribunal does not have jurisdiction to hear a claim of unfair dismissal if presented outside the time limit. Even if the employer offers to waive its right to object to the employee's late presentation of the claim, the tribunal would simply be unable to hear the claim given the limits of its statutory jurisdiction. Thus, if it appears to a tribunal that a claim has not been presented in time, it will raise the issue even if the respondent has not done so. (The practicalities and implications of the various time limits that apply to employment tribunal claims are considered in Chapter 5, 'Time limits'.)

In practice, it should be rare for a claim to get to the final hearing without a jurisdictional question being considered. The respondent will usually be astute enough to take the point at the preliminary stage. Furthermore, rule 26 of the Tribunal Rules 2013 now makes specific provision for a judicial 'sift' of all claims, at which stage an employment judge is required to consider whether there is an arguable claim (or defence) within the tribunal's jurisdiction – see Chapter 7, 'Judicial sift', under 'Grounds for dismissal following initial consideration – grounds for dismissal of the claim (or part)'. There is also the possibility of a preliminary hearing under rule 53, which may raise jurisdictional issues – see Chapter 11, 'Case management', under 'Preliminary hearings'. Thus, where there is some doubt over whether the tribunal has jurisdiction to hear a claim, there are several opportunities for this to be flushed out before the final hearing.

12.133 However, in the event that the point has not been dealt with by the time of the final hearing, it is fully open to a tribunal to raise it. In Radakovits v Abbey National plc 2010 IRLR 307, CA, R brought a claim of unfair dismissal one day out of time. The tribunal arranged a pre-hearing review (which would now be a preliminary hearing under the Tribunal Rules 2013) to consider whether the claim should be accepted but, after the employer indicated that it did not intend to contest this point, an employment judge vacated the PHR and issued case management orders. However, when it came to the full hearing, the tribunal decided that it should give full consideration to the time point. It went on to conclude that the claim was out of time and could not proceed. The EAT rejected R's appeal against that decision, holding that, since the issue was one of jurisdiction, the tribunal was required to consider it of its own motion if it was unsure whether it could properly deal with the case. The Court of Appeal rejected R's further appeal, holding that the vacation of the PHR could not be treated as a binding judgment in which the tribunal accepted jurisdiction.

Lord Justice Elias, giving judgment in Radakovits, went on to comment on the extent of an employment tribunal's obligation to raise a jurisdictional issue such as this, which has been overlooked by the parties. He stated that, while tribunals are obliged to raise the issue of jurisdiction even though it has not been identified in order to guard against exercising a jurisdiction when the statutory conditions are not met, tribunals are not 'bloodhounds who have to sniff out potential grounds on which jurisdiction can be refused'. His view was that if, for example, the parties agree that a particular claimant is an employee, there would have to be good reason for the tribunal to doubt that that was the case and to require a preliminary hearing to investigate the matter. If, on the face of it, it appears that the tribunal does have jurisdiction or if there appears to have been a satisfactory explanation for extending what would be the usual time limits, then the tribunal can properly act on that. It does not have to explore fully every case where a jurisdictional issue could potentially arise.

Assisting parties with giving evidence

12.134

It is not just in the presentation of the legal issues that unrepresented parties may desire assistance from a tribunal. Litigants in person may also struggle with the presentation of evidence, either through oversight of important facts or through a failure to appreciate the need to establish a particular point. This is indeed recognised in the Tribunal Rules 2013, as rule 41 allows the tribunals to question the parties so far as appropriate to clarify the issues or 'elicit the evidence'. However, just as there is no formal duty on tribunals to assist the parties in presenting the legal issues, so there is no formal duty to assist in presenting the evidence.

Nonetheless, there are circumstances in which the tribunal will be under a duty to warn a party about the effect on his or her case of failing to present evidence on a particular point. In Radakovits v Abbey National plc 2010 IRLR 307, CA (considered under 'Issues going to jurisdiction' above), Lord Justice Elias commented that it might be proper for a tribunal to explain to an unrepresented party the issue that it has to determine and explain why, for example, that party may be prejudiced if he or she fails to give evidence. He went on to note, however, that the tribunal must not say anything about the evidence the party should give in order to sustain his or her case.

The EAT applied Radakovits in Bozeat-Manzi v Telefonica UK Ltd EAT 12.135 0389/12. There, the claimant, BM, was suffering from depression and unable to present his claims of unfair dismissal, disability discrimination and breach of contract in person. His father, B, conducted the claim on his behalf. The claims were lodged one day out of time and so the tribunal convened a pre-hearing review (now a 'preliminary hearing' under rule 53) to consider whether time should be extended. At the PHR, the employment judge told B that, normally, the claimant could be expected to give evidence on a time point. B confirmed that BM was too ill to attend and was content that the hearing should proceed in his absence. The PHR accordingly proceeded on the basis of written submissions and the judge decided that time should not be extended. On appeal, the EAT held that, in proceeding without indicating to B that he himself could

705

give relevant evidence and that BM's case might suffer if he did not do so, the judge was in error of law.

In contrast, in Senator Hotels Ltd v Ratkowski EAT 0318/12 the EAT rejected the suggestion that the unrepresented employer, who had ignored a case management order to produce a witness statement because he saw no value in doing so, should have been offered an adjournment on the day of the hearing so that he could remedy the lack of evidence. If the employer was to be allowed to remedy his failure to provide a witness statement, the time for any remedy was that very day. Nor was the tribunal obliged to ensure that the employer adduced evidence in support of his case – if anything, the tribunal had been generous in highlighting the importance of adducing evidence and offering him the opportunity to do so on the day.

'No case to answer'

12.136

By the time all the evidence has been given, the party going first will hope at least to have proved those facts absolutely essential to his or her case. If by then the opponent believes that the fundamental facts have not been proved, he or she may consider making a submission of 'no case to answer'. This may be appropriate, for example, where it is felt that an employee who claims constructive dismissal has failed to show any conduct by the employer that justified him or her in resigning or walking out. It may also be the case where the claimant simply fails to produce the requisite standard of evidence. In Fitzke v AEG Europe ET Case No.2328223/08 the claimant, F, had been ordered at a pre-hearing review to exchange a written witness statement with AEG by 25 August. On 23 August she wrote to the tribunal stating that she was not to be a witness in her case. At the outset of the hearing she reiterated her refusal to give evidence, take an oath or subject herself to cross-examination as she wanted her case to proceed solely on the basis of AEG's evidence and her cross-examination of its witnesses. AEG made a submission of no case to answer and the tribunal acceded to this, as a result of which it dismissed the claim. In the tribunal's assessment, F's allegations concerned spoken words and actions that could only be established by oral evidence. Her refusal, therefore, to give evidence and to submit to cross-examination meant that she had provided no evidence for AEG to answer.

If a submission of 'no case to answer' is accepted by the tribunal, the party making it will not be required to present his or her evidence and the claim or, as the case may be, defence will fail. The approach has been sanctioned by the EAT on several occasions and, in Clark v Watford Borough Council EAT 43/99, the Appeal Tribunal summarised the general principles thus:

- there is no inflexible rule of law and practice that a tribunal must always hear both sides, although that should normally be done

706

- the power to stop a case at 'half-time' must be exercised with caution

- it may be a complete waste of time to call upon the other party to give evidence in a hopeless case

- even where the onus of proof lies on the claimant, as in discrimination cases, it will only be in exceptional or frivolous cases that it would be right to take such a course of action

- where there is no burden of proof, as under S.98(4) of the Employment Rights Act 1996 (reasonableness of dismissal), it will be difficult to envisage arguable cases where it is appropriate to terminate the proceedings at the end of the first party's case.

This summary was later approved explicitly by the Court of Appeal in Logan v Commissioners of Customs and Excise 2004 ICR 1, CA. The Court went on to observe that the fourth point above in relation to discrimination cases applies equally to constructive dismissal cases, and noted that it should be 'rare for the submission to be made and rare for the submission to succeed'. The EAT in Boulding v Land Securities Trilliam (Media Services) Ltd EAT 0023/06 later held that whistleblowing victimisation is a form of discrimination and that such claims should also normally be heard in full. **12.137**

It is notable, though, that many of the cases in which the submission has been accepted were decided at a time before tribunals had a specific power to strike out a case on the ground that it has no reasonable prospect of success. Such a power was introduced for the first time in 2001 and is currently found in rule 37(1) of the Tribunal Rules 2013. This states clearly that the power to strike out may be exercised at any stage of the proceedings, either on the tribunal's own motion or in response to a party's application, and so this may seem a more natural channel for the assertion that a case is manifestly doomed to fail. The EAT has recognised that tribunals must proceed with greater caution in relation to submissions of 'no case to answer' now that there are specific procedures available for weeding out hopeless claims before they get to a hearing – Wiggan v RN Wooler and Company Ltd EAT 0542/06. The EAT made this observation at a time when the Tribunal Rules 2004 were in force. It must also apply (possibly with increased vigour) under the 2013 Rules, which introduce, among other things, a preliminary sift designed to identify weak claims – see Chapter 7, 'Judicial sift'.

The EAT in Wiggan also recognised that the same substantive considerations apply to a submission of 'no case to answer' as to an application for strike-out made midway through proceedings on the basis that the claim has no reasonable prospect of success. The difference between the two kinds of submission is merely one of label. Thus, recent cases exhorting tribunals to be reluctant to accede to such strike-out applications must also restrict the scope for tribunals to accept submissions of 'no case to answer'. **12.138**

707

One of the leading cases on striking out halfway through proceedings is the decision of the EAT, under its President, Mr Justice Langstaff, in Williams v Real Care Agency Ltd 2012 ICR D27, EAT. Although the EAT did not refer to the authorities on 'no case to answer', such as Logan v Commissioners of Customs and Excise (above), the application for a strike-out was a submission of 'no case to answer' in all but name. The claim was one of unfair dismissal, where W was accused of falsely over-stating the hours she had worked as a care worker, with the result that she was overpaid and her employer overcharged its clients. Her defence was that this was a common practice, which was endorsed by the employer. At the tribunal, after three days of hearing, by which time the employee had given evidence-in-chief and been cross-examined in part, but had not called any of her witnesses, the tribunal acceded to the respondent employer's application for strike-out on three grounds: (1) it was inevitable that it would find that W's contract of employment had been performed illegally, meaning that she had no contract on which to base her claim; (2) W's credibility had been severely undermined in the course of her giving evidence; and (3) W could not realistically expect to be awarded compensation given the extent to which she had profited from the over-charging. On appeal, the EAT held that the tribunal had erred in law. It had to be recognised that the circumstances would be very exceptional indeed, to the point of the instances of it being vanishingly small, that a claim could ever legitimately be struck out mid-hearing on the basis that the evidence is lacking. The EAT also noted that the hearing of an application for strike-out during the course of the proceedings will itself take up the tribunal's time, which could otherwise be better spent hearing evidence. Such a procedure would therefore run counter to the overriding objective in that it would cost time, money and resources, cause inconvenience to the parties and risk giving the impression to a litigant that he or she has been wrongly shut out from telling his or her story in a public forum.

12.139 As noted above, the EAT in Williams was expressly dealing with a strike-out application under what was then rule 18(7) of the 2004 Rules (now rule 37(1) of the 2013 Rules), and not a submission of 'no case to answer'. However, given that both applications involve a submission of what Langstaff P in Williams termed 'evidential insubstantiability', the same considerations must surely apply. Indeed, the EAT in Timbo v Greenwich Council for Racial Equality 2013 ICR D7, EAT, considered the authorities relating to strike-out and those relating to 'no case to answer' and accepted that the position in relation to both is fundamentally the same. There, the tribunal granted an application for strike-out after three days of hearing in a discrimination claim, having heard the claimant's case but no evidence from the respondent apart from the witness statements. The EAT held that it was wrong to do so. Having properly recognised that, to a very significant extent, the claimant's case depended on her credibility as a witness, the tribunal should have heard all the evidence and evaluated it. It is one thing to reach a provisional view at the halfway point that a witness's evidence is unsatisfactory and that it is unlikely to be accepted if there is evidence to the contrary, but another thing altogether to reach a concluded view that a witness's evidence must inevitably be rejected in its entirety even if there is no evidence to contradict it.

The grounds on which a claim may be struck out and the restrictions on the use of the power are discussed more generally in Chapter 11, 'Case management', under 'Striking out'.

In so far as the submission of 'no case to answer' still has some place in the **12.140** modern tribunal, tribunals should not of their own motion invite a party to make such a submission, since it destroys the appearance of justice and impartiality – see Harper v Mothercare Ltd EAT 153/84. A more discreet and usual way to encourage a saving in time and money where a party's case seems hopeless is for the tribunal to suggest to the parties that they try to settle. If necessary, some tribunals will adjourn for this to be done and then tell the parties' representatives in private that, due to the weakness of one side's case, a withdrawal or settlement would seem appropriate.

Where a party makes an unsuccessful submission of 'no case to answer', he or she will not usually be prevented from calling his or her own evidence – Walker v Josiah Wedgwood 1978 ICR 744, EAT. This contrasts with the position in ordinary civil courts, where a judge will not normally rule on any such submission unless the party making it undertakes not to pursue his or her own case if the submission fails. However, where a party to tribunal proceedings specifically states that he or she will not call evidence, that party will be bound by this statement if the submission of 'no case' is rejected – Stokes v Hampstead Wine Co Ltd 1979 IRLR 298, EAT. Care should therefore be taken over this manoeuvre.

Closing statements and legal submissions   12.141

By the time the parties come to present their closing speeches, the examination-in-chief, cross-examination and re-examination of the parties and their witnesses will have been completed and the tribunal will have heard all the evidence from both sides (at least, all that relates to liability). It has generally been thought that, in contrast to opening statements, parties have the right to make closing statements to the tribunal. Such statements in the ordinary courts are customarily called 'addresses' and, until recently, the tribunal rules have contained an express rule stating that a party is entitled to 'address' the tribunal. Indeed, failure to allow a closing speech has been a ground for appeal – Camden and Islington Health Authority v Fenwick unreported 18 April 2000, CA (although the appeal did not succeed on the facts).

However, the position is less clear-cut under the Tribunal Rules 2013 as there is no longer any specific right for a party to 'address' the tribunal. This right has

709

been part of the rules of procedure for a long time. The appeal in Fenwick relied on rule 9(2) of Schedule 1 to the Industrial Tribunals (Constitution and Rules of Procedure) Regulations 1993 SI 1993/2687, which stated that 'a party shall be entitled to give evidence, to call witnesses, to question any witness and to address the tribunal'. That rule was re-enacted in 2001 and again in 2004, appearing in materially identical form at rule 27(1) of the Tribunal Rules 2004. However, there is no equivalent in the 2013 Rules and, if anything, the current incarnation of the Employment Tribunal Rules of Procedure is weighted away from any specific right to be heard and towards tribunals having a discretion to control the amount of time given over to advocacy. For instance, rule 45 specifically provides that 'a tribunal may impose limits on the time that a party may take in presenting evidence, questioning witnesses or making submissions, and may prevent the party from proceeding beyond any time so allotted'. Of course, tribunals were always able to do this under the previous rules but, as noted under 'Presenting the evidence' above, the specific statement of this power in the 2013 Rules is intended to embolden tribunals to take robust case management decisions. Accordingly, in so far as there is any right to make a closing statement, parties and advocates must be prepared to limit their submissions to the time made available by the tribunal.

12.142 In England and Wales, tribunals will usually follow the ordinary court procedure of allowing the party upon whom the burden of proof lies to have the benefit of addressing the tribunal last. In discrimination cases, where the burden of proof may shift from claimant to respondent, the usual practice is for the claimant to go last. In Scotland the practice is for closing speeches to be made in the same order as that in which the evidence was led. Given their discretion over procedure, it would seem that where tribunals do not follow the usual order, their proceedings will not necessarily be regarded as irregular – see Peters v Science Museum, unreported 29.11.79, CA. Indeed, in Glencross and anor v Dymoke 1979 ICR 536, EAT, the EAT declined to make a ruling on the order in which closing speeches should be made.

The purpose of closing statements is to relate the evidence to the relevant law with a view to persuading the tribunal to decide the case, on the balance of probabilities, in favour of one's own party. In most cases, closing speeches may be helpful but not decisive. The tribunal will by now know all the relevant issues and the application of the law to those issues will rarely be a difficult task for experienced employment judges. Occasionally, however, the case is so complex – factually or legally – that a party's final address may be decisive in persuading the tribunal of what law is relevant, how it should be applied to the facts and the conclusion which should ultimately be reached. In any case, a succinct and cogent closing address should do all of the following:

- remind the tribunal of the legal issues involved, referring briefly to the relevant statutory provisions

710

- review the most salient evidence

- present legal submissions as to why the tribunal should find in favour of the party making the address. (This may include relying on legal precedents – see below)

- clearly relate the evidence and legal submissions to pleas in the alternative where these exist

- attempt to deal with the other party's case and explain how the facts and law combine to defeat it.

It is important to note that there will be no need to review all the evidence in the case. To do so will simply irritate the tribunal. A closing speech should not include matters that have not been given in evidence – for example, where evidence had been omitted by mistake or the witness had not come up to proof. Nor should they seek to introduce a ground of claim not already raised, as the tribunal will not be able to hear it – see, for example, Olasehinde v Panther Securities plc EAT 0554/07. What ought to be highlighted are the vital aspects of the evidence and those facts which are not challenged by the other side. Any inconsistencies and weaknesses should also be pointed out. And it may be appropriate in an unfair dismissal case to suggest how a reasonable employer would have handled the dismissal. **12.143**

In complex cases, tribunals may request written submissions from the parties, summing up their respective cases, before hearing closing oral submissions. The EAT approved this procedure in Sinclair Roche and Temperley and ors v Heard and anor 2004 IRLR 763, EAT, but cautioned that the parties and, maybe more importantly, the tribunal should have ample time to read and assimilate the written statements before oral submissions are heard. In that case, extensive written submissions – running to 97 pages from the respondent and 67 from the claimant – were received by the parties and the tribunal on the same day that oral submissions were due to start. Neither party, nor the tribunal, would have had time to read, let alone understand, the written submissions, and that detracted much from the value of the oral submissions.

Although, as noted above, tribunals are entitled to place time limits on the length of closing addresses, too short a limit may give rise to a legitimate ground of appeal. In Ahmed v London Borough of Hackney and anor EAT 120/99 written closing statements were submitted by the parties and the tribunal heard additional oral submissions which it limited to 30 minutes each. The EAT held that this is perfectly acceptable and is common practice all over the country. However, in Hulmes v British Telecommunications plc EAT 475/86 the tribunal chairman limited final speeches at the end of a two-day hearing to ten minutes each in order avoid the necessity of an adjournment. The EAT overturned the tribunal's decision, holding that, on the facts, the claimant's representative had not been given time enough to develop his arguments and justice had clearly

711

not been seen to be done. Although the EAT refused to lay down any general guidance to tribunals on the issue, it did comment that the injustice to the claimant was not remedied by placing a similar limit on the respondent's closing speech. The continued authority of this case may be in question now that rule 45 of the Tribunal Rules 2013 specifically empowers a tribunal to limit the amount of time a party takes in making submissions. However, any power that the tribunal exercises under the Tribunal Rules must be exercised judicially and not in such a way as to deprive either side of a fair hearing, and so a complaint about insufficient time being allocated to closing submissions might still be heard on this ground.

12.144 Precedents and the law

Careful use of precedents from decided cases can be made as part of any legal submission. Decisions of a superior court are binding on employment tribunals, so if a decision of a higher court cannot be distinguished in its application of principle to the facts of the case before it, the tribunal must follow that decision. Employment tribunals are bound by previous decisions of the Supreme Court (and its predecessor, the House of Lords), Court of Appeal, High Court and EAT (and its predecessors).

Employment tribunals are not bound by other tribunal or county court decisions, although these may be of persuasive value if the facts are similar and the decision soundly structured in law. Conversely, the decisions of employment tribunals themselves may be binding on the civil courts in respect of their findings of fact (but not propositions of law), since such decisions may give rise to 'issue estoppel' so long as they relate directly to proceedings between the same parties – O'Laoire v Jackel International Ltd (No.2) 1991 ICR 718, CA. Issue estoppel is considered in Chapter 2, 'Tribunals' jurisdiction', under 'Relitigation: res judicata and abuse of process'.

12.145 Problems can arise where there are two conflicting EAT decisions on the same point. Where this happens, as a matter of ordinary precedent and practice the tribunal can be expected to follow the more recent decision, although it should normally look at the matter in detail and come to its own conclusion on which authority is to be preferred, using the chronology of the cases to tip the balance only if there is nothing between them – Blue Diamond Services Ltd v McNeish and ors EAT 1354/01.

Most tribunals prefer parties to argue from principle and statute, not previous case law. In any event, the relevant law will usually be known to the tribunal, who will be well-versed in how to apply it to multifarious factual situations. Indeed, the EAT has been keen to dissuade parties from over-reliance on reported case authorities. In Anandarajah v Lord Chancellor's Department 1984 IRLR 131, EAT, for example, the then President of the EAT stated that: 'The days are passing... when [employment] tribunals were to be treated as dependent for the

712

discharge of their fact-finding role upon judicial "guidelines" sought to be extracted from reported decisions... Sometimes the judgment in a particular case [expresses] in concise and helpful language some concept which is regularly found in [the field of employment law] and it becomes of great illustrative value. But reference to such a case can never be a substitute for taking the explicit directions of the statute as the guiding principle.' And in Clark v Clark Construction Initiatives Ltd and anor 2009 ICR 718, CA, the Court of Appeal criticised the employment tribunal for referring in its judgment to authorities that had not been canvassed at the hearing and which were untraceable by the parties. However, the tribunal's decision was sufficiently reasoned and clear despite these flaws – the Court noted that, while there is no universal test of procedural irregularity, a tribunal's determination is not vitiated by reference to uncanvassed authorities if these have not been central to and influential in the eventual decision.

There can be said to be an obligation on a tribunal to raise with the parties an **12.146** authority that the tribunal believes to be relevant, significant and material to its decision but which neither party has referred to. In Albion Hotel (Freshwater) Ltd v Maia e Silva and anor 2002 IRLR 200, EAT, it was held that a failure to do so can amount to a breach of natural justice and of the right to a fair hearing – see 'Natural justice and the right to a fair hearing – knowing the case which has to be met' below.

Precedent is most useful where the law is new or particularly complex so that every decision has potential interpretative value, or where an unforeseen problem in 'old' law arises in circumstances where principles must be identified to help apply that law to the new facts. If case law is used to support a party's arguments, it is necessary for that party to know the cases thoroughly rather than simply relying upon headnotes or parts of judgments which seem to be in the party's favour.

Natural justice and the right to a fair hearing   12.147

The principle that justice must not only be done but must be seen to be done is more than a legal maxim. It forms the essential basis of many decisions by the appellate courts allowing appeals from employment tribunals that have breached the principles of natural justice. These principles constitute fundamental procedural safeguards in all contentious litigation conducted in an adversarial environment. Essentially they require that:

- both parties must be permitted to present their cases fully and openly

- each party is entitled, so far as is consistent with fairness, to know the case he or she has to meet in order to succeed

- neither party should be denied the right to present relevant evidence, call witnesses or cross-examine opposing witnesses

713

- the judicial body hearing the case must be free from bias and must do nothing which could reasonably create the impression of partiality.

Furthermore, since the Human Rights Act 1998 came into force on 2 October 2000, parties before courts and tribunals in the UK have been able to rely on the right to a fair hearing enshrined in Article 6 of the European Convention on Human Rights, which provides that 'in the determination of his civil rights and obligations... everyone is entitled to a fair and public hearing within a reasonable time by an independent and impartial tribunal established by law'. UK courts and tribunals must therefore take account not only of previous domestic cases but also of decisions of the European Court of Human Rights.

12.148 The ideals of justice and fairness are in any case expressly imposed upon tribunals (and indeed the parties themselves) by virtue of the 'overriding objective' to deal with cases fairly and justly, which is contained in rule 2 of the Tribunal Rules. In Bache v Essex County Council 2000 ICR 313, CA, Lord Justice Mummery made the following comments:

- at the hearing the employment tribunal must follow a procedure that is fair to both sides. It must normally allow each party to call relevant evidence, to ask relevant questions of the other side's witnesses and to make relevant submissions on the evidence and the law

- the tribunal is responsible for the fair conduct of the hearing. It is in control. Neither the parties nor their representatives are in control of the hearing

- procedural fairness applies to the conduct of all those involved in the hearing. Just as the tribunal is under a duty to behave fairly, so are the parties and their representatives. The tribunal is accordingly entitled to require the parties and their representatives to act in a fair and reasonable way in the presentation of their evidence, in challenging the other side's evidence and in making submissions. The rulings of the tribunal on what is and is not relevant and on what a fair and appropriate procedure requires ought to be respected even by a party and his representative who do not agree with a particular ruling. If the party and his or her representative disagree with a ruling, an appeal lies against it if the tribunal has made an error of law.

These prerequisites for a fair hearing are discussed below. The right to a public hearing, enshrined in Article 6, is also discussed under 'Hearings in private' above.

12.149 Hearing both sides

As a general rule, justice can rarely be seen to be done if a body purporting to act in a judicial way fails to hear both sides of the dispute. This does not, of course, mean that a court or tribunal is expected to allow the parties to run their cases exactly as they wish – see, for example, the reservations expressed by the Court of Appeal in Yeboah v Crofton 2002 IRLR 634, CA. But natural justice does require, for the most part, that each party is given an opportunity to present relevant evidence and to examine and cross-examine witnesses in a manner conducive to ensuring that the issues and contentions are exhaustively put before the tribunal.

In the context of employment tribunals, the EAT and the appellate courts have shown themselves to be acutely aware of the fact that the parties are frequently unrepresented. And sometimes, more important than the prospect of obtaining or paying compensation, parties are driven by the need to give vent to the sense of grievance caused by the dispute which gave rise to the proceedings. Consequently, tribunals are expected to have fully in mind their duty to hear both sides and to be conscientious in conducting the hearing so as to avoid any impression that conclusions are reached prematurely or on the basis of an unfair advantage being given to one side over the other.

12.150 As noted earlier in this chapter, tribunals may in rare circumstances accept submissions of 'no case to answer' where a claimant wholly fails to make out any viable grounds for supporting his or her claim – see 'No case to answer' above. Acceptance of such a submission avoids the necessity of the respondent presenting his or her evidence and so denies the claimant any opportunity to cross-examine the respondent's witnesses or to challenge the documentary evidence which the respondent would have produced in defence of the claim. Because of the risk that a tribunal might have been influenced by evidence or testimony that it would not have an opportunity to hear if a submission of 'no case' is accepted, the appellate courts have enjoined tribunals to be most reluctant to accept such submissions and to do so only where the claimant has failed to establish in law or fact that he or she has any basis at all for making the complaint – see, for example, Logan v Commissioners of Customs and Excise 2004 ICR 1, CA. Furthermore, the appropriateness of a 'no case to answer' submission is increasingly in doubt now that there are various mechanisms within the Tribunal Rules designed to weed out hopeless cases at an early stage.

12.151 **Equality of arms.** The jurisprudence from the European Court of Human Rights clearly establishes that 'equality of arms' is one aspect of the Article 6 protection. In general, this means that a party must not be placed at a substantial disadvantage compared to his or her opponent. However, this principle cannot go so far as to demand an entirely level playing field – for example, a party represented by an experienced employment barrister will have an advantage over a litigant in person, but this is not an advantage that will generally detract from the fairness of proceedings. In Millin v Capsticks LLP and ors 2013 ICR D35, EAT, the EAT observed that a complaint that the tribunal did not ensure equality of arms is really an allegation that the tribunal was biased against one party or in favour of another – i.e. it did not treat the parties fairly and evenly.

715

It also noted that one cannot 'siphon off' equality of arms as a rule in itself; it must be looked at in the context of the trial as a whole.

In the Millin case, the claimant lost complaints of sex discrimination because the employment tribunal, in general, preferred the respondent's evidence. Although it did not find that the claimant was lying, her inconsistent recollection of events and the difference between her perception of events and other people's led the tribunal to find her evidence unreliable. It also noted that some of her written submissions did not accord with the evidence. On appeal, the claimant complained that the tribunal had held it against her that she had made submissions that were not supported by the evidence. She argued that this meant that she was disadvantaged by the inequality of arms, since a tribunal would not hold it against a represented party's credibility that his or her representative had sought to advance an untenable proposition. The EAT dismissed her appeal. It held that the tribunal had made adequate findings on which to doubt the claimant's credibility, quite apart from any adverse inference that it might have drawn from her submissions. But, in any event, the tribunal was entitled to hold it against her that she had advanced a proposition that was not credible in her witness statement or oral evidence. The EAT noted that, while counsel is bound by professional rules as to what he or she can say and do, the litigant in person is not. If the litigant in person does something that is not professionally available to counsel – e.g. puts forward a wholly unarguable point – there is no breach of the right to a fair trial if the tribunal finds her not to be reliable or credible in putting forward such a contention.

12.152 Tribunal giving a preliminary view
The appearance of justice can be jeopardised even where employment tribunals do not go so far as to make a premature decision on the case before them but nonetheless give some indication of having reached a conclusion or demonstrate in some way that their mind is made up. A party may be permitted to continue presenting his or her case but, if it is reasonably obvious that the tribunal's eyes and ears are already closed to what he or she and his or her witnesses have to say, then the indulgence granted by the tribunal will have become merely a charade. Any indication that the tribunal has prejudged a matter before giving both sides the fullest opportunity to put their case risks breaching the fundamental principle that justice must not only be done but must be seen to have been done. Two examples:

- **Ellis v Ministry of Defence** 1985 ICR 257, EAT: E complained that her dismissal was unfair. The tribunal heard evidence from the respondents over a two-day period but before E had presented any evidence herself the chairman stated that, while the tribunal had reached no conclusion about the unfairness of the dismissal, it was satisfied that it was a case where no compensation should be awarded. E's claim was eventually dismissed. On appeal, the EAT held that although it was permissible for a tribunal in mid-hearing to give a tentative indication of its view for the sake of saving time or promoting a settlement, the discretion to do so had to be exercised with care. Such a preliminary expression of opinion ought never to be allowed to become a concluded decision where there was still evidence to be received and arguments to be heard. The tribunal in the instant case was in breach of the principles of natural justice so as to justify setting aside its decision

- **Chris Project v Hutt** EATS 0065/05: before the hearing of an unfair dismissal claim and having looked at the case on the papers alone, the tribunal chairman indicated to the employer that it would be an 'uphill struggle' to prove that the claimant was not dismissed. On the basis of that comment, the employer's representative conceded the fact of dismissal and the claimant went on to succeed in his claim. The EAT allowed the employer's appeal against the tribunal's decision, noting that there could be few occasions on which a tribunal could properly comment on the difficulties in a case before having heard any evidence. To make such a comment would plainly risk giving the parties the impression of pre-judgement, unless it is made clear that the view expressed is only provisional, which was not the case here. The employer would therefore be allowed to withdraw the concession and the case would be remitted to a freshly constituted tribunal.

These examples are fairly unusual, however, and in general there is no objection to an employment judge indicating which way the proceedings are going, so long as the view is clearly open to change as more evidence is presented. In London Borough of Southwark v Jiminez 2003 ICR 1176, CA, the claimant complained of unfair constructive dismissal and disability discrimination. After ten days of hearing, by which time all significant witnesses had been heard, the tribunal chairman indicated in a discussion with counsel that he felt that the Council had treated the claimant appallingly; had treated him less favourably for a reason related to his disability; and had failed to explain conduct amounting to a serious breach of the unfair dismissal provisions. The tribunal went on to find against the Council, which appealed on the basis that the chairman's comments indicated that the tribunal had already formed a concluded view hostile to its case, and that this represented a very real risk of bias. The EAT agreed and allowed the appeal. The Court of Appeal, however, overturned that decision and restored the decision of the tribunal. The Court held that the chairman was entitled to indicate the need for unusually compelling evidence in relation to a feature of a party's case that struck him as inherently improbable, provided that he did not thereby convey an unwillingness to be persuaded of a factual proposition whatever the evidence may be. Although the opinion expressed by the chairman was a strong one, the parties should not have been in any doubt that it was only a provisional opinion and by no means final.

Similarly, there is generally nothing wrong with the tribunal or employment **12.153** judge giving an early view on the value of the claim. In Abegaze v Shrewsbury

717

College of Arts and Technology EAT 0176/07 the claimant appealed against an employment judge's decision to strike out his claim, complaining that the judge had expressed a view on the likely amount of compensation at an aborted remedy hearing. The EAT rejected the argument that there was any suggestion of unfair pre-judgement. The employment judge had indeed remarked that the employer faced a claim for 'substantial' compensation. However, this was not a negative view and so could not be a ground on which the claimant could properly complain of bias. The EAT went on to give the obiter opinion that an employment judge holding a preliminary view about the value of a claim will not ordinarily warrant recusal. The EAT noted that it is not surprising that, during or at the end of several days of hearing and discussion, an employment judge finding in favour of a claimant looks forward to the remedy stage, especially given that modern litigation requires the presentation of evidence and a schedule of loss at the outset. The EAT applied Lord Justice Ward's observation in the family law case El-Farargy v El-Farargy and ors 2007 EWCA Civ 1149, CA, that the fair-minded observer would know that judges are trained to have an open mind and that they frequently do change their minds during the course of any hearing. Thus, there are times in any trial and in any pre-trial review where a judge is entitled to express a preliminary view. A judge can even hold a strong preliminary view – he or she is best advised not to express it but, if he or she does, that does not call for recusal. (The EAT's decision to reject the bias appeal was endorsed by the Court of Appeal in the subsequent case of Abegaze v Shrewsbury College of Arts and Technology 2010 IRLR 238, CA.)

Two further examples of unobjectionable preliminary comments:

- **Choudhury v Inkfish Call Centres** EAT 0104/04: the claimant brought a complaint of unfair dismissal. At the start of the hearing, the tribunal chairman indicated that the panel would read the parties' witness statements and bundle of documents and give a preliminary view on them. This view was that it would be 'a virtually impossible task for the applicant to succeed in this claim'. The claim was eventually rejected and the claimant appealed on the ground of, among other things, procedural irregularity in the tribunal giving a preliminary view. The EAT dismissed the appeal on that point – referring to the Court of Appeal's guidance in London Borough of Southwark v Jiminez (above), it was satisfied that the tribunal had qualified its view as 'preliminary' and, more importantly, that it had not given the impression of having conclusively made up its collective mind

- **Roberts v Carlin** EAT 0183/09: the EAT rejected a charge of apparent bias based on an employment judge's comment, at the end of the claimant's evidence, that the respondent had a 'very steep hill to climb'. The judge had also remarked, in relation to the respondent's decision to proceed with the claim instead of settling, 'let's hope they don't rue the day'. The EAT held that these comments fell 'very close to the borderline' between a helpful provisional view, designed to assist the parties in resolving their differences by a mutually agreed settlement, and the manifestation of a closed mind before hearing the whole of the evidence and argument. However, it took into account that this was a complaint of sex discrimination, where the undisputed facts were that the claimant was suspended and summarily dismissed shortly after revealing her pregnancy. She had therefore raised a prima facie case, requiring the respondent to show that the dismissal was in no way whatsoever connected to the fact of her pregnancy. Any respondent, in such a case, would have a hill to climb.

The danger of displaying apparent bias is also present when a view is expressed **12.154** on liability before any evidence is even heard. In Ezsias v North Glamorgan NHS Trust 2007 ICR 1126, CA, the Court of Appeal held that a tribunal chairman had given the appearance of bias when, at a hearing to determine whether the claimant should be ordered to pay a deposit, she stated her opinion that the claimant's claim of unfair dismissal for having made a protected disclosure had no reasonable prospect of success. She relied on the fact that the employer's asserted reason for dismissal – namely, breakdown in working relationships – was supported by statements from all nine of the claimant's colleagues; and that the dismissal procedure was manifestly reasonable in the circumstances. The chairman later struck out the claim on the same basis but insisted that her comments at the deposit stage reflected merely an interim opinion. The Court of Appeal rejected that characterisation. The chairman's comments at the time were not stated to be a preliminary or provisional view but rather were clearly expressed in concluded terms. Although her later explanation sufficed to acquit her of any suggestion of actual pre-determination, it could not displace the perception that any fair-minded and informed observer would have formed that there was a real possibility that she had a concluded view or a closed mind as regards the claimant's prospects of success.

Knowing the case that has to be met
12.155

It is a principle of all litigation that each party is entitled to know – at least in general terms – the case he or she must meet in order to succeed. That said, there is no rule that a party should not have to expect to deal with any issue not identified in case management – Wilcox v Birmingham CAB Services Ltd 2011 EqLR 810, EAT. The EAT applied this approach in North Bristol NHS Trust v Harrold EAT 0548/11, where it rejected the respondent's argument that, since the claimant had put her case of discrimination and victimisation on the basis of a named comparator, the employment tribunal was not entitled to assess her claim by reference to a hypothetical comparator.

New points sometimes arise during the course of proceedings when the tribunal identifies something overlooked by the parties. In Taskmaster Resources v Kanyimo EAT 0441/06 the EAT set out what it considered to be the legal

719

principles applicable where a tribunal raises a new point of its own volition. It stated, among other things, that a tribunal is under a statutory duty to enquire into the matters before it. If it comes up with a point that has not previously occurred to the parties or been raised at the preliminary stage, it must take particular care – especially when the parties are not legally represented – to ensure that a full opportunity is given for the point to be considered. This may require an adjournment. However, in BAE Systems (Operations) Ltd v Paterson 2013 ICR D3, EAT, the EAT in Scotland expressed doubts about the existence of a duty to enquire. It noted that tribunal procedure is adversarial and that represented parties must generally be assumed to have considered carefully what findings of fact are relevant to the issues of law in the case. If a point has not been taken it may well be because the parties, for their own purposes, have concluded it should not be taken. The EAT stated that it would not wish to endorse, without further argument, a principle entitling a tribunal in general terms to raise whatever issue it wishes, rather than to determine the issues that the parties wish to have determined.

12.156   If a matter of substance is raised suddenly without having been pleaded in the claim form or response, it is important that the opponent (or both parties, if the matter is raised by the tribunal) be given an opportunity to consider it and to make representations. A failure to do this will amount to a breach of natural justice. Where the party is unable to deal with the fresh allegation there and then, the tribunal should consider adjourning the hearing and giving directions for the further conduct of the case. Furthermore, where the new issue involves a new ground of claim being raised, it is of paramount importance that any proposed amendment of the ET1 is set out in writing so that the parties and the tribunal are all clear about the ambit of the new point, and submissions can be made on whether it should be allowed – Care First Health Care Ltd v McLaren EAT 0982/03. It is inappropriate for the tribunal to draft the amendment itself – Margarot Forrest Care Management v Kennedy EATS 0023/10 (discussed under 'Assistance by the tribunal – issues not raised by the parties' above).

Often a failure to allow an opponent (or both parties, where relevant) the opportunity to consider a new matter and make representations arises because the tribunal bases its conclusions on a factor which was not argued fully or at all before it. In Haxey Engineering Ltd v Turner EAT 268/78, for example, the tribunal found a dismissal to be unfair on the ground that the procedure adopted for dismissing the claimant had been infelicitous and unfair. Neither party had made any submissions on this issue. The EAT held that although the employment tribunal was at liberty to raise the question of procedural propriety in considering the 'reasonableness' of the dismissal, having raised the matter for consideration of its own motion, it was incumbent on it to let the parties know that it was a consideration to which some importance was attached and accordingly to allow the parties to make representations about it.

However, the principle that unexpected findings of the tribunal must always be **12.157** put to the parties for them to make representations is not without limits. In Judge v Crown Leisure 2005 IRLR 823, CA, one of the central factual issues was whether the employer had promised the claimant a pay increase. The claimant contended that such a promise had been made during a conversation at a Christmas party; the employer, on the other hand, denied the conversation took place. The tribunal found that there may well have been a casual conversation between the two about the issue of pay, and that the employer may have given the claimant 'words of comfort and assurance' regarding his remuneration, but there was no intention to enter into any binding agreement. The claimant appealed to the EAT on the ground, inter alia, that the tribunal had not been entitled to come to that finding of fact as neither party had argued for it. The EAT rejected that ground of appeal, and the point was not pursued further. However, before the Court of Appeal, the claimant argued instead that as the finding of fact was not contended for by either party, it had been procedurally unfair for the tribunal not to give the parties an opportunity to make submissions on the legal effect of that finding. Lady Justice Smith, giving an opinion with which the rest of the Court concurred, accepted the general proposition that it was a cardinal principle of fairness that the parties should be heard on any issue that is likely to be relevant to the decision. Her Ladyship noted, further, that if a tribunal foresees that it is likely to make a finding of fact that neither side has contended for, it is highly desirable that it raise that issue in closing submissions. However, giving such an opportunity was not an invariable requirement – it was well within the tribunal's wide discretion to regulate its own procedure under what was then rule 14(3) of the Tribunal Rules 2004 (now rule 41 of the Tribunal Rules 2013) to consider whether or not such an opportunity need be given. In a case such as this, where the legal effect of the finding was obviously and unarguably clear, no injustice is done if submissions are not invited on that point. The appeal was therefore dismissed.

More generally, some issues are so common and/or obvious that experienced representatives may be expected to be able to deal with them without notice. For example, in North Bristol NHS Trust v Harrold EAT 0548/11 the EAT held that there could be no objection to a tribunal considering a victimisation claim on the basis of a comparison with a hypothetical comparator even though the claimant had only put her case on the basis of a named comparator. The EAT held that there was no question of any unfairness being suffered by the employer since its representative – an experienced employment lawyer – would have been able, and indeed was able, to deal with the case on that basis. The EAT went on to suggest that the tribunal was in fact obliged, under the Equality Act 2010, to consider the position of a hypothetical comparator, since it was central to the definition of unlawful victimisation.

In contrast, where the new point might affect the parties' presentation of their **12.158** cases, it is likely to require notice to the parties and an opportunity to make

721

submissions. In Sheibani v Elan and Co LLP 2012 ICR D38, EAT, the employment tribunal rejected claims for unfair dismissal, breach of contract and unpaid holiday pay on the basis that the contract of employment had been performed illegally because the claimant was receiving half of his salary 'off the books'. Neither party had raised illegality as an issue. The tribunal decided to deal with it of its own motion, basing itself on authorities that it only cited when giving judgment and on which the parties had not been able to make submissions. On appeal, the EAT held that the tribunal's procedure was legally flawed. What had happened was, in effect, that the tribunal determined that the claimant was acting fraudulently without first warning him that it had this in mind and permitting him to try to explain such a serious matter. Had the tribunal allowed the parties to deal with the question of whether they had acted so as to defraud the Revenue, they might have produced further evidence which could have led to different factual conclusions. Furthermore, where potential criminal offences may be under consideration, it is an essential matter of justice and procedure that a party should be warned by the tribunal that he or she need not answer a question, if to do so might incriminate him or her.

Tribunals will also be particularly sensitive to allegations of fraud or misconduct that are made without notice. For example, in the unfair dismissal case Hotson v Wisbech Conservative Club 1984 ICR 859, EAT, the employer initially relied on inefficiency as the reason for dismissal, but changed this to dishonesty during the hearing. The EAT held that this failure to give the employee the fullest opportunity to consider the implications of the allegation and to answer it was a denial of natural justice, which vitiated the tribunal's decision. Although employers are not tied to the label they initially attach to the reason for dismissal (assuming the facts relied on are the same), the substitution of dishonesty for capability as the reason went beyond a mere change of label. And in Panama v London Borough of Hackney 2003 IRLR 278, CA, the Court of Appeal stated that it was doubtful that the employee had had a fair hearing when the employment tribunal decided that she was not entitled to compensation for unfair dismissal because it was more likely than not that she would have been summarily dismissed for fraud. The allegation of fraud arose for the first time during cross-examination of the employee at the tribunal. It was therefore doubtful that the allegation had been put to her sufficiently formally and early to give her a full opportunity to answer it.

12.159 Right to cross-examine and present evidence
Although rule 41 of the Tribunal Rules confers upon employment tribunals a broad discretion to conduct their proceedings in the manner that seems most fair, they are not entitled to eschew the ordinary processes by which courts receive testimony and evidence. For example, a denial of the right to cross-examine witnesses will, in most cases, amount to a breach of natural justice – see McBride v British Railways Board and ors 1972 ITR 84, NIRC. However,

as previously indicated, natural justice does not require tribunals to be completely passive over matters concerning the conduct of a party's case. If evidence is irrelevant or repetitive, or cross-examination is wholly unhelpful, there is no reason why the tribunal should not intervene to require the party responsible to desist in the course he or she is taking.

The range of issues that may be raised in cross-examination is a matter for the tribunal to consider as part of its general discretion in conducting the proceedings. If the tribunal considers that a party's cross-examination is straying into irrelevant territory, then it is entitled to curtail it. Thus, in Zurich Insurance Co v Gulson 1998 IRLR 118, EAT, the EAT held that an employment tribunal is not obliged to allow 'lengthy and detailed cross-examination on matters that do not appear to the tribunal to be of assistance'. This decision was applied by EAT in the subsequent decision of Kennedy t/a Snappy Snaps v Warwick EAT 0118/04, where it was held that a tribunal's conduct in restricting the employer's cross-examination of the employee betrayed no error of law. The employer was questioning the employee on why he had initially brought claims of disability discrimination and automatically unfair dismissal for having asserted a statutory right but withdrawn them before the hearing. The employer asserted that the employee had simply added these claims in order to be vexatious or malicious. The EAT held that this issue went only to credit and the tribunal was entitled to limit cross-examination on the allegation because it was not borne out by the evidence.

12.160 The principle identified in Zurich Insurance Co v Gulson (above) was endorsed and elaborated upon by another division of the EAT in Jones v London Borough of Havering and anor EAT 1099/01, where it held that an employment tribunal had been wrong to halt the claimant's cross-examination of a witness when it did so in the mistaken belief that the claimant was thereby trying to introduce new evidence. While the claimant was seeking to explore an issue that she had not herself given evidence about, the EAT thought it a well-established principle that cross-examination on behalf of a party who has given evidence-in-chief is not limited to matters that that party has already put forward in evidence. Provided the matters raised in cross-examination went to relevant issues, it was not within the tribunal's discretion under what is now rule 41 to exclude them, unless they had been left out of evidence-in-chief for tactical reasons – see Aberdeen Steak Houses Group plc v Ibrahim 1988 ICR 550, EAT.

Bias

12.161

It is axiomatic that a judicial body, in exercising its functions, must be completely above any reasonably held suspicion of bias or partiality. Bias in this context means that a tribunal is 'predisposed or prejudiced against one party's case for reasons unconnected with the merits of the issue' – R v Inner West London Coroner ex parte Dallaglio and anor 1994 4 All ER 139, CA. Bias may relate

723

to the way in which a hearing is conducted ('conduct bias') or to any personal interest or other factors which may cause the decision-maker to be inclined to favour one side or the other ('interest bias') or to both.

The leading case on the test for bias is the House of Lords' judgment in Porter v Magill 2002 2 AC 357, HL. Lord Hope of Craighead reviewed the case law on impartiality of courts and tribunals and considered the influence of Article 6 of the European Convention on Human Rights, which is incorporated into domestic law by the Human Rights Act 1998. His Lordship noted that the concept of impartiality required not only that the court or tribunal be truly independent and free from actual bias – which is likely to be very difficult to prove – but also that it must not appear in the objective sense to lack these essential qualities, i.e. it must also be free from apparent bias. In order to establish whether there was apparent bias in any case, the court or tribunal must consider whether the circumstances would lead a fair-minded and informed observer to conclude that there was a real possibility that the tribunal was biased. This hypothetical observer would be apprised of all the relevant circumstances, including matters not necessarily known to the parties at the time of the hearing, as well as the employment judge's or member's explanations. Furthermore, the hypothetical observer need not apprehend that bias actually existed, nor even that it was 'likely' or 'probable', only that there was a risk that was more than minimal – see the Dallaglio case (above).

12.162 Allegations of apparent bias frequently fail, often because the parties in the proceedings have failed to distinguish between disappointment or frustration and a belief that the tribunal was unfairly disposed against them – note the comment of Lord Justice Rimer in the Court of Appeal in Kennaugh v Lloyd-Jones t/a Cheshire Tree Surgeons 2013 EWCA Civ 1, CA, that assertions by self-represented litigants of judicial bias are 'tediously common'. Furthermore, employment tribunals (as with all judicial bodies) have the benefit of a presumption in favour of their impartiality. That presumption can be rebutted, but only by making out a cogent case that bias has actually occurred or that there are objective grounds for suggesting that it might have occurred. The problems inherent in making out a case of bias were acknowledged by the EAT in Ansar v Lloyds TSB Bank plc and anor EAT 0152/06, where it highlighted the very real risk noted at para 11.6 of the EAT Practice Direction 2004 that firm case management by a chairman will be seen or characterised by a party as unfairness. (Note that this case has been the subject of an appeal to the Court of Appeal on different grounds – see 'Personal interest' below.) The EAT also underlined the evidential problems, inherent in hearing appeals based on an allegation of bias, of reconstructing exactly what happened before the employment tribunal. However, the EAT endorsed para 7.3 of the 2004 Practice Direction, which set down a procedure for the parties to an appeal requiring them to cooperate in agreeing a statement or note of the relevant evidence within a given time period, as a good substitute for an accurate record of the proceedings. The 2004 Practice Direction has since been replaced – the currently applicable Practice Direction is the one that came into force on 29 July 2013. This does not specifically note the risk of firm case management being seen as bias but it does set down a more detailed procedure for would-be appellants to follow when asserting bias. It also warns, at para 13.6.3, that 'unsuccessful pursuit of an allegation of bias or improper conduct, particularly in respect of case management decisions, may put the party raising it at risk of an order for costs against them'.

Conduct bias

12.163

Occasionally, an employment tribunal will be chastised by the EAT for conducting a hearing without due regard to the right of parties to present their cases in the manner they think fit. A persistently bad-tempered judge who frequently interrupts or cajoles a party may be brought to task if the EAT takes the view that the tribunal's interventions have caused injustice. The effect of such conduct on unrepresented parties should be especially borne in mind since, within reason, tribunals are expected to be indulgent rather than intimidatory about a party's lack of experience.

Trained legal representatives, on the other hand, will largely be expected to take difficult conduct by a tribunal in their stride. For example, in UK Inspection Ltd v Ashley EAT 94/97 the EAT recognised that where only one party is legally represented, the tribunal often has to adopt a more inquisitorial role than would have been appropriate if both parties were represented. In that case the appellant company complained that the employment judge's constant interruptions distracted the witnesses from presenting its case and that its solicitor was so harassed that he was unable to present the case as he had wished. The EAT held that an employment judge may intervene to the extent necessary to ensure a proper understanding of the issues and the relevant facts, and has to regulate the proceedings so as to ensure time is not wasted with irrelevancies. If a witness or advocate is reluctant to accept the judge's control, there is likely to be a souring of the atmosphere, but this does not necessarily mean that the tribunal's impartiality may be impugned. Similarly, in Bird v Sylvester EAT 0037/06, the EAT held that the tribunal chairman telling a solicitor to 'get on with it' did not even arguably taint the fairness of the hearing. The comment was made to the claimant's solicitor during a break in hearing the claimant's evidence, when the solicitor was in discussion with the respondent's solicitor. In the EAT's view, if advocates have a private conversation, whether about the case or not, while a witness is trying to read her witness statement, they must expect to be told to get on with it.

However, a complaint of conduct bias may succeed if the conduct of the tribunal   12.164
panel members suggests that they might have formed a premature view without hearing the evidence and therefore did not have an open mind to the issues. For example, in Harada Ltd (t/a Chequepoint Ltd) v Turner 2001 EWCA Civ 599,

725

CA, the tribunal chairman, prior to the hearing, called the parties' representatives into a private meeting, where he remarked that the employer was well known to the tribunal as this was the seventh time that the company had been in the tribunal in six months. He criticised the manner in which the employer had conducted previous cases and suggested that the employer was using spurious arguments over jurisdiction simply in order to avoid going to trial. He went on to suggest that the parties might benefit from ten minutes to discuss the matter (presumably to reach a settlement). The employer withdrew from proceedings and appealed, alleging bias. The Court of Appeal commented that there was nothing wrong with a tribunal indicating before or during a hearing the difficulties that a party may face arguing one or more of the points at issue and that there is nothing wrong with a chairman suggesting that parties might like some time to discuss settlement. However, the remarks in this case were not directed towards any particular issue and merely involved a general slur upon the employer. The Court could only conclude that there was a real danger of the tribunal looking generally with disfavour on any case that the employer might care to advance that day and the case was remitted to a fresh tribunal. This form of conduct bias is discussed in more detail under 'Natural justice and the right to a fair hearing – tribunal giving a preliminary view' above.

A different form of conduct 'bias' arises where a member of the tribunal panel appears not to be giving his or her fullest attention to the case being heard. Although incidents of tribunal members falling asleep are, thankfully, rare, they do occur, and it has been established – for example, in Stansbury v Datapulse plc and anor 2004 ICR 523, CA – that this is liable to render a decision unfair. The fact that the decision was unanimous or reserved will not alter this position. In Stansbury, not only was there evidence to suggest that a member had fallen asleep during the hearing, there was also evidence to suggest that the cause was that he had been drinking. The Court of Appeal therefore concluded that the requirement that a hearing must be seen to be fair had not been satisfied and it remitted the case for rehearing before a differently constituted tribunal.

12.165 Two further examples of the conduct of lay members coming in for scrutiny:

- **Ross v Micro Focus Ltd** EAT 0304/09: the claimant, who was unsuccessful before the employment tribunal in her unfair dismissal claim, appealed on the ground of bias, alleging that the employer-side lay member's body language throughout her representative's questioning of the chairman of the employer made it clear that she was impatient with the line of questioning. The EAT rejected the complaint. Although it accepted that the lay member's behaviour was intemperate and discourteous, and that she had made clear her agreement with the answers being given by the chairman, it did not consider that this betrayed a closed mind. The lay member disagreed with the propositions being put by the claimant's representative because, as she knew from her own experience of chairing a large company, the line of questioning betrayed a misunderstanding of the role of a company chairman. Furthermore, although the lay member did not accept that she had displayed overt disapproval of the questioning, she did apologise for her discourtesy

- **Aziz-Mir v Sainsbury's Supermarkets plc** EAT 0415/07: the claimant had been dismissed for misconduct but was reinstated after a successful internal appeal. He nonetheless went on to bring various claims, including race discrimination and trade union victimisation, on the basis that the dismissal followed by eventual reinstatement amounted to a detriment. At the beginning of the tribunal hearing, before any evidence was led, a lay member made a comment about the claimant's case, to the effect that 'he's been reinstated, what more does he want?' The EAT did not consider that this gave rise to an appearance of bias. It accepted the tribunal's account of the context in which the remark was made – namely, that the lay member may well have missed the full nuance of the discrimination claim and, if so, he was put on the right lines by the tribunal chairman. The EAT saw no reason to believe that any such misconception was carried forward in the lay member's mind when listening to the evidence and argument and in final deliberations.

It is worth noting that in Ross v Micro Focus Ltd (above) the EAT approved the appellant's summary of ground rules for tribunal members. These were as follows:

- tribunal members should avoid overt signs of friendliness or hostility towards either party or representative

- although it will sometimes be necessary for the employment judge to be firm with a witness or representative, tribunal members should at all times act respectfully and courteously towards those who appear before them

- tribunal members should keep to a minimum demonstrative reactions to evidence or submissions (whether by way of facial expressions, gestures, the making of noises or body language), save in the form of direct questions

- tribunal members should avoid 'asides', comments and remarks, unless formulated as direct questions to the employment judge, a witness or the representatives.

Discrimination cases. Any suggestion of stereotyping or prejudice related to a **12.166** protected characteristic will surely give rise to an appearance of bias. Two examples that arose in race discrimination cases:

- **Diem v Crystal Services plc** EAT 0398/05: the claimant complained of race discrimination, victimisation and unfair dismissal against her former employer. With regard to her race discrimination complaint, she argued that she had been treated less favourably contrary to S.1(1)(a) of the Race Relations Act 1976 (since repealed and re-enacted in the Equality Act 2010)

727

on the ground of her Vietnamese ethnic or national origin. During the course of the hearing, the tribunal chairman asked her whether she wished to expand her race discrimination claim to include an allegation that she had been treated less favourably on the ground of her colour. He enquired whether she was claiming to be non-white, and commented that her skin colour was 'as white as the English'. He also pointed to the skin on his own hand, adding that 'your skin looks whiter than mine'. Her claims were dismissed and she appealed to the EAT. The EAT noted that, although the chairman's desire to establish whether the claimant was departing from her case as outlined at the beginning of the hearing was perfectly legitimate, and that he did not intend to cause offence, complaints of race discrimination require sensitive handling by tribunals and high standards of communication by judicial officers are rightly expected. In the EAT's view, the chairman crossed the line in his prolonged questioning of the claimant with regard to how she viewed her skin colour, and in making comparisons with his own. The EAT decided that a fair-minded observer would have concluded that the chairman's remarks were likely to cause the claimant to feel unsettled, humiliated and embarrassed, and went on to hold that there was a real possibility of unconscious bias in this case

- **Lewis v New College Oxford** EAT 0533/10: the claimant, a black man of Afro-Caribbean descent, argued that his dismissal was motivated by race discrimination. It was part of his case that the employer took a stereotypical view of black Afro-Caribbean men as lazy and stupid. The employment judge did not accept that that was the stereotypical view of black Afro-Caribbean men but said that 'they may have a more "relaxed" approach to life than other ethnic groups'. The EAT held that the judge thereby at least gave the appearance of holding a stereotypical view, which was inappropriate.

In Tchoula v Netto Foodstores Ltd EAT 1378/96 the unsuccessful claimant in a race discrimination case made a number of complaints to the EAT about the way in which the tribunal had conducted the hearing. These included allegations that one of the lay members had closed her eyes and appeared to be thoroughly bored and that the tribunal had reprimanded the claimant for asking leading questions, had put a time limit on his cross-examination and had made a number of gratuitous and unnecessary personal comments, both during the hearing and in the written decision. The EAT concluded nonetheless that an objective observer would not have gained the impression of bias.

12.167 Recognising that there was an increasing number of appeals being launched about the way in which tribunals had conducted themselves, and also that such appeals were very rarely successful, the EAT laid down some guidance for tribunals to help them avoid giving the wrong impression:

- whether justified or not, many people from ethnic minorities distrust the judicial system and tribunals should be particularly careful to give no grounds for this distrust and should avoid making any comment which, however well-intentioned, might confirm the worst fears of a suspicious litigant

- tribunals should be well prepared for hearings and should hold a preliminary hearing in more complicated discrimination cases, which will help identify the real issues and therefore give the parties confidence that the tribunal is well informed and understands the matters at issue

- tribunals should show respect for litigants and avoid making personal remarks or judgments about someone as a person

- tribunals should seek to minimise the natural fear of unrepresented parties, who may feel something of an outsider if the other party is represented. Often unrepresented parties have taken great pains to prepare themselves and may feel patronised if the tribunal assumes that the party will not be able to give as much help to the tribunal as the other party's representative

- the panel should always appear alert and interested – if proceedings are not making any progress it is better that the tribunal should say so. Assuming an air of bored indifference is not an appropriate signal to give a party who is unrepresented

- in its decision, a tribunal should state its findings of fact in a sensible order, indicating in relation to any significant finding the nature of the conflicting evidence and the reason why one version has been preferred to another. A bald statement that wherever there was a conflict, X's evidence was preferred to Y's is implausible and unreasoned, and therefore unacceptable

- tribunals should give reasons for their decisions, and where the reasons are essentially those put forward in the submissions of one of the parties, which have been set out in full in the decision, then the tribunal should make it clear that it has accepted all those reasons in arriving at its conclusion.

The Court of Appeal approved this guidance in relation to the need to give sufficiently detailed reasons in Anya v University of Oxford and anor 2001 ICR 847, CA.

Personal interest   12.168

A judge is automatically disqualified from sitting on cases in which he or she has a financial or proprietary interest – for example, shares in the respondent company – or in which there is no pecuniary interest but the decision will lead to the promotion of a cause in which the judge is involved – R v Bow Street Metropolitan Stipendiary Magistrates ex parte Pinochet Ugarte (No.2) 1999 2 WLR 272, HL. The same rules apply to employment tribunal members, although the latter category of case was so narrowly defined by the House of Lords that it should rarely, if ever, occur in an employment context. Indeed, the EAT in Hamilton v GMB (Northern Region) 2007 IRLR 391, EAT, confirmed that interest bias is usually pecuniary or proprietary, and only in exceptional cases will some non-financial interest attract the application of the automatic rule.

Apparent interest bias is much more common, arising wherever the reasonable, objective observer would see a real risk of a tribunal member being swayed by personal considerations. The Hamilton v GMB case is one such example. There, H was a union member who claimed sex discrimination by the GMB union when it disciplined him for going against the union's strategy in pursuing equal pay claims on behalf of its members. The employee-side lay member hearing the claim had formerly been a senior official in the union, which had adopted the same policy as the GMB with regard to equal pay claims. H applied for the tribunal to recuse itself because of this association but it refused to do so. On appeal, the EAT held that the tribunal had erred, considering it to be highly significant that the legality of the equal pay strategy, which was commonly shared by both unions, was under consideration. The EAT thought it legitimate to infer that the lay member would at least have been involved in discussions about Unison's equal pay strategy and would have wanted to support it. These circumstances gave rise to apparent bias and so the tribunal should have recused itself.

12.169 Two further examples where the EAT has held that tribunal members should have declared their interests and recused themselves:

- **University College of Swansea v Cornelius** 1988 ICR 735, EAT: one of the lay members was the mother-in-law of a professor who had sat on the internal appeal committee that had upheld the claimant's dismissal

- **Source Publications Ltd v Ellison** EAT 872/83: one of the lay members had a domestic dispute about a bill with the appellant company.

However, not all previous connections will necessarily lead to an inference of apparent bias. In Locabail (UK) Ltd v Bayfield Properties Ltd and other cases 2000 IRLR 96, CA, the tribunal chairman admitted that he had worked for the respondent employer in a junior position over 30 years ago. The Court of Appeal held that it was 'fanciful' to suggest that this could have affected his view of the proceedings. While recognising that everything will depend on the facts of the case, and that it would be 'dangerous and futile' to attempt to define the factors which may or may not give rise to a real danger of bias, the Court listed a number of factors which, ordinarily at any rate, should not be objected to:

- a tribunal member's social, educational, service or employment background or history (or that of any member of his or her family)

- a tribunal member's previous political associations

- a tribunal member's membership of social, sporting or charitable bodies or Masonic associations

- a tribunal member's previous judicial decisions or extra-curricular utterances (whether in text books, lectures, speeches, articles, interviews, reports or responses to consultation papers)

- a tribunal member's previous receipt of instructions to act for or against any party, solicitor or advocate engaged in a case before him or her; or his or her membership of the same Inn, circuit, local Law Society or chambers as a party's representative.

In Williams v Cater Link Ltd EAT 0393/08 the EAT confirmed the final point **12.170** in this list (although without specifically referring to the Locabail case). It rejected an allegation of bias based on the fact that the employment judge, when a practising solicitor, had instructed the respondent's counsel. The EAT firmly rejected the proposition that there should be automatic disqualification by reason of this professional relationship. Each case must be taken on its particular facts. If the professional relationship was extensive, lengthy, recent and/or ongoing, different considerations might apply. However, in the present case, the judge had previously instructed counsel a year or so earlier on two matters, each of them very short. There was no reason for him to recuse himself.

Where the Court in Locabail refers to the tribunal member's 'social' background, this should also include any considerations of race and religion, which should not provide grounds for an inference of bias. For example, an objection by a Sikh, bringing a race discrimination claim against a Muslim, to the presence of a Muslim on the tribunal panel on the ground that the member's religion would be likely to make him biased against the claimant was not well-founded – Singh v Bristol City Council and anor ET Case No.5300263/00.

An example of apparent personal interest through employment was provided **12.171** in Peninsula Business Services Ltd and anor v Rees and ors EAT 0333/08, where the part-time employment judge was a practising solicitor and partner in a law firm. The firm's recent advertising in the local press had denigrated unqualified employment law consultants. The respondent in the case, PBS Ltd, was the largest employment law consultancy in England. After it lost the case in the employment tribunal it appealed to the EAT on the ground of apparent bias. The EAT allowed the appeal, holding that the judgment would have to be set aside on the basis that the employment judge had been associated with the expression of trenchant, derogatory views about unqualified employment law consultants, of which PBS Ltd was a well-known employer. A fair-minded and objective observer would be likely to consider that the judge held the views expressed in his firm's advertisement.

Apparent bias in 'extra-curricular utterances' arose in City and County of Swansea v Honey EAT 0030/08, where the union-side lay member had been

731

involved in a well-publicised campaign against the local council on behalf of his trade union members. Among other things, he had been quoted in a newspaper report as saying that the council's case was extremely biased and that its leadership was poor and inefficient. In short, it was plain that he held a thoroughly negative view of the council, which the fair-minded observer would consider to give rise to a real possibility of bias. The EAT rejected the argument that the logical extension of this decision would place an unduly burdensome responsibility on union-side lay members to identify prior involvements. It pointed out that union officials will know if they have been involved in dealings which have been in any way contentious and if, wearing their union official's 'hat', they have articulated public criticism of the employer. In such circumstances, the member should have no difficulty in identifying that there could be a problem.

12.172 As for membership of associations, in Martin v Co-Operative Group EATS 0061/10 the EAT doubted whether it had really been necessary for the employment judge to declare his membership of the Co-operative Society in a claim against a Co-operative Pharmacy. The EAT observed that the link was so minor that it was not at all convinced that it was something that the employment judge was required to raise. In any event, the judge had raised it in the proper manner and the claimant had had ample opportunity to object and did not do so, and so there could be no complaint of apparent bias.

12.173 Previous judicial decisions
As noted in relation to 'Personal interest' above, a tribunal member's previous judicial decisions will not normally be thought to have a bearing on his or her partiality in any particular case. The EAT confirmed this in Lodwick v Southwark London Borough Council EAT 0116/05. There, the claimant had appeared before the same chairman as a trade union representative on behalf of a claimant in a race discrimination claim four years previously. The respondent to that claim was the same as the respondent in the present case, and the chairman had made a costs order against the present claimant for the way in which he had conducted those race discrimination proceedings. The claimant objected to the chairman sitting in the present case, arguing that he could not have a fair hearing. The chairman refused to stand down, however, reasoning that he had no recollection of the race discrimination claim years earlier. The EAT rejected the appeal against that refusal, holding that the case fell comfortably within the bounds of conspicuous impartiality described in Locabail (UK) Ltd v Bayfield Properties Ltd and other cases 2000 IRLR 96, CA. The EAT noted that Lord Justice Pill had, in that case, referred to the need for 'something more' than the simple fact that the impugned member had heard proceedings in which the party was previously involved, and decided that 'something more' was not present here.

The clearest guidance on this kind of case is now to be found in Ansar v Lloyds TSB Bank plc and ors 2007 IRLR 211, CA, where the Court of Appeal

732

summarised a number of points of general application. It emphasised that the mere existence of a complaint against a particular tribunal member cannot give rise to an automatic decision to recuse. It is important to consider the nature of the complaint made, and to ask whether its having been made rendered it inappropriate for the same judge to sit in later proceedings. Although the nature of the complaint may in some cases be decisive, even an allegation of wholly outrageous misconduct would not necessarily be grounds for recusal if the allegation was manifestly fanciful or unfounded. In the present case, where the applicant had put forward as 'one of the clearest examples of apparent bias' the fact that when rising for a morning break the chairman had nodded to the opposing counsel only and not to him, the nature of the allegations clearly did not require the chairman to recuse himself from later proceedings.

Two contrasting cases where a judge's handling of an earlier case involving the **12.174** same claimant led to applications for recusal:

- **Breeze Benton Solicitors (a partnership) v Weddell** EAT 0873/03: the respondent firm before the tribunal had been before the same tribunal chairman in earlier proceedings, following which the firm had written to the Regional Chairman and then to the Lord Chancellor's Department (now the Ministry of Justice) to complain of the chairman's conduct in those proceedings. The conduct complained of related to 'stinging comments' the chairman was alleged to have made during the proceedings about the respondent's business. The respondent firm applied, in the present proceedings, for the chairman to recuse himself, but the application was refused. On appeal, the EAT held that the chairman should have acceded to the application. Although the facts of the earlier complaint of conduct bias were not proved, it was clear that, in that earlier case, the respondent firm had a genuinely held belief that the chairman was biased against it. Furthermore, the very fact that the firm had complained about the chairman's conduct after the earlier proceedings made it inappropriate that the chairman should sit in the later case. It was also significant that the factual connection between the two cases was similar, and that there was little time between them

- **Aziz v Crown Prosecution Service** EAT 0027/13: the EAT held that an employment tribunal should not have recused itself from hearing a successful claimant's application for costs and exemplary damages. The recusal was based on a contretemps between the respondent's former counsel and the employment judge, which had occurred at a hearing three years earlier and which had led to the judge criticising the former counsel's conduct. The costs application relied in part on counsel's conduct at this hearing. Although the EAT accepted that the employment judge still recalled the incident with displeasure, it did not believe that a fair-minded and impartial observer would consider that there was a real risk of unfairness. In any

733

event, even if there were an appearance of bias, the tribunal should have explored what it could do to avoid recusal – it could at least have asked the claimant what weight she attached to the conduct in her costs application before recusing itself from long-running litigation over which it had presided at so many hearings.

Furthermore, even where the tribunal member has acceded to a recusal application in a previous claim it does not necessarily mean that he or she cannot fairly sit in later proceedings involving the same party or parties – Balamoody v Nursing and Midwifery Council EAT 0115/08. In that case, a tribunal chairman stepped down from a pre-hearing review when the claimant pointed out that he (the chairman) had decided an interlocutory application in a different case brought by the claimant many years before. The chairman did not consider that this was sufficient reason to recuse himself but withdrew anyway because he had other matters to attend to and another chairman was available. When the chairman who had withdrawn came to hear the substantive claim, he refused the claimant's further application for recusal. The EAT held that he was right to do so. It rejected the claimant's argument that, given the earlier recusal, there was apparent bias in the chairman's refusal to stand down at a subsequent hearing. The fair-minded and informed observer would have realised that the earlier recusal was not reasoned and not based on argument but was acceded to on purely pragmatic grounds.

12.175 Declaring an interest

In University College of Swansea v Cornelius 1988 ICR 735, EAT, the EAT suggested that the importance of disclosing any connection with persons or bodies involved in proceedings before an employment tribunal should be impressed upon lay members prior to any hearing. In that case, one of the lay members was the mother-in-law of a member of the employer's internal appeal panel that heard and dismissed the claimant's appeal against her dismissal.

In London Underground Ltd v Ayanbadejo EAT 1160/97 the EAT held that a lay member of a tribunal should have disclosed in advance the fact that he had previously worked for the old London Transport Executive. This was so notwithstanding the lapse of time (12 years) since his retirement, the fact that his employment had been with the London Transport Executive and not London Underground Ltd, the fact that he could have had no direct connection with anyone involved in the case, and the fact that no objection had been made until after the tribunal's decision had been reached. And in Corus UK Ltd v Young EAT 0114/05 the EAT held that a lay member should have disclosed that he was a former employee of CUK Ltd. It was relevant that, during his time at the company, he had acted as a union official representing employees and had had a difficult relationship with a particular HR manager who was referred to in the claimant's particulars of claim. The lay member did eventually recuse himself but only after CUK Ltd raised the issue and the tribunal went on to award costs against CUK Ltd for the hearing day lost as a result. The EAT held that the tribunal should not have made the costs order, given the lay member's responsibility for this turn of events.

The importance of members declaring their interests, or apparent interests, as **12.176** early as possible was highlighted in British Car Auctions Ltd v Adams 2013 ICR D25, EAT. In that case a lay member, K, lived three miles away from the BCA Ltd workplace where the events in the case occurred, and his son had worked there. Furthermore, K's daughter-in-law's step-brother, M, was a witness in the case. However, K did not raise these matters with the employment judge before the hearing began. They only became apparent when a branch manager for BCA Ltd heard of a conversation between K, his son and a third man about the poor quality of some of the evidence given in the case. BCA Ltd applied for recusal, not so much because it feared not getting a fair hearing but because it was concerned that, if A lost his case, he would assert bias and drag BCA Ltd into further litigation. The tribunal considered the application and refused it, but without reporting any of the views or evidence that K had given – it merely accepted his assurance that his impartiality was intact. The EAT allowed an appeal against the tribunal's decision not to withdraw. It held that K knew of his family relationship with BCA Ltd; knew that he ought to avoid cases where he knew people who might feature in the evidence; knew that that was a real risk; knew that M had been named in the papers in a significant way; and should have known that he ought to disclose those facts at the outset of the hearing. The fair-minded observer would think that K was consciously hiding his connection with BCA Ltd. Furthermore, the tribunal's procedure in dealing with the application was materially irregular. Although it was entitled to accord little weight to the branch manager's evidence, which was uncorroborated, third-hand hearsay, it should have been more transparent, making clear K's comments on the accusation and giving the parties a chance to respond before making a decision.

The message of such cases is that it is better to err on the side of caution and bring any potential interest or appearance of potential interest out into the open. The test formulated in University College of Swansea v Cornelius (above), and approved in Corus UK Ltd v Young (above), is whether a person acting in a judicial capacity would think that the situation should have been made known to the parties in case they wish to take objection. If so, then whether the member should in fact stand down will depend on any submissions the parties wish to make and, ultimately, the judgement of the tribunal.

Procedure where bias is alleged 12.177

Although an employment tribunal is not entitled to withdraw from a case simply because one of the parties alleges a lack of confidence in it during the hearing – see Automobile Proprietary Ltd v Healy 1979 ICR 809, EAT – it is right that whenever the possibility of an impression of bias arises, the tribunal should at least bring the matter out into the open at once so that all sides have an opportunity to discuss how best to proceed. It is always possible for the party with the right to object to waive that right, provided that such waiver is unequivocal and made in full knowledge of the relevant facts – Locabail (UK) Ltd v Bayfield Properties Ltd and other cases 2000 IRLR 96, CA.

The leading guidance on the steps that a tribunal should take in cases where bias is alleged was given by the Court of Appeal in Jones v DAS Legal Expenses Insurance Co Ltd and ors 2004 IRLR 218, CA. In that case, the tribunal chairman told the claimant that her (the chairman's) husband was a barrister in chambers that undertook work for the employer, DAS. The claimant chose to continue with the hearing, which he eventually lost. He later complained to the Regional Chairman of bias, claiming that the chairman had not made clear that her husband personally undertook work for DAS. He was refused a review of the decision, and his appeal to the EAT was dismissed on the ground that he had known about the chairman's connection and had waived his right to complain. The Court of Appeal dismissed his appeal against the EAT's decision, holding that there was no appearance of bias sufficient to pass the 'fair-minded and informed observer' test. In any case, even if there had been apparent bias, the claimant had waived his right to complain. Furthermore, his waiver was fully informed, as the principle in Locabail (UK) Ltd v Bayfield Properties Ltd and other cases (above) requires. The Court then went on to suggest some steps that an employment judge might take in similar circumstances:

- the judge should ascertain whether someone else is available to hear the case, as it is better to transfer a case than risk an allegation of bias

- the judge should prepare a full explanation of his or her interest and of why the problem has arisen so late in the day. The explanation should be mechanically recorded if possible, or carefully noted

- the parties should be informed of their options, namely either continuing with the judge or applying for the judge to recuse him or herself. The parties should be reassured that the court will not take it amiss if such an application is made

- the parties should be given time to reflect before they decide whether to object to the judge's hearing the case. An unrepresented claimant could be directed to the Citizens Advice Bureau for assistance, if required, or to the chief clerk or listing officer

- if the judge decides to stand down, the parties should be told the likely dates on which the matter might be relisted.

12.178 However, the Court emphasised that it was not setting down a mandatory checklist. It said: 'Sometimes some of these suggestions may be adopted, sometimes none of them may apply. We wish strongly to disabuse any disgruntled litigant of the idea that he may seize upon this judgment and use it as the mantra for complaint about ill-treatment. Any attempt to do so will receive short shrift.'

An indication of the shortness of the shrift can be gleaned from the Court of Appeal's refusal of permission to appeal in Donovan v London Borough of Barking and Dagenham 2012 EWCA Civ 1375, CA. The appeal related to tribunal proceedings in which the employment judge had revealed that she was a personal friend of the respondent's in-house lawyer, who had conduct of the case for the respondent but did not represent it at the tribunal. The claimant agreed to proceed but, when she lost, she appealed on the basis that she had not been given a fair opportunity to object to the case being heard by the employment judge. The EAT comprehensively rejected that argument. It accepted that the judge did not tell the claimant explicitly that she had a right to ask for recusal, and that if she continued with her case she could be taken to have waived her right to object, but considered that these points would have been obvious. It also held that there was no error of law in the employment judge failing to tell the claimant that, if she did apply for recusal, the tribunal would not take it amiss. In any event, there was no suggestion that the claimant actually thought that it would be held against her if she did object. The Court of Appeal refused the claimant permission to appeal against this 'manifestly sound' reasoning.

Raising the issue of bias   12.179
A distinction may be drawn between 'interest' and 'conduct' type cases when it comes to determining whether a party should raise an allegation of bias with the employment tribunal itself. In Cleveland Transit Ltd v Walton EAT 578/91 the allegation was that the tribunal chairman, in his capacity as a partner of a firm of solicitors, had a professional interest in the employer's business. The EAT held that where such allegations are made, they should be raised with the tribunal at the earliest opportunity. Indeed, the EAT warned that if a point of law such as this is not raised at first instance (assuming the facts are known) then it could not properly be raised on appeal.

It may seem unsatisfactory that it is for the tribunal accused of bias (or apparent bias) to decide for itself whether the accusation warrants recusal – i.e. in effect being judge in its own cause. However, the EAT has rejected the suggestion that the matter should be referred elsewhere, such as to a Regional Employment Judge or some other tribunal. In British Car Auctions Ltd v Adams 2013 ICR D25, EAT, it held that a tribunal cannot 'duck' the issue by passing the decision on to some other body, since that other body is unlikely to have the familiarity with the case that the application demands. The tribunal must put itself in the position of not answering for itself but asking what the view of the fair-minded, objective observer would be. This is so whether the application relates to the conduct of the tribunal as a whole or one of its members. Nor, in the case where

737

the conduct impugned is that of one member, should that one member be excluded from discussions. Furthermore, if the party making the application then seeks a review of the decision (now called a 'reconsideration' under the Tribunal Rules 2013 – see Chapter 15, 'Reconsideration of tribunal judgments and decisions'), that too should be heard by the same employment judge or tribunal in the normal way.

12.180 This contrasts with allegations of bias based upon the manner in which a tribunal conducts a hearing. The EAT recognised that in a conduct bias case, to raise the issue before the tribunal may only serve to exacerbate the situation and that the matter might properly be dealt with by way of appeal to the EAT. In Peter Simper and Co Ltd v Cooke 1986 IRLR 19, EAT, a conduct bias case, the EAT said that it is undesirable that the tribunal accused of giving the impression of bias should be asked to adjudicate on that matter itself. The case was cited with apparent approval, both by the EAT in Cleveland Transit Ltd v Walton (above) and by the Court of Appeal in Harada Ltd (t/a Chequepoint Ltd) v Turner 2001 EWCA Civ 599, CA.

The EAT went further in Kudrath v Ministry of Defence EAT 422/97, holding that in the context of employment tribunals, where one party is often unrepresented, it would be a denial of justice for the EAT to refuse to intervene where a tribunal chairman appeared to fall asleep, just because no complaint had been made at the time (although clearly it is preferable if the complaint is made at the time). The Court of Appeal later approved this decision in Stansbury v Datapulse plc and anor 2004 ICR 523, CA, and rejected the argument that, as the claimant had been represented by counsel at the tribunal hearing and had not raised an objection then about the member's conduct, the EAT should have declined to hear the complaint. The Court of Appeal recognised the difficulty, even for legal representatives, in raising a complaint about the behaviour of a member who, if the complaint were not upheld, might be part of the tribunal ruling on the case. Therefore, although a professional advocate might be expected to raise an objection during the course of the allegedly unfair hearing, this should not be a precondition to the matter being raised on appeal.

12.181 Following Stansbury, it would appear to make little difference whether a complaint about an inattentive member is raised during the hearing itself or on appeal, as there should be no bar to the EAT hearing such a complaint. However, if the issue is raised and dealt with before the tribunal and the parties and the employment judge agree to continue with the hearing, this will usually mean the party has waived his or her right to complain about the matter on appeal unless there is some further incident. In Fordyce v Hammersmith and Fulham Conservative Association EAT 0390/05 counsel for the respondent noticed that a lay member appeared to be asleep and agreed with counsel for the claimant to raise the matter jointly with the tribunal. This was done and, after enquiries were made of the member in question, all parties agreed to continue. However the member, despite the reassurances he had given to the parties and the tribunal chairman, appeared to continue dropping off after the resumption. No further complaint was made, but the respondent, on losing the case, complained to the EAT of an unfair hearing. The EAT held that it had no choice but to remit the matter to a differently constituted tribunal, despite acknowledging that this might be perceived as allowing the respondent a 'second bite at the cherry'. The essence of a tribunal decision is that it is the decision of all three members, and if one of those members has been asleep for a substantial period of time, that member cannot have played a full part in the decision that was made. However, had there been no further incident after the parties had agreed to continue, the EAT indicated that it would have held that neither party would have had any right to complain.

Withdrawal by party
12.182

Where a party has made a complaint of bias at the hearing and the tribunal has declined to withdraw from the case, that party may feel that a fair hearing is impossible and see no point in continuing. However, the Court of Appeal in Harada Ltd (t/a Chequepoint Ltd) v Turner 2001 EWCA Civ 599, CA, discouraged litigants from withdrawing unilaterally in such circumstances, preferring the approach advocated in Peter Simper and Co Ltd v Cooke 1986 IRLR 19, EAT, of waiting until the end and appealing against the decision. Nonetheless, the Court did indicate that there may be cases where it simply would not be appropriate to carry on, due; for example, to the nature of the tribunal's conduct, or where the point arises very early on in a long hearing.

Appeals
12.183

If an appeal is taken to the EAT on the ground of bias by an employment tribunal, the notice of appeal must give full particulars of each complaint: general allegations of bias will not be countenanced. The notice of appeal will then be sifted by a judge or the Registrar, who will usually direct that the parties or their advisers swear affidavits as to the facts that form the basis of the complaint. These statements of fact, together with the notice of appeal, may then be sent to the employment judge so that he or she, and if appropriate the lay members of the tribunal, will have the opportunity of commenting on them, and their comments will then be supplied to the parties. The procedure is set out in full at para 13 of the EAT Practice Direction 2013. If this procedure is not complied with, no complaints of bias will be entertained at the hearing of the appeal. The Practice Direction also goes on to state that challenges to the tribunal's conduct in exercise of its discretion under the Tribunal Rules are less likely to succeed, and that unsuccessful pursuit of an allegation of bias or improper conduct, particularly in respect of case management decisions, may put the party raising it at risk of an order for costs. (For full details of the procedure for appealing tribunal decisions based on allegations of bias, see

739

Chapter 16, 'The Employment Appeal Tribunal', under 'Grounds of appeal – conduct of the tribunal: bias, procedural irregularity or delay'.)

Where there is a sharp conflict of primary fact, the resolution of which will play a material part in the EAT's decision on the question of bias, the EAT may, if it is essential for a just decision, invite sworn affidavits from the employment judge or lay members and may draw adverse inferences where a judge or lay member declines to give such evidence without good reason. However, tribunal members cannot be orally cross-examined, even where they consent to it – Facey v Midas Retail Security and anor 2001 ICR 287, EAT (later approved by the Court of Appeal in Stansbury v Datapulse plc and anor 2004 ICR 523, CA).

12.184 An employment judge's statement that neither he or she nor the lay members felt subject to any bias cannot be conclusive. Indeed, in Locabail (UK) Ltd v Bayfield Properties Ltd and other cases 2000 IRLR 96, CA, the Court of Appeal said that owing to the 'insidious nature of bias', such comments will be of little value and it is for the appellate court, and not the first-instance tribunal, to assess the risk that some extraneous consideration may have influenced the decision. The courts recognise that a person may be unconsciously affected by bias even though he or she believes in good faith that he or she is acting impartially. Moreover, the issue is frequently not so much whether the tribunal was actually biased but whether a fair-minded and informed observer would have concluded that there was a real danger of bias – Harada Ltd (t/a Chequepoint Ltd) v Turner 2001 EWCA Civ 599, CA.

The appellate body is, however, entitled to take into account its own knowledge of the judge in question. In Abegaze v Shrewsbury College of Arts and Technology EAT 0176/07 the EAT gave the obiter view that the judge's 'court room style' and reputation are relevant factors, following cases on bias in the civil courts such as El-Farargy v El-Farargy and ors 2007 EWCA Civ 1149, CA. In Abegaze, all three members of the EAT had previously heard appeals from the judge in question and they had no doubt about his impartiality. The EAT also thought it relevant to take into account the track record of the complainant, noting that this particular complainant frequently abused the judiciary and made unfounded allegations of bias.

12.185 Where the employment judge or lay members have been asked for their comments on the allegations, there is no rule that the tribunal's recollection of events at the hearing should unquestioningly be preferred to that of a party or his or her representative – Facey v Midas Retail Security and anor (above). Despite a number of earlier EAT cases suggesting such a rule – see, for example, Roberts v United Friendly Insurance plc EAT 436/95 – the EAT in the Facey case rejected the proposition, relying on the Court of Appeal's judgment in Jones v Secretary of State for Wales and ors 1995 70 P and CR 211, CA, which involved allegations of impropriety against a planning inspector acting in a quasi-judicial role.

However, where the dispute concerns the accuracy of the employment judge's contemporaneous notes of the hearing, a party will not be allowed to put in evidence their own (or their representative's) notes of the hearing as a means of challenging the accuracy of the employment judge's notes. Unless both parties agree an alternative version, the employment judge's notes will prevail – Saga Petroleum v Bourgeois EAT 327/99.

13 Evidence

In contentious litigation, both sides are intent on proving their respective **13.1** versions of events. Rarely will they be in complete accord with each other about the facts of a case – if they are, then the matter will remain contentious only if there is a dispute about the interpretation of the relevant law or its application to the agreed facts. In the majority of cases, however, what is in dispute between the parties is the veracity of each other's contentions about what happened. It follows that the presentation of evidence is a vital aspect of any tribunal hearing.

In the ordinary courts, complex rules govern the admissibility and sufficiency of evidence. By and large these are inapplicable in employment tribunal proceedings, where the emphasis is on greater flexibility and informality. Indeed, rule 41 of the Tribunal Rules 2013, as set out in Schedule 1 to the Employment Tribunals (Constitution and Rules of Procedure) Regulations 2012 SI 2013/1237 ('the Tribunal Rules 2013'), expressly states that the tribunal 'is not bound by any rule of law relating to the admissibility of evidence in proceedings before the courts'.

However, this does not mean that the ordinary rules can be totally ignored. Just **13.2** like the ordinary courts, tribunals must assess and weigh the evidence they receive in a manner that is neither arbitrary nor cavalier. Indeed, as the EAT commented in Aberdeen Steak Houses Group plc v Ibrahim 1988 ICR 550, EAT, 'the rules of procedure and evidence have been built up over many years in order to guide courts and tribunals in the fairest and simplest way of dealing with and deciding issues... total informality and absence of generally recognised rules of procedure and evidence can be counter-productive in that parties may not feel that their cases have been fairly and appropriately dealt with.'

In this chapter we discuss the means by which tribunals seek to strike the difficult balance between observing the spirit of the civil courts' rules of evidence while not being hidebound by them. First, we consider the burden of proof and standard of proof in the employment tribunal, before looking at how the quality of evidence should be assessed. We then turn to the question of the weight that it is permissible to accord to evidence and whether various kinds of evidence are even admissible in an employment tribunal. Finally, we consider

743

the grounds on which evidence of discussions between employer and employee about the termination of the employment relationship may be shielded from consideration by the tribunal.

13.3 Burden of proof and standard of proof

Where facts are in dispute, the law uses the concept of 'burden of proof' to determine which side has the ultimate responsibility of proving his or her case to the tribunal. The burden of proof determines which side would win on that point if no evidence were adduced on either side, or if the evidence were so finely balanced that the tribunal could not decide which side to favour. Where dismissal is admitted in an unfair dismissal case, for example, the claimant would win if no evidence were adduced, since the employer will be taken to have unfairly dismissed the employee unless it can adduce evidence to show what the reason for dismissal was and demonstrate that that reason fell within the category of potentially valid reasons – S.98(1) Employment Rights Act 1996 (ERA). As a result, the employer will usually lead its evidence first in such a case (see Chapter 12, 'The hearing', under 'Starting the hearing – which side starts?').

As a general rule, however, except in cases where an essential fact is admitted (such as where the employer concedes that there has been a dismissal), the primary onus of proving a case, at least initially, rests with the claimant. It is he or she who must satisfy the tribunal that it has jurisdiction to entertain the claim, that he or she qualifies for the relief sought and that, in the circumstances of the case, he or she is entitled to that relief. So in cases where dismissal is not admitted – for example in a constructive dismissal case – the essential fact to be proved first is that there was a dismissal at law: consequently, the burden of proof rests on the employee. However, the law frequently provides that once the claimant has made out certain elements of his or her case, the respondent then takes on the burden of proof in relation to particular aspects of its defence. For instance, a female claimant for equal pay who claims that she is engaged on 'like work' with a male comparator would lose if she brought no evidence, as the onus of establishing that she is entitled to equal pay will not have been satisfied. If, however, it is proved that she is engaged on like work and that she receives less pay than her comparator, the burden of proof shifts, and it is then for the employer to show that any variation between the claimant's contract and her comparator's is genuinely due to a material difference, reliance on which is not discriminatory – S.69 Equality Act 2010 (EqA).

13.4 It will be rare that the legal burden of proof becomes an issue in tribunal proceedings (with the possible exception of cases invoking the EqA – see 'Burden of proof in discrimination cases' below). Occasionally a case may be decided against the party on whom the burden lies in circumstances in which the tribunal is simply unable to decide which of the parties' conflicting versions

744

of the facts to believe – Morris v London Iron and Steel Co Ltd 1987 ICR 855, CA. However, the Court in Morris, and the EAT in several subsequent cases, have confirmed that it should be exceptional for a tribunal to be unable to make a finding on the evidence and to have to fall back on the burden of proof. Furthermore, the Court of Appeal in Stephens and anor v Cannon and anor 2005 EWCA Civ 222, CA, has held that where a court relies on the burden of proof, it must ensure that others can discern that it has striven to make a finding in relation to a disputed issue and can understand the reasons why it has concluded that it cannot do so. In other words, it must give sufficiently detailed reasons for its approach, so that the parties can know why they have won and lost.

Burden of proof in discrimination cases

13.5

It is generally accepted that discrimination cases are difficult to prove since employers will rarely oblige complainants with overt and unequivocal 'proof' of discrimination. More usually, discrimination takes a disguised form and the evidence available to prove it often does nothing more than hint at logical inferences that can be drawn from the proven facts. Following a number of decisions of the European Court of Justice that recognised the particular difficulty faced by sex discrimination complainants in proving an act of discrimination, the EU Burden of Proof Directive (No.97/80) was passed into law, requiring EU Member States to take measures aimed at ensuring that once a complainant of sex discrimination establishes 'facts from which it may be presumed that there has been direct or indirect discrimination, it shall be for the respondent to prove that there has been no breach of the principle of equal treatment'. The Directive has since been subsumed into the recast EU Equal Treatment Directive (No.2006/54). A similar requirement was imposed on Member States in relation to race discrimination by the EU Race Directive (No.2000/43), and the EU Equal Treatment Framework Directive (No.2000/78) then prescribed an identical approach in respect of disability, religion/belief, sexual orientation and age, all of which have now been the subject of implementing legislation.

The mechanism is now set out in domestic law by S.136 EqA, which applies to all of the above protected characteristics. S.136 provides, in essence, that where a claimant proves facts from which a tribunal could conclude in the absence of an adequate explanation that the respondent has unlawfully discriminated against the claimant (i.e. a 'prima facie case'), the tribunal must uphold the complaint unless the respondent proves that he or she did not discriminate. In other words, if an employee establishes a prima facie case of differential treatment from which a tribunal could properly draw an inference that the treatment was because of one of the protected characteristics, then it will be for the employer to prove that there was some other ground for the treatment (or that one of the exceptions, such as a genuine occupational requirement,

745

applied). These counter-intuitive provisions have been the subject of detailed examination by courts and tribunals and there is now a substantial body of case law on the evidence required to establish a prima facie case and the point at which the burden ought to shift. This case law is discussed in detail in IDS Employment Law Handbook, 'Discrimination at Work' (2012), Chapter 32, 'Burden of proof'.

13.6 More generally, the question of the kind of evidence that is admissible in discrimination cases, and the particular problems inherent in proving discrimination, are considered in IDS Employment Law Handbook, 'Discrimination at Work' (2012), Chapter 33, 'Proving discrimination', under 'Admissibility and quality of evidence'.

13.7 Balance of probabilities

In the majority of cases, the tribunal will decide the outcome not by resting its decision on a failure by the party upon whom the burden of proof lies to discharge that burden, but on conclusions reached about the quality and sufficiency of the evidence presented by both sides. In this respect, both parties must adduce evidence sufficient to prove those facts necessary to determine the case in their favour. Lawyers speak of the degree of cogency that evidence must reach in order that it may discharge the legal burden of proof. What this essentially boils down to is a consideration of the strength of the evidence of the respective parties. Once all the evidence has been presented, it is the tribunal's task (in common with all other courts in civil proceedings) to determine the case 'on the balance of probabilities'.

In Miller v Minister of Pensions 1947 2 All ER 372, Div Ct, Mr Justice Denning (as he then was) defined the civil standard of proof in the following terms: '[The degree of cogency] is well settled. It must carry a reasonable degree of probability, but not so high as is required in a criminal case. If the evidence is such that the tribunal can say: "we think it more probable than not", the burden is discharged, but if the probabilities are equal, it is not.' In other words, if the party on whom the legal burden of proof lies is able to convince the tribunal that the evidence which he or she has provided makes it more likely than not that his or her version of the facts is correct, then the tribunal will find those facts to be as asserted by that party. Anything less and the party will have failed to make out his or her case.

13.8 It should be clearly noted that the standards of proof applicable in civil and criminal proceedings are different. Whereas civil proceedings are decided on the 'balance of probabilities', the criminal standard of proof is that a charge must be proved 'beyond reasonable doubt'. The latter is a much more exacting standard and the prosecution in any criminal trial has the duty to discharge the burden of proving the defendant's guilt by providing evidence that is sufficiently cogent to allay any reasonable doubts that the jury might have over the question of guilt. It is unlikely, to the point of being unthinkable, that a tribunal would ever apply the wrong standard of proof and so this distinction will rarely trouble the appellate courts. In Turner v South Central Ambulance Service NHS Trust EAT 0383/12 the EAT dismissed an appeal against an employment judge's decision that the claimant was not disabled, where the judge had asked whether the claimant was 'clearly' a disabled person and noted that he felt unable to answer that question 'with certainty'. The EAT held that to suppose that the judge was thereby indicating that he was actually applying a standard of proof higher than that necessary would be to hold that he was committing one of the most basic errors, which was improbable.

There have been suggestions that a higher standard of proof may be required to prove certain facts. For example, an industrial tribunal in Singh v British Steel Corporation 1974 IRLR 131, IT, held that a claimant would have to show 'strict proof' in order to benefit from a term he or she claimed to have been implied by custom, which suggests a different, higher standard of proof for the implication of terms into an employment contract by custom or practice. The Court of Appeal has since held that use of the word 'strict' in this context is inappropriate, but went on to note that 'clear evidence of practice is, however, required to establish something as potentially nebulous as custom and practice, and there should be a scrutiny commensurate with the particular circumstances' – Henry and ors v London General Transport Services Ltd 2002 ICR 910, CA.

13.9 It is unlikely that any intermediate standard of proof, higher than the 'balance of probabilities' but lower than 'beyond all reasonable doubt', was realistically being proposed by either the tribunal in Singh or the Court of Appeal in Henry. Instead, these cases demonstrate the courts' recognition that certain facts are more difficult to prove than others. This has been well established by cases in the ordinary civil courts, particularly in those brought under family and childcare law jurisdictions that involve allegations of sexual abuse. In one such case – Re H (minors) 1996 AC 563, HL – Lord Nicholls commented that 'the inherent probability or improbability of an event is itself a matter to be taken into account when weighing the probabilities and deciding whether, on balance, the event occurred. The more improbable the event, the stronger must be the evidence that it did occur before, on the balance of probability, its occurrence will be established.' His Lordship went on to make clear that he was not proposing a general principle that serious cases, such as those concerning allegations of sexual assault or harassment, require a higher standard of proof than other less serious matters. Rather, the more serious the allegation, the less likely it is to be true and therefore the more cogent will the evidence need to be for the tribunal to be satisfied that the event was more likely than not to have occurred.

In B v A and anor EAT 0505/07 the EAT rejected the argument that an employment tribunal had got the Re H guidance the wrong way round when it apparently referred to the seriousness of allegations as supporting their likely

747

truthfulness. The case involved claims of serious sexual harassment made by C against B. Among other things, C alleged that B had raped her at the school where they worked. B denied all the allegations and it was part of his defence that C had made up the allegations against him in response to an incident at work when he had belittled her in public. The tribunal rejected that defence, noting that it would be massively disproportionate to manufacture allegations of this enormity as a reaction to such an event. On appeal, the EAT could find no fault with the tribunal's analysis. If the tribunal had directed itself that these allegations were so grievous and serious that they could not have been made up then that would manifestly be a fundamental misdirection. However, this was not what the tribunal was saying. It was responding to a specific argument advanced by B. Although there was no burden on him to provide a motive as to why C may have concocted her story, he had sought to provide a possible explanation, as he was entitled to do, and the tribunal was entitled to be unconvinced by it.

13.10 Even if the evidence is not accepted as proving precisely that which a party asserts, it may nonetheless be helpful to that party's case. In Woodhouse School v Webster 2009 ICR 818, CA, the factual dispute centred on whether M, the owner of the school at which W worked, had instructed W to dismiss a deaf teacher because of her deafness. W relied on this instruction as part of his reason for resigning and claiming constructive dismissal. The tribunal rejected W's case that M had expressly instructed him to dismiss the teacher for that reason but found that there was an implied instruction to this effect. The school appealed, arguing, among other things, that neither side had given evidence of an implied instruction and so it was wrong of the tribunal to make a finding based on a case that neither side had advanced. The EAT rejected this argument and so did the Court of Appeal. The Court held that, although it is good practice for a tribunal to warn the parties and give them an opportunity to make submissions if it prefers an interpretation of the evidence that neither has contended for, there was no procedural unfairness where the parties had in fact had a fair opportunity to address the tribunal on the substance of the evidence. It had been open to the tribunal to find, on the balance of probabilities, that W's reason for resigning was that he had been instructed to dismiss the deaf teacher, even though it did not accept his evidence that there was ever an explicit instruction. Lord Justice Mummery noted that oral evidence does not have to attain standards of perfection, only to be more probably true than the evidence given on the other side.

13.11 Legal presumptions

The obligation to produce sufficient evidence to discharge the burden of proving a case on the balance of probabilities can, in some limited circumstances, be assisted by legal or evidential presumptions in favour of certain crucial facts. A legal presumption generally requires that a particular fact be inferred in the absence of evidence which is sufficient (on the balance of probabilities) to persuade the tribunal to the contrary. This is called a 'rebuttable presumption'. Occasionally, however, the effect of the presumption goes even further by conclusively presuming a fact in favour of a party irrespective of evidence (no matter how cogent) to the contrary. This is then called an 'irrebuttable presumption'.

The law of presumptions tends to apply mostly in criminal proceedings and generally derives from the common law. However, in the context of employment tribunals, certain presumptions are imposed, both as part of the substantive law contained in statutory provisions and as part of common law principles of construction. The most important are listed below.

Rebuttable presumption of continuity of employment. By virtue of S.210(5) **13.12** ERA, 'a person's employment during any period shall, unless the contrary is shown, be presumed to have been continuous'. This is important because entitlement to many statutory rights is dependent on a specified period of continuous employment. The presumption as to continuity has the effect of casting the evidential burden of disproving the fact onto the employer whenever it is contested that the claimant has sufficient continuous service to entitle him or her to bring a claim – Nicoll v Nocorrode Ltd 1981 ICR 348, EAT. However, the EAT has commented that a tribunal should not readily resort to the presumption in a case where there is a good deal of evidence as to a particular alleged break in continuity, and that it is only in rare cases that the evidence will be so finely balanced that the presumption comes into play – Mark Insulations Ltd v Bunker EAT 0331/05.

Rebuttable presumption against the extra-territorial application of UK 13.13 enactments. The EAT in Jackson v Ghost Ltd and anor 2003 IRLR 824, EAT, endorsed a general presumption of statutory construction that domestic statutes do not ordinarily apply outside the territory to which they extend. That case was concerned with the territorial application of the unfair dismissal provisions of the ERA. The issue as it relates to unfair dismissal has since been comprehensively examined by the House of Lords in Lawson v Serco Ltd and two other cases 2006 ICR 250, HL, where their Lordships held that expatriate employees working wholly outside Great Britain could nonetheless bring claims under the ERA in certain circumstances. Lord Hoffmann noted, however, that 'the general principle of construction is, of course, that legislation is prima facie territorial', and so the rebuttable presumption remains the starting point for examining the geographical scope of legislation. For a full discussion of the territoriality issue, see Chapter 2, 'Tribunals' jurisdiction', under 'Territorial limitations'.

Rebuttable presumption that documents sent by post, fax or other form of 13.14 electronic communication are received on a certain date. Service of documents by post in ordinary civil claims has long been subject to the 'ordinary course of post' rule, under which a document sent by first-class post is presumed

749

to arrive on the second day after it was posted (excluding Sundays and bank holidays). The Court of Appeal in Consignia plc (formerly the Post Office) v Sealy 2002 ICR 1193, CA, expressly applied this rule to the postal presentation of an ET1 form. The presumption is now included in rule 90 of the Tribunal Rules 2013, which states that a document sent by post shall, unless the contrary is proved, be taken to have been received by the addressee on the day on which it would be delivered in the ordinary course of post. Furthermore, a notice or document transmitted by means of electronic communication shall, unless the contrary is proved, be presumed to have been received on the day on which it is transmitted. The rules governing delivery and service are discussed fully in Chapter 10, 'Service of notices and documents'.

13.15 **Rebuttable presumption of redundancy.** By virtue of S.163(2) ERA, for the purpose of any claim for a redundancy payment, 'an employee who has been dismissed by his [or her] employer shall, unless the contrary is proved, be presumed to have been so dismissed by reason of redundancy'. However, this does not necessarily mean that there is an 'onus' on the employer to rebut the presumption of redundancy. The tribunal must make a decision on the reason for dismissal based on all the facts, including those agreed between the parties and those found on the evidence from both sides – Greater Glasgow Health Board v Lamont EATS 0019/12. It is important to note, however, that in claims for unfair dismissal an employer, in seeking to discharge the burden imposed on it by S.98(1) ERA to show what the reason for dismissal was, is not entitled to rely on the presumption that a dismissal is by reason of redundancy – Elliott Turbomachinery Ltd v Bates 1981 ICR 218, EAT.

13.16 **Rebuttable presumption that a judgment certified by tribunal staff is a true copy.** Reg 14(3) of the Employment Tribunals (Constitution and Rules of Procedure) Regulations 2013 SI 2013/1237 stipulates that 'a document purporting to be certified by a member of staff of a Tribunal to be a true copy of an entry of a judgment in the register shall, unless the contrary is proved, be sufficient evidence of the document and its contents'. This is a change from the antecedent Reg 18 of the Employment Tribunals (Constitution and Rules of Procedure) Regulations 2004 SI 2004/1861, which conferred the presumption only on documents purporting to be certified by the Secretary.

13.17 **Rebuttable presumption that a collective agreement is not intended to be legally binding**. This presumption is laid down by S.178 of the Trade Union and Labour Relations (Consolidation) Act 1992 and can only be rebutted if the agreement is in writing and includes a statement that the parties intend that the agreement shall be a legally enforceable contract.

13.18 **Irrebuttable presumption of truth of matters stated in a Minister's Certificate.** Various provisions in employment legislation provide that a certificate signed by or on behalf of a Minister of the Crown will be conclusive evidence of the truth of specific facts stated therein. For example, in claims made under S.183 TULR(C)A (failure to disclose information to a trade union) a certificate from the Secretary of State for Employment certifying that a request for information could not have been complied with other than by disclosing information contrary to the interests of national security will be conclusive evidence of that fact – S.183(6). There is also a rebuttable presumption that any document purporting to be such a certificate is authentic unless proved otherwise.

Irrebuttable presumption of trade union independence. A certificate of **13.19** independence issued by the Certification Officer is conclusive evidence that a trade union is independent (and a refusal, withdrawal or cancellation of such a certificate is conclusive evidence that a trade union is not independent) – S.8(1) TULR(C)A. There is also a rebuttable presumption that any document purporting to be a certificate of independence is authentic unless proved otherwise – S.8(2).

Assessing the weight of evidence   13.20

An employment tribunal can only decide whether a party has discharged the evidential burden of proving his or her case once the evidence is complete, and thus only after it has come to some conclusion about the quality of the evidence presented. This assessment involves ascribing weight to items of evidence in order to decide what influence (if any) such items bear on the matters to be decided. The question of the weight to be attached to evidence is one for the tribunal to decide as the fact-finding body or 'industrial jury'. An appeal against a tribunal's assessment will only succeed if it can be shown, for example, that the tribunal ignored relevant evidence, took into account irrelevant evidence, or came to a conclusion that was perverse. Although the criteria by which a tribunal will assess the weight of evidence are somewhat vague, it is possible to suggest the kinds of factor that may influence a tribunal in making such an assessment. These include the volume of evidence, the credibility of witnesses, effectiveness of examination and cross-examination and veracity and cogency of evidence.

Volume of evidence. If there is a preponderance of evidence on one side, as **13.21** against a lesser amount of equally good or bad evidence on the other, a tribunal may well be impressed simply by the volume of evidence in favour of one party. But simply because, say, five witnesses are called to give evidence on the same point does not necessarily enhance a party's case. As a general rule, it is quality not quantity that matters most when assessing the weight to be given to the parties' evidence.

Credibility of witnesses. The advantage of hearing and seeing witnesses give **13.22** oral testimony is never underestimated by tribunals. For that reason written statements and submissions unaccompanied by oral testimony are always

751

regarded as second-best evidence if, indeed, they are accepted at all. Factors such as the demeanour of a witness and the coherence of his or her evidence are taken into account by the tribunal in assessing credibility. There is no requirement for any evidence given to be corroborated: it is simply for the tribunal to assess, as a matter of common sense and judgement, the extent to which it finds the evidence of a witness satisfactory and reliable – Peart v Dixons Store Group Retail Ltd EAT 0630/04. It is well established that a tribunal may properly have regard to the witness's credibility on a collateral matter when deciding whether to accept his or her evidence on a central issue – see, for example, London Clubs Management Ltd v Rooney EATS 0019/11.

13.23 **Examination and cross-examination.** The inroads that can be made into revealing the strengths or weaknesses of a witness's testimony depend largely upon the effectiveness of the examination and, even more so, the cross-examination of the witness. These techniques of advocacy are discussed in Chapter 12, 'The hearing', under 'Presenting the evidence – cross-examination'. A tribunal may legitimately draw an adverse inference if there is an omission to call an obvious witness. Moreover, if a crucial matter is not raised in cross-examination, the tribunal may also take such omission into account – although, of course, it may always question the witness itself on any matter not raised by either of the parties, and may recall a party who has already given evidence for this purpose.

13.24 **Evidence that would ordinarily be inadmissible.** Evidence that would ordinarily be inadmissible under the rules governing the ordinary courts may be admitted by a tribunal in the exercise of its discretion under rule 41 of the Tribunal Rules 2013. Even so, the weight attached to such evidence may, in the event, be slight, having regard to the doubts about the veracity or cogency of the evidence that would be raised before an ordinary court. Specific issues concerning the admissibility of evidence are discussed later in this chapter – see 'Admissibility of evidence' below.

As with most aspects of practice and procedure, tribunals have a wide discretion to make their own judgement about the weight that it is proper to attach to various pieces of evidence, and the appeal courts will interfere in such a decision only very reluctantly. In Erhayiem v Stockport and High Peak TEC Ltd and anor EAT 705/01, for example, there was found to be no error of law in a tribunal's decision that even though the respondent had been held to have forged the claimant's signature on documents relevant to his claim of race discrimination, the documents were not crucial pieces of evidence and so the respondent's case was not seriously undermined. In contrast, in the sexual harassment case B v A and anor EAT 0505/07, where B was accused of a serious sexual offence in the school where he worked, his response was that he was not even present on that day. The tribunal found, on the basis of other witness evidence, that in fact he was present that day. It took this into account as seriously undermining B's credibility in relation to his response to the claims in general. The EAT dismissed an appeal against the tribunal's weighing of the evidence.

Note that, even when a witness is entirely credible, his or her evidence does not have to be accepted in its totality. This is because courts and tribunals draw a distinction between credibility and reliability. As the Scottish EAT put it in Netintelligence Ltd v McNaught EATS 0057/08, 'for any fact-finder to be entitled to accept evidence, it requires to be satisfied that not only is the witness's evidence on the point credible but also that it is reliable. A witness may be credible in the sense that the fact-finder is satisfied that they are honest and doing their best to tell the truth but their evidence may not be reliable for a whole host of reasons which involves looking at how the witness gave [his or] her evidence, at conflicts in [his or] her evidence, on the clarity of [his or] her evidence or the lack thereof and beyond what the witness has said to the whole evidence in the case.'

Parties' responsibilities in matters of evidence 13.25
Relatively informal though they may be, tribunals are under no duty to advise a party (even if unrepresented) about whether that party should or should not call any particular evidence – Hawker Siddeley Power Engineering Ltd v Rump 1979 IRLR 425, EAT. The EAT stated in Dimtsu v Westminster City Council 1991 IRLR 450, EAT, that it 'would not wish to cast any doubt on the propriety of the long-established practice whereby chairmen of [employment] tribunals give assistance where it is needed in the formulation and presentation of the cases of persons before them... But this must be a matter for the judgment of the [employment] tribunal in each individual case and should not be erected into an obligation which if not fully complied with leads to a conclusion that an error in law has been committed.' This topic is discussed in more detail in Chapter 12, 'The hearing', under 'Assistance by the tribunal'.

The responsibility to ensure that relevant evidence is adduced means that a party cannot usually open up issues on appeal that were not raised by him or her during the tribunal proceedings – Hellyer Brothers Ltd v McLeod and ors and another case 1987 ICR 526, CA. Consequently, parties must endeavour to present their cases in a coherent way so that all the issues that arise are actually addressed and all evidence that is relevant to those issues is introduced at the right time and in a way that makes it apparent why the evidence is being called. There is limited scope for introducing fresh evidence on appeal in situations where the evidence could not, with reasonable diligence, have been obtained before the tribunal, the evidence is sufficiently relevant that it is potentially influential on the result and the evidence is apparently credible – Wileman v Minilec Engineering Ltd 1988 ICR 318, EAT. The rules governing the introduction of new evidence on appeal are considered in detail in Chapter 18, 'EAT hearings and decisions', under 'Evidence – admission of new evidence on appeal'.

753

13.26 ## Admissibility of evidence

The provision in rule 41 of the Tribunal Rules 2013 enabling employment tribunals to admit evidence that would not be admissible before the ordinary courts serves two functions. First, it allows the tribunal to be the arbiter of whether any particular item of evidence should be admitted and, if so, what degree of weight should be attached to it. Secondly, it avoids the necessity for parties appearing before tribunals to be experts in the complicated rules of admissibility applicable in the civil courts. The discretion granted by rule 41 does not always prevent complicated and time-consuming arguments on admissibility from arising. This often occurs in the form of a preliminary hearing, although recent cases have doubted the appropriateness of dealing with the question of admissibility at the preliminary stage – see, for example, the comments of Mr Justice Underhill (then President of the EAT) in HSBC Asia Holdings BV and anor v Gillespie EAT 0417/10. (The range of matters suitable to be decided as preliminary issues is considered in Chapter 11, 'Case management', under 'Preliminary hearings'.) Where problems do arise, it may be more pragmatic for the tribunal to admit potentially excludable evidence in pursuance of its discretion and then ascribe such weight to it as it thinks fit, having regard to the fact that such evidence would (or might) ordinarily be inadmissible in other proceedings. Indeed, a tribunal may properly admit evidence but accord it no weight – Manning and anor v Middleton Miniature Mouldings EAT 0439/09.

What follows in this section is a discussion first of the general principle that evidence must be relevant in order to be admissible, and then of a number of categories of evidence to which particular rules may apply and which may be inadmissible in certain circumstances. It is worth noting at this stage that there is a further category of inadmissible evidence, falling under the rubric of 'privilege', which is not discussed in this chapter. This category includes 'legal advice privilege' and 'litigation privilege', which may prevent courts seeing documents relating to earlier legal disputes. The various grounds on which 'privilege' can be claimed in respect of documentary evidence are discussed in Chapter 9, 'Responding to opponent's case', under 'Disclosure and inspection of documents – privilege'. There is also the significant category of evidence excluded by the 'without prejudice' rule or by the statutory restriction on introducing evidence of pre-termination discussions in unfair dismissal cases. This is discussed separately at the end of this chapter, under 'Evidence of settlement negotiations'.

13.27 ### Relevance
The overarching factor that governs the admissibility of all kinds of evidence is relevance. For any evidence to be admissible it must be relevant to the issues that require adjudication by the tribunal. 'Relevant', in this context, means that

the evidence is 'logically probative or disprobative of some matter which requires proof', per Lord Bingham in O'Brien v Chief Constable of South Wales Police 2005 2 AC 534, HL. However, it is not enough that the evidence just falls within this definition – it must achieve a minimum standard of relevance. Mr Justice Underhill (then President of the EAT), sitting alone in HSBC Asia Holdings BV and anor v Gillespie (above), held that 'evidence may be, as it is sometimes put, "logically" or "theoretically" relevant but nevertheless too marginal, or otherwise unlikely to assist the court, for its admission to be justified'. Tribunals therefore have a discretion not to admit evidence that is only marginally relevant or unnecessarily repetitive.

This discretion is a manifestation of the tribunal's general power to regulate its own proceedings in the furtherance of the overriding objective (rule 2). Underhill P in Gillespie referred to Lord Justice Henry's judgment in Noorani v Merseyside TEC Ltd 1999 IRLR 184, CA, where he stated that employment tribunals should be even more willing than the civil courts to exclude marginally relevant evidence, given the greater emphasis on informality in the tribunal. It would be incompatible with the overriding objective if tribunals were unable to exclude otherwise relevant evidence. For this reason, Rosedale Mouldings Ltd v Sibley 1980 ICR 816, EAT, is no longer good law. In that case, the EAT held that industrial tribunals (the forerunners to employment tribunals) had no discretion to refuse to admit evidence that is admissible and probative of one or more of the issues before it. Underhill P noted that that proposition had more than once been doubted on an obiter basis, and that it had been disapproved as a matter of ratio in Digby v East Cambridgeshire District Council 2007 IRLR 585, EAT. The decision was therefore out of line with the current state of the law.

The discretion to exclude evidence that is only marginally relevant must be **13.28** exercised judicially and so there may be (limited) scope for appeal against any such decision. The Digby case is a rare example of a tribunal erring in this regard, where the EAT allowed an appeal against the tribunal's decision to exclude evidence of the circumstances in which a dismissed employee was given a final warning. The ex-employee was complaining of unfair dismissal and it was part of his case that it was unfair of the employer to rely on the warning in question. The tribunal had assumed that there was no reason to doubt the appropriateness of the warning and so refused to hear evidence relating to it. This was an error of law.

It may be particularly difficult for tribunals to draw the line between relevant and irrelevant (or only marginally relevant) evidence in discrimination cases. Given that it is notoriously difficult to find direct evidence of discrimination, claimants often rely on evidence of incidents which, although not complained about in their own right, are said to shed light on the reason for later, allegedly discriminatory, acts. Mr Justice Mummery (as he then was) in Qureshi v Victoria University of Manchester and anor 2001 ICR 863, EAT, observed

755

that, in some cases, such a volume of background material is introduced that the actual issues in the case may be obscured or even eclipsed. In Anya v University of Oxford 2001 ICR 847, CA, evidence of the 'background' of the working relationship between the claimant and his supervisor was held to be relevant to the claimant's assertion that a recruitment panel, which included the supervisor, discriminated against him in rejecting his application for a new post. The claimant's case was that the background indicated a preconceived hostility towards him and it was material from which the tribunal could properly draw an inference of discrimination. This case was later distinguished in HSBC Asia Holdings BV and anor v Gillespie (above), which also had to consider whether 'background' material should be admitted. There, the claims were of discrimination and harassment at the employer's London office. The EAT held that the claimant should not have been allowed to present evidence relating to allegations of harassment involving different perpetrators and taking place several years previously at an overseas office. Whereas in Anya the background information related to the alleged discriminator himself and had the potential to shed light on his motivation, in Gillespie the background allegations were only marginally relevant. The particular problems that arise in showing evidence of discrimination are considered in detail in IDS Employment Law Handbook, 'Discrimination at Work' (2012), in Chapter 33, 'Proving discrimination'.

13.29 It is worth noting that, in his summary of the law on tribunals' power to exclude insufficiently relevant evidence, Underhill P in HSBC Asia Holdings BV and anor v Gillespie (above) stated that the position is in principle no different to that obtaining in the civil courts under the Civil Procedure Rules 1998 SI 1998/3132. He also warned that just because evidence is insufficiently relevant, that does not mean that the tribunal must take steps to exclude it in every case, and certainly not at an interlocutory stage or at the outset of a hearing. He noted that tribunals are constantly presented with irrelevant evidence but most often it is better to 'make no fuss and simply disregard it or, if the evidence in question is liable to prejudice the orderly progress of the case, to deal with it by a ruling in the course of the hearing'. Underhill P observed that, in general, the cost and trouble involved in a pre-hearing ruling are unjustified and, where there is genuine room for argument about the admissibility of the evidence, a tribunal at a preliminary hearing may be less well placed to make the necessary assessment. However, the situation may be different for discrimination cases, in which there is a tendency for claimants to adduce evidence of very many incidents extending over long periods of time, which may overburden the tribunal and the parties and obscure the real issues. In such cases, it may be appropriate to decide questions of admissibility in advance of the full hearing. The procedure at preliminary hearings is considered in detail in Chapter 11, 'Case management', under 'Preliminary hearings'.

Hearsay

The Civil Evidence Act 1995 defines hearsay as 'a statement made otherwise than by a person while giving oral evidence in the proceedings which is tendered as evidence of the matters stated' – S.1(2)(a). Hearsay evidence is commonly (but incorrectly) defined as being evidence of something a third party has said or written. The crucial omission in this definition is that it is hearsay only if the evidence is adduced in order to prove the truth of what was said or written. It is not hearsay if it is adduced in order merely to prove, for example, that the words were spoken, or that the person making the statement must have been in a certain place at a certain time to have spoken those words.

Hearsay is generally divided into two forms, or 'degrees'. First-degree hearsay comprises an oral or written statement previously made by a person, which is proved by the production of the document in which he or she made it, or by the direct oral evidence of a witness who heard him or her make it, or by that person's own direct oral evidence that he made the statement. Second-degree hearsay (or 'double-hearsay') comprises the situation where, for example, witness A swears that B told him that C had said something. In this case, A's testimony as to the facts stated by C is second-hand hearsay. The same applies if a document asserts that the author of the document was told something by another.

The complex rules relating to the admissibility of hearsay evidence in civil proceedings were abolished by the Civil Evidence Act 1995, which states in S.1 that 'in civil proceedings evidence shall not be excluded on the ground that it is hearsay'. Even prior to this, employment tribunals – by virtue of the equivalent of what is now rule 41 of the Tribunal Rules 2013 – were not subject to the rule against hearsay and, in practice, tribunals often have to admit first-hand hearsay statements in order to determine the facts and the areas of contention that lie behind those facts. For example, confidential allegations by an informant about an employee's conduct may be made to an HR officer. The employee may as a result be dismissed and the HR officer called to give evidence in the ensuing tribunal proceedings. Although the HR officer's report of what he or she was told by the informant would be hearsay, it would nevertheless be vital in order to enable the tribunal to assess whether the employer had reasonable grounds for dismissing. Indeed, the refusal to admit hearsay evidence in dismissal cases may even amount to an error of law. In Coral Squash Clubs Ltd v Matthews and anor 1979 ICR 607, EAT, the company sought to adduce information about an employee that was given to it by a colleague. The tribunal refused to admit the information into evidence but on appeal the EAT held that it had been wrong to do so. It was information that had influenced the company in its decision to dismiss and was therefore relevant. The fact that the person who gave the information to the employer was not called to give evidence (even though this would have been possible) was a matter that went to the weight of the evidence and not to its admissibility. However, a tribunal will not act unlawfully in excluding hearsay if its admission 'could in some way adversely affect the reaching of a proper decision in the case'.

Whenever tribunals admit hearsay evidence it is important that they do not lose sight of the problems associated with such evidence. The drawback is essentially that the maker of the statement that is being reported second-hand is rarely called to give evidence him or herself and so the veracity of that statement cannot be tested by cross-examination of the person who made it. Tribunals should therefore pay careful regard to assessing the quality of the hearsay and should determine the extent to which (i) the evidence is credible, and (ii) the statement of the person is being accurately and authentically reported. A tribunal that decides a case in favour of a party whose entire evidence is hearsay may well find that the appellate courts have such doubts about the quality of that evidence as to overturn the decision. In Etherington v Henry J Greenham (1929) Ltd 1969 ITR 226, Div Ct, the tribunal rejected a claimant's claim for a redundancy payment solely on the evidence of a manager who had been told by a director that the claimant was to be replaced by a younger man. The Divisional Court pointed out that such evidence was hearsay and that, although tribunals were not bound by the civil courts' rules against hearsay that were in place at the time, the hearsay evidence of the manager was not sufficient to overturn the statutory presumption that a dismissal was due to redundancy. And in Tidman v Aveling Marshall Ltd 1977 ICR 506, EAT, the EAT remitted a case to a fresh tribunal after the original tribunal had limited the period of compensation for unfair dismissal to four months by relying entirely on hearsay evidence to the effect that the claimant would in any event have been made redundant within that time.

13.32 Nonetheless, there are plenty of examples of tribunals giving weight to hearsay evidence in appropriate circumstances, and of the EAT approving their right to do so. Two instances:

- **Abiodun v Crystal Services plc and ors** EAT 1266/02: the EAT saw no error of law in an employment tribunal relying on a hearsay statement from a witness whom the respondent had chosen not to call. The tribunal was plainly aware that the evidence was hearsay and took it into account only as one of the reasons leading it to prefer the respondent's evidence over the claimant's

- **Locke v Tabfine Ltd t/a Hands Music Centre** EAT 0517/10: an employment judge erred in finding that the claimant, who had presented an out-of-time claim, had not discharged the burden of proving that it was not reasonably practicable for him to present the claim in time. The employment judge appeared to have reached this conclusion without in any way rejecting the account given by the claimant in his witness statement of the medical problems that hindered him in presenting his claim. The statement accorded with the medical evidence and, although it was untested and therefore hearsay, it should have been given some weight.

Hearsay evidence can be of particular use in supporting the credibility of a **13.33** claimant or a witness in a complaint of harassment, where the claimant is likely to have trouble establishing, in the absence of witnesses, cogent evidence that an incident of sexual harassment took place. For example, the claimant might call a witness to give evidence that the claimant complained to him or her of the incident at the time. This kind of evidence can be relevant under the common law doctrine of 'recent complaint', which acknowledges that it may be relevant to the assessment of the credibility of the person making an allegation that he or she complained about it to a third party at or close to the time of the incident – see, for example, Peart v Dixons Store Group Retail Ltd EAT 0630/04.

Note that the EAT in Harlington Hospice Association v Mitchell EAT 0424/07 accepted the submission that 'if the tribunal is going to prefer hearsay to direct evidence, then it ought, albeit briefly, to indicate why it has reached that conclusion'. The tribunal had made a finding that accorded with the evidence given in two untested witness statements, and which contradicted the oral evidence given by the claimant, but without stating that it preferred the hearsay evidence over the oral evidence. The EAT held that it would be perfectly proper for the tribunal to weigh the evidence in this way but that it had not given sufficient reasons for its finding. This matter would therefore have to be remitted. The EAT commented that it did not think that the explanation would have to be detailed.

Credibility and collateral issues
13.34

Collateral evidence is evidence which is not probative of any of the issues that a party must prove (or disprove), but which is sought to be introduced to cast doubt on either the character or credibility of a witness for the other side – for example, to show that the witness has done wrong on a previous occasion and so is likely to have done wrong on the occasion in question. The EAT in Fox v Anago Ltd EAT 32/92, under its then President, Mr Justice Mummery, accepted a number of propositions as to the state of the law on admissible evidence. One of the propositions was that 'evidence can be relevant which goes to an issue of the credit of a witness. It is always possible in proceedings to give evidence to the effect that a witness cannot be believed and anything which goes to affect the credibility of that witness is relevant to an issue before the court and cannot properly be disregarded by the tribunal.' However, the EAT did not, in the end, give a judgment on the appeal and so this endorsement is obiter.

In Burford v Servispak Ltd and anor ET Case No.1300511/05 an employment tribunal allowed the claimant in a sexual harassment case to call witnesses to give evidence that the alleged harasser had also sexually harassed them. The tribunal admitted the evidence on the basis that the tribunal members were

759

experienced in dealing with material of that nature and would be capable of distinguishing between matters of primary importance and peripheral considerations. In contrast, in A v B 2013 IRLR 434, EAT, an employment judge doubted whether evidence of the claimant's historical conviction for kerb-crawling could be relevant, on the ground of either propensity or credibility, to the employer's case that it had dismissed him because of alleged inappropriate conduct towards female colleagues. The judge observed that the fact that an individual has an inclination to solicit prostitutes may not go far in proving any particular attitude towards women, such as to indicate propensity to do the acts alleged. (The judge did, though, allow the evidence to be admitted on other grounds, even though it would ordinarily have been rendered inadmissible by the statutory exclusion of evidence relating to spent convictions. This aspect of the case is discussed under 'Criminal records' below.)

13.35 More commonly, evidence on a collateral matter is relevant because it has the potential to undermine a party's credibility on a central issue in the case. In Scottish Shellfish Marketing Group Ltd v Connelly EATS 0008/06 the EAT gave the obiter view that the employment tribunal had been wrong to refuse to review its finding of unfair dismissal on the basis of later-discovered evidence that undermined the claimant's credibility. The tribunal had found that C was unfairly dismissed when, after a road traffic accident, SSMG Ltd took the view that he was no longer capable of doing his job, which involved heavy manual work. Following that decision, evidence came to light that the claimant was lying when he told the tribunal that the accident was not his fault. Although his liability for the accident may not have affected the fairness of the dismissal, the claimant's credibility was critical, since there was a clear dispute of fact between the claimant and the employer as to the content of the claimant's job. The EAT noted that it is a standard and proper advocacy technique to attack credibility by reference to a collateral matter and that no reasonable employment judge would have refused the application.

Although collateral matters can be pursued in cross-examination, the party cross-examining will usually be bound by the answers given and cannot bring evidence to contradict them – Snowball v Gardner Merchant Ltd 1987 ICR 719, EAT. Case law in the Appeal Tribunal is divided on the question of whether the rule applies equally where credibility is in issue. In Aberdeen Steak Houses Group plc v Ibrahim 1988 ICR 550, EAT, the EAT held that when questions put in cross-examination are relevant only to the credibility of the witness, the party cross-examining will not be allowed to introduce evidence to rebut the answers given. However, in the Snowball case (above), the EAT held that anything that goes to the credibility of a witness is relevant to the issue before the tribunal and is not to be disregarded as a side issue. Although in neither case was a ruling on that issue essential to the disposal of the appeal (and so both opinions are obiter dicta), most learned commentary seems to favour the view in Ibrahim on this point.

Evidence inadmissible in criminal proceedings

13.36

As a general rule, evidence that is inadmissible in a criminal court will not be excluded for that reason alone from tribunal proceedings. The converse is also true: just because evidence might be admissible in a criminal trial does not mean that the same evidence will be relevant before a tribunal, even if both sets of proceedings arise out of the same facts. For example, it might be proper for a tribunal to disallow cross-examination of a party as to whether he or she has been convicted of a charge arising out of the facts that led to the dismissal in a case where the issue is not whether a criminal offence has been committed but whether the employer had reasonable grounds for suspecting such an offence to have been committed – Wagstaff v The Trade and Industrial Press Ltd 1968 ITR 1, Div Ct.

In deciding on the admissibility in tribunal proceedings of evidence that may be of relevance in related criminal proceedings, tribunals must always bear in mind the different nature of the two sets of proceedings. In particular, the relevant issues will usually vary, as will the relevant standards of proof. The following cases illustrate this:

- **Morley's of Brixton Ltd v Minott** 1982 ICR 444, EAT: M, who was suspected of fraud, admitted in an interview with her manager that she had failed to record some money on the till and had kept it herself. Following her dismissal, a tribunal held that her confession had been made in response to a suggestion that no action would be taken against her if she admitted the theft. The tribunal held that the confession was inadmissible in that it was contrary to the Judges' Rules, which require a confession to have been made voluntarily and not obtained by hope of advantage held out by a person in authority. The tribunal concluded that the employer had acted unreasonably in dismissing M and awarded her compensation. On appeal, the EAT observed that the Judges' Rules were inappropriate in civil litigation and were in any case irrelevant to the issue before the tribunal; namely, whether the employer had reasonable grounds for believing that M was guilty. Accordingly, the tribunal had erred in excluding M's confession, since it was the basis for the employer's belief in her guilt

- **Dhaliwal and ors v British Airways Board** 1985 ICR 513, EAT: D and others, who were airport baggage handlers, were dismissed for alleged dishonesty. At the internal disciplinary investigation the employer relied heavily on confessions that the police had obtained, but which in criminal proceedings against the employer had been ruled to be inadmissible because the judge was not satisfied that they had not been obtained by duress. The employees were acquitted of the criminal charges but the tribunal nonetheless found that their dismissal for gross misconduct was fair. The EAT upheld that decision, commenting that it was not inherently unfair for statements ruled inadmissible in criminal proceedings to be used as the

761

basis for the employer's decision to dismiss, and that the tribunal had been correct, when assessing the reasonableness of the employer's conduct, to consider the weight to be attached to the police statements rather than to rule that such evidence was in itself inadmissible.

13.37 The lesson to be drawn from the above cases is that the proper approach for tribunals, when considering the admissibility of evidence that may be inadmissible in related criminal proceedings, is to determine for themselves the relevance of such evidence while paying close regard to the different issues that arise in the two sets of proceedings. The crucial task for tribunals lies in the weighing of evidence: where doubtful or contentious evidence is admitted, the tribunal should always consider most carefully the quality of the evidence and assess the importance to be attached to it.

13.38 Privilege against self-incrimination

The common law recognises a privilege against self-incrimination. This rule, which applies in both criminal and civil proceedings, asserts that a witness is not bound to answer any question put to him or her if the answer thereto would expose that witness to the likely risk that he or she would be subjected to criminal proceedings. The rule extends to documentary evidence, so that a document may be 'privileged' (and thus immune from inspection) on the ground that it has a tendency to incriminate. The rule against self-incrimination does not, however, apply if the risk is that the witness will be rendered liable to a civil action.

The rule's applicability in the employment tribunal was recognised by the EAT in Osborne v Valve (Engineering) Services Ltd and anor EAT 393/00, although it held that there was no breach of it when a tribunal ordered the claimant to produce a transcript of the recording she had made of a meeting between herself and her employer. She sought to rely on things said in that meeting as evidence of sex discrimination but did not want to produce the transcript because, during the meeting, she had allegedly attempted to blackmail the company. The EAT observed that the case authorities on self-incrimination suggest that the tribunal must decide whether there are grounds to apprehend danger to the witness as a result of the disclosure, and that those grounds must be reasonable, rather than fanciful, if the rule is to be engaged. Taking into account the very small likelihood that any criminal proceedings would result, and having regard to the undertaking given by the employer not to use or disclose the tape-recording or transcript for any purpose unconnected with the tribunal proceedings, the EAT held that the tribunal had been right to order production. The EAT also noted that Article 6 of the European Convention on Human Rights made it less likely that the Crown would be able to rely on the material if it did decide to bring criminal proceedings. Although the case was decided before the Human Rights Act 1998 was in force, the Act's commencement was then imminent and the EAT took the European Court of Human Rights authorities into account.

In practice, the privilege is very rarely cited in the employment tribunal. His **13.39** Honour Judge McMullen QC accepted in Ali v Sovereign Buses (London) Ltd EAT 0274/06 that the exclusion of evidence on the basis of the privilege against self-incrimination is more naturally the domain of the Crown Court than the employment tribunal. The Crown Court has power to exclude evidential material acquired in such circumstances that its admission would render the criminal proceedings unfair – see, for example, S.78 of the Police and Criminal Evidence Act 1984. If these protections are insufficient to safeguard an employee giving information in an employment situation, that is a matter that will arise in the Crown Court but not in the employer's disciplinary process or the employment tribunal. Furthermore, any concerns of prejudicing an employee's right to a fair hearing where he or she is facing a criminal trial in respect of the same facts that form the basis of his or her employment tribunal claim might more effectively be mitigated by staying the tribunal claim until any criminal proceedings are completed. The circumstances in which such a stay may be ordered are discussed in Chapter 11, 'Case management', under 'Stay of proceedings – stay pending criminal proceedings'.

Criminal records **13.40**

The Rehabilitation of Offenders Act 1974 makes provision for excluding evidence of 'spent' convictions from proceedings before a 'judicial authority', the definition of which is wide enough to encompass employment tribunals. The Act provides for certain criminal convictions to become 'spent' – in effect, wiped off the record – after a designated 'rehabilitation' period, provided the offender has complied with the sentence or order handed down and has not committed a further offence during the rehabilitation period. The rehabilitation period varies in accordance with the sentence rather than the type of offence, ranging from two to seven years (in addition to the length of the sentence) for custodial sentences of up to four years. In the case of a fine, there is a fixed period of one year from the date of conviction. Some rehabilitation periods are halved for persons under 18. Certain sentences are excluded and can never become spent: life imprisonment, life custody, detention for life or during Her Majesty's pleasure, and custodial sentences over four years. Orders that impose any disqualification, disability, prohibition or other penalty – such as a driving ban – are spent when the order ceases to have effect. But if such an order is accompanied by a fine, as it normally will be, the usual one-year rehabilitation period applicable to fines will apply. If someone is subject to more than one sentence at once, the longest rehabilitation period operates.

Once a conviction has become 'spent', the Act restricts the admissibility of evidence relating to it. S.4(1) provides that (a) in any proceedings before a judicial authority, no evidence shall be admissible to prove that a rehabilitated

763

person has committed, or been charged with, or prosecuted for, or convicted of, or sentenced for any offence which was the subject of a spent conviction; and (b) a person shall not, in any such proceedings, be asked, and if asked shall not be required to answer, any question relating to his or her past which cannot be answered without acknowledging or referring to a spent conviction or spent convictions or any circumstances ancillary thereto. S.4(1) does not, however, apply where either the rehabilitated person gives consent to evidence about the conviction being admitted, or where it is necessary for such evidence to be admitted in order for justice to be done, or where the Home Secretary has made an Order excluding the application of the provision in respect of certain classes of persons – S.7(2)–(4).

13.41 There are few cases on the general application of S.4 in the employment context but the EAT gave a notable judgment on one of the exceptions under S.7 in A v B 2013 IRLR 434, EAT. In that case, A was dismissed because he was thought to have 'rated' female colleagues by reference to their attractiveness, sex appeal and willingness to engage in sexual encounters. One of the women, who reported to A, was said to have felt so uncomfortable about working with A in these circumstances that she wanted to distance herself from him. For his part, A claimed that he had been discriminated against throughout his employment because of his British Asian ethnicity and sought to claim, among other things, unfair dismissal and race discrimination. In its defence to the claims, the employer wished to put in evidence that the relevant actors in the alleged discrimination and dismissal knew of A's spent conviction for kerb-crawling. This knowledge might have meant that A was less respected at work than other people, which might provide a non-discriminatory explanation for any difference in treatment as between A and an appropriate comparator. An employment judge decided to admit this evidence under S.7(3), which allows for the admission of evidence that would otherwise be excluded by S.4 if justice cannot be done in the case without it. The judge considered that if the employer's witnesses could not give evidence about their knowledge of A's conviction and the extent to which it affected their relationship and dealings with A, they would not be able to give full and honest evidence and the tribunal would not be able fairly to determine 'why' the relevant events occurred.

The EAT dismissed A's appeal against the judge's decision. In doing so, it made a number of points about the scope of the S.7(3) exception. It observed that the critical question under S.7(3) is whether the admission of the evidence is the only way in which justice can be done. It is also relevant to take into account the prejudice to the rehabilitated party. Following the Court of Appeal's decision in Thomas v Commissioner of Police of the Metropolis 1997 QB 813, CA, the tribunal must balance the relevance of the conviction against the degree of the prejudice which its admission into the evidence would cause.

Written statements   13.42

Under rule 42 of the Tribunal Rules 2013, parties may opt to rely on written representations as an alternative to attending the tribunal to give oral testimony. They must deliver such representations to the tribunal not less than seven days before the hearing and a copy must be sent to all other parties. If this rule is complied with then the written representations are clearly admissible and must be taken into account – rule 42 states that the tribunal 'shall' consider any written representations delivered in this way.

Although written representations are required to be considered, the tribunal is still entitled to accord them limited weight. It is well recognised that untested written evidence is entitled to less weight than oral evidence that has been subjected to cross-examination. However, such evidence is nonetheless entitled to some weight and there are circumstances in which it may prove decisive. These are considered in Chapter 12, 'The hearing', under 'Non-attendance'.

Documentary and 'real' evidence   13.43

In the civil courts, photocopies of documents are now acceptable as evidence. However, if one party doubts the authenticity of a copy, it may require the other party to 'prove' the document by producing the original. For example, in Nicholls v CLI Ltd EAT 0504/03, where the claimant challenged the genuineness of financial documents disclosed by the respondent in support of its economic reason for dismissing him, the EAT ordered disclosure by the respondent's bank of financial reports submitted to it by the respondent. It relied on the tribunal's power under what was then rule 4(5)(a) of Schedule 1 to the Employment Tribunal (Constitution and Rules of Procedure) Regulations 2001 SI 2001/1171 to order any person (including a non-party) to attend a tribunal hearing and produce documents. An equivalent power is now found at rule 32 of the Tribunal Rules 2013.

'Real' evidence is anything other than testimony, hearsay or a document, the contents of which are offered as testimonial evidence as a means of proof. Such evidence is most commonly adduced in criminal trials. The kinds of real evidence that may occasionally be served up before tribunals include audio and video recordings, whether made on tape, computer, or some other digital format.

It will usually be necessary for a party seeking to introduce such evidence to   13.44
provide transcripts, tapes, and a clear explanation of why the recording – or particular parts of it – is relevant. In Vaughan v London Borough of Lewisham and ors EAT 0534/12, where the claimant sought to introduce 39 hours of recorded material, the EAT doubted the correctness of the tribunal's suggestion that the recordings would have to be independently transcribed in their entirety before they could be admissible. It should have been sufficient for the claimant to serve on the respondent her own transcripts, along with the underlying tapes. Only then could a sensible view be taken on whether the respondent

765

would need or wish to dispute the accuracy of the transcription, in whole or in part. And only if the respondent wished to dispute the accuracy of some passage of sufficient importance and potential relevance might it be necessary for an independent third party to be instructed to listen and produce an authoritative view.

13.45 Covert recordings

As noted under 'Documentary and "real" evidence' above, admissible evidence can include audio and video recordings. Where such recordings are made covertly, a question may arise over their admissibility. Although the clandestine nature of such recordings would be likely to present a significant problem in the civil or criminal courts, the EAT's decision in Chairman and Governors of Amwell View School v Dogherty 2007 ICR 135, EAT, is authority for the proposition that such recordings are not, simply because of their covert origins, inadmissible in the employment tribunal. There, the EAT allowed the unfair dismissal claimant to adduce clandestine recordings of the open part of the disciplinary hearing before the school governors that led to her dismissal. The EAT saw no reason, based on either public policy or the right to privacy, why evidence of a hearing of which it was always intended that there would be a written record should not be admitted. However, it went on to hold that the claimant could not adduce secretly obtained recordings of the governors' private deliberations. It stated that there is an important public interest in parties before disciplinary and appeal proceedings complying with the 'ground rules' – in this case, the understanding that the panel's deliberations would be conducted in private and remain private. The EAT noted that this decision was particular to the facts of the instant case, where the disciplinary panel had asked all parties, including the claimant and her representative, to withdraw, and they had accepted that invitation without demur on the premise that by doing so they would disable themselves from having any record of what might be said. The EAT emphasised that it was not seeking to create a 'new broad class of common-law public interest immunity' in relation to the recording of privately held deliberations. Indeed, it went on to note that it might have decided differently if facts were present that swung the public interest balance towards admitting the recording of the private deliberations. One example would be if the claim were one of discrimination and the inadvertent recording of private deliberations produced the only evidence.

It is worth noting that, in Dogherty, the EAT also rejected the argument that the disciplinary panel proceedings were protected by judicial privilege. There was no evidence that the school governors were thereby conducting judicial or quasi-judicial proceedings. Judicial privilege is considered in more detail in relation to documentary evidence in Chapter 9, 'Responding to opponent's case', under 'Disclosure and inspection of documents – privilege'.

The EAT was prepared to admit covertly recorded material in Vaughan v **13.46** London Borough of Lewisham and ors EAT 0534/12, where V had brought claims of discrimination, detriment on account of having made a protected disclosure, and unfair dismissal. She applied to adduce as evidence approximately 39 hours of covert recordings of interactions between herself and colleagues and managers, which she had made using a dictaphone and then transferred to an iPod. The tribunal refused, stating that it was impossible for it to be persuaded of the relevance of any of the recorded material without V first providing a transcript. The EAT dismissed an appeal against that decision, holding that this was a proper basis for refusing to admit otherwise admissible evidence. It went on to note that V could make a fresh application to the tribunal, seeking permission to adduce a much more limited quantity of transcripts and recordings, accompanied by a clear explanation of why they are relevant. V did, in the end, make such an application and was permitted to adduce material relating to five of the 39 recorded hours.

Similarly, in Punjab National Bank v Gibson EAT 0003/14 the EAT held that an employment judge had been entitled to distinguish Chairman and Governors of Amwell School v Dogherty (above) when ordering that a covert tape-recording made during an employer's private deliberations concerning a grievance and disciplinary hearing should be admitted into evidence. The judge had properly balanced the competing interests between the relevance of the evidence on the one hand and the public interest in preserving confidentiality of private deliberations on the other when making her order.

In contrast, the EAT held that an employment tribunal was correct to refuse to **13.47** admit covertly recorded evidence in Williamson v Chief Constable of Greater Manchester Police EAT 0346/09. There, W was subject to disciplinary proceedings. During a disciplinary hearing, W left his mobile phone in the room to record what was being discussed while he and his representative were outside. He sought leave to introduce a transcript of the recording into evidence in support of his subsequent tribunal claim for disability discrimination. An employment judge, having listened to sections of the recording in private, refused to admit it. The recording was clandestine, the parties to the discussion believed that they were having a private discussion and it was perfectly understandable that things would be said that would not be said in public. The judge also considered that the evidence was insufficiently relevant and that there had to be some very cogent reason why the normal principle of excluding such evidence should be overruled, such as an obvious statement showing that one of the parties to the discussion was thinking or acting in a discriminatory way. There was no such statement in the recording. The EAT endorsed the judge's decision on appeal. The employment judge had correctly applied the balancing test set out by the EAT in Dogherty (above). The EAT also rejected W's argument that Dogherty suggested that, in a discrimination case, the balancing test must be exercised in favour of disclosure. The obiter view given

767

in Dogherty was that an inadvertent recording of closed proceedings might be admitted if it were the only evidence of discrimination and if the evidence were incontrovertible – such was not the case here.

Note that objections to the admission of covertly recorded material often rely on the right to a private life as protected by Article 8 of the European Convention on Human Rights. The human rights implications of admitting such material are considered under 'Human rights issues' below.

13.48 **Admission of Hansard for purposes of statutory construction**
It used to be that the admission of Parliamentary debates as contained in Hansard for the purpose of construing statutory provisions was strictly forbidden. This rule was based on the constitutional propriety of leaving Parliament to legislate in words and the courts to construe the meaning of those words as finally enacted. However, in Pepper (Inspector of Taxes) v Hart 1993 ICR 291, HL, the House of Lords held that the rule excluding reference to Parliamentary material should be relaxed to permit such reference, but only where (i) the legislation in question is ambiguous or obscure or where its literal meaning leads to absurdity; (ii) the material relied upon consists of a statement or statements by a Minister or other promoter of the Bill, together with such other Parliamentary material as is necessary to understand such statements and their effect; and (iii) those statements are clear. The rationale behind this relaxation of the exclusionary rule, as cogently explained by Lord Browne-Wilkinson, was that the court's duty in interpreting the words of a statute is to give effect to the intention of Parliament. Where words are capable of bearing two meanings, and the intended meaning has been expressly considered by Parliament, then the courts should not blind themselves to a clear indication of Parliament's intention.

The rule in Pepper v Hart is occasionally referred to in employment tribunals and the EAT but there are few examples of parliamentary material making a significant difference. The EAT referred to the rule in Mason v Governing Body of Ward End Primary School 2006 ICR 1128, EAT, when considering the extent to which Parliament intended that the now-repealed S.98A ERA should reverse the long-established rule that an employer cannot defend a procedurally unfair dismissal on the basis that a fair procedure would have made no difference to the outcome. The EAT eventually declined to rely on Pepper v Hart because it did not agree that the particular provision was ambiguous.

13.49 The scope for applying the rule in the employment sphere is further reduced by the fact that much of employment law is derived from the European legislature. In Secretary of State for Business, Innovation and Skills v McDonagh and ors 2013 ICR 1177, EAT, Mr Justice Langstaff, President of the EAT, made the point that when construing the intention behind a statutory provision implementing an EU Directive – in this case, the Insolvency Act 1986, which amended provisions of what is now the ERA – the relevant purpose is the purpose of the Directive, not of Parliament. That said, there may be cases in which the parliamentary material shows that Parliament intended to give more favourable protection than required by EU law – see, for example, Royal Bank of Scotland plc v Harrison 2009 ICR 116, EAT, although the EAT there doubted whether there was sufficient ambiguity in the word 'unexpected', as used in S.57A(1) ERA, to warrant reliance on Pepper v Hart.

Documents relating to appealed decision 13.50

A special case arises where the employment tribunal proceedings are the result of a successful appeal against an earlier decision. The situation was considered in Varma v North Cheshire Hospitals NHS Trust EAT 0178/07, a case in which the claimant lost claims of sex and race discrimination, unfair constructive dismissal, breach of contract and detrimental treatment for having made protected disclosures. He appealed successfully against the rejection of his unfair dismissal claim only and the EAT ordered that this claim be reheard entirely afresh. When the remitted hearing came on for case management directions, a dispute arose as to the extent to which the tribunal could consider documents placed before and produced by the first tribunal. The tribunal chairman ruled that documents including the parties' original submissions, the original tribunal's decision, its decisions dismissing the claimant's application for review, the notice of appeal and response, and the EAT's judgment, should all be in the bundle for the remitted hearing. The claimant appealed against that decision.

The EAT allowed the appeal, holding that, since the remission was intended to achieve a complete rehearing of the constructive dismissal claim only, most of the documents to which the chairman referred were irrelevant and inadmissible. The only documents that should be admitted at the rehearing were the original tribunal's directions and the EAT's judgment. Furthermore, if a witness at the new hearing were to give evidence inconsistent with evidence that he or she gave before the original tribunal, any document tending to establish that inconsistency would be admissible in the same way that evidence given at a first criminal trial is admissible at a retrial as evidence of a previous inconsistent statement. The EAT went on to note that it would be for the new tribunal to consider any application by the respondent to exclude matters that were not raised by the claimant before the original tribunal.

Decisions of other tribunals 13.51

The central facts of a claim brought before an employment tribunal can also be the subject of proceedings in other courts and tribunals. This is particularly so in the area of disability discrimination, where the factual question of whether an individual is disabled can be relevant to that individual's entitlement to social security benefits as well as to protection from discrimination. Although

769

this issue is approached differently in different tribunals, and decided according to different statutory tests, the finding of one tribunal on that issue can be relevant evidence before an employment tribunal. Two examples:

- **Abadeh v British Telecommunications plc** 2001 ICR 156, EAT: A's complaint of disability discrimination was rejected by an employment tribunal, which found as a preliminary point that he was not disabled for the purposes of the Disability Discrimination Act 1995 (DDA) (since repealed and re-enacted in the EqA). He appealed against that decision arguing, among other things, that the tribunal had erred in failing to take account of the finding of a Medical Appeal Tribunal (MAT) that he suffered from an 18 per cent disablement. The EAT allowed the appeal. Although the MAT's assessment was carried out for the purpose of deciding whether A was entitled to industrial disablement benefit, and was not directed to the specific test under the DDA, that did not make it wholly irrelevant. It was clearly relevant evidence, although it was entirely up to the tribunal to decide what weight should be attached to it

- **Hill v Clacton Family Trust Ltd** 2005 EWCA Civ 1456, CA: H was awarded disability living allowance by the Social Security Appeals Tribunal (SSAT) on the basis that she was suffering from post-traumatic stress disorder. Nevertheless, an employment tribunal dismissed her disability discrimination claim on the ground that she had not been suffering from a clinically well-recognised illness at the time of her dismissal, and thus did not have a 'mental impairment' falling within the definition of 'disability' then contained in the DDA. Her claim was therefore rejected, and her appeal to the EAT against that decision was dismissed. The Court of Appeal, considering the weight to be attached to the SSAT's decision, accepted that it was unfortunate that two public bodies – the employment tribunal and the SSAT – could reach different conclusions as to whether or not H was disabled. However, in its view, the decision of the SSAT was in no way conclusive of the issue of whether H had a disability for the purposes of the DDA. There is no rule or principle of law that an employment tribunal is bound to follow decisions of the SSAT, and it was for the tribunal to make up its own mind on the evidence before it.

13.52 These cases indicate that decisions of other tribunals are likely to be relevant but do not need to be followed. That being so, the employment tribunal should usually give an explanation for reaching a different conclusion. In Mahon v Accuread Ltd EAT 0081/08 the EAT allowed an appeal against a tribunal's decision that the claimant was not disabled for the purposes of the DDA. The main reason for the EAT's decision was that the tribunal's conclusion was untenable in the face of the medical evidence. However, the EAT also expressed surprise that the tribunal had departed from the view of the SSAT, consisting of a chairman and a medically qualified member, without explaining why. The

EAT acknowledged that the tribunal was not bound by the SSAT's decision but, given that the decision was available to the tribunal, it was very surprising that the tribunal did not refer to it, even if only to explain the basis for its disagreement.

Expert evidence   13.53

Given the complexity of some of the issues that tribunals are called upon to adjudicate, it is no surprise that expert evidence may have some part to play in establishing a case and its use is now fairly routine. Nonetheless, a tribunal must be careful only to admit evidence that is relevant and not to let an expert pronounce on the legal or factual matters that are properly the province of the tribunal (or judge). So, for example, in a case where the question to be determined is whether the claimant is or was 'disabled' within the meaning of S.6 EqA, expert evidence may be admissible on the extent to which the claimant's condition affects his or her ability to carry out normal day-to-day activities, but not on the question of whether any particular condition satisfies the statutory definition.

A party who intends to rely upon expert evidence should usually explore with the tribunal whether the evidence is likely to be acceptable, either in correspondence or at a preliminary hearing. The issues that may require canvassing will generally include the relevance and admissibility of the evidence, and the qualifications and independence of the proposed expert. A tribunal's failure to address these issues may lead it to place too much weight on the evidence or to let the expert stray into areas that are outwith his or her expertise. For example, in Sharpe v Worcester Diocesan Board of Finance Ltd EAT 0243/12 the question was whether S, a Church of England minister, could bring claims as either an 'employee' or a 'worker'. This issue turned on the nature of S's contract with the Church, if indeed he had one. An employment judge allowed the Church to rely on evidence provided by an expert in ecclesiastical law and the structure of the Church of England. The judge accepted much of the expert's evidence uncritically and decided that there was no relationship between S and the Church that gave rise to employment rights. The EAT allowed an appeal against this decision, holding, among other things, that the judge had failed to consider the evidence's admissibility and to treat it with due caution. For one thing, the expert had chaired a committee convened by the Church to investigate the employment status of the clergy, which had concluded that the clergy enjoyed no employment status and recommended against changing the current position. For another, the expert had not confined himself to matters within his expertise. Indeed, the judge had noted that the evidence included 'a good deal of opinion that effectively amounted to submissions about the claimant's relationship with his Church being other than one based in contract. As one might expect, such opinion was given from the viewpoint of someone who had made a study and was justifying the conclusion he had

771

reached.' The EAT held that the judge had erred in allowing expert evidence to be advanced on the very questions that he himself had to determine.

13.54 **Evidence in disability discrimination cases.** Expert medical evidence plays a particularly important role in disability discrimination claims, where the claimant often has to surmount the initial hurdle of satisfying the specific definition of 'disability' set out in S.6 EqA. Such evidence can be relevant not only in relation to the nature of the impairment suffered by the claimant, but also in relation to its effects and, if the condition has not lasted 12 months, whether it is likely to last that long. Sometimes there may be conflicting medical reports regarding diagnosis and prognosis presented by either side. Tensions are also created where the legal concepts of impairment and disability for the purposes of the EqA are different from the accepted medical concepts of those terms. Clearly, it is important that tribunals attach the correct weight to medical evidence and that they know what they are free to accept and what they are free to reject.

The major concern regarding the use of medical evidence is that the instruction of one or more experts to prepare a report on, for example, the extent of a claimant's psychiatric illness adds expense and complexity to the proceedings, so detracting from the principle of informality on which the employment tribunal system was founded. The EAT in De Keyser Ltd v Wilson 2001 IRLR 324, EAT, was sufficiently exercised by this concern to issue guidelines on the use of independent medical experts, the principal points of which can be summarised as follows:

- joint instruction of experts is preferable

- a letter of instruction should specify in detail any particular questions that the expert is to answer and any general subjects which he or she is to address

- instructions to medical experts should avoid partisanship. It is important not to beg the very questions that are raised. The letter should emphasise the expert's non-partisan duty to the tribunal

- separately instructed experts should attend a 'without prejudice' meeting in an attempt to resolve conflict

- if a party fails to comply with these guidelines, the tribunal may wish to consider whether its power to award costs against that party on the ground of unreasonable conduct has been engaged.

13.55 The EAT was careful to stress, though, that this guidance is no more than that, and should not be read as laying down any concrete rules of evidence.

For further cases on the assessment of expert evidence in disability cases see IDS Employment Law Handbook, 'Discrimination at Work' (2012), Chapter 6, 'Disability', under 'Medical evidence'.

Expert evidence in equal pay cases. Schedule 3 to the Employment Tribunal **13.56** (Constitution and Rules of Procedure) Regulations 2013 SI 2013/1237 lays down special rules of procedure in 'equal value' claims – i.e. claims for equal pay that turn on the claimant's assertion that he or she is performing work of equal value to that of his or her chosen comparator. These rules include special provision for the tribunal to require an independent expert to prepare a report on the issue of whether the jobs performed by the claimant and the comparator are of equal value. Such a report has to be based only on facts that the parties, or the independent expert him or herself, have agreed to be relevant to the question of equal value and, once made, it must be admitted into evidence unless the tribunal determines that the report is not based on those facts – rule 8(1) Equal Value Rules. In proceedings in which an independent expert has been required to submit such a report, no other expert report will be admissible unless it is based on the facts determined to be relevant to the issue by the parties, the independent expert and/or the tribunal – rule 10(4).

The rules of procedure in 'equal value' cases are discussed in detail in IDS Employment Law Handbook, 'Equal Pay' (2011), Chapter 7, 'Work of equal value', under 'Equal value procedure'.

Human rights issues
13.57
Since the coming into force of the Human Rights Act 1998 on 2 October 2000, the rights enshrined in the European Convention on Human Rights (ECHR) have played a more significant role in evidential matters. This is because, under S.6(1) of the HRA, it is unlawful for public authorities – including courts and tribunals – to 'act in a way which is incompatible with a Convention right'. Furthermore, S.3(1) imposes the requirement on courts and tribunals that, so far as it is possible to do so, 'legislation must be read and given effect in a way which is compatible with the Convention rights'. The effect of these provisions is that it is now possible to argue that action taken by an employment tribunal, such as making orders for disclosure or ruling on the admissibility of evidence, impinges upon the Convention rights of one of the parties. Two Articles in particular – the Article 6 right to a fair trial, and the Article 8 right to respect for one's private and family life – often come into conflict before the tribunal, which is obliged to attempt to strike a balance between them. Three examples:

- **Jones v University of Warwick** 2003 3 All ER 760, CA: an enquiry agent, acting for the defendant employer's insurers, obtained access to J's home by posing as a market researcher and filmed her using a hidden camera. J had made a personal injury claim against the defendant, in which she alleged significant continuing disability and claimed substantial damages. The defendant sought to use the video footage as evidence that J had virtually recovered. The Court of Appeal ruled that the video footage, which had been obtained in clear breach of J's Article 8 right to a private life, should nevertheless be admitted. The conduct of the insurers had not been so

773

outrageous that the employer's defence should be struck out, and it would be artificial and undesirable for evidence that was relevant and admissible not to be considered by the trial judge. However, where, as in the instant case, the insurers had been responsible for trespass and for contravention of a claimant's privacy, in violation of Article 8 of the ECHR, that was a relevant consideration for a court to take into account when making case management orders. In this case, it was appropriate to reflect disapproval of the insurers' conduct by ordering the defendant to pay the costs of the proceedings relating to the admissibility of the evidence at all stages up to and including the Court of Appeal hearing

- **XXX v YYY and anor** 2004 IRLR 471, CA: a nanny, in support of a sex discrimination case against her former employer, sought to submit a video recording that she made secretly in the family home that included shots of a child. The employment tribunal held that the video was not admissible. On appeal, the EAT held that it was necessary to admit the evidence to protect the nanny's right to a fair and public hearing, but that the admission of the video recording in a public hearing would infringe the child's Article 8 rights. In these circumstances, the rights of all the parties would be protected if the video evidence were considered in private. However, on further appeal, the Court of Appeal overturned the EAT's decision. It noted that the employment tribunal – the only court to have seen the video recording – had concluded that it did not assist the employee's case. Therefore, in its view, the footage was not relevant to the issues and, accordingly, did not affect the balance struck between Articles 6 and 8

- **Avocet Hardware plc v Morrison** EAT 0417/02: an employment tribunal found that allowing AH plc to introduce evidence acquired by intercepting a telephone call that M, a telesales worker, had placed to a customer, would interfere with M's right to respect for his private life. The tribunal took into account that the interception was in breach of the Regulation of Investigatory Powers Act 2000 since AH plc made insufficient efforts to inform employees that their calls might be intercepted. The EAT allowed an appeal against this decision, holding that if there was any interference with M's Article 8 right, it would be justified under Article 8(2). It also noted that the exclusion of the evidence would result in a breach of AH plc's right to a fair trial under Article 6, in that, for all practical purposes, it would be 'required to go into the forensic arena with its hands tied behind its back'.

13.58 The courts have thus been willing to find, where appropriate, that the Article 6 right to a fair trial can trump the Article 8 right to a private life where the importance of the evidence in question to the fair hearing of the case outweighs the other party's right to privacy. The question is always, however, one of balance between the two.

Evidence of settlement negotiations

As discussed in Chapter 9, 'Responding to opponent's case', under 'Disclosure and inspection of documents', a party to employment tribunal proceedings may refuse to disclose documents on the basis that their content is 'privileged'. The law recognises a public interest in not obliging parties to disclose documents that contain, among other things, confidential information or information that relates to discussions between a lawyer and a client. The law also recognises a public interest in promoting the resolution of disputes without resort to the court system and so provides for a further category of evidence (both documentary and otherwise) that does not require to be disclosed. This kind of evidence is generally referred to as 'without prejudice' and covers negotiations aimed at settling or resolving a dispute. The 'without prejudice' rule is a creation of the common law and, although tribunals are not generally bound by the formal rules of evidence, it has been established that the 'without prejudice' principle applies in the employment tribunal – Independent Research Services Ltd v Catterall 1993 ICR 1, EAT. The scope of the rule and its exceptions are considered under 'Without prejudice negotiations' below.

There is a more recent addition to the categories of evidence that are excluded from consideration in employment tribunal proceedings. By virtue of an amendment made by S.14 of the Enterprise and Regulatory Reform Act 2013, the ERA now renders evidence of pre-termination negotiations inadmissible in unfair dismissal proceedings, subject to certain criteria. This new rule is discussed under 'Pre-termination negotiations'.

'Without prejudice' negotiations
Parties conducting settlement negotiations will usually do so on a 'without prejudice' basis. The purpose of the 'without prejudice' rule is to encourage parties to settle their disputes without resort to litigation. The principle is that where there is a dispute between the parties, any written or oral communications between them that comprise genuine efforts to resolve their dispute will not generally be admitted in evidence at a subsequent hearing of the claim. This enables parties to negotiate fully and frankly without the risk that anything they say or write in the course of negotiations will be used against them in legal proceedings if the negotiations fail.

While it might assist employers to discuss settlements on a 'without prejudice' basis, they should not assume that simply because an offer or discussion is described as being 'without prejudice' the rule will actually apply to it. There is no magic in the words 'without prejudice' and if there is no extant dispute, and/ or there are no genuine efforts at resolving the dispute, the rule will not apply, regardless of the label that the parties place on the communications. Conversely, the absence of the words 'without prejudice' will not be fatal if the negotiations meet these criteria. For example, in Hawkes v Brewin Dolphin Securities Ltd ET Case No.2305111/05 an employment tribunal accepted that a conversation described as 'off the record' was clearly conducted on a 'without prejudice' basis, despite the fact that these specific words had not been uttered.

13.61 While it is usually the employer who seeks the protection of the 'without prejudice' rule in relation to settlement negotiations, the rule applies both ways and there may be occasions on which it is the employee who seeks to exclude evidence that might otherwise harm his or her case. For example, in Shah v Smartest Energy Ltd ET Case No.2202929/07 the tribunal found that correspondence exchanged between employer and employee before the employee resigned and claimed constructive dismissal was privileged by the 'without prejudice' rule. It therefore acceded to the employee's application for the material to be excluded. In contrast, in Milne v Andrew Granger and Co LLP ET Case No.1901594/06 the tribunal rejected M's attempt to rely on the 'without prejudice' rule in relation to a letter she had sent to her employer regarding her complaint of bullying and harassment by a colleague. Although the claimant had marked the letter 'without prejudice', at the point that she sent it there was no extant dispute about the termination of her employment, on which her tribunal claim relied.

13.62 **'In dispute'.** The protection of the 'without prejudice' rule only arises if and when the parties are 'in dispute' with one another. This means that the parties must be conscious of at least the potential for litigation, even if neither side intends it as an outcome. In Portnykh v Nomura International plc 2014 IRLR 251, EAT, the EAT considered whether the mere fact that an employer and an employee are in negotiations might suffice to trigger the application of the rule. It acknowledged that an argument could be made for applying the rule to negotiations if the parties have expressly or impliedly agreed that the privilege will apply. The EAT did not rule out the possibility that parties may, in a factual context unconnected with litigation, agree that conversations or correspondence will not be admissible before a court if litigation should arise, even though litigation is not at the time within their reasonable contemplation. However, it did not need to decide this point in the present case.

The EAT in Portnykh did, however, give a clear ruling on the existence of a 'dispute' once dismissal has been proposed. There, NI plc told P that he would be dismissed for misconduct but that it would be agreeable to presenting the termination as a resignation. There then followed correspondence about the possibility of structuring the dismissal as a redundancy with a termination payment, a course of action that NI plc maintained had been suggested by P. When P later brought a claim of automatically unfair dismissal for having made protected disclosures, NI plc sought to rely on this correspondence in support of its asserted reason for dismissal. The EAT held that the 'without prejudice' rule applied and so the correspondence could not be admitted into evidence.

776

Looking at the factual matrix prior to the exchange of correspondence, there was clearly a 'dispute' in existence. His Honour Judge Hand QC, sitting alone, stated that although there is not axiomatically a dispute whenever a compromise agreement is offered and considered, if the employer announces an intention to dismiss the employee for misconduct and there are then discussions about an alternative manner of dismissal, it seems beyond argument that there is either a present dispute or the potential for a future dispute. Even without taking account of the facts prior to the correspondence, the existence of at least a potential dispute was evident from the correspondence itself. It is not necessary for any proceedings to be extant, nor for any specific complaint to have been raised – such as an explicit allegation of unfair dismissal – for there to be a potential dispute.

It is less clear cut when a 'dispute' will arise where the employee raises a **13.63** grievance, as will commonly be the case. In BNP Paribas v Mezzotero 2004 IRLR 508, EAT, the EAT held that the employee's raising of a formal grievance did not bring subsequent negotiations between employer and employee within the 'without prejudice' rule. The facts of the case were as follows. M raised a formal grievance on her return to work from maternity leave, claiming that before and on return from her leave she was singled out for demotion and publicly humiliated. In January 2003 she was called to a meeting by her employer. Upon entering the room she was informed that the discussion would be 'without prejudice' and that the meeting was independent of her formal grievance. M was told that her job was no longer viable, that there was no other position available in the bank, and that it would be best for both parties if her contract was terminated. She was also told that the matter would be regarded as a redundancy rather than a termination, and was offered a settlement package. M did not agree to the package and in March 2003 brought several claims, including sex discrimination. She sought to rely upon the 'without prejudice' meeting as evidence and BNP objected. The tribunal found in M's favour on this point. It held that the meeting between M and her employer had not been genuinely aimed at settling M's grievance. Rather, the meeting had been intended to achieve the termination of M's employment. The tribunal concluded that it would therefore be an abuse of the rule to exclude details of the meeting. BNP appealed to the EAT.

In the EAT's view, the act of raising a grievance does not by itself mean that parties to an employment relationship are necessarily 'in dispute'. A grievance might be upheld, or alternatively dismissed for reasons that the employee finds acceptable, in which case the parties never reach the stage where they could properly be said to be in dispute. M's grievance did not raise any complaint that a decision had been taken to terminate her employment, although she was concerned about her employer's treatment of her. In fact, the employer had made it clear at the meeting that the grievance was going to continue 'independent of any termination'. The EAT also thought it unrealistic to conclude that the parties had expressly agreed to speak 'without prejudice' given their unequal relationship, the vulnerable position of the claimant in such a meeting, and the fact that the suggestion was made by the employer only once that meeting had begun. The EAT therefore held that the tribunal was entitled to conclude that by the time of the meeting there was no existing dispute between the parties. The meeting was not a genuine attempt to settle, as M's grievance concerned her discriminatory treatment, whereas the meeting was concerned with terminating her employment. The 'without prejudice' rule did not, therefore, apply to prevent the statements made at the meeting being admissible in evidence before the tribunal.

13.64 In Barnetson v Framlington Group Ltd and anor 2007 ICR 1439, CA, the Court of Appeal addressed the question of the point at which, in escalating exchanges between employer and employee, a 'dispute' can be said to have arisen. Lord Justice Auld, who gave the leading judgment, began by repeating the well-established principle that the 'without prejudice' rule will be engaged where there is a dispute between the parties notwithstanding that litigation has not yet begun. As for what amounts to a dispute, he held that this occurs when the nature of the exchanges is such that the parties have contemplated, or could reasonably be expected to have contemplated, litigation if they did not agree. On the facts of the case, that point was reached when B, a senior executive, was informed by the employer that it intended to terminate his contract early, even though formal notice was not given until nearly two months later. Essentially, the dispute crystallised when the threat of termination was made. At that point litigation – even though not threatened by B – must have been in both parties' contemplation. As a result of the Court of Appeal's ruling, B had to re-serve his witness statement, omitting references to negotiations made following the date he was informed he was going to be dismissed as these were covered by the 'without prejudice' rule.

At first glance, there may appear to be inconsistency between the Court of Appeal's decision in Barnetson and the EAT's decision in Mezzotero. The former appears to suggest that most parties can reasonably be expected to have contemplated litigation by the time a formal grievance has been raised, whereas the latter suggests that the mere fact that a grievance has been raised does not necessarily mean that there is a dispute in existence. However, any difference is best explained by concluding that the 'without prejudice' rule can only apply in relation to correspondence that seeks to settle the particular dispute that has been raised. In Barnetson, the 'without prejudice' correspondence related to B's claims arising out of the termination of his employment. The dispute related to B's employer's proposal to terminate his employment early and so, if the parties contemplated litigation in relation to the dispute, it would have been about termination of employment. In BNP Paribas v Mezzotero (above), by contrast, if there was an extant 'dispute' at the time of the meeting, it arose out of M's grievance about her perceived treatment on return from maternity leave. The employer therefore could not invoke the 'without prejudice' rule in relation to its out-of-the-blue proposal to terminate her employment. In so far as M might have contemplated any litigation at that stage, it would have been a claim of discrimination, which would not depend on the termination of her employment. Thus, although there might have been an extant dispute about discrimination, there was no extant dispute about termination, and so the employer could not claim 'without prejudice' protection.

An employment tribunal relied on this distinction in Leclerc v BSI Products **13.65** Services Ltd ET Case No.1201504/07. There, L raised an informal grievance about race discrimination, among other matters. She was dissatisfied with the outcome and went on to raise a formal grievance about race and sex discrimination. The grievance meeting was due to take place in January 2007 but, in December 2006, one of the company directors had a meeting with her to discuss complaints made against her by colleagues and her alleged team-working failures. There was then a further meeting, before the grievance hearing took place, at which L and the director agreed exit terms. When L later brought claims of victimisation and unfair constructive dismissal, among other things, the question arose whether the later meeting attracted 'without prejudice' privilege. The tribunal found that it did not. Even if L's raising of a grievance could be characterised as giving rise to a dispute, it related to her alleged discriminatory treatment and not the termination of her employment. The meeting could not, therefore, have been a genuine attempt to settle that dispute. The tribunal also took into account – as did the EAT in Mezzotero – that there was no clear agreement between L and her employer that the meeting would be held on a 'without prejudice' basis.

The timing of settlement discussions in terms of relying on the 'without prejudice' rule proved crucial in A v B and anor EAT 0092/13. In September 2011 A, who taught at a school for children with behavioural difficulties, attended a disciplinary hearing following disclosures by the police that he appeared to have had inappropriate relationships with female pupils. The disciplinary panel decided to issue A with a final written warning but he was not immediately notified of the decision. Instead, discussions expressed to be 'without prejudice' and 'off the record' began between D, his trade union representative, and F, a member of the school's human resources team, with a view to terminating A's employment via a settlement agreement. During these discussions, F told D that the panel had wanted to dismiss A but had changed this to a final written warning after F advised it against dismissal. D then told A. Two weeks later, A was formally notified that the panel had decided to issue him with a final written warning and he remained at the school. However, A was eventually dismissed in March 2012 after a second disciplinary hearing, which had been convened following further information from the police. A complained of unfair dismissal and, in support of his claim, sought to rely on the content of the settlement discussions that took place between D and F.

779

13.66 The tribunal found that the discussions were conducted on a 'without prejudice' basis and so were not disclosable as evidence. The EAT, however, allowed the appeal in part. Referring to the Court of Appeal's decision in Barnetson v Framlington Group Ltd and anor (above), it considered that at the time the settlement discussions commenced A must have believed that there was a very real possibility that he would be dismissed. Given that dismissal in these circumstances would have effectively ended his teaching career, he must have reasonably contemplated litigation in such an event. That state of mind continued until D informed him that the panel had decided that he would not be dismissed. Consequently, the EAT concluded that any documents relating to the settlement discussions up to the point in time when A was told of the panel's decision were protected under the 'without prejudice' rule, but that any documents that related to the period thereafter were admissible in evidence.

In reaching this conclusion, the EAT also accepted (albeit without argument) that it was sufficient for the 'without prejudice' rule to apply that only one of the parties – i.e. A – had reasonably contemplated litigation if the dispute could not be settled. According to the EAT, the school could not reasonably have contemplated litigation at the time the settlement discussions were taking place between D and F because it knew then that he would not be dismissed. This point was not addressed by Lord Justice Laws in the Court of Appeal in Barnetson (above) because, on the facts of that case, 'both [parties] were clearly conscious of the potential for litigation if they could not resolve the dispute without it'. In the present case, by contrast, the tribunal proceeded on the basis that it is sufficient for the 'without prejudice' rule to apply that only one of the parties contemplated litigation. On appeal, the EAT noted that it had not been suggested before it that such a view was erroneous in law and so it did not interfere with the tribunal's decision on this point.

13.67 **Waiver of privilege.** Where the 'without prejudice' doctrine applies to communications, it is possible for the parties to agree to waive the privilege. Waiver requires the agreement of both parties. Although in many cases where legal privilege exists it can be waived by the party entitled to the benefit of it, this is not the case with the 'without prejudice' rule – Cowen v Rentokil Initial Facility Services (UK) Ltd (t/a Initial Transport Services) EAT 0473/07. Furthermore, the waiver will usually need to be unequivocal. In Pedropillai v PricewaterhouseCoopers LLP ET Case No.2300068/10 an employment tribunal rejected the argument that the employer had waived privilege in respect of the contents of a document that it had accidentally included in the hearing bundle. In the context of the huge volume of evidence in the case, it was clear that the inclusion of the document was a mistake, which the employer immediately tried to rectify when it came to light.

In Brunel University and anor v Vaseghi and anor 2007 IRLR 592, CA, however, the Court of Appeal held that, in some exceptional circumstances, bilateral waiver may be implied from the parties' conduct. There, V and W brought race discrimination claims against the University. There were settlement discussions, which came to nothing, and both eventually failed in their claims at the tribunal. The University's Vice-Chancellor subsequently made reference in his quarterly newsletter to the fact that the University had spent in excess of £60,000 defending two particular claims and stressed that the University would 'defend its reputation against unfounded allegations, especially when these are accompanied by unwarranted demands for money'. V and W both lodged grievances, contending that it was the University that had initiated discussions over money in the settlement negotiations. An independent committee convened by the University rejected the grievances, after having heard oral evidence as to what had been said and done in the settlement negotiations. V and W then brought claims of victimisation based on the newsletter comments. They included an account of the settlement discussions in their ET1s and the University annexed the grievance committee's report to its ET3. When the tribunal considered whether evidence of the settlement discussions was admissible, it decided that references to the discussions in V and W's evidence were inadmissible because of 'without prejudice' privilege, but that the grievance reports appended to the University's ET3, which referred to those same discussions, were admissible. This was because the University had waived its right to claim privilege by hearing evidence of those discussions at the grievance hearing and putting the findings into the panel's reports. The tribunal observed that if the University had wished to retain privilege, it should have made its position clear at the grievance stage.

On appeal, the EAT held that the conduct of both parties throughout the **13.68** grievance hearings was totally inconsistent with the maintenance of 'without prejudice' privilege and concluded that there had been an implied bilateral waiver of privilege in respect of all references to the settlement discussions – not just those in the grievance reports, as had been held by the tribunal. The Court of Appeal agreed. In most cases, where a grievance meeting takes place in the usual way, internally, there will be no question of waiver if the parties mention matters covered by 'without prejudice' privilege. But in the particular and unusual facts of this case, where the grievance proceedings were in effect a trial of V and W's victimisation complaints by an independent panel and where both parties gave or called evidence of the previous negotiations, the EAT had been entitled to conclude that the privilege had been bilaterally waived. The University's appeal on this point was therefore dismissed.

Exceptions. If the 'without prejudice' rule applies to a particular piece of **13.69** evidence, a tribunal is usually unlikely to be persuaded that it should hear it. However, there are a number of exceptional circumstances where justice requires that a party be prevented from relying on the rule. The Court of Appeal listed what it considered to be the most important of these circumstances in Unilever plc v Procter and Gamble Co 2000 1 WLR 2436, CA, a commercial

781

case. These include cases where there is an issue as to whether an agreement has actually been reached; where the evidence is required to show that an agreement apparently concluded between the parties should be set aside on the ground of misrepresentation, fraud or undue influence; and where exclusion of the evidence would otherwise act as a cloak for perjury, blackmail or other 'unambiguous impropriety'.

In addition, the Supreme Court in Oceanbulk Shipping and Trading SA v TMT Asia Ltd and ors 2010 3 WLR 1424, SC, added a new exception – the 'interpretation exception' – and formally recognised the 'rectification exception', which was not listed by the Court of Appeal in Unilever. The 'interpretation exception' makes it permissible to refer to evidence communicated in the course of 'without prejudice' negotiations where this is necessary to enable the settlement agreement to be properly construed. The 'rectification exception' provides that the 'without prejudice' veil may be lifted where it is alleged that, through error, the settlement terms do not accurately reflect the agreement of the parties. In establishing the new 'interpretation exception', the Supreme Court recognised that the 'without prejudice' rule serves the important public policy of encouraging litigants to settle their differences and therefore should not be lightly eroded. However, the application of the same interpretation process in both open and 'without prejudice' cases would not undermine the 'without prejudice' rule's objective. Rather, settlement would be encouraged if parties to a negotiation knew that in the event of a dispute about what a settlement contract meant, objective facts which emerged during negotiations would be admitted to ascertain their true intentions. The Court also agreed that refusing to admit 'without prejudice' communications in such circumstances would be inconsistent with two of the existing exceptions to the 'without prejudice' rule: that of resolving the issue of whether there is a concluded settlement agreement and for the purpose of rectification. For these reasons, justice clearly demanded that the need for 'interpretation' should be recognised as an exception to the 'without prejudice' rule.

13.70 It is the 'unambiguous impropriety' exception that is most commonly cited in employment cases – this is dealt with separately under 'Unambiguous impropriety' below. If a case cannot be brought within one of the recognised exceptions then the privilege will apply. In Independent Research Services Ltd v Catterall 1993 ICR 1, EAT, the EAT held that the 'without prejudice' rule applied to a letter, written by the employee, which included an offer to remain a full-time employee. The employer argued that the letter was inconsistent with the employee's assertion that the relationship of trust and confidence had been undermined. The EAT held that the letter did not come within a recognised exception – it could not be said that refusing to admit the letter would enable the employee to prosecute a dishonest case. Similarly, in Portnykh v Nomura International plc 2014 IRLR 251, EAT, the EAT held that there was no impropriety in excluding evidence that tended to show that the employee, who was claiming automatically unfair dismissal for having made a protected disclosure, had suggested to the employer that his employment be terminated by reason of redundancy, along with a termination payment. In contrast, in Hawick Jersey International Ltd v Caplan, *The Times*, 11 March 1988, QBD, C secretly tape-recorded a without prejudice meeting in which HJI Ltd accepted that a transaction between it and C was not a loan. The High Court allowed this to be admitted as evidence because it proved that the whole of HJI Ltd's claim for repayment was based on a lie – namely, its assertion that the transaction was a loan.

'Unambiguous impropriety'. The protection of the 'without prejudice' **13.71** rule may be removed in cases where the rule would otherwise serve as a cloak for 'unambiguous impropriety'. In short, the court will not protect a party who has abused the privilege usually afforded by the 'without prejudice' rule. Non-employment case law suggests that a high threshold of seriousness must be reached before the abuse will warrant withholding 'without prejudice' protection – see, for example, Savings and Investment Bank Ltd (in liquidation) v Fincken 2004 1 WLR 667, CA.

In employment cases, 'unambiguous impropriety' is most commonly asserted where the 'without prejudice' rule would otherwise exclude evidence of alleged discrimination. Mrs Justice Cox, sitting alone in the EAT, considered such an argument on an obiter basis in BNP Paribas v Mezzotero 2004 IRLR 508, EAT. There, M raised a grievance about the way she had been treated in relation to her maternity leave. She was invited to a meeting, which she was told was being held on a 'without prejudice' basis, at which she was told that her job was no longer viable, and that it would be best for both parties if her contract was terminated. She was also told that the matter would be regarded as a redundancy rather than a termination and was offered a settlement package. When M brought tribunal proceedings in respect of a number of matters, including sex discrimination, the tribunal refused BNP's application to exclude evidence of the meeting. The tribunal found that the meeting had not been genuinely aimed at settling M's formal discrimination complaint and so the 'without prejudice' rule did not apply. On appeal, Cox J in the EAT held that the tribunal was entitled to find that the 'without prejudice' rule was not engaged because there was no extant 'dispute' between the parties at the time.

Although that was sufficient to determine the appeal, Cox J went on to give the **13.72** view that, even if the rule were engaged, BNP's conduct would have fallen within the 'unambiguous impropriety' exception. She noted that the sex and race discrimination legislation seeks to eradicate the 'very great evil' of discrimination and, as such, it is in the public interest that allegations of unlawful discrimination in the workplace are heard and properly adjudicated – particularly as discrimination cases can only properly be determined after full consideration of all the facts. Cox J therefore suggested that remarks alleged to

783

be discriminatory cannot be protected by the 'without prejudice' rule. If they were, the logical result would be that an employer could say at a without prejudice meeting, 'we do not want you here because you are black', and then seek to argue that the discussions should be excluded from consideration by a tribunal hearing a complaint of race discrimination.

The Mezzotero case gave rise to speculation that a new rule had been introduced that allowed discrimination claimants special rights to refer to what was said during discussions with their employer to resolve a discrimination complaint, even where those discussions were conducted on a 'without prejudice' basis. One interpretation of the case was that a new strand of the 'unambiguous impropriety' exception had been identified: that any comments made during the course of settlement discussions which were alleged to be discriminatory would no longer benefit from the 'without prejudice' rule. The Court of Appeal appeared to lend some weak support to this view when it acknowledged, obiter, in Brunel University and anor v Vaseghi and anor 2007 IRLR 592, CA, that it might sometimes be difficult to prove victimisation cases if the 'without prejudice' rule was applied across the board. This speculation was laid to rest, however, by the EAT's ruling in Woodward v Santander UK plc 2010 IRLR 834, EAT, where it held that the 'unambiguous impropriety' exception did not apply in the absence of blatant discrimination, and refused to extend the exception to include comments from which an inference of discrimination might be drawn. The EAT could not accept that Cox J had intended to say in Mezzotero that it was unnecessary, in a discrimination case, to find 'unambiguous impropriety'. Rather, she had placed her view that the 'without prejudice' rule should not protect discriminatory acts in the context of 'the abuse principle' – i.e. as part of the existing 'unambiguous impropriety' rule.

13.73 The EAT in Woodward went on to set out the scope of the 'unambiguous impropriety' exception in discrimination cases. It held that while words that are unambiguously discriminatory – such as a refusal to continue to employ someone because he or she is black – should be admissible as an exception to the 'without prejudice' rule, words that only *could be* discriminatory should not. While it accepted that, at first sight, it may seem unattractive to exclude evidence from which an inference of discrimination could be drawn, the EAT considered that it would inhibit the ability of the parties to speak freely in negotiations if one or the other could subsequently 'comb through the content of correspondence or discussions' for equivocal words or actions to support an inference of discrimination. Consequently, it rejected W's submission that there should be a wider exception to the 'without prejudice' rule when discrimination is alleged. It confirmed that the policy underlying the 'without prejudice' rule applies with as much force to cases where discrimination has been alleged as it applies to any other form of dispute and noted that it may even be said to apply with particular force in cases where the parties are seeking to settle a discrimination claim. Discrimination claims often place heavy emotional and financial burdens on claimants and respondents alike, and it is important that parties should be able to settle their differences (whether by negotiation or mediation) in conditions where they can speak freely.

The EAT's decision in Woodward is helpful in clarifying the application of the 'without prejudice' rule in discrimination cases but there is still some room for doubt over what is a 'blatantly' or 'unambiguously' discriminatory statement. Furthermore, it surely cannot be the case that, simply because a claim involves blatant or unambiguous discrimination, the rule is automatically disapplied. It must be remembered that the whole purpose of the rule is to allow the parties to discuss the merits of a claim frankly and openly, and to seek to reach agreeable terms without recourse to the court. Thus, if the dispute itself involves an allegation that the employer has blatantly discriminated against the employee, the rule should not be excluded simply because the employer admits the basis of the claim in negotiation discussions. As Lord Justice Rix stated in Savings and Investment Bank Ltd (in liquidation) v Fincken 2004 1 WLR 667, CA, 'it is not an abuse of the privilege to tell the truth, even where the truth is contrary to one's case'. And in Portnykh v Nomura International plc 2014 IRLR 251, EAT, HHJ Hand QC observed that 'unambiguous impropriety' means 'something far more than being disadvantaged by the exclusion of evidence'. In other words, there is nothing wrong in an employer admitting the truth of the employee's claim in 'without prejudice' discussions but then seeking to defend that claim later on if the discussions produce no settlement. Accordingly, if the claim is one of discrimination, the fact that the employer admits to it during 'without prejudice' discussions should not mean that those discussions are admissible under the 'unambiguous impropriety' exception. For example, imagine that an employee brings a claim of discrimination based on a racist comment made by a colleague. If the employer tries to settle the claim, it might offer the employee an apology for failing to prevent the incident and a sum in settlement – in other words, it might thereby concede the factual basis of the claim. On a straight application of the 'without prejudice' principle, the employer should not be held to that concession if the case proceeds to a tribunal hearing. So the mere fact that the claim is one of discrimination does not mean that even a blatant admission of discrimination must always escape the 'without prejudice' rule.

In practice, employment tribunals are well able to draw the line between **13.74** impropriety amounting to abuse and legitimate suggestions of settlement in discrimination proceedings. In Pedropillai v PricewaterhouseCoopers LLP ET Case No.2300068/10 the tribunal found that it was an unambiguous act of victimisation under the Race Relations Act 1976 (since repealed and re-enacted in the EqA) for P to be told in a meeting that he would not be able to continue as a partner in the company if he continued with his race discrimination proceedings. In the tribunal's view, it was possible to infer that P was being threatened with expulsion from the partnership if he continued to prosecute his

785

claim. This was an act of victimisation that triggered the 'unambiguous impropriety' exception. In contrast, in Sud v London Borough of Ealing ET Case No.3300384/08 an employment tribunal found that the 'unambiguous impropriety' exception did not apply to a conversation in which a member of the employer's human resources team spoke to an employee's trade union representative with a view to ascertaining whether the employee would consider settling her numerous tribunal claims, including discriminatory dismissal. During the conversation, the HR representative mentioned that the employee's manager had threatened to leave if the employee returned to her department. The tribunal rejected the suggestion that this indicated any kind of unlawful discrimination. (Although both of these cases were decided before the EAT in Woodward v Santander UK plc (above) clarified the scope of the 'unambiguous impropriety' exception, neither tribunal relied on BNP Paribas v Mezzotero (above) on this point and so their conclusions still stand up to scrutiny today.)

Although it is in discrimination cases that the 'unambiguous impropriety' exception is most commonly raised, the exception is not necessarily confined to this setting. In Brodie v Ward t/a First Steps Nursery EAT 0526/07 the EAT considered whether the 'unambiguous impropriety' exception could be extended to allow a claimant bringing a constructive dismissal case to rely on the contents of a privileged letter containing an offer of settlement arising out of a different dispute with her employer. The letter proposed a settlement agreement to settle her sick pay complaint in return for her resignation. B, however, resigned without signing the settlement agreement and brought a further tribunal claim against FSN for unfair constructive dismissal, citing the solicitor's letter as the 'last straw' in a series of actions by FSN calculated to destroy trust and confidence. B contended that if she could not give evidence about the contents of the letter, she would not be able to prove that it amounted to the 'last straw' entitling her to resign, and so her claim for constructive dismissal would be fatally damaged. She argued that the 'without prejudice' rule should not be allowed to suppress evidence in such circumstances, and that FSN was using the rule for the purposes of dishonesty and 'unambiguous impropriety'.

13.75 The EAT, however, was unwilling to extend the exception to constructive dismissal on the facts of the present case. Following the relevant authorities, it held that the solicitor's letter could not possibly be construed as 'unambiguous impropriety' in the sense of 'fraud, blackmail or perjury', or indeed as impropriety of any kind. It was a perfectly proper attempt to settle the tribunal claim arising out of the sick pay complaint. This was so despite B's contention that the rule prevented her putting her constructive dismissal claim fully. She was not barred from putting her case forward – her essential objection was that she could not present her case in the way that she would like, but that was simply the result of the normal operation of the 'without prejudice' rule. B's appeal was accordingly dismissed.

Costs. Once a tribunal claim has been brought, the process of preparing for the 13.76 hearing frequently runs in parallel with negotiations to settle. As part of this process, parties sometimes make an offer of settlement marked 'without prejudice save as to costs', also known as a 'Calderbank offer' (following Calderbank v Calderbank 1975 3 All ER 333, CA). The idea is that the offer of settlement will be kept from the tribunal's knowledge during the substantive hearing but, if the claimant is successful, the respondent may bring the offer to the tribunal's attention when the issue of costs is being discussed. In the civil court system, where the claimant obtains an award that is equivalent to or less than the amount that the other side had offered by way of settlement, he or she will usually have to bear the respondent's costs incurred after the deadline for acceptance – the principle being that the claimant was wasting everyone's time in pursuing the claim when he or she could have accepted the offer. In Kopel v Safeway Stores plc 2003 IRLR 753, EAT, the EAT held that this rule does not apply to employment tribunals but that a tribunal can take into account a claimant's refusal of any settlement offer in deciding whether it should award costs on the basis of unreasonable conduct under what is now rule 76(1)(a) of the Tribunal Rules 2013. Costs awards on this basis are discussed in Chapter 20, 'Costs and penalties', under 'Factors relevant to tribunal's discretion – rejection of settlement offer'.

Pre-termination negotiations 13.77

As of 29 July 2013, any settlement negotiations conducted between an employer and an employee with a view to ending the employment relationship on agreed terms cannot be relied upon in any subsequent unfair dismissal claim. Confidentiality in these circumstances is guaranteed (subject to some exceptions) by S.111A ERA, which was inserted by the Enterprise and Regulatory Reform Act 2013. In its 'Ending the Employment Relationship' consultation in September 2012, the Government stated that the section was intended 'to facilitate open discussions between employers and employees' where the employment relationship was not working out 'without the concern that this could be used against either party in the event of an unfair dismissal claim'. The Government believed that the provision would offer both sides the option of swiftly and amicably agreeing to go their separate ways.

Acas has produced a statutory Code of Practice on Settlement Agreements ('the Code') to help employers and employees understand the implications of S.111A. While the Code is not binding, it will be relied on by employment tribunals when considering relevant cases. The Code was issued under Acas's general power in S.199 of the Trade Union and Labour Relations (Consolidation) Act 1992 (TULR(C)A), which means, pursuant to S.207, that the Code is admissible in evidence and 'any provision of the Code which appears to the tribunal... to be relevant to any question arising in the proceedings shall be taken into account in determining that question'. Additional guidance on the confidentiality

787

of pre-termination settlement negotiations can be found in the non-statutory Guide on Settlement Agreements ('the Guide'), also produced by Acas, which contains template letters that can be used to initiate settlement discussions under S.111A and a model settlement agreement recording the terms agreed.

13.78 The Foreword to the Code states that failure to follow the Code will not lead to an adjustment in any compensation awarded by the tribunal. This is a reference to S.207A TULR(C)A, which allows a tribunal to increase or reduce compensation by up to 25 per cent to reflect an employer's or employee's unreasonable failure to follow a relevant Code of Practice. This suggests that Acas takes the view that the Code of Practice on Settlement Agreements is not a 'relevant Code of Practice' for this purpose. This is a surprising interpretation, since S.207A(4) defines a relevant Code of Practice as one that relates 'exclusively or primarily to procedure for the resolution of disputes'. This phrasing seems apt to describe a pre-termination negotiation aimed at producing a settlement agreement.

13.79 **When does S.111A ERA apply?** Section 111A(1) ERA provides that any evidence of pre-termination negotiations is inadmissible in any proceedings on a complaint under S.111 ERA, i.e. a complaint of unfair dismissal. In other words, any settlement negotiations that are conducted between the employer and the employee with a view to terminating the employment relationship will not normally be admissible as evidence before a tribunal in any unfair dismissal claim. Such discussions are often described as 'protected conversations'.

The Guide gives several practical examples of the circumstances in which S.111A may apply. These include the employer offering a settlement agreement to an employee who has been the subject of previous disciplinary proceedings and whose behaviour has not improved. Upon receiving the offer, the employee may respond by immediately resigning and claiming unfair constructive dismissal on the basis that the offer breached the implied term of mutual trust and confidence between them. If S.111A applies, the employee will not be able to refer to the discussion in which the offer was made before the tribunal. Alternatively, if the employee declines the settlement offer and is later dismissed after further disciplinary action, he or she will not be able to refer to the earlier offer to end the relationship, or any settlement discussions, in any subsequent unfair dismissal claim. Accordingly, when determining whether the employer's decision to dismiss fell within the range of reasonable responses and was thus fair, the tribunal will not be able to have regard to the employer's earlier proposal to terminate the employment.

13.80 However, there are a few important limitations on the applicability of S.111A. The provision only applies where the employee is complaining of 'ordinary' unfair dismissal. Claims for automatically unfair dismissal are expressly excluded by virtue of S.111A(3). Accordingly, where the employee alleges that the dismissal occurred for a reason relating to, for example, their pregnancy or trade union membership, S.111A will have no application. The full list of automatically unfair reasons for dismissal is set out in IDS Employment Law Handbook, 'Unfair Dismissal' (2010), Chapter 10, 'Automatically unfair dismissals', under 'List of automatically unfair reasons'.

In addition, S.111A does not apply to any other type of claim, such as breach of contract or discrimination claims, even if those other claims are brought together with the unfair dismissal claim. The Guide explains that where a claimant raises an allegation of unfair dismissal together with other allegations, settlement discussions may be inadmissible under S.111A in relation to the unfair dismissal claim but admissible in relation to the other claims (unless otherwise covered by the 'without prejudice' rule – see 'Overlap with "without prejudice" rule' below). The position therefore appears to be that a tribunal cannot have regard to the settlement discussions when determining the question of the fairness of the employee's dismissal but it can have regard to the discussions when deciding whether the employee's other claims are well founded. Employers will therefore need to be aware that, if the employee rejects a settlement offer and later brings a complaint other than ordinary unfair dismissal, S.111A will not prevent the conversation in which the employer offered the employee a sum of money in return for leaving the employment from being adduced as evidence in relation to the employee's other claim. For instance, an employee who receives an offer of compensated termination shortly after returning to work from maternity leave is likely to argue that the offer should be taken into account by the tribunal when considering whether there is evidence from which the tribunal could infer discrimination. Employers may therefore be reluctant to make a settlement offer where, absent any pre-existing dispute with the employee that would ensure confidentiality under the 'without prejudice' rule, there is a possibility that the offer would have to be disclosed in all proceedings apart from unfair dismissal.

Finally, S.111A also does not apply where there has been 'improper behaviour' with regard to anything said or done in relation to the settlement negotiations – see 'Improper behaviour' below.

Scope of S.111A ERA. The term 'pre-termination negotiations' is defined in S.111A(2) as encompassing 'any offer made or discussions held, before the termination of the employment in question, with a view to it being terminated on terms agreed between the employer and the employee'. **13.81**

There are several things to note about the section's scope. It is not necessary, in order for the exception to be engaged, that the employer make a specific monetary offer to the employee – any 'discussions' that relate to termination on agreed terms are capable of being caught by S.111A. Nor is it necessary for the employer and the employee actually to reach agreement as to termination. Even if the employee declines any or all offers made, confidentiality will still be preserved by virtue of S.111A. Furthermore, there is no requirement for there to be any existing workplace dispute or any concern about the employee's performance or conduct at work. It is therefore open to the employer to ask the employee to leave at any stage of the employment relationship. That said, the Guide notes that employers may want to think carefully about what a settlement offer, particularly one that is perceived by the employee as coming entirely 'out of the blue', would mean for the ongoing working relationship if it is declined.

13.82 The protection of S.111A ERA is not restricted to cases where the employer initiates the settlement discussion. Although it will usually be the employer who does this, it is entirely possible for the first approach to be made by the employee. The Guide cites the example of an employee who does not personally get on with another colleague, where this 'personality clash' is having an adverse effect on the performance of the other members of the team. If the situation does not improve, the employee may approach the employer about the possibility of leaving with a good reference and a payment. In these circumstances, a settlement agreement may be reached on mutually agreeable terms and S.111A would apply irrespective of the fact that the settlement negotiations were initiated by the employee rather than the employer. This may be to the employee's benefit if, for example, he or she later wishes to deny in an unfair dismissal claim that there was any good reason for dismissing him or her.

When the idea of legislating in this area was first mooted, it was proposed that confidentiality would attach to any discussions between the employer and the employee, whatever the subject matter. The idea behind these so-called 'protected conversations' was that employers could approach employees to discuss a range of workplace issues without this potentially forming part of the employee's evidence in any tribunal claim brought later on. It was envisaged that the employer could, for example, ask the employee about his or her retirement plans without fear of that conversation being relied upon before a tribunal in any subsequent age discrimination claim. However, following consultation, this proposal was not taken forward. Accordingly, S.111A only covers discussions that take place *with a view to the employment being terminated*, and only in relation to *unfair dismissal*. In other words, any discussion between the employer and the employee that proceeds on the basis that the employment relationship is going to continue will not fall within S.111A and so will be admissible.

13.83 **Procedural steps.** It is not necessary for an employer to have followed any particular procedure prior to offering settlement terms in order to attract the S.111A protection. The Code has some recommendations in relation to specific aspects of the pre-termination discussion. In relation to the employer making an offer of settlement, it notes that it may be helpful if reasons for the proposal are given when the proposal is made (para 11). It states that a proposal may be oral but notes that a valid settlement agreement will need to be reduced into writing at some point. If an offer is made, the employee should be given a reasonable period of time to respond to it. The Code states that, while what constitutes a reasonable period will depend on the circumstances, a minimum of ten calendar days should generally be allowed to consider the proposed formal written terms of a settlement agreement and to receive independent advice, unless the parties agree otherwise (para 12). The Code also states that, while there is no statutory right to be accompanied at a meeting to discuss a settlement agreement, as a matter of good practice, the employer should allow the employee to be accompanied at the meeting by a work colleague or trade union official or representative if he or she requests, as this may help to progress the settlement discussions (para 13). If and when a settlement is agreed, the details of any payments due to the employee and their timing should be included in the agreement (para 14).

The non-binding Guide also indicates some best practice points in relation to settlement negotiations under S.111A. It states that, at the start of the meeting, it is advisable to make sure that those involved are aware that any discussions about a proposed settlement agreement are expected to be inadmissible in relevant legal proceedings. It should also be made clear that the discussions will have no bearing on any disciplinary or capability procedure in the event that agreement is not reached. The Guide also points out that the discussion process is voluntary and that either party is free to pull out at any time. Furthermore, the Guide reminds employers that refusing a request to be accompanied may amount to unlawful discrimination. For example, it may be a reasonable adjustment to allow a disabled employee to be accompanied because of the nature of their disability.

'Improper behaviour'. The protection in S.111A(1) will not apply where **13.84** there is some improper behaviour, on the part of the employer or the employee, in relation to the settlement negotiations. S.111A(4) provides that the inadmissibility provided for by S.111A(1) will only apply to anything said or done which in the tribunal's opinion was improper, or connected with improper behaviour, to the extent that the tribunal considers just. Essentially, the tribunal is asked to go through two separate stages in order to decide whether the inadmissibility rule still applies. It must first consider whether there was improper behaviour by either party during the settlement negotiations. In the event that it finds any improper behaviour, it is then up to the tribunal, at the second stage, to decide the extent to which confidentiality should be preserved in respect of the settlement negotiations. Importantly, the provision is not phrased in such a way as to make the settlement negotiations *as a whole* admissible whenever the tribunal finds that a party acted improperly. Rather, it is left to the tribunal's discretion to decide whether it is just for any improper behaviour or anything said or done that is connected with improper behaviour to form part of the evidence before the tribunal. For example, if the employee is offered a settlement agreement for a discriminatory reason, such as that he or she is close to pensionable age, the tribunal may decide that it is just for the entirety of the settlement negotiations to be admissible in an unfair dismissal claim. Conversely, if, during the discussion, the employer uses derogatory language about the employee that goes beyond what is reasonable in the context of a workplace discussion, the tribunal might admit evidence of the employer's treatment of the employee but exclude some detail of the proposed settlement. Unfortunately, Acas does not give any examples, either in the Code or the Guide, of the circumstances in which total or partial exclusion of such evidence will be appropriate, and so it will be for case law to develop guidance on this point.

What amounts to improper behaviour for the purposes of S.111A(4) is ultimately for the tribunal to decide on the facts and circumstances of each case. Para 17 of the Code states that improper behaviour will include, but is not limited to, behaviour that would be regarded as 'unambiguous impropriety' under the 'without prejudice' rule – see 'Without prejudice negotiations – unambiguous impropriety' above. However, the concept of 'unambiguous impropriety' has always been narrowly construed by the courts and it appears that the concept of 'improper behaviour' is capable of a wider application. The Code, at para 18, contains a non-exhaustive list of what would be considered improper behaviour:

- harassment, bullying and intimidation, including through the use of offensive words or aggressive behaviour
- criminal behaviour, such as the threat of physical assault
- victimisation
- discrimination because of age, sex, race, disability, sexual orientation, religion or belief, transgender, pregnancy and maternity and marriage or civil partnership
- putting undue pressure on a party.

13.85 In terms of putting undue pressure on a party, the Code explains that this may include not giving an employee a reasonable period of time to consider any proposed settlement offer, an employer saying before any form of disciplinary process has been commenced that the employee will be dismissed if he or she rejects a settlement proposal, or an employee threatening to undermine an organisation's public reputation if the organisation does not sign a settlement agreement (unless the provisions of the Public Interest Disclosure Act 1998 apply).

While it is uncontroversial that the above examples amount to improper behaviour, other situations may be more difficult to assess. The Code states that setting out the reasons that have led to the proposed settlement agreement 'in a neutral manner' or 'factually stating' the possibility of starting a disciplinary process as a likely alternative if an agreement is not reached will not amount to

792

improper behaviour (para 19). The Guide adds that the following may also *not* be considered improper:

- factually stating that if an employee refuses a settlement agreement and any subsequent disciplinary action results in dismissal then the employee may not be able to leave on the same terms as set out in the proposed settlement agreement

- not agreeing to provide a reference

- not paying for independent advice for the employee; or

- encouraging an employee, in a non-threatening way, to reconsider a refusal of a proposal.

The Code goes on to explain that, while the test of 'improper behaviour' in **13.86** S.111A(4) is not intended to interfere with existing and acceptable negotiating practices, employers should consider whether their presentation of an offer could be perceived by a tribunal to fall within that category. For example, adopting a negotiating tactic that the amount offered reduces progressively while the employee is considering the offer may amount to undue pressure on the individual to rush a decision and could be improper behaviour. Given the difficulty of predicting with confidence which side of the dividing line negotiations tactics will fall on, it seems likely that this will be an area where case law is going to develop.

Where the tribunal decides that settlement negotiations should be disclosed as a result of the employer's improper behaviour, this does not necessarily mean that it will go on to find the employee's dismissal unfair. The test is still whether, taking into account all the circumstances, the employer's decision to dismiss fell within the range of reasonable responses. However, where the employee relies upon constructive dismissal to found a claim of unfair dismissal – particularly where he or she alleges that a series of incidents have affected trust and confidence in the employment relationship – any improper behaviour during pre-termination negotiations might be used to bolster the employee's claim. Furthermore, it is conceivable that an employer's improper behaviour may itself constitute the basis for a claim – for example, offering an employee a settlement agreement because she is pregnant will give rise to a sex discrimination claim or a discrimination claim alleging unfavourable treatment based on pregnancy and maternity.

Overlap with 'without prejudice' rule. As discussed under 'Without prejudice **13.87** negotiations' above, any discussion between employer and employee entered into on a 'without prejudice' basis to settle an existing employment dispute cannot be disclosed in any subsequent legal proceedings. However, the 'without prejudice' rule only applies where there is an existing dispute between the parties and it is therefore unlikely that any conversation initiated by the

793

employer to 'test the waters' as to whether there is scope for a consensual parting of the ways by means of a settlement agreement will be covered by it. In these circumstances, S.111A ERA, which runs alongside the 'without prejudice' rule, comes into play – it effectively extends the rule to situations where no formal dispute has yet arisen. That said, it is worth emphasising that the 'without prejudice' rule – if applicable – covers any type of claim. By contrast, S.111A only ensures that any evidence from pre-termination negotiations is inadmissible in a claim for ordinary unfair dismissal.

The Guide includes a flowchart in Annex 6 of how the 'without prejudice' rule and S.111A work together in practice in determining the admissibility of settlement agreement negotiations in unfair dismissal cases.

13.88 **Costs.** Section 111A(5) ERA provides that the protection provided for in S.111A(1) does not affect the admissibility of any evidence relating to an offer that was made on the basis that the right to refer to it on a question as to costs or expenses was reserved. This effectively replicates the position that exists in respect of offers of settlement that are marked 'without prejudice save as to costs', discussed under 'Without prejudice negotiations – costs' above. Accordingly, while the offer of settlement will be kept from the tribunal's knowledge during the substantive hearing, the employer may, if the claimant is successful, bring the offer to the tribunal's attention when the issue of costs is being discussed. The employee's refusal of the offer may then be a factor in the tribunal's assessment of whether the employee was unreasonable to bring the claim. Costs awards are discussed in Chapter 20, 'Costs and penalties', under 'Grounds for making orders against a party'.

14 Tribunal judgments

Rules 60–69 of the Employment Tribunals Rules of Procedure ('the Tribunal **14.1** Rules') – contained in Schedule 1 to the Employment Tribunals (Constitution and Rules of Procedure) Regulations 2013 SI 2013/1237 ('the Tribunal Regulations') – govern the power of employment tribunals to make decisions and their obligation to give reasons for those decisions. The majority of these rules apply to *any* decision made by an employment tribunal, including tribunal orders such as case management orders. However, in this chapter we focus on how these rules apply to tribunal judgments. A 'judgment' is defined by rule 1(3)(b) as 'a decision, made at any stage of the proceedings (but not including a decision under rule 13 or 19), which finally determines –

- a claim, or part of a claim, as regards liability, remedy or costs (including preparation time and wasted costs);

- any issue which is capable of finally disposing of any claim, or part of a claim, even if it does not necessarily do so (for example, an issue whether a claim should be struck out or a jurisdictional issue); or

- the imposition of a financial penalty under S.12A of the Employment Tribunals Act 1996.'

(Rule 13 deals with reconsideration of rejected claims and Rule 19 is concerned with reconsideration of rejected responses – Chapter 15, 'Reconsideration of tribunal judgments and decisions'.)

This definition of a 'judgment' is not too dissimilar from that found in **14.2** rule 28(1)(a) of the Tribunal Rules 2004 (contained in Schedule 1 to the Employment Tribunal (Constitution and Rules of Procedure) Regulations 2004 SI 2004/1861), which defined a judgment as 'a final determination of the proceedings or of a particular issue in those proceedings; it may include an award of compensation, a declaration or recommendation and it may also include orders for costs, preparation time or wasted costs'. Given the similarities, cases decided under the old rules continue to be of value in interpreting the provisions of the current rules and we refer to them when appropriate.

Note that default judgments – now known as 'rule 21 judgments' – are discussed in Chapter 6, 'Defending a claim', under 'Rule 21 – "default judgments"'.

795

14.3 Promulgating judgments

Any judgment made without a hearing must be communicated to the parties in writing, and the employment judge who made the decision must be identified – rule 60. Where a hearing is held, a tribunal can either announce its judgment orally at the hearing, or reserve it to be given in writing at a later date – rule 61(1). If a judgment is announced at a hearing, a written record of the decision will be provided to the parties as soon as practicable. If the proceedings were referred to the employment tribunal by a court, a copy of the written record of the decision will also be sent to that court – rule 61(2).

14.4 Reserving judgment

When judgment is reserved, a written judgment must be sent to the parties as soon as practicable – rule 61(1). Reserving judgment would have been the best option in Anglian Home Improvements v Kelly 2005 ICR 242, CA, where the tribunal members could not agree on the correct outcome of the complaint. In the event, the two lay members of the tribunal found that the claimant had been unfairly dismissed, but the chairman came to the opposite conclusion. The Court of Appeal said that, in the circumstances, especially since the majority consisted of the two lay members, it would have been preferable for the chairman (who had the task of writing the judgment) to reserve the judgment to be given in writing at a later date. That would have given the two lay members the opportunity of ensuring that their views were correctly expressed in the document prepared by the chairman.

14.5 Delay in giving reserved judgment.
Although there is no absolute time limit within which the tribunal is required to give its final determination, in Kwamin v Abbey National plc and other cases 2004 ICR 841, EAT, the Appeal Tribunal expressed the view that, even allowing for the difficulties and necessity of communication between the three members of a tribunal, three-and-a-half months should be the maximum time necessary for the preparation and promulgation of all but the most complicated and lengthy judgments. In that case the EAT, hearing conjoined appeals, found that serious delays of seven-and-a-half, twelve and fourteen-and-a-half months respectively meant that the tribunal judgments were unsafe, owing to factual errors and omissions, and should be set aside. However, when one of those cases went to the Court of Appeal – Connex South Eastern Ltd v Bangs 2005 ICR 763, CA – the Court held that the EAT had erred in overturning the tribunal's decision. The Court stressed that unreasonable delay by a tribunal does not automatically amount to a serious procedural error giving rise to a ground for appeal. The key question is whether, owing to the unreasonable delay, there is a real risk that a party has been denied his or her right to a fair trial and whether it would be unfair and unjust to allow the tribunal's determination to stand.

In Grosvenor v Governing Body of Aylesford School and ors and other cases EAT 0001/08 the hearing, originally listed for 15 days, occupied some 40 days between 7 November 2005 and 13 October 2006. The employment tribunal then spent a total of 26 days deliberating in private before promulgating the judgment and reasons. The first meeting in chambers was held on 30 October 2006 and the last on 3 September 2007. The employment tribunal's judgment and reasons, together with appendices (which totalled 378 pages), was completed and signed off by the chairman on 28 September 2007. The EAT held that while a delay of one year in promulgating an employment tribunal judgment ought never to happen, the unusual feature of this case was the number of days spent by the employment tribunal considering the matter. It was not a case where there was a large gap in time between the tribunal's deliberations and production of the judgment and reasons. The last meeting in chambers took place three weeks before the chairman completed the final judgment and reasons. The EAT held that, in the absence of perversity, the mere fact of delay was not in this case, of itself, a free-standing ground of appeal. (Note that an appeal to the Court of Appeal is outstanding in this case.)

For further discussion on the question of how delay can impact upon an employment tribunal's decision, see Chapter 16, 'The Employment Appeal Tribunal', under 'Grounds of appeal'.

Judgment must be signed   14.6
The written record of an employment tribunal's judgment must be signed by the employment judge who made the decision – rule 61(3). If the judge is unable to sign owing to death, incapacity or absence, it can instead be signed by the other member or members of the tribunal hearing panel (where the case was heard by a full tribunal) or by the President, Vice-President or a regional employment judge (where the case was heard by an employment judge sitting alone) – rule 63. (Note that under old rule 31 of the Tribunal Rules 2004, any person who signed a document on a judge's behalf had to certify that the judge was unable to do so. This is no longer a requirement under the 2013 Rules, although it would be best practice for the person who is signing the judgment on an employment judge's behalf to make this clear on the document.)

Majority decisions   14.7
In most cases, the tribunal members agree on the judgment to be made. Nevertheless, rule 49 allows for decisions to be made by a majority where the tribunal is composed of three members. If a tribunal comprises only two members (one of whom must be an employment judge), the judge has a second or casting vote to avoid deadlock. The Court of Appeal has stressed, however, that although a split decision may be inevitable in some cases, a tribunal should always aim to reach a unanimous decision. It should make every effort, and if need be allow extra time by reserving its decision, to come to an agreement on

797

the issues before it – Anglian Home Improvements v Kelly 2005 ICR 242, CA. If a unanimous decision cannot be reached, it is good practice to set out the view of the minority member in the judgment. However, departure from this good practice is not a ground for appeal in itself – Morgan v Welsh Rugby Union 2011 IRLR 376, EAT.

14.8 Consent judgments

If the parties agree in writing upon the terms of a judgment, a tribunal is, by virtue of rule 64, empowered to make such a judgment if it thinks fit. This generally occurs where the parties have agreed settlement. The judgment will be identified as having been made by consent. Consent judgments of this kind usually specify the terms of the agreement between the parties. For a full discussion of settlements, see Chapter 3, 'Conciliation, settlements and ADR'.

14.9 Remitting case to another tribunal

In rare circumstances a tribunal may decide not to give judgment and instead remit the case for a rehearing by another tribunal. This happened in R v Industrial Tribunal ex parte Cotswold Collotype Co Ltd 1979 ICR 190, QBD, where a tribunal heard three claims for unfair dismissal compensation and/or redundancy payments, but the tribunal members were hopelessly split. One thought that the claimants had been unfairly dismissed but were not redundant; the second thought that they had not been unfairly dismissed but were redundant; and the third thought that they were neither unfairly dismissed nor redundant. In the circumstances, the tribunal decided that the case should be heard again by a different tribunal. The employer applied for judicial review (rarely invoked against employment tribunals) to prohibit a rehearing and to direct that the original decision – which showed majorities against both unfair dismissal and redundancy findings – should be recorded as final. The High Court, however, held that the tribunal had an inherent power to refer the case to another tribunal and that it was entitled in the circumstances to hold that its own findings were inconclusive. Although there were tribunal majorities against unfair dismissal compensation and redundancy payments, the majority was in favour of some form of compensation for the loss of employment.

The power to order a rehearing before a different tribunal is now conferred on tribunals by virtue of rules 29 (the power to make case management orders) and 41 (the power to regulate procedure). However, the EAT in Charman v Palmers Scaffolding Ltd 1979 ICR 335, EAT, stressed that a tribunal's power to order a rehearing should be exercised very sparingly and only for very good reasons. In that case, the fact that a tribunal chairman had adjourned proceedings and advised an unrepresented employee to take legal advice and reconsider his or her position did not warrant a rehearing.

14.10 In Automobile Proprietary Ltd v Healy 1979 ICR 809, EAT, the tribunal ordered a rehearing by a differently constituted tribunal because the claimant said that he had no confidence in the fairness of the proceedings. The EAT ruled that the tribunal had misdirected itself in law. The mere fact that a claimant disliked the way that the hearing was going could not possibly be a ground for asking for the hearing to be discontinued in the hope that he or she would fare better before a different tribunal.

When a judgment takes effect

An employment tribunal judgment takes effect from the day when it is given or made, or on such later date as specified by the tribunal – rule 65. Therefore, if a tribunal's judgment is announced at a hearing, it will, by virtue of rule 65, take effect immediately (unless otherwise specified by the tribunal). Technically speaking, this means that it will be enforceable immediately, even before the written record of the judgment is sent to the parties. However, in the case of a judgment for the payment of an amount of money, rule 66 provides that a party has 14 days within which to comply, unless the judgment, or any of the rules, specifies a different date for compliance, or the tribunal has stayed (or, in Scotland, sisted) the proceedings or judgment. The Government has stated that the 14-day time limit for payment shows that a tribunal expects prompt payment of the award but also 'signals when it is legitimate for a party to start pursuing enforcement action'. Therefore, even though a judgment is enforceable as soon as it is given or made, in most cases it is expected that the party in whose favour the judgment was made will wait 14 days before commencing enforcement action. For discussion as to how tribunal judgments can be enforced, see Chapter 21, 'Enforcement of tribunal awards'.

Interest

Article 3(1) of the Employment Tribunals (Interest) Order 1990 SI 1990/749 ('the 1990 Order') provides that interest accrues on any amount to be paid by virtue of an employment tribunal decision from, and including, 'the calculation day'. The calculation day used to be the day immediately following the expiry of the period of 42 days beginning with the relevant decision day, meaning that interest only began to accrue on an unpaid tribunal award after 42 days. However, Article 2 of the Employment Tribunals (Interest) Order (Amendment) Order 2013 SI 2013/1671 ('the 2013 Amendment Order'), which came into force on 29 July 2013, amended the definition of 'the calculation day' so that, for all claims issued on or after 29 July 2013, it is the day immediately following the relevant decision day. For the purposes of these provisions, 'decision day' means the day 'signified by the date recording the sending of the document which is sent to the parties recording the tribunal's award' and the 'relevant decision day' means, save for in certain circumstances where the tribunal's decision is reconsidered, remitted or appealed, the day so signified in relation to a relevant decision – Article 2(3) 1990 Order. This means that, in most cases, interest will start to accrue from the day after the relevant decision is made.

14.11

14.12

799

The written record of the tribunal's judgment will specify the decision day, the stipulated rate of interest and the calculation day in respect of the decision concerned – Article 12(2) 1990 Order. However, if a tribunal fails to provide this information correctly or at all it will not affect the liability of one party to pay to another party the sum ordered – Article 12(3). The current rate of interest is 8 per cent – S.17 Judgments Act 1838.

14.13 While interest now accrues from the day immediately after the date the relevant decision is made, Article 3(4) of the 1990 Order (which was inserted by the 2013 Amendment Order) provides that the interest accrued is not payable if payment of the full amount of the award (including any interest under Reg 2 of the Employment Tribunals (Interest on Awards in Discrimination Cases) Regulations 1996 SI 1996/2803) is made within 14 days after the relevant decision day, i.e. within the time period set out in rule 66 – see 'When a judgment takes effect' above.

14.14 Reasons for judgments

Where a tribunal makes a decision on any disputed issue, whether on a substantive point of law or fact or a point of procedure (including any decision on an application for reconsideration or for orders for costs, preparation time or wasted costs), it must give reasons for its decision – rule 62(1). This requirement is based on the fundamental principle that justice must not only be done but must also be seen to be done. Reasons are required if decisions are to be acceptable to the parties and to members of the public. Furthermore, as Lord Justice Henry observed in Flannery and anor v Halifax Estate Agencies Ltd (t/a Colleys Professional Services) 2000 1 WLR 377, CA (a case concerning professional negligence), fairness requires that the parties, especially the losing party, should be left in no doubt as to why they have won or lost. Without reasons the losing party will be unable to ascertain whether the court has misdirected itself, and thus whether he or she might have grounds to appeal on the substance of the case. Furthermore, the requirement to give reasons concentrates the mind of the judge and the resulting decision is more likely to be soundly based on the evidence.

14.15 Oral and written reasons

Where a tribunal's decision is given in writing (for instance, where a tribunal reserves its judgment to be given at a later date or where a tribunal enters a 'default judgment' without holding a hearing in accordance with the terms of rule 21), the reasons for that decision must also be given in writing. If the decision is announced at a hearing the reasons may be given orally at the hearing, or reserved to be given in writing at a later date. Where reserved, the reasons need not be given in writing as part of the written record of the decision. The reasons can be delivered separately – rule 62(2).

Where reasons have been given orally at a hearing, the employment judge is required to announce that written reasons will not be provided unless they are asked for by a party, either at the hearing itself or in writing within 14 days of the date on which the written record of the decision is sent to the parties. The written record of the decision will repeat that information. If no such request is received, the tribunal will provide written reasons only if required to do so by the EAT or a court – rule 62(3).

A party will almost certainly require written reasons if he or she wishes to **14.16** appeal to the EAT against an employment tribunal's decision (for further details, see Chapter 17, 'Processing an appeal', under 'Instituting an appeal – written reasons'). As stated above, a request for written reasons must be made by a party either orally at the hearing itself or in writing within 14 days of the date on which the judgment was sent to the parties. The date on which the judgment was sent will be endorsed on the written record of the decision. In calculating the time limit, that date is not included – rule 4(3).

It used to be the case under old rule 30(5) that where a party had failed to request written reasons within the 14-day window permitted, the tribunal had discretion to extend the time limit where it considered that it was just and equitable to do so. This provision is not replicated in the Tribunal Rules 2013. Rule 62(3) provides that if no request for written reasons is received, the employment tribunal will *only* provide them if requested to do so by the EAT or a court. The wording of this rule suggests that a tribunal may not even be able to rely on its general discretion under rule 5 to extend the time limit and accede to a request for written reasons. Having said that, the restriction in rule 63(2) only applies where 'no such request is received', i.e. no request is received at all. Arguably, therefore, where a request *is* received, but outside the 14-day time limit, a tribunal can exercise its discretion to extend time and grant the request.

Written reasons for a judgment must be provided if requested by the EAT – **14.17** rule 62(3). The EAT made use of this power in NSM Music Ltd v Leefe 2006 ICR 450, EAT, to obtain written reasons where the tribunal had initially declined to provide them. In that case, the respondent company had failed to submit a timeous response to the employee's unfair dismissal claim. The company was thus barred, by virtue of old rule 9 of the Tribunal Rules 2004, from taking any further part in the proceedings save for extremely limited purposes. In the event, the employee's claim was successful and the company, wishing to appeal to the EAT, applied to the tribunal for its written reasons. The tribunal decided that, owing to the rule 9 restrictions, the company was not permitted to make such a request. The tribunal therefore refused to provide written reasons and the company appealed to the EAT against that refusal. The EAT agreed with the tribunal's analysis of rule 9. However, in the circumstances, it decided to make use of its power (then set out in rule 30(3)(b)) to request the

801

written reasons itself. In deciding to take that course of action, Mr Justice Burton, then President of the EAT, noted that the Appeal Tribunal, on its sift, makes use of this power on a regular basis where there are no written reasons provided by a tribunal, either because they have not been sought or because they have been sought and refused. An appropriate case, he continued, 'is where it appears to the appeal tribunal... that there might be something in the appeal'.

Reasons given orally at a hearing are normally recorded on tape. If a party requests written reasons, a transcript of the oral reasons is provided to the employment judge as a first draft to be edited, signed and sent to the parties. In Trollope and Colls Construction Ltd v Sharp EAT 812/92 the employer, which wished to appeal against the employment tribunal's judgment, requested a written copy of the reasons that had been given orally at the hearing. However, the tape-recording of the tribunal's oral reasons had been lost and the tribunal was therefore only able to produce a reconstructed statement, which it knew could not be a true record of its reasoning. The EAT ordered a fresh hearing of the case by a different tribunal on the basis that the employer could not found an appeal on the reconstructed statement.

14.18 When written reasons are supplied they constitute the sole authoritative statement of the tribunal's reasons and any oral reasons that were given are superseded – Partners of Haxby Practice v Collen EAT 0120/12. In that case, a tribunal found in favour of the claimant but gave different reasons for its decision in its oral and written reasons. The EAT held that although the details of the tribunal's reasoning (in both the oral and the written reasons) could be criticised, its substantive decision was unarguably right. It held that a divergence between a tribunal's oral and written reasoning, where there was no change in the decision itself, did not constitute an error of law. In the course of giving its judgment, the EAT commented that it is unsurprising that the process of producing written reasons will occasionally modify an employment judge's detailed thinking. Employment judges would be in a very awkward position if they were obliged to continue to justify a decision on the basis of oral reasoning which they had come conscientiously to believe was wrong. Furthermore, if parties were enabled to advance an appeal on the basis of supposed divergences between a tribunal's oral reasons and its subsequent written reasons, it would be all too easy for appellants – not necessarily in bad faith – to raise such grounds given the absence of any authoritative record of the oral judgment. Such disputes could only be resolved by obtaining a transcript of the oral reasons, which, the EAT held, would undermine the entire scheme of the requirement to provide reasons.

14.19 **Form of written reasons**

If provided, the written reasons must be signed by the employment judge responsible for the decision – rule 62(2). As with the judgment itself, where it is impossible or impracticable for the employment judge to sign the written reasons owing to death, incapacity or absence, rule 63 provides that the written reasons can be signed by the other member or members (in the case of a full tribunal) or by the President, Vice-President or a regional employment judge (in the case of a judge sitting alone).

In Rustamova v Governors of Calder High School EAT 0214/13 the majority judgment and reasons were produced and signed by the lay members, but were not signed by the dissenting employment judge. This did not meet the mandatory requirements in what are now rules 61(3) and 62(2). The EAT referred to the guidance provided by the Court of Appeal in Anglian Home Improvements v Kelly 2005 ICR 242, CA, to the effect that where the lay members of a tribunal are in the majority, it would be preferable for the minority employment judge to write the majority reasons with the approval of the members. The appeal in this case was therefore adjourned until the employment judge had produced a judgment and reasons, with the approval of his lay colleagues, duly signed by him.

14.20 Once signed, a copy of the written reasons will be sent to all parties to the proceedings. The date on which they are sent by the tribunal will be endorsed on the document itself.

Note that in Kirkcaldy Out Of Hours GP Co-Operative v Goyal and ors EAT 0083/03 Mr Justice Burton, then President of the EAT, urged tribunal judges to number the paragraphs in their written judgments to aid clarity. He pointed out that a lengthy set of reasons that does not contain paragraph numbers makes it very difficult for both parties to identify those parts to which particular attention is drawn on appeal. Furthermore, Burton P continued, judgments should not contain 'massive numbers of sub-paragraphs and sub-sub-paragraphs'. If these are necessary, it is preferable to use consecutive paragraph numbering (e.g. 12.1, 12.2, 12.3, 12.4, etc).

Content of written reasons
14.21

Parties pursuing an appeal commonly allege that the tribunal's reasons were inadequate, and that this led to an error of law. The case most often quoted in this context is Meek v City of Birmingham District Council 1987 IRLR 250, CA, where the Court of Appeal held that although a tribunal's reasons are not required to be an elaborate formalistic product of refined legal draftsmanship, they must nonetheless contain:

- an outline of the facts of the case that gave rise to the complaint

- a summary of the tribunal's basic factual conclusions, and

- a statement of the reasons which led it to reach its conclusions on the facts as found.

803

The Court of Appeal emphasised that the parties are entitled to be told why they have won or lost, and the tribunal's decision must give a sufficient account of the facts and of the reasoning to enable an appellate court to determine whether any question of law arises.

14.22 The Meek decision became the benchmark against which other cases were judged to the extent that if a decision was inadequately reasoned it was said not to be 'Meek-compliant'. Two examples:

- **Chapman and anor v Simon** 1994 IRLR 124, CA: a tribunal held that the claimant, S, had been discriminated against on the ground of race. However, the Court of Appeal stated that the tribunal had made no findings of fact from which its inference that there was subconscious racial prejudice could have been drawn. The Court held that the tribunal had erred in law, stating that, in order to justify an inference of discrimination, a tribunal must first make findings of fact from which it is legitimate to draw such an inference. The Court therefore allowed the employer's appeal and dismissed S's claim

- **Moore v Travelsphere Ltd and ors** EAT 738/97: M, a claimant of Afro-Caribbean origin, claimed race discrimination on the basis that she had been disciplined for her poor performance whereas white employees who performed in a similar way had not faced disciplinary proceedings. The tribunal stated: 'We have considered the facts and the submissions very carefully. We do not find any evidence of racial discrimination.' The EAT held that the tribunal had not made sufficient findings of fact and, accordingly, had not been in a position to decide what inferences should be drawn. Furthermore, the EAT held that M could justly say that she did not know why she had lost. Accordingly, the EAT remitted the matter to a freshly constituted tribunal.

14.23 Note that when Meek v City of Birmingham District Council (above) was decided, the relevant tribunal rules provided only that 'a tribunal shall give reasons, which may be in full or in summary form, for its decision' – rule 9(3), Sch 1 Industrial Tribunals (Rules of Procedure) Regulations 1985 SI 1985/16. The succeeding paragraphs of the rule went on to indicate the circumstances in which full reasons should be given, but the concepts of 'full' and 'summary' were not defined and the rules did not set out what a tribunal's reasons should include. Subsequent versions of the rules, however, have provided increasingly more detail in this regard and rule 62(5) of the Tribunal Rules 2013 (which is almost identical to old rule 30(6) of the Tribunal Rules 2004) now provides that the reasons given for any employment tribunal judgment must:

- identify the issues which the tribunal has determined

- state the findings of fact made in relation to those issues

- concisely identify the relevant law

804

- state how that law has been applied to those findings in order to decide the issues, and

- where the judgment includes a financial award the reasons must identify, by means of a table or otherwise, how the amount to be paid has been calculated.

Additionally, in discrimination and equal pay cases a tribunal's written reasons must also contain a statement of the amount of any interest awarded, and either a table showing how it has been calculated or a description of the manner in which it has been calculated – Reg 7 Employment Tribunals (Interest on Awards in Discrimination Cases) Regulations 1996 SI 1996/2803.

In Fisher v Hoopoe Finance Ltd EAT 0043/05 the EAT held that the requirements **14.24** of rule 62(5) (rule 30(6) as it was then) do not supersede Meek v City of Birmingham District Council (above). It held that the provisions of the rule helpfully spell out in clear terms what an employment tribunal is required to do in order to make its decision Meek-compliant. The EAT stated that 'it is clear that for an employment tribunal to be Meek-compliant it *must* comply with rule [62(5)]' (EAT's stress). However, contrary to the EAT's opinion in Fisher – and despite the seemingly mandatory wording of the rule – the EAT in Commotion Ltd v Rutty 2006 ICR 290, EAT, stated obiter (i.e. without binding force) that it did not think that adherence to the rule was compulsory.

The issue was revisited by the Court of Appeal in Balfour Beatty Power Networks Ltd and anor v Wilcox and ors 2007 IRLR 63, CA, where it advised tribunals to recite the terms of the rule and to indicate serially how their determinations fulfil its requirements. Nevertheless, in the Court's view, 'the rule is surely intended to be a guide and not a straitjacket' and, provided it can be reasonably spelled out from the determination of the tribunal that the requirements of the rule have been complied with, no error of law will have been committed.

The Court of Appeal's decision was followed in Greenwood v NWF Retail Ltd **14.25** 2011 ICR 896, EAT, where the EAT held that compliance with the requirements of the rule is mandatory and, while a judgment will not be erroneous in law simply because the structure of the rule is not explicitly visible, the judgment must demonstrate substantial compliance. It said that employment tribunals, while not confining themselves in a straitjacket, should set out judgments in a structure that clearly recognises and demonstrates both the formal and substantial requirements of the rule in sufficient detail in respect of each of the rule's components to enable a party to understand the conclusion reached. The judgment in this case was erroneous because it failed to articulate the issues as fully the rule required, failed to set out the facts relating to those issues and failed to adequately explain its reasons for reaching its conclusion.

The EAT rejected a submission that Meek v City of Birmingham District Council (above) is to be equated with the common law position espoused by

805

Lord Justice Phillips in English v Emery Reimbold and Strick Ltd and other cases 2003 IRLR 710, CA, and that the adequacy of reasons should therefore be judged in accordance with that position, rather than rule 30(6). Meek was not referred to in English, which, the EAT held, was not at all surprising given that Meek was a judgment reached in the employment law jurisdiction, which is created and controlled by legislation, whereas English was about the extent to which the common law requires a reasoned judgment to be given in the civil courts. The EAT held that, however closely Meek appeared to resemble English, employment tribunals would be better to refer to Meek, which is the Court of Appeal decision relevant to an employment tribunal's jurisdiction. It held that Meek remained a helpful guide as to whether rule 30(6) (and now rule 62(5)) has been complied with.

14.26 The Greenwood case was referred to in Uche v Oxfordshire County Council EAT 0348/12, where the EAT held that while the employment tribunal had not made specific reference to the relevant legislation under which the claimant's claims had been brought, it was clear that the law had been applied correctly. Furthermore, it did not think it should take too technical a view as to how the employment tribunal had expressed itself and was satisfied that the tribunal had substantially complied with the requirements of rule 30(6) (now rule 62(5)). However, the EAT stated that when giving judgment, tribunals would be well advised to follow the Court of Appeal's guidance in Balfour Beatty Power Networks Ltd and anor v Wilcox and ors (above) and recite the terms of rule 30(6) (now rule 62(5)) indicating serially how their determination fulfils its requirements.

Employment tribunals should make it clear that they have considered the arguments made on behalf of both parties. In University of Manchester v Faulkner EAT 0081/10 the EAT held that a tribunal's judgment was not Meek-compliant because, although it had set out the arguments and evidence that had been advanced on behalf of the claimant, it had failed to set out the arguments and evidence that had been advanced on behalf of the respondent or to indicate a proper evidential basis for the conclusions that it had reached. The judgment was therefore set aside and the claim remitted to a fresh tribunal for a rehearing. Similarly, in English v Royal Mail Group Ltd and anor EAT 0027/08 the EAT held that an employment tribunal's judgment could not stand because it simply repeated verbatim (save for some grammatical changes) the closing written submissions of the respondent and ignored entirely the claimant's closing submission. In doing so, it had not made a clear distinction between submissions and findings of fact and had failed to comply with the requirements of due process and of rule 30(6) (now rule 62(5)). The case was remitted to a differently constituted tribunal.

14.27 Where a set of reasons deals with more than one claim, those reasons must be sufficient to enable the EAT to establish whether or not there has been an error of law in relation to each individual claim. In HJ Heinz Co Ltd v Kenrick 2000 ICR 491, EAT, the employee claimed both unfair dismissal and disability discrimination. The tribunal found that the dismissal fell foul of the Disability Discrimination Act 1995 (now repealed and re-enacted in the Equality Act 2010), and then seemed to move automatically to a finding of unfair dismissal. The EAT noted that there is no enacted provision which states that an unjustified disability-related dismissal is, without more, automatically unfair. The fairness of any such dismissal must be determined by reference to S.98 of the Employment Rights Act 1996. Accordingly, since the employment tribunal had not set out in its reasons a separate consideration of S.98, its decision as to the fairness of the dismissal was set aside. The question was remitted to the tribunal for further consideration.

Language used when giving reasons. Tribunals should be careful to use **14.28** appropriate language when giving reasons. Using language that is stronger than would normally be considered necessary leaves the employment judge open to the charge that he or she has lost his or her objectivity. The use of moderate language, on the other hand, indicates that an employment judge has approached matters in a measured way – Co-Operative Group Ltd v Baddeley EAT 0415/12 and Governing Body of Story Wood School and Children's Centre v Jones EAT 0522/12. In both cases, the language used by the tribunal judge was unusually robust. For example, in the Baddeley case, the judgment talked of the claimant becoming 'enmeshed' in 'a somewhat insidious catalogue of events', as a result of the respondent's 'malice' towards him, which arose because 'of his insistence to speak his mind rather than stay silent on what he saw was wrong'. Similarly strong language was used in the Jones case. In both cases – the judgments for which were delivered on the same day – the EAT held that it was unwise for employment tribunal judgments to be expressed in a way that was less than judicious. The robustness of the language used had caused the EAT to subject the judgments to even greater scrutiny than might otherwise have been justified. It is one thing, the EAT said in the Jones case, for employment judges to want to tell it how it is, but it is quite another to do so in a way which leads people to think that the judge has abandoned his or her detachment, and has an agenda of his or her own. Having said that, in these cases the EAT was satisfied that the tribunals had not lost their objectivity such that the judgments should be set aside on that basis. (Note that an appeal to the Court of Appeal is outstanding in the Baddeley case.)

Reasons must be proportionate. Rule 62(4) states that 'the reasons given for **14.29** any decision shall be proportionate to the significance of the issue and for decisions other than judgments may be very short'. This is a new provision. In the case of a judgment, what will be proportionate reasoning will depend on the nature and complexity of the case in hand. It will not depend on the constitution of the tribunal, however. An employment judge sitting alone is not

807

required to provide fuller reasoning than if he or she was sitting with two lay members – Disotto Food Ltd v Santos EAT 0623/12.

14.30 Clarification of reasons

Where the EAT considers a tribunal's written reasons for its judgment to be inadequate, it can invite the tribunal to clarify, supplement or provide its reasoning. This is known as the 'Burns/Barke procedure' after the case of Burns v Royal Mail Group plc (formerly Consignia plc) and anor 2004 ICR 1103, EAT, in which Mr Justice Burton, then President of the EAT, held that this practice was lawful. The practice is not codified in the Employment Appeal Tribunal Rules 1993 SI 1993/2854, but was confirmed by the Court of Appeal in Barke v SEETEC Business Technology Centre Ltd 2005 ICR 1373, CA. We consider the Burns/Barke procedure in greater detail in Chapter 17, 'Processing an appeal', under 'Interlocutory procedures – miscellaneous powers'.

14.31 Split hearings

A split hearing occurs where a tribunal directs that the issue of liability and remedy should be dealt with in separate sessions, or where a decision in favour of a claimant is reached but there is insufficient time to decide on compensation.

Tribunals have a discretion whether or not to give reasons for a decision on liability before holding a hearing on compensation or other remedies. The EAT has said, however, that it would be prudent for a tribunal judge who decides not to give a reasoned decision on liability before a separate compensation hearing to explain why he or she considers this unnecessary – Metropole Casinos (UK) Ltd v Brown EAT 539/87.

14.32 Registration of judgments

Regulation 14(1) of the Tribunal Regulations states that the Lord Chancellor will maintain a register containing a copy of all judgments and written reasons issued by an employment tribunal which are required to be entered in the Register by virtue of any of the rules set out in Schedules 1–3. Rule 67, contained in Schedule 1 to the Regulations, confirms that a copy of any judgment and any written reasons for a judgment will be entered in the Register. The Register of judgments for England and Wales is currently held in Bury St Edmunds, while the Scottish Register is held in Glasgow.

The entry in the Register of any judgment and of any written reasons is subject to rules 50 ('Privacy and restrictions on disclosure') and 94 ('National security proceedings') – rule 67. Under rule 50(3)(b) tribunals are vested with a discretion to omit the identity of any persons from the Register of judgments – by way of an anonymity order or otherwise – where it is necessary in the interests of justice to protect the Convention rights of any person or in any of the circumstances listed in S.10A of the Employment Tribunals Act 1996. This discretion may be exercised, for example, in cases involving allegations of sexual misconduct. For more information about employment tribunals' powers as regards privacy and restrictions on disclosure, see Chapter 11, 'Case management', under 'Privacy and restrictions on disclosure'.

Under rule 94(1), where, in relation to Crown employment proceedings, a Minister considers it expedient in the interests of national security to do so, he or she may direct the tribunal to (a) conduct all or part of the proceedings in private, (b) exclude a person from all or part of the proceedings, and/or (c) take steps to conceal the identity of a witness in the proceedings. Rule 94(2) gives tribunals a general power to do anything that they can be required to do under rule 94(1)(a)–(c), as well as the power to order a person not to disclose any document (or the contents of any document) provided for the purposes of the proceedings. (This general power applies to any proceedings, not just Crown employment proceedings.) Directions or orders made under rule 94(1) or (2) can include the omission of certain information from the Register of judgments. For further information, see Chapter 12, 'The hearing', under 'National security'. **14.33**

A document certified by a member of tribunal staff as being a true copy of an entry of a judgment in the Register will be sufficient evidence of the document and its contents, unless proven otherwise – Reg 14(3).

When is a judgment final?
14.34

Once a judgment has been entered in the Register, it is final in the sense that the tribunal has no power to vary it, subject to two exceptions. These are:

- the power of an employment judge to correct clerical mistakes and accidental slips or omissions under what is commonly known as the 'slip rule' – rule 69, and

- a tribunal's power to formally reconsider any judgment where it is necessary in the interests of justice to do so – rule 70.

Both of these powers are discussed in Chapter 15, 'Reconsideration of tribunal judgments and decisions'.

The question of whether or not a decision can be varied *before* entry in the Register was dealt with by the EAT in Hanks v Ace High Productions Ltd 1978 ICR 1155, EAT. In that case Mr Justice Phillips held that an employment tribunal's judgment is not 'perfected' until it has been drawn up and entered in the Register. Until that happens, the tribunal retains the power to recall the parties to provide additional argument in the case for its consideration.

However, this power cannot be exercised merely to rehear the case or invite fresh argument on matters on which the tribunal has already made a clear finding. It should be used only where there has been a clear error or omission on the part of the tribunal and, in this regard, the tribunal's notice of recall to **14.35** the parties should give a clear indication as to why the matter has been reopened. The Appeal Tribunal in CK Heating Ltd v Doro 2010 ICR 1449, EAT, held that the ultimate question in deciding whether to exercise the power of recall is whether the tribunal believes that it is necessary to do so in the interests of justice having regard to the overriding objective (to deal with cases fairly and justly – see rule 2).

A tribunal must not change a decision without inviting representations from the parties. In Arthur Guinness Son and Co (Great Britain) Ltd v Green 1989 ICR 241, EAT, a tribunal announced orally, after hearing submissions, that the cut-off date for a claimant's unfair dismissal compensation would be 31 March. In the tribunal's written reasons, which were promulgated without hearing any further representations from the parties, the tribunal varied the cut-off date to a date 12 weeks after 13 May (the date of the judgment). The EAT overruled the tribunal and restored the oral judgment. It said that a tribunal should not depart from a previous oral judgment without informing the parties of what it was proposing to do and giving them an opportunity to make representations.

14.36 However, in light of new rule 65, under which a judgment takes effect 'from the day when it is given or made, or on such later date as specified by the tribunal', it may now be the case that the power of recall can only be exercised where a tribunal reserves its judgment or specifies a later date on which the judgment will take effect. A judgment delivered orally at the hearing will take effect – or to use the language of Phillips J in the Hanks case above, be 'perfected' – under rule 65 as soon as it is made (unless the tribunal indicates otherwise). In these circumstances, the tribunal may no longer have the freedom to simply recall the parties in order that they can make additional representations and the only option may be for the tribunal to exercise its power to formally reconsider the judgment on its own initiative in accordance with rules 70 and 73. For more information on a tribunal's power to reconsider its judgments see Chapter 15, 'Reconsideration of tribunal judgments and decisions'.

14.37 Information to Commission for Equality and Human Rights
By virtue of rule 103, an employment tribunal is required to send copies of all judgments and reasons relating to complaints made under S.120, S.127 or S.146 of the Equality Act 2010 to the Commission for Equality and Human Rights. These sections set out the employment tribunals' jurisdiction to hear complaints of discrimination that arise under that Act. This obligation does not apply in proceedings where a Minister of the Crown has given a direction, or an employment tribunal has made an order, under rule 94 ('National security proceedings') *and* the Security Service, the Secret Intelligence Service or the Government Communications Headquarters is a party to the proceedings.

15 Reconsideration of tribunal judgments and decisions

Reconsideration of a tribunal judgment

Grounds for reconsideration

Applying for reconsideration

Procedure for reconsideration

Powers of tribunal on reconsideration

Challenging other tribunal decisions and orders

Correcting mistakes

An employment tribunal judgment can be challenged in two ways. In some **15.1** circumstances, an appeal to the EAT is appropriate (we examine the law relating to appeals in Chapters 16 to 18). In others, a tribunal judgment should be challenged by seeking a 'reconsideration'. Rules 70–73 of the Employment Tribunal Rules of Procedure ('the Tribunal Rules 2013') contained in Schedule 1 to the Employment Tribunals (Constitution and Rules of Procedure) Regulations 2013 SI 2013/1237 ('the Tribunal Regulations') set out the procedure for tribunals to 'reconsider' judgments. It is similar to the 'review' procedure that existed under old rules 33–36 of the Tribunal Rules 2004. However, there are some differences, which we discuss where relevant.

In most cases, a reconsideration will deal with the issue more quickly and at less expense than an appeal to the EAT. Having said that, both means of challenging a judgment now attract the payment of a fee by the applying party under the Employment Tribunals and the Employment Appeal Tribunal Fees Order 2013 SI 2013/1893. We discuss this where relevant below.

In this chapter we examine the provisions for a reconsideration of a tribunal judgment, including the procedure for applying for a reconsideration. We also discuss how other tribunal decisions and orders can be challenged under the rules, and how some employment tribunal mistakes can be rectified without the necessity of undergoing a formal reconsideration or appeal procedure.

Reconsideration of a tribunal judgment

15.2

Rule 70 of the Tribunal Rules 2013 provides an employment tribunal with a general power to reconsider any judgment where it is necessary in the interests of justice to do so. This power can be exercised either on a tribunal's own

_____

811

initiative or on the application of a party. Rules 71–73 set out the procedure by which this power can be exercised, which we discuss in detail below. Only a 'judgment' can be reconsidered using this power.

15.3 What decisions constitute a 'judgment'?

A 'judgment' is defined in rule 1(3)(b) of the Tribunal Rules 2013 as 'a decision, made at any stage of the proceedings (but not including a decision under rule 13 or 19), which finally determines –

- a claim, or part of a claim, as regards liability, remedy or costs (including preparation time and wasted costs);

- any issue which is capable of finally disposing of any claim, or part of a claim, even if it does not necessarily do so (for example, an issue whether a claim should be struck out or a jurisdictional issue); or

- the imposition of a financial penalty order under S.12A of the Employment Tribunals Act 1996.'

Note that it is only a decision which finally determines a *claim* or any issue in a claim that can constitute a judgment for the purposes of a reconsideration under rule 70. A 'claim' is defined in rule 1(1) as 'any proceedings before an Employment Tribunal making a complaint'. In turn, a 'complaint' means anything that is referred to as a 'claim, complaint, reference, application or appeal in any enactment which confers jurisdiction on the Tribunal'. The new definition of a 'judgment' is not too dissimilar from the definition that was set out under old rule 28(1)(a) of the Tribunal Rules 2004, which defined this in terms of 'a final determination of the proceedings or of a particular issue in those proceedings; it may include an award of compensation, a declaration or recommendation and it may also include orders for costs, preparation time or wasted costs'.

15.4

A decision that relates solely to the response to a claim – for example, the striking out of the response (or part of the response) under rule 37 of the Tribunal Rules 2013 because it has not been actively pursued – will not be open to reconsideration in accordance with the power provided by rule 70. This is because the decision to strike out the response does not of itself finally determine the claim or any issue which is capable of finally disposing of the claim. It therefore does not fall within the definition of a 'judgment' for the purposes of a reconsideration under rule 70. But any decision made in determination of the claim following the rejection, striking out or dismissal of a response (including what is commonly referred to as a default judgment) will constitute a 'judgment' and therefore may be challenged under the rule 70 reconsideration procedure – see 'Reconsideration of a default judgment' below.

However, while a decision may not (depending on the above) constitute a judgment and therefore may not be challenged under the reconsideration procedure set out in rules 70–73, it may nevertheless be challenged under separate provisions in the Tribunal Rules. This is discussed under 'Challenging other tribunal decisions and orders' below.

Reconsideration of decision to reject claim, response or counterclaim 15.5

Under the old Tribunal Rules 2004, a decision not to accept a claim, response or counterclaim was specifically listed as being a reviewable decision – old rule 34(1)(a). Such decisions are not expressly included as being open to reconsideration under the general power now set out in rule 70 of the Tribunal Rules 2013. Instead, separate express provisions exist for the reconsideration of such decisions: in particular, the reconsideration of a decision to reject a claim (including a counterclaim) falls under rule 13; and the reconsideration of a decision to reject a response falls under rule 19. These provisions are discussed in detail in, respectively, Chapter 4, 'Starting tribunal proceedings', under 'Processing the claim form – reconsideration of rejection', and Chapter 6, 'Defending a claim', under 'Processing the response – reconsideration of rejection of response'. Suffice it to say here that they allow for the reconsideration of a decision to reject a claim, response or counterclaim where the original decision to reject was wrong or where the notified defect (such as failure to include minimum information or failure to use the prescribed form) can be rectified. In order to bring an application for the reconsideration of a claim, response or counterclaim within rule 70, the claimant or respondent will have to satisfy the tribunal that the initial decision to reject falls within the strict definition of 'judgment' under rule 1(3)(b), as set out under 'What decisions constitute a "judgment"?' above.

Rejection of a claim. A decision to reject a claim may be open to reconsideration 15.6 under rule 70. A claim (or part) is treated as having been rejected if the claimant fails to include the necessary minimum information, fails to use the prescribed form, fails to pay the claim fee (or submit a remission application), or an employment judge considers that the claim is one which a tribunal has no jurisdiction to consider, is in a form that cannot sensibly be responded to, or is otherwise an abuse of process (rules 10, 11 and 12). It could be argued that a decision to reject a claim on any of these grounds involves the determination of 'any issue' which is capable of finally disposing of the claim within the terms of rule 1(3)(b), and thus that it constitutes a judgment for the purposes of the reconsideration power in rule 70.

Rejection of a counterclaim. Rule 23 of the Tribunal Rules 2013 provides that 15.7 an employer's contract claim (i.e. a counterclaim) may be rejected on the same basis as a claimant's claim may be rejected under rule 12 – namely, that an employment judge considers that the counterclaim is one which a tribunal has no jurisdiction to consider, is in a form that cannot sensibly be responded to, or is otherwise an abuse of process – in which case rule 13, 'Reconsideration of a

813

rejection', applies. Therefore, a decision to reject a respondent's counterclaim is treated in the same way as a decision to reject a claimant's claim for the purpose of reconsideration. The definition of a 'claim' in rule 1(1) can include a respondent's counterclaim – referred to as an 'employer's contract claim' – and so, like a claimant's claim, it could possibly be argued that a decision to reject an employer's contract claim involves the determination of 'any issue' that is capable of finally disposing of that claim such as to constitute a 'judgment' for the purposes of rule 1(3)(b). If that contention were to be accepted, the rejection of the contract claim would be open to reconsideration under the general power in rule 70.

15.8 **Rejection of a response.** The rejection of a response, on the other hand, does not of itself finally determine the claim, or part of the claim, as regards liability, remedy or costs, or any issue which is capable of finally disposing of any claim, or part of a claim, for the purposes of the definition of 'judgment' in rule 1(3)(b). This only occurs when, following the rejection of the response, the tribunal proceeds to make an actual determination of the claim and, where appropriate, issues a judgment accordingly. It follows that a further process is necessary following the rejection of a response before the relevant claim can be regarded as having been determined or disposed of. A respondent's only course of action in a case where its response has been rejected may be to seek a reconsideration under rule 19 on the basis that the decision to reject the response was wrong or that the notified defect can be rectified, failing which an appeal may be pursued to the EAT.

15.9 **Relying on alternative bases for securing reconsideration.** If a party believes without being absolutely certain that a decision to reject a claim, response or counterclaim does fall within the definition of 'judgment', it will be open to it to apply for reconsideration of the decision on alternative bases (i.e. pursuant to the general power to reconsider a judgment under rule 70 and the power to reconsider a decision to reject the claim (including a counterclaim) or response under rules 13 or 19 respectively). This could be beneficial where the claimant or respondent is unable to satisfy the test set out in rule 13 or rule 19 – i.e. that the original decision to reject was wrong or that the notified defect, such as failure to include minimum information or failure to use the prescribed form, can be rectified – but is nonetheless able to satisfy the more general 'interests of justice' test under rule 70 – see 'Grounds for reconsideration' below. And even if the challenge cannot be brought under rule 70 in the alternative, this may not be the end of the party's capacity to challenge the rejection on the interests of justice ground – see discussion under 'Challenging other tribunal decisions and orders' below.

15.10 **Reconsideration of prior reconsideration.** The question may arise of whether a party who is disappointed by a decision regarding a reconsideration – whether that be the refusal of an application for a reconsideration or the actual

814

conclusion reached by the tribunal after conducting a reconsideration of a prior judgment – can apply for that decision itself to be reconsidered. In answering this, it has again to be borne in mind that only 'judgments' (and not mere 'decisions') are susceptible to reconsideration within the terms of rule 70. As mentioned above, rules 13 and 19 deal separately with the reconsideration of a decision to reject a claim, response or counterclaim (or part of a claim, response or counterclaim). The exclusion of a decision made under these rules from the definition of 'judgment' in rule 1(3)(b) is no doubt intended to stop a claimant or respondent from applying for a 'reconsideration of a prior reconsideration'. In other words, if a party's application for a reconsideration of a tribunal's decision to reject a claim or counterclaim (under rule 13) or response (under rule 19) is unsuccessful, it cannot then seek reconsideration of that decision under rule 70. Equally, it would seem bizarre if, having undertaken a reconsideration of a judgment, a tribunal's conclusion confirming, varying or revoking that judgment were to be regarded as a 'judgment' so as to allow a party to apply for a further reconsideration under that rule. Such a potentially never-ending loop would stray into the world of Alice in Wonderland. In either of the situations mentioned above, the disappointed party's only option is to pursue an appeal to the EAT, assuming that an error of law can be identified and that the time limit for lodging an appeal has not expired.

Reconsideration of rejection of claim for failure to pay fee   15.11
Rule 13 of the Tribunal Rules 2013 stipulates that a claimant whose claim has been rejected under rules 10 or 12 may apply for a reconsideration of that decision on the basis that it was wrong or that a notified defect in the application can be rectified. Those rules deal with the rejection of claims because of the failure to use the prescribed form, failure to supply mandatory information or because of some substantive defect in the ground of the claim. It is notable that rule 13 does not apply to the rejection of claims pursuant to rule 11, which deals with decisions to reject because the claim was not accompanied by a tribunal issue fee or fee remission application.

So if rule 13 does not apply, is there any other basis by which a claimant can seek a reconsideration of the decision to reject his or her claim owing to non-payment of the appropriate fee or failure to apply for remission of the fee? Certainly, rule 11 itself, in providing that 'the tribunal shall reject a claim if it is not accompanied by a tribunal fee or a remission application', makes no specific provision for the claimant to apply for a 'reconsideration' of a tribunal's decision to reject. Furthermore, rule 40 – which states that where a party has not paid a 'relevant Tribunal fee', the tribunal will send the party a notice specifying a date for payment – is expressed to be 'subject to rule 11'. In other words, rule 40 applies to all fees except issue fees. This suggests that a claimant has no second chance to pay the issue fee once the time limit for presenting the claim has expired, and the rejection of a claim for non-payment would appear

815

to be the end of the road, so far as proceedings in the employment tribunal are concerned.

15.12 The only option a claimant has to apply for a reconsideration of a decision to reject the claim pursuant to rule 11 is to argue that such a decision can be reconsidered under the general power contained in rule 70. However, as discussed above, that rule only applies in respect of 'judgments' as defined by rule 1(3)(b). It is far from clear that a decision to reject owing to a failure to pay the appropriate fee or apply for remission would constitute a 'judgment' for those purposes. At a pinch, such a decision might be argued to be 'an issue which is capable of finally disposing of any claim' within the terms of rule 1(3)(b)(ii) and thus constitute a 'judgment', but we regard this as unlikely. Rule 1(3)(b)(ii) itself gives two examples of such an 'issue' – namely, whether a claim should be struck out, or an issue affecting the tribunal's jurisdiction. It takes some stretch of the imagination to regard a decision to reject a claim for non-payment as being analogous to these kinds of issue. It may be, therefore, that if a claimant fails to pay the fee he or she cannot in any circumstances obtain a reconsideration of a decision to reject.

Of course, if the time limit for presenting the claim has yet to expire, the claimant will have the opportunity to present a further claim with the appropriate fee (or remission application). It is also perhaps worth noting that if the rejection of the claim for non-payment/failure to submit a remission application is due to a 'clerical mistake' or 'accidental slip', an employment judge 'may at any time' correct this under rule 69 – see 'Correcting mistakes' below.

15.13 Reconsideration of automatic strike-out/dismissal of claim or response

Rule 38(1) of the Tribunal Rules 2013 provides that an order of an employment tribunal may specify that unless it is complied with by a specified date the claim or response (or part of it) will be dismissed without further order. For more information about these so-called 'unless orders' see Chapter 11, 'Case management', under 'Unless orders'. Rule 39(1) further provides that where at a preliminary hearing a tribunal considers that any specific allegation or argument in a claim or response has little reasonable prospect of success, 'it may make an order requiring a party ("the paying party") to pay a deposit not exceeding £1,000 as a condition of continuing to advance that allegation or argument'. Where the relevant party fails to pay by the date specified, the specific allegation or argument to which the deposit order relates will be struck out – rule 39(4). Such 'deposit orders' are also discussed in Chapter 11, 'Case management', under 'Deposit orders'. The issue of whether and to what extent a party may challenge either of these types of order by way of an application for reconsideration is discussed immediately below.

Unless orders. In Uyanwa-Odu and anor v Schools Offices Services Ltd and 15.14 anor EAT 0294/05 (a case decided under the Tribunal Rules 2004) the EAT held that an unless order is akin to a conditional judgment that becomes a final determination of proceedings if and when the party fails to comply with the order, and was therefore open to review (now 'reconsideration' under rule 70). However, in the later case of North Tyneside Primary Care Trust v Aynsley and ors 2009 ICR 1333, EAT, the EAT held that this only applies in relation to the dismissal of a claim, as opposed to a response, following non-compliance with an unless order. That case involved equal pay claims brought by female nurses against a primary care trust. An employment judge ordered that the Trust's response would be struck out if it failed to comply with an earlier order for disclosure of claimants' and comparators' employment details. Following non-compliance, the Trust's response was automatically struck out and an employment judge subsequently rejected an application to review the strike-out. On appeal, the EAT held that the decision to strike out a response for non-compliance with an unless order is not a 'judgment' as it does not give rise to a final determination of the proceedings. Therefore, it was not capable of being reviewed. Instead, the Trust was in the same position as a respondent who had failed to present a response and was liable to have a default judgment issued against it. Since the judge had not made a default judgment, the review provisions did not come into play.

In the light of the above decisions, a claimant whose claim is dismissed for non-compliance with an unless order issued in accordance with rule 38 may apply for a reconsideration under rule 70 on the basis that when the order's operation is triggered by non-compliance the resulting dismissal of the claim represents a final determination of the claim (i.e. a judgment) within the meaning of rule 1(3)(b). However, a respondent whose response is dismissed for non-compliance with an unless order cannot apply for a reconsideration under rule 70 because the dismissal of the response does not fall within the meaning of a 'judgment'.

Having said that, rule 38(2) specifically provides that a party whose claim or 15.15 response has been dismissed in whole or in part for non-compliance with an 'unless order' may apply to have the order set aside on the basis that it is in the interests of justice to do so. Such an application has to be made in writing within 14 days of the date that notice of the dismissal was sent to the parties.

Despite the distinction drawn between an 'order' and a 'judgment' for the purpose of determining under which provisions the dismissal of the response for non-compliance can be challenged, it is worth noting that the test a tribunal is required to apply when considering whether to vary, suspend or set aside an unless order under rule 38(2) is in fact the same as the test it is required to apply for reconsideration of a judgment under rule 70 – i.e. that it is 'necessary in the interests of justice'. It follows that it is of little consequence that a respondent is unable to challenge the dismissal of its response by applying for a

817

reconsideration under rule 70 given that the same thing can more or less be achieved by an application pursuant to rule 38(2).

15.16 The striking out of a claim or a response following non-compliance with an unless order may also be appealed to the EAT provided that an error of law can be identified and the appellant pays the appropriate appeal fee.

15.17 **Deposit orders.** There is no right to apply for reconsideration pursuant to rule 70 of an employment tribunal's decision to issue a deposit order in accordance with rule 39(1) requiring a party to pay a deposit as a condition for pursuing an allegation or argument that is thought to have little reasonable prospect of success. Nor is it possible to ask for the amount ordered to be deposited to be reconsidered. Neither decision constitutes a 'judgment' within the meaning of rule 1(3)(b). However, a tribunal is empowered to 'vary, suspend or set aside an earlier case management order' under rule 29 (which would include a decision to impose a deposit order). Accordingly, something very akin to reconsideration can be achieved by applying for the deposit order to be varied, suspended or set aside under rule 29. For more information, see the discussion under 'Challenging other tribunal decisions and orders' below.

The position regarding the applicability of the reconsideration process is very different in respect of a decision to dismiss a claim or response for non-compliance with a deposit order once made. In Sodexho Ltd v Gibbons 2005 ICR 1647, EAT, the EAT held that the definition of a 'judgment' that existed under rule 28(1)(a) of the Tribunal Rules 2004 – namely, 'a final determination of the proceedings or of a particular issue in those proceedings' – covered the striking out of a claim for non-payment of a deposit and that, therefore, such a striking out was reviewable. His Honour Judge Peter Clark rejected the claimant's argument that a striking out on this ground is merely an administrative act rather than a judicial decision because the employment judge has no discretion as to whether a claim should be struck out for non-payment of a deposit and there is no consideration of the merits of the claim. On the basis of the decision in Sodexho, it would seem that a striking out of a claim following a claimant's failure to comply with an order to pay a deposit is a 'judgment' for the purposes of rule 1(3)(b) of the Tribunal Rules 2013, and therefore can be the subject of a reconsideration under rule 70.

15.18 However, for the same reasons as were discussed above in respect of 'unless orders', the striking out of a response following a respondent's failure to comply with an order to pay a deposit would not constitute a 'judgment' for the purposes of the provisions on reconsideration – see North Tyneside Primary Care Trust v Aynsley and ors (above). It is merely an 'order' – more particularly, an 'automatic' strike-out order. In contrast, however, to the provisions of rule 38 dealing with unless orders, rule 39 contains no express provision under which the parties can challenge the striking out of a claim or response for failure to pay a deposit. Having said that, in the Aynsley case the EAT held that the automatic strike-out of the response was an order that could be revisited in accordance with the employment tribunal's general power to vary, suspend or revoke case management orders under what was then rule 10(2)(n) of the 2004 Rules and is now rule 29 of the Tribunal Rules 2013. A respondent should therefore be entitled to apply under rule 30 for the order to be varied, suspended or set aside – see 'Challenging other tribunal decisions and orders' below. The automatic strike-out of a claim or a response, or part of a claim or response, under rule 39 may also be appealed to the EAT where an error of law can be identified and the appropriate appeal fee (if applicable) is paid.

Reconsideration of a default judgment   15.19
Unlike under the old Tribunal Rules 2004, there is no separate rule in the Tribunal Rules 2013 providing for the reconsideration of 'default judgments'. In fact, the term 'default judgment' is not used in the Rules. However, rule 21 makes similar – albeit less draconian – provision for judgment against and debarring of respondents consequent on failure to present a response, and for where a received response is rejected or where the respondent has stated that no part of the claim is contested. In any of these cases an employment judge will decide whether, on the available material, a determination can properly be made of the claim. If a determination can be made, then a judgment will be issued accordingly. Otherwise a hearing will be fixed before a judge alone – rule 21(2). The respondent will be sent notice of any hearings and decisions of the tribunal but, unless and until an extension of time for submitting a response is granted, shall only be entitled to participate in any hearing to the extent permitted by the judge – rule 21(3).

While there is no specific power reserved for the reconsideration of rule 21 judgments, the tribunal's general power under rule 70 applies: the definition of 'judgment' for this purpose (see 'What decisions constitute a "judgment"?' above) is wide enough to include judgments made under rule 21 and, unlike the old default judgments, they are not expressly excluded from the general power of reconsideration. This is confirmed by the Presidential Guidance on Rule 21 Judgments issued on 4 December 2013, which states that any party wishing to seek a reconsideration of a decision in connection with the grant or refusal to grant a rule 21 judgment must make an application in accordance with the provisions of rules 70–72 – para 7.

Grounds for reconsideration   15.20

Under old rule 34 of the Tribunal Rules 2004, there were five grounds upon which a tribunal could review a judgment (not including a default judgment). These were:

- that the decision was wrongly made as a result of an administrative error – old rule 34(3)(a)

819

- that a party did not receive notice of the proceedings leading to the decision – old rule 34(3)(b)

- that the decision was made in the absence of a party – old rule 34(3)(c)

- that new evidence had become available since the conclusion of the tribunal hearing to which the decision related, the existence of which could not have been reasonably known of or foreseen at that time – old rule 34(3)(d); and/or

- that the interests of justice required a review – old rule 34(3)(e).

(In the case of a default judgment, old rule 33(2) required the party making the application to show good reason why the default judgment should be varied or revoked.)

15.21   Under the Tribunal Rules 2013 only one of these grounds is carried forward – namely, that a reconsideration *is necessary in the interests of justice*. The absence of official commentary to explain this significant change to the rules is surprising, especially as the other specific grounds for review had been retained through a number of previous versions of the Rules. However, while there is no official line as to whether it is intended that those other grounds now fall within the remit of the 'interests of justice', and while some of the old case law suggests that this ground should not be viewed simply as a catch-all, it is generally accepted that this ground for a reconsideration is broad enough to embrace the other four specific grounds upon which a review could previously be based. This proposition is supported by the fact that it was, in fact, commonplace for parties making applications for a review based on one of these grounds to rely additionally or in the alternative on the 'interests of justice' ground and indeed for tribunals to cite that ground as justifying a review in addition to one of the other more specific grounds.

There is an underlying public policy principle in all proceedings of a judicial nature that there should be finality in litigation. Reconsiderations are thus best seen as limited exceptions to the general rule that employment tribunal decisions should not be reopened and relitigated. It is not a method by which a disappointed party to proceedings can get a second bite of the cherry. In Stevenson v Golden Wonder Ltd 1977 IRLR 474, EAT, Lord McDonald said of the old review provisions that they were 'not intended to provide parties with the opportunity of a re-hearing at which the same evidence can be rehearsed with different emphasis, or further evidence adduced which was available before'. Courts and tribunals will no doubt view the reconsideration provisions in the same manner.

15.22   **'Interests of justice'**
Under rule 70 of the Tribunal Rules 2013, a judgment will only be reconsidered where it is 'necessary in the interests of justice to do so'. This ground gives an

employment tribunal wide discretion, but the case law that considered the same ground under the old review procedures suggests that it will be carefully applied. It does not mean that in every case where a litigant is unsuccessful he or she is automatically entitled to a reconsideration: virtually every unsuccessful litigant thinks that the interests of justice require the decided outcome to be reconsidered. The ground only applies where something has gone radically wrong with the procedure involving a denial of natural justice or something of that order – Fforde v Black EAT 68/80.

This basis for a reconsideration can be used to correct errors that occur in the course of proceedings regardless of whether the error was a major or a minor one – Trimble v Supertravel Ltd 1982 ICR 440, EAT. In that case, the employment tribunal found that the claimant had been unfairly dismissed and, without hearing her solicitor on the issue of compensation, announced that she would get no compensatory award because of failure to mitigate her loss. The alleged failure to mitigate was based entirely on the claimant's conduct before dismissal, whereas, in law, mitigation of loss is focused on events that follow dismissal rather than those that precede it. The tribunal thought it had no jurisdiction to review its decision since the point raised was a major point of law that should be taken on appeal to the EAT. The EAT agreed that a tribunal's error as to the nature of the duty to mitigate was usually a matter best dealt with by way of appeal but said that it was clear that the tribunal in this case had reached its finding without allowing the claimant's solicitor to make submissions on the point. This amounted to a procedural mishap which the tribunal should have rectified by granting a review. In so holding, the EAT made the following observations:

- it is irrelevant whether a tribunal's alleged error is major or minor

- what is relevant is whether or not a decision has been reached after a procedural mishap

- since, in the instant case, the tribunal had reached its decision on the point in issue without hearing representations, it would have been appropriate for it to hear argument and to grant the review if satisfied that it had gone wrong

- if a matter has been ventilated and properly argued, then any error of law falls to be corrected on appeal and not by review.

Are exceptional circumstances required? More recent case law, however, **15.23** suggests that the 'interests of justice' ground should not be construed as restrictively as it was prior to the introduction of the 'overriding objective' by the Tribunal Rules 2001, which is now set out in rule 2 of the Tribunal Rules 2013. This requires an employment tribunal to seek to give effect to the overriding objective (to deal with cases fairly and justly) whenever it exercises a power conferred by the rules or is required to interpret its provisions. (For

821

more information about the overriding objective see Chapter 1, 'Employment tribunals', under 'What are employment tribunals? – employment tribunal rules'.) In Williams v Ferrosan Ltd 2004 IRLR 607, EAT, the EAT had the opportunity to reconsider earlier case law that had stressed that a review on the basis of the 'interests of justice' ground was only appropriate in 'exceptional circumstances'. Such cases preceded the introduction of the overriding objective. The EAT held that, in light of the overriding objective, there was, in fact, no reason for an 'exceptionality hurdle' and that 'there is a difference between saying that a case to which [the interests of justice ground] applies will in practice be unusual or exceptional and saying that [the interests of justice ground] should be read as if inserted into it are the words "exceptional circumstances"'. In this particular case the EAT granted a review where the calculation of compensation was based on a mistaken view about the taxation of future loss of earnings by both parties and the tribunal chairman.

Applying the approach taken in Williams v Ferrosan Ltd, the EAT in Sodexho Ltd v Gibbons 2005 ICR 1647, EAT, held that an employment judge in that case had been entitled to review the striking out of a claim following the claimant's failure to comply with a deposit order on the basis that it was in the interests of justice. Although in the past this ground for review had been restrictively construed, the employment judge had acted properly in the light of the overriding objective of dealing with cases justly by balancing the interests of both parties. The judge had thus been entitled to carry out a review of the decision to strike out, and to revoke it.

15.24   The EAT again considered the extent to which a review was in the interests of justice in Newcastle upon Tyne City Council v Marsden 2010 ICR 743, EAT. That case concerned a claimant who was wrongly advised by counsel not to attend a pre-hearing review which was held to determine whether or not he had a disability within the meaning of the Disability Discrimination Act 1995. In his absence, an employment judge found that the claimant had failed to provide evidence to establish that the effects of his injury were long term and, consequently, that he did not have a disability within the meaning of the DDA. The judge therefore dismissed the claim. On review, the judge revoked his original decision when it became clear that counsel had misled the tribunal by failing to tell it that it was his advice that had caused the claimant not to attend the PHR and that counsel should have sought an adjournment, which in the circumstances would have been granted. In doing so, the judge observed that the overriding objective meant that the interests of justice ground for granting review did not have to be construed restrictively, as earlier case law had suggested. The judge regarded such case law as having been superseded by the introduction of the overriding objective.

On the employer's appeal the EAT accepted that the employment judge had gone too far in asserting that the interests of justice ground did not have to be construed restrictively, since the overriding objective to deal with cases justly required the application of recognised principles. These included finality of litigation, which was in the interests of both parties. The EAT went on to observe that the cases of Williams v Ferrosan Ltd (above) and Sodexho Ltd v Gibbons (above) clearly showed that the earlier extensive case law in relation to the 'interests of justice' ground should not be regarded as requiring tribunals to apply particular, and restrictive, formulae when considering applications for review under that head. However, the EAT also stressed that, while cases such as Lindsay v Ironsides Ray and Vials 1994 ICR 384, EAT, and Flint v Eastern Electricity Board 1975 ICR 395, QBD (discussed below), should not be regarded as establishing propositions of law that drive towards the same conclusive answer in every apparently similar case, the principles underlying those decisions remain valid.

Turning to the facts of the particular case in front of it, the EAT concluded that **15.25** the importance of maintaining finality of litigation was outweighed by the injustice to the claimant and the employment judge's substantive decision to grant a review was therefore correct. Given that the judge had found that the claimant's counsel had been guilty of misconduct in misleading the tribunal and had deprived his client of the advantage of an adjourned hearing, this amounted to an exceptional circumstance distinguishable from the ordinary case of a party being wrongly advised by his representative, where the overall interests of justice might well require that party to bear the consequences. Given that the employer had suffered no prejudice beyond the fact that the case would have to be reopened, the EAT held that it was appropriate to revoke the original decision.

Interests have to be seen from both sides. It is clear that the interests of justice **15.26** as a ground for reconsideration relate to the interests of justice to both sides. In Redding v EMI Leisure Ltd EAT 262/81 the claimant appealed against an employment tribunal's rejection of her application for a review of its judgment. She argued that it was in the interests of justice to do so because she had not understood the case against her and had failed to do herself justice when presenting her claim. The EAT observed that: 'When you boil down what is said on [the claimant's] behalf, it really comes down to this: that she did not do herself justice at the hearing, so justice requires that there should be a second hearing so that she may. Now, "justice" means justice to both parties. It is not said, and, as we see it, cannot be said that any conduct of the case by the employers here caused [the claimant] not to do herself justice. It was, we are afraid, her own inexperience in the situation.' Accordingly, the claimant's appeal failed.

Article 6 ECHR. The interests of justice must be exercised consistently with **15.27** the right to a fair trial under Article 6(1) of the European Convention on Human Rights, which is incorporated into UK law by the Human Rights Act

823

1998. This includes the need for judges to be independent and impartial in order to preserve public confidence in the administration of justice. In City and County of Swansea v Honey EAT 0030/08 the EAT referred to this fundamental principle when determining whether a review should have been granted in a case where an allegation of bias was being made against one of the lay members who had participated in the employment tribunal hearing. In that case, one of the tribunal lay members was District Secretary of the RMT trade union and, at the time of the hearing of the case, was involved in that capacity in a dispute with the respondent regarding the licensing of taxi cabs. He had criticised the respondent openly in a press statement and was reported by the local press as having 'blasted' the respondent's explanation of the dispute as 'extremely biased' and as having shown 'very poor leadership and inefficiency'. The respondent's legal services department did not become aware of the lay member's involvement in the taxi licensing dispute until after the tribunal merits hearing, at which point the legal advisers unsuccessfully sought a review (now a reconsideration) on the interests of justice ground citing apparent bias.

On appeal, the EAT held that there was a clear case of apparent bias on the part of the tribunal lay member and it should have been quite plain to the lay member that he was required to recuse himself from participating in the hearing. The demands of impartiality therefore required a review of the tribunal's decision. The EAT said that if grounds exist that are sufficient to create in the mind of the fair-minded and informed objective observer a doubt about a judge's impartiality then there is apparent bias which amounts to a breach of Article 6. The fundamental duty to afford parties a fair hearing before an impartial tribunal – i.e. a tribunal that is free of not just real but apparent bias – must be borne in mind, and the practical difficulties in identifying problematic circumstances in advance are as irrelevant to the question of whether or not that duty has been performed as are questions of the inconvenience, expense and delay involved in starting the hearing again.

15.28 **Errors by parties' representatives.** Ordinarily, it will not be in the interests of justice to reconsider a judgment because of an error made by a party's representative. In Lindsay v Ironsides Ray and Vials 1994 ICR 384, EAT, an employment tribunal had reviewed its decision that an application was presented out of time on the basis that the claimant's representative had not made any submissions on the issue of the tribunal's discretion to allow a late application. The EAT ruled that failings of a party's representative – professional or otherwise – would not usually constitute a ground for review. If it were otherwise, there would be the risk that disappointed claimants would be encouraged to re-argue their cases by blaming their representatives. This would mean that tribunals would have to investigate the competence of representatives who would not be given the opportunity of defending themselves. Complaints about the conduct and competence of representatives should not be dealt with by way of tribunal proceedings.

This case can be distinguished from Newcastle upon Tyne City Council v Marsden (discussed under 'Are exceptional circumstances required?' above), in which an employment tribunal allowed a review on the basis of the claimant's representative's error. Once the tribunal in Marsden was aware that the claimant's counsel had advised him not to attend the hearing, it was within the tribunal's knowledge that it had been misled by that counsel, who had not made the tribunal aware of this. It therefore did not need to investigate the representative's conduct.

A reconsideration might be justified, however, if a 'procedural mishap' occurs **15.29** due to the conduct of the other party's representative. In Shortall t/a Auction Centres v Carey EAT 351/93 the employment tribunal felt that it was in the interests of justice to review a decision on compensation. The initial decision had been made without reference to the provision that is now contained in S.122(2) of the Employment Rights Act 1996 allowing a tribunal to reduce the basic award for unfair dismissal where there has been misconduct on the part of the employee. Although the failure to consider the statutory provision was an error of law, the EAT held that it was perfectly proper for the tribunal to conduct a review because the relevance of the subsection was not brought to its attention in the course of the hearing. The employer was not legally represented and the barrister representing the employee should, according to the Bar's code of conduct, have referred the tribunal to the provision even though to do so would not have been in his client's interest.

Another example of a procedural mishap is found in Smith v Clarke EAT 617/84. In that case the employment tribunal reached a decision on both liability and compensation in relation to unfair dismissal having heard evidence only on liability. Because nothing had been said during the hearing about assessment of compensation, the claimant's representative assumed that there would, if necessary, be a separate hearing on that issue. In fact, the tribunal took the view that as nothing had been said about compensation it had carte blanche to make whatever order it thought fit. The EAT held that it was essential that the parties to a case were left in no doubt as to the procedure that the tribunal intended to follow. In this particular case there had been a very striking misunderstanding and the interests of justice required a review.

In Obonyo v Wandsworth Primary Care Trust EAT 0237/07 the EAT held that **15.30** a review should have been allowed in the interests of justice to clarify the terms of a consent order. After an initial tribunal award to O in the net sum of £108,000 had been set aside in part on appeal to the EAT and remitted, a consent order made by a second tribunal for £104,000 failed to specify whether it was net or gross. On appeal, the EAT held that the tribunal had wrongly refused an application for review (either to set aside the consent order on the ground of mistake or to clarify it). The EAT set aside the tribunal's decision and

825

substituted a decision that the consent order was on the same terms as the original award – i.e. net and without deduction of tax by the employer.

15.31 **Events occurring after the tribunal hearing.** Events that occur subsequent to a hearing may justify a reconsideration in the interests of justice. Two examples of cases decided in relation to the old procedure of 'review' that would arguably justify a reconsideration under rule 70 of the Tribunal Rules 2013:

- **Help the Aged Housing Association (Scotland) Ltd v Vidler** 1977 IRLR 104, EAT: V was awarded unfair dismissal compensation based on two years' loss of salary because the employment tribunal thought that, at the age of 60, he was unlikely to find another job. But V did find another job two weeks later. The EAT held that the substratum of the tribunal's reasoning in assessing compensation had disappeared and that it should have reviewed its decision in the light of this new evidence

- **Ladup Ltd v Barnes** 1982 ICR 107, EAT: B was arrested and charged with cultivation and possession of cannabis. His employer promptly dismissed him without further investigation. An employment tribunal found the dismissal to be unfair and awarded compensation on the basis that B had not contributed to it. Shortly afterwards, B was convicted in the Crown Court of possessing cannabis but the employment judge refused to review the decision. The EAT held that this refusal created a blatant injustice and substituted a finding that B had contributed 100 per cent to his dismissal.

15.32 However, not every change in circumstances after a decision has been reached will justify a reconsideration. In Yorkshire Engineering and Welding Co Ltd v Burnham 1974 ICR 77, NIRC, the National Industrial Relations Court held that the test for tribunals considering applications for review of remedies decisions in which the compensation awarded includes an element of future loss was whether the forecasts that were the basis for the decision have been falsified to a sufficiently substantial extent to invalidate their assessment and whether the falsification occurred so soon after the decision that a review is necessary in the interests of justice. In that case the claimant had testified that he expected to get a new job at not more than £36.50 a week and the tribunal calculated unfair dismissal compensation accordingly. In the event he secured a job at £40.38 a week. The NIRC said that this difference was not sufficiently substantial to warrant a review of the tribunal's decision. The tribunal's errors fell well within the range of error inherent in any form of forecasting.

15.33 **Decision wrongly made as a result of administrative error.** Old rule 34(3)(a) of the Tribunal Rules 2004 provided that a decision could be reviewed on the ground that it 'was wrongly made as a result of an administrative error'. In Sodexho Ltd v Gibbons 2005 ICR 1647, EAT, the claimant had given the wrong post code for his solicitor when completing the ET1, and this led to a delay in serving a deposit order on the claimant's solicitor which ultimately led to the tribunal striking out the claim for non-payment of the deposit. In upholding the tribunal's decision to review the striking-out order, the EAT held that 'administrative error' included errors by the parties as well as by tribunal staff (but not tribunal judges). The dictionary definition of 'administrative' as 'pertaining to the management of affairs' was apt to include completion of the ET1 form by the claimant. Therefore, the tribunal was entitled to review the decision on this ground.

Although there no longer exists a separate ground for reconsideration of a judgment on the basis that it was wrongly made as a result of an administrative error, such an argument could form the basis of the grounds used to satisfy the interests of justice test. In fact, in the Sodexho case the employment tribunal had found that, in the alternative, the interests of justice required a review. The EAT held, by having regard to the overriding objective and balancing the interests of both parties, that the tribunal judge had correctly adopted an approach consistent with the overriding objective.

15.34 It is worth noting here that some errors, even though clerical mistakes by the tribunal staff, may be more appropriately dealt with under the 'slip rule' (see 'Correcting mistakes' below).

15.35 **Non-receipt of notice of proceedings.** Under the Tribunal Rules 2004, if a party did not receive the notice of a hearing and this led to a judgment being made at the hearing in his or her absence, this provided a legitimate ground for a review – old rule 34(3)(b). This may provide an equally legitimate basis for a reconsideration under the interests of justice ground under rule 70 of the Tribunal Rules 2013.

However, it can often be difficult to establish non-receipt of a notice in practice. In nearly all cases notices of hearing are sent by the tribunal via first-class post, which means that the provision as to deemed service in rule 90 applies. This stipulates that, once it is established that a document was properly addressed, stamped and posted, it will be presumed – unless the contrary is proved – that it was received by the party to which it was sent on the day on which the notice 'would be delivered in the ordinary course of post', unless the contrary is proved. This means on the second day after posting (excluding Sundays and bank holidays) in the case of first-class mail. The burden is on the party alleging that the document was not received to prove that this was so. It is usually difficult to prove the negative and rebut the presumption.

15.36 In T and D Transport (Portsmouth) Ltd v Limburn 1987 ICR 696, EAT, the EAT confirmed that, where it can be shown that a notice was properly sent, the applying party must satisfy the tribunal that the notice was not properly received. This decision was made under antecedent rules of procedure but the same principles still apply. While the notice must be properly addressed for the presumption of effective service to apply, this is treated in a commonsense way

827

by tribunals. For example, in Genevieve Restaurants Ltd v Koura EAT 254/84 the employer appealed against the tribunal's decision, arguing that the omission of the word 'Limited' from its name on notices meant that the notices had not been properly served. In upholding the tribunal's decision, the EAT held that the employer's appeal was unreasonable and made an order for costs.

Furthermore, the inclusion of new rule 91, which deals with irregular service and states that a tribunal may treat any document as delivered notwithstanding non-compliance with the provisions for service in rules 86–88 provided that it is satisfied that the document (or its substance) has in fact come to the attention of the party, may make it even more difficult to secure a reconsideration in the interests of justice on the basis of non-receipt of a notice of proceedings.

15.37 **Judgment made in absence of a party.** Old rule 34(3)(c) of the Tribunal Rules 2004 provided that a judgment could be reviewed on the ground that it 'was made in the absence of a party'. However, this did not mean that a party could simply decline to attend the hearing, rely on written submissions and then apply for a review if the employment tribunal's decision was unfavourable. To succeed on this ground the party had to have a good reason for his or her absence from the hearing, such as illness or accident, or a genuine mistake about the hearing date. In Morris v Griffiths 1977 ICR 153, EAT, the Appeal Tribunal reviewed an employment tribunal judgment and ordered a rehearing when it accepted as genuine that the respondent employer had fallen ill on the way to the tribunal and had had to return home.

However, in Lewes Associates Ltd t/a Guido's Restaurant v Little EAT 0460/08 the EAT held that an employment tribunal was unarguably correct in refusing to revoke its decision to uphold the claimant's claim in the absence of the respondent, who had told the tribunal that she was unable to attend the hearing because of a bad back. The medical evidence subsequently provided stated only that she should refrain from work for a few days, not that she was unable to attend the hearing. A party who makes a conscious choice not to appear must take the consequences of that decision – Fforde v Black EAT 68/80.

15.38 In Lawton v British Railways Board EAT 29/80 the claimant arrived a day late for a tribunal hearing although he had received due notice. The tribunal held that this was 'carelessness of the grossest sort' and refused an application for review. The EAT held that this was wrong. The claimant had made a 'perfectly honest and genuine mistake' and the tribunal should have given due weight to this and granted a review hearing.

However, in GBM Services Ltd v Oyeghe EAT 402/92 a different division of the EAT adopted a stricter approach in respect of a party who was legally represented. In that case the employer failed to attend the hearing as it was under the impression that the hearing had been postponed. The employer's representative had reached an agreement with the employee that an application

828

for a postponement would not be opposed. The representative then sent the application for postponement by fax. Unfortunately, it was sent to the central office rather than to the appropriate regional office of the employment tribunals. As a result, when the time came for the hearing, the employer was not present and no application for a postponement had been received. The EAT held that the tribunal had been right not to order a review of the judgment reached at the hearing. The tribunal had clearly taken into account the fact that the employer's representative had been careless in not checking that the application for a postponement had been received and approved.

Many of the cases heard on this previous separate ground turned on whether **15.39** the tribunal believed that the reason for the absence was genuine. In Morris v Griffiths (above), the claimant appeared in person at the EAT with regard to his appeal against the tribunal's decision not to review its earlier judgment and the EAT decided that he was honest in his explanation for the absence from the employment tribunal hearing. This influenced its decision to order a review. The applying party's honesty will be just as relevant to the question of whether, pursuant to rule 70 of the Tribunal Rules 2013, it is in the interests of justice to reconsider a judgment made in that party's absence.

The existence now of only a sole ground for a reconsideration (namely, the 'interests of justice') is unlikely to mean that tribunals will become more favourably disposed to granting reconsideration applications based on the fact that a decision was made in the absence of a party than they were under old rule 34(3)(c). A tribunal will still require the applying party to provide a good reason for his or her absence along with any supporting evidence, and the tribunal will form a judgement about whether that reason is genuine. In addition, under rule 70, the party will also have to satisfy the tribunal that, owing to the reason for the original absence, it is *necessary* in the interests of justice for the tribunal's judgment to be reconsidered. This was not required under old rule 34(3)(c). As discussed above, 'the interests of justice' relates to the interests of justice to *both* parties. It is therefore possible that a tribunal may find that a party had a genuine good reason for failing to attend the hearing yet conclude that it is not in the interests of justice to reconsider the decision made in the absence of that party.

New evidence has become available. Old rule 34(3)(d) of the Tribunal Rules **15.40** 2004 provided a ground for review if 'new evidence [had become] available since the conclusion of the hearing to which the decision relates, provided that its existence could not have been reasonably known of or foreseen at that time'. This provision reflected the well-known principles for admission of new evidence on appeal in civil litigation set down by the Court of Appeal in Ladd v Marshall 1954 3 All ER 745, CA.

Seeking to adduce fresh evidence was one of the more frequent grounds for applying for a review under the previous Rules. Similarly, a party may argue

829

under the 2013 Rules that it is in the interests of justice to reconsider a judgment where new evidence has come to light. But though the Rules no longer contain a specific limitation to the effect that the new evidence must be shown not to have been reasonably known or foreseen at the time of the original hearing, it is highly likely that such limitations will still be rigorously applied even under the ostensibly more flexible 'interests of justice' ground for reconsidering a judgment. Tribunals will remain mindful of the fact that it is not generally in the interests of justice that parties in litigation should be given a second bite of the cherry simply because they have failed as a result of oversight or a miscall in their litigation strategy to adduce all the evidence available in support of their cases at the original hearing.

15.41 Furthermore, the employment tribunal will refuse an application for reconsideration on the 'interests of justice' ground unless the new evidence is likely to have an important bearing on the result of the case. In Wileman v Minilec Engineering Ltd 1988 ICR 318, EAT, the EAT said that the reason for this requirement is that unless the new evidence is likely to influence the decision, then 'a great deal of time will be taken up by sending cases back to an [employment] tribunal for no purpose'.

No doubt the same expectations as previously applied to applications for a review under the old Rules will continue to operate whenever a party seeks to apply for a reconsideration under rule 70 based on the availability of new evidence. Case law establishes that any such application should be accompanied by details of the evidence that is sought to be adduced – Vauxhall Motors Ltd v Henry EAT 846/77. The applicant should also explain why the evidence was not produced beforehand and why it is now in the interests of justice to consider that evidence.

15.42 New evidence generally takes the form of newly discovered documents or witnesses, but that is not always the case. For example, in Qureshi v Burnley Borough Council EAT 916/92 a successful claimant was alleged to have admitted to his employer that he had lied on oath when giving evidence to the tribunal. On conducting a review, the tribunal revoked its decision and ordered a fresh hearing, since the original decision had been reached on the basis that, where there were conflicts in evidence, these were to be resolved in the employee's favour. The EAT upheld that finding, equating the discovery that the evidence of the employee was unreliable with the discovery of new evidence that had direct bearing on the case.

15.43 *Better to appeal or apply for reconsideration?* Where new evidence relates to a crucial finding of fact, it is clear that the appropriate course is to apply for a reconsideration rather than to appeal to the EAT. In Adegbuji v Meteor Parking Ltd EAT 1570/09 the EAT stated that the correct course for a party seeking to challenge a tribunal decision on the basis of fresh evidence would almost always be to apply to the original tribunal for a review (now a reconsideration) rather than appeal against its decision. In such circumstances, a party should appeal to the EAT only if an application for reconsideration is refused. However, in Aslam v Barclays Capital Services and ors EAT 0405/10 the EAT revisited the guidance in Adegbuji and concluded that, in the particular circumstances of that case, a review would not be appropriate – the tribunal had made findings as to the credibility of witnesses that would be difficult for it to revisit – and the case should be remitted for a complete rehearing before a differently constituted tribunal. The Aslam case is a rare example of a fresh evidence challenge in which it would have been inappropriate for the original tribunal to conduct a review.

Two other illustrations which, though brought under the old review procedure, demonstrate the importance of pursuing the correct avenue for challenging a tribunal's prior judgment:

- **Green and Symons Ltd v Shickell and anor** EAT 528/83: the claimants had produced new evidence at the employment tribunal hearing. This was accepted and led to unfair dismissal findings in their favour. A subsequent investigation showed that the evidence was incorrect and the employer appealed to the EAT. The EAT dismissed the appeal: there was no error of law in the tribunal's decision and it had not been perverse on the evidence available to it. The employer should have applied for a review and £100 costs were awarded against it for bringing an unnecessary appeal

- **William P Harrower Ltd v Hogg** EAT 215/78: as a result of a police investigation, new evidence came to light that suggested that the successful claimant in an unfair dismissal case had committed perjury. The employer appealed to the EAT. The EAT thought that the interests of justice required the case to be remitted for a rehearing – but awarded costs against the employer for bringing an unnecessary appeal when the proper procedure was an application for review.

In Governing Body of St Andrew's Catholic Primary School v Blundell 2012 **15.44** ICR 295, CA, the Court of Appeal accepted that, in accordance with the EAT's guidance in Adegbuji v Meteor Parking Ltd (above), it is normally better to pursue a fresh evidence point by way of review rather than appeal. However, in that particular case the application to consider new evidence was bound up with an appeal by the employer against the tribunal's failure to deal with its application – made during legal submissions at the hearing – for disclosure of the item of new information that constituted the new evidence in question. The Court of Appeal therefore thought it right to consider the significance of fresh evidence in the context of the other ground of appeal. The fresh evidence in question (which was only obtained after the tribunal's judgment had been issued) revealed that the claimant was following an MA course during a period for which she had been awarded compensation on the ground that she was unable to work. The Court of Appeal concluded that justice required that the

831

award of compensation be reassessed in the light of this new evidence since it could materially alter the tribunal's assessment of the facts and its award of compensation. The issue was accordingly remitted to the same tribunal to conduct this exercise.

15.45 *Evidence available but not used.* There are many examples of applications for review under old rule 34(3)(d) being refused on the basis that the evidence was, in fact, available though deliberately or inadvertently not used. For example, in Flint v Eastern Electricity Board 1975 ICR 395, QBD, the employee was claiming a redundancy payment but did not disclose a medical condition that was relevant to whether or not he had unreasonably refused an offer of suitable employment, and sought to raise his medical condition on review as new evidence. It was held that he was not entitled to a review as the medical evidence was available at the time of the original hearing. Similarly, in General Council of British Shipping v Deria and ors 1985 ICR 198, EAT, the Appeal Tribunal decided that the claimants in a racial discrimination case who wanted their complaints reheard to take into account certain documentary evidence should be refused a review because the documents were available at the time of the original hearing.

However, in the Flint v Eastern Electricity Board case (above) it was held that, in theory, it was possible to obtain a review under the 'interests of justice' ground in order to introduce evidence that was available but not used, though only in exceptional circumstances. This means that it may be possible to argue that it is in the interests of justice to reconsider a judgment where evidence was available. Having said that, it is not entirely clear what 'exceptional circumstances' will qualify. In General Council of British Shipping v Deria (above) the EAT held, following the Flint case, that the circumstances must involve some mitigating factor relating to the failure to produce evidence in the first place. It was not enough that the so-called new evidence would probably have won the day for the claimant or that an issue of widespread public importance was involved.

15.46 The EAT's decision in Evans v Parasol Ltd and anor EAT 0536/08 may, it is contended, constitute an example of the 'special circumstances' mentioned above. In that case the claimant sought to pursue a claim for one month's contractual notice pay. However, the employment tribunal struck out the claim as having no reasonable prospect of success because her contract, presented to the tribunal by the respondent, stated that she was only entitled to one week's notice, which had been paid to her. After the decision to strike out had been made the claimant found an e-mail contradicting the terms of the contract and stating that she was entitled to one month's notice. The tribunal refused an application for a review of the strike-out decision based on the 'new' evidence but this refusal was subsequently overturned on appeal. The EAT noted that the strike-out decision had been made at a stage in the proceedings before any order for disclosure had been made. Had such an order been issued, it would have required the parties to disclose documents in their possession upon which they sought to rely (which would have embraced documents that weakened their own case). The effect of the strike-out was that the case never got as far as making the normal disclosure order. The EAT therefore held that it had been in the interests of justice for the tribunal to grant a review and, had it done so, the decision to strike out would inevitably have been set aside in the light of the e-mail evidence. The EAT therefore remitted the case for a full merits hearing.

Occasionally a party will be allowed to adduce 'new' evidence at a reconsideration **15.47** hearing where he or she was taken by surprise at the original tribunal hearing. Two examples:

- **Grieves v Coldshields Windows Ltd** EAT 218/82: the employer claimed for the first time at the employment tribunal hearing that G had been selected for redundancy largely because of his attitude to customers. G could have produced convincing rebutting evidence had he been prepared for the employer's change of tack. The tribunal dismissed his application for a review. However, on appeal the EAT held that, at the main hearing, the tribunal should have suggested an adjournment of the case to enable him to deal with the allegation suddenly raised and, accordingly, that G's application for review should have been granted

- **Mahmood v Barker t/a Derby Transit Ltd** EAT 224/00: on the morning of the employment tribunal hearing, M, who was unrepresented, was handed a bundle of 30 or more pages of documents in which the employer made a number of allegations against him. It was possible, although the facts were somewhat unclear, that M was then first shown the employer's accounts, which were relevant to the proceedings, during the hearing itself. In the event, M's claims were dismissed. M argued that the interests of justice required a review since he had not had the opportunity to assimilate the information that had been given to him on the day of the hearing. The tribunal refused M's application because he had stated at the start of the hearing that he was prepared to proceed. The EAT, allowing his appeal, held that the tribunal had been wrong to refuse a review. It was likely that, had he been represented, M would have asked for an adjournment. The EAT held that M should be given the opportunity to bring evidence at a review hearing.

However, it is clear that if a party is genuinely taken by surprise by an allegation or item of evidence that has not previously been made or disclosed, the proper course will be for that party to ask the tribunal for an adjournment. Where the aggrieved party is legally represented and does not request an adjournment, it is unlikely that the tribunal will accede to an application for reconsideration at a later date simply by reason of having been taken by surprise – Douglas Water Miners Welfare Society Club v Grieve EAT 487/84.

833

15.48 Applying for reconsideration

An application for reconsideration of a judgment can be made during the course of a hearing. If the application is not made at a hearing, it must be presented to the employment tribunal in writing and copied to all the other parties – rule 71.

15.49 **Reconsideration on tribunal's own initiative.** Note that a tribunal is empowered by rule 73 to reconsider a judgment on its own initiative, i.e. without an application having been made. One scenario where this might occur is where the EAT has requested the tribunal to consider conducting a reconsideration following an appeal. For more information, see 'Reconsideration on tribunal's own initiative', under 'Procedure for reconsideration' below.

15.50 Preliminary considerations

As a general rule *any* party to the proceedings may apply under rule 71 to have a judgment reconsidered. This differs from an application for reconsideration of a rejection of a claim, response or counterclaim under rule 13 or 19 that can only be made by the party against whom the rejection was made.

15.51 **Employment tribunal fees.** Under the Employment Tribunals and the Employment Appeal Tribunal Fees Order 2013 SI 2013/1893, which came into force at the same time as the Tribunal Rules 2013, certain applications attract a fee and these include applications for reconsideration of a 'default judgment' and applications for reconsideration of a judgment following a final hearing. For a 'default judgment', the fee is currently £100. For a final hearing judgment, the fee is £100 or £350 depending on whether the claim at issue is Type A or Type B. These two categories of claim are explained in Chapter 19,' Fees'. Interestingly, the term 'default judgment' has been retained in the 2013 Order, but has not been retained in the Rules. This means that, on a literal reading, there is no requirement to pay a fee for reconsideration of a judgment made under rule 21 (which deals with judgments following the non-presentation or rejection of a response), even though it can clearly be perceived from the Order that it is intended that a fee should be payable. It would be unsafe for parties to rely upon this technicality as a basis for not paying the appropriate fee when applying for a reconsideration.

There is no set deadline for payment of the fee. It is not specifically payable with the application itself – Article 4(2) of the Order simply provides that the fee is payable 'on a date specified by the Lord Chancellor in a notice following the making of the application'. A remission system, like that which operates in the civil courts, exists so that those on low incomes will be excused payment (either in whole or in part).

834

Where a reconsideration of a default judgment or a final hearing judgment is **15.52** ordered on the initiative of the employment tribunal or at the behest of the EAT, no application-specific fee is payable. In the latter case, however, it is likely that the applying party will have already paid a fee for an unsuccessful reconsideration application, which led to the EAT proceedings for which a fee would also have been payable. (To appeal any decision to the EAT, the appellant is required to pay a fee of £400 with a further fee of £1,200 payable when the appeal proceeds to an oral hearing.) For further details about the employment tribunal and EAT fees regime, see Chapter 19, 'Fees'.

Costs implications. Where a party applies for a reconsideration under rule 71, **15.53** it is likely that the tribunal will order the costs of any reconsideration hearing to be paid by him or her. This is particularly so in circumstances where the party wishes to make an application for reconsideration against a judgment that was made in consequence of its own default – for instance, where the respondent failed to comply with the requirement to submit a response in time. Given that it is the respondent's default that will have led to the judgment being issued in the first place, it is that default that will have necessitated the application for a review. Had the respondent complied with the requirement to submit the response in time, no reconsideration hearing would have been necessary. Therefore, the respondent may well be ordered to pay the costs of the application. Note that rule 76(1)(a) of the Tribunal Rules 2013 specifically states that an employment tribunal may make a costs order (in favour of a party who is represented) or a preparation time order (in favour of a non-represented party), where proceedings have been conducted unreasonably. A tribunal may also make such an order where a party has been in breach of any order or Practice Direction – rule 76(2). Furthermore, rule 80 provides that a 'wasted costs order' may be made against a representative in favour of any party where that party has incurred costs as a result of any improper, unreasonable or negligent act or omission on the part of the representative, or which, in light of any such act or omission occurring after the costs were incurred, the tribunal considers it unreasonable to expect the receiving party to pay. So, for example, in Miles v Johnsons Apparelmaster Ltd ET Case No.1902136/04 the tribunal made a wasted costs order on the ground that the respondent's legal representative had been solely responsible for the non-compliance with the tribunal rules of procedure necessitating a review application.

A party may be vulnerable to similar costs orders being made against him or her if he or she unreasonably institutes an appeal against the refusal of a reconsideration application. In British School of Motoring v Fowler EAT 0059/06 the respondent appealed against a decision of the employment tribunal rejecting an application for a review of a decision that since no response had been received to the claim brought by the claimant it should take no part in the proceedings. The EAT ordered the respondent to pay the costs of the appeal hearing on the ground that the appeal proceedings had been caused by

835

unnecessary errors on the part of the respondent and his legal representatives. His Honour Judge Peter Clark's reasoning was that, if the case had been dealt with properly in the first place when the proceedings were served and sent in good time to the respondent's representatives, there would have been no need for an appellate decision.

15.54 Notwithstanding the potential liability to pay the other party's costs, or to pay an application-specific fee – see 'Employment tribunal fees' above – it will generally be less costly to the applying party to pursue an application for reconsideration rather than an appeal to the EAT. This fact of itself may influence parties to make a reconsideration application wherever possible.

For a detailed discussion on costs in the employment tribunal and the EAT, see Chapter 20, 'Costs and penalties'.

15.55 Making and timing of application

Except where made at a hearing, an application for reconsideration must be presented in writing and copied to all other parties within 14 days of the date on which the written record, or other written communication, of the original decision was sent to the parties, or within 14 days of the date that written reasons were sent (if later). In addition, the application must set out why a reconsideration of the original decision is necessary – rule 71. On the wording of rule 71, an application made 'in the course of a hearing' can be made orally at any point during that hearing, and without providing accompanying reasons, though, of course, the applying party would be well advised to provide oral and/or written submissions in support of its application.

Interestingly, rule 71 provides that an application must set out why reconsideration of the original decision is 'necessary', not why it is 'necessary in the interests of justice'. However, in light of the fact that rule 70 specifies the interests of justice as the sole ground upon which an employment tribunal may reconsider a prior judgment, the applicant should ensure that he or she sets out why reconsideration is in the interests of justice.

15.56 In addition, in PJ Drakard and Sons Ltd v Wilton 1977 ICR 642, EAT – a case concerning the previous 'review' provisions – the EAT established that, as a matter of practice, when applying for a review the party should set out not only the grounds upon which the review is sought but also the grounds for contending that the decision of which he or she seeks review is wrong. This also applies to the new procedure for reconsideration: a party applying for a reconsideration under the Tribunal Rules 2013 should set out not only why it is necessary in the interests of justice for the original decision to be reconsidered but also why the original decision is regarded as wrong.

When making an application for a review of a default judgment under old rule 33 of the Tribunal Rules 2004, the respondent was required to include a completed ET3 form, an application for an extension of the time limit for presenting the response and an explanation of why the response or an extension application was not submitted in time. While there is no such requirement under the new rules, a respondent would nonetheless be wise to provide these when applying for a judgment issued under rule 21 of the Tribunal Rules 2013 (i.e. the current equivalent of a default judgment) to be reconsidered pursuant to rule 71 in order to satisfy the tribunal that it is necessary in the interests of justice to grant the reconsideration.

Application for extension of time. The 14-day time limit may be extended (or **15.57** indeed shortened) by virtue of the employment tribunal's general power to do so under rule 5 of the Tribunal Rules 2013. Although a party would be well advised to make any application for an extension of this time limit before it expires, such an application can be granted even where the initial 14-day time limit has already expired. There is no requirement that the party should demonstrate that compliance with the time limit was 'not reasonably practicable' or, as was the case in relation to an application for a review of a default judgment under the previous Rules, that it is 'just and equitable' to extend the time limit. In light of this the EAT has on occasion suggested that a late application for a review would be a more suitable way of dealing with a case than an appeal. In Green and Symons Ltd v Shickell and anor EAT 528/83 the Appeal Tribunal, having held that the employer had been wrong to lodge an appeal, expressed the view that even at such a late stage the employment tribunal ought to exercise its discretion to extend the time for applying for a review of its judgment.

Repeat applications for reconsideration. A party may make more than one **15.58** application for reconsideration, since nothing in the Tribunal Rules 2013 expressly prohibits this, although a second application when a first application has been properly refused is only likely to succeed in exceptional circumstances – Raybright TV Services Ltd v Smith 1973 ICR 640, NIRC. In fact, rule 72(1) provides that where an application for a reconsideration has previously been refused on the basis that there is no reasonable prospect of the original decision being varied or revoked, a second application that is substantially the same as the first will be refused 'unless there are special reasons'. Presumably, this could also include a situation where an application for reconsideration of a rejected claim/response has been made and refused under rules 13 or 19 – see 'Reconsideration of tribunal judgment – reconsideration of decision to reject a claim, response or counterclaim' above. In such a case, therefore, the application would need to show 'special reasons' why it should be allowed to proceed under the general reconsideration procedure instead.

These 'special reasons' would, of course, have to satisfy the 'interests of justice' test set out in rule 70. Such circumstances existed in Raybright TV Services Ltd v Smith (above), where the NIRC allowed an appeal against a refusal of a

837

second application under the old procedure for a review. The employer's first application concerned the fact that no one from the company had had a chance to attend the hearing and defend the claim but it failed to set out the basis upon which the employer intended to defend the claim. However, its second application was much more cogent and was supported by evidence. The court held that the interests of justice required that the matter be examined afresh and remitted the case for a complete rehearing by a different tribunal.

15.59 **Simultaneous appeal to the EAT.** Occasionally, a party may wish to appeal against a judgment to the EAT on a point of law while at the same time applying for a reconsideration of the tribunal's decision. There is no legal reason why this cannot be done, provided the circumstances warrant it. In Blackpole Furniture Ltd v Sullivan and anor 1978 ICR 558, EAT, the EAT observed that if either the tribunal judge or one of the parties felt that it was, in the circumstances, undesirable for a review to take place while an appeal was pending, then the judge should contact the Registrar of the EAT to discuss the best course to take. The EAT made it clear that, even when a review was applied for, the time limit for lodging an appeal (as to which see Chapter 17, 'Processing an appeal', under 'Time limit for lodging an appeal') still ran from the date of the original decision. Similarly, an application for reconsideration will not affect the time limit for lodging an appeal to the EAT.

As discussed above, the costs of a reconsideration are likely to be less than those of an EAT appeal, and this factor, of itself, may influence parties to make a reconsideration application wherever possible instead of pursuing an appeal to the EAT.

15.60 ## Procedure for reconsideration

Rule 72 of the Tribunal Rules 2013 sets out the procedure that an employment tribunal will follow upon receipt of an application for reconsideration. This is similar to the procedure that applied to reviews under the previous rules. First, the application will be put before an employment judge – rule 72(1). If he or she considers that there is no reasonable prospect of the original decision being varied or revoked, the application will be refused and the tribunal will inform the parties accordingly.

If the application is not refused, the tribunal will send a notice to the parties setting a time limit for any response to the application by the other parties and seeking the parties' views on whether the application can be determined without a hearing – rule 72(1). The notice may also 'set out the judge's provisional views on the application', although it does not have to do so. The matter will then proceed to a hearing, unless the employment judge considers, having regard to any response to the application, that a hearing is 'not necessary in the interests of justice' – rule 72(2). If the reconsideration proceeds without a hearing, the parties shall be given a reasonable opportunity to make further written representations – rule 72(2). It is clearly the policy intention underlying rule 72 that applications for reconsideration will be dealt with on the papers alone wherever possible, thereby saving time, expense and resources.

Rule 72(3) provides that, where practicable, stage one of the process – i.e. the **15.61** initial consideration of the application under rule 72(1) – will be carried out by the judge who made the original decision (or who chaired the tribunal which made it). Furthermore, where practicable, stage two – i.e. the hearing stage (unless a hearing is not necessary) – shall also be carried out by that judge or, as the case may be, the full tribunal that made the original decision. Where that is not practicable, another judge will be appointed by the President, Vice President or a Regional Employment Judge. Alternatively, in the case of a decision of a full tribunal, one of the above shall either direct that the reconsideration be by such members of the original tribunal as remain available or reconstitute the tribunal in whole or in part.

Reconsideration of a default judgment. The same procedure now applies to **15.62** the reconsideration of judgments issued under rule 21 of the Tribunal Rules (i.e. the equivalent of default judgments). Old rule 33(5) of the 2004 Tribunal Rules stated that a default judgment had to be revoked where, before the judgment was issued, the whole of the claim was satisfied or the parties had settled. Thus, in these particular circumstances, the judge had no discretion but to allow the review and order revocation. While no such provision exists under the Tribunal Rules 2013, common sense suggests that in such circumstances a tribunal will exercise its discretion and revoke the rule 21 judgment.

Is a hearing necessary?
15.63
As mentioned above, it is clearly the Government's intention that applications for reconsideration will be dealt with on the papers alone wherever possible, thereby saving time, expense and resources. The reconsideration provisions also provide that there is no need to hold a hearing to carry out the reconsideration itself. In Opara v Partnerships in Care Ltd EAT 0368/09 the EAT held that the scope of the hearing will depend on the subject matter of the review (reconsideration). If the issue at stake is minor, the parties may content themselves with written submissions. But where there is a fully contested application, the tribunal should not dispense with a hearing. In this particular case, the EAT held that the employment tribunal ought to have convened a hearing as it was being invited to make a finding tantamount to dishonesty on the part of the claimant, and no tribunal should make such a serious finding without according to the person concerned a full and proper opportunity to be heard upon it.

The same approach was adopted in Ogedegbe v Stag Security Service Ltd EAT 0001/12, where the EAT held that it was inappropriate for an employment

839

judge to conclude solely on the basis of written material that fresh evidence adduced by a claimant on an application for a review was forged. An allegation of that seriousness should have been specifically put to the claimant at the hearing before it was upheld. Similarly, in Patel v Babcock Airports Ltd EAT 0037/12 the EAT found that an employment judge had been wrong to refuse a review without a hearing on the ground that the claimant was not telling the truth when he said he had not received an e-mailed letter from the tribunal advising him that the judge was considering striking out his claim.

15.64 Under the old rules, a review of a default judgment had to be conducted by a tribunal judge in public – rule 33(3) Tribunal Rules 2004. No such provision has been carried into the Tribunal Rules 2013. However, an employment judge may find that it is necessary in the interests of justice to hold a hearing in public in cases concerning the reconsideration of a rule 21 judgment (the current equivalent to a default judgment under the old Rules).

Finally, where the reconsideration involves the consideration of contested medical evidence, a hearing will certainly be required – Royal Bank of Scotland v Soper EAT 0080/07.

15.65 Procedure at reconsideration hearing
A reconsideration hearing will be held in accordance with the general rules for hearings – see Chapter 12, 'The hearing'. In practice, much will depend on the particular basis upon which the applying party seeks to satisfy the interests of justice ground as to what, if any, evidence and witnesses will be required, or whether oral submissions alone may be adequate. For instance, where the applying party seeks a reconsideration on the basis that it is necessary in the interests of justice because new evidence is available, it will be intrinsic that the new evidence be placed before the tribunal together with an explanation as to why it was not and could not have been made available at the original hearing. The normal tribunal rules apply and the party resisting the application will be entitled to produce his or her own evidence and to cross-examine witnesses.

15.66 Reconsideration on tribunal's own initiative
An employment tribunal may also reconsider a judgment on its own initiative, i.e. without an application having been made. Rule 70 stipulates that this may also be done at the behest of the EAT. One situation where this might occur is where, following an appeal against the tribunal's decision to refuse an application for a reconsideration of its judgment, the EAT allows the appeal and remits the case to the tribunal to enable it to carry out the reconsideration. Another situation where reconsideration may be ordered at the behest of the tribunal is where the tribunal realises after giving judgment that it has omitted to deal with a crucial point or failed to take into account binding case authorities.

Where a tribunal proposes to reconsider a decision on its own initiative, the process is slightly different. For one thing, the tribunal must inform the parties of the reasons why the decision is to be reconsidered – rule 73. In accordance with rule 70, the reconsideration must be necessary in the interests of justice, so the reasons the tribunal gives must satisfy this test.

Rule 73 goes on to stipulate that the decision will be reconsidered in accordance **15.67** with rule 72(2) (i.e. as if an application had been made and not refused). In other words, the employment judge will convene a hearing to reconsider the original decision unless he or she considers, having regard to any response to the notice of his or her intention to reconsider the judgment, that a hearing is not necessary in the interests of justice. If the reconsideration proceeds without a hearing the parties shall be given a reasonable opportunity to make further written representations.

Unlike old rule 36(2)(b) of the Tribunal Rules 2004, there is no time limit for a tribunal to conduct a reconsideration on its own initiative under the Tribunal Rules 2013. It need not, for instance, notify the parties of its intention to conduct a reconsideration within a specified period after the judgment has been delivered – unlike in the case of an application for reconsideration by a party, which must be made within 14 days of the date upon which the original decision (or, if later, the written reasons for the decision) was sent to the parties – see 'Applying for reconsideration – making and timing of application' above.

Powers of tribunal on reconsideration   15.68

Upon reconsideration of a judgment, the employment judge or tribunal (as the case may be) may confirm, vary or revoke the original decision and, if revoked, the decision may be taken again – rule 70. Under old rule 36(3) of the Tribunal Rules 2004, if a decision was ordered to be taken again and the original decision was taken by a judge without a hearing, the new decision could be taken without hearing the parties. But if the original decision was taken at a hearing, a new hearing had to be held. No equivalent provisions exist in the Tribunal Rules 2013. Therefore, where a decision is ordered to be taken again it is left to the tribunal's discretion as to whether a hearing should be held.

If the employment tribunal rejects an application for reconsideration or confirms the original decision, there is no further recourse for the applicant, short of repeating the reconsideration application (which, as previously mentioned, will usually be of little merit) or submitting an appeal against the decision to the EAT against the tribunal's original judgment and/or its decision following the reconsideration, assuming of course that an error of law can be identified and the time limit for appeal has not expired.

The power of a tribunal to vary a decision is not limited to minor amendments. **15.69** It includes the power to substitute a completely different decision if the material

---

841

before it on the reconsideration justifies this – even though this may seem to amount to revoking the decision and failing to order a full rehearing. A tribunal need not order a rehearing in these circumstances. In Stonehill Furniture Ltd v Phillippo 1983 ICR 556, EAT, an employment tribunal made a finding that the claimant had been fairly dismissed for redundancy. The claimant then discovered fresh evidence that a person had been recruited to do his job. The tribunal reversed its earlier decision, substituting findings that there had been no redundancy, that the claimant had been unfairly dismissed and that he was entitled to £6,380 in compensation. On appeal by the employer, the EAT held that the tribunal had been entitled to do all of this. In its view: '[The] tribunal can... decide that at the original hearing the decision it came to was wrong, and the right answer is so obvious that it can go straight to that right answer.'

In most cases, however, the right answer is not so obvious and tribunals should not reach a fresh conclusion on a case too readily. A tribunal has the power to reconsider the whole of a decision and not just the part of it that prompted the application for reconsideration. However, the tribunal should not reach a new conclusion without giving the parties an opportunity to prepare submissions on the point – Estorffe v Smith 1973 ICR 542, NIRC.

15.70 Most successful applications result in a variation of the original decision – e.g. by a reassessment of compensation. But a tribunal may revoke a decision and order a rehearing. This will typically happen where new evidence is admitted that casts doubt on the original decision such that it is necessary in the interests of justice to reconsider it but it falls short of being conclusive evidence that the initial judgment was wrong.

Where an employment judge decides that a judgment issued under rule 21 following the failure to present or rejection of a response should be varied or revoked, with the consequence that the respondent is allowed to put in a response to the claim, then so long as the response is submitted in accordance with the judge's instruction, the claim will proceed in the usual way.

15.71 Challenging other tribunal decisions and orders

As previously explained, only a 'judgment' (as defined by rule 1(3)(b) of the Tribunal Rules) may be reconsidered in accordance with an employment tribunal's general power under rule 70 – see 'Reconsideration of a judgment – what decisions constitute a "judgment"?' above. This therefore excludes any decision that does not comprise a final determination of a claim, or part of a claim, as regards liability, remedy or costs; any issue which is capable of finally disposing of any claim, or part of a claim, or the imposition of a financial penalty. More specifically, it excludes any case management order, this being 'an order or decision of any kind in relation to the conduct of proceedings, not

842

including the determination of any issue which would be the subject of a judgment' – rule 1(3)(a).

Challenging case management orders

15.72

Much of the case law decided under old tribunal rules of procedure remains relevant to the question of what constitutes a 'case management order' and is thus excluded from the power of reconsideration under rule 70 of the Tribunal Rules 2013. For example, in Reddington and ors v S Straker and Sons Ltd and ors 1994 ICR 172, EAT, the Appeal Tribunal held that a joinder order was an interlocutory order and so was not covered by the old review provisions. Such an order will also be excluded from the reconsideration provisions as it does not fall within the definition of a 'judgment' for the purposes of rule 1(3)(b). Similarly, the making of, or refusal to make an order for, a deposit is not within the scope of the reconsideration provisions – Maurice v Betterware UK Ltd 2001 ICR 14, EAT. This is to be contrasted with the striking out of a claim (but not a response) on the ground that the claimant failed to pay a deposit: as we have seen under 'Reconsideration of a tribunal judgment – reconsideration of automatic strike-out/dismissal of claim or response' above, such a decision is a 'judgment' that is susceptible to reconsideration in accordance with rule 70 – Sodexho Ltd v Gibbons 2005 ICR 1647, EAT.

Other types of case management order that cannot be reconsidered under rule 70 include orders for additional information, disclosure, postponements and adjournments, witness orders, unless orders, orders requiring the provision of written answers and the consolidation of proceedings.

However, although such case management orders cannot be reconsidered under **15.73** the general power under rule 70, rule 29 provides that an employment tribunal may 'at any stage of the proceedings... vary, suspend or set aside an earlier case management order where that is necessary in the interests of justice, and in particular where a party affected by the earlier order did not have a reasonable opportunity to make representations before it was made'. Rule 30, in turn, allows the parties to apply for a particular case management order, including an order to vary, suspend or set aside a previous order, either at a hearing or in writing to the tribunal. These rules can therefore be relied upon effectively to ask the tribunal to revisit the order without necessitating an appeal to the EAT, which would require the relevant party to identify an error of law. It is striking that, as with the general power in rule 70, the ground varying, suspending or setting aside a previous case management order is that this is necessary 'in the interests of justice'. So very similar considerations will apply to those that are relevant when determining whether to grant an application to review a judgment.

While in theory there is no limit to the number of times a tribunal can revisit one of its case management orders, in practice it will be extremely rare to revisit an order unless there has been some change of circumstance. However, in an

843

exceptional case, revisiting a case management order may be justified where a party wishes to argue a potentially significant point that could have been, but was not, advanced at an earlier hearing, even without any change in circumstance – Hart v English Heritage (Historic Buildings and Monuments Commission for England) 2006 ICR 655, EAT.

15.74 Case management order *or* judgment?

Rule 1(3) of the Tribunal Rules 2013 states that 'an order or other decision of the tribunal is either (a) a "case management order"... or (b) a "judgment"'. It is not clear whether the draftsman's intention was that a tribunal decision must be one or the other. And this therefore raises the question of whether certain types of decision that have the 'flavour' of a final determination of the claim might be both 'orders' and 'judgments' and thus subject to the general provisions relating to a reconsideration of a judgment in rules 70–73. Such orders would include a decision to reject a claim, response or counterclaim and the dismissal or strike-out of a response for failure to pay a deposit.

The question of whether these kinds of order are 'judgments' has been considered elsewhere in this chapter – see 'Reconsideration of a tribunal judgment – reconsideration of decision to reject claim, response or counterclaim' above – so the discussion will not be repeated here. Suffice it to say, however, that even if any decision of the kind just mentioned does not constitute a 'judgment' within the meaning of rule 1(3)(b) but rather is to be regarded solely as a case management order, such an order can be revisited by the tribunal either on its own initiative or on application by the relevant party pursuant to rule 29. That rule – as previously outlined (see 'Case management orders' above) – allows the tribunal to vary, suspend or set aside any earlier case management order where it is necessary in the interests of justice to do so.

15.75

It therefore appears that the difference between a 'case management order' and a 'judgment' for the purposes of challenging a tribunal's decision on the basis that it is in the interests of justice to do so is somewhat academic. An application can be made for the tribunal either to revisit its decision in accordance with its power under rule 29, or to reconsider its decision in accordance with its power under rule 70. Either way, the tribunal is required to apply the interests of justice test.

15.76 Correcting mistakes

There are two situations in which tribunal errors may be corrected without the need for a formal appeal or a reconsideration.

15.77 Recalling the parties

In Hanks v Ace High Productions Ltd 1978 ICR 1155, EAT, an employment tribunal, having made a finding on a claimant's entitlement to a redundancy payment, wrote to the parties informing them that the chairman wanted to hear additional argument on the matter, specifically about a cited case that had not been covered fully in argument. In the EAT, Mr Justice Phillips accepted that the tribunal was entitled to take this course. He held that a tribunal's decision is not 'perfected' until it has been drawn up and entered in the Register. Until that happens, the tribunal retains the power of recall. He went on to say, however, that it would be wrong to use this power merely to rehear the case or invite fresh argument on matters upon which the tribunal has already made a clear finding. It is envisaged that it will be used only where there has been a clear error or omission on the part of the tribunal and, in this regard, the tribunal's notice of recall to the parties should give a clear indication as to why the matter has been reopened.

The reasoning in the Hanks case was applied in CK Heating Ltd v Doro 2010 ICR 1449, EAT, where an employment tribunal, having found that the claimant had been unfairly dismissed but that a 30 per cent reduction in compensation should be applied for contributory conduct, sought further representations from the parties on this issue before the decision was drawn up and registered. In holding that the tribunal was entitled to take this approach, the EAT observed that the ultimate question in deciding whether to exercise the power of recall is, like the power to review (now reconsider) a judgment, whether the tribunal judges that it is necessary to do so in the interests of justice having regard to the overriding objective.

Although a tribunal may thus, in certain circumstances, reopen the case at any **15.78** time before its decision is 'perfected', it is clear that what it must not do is change a decision without first inviting representations from the parties. In Arthur Guinness Son and Co (Great Britain) Ltd v Green 1989 ICR 241, EAT, the Appeal Tribunal stated that a tribunal should not depart from a previous oral decision without informing the parties of what it was proposing to do and giving them an opportunity to consider the position.

However, it is important to note that a new provision inserted into the Tribunal Rules 2013 now expressly stipulates when a judgment or order is to be regarded as taking effect. Under rule 65 a judgment takes effect, or – to use the language of Phillips J in Hanks v Ace High Productions Ltd (above) – is 'perfected' on 'the day when it is given or made, or on such later date as specified by the tribunal'. This being the case, it appears that the power of recall can only be exercised where a tribunal reserves its judgment to be given at a later date. By way of contrast, a judgment delivered orally at the hearing will, under the terms of rule 65, take effect as soon as it is made unless the tribunal indicates otherwise, in which case the tribunal will not now have the latitude of simply recalling the parties to enable them to make further representations. The only option for securing further representations in such a case would appear to be for the tribunal to exercise its power to formally reconsider the judgment on its own initiative in accordance with rules 70 and 73 – see 'Procedure for reconsideration – reconsideration on tribunal's own initiative' above for further details.

845

15.79 **Correction – the 'slip rule'**

Once a decision has been entered in the Register, major errors or omissions must be dealt with by way of either reconsideration or appeal. However, a reconsideration is not necessary if the mistake complained of is merely a clerical error, or one arising from an accidental slip or omission. In such circumstances rule 69 of the Tribunal Rules provides that 'an Employment Judge may at any time correct any clerical mistake or other accidental slip or omission in any order, judgment or other document produced by the tribunal'.

This power – known as the 'slip rule' – is most commonly used to correct names or numerical errors in calculating compensation. It should only be used for matters which are not the subject of any dispute between the parties. Contentious issues should be dealt with by way of appeal or application for reconsideration. In Babcock Wanson UK Ltd v Wright EAT 0485/06 an employment tribunal was found to have erred in law by using the slip rule to amend a calculation of loss of pension rights. It had failed to take into account the counter schedules of loss that had been advanced by the parties as to what multiplier should have been used in the calculation, and the EAT held that the only proper course was to set aside the amended judgment and to invite the tribunal to reconsider the issue and to give reasons as to the appropriate method of calculation. Similarly, in Bone v Newham London Borough Council and ors 2008 ICR 923, CA, the Court of Appeal held that an employment tribunal had erred in law by using the slip rule to amend its previous judgment to insert an additional finding that the claimant's constructive dismissal was also an act of sex discrimination and victimisation, even though it was evident that the tribunal had intended to make this finding. Such went far beyond a 'clerical' or 'accidental' slip.

15.80 In Times Newspapers Ltd v Fitt 1981 ICR 637, EAT, the EAT held that the 'slip rule' covered not only mistakes by the employment tribunal but also mistakes made by one of the parties to the proceedings. It also decided that where an alteration under the slip rule might affect another party to the proceedings, the tribunal should give that party the opportunity to make representations about the issue and a failure to do so would invalidate any alteration that had been made.

There is no time limit covering the issue of a correction pursuant to rule 69. Where a correction is made, any published version of the document will be corrected and a copy of the corrected version, signed by the judge, will be sent to all the parties. If 'as a result of death, incapacity or absence', the employment judge is unable to sign the corrected document, then it will be signed by the other member or members (in the case of a full tribunal) or by the President, Vice President or a Regional Employment Judge (in the case of a judge sitting alone) – rule 63.

16 The Employment Appeal Tribunal

What is the EAT?

EAT Rules, Practice Directions and Practice Statements

Composition of the EAT

Jurisdiction of the EAT

Grounds of appeal

The main function of the Employment Appeal Tribunal (EAT) is to hear **16.1** appeals from decisions made by employment tribunals. Established by S.87 of the now-repealed Employment Protection Act 1975, the EAT started operating on 31 March 1976 as a successor to the National Industrial Relations Court. Its powers are derived from S.20(1) of the Employment Tribunals Act 1996 (ETA), and from April 2006 until April 2011 it was part of the Tribunals Service – an executive agency of the Ministry of Justice. Then, on 11 April 2011, the Tribunals Service merged with Her Majesty's Courts Service to form a new organisation entitled 'HM Courts and Tribunals Service', which is responsible for the administration of the criminal, civil and family courts and tribunals in England and Wales, in addition to the non-devolved tribunals in Scotland and Northern Ireland.

The stated aim of HM Courts and Tribunals Service is to ensure that 'all citizens receive timely access to justice'. The EAT was the subject of criticism in the early 1990s for serious delays in the hearing of appeals in England and Wales, and since then various procedural reforms have been implemented in order to address this. Those reforms are incorporated into the statutory and non-statutory procedural rules that apply to the EAT (see 'EAT Rules, Practice Directions and Practice Statements' below). These – together with an increase in the number of EAT sittings – have all contributed to the EAT now reaching its efficiency targets. The Employment Tribunals and EAT statistics for April 2011 to March 2012 – produced by the Ministry of Justice – reveal that, in that year, 2,170 appeals were received and 2,220 disposed of. This compares with 2,050 receipts and 2,000 disposals the previous year. Of the appeals that were received in 2011/12, 510 were disposed of at a full hearing, compared with 360 the previous year.

This chapter starts by explaining the statutory and non-statutory provisions **16.2** that govern EAT procedure before considering the position of the EAT within the judicial system and explaining its composition. It then goes on to deal with the EAT's jurisdiction – i.e. its powers to hear and decide cases. The next two chapters are concerned with the way in which tribunal decisions may be challenged by appealing to the EAT.

16.3 What is the EAT?

The EAT has the status of a superior court of record – S.20(3) ETA – which means that it has equivalent status to the High Court and that its decisions have precedent value. However, note that designation as a court of superior record does not prevent a court or tribunal from being susceptible to judicial review, although the circumstances in which this will be appropriate are very limited – see R (on the application of Cart) v Upper Tribunal 2012 1 AC 663, SC. The EAT has the same powers, rights, privileges and authority in respect of the attendance of witnesses, production of documents and 'all other matters incidental to its jurisdiction' as the High Court in England and Wales and the Court of Session in Scotland – S.29(2) ETA. The EAT is not, however, a 'court' within the meaning of S.4(5) of the Human Rights Act 1998, meaning that it does not have jurisdiction to determine the question of whether legislation is compatible with rights under the European Convention on Human Rights – Whittaker v P and D Watson (t/a P and M Watson Haulage) and anor 2002 ICR 1244, EAT. Note also that the EAT is an 'added tribunal' for the purposes of S.42 of the Tribunals, Courts and Enforcement Act 2007, meaning that, under this provision, the Lord Chancellor can make an order imposing fees for anything that the EAT deals with – see Reg 2 Added Tribunals (Employment Tribunals and Employment Appeal Tribunal) Order 2013 SI 2013/1892.

16.4 Venue

Section 20(2) ETA establishes a central office of the EAT in London, but empowers the EAT to hear cases anywhere in Great Britain. Its choice of venue is a matter of its own discretion, although in practice the EAT sits permanently in London (currently at Fleetbank House, 2–6 Salisbury Square, London EC4Y 8JX) and in Edinburgh (at 52 Melville Street, Edinburgh EH3 7HF), and only occasionally elsewhere. In Williams v Cowell and anor 2000 ICR 85, CA, the EAT refused to exercise its discretion to sit in Wales and the Court of Appeal upheld this decision, finding that the EAT had not exercised its discretion in conflict with or in disregard of the appellant's human rights to due process and a fair procedure.

There is an exception to the rule that the EAT may hear cases anywhere in Great Britain at its own discretion. The following regulations all specify that certain proceedings must be heard in either England and Wales or Scotland in certain circumstances:

- Reg 34 of the Transnational Information and Consultation of Employees Regulations 1999 SI 1999/3323

- Reg 35 of the European Public Limited-Liability Company (Employee Involvement) (Great Britain) Regulations 2009 SI 2009/2401

- Reg 36 of the Information and Consultation of Employees Regulations 2004 SI 2004/3426

- Reg 58 of the Companies (Cross-Border Mergers) Regulations 2007 SI 2007/2974, and

- Reg 37 of the European Cooperative Society (Involvement of Employees) Regulations 2006 SI 2006/2059.

Doctrine of binding precedent   16.5
Although the EAT sits in both England and Scotland, it is a single appellate court. This is reflected in the fact that the EAT's decisions are binding on all employment tribunals, whether those decisions are made in England or Scotland.

The EAT is not, however, bound by its own decisions or those of other branches of the High Court. Although it will normally follow such decisions, it can depart from them 'in exceptional circumstances, or where there are previous inconsistent decisions' – Secretary of State for Trade and Industry v Cook and ors 1997 ICR 288, EAT. By way of an example, in Woodward v Abbey National plc (No.2) and another case 2005 ICR 1702, EAT, Mr Justice Burton, then President of the EAT, departed from his earlier decision in Clark v Midland Packaging Ltd 2005 2 All ER 266, EAT, on the ground that the Midland Packaging case was wrongly decided. Where a later division of the EAT has reservations about an earlier EAT decision then it is permissible, in the interests of comity, to follow that earlier decision and leave it to the Court of Appeal to correct any error in approach – Duncombe v Secretary of State for Children, Schools and Families EAT 0433/07.

Faced with two inconsistent decisions, the EAT's practice, following its decision **16.6** in Digital Equipment Co Ltd v Clements (No.2) 1997 ICR 237, EAT, is to direct employment tribunals as to which of the two decisions they should follow.

The decisions of higher courts are binding on the EAT under the doctrine of precedent. The EAT is bound, therefore, to follow decisions of the Supreme Court. It must also follow decisions of the Court of Appeal (when hearing an appeal instituted in England) and the Court of Session (Inner House) (when hearing an appeal instituted in Scotland). The fact that the EAT in England need not follow the Court of Session and the EAT in Scotland need not follow the Court of Appeal can cause inconsistencies. In Marshalls Clay Products Ltd v Caulfield and ors 2004 ICR 436, EAT, for example, the EAT in England declined to follow the Court of Session's construction of the Working Time Regulations 1998 in MPB Structures Ltd v Munro 2004 ICR 430, Ct Sess (Inner House), causing uncertainty at the time as to whether an employer's

849

payment of 'rolled-up' holiday pay is lawful. However, when the Court of Appeal gave judgment in Caulfield, Lord Justice Laws said that as a matter of 'pragmatic good sense' the English and Scottish EATs are expected to follow decisions of the higher appeal court in the other jurisdiction where the point confronting them is indistinguishable from what was decided by that appeal court – Marshalls Clay Products Ltd v Caulfield and ors and another case 2004 ICR 1502, CA. In Airbus UK Ltd v Webb 2007 ICR 956, EAT, the EAT endorsed Laws LJ's comments in Caulfield and went on to say that his guidance should be followed even where there were narrow grounds for distinguishing the appeal court's judgment in the other jurisdiction. On further appeal, the Court of Appeal agreed with the EAT's approach, Lord Justice Mummery saying that a contrary approach where lower courts and tribunals in England and Wales did not feel themselves bound by decisions of the Court of Session (Inner House) and vice versa would lead to a confused situation where the law in England and Wales would differ from that in Scotland on the meaning of provisions within statutes that extend to all parts of Great Britain (such as the Employment Rights Act 1996) – Airbus UK Ltd v Webb 2008 ICR 561, CA.

16.7 EAT Rules, Practice Directions and Practice Statements

The statutory rules that govern EAT procedure are currently the Employment Appeal Tribunal Rules 1993 SI 1993/2854 ('the EAT Rules'). These originally came into force on 16 December 1993 but have been the subject of substantial amendments in 2001, 2004, 2005 and 2013. The latest set of amendments are the Employment Appeal Tribunal (Amendment) Rules 2013 SI 2013/1693. These regulations, which came into force on 29 July 2013, made changes to the EAT Rules to take account, among other things, of the introduction of fees in the EAT pursuant to the Employment Tribunals and the Employment Appeal Tribunal Fees Order 2013 SI 2013/1893, which was also introduced on 29 July 2013. For further discussion of the introduction of fees in the EAT, see Chapter 19, 'Fees', under 'EAT fees'.

The EAT has the power to regulate its own procedure, subject to the provisions of the EAT Rules and any Practice Directions issued by the President of the EAT or Senior President of the Tribunals – S.30(3) ETA. Therefore, the EAT Rules must be read in conjunction with Practice Directions that are issued by the President of the EAT from time to time. These Directions supplement the EAT Rules and will govern procedure in all instances where the Rules themselves make no specific provision. However, if there is any conflict between the EAT Rules and a Practice Direction, the Rules will prevail. Practice Directions were previously handed down in 2002, 2004 and 2008. All of these have now been

850

superseded by the latest Practice Direction (2013 ICR 1382), which came into force on 29 July 2013 and was issued by the EAT's current President, Mr Justice Langstaff. The provisions of this Practice Direction are referenced extensively throughout the remainder of this chapter and in the following two chapters.

The EAT occasionally also issues Practice Statements covering specific topics. **16.8** Although there is no direct provision authorising such statements in either the EAT Rules or the 2013 Practice Direction (or its 2008 predecessor), it would seem that the EAT adopts the practice of making these occasional statements as part of its general power to regulate its own procedure under S.30(3) ETA. Sometimes, such Practice Statements are issued and reported as part of a judgment in a particular case; at other times they are issued as an independent, discrete document by (or with the authorisation of) the President of the EAT. An example of the former is the statement issued by His Honour Judge Peter Clark on the express authority of the EAT's then President, Mr Justice Elias, in Sage (UK) Ltd v Bacco EAT 0597/06 regarding the citation of reported cases during EAT hearings. This particular statement was subsequently incorporated into a more detailed Practice Statement on the subject issued in amended form by the EAT's current President, Mr Justice Langstaff, on 23 April 2012.

The two Practice Statements extant at the time of writing are:

- EAT Practice Statement of 3 February 2005 – issued by Mr Justice Burton (President) regarding the consequences of failing to lodge within the 42-day appeal time limit the documents required by the Rules in addition to the notice of appeal (e.g. the original ET1 and ET3 and the tribunal's written reasons). This particular statement made it clear that, from the date of issue, the EAT would not permit ignorance or misunderstanding of these requirements to excuse late compliance with this requirement even if a party is unrepresented

- EAT Practice Statement of 17 April 2012 (as amended on 23 April 2012) – issued by Langstaff P regarding two separate matters: (i) the limited circumstances in which the EAT will consider evidence not previously placed before the employment tribunal and the procedure for applying to have such fresh evidence considered; and (ii) the citation of case authorities in EAT proceedings. Both these matters are discussed in further detail in Chapter 18, 'EAT hearings and decisions', under 'Documents and authorities' and 'Evidence – admission of new evidence on appeal' respectively.

Although the matters dealt with in both of these Practice Statements are also **16.9** covered by the 2013 Practice Direction, the statements go into greater detail and therefore can be seen as expanding upon the provisions of the Practice Direction.

851

16.10 Composition of the EAT

The EAT comprises a panel of legal members made up of qualified judges and a panel of lay members, as detailed below.

16.11 The legal members

The legal members are such judges of the High Court and the Court of Appeal as may be nominated from time to time by the Lord Chief Justice after consultation with the Lord Chancellor. They include at least one judge of the Court of Session, nominated from time to time by the Lord President of the Court of Session – S.22(1) ETA.

In addition, there is a power contained in S.24 for the Lord Chief Justice, at the request of the Lord Chancellor, to appoint additional judges to sit as temporary EAT judges in England and Wales in order to facilitate the disposal of business. Such a judge must be a 'qualified person' – i.e. one who is already a High Court or Court of Appeal judge or at least is qualified for appointment as a High Court judge under S.10 of the Senior Courts Act 1981 – S.24(2) ETA. Such persons include circuit judges who have held office for at least two years and persons who satisfy the judicial-appointment eligibility condition on a seven-year basis. In practice, several such judges regularly sit at the EAT. A temporary judge has all the powers of a permanent judge, and will be appointed for such period and on such occasions as the Lord Chief Justice determines – S.24(1B) and (3).

16.12 Since comments made by the House of Lords in Lawal v Northern Spirit Ltd 2003 ICR 856, HL, the practice of permitting practising QCs to sit as part-time legal members has been restricted. In that case, the House of Lords found that there was an appearance of bias where the employer's counsel had previously sat as the presiding EAT judge with one of the lay members. This practice was held to undermine public confidence in the judicial system and was modified to match that in the employment tribunal. Part-time judges are now restricted from appearing as counsel before a panel of the EAT consisting of one or two members with whom they have previously sat judicially.

One of the members of the legal panel must be appointed as the President of the EAT – S.22(3) ETA, usually for a term of three years. That post has been held by Mr Justice Langstaff since 1 January 2012 and prior to that by Mr Justice (now Lord Justice) Underhill. The President presides over cases in the same way as any other judge but also has administrative responsibilities including the allocation of EAT members to particular cases or sittings. Provision is made in S.23(1) and (4) for another suitable judge to be nominated temporarily as President and to exercise all the functions of that office if the office falls vacant or if the current President is temporarily absent or unable to act.

The lay members 16.13

The panel of lay members – referred to in the legislation as the 'appointed members' – consists of part-timers who 'appear to the Lord Chancellor and the Secretary of State to have special knowledge or experience of industrial relations either (a) as representatives of employers, or (b) as representatives of workers' – S.22(2) ETA. While lay members are formally appointed by the Queen on the recommendation of the Lord Chancellor and the Secretary of State, the Judicial Appointments Commission is responsible for the selection of candidates to lay membership.

With effect from 3 April 2006, responsibility for carrying out statutory functions relating to tribunals under the ETA passed from the Department for Trade and Industry to the Ministry of Justice (formerly the Department for Constitutional Affairs). Thus, the relevant Secretary of State for the purposes of S.22(2) is now the Secretary of State for Justice.

The Registrar 16.14

The Registrar is the principal administrative officer of the EAT, and the definition of 'Registrar' includes any officer of the Appeal Tribunal authorised by the President to act on behalf of the Registrar – rule 2(1) EAT Rules. The Registrar's responsibilities are mainly administrative – such as receiving all correspondence or other documentation directed to the EAT – but he or she also performs certain quasi-judicial functions. For instance, the Registrar has the power to reject notices of appeal on jurisdictional grounds and to dispose of interim (i.e. interlocutory) applications. Under rule 20 every interim application, save for two specific exceptions, will be considered in the first instance by the Registrar and be disposed of by him or her except where he or she thinks that the application should properly be decided by the President or a judge. The two exceptions are: (i) applications relating to restricted reporting orders, and (ii) applications to be permitted to institute or continue proceedings before an employment tribunal or the EAT by a person who is the subject of a 'restriction of proceedings order' pursuant to S.33 ETA, having been declared to be a vexatious litigant. In either of these cases, the application must be disposed of by the President or a judge or, if he or she so directs, by a full division of the EAT – rules 20(3) and (4). In the particular case of an application in connection with a restriction of proceedings order, para 3.10 of the Practice Direction stipulates that this will be considered on paper by a judge who may make an order granting, refusing or otherwise dealing with the application.

Rule 21(1) provides that where any party is aggrieved by a decision of the Registrar disposing of an application, that party may appeal to a judge, who may determine the appeal him or herself or refer the matter (in whole or in part) for decision to the EAT. Such an appeal can be made orally or in writing and must be lodged within five days of the Registrar's decision – rule 21(2).

853

16.15 **Sittings of the EAT**
At hearings where a judge sits with appointed members, it is normally the case that two such members will sit, although in rare cases the EAT can direct that four members should do so. In this regard, S.28(2) ETA (as amended by the Enterprise and Regulatory Reform Act 2013 (ERRA)) stipulates that a 'judge may direct that proceedings are to be heard by a judge and either two or four appointed members', and where this happens S.28(4) makes it clear that the number of employer-representative and worker-representative members must be equal. Similar provision was made in the unamended version of S.28. What is different as a result of the ERRA amendment – which came into effect on 25 June 2013 – is that the default position for all EAT hearings is now that a judge will sit alone (i.e. without members). This reverses the position as it had existed ever since the EAT's inception in 1976 whereby EAT hearings would, by default, be constituted by a panel comprising a judge and two appointed members. The details of this change are examined further below. Suffice it to say here that, although the EAT retains a power to direct in any case that a hearing will be conducted by a judge sitting with two or four appointed members, many more hearings (including substantive appeal hearings) are now likely to be conducted exclusively by a judge alone.

16.16 **Hearings where only one member sits.** Section 28(4) ETA (as amended) provides that: 'A judge may, with the consent of the parties, direct that proceedings are to be heard by a judge and either one or three appointed members.' This addresses the occasional difficulty of where, owing to illness, delay or concern about a conflict of interest, one of the appointed members scheduled to sit on the appeal hearing expectedly becomes unavailable to sit. In such circumstances, provided that all parties give their consent, the EAT can direct that the hearing should proceed with an imbalance of members (i.e. with one member down).

In de Haney v Brent MIND and anor 2004 ICR 348, CA, the Court of Appeal made it clear that the power in what is now S.28(4) ETA is an exceptional one and must be exercised carefully. In that case the appellant, who was a litigant in person, arrived at the EAT to be confronted with the news that one of the appointed members due to sit on her appeal had recused himself because he had a conflict of interest in that he had been previously connected with the respondent charity. Both parties were informed of this by the judge, through the court's usher, and both gave their oral consent to proceeding with one member down. However, just before the hearing began, the appellant learned that the appointed member now left sitting was the employer's representative, at which point she withdrew her consent to the hearing proceeding. The EAT took the view that sufficient consent had already been forthcoming and directed that the hearing should go ahead. On appeal, the Court of Appeal ruled that, even though it was tolerably clear that a certain amount of information had been relayed to the appellant sufficient for her to know that the EAT habitually sat with employer- and worker-representative members, that information had not specifically included the fact that the member left sitting was the employer-representative. This meant that the appellant's consent was not *informed* consent, as the Court of Appeal ruled it had to be to satisfy S.28(4). Therefore, in accordance with rule 52.11(3) of the Civil Procedure Rules, the Court was bound to allow her appeal and set aside the EAT's decision because that decision was unjust in view of the serious procedural irregularity in the Appeal Tribunal's proceedings.

Hearings conducted by judge sitting alone. Prior to June 2013 the majority **16.17** of cases before the EAT were heard by a member of the legal panel and two lay members – one experienced in representing employees and the other experienced in representing employers. Under the relevant statutory provisions as they existed before this date, there were only two exceptions to this rule as set out in the unamended versions of Ss.28(4) and 30(2)(f) ETA. These allowed the EAT to be composed of a single judge when determining any matter on appeal that had itself been considered by a single employment judge at the employment tribunal and for a single judge (or the Registrar) to determine interlocutory matters. Pursuant to these statutory exceptions, rule 3(7) and (10) of the EAT Rules provided that the Registrar or a single judge should determine whether the Notice of Appeal disclosed reasonable grounds for the appeal, and if they did not to take no further action on the appeal (i.e. effectively to dismiss it at this stage). This practice, however, was subjected to a legal challenge in Francis v Pertemps Recruitment Partnership Ltd 2011 CSIH 40, Ct Sess (Inner House), where it was argued that rule 3(7) and (10) were ultra vires on the basis that Ss.28 and 30 ETA envisaged the Registrar or a sole judge only determining genuine interlocutory matters, whereas the dismissal at the sift stage of an appeal constituted a final decision that should be determined by a full EAT comprising a judge sitting with appointed members. Rejecting this contention, the Inner House of the Court of Session concluded that rule 3(7) and (10) sanctioned the practice of a single judge or the Registrar dismissing an appeal at the sift stage since it constituted a genuinely interlocutory matter and that that rule was not therefore ultra vires the ETA.

With effect from 25 July 2013, S.28 ETA has now been amended by the ERRA in order to make it the default position that all proceedings before the EAT are heard by a judge alone – see S.28(2) ETA (as amended). So not only will interlocutory and sift decisions continue to be made by the Registrar or a single judge, but also a single judge may now determine substantive appeals. However, the 'single judge' rule is subject to the following exceptions:

- where a judge directs that proceedings are to be heard by a judge and either two or four appointed members (who must constitute an equal number of employer- and worker-related representatives) (see, for example, Z v A EAT 0203/13)

855

- where a judge, with the consent of the parties, directs that proceedings are to be heard by a judge and either one or three appointed members

- where the Lord Chancellor makes an order for the proceedings described in the order to be heard by a judge and either two or four appointed members – S.28(3)–(5) (as amended).

16.18 Transitional provisions provide that the single judge default rule will not apply to proceedings that are already in the process of being heard by the EAT on the date that the revised statutory provisions came into force (i.e. 25 July 2013) – see S.24(2) ERRA. We take this to mean that the rule will not apply to those appeals that have been listed for hearing or where hearings have already commenced, but that the rule will now apply in the case of any appeal that, though already lodged before 25 July 2013, has not yet reached the listing stage.

The Government's thinking behind this change in the default constitution of the EAT when determining appeals was that the input of lay members should be reduced given that the Appeal Tribunal has no fact-finding remit and deals only with points of law. Accordingly, the changes were designed to make the system more efficient and streamlined, especially in light of the Government's estimation that lay members were costing the EAT around £300,000 per year.

16.19 Jurisdiction of the EAT

The EAT is mainly an appellate court. Its principal function is to hear appeals on a question of law arising from decisions of employment tribunals and it is empowered to do so by various statutory sources. However, it does not have an exclusively appellate jurisdiction as it also has original jurisdiction to determine specific complaints and applications under:

- Reg 21(6) of the Transnational Information and Consultation of Employees Regulations 1999 SI 1999/3323 (the TICE Regulations)

- Reg 20(6) of the European Public Limited-Liability Company (Employee Involvement) (Great Britain) Regulations 2009 SI 2009/2401 (the EPLLC(EI) Regulations)

- Reg 22(6) of the Information and Consultation of Employees Regulations 2004 SI 2004/3426 (the ICE Regulations)

- Reg 22(6) of the European Cooperative Society (Involvement of Employees) Regulations 2006 SI 2006/2059 (the ECS(IE) Regulations), and

- Regs 53(6) and 54(5) of the Companies (Cross-Border Mergers) Regulations 2007 SI 2007/2974 (the C(CBM) Regulations).

In such cases, the EAT performs a role akin to that of the employment tribunal as an arbiter of fact.

Appellate jurisdiction   16.20

The EAT's appellate jurisdiction is derived mainly from the Employment Tribunals Act 1996. Specific statutes – namely the Transfer of Undertakings (Protection of Employment) Regulations 2006 SI 2006/246 (TUPE) and the Trade Union and Labour Relations (Consolidation) Act 1992 (TULR(C)A) – also confer jurisdiction on the EAT to hear appeals from the employment tribunal.

The EAT has what is called 'limited jurisdiction' – i.e. it has no inherent jurisdiction to hear appeals arising from legislation that is not listed in S.21(1) ETA, unless jurisdiction is conferred by another piece of legislation. In Refreshment Systems Ltd (t/a Northern Vending Services) v Wolstenholme EAT 0608/03 an employer sought to appeal against a tribunal's decision that it was in breach of S.11 of the Employment Relations Act 1999 (ERelA) (right to be accompanied at a disciplinary hearing). At the time of the appeal the ERelA was not listed in S.21(1) ETA. As a result, the EAT declined jurisdiction, stating that 'if Parliament has not legislated to provide a right of appeal, respect for the democratic process requires a court of limited jurisdiction to take a point concerning its jurisdiction'. S.21(1) ETA was subsequently amended by S.38 of the Employment Relations Act 2004 to include the ERelA with effect from 1 October 2004.

Where neither S.21(1) ETA nor an individual statute confer jurisdiction upon 16.21 the EAT to hear an appeal against a decision of an employment tribunal, an appeal on a question of law lies to the High Court under S.11 of the Tribunals and Inquiries Act 1992 and the Civil Procedure Rules 1998 SI 1998/3132. Such an appeal would be heard by a judge alone in the Queen's Bench Division.

Employment Tribunals Act 1996. Section 21(1) ETA provides that an appeal 16.22 lies to the EAT on a question of law arising from a decision of, or proceedings before, an employment tribunal hearing a case brought under or by virtue of:

- the Trade Union and Labour Relations (Consolidation) Act 1992
- the Employment Rights Act 1996
- the Employment Tribunals Act 1996
- the National Minimum Wage Act 1998
- the Employment Relations Act 1999
- the Equality Act 2006
- the Pensions Act 2008

857

- the Equality Act 2010

- the Working Time Regulations 1998 SI 1998/1833

- the Transnational Information and Consultation of Employees Regulations 1999 SI 1999/3323

- the Part-time Workers (Prevention of Less Favourable Treatment) Regulations 2000 SI 2000/1551

- the Fixed-term Employees (Prevention of Less Favourable Treatment) Regulations 2002 SI 2002/2034

- the Merchant Shipping (Working Time: Inland Waterways) Regulations 2003 SI 2003/3049

- the European Public Limited-Liability Company Regulations 2004 SI 2004/2326

- the Fishing Vessels (Working Time: Sea-fishermen) Regulations 2004 SI 2004/1713

- the Information and Consultation of Employees Regulations 2004 SI 2004/3426

- the Schedule to the Occupational and Personal Pension Schemes (Consultation by Employers and Miscellaneous Amendment) Regulations 2006 SI 2006/349

- the European Cooperative Society (Involvement of Employees) Regulations 2006 SI 2006/2059

- the Companies (Cross-Border Mergers) Regulations 2007 SI 2007/2974

- the Cross-border Railway Services (Working Time) Regulations 2008 SI 2008/1660

- the European Public Limited-Liability Company (Employee Involvement) (Great Britain) Regulations 2009 SI 2009/2401

- the Employment Relations Act 1999 (Blacklists) Regulations 2010 SI 2010/493, or

- the Agency Workers Regulations 2010 SI 2010/93.

16.23 Note that the jurisdiction of the EAT to hear appeals from the Equality Act 2010 was effected by para 32(b) of Schedule 26 to the EqA. However, the EAT continues to have jurisdiction to hear appeals under the antecedent discrimination legislation – Article 15 Equality Act 2010 (Commencement No.4, Savings, Consequential, Transitional, Transitory and Incidental Provisions and Revocation) Order 2010 SI 2010/2317. The antecedent discrimination statues are:

- the Equal Pay Act 1970

- the Sex Discrimination Act 1975

- the Race Relations Act 1976

- the Disability Discrimination Act 1995

- the Employment Equality (Religion or Belief) Regulations 2003 SI 2003/1660

- the Employment Equality (Sexual Orientation) Regulations 2003 SI 2003/1661, and

- the Employment Equality (Age) Regulations 2006 SI 2006/1031.

TUPE Regulations 2006. Regulation 16(2) of the Transfer of Undertakings **16.24** (Protection of Employment) Regulations 2006 SI 2006/246 provides that an appeal from any decision of an employment tribunal made under those Regulations is subject to an appeal to the EAT on a question of law.

Trade Union and Labour Relations (Consolidation) Act 1992. The EAT has **16.25** jurisdiction under the TULR(C)A to entertain appeals from certain decisions of the Certification Officer, as follows:

- Section 9 TULR(C)A provides that an organisation which is aggrieved by the refusal of the Certification Officer to enter its name in the list of trade unions; by his or her decision to remove its name from the list; or by his or her refusal to issue it with a certificate of independence or by his or her decision to withdraw its certificate, may appeal to the EAT on 'any appealable question'. S.126 gives the EAT corresponding jurisdiction for decisions on the listing of employers' associations. Note that an 'appealable question' is 'any question of law arising in the proceedings before, or arising from the decision of, the Certification Officer' and does not extend to questions of fact. Prior to 5 April 2005 appeals under S.9 or S.126 could be made to the EAT on a question of fact, but this was changed by S.51(1) of the Employment Relations Act 2004

- the TULR(C)A also provides that an appeal lies to the EAT on a question of law arising from decisions of the Certification Officer in respect of trade union administration (S.45D); compliance with trade union election requirements (S.56A); application of union funds for political purposes (S.95); trade union amalgamation or transfer of assets (S.104); and alleged breach of union rules (S.108C).

The EAT no longer has original jurisdiction to hear claims for compensation relating to the unjustifiable disciplining of a trade union member or in respect of claims for compensation for unlawful exclusion or expulsion from a trade union. The relevant sections of the TULR(C)A – S.67(1) and S.176(2)

859

respectively – were repealed by S.34 of the Employment Relations Act 2004, which transferred this jurisdiction to employment tribunals.

16.26 **Declarations or orders of the Central Arbitration Committee.** The EAT has jurisdiction to hear appeals on a question of law against any declaration or order of the Central Arbitration Committee (CAC) under:

- Reg 38(8) of the TICE Regulations

- Reg 35(6) of the ICE Regulations

- Reg 57(6) of the C(CBM) Regulations

- Reg 34(6) of the EPLLC(EI) Regulations, and

- Reg 36(6) of the ECS(IE) Regulations.

16.27 ## What types of decision can be appealed?
Section 21(1) ETA provides that an appeal lies to the EAT arising from 'any decision of, or arising in any proceedings before, an employment tribunal'. Below, we examine types of decision or aspects of decision-making in respect of which it is not immediately obvious whether S.21 applies.

16.28 **Interim orders.** In Haydock v GD Cocker and Sons Ltd EAT 1143/99 the EAT considered whether it had jurisdiction to hear an appeal against a tribunal's order refusing to grant a witness order sought by the employee. It concluded that the use of the expression 'decision of, or arising in any proceedings' in S.21(1) must include not only decisions of the tribunal (as then defined in Reg 2(2) of the Employment Tribunal Rules 2001), but also its interim orders. This decision is reflected in the EAT Rules, which make explicit reference to appeals from 'an order of an employment tribunal' – rule 3(1)(e). The Haydock decision also clarified that the EAT has jurisdiction to hear an appeal against an interim order even where the tribunal had not provided extended written reasons for its order. Once again, this point has been clarified by rule 3(1)(e) of the EAT Rules. However, note that where the EAT determines that an employment tribunal has correctly struck out a claim, it has no jurisdiction to hear an appeal against an interim order pursuant to that claim – Edem v Ajilon (UK) Ltd and another case EAT 1600/06. This approach was subsequently approved by the Court of Appeal in its decision refusing leave to appeal – see Edem v Ajilon UK (Ltd) and anor 2007 EWCA Civ 394, CA. In the past it was believed that, when determining appeals against the interim decisions of employment tribunals, the EAT had jurisdiction to determine any interim matter afresh. The belief derived from the decision in British Library v Palyza and anor 1984 ICR 504, EAT, where the EAT held that, when considering an appeal from an employment tribunal's order granting or refusing discovery, it was not restricted to setting aside the order only where the employment tribunal had exercised its discretion on wrong principles. Rather, the EAT could freely review the decision and

860

substitute its own discretion. However, in the subsequent case of Medallion Holidays Ltd v Birch 1985 ICR 578, EAT, another division of the EAT ruled that the Appeal Tribunal's appellate jurisdiction in relation to employment tribunals' interim decisions is the same as that which applies to employment tribunals' final determinations. Thus, the EAT has no power to interfere with such decisions or review their merits unless it can be shown that the discretion exercised by the employment tribunal was erroneous in law (for further details see 'Grounds of appeal – failure to exercise discretion' below). The Medallion Holidays case was subsequently approved by the Court of Appeal in Ashmore v British Coal Corporation 1990 ICR 485, CA. So, it is now clear that an employment tribunal's discretion is only challengeable where it has erred in law or where its conclusion 'was outside the generous ambit within which a reasonable disagreement is possible' – Noorani v Merseyside TEC Ltd 1999 IRLR 184, CA. Uniformity has thus been brought to the appeal procedure, which now makes no distinction between appeals concerning interim orders and appeals about other matters.

Other EAT decisions. The EAT has no power to overrule its own decisions. **16.29** This principle was illustrated in Asda Stores Ltd v Thompson and ors (No.2) 2004 IRLR 598, EAT. In that case, the EAT issued an order regarding the disclosure of confidential statements. The employer was unhappy about the way this order was applied by the employment tribunal and it appealed to the EAT against the tribunal's decision. The EAT (presided over by Mr Justice Wall) remitted the matter to the same employment tribunal with directions as to how the case should proceed. However, it was felt by all sides that the scope of the EAT's order was ambiguous, which led to the exchange of copious amounts of correspondence between the parties and the tribunal and even between the tribunal and the EAT, culminating in an appeal by the employer and a cross-appeal by the claimants against the employment tribunal's eventual further directions. In effect, the cross-appeal raised the question of whether it was open to the EAT (now presided over by Mr Justice Burton) to revisit the Order made by Wall J to permit it to clarify matters and reach a fresh decision as to how disclosure of the confidential statements should be handled. The cross-appellants argued that the EAT has residual jurisdiction to intervene, interfere and overrule one of its own earlier decisions, or to indicate that it should not be followed, should it take the view that the earlier decision in the same case is either unclear or wrong. In so arguing, they drew an analogy with the undoubted – although exceptional – power of the EAT not to follow its own earlier decision if it concludes that that decision is wrong – see Secretary of State for Trade and Industry v Cook 1997 ICR 288, EAT. Rejecting this argument, Burton J held that, unlike the Court of Appeal – which may be prepared to reopen one of its decisions in exceptional circumstances – the EAT has no power to do so. A party who believes a decision of the EAT to be wrong or unclear should take his, her or its case to the Court of Appeal. His Lordship

861

concluded: 'We think it very important that this Tribunal should be able to carry on with its job as speedily as it can by way of appeal from employment tribunals, and, once it has decided the matter, to leave it where it is; and that the aim of this Tribunal to give as speedy justice as possible should not be put at risk by cases coming back and back to it, unless of course on remission to it as a result of a successful appeal to a higher court.'

Interestingly, nowhere in the EAT's extensive judgment in the Asda Stores case is there any mention of the power – conferred by rule 33 of the EAT Rules – for the Appeal Tribunal to review its own decisions and/or correct errors. Perhaps this is not surprising given that this power – considered in detail in Chapter 18, 'EAT hearings and decisions', under 'Review of EAT decisions and further appeals' – has been very narrowly confined in cases where its scope has been considered. In the main, the power is limited to correcting some form of mistake, and this suggests that it would not be apt to cover the attempt by the cross-appellants in the Asda case to get another division of the EAT to revisit the decision made previously by a different division of the EAT in the same proceedings to obtain clarification/reconsideration of that EAT's original Order.

16.30 All this being said, the EAT – through the 2013 Practice Direction – has sought to make provision for the situation where there is genuine lack of clarity as to the scope of an order remitting the case to the employment tribunal. Para 23.1 of the Practice Direction states that where the EAT orally makes an order remitting the case or part of it to an employment tribunal for further hearing or a rehearing, the parties must immediately raise any uncertainty any of them has as to the precise scope of the remission. It is the obligation of each party to ensure that the scope as set out in the EAT's order corresponds with their understanding and to raise the question without delay if it appears not to do so. Para 23.2 goes on to state that if, at the later employment tribunal hearing, an issue arises as to the scope of remission, the *tribunal* may invite the EAT to give whatever clarification is thought necessary, and if so given any such clarification will be conclusive.

16.31 **Academic appeals.** Appeals only lie to the EAT against a substantive decision of a tribunal. The EAT will not consider appeals brought on an issue of principle or consider hypothetical questions that do not have concrete consequences for the participants. There must be a dispute to resolve. Four illustrations:

- **Baker and ors v Superite Tools Ltd** 1986 ICR 189, EAT: the claimants had been assessed for tax purposes as self-employed but the Inland Revenue reclassified them as employees and said that they should be taxed under PAYE. The claimants applied to a tribunal for a determination of their particulars of employment and the tribunal held that they were not employees but self-employed – a decision with which the 'employer' agreed. Although there was no dispute between the parties, the claimants appealed to the EAT in order to give greater weight to the tribunal's decision. The

862

EAT held that the appeals were 'a misuse of the appellate procedure laid down by Parliament for the resolution of genuine disputes on a genuine appeal on an issue of law from a decision of a tribunal'. In any case, there were special procedures for resolving disputes between taxpayers and the Inland Revenue, and nothing that the EAT could say would bind the Inland Revenue. It would not be right to entertain the appeals

- **Biwater Ltd v Bell EAT** 218/89: B Ltd raised a preliminary objection to B's unfair dismissal claim, arguing that he was excluded from the right to claim by S.196 ERA (a provision which has now been repealed) because he ordinarily worked outside Great Britain. The tribunal ruled against the company on this point. B Ltd then reached a settlement of B's claim, which was agreed to be legally binding. However, the company appealed because it wanted a binding decision on the type of contract under which B worked since a number of other employees worked under similar arrangements. The EAT held that there was no remaining dispute between the parties. It would be contrary to principle for the EAT to hear an appeal simply in order to give legal advice to the employer about the drafting of contracts, even if a genuine point of law was involved

- **IMI Yorkshire Imperial Ltd v Olender and ors** 1982 ICR 69, EAT: a tribunal found that four men had been unfairly dismissed and ordered their reinstatement plus the payment of compensation. The employer complied with the order, but appealed against the decision as a matter of principle. The EAT dismissed the appeal, concluding that it was not right for it to hear an appeal which no longer involved any practical consequences for the parties

- **Laing v Partnership in Care (t/a The Spinney)** EAT 0027/09: in dismissing L's race discrimination claim, an employment tribunal made strong criticisms of his conduct during the hearing and at a subsequent hearing ordered that he should pay costs totalling more than £9,000. L commenced an appeal to the EAT but before the hearing the employer conceded that the costs order had not been justified and should be rescinded. However, L submitted that he would only agree to the disposal of the appeal by consent if the criticisms of his conduct by the employment tribunal were removed. The EAT ruled that it was inappropriate to allow an appeal by consent in circumstances where no error on the part of the employment tribunal had been demonstrated. Furthermore, L's submission required the EAT to make positive findings that the tribunal's criticisms of him were wrong. But that was not a request the EAT could accede to, since it was not part of the Appeal Tribunal's function to resolve issues that were no longer material to any actual legal liability of the parties, and it would be wrong in principle to keep the costs order alive simply as a vehicle for an examination of whether the criticisms of L were justified. In addition, the tribunal's findings concerning L's conduct were

863

made in the context of the substantive decision on his discrimination claim and his appeal against that decision had been made out of time. In those circumstances it was even less acceptable for the instant appeal to be used as an artificial vehicle for examination of those criticisms. However, it was clear that both parties wished to see the costs order revoked and the EAT therefore exercised its powers under S.35(1)(a) ETA to review the original costs order. Once the tribunal's order had been revoked, the only live aspect of L's appeal fell away.

16.32 Who can bring an appeal?

Any party to proceedings in the tribunal may appeal against an adverse decision. This includes a would-be tribunal claimant who wishes to appeal against a tribunal's decision not to accept his or her claim form – Richardson v U Mole Ltd 2005 ICR 1664, EAT – and a would-be respondent who has failed to present a response to a tribunal claim – Atos Origin IT Services UK Ltd v Haddock 2005 ICR 277, EAT. In the latter case, the EAT held that although rule 3(3) of the 2001 Tribunal Rules prevented a party who had failed to enter its response from taking 'any further part in proceedings', this rule referred to proceedings in the employment tribunal and not in the EAT. A party's entitlement to appeal is governed by the EAT Rules and by its Practice Directions. Neither of these purported to restrict a party's right to participate in an appeal as a consequence of failing to submit a notice of appearance.

In fact, para 19 of the 2013 Practice Direction now specifically addresses appeals by a party who has not presented a response to the tribunal. Such a party must state in the notice of appeal: (a) whether there was a good excuse for his or her failure to present a response or (if appropriate) apply for an extension of time; and (b) whether he or she has a reasonably arguable defence to the claim. A witness statement in support must also be provided.

16.33 Appeals by consent

Rule 6(5) of the EAT Rules provides that 'where the respondent does not wish to resist an appeal, the parties may deliver to the Appeal Tribunal an agreed draft of an order allowing the appeal and the Tribunal may, if it thinks it right to do so, make an order allowing the appeal in the terms agreed'. Para 18.3 of the 2013 Practice Direction stipulates that if the parties reach an agreement that the appeal should be allowed by consent, and that an order made by the employment tribunal should be reversed or varied or the matter remitted to the tribunal on the ground that the decision contains an error of law, it is usually necessary for the matter to be heard by the EAT to determine whether there is a good reason for making the proposed order. On notification by the parties, the EAT will decide whether the appeal can be dealt with on the papers or by a hearing at which one or more parties or their representatives should attend to argue the case for allowing the appeal and making the order that the parties

864

wish the EAT to make. In fact, the attendance of the parties will usually be required so that the Appeal Tribunal can satisfy itself that the consent order is truly 'consensual' and that it is appropriate for it to be issued in the circumstances – see Mowels v Vox Displays Ltd EAT 0122/07.

The EAT considered its general power to allow appeals by consent in the following cases:

- **J Sainsbury plc v Moger** 1994 ICR 800, EAT: M applied to an employment tribunal for a declaration of the terms of her employment. She also brought a claim under the now-repealed Wages Act 1986 and claimed unfair dismissal in the alternative. The tribunal ordered a preliminary hearing to determine whether M had been dismissed. M's case was that S plc had simply purported to vary the terms of her employment contract. S plc argued that M's original contract had been terminated and that she had accepted a new contract on new terms. At the preliminary hearing the tribunal found that M had not been dismissed. Although this finding precluded M from pursuing her unfair dismissal claim, S plc appealed. Before the EAT, both parties argued that the appeal should be allowed by consent, that a finding of dismissal should be substituted and that the case should be remitted for consideration of the other issues. The EAT, however, took the view that it was generally inappropriate to grant such a request where there was no overall settlement of the dispute. Furthermore, the EAT found that it only had the power to reverse the decision of a tribunal on a point of law. Nevertheless, having heard arguments, the EAT allowed the appeal on the ground that, in the circumstances, the tribunal chairman had erred in law by ordering a preliminary hearing on the issue of dismissal

- **Ansells Ltd v Walford** EAT 592/94: an employment tribunal upheld W's complaint under the now-repealed Wages Act 1986 as well as his claim of unfair dismissal. The parties then reached a settlement on compensation before A Ltd's appeal to the EAT was heard. The parties agreed that the appeal should be allowed by consent. A copy of the compromise agreement was sent to the EAT in which it was stated that W would consent to an order that the appeal be allowed. The EAT found itself in a 'constitutional difficulty in deciding how to deal with this matter'. It noted that, if the tribunal had made no error of law, the EAT had no right to allow an appeal even where the parties took the view that there had been an error of law. Furthermore, even if the EAT decided that there had been an error of law, for it to remit the case to the tribunal would be futile since W was contractually precluded from continuing with the proceedings. In the event, the EAT decided that it should make no order on the appeal.

The point made in the Ansells case – that if the tribunal had made no error of **16.34** law, the EAT had no right to allow an appeal even where the parties took the view that there had been an error of law – was reiterated by the EAT in Sakharkar

865

v Northern Foods Grocery Group Ltd t/a Fox's Biscuits EAT 0314–15/12. In that case, S appealed against his compensatory award and against the tribunal's refusal to grant him a review (now referred to as a 'reconsideration') of its decision. The EAT began by hearing oral evidence on the compensatory award appeal, but at the end of that evidence there was no time to proceed to argument and the appeal had to be adjourned. Before the resumption of the appeal, the parties agreed that the compensatory award appeal should be allowed and that the question of remedy be remitted to the tribunal to be considered afresh. The EAT held that the parties to an appeal could not of themselves agree that an appeal should be allowed. The judgement of a court or tribunal could only be overturned by the judgment of an appellate court or tribunal.

The EAT emphasised in Dozie v Addison Lee plc 2013 ICR D38, EAT, that the general practice is for the EAT not to routinely allow appeals by consent without first giving close scrutiny to the matter. The various reasons why this is so were helpfully summarised by His Honour Judge David Richardson in that case. First, judgments and orders of the employment tribunal and of employment judges are entitled to respect and it is in the interests of justice and good order that they should stand unless there is good reason for upsetting them. Secondly, parties sometimes agree to the setting-aside of judgments or orders for purely tactical reasons. These are not in themselves good reasons for setting aside judgments and orders. Thirdly, parties do not always think through the consequences of allowing an appeal. There may easily be a misunderstanding as to the effect of doing so or the scope of what the tribunal will decide after the appeal is allowed. This is why the EAT proceeds with caution before sanctioning a draft consent order. And fourthly, there is sometimes a wider public interest in a judgment beyond the interests of the parties to the litigation in question. This is something the Appeal Tribunal will take into account when deciding whether to allow the appeal by consent.

16.35 Grounds of appeal

The scope for appealing against employment tribunal decisions is relatively narrow, although at present there is no statutory requirement for a party to seek permission to appeal to the EAT (in contrast with the requirement to seek leave to appeal to the Court of Appeal). An appeal from a tribunal lies only on a 'question of law' – S.21(1) ETA. An argument that the tribunal misunderstood or misapplied the *facts* does not give a party a ground of appeal in its own right. Such an argument may only form the basis of an appeal where it is part of an argument that the decision was wholly unsupported by any evidence or that the tribunal's decision was perverse (see 'Perversity' below) – British Telecommunications plc v Sheridan 1990 IRLR 27, CA.

Questions of law and questions of fact   16.36

Since an appeal from an employment tribunal lies only on a 'question of law', the distinction between questions of law and questions of fact is clearly crucial. However, it is not always an easy distinction to make. In Brent London Borough Council v Fuller 2011 ICR 806, CA, Lord Justice Mummery said that 'appellate bodies learn more from experience than from precept or instruction how to spot the difference between a real question of law and a challenge to primary findings of fact dressed up as law'.

Obvious examples of a question of law would be where the tribunal asked itself the wrong question; misconstrued a statutory provision; ignored a legal requirement; or failed to apply the correct legal test. Also included are cases where the tribunal gave no or inadequate reasons for its decision; failed to exercise a discretion or exercised it on wrong principles; or committed procedural errors that breached the rules of natural justice.

The EAT and the Court of Appeal have adopted a generally restrictive approach   16.37 to identifying errors of law. The following, for instance, have all been held to be largely determined by questions of fact:

- whether or not workers are employees – Hellyer Brothers Ltd v McLeod and ors and another case 1987 ICR 526, CA

- whether or not termination of employment was a dismissal – Martin v Glynwed Distribution Ltd 1983 ICR 511, CA

- whether or not an employer's conduct amounted to a fundamental breach of contract justifying an employee in resigning and claiming constructive dismissal – Woods v WM Car Services (Peterborough) Ltd 1982 ICR 693, CA

- the assessment of fairness in unfair dismissal cases – Earl v Slater and Wheeler (Airlyne) Ltd 1972 ICR 508, NIRC

- whether or not an employee was taking part in industrial action – Naylor and ors v Orton and Smith Ltd and anor 1983 ICR 665, EAT

- whether an individual is disabled – Bourne v ECT Bus CIC EAT 0288/08

- what constitutes a fair and proper consultation in the context of redundancy – Slingsby v Griffith Smith Solicitors EAT 0619/07.

Nevertheless, questions of law are also clearly involved in the situations outlined   16.38 above. For example, the question of what is capable of amounting to a fundamental breach of contract is a question of law, but whether or not a breach which is capable of being fundamental actually does go to the heart of the contract is a question that can best be determined by the tribunal on the evidence presented by the parties and is one of fact. Particular difficulty has been caused by the question of employee status. On the face of it, the category into which an

867

agreement falls should be a question of law. Courts have held, however, that in most cases the legal test involves an analysis of a wide range of circumstances – such as control, method of payment and the existence of mutual obligations – which can best be categorised as questions of fact. For further details of these issues see IDS Employment Law Handbook, 'Contracts of Employment' (2009), Chapter 1, 'Basic requirements', under 'Who is an employee?'.

When the issue in question purely concerns the interpretation of a legal document – such as a written contract – then it has been held that higher courts can interfere with a tribunal's decision because the meaning of a legal document is a question of law – Davies v Presbyterian Church of Wales 1986 ICR 280, HL. The interpretation of a statute is also a question of law. However, the question of what is 'reasonable' is a question of fact for tribunals, as is whether or not a provision, criterion or practice is 'justified' in complaints of indirect discrimination. Similarly, the extent to which a claimant is held to have contributed to his or her own dismissal is a matter for the tribunal and not for the EAT. The inevitable result of this is that different tribunals may reach different conclusions on facts that appear virtually identical, but that each decision may well be equally 'right'. Furthermore, the EAT may be confronted with findings of fact made by a tribunal with which it disagrees. In such circumstances, provided there was some evidence on which the tribunal's findings were based, the EAT should not interfere. As Mr Justice Browne-Wilkinson (as he then was) put it in Ellett v Welsh Products Ltd EAT 652/82, 'there is no error of law where there is some evidence pointing in one direction and some evidence pointing in the other direction, and the [employment] tribunal has preferred one set of evidence to the other. A finding contrary to the weight of the evidence is not a question of law.'

16.39 The importance of respecting the tribunal's role as the arbiter of fact was emphasised in the case of Martin v Glynwed Distribution Ltd 1983 ICR 511, CA, in which the then Master of the Rolls, Sir John Donaldson, said: 'It is very important, and sometimes difficult, to remember that where a right of appeal is confined to questions of law, the appellate tribunal must loyally accept the findings of fact with which it is presented and where, as can happen from time to time, it is convinced that it would have reached a different conclusion of fact, it must resist the strong temptation to treat what are in truth findings of fact as holdings of law or mixed findings of fact and law. The correct approach involves recognition that Parliament has constituted the [employment] tribunal the only tribunal of fact and that conclusions of fact must be accepted unless it is apparent that, on the evidence, no reasonable tribunal could have reached them. If such be the case, and happily it is a rarity, the tribunal, which is to be assumed to be a reasonable tribunal, must have misdirected itself in law and the Employment Appeal Tribunal will be entitled to intervene.'

Misdirection or misapplication of the law

16.40

An appellant may have a number of criticisms of an employment tribunal's decision, such as that the tribunal asked itself the wrong legal question; applied the wrong legal test; failed to follow a binding authority; misinterpreted or failed to apply an applicable statutory provision; or identified the wrong comparator for the purposes of a discrimination claim. The EAT must identify the error of law before upholding the appeal. As previously explained, it should not interfere with a tribunal's decision simply on the ground that it would have reached a different decision on the facts. Nor should it conclude that a tribunal has overlooked a point simply because it has not expressly mentioned it in its decision. Indeed, in Brent London Borough Council v Fuller 2011 ICR 806, CA, the Court of Appeal said that 'the reading of an Employment Tribunal decision must not... be so fussy that it produces pernickety critiques. Over-analysis of the reasoning process; being hypercritical of the way in which the decision is written; focusing too much on particular passages or turns of phrase to the neglect of the decision read in the round: those are all appellate weaknesses to avoid.'

Note that a tribunal will not be regarded as having committed an error of law if it fails to apply a statutory provision that was not in force at the date of its decision unless that provision has retrospective effect – Vakante v Governing Body of Addey and Stanhope School (No.2) 2005 ICR 231, CA.

Inadequate reasons for decision

16.41

If an employment tribunal fails to give adequate reasons for its decision, this can amount to an error of law giving rise to an appeal to the EAT. The case almost always quoted in such circumstances is that of Meek v City of Birmingham District Council 1987 IRLR 250, CA, in which the Court of Appeal held that, although a tribunal decision is not required to be an elaborate formalistic product of refined legal draftsmanship, it must nonetheless contain an outline of the facts of the case, a summary of the tribunal's basic factual conclusions, and a statement of the reasons that led it to reach its conclusions on the facts as found. The parties are entitled to be told why they have won or lost, and the tribunal's reasoning must enable an appellate court to determine whether any question of law arises.

In Fisher v Hoopoe Finance Ltd EAT 0043/05 the EAT held that rule 30(6) of the Employment Tribunal Rules 2004 spelt out clearly what a tribunal was required to do to make its decision 'Meek-compliant'. Rule 30(6) required that the tribunal set out, among other things, the issues it had identified as relevant and, if some of those issues were not determined, what those issues were and why they were not determined. However, rule 62(5) of the Employment Tribunal Rules 2013 – which is the equivalent of old rule 30(6) – does not require the tribunal to set out all relevant issues and explain why

— 869

only some have been decided. Rule 62(5) provides that the reasons given for a judgment must:

- identify the issues which the tribunal has determined

- state the findings of fact made in relation to those issues

- concisely identify the relevant law and state how that law has been applied to those findings in order to decide the issues, and

- where the judgment includes a financial award, identify (by means of a table or otherwise) how the amount to be paid has been calculated.

16.42 We presume that if a tribunal decision meets the criteria of rule 62(5) then it will still be 'Meek-compliant' notwithstanding that less detail is now required.

Note that rule 62(5) only applies to 'judgments', defined by rule 1(3) of the Employment Tribunal Rules 2013 as any decision that finally determines liability, remedy or costs, or which is capable of finally disposing of a claim or part of a claim. Therefore, this level of detail is not required for procedural decisions such as case management orders. For further details, see Chapter 14, 'Tribunal judgments', under 'Reasons for judgments – content of written reasons'.

16.43 Employment tribunals must discharge their responsibility to make findings about specific facts. In Peart v Dixons Store Group Retail Ltd EAT 0630/04 the EAT held that statements such as 'we are therefore unable to make any finding' or 'we cannot find that' were an unsatisfactory formula for dealing with undisputed facts. This was because:

- it is the duty of an employment tribunal, faced with a decision as to whether a particular event occurred or not, to find as fact whether it occurred. If there is evidence both ways, it can decide either way. There will be rare occasions when the evidence is so finely balanced that the tribunal is unable to make up its mind as to whether the event occurred or not. In that rare event, the tribunal should say so, and the burden of proof will decide the issue

- the use of the word 'cannot' or 'unable' may suggest that the tribunal thought that there was some legal bar to a particular result. There is no legal bar to the tribunal believing one witness as opposed to another or to a number of other witnesses

- at the end of the case the parties are entitled to know why they have won or lost.

These comments were endorsed in the later EAT decision of Jocic v Hammersmith and Fulham LBC EAT 0194/07.

16.44 **Clarification and/or expansion of reasons – the 'Burns/Barke procedure'.** Note that where the EAT considers an employment tribunal's written reasons

870

for its decision or order to be inadequate, it can invite the tribunal to clarify or supplement its original reasoning or even provide reasoning that was absent altogether. This practice has come to be known as the 'Burns/Barke procedure' because it is based on the reasoning of the EAT in Burns v Royal Mail Group plc (formerly Consignia plc) and anor 2004 ICR 1103, EAT, as subsequently approved by the Court of Appeal in Barke v SEETEC Business Technology Centre Ltd 2005 ICR 1373, CA. The approval of this power to require a tribunal to add to the reasoning set out in its original judgment was given even though it is not part of the statutory framework governing the EAT and has no explicit statutory authorisation. The practice is, however, now codified in para 11.3 of the 2013 Practice Direction. We consider the Burns/Barke procedure in greater detail in Chapter 17, 'Processing an appeal', under 'Interlocutory procedures – miscellaneous powers'.

Failure to exercise discretion 16.45
An error of law will have been committed if an employment tribunal either fails to exercise a discretion or exercises that discretion based on wrong principles – Carter v Credit Change Ltd 1979 ICR 908, CA. Employment judges are often vested with discretion in the exercise of their powers (e.g. the discretion to extend time for complying with interlocutory orders, grant adjournments/postponements and order disclosure/inspection of documents and attendance of witnesses). Although the challenge to such decisions is frequently argued as part of a perversity appeal, the test is, in fact, stricter than that for perversity. An appellant will only succeed if he or she establishes that the tribunal took an improper factor into account; failed to take a proper factor into account; or reached a perverse decision on the exercise of its discretion (i.e. one that no reasonable tribunal could have reached) – Bastick v James Lane (Turf Accountants) Ltd 1979 ICR 778, EAT.

Conduct of the tribunal: bias, procedural irregularity or delay 16.46
Article 6 of the European Convention on Human Rights (ECHR), incorporated into UK law by the Human Rights Act 1998, requires courts and tribunals to ensure that they operate a fair procedure. An allegation by an appellant that he or she did not receive a proper hearing from the tribunal on the ground that there was bias, apparent bias or improper conduct on the part of the tribunal is therefore a ground of appeal to the EAT. An extensive discussion about bias as a ground for appeal can be found in Chapter 12, 'The hearing', under 'Bias'.

Note that para 13 of the 2013 Practice Direction sets out a detailed procedure that must be followed by an appellant who intends to complain about the conduct of the employment tribunal or, indeed, of the EAT itself. A party will not usually be allowed to present allegations about the conduct of the tribunal unless the correct procedure has been complied with (para 13.6.1). This procedure serves to emphasise to the appellant the gravity of the allegations

871

that the party is making. The EAT will look very disapprovingly upon allegations as to the conduct of the tribunal that are made lightly or untruthfully. Further details of the procedure as set out in the Practice Direction are provided below.

16.47 **Bias.** Paragraph 13(1) of the EAT Practice Direction stipulates that an appellant intending to complain about the conduct of the employment tribunal (e.g. bias, apparent bias or improper conduct by the employment judge, lay members or any material irregularity at the hearing) must include in the Notice of Appeal full details of each complaint. At the sift stage, a judge or the Registrar may direct that the appellant or the appellant's representative provide an affidavit or statement setting out full particulars of all allegations of bias or misconduct relied upon – para 13.2.

If a decision is taken at the sift stage to proceed with the appeal, the EAT may take the following steps prior to the hearing within a time limit set out in the relevant order:

- require the appellant (or representative) to provide an affidavit or statement fully particularising the complaint if this has not already been provided

- require any other party, representative or other person present at the tribunal hearing to give an affidavit or provide a witness statement giving their account of the events as set out in the appellant's or representative's own affidavit

- seek the comments of the relevant employment judge and/or lay members upon all affidavits or witness statements received and other relevant documents including the Notice of Appeal. Copies of such comments will then be supplied to the parties – para 13.3.

16.48 Any respondent seeking to make a complaint of bias or irregularity in its Notice of Appeal or by way of cross-appeal must provide full particulars of the complaint following which the procedure as set out above will be followed – para 13.4.

Paragraph 13.6 of the Practice Direction explicitly draws the parties' attention to the fact that the EAT will not permit bias and irregularity complaints to be raised or developed at the hearing of the appeal unless the procedure as outlined above has been followed. The Practice Direction also expressly recognises that employment judges and employment tribunals are given wide powers and duties in relation to case management so that appeals in respect of the conduct of a tribunal when exercising such powers and duties are less likely to succeed. Finally, para 13.6.3 warns that the unsuccessful pursuit of an allegation of bias or improper conduct – particularly in respect of case management decisions – may expose the party raising the complaint to an order for costs.

16.49 **Procedural irregularities.** Irregularity will be taken to have occurred where the employment tribunal relies on matters after the hearing that had not been mentioned or treated as relevant during the hearing. In Neale v Hereford and Worcester County Council 1986 ICR 471, CA, Lord Justice Gibson said that 'it would be unwise and potentially unfair for a tribunal to rely upon matters which occur to members of the tribunal after the hearing and which have not been mentioned or treated as relevant without the party, against whom the point is raised, being given the opportunity to deal with it unless the tribunal could be entirely sure that the point is so clear that the party could not make any useful comment in explanation'.

Reliance on uncited case authorities. In Stanley Cole (Wainfleet) Ltd v **16.50** Sheridan 2003 ICR 1449, CA, the Court of Appeal made the general point that it was impossible to lay down a rigid rule as to where the boundaries of procedural irregularity lie or what makes a hearing unfair – everything depends on the subject matter and the facts and circumstances of each case. However, it did give the following guidance in relation to the consideration and reliance on case authorities that have not been cited to the tribunal in the course of the parties' legal submissions or in the pleadings:

- where an employment tribunal considers that an authority is 'relevant, significant and material' it should alert the parties to that authority and invite them to give submissions before concluding its decision. Failure to do so may amount to a breach of natural justice and of the right to a fair hearing – Albion Hotel (Freshwater) Ltd v Maia e Silva 2002 IRLR 200, EAT

- a case authority will only be relevant, significant and material if it is central to the decision and not peripheral to it. It must play an influential part in shaping the judgment

- the test is whether what happened was 'seriously irregular and unfair'. For example, there is no serious irregularity simply because an employment judge cites in his or her judgment cases that had not been referred to in the course of the hearing. Judicial research would be stultified if that were so

- there must be 'material injustice' as a result of what happened – Nelson v Carillion Services Ltd EAT 837/01. For example, there will be no material injustice if the case authority would have made no difference to the outcome of the tribunal's decision had it been referred to the parties during the hearing.

Delay. Article 6(1) ECHR provides that 'in the determination of his civil rights **16.51** and obligations... everyone is entitled to a fair and public hearing within a reasonable time by an independent and impartial tribunal established by law'. A delay by the tribunal in promulgating its decision *may* therefore give rise to grounds for appeal under the terms of the ECHR. However the Court of Appeal stressed in Bangs v Connex South Eastern Ltd 2005 ICR 763, CA, that this type of delay by the tribunal does not automatically amount to a serious procedural error giving rise to a question of law within the meaning of S.21(1) ETA. The key question is whether, owing to the unreasonable delay, there is a real risk

873

that a party has in substance been denied or deprived of the Article 6 right to a fair trial and whether it would be unfair and unjust to allow the delayed decision to stand.

The EAT considered the time frame within which it would be reasonable to expect a tribunal to deliver its decision in Kwamin v Abbey National plc and other cases 2004 ICR 841, EAT. As a starting point, it noted that the High Court was expected to deliver a judgment within three months of the end of a hearing. There, the judgment was the responsibility of the judge alone. Allowing for the difficulties of, and the necessity of, communication between the three members of a tribunal, the EAT stated that there ought to be no reason why three-and-a-half months should not be the maximum time after the end of a case for preparation and promulgation of all but the most complicated and lengthy judgments.

16.52 In Grosvenor v Governing Body of Aylesford School and ors and other cases EAT 0001/08 an employment tribunal case that was originally listed for 15 days actually lasted 40. Thereafter, the tribunal spent a total of 26 days deliberating the case before delivering its judgment approximately one year from the end of the hearing. Having considered Bangs (above) the EAT held that, although a delay of one year in promulgating a judgment ought never to happen, the unusual feature in this case was the amount of time spent by the tribunal considering the matter. Given that there was not a large gap in time between the tribunal's deliberations and delivery of its judgment, the mere fact of delay in this case did not, of itself, constitute a free-standing ground of appeal.

In Somjee v United Kingdom 2002 IRLR 886, ECtHR, the European Court of Human Rights considered what factors should be taken into account when assessing the reasonable length of proceedings. The claimant in that case had launched three sets of proceedings against her employer. These had taken eight years and nine months, seven years and eleven months and eight years and eight months respectively to resolve. The Court noted that some of the issues to be determined had been complex and that some of the delay could be attributed to the claimant. These factors reduced the period of time for which the tribunal and the EAT – and ultimately the UK Government – could be held accountable. However, as the conduct of the tribunal and the EAT had contributed directly to the length of the proceedings, there had been a violation of Article 6(1) ECHR.

16.53 **No evidence supporting factual findings**

A party may seek to appeal to the EAT on the basis that there was no evidence to support a finding of fact by the tribunal. Where there *is* some evidence to justify a finding, but the appellant considers that evidence to be insufficient, the appeal should be made on the ground that the tribunal's decision was perverse (see 'Perversity' below). In this regard, it should be borne in mind that a tribunal's finding that is contrary to the *weight* of evidence does not amount to a question of law capable of being appealed – Ellett v Welsh Products Ltd EAT 652/82. Mr Justice Browne-Wilkinson (as he then was) observed in that case: '[The EAT's] jurisdiction is limited to correcting errors of law only. An error of law can be shown if a tribunal has failed to make a finding of fact as to which there was uncontroverted evidence, or has made a finding of fact contrary to all the evidence. It is equally clear that there is no error of law where there is some evidence pointing in one direction and some evidence pointing in the other direction, and the [employment] tribunal has preferred one set of evidence to the other... It is for the... tribunal to make its decision as to the weight of the evidence and to make the findings as to what the position was.'

Nor is it an error of law for a tribunal to fail to refer to all of the evidence (or submissions by the parties) in its judgment – see the judgment of Lord Justice Buxton in Balfour Beatty Power Networks and anor v Wilcox and ors 2007 IRLR 63, CA, and the EAT's decision in Blitz v Vectone Group Holdings Ltd EAT 0253/10. Indeed, the EAT has ruled that it is its duty to assume in an employment tribunal's favour that all the relevant evidence and all the relevant factors were in the tribunal's mind, whether express reference to that appears in its final decision or not – see Royal Society for the Protection of Birds v Croucher 1984 ICR 604, EAT.

Perversity   16.54

An appeal against a tribunal's decision (or its interim order – see Younas v Chief Constable of Thames Valley EAT 795/00) will succeed where it is shown that that decision was perverse. The precise nature of such 'perversity', however, has proved somewhat elusive. A commonly quoted statement in this context is that of Lord Justice May in Neale v Hereford and Worcester County Council 1986 ICR 471, CA: 'Deciding these cases is the job of [employment] tribunals and when they have not erred in law neither the Appeal Tribunal nor this court should disturb their decision unless one can say in effect: "My goodness, that was certainly wrong".'

In the later case of Stewart v Cleveland Guest (Engineering) Ltd 1996 ICR 535, EAT, Mr Justice Mummery (as he then was) gave further examples of when a decision might be considered perverse: namely, when on the evidence it concludes that the decision is 'irrational, offends reason, is certainly wrong or is not a permissible option or is fundamentally wrong or is outrageous or makes absolutely no sense or flies in the face of properly informed logic'.

In Piggott Brothers and Co Ltd v Jackson and ors 1992 ICR 85, CA, the Court   16.55
of Appeal warned that there was a danger that an appellate court could easily persuade itself that, because it would not have reached the same conclusion, the tribunal's decision must certainly be wrong. Here, the Court stressed that what mattered was whether the decision under appeal was a *permissible option*. If

875

the EAT was inclined to find that it was not, then it would almost certainly be possible to identify a finding of fact which was unsupported by any evidence or a clear misdirection by the tribunal as to the law to be applied. If the EAT could identify no such finding or misdirection, said the Court, then it would have to 're-examine with the greatest care' its conclusion that the tribunal's decision was perverse.

Appeals on the ground of perversity were analysed further by Lord Justice Mummery in Yeboah v Crofton 2002 IRLR 634, CA. There, an employment tribunal made findings of fact from which it drew inferences leading to a conclusion that the claimant had been discriminated against on the ground of his race. That decision was appealed on many grounds, including that it was perverse in that it excluded or disregarded important evidence. The EAT agreed that the tribunal's findings had not been supported by evidence and it overturned the decision. The employee then appealed to the Court of Appeal, which held that the EAT had been unjustified in concluding that specific findings of fact and ultimate decisions on liability by the tribunal had been perverse, as the EAT had considered only part of the vast expanse of evidence that had been available to the tribunal (the tribunal hearing had lasted 104 days). Furthermore, the EAT had reached its decision in response to a largely unparticularised notice of appeal and in the absence of counsel representing either party.

16.56 Giving the lead judgment of the Court, Lord Justice Mummery made some general observations about perversity appeals, commenting that they 'ought only to succeed where an overwhelming case is made out that the employment tribunal reached a decision which no reasonable tribunal, on a proper appreciation of the evidence and the law, would have reached'. Accordingly, it is very difficult for a claimant to succeed in a perversity appeal. Mummery LJ also cautioned that the EAT should not allow appeals to be turned into a rehearing of parts of the evidence, observing that this might lead it to substitute its own assessment for that of the tribunal. This would not be appropriate given that only the employment tribunal hears all the relevant evidence first hand, and that the evidence available to the EAT is always incomplete. Indeed, in Perry v Imperial College Healthcare NHS Trust EAT 0473/10 the EAT acknowledged that the high threshold for perversity challenges has been referred to by the Court of Appeal numerous times, which serves as a warning that the EAT should not too easily substitute its decision for that of the tribunal on the ground of perversity.

In Bowater v North West London Hospitals NHS Trust 2011 IRLR 331, CA, B, a staff nurse, was dismissed for gross misconduct following a suggestive comment she made while straddling the naked genitals of a patient who was suffering from a fit. The tribunal held that B was unfairly dismissed, finding that, at worst, the comment could have been described as lewd and that a 'large proportion of the population' would have considered it merely humorous. The

EAT allowed the employer's appeal, holding that the tribunal should have considered how a reasonable NHS Trust would have treated that comment. In restoring the tribunal's decision, the Court of Appeal held that the EAT had been overcritical and stated that the EAT should pay 'proper respect' to tribunals' decisions, since Parliament has entrusted them with the responsibility of making difficult and borderline decisions in relation to the fairness of a dismissal. Given that an appeal to the EAT lies only on a point of law, it was important that the EAT did not, under the guise of a charge of perversity, substitute its own judgment for that of the tribunal.

Appeals against strike-out. In Riley v Crown Prosecution Service EAT 0043/12 **16.57** the EAT commented that there was a potential disconnect between two lines of authority emanating from the Court of Appeal in relation to the approach that should be taken by the EAT in strike-out appeals. One view – exemplified by cases such as Teinaz v London Borough of Wandsworth 2002 ICR 1471 – was that the EAT could interfere on the ground of 'Wednesbury reasonableness' (or perversity, as it is often called). This principle, which arose out of the Court of Appeal's decision in Associated Provincial Picture Houses Ltd v Wednesbury Corporation 1948 1 KB 223, CA, is that a public body will breach its duty to make reasonable decisions if it makes a decision so unreasonable that no reasonable decision-maker could have arrived at it. The other view, exemplified by the Court of Appeal in Terluk v Berezovsky 2010 EWCA Civ 1345, CA, required the tribunal to reach the 'right' conclusion on the question of whether it was 'fair' to strike out the proceedings and, if the EAT considered that it had reached the wrong decision, then that decision would be set aside.

In O'Cathail v Transport for London 2013 ICR 614, CA, Lord Justice Mummery resolved this apparent conflict in favour of the Wednesbury test. He observed: 'The crucial point of difference from Terluk's case is that decisions of the employment tribunal can only be appealed on questions of law, whereas under the [Civil Procedure Rules] the appeal is normally by way of review and the decision of a lower court can be set aside, if it is wrong, or if it is unjust by reason of a serious procedural or other irregularity in the proceedings. In relation to case management the employment tribunal has exceptionally wide powers of managing cases brought by and against parties who are often without the benefit of legal representation. The tribunal's decisions can only be questioned for error of law. A question of law only arises in relation to their exercise, when there is an error of legal principle in the approach or perversity in the outcome. That is the approach, including failing to take account of a relevant matter or taking account of an irrelevant one, which the Employment Appeal Tribunal should continue to adopt rather than the approach in Terluk.'

Procedural requirements. In Yeboah v Crofton 2002 IRLR 634, CA, Mummery **16.58** LJ emphasised that an appeal based on perversity should always be fully particularised in order that the respondent can be prepared to meet it, and also

877

in order to deter hopeless appeals on factual points. This guidance is reflected in the 2013 Practice Direction, para 3.8 of which provides that, in any appeal brought on the ground of perversity, an appellant may not 'state as a ground of appeal simply words to the effect that "the judgment or order was contrary to the evidence," or that "there was no evidence to support the judgment or order", or that "the judgment or order was one which no reasonable tribunal could have reached and was perverse" unless the Notice of Appeal also sets out full particulars of the matters relied on in support of those general grounds'. Further, in Inland Revenue Commissioners v Millar EATS 0003/08 the EAT said that if a perversity case is to be made, then it is necessary for the Appeal Tribunal to have either notes of the evidence that are agreed by the parties, or the employment judge's notes of evidence. In the absence of such notes, the EAT cannot with confidence make a finding that a decision was made without evidence. For example, the tribunal may have heard live evidence from the witnesses that provides a proper basis for its conclusions, even though on the face of it their evidence appears to be at odds with documentary material.

The EAT is entitled to refuse to allow a full hearing of a notice of appeal that does not properly and relevantly focus on a question of law. In Krishna v Argyll and Bute Council and ors 2005 CSIH 52, Ct Sess (Inner House), the Court of Session considered an employee's contention that, once she had identified perversity in her notice of appeal, the EAT had no discretion to refuse to entertain it. Her appeals (she submitted two) had been rejected by the Registrar. The employee resubmitted her appeals under rule 3(10) of the EAT Rules (which at the time meant that the Registrar had to place the papers before the President or a judge where the appellant was dissatisfied with his or her decision), and the revised appeals were refused once again. Hearing her appeal, the Court of Session held that the fact that her notices of appeal identified perversity as a ground of appeal did not automatically entitle her to a full hearing. It also rejected the employee's argument that the EAT's procedure for accepting appeals in effect imposed an unauthorised 'leave to appeal' requirement on would-be appellants. On the contrary, it observed that an appeal is 'instituted' as soon as a timeous notice of appeal arrives at the EAT's offices, and is in existence and being processed while it is being considered by the Registrar (or a judge under the rule 3(10) procedure). The sift procedure was not therefore inconsistent with the fact that leave to appeal is not a requirement or precondition for lodging appeals to the EAT.

16.59 Note that, following the 2013 amendments to the EAT Rules, an appellant is no longer automatically entitled to a rule 3(10) hearing where he or she is dissatisfied with the Registrar's decision. For further details, see Chapter 17, 'Processing an appeal', under 'The sift – rule 3(7) cases (no valid grounds of appeal)'.

17 Processing an appeal

17.1 This chapter examines the procedures involved in bringing an appeal before the EAT, from the lodging of the notice of appeal to the interim matters that may arise before the appeal proper is heard.

The appeal process is governed by the Employment Appeal Tribunal Rules 1993 SI 1993/2854 ('the EAT Rules'), which came into force on 16 December 1993. These were subsequently amended by the Employment Appeal Tribunal (Amendment) Rules 2004 SI 2004/2526; the Employment Appeal Tribunal (Amendment) Rules 2005 SI 2005/1871; and most recently the Employment Appeal Tribunal (Amendment) Rules 2013 SI 2013/1693.

17.2 Supplementing the statutory rules, the EAT is empowered to issue Practice Directions. The current Practice Direction (2013 ICR 1382) came into force on 29 July 2013 and its provisions are referenced extensively in this chapter. In addition, the EAT occasionally issues 'Practice Statements' on specific aspects of procedure. The latest of these is the statement issued in amended form on 23 April 2012 by the current President of the EAT, Mr Justice Langstaff, dealing with the citation of case authorities and the admission of evidence on appeal not previously placed before the employment tribunal.

Subject to the EAT Rules, EAT Practice Directions, and directions given by the President of the Appeal Tribunal, the EAT has the power to regulate its own procedure – S.30(3) Employment Tribunals Act 1996.

879

17.3 Note that the scope of this chapter is restricted to the procedure involved in appeals against decisions of employment tribunals. It does not cover in detail the procedure applying to first instance proceedings before the EAT under:

- the Transnational Information and Consultation of Employees Regulations 1999 SI 1999/3323 ('the TICE Regulations')

- the European Public Limited-Liability Company Regulations 2004 SI 2004/2326 ('the EPLLC Regulations')

- the European Public Limited-Liability Company (Employee Involvement) (Great Britain) Regulations 2009 SI 2009/2401 ('the EPLLC(EI) Regulations')

- the Information and Consultation of Employees Regulations 2004 SI 2004/3426 ('the ICE Regulations')

- the Companies (Cross-Border Mergers) Regulations 2007 SI 2007/2974 ('the C(CBM) Regulations'), and

- the European Cooperative Society (Involvement of Employees) Regulations 2006 SI 2006/2059.

Nor does it cover proceedings arising from decisions of the Certification Officer under the Trade Union and Labour Relations (Consolidation) Act 1992. In most cases the procedure to be followed by an appellant in such cases does not differ much from that outlined in this and the next chapter (Chapter 18, 'EAT hearings and decisions'). However, subscribers should consult the specific provisions in the EAT Rules and 2013 Practice Direction for further information.

17.4 Also note that this chapter does not deal with the special steps applying to 'national security proceedings' – i.e. proceedings that have been identified as such by either a Minister of the Crown or an employment tribunal under rule 94 of Schedule 1 to the Employment Tribunals (Constitution and Rules of Procedure) Regulations 2013 SI 2013/1237 (the Tribunal Rules 2013). Once again, reference should be made to the EAT Rules and the Practice Direction.

17.5 Overriding objective

Although formally introduced by way of amendment to the EAT Rules in 2004 – to bring them into line with the Tribunal Rules 2004 – the overriding objective has actually been part and parcel of EAT procedure since a Practice Statement issued in 2002 (now incorporated into the current 2013 Practice Direction). Its purpose is to enable the EAT to deal with cases 'justly' – rule 2A EAT Rules. Rule 2A and para 1.5 of the Practice Direction explain that dealing with a case justly includes, so far as practicable:

- ensuring that the parties are on an equal footing

- dealing with the case in ways which are proportionate to the importance and complexity of the issues

- ensuring that the case is dealt with expeditiously and fairly, and

- saving expense.

The EAT must seek to give effect to the overriding objective when exercising any power given to it by the EAT Rules. Also, the parties are under a duty to assist the EAT to further the overriding objective – rule 2A(3). Para 1.6 of the Practice Direction explains that dealing with a case justly includes safeguarding the EAT's resources so that each case receives its fair share of available time but no more.

A number of changes to procedure brought about by the 2004 amending **17.6** regulations clearly have furtherance of the overriding objective in mind. One consequence of the amendments was that the EAT began applying an initial vetting of appeals at an early stage (termed 'the sift') in order to determine whether it has jurisdiction to hear the appeal. One aspect of the sift – as expressly reflected in the previous 2008 Practice Direction – was that of appeals being allocated to one of the following four tracks to help promote effective and appropriate case management:

- rule 3(7) cases

- preliminary hearing cases

- full hearing cases, and

- fast-track full hearing cases.

Although the 2013 Practice Direction does not list these four tracks in the same explicit way, the heading of para 11 is 'The Sift of Appeals: Case Tracks and Directions', and it is clear upon reading the contents of that rule that the allocation of an appeal to one of these four tracks continues to be part of the sift process. For further discussion of each of the four case tracks, see 'The sift' below.

In addition, the 2013 Practice Direction specifically requires the parties to **17.7** agree as much as possible before the hearing – such as the preparation of a core bundle to ensure that documentation is confined to that which is necessary and relevant (para 8.1) and cooperation as to the case authorities being relied upon (para 17.2).

Note that the overriding objective influences not just the EAT's application of its own Rules but also its assessment of tribunals' decisions. In Williams v Ferrosan Ltd 2004 IRLR 607, EAT, for example, the EAT held that an employment tribunal had been wrong to refuse to use the review procedure to correct an error made by the employment judge and the parties. In the EAT's

881

view, reviewing the decision rather than appealing it was the correct route to take, as it provided a quicker and less expensive remedy for the parties. It was therefore in the interests of justice and in furtherance of the overriding objective for the tribunal's decision to be reviewed rather than appealed.

17.8 Instituting an appeal

Every appeal must be instituted by the appellant lodging a notice of appeal, together with appropriate supplemental documents and fee, at the EAT. Below, we set out what exactly is required and examine the form which a notice of appeal should take.

17.9 Documents required

The 2004 amendments to the EAT Rules extended the list of supplemental documents that an appellant must lodge with the EAT along with his or her notice of appeal. As discussed below, the requirements differ depending on whether the appeal is against a tribunal *judgment* or a tribunal *order*.

17.10 Judgments and orders. Rule 1(3)(a) of the Tribunal Rules 2013 defines an 'order' as being an order or decision of any kind in relation to the conduct of proceedings. Rule 1(3)(b) of those Rules defines a 'judgment' as a decision, made at any stage of the proceedings (but not including the reconsideration of a decision to reject a claim) that finally determines liability, remedy or costs, or which is capable of finally disposing of a claim or part of a claim (or which finally determines the imposition of a financial penalty under S.12A ETA).

17.11 All appeals. In all cases, a notice of appeal in accordance (or substantially in accordance) with form 1, 1A or 2 in the Schedule to the EAT Rules is required. Form 1 is a notice of appeal from an employment tribunal decision; form 1A is a notice of appeal from a decision, declaration or order of the Central Arbitration Committee made under the TICE Regulations, the EPLLC(EI) Regulations, the ICE Regulations, or the C(CBM) Regulations. Form 2 is a notice of appeal from a decision of the Certification Officer. The notice must identify the date of the judgment, decision or order being appealed (para 3.1 of the Practice Direction). Requirements as to the actual content of the notice of appeal – in particular, the setting out of the substantial grounds of appeal – are discussed under 'Grounds of appeal' below.

(Note that a number of forms mentioned in this chapter are available on the EAT's website (www.justice.gov.uk/forms/hmcts/employment-appeals).)

17.12 Appeals from judgments and appeals from orders. Rule 3(1) of the EAT Rules distinguishes between appeals against tribunal *judgments* and appeals against tribunal *orders*. In the case of an appeal from a *judgment* of an employment tribunal, an appellant must provide, in addition to the notice of appeal:

882

- a copy of any claim or response in the proceedings before the tribunal or an explanation as to why either is not included – rule 3(1)(b), and

- a copy of the judgment which is the subject of the appeal together with a copy of the written reasons for the tribunal's judgment (or explanation as to why written reasons are not included) – rule 3(1)(c).

If the tribunal records its reasons in two separate judgments, both must be served with the notice of appeal. Failure to do this will result in the appeal being rejected – Yorkshire Window Co Ltd v Parkes EAT 0484/09. Furthermore, where the tribunal has used the slip rule to revoke its judgment (either in full or in part) and issues a new or revised one in its place, that new or revised judgment must be attached to the notice of appeal in order for it to be validly lodged – Kennaugh v Lloyd-Jones t/a Cheshire Tree Surgeons EAT 0710/07. The 'slip rule' – rule 69 of the Tribunal Rules 2013 – enables an employment tribunal to rectify any clerical mistake in a decision, order or judgment caused by an accidental slip or omission.

The means by which an appellant can obtain the written reasons for a tribunal's **17.13** decision (if these have not been automatically provided) are explained below, under 'Written reasons'.

Where an appeal relates to an *order* of an employment tribunal as opposed to a judgment, rule 3(1) suggests that the requirements are less stringent. Rule 3(1)(e) states that an appellant must provide, in addition to the notice of appeal, a copy of the written record of the order of the tribunal and, 'if available', the written reasons for the order. There is no requirement that an appellant provide an explanation as to why written reasons are not included. Furthermore, there is nothing in rule 3(1) to suggest that a copy of the claim or response forms from the tribunal proceedings must be lodged with an appeal against an order.

Importantly, however, and in contrast with rule 3(1), the Practice Direction **17.14** makes *no* distinction between appeals against judgments and appeals against orders, suggesting that the requirements are the same with regard to both. Para 3.1 of the Practice Direction states that 'copies of the *judgment, decision or order* appealed against must be attached, as must be the Employment Tribunal's written reasons, together with a copy of the claim (ET1) and the response (ET3), or if not, a written explanation for the omission of [any of these documents] must be given' (our stress). Bearing in mind that the para 3.1 requirements were emphasised by Mr Justice Burton in a Practice Statement issued in 2005, parties wishing to bring appeals against tribunal orders – whether they be legally represented or litigants in person – would be wise to comply with them. (For further information on Practice Statements, see Chapter 16, 'The Employment Appeal Tribunal', under 'EAT Rules, Practice Directions and Practice Statements').

883

17.15 *Other relevant documents.* The following documents should also be included with a notice of appeal, if relevant:

- a copy of any application to an employment tribunal for reconsideration of its judgment together with the judgment and written reasons of the tribunal in respect of that application, or a statement that these documents are awaited, and

- copies of any orders, including case management orders, made by the employment tribunal to the extent that these are relevant to the appeal – paras 3.2 and 3.3 Practice Direction.

Note that if an appellant wants to appeal against both the reconsideration decision and the original decision, he or she should use two separate notices of appeal.

17.16 Prior failure to defend claim in employment tribunal

It sometimes happens that a respondent to the original employment tribunal proceedings fails to defend those proceedings by submitting a response to the claim (ET3), or fails to apply for an extension of the deadline for submitting such a response, as a result of which it is barred from taking any active part in the tribunal proceedings. In such a case, where that party subsequently seeks to appeal to the EAT against the tribunal's judgment or order, it must comply with the following specific requirements:

- the grounds of appeal must include particulars directed at determining (a) whether there is a good excuse for failing to present the ET3 and, if that is the case, for further failing to apply for an extension of time; and (b) whether there is a reasonably arguable defence to the original tribunal claim (ET1)

- accompanying the notice of appeal, the appellant must present the EAT with a witness statement detailing the circumstances in which there has been a failure to serve the ET3 in time or to apply for an extension of time, the reason for that failure and the facts and matters relied upon for contesting the employment tribunal claim on the merits

- all other relevant documents together with a completed draft ET3 must be exhibited to the aforementioned witness statement – para 19 Practice Direction.

17.17 Fees

On 29 July 2013 – by virtue of the Employment Tribunals and the Employment Appeal Tribunal Fees Order 2013 SI 2013/1893 ('the Order') – a fee regime was introduced simultaneously in employment tribunals and the EAT. Part 3 of the Order deals with the fees applicable to EAT proceedings. Potentially, two different types of fee are now payable: one in connection with the submission of a notice of appeal (or cross-appeal), and the other in connection with hearings. In order to institute an appeal and thereafter for there to be a hearing of the appeal, it is a precondition that the appropriate fee has been paid (or for the appellant to demonstrate that remission of the fee has been authorised). For full details, see Chapter 19, 'Fees', under 'EAT fees'.

Failure to lodge the required documents   17.18
A notice of appeal lodged at the EAT without all the required supplemental documentation will not be valid. Previously, the EAT's practice had been to accept a timely notice of appeal despite incomplete documentation. However, this practice was stopped by a combination of the EAT's decision in Kanapathiar v London Borough of Harrow 2003 IRLR 571, EAT, and changes that were made to rule 3 of the EAT Rules and the then applicable 2004 Practice Direction. In Kanapathiar – a decision reached prior to the 2004 amendments to the Rules – Mr Justice Burton insisted that henceforth a notice of appeal served without the tribunal's written reasons was invalid and would have the same status as a notice that had not been submitted at all. His subsequent 2005 Practice Statement clarified that the rule in Kanapathiar applied equally to the additional supplemental documentation now explicitly required under the Rules.

Form of notice of appeal   17.19
As explained under 'Documents required' above, the EAT Rules require that every appeal to the EAT be instituted by serving on the EAT a notice of appeal in, or substantially in, accordance with form 1, 1A or 2 as set out in the Schedule to the Rules – rule 3(1)(a).

From the wording of rule 3(1)(a) it is clear that the Rules do not lay down an absolute requirement for the proper forms to be used when lodging an appeal. They merely require that there should be 'substantial accordance' with one of the appropriate forms. This can be contrasted with proceedings in the employment tribunal, where an ET1 must be used by a person wishing to bring a claim, and an ET3 by a person wishing to respond to it.

As the case of Martin v British Railways Board 1989 ICR 24, EAT, indicates,   17.20
however, this does not mean that the Appeal Tribunal will tolerate significant departures from the prescribed appeal method. There, the appellant's notice of appeal was five days late, but he argued that a letter written by his solicitors saying that 'our client wishes to appeal against the decision of the industrial tribunal' should be treated as a notice of appeal and that, in any case, latitude was to be encouraged in this jurisdiction because appellants were often unrepresented. Mr Justice Wood, then President of the EAT, said that the letter could not be deemed a proper notice of appeal and that it was only in 'clearly exceptional' cases that a document other than an EAT prescribed form could be admitted. Where a proper form was not used, the document containing the notice of appeal should show 'the efforts made to acquire such a form; the

885

names and addresses of each of the parties; the date and content of the decision; the identity of the tribunal; and sufficiently defined grounds of appeal', together with a copy of the full reasons for the tribunal's decision.

17.21 Written reasons

In the discussion under 'Documents required' above, we explained that an appellant must provide the EAT with the employment tribunal's written reasons for the judgment or order under appeal or, failing that, with an explanation as to why such reasons are not being provided – para 3.1 Practice Direction. Below, we examine how a party can get hold of a tribunal's written reasons and the consequences of his or her failing to do so. For an explanation of what a tribunal must include in a set of written reasons, see Chapter 14, 'Tribunal judgments', under 'Reasons for judgments – content of written reasons'.

17.22 **Obtaining written reasons.** Rule 62(1) of the Employment Tribunal Rules 2013 provides that a tribunal shall give reasons for its decision on any disputed issue, *whether substantial or procedural*, including any decision on an application for reconsideration (formerly known as a 'review'), or orders for costs, preparation time or wasted costs.

17.23 *Decision given in writing.* In the case of a decision given in writing the reasons shall also be given in writing – rule 62(2).

17.24 *Decision announced at the hearing.* In the case of a decision announced at a hearing, the reasons may be given orally at the hearing or reserved to be given in writing later (which may, but need not, be as part of the written record of the decision) – rule 62(2). Where reasons have been given orally, the employment judge shall announce that written reasons will not be provided unless they are asked for by any party at the hearing itself or by a written request presented by any party within 14 days of the sending of the written record of the decision – rule 62(3).

17.25 **Where no written reasons are available.** Where an appellant has failed to obtain the tribunal's written reasons for a judgment or order, it goes without saying that he or she will not be able to send such reasons to the EAT. Para 3.1 of the Practice Direction states that, in such circumstances, the appellant must, together with his or her notice of appeal, provide an explanation as to why written reasons are not being provided. Para 3.4 of the Practice Direction clarifies the position further, explaining: 'Where written reasons of the Employment Tribunal are not attached to the Notice of Appeal, either (as set out in the written explanation) because a request for written reasons has been refused by the Employment Tribunal or for some other reason, an appellant must, when presenting the Notice of Appeal, apply in writing to the EAT to exercise its power to hear the appeal without written reasons or to exercise its power [under rule 62(3)] to request written reasons from the Employment Tribunal, setting out the full grounds of that application.'

As stated above, rule 62(3) of the Employment Tribunal Rules provides that the EAT can request written reasons for an order or a judgment at any time. A party who has failed to obtain written reasons should, when submitting his or her notice of appeal, attempt to persuade the EAT to use this power. As Mr Justice Burton, then President of the EAT, noted in NSM Music Ltd v Leefe 2006 ICR 450, EAT, this is not a jurisdiction that the Appeal Tribunal would wish to exercise very often. Nevertheless, he continued, the EAT now does, on its sift, make use of rule 30(3) of the Employment Tribunal Rules 2004 (now rule 62(3) of the Employment Tribunal Rules 2013) in appropriate cases where there are no reasons provided by a tribunal either because they have not been sought or because they have been sought and refused.

Grounds of appeal   17.26

We saw under 'Documents required' above that a notice of appeal must be set out in accordance (or substantially in accordance) with form 1, 1A or 2 in the Schedule to the EAT Rules. Form 1 – the appropriate form for an appeal against an employment tribunal decision – requires the appellant to state the grounds upon which the appeal is brought.

Particulars. The notice of appeal must identify the grounds of appeal clearly. **17.27**
In Dass v Tower Hamlets College EAT 127/98 the EAT refused to accept D's appeal because his notice of appeal, which was spread over 17 pages of single-spaced typewriting, did not comply with para 2.3 of the 1996 Practice Direction. This stated that 'the Notice of Appeal must clearly identify the point of law which forms the ground of appeal from the decision of the Employment Tribunal to the EAT. It may also state the Order which the Appellant will ask the EAT to make at the hearing.' The EAT held that, largely because of its size, the notice of appeal failed to identify clearly the points of law that D had sought to rely upon. Accordingly, the EAT adjourned so that D could be given the opportunity to amend his notice of appeal in this regard. Note that para 3.5 of the 2013 Practice Direction contains an almost identical obligation to that found in para 2.3 of the 1996 version. Para 3.6 also stipulates that 'A Notice of Appeal should be no longer than the making of a clear statement of the ground of appeal requires... [I]t should not set out detailed argument and citation from case law unless this is essential for understanding.'

The EAT's decision in Tran v Greenwich Vietnam Community Project EAT 185/00 is another case in which the Appeal Tribunal decided that an employee had failed to properly particularise his appeal. The employee appealed against an employment tribunal's decision that he had not been unfairly dismissed and, during the appeal hearing, the employee's representative sought to advance the argument that the tribunal had failed to explain the reason for its findings. The EAT noted, however, that the notice of appeal had simply referred to the lack of a clear reason on the part of the employer for its decision and not to a lack of clarity by the tribunal. Furthermore, the employee's skeleton argument did

887

not develop any clear complaint against the tribunal. The EAT held that, therefore, the employee had not developed any clear ground of appeal.

17.28 **Perversity appeals.** As explained in Chapter 16, 'The Employment Appeal Tribunal', under 'Grounds of appeal – perversity', appeals to the EAT that are founded on the argument that a tribunal's decision was 'perverse' are subject to para 3.8 of the Practice Direction. This makes it clear that 'an appellant may not state as a ground of appeal simply words to the effect that "the judgment or order was contrary to the evidence," or that "there was no evidence to support the judgment or order", or that "the judgment or order was one which no reasonable tribunal could have reached and was perverse" unless the Notice of Appeal also sets out full particulars of the matters relied on in support of those general grounds'. This requirement was emphasised by Lord Justice Mummery in Yeboah v Crofton 2002 IRLR 634, CA. Essentially, this amounts to a check on parties pursuing hopeless appeals on the ground of perversity.

The Practice Direction appears to contemplate that the length of the Notice of Appeal may be greater in perversity or bias appeals than in other types of appeal, presumably owing to the need to explain evidential and other issues in such appeals as opposed to most other grounds of appeal where it is simply necessary to outline the alleged error(s) of law relied upon – see para 3.6.

17.29 **Amending a notice of appeal.** The grounds specified by a party in its notice of appeal will, in most cases, define the scope of the appeal hearing. Unless there are exceptional circumstances, the EAT will not allow appellants to raise new grounds of appeal at a later stage. Para 3.10 of the Practice Direction states that it is not open to parties to 'reserve the right' to amend, alter or add to a notice of appeal or a respondent's answer, and goes on to provide that a party wishing to amend its notice of appeal or answer must make an application for leave to amend as soon as practicable. Such an application must be accompanied by a draft of the amended pleading that makes clear the precise amendments for which permission is sought.

The case of Khudados v Leggate and ors 2005 ICR 1013, EAT, outlines the matters that will be considered by the EAT in deciding an application for leave to amend a notice of appeal. The starting point is the overriding objective to deal with cases justly. The EAT noted that justice includes fairness to all sides, and to the interests of the public in the efficient administration of courts and tribunals. In addition, the EAT will take into account the following:

- whether the appellant has complied with the requirements of para 3.10 of the Practice Direction. This is of considerable importance. The requirement to make an application for leave to amend as soon as possible is not simply aspirational or an expression of hope

- whether the EAT has received a full, honest and acceptable explanation for any delay or failure to comply with the EAT Rules or Practice Direction

- the extent to which the proposed amendments, if allowed, will cause any delay. Proposed amendments which fill in existing grounds of appeal are more likely to be allowed than wholly new grounds of perversity raising issues of complex fact, which, if allowed, are bound to cause delay and extra expense

- whether allowing the amendments will cause prejudice to the opposite party, and whether refusing the amendments will cause prejudice to the appellant by depriving him or her of fairly arguable grounds of appeal

- in some cases, the merits of the proposed amendments. The amendments, as a general rule, must raise a point of law that gives the appeal a reasonable prospect of success at a full hearing

- the public interest in ensuring that business in the EAT is conducted expeditiously and its resources used efficiently.

17.30 The EAT takes a strict view of anything, including proposed amendments, that might delay a final hearing, especially in cases where there has been a failure to comply with a rule or with the Practice Direction. This approach is consistent with the fact that the period within which most claims can be brought in employment tribunals is significantly shorter than the relevant period of limitation for most civil claims.

That said, the EAT rejected the contention made by the respondent in the Khudados case that the strict principles applied by the EAT to extension of time applications (which we discuss at length under 'Time limit for lodging an appeal' below) should be applied to amendment applications.

Time limit for lodging an appeal

17.31

Rule 3(3) of the EAT Rules sets down a 42-day time limit for lodging an appeal against a judgment, decision or order of a tribunal. Below, we consider when time starts to run for the purposes of this limit, when the limit expires, and the circumstances in which time might be extended.

When does time start to run?

17.32

Precisely when time starts to run for the purposes of the 42-day limit depends upon whether the appeal is against a tribunal judgment or against a tribunal decision or order.

Judgments. As stated under 'Documents required – judgments and orders' **17.33** above, an employment tribunal judgment is defined as a decision that finally determines a claim, or part of a claim, as regards liability, remedy or costs, or which finally determines any issue capable of disposing of any claim or part of a claim – rule 1(3)(b) Employment Tribunal Rules 2013. In the following three circumstances, rule 3(3)(a)(i) of the EAT Rules provides that an appeal against

889

a tribunal judgment must be instituted within the 42-day period from the date on which *written reasons* for that judgment were sent to the parties:

- where written reasons were requested orally at the hearing

- where written reasons were requested within 14 days of the date when the written record of the judgment was sent to the parties, or

- where reasons for the judgment were reserved and given in writing by the tribunal.

In light of the requirement that an appellant submit a copy of the tribunal's written reasons along with his or her notice of appeal, it is likely that one of the above will occur in most cases. If not, however, the appeal must be instituted within the 42-day period from the date on which the *written record* of the judgment was sent to the parties – rule 3(3)(a)(iii).

17.34 **Decisions or orders.** An appeal against an order must be instituted in the 42-day period from the date of the order, direction or decision – rule 3(3)(b) EAT Rules. Para 5.2 of the Practice Direction clarifies that the date of an order, direction or decision is the date when it was sent to the parties. Para 5.2 also clarifies that where a tribunal refuses to give written reasons for a decision or order, the EAT will treat that refusal as itself constituting a decision or order.

17.35 **'Sent to the parties'.** As stated above, the 42-day period for bringing an appeal begins when the judgment, the written reasons for the judgment, or the order is 'sent to the parties'. For some time there was confusion over whether, for the purposes of the rule 3 time-limit provisions, a document is 'sent' on the date on which it is put in the post or the date on which it is deemed to arrive.

In Mock v Commissioners of the Inland Revenue 1999 IRLR 785, EAT, the appellant pointed out that, under rule 35 of the EAT Rules (which is headed 'Service of documents') and S.7 of the Interpretation Act 1978, service of a document sent by post is deemed to be effected when the document would be delivered in the normal course of post. However, Mr Justice Morison, then President of the EAT, held that neither rule 35 nor S.7 were relevant to the correct interpretation of rule 3(3), which was not concerned with the service of documents. Rule 3(3) simply deals with the calculation of the date from which time starts to run for the purposes of instituting the appeal. A similar conclusion was reached by the EAT in London Borough of Hammersmith and Fulham v Ladejobi 1999 ICR 673, EAT, but the EAT expressed a contrary view on this point in both Immigration Advisory Service v Oommen 1997 ICR 683, EAT, and Scotford and anor v Smithkline Beecham 2002 ICR 264, EAT. This matter was settled by the Court of Appeal in Gdynia American Shipping Lines (London) Ltd v Chelminski 2004 ICR 1523, CA, which favoured the Mock and Ladejobi reasoning, holding that the 42-day period runs from when the relevant document is actually sent out by the tribunal.

890

In Tasneem v Dudley Group of Hospitals NHS Trust EAT 0496/09 His Honour **17.36** Judge Serota QC held that the sent date recorded on an employment tribunal judgment creates a strong *but not irrebuttable* presumption that it was sent on that date. Consequently, as the would-be appellant in that case had proved on the balance of probabilities that the judgment was posted later than the recorded sent date, his notice of appeal had been lodged within the prescribed 42-day time limit. Notwithstanding his decision, HHJ Serota expressed concern about the fact that the sent date recorded on a tribunal judgment was open to challenge, as he recognised that it could lead to unmeritorious claims of a judgment being sent after the date it was recorded as having been sent. Consequently, he said that he expected all employment tribunals to have procedures in place giving effect to rule 30(4) of the Employment Tribunal Rules 2004, which at that time required that, when written reasons were provided, the Secretary had to send a copy of the reasons to all the parties 'and record the date on which the reasons were sent'. This way, it would be clearly shown that a document was delivered to the post office on the date recorded in that document. Further, HHJ Serota believed that such procedures must be strictly followed so that in future cases where the date of sending was challenged tribunals could, if requested, supply evidence on this issue.

Note that the wording of rule 30(4) of the 2004 Rules is not replicated in the Employment Tribunal Rules 2013. Rule 4(6) of these Rules states that 'where time is specified by reference to the date when a document is sent to a person by the tribunal, the date when the document was sent shall, unless the contrary is proved, be regarded as the date endorsed on the document as the date of sending or, if there is no such endorsement, the date shown on the letter accompanying the document'.

Where the tribunal issues a certificate of correction to its original judgment **17.37** under the slip rule (rule 69 of the Employment Tribunal Rules 2013), then the certificate will not start time running again. However, different considerations apply where the tribunal issues a certificate rescinding the *whole* of its written reasons and provides new written reasons in their place. In those circumstances, the time limit for appealing runs from the date that the corrected judgment was issued, not the date on which the parties were originally informed of the decision – see Kennaugh v Lloyd-Jones t/a Cheshire Tree Surgeons EAT 0710/07. In that particular case, the EAT upheld its earlier decision in Aziz-Mir v Sainsbury's Supermarkets plc EAT 0537/06 to the effect that, where a correction is issued by way of a fresh judgment, time starts to run from the date that the corrected judgment was issued. Indeed, in Aziz the EAT discouraged tribunals from rescinding the whole of its original judgment under the slip rule because of the confusion that could ensue.

Separate decisions on liability and remedy. Confusion over time limits can **17.38** arise if a claim involves more than one tribunal decision, e.g. separate decisions

891

on liability and remedy. However, it is clear from para 5.4 of the Practice Direction that time for appealing runs 'even though the question of remedy and assessment of compensation by the Employment Tribunal has been adjourned', unless, of course, it is the remedies decision which is being appealed.

In rare cases it may be that, notwithstanding a 'split' hearing on issues of liability and remedy which results in the promulgation of separate decisions by the tribunal, an appellant may be justified in delaying the commencement of an appeal against the liability finding until he or she receives written reasons covering both matters. In Stocks v Solihull Metropolitan Borough Council EAT 72/94 the employment tribunal's summary reasons for its decision on compensation were sent to the parties before the decision on liability. The employee – who won on the question of unfair dismissal – only put in an appeal relating to the decision on compensation once the decision on liability was sent. Mr Justice Mummery held that, on these facts, the time limit for appealing did not start to run until the whole of the tribunal's decision had been sent out in extended form, as it was reasonable and responsible for the appellant to wait until he received the entirety of the tribunal's reasons before making a final decision on whether to appeal. Consequently, his appeal was not out of time.

17.39 **Multiple claims.** It appears that a party should not delay lodging its appeal on the ground of having received written reasons for some, but not all, of the matters decided by the tribunal. In Hooper v Hertfordshire County Council and anor 2004 All ER (D) 75, EAT, an employment tribunal sent out summary reasons (as was the practice under the then applicable Employment Tribunal Rules 2001) for two of the three substantive issues raised at a hearing on 13 August 2003. On 20 October the tribunal confirmed that the employment judge's summary reasons were his extended reasons on these two points. Extended reasons for the third issue, however, were not promulgated until 30 October 2003. The employee posted a notice of appeal in respect of all three issues on 30 November 2003, which arrived at the EAT on 2 December 2003. The Registrar rejected the appeal with regard to the first two issues, deciding that it was out of time. When the matter came before a judge in chambers, the employee appears to have argued that time for an appeal on these points did not start to run until 30 October – the date on which extended reasons were given on the third issue. His Honour Judge Ansell rejected this argument, however, finding that the three issues were clearly divisible, and that time had started to run in respect of the first two matters on 20 October – the date on which the tribunal confirmed that its summary reasons on those matters amounted to its extended reasons.

17.40 **Reconsiderations.** In Blackpole Furniture Ltd v Sullivan and anor 1978 ICR 558, EAT, the EAT stressed that time for serving an appeal continues to run irrespective of the progress of an application for a review (now known as a 'reconsideration') of a tribunal decision – a point confirmed in para 5.4 of the

EAT Practice Direction. To illustrate, in Priory Products v Ball EAT 170/80 the EAT refused to accept a late appeal even though there had been an application for review and the review decision had not been given until after the 42-day appeal period had expired. For further information about the reconsideration process, see Chapter 15, 'Reconsideration of tribunal judgments and decisions'.

Appeals lodged early. Note that by virtue of rule 39(2) and (3) of the EAT **17.41** Rules, the EAT may authorise the institution of an appeal *before* the 42-day period prescribed by the Rules has started – i.e. in respect of judgments before full written reasons have been sent by the employment tribunal.

When does time expire? 17.42

Although the date on which the tribunal *sends* the judgment, order or reasons to the parties is that which triggers the rule 3 time-limit provisions, that date is *not* counted as one of the 42 days within which an appeal must be lodged. Para 1.8.1 of the Practice Direction states: 'For the purpose of serving a valid Notice of Appeal under... para 3 below, when an Employment Tribunal decision is sent to parties on a Wednesday, that day does *not* count and the Notice of Appeal must arrive at the EAT by 4.00 pm on or before the Wednesday 6 weeks (i.e. 42 days) later.'

The 4 pm deadline is reinforced by rule 37(1A) of the EAT Rules, which provides that 'where an act is required to be done on or before a particular day it shall be done by 4 pm on that day'. Therefore, the 42-day time limit will expire at 4 pm on the final day for lodging the appeal. This means that the notice of appeal and all supporting documents must be lodged in their entirety by 4 pm. Where documentation is being lodged by fax, the time of transmission is determined by reference to the EAT's fax machine. The EAT's decision in Woodward v Abbey National plc (No.2) and another case 2005 ICR 1702, EAT, clarified that transmission of the notice of appeal and supporting documents must be complete by 4 pm – where documentation is still being received at the 4 pm deadline, the appeal will be out of time. The EAT in Woodward disapproved its earlier decision in Midland Packaging v Clark 2005 2 All ER 266, EAT – where it held that the time of receipt of an appeal would be the time that the machine started to transmit the documents – and made it clear that the Midland Packaging case should not be followed.

If the deadline for lodging an appeal falls on a public holiday, the period for **17.43** lodging an appeal is automatically extended to the next day on which the office is open – rule 37(2). Furthermore, the EAT website states that if the deadline falls on a day when the EAT office is closed, it is extended to the next working day, and – for appeals delivered by Royal Mail only – if the deadline falls on a day on which there is a national postal strike, then it is extended to the next working day.

893

17.44 **Electronic forms.** In the Woodward case (above), the EAT held that the 4 pm deadline was consistent with the operation of e-mail because not only would there be a record at the EAT of when the e-mail arrives, but the e-mail – assuming it has the relevant attachments – would be a complete document the moment it arrives. In Patel v South Tyneside Council EAT 0917/11 the EAT ruled that an e-mailed notice of appeal was received when the sender received a 'successful delivery' message. Whether the e-mail was received depended on whether it 'hit' the EAT's server and the fact that the message failed to appear in the EAT's inbox did not matter. In that case, P's representatives e-mailed a notice of appeal to the EAT on 17 June 2011 and received a 'successful delivery' notice. When they contacted the EAT on 22 June they discovered that no notice of appeal had appeared in the EAT's inbox and the resubmitted appeal had been received out of time. On this basis, the Registrar rejected the appeal. On appeal to a single judge, it was common ground that the e-mail address 'londoneat@hmcts.gsi.gov.uk' had received 'successful delivery' of the notice of appeal. However, the Council argued that the delivery notification was not evidence of receipt by the EAT, as it was sent from 'DAEMON', a third party.

Rejecting this argument, the EAT followed the decision in Yellow Pages Sales Ltd v Davie 2012 ICR D11, EAT, where it was held in the context of employment tribunal proceedings that a tribunal had received a claim when its fax machine received 'data packets' but failed to convert them into a fax printout – the written document had been transmitted but, in effect, lost at the tribunal's end. In Patel, the EAT thought it immaterial that the delivery notification was sent from a third party. It was triggered because there had been successful delivery to the EAT's e-mail address – i.e. it had 'hit' the EAT server. Consequently, the notice of appeal had been received in time. The EAT noted that even if the notice of appeal was not in time, the EAT would have extended time in the exceptional circumstances of the case as the appellant was not at fault and, having received a successful delivery notification, his advisers were not at fault either because they had been entitled to assume that the notice of appeal had been properly served on the EAT.

17.45 **Extending the time limit for appeals**

Rule 37(1) of the EAT Rules states: 'The time prescribed by these Rules or by order of the Appeal Tribunal for doing any act may be extended (whether it has already expired or not) or abridged, and the date appointed for any purpose may be altered, by order of the Tribunal.' This appears to give the EAT very wide latitude in allowing late appeals. In practice, however, late appeals are only accepted in limited circumstances. This was emphasised in Muschett v Hounslow London Borough Council and other cases 2009 ICR 424, EAT, where the EAT held that certainty and finality of legal proceedings are in the interests of the parties and of the public, so courts should be more strict about time limits on appeal than at first instance.

894

The EAT Practice Direction states the following with regard to late appeals:

- a notice of appeal must be lodged with the EAT. An application for an extension of time cannot be considered until this is done – para 5.5

- an application for an extension must be made as an interim application to the Registrar, who will normally determine the application after inviting and considering written representations from each side. An interim appeal lies from the Registrar's decision to a judge – para 5.6

- in determining whether to extend the time for appealing, particular attention will be paid to whether any good excuse for the delay has been shown, and to the guidance of the EAT and Court of Appeal respectively in United Arab Emirates v Abdelghafar and anor 1995 ICR 65, EAT, Aziz v Bethnal Green City Challenge Co Ltd 2000 IRLR 111, CA, and Jurkowska v Hlmad Ltd 2008 ICR 841, CA (for more on these cases, see below) – para 5.7

- it is not usually a good reason for a late appeal that a party is awaiting the result of an application for legal aid; or that support is being sought from some body such as the Equality and Human Rights Commission; or that the appellant is awaiting the result of an application for reconsideration of the tribunal's decision; or that negotiations between the parties are continuing – para 5.8

- where there is any doubt or difficulty, a notice of appeal should be served in time and an application made to the Registrar for directions – para 5.9.

17.46 Note that where the Registrar has considered an application for an extension of time for an appeal but has rejected it, the appellant may appeal to a judge within five days of the Registrar's decision. Similarly, if the Registrar has allowed an extension of time for appealing, the respondent may appeal against that decision within five days. The judge may determine the appeal him or herself, or refer it to a full division of the EAT – rule 21(1) EAT Rules. Notice of such an appeal may be given either orally or in writing to the EAT and the Registrar is then responsible for notifying the other parties concerned – rule 21(2). A further appeal lies to the Court of Appeal.

17.47 **Relevant case law.** As stated above, para 5.7 of the Practice Direction states that in considering applications for an extension of time to serve a notice of appeal, the EAT will pay particular attention to the guidance contained in the cases of United Arab Emirates v Abdelghafar and anor (above), Aziz v Bethnal Green City Challenge Co Ltd (above), and Jurkowska v Hlmad Ltd (above).

17.48 *United Arab Emirates v Abdelghafar.* In United Arab Emirates v Abdelghafar and anor 1995 ICR 65, EAT, Mr Justice Mummery (as he then was) conducted a thorough review of principles arising from cases in which parties had been late to comply with procedural requirements. From these cases – in particular, two Court of Appeal cases outside the employment field – Mummery J identified,

895

'with reasonable precision', the general principles that govern the exercise of the Appeal Tribunal's discretion to extend time. He stated that the discretion to grant or refuse an extension of time was to be exercised in a principled manner after weighing and balancing all relevant factors. In his view, the approach should be modified according to the stage which the relevant proceedings have reached. Extensions of time are more likely to be granted where appeals are against an interim decision and the question of liability had yet to be decided. This is because public policy favoured allowing proceedings to go to a full hearing on their merits. It was quite a different matter when a hearing on the merits has taken place and liability has been determined. In such circumstances, it is incumbent upon the party aggrieved by the result of the liability hearing to act promptly. Mummery J also made the point that an extension of time is an indulgence granted by the court to a party who is at fault. There should be no expectation on the part of such a litigant that the indulgence would be granted, even if the opposing party would suffer no prejudice as a result. Finally, it is incumbent upon the applicant for an extension of time to provide a full, honest and acceptable explanation of the reasons for the delay. He or she cannot reasonably expect the EAT's discretion to be exercised in his or her favour, as a defaulter, unless he or she provides an explanation for the default.

17.49 Mummery J then went on to offer guidance as to how the above general principles should be applied by the EAT. We set this out below and, where appropriate, refer to subsequent case law either clarifying or developing the guidance:

- time limits will only be relaxed in *rare and exceptional cases* where the EAT is satisfied that there is a reason that justifies the departure from a time limit laid down in the EAT Rules. Although more sympathy would be shown if the party in question was unrepresented, there was, nevertheless, no excuse for ignorance of the time limit or of the importance of compliance. In Jurkowska, the Court of Appeal held that it did not interpret this part of the guidance as meaning that the appellant must prove his or her case to be a rare and exceptional one. In its view, it meant no more than that only in rare and exceptional cases will it be appropriate to extend time. Furthermore, in Hine t/a Hine Marketing Partnership v Talbot EAT 1783/10 the EAT held that 'the purpose of a discretion is to acknowledge cases where there is venial fault or a very convincing explanation'

- the EAT's discretion will not be exercised unless a full and honest explanation for non-compliance is provided. If the explanation satisfies the EAT that there is a *good excuse* for the default, an extension of time may be granted. However, in most cases the explanations offered do not excuse the delay that has occurred. For example, the EAT found the following explanations not to amount to excuses for delay: ignorance of the time limit; oversight of the passing of the limit; prior notification to the EAT or the other party of an intention to appeal; the existence of pending applications for reconsideration or for remedies hearings; and delay in applications for legal aid or other assistance. It is always possible in cases where there may be unavoidable delay for an extension to be granted *before* the 42-day period has expired, or for a notice of appeal to be lodged within the time limit with a covering letter saying that it may be necessary to apply to amend it at a later stage (note, however, that para 3.10 of the Practice Direction precludes parties from reserving the right to amend, alter or add to any pleading. Whether a party will be allowed to do so will, once again, be a matter for the EAT's discretion)

- if an explanation for the delay is offered, then *other factors* – such as the length of the delay that has occurred, questionable tactics, or intentional default – *may be* relevant to the EAT's decision whether to extend time. The merits of the appeal may be relevant, but are usually of little weight – it is not appropriate for the EAT to be asked to investigate in detail the strength of an appeal. Equally unimportant is the fact that the other party would suffer no prejudice by an extension of time, although if prejudice *would* be suffered, this strengthens the opposition to an application for an extension.

17.50 The second point set out by Mummery J in the guidance outlined above – i.e. that the EAT's discretion to extend the time limit for appealing will not be exercised in the absence of a full and honest explanation for non-compliance with the ordinary time limit – was the focus of further attention by the EAT in Muschett v Hounslow London Borough Council and other cases 2009 ICR 424, EAT. In that case the EAT held that an excuse will not be sufficient unless the explanation covered the entire period in which a notice of appeal could have been lodged, and that an analytical approach should be used when looking at different parts of the 42-day period. His Honour Judge McMullen used the following example to illustrate this point: suppose a claimant receives the judgment and resolves to appeal in week one but suffers a stroke and is physically unable to lodge an appeal in time. A sympathetic approach would be forthcoming not only for the period of incapacity, but also for the first week, as it would not be just to debar someone for not acting immediately on receipt of a judgment. But a less sympathetic approach to the first segment might be taken if the stroke occurred in week six. Then it would depend on what evidence was put forward in explanation for the claimant not acting in the preceding five weeks.

In Westmoreland v Renault UK Ltd EAT 1571/08 HHJ McMullen clarified that his approach on this issue was different from that previously adopted by Mr Justice Burton in Woodward v Abbey National plc (No.2) and another case 2005 ICR 1702, EAT, who said that the excuse should show 'why for the entirety of the six weeks it was not possible to put in a notice of appeal'. Indeed, Burton J held that this was what was required by United Arab Emirates v Abdelghafar and anor and in Aziz v Bethnal Green City Challenge Co Ltd (see below). However, in Westmoreland, HHJ McMullen pointed out that those

897

cases did not support Burton J's approach, nor was that approach cited or reflected in Jurkowska v Hlmad Ltd (see below). HHJ McMullen continued that 'it is wrong to require an appellant to show that throughout the entire 42 days it was impossible, or not reasonably practicable, to lodge an appeal, or to withhold discretion if there was a stage in the 42 days when the notice of appeal could have been lodged... What is required is an acceptable explanation, excusing inaction or imperfect lodging of the appeal, during each stage within the 42 days, or a compelling other reason.'

17.51 HHJ McMullen applied this approach in one of the three cases heard alongside Muschett, Ogbuneke v Minster Lodge and ors 2009 ICR 424, EAT, and determined that the appellant there, who had submitted her appeal 34 days late, had provided a good excuse in the circumstances as she, among other things, had a very poor command of English and could only access help from a law centre following expiry of the time limit. Similarly, in Hakim v Italia Conti Academy of Theatre Arts EAT 1444/08 the EAT, applying Muschett, held that an appellant with severe dyslexia had an exceptional reason for presenting his appeal one day late. Although Muschett and Woodward represent conflicting authorities at EAT level on this point (for which definitive guidance from the Court of Appeal would be welcome) we would respectfully argue that the Muschett approach is more compelling than the stricter approach adopted in Woodward since the former has been specifically adopted and applied in subsequent case law. Indeed, in O'Cathail v Transport for London 2013 ICR D2, CA, the Court of Appeal included Muschett in the list of authorities it said represented 'the EAT's general approach to applications to extend the generous time limit allowed for appealing from the Employment Tribunal'.

In that particular case, the appellant was late in lodging the necessary documents (including a copy of the employment tribunal's judgment) within the 42-day time limit even though his actual notice of appeal was presented in time. He alleged that this was the result of a disability comprising depression, anxiety and panic attacks. However the EAT refused to extend time and the Court of Appeal upheld that decision. Although the documents were lodged only one day out of time and the length of the delay was a material factor, the crucial issue was whether there was a good excuse for the delay, rather than whether it was long or short. The Court of Appeal found that the appellant was not disabled from lodging his appeal within the relevant period as he had produced long and complex grounds of appeal and had, in fact, submitted these in time. His disability did not explain or excuse his failure to attach the required documentation. Although it had been a contributory factor in his inability to travel to the EAT on the day on which the time limit expired, his failure to lodge the additional documents was not referable to and did not arise out of his disability. In particular, his disability did not mean that he had been unable to lodge all the documents in advance of the deadline. In addition, it was relevant that the documents did not have to be lodged in person: other methods could have been used and were in fact used, but too late, because he had left taking the necessary steps until the very end of the six-week limitation period.

Returning to the general guidance provided in United Arab Emirates v **17.52** Abdelghafar and anor, Mummery J neatly abbreviated the questions to be asked by the EAT when considering an application to extend time as follows: '(a) what is the explanation for the default? (b) does it provide a good excuse for the default? (c) are there circumstances which justify the tribunal taking the exceptional step of granting an extension of time?'

Note that, on the facts of the United Arab Emirates case, there was an exceptional factor, in that the party seeking to appeal was a sovereign country covered by the State Immunity Act 1978. This meant that the overriding duty of the EAT was to give effect to the particular state's immunity from any civil suit covered by the 1978 Act. If the tribunal had erred in concluding that immunity from suit did not apply, then it was the duty of the EAT to intervene even if the time limit for lodging an appeal had not been complied with.

Aziz v Bethnal Green City Challenge Co Ltd. The second case referred to in **17.53** para 5.7 of the Practice Direction is that of Aziz v Bethnal Green City Challenge Co Ltd 2000 IRLR 111, CA, in which the Court of Appeal considered how the guidance set out by Mummery J in United Arab Emirates v Abdelghafar and anor (above) could be reconciled with the Court of Appeal's own approach to extension-of-time cases. In the Aziz case, A's confusion about the date-stamp on the tribunal's extended reasons led him to present his notice of appeal to the EAT three days out of time. The Registrar refused A's application to extend time and, on appeal, Mr Justice Morison (then President of the EAT) upheld the Registrar's decision. In Morison P's view, although A's explanation for the delay was honest and full, it was not acceptable. A appealed to the Court of Appeal, arguing that the EAT had failed to take into account factors such as the length of the delay, the prejudice to the other side and the merits of the case, that would have been taken into account by the Court of Appeal in deciding whether to grant an extension of time. He contended that there was no apparent justification for the EAT taking a different approach.

Lady Justice Butler-Sloss, who delivered the leading judgment in the Court of Appeal, rejected A's argument, pointing to the importance of the distinction between the jurisdiction of the EAT and that of the Court of Appeal. First, she noted that the Court of Appeal can, in some instances, hear appeals on facts, whereas the EAT can only hear appeals from employment tribunals based on law. Secondly, she highlighted the fact that the EAT has the power to regulate its own procedure under S.30(3) ETA, and may have its own good reasons for requiring parties to present their appeals on time. Butler-Sloss LJ thought that the guidelines set out by Mummery J in the United Arab Emirates case provided a perfectly acceptable formula for use by the EAT in determining whether to

899

grant an extension of time, and concluded that the EAT in the instant case had not erred in following that approach.

17.54 *Jurkowska v Hlmad Ltd.* The final case referred to in para 5.7 of the Practice Direction is Jurkowska v Hlmad Ltd 2008 ICR 841, CA, which approved United Arab Emirates, having taken account of the overriding objective now to be found in rule 2A of the EAT Rules and discussed under 'Overriding objective' above. This principle was not in effect when Mummery J gave the EAT's judgment in that case. Indeed, Lord Justice Rimer, who gave the lead judgment in Jurkowska, dismissed the idea that rule 2A had 'somehow trumped the Abdelghafar guidelines so as to require the EAT to put them on one side and instead approach extension applications by reference to some wholly undefined and unprincipled appeal to justice'. In Jurkowska, the Court of Appeal held that the EAT did not err in extending by 33 minutes the 42-day time limit for lodging an appeal in circumstances where the only appeal document lodged out of time was a copy of the tribunal judgment. The notice of appeal to the EAT and the written reasons for the employment tribunal's decision had both been lodged by H Ltd in time, and the EAT was entitled to conclude that the employer's representatives had only failed to include the judgment itself because they had never received it. Rimer LJ, giving an opinion with which the rest of the Court agreed, held that, strictly speaking, the solicitors acting for the employer should have known that written reasons for a judgment do not count as the judgment itself – rule 3(1)(c) of the EAT Rules clearly differentiates between the two. In this case, however, Mr Justice Underhill, sitting alone in the EAT, had explained why he regarded the solicitors' excuse to be acceptable: in the absence of a separate judgment, they believed that the written reasons incorporated it. In addition, very prompt action had been taken to remedy the error once it was known. In Rimer LJ's view, Underhill J was entitled to come to this decision because he clearly had the Abdelghafar principles in mind, even if Rimer LJ indicated that he himself might have reached a different conclusion. J's appeal was therefore dismissed.

17.55 **Discretion to extend time limit where written reasons received late.** The following three cases concern the EAT's discretion to extend the 42-day time period for lodging a notice of appeal where the parties had received the tribunal's written reasons late:

• **Rhondda Cynon Taff County Borough Council v Griffiths** EAT 1477/05: on 12 September 2005 an employment tribunal sent out written reasons for its judgment against the employer. The employer, however, did not receive these reasons, and discovered only on 8 November that they had been dispatched. On 1 December 2005 the employer eventually lodged an appeal against the tribunal's decision, but the Registrar rejected the appeal because it was out of time. The employer appealed to the EAT, arguing that an extension of time should have been granted. The EAT was satisfied that the employer had not been aware of the existence of written reasons until 8 November, and that there was, therefore, an acceptable reason why the employer had not lodged its notice of appeal before that date. However, the employer had no acceptable reason for failing to lodge its notice for a further 24 days. The EAT pointed out that where a party receives late notification of written reasons, it is important that it does everything possible to ensure that the relevant notice of appeal is lodged at the earliest opportunity. Here, the employer had not appreciated the need to galvanise itself urgently to do so. In particular, the EAT was critical that it had taken the employer until 21 November to instruct counsel to draft the grounds of appeal, and that, owing to pressure of work, it had taken counsel until 29 November for the notice of appeal to be completed. The EAT accordingly dismissed the employer's appeal

- **Leggott v Trafalgar House Services Ltd** EAT 1051/95: extended written reasons for a tribunal's decision were sent to the parties on 3 March 1995, but L did not receive a copy until 1 July. L, who was by that stage without representation, then entered into lengthy and somewhat confused correspondence with the tribunal, requesting information on the appeal procedure. His notice of appeal was finally received by the EAT on 5 September, some 145 days late. The EAT upheld the Registrar's decision to refuse an extension of time. Mummery J accepted that L had not received the extended written reasons until 1 July. He also accepted L's explanation that he had not contacted the tribunal to see where the reasons were because, as an unrepresented claimant, he had assumed that a delay was to be expected. Mummery J was, therefore, of the view that it was not unreasonable for L to have delayed in making his appeal until he received the reasons in July. He did not, however, think that L had a reasonable excuse for delaying once he had received the extended reasons. Mummery J stressed that, although some allowance is given to the fact that a party is unrepresented, ultimately the same time limit rules apply

- **Dodd v Bank of Tokyo-Mitsubishi Ltd** EAT 0480/05: despite the appellant's contact with the tribunal with a view to obtaining written reasons, such reasons were not received until the last day for lodging the notice of appeal. The appellant's solicitor sought instructions, settled the notice of appeal with counsel and lodged it within 14 days. The EAT exercised its discretion to allow the notice of appeal to be validated, acknowledging that the appellant had given up a 'six-week period provided by the Rules in exchange for a two-week period'.

Postal problems. Failure to meet the EAT's deadline as a result of postal **17.56** problems was considered by the Court of Appeal in Peters v Sat Katar Co Ltd (in liquidation) 2003 ICR 1574, CA. In that case, P, an unrepresented appellant, posted her notice of appeal on 28 March 2002, well before the 42-day deadline of 12 April. Having received no response, she telephoned the EAT on 23 April – 11 days after the deadline had passed – and discovered that her notice of appeal had not been received. The Registrar refused to extend time on the basis that the disappearance of documents in the post was not an acceptable reason for delay. The EAT judge hearing the matter on appeal agreed, taking the view that it was the responsibility of the appellant to ensure that the notice of appeal arrived in time. The Court of Appeal, however, allowed P's appeal against the EAT's decision not to extend time. In doing so, the Court stated that a highly relevant factor to be taken into account by the EAT in considering whether to allow a late appeal is whether the applicant acted reasonably in the steps he or she took to institute the appeal within the time limit. Here, P had acted entirely reasonably. She had posted the notice of appeal well before the time limit expired. Furthermore, as an unrepresented litigant with no knowledge or experience of the EAT system, she should not be expected to verify receipt by the EAT of her notice of appeal unless specifically alerted to this requirement – she was entitled to rely on the presumption of receipt under rule 35(3) of the EAT Rules. Moreover, she was not put on notice to expect an acknowledgement from the EAT. The Court went on to note that, had P been receiving legal advice, it would have been arguable that she had not acted reasonably in waiting until four weeks after the date of posting to check whether her appeal had been received. However, in the circumstances of the case P could not be said to be at fault for this. Once told of the non-delivery she acted without delay in faxing the notice of appeal to the Appeal Tribunal.

In Gavin v Commission for Racial Equality EAT 0221/10 His Honour Judge McMullen noted that it was because of the ruling in the Peters case (above) that the EAT Rules and Practice Directions were subsequently amended so that full information is given to potential litigants about the appeal process. He also noted that unlike at the time of the Peters judgment, the EAT now has a fully functioning website giving clear information. The website states, for example, that 'if you use the post you should bear in mind the likelihood of delay or loss and should contact the EAT if you have received no acknowledgement after seven days'. Given these changes, it is perhaps unlikely that the decision reached in Peters would be repeated in a similar case today. This view is reinforced by the EAT's guidance in Muschett v Hounslow London Borough Council and other cases 2009 ICR 424, EAT, that the rules on deadlines apply equally to litigants in person, as was made expressly clear in the 2005 Practice Statement. However, note that where the appellant has relied on out-of-date information on the EAT website, discretion has been exercised in favour of extending time on the basis that the appellant was blameless in this situation – Fazal v Thames Water Utilities Ltd EAT 0058–60/12.

17.57 The issue of postal delays occurred again in the case of Bost Logistics Ltd v Gumbley and another case EAT 0013/08. There, B Ltd was sent the judgment and reasons of an employment tribunal, which found against it, on 22 November

2007. The 42-day time limit for appealing to the EAT subsequently expired on 3 January 2008. B Ltd's representative waited for five weeks before drafting an appeal on 27 December. The appeal should have left the post room on 28 December, but was in fact not picked up by the Royal Mail until 31 December. B Ltd's representative was made aware of the delay the same day but opted not to send the appeal by an alternative method such as courier or fax. Nor did he make any further attempt to ensure that the appeal had been received on either 2 or 3 January. In the end, the appeal was received by the EAT on 4 January and was rejected by the Registrar as being out of time. B Ltd appealed against the Registrar's decision, pointing to the postal rule in rule 6.7 of the Civil Procedure Rules, which provides that when documents relating to a claim are posted first class they are deemed to be received on the second day after posting irrespective of the date on which they were actually received. This rule, though technically only applicable to claims in the county court or High Court, was extended to the lodging of claims within employment tribunals by the Court of Appeal's decision in Consignia plc (formerly the Post Office) v Sealy 2002 ICR 1193, CA. Since the rule applies to employment tribunals, B Ltd reasoned, it should also apply to lodging appeals with the EAT.

However, the EAT dismissed B Ltd's appeal, holding that there was a distinction to be drawn between the lodging of claims at first instance, which was the scenario before the Court of Appeal in Sealy, and the lodging of appeals. At the appeal stage, the party concerned has already had a trial. Furthermore, the appeal in Sealy concerned the test in S.111(2)(b) of the Employment Rights Act 1996, which applies where it is not 'reasonably practicable' to present an unfair dismissal claim in time; i.e. it was concerned with an escape clause from the rules concerning the service of tribunal claims. In the EAT, there is no escape clause on the ground of reasonable practicability or on any other grounds. Appeal Tribunals have a discretion to allow out-of-time appeals, but only in exceptional circumstances. Furthermore, nowhere in authorities such as United Arab Emirates v Abdelghafar and anor 1995 ICR 65, EAT, Aziz v Bethnal Green City Challenge Co Ltd 2000 IRLR 111, CA, and Woodward v Abbey National plc (No.2) and another case 2005 ICR 1702, EAT (see 'Relevant case law' above), is there any reference to a postal rule of deemed service. If such a rule existed – the effect of which would be that a posted appeal which was never received by the EAT would be deemed to have been lodged two days after it was posted – it would be fair to assume that it would be contained in one of the authorities.

17.58 As noted above, the EAT's website states that, for appeals delivered by Royal Mail only, if the appeal deadline falls on a day on which there is a national postal strike, then it is extended to the next working day.

17.59 **Representatives at fault.** As part of its guidance given in Muschett v Hounslow London Borough Council and other cases 2009 ICR 424, EAT, the EAT referred to Steeds v Peverel Management Services Ltd 2001 EWCA Civ 419, CA (a personal injury case), where the Court of Appeal held that it would be inequitable to bar a claimant where failure to enter proceedings in time was the fault of his or legal adviser. His Honour Judge McMullen QC, who sat alone in Muschett, reasoned that while this rule does not apply directly in the EAT, it is a factor which, when combined with others, might contribute to the exercise of discretion. But emphasis should be placed on the word *might*. In Bost Logistics Ltd v Gumbley and another case (above), for example, the EAT was critical of the conduct of B Ltd's representative – who had done nothing for five weeks after receiving the employment tribunal's written judgment, and had then posted the notice of appeal during the festive period when he should have known there would be issues with the speed of delivery. The EAT concluded that there were no exceptional circumstances justifying the exercise of its discretion to allow the appeal in that case to proceed.

Here are two more examples of cases where appellants have sought time extension due to fault on the part of their representatives:

- **Duke v Prospect Training Services Ltd** 1988 ICR 521, EAT: the appellant's notice of appeal was one day late because of unusual pressure of work on her solicitor. The Registrar allowed an extension of time but the employer appealed against the Registrar's decision on the ground that there were no exceptional circumstances to justify it. The EAT allowed the employer's appeal. Mr Justice Popplewell said that pressure of work on the solicitor was only an 'explanation' for the delay and could not 'possibly constitute a proper excuse or be an exceptional circumstance'. The EAT added that the fact that the appeal may have had some merit, and that the employer would be unlikely to suffer any prejudice, was irrelevant to the key issue – which was whether there were 'exceptional circumstances' which could excuse the delay. Popplewell J stated that 'the principle that 42 days means 42 days is to be upheld, save in exceptional circumstances'

- **Mock v Commissioners of the Inland Revenue** 1999 IRLR 785, EAT: an appeal was presented one day out of time owing to a computer failure of the barrister representing the appellant. The EAT refused to extend the time limit. Mr Justice Morison took the view that the reason given for the delay did not provide a satisfactory explanation or excuse because there were alternative means by which the appeal could have been presented in time. He went on to stress that the time limit is a limit and not a target.

17.60 **Interim orders.** In United Arab Emirates v Abdelghafar and anor 1995 ICR 65, EAT, Mr Justice Mummery (as he then was) explained that an extension of time is more likely to be granted in respect of an appeal against an *interim order* than an appeal against a judgment with regard to liability. The case of London Borough of Southwark v Savona EAT 1009/95 demonstrates this point. There, the employment tribunal ordered an employer to give discovery and inspection of certain documents which the employer argued were subject to public interest immunity. The employer sought to appeal against this interim order, but miscalculated the deadline and thus presented the notice of appeal 11 days out of time. The employer's appeal for an extension of time went straight to the EAT for determination because of an unusual point regarding public interest immunity raised in the appeal. Mummery J did not think that the explanation given by the employer amounted to a good excuse for the delay. However, referring to the guidelines he had laid down in the United Arab Emirates case, he noted that the appeal was against an interim order of the tribunal as opposed to a final decision, and that in such circumstances an extension would be more readily granted. He also noted that the appeal raised an unusual and reasonably arguable point of law on public immunity – not unlike the issue of state immunity in the United Arab Emirates case – and as such there were exceptional circumstances that warranted the granting of an extension of time. The employer was, however, ordered to pay costs on the basis that it had not shown a good excuse for its delay in bringing the appeal.

Change in the law. Where the law has changed since the date of the employment **17.61** tribunal's decision following a higher court decision, it was the obiter view of the EAT in Foster v South Glamorgan Health Authority 1988 ICR 526, EAT, that it would treat an application for an extension of time in accordance with the exact same principles that tribunals should adopt when deciding whether it was just and equitable to extend time for the late presentation of a tribunal complaint. Popplewell J, who gave the EAT's judgment, said that in this type of case the EAT would decide each application for an extension of time on its merits, taking into account the period of delay and the reasons behind the appeal not being brought in time.

In Setiya v East Yorkshire Health Authority 1995 ICR 799, EAT, the appellant attempted to bring an appeal some two years after an adverse employment tribunal decision, on the basis that the provision relied upon by the tribunal in rejecting his claim had been found to be contrary to European law. His unfair dismissal claim was dismissed by a tribunal in 1992 on the ground that he worked fewer than eight hours per week. This meant that he did not qualify to bring a claim under the law as it then stood. In 1994, however, the House of Lords held that the part-timer qualification provisions upon which the tribunal's decision had been based were sex discriminatory and contrary to European law. The appellant lodged an appeal against the 1992 tribunal decision on 3 August 1994, arguing, with reference to the European Court of Justice's decision in Emmott v Minister for Social Welfare and anor 1993 ICR 8, ECJ, that the time for appealing did not begin to run until the offending legislation was amended. The EAT disagreed, holding that the principles laid down in the Emmott case – to the effect that the state or an employer who is an emanation of the state may not rely upon an individual's delay in bringing proceedings to protect rights conferred by European law until that law has been fully transposed into domestic law – related only to time limits for initiating proceedings, and had no application to the time limit for appealing against a tribunal's decision. Furthermore, the EAT did not accept that there were exceptional circumstances that would justify the exercise of the EAT's discretion to extend the time limit in this case. The mere fact that a later decision of a higher court establishes that the decision sought to be appealed was wrongly decided was not of itself a sufficient reason for granting an extension of time, particularly where the original decision did not have continuing consequences for the parties.

17.62 The sift

In October 1997 a filtering process was adopted by the EAT with the purpose of weeding out appeals that did not raise a question of law. Between 1997 and 2002 the EAT routinely listed all appeals for a preliminary hearing. This practice, however, was altered by a Practice Direction issued in 2002 and pertains under the current 2013 Practice Direction. In place of a preliminary hearing, the Registrar or a judge now carries out a sift of all notices of appeal to determine that the notice discloses reasonable grounds for bringing the appeal and, assuming it does, to give directions for case management in pursuance of the overriding objective so that a case can be dealt with quickly, or be better considered, and in the most effective and just way – paras 11.1 and 14.1 Practice Direction. This system works effectively in the EAT, which only hears appeals on questions of law, and many perversity appeals fall at this hurdle.

A similar sift applies to the statement of grounds for a cross-appeal contained in a respondent's Answer to an appeal – see 'Answer and cross-appeals' below.

17.63 Once a Notice of Appeal has been received, properly instituted, and any applicable fee has been paid (or remission granted) within time, it will be sifted by a judge or the Registrar – para 11.1 Practice Direction. However, the judge or Registrar may stay (or 'sist' in Scotland) the sift of the appeal for a period of 21 days pending the making or the conclusion of an application by the appellant to the employment tribunal for a reconsideration of its decision – para 11.3.

17.64 **Allocation of case track.** The sift results in a decision as to which 'case track' the appeal will occupy. There are four such tracks:

- rule 3(7) cases: where it appears to the Registrar or a judge that the stated grounds of appeal do not give the EAT jurisdiction

- preliminary hearing cases

- full hearing cases, and

- fast-track full hearing cases.

The detailed procedures relevant to each case track, which are contained in para 11 of the Practice Direction, are explained below.

Review of sift decisions. It is possible for the EAT to revisit a decision to allow **17.65** an appeal through at the sift stage using its general powers to review its own decisions. But this is a power that will be exercised only very rarely. For more details, see Chapter 18, 'EAT hearings and decisions', under 'Review of EAT decisions and further appeals'.

Rule 3(7) cases (no valid grounds of appeal)   **17.66**
An appeal falls within this case track where it appears to the Registrar or a judge from the papers that the stated grounds of appeal do not give the EAT jurisdiction because no question of law can be discerned (rule 3(7)(a) EAT Rules) or because the appeal is an abuse of process or is otherwise likely to obstruct the just disposal of proceedings (rule 3(7)(b)). In such circumstances the following procedure is adopted:

- the Registrar writes to the appellant informing him or her as to reasons why the Registrar or judge intends to take no further action in respect of the appeal – rule 3(7)

- in the event that the appellant is dissatisfied with the Registrar or judge's decision and considers that he or she has a perfectly arguable case, the appellant may request an oral hearing before a judge under rule 3(10) of the EAT Rules provided he or she does so within 28 days of the date on which the rule 3(7) notification was sent. (We stress the word 'may' because, following the 2013 changes to the EAT Rules, there is no longer an automatic entitlement to a rule 3(10) hearing)

- where a judge or the Registrar has taken a decision under rule 3(7) and also considers that the notice of appeal is *totally without merit*, the judge or Registrar may order that the appellant is not entitled to have the matter heard before a judge – rule 3(7ZA). In that case, the appellant's only recourse would be to appeal against such order to the Court of Appeal – see para 11.1(c) Practice Direction.

Note that the 2013 changes to the EAT Rules deleted old rule 3(8) and 3(9), which previously stated that, where rule 3(7) applied, a fresh appeal could be served setting out valid grounds for appeal within the period allowed for filing the original appeal or within 28 days from the date on which the rule 3(7) notification was sent to the appellant. The fresh notice of appeal would then have been treated by the Registrar or judge as if it were the original notice of appeal.

In the absence of rules 3(8) and (9), it might be wondered whether an appellant **17.67** or cross-appellant is still entitled to resubmit a notice of appeal/cross-appeal – duly revised – within the 42-day time limit in any case where the Registrar has rejected the original notice under rule 3(7) as disclosing no arguable grounds for bringing the appeal or as amounting to an abuse of process. Nothing in the

907

EAT Rules as revised imposes a limit on how many notices of appeal may be filed within the 42-day time limit so, in these circumstances, the appellant would appear to be entitled to serve a fresh appeal within the time limit subject to payment of a further issue fee. To avoid the requirement to pay this additional fee, the alternative approach in a case where the Registrar or judge has rejected the ground of appeal under rule 3(7) but has not specifically ruled that these are totally without merit under rule 3(7ZA) would be for the appellant to request a rule 3(10) hearing and apply in advance of that hearing for permission to amend the original notice of appeal. There would, of course, be no guarantee that the amendment would be allowed as this is a matter of discretion for the EAT. The judge may well be particularly reluctant to exercise such discretion in the appellant's favour if the revised grounds of appeal are substantially different from the original grounds.

17.68　**Rule 3(10) hearings.** As mentioned above, where the Registrar or a judge determines that no further action should be taken in respect of an appeal or cross-appeal because the Notice of Appeal discloses no reasonable grounds for bringing the appeal or comprises an abuse of process, the appellant may – subject to rule 3(7ZA) – appeal to a single judge against that determination – rule 3(10) EAT Rules. If such a hearing takes place, the EAT may seek a response from the respondent at this point – see, for example, Bladen v Cardiff University EAT 0071/05. At the hearing, which will normally last not more than one and a half hours, the judge will give directions as to whether any further action should be taken on the notice of appeal. The judge may confirm the Registrar's decision to reject the appeal, or order that it proceed to a preliminary or full hearing – para 11.6 Practice Direction.

As mentioned earlier, the time limit for a rule 3(10) request is 28 days from the date that the Registrar *sent* notification to the party that their notice of appeal has been rejected. Accordingly, in Echendu v William Morrison Supermarkets plc EAT 1675/07, where the claimant requested such a hearing within 28 days of the date he *received* the notification, the application was held to be out of time and the EAT saw no grounds on which to grant an extension of the time limit. Where the matter does proceed to a hearing in front of a single judge, the appellant can amend his or her grounds of appeal at the oral hearing. The principles that govern a notice to amend were set down by the EAT in Khudados v Leggate and ors 2005 ICR 1013, EAT – see 'Instituting an appeal' above, under 'Grounds of appeal – amending a notice of appeal'. In Readman v Devon Primary Care Trust EAT 0116/11 the EAT held that it will usually be in the interests of justice to approve applications for permission to amend at a rule 3(10) hearing provided that the amendment is reasonably arguable.

17.69　If an appellant's case is allocated to the rule 3(7) track by the Registrar, then he or she is at liberty to appeal that decision to the Court of Appeal rather than serve a fresh notice of appeal or express dissatisfaction at the decision in accordance with rule 3(10) of the EAT Rules. This is confirmed by para 11.1(c) of the Practice Direction. In Barreto v Wincanton Group Ltd EAT 0659/10 the appellant in these circumstances did just that. However, the Court of Appeal declined jurisdiction on the basis that B had not exhausted his right to appeal in the EAT – he could still seek an oral hearing under rule 3(10). B then expressed dissatisfaction under rule 3(10), but did so out of time and the Registrar refused to extend time. Upon hearing his appeal, His Honour Judge McMullen QC, sitting alone, held that S.37(1) ETA – which provides that an appeal on any question of law lies from the EAT to the relevant appeal court subject to leave being granted by either body – is unlimited and allows an appellant to apply for permission to appeal against an opinion under rule 3(7) and 3(8) of the EAT Rules. (As previously stated, it should be borne in mind that rule 3(8) – which allowed an appellant to serve a fresh notice of appeal with a view to meeting the objections of the Registrar following a rule 3(7) notification – has now been deleted from the EAT Rules by virtue of the 2013 amendments.)

An appellant may also appeal to the Court of Appeal – again subject to leave from the EAT or the Court – if he or she is unsuccessful at a rule 3(10) hearing. In Scotland, an appeal lies to the Court of Session. The Court of Session in Francis v Pertemps Recruitment Partnership Ltd 2011 CSIH 40, Ct Sess (Inner House), held that the EAT's decision to refuse leave in that case was 'a decision or order of the Appeal Tribunal' under 37(1) ETA. Consequently, F was entitled to apply to the Court of Session for leave to appeal and did not have to challenge the EAT's refused permission by way of judicial review.

Preliminary hearing cases   17.70
The purpose of a preliminary hearing is to determine:

- whether the grounds in the notice of appeal raise a point of law which gives the appeal a reasonable prospect of success at a full hearing, or

- whether the appeal should be heard for some other compelling reason – for example, that the appellant seeks a declaration of incompatibility under the Human Rights Act 1998, or to argue that a decision binding on the EAT should be considered by a higher court – para 11.8.2 Practice Direction.

Paragraphs 11.8–11.19 of the Practice Direction set out the procedure applying when a case has been allocated to the preliminary hearing track:

- the notice of appeal will be sent to all respondents and automatic directions will precede the preliminary hearing. These will include a direction requiring or enabling the respondent to lodge and serve written submissions in response to the notice of appeal within 14 days of the order (unless otherwise directed) – para 11(9)

- a respondent wishing to cross-appeal must lodge and serve this, together with written submissions, within 14 days of service of the notice of appeal. The respondent must explain whether or not the cross-appeal is conditional on the appellant succeeding. If a cross-appeal is lodged, the respondent is entitled to attend the preliminary hearing, which will also amount to a preliminary hearing of the cross-appeal, and make submissions – para 11.10

- all parties will be notified of the date of the preliminary hearing. Normally, only the appellant should attend and make submissions to the EAT on the issue of whether the Notice of Appeal raises any reasonable ground for bringing the appeal. However, it is open to the respondent to observe the proceedings, and although it will not normally be permitted to take part in them, the respondent may do so if the judge considers it desirable – para 11.11

- the preliminary hearing, including judgment and directions, will normally last no more than an hour, and therefore arguments should be carefully planned so that this time is not exceeded. If it is, the Appeal Tribunal may impose a guillotine on further argument in order to ensure that the case does not take a share of the Appeal Tribunal's resources which is disproportionate to that taken by other appeals yet to be heard – para 11.13

- if satisfied that the appeal should be heard, the EAT will give directions for further conduct of the matter – para 11.14. It will also, under para 11.19, assign one of the following listing categories to the case:

  – P (recommended to be heard in the President's list)

  – A (complex and raising point(s) of law of public importance)

  – B (any other cases).

  The President reserves the discretion to alter any relevant category as circumstances require

- the EAT will determine the grounds (if any) upon which the appeal is permitted to proceed. If the appeal is not permitted to proceed on any grounds it will be dismissed and a judgment setting out the reasons for doing so provided – para 11.16

- if an appeal is permitted to go forward on all grounds a judgment will not be supplied – para 11.17

- if the parties become aware that a similar point is being raised in other proceedings before the employment tribunal or the EAT, they will be encouraged to cooperate in bringing this to the Registrar's attention so that consideration can be given to the possibility of hearing the cases together – para 11.18.

There have been a number of cases dealing with appeals in which some, but not **17.71** all, of the grounds of appeal have been judged to give rise to an arguable case. In Younas v Chief Constable of Thames Valley Police 2001 EWCA Civ 1936, CA, the Court of Appeal stressed that where a preliminary hearing has dealt with more than one ground of appeal, the EAT should make it clear which ground merits going forward to a full hearing. The EAT's jurisdiction at the full hearing is then limited to the stated ground or grounds of appeal – Miriki v General Council of the Bar and anor 2002 ICR 505, CA. However, Lord Justice Pill, giving judgment in Vincent v MJ Gallagher Contractors Ltd 2003 ICR 1244, CA, urged the EAT to be cautious before adopting an approach whereby it permits an appeal to proceed on one ground but not another. In that case, V appealed against an employment tribunal's finding that her employer had adequately consulted with her about her redundancy, and the EAT dismissed three of her five grounds of appeal at the preliminary hearing stage. When the case reached the Court of Appeal, Lord Justice Pill described it as having a 'comparatively narrow compass'. All five grounds of appeal related to the employer's consultation procedure, and it would have been appropriate for the EAT to allow the appeal to proceed on all these grounds.

Full hearing cases
17.72

If a judge or the Registrar determines that an appeal should proceed without the need for a preliminary hearing, he or she will give appropriate directions for the future conduct of the case. These might relate to amendment, further information, a procedure in respect of matters of evidence at the employment tribunal not sufficiently appearing from the written reasons, allegations of bias, apparent bias or improper conduct, provisions for skeleton arguments, appellant's chronology and bundles of documents and of authorities, time estimates and listing category – para 11.20 Practice Direction. For listing categories, see 'Preliminary hearing cases' above.

Fast-track full hearing cases
17.73

Full hearing cases are usually heard in the order in which they are received by the EAT. However, cases will be expedited – that is, placed in the fast track to be heard as soon as they can be fitted into the list – at the discretion of a judge or the Registrar. Para 11.21 of the Practice Direction states that fast-track full hearing cases will normally fall within one of the following categories:

- appeals where the parties have made a reasoned case on the merits for an expedited hearing

- appeals against interim orders or decisions of the tribunal, particularly those which involve the taking of a step in the proceedings within a specified time

- appeals where the outcome affects other claims before tribunals, the EAT or civil courts

911

- appeals where a reference to the ECJ or declaration of incompatibility under the Human Rights Act 1998 is sought, or

- appeals involving applications for reinstatement, re-engagement or interim relief.

Cases allocated as Category B (i.e. those involving well-settled legal principles) may also be placed in the fast track where they have a time estimate of less than two hours – para 11.22 Practice Direction.

17.74 Serving notice on the parties

Once an appellant's notice of appeal has passed through the initial sift procedure and been accepted, and the required hearing fee has been paid (or remission granted), the Registrar seals it with the EAT's seal and serves a sealed copy on:

- the appellant

- all respondents to the appeal

- the Secretary of the Employment Tribunals (if the appeal is from an employment tribunal)

- the Secretary of State for Work and Pensions in a case brought under Chapter II of Part IV of the Trade Union and Labour Relations (Consolidation) Act 1992 (industrial relations – procedure for handling redundancies)

- the Secretary of State for Work and Pensions if the appeal involves payments out of the National Insurance Fund and he or she has not been named as a respondent

- the Certification Officer or Chairman of the Central Arbitration Committee in appropriate cases – rule 4 EAT Rules.

In the case of appeals from employment tribunals, all parties to the tribunal proceedings other than the appellant are regarded as respondents to the appeal and will be served with a copy of the notice of appeal accordingly – rule 5(a). This means that the Secretary of State will be a respondent if he or she was named as a party to the tribunal proceedings.

17.75 Answer and cross-appeal

Once an appellant's appeal has been accepted, the next stage is for the respondent to the appeal to provide an *answer* to the appellant's notice of appeal. The respondent will be notified by the Registrar of the date by which an answer to the notice of appeal must be delivered – rule 6(1). Para 12.1 of the Practice Direction states that the respondent will have 14 days from the seal date of the EAT's order to lodge an answer at the EAT and serve a copy on the other parties. If a respondent needs an extension of time in which to lodge his or her answer then general discretionary principles apply. In Slingsby v Griffith Smith Solicitors EAT 0619/07 the EAT held that while the time limit for instituting an appeal to the EAT should be strictly enforced, a more liberal view can be taken in relation to the time limit for presenting an answer in response to a notice of appeal.

Paragraph 12.3 of the Practice Direction makes it clear that a respondent who wishes to resist the appeal and/or cross-appeal but who fails to deliver a respondent's answer may be barred from taking part in the appeal unless permission is granted to serve an answer out of time. In all cases, the answer should state the grounds (if any) upon which the appeal is to be resisted (which may involve, for example, simply stating that the respondent relies upon the reasoning of the employment tribunal). The answer should be in writing and in accordance with (or substantially in accordance with) form 3, which is set out in the Schedule to the EAT Rules – rule 6(2). In practice, a copy of form 3 will be sent to the respondent(s) together with the notice of appeal.

17.76 After presentation and service of the respondent's answer, the Registrar may, where necessary, invite applications from the parties in writing for directions (provided that notice of any such application is given to the other side), and he or she may give any appropriate directions based on the papers or may fix a day when the parties should attend for an appointment for directions (as to which, see 'Interlocutory procedures – directions' below) – para 12.4 Practice Direction.

A respondent to an appeal may also choose to lodge a cross-appeal. This allows a party to challenge some aspect of a decision even though, taken as a whole, the tribunal found in that party's favour. For example, an employer may appeal against a tribunal's finding of unfair dismissal. The respondent (the ex-employee) will normally resist the appeal, perhaps simply relying on the grounds set out by the tribunal in its decision. He or she may, however, wish to cross-appeal against the tribunal's decision on compensation – e.g. arguing that compensation was set too low or contributory conduct was set too high. Note that a cross-appeal must arise out of the same decision that the appellant is contesting. If the respondent wishes to challenge a different decision, even if it concerns the same parties, then that constitutes an independent appeal – Asda Stores Ltd v Thompson and ors (No.2) 2004 IRLR 598, EAT. The EAT there held that, if a cross-appeal falls into this category, that of itself may well be a good justification for relaxing the normally strict principles governing an extension of time.

17.77 The cross-appeal is then subject to the same sift procedure as applies in respect of the notice of appeal as described under 'The sift – rule 3(7) cases (no valid grounds of appeal)' above. The sift procedure applicable to cross-appeals is set out in rules 6(12)–(16) of the EAT Rules. If the cross-appeal is accepted, it will be dealt with in accordance with directions given by the judge or Registrar (see 'Interlocutory procedures' below). In this regard, note that following the 2013 changes to the EAT Rules, a new rule 6(12A) has been added. This provides that, where a judge or the Registrar has decided under rule 6(12) that the cross-appeal discloses no reasonable ground for bringing the cross-appeal or is an abuse of process, and also decides that the cross-appeal is totally without merit, the judge or Registrar may order that the respondent is not entitled to have the matter heard before a judge under rule 6(16). In that case the cross-appellant's sole remedy lies in an appeal to the Court of Appeal.

The 2013 changes also removed old rule 6(14) and (15). These previously stated that, where a judge or the Registrar decided under rule 6(12) that the stated grounds of cross-appeal did not disclose any reasonable grounds for bringing the cross–appeal or were an abuse of process, a fresh cross-appeal could be served within the original time limit under rule 6(1) or within 28 days from the date that the notice was given under rule 6(12), whichever was the longer. The fresh cross-appeal would then be treated as if it were contained in the respondent's original answer. The position now is that, where rule 6(12) applies to the respondent's cross-appeal – but not rule 6(12A) – and the respondent has requested an oral hearing under rule 6(16), the respondent can apply for permission to amend the cross-appeal in advance of that rule 6(16) hearing.

17.78 According to para 12.2 of the Practice Direction, the respondent must pay a fee in respect of any cross-appeal contained within an answer to an appeal in the same way that an appellant pays a fee in respect of the appeal. However, this does not accord with Article 13 of the Employment Tribunals and the Employment Appeal Tribunal Fees Order 2013 SI 2013/1893, which states that a 'fee… is payable by an appellant on the date specified in a notice issued by the Lord Chancellor, following the receipt by the Employment Appeal Tribunal of a *notice of appeal*' (our stress). 'Notice of appeal' is defined in the Order as a notice referred to in rule 3(1)(a) of the EAT Rules, which does not include a cross-appeal contained within an answer under rule 6 of the EAT Rules. Moreover, guidance produced by HM Courts and Tribunals Service entitled 'Employment Appeal Tribunal Fees' (Form T437) provides that no fees are payable by a respondent who cross-appeals. As para 4.1 of the Practice Direction makes clear that the Practice Direction is subject to the Order, we would respectfully suggest that a respondent is *not* liable to pay either an issue or a hearing fee in respect of a cross-appeal. For further discussion on fees in the context of appeals to the EAT, see Chapter 19, 'Fees', under 'EAT fees'.

If there is a cross-appeal, then the other party (who technically becomes a respondent to the cross-appeal) should provide a *reply* stating the grounds upon which the cross-appeal is to be resisted – rule 6(3) EAT Rules. It is for the Registrar to specify a time within which this document should be served. The notice of appeal, the answer, the cross-appeal, and the reply to the cross-appeal constitute what are known as 'the pleadings'. They are all sent to the Registrar, whose job it is to send copies to each of the other parties.

If a respondent does not wish to contest an appeal, rule 6(5) provides that the **17.79** parties may deliver to the EAT an agreed draft of an order allowing the appeal and the EAT may make an order allowing the appeal in the terms agreed. The EAT will only do so, however, if it appears to be the right thing to do, and parties to an appeal should not take the EAT's acquiescence to any agreement between the parties for granted. This point was made in Sakharkar v Northern Foods Grocery Group Ltd t/a Fox's Biscuits EAT 0314–15/12, where the EAT held that the parties to an appeal could not of themselves agree that an appeal should be allowed – the judgment of a court or tribunal could only be overturned by the judgment of an appellate court or tribunal.

In certain circumstances, the EAT, in the exercise of its power under rule 6(5), has allowed appeals by consent without requiring the parties to attend a hearing – for example, where the parties have reached an overall settlement of their dispute and have agreed as part of the settlement that the decision of the tribunal was wrong. In such circumstances, the EAT will examine the facts of the case and, if satisfied that the parties are fully aware of the situation and that it is an appropriate case for allowing the appeal, will make a consent order on the basis of the parties' written representations – see British Publishing Co Ltd v Fraser 1987 ICR 517, EAT. However, in J Sainsbury plc v Moger 1994 ICR 800, EAT, the EAT made it clear that it will not, in general, make an order by consent where there is no overall settlement of the dispute and where the parties ask that the case be remitted to the same or a different tribunal for rehearing. In these circumstances, the EAT will need to hear the matter to determine whether there is a good reason for making the order – para 18.3 Practice Direction. For further discussion about the general principles that apply to allowing appeals by consent, see Chapter 16, 'The Employment Appeal Tribunal', under 'Jurisdiction of the EAT – appeals by consent'.

Interlocutory procedures   17.80

Once the formalities have been completed for the notice of appeal, the respondent's answer and cross-appeal, and the reply to the cross-appeal, the Registrar will give notice of the arrangements for hearing the appeal to the interested parties (who are the same as those on whom he or she served copies of the original notice of appeal – see 'Serving notice on the parties' above) – rule 7 EAT Rules. However, a number of interim steps may need to be taken before the full appeal can be heard. Examples of these are outlined below:

- amendment of the notice of appeal or answer
- admission of facts or documents not cited at the original tribunal hearing

915

- joinder of a new party to the proceedings or removal of an existing party from the proceedings

- applications to strike out pleadings or to debar a party from taking any further part

- the manner in which evidence is to be given at the hearing of the appeal

- consolidation of the proceedings with any other proceedings pending before the EAT

- deciding the place and date of the hearing (including applications for postponement).

The EAT may raise all such matters of its own motion or they may surface because of an application by a party.

17.81 Directions

Once an appeal is allowed to proceed to a full hearing, the EAT will invite applications from parties in writing, on notice to all other parties, for directions. It may either give appropriate directions in writing or fix a day when the parties should attend the EAT on an 'appointment for directions' – para 12.4 Practice Direction.

The EAT may, on its own motion, or following the application of the parties under rule 19 of the EAT Rules, make arrangements for a meeting for directions at any stage of proceedings – rule 24(1). When a meeting for directions is called, the Registrar must give each party notice of the date on which directions are to be given and any party who intends to ask for particular directions should, if practicable, give notice of these to the EAT before that date – rule 24(2). The Registrar should inform every party of any directions that have been applied for by one of the other parties – rule 24(3).

Under rule 24(5), the EAT is expressly empowered to give directions relating to:

- the amendment of notices, answers or other documents

- the admission of any facts or documents

- the admission of documents into evidence

- the way in which evidence will be presented at the hearing

- the consolidation (joining together) of separate proceedings

- the place and date of the hearing.

In addition to the above, the EAT may also give directions relating to any other matters which seem appropriate to secure the 'just, expeditious and economical disposal of the proceedings' – rule 24(4). Para 14.1 of the Practice Direction states that 'consistent with the overriding objective, the EAT will seek to give directions for case management so that the case can be dealt with quickly, or better considered, and in the most effective and just way'.

Note that the EAT's power to give directions includes the power to order parties to take particular steps in relation to the proceedings – rule 25.

Challenging an order for directions. If directions have been given by a **17.82** Registrar, parties have the right of appeal to a judge – para 14.2 Practice Direction. A party may also apply to vary or discharge an order, or seek an extension of time to comply with it – para 14.5. Such an application must be lodged with the EAT within the time limit for compliance with the direction. A party opposing the application must submit written representations within the period required by the EAT (usually 14 days) to the EAT and other parties.

Failure to comply with an order for directions in time or at all may result in the EAT exercising its powers for dealing with non-compliance under rule 26 – namely, it may: strike out the appeal, cross-appeal or respondent's answer; debar a party from taking any further part in the proceedings; or make any other order it thinks fit, including an award of costs – para 14.2.

Disposing of interim applications

17.83

Not all interim applications need to be dealt with by way of a meeting for directions, and the EAT Rules set out a procedure whereby such applications can be dealt with by the Registrar in the first instance. There is a right of appeal to a judge from a decision of the Registrar disposing of an interim application – para 6.3 Practice Direction – and the notice of appeal must be given within five days of the decision appealed from but such notice may be given either orally or in writing.

An interim application should be in writing and should specify the order or direction being sought – rule 19(1) EAT Rules. The application will go first to the Registrar, who, in addition to serving a copy on every other party to the proceedings who appears to be concerned in the matter to which the application relates (rule 19(2)), will consider how it may be justly and economically disposed of, bearing in mind the expense that may be involved if the parties have to attend an oral hearing – rule 20(1). After considering the papers, the Registrar may determine not to deal with it him or herself but to refer the matter to the President or a judge.

Until recently, it was possible that interim applications referred by the Registrar **17.84** to the President or a judge could either be disposed of by the President or judge him or herself, or referred in whole or part to a full Appeal Tribunal. Likewise, applications for 'restricted reporting orders' or 'restriction of proceedings orders' – which Registrars are not permitted to hear – could also be referred to a full Appeal Tribunal if they were not disposed of by the President or a judge. However, changes made to S.28 of the ETA by the Enterprise and

917

Regulatory Reform Act 2013 now mean that Appeal Tribunal hearings will be composed, by default, of a single judge unless a contrary direction is specifically given – for further information, see Chapter 16, 'The Employment Appeal Tribunal', under 'Composition of the EAT – sittings of the EAT'. It should also be noted that cases involving a restricted reporting order will not necessarily be dealt with in the absence of oral argument, since rule 23(5) stipulates that such an order cannot be made until each of the parties to the proceedings has been given an opportunity to advance oral argument at a hearing if they so wish. For information on restricted reporting orders and restriction of proceedings orders, see 'Sexual misconduct and disability cases' and 'Vexatious proceedings' below.

The EAT may sit either in public or in private to hear an interim application – rule 22(1). However, in cases concerning national security, a Minister of the Crown may direct, or the Appeal Tribunal may order, that the EAT sit in private.

17.85 Miscellaneous powers

There are certain matters, which will arise at an interim stage, over which the EAT has specific powers under the EAT Rules.

17.86 Witness orders. As appeals from employment tribunals may only be brought on questions of law, hearings before the EAT normally only involve the making of legal submissions. The EAT nevertheless has the power to order any person to attend a hearing as a witness or to produce any document. Individuals who are so ordered are only obliged to comply if they are paid a sum of money to cover the costs of their compliance – rule 27. Failure to attend in compliance with a witness order issued by the EAT will constitute a contempt of court – S.29(2) ETA.

17.87 Waiver of the Rules. Under rule 39 the EAT may overlook failure to comply with any of the EAT Rules. The EAT may also dispense with any step required by the Rules or direct that the procedure laid down by the Rules should be varied – rule 39(2). In China National Star Petroleum Corp v Thain EAT 236/01 the EAT relied on this power to allow a firm of solicitors, which was not a party to the proceedings but which was affected by an employment tribunal's decision, to challenge that decision before the EAT.

17.88 Extension of time. The EAT has the power under rule 37(1) to extend or abridge any time limit provided for under the Rules. Any application for an extension of time in relation to a case management order must be notified to the other parties to the appeal and must be served on the EAT within the time fixed for compliance – para 14.5 Practice Direction. Any opposing party who wishes to resist the application has to submit representations to the EAT and the other parties within 14 days (or such shorter period as may be ordered) of receiving the application – para 14.6 Practice Direction.

918

Joinder of parties. Under rule 18 the EAT may direct that a person who is not **17.89** a party to the proceedings be added as a party. This can be done even if the new party has no strict legal liability – e.g. Acas could be joined as a party in a case where an appellant is attacking the validity of a conciliated settlement reached under the auspices of Acas. Conversely, the EAT may direct that any party should cease to be a party to the proceedings.

Conciliation. A judge may at any time, upon consideration of the papers, or at **17.90** a hearing, take such steps as he or she thinks fit to enable the parties to make use of opportunities for conciliation, compromise, mediation or a reference to Acas – para 12.5 Practice Direction. This could include giving appropriate directions (rule 24(4)) or adjourning the proceedings (rule 36). Furthermore, para 26 of the Practice Direction states that the parties should – and when so directed must – consider conciliation of their appeals. Such a direction could be given at any stage by either the Registrar or a judge, who may also require the parties to report on steps taken to effect a conciliated settlement with the assistance of an Acas officer.

Obtaining enhanced written reasons – the 'Burns/Barke procedure'. Where **17.91** an EAT judge considers an employment tribunal's written reasons for its judgment, decision or order to be inadequate, he or she can remit the matter to the tribunal, inviting it to clarify, supplement or provide its reasoning. This is known as the 'Burns/Barke procedure' after the cases of Burns v Royal Mail Group plc (formerly Consignia plc) and anor 2004 ICR 1103, EAT, in which Mr Justice Burton, then President of the EAT, decided that this practice is lawful, and the approval of that case by the Court of Appeal in Barke v SEETEC Business Technology Centre Ltd 2005 ICR 1373, CA. In Woodhouse School v Webster 2009 ICR 818, CA, the Court of Appeal stressed that it is necessary for the EAT to identify correctly the point on which the tribunal's reasons may be inadequate. Furthermore, the Court continued, it is not desirable for the tribunal to do more than answer the request. For example, it should not advance arguments in defence of its decision.

Although the Burns/Barke procedure is not specifically codified in the EAT Rules, para 11.3 of the Practice Direction now states that a judge or the Registrar may stay the appeal pending the response by the employment tribunal to an invitation to clarify, supplement or give its written reasons.

Burton P's decision in the Burns case turned on his interpretation of S.35(1) **17.92** ETA. This provides that 'for the purpose of disposing of an appeal, the Appeal Tribunal may remit the case' to the employment tribunal. This reasoning has now been superseded by the Court of Appeal's decision in Barke. There, the Court agreed that the EAT had power to remit a case to the tribunal for fuller reasons at any time in the proceedings. However, it based its decision not on S.35 ETA, but on the following two statutory provisions:

- rule 30(3)(b) of the Employment Tribunal Rules of Procedure 2004 (now rule 62(3) of the Tribunal Rules 2013), which expressly permits the EAT to request written reasons in relation to a judgment or order at any time (see 'Instituting an appeal – written reasons' above), and

- S.30(3) ETA, which gives the EAT the general power to regulate its own procedure.

The Court of Appeal in Barke also considered the extent of the EAT's power to remit a matter to the employment tribunal. It rejected the contention that the Burns/Barke procedure should only be used in limited circumstances, saying that to apply such restrictions would frustrate the overriding objective to deal with cases justly. The purpose of the procedure was to avoid the cost and delay of a full hearing before the EAT in cases where these might be avoided should the parties be furnished with fuller reasons for the tribunal's decision. The Court did, however, identify some limits to the procedure. First, it noted that the EAT could not require the tribunal to supplement its reasons – it could only *invite* it to do so. Secondly, it agreed that there might be circumstances – such as where a tribunal's reasons were wholly inadequate – when it would be inappropriate to seek further reasons from the tribunal because of the risk that the tribunal might construct reasons that had not existed at the time. Thirdly, the Court warned that the EAT should be aware of the possibility that the tribunal might tailor its response so as to cast its decision 'in the best possible light'.

17.93 Note that simply because the EAT seeks answers to a large number of questions with regard to the employment tribunal's reasons for its decision does not itself constitute a valid basis for contending that the EAT's use of the Burns/Barke procedure is impermissible. In Korashi v Abertawe Bro Morgannwg University Local Health Board 2011 EWCA Civ 187, CA, the EAT asked 187 questions of a tribunal that had conducted an eight-week hearing and produced a 55-page judgment. The Court of Appeal ruled that, although the EAT's inquiry was close to the limit, it was permissible in the circumstances. Lord Justice Mckay, who gave the lead judgment, held that the questions posed had to be seen in the context of a long and multi-faceted tribunal hearing.

It is the EAT's practice, when making an order that the tribunal be invited to provide reasons pursuant to the Burns/Barke procedure, to give the respondent liberty to apply on notice for the EAT to vary or discharge the order. This practice was endorsed by the Court of Appeal in the Barke case. Accordingly, a respondent who is unhappy with the fact of an order made pursuant to the Burns/Barke procedure or with its terms will normally be required to apply to the EAT before considering an appeal to the Court of Appeal. In UPVC Designs Ltd t/a Croston Conservatories v Latimer EAT 0431/07 the appellant criticised the procedure on the basis that sometimes the employment judge will have responded to the order of amplified reasons before the respondent has had the opportunity to apply for that order to be set aside. His Honour Judge Richardson accepted that there was some force in this criticism. However, he held that it was important that the employment tribunal should, if asked to give further reasons, consider the matter as soon as possible, since to do otherwise would cause delay in circumstances where time considerations are important. Moreover, applications to set aside are rare and it is even rarer for the employment judge to respond before such an application is made.

Stay of appeal. A judge or the Registrar may stay ('sist' in Scotland) an appeal **17.94** for a period, normally 21 days, pending:

- the making or conclusion of an application by the appellant to the employment tribunal for a reconsideration of its decision even if this is made out of time

- a response by the tribunal to an invitation by the judge or Registrar to clarify, supplement or give its written reasons (as explained above) – para 11.3 Practice Direction.

Enforcing EAT procedures

17.95

The EAT has the power, by virtue of rule 26 of the EAT Rules, to penalise parties who fail to provide an answer to a notice of appeal within the proper time or who fail to comply with any order or direction that the EAT gives by ordering that such parties be debarred from taking part in the proceedings. Two examples:

- **Melstar Ltd v Rix** EAT 0701/04: M Ltd appealed against a tribunal's finding of sex discrimination. However, the company, which purported to be in financial difficulty, did not comply with a number of the EAT's orders, including an order to provide bundles for a hearing. M Ltd's appeal was struck out pursuant to rule 26. The fact that the company could not afford representation; that its directors were based abroad; and that it faced going into administration, did not constitute grounds to delay the hearing of the case, nor to allow it to continue with the appeal in light of its breaches

- **Lewis v Tesco Stores Ltd** EAT 0995/03: the appellant's conduct during the tribunal and appeal proceedings demonstrated a refusal to comply with court orders. The EAT accordingly exercised its power to dismiss the appeal and debar the appellant from taking any further part in it. The interesting point to note in this case is that the EAT took into account the appellant's conduct in the earlier tribunal proceedings in reaching its decision.

Note that rule 26 also provides that the EAT can take action short of actually preventing a defaulting party from proceeding by making any other order that it thinks just.

921

17.96 **Withdrawal**

Paragraph 18.1 of the Practice Direction states that where an appellant withdraws an appeal or the parties agree to settle proceedings the parties must inform the EAT as soon as possible. If the appellant does not decide to withdraw until close to the hearing date, the EAT may require the appellant (or his or her representative) to attend a hearing to provide an explanation for the delay in making a decision not to pursue the appeal – para 18.5.

The case of Yell Ltd v Garton 2004 EWCA Civ 87, CA, provides an indication of how late notification of withdrawal or settlement is viewed by the courts. There, the Court of Appeal criticised the representatives of the parties (and the barristers' clerks) for failing to notify the Court that a settlement had been reached at 6 pm on the Friday before a hearing that was due to start on the following Monday morning. The Court stressed that the court office should be notified when serious settlement negotiations are proceeding. It also pointed out that in the case of the Court of Appeal, there is a 24-hour switchboard that would, at the very least, have been able to get a message to the clerk of the judges. Lord Justice Peter Gibson went on to warn that 'there is a professional obligation on those advising parties to litigation to notify the court if there is a likelihood that judicial time will be wasted in preparing for an appeal which has either been settled or is subject to negotiations which may well lead to settlement'.

17.97 The appellant (or a representative) wishing to withdraw must sign and submit a letter to the EAT asking for permission to do so and requesting a consent order dismissing the appeal in the form of an attached draft. The respondent must also countersign the letter and suggested draft order – para 18.1 Practice Direction. If a respondent does not agree the terms of the draft order – perhaps because he or she wishes to raise the question of costs – written submissions should be lodged with the EAT and served on the other parties. The matter will then be determined by the EAT either on paper or at a hearing – para 18.2. In addition, where the parties seek an order that a tribunal's order should be reversed or varied, or the matter remitted to the tribunal, it is usually necessary for the matter to be determined at a hearing – para 18.3.

In Dozie v Addison Lee plc 2013 ICR D38, EAT, the EAT made it clear that it does not allow appeals to be dealt with by consent without scrutiny of the terms of the proposed consent order. There were several good reasons for this: first, that judgments and orders of the employment tribunal were entitled to respect and it was in the interests of justice and good order that they stand unless there is a good reason for upsetting them. Secondly, parties sometimes sought to agree to the setting-aside of judgments or orders for purely tactical reasons and did not always think through the consequences of an appeal. Finally, there was sometimes a wider public interest in a tribunal judgment beyond the interests of the parties to the litigation in question.

922

If the parties agree to a settlement and the EAT then makes an order withdrawing   **17.98**
the appeal, the EAT has no power to subsequently set aside the agreement if the
appellant changes his or her mind and wants to go ahead with the appeal after
all – Eden v Humphries and Glasgow Ltd 1981 ICR 183, EAT.

Sexual misconduct and disability cases   **17.99**

In cases involving sexual misconduct or disability discrimination employment
tribunals have the power to make restricted reporting orders (see Chapter 11,
'Case management', under 'Privacy and restrictions on disclosure – restricted
reporting orders'. Special rules apply where there is an appeal to the EAT
against a tribunal's decision to make or not to make such an order, or against
any interim decision of a tribunal where an order has been made and not
revoked, or where the EAT decides to make this order of its own volition.
These are contained in Ss.31 and 32 ETA and rules 23 and 23A of the EAT
Rules, as discussed in the sections on 'Sexual misconduct cases', 'Cases not
involving sexual misconduct' and 'Disability cases' below.

Sexual misconduct cases   **17.100**
Section 31 ETA makes provision for the restriction of publicity in cases involving
sexual misconduct.

Omission and deletion of 'identifying matter'. If it appears to the Registrar   **17.101**
that an appeal brought before the EAT involves allegations that a sexual offence
has been committed – i.e. a criminal offence contrary to one of the sexual
offences Acts (S.31(8) ETA) – then he or she must omit from the public register
kept by the EAT, or delete from any order, judgment or other document
available to the public, any 'identifying matter' which is likely to enable any
member of the public to identify the person making the allegation or any person
affected by it – rule 23(2) EAT Rules.

When determining whether or not a case appeared to involve allegations of the
commission of a sexual offence, an employment tribunal was not limited to
consideration of the pleadings but should take account of everything that it had
heard or read. The allegations did not have to be the basis of the cause of action
or even central to the question of whether the case appeared to involve
allegations of the commission of a sexual offence or of sexual misconduct
decision-making. To be justified in making an RRO, the tribunal simply had to
satisfy itself that the case would involve such allegations – see X v Commissioner
of Metropolitan Police 2003 ICR 1031, EAT. In that particular case, X
contended that she had been refused a post with the Metropolitan Police
because she was a post-operative male-to-female transsexual, and lodged a sex
discrimination claim against the Commissioner. Among other things, she made
an application for a 'register deletion order' (see below). An employment judge
cited the decision in Chief Constable of the West Yorkshire Police v A 2001

923

ICR 128, EAT, as authority for the proposition that neither the tribunal nor the EAT could make a restricted reporting order where there were no allegations of sexual misconduct. In light of this, the judge in the Commissioner of Police of the Metropolis case concluded that she lacked power to make a register deletion order. On appeal, the EAT held that the reference to 'allegations appearing to involve the commission of a sexual offence' in rule 15(6) of the Tribunal Rules 2001 was not limited to the pleadings and could cover facts arising from witness statements or submissions made to the tribunal. The EAT also construed 'involve' widely, holding that allegations 'involved' need not form part of the claim or be central to the issue of liability.

17.102 Note that prior to the introduction of the Tribunal Rules 2004, tribunals had a separate power to make a register deletion order where allegations of a sexual offence were involved. This had the effect of requiring that the public register of judgments and any other public documents generated in the proceedings were modified or redacted to prevent identification of the persons making, or affected by, the allegation. However, under rule 50(3)(b) of the Employment Tribunal Rules 2013 a tribunal may now simply order that the identities of specified parties, witnesses and other persons referred to in proceedings should not be disclosed to the public, whether in the course of any hearing or in its listing or in any documents entered on the Register or otherwise forming part of the public record.

17.103 **Restricted reporting orders.** In cases involving allegations of sexual misconduct – i.e. the commission of a sexual offence (see above), sexual harassment or other adverse conduct related to sex, gender or sexual orientation (S.31(8) ETA) – the EAT may at any time, on the application of either party or of its own motion, make a restricted reporting order – rule 23(3) EAT Rules. The order is effective either until it is revoked by the EAT, or until its decision is promulgated – whichever is the sooner. For these purposes a decision is 'promulgated' when the order finally disposing of the appeal is sent to the parties – rule 23(9). The order prohibits the publication in Great Britain of any matter (written or broadcast) likely to lead members of the public to identify an individual as a person affected by or making the allegation – S.31(7) and (8) ETA. It must specify the individuals who may not be identified – rule 23(4).

In Tradition Securities and Futures SA and ors v Times Newspapers Ltd and ors 2009 IRLR 354, EAT, the EAT held that under the Employment Tribunal Rules 2004 that then governed employment tribunal procedure (and so, by extension, the EAT Rules) it may, in principle, be appropriate to include a claimant in a restricted reporting order to protect the identity of an alleged perpetrator.

17.104 Subject to its powers to make a temporary restricted reporting order (see below), the EAT must not make a restricted reporting order without first giving each party the opportunity of presenting oral argument at a hearing, if they so wish – rule 23(5). Note that unlike rule 50(4) of the Employment Tribunal

Rules 2013, which allows an interested third party to make representations at such a hearing, the EAT Rules do not permit submissions by anyone other than parties to the proceedings.

When a restricted reporting order has been made, the Registrar must ensure that a notice stating that fact is displayed on the EAT notice board and on the door of the room in which the case is being heard, and is attached to any list of the proceedings taking place before the EAT – rule 23(8). Once made, a restricted reporting order can be revoked by the EAT at any time – rule 23(7).

Section 31(3) ETA provides that if any identifying matter is published in **17.105** contravention of a restricted reporting order, then an offence will have been committed by:

- in the case of publication in a newspaper or periodical – any proprietor, any editor and any publisher of the newspaper or periodical

- in the case of publication in any other form – the person publishing the matter, and

- in the case of matter broadcast in a relevant programme – any corporate body (and any officer of the company conniving in the broadcast) engaged in providing the service in which the programme is included and any person who has a function in relation to that programme corresponding to that of an editor of a newspaper.

The offence will be punishable by a fine not exceeding level 5 on the standard scale. It will, however, be a defence for any of the persons listed above to prove that he or she was not aware, and had no reason to suspect, that the publication or programme in question included the matter covered by the order. This appears to be a very limited defence. It would not, for instance, assist an individual who did not know of the order itself. The ignorance can only relate to the contents of the publication or broadcast in question.

Temporary restricted reporting orders. The 2004 Amending Regulations **17.106** altered the EAT Rules to confer on the EAT the power to make temporary restricted reporting orders in cases involving allegations of sexual misconduct. These may be made by the EAT on its own initiative and without a hearing – rule 23(5A) EAT Rules.

A temporary restricted reporting order will have effect for 14 days, after which time it will lapse unless either party has applied to have it converted into a full order within this time. If such an application has been made, the temporary order will continue to have effect until the hearing at which the application is considered – rule 23(5C). A party may also apply to have the temporary order revoked – again within 14 days of the date of the order – rule 23(5B).

925

17.107 **Cases not involving sexual misconduct**

The provisions for the making of a restricted reporting order outlined immediately above only apply in cases involving allegations of sexual misconduct. However, the EAT has made a restricted reporting order in a case which did not involve allegations of sexual misconduct, in order to protect the identity of a transsexual bringing a claim of sex discrimination. In Chief Constable of the West Yorkshire Police v A 2001 ICR 128, EAT, the then President of the EAT, Mr Justice Lindsay, noted that the EAT could not make a restricted reporting order under rule 23 because of the absence of allegations of sexual misconduct. He held, however, that the EAT had jurisdiction derived from European law to make such an order. The appellant could rely directly on the EU Equal Treatment Directive (No.76/207) (now consolidated into the recast EU Equal Treatment Directive (No.2006/54)) in bringing her claim of sex discrimination because the claim was against the police as an emanation of the state. Under Article 6 of Directive No.76/207 (now Article 17 of the 2006 Directive) the UK is obliged to ensure that the appellant has an effective remedy for breaches of the Directive. The EAT thought that there was strong evidence that she would have refrained from bringing a claim had her identity not been protected. The EAT also concluded that the appellant would have been denied an effective remedy for breach of the Directive if a restricted reporting order were not made.

In X v Commissioner of Metropolitan Police 2003 ICR 1031, EAT – another sex discrimination case – an employment tribunal's decision not to make, among other things, a restricted reporting order was overturned because the relevant criteria for making such an order as set out in the Employment Tribunal Rules had been satisfied. However, the EAT went on to decide that it *and the employment tribunal* could, in any case, have made such an order under Article 6 of the 1976 Directive based on the claimant's contention that she would otherwise have been deterred from proceeding if she had been forced to air in public details relating to her transgender status. But, unlike the EAT in Chief Constable of the West Yorkshire Police v A, which held that Article 6 directly conferred the necessary jurisdiction on the EAT, the EAT in X v Commissioner of Metropolitan Police thought that provisions enabling the EAT and the tribunal to regulate their own procedure were the key to achieving this aim. It held that S.30(3) ETA provides the EAT with power to regulate its own procedure and a similarly wide power is granted to tribunals under what is now rule 41 of the Employment Tribunal Rules 2013. The EAT was satisfied that this empowered both the employment tribunal and the EAT to make orders analogous to, but wider than, restricted reporting orders in circumstances where the facts of the case did not fall within the narrow definitions contained in the respective procedural rules to ensure anonymity where the applicant would otherwise be deterred from bringing a claim.

17.108 **European Convention on Human Rights.** The question of whether restricted reporting orders could be issued other than in accordance with the normal

procedural rules was also considered by the EAT in A v B 2010 ICR 849, EAT. There, the employment tribunal made a restricted reporting order in an unfair dismissal claim concerning the unsolicited disclosure by the police of allegations of child sex abuse in respect of an employee whose job did not bring him into contact with children. When the tribunal's decision was heard on appeal, the EAT made an order similar to a restricted reporting order but at the same time expressed anxiety about the basis of its jurisdiction to do so. In a supplementary judgment handed down to address this concern, the EAT held that the reasoning applied in Chief Constable of the West Yorkshire Police v A (above) and in X v Commissioner of Metropolitan Police (above) was not available to it because the claim in Av B was not based on any right deriving from EU legislation. The EAT then considered whether there was an analogous route to establishing jurisdiction by reference to the Human Rights Act 1998. In this regard, it noted that if the loss of a claimant's anonymity involved a breach of his or her rights under the European Convention on Human Rights, then it would be the duty of the EAT under S.6 HRA to interpret its powers so as to protect that anonymity. Furthermore, it was well-established that the 'right to be protected in one's honour and reputation' fell within the scope of Article 8 of the Convention – the right to respect for private and family life. The EAT observed that the use of anonymisation orders to protect the Article 8 rights of litigants had been considered in In re Guardian News and Media Ltd and ors 2010 2 WLR 325, SC, a case in which the Supreme Court held that where full publication of the proceedings before a court is liable to impact on the Article 8 rights of a party the court would have to conduct a balancing exercise between that right and those protected by Article 10 – the right to freedom of expression. Against this background, the EAT decided that the balance in that case came down clearly in favour of preserving the claimant's anonymity. In circumstances where nothing had ever been proved against him, the Appeal Tribunal saw no public interest that would outweigh the damage which it was reasonable to assume would ensue if the allegations against the claimant were put into the public domain. Consequently, the effect of Article 8 was that the EAT should, in the exercise of its powers to regulate its procedure under S.30(3) ETA, confirm the steps it had already taken to protect the claimant's identity.

The EAT's reasoning in A v B was applied in the subsequent case of F v G 2012 ICR 246, EAT. In that case, F worked as a carer in a college of further education with special facilities for disabled students. In 2008, following a recommendation from the Commission for Social Care Inspection, the college introduced a formal 'Relationships and Sexuality Policy' (the policy) relating to its students. One of the policy's elements was a recognition that disabled male students who were physically unable to masturbate should be entitled to some assistance in doing so. The assistance did not involve any member of staff masturbating students or being present while masturbation took place. Rather, it took the form of a relevant member of staff helping to apply an appropriate aid and to take it off

927

afterwards. The policy stated that no member of staff would be required to provide such assistance. F alleged that on two occasions she was asked to wash a male student very shortly after assisted masturbation had taken place. Although the student should have been helped by the volunteer who had been assisting, F nevertheless felt that washing him so soon after masturbation associated her with the act, and she found it repugnant. After pursuing various internal processes, F resigned and submitted claims for direct sex discrimination, sexual harassment and unfair constructive dismissal. Among other things, an employment tribunal judge granted the college a permanent anonymity order under rule 49 of the Tribunal Rules 2004, a decision which F appealed against. Mr Justice Underhill – then President of the EAT – held that the tribunal did not have the power to grant a permanent anonymity order under rule 49, as F's complaint did not involve the commission of a sexual offence.

17.109 The tribunal had, however, also considered the Article 8 rights of the parties and others directly affected by the case. Therefore, Underhill P had to examine whether the tribunal had made a properly reasoned decision in accordance with the principles laid down in the A v B case. In this regard, he noted that the tribunal had found that it was G's students and staff whose rights potentially required protection (given that F did not want anonymisation). As they were persons affected by the case, Underhill P held that the tribunal had been obliged to consider whether publication of information about them would interfere with their rights under Article 8. He also held that the identities of F and G could be withheld if the students and staff required protection as their identities could be gleaned from the disclosure of F and/or G's names. Underhill P concluded that to identify an individual student as having received assistance to masturbate would disclose his sexual behaviour, which was a central aspect of an individual's private life. Naming individual students would, therefore, interfere with their rights under Article 8. In respect of staff, he held that volunteering to assist students in such a personal way should be regarded as an aspect of their private life, even though this activity was carried out at work. Thus, identifying individual members of staff would interfere with their rights under Article 8. Furthermore, there was no public interest that could justify, or outweigh, the interference with the relevant individuals' rights under Article 8, and so their identities should be protected. On this basis, Underhill P agreed with the findings of the tribunal and upheld its order.

17.110 Disability cases

Provisions concerning the restriction of publicity in disability cases brought under the Equality Act 2010 are contained in S.32 ETA and rule 23A of the EAT Rules. These are very similar to the rules on restricted reporting orders in sexual misconduct cases, and include a power to make temporary orders. The provisions apply to cases in which evidence of a personal nature is likely to be heard. 'Evidence of a personal nature' is defined by S.12(7) ETA as 'any evidence of a medical, or other intimate, nature which might reasonably be assumed to be likely to cause significant embarrassment to the complainant if reported'.

Guidance

In F v G 2012 ICR 246, EAT, Mr Justice Underhill set out a suggested procedure in cases where restricted reporting orders or anonymity orders are sought. Although this guidance relates to the issuing of such orders in accordance with the Employment Tribunal Rules then in place, it is equally applicable to the power of the EAT to issue such orders:

- the starting point is to consider whether an anonymity order rule applies. If it does, anonymisation is mandatory

- subject to the above, the best starting-point is to consider whether restrictions on reporting and/or anonymisation are required in order to protect the rights of a party or other affected person under Article 8 ECHR, other Articles of the ECHR, or EU law. In considering this, employment tribunals must pay full regard to the importance of open justice and consider the extent of any measures. It will be necessary to consider not only what restrictions are proportionate but for how long they need remain in place: permanent protection may or may not be appropriate

- if protection is required and the necessary measures can be taken pursuant to procedural rules, they should be so taken

- where these rules have no application – say, because there is no allegation of the commission of a sexual offence or of sexual misconduct, nor any disability issue – the employment tribunal should issue the necessary measures pursuant to its general power in accordance with the reasoning in X v Commissioner of Metropolitan Police 2003 ICR 1031, EAT, and A v B 2010 ICR 849, EAT (discussed under 'Cases not involving sexual misconduct' above)

- for cases within the scope of the rule governing restricted reporting orders, where the relief available under that rule is too limited – e.g. if restriction of reporting is required beyond the end of the proceedings – the employment tribunal should make clear what it is doing under the rule and what extra it is doing under the wider powers recognised in X v Commissioner of Metropolitan Police and A v B

- if there is no entitlement to protection under the Convention, the case must be dealt with solely within the terms of the procedural rules

- except in cases where an anonymisation order applies, an employment tribunal does not have to make a 'once and for all' judgment on anonymisation at the beginning of proceedings. It can make an interim order for anonymity, with a final decision being made when the judgment is delivered.

929

17.112

Vexatious proceedings

The EAT has the power under the ETA to prevent 'vexatious litigants' from instituting or continuing with tribunal proceedings. S.33 of that Act provides that the EAT may, on the application of the Attorney General (or, in Scotland, the Lord Advocate) make a restriction of proceedings order in relation to an individual. The application must be accompanied by an affidavit in support – rule 13 EAT Rules. Such an order would prevent that individual from bringing, continuing with or making an application in any proceedings before a tribunal or the EAT without the EAT's leave. The EAT may only grant a person who is the subject of such an order leave to bring proceedings if it is satisfied that the proceedings in question are not an abuse of process and that there are reasonable grounds for bringing them – S.33(4) ETA. Note that while an individual has the right of appeal against a restriction of proceedings order (see Attorney General v Wheen 2001 IRLR 91, CA, below), once such an order is in place the individual has no right of appeal against the EAT's decision not to grant leave to bring or continue proceedings.

This draconian order may only be made if the EAT is satisfied that the individual in question has habitually, persistently and without any reasonable ground either instituted vexatious proceedings before a tribunal or the EAT against the same person or against different persons (S.33(1)(a)), or made vexatious applications in any such proceedings (S.33(1)(b)). The individual has a right to present oral argument to the EAT before any such order can be made. A restriction of proceedings order may provide that it is to cease to have effect at the end of a specified period, but will otherwise remain in force indefinitely – S.33(3).

17.113 In Attorney General v Tyrrell EAT 0236/03 the EAT rejected the appellant's contention that a restriction of proceedings order made under S.33 ETA breached the right to a fair trial and due process guaranteed by Article 6 of the European Convention on Human Rights. The EAT held that such an order did not prevent the subject of it from bringing further proceedings, but merely imposed a threshold condition of showing that the bringing of such proceedings was reasonable and soundly based.

Three examples of circumstances in which the EAT has exercised its discretion to make an unlimited restriction of proceedings order:

- **Attorney General v Roberts** EAT 0058/05: R made at least 24 claims to employment tribunals, most alleging that he had been refused employment by different respondents on the ground of his trade union membership. The EAT found that R had habitually, persistently and unreasonably instituted vexatious proceedings within the meaning of S.33(1)(a) ETA and had made vexatious applications in proceedings within the meaning of S.33(1)(b) of that Act. In particular, R habitually sought to adjourn hearings at short notice and frequently failed to attend hearings. The fact that R's claims had mostly been brought against different respondents did not alter the EAT's finding. Indeed, the EAT noted that this was usually true of vexatious litigants in the employment field

- **Attorney General v Kuttappan** EAT 0478/05: between 1996 and April 2005 K commenced at least 33 claims, all but nine of which arose from failed job applications. These claims went on to occupy over 125 days of tribunal time. By the time that the Attorney General's application for a restriction of proceedings order was heard, K accepted that he had abused the tribunal's process, and offered an undertaking not to pursue proceedings without leave of the EAT. The EAT nevertheless made an objective assessment of the number, nature and outcome of K's claims and concluded that the conditions for the exercise of its discretion to grant a restriction of proceedings order had been satisfied. This was so even though it acknowledged that the primary motivation behind the majority of K's claims was his pursuit of an equality campaign. The EAT agreed with the Attorney General that it was in the public interest that a proper control be imposed over K's future conduct and that this would best be achieved by means of an order against K rather than receipt of an undertaking from him

- **Attorney General v Bentley** EAT 0556/11: B pursued a 'campaign' by way of bringing age discrimination claims before the employment tribunal. He would apply for a job with the respondents and, if rejected, habitually issue claims for age discrimination (and sometimes disability discrimination). Between June 2009 and September 2011, B made 29 tribunal claims, but never attended a single hearing. In granting the restriction of proceedings order, the EAT held that it was necessary to 'protect the reputation of the system and to protect potential respondents'.

In Attorney General v England EAT 367/00, however, the EAT adjourned the **17.114** Attorney General's application for a year rather than make a restriction of proceedings order. It did so in light of the fact that both parties agreed to this approach, and because E was aged 64 and professed that he did not intend to seek employment in the future. The EAT accepted that the circumstances that had given rise to most, if not all, of E's previous claims to the tribunal would not arise in the future.

As explained above, an individual can, in theory, appeal against the EAT's decision to grant a restriction of proceedings order. However such an appeal is unlikely to succeed as the matter is one which is at the discretion of the EAT. In Attorney General v Wheen 2001 IRLR 91, CA, the Court of Appeal heard an appeal from an order made by the EAT under S.33 ETA. The appellant had commenced 15 sets of tribunal proceedings between July 1997 and April 1998 against various respondents, all of which were unsuccessful. Some of the

931

applications were described by the tribunal as frivolous or vexatious, while others were considered to have no reasonable prospect of success. The appellant brought appeals against a number of the tribunals' decisions. Five of these appeals were heard and dismissed by the EAT, which described them as being an abuse of process. In October 1999 the Attorney General applied to the EAT for a restriction of proceedings order under S.33. The EAT held that the requirements of S.33 had been made out and exercised its discretion to make an indefinite order. The Court of Appeal granted leave for W to appeal.

17.115   W put forward a number of arguments before the Court of Appeal. First, he argued that the EAT had been wrong to exercise its discretion in view of the lapse in time between his last tribunal claim on 3 April 1998 and the Attorney General's application for the S.33 order on 22 October. This, argued the appellant, indicated that he was unlikely to institute any further proceedings and that, therefore, the order was unnecessary. The Court of Appeal rejected this argument. The Court thought that, although the appellant had not instituted any new proceedings between April and October, he had nonetheless taken steps to appeal against tribunal decisions. The Court added that there was no evidence to indicate that the appellant had undergone a change of heart rendering him unlikely to continue to make vexatious applications if free to do so. The Court also noted that the wording of S.33 was capable of including a person who is not currently instigating vexatious proceedings and has not done so for some time.

The appellant next contended that all his applications had been arguable and that, therefore, the EAT had erred in holding that his behaviour had been vexatious within the meaning of S.33. The Court of Appeal disagreed. In the Court's view, the EAT had properly based its decision on the fact that the appellant had repeatedly brought proceedings which tribunals found had no reasonable prospect of success or were frivolous, vexatious or an abuse of process. On an application under S.33 it was not open to the appellant to reopen the merits of the cases that had been struck out by the tribunals. Finally, the appellant argued that the restricted proceedings order amounted to a breach of his human rights. Although the Court of Appeal accepted that the appellant had a right to a fair trial under Article 6 of the European Convention on Human Rights (as incorporated into UK law by the Human Rights Act 1998), it noted that it was not an absolute right but, rather, required a balance to be struck between the right of the individual citizen to use the courts and the rights of others and the courts not to be troubled by wholly unmeritorious claims. It also pointed out that a S.33 order does not prohibit access to the tribunal but simply provides that such access is only possible if leave is obtained. The Court, therefore, ruled that there was no conflict between S.33 and the Convention. Accordingly, the Court of Appeal held that the EAT had correctly exercised its discretion to make a restricted proceedings order under S.33 and dismissed the appeal.

18 EAT hearings and decisions

Listing of appeals

Skeleton arguments

Documents and authorities

Evidence

New points of law

EAT hearings

EAT decisions

Review of EAT decisions and further appeals

When an appeal has been accepted as valid and the respondent's answer has **18.1** been received, the EAT will list the case for hearing. The parties then have a period of time to prepare for the hearing, during which they will draft skeleton arguments and agree the documentation and authorities that will be referred to. We discuss these steps below, before moving on to look at the real business of challenging tribunal decisions – the EAT hearing and its outcome.

In this chapter, references to the 'EAT Rules' are, unless otherwise stated, to the Employment Appeal Tribunal Rules 1993 SI 1993/2854, as amended, and references to the 'Practice Direction' are, unless otherwise stated, to the Practice Direction (Employment Appeal Tribunal – Procedure) 2013.

Listing of appeals
18.2

All parties are consulted as to possible dates for a hearing. The Listing Officer will try to accommodate any requests (including requests for dates that are compatible with representatives who appeared for the parties before the employment tribunal), but is not bound to do so. Once the date has been fixed it is 'set down in the list' – para 15.5 Practice Direction (2013 ICR 1382). At that point, the hearing can only be rearranged following an application to the Listing Officer – para 15.5. The other parties must submit their own views as to the application for a rearrangement of the date of hearing within seven days of receiving notice of the application – para 15.6.

Estimate of length of hearing. Parties are required to provide an estimate of **18.3** the time they think it will take to conduct a hearing, taking into account that the EAT will have pre-read the papers. The estimate should include the time it will take for the EAT to deliberate its decision and the time for the judgment to

933

be considered and delivered orally on the day of hearing – paras 15.1 and 15.2 Practice Direction. Although it is not expressly mentioned, it is sensible for the parties to agree between themselves an estimate of the length of the hearing and submit a single figure to the EAT rather than submit their own separate estimates. Para 15.1 of the Practice Direction specifically draws attention to the importance of these estimates in cases where lay members are scheduled to sit, since if a hearing overruns and thus goes part-heard, it can be logistically difficult within a short timeframe to reconvene the same judge and lay members for the resumed hearing or for deliberation of the outcome.

If the EAT concludes that the hearing is likely to exceed the estimate or if, for other reasons, it is likely that the hearing will not be concluded within the allotted time, the parties may be placed under appropriate time limits requiring them to complete the presentation of submissions within the estimated or available time – para 15.3. During the hearing, a judge may, with a view to achieving the overriding objective – see Chapter 17, 'Processing an appeal', under 'Overriding objective' – require submissions to take place in whatever order and within whatever time limit he or she considers appropriate – para 15.4.

18.4 **Warned list.** In addition to the above 'fixed date' procedure, the EAT also operates a 'warned list', which is updated weekly in respect of the following week's appeals and includes any changes made to listed appeals (including the specifying of cases that have been given fixed dates) – paras 15.7 and 15.9 Practice Direction. The warned list, which is published on the EAT's website, contains cases identified by the Registrar or a judge as being suitable to be heard on short notice. Ordinarily these are cases with a short time estimate or those which it is agreed should be expedited. Other cases can be placed on the warned list with the parties' consent, usually where the appeal has been settled or withdrawn or where it appears that it will take less time than originally estimated – para 15.8. A party who does not agree to the appeal being placed on the warned list should make representations to the Listing Officer. A right of appeal to a judge or the Registrar exists against the Listing Officer's decision.

18.5 Skeleton arguments

Paragraph 16.1 of the Practice Direction states that skeleton arguments must be provided by all parties in respect of all hearings. This rule is subject to the following exceptions:

• the requirement to submit a skeleton argument does not exist in respect of appeals being heard in Scotland, unless the EAT in Edinburgh directs otherwise (see further under 'Scottish appeals' below)

• there is no need to supply a skeleton where a party has notified the EAT that the notice of appeal, answer or the relevant application contains his or her entire argument

- on rare occasions the EAT may also direct a party not to supply a skeleton argument.

The purpose of a skeleton argument, as articulated by para 16.1 of the Practice Direction, is to help the EAT and the parties 'to focus on the point(s) of law required to be decided and so makes the oral hearing more effective'.

Format. Paragraph 16 of the Practice Direction gives precise instructions as to the form that a skeleton argument should take: **18.6**

- it should be 'concise' and 'identify and summarise the point(s) of law, the steps in the legal argument and the statutory provisions and authorities to be relied upon, identifying them by name, page and paragraph and stating the legal proposition sought to be derived from them'. It should not, however, argue the case on paper in detail – para 16.3

- it should, if possible, be in print rather than hand-written, using A4 paper, 12-point standard font typescript, and arranged in consecutive paragraph numbers with each paragraph separated by a double space – para 16.3

- it should state the form of order which the party will ask the EAT to make at the hearing – para 16.5

- documents referred to in the skeleton argument should be identified by reference to pagination in the appeal bundle – para 16.7

- where a note of the evidence at the tribunal has been produced (usually by the employment judge), the argument should identify the parts of the note that will be referred to – para 16.7.

Chronology of events. Skeleton arguments must be accompanied by a **18.7** chronology of events relevant to the appeal – preferably one agreed by the parties, since the chronology will usually be taken to be an uncontroversial document unless corrected by another party or the EAT – para 16.6 Practice Direction. It is good practice for the chronology to provide references to relevant paragraph numbers in the employment tribunal's decision and the agreed appeal bundle of documents.

Submission of skeleton arguments. Skeleton arguments can be lodged with **18.8** the appellant's notice of appeal or with the respondent's answer – para 16.10 Practice Direction. If they are not, they must be lodged in accordance with the time limits prescribed by para 16.11 as follows:

- in the case of a preliminary hearing, an appeal against a Registrar's order, a rule 3(10) hearing or an Appointment for Directions, skeleton arguments must be lodged no later than ten days before the hearing. If, however, the hearing is fixed with less than seven days' notice, the skeleton arguments must be lodged as soon as possible after the hearing date has been notified

935

- in the case of a full hearing, skeleton arguments must be lodged not less than 14 days before the hearing

- in warned list and fast-track full hearing cases (see 'Listing of appeals' above, and Chapter 17, 'Processing an appeal', under 'The sift' for details), skeleton arguments must be lodged as soon as possible and, in any event, within seven days of the parties' being notified that the case is expedited or on the warned list (unless, that is, the hearing date is less than seven days after such notification).

In all the above instances, skeleton arguments must be exchanged with the other parties at the same time as being lodged with the EAT.

18.9 Failure to follow the above procedure may lead to adjournment of the appeal or to dismissal of the appeal for non-compliance pursuant to rule 26 of the EAT Rules and to an award of costs – para 16.12. The defaulting party may also be required to attend before the EAT to explain its failure and, in any event, will be required to dispatch the late skeleton argument to the EAT by hand, fax or e-mail, and to bring sufficient copies (a minimum of four, and six if the appeal hearing is to be heard by a judge with lay members) along with copies of any case authorities to be relied upon unless these are contained in the 'familiar authorities' bundle (see 'Documents and authorities – documents bundle' below).

18.10 **Scottish appeals.** The practice of automatic presentation of skeleton arguments is not one that is adopted by the EAT in Scotland. Although skeleton arguments are considered to be helpful, the parties are at liberty to decide – subject to any specific direction by the EAT – whether or not to present such outline arguments – para 16.13 Practice Direction. If they choose to do so (and one party is entitled to present a skeleton argument even if the other declines to do so) a copy must be served on all other parties and the EAT at the same time at least seven days prior to the scheduled hearing date. The EAT reserves the right not to read any skeleton argument that is presented late.

18.11 Documents and authorities

In the past the EAT was responsible for preparing bundles for use at hearings. Under the previous 2002 Practice Direction this responsibility moved to the appellant, who is now charged with preparing the bundle once agreement has been reached with the other parties as to its content.

18.12 **Documents bundle.** Paragraph 8.2 of the 2013 Practice Direction identifies the core documents that should be included in the agreed bundle of papers and the order in which the bundle should be compiled, as follows:

- judgment, decision or order appealed from and written reasons

- sealed notice of appeal

- respondent's answer (if full hearing) or respondent's submissions (if preliminary hearing)

- ET1 claim (and any additional information or written answers)

- ET3 response (and any additional information or written answers)

- questionnaire and replies (in discrimination and equal pay cases)

- relevant orders, judgments and written reasons of the tribunal

- relevant orders and judgments of the EAT

- affidavits and employment tribunal comments (where ordered)

- any documents agreed or ordered pursuant to para 8.3 of the Practice Direction (for which, see 'Evidence' below).

Other documents relevant to the hearing may be included after these core documents, provided the total number of these additional pages does not exceed 50. Parties whose bundle exceeds that limit will have to seek the permission of the Registrar or a judge, and such permission will not be granted if the relevant party fails also to submit an 'essential reading list' as soon as practicable after submitting its application – para 8.3. If permission is granted, any additional documents not already included in the main bundle should be included in a paginated additional bundle.

The Practice Direction contains strict instructions to appellants and their **18.13** advisers to include only those documents that are strictly necessary to the point(s) of law raised in the appeal and which are likely to be referred to at the hearing – para 8.1. Any problems that arise in agreeing a bundle can be resolved by means of an application to the Registrar for appropriate directions – para 8.8.

With the sole exception of proceedings concerning national security (as governed by rule 30A of the EAT Rules), the EAT will not accept documents or communications asserted to be confidential and therefore non-disclosable to the other parties. All documents presented by one party to an appeal are disclosable to the other(s), and the parties must expect that to be the case – para 8.9.

Lodging the bundle. The Practice Direction prescribes the number of copies **18.14** required and the time frame for lodging the bundle:

- for a preliminary hearing, an appeal against a Registrar's order, a rule 3(10) hearing (see Chapter 17, 'Processing an appeal', under 'The sift – rule 3(7) cases (no valid grounds of appeal)') or an Appointment for Directions, two copies (increased to four where the judge has directed a sitting with lay members) of the bundle must be lodged as soon as possible after service of the notice of appeal and no later than 28 days from the seal date of the relevant order – para 8.5

- for a full hearing, two copies (increased to four where the judge has directed a sitting with lay members) of the bundle must be lodged by no later than 28 days from the seal date of the relevant order – para 8.6

- for a fast-track case, the bundles must be lodged as soon as possible and in any event within seven days after the parties have been notified that the case is expedited – para 8.7.

18.15 **Case authorities.** The parties are also required to produce a bundle containing any authorities upon which they wish to rely. Para 17 of the Practice Direction sets out the procedural rules relating to the compilation of an agreed bundle and the obligations on parties when citing authorities in support of their submissions. The parties must cooperate in agreeing this list of authorities – para 17.2.

In Sage (UK) Ltd v Bacco EAT 0597/06 the EAT issued a Practice Statement on citing authorities in the course of its judgment. This provides that where a case is featured in the Industrial Cases Reports (ICR) or the Industrial Relations Law Reports (IRLR), parties should ensure that the bundle contains copies of these reports and not simply a transcript of the judgment. The reason for this is twofold: first, when pre-reading a case, it helps the EAT to refer to a headnote of an authority – it is not a sensible use of time to read the entire judgment in order to assimilate the basic facts and conclusions of a case. Secondly, it is useful for the readers of EAT judgments to see precise references to the earlier decisions cited. This Practice Statement is now reflected in para 17.4 of the 2013 Practice Direction.

18.16 The EAT's latest Practice Statement – which was issued in amended form on 23 April 2012 by the current President of the EAT, Mr Justice Langstaff – also includes guidance on the citation of authorities. As well as repeating the importance of using formal ICR or IRLR reports (as opposed to electronic reports such as from the British and Irish Legal Information Institute (BAILLI)) that was stressed in Sage (UK) Ltd v Bacco (above), the Practice Statement also states that it is best practice to use photocopies or online copies of these law reports, rather than copies from other online sources. Additionally, the reports should be presented in chronological order, with the relevant passages highlighted clearly, and ring binders should be properly tabulated. The Practice Statement refers to the Practice Direction in respect of civil appeals in England and Wales, issued by the Lord Chief Justice and Heads of Division on 23 March 2012, which parties are advised to consider as applicable to EAT appeals subject to any necessary adaptations. The Lord Chief Justice's Practice Direction states that reference should be made to no more than ten authorities unless the scale of the appeal warrants more extensive citation. This stipulation is expressly reflected in para 17.6 of the Practice Direction.

18.17 *Familiar authorities list.* The EAT's 2012 Practice Statement (and para 17.5 of the Practice Direction) provides that a number of familiar authorities are so frequently cited to the EAT that sufficient copies of them will be maintained at every EAT venue. This avoids unnecessary work for the parties, as well as overuse of paper and copying resources. The Practice Statement continues that a list of these cases will be maintained on the EAT's website, and that any case named on it should not be photocopied. Instead, the case may be relied on in argument before the EAT and, when doing so, it will be sufficient for a party relying on the case to identify the principle contended for by reference to the paragraph in the applicable formal case report.

In furtherance of this guidance, the EAT published its Familiar Authorities Bundle, which contains 24 cases, in June 2012. Notes accompanying the list state, among other things, that the list will be kept under review and that parties should always check the current version of the list before assembling their own bundles.

At the time of publication, the familiar authorities bundle list comprised the **18.18** following well-known authorities:

- *Amendment (notice of appeal – whether to grant)*
  - Khudados v Leggate and ors 2005 ICR 1013, EAT
  - Readman v Devon Primary Care Trust 2011 EAT 0116/11
- *Bias (allegations – EAT procedure)*
  - Facey v Midas Retail Security and anor 2001 ICR 287, EAT
- *Bias (test for)*
  - Porter v Magill 2002 2 AC 357, HL
- *Deciding a case on ground not argued*
  - Chapman and anor v Simon 1994 IRLR 124, CA
- *Error of law (jurisdiction of EAT)*
  - British Telecommunications plc v Sheridan 1990 IRLR 27, CA
  - Brent London Borough Council v Fuller 2011 ICR 806, CA
- *New points of law (taken for first time at the EAT)*
  - Kumchyk v Derby City Council 1978 ICR 1116, EAT
  - Jones v Governing Body of Burdett Coutts School 1999 ICR 38, CA
  - Glennie v Independent Magazines (UK) Ltd 1999 IRLR 719, CA
  - Secretary of State for Health v Rance 2007 IRLR 665, EAT
- *New points (taken for first time during an employment tribunal hearing)*
  - Ladbrokes Racing Ltd v Traynor EATS 0067/06

939

- *Perversity*
  - Yeboah v Crofton 2002 IRLR 634, CA
- *Polkey*
  - Polkey v AE Dayton Services Ltd 1988 ICR 142, HL
- *Reasons (duty to give)*
  - Meek v City of Birmingham District Council 1987 IRLR 250, CA
  - English v Emery Reimbold and Strick Ltd 2003 IRLR 710, CA
  - Greenwood v NWF Retail Ltd 2011 ICR 896, EAT
- *Reasons (EAT power to ask for further reasons)*
  - Barke v SEETEC Business Technology Centre Ltd 2005 ICR 1373, CA
- *Remission (whether to the same or differently constituted tribunal)*
  - Sinclair Roche and Temperley v Heard 2004 IRLR 763, EAT
- *Time limits (whether to grant an extension of time for appealing)*
  - United Arab Emirates v Abdelghafar 1995 ICR 65, EAT
  - Aziz v Bethnal Green City Challenge Co Ltd 2000 IRLR 111, CA
  - Jurkowska v Hlmad Ltd 2008 ICR 841, CA
  - Muschett v London Borough of Hounslow 2009 ICR 424, EAT
- *Striking-out (exercise of employment tribunal's powers)*
  - Tayside Public Transport Co Ltd v Reilly 2012 IRLR 755, Ct Sess (Inner House)

18.19 Evidence

Appeals to the EAT generally lie only on a point of *law*. That being so, in the vast majority of cases the main (and sometimes only) document considered by the EAT is the decision of the employment tribunal against which the appeal is brought. However, in some circumstances a party may wish to apply to the EAT for permission to adduce evidence that was raised before the tribunal but not articulated in the tribunal's written reasons, or to adduce new evidence that the tribunal did not have the opportunity to consider. The EAT has the power to allow the admission of additional evidence in both circumstances, as explained in detail below. Whenever entirely fresh evidence is admitted in the course of an appeal hearing, the EAT may, either of its own motion or on application by one of the parties, require it to be given on oath – rule 28 EAT Rules.

940

Evidence before the tribunal and employment judge's notes 18.20

Where an appellant or respondent believes that the employment tribunal's written reasons do not (or do not sufficiently) articulate a point of evidence which forms part of the notice of appeal or answer, then the relevant party can apply to the EAT either for that evidence to be admitted or for relevant parts of the employment judges's notes of evidence to be produced. As discussed below, para 9 of the Practice Direction prescribes the procedure by which such an application should be made.

Note that the employment judge's notes record the details of the oral and documentary evidence called by the parties at a tribunal hearing, and will usually also record the details of the submissions made by each side once all the evidence has been heard.

Application. An application by an *appellant* to admit evidence that was before 18.21 the tribunal or for production and admission of the employment judge's notes of evidence should ordinarily be made with the notice of appeal – para 9.1 Practice Direction. The application can, however, be made at a later date. If a preliminary hearing is ordered, the application can be made in the skeleton argument or written submissions lodged prior to the preliminary hearing. If no preliminary hearing is ordered, the application can be made no later than 14 days after the order directing a full hearing. A *respondent* wishing to adduce evidence or obtain the employment judge's notes must make an application as soon as possible and, in any event, no later than when lodging the respondent's answer.

The application must explain why the evidence or notes are necessary in order to argue the point of law raised in the notice of appeal or answer. It must therefore identify:

- the relevant issue
- the names of the witness(es) whose evidence is relevant
- the part of the hearing when the evidence was given
- the gist of the evidence alleged to be relevant, and
- any record of the evidence, explaining who composed the record and when, or alternatively an extract from a witness statement given in writing at the hearing – para 9.2.

The application will be considered either by the Registrar or a judge, either on 18.22 the papers or at a preliminary hearing. Para 9.3 of the Practice Direction indicates that, ordinarily, an order requiring the parties to prepare an agreed note of the relevant evidence will be made, accompanied by a set timeframe – usually 21 days – to comply with the order. In the absence of agreement, any party may seek directions from the EAT within seven days of the expiry of the

941

21-day timeframe – para 9.4. In doing so, the party must enclose all relevant correspondence and give notice to the other parties. The EAT may then direct the parties to resolve any disagreement or direct a request for information to be administered to a party or the employment judge. Alternatively, if the EAT is satisfied that the employment judges's notes are necessary, it may request the employment judge to produce his or her notes of evidence in whole or part.

18.23 **When will the EAT admit an employment judge's notes?** An employment judge's notes will not be admitted or produced to the parties as a matter of course. As clarified by His Honour Judge Peter Clark in Henry v UNISON EAT 0693/03, 'in practice, [employment judges'] notes of evidence will only become relevant where it is alleged that there is no evidence to support a material finding of fact, or that the employment tribunal failed to make a relevant finding of fact, or that a finding of fact is perverse'. Para 9.7 of the Practice Direction makes it clear that a note of evidence will not be produced in order to allow the parties to embark on a 'fishing expedition' to establish grounds of appeal.

Another reason for discouraging the too-frequent use of employment judges' notes is the delay, expense and inconvenience that their production entails. In Henderson Joiners v Murphy EAT 285/81 the EAT was persuaded to order the production of the employment judge's notes, but in the end found them to be of little help in disposing of the appeal. Pointing out that considerable expense had been incurred, Lord McDonald said: 'The use of [employment judges'] notes in these appeals is of very limited application and we deprecate any practice whereby this Appeal Tribunal is invited to analyse the rough notes taken by [an employment judge] at [a] tribunal hearing and to construe these as if they were a formal legal document.' A similar view was expressed in Wilson v Metropolitan Borough of Knowsley EAT 430/88. In that case, the appellant's advisers were granted a full transcript of 100 pages of the employment judge's notes of evidence but, in the event, only a single paragraph from one page of the notes was referred to in the appeal hearing. Mr Justice Wood felt that the cost involved in having the notes prepared was a waste of public money. Had he the power to do so, he would have ordered that the costs of preparing the notes be paid by the offending party. He regretted that he only had power to make an award in respect of costs incurred by another party and not by the public purse. The EAT's power to award costs is covered in Chapter 20, 'Costs and penalties'.

18.24 The EAT considered the question of what could amount to good cause for the production of a employment judge's notes in Webb v Anglian Water Authority 1981 ICR 811, EAT. There, it confirmed that where an appeal is purely on a question of law, there should generally be no reason for going behind the facts set out in the tribunal's extended reasons for its decision. It was only when those findings of fact were themselves attacked by one of the parties that it might be permissible to investigate the basis upon which those findings had been reached (for a discussion of the grounds upon which a tribunal's findings of fact can be challenged, see Chapter 16, 'The Employment Appeal Tribunal', under 'Grounds of appeal – no evidence supporting factual findings'). The EAT held that the application for the production of the employment judge's notes should specify precisely which findings of fact are to be challenged – a generalised allegation will not be sufficient. It will then be for the EAT to decide whether all of the employment judge's notes are required or only those relating to the specific issues.

In Cheapside (SSL) Ltd (formerly Schroder Securities Ltd) v Bower EAT 0678/01 the EAT ordered only specific parts of the employment judge's notes to be produced. The Registrar had initially ordered the employment judge to produce the whole of his notes of evidence, but when the judge pointed out the work involved in producing a note of a lengthy hearing, the Registrar referred the matter to an EAT hearing. HHJ Peter Clark considered each ground of the notice of appeal in detail, and made an order requesting specific parts of the employment judge's notes as were necessary for the appeal's disposal.

18.25 While there is no absolute right for a party to have access to the employment judge's notes of evidence, it is unlikely that any appeal based on perversity or mistake of fact will be able to succeed without them. This was accepted by the EAT in SGB plc v Fletcher EAT 642/90, where it was held that an allegation that a finding was perverse could not properly be considered without the employment judge's notes of evidence. However, the onus was placed firmly upon the party appealing to make the necessary application to have the notes produced. Moreover, where a party is alleging perversity, the employment judge's notes will not be produced unless that party can show that there are reasonable grounds for believing that the finding of fact under challenge may be shown to be perverse on the basis of the notes produced. In Gilbert v Portsmouth Publishing and Printing Ltd EAT 63/93 His Honour Judge Peppitt QC refused to order the production of the employment judge's notes because it was clear that even if the points raised by the appellant were substantiated, this would still not justify a finding that the employment tribunal's decision was perverse. This order was based substantially on the inconvenience caused to the employment judge by being ordered to type up and produce the notes of a three-day hearing. When the appellant at a later hearing pointed out that, because he was profoundly deaf, a verbatim transcript of the tribunal hearing had been produced as the hearing progressed and displayed on a screen for him to read, and that a full note of the evidence had been taken which could be easily accessed at any time, the EAT was prepared to change its mind and order that the notes of evidence be produced. Para 9.6 of the Practice Direction does, however, make it clear that where proceedings in the tribunal were tape recorded and a transcript is thus readily available, the EAT will still apply the

943

principles outlined in para 9 in deciding whether to grant an application for production of a note of evidence.

It has also been recognised that allegations of perversity on appeal may take different forms, not all of which will require production of the employment judge's notes. In Hawkins v Ball and anor 1996 IRLR 258, EAT, the employer appealed against the preliminary decision of an employment tribunal to allow an employee to bring a claim for sex discrimination out of time on the ground that it would be 'just and equitable' to do so. Before the EAT, the employer requested a copy of the employment judge's notes, arguing that they were necessary because the appeal challenged the tribunal's decision on the ground of perversity. The EAT dismissed the employer's application, holding that it was not necessarily the case that the employment judge's notes would automatically become available where a party alleges perversity. The EAT thought that, although the employment judge's notes would be likely to be necessary in cases where the allegation of perversity requires a consideration of all the evidence (e.g. where a party alleges perversity on the basis that there was no evidence to support a tribunal's findings), this was not such a case. The instant case involved an allegation of perversity resting on a specific and limited platform for which the employment judge's notes were not required for the appeal to be properly heard.

18.26 **Request for employment judge's notes by EAT of its own motion.** In his examination of the procedure relating to the request of an employment judge's notes of evidence in Henry v UNISON (above), HHJ Peter Clark pointed out that there are three occasions on which the EAT may itself take action with regard to the employment judge's notes. First, at the 'sift' stage (see Chapter 17, 'Processing an appeal', under 'The sift') a judge may, under para 11.3 of the Practice Direction, postpone his or her decision as to which track an appeal should occupy until after the employment judge's notes have been received. Furthermore, a judge presiding over a hearing to determine whether an appellant has reasonable grounds of appeal has the power to request the employment judge's notes of evidence for the purposes of a preliminary hearing or full hearing, or to adjourn the hearing pending their receipt.

18.27 **Where employment judge's notes do not reflect the tribunal hearing.** A situation may arise in which the employment judge's notes of evidence have been produced and one of the parties believes that they do not accurately reflect what was said at the employment tribunal hearing. Unless both sides agree that the notes are inaccurate, however, there is not much that can be done. In Dexine Rubber Co Ltd v Alker 1977 ICR 434, EAT, the EAT suggested that where criticism is made of the employment judge's notes, the party making the criticism should first broach the matter with the other party and then submit the criticisms to the employment judge for his or her comments. This will assist the employment judge in determining whether there is a risk acknowledged by both sides that his or her notes might not be accurate or complete. If the parties are not agreed that the notes are inaccurate, then the employment judge's response to the criticisms must be accepted.

Conflict between employment judge's notes and findings of fact. It should **18.28** be borne in mind that the employment judge's notes are just notes and not a verbatim record of the evidence. If there is a conflict between the findings of fact set out in the employment tribunal's decision and the notes taken by the employment judge, then the decision will be regarded as being the accurate version 'unless there are compelling circumstances which lead... to the conclusion that the reasons may inaccurately state the substance of the evidence' – Ogidi-Olu v Guys Hospital Board of Governors 1973 ICR 645, NIRC.

Compelling circumstances were found to exist in Creighton v Personnel Facilities Management Ltd, unreported 6.2.85, CA, where the employment judge's notes were used to overturn an employment tribunal decision. The tribunal had found that the employee was unfairly dismissed but that she was 75 per cent to blame for her dismissal because she had failed to report to senior management that she was overworked. The EAT dismissed her appeal but, on appeal to the Court of Appeal, the employment judge's notes of evidence were produced showing that the employee had in fact complained to her immediate superior that her work was too much for her. The Court of Appeal held that the tribunal could not have reached the conclusion that it did reach concerning contributory conduct if it had had that evidence in mind. Since failure to complain was the only reason for reducing the employee's compensation, the Court accordingly set aside the finding of contributory fault.

Evidence made by parties' representatives. It is only in the most exceptional **18.29** circumstances that notes of evidence made by one of the parties' representatives will be ruled admissible on appeal. In Owen and Briggs v James 1981 ICR 377, EAT, the EAT ruled that the point at issue would have to turn on the precise evidence that was given and both sides would have to agree that the employment judge's notes were either inaccurate or incomplete. If agreement cannot be reached, then the employment judge's notes will be regarded as remaining 'supreme' – Aberdeen Steak Houses Group plc v Ibrahim 1988 ICR 550, EAT. This was later confirmed in Saga Petroleum v Bourgeois EAT 327/99, where the EAT refused the appellants' request that an appeal be considered on the basis of the notes made by their representative rather than the notes of the employment judge. The EAT reached this decision despite accepting that the employment judge's notes were lacking in some respects. The wariness to admit the parties' own notes of evidence also extends to situations where the employment judge's notes record a comment made in evidence on the say-so of the lay members in circumstances in which the employment judge did not him or herself hear the comment.

945

18.30 Admission of new evidence on appeal

As discussed in Chapter 15, 'Reconsideration of tribunal judgments and decisions', in the section 'Grounds for reconsideration', under '"Interests of justice" – new evidence has become available', the discovery of new evidence germane to an employment tribunal's already announced decision should ordinarily be dealt with by way of an application to the employment tribunal for reconsideration (formerly, review) of its own decision rather than appeal to the EAT. This accords with guidance given in the EAT 2012 Practice Statement issued by Mr Justice Langstaff, President, on 17 April 2012 (as revised on 23 April 2012).

Furthermore, in Adegbuji v Meteor Parking Ltd EAT 1570/09 Mr Justice Underhill, then President of the EAT, held that the reconsideration procedure in employment tribunals will normally be much more appropriate for deciding the fresh evidence issue as it is normally better placed than the EAT to deal with the second and third questions identified in Ladd v Marshall 1954 3 All ER 745, CA – namely, whether the evidence would probably have had an important influence on the result of the case, and whether it is apparently credible. It is for this reason that fresh evidence appeals are generally stayed at the 'sift' stage (see Chapter 17, 'Processing an appeal', under 'The sift') to allow the appellant to make a reconsideration application to the tribunal that originally heard the claim. Underhill P in Adegbuji also commented that although it was very common for fresh evidence appeals to be stayed pending a reconsideration application, it was not universal practice. However, he hoped that it would become so following his judgment, at least in cases where the fresh evidence issue stands alone or is easily separable.

18.31 Notwithstanding the above, the EAT does not always insist that a reconsideration take place in fresh evidence appeals, as it does have a discretion to allow evidence that was not before the tribunal to be admitted on appeal. This discretion is derived, as was made clear by the EAT in International Aviation Services (UK) Ltd v Jones 1979 ICR 371, from two different provisions contained in the ETA. The first is S.35, which stipulates that, for the purpose of disposing of an appeal, the EAT may exercise the same powers as the employment tribunal – including, of course, the power to admit evidence. The second provision is S.29(2), which confers upon the EAT the same powers, rights, privileges and authority as the High Court or Court of Session in relation to the attendance and examination of witnesses. The power of the High Court to admit fresh evidence on an appeal is contained in para 52.11 of the Civil Procedure Rules 1998 SI 1998/3132 (CPR).

The problem, however, is not whether the EAT as a body has the general power to admit fresh evidence, but whether the scope of the EAT's jurisdiction will ordinarily allow it properly to interfere with a tribunal's determination of fact. As has been repeatedly stated throughout this chapter, the EAT's jurisdiction is confined almost exclusively to appeals on questions of law. In Aslam v Barclays Capital Services Ltd and ors EAT 0405/10 the EAT held that admission of further evidence may be relevant on appeal to a question of law if it raises questions about the fairness of the hearing process at tribunal level. It was part of the EAT's task to ensure that that process met the requirements of due process at common law and of Article 6 of the European Convention on Human Rights, both of which guarantee a fair hearing. The EAT stressed that, in general, the mere fact that fresh evidence has come to light would not imperil the fairness of proceedings, as employment tribunal procedure – including the power to grant a reconsideration – can encompass most circumstances in which fresh evidence has emerged and deal with it in a way that is both fair and proportionate. Occasionally, however, this will not be possible and the EAT must intervene.

Notwithstanding that the EAT's jurisdiction is confined to questions of law **18.32** when hearing appeals from employment tribunals, case law shows that the EAT is not prevented from allowing new evidence to be admitted that has the effect of undermining an employment tribunal's decision, even though that decision was a proper one reasonably reached on the basis of the evidence actually presented. Indeed, in International Aviation Services (UK) Ltd v Jones (above), the EAT expressly rejected the argument that its discretion to admit new evidence could only be exercised in cases where the evidence in question related either to what happened in the course of the employment tribunal hearing or to matters which have arisen since the tribunal hearing. It ruled that fresh evidence other than that relating to what had occurred in the course of the tribunal hearing or after the decision could, in the exercise of its discretion, be admitted on appeal, so long as the party seeking to adduce that evidence could satisfy the well-established stringent conditions for the admissibility of new evidence in appellate jurisdictions (as to which see 'Admission of evidence in cases under EAT's original jurisdiction' below).

However, in Adegbuji v Meteor Parking Ltd EAT 1570/09 Underhill P, by way of an obiter comment, queried whether the EAT could hear such fresh evidence appeals given the limit of its jurisdiction to correct errors of law on the part of employment tribunals as specified in S.21(1) ETA. The former EAT President, who did not refer to the International Aviation Services case, declined to accept that an employment tribunal that decides a case properly on the evidence before it could be said to have made an error of law simply because evidence is subsequently produced which suggests that its decision was wrong. He also believed that 'any analogy with fresh evidence appeals in the Court of Appeal or appeals from the High Court seems to me flawed, because the Court of Appeal has in principle jurisdiction to entertain an appeal on an issue of fact'. Underhill P continued that this was a 'novel point' which may need to be decided on a future occasion, although for the purposes of the particular appeal in Adegbuji, he was prepared to assume that the EAT had jurisdiction to hear fresh evidence appeals.

18.33 Underhill P's doubts on this point are reinforced by the EAT's 2012 Practice Statement, which states that 'the Employment Appeal Tribunal has a jurisdiction which is limited to appeals on a question of law. It will be rarely (if at all) that an Employment Tribunal will be in error of law by failing to have regard to evidence which was not placed before it by one or other party, where no attempt was made to invite the Employment Tribunal to pay regard to evidence which it then declined to hear. It has no jurisdiction on fact, save where the Employment Tribunal makes a decision which is perverse, or which materially misapprehends a relevant fact before it.' Para 10.1 of the Practice Direction builds on this strong presumption that employment tribunals are the appropriate forum to consider fresh evidence appeals by stating the following: 'It remains open to an intending appellant to contend that there has been an error of law if the Employment Tribunal is in error of law in refusing to reconsider its decision, and if so then to refer to evidence which was not placed before the Employment Tribunal at the time it made its initial decision but was placed before that tribunal for the purposes of seeking or hearing a reconsideration of its decision.'

Given the above conflict in case law at EAT level, it is clear that the question of whether the EAT has the appropriate jurisdiction to hear fresh evidence appeals needs to be definitively resolved by the Court of Appeal.

18.34 **Application.** The procedure applying where a party wishes to introduce new evidence is set out in para 10 of the Practice Direction. The party must make an application to the EAT at the time of lodging the notice of appeal or respondent's answer as appropriate. The application must be accompanied by copies of the documents sought to be admitted. In the case of oral evidence, the application should be accompanied by a document setting out the nature and substance of the evidence together with an explanation as to when the party first became aware of the evidence, along with a witness statement from the relevant witness with a signed statement of truth. The application and copy should be served on the other parties – para 10.2. A party wishing to resist such an application must, within 14 days of its being sent, submit any representations to the EAT and the other parties – para 10.4.

18.35 **When will the EAT admit new evidence?** In Wileman v Minilec Engineering Ltd 1988 ICR 318, EAT, Mr Justice Popplewell stated that the principles to be applied when determining whether the EAT should allow new evidence on appeal should be the same as those set out for the admissibility of fresh evidence before the Court of Appeal in the case of Ladd v Marshall 1954 3 All ER 745, CA. Under those principles, a party seeking to introduce new evidence must show that:

- the evidence sought to be introduced could not with *reasonable diligence* have been obtained for use before the tribunal

- the evidence is so relevant that it would probably have had an *important influence* on the result of the case, although it need not be decisive in itself, and

- the evidence is apparently *credible*, though it need not be incontrovertible.

With regard to the first limb of this test, Popplewell J in Borden (UK) Ltd v Potter 1986 ICR 647, EAT, said that this approximated to the test applied by employment tribunals when deciding to accept an application for review under the Employment Tribunal Rules 2004 (now termed an application for reconsideration under the Employment Tribunal Rules 2013). That test entails asking whether the existence of new evidence, which has become available since the hearing ended, could not have been reasonably known or foreseen at the time of the hearing. Also regarding this first limb, note that where a party has decided not to admit a particular piece of evidence into tribunal proceedings, that party will be bound by its decision and will be prevented from later arguing that the evidence could not have been obtained with reasonable diligence – Bingham v Hobourn Engineering Ltd 1992 IRLR 298, EAT.

18.36 The guidance in the Ladd decision is now enshrined in para 10.3 of the Practice Direction, which states that 'in exercising its discretion to admit any fresh evidence or new document, the EAT will apply the principles set out in Ladd v Marshall... having regard to the overriding objective'. For discussion of the overriding objective, see Chapter 17, 'Processing an appeal', under 'Overriding objective'.

It is clear that the cumulative nature of the above test makes the scope for admitting new evidence on appeal very narrow in practice. Furthermore, if an appellant cannot convince the EAT of the need to admit new evidence because it fails to satisfy the exacting criteria, then it is not open to the EAT to get round this by remitting the case to a tribunal for a rehearing so that the evidence can then be called – Kingston v British Railways Board 1984 ICR 781, CA. Similarly, where a case has been remitted to the tribunal following a successful appeal, a party will not be permitted to argue its case on a basis that was not argued at the original hearing.

18.37 Most applications to admit fresh evidence fail on the ground that the evidence was available and could have been put forward at the time of the original tribunal hearing. Three examples:

- **Borden (UK) Ltd v Potter** (above): the employer sought to adduce a medical report which, the EAT agreed, would have been credible and likely to have an effect on the employment tribunal's decision. But the EAT nevertheless refused to allow the report to be admitted as evidence on the appeal. It had been reasonably foreseeable at the time of the tribunal hearing that the report would be needed, and the report could have been obtained at that time

949

- **Taylor and ors v John Webster, Buildings Civil Engineering** 1999 ICR 561, EAT: an employment tribunal held that three employees had been unfairly dismissed and calculated compensation on the basis of a basic award, a sum for the period from the date of dismissal to the tribunal hearing and for future loss of earnings. The tribunal went on to reduce their compensation because there was a 40 per cent chance that they would have been made redundant had they not been unfairly dismissed. The employees appealed against the reduction and the employer cross-appealed. In doing so, the employer sought to introduce fresh evidence that the employees had found new employment soon after their employment terminated and that their compensation should therefore be reduced to reflect that fact. This evidence related to periods both before and after the tribunal hearing. It was the EAT's view that evidence as to whether the employees had worked after the date of the hearing was irrelevant, as tribunals must calculate compensation at the date of the hearing with the information available at the time. The EAT therefore concluded that this evidence would have failed the Ladd v Marshall test as, although the evidence may have been credible, it would not have had any influence on the amount of compensation. Turning to the evidence in relation to the period between dismissal and the date of the tribunal hearing, the EAT held that this evidence too failed the test since there was no reason why the evidence could not, with reasonable diligence, have been provided to the employment tribunal

- **Adegbuji v Meteor Parking Ltd** EAT 1570/09: A brought a number of claims against his former employer, including unfair dismissal, breach of contract, and race discrimination. At the time, those claims were governed by the (now repealed) statutory dismissal, disciplinary and grievance procedures introduced by the Employment Act 2002. S.32 of that Act required that, in respect of certain claims, the employee must first initiate the statutory grievance procedure and wait 28 days before presenting a tribunal claim. The employer argued that the tribunal did not have jurisdiction to hear A's claims as he had not complied with S.32 by first lodging a grievance, a contention upheld by an employment judge. A then lodged an appeal before the EAT in which he sought to introduce fresh evidence in the form of a witness statement from his supervisor, K, confirming that K had passed the grievance letter on to A's manager. The EAT rejected that application. In its view, A knew at an early stage that K's evidence would be crucial to his case and he had not done all he could to secure K's appearance.

18.38 The third element of the three-point test in Ladd v Marshall (above) for admission of new evidence goes to the credibility of the evidence. Note that in determining whether this element is satisfied, the EAT has only to decide whether the evidence is 'apparently' credible. In this regard, the EAT will not have the opportunity to cross-examine witnesses, and will only assess the evidence at face value. In Martin v JF X-press Ltd EATS 0010/04 the EAT refused to accept new evidence owing to its lack of apparent credibility. In that case, the employment tribunal had reluctantly found that the employee had been fairly dismissed, deciding that his employer had acted reasonably in dismissing him after receiving pressure to do so from a customer. On appeal, the employee sought to admit an affidavit from a third party which supported his case that the employer had acted unfairly in not discussing the matter with the customer's senior management. The affidavit referred to letters from a manager at the customer to the employer. However, the EAT had seen these letters, and did not believe that they were in the terms described by the affidavit. It concluded that, in the absence of cross-examination to the contrary, it did not consider the affidavit to be 'apparently credible', feeling that it would be subject to a 'forceful attack' by the employer. For this reason the EAT refused to admit the affidavit as new evidence.

In Lancaster v DEK Printing Machines Ltd EAT 623/99, however, the EAT did allow new evidence to be admitted. The employee's claim arrived at the employment tribunal late because of problems with the Christmas post. The tribunal held that it had been reasonably practicable for him to present his claim within the three-month time limit, and thus declined to hear the claim. On appeal to the EAT, the employee sought to introduce new evidence in the form of two letters in which the Post Office apologised and accepted full blame for the postal failure. The EAT held that since the evidence could not reasonably have been obtained before the hearing (because the employee was not aware that the claim had arrived late until the day of the hearing); the evidence would clearly have a significant impact on the outcome of the appeal; and there was no question as to the credibility of the evidence, the test for admission of the new evidence had been met.

18.39 Evidence that simply attacks the credibility of a witness is unlikely to be admitted if it seems peripheral to the main issue – Temblett v Avon County Council EAT 212/80. But it will be different if the credibility of a party is central to the case. In Bartlett v Blackman EAT 463/82 there was an almost total conflict of evidence between the employer and the employee, who claimed to have been unfairly dismissed. A good deal of the employer's case concerned the alleged complaints of customers about the employee's workmanship, but this evidence was hearsay as the customers were not called as witnesses, and in some cases even their names had not been revealed before the hearing. The tribunal majority accepted the employer's case and found the dismissal fair. After the hearing the employee discovered that, had they been called as witnesses, the customers concerned would have given evidence that contradicted the views attributed to them by the employer. The EAT held that this new evidence, which was ostensibly credible, could well cast doubt on the employer's credibility as a whole. Accordingly, the interests of justice required the case to be reconsidered by a fresh tribunal.

If, during an appeal, one party makes an admission to the EAT that conflicts with the evidence that that party gave to the employment tribunal, the EAT may allow the other party to admit fresh evidence relevant to the admission even if the evidence would have faced rejection for lack of credibility had it been considered in isolation. In Photostatic Copiers (Southern) Ltd v Okuda and Japan Office Equipment Ltd (in liquidation) 1995 IRLR 11, EAT, the employee admitted to the EAT that he had received a payment from a rival firm. The EAT held that this admission would have had an important influence on the tribunal's decision as regards compensation. In that regard, it allowed the employer to admit fresh evidence relating to alleged payments to the employee even though the authenticity of that evidence was questionable. In the EAT's view, the employment tribunal on remission needed to hear all the evidence on this issue and re-evaluate its decision regarding compensation in the light of it.

18.40 **The EAT may consider the effect of the evidence.** If the Ladd v Marshall test for admitting new evidence on appeal is satisfied, the EAT may decide not only to admit the evidence for the purposes of the appeal but also to consider the nature and effect of that evidence, rather than remit the matter to the employment tribunal. Two examples show, however, that this will only be done in exceptional circumstances:

- **DG Moncrieff (Farmers) v MacDonald** 1978 IRLR 112, EAT: an employment tribunal found that M had been unfairly dismissed. The employer then received evidence pointing to conduct on his part that may have had an effect on the compensation awarded. The employment judge refused an application for a review and the employer made allegations of bias against him – which it later withdrew. The EAT felt that it was inappropriate to remit the case to the same tribunal because of the (unfounded) allegations that had been made against the employment judge. It was also inappropriate to remit the matter to a different tribunal because the new evidence only had relevance to a small part of the overall decision. The EAT decided that the only proper course was to hear the evidence itself

- **Oliver v JP Malnick and Co** 1983 ICR 708, EAT: the point at issue was whether O, a solicitor's articled clerk, was employed only by the solicitor to whom she was articled or by the firm of solicitors as a whole. The firm raised the issue for the first time at the employment tribunal hearing, taking O by surprise, and persuaded the tribunal to find that she was employed solely by the partner. On appeal, the EAT allowed O to produce an affidavit from the Law Society that indicated the contrary. Because the fresh evidence was, in the EAT's view, decisive, there was no need to remit the point to the tribunal.

18.41 **State immunity.** The EAT will usually admit new evidence as a matter of course where the case involves state immunity. In Arab Republic of Egypt v

Gamal-Eldin and anor 1996 ICR 13, EAT, it was held that where a tribunal has committed an error of law and as a result failed to enforce the immunity that is properly enjoyed by a foreign state, it is the EAT's duty to correct that error and grant immunity 'even where that involved a departure from the rules normally applying to the admission of new evidence on appeal'.

Admission of evidence in cases under EAT's original jurisdiction 18.42
As noted in Chapter 16, 'The Employment Appeal Tribunal', under 'Jurisdiction of the EAT', the EAT's jurisdiction is not exclusively confined to appeals. In some cases it has what is known as 'original jurisdiction', whereby it can hear evidence and make findings of fact. The EAT has such jurisdiction in respect of complaints brought under Reg 21(6) of the Transnational Information and Consultation of Employees Regulations 1999 SI 1999/3323 (the TICE Regulations), Reg 20(6) of the European Public Limited-Liability Company (Employee Involvement) (Great Britain) Regulations 2009 SI 2009/2401 (the EPLLC(EI) Regulations), Reg 22(6) of the Information and Consultation of Employees Regulations 2004 SI 2004/3426 (the ICE Regulations), Reg 22(6) of the European Cooperative Society (Involvement of Employees) Regulations 2006 SI 2006/2059 (the ECS(IE) Regulations), and Regs 53(6) and 54(5) of the Companies (Cross-Border Mergers) Regulations 2007 SI 2007/2974 (the C(CBM) Regulations).

It used to be the case that the EAT had jurisdiction to hear appeals on questions of law and fact against decisions of the Certification Officer relating to the listing of trade unions and employers' associations or the certification of independence – Ss.9 and 126 Trade Union and Labour Relations (Consolidation) Act 1992 (TULR(C)A). However Ss.9 and 126 were amended by S.51(1) of the Employment Relations Act 2004, with the effect that appeals to the EAT against these decisions can only be on an 'appealable question', which is defined in the Act as a question of law. Thus, the EAT can no longer consider evidence in addition to that which was before the Certification Officer. The same is true for other appeals against decisions of the Certification Officer under Ss.45D, 56A, 95, 104 and 108C TULR(C)A, as well as appeals from any declaration or order of the Central Arbitration Committee under the TICE, ICE, C(CBM), EPLLC(EI) and ECS(IE) Regulations.

New points of law 18.43

The principles to be applied when a party seeks to have fresh evidence on a question of fact admitted on appeal were discussed in the section on 'Evidence' above. Problems also arise, however, when a party seeks to raise legal argument before the EAT that was not presented to the employment tribunal at first instance.

953

18.44   **Restrictive test for raising new point of law.** The general rule is that a party will not be permitted to raise points or issues of law that were not part of the submissions made to the employment tribunal. The reason for this is the natural reluctance felt by any appellate court to hear substantially new legal arguments that have not had the benefit of being considered by the parties and by the court below. Furthermore, the Court of Appeal in Slack and ors v Cumbria County Council 2009 ICR 1217, CA, held that such a policy was 'in the interests of doing substantive justice to both parties, of saving legal costs and of achieving efficiency and finality in litigation in the public interest'.

This general rule was upheld by the Court of Appeal in Jones v Governing Body of Burdett Coutts School 1999 ICR 38, CA, where the Court overruled the EAT's decision to allow the employee to argue a point of law that had already been conceded by his advocate before the employment tribunal. The Court held that the discretion to allow a new point of law to be raised, or a conceded point reopened, should only be exercised in exceptional circumstances – particularly where, in doing so, it would be necessary to open new issues of fact which had not been investigated sufficiently, or at all, before the tribunal. Lord Justice Walker, one of the judges in Jones, acknowledged that this approach sometimes results in a case being decided on a basis of law 'that is not merely arguably, but demonstrably, wrong by the time it reaches the appellate court'.

18.45   The constitutional basis for the exercise of the EAT's discretion was explained by the Court of Appeal in Miskovic v Secretary of State for Work and Pensions 2011 EWCA Civ 16, CA, when it said that 'the Court of Appeal exists, like every other court, to do justice according to law. If justice both requires a new point of law to be entertained and permits this to be done without unfairness, the court can and should entertain it unless forbidden to do so by statute'.

Note that, if the new point of law raised on appeal concerns a principle that is so well established that an employment tribunal should be expected to have considered it as a matter of course, then this may well lead the EAT to exercise its discretion and allow the new point of law to be raised – Langston v Cranfield University 1998 IRLR 172, EAT. In that case, His Honour Judge Peter Clark identified the legal issues that a tribunal will ordinarily be expected to consider as a matter of course in certain types of case:

- in unfair redundancy dismissals, whether the unfairness incorporates unfair selection, lack of consultation, and failure (by the employer) to seek alternative employment

- in cases of alleged misconduct dismissals, the threefold test set down in British Home Stores Ltd v Burchell 1980 ICR 303, EAT – namely, whether the employer had a genuine belief in the employee's guilt, held on reasonable grounds following a reasonable investigation

- in assessing unfair dismissal compensation, the four heads of claim identified in Norton Tool Co Ltd v Tewson 1972 ICR 501, NIRC, i.e. immediate loss of wages; the manner of dismissal (where this causes financial loss); future loss of wages; loss of protection from unfair dismissal; and redundancy. The tribunal should also consider loss of pension rights – Tidman v Aveling Marshall Ltd 1977 ICR 506, EAT – and, where it is alleged that the employee was paid less than the minimum wage, the tribunal should investigate this even though no claim has been made under the National Minimum Wage Act 1998; Paggetti v Cobb 2002 IRLR 861, EAT. Furthermore, when assessing compensation, the tribunal should also consider the principle established in Polkey v AE Dayton Services Ltd 1988 ICR 142, HL, i.e. whether the employee's compensation should be reduced to reflect the likelihood that he or she would still have been dismissed in any event had a proper procedure been followed.

Legal points affecting employment tribunal's jurisdiction, etc. The grounds **18.46**
on which the EAT is most often prepared to entertain new points of law are:

- where the point in question goes to the jurisdiction of the employment tribunal

- where a decision of the Court of Appeal or the Supreme Court decided subsequent to the tribunal decision suggests that that decision was wrong, or

- where a party wishes to argue that European law is directly applicable to the point in issue.

Of these, the ground that has perhaps caused the most difficulty is that relating to raising new points of law concerning the jurisdiction of the employment tribunal. If the tribunal had no jurisdiction to hear the case, then its decision is a nullity and should not be allowed to stand, whether or not the point on jurisdiction was specifically raised before it. In British Midland Airways Ltd v Lewis 1978 ICR 782, EAT, the EAT said 'this being a question as to jurisdiction, the... tribunal should have taken the point themselves even if the parties did not; and they cannot merely by silence confer upon themselves a jurisdiction which they do not have'.

However, the Court of Appeal has stressed that the EAT's discretion whether or **18.47**
not to allow a new point of law to be brought on a jurisdictional issue is not unfettered. In Glennie v Independent Magazines (UK) Ltd 1999 IRLR 719, CA, the Court overruled the EAT's decision that it would be in the interests of justice to allow an appellant to present a new point of law in relation to the effective date of termination of her employment – an issue relevant to the applicable time limit for bringing her claim. The Court of Appeal was of the view that the EAT had been misled by the judgment in an earlier case (Barber v Thames Television plc 1991 ICR 253, EAT) into thinking that it had an

955

unfettered discretion to decide, on balance, whether the new point as to jurisdiction should be allowed to be taken. The Court could envisage circumstances where, in the case of an unrepresented party, justice might demand that the EAT correct what appeared to be a glaring injustice, despite the fact that the evidence on which the unrepresented party sought to rely would have been available before the tribunal. However, the Court did not think that when 'a represented party has fought and lost a jurisdictional issue on agreed facts before the tribunal, it should then be allowed to resile from its agreement and seek a new tribunal hearing in order to adduce evidence which would then be challenged, and invite the tribunal to decide the question of jurisdiction all over again'.

The restrictive approach advocated by the Court of Appeal in Glennie is reflected in the EAT's decision in Mingeley v Pennock and anor (trading as Amber Cars) EAT 1170/02. There, an employment tribunal decided that it did not have jurisdiction to hear an individual's race discrimination claim on the ground that he was not employed by the respondent within the meaning of S.78(1) of the former Race Relations Act 1976. On appeal, the claimant sought to raise the new argument that, if he was not an employee, the tribunal nevertheless had jurisdiction to hear his claim under S.14 RRA because the respondent was an 'employment agency' within the meaning of that Act. The EAT refused permission to add the new ground of appeal on the basis that, although it went to the issue of the tribunal's jurisdiction, it could not be determined without further fact-finding. It was not an exceptional case, as demanded by the test in Jones v Governing Body of Burdett Coutts School 1999 ICR 38, CA (see above), and it would not be right to allow the appellant to take this point for the first time on appeal – particularly as he had been represented before the tribunal.

18.48 **Confusion as to current state of law.** A further point made by the Court of Appeal in Jones v Governing Body of Burdett Coutts School (above), was that, in the absence of exceptional circumstances, confusion over the state of the relevant law at the time of the employment tribunal hearing will not be a sufficient reason for the EAT to allow a new point of law to be argued before it. Similarly, inexperience of a party's advocate will not suffice. This point was emphasised by the EAT in Caspersz v Ministry of Defence EAT 0599/05. There, the appellant argued that it was unfair for a litigant who was represented by a lay representative to be expected to raise the points of argument before an employment tribunal with the same thoroughness as a professional lawyer might. The EAT had some sympathy with that contention, but held that it was bound by case law to reject the argument. It went on to express the view that the rule in Jones makes perfect sense, as 'any other rule would have the effect that those who are professionally represented would not be able to take a point on appeal which had not been run below whereas those who are not professionally represented would be free to do so'. This, in the EAT's view, would represent an injustice to those who are legally represented and 'would also permit a second bite at the cherry and open up the system to the possibility of procedural manipulation'.

The general rule in the Jones case was reiterated by the Court of Appeal in Leicestershire County Council v UNISON 2006 IRLR 810, CA. There, the Council appealed against the EAT's decision not to allow it to raise a new point on appeal. The point at issue related to the construction of the requirement to consult with potentially redundant employees 'in good time' under S.188 TULR(C)A. The Council argued that it should be allowed to raise the new point because there were exceptional circumstances for doing so. These were: (i) that there was a public interest in the point being decided; (ii) that there was a large amount of money at stake given the value of the award which might be payable to the employees concerned; and (iii) no new findings of fact would be required if the Council was allowed to raise the point. The Court of Appeal disagreed with the Council's submission that determination of the new point would require no further fact-finding on the part of the tribunal, and noted that the Court in the Jones case had attached particular importance to this question. Despite acknowledging that there was a public interest in the construction of S.188 TULR(C)A, the Court felt that the Council's argument was 'greatly undermined' by the fact that the matter would have to be remitted to the tribunal for findings of fact. The Court also dismissed the idea that the value of the claim could have any bearing on whether there were exceptional circumstances justifying the admission of a new point on appeal. The Court thus upheld the EAT's decision to refuse the Council to raise the new point of law.

Novel points of law. In Blackpool Fylde and Wyre Society for the Blind v 18.49
Begg EAT 0035/05 the EAT held that it was particularly important that any wholly novel point be raised before the employment tribunal. In that case the employer raised an interesting argument before the EAT that, pursuant to the Law Reform (Contributory Negligence) Act 1945, the employee's contributory conduct should have been taken into account in the assessment of his compensation for disability discrimination. The EAT refused to allow the employer to pursue this novel argument before it, expressing concern that the employee had been denied his right to a first instance hearing by a specialist employment tribunal on this matter.

Reopening concessions previously made by a party. Sometimes – as in Jones 18.50
v Governing Body of Burdett Coutts School 1999 ICR 38, CA (discussed at length above) – a party will seek to revisit a point that has been conceded before the employment tribunal. Below, we consider two cases in which the EAT did allow such points to be reconsidered:

- **Embleton v Rapid Fire Services Ltd** EAT 129/99: the EAT held that an employer cross-appealing against a finding of unfair dismissal could withdraw a concession made at the employment tribunal that the employee's dismissal could not be said to have been for redundancy. The EAT reached this decision because the employer's concession had not affected the leading of evidence before the tribunal. The question that prompted the concession had been put by the employment judge after the conclusion of evidence, and the tribunal had not focused on the issue of whether the dismissal had been by reason of redundancy or not. The EAT decided that the best course of action would be to allow the concession to be withdrawn and to remit the matter to the tribunal

- **Lipscombe v Forestry Commission** EAT 0191/06: when submitting an unfair constructive dismissal claim to an employment tribunal, L answered 'No' to the question of whether he had submitted the requisite statutory grievance. The tribunal eventually rejected his claim on the basis that no such grievance had been raised. L appealed to the EAT, seeking to argue, with reference to his resignation letter, that he had in fact raised a grievance with his employer prior to bringing his tribunal claim. The EAT held that even if the tribunal had been correct to hold that L had conceded that he had not raised a grievance, there were exceptional circumstances allowing the matter to be reopened. L was a litigant in person who, although articulate in his approach, was suffering from a mildly severe stress disorder. In the EAT's opinion, allowance should be made for that. The EAT went on to state that its path to allowing L to raise the grievance point once more 'has been made easier by [the employer's] concession that the written material would constitute a grievance if that point were put'. In the event, the EAT allowed L's appeal and remitted the matter to the tribunal for a full hearing – a decision which was subsequently approved by the Court of Appeal (2007 EWCA Civ 428, CA).

18.51 **New points of law asserted by respondent to appeal.** The position regarding the admission of a new point of law on appeal is somewhat different when it is the respondent to the appeal who seeks to introduce the new point in order to defend, rather than attack, the employment tribunal's decision. It may be that the point raised by the respondent, while not dealt with specifically at the tribunal hearing, may be implicit in the reasons for the tribunal's decision. Nevertheless, the EAT and the higher courts will generally refuse to allow respondents to argue such points unless it is very clear that no new evidence will have to be called and that no further investigation of the evidence that has already been adduced will have to take place – Hellyer Brothers Ltd v McLeod and ors and another case 1987 ICR 526, CA. In the McLeod case, a tribunal held that a group of fishermen were employed under a 'global' contract of employment, the termination of which amounted to a dismissal. This finding was challenged on appeal to the EAT, where the fishermen sought to argue that the tribunal's decision could be supported on the basis that, even if there were no global contract, they were nonetheless employed under a series of fixed-term contracts and a dismissal could be deemed to have taken place when the last such contract expired without being renewed. The Court of Appeal upheld the EAT's refusal to allow this point to be argued on the ground that it could not be sustained without further investigation of the evidence and without further findings of fact.

Summary. The general principles surrounding the EAT's discretion to allow a **18.52** new point of law to be argued were comprehensively summarised by the EAT in Secretary of State for Health and anor v Rance and ors 2007 IRLR 665, EAT. His Honour Judge McMullen reviewed a number of the main authorities in this area, including Leicestershire County Council v UNISON 2006 IRLR 810, CA, Glennie v Independent Magazines (UK) Ltd 1999 IRLR 719, CA, and Jones v Governing Body of Burdett Coutts School 1999 ICR 38, CA, and then set out the following guidelines:

- there is a discretion to allow a new point of law to be argued in the EAT but it is tightly regulated

- the discretion covers new points and the reopening of conceded points

- the discretion is only exercised in exceptional circumstances

- it would be even more exceptional to exercise the discretion where fresh issues of fact would have to be investigated

- where the new point relates to jurisdiction, this is not a trump card inevitably requiring the point to be allowed to be raised for the first time on appeal

- the discretion to allow in the new point of law may be exercised in the following circumstances –

  - where it would be unjust to allow the other party to get away with some deception or unfair conduct which meant that the point was not taken by the employment tribunal

  - if the EAT is in possession of all material necessary to dispose of the matter fairly without recourse to a further hearing

  - the new point enables the EAT plainly to say from existing material that the employment tribunal judgment was a nullity. In this situation it is the EAT's duty to put right the law on the facts available to the Appeal Tribunal

  - the EAT can see an obvious 'knock out' point

  - the issue is a discrete one of pure law requiring no further factual enquiry, or

  - it is of particular public importance for a legal point to be decided provided that no further factual investigation by the employment tribunal is required

- the discretion will not be exercised in the following circumstances –

    - where, notwithstanding that the new point concerns the jurisdiction of the employment tribunal, in order to make out that point it would be necessary to call fresh evidence

    - the issue arises as a result of lack of skill by a represented party

    - the point was not taken in the employment tribunal as a result of a tactical decision by a representative or a party

    - all the relevant material is before the EAT but what is required is an evaluation and an assessment of that material (and an application of the law to it) by the employment tribunal as the fact-finding forum

    - a represented party has fought and lost a jurisdictional issue and now seeks a new hearing. This applies whether the jurisdictional issue is the same as that argued before the employment tribunal, or different

    - where the factor relied upon for being permitted to raise the new point is the high value of the case.

18.53 EAT hearings

Subject to the comments made above relating to the admission of evidence – see 'Evidence' above – appeal hearings conducted by the EAT are confined to arguments about the questions of law that underlie the grounds for appeal. The onus is on the appellant to show that the employment tribunal's decision is flawed and so it is usually the appellant who will start. However, subject to the EAT Rules, EAT Practice Directions, and directions given by the President of the Appeal Tribunal, the EAT has the power to regulate its own procedure – S.30(3) ETA. Consequently, it is open to it to require the respondent to begin if that appears to be the most appropriate course.

18.54 Private hearings

In general, hearings of the EAT at which any proceedings are finally disposed of must take place in public – rule 29(1) EAT Rules. However, a Minister of the Crown may direct (or the EAT may of its own initiative order) that the hearing be conducted in private where he or she considers it to be in the interests of national security – rule 30A(1) and (2). In addition, in cases where the EAT exercises its discretion to hear evidence itself, it may sit in private to hear the evidence given by a particular witness if, in its opinion, such evidence is likely to consist of:

- information that the witness could not disclose without breaking the law, e.g. the Official Secrets Acts

- information communicated to the witness in confidence, or as a result of the confidence placed in him or her by another person, or

- information that may, for reasons other than its effect on negotiations, have such an effect on a collective agreement or collective bargaining (as defined by S.178(2) TULR(C)A) that its disclosure could lead to substantial injury to the witness's undertaking, or any undertaking in which he or she works.

Video and telephone hearings   18.55

Exceptionally, short preliminary hearings and appointments for directions can be conducted by video or telephone link upon the written application of one of the parties if they or their representative has a disability – para 20.2 Practice Direction. Such an application must be supported by appropriate medical evidence and will only be acceded to by the Registrar or a judge if all parties participate in the hearing and are legally represented. The applicant party may be asked to bear the call charges incurred by conducting the hearing in the form of a telephone conference.

Hearings will not normally be recorded except for the giving of any judgment – para 20.3.

Length of hearings   18.56

The parties will be asked to give an estimate of the time it will take the EAT to hear the case, or the EAT may itself come up with an estimated length of hearing. Estimates should take into account the fact that the EAT will have pre-read the papers and do not need to factor in the time it will take for the EAT to give its decision – see further under 'Listing of appeals' above. Serious administrative difficulties can result if the estimated length of the hearing proves to be considerably shorter than the length of time the hearing actually takes. Such cases have to be adjourned and reconvened on another date. This may involve a considerable delay as the EAT's next day of business will almost certainly be the subject of a full schedule and, in any event, the lay members – who are all part time – do not attend the EAT every day but come in on pre-arranged dates according to when they are available. It may therefore be some time before all the members of the EAT panel are available again. However, in this regard, note that changes made to the ETA by the Enterprise and Regulatory Reform Act 2013 now mean the default position is that proceedings before the EAT are to be heard by a judge alone – S28(2) ETA. For further details, see Chapter 16, 'The Employment Appeal Tribunal', under 'Composition of the EAT – sittings of the EAT'.

Representation   18.57

In keeping with the aim of the tribunal system to be accessible to those who cannot afford or do not want legal representation, there is no requirement that parties instruct a solicitor or barrister to act for them either during the interim

961

stages of proceedings or during the hearing itself. S.29 ETA states that 'a person may appear before the Appeal Tribunal in person or be represented by – (a) counsel or a solicitor, (b) a representative of a trade union or an employers' association, or (c) any other person whom he desires to represent him'.

Note that 'Legal Help' or 'Help at Court' (formerly called legal aid) are types of legal aid administered by the Legal Services Commission. The scope for providing such assistance for the purposes of pursuing or defending both employment tribunal and EAT proceedings has been drastically narrowed since April 2013 as a result of reform of legal aid introduced by the Legal Aid, Sentencing and Punishment of Offenders Act 2012. However, such assistance continues to be potentially available to individuals pursuing appeals from employment tribunal decisions, subject to the normal conditions – see the Civil Legal Aid (General) Regulations 1989 SI 1989/339 (as amended) – the amendments made by the 2012 Act in effect confine the legal aid available in EAT proceedings to discrimination and harassment claims, in respect of which such aid can cover both advice and advocacy – see Parts 1 and 3 of Schedule 1 to the 2012 Act. A number of schemes with different eligibility criteria exist to offer advice, and in some cases free representation, to those who are not eligible for legal aid. Further information can be obtained from the Bar Council and the Free Representation Unit.

18.58 ## EAT decisions

When the hearing of the appeal has been completed, the EAT retires to consider its judgment. This may be given after a short adjournment or, alternatively, the EAT can adjourn altogether and reconvene at a later date to give its judgment – known as a 'reserved judgment'. The decision must usually be given within three and a half months of the last hearing or submission – Kwamin v Abbey National plc and other cases 2004 ICR 841, EAT.

The EAT will usually give a full reasoned judgment to accompany its formal order following the substantive appeal hearing. Often, however, it will give an immediate indication of the order that it is minded to make and inform the parties that a full reasoned judgment will be sent to them in due course. If, following the hearing, the EAT does not indicate an intention to produce a full judgment, any party may request it to give reasons for its order. Such a request must be made within 14 days of the making of the order – rule 31(2) EAT Rules and para 21.4 Practice Direction. On occasion a judge will agree to provide the parties with an advance copy of the decision, subject to its remaining confidential – para 21.5.

18.59 The Practice Direction also outlines what the parties can expect regarding the provision of reasoned judgments in respect of interim decisions. Where, as part of the initial 'sift', an appeal is allowed to go forward to a preliminary or full hearing, reasons will be given in the form of either a short judgment or note made by the judge, a copy of which will be provided to all parties – para 21.3.3. If a judgment is given orally, it will be transcribed and a transcript provided to the parties unless the judge considers a written note of his or her reasons to be sufficient.

Judgment hand-down. In order to save the time and inconvenience involved **18.60** in reconvening the full tribunal in cases where reserved judgment is given, the EAT will inform the parties of the day on which judgment will be handed down – para 21.1 Practice Direction. This will normally entail the parties (or their representatives) merely turning up on that day and being given the judgment to read, although the attendance of the parties is not compulsory. The judgment will be pronounced without being read aloud by the judge who conducted the appeal or by another judge on his or her behalf.

In Scotland judgments are normally reserved and are handed down as soon as practicable on a provisional basis to the parties. Parties then have 14 days to make any representations about expenses, leave to appeal or any other relevant matter. Once the 14-day period has expired and any representations have been dealt with, an order is issued to conform to the original judgment – para 21.6.

Consequential applications. A party who wishes to make an incidental **18.61** application (such as an application for costs or leave to appeal) must give the EAT and the other parties notice of this fact 48 hours before the judgment is due to be handed down. Notice of the application should be accompanied by the appropriate documents, such as a schedule of costs or a draft notice of appeal. Once the judge has pronounced the reserved judgment, he or she will deal with any applications, either by making a decision or referring it to the judge or EAT tribunal who heard the appeal. Every order of the EAT is drawn up by the Registrar, stamped with the EAT's seal and served by the Registrar on all relevant parties – rule 31(1). The judgment is also served on the Secretary of Employment Tribunals or, where relevant, the Certification Officer, the Secretary of State or the Chairman of the CAC. Also, note that all judgments which are transcribed or handed down are posted on the EAT website – para 21.7 Practice Direction.

Appeal outcomes. The EAT's powers in determining an appeal are as wide as **18.62** the powers of the body or officer from whom the appeal is brought – S.35 ETA. Where the EAT is sitting as a full tribunal, the decision must be reached by a majority, but this does not have to include the legally qualified member of the panel. For discussion on the composition of the EAT, including reforms that have been implemented in this area, see Chapter 16, 'The Employment Appeal Tribunal', under 'Composition of the EAT'.

In practical terms, an appeal from an employment tribunal decision can have one of three possible outcomes:

- the appeal may be dismissed

- the appeal may be allowed with the EAT substituting its own decision for that of the tribunal

- the appeal may be allowed and the case remitted to the same tribunal or a different tribunal for either a complete rehearing or fresh consideration of a particular point in the light of the EAT's ruling on the law.

Note that, in respect of the last two outcomes, the EAT can also order a respondent to a successful appeal to reimburse the appellant in respect of the EAT fees – rule 34A(2A) EAT Rules (for further details of reimbursement of fees, see Chapter 19, 'Fees', under 'EAT fees').

We shall deal with each of the possible outcomes listed above in turn.

18.63 Dismissing the appeal

Dismissing an appeal has the effect of confirming the decision of the employment tribunal. The EAT *must* dismiss an appeal unless the tribunal has made an error of law, or its decision is one which no reasonable tribunal properly directing itself on the facts could have reached (i.e. the decision is 'perverse' – see Chapter 16, 'The Employment Appeal Tribunal', under 'Grounds of appeal – perversity').

In very rare cases, the EAT may dismiss an appeal even though it finds a significant error of law on the part of the tribunal. For example, in Peters v Science Museum, unreported 29.11.79, CA, P claimed constructive dismissal but the employment tribunal treated her claim as one of express dismissal, which it found to be fair. While the Court of Appeal agreed with the EAT that this amounted to a significant error of law, it upheld the decision on the ground that no reasonable tribunal, howsoever the case was put to it, would have found the dismissal unfair. The principle here is that a decision of a tribunal that has been reached under a mistake of law can nevertheless be allowed to stand provided that it is *plainly and unarguably right*, despite the misdirection – Dobie v Burns International Security Services (UK) Ltd 1984 ICR 812, CA. This is also the approach where the tribunal's error is procedural – Bache v Essex County Council 2000 ICR 313, CA.

18.64 Note that in Hellyer Brothers Ltd v McLeod and ors and another case 1987 ICR 526, CA, the Court of Appeal held that the principle in Dobie is subject to an implicit qualification; namely, that if the EAT is satisfied that a tribunal's decision, reached as a result of a misdirection, is plainly and unarguably wrong on the facts, and those facts do not require further amplification or reinvestigation by the EAT, then the EAT is entitled and bound to substitute its own conclusion as to what those findings require in law.

Substituting the tribunal's decision   18.65

The EAT has the power to overturn an employment tribunal decision and substitute one of its own. However, it should not do so as a matter of course. In O'Kelly and ors v Trusthouse Forte plc 1983 ICR 728, CA, the Court of Appeal held that if the EAT detects an error of law in the tribunal's decision, it may only substitute its own decision if the tribunal *must* – but for that error – have reached the same conclusion as the one that the EAT feels minded to reach. If, however, it is an open question as to what the tribunal would have concluded had it not erred in law, or if the tribunal's reasons are simply unclear or inadequate, then the EAT cannot avoid remitting the matter for further consideration. In Tilson v Alstom Transport 2011 IRLR 169, CA, Lord Justice Elias opined that there was a strong argument for the relaxation of the O'Kelly principle. He observed that 'the overriding objective set out in the EAT rules seeks to save costs, amongst other matters, and it is not necessarily in the parties' interests to disable the appellate court from reaching a decision on the same evidence as would be available to the judge'. However, as he was not addressed on this issue by the parties , Elias LJ did not believe that it was an appropriate opportunity to attempt any modification of the O'Kelly principle.

Often an employment tribunal is aware of the fact that it is ruling on a matter that may well become the subject of challenge on appeal. In such cases, it often makes alternative findings in the event that its initial decision is held to be wrong in law. In Stacey v Babcock Power Ltd EAT 1986 ICR 221, EAT, for instance, the tribunal had given a clear indication that it would have found the employee's dismissal unfair had it considered itself free to do so in law. The EAT held that the tribunal was mistaken about the law and was free to find that the dismissal was unfair. In view of the tribunal's alternative finding, the EAT saw no reason to remit the case on liability and substituted a finding that the dismissal was unfair.

If the decision of an employment tribunal is successfully challenged on the **18.66** ground that it is perverse, then it is axiomatic that it cannot be right and must be overturned. In Holden v Bradville Ltd 1985 IRLR 483, EAT, the EAT held that the tribunal had reached a perverse conclusion in finding that consultation prior to a redundancy would have been impracticable. It also held that there was no evidence to support a further tribunal finding that consultation would have made no difference to the decision to dismiss. The EAT went on to hold that 'there does not appear to be any such uncertainty as to the facts or any incompleteness in the findings requiring us to order a re-hearing'.

If the EAT reverses a finding of fair dismissal and holds that an employee was unfairly dismissed, then clearly that does not dispose of the matter because the question of compensation remains to be determined. In such circumstances the proper course is for the EAT to remit the case on the question of compensation – unless it is clear that only one outcome would be inevitable. For example, the

EAT may decide that a dismissal was procedurally unfair but that a tribunal would be bound to find that the employee had contributed to the dismissal to such an extent that no compensation would be awarded. In that case, the EAT would be entitled to make the order that no compensation should be paid.

18.67 The findings contained in the tribunal's extended reasons for dismissal may also allow the EAT to make a finding as to the amount of compensation that should be awarded. In cases of redundancy, for example, the EAT may hold that the tribunal should have confined compensation to the length of time that reasonable consultations would have taken. If the tribunal has made a finding as to the length of the period that would be reasonable to allow for compensation, then there is no reason why the EAT cannot determine the matter itself. However, the EAT should not decide the length of reasonable consultation itself and if the tribunal made no finding on the point then the case should be remitted – Christie and Co v Blacklaw EAT 175/92.

Appeals by consent are covered by rule 6(5) of the EAT Rules, which provides that 'where the respondent does not wish to resist an appeal, the parties may deliver to the Appeal Tribunal an agreed draft of an order allowing the appeal and the Tribunal may, if it thinks it right to do so, make an order allowing the appeal in the terms agreed'. Para 18.3 of the 2013 Practice Direction stipulates that if the parties reach an agreement that the appeal should be allowed by consent, and that an order made by the employment tribunal should be reversed or varied or the matter remitted to the tribunal on the ground that the decision contains an error of law, it is usually necessary for the matter to be heard by the EAT to determine whether there is a good reason for making the proposed order. For more in-depth discussion on appeals by consent, see Chapter 16, 'The Employment Appeal Tribunal', under 'Jurisdiction of the EAT – appeals by consent'.

18.68 Remitting to employment tribunal

This is the most common outcome of successful appeals, since a correction of a legal error will not usually be enough to resolve the case. In choosing to remit, the EAT has the option of remitting the case to be considered by the same tribunal that made the original decision or to a new tribunal presided over by a different judge and members.

In Sinclair Roche and Temperley and ors v Heard and anor 2004 IRLR 763, EAT, the then President of the EAT, Mr Justice Burton, provided the following non-exhaustive list of factors relevant to the question of whether the EAT should remit a matter to the same or a different tribunal:

- *proportionality* – whether sufficient money is at stake that the additional costs to both parties of a fresh hearing do not offend on the ground of proportionality

- *passage of time* – a matter should not be remitted to the same tribunal if there is a real risk that the tribunal will have forgotten about the case

- *bias or partiality* – it would not be appropriate to send a matter back to the same tribunal where there is a question of bias or the risk of prejudgment or partiality (this is obviously the case where the basis of the appeal depends upon bias or misconduct, but is not limited to such a case)

- *totally flawed decision* – it would not ordinarily be appropriate to send a matter back to the same tribunal where, in the conclusion of the EAT, the first hearing was completely flawed or mishandled

- *second bite* – the EAT should only remit a matter to the same tribunal if it has confidence that, with guidance, the tribunal would be prepared to look fully at further matters and be willing, if appropriate, to reach a different conclusion

- *tribunal professionalism* – in the absence of clear indications to the contrary, it should be assumed that a tribunal is capable of a professional approach to dealing with a matter on remission.

Applying these factors to the Sinclair Roche case, the EAT decided to remit the **18.69** matter to the same tribunal. Although there were concerns over the tribunal's handling of the case, there had not been a 'complete mishandling' and there was no evidence of bias or partiality. In the EAT's view, the tribunal would be able to 'approach its renewed task free of preconceptions and with an open mind'. However, following delay and other incidents of mishandling by the tribunal once the case had returned to it, the EAT subsequently reviewed its decision to remit the matter to the same tribunal – see Sinclair Roche and Temperley v Heard and anor EAT 0637/05. At the review, the EAT revisited its guidelines and concluded that there was evidence that the employment judge lacked professionalism, that he had a closed mind towards the respondents and that there was a real risk that he was biased. Even though remitting the case to a different tribunal would mean a delay of four months, this disadvantage had to be weighed up with the other relevant factors. Accordingly, the EAT concluded that the matter should after all be reheard by a different tribunal.

The guidelines laid down by Burton P in Sinclair Roche and Temperley and ors v Heard and anor 2004 IRLR 763, EAT, mark a departure from the EAT's previous practice. At the review hearing in the Sinclair Roche proceedings, Burton P stated that 'there is no doubt that the [EAT's] previous practice for many years had been solidly in favour of remitting to a different tribunal, simply on the basis that, otherwise, justice may not be seen to be done'. He also noted that none of the previous EAT decisions on the question attempted 'to analyse the factors which ought to be considered if a decision needed to be made as to whether to send it back to the same or a different tribunal'. Although Burton P stressed that his guidance should not 'be regarded as anywhere near

967

holy writ or, in any event, as exclusive of the considerations which may be relevant', it will now doubtless be the EAT's first point of reference in making a decision about remittance. Indeed, the guidelines were referred to, without disapproval, by the Court of Appeal in Barke v SEETEC Business Technology Centre Ltd 2005 ICR 1373, CA.

18.70 Scope of a remitted hearing. As a general rule, when the EAT has remitted a case to a differently constituted tribunal, the employment tribunal will be entitled to reconsider the entire case afresh and will not be bound by any findings of fact or evidence made by or presented to the original tribunal. In contrast, where the remission is to the same tribunal, the scope of the hearing will usually be confined to argument and/or evidence on specific points in accordance with the directions given by the EAT.

This was confirmed by the Court of Appeal in Aparau v Iceland Frozen Foods plc 2000 ICR 341, CA, where the Court held that a tribunal had acted outside of the scope of its remit and, therefore, its jurisdiction. The EAT had remitted the case to the tribunal for the sole purpose of reconsidering whether an employee had been constructively dismissed, but the tribunal went on to consider the fairness of the dismissal. The Court of Appeal noted that employment tribunals are bodies established by statute with their constitution and procedure being governed by the Employment Tribunal Rules. The relevant rule applicable at the time (rule 13 of the Employment Tribunal Rules 2001) gave the tribunal only a limited power to review its decision with no power to reopen proceedings once they had been disposed of by a final decision. That remains the case under the rules relating to the reconsideration of judgments in rules 70–73 of the Employment Tribunal Rules 2013. The Court of Appeal held that, as a result of this limited power of review, a tribunal has exhausted its jurisdiction once it has delivered a final decision and has no power to reopen a hearing or reconsider a decision unless the matter is remitted to it for that purpose by the EAT. Accordingly, the extent to which a tribunal's jurisdiction is revived by an order remitting the matter to it depends entirely on the scope of the remission as set out in the EAT's order. Moreover, since the jurisdiction of tribunals derives entirely from statute, and is exercised within the framework of the statutory rules of procedure, the Court further held that it was not open to the parties to argue that they had acquiesced or consented to the tribunal's assuming a jurisdiction it would not otherwise possess. The Court of Appeal concluded that the tribunal in this case did not have jurisdiction to consider the issue of the fairness of the employee's dismissal, and accordingly that its decision on that point was a nullity.

18.71 Where the EAT orally makes an order remitting a case or part of it to a tribunal for a further hearing or rehearing, the parties must immediately raise any uncertainty that they have as to the precise scope of the remission – para 23.1 Practice Direction. This paragraph goes on to state that the scope of remission will be recorded in the EAT's order following a hearing and that it is the obligation of each party to ensure that the scope corresponds with their understanding of it.

As stated above, the EAT's power to remit a case can be used to require an employment tribunal to reconsider an entire case afresh without being bound by any findings of fact or any evidence. But note that the EAT can also require a tribunal to reconsider a particular point even if no question of law about that point had been raised before the EAT. In Prestcold v Irvine 1981 ICR 777, CA, the EAT remitted a case to the employment tribunal for reconsideration of compensation under the former Sex Discrimination Act 1975 (now consolidated into the Equality Act 2010). The Court of Appeal held that the EAT was entitled to do this. The fact that no question of law about the correctness of compensation had been raised before the EAT did not deprive it of jurisdiction to remit the matter.

Reference to the European Court of Justice 18.72
In recent years, the influence of European law over certain areas of UK employment law has been growing rapidly. When the EAT (or any other court) is considering a case relating to domestic legislation that has been enacted in order to implement European law – for example, in the areas of discrimination, equal pay, working time, transfer of undertakings or collective consultation over redundancies – it must ensure that its decision is in accordance with that law.

When questions arise as to the interpretation of European law, the EAT *may* request a ruling from the European Court of Justice (ECJ). However, the EAT is not obliged to make a reference to the ECJ – it may instead allow the appeal to proceed to a higher court, which can make the reference if it considers this to be the appropriate course. The costs implications of a reference to the ECJ are considered in Chapter 20, 'Costs and penalties', under 'Costs beyond the EAT – references to the ECJ'.

Enforcement of EAT decisions 18.73
Any decision or award of the EAT in its appellate capacity has the same effect and may be enforced in the same manner as a decision or award of the employment tribunal, as to which see Chapter 21, 'Enforcement of tribunal awards'.

Review of EAT decisions and further appeals 18.74

The EAT, like employment tribunals, can review its decisions either of its own motion or on the application of one of the parties – rule 33(1) EAT Rules. On review, the EAT may revoke or vary the order that it has made on the ground that:

969

- the order was wrongly made as a result of an error on the part of the EAT or the EAT's staff – rule 33(1)(a)

- one of the parties did not receive proper notice of the proceedings leading to the order – rule 33(1)(b), or

- the interests of justice require such a review – rule 33(1)(c).

A review application must be made within 14 days of the date of the decision which is to be reviewed – rule 33(2). A merely clerical slip or omission in the drawing up of an EAT's order may, however, be corrected at any time on the authority of a judge or EAT member – rule 33(3).

18.75 Rule 33(4) was inserted into the EAT Rules in 2004. It provides that 'the decision to grant or refuse an application for review may be made by a judge'. The Practice Direction clarifies the extent of this rule, at para 24. Where a judge heard the original appeal or made the original order alone, he or she may make such order as he or she thinks fit. This can involve granting, refusing, adjourning or otherwise dealing with an application for review. If the original order was made by the judge with the lay members, the judge can refuse an application for review without consulting the lay members. However, before a judge grants such an application, he or she must give notice to the other parties and refer the matter to the lay members for their consideration of the matter, either on paper or at a hearing. For discussion on the composition of the EAT, including recent reforms in this area, see Chapter 16, 'The Employment Appeal Tribunal', under 'Composition of the EAT'.

Note that there are fewer grounds for reviewing an EAT decision than there are for reconsidering a tribunal judgment (for reconsideration of tribunal judgments, see Chapter 15, 'Reconsideration of tribunal judgments and decisions', under 'Grounds for reconsideration'). It is actually very rare for the EAT to review a decision. One of the main reasons for this, as the EAT itself has acknowledged, is that the facts of the case have already been disposed of at tribunal level, and if a party has any objection to the way in which the EAT has dealt with the law then it is probably more appropriate to pursue an appeal to the Court of Appeal than to seek a review – Stannard and Co (1969) Ltd v Wilson 1983 ICR 86, EAT.

18.76 In Blockleys plc v Miller 1992 ICR 749, EAT, the EAT decided that a review should only be brought on very narrow grounds. It was not a method by which to reargue or rehear a case. The EAT clarified that the error envisaged in rule 33(1)(a), for example, covered only the situation in which some alteration was necessary to the form of the order, and the 'interests of justice' provision in rule 33(1)(c) was applicable only in cases where it was necessary to 'repair an error in jurisdiction or a defect in the process of the appeal'.

Some further guidance on the question of when a review should be granted under the 'interests of justice' provision in rule 33(1)(c) was given in Vadehra v UK Project Support Ltd EAT 603/99. In that case the EAT granted the appellant's request that the appeal be listed as a matter of urgency, in view of the imminent listing of another related claim in the employment tribunal. The appellant, however, failed to attend the appeal hearing and the matter was heard in his absence. The EAT dismissed the appeal and the appellant sought a review of its decision under rule 33(1)(c). The EAT stated that, in considering whether it would be in the 'interests of justice' to grant a review, it should first ask itself whether the appellant had shown a good and genuine reason for his absence from the appeal hearing and, secondly, whether there was any real prospect of the review succeeding on its merits if it were granted. In answering the first question, the EAT accepted that the appellant's reason for being absent – namely, that he was away from his usual address when the notice of the hearing arrived and did not learn of the date until after the hearing – was genuine. However, the EAT did not think this was a good reason for his absence. The appellant had requested an urgent hearing and it was his responsibility to maintain contact with the EAT to ensure that he was made aware of the hearing date. In view of the answer to the first question, the EAT did not think it necessary to go on to consider the second question concerning the merits of the review application.

18.77 In Zinda v Governors of Barn Hill Community High and ors EAT 1146/09 the EAT reviewed a number of authorities on the subject of EAT reviews and set down the following principles:

- reviews by the EAT of its judgments, decisions and orders will be rare

- the interests of justice can include consideration of whether the admission of fresh evidence should be considered

- the underlying purpose of a review by the EAT is the correction of mistakes

- a review is not, and cannot be used as, a substitute for an appeal, and the EAT must not conduct a review which amounts to an appeal of its own decision

- it may be an abuse of process to seek a review while a further appeal is pending, particularly where the same issues have been, or could have been, raised in a pending appeal

- there may, however, be cases where it will be preferable for the EAT to conduct a review rather than compel an applicant for review to pursue an appeal

- where the interests of justice require it, the time for a review can be extended.

971

In Bass Leisure Ltd v Thomas 1994 IRLR 104, EAT, the Appeal Tribunal held that if a case was not appropriate for a review, the EAT nevertheless has the power to reconsider its judgment at any time before it was perfected by relying on its powers as a superior court of record. In that case, the EAT realised just after delivering an oral judgment that further consideration needed to be given to a particular point. However, many commentators are of the view that the procedure adopted by the EAT in the Bass case was invalid, in that the EAT sought to bypass the narrow grounds on which it could order a review under the EAT Rules. It has been suggested that if the EAT Rules do not provide a mechanism for allowing such a case to be drastically reconsidered, the EAT should not invent one.

18.78 In exceptionally rare circumstances, the EAT may decide to use its general powers to review its own decisions to allow it to revisit a decision made at the sift stage when allowing the appeal to proceed to a full hearing. In Jamieson v Nationwide Building Society EATS 0028/13 the appellant had failed in her unfair dismissal claim before the employment tribunal on the basis that she had resigned rather than, as she contended, been unduly pressured to resign in circumstances that amounted to dismissal. The advice to resign had come from someone acting as her trade union adviser. On appeal, the appellant managed to proceed through the sift after asserting that the adviser was, in fact, a person employed by the respondent employer and that in the light of this her resignation had not been truly voluntary. It subsequently came to light that the appellant had been untruthful in the assertion that her adviser was an employee of the respondent and, on that basis, the EAT granted the employer's application for review under rules 33(1)(a) and (c) of the EAT Rules on the grounds that the order permitting the case to proceed to a full hearing had been wrongly made as a result of error on the part of the EAT and that the interests of justice required a review.

In so holding Mr Justice Langstaff (President of the EAT) accepted that the grant of a review of a sift decision will be rare, but that there was nothing explicitly in the EAT to prevent this. Regarding the 'error' ground relied upon by the employer in this particular case, his Lordship acknowledged that the expression 'error on the part of the Tribunal' in rule 33(1)(a) usually looks to an error that the EAT itself or its staff has made, but concluded that the phrase was apt to cover an error precipitated by fault on the part of the claimant with regard to the assertions made in the Notice of Appeal. Langstaff P also found that the 'interest of justice' was also plainly made out given that the EAT had been misled in a material respect. Having allowed the review, however, his Lordship ended up confirming the original decision that the case should proceed to a full hearing since there remained issues of law to be determined.

18.79 Note that the EAT's refusal to grant a review is not 'an order finally disposing of any proceedings' within the meaning of rule 31(2) of the EAT Rules.

Consequently, it does not have to provide written reasons for its refusal – Persson v Matra Marconi Space UK Ltd EATRF 95/1565–66/B, CA. However, in that case the Court of Appeal held that it would nevertheless be good practice for the EAT to give brief reasons when rejecting an application for review.

Appeals from the EAT   **18.80**

A further appeal will lie from the EAT on any question of law to the Court of Appeal in England and Wales or to the Court of Session (Inner House) in Scotland – S.37 ETA. Appeals to the Court of Appeal are governed by Part 52 of the Civil Procedure Rules 1998 SI 1998/3132 (CPR).

The traditional view is that, in considering an appeal, the question for the Court of Appeal is whether the employment tribunal made an error of law or reached a perverse conclusion, as opposed to whether the EAT's decision was correct – Campion v Hamworthy Engineering Ltd 1987 ICR 966, CA. However, in Balfour Beatty Power Networks Ltd and anor v Wilcox and ors 2007 IRLR 63, CA, Lord Justice Buxton suggested that this traditional view is incorrect. He stated that 'the jurisdiction of this court... is to hear appeals from the Employment Appeal Tribunal and not from the Employment Tribunal. While it will be necessary, because of the form of the submissions before us, and to some extent because of the existing jurisprudence of this court, to revert at some length to what the Employment Tribunal said and did, I do not lose sight of the real question, which is whether the Employment Appeal Tribunal erred in law in the judgment under appeal.'

Leave (i.e. permission) to appeal. An appeal can only be made with the leave   **18.81**
of the EAT, to which an application should be made initially, or with the leave of the Court of Appeal if the EAT refuses to grant such leave. A would-be appellant must show an arguable case that there has been an error of law which should be considered by the higher court.

The procedure for applying for leave to appeal differs depending on whether the appeal was heard in England and Wales or in Scotland. For appeals heard in England and Wales, an application for leave to appeal must be made to the EAT at the hearing or at the time when the reserved judgment is handed down. If an application for leave to appeal is not made then, or is refused by the EAT, an application should be made to the Court of Appeal within 14 days of the date of the sealed order. The EAT has jurisdiction to extend the time available for making an application for leave to appeal so long as the extension application is made before the expiry of the normal time-limitation period – Tether v Financial Times Ltd 1980 ICR 447, EAT. Para 25.1 of the Practice Direction states that the EAT will consider an extension of time application where 'a case is made out to the satisfaction of a judge or Registrar that there is a need to delay until after a transcript is received'. The Practice Direction goes on to say,

973

however, that applications for an extension of time for permission to appeal should 'normally' be made to the Court of Appeal.

18.82 An application for permission to appeal to the Court of Session in respect of an appeal heard in Scotland must be made within 42 days of either the date of the hearing (when judgment was delivered at the hearing) or the date when the judgment was sent to the parties – para 25.3 of the Practice Direction.

The party seeking permission to appeal must state the point of law to be advanced and the grounds of appeal. In weighing up the application, the EAT has to be satisfied that the party seeking leave has a real prospect of success in the appeal or some other compelling reason why the appeal should be heard – para 52.3 CPR.

18.83 In Home Office v Bailey and ors EAT 0706/04 counsel referred the EAT to the Court of Appeal's decision in Cooke v Secretary of State for Social Security 2002 3 All ER 279, CA, in which the Court considered the test it should apply when considering permission to appeal applications. There, Lady Justice Hale noted that applications for leave to appeal against the Social Security Commissioner should be dealt with robustly in light of the fact that the Commissioner was a 'specialist body'. In the Home Office v Bailey case, counsel argued that the same test should apply to appeals from the EAT. The EAT, however, felt that a distinction could be drawn between the Social Security Commissioner and the EAT because the former dealt with appeals which had a wide public significance. The EAT's view was that, in order to grant leave to appeal, 'we should be satisfied that there is a real prospect of success in the appeal or some other compelling reason for granting permission to appeal, but we accept... that in deciding that question, we should take a robust view'.

Note that in certain circumstances the Court of Appeal may, before hearing an appeal, remit a case to the EAT for it to hear legal submissions and make a judgment which would assist the Court of Appeal in reaching its decision. For example, in Grady v Prison Service 2003 ICR, 753, CA, the Court overturned the EAT's rejection of G's appeal for lack of jurisdiction, but would not hear the substantive arguments in the case without first receiving a reasoned judgment from the EAT.

18.84 **Exposure to costs.** Those contemplating an appeal from the EAT should be aware that the losing party before the Court of Appeal will usually be required to pay the winner's costs. Formal legal advice is strongly suggested before pursuing such an appeal. For a detailed discussion of the exposure to costs in respect of appeals beyond the EAT, see Chapter 20, 'Costs and penalties', under 'Costs beyond the EAT'.

18.85 **Further appeal to Supreme Court.** A further appeal lies from the Court of Appeal or the Court of Session to the Supreme Court, but only with the leave of the court from whose decision the appellant is seeking to appeal or the

Supreme Court. Leave will only be given when the grounds for appeal raise a point of law of general public importance. Appeals to the Supreme Court are covered by the Supreme Court Rules 2009 SI 2009/1603, which are available on the UK Parliament website. Note that the overriding objective of the Supreme Court is 'to secure that the court is accessible, fair and efficient'.

19 Fees

Fees for bringing employment tribunal claims (and appeals to the EAT) were **19.1** introduced by the Employment Tribunals and the Employment Appeal Tribunal Fees Order 2013 SI 2013/1893 ('the Fees Order') on 29 July 2013, the same day on which the Employment Tribunal Rules 2013 ('the Tribunal Rules'), contained in the Employment Tribunals (Constitution and Rules of Procedure) Regulations 2013 SI 2013/1237 ('the Tribunal Regulations'), came into force. For the first time, all potential employment tribunal claimants and EAT appellants are required to pay a fee in order to bring and pursue their tribunal claims and appeals, unless they qualify for fee remission (which is generally only available to those on very low incomes). In the employment tribunal, a claimant has to pay:

- an issue fee to bring a claim, and

- a hearing fee to pursue it to hearing.

These fees are discussed under 'Tribunal issue fee' and 'Tribunal hearing fee' respectively below. Different fee levels apply for claimants bringing so-called 'fee group' claims – see '"Fee group" claims' below. There is little scope for reimbursement of these fees, at least by the employment tribunal. However, it may be prepared to order the other side to reimburse the fee in the event of a successful claim/application. This is dealt with under 'Reimbursement' below.

977

19.2 Although the burden of paying employment tribunal fees rests primarily on claimants (in the form of the issue fee and the hearing fee), there are also 'application-specific fees' payable by the party who makes the application – see 'Application-specific tribunal fees' below. Furthermore, respondents will be required to pay a fee for issuing an employer's contract claim – the equivalent to a 'counterclaim' under the old Tribunal Rules 2004 – or if the parties decide to pursue judicial mediation. These fees are discussed under 'Fee for employer's contract claim' and 'Judicial mediation fee' respectively below.

A party wishing to appeal to the EAT must pay:

• an appeal fee on submission of the notice of appeal, and

• an appeal hearing fee when the matter proceeds to a full hearing.

These are discussed under 'EAT fees' below.

19.3 The final section in this chapter deals with fee remission – the system of fee waivers and reductions, known as the remission system, which is available to those on low incomes who may have difficulty paying employment tribunal and EAT fees.

Note that fees are only payable in respect of employment tribunal claims presented and appeals received on or after 29 July 2013 – Article 15 Fees Order.

19.4 **Legal challenge to fees regime.** In June 2013 the trade union UNISON applied to the High Court for judicial review of the Ministry of Justice's decision to introduce employment tribunal and EAT fees, arguing that these charges would make it 'virtually impossible' for workers to exercise their employment rights. The application was heard in October 2013 and judgment rejecting the challenge was delivered on 7 February 2014 – R (on the application of UNISON) v Lord Chancellor (Equality and Human Rights Commission intervening) 2014 IRLR 266, QBD. The main stumbling block for the union was a lack of evidence proving that fees deter claimants on low incomes from bringing tribunal claims and appeals to the extent that they are effectively prevented from enforcing their EU-derived employment rights. The High Court preferred to adopt a 'wait and see' approach to allow any problems that might arise to be addressed by the Lord Chancellor. It ruled, however, that because the Lord Chancellor had accepted that the claim was premature, UNISON would not be prevented from bringing a fresh challenge further down the track. In any event, UNISON has indicated that it will appeal against the High Court's decision so we have not heard the last of it.

Note that a similar application was made by the law firm Fox and Partners to the Court of Session in respect of fees that were introduced in employment tribunals and the EAT in Scotland. This challenge was stayed pending a decision in the UNISON case but there has been nothing to indicate that it will be dropped. Indeed, such a move would be unlikely given UNISON's plan to appeal against the High Court's decision.

Types of tribunal claim subject to fees 19.5

The new rules on fees apply to *all* employment tribunal claims, meaning that no claim is exempt, even low or zero value claims (such as national minimum wage claims, claims where no financial remedy is sought, and holiday or notice pay claims). Claims are, however, divided into two categories – 'Type A' and 'Type B' – for the purpose of assessing the level of fee payable. For example, the issue fee for a Type A claim is £160 and for a Type B claim £250 – see 'Tribunal issue fee' below.

Type A claims 19.6
Type A claims (which attract the lower fee) are listed in Table 2 of Schedule 2 to the Fees Order 2013 – see the Appendix to this chapter. In the main, they are straightforward claims for defined sums, such as unauthorised deductions from wages, redundancy payments and holiday pay. Other notable examples include claims for a protective award in cases of collective redundancy, claims for further and better particulars, claims for failure to allow time off for trade union or safety representative activities and claims against the Secretary of State for a payment from the National Insurance Fund where the employer is insolvent.

Type B claims 19.7
Any claim *not* listed in Table 2 is a Type B claim – Article 7. Type B claims include unfair dismissal, discrimination, equal pay and whistleblowing – in other words, claims which (generally) involve more complex issues, although not necessarily higher compensation.

Tribunal issue fee 19.8

A claimant must now pay an issue fee in order to bring an employment tribunal claim. The fee is payable when the claim form is presented to the employment tribunal – Article 4(1)(a) Fees Order.

Amount of issue fee 19.9
There are two levels of issue fee in the employment tribunal, depending upon whether the claim is a Type A or Type B claim – see 'Types of tribunal claim subject to fees' above. The issue fee for:

• Type A claims is £160 – Article 6 Fees Order

979

- Type B claims is £250 – Article 7 Fees Order.

A claimant only has to pay a single issue fee irrespective of the number of claims being brought. If all the claims are Type A, the standard Type A fee is payable – Article 9(b). Where at least one of the claims is Type B, the issue fee is charged at the standard Type B rate – Article 9(a). For example, a claim containing a complaint of unpaid wages (a Type A claim) and unfair dismissal (a Type B claim) would be charged a single issue fee at the Type B rate (i.e. £250).

19.10 **Timing and method of payment of issue fee**

Article 4(1)(a) of the Fees Order states that an issue fee is payable 'when a claim form is presented to an employment tribunal'. More specifically, rule 11 of the Tribunal Rules states that the claim form must be 'accompanied' by the fee (or a remission application – see 'Remission' below), otherwise it will be rejected. The methods by which a claim form can be presented are prescribed in two Presidential Practice Directions on the 'Presentation of claims', one for England and Wales and one for Scotland. They provide that the claim form (and therefore the accompanying fee) may be presented:

- online using the online form submission service provided by HMCTS

- by post to a central office, or

- in person to one of the employment tribunal offices listed in the schedule to the relevant practice direction.

For further details, see Chapter 4, 'Starting tribunal proceedings', under 'Making a claim – the claim form (ET1)'.

19.11 Guidance issued by HMCTS, 'Employment tribunal fees for individuals' (T435) ('HMCTS fees guidance'), gives additional information on the payment of the issue fee. It provides that if the claim is being submitted online, payment can only be made by debit or credit card. If the claim is being sent by post, payment can be made by cheque (payable to HM Courts and Tribunals Service) or postal order. The guidance states that cash should not be sent by post as there is no guarantee it will arrive safely. Furthermore, the additional information appended to the Scottish Practice Direction notes that cash cannot be accepted at local employment tribunal offices in Scotland.

The guidance advocates use of the online system on the basis that it provides 'a quick, simple and convenient method to send us your claim' and will calculate the correct amount to pay. Similarly, the additional information attached to the Practice Directions advises that 'the speediest and most efficient method of presenting a claim will normally be by using the online submission service. The online system will assist in calculating the fee which is due, will ensure that a claimant does remember to pay or apply for remission (since it will not allow the claim to be submitted otherwise) and will reach the fee processing centre very quickly. It also leaves no room for doubt about when the claim was presented since this is recorded electronically. That may be important if the claim is being presented close to the end of the limitation period.'

Consequence of non-payment of issue fee   19.12
Rule 11 of the Tribunal Rules provides that 'the tribunal shall reject a claim if it is not accompanied by a *tribunal fee* or a remission application' (our stress). 'Tribunal fee' is defined in rule 1(1) as 'any fee which is payable by a party under any enactment in respect of a claim, employer's contract claim, application or judicial mediation in an employment tribunal'. Therefore, if the claimant makes no payment whatsoever, the claim form will be rejected and returned to him or her – with a notice of rejection explaining why (see rule 11(4)). Note that it is the employment tribunal staff – not employment tribunal judges – who deal with rejections under rule 11.

Can the claimant apply for a reconsideration? There is no provision allowing 19.13
a claimant to apply for a 'reconsideration' (i.e. a review) of an employment tribunal's decision to reject a claim on the basis of non-payment of fees (or failure to present a remission application). Rule 13, which provides for rejected claims to be reconsidered by a tribunal in certain circumstances, does not apply to a claim rejected under rule 11. Furthermore, rule 40 – which states that where a party has not paid a 'relevant tribunal fee', the tribunal will send the party a notice specifying a date for payment – is expressed to be 'subject to rule 11'. In other words, rule 40 applies to all fees *except* issue fees. This suggests that a claimant would not be given a second opportunity to pay the fee once the time limit for presenting the claim has expired. If this is right, then the rejection of a claim for non-payment is effectively the end of the road, at least so far as proceedings in the employment tribunal are concerned. (Note that if the time limit for presenting the claim has *not* expired, the claimant would be able to resubmit the claim with the relevant payment.)

One possible lifeline for claimants is rule 70. This provides that 'a tribunal may, either on its own initiative... or on the application of a party, reconsider any judgment where it is necessary in the interests of justice to do so'. In order to rely on this provision, it would have to be shown that a decision to reject a claim under rule 11 amounts to a 'judgment', which is defined in rule 1(3)(b) as 'a decision, made at any stage of the proceedings (but not including a decision under rule 13 or 19), which finally determines –

- a claim, or part of a claim, as regards liability, remedy or costs (including preparation time and wasted costs)

- any issue which is capable of finally disposing of any claim, or part of a claim, even if it does not necessarily do so (for example, an issue whether a claim should be struck out or a jurisdictional issue)

981

- the imposition of a financial penalty under S.12A of the Employment Tribunals Act 1996'.

19.14 While it is perhaps not immediately obvious that a decision to reject a claim under rule 11 falls within this definition of 'judgment', it is not specifically excluded from the definition, unlike decisions under rule 13 or rule 19 (which provide for rejected claims and responses to be reconsidered in certain circumstances). For further discussion, see Chapter 15, 'Reconsideration of tribunal judgments and decisions', under 'Reconsideration of a tribunal judgment – reconsideration of rejection of claim for failure to pay fee'. Failing reconsideration under rule 70, it seems that the only option for a claimant would be to appeal to the EAT against the tribunal's decision not to accept the claim, in which case an additional £400 issue fee and a £1,200 hearing fee would be payable – see 'EAT fees' below.

As mentioned above, if the time limit for presenting the claim has yet to expire, the claimant will be able to present a further claim with the appropriate fee (or remission application). It is also perhaps worth noting that if the rejection of the claim for non-payment/failure to submit a remission application is due to a 'clerical mistake' or 'accidental slip', an employment judge 'may at any time' correct this under rule 69 – see further Chapter 15, 'Reconsideration of tribunal judgments and decisions', under 'Correcting mistakes'.

19.15 Paying the wrong amount
As noted above, rule 11(1) provides that 'the tribunal shall reject a claim if it is not accompanied by *a* tribunal fee or a remission application' (our stress). 'Tribunal fee' is defined by rule 1(1) as 'any fee which is payable by a party under any enactment in respect of a claim, employer's contract claim, application or judicial mediation in an employment tribunal'. Therefore, so long as the claimant pays one of these types of fee, the claim will not be rejected outright. The claim form will, however, only be *accepted* if the correct issue fee is paid – i.e. £160 for a Type A claim and £250 for a Type B claim. If another type of tribunal fee is mistakenly paid and this is lower than the correct fee – for example, a Type A fee for a Type B claim – rule 11(2) provides that the tribunal will send the claimant a notice specifying a date for payment of the additional amount due. If the amount due is not then paid by the date specified, the claim (or the part of it in respect of which the relevant tribunal fee has not been paid) will be rejected by the tribunal. So, for example, if a claimant is bringing both a Type A claim (such as unlawful deduction from wages) and a Type B claim (such as disability discrimination) but has only paid a Type A fee, the Type B claim will be rejected. Again, the rules make no provision for a claimant to apply for this decision to be reconsidered – see further 'Consequence of non-payment of issue fee' above.

Therefore, while rule 11(2) provides some latitude for claimants who have not paid the correct fee, its scope is limited. It would seem only to apply where the claim is accompanied by a 'tribunal fee' (i.e. as defined by rule 1(1)) of some sort, albeit the wrong sort. This means that an employment tribunal will only be able to issue a notice to pay under rule 11(2) in very narrow circumstances – that is, where the wrong type of fee has been paid. If the claimant has simply made a mistake and submitted the wrong amount, rather than the wrong fee, it will not be a recognised 'tribunal fee' for the purposes of rule 11(1). Accordingly the claim will simply be rejected if only part of a 'tribunal fee' has been paid.

19.16 The Tribunal Rules are silent as to what happens if the claimant pays an amount that is *more* than the prescribed fee (and which is not a recognised tribunal fee). Strictly speaking, and by analogy with the above, the claim form is not accompanied by a 'tribunal fee' as defined and should therefore be rejected. However, it seems more likely that the tribunal would accept the claim and reimburse the surplus. But if such latitude can be allowed when the claimant pays too much, it is hard to see why some latitude should not be allowed if the claimant pays too little, particularly in view of the tribunal's overriding objective, which is to deal with cases 'fairly and justly' (see rule 2).

Given that the online system is set up to automatically calculate the fee (in response to the data inputted by the claimant), the likelihood of the wrong fee being paid electronically is low. That said, the system is not foolproof and there are potential pitfalls for claimants, particularly for those without the benefit of representation. It is, however, extremely unlikely that anything other than a recognised 'tribunal issue fee' will be paid when submitting the claim online, since the system is programmed only to calculate the issue fee for Type A and Type B claims respectively and it is not possible for the claimant to opt to pay a different amount. At worst, therefore, it seems that the claimant could end up paying a Type A fee for a Type B claim (or vice versa). Should this happen the claimant would be sent a notice under rule 11(2) to pay the £90 shortfall.

19.17 There is, perhaps, greater potential for error – at least so far as litigants in person are concerned – when submitting the claim form by post. In that case, although the claimant is provided with some information about fee levels (and is referred to the HMCTS fees guidance for further details), it is up to him or her to work out how much the fee is and draw up a cheque (or postal order) accordingly. It seems that if he or she sends an amount that is less than the required fee, even if by just £1, the claim form will – on a literal interpretation of rule 11(2) – be rejected *unless* the amount sent happens to be a recognised tribunal fee, which seems unlikely.

Impact of issue fee on tactical claims
19.18 It is not uncommon for claimants to issue tactical claims to protect their position. For example, if the employer and employee are still negotiating the

terms of a settlement agreement on the day of limitation, it is generally considered advisable for the claimant to submit a 'holding' tribunal claim pending the anticipated conclusion of the agreement. Under the new regime the claimant will have to pay an issue fee in order to do so with no hope of the employment tribunal reimbursing the fee in the likely scenario that the claim is subsequently withdrawn – see 'Reimbursement – reimbursement by employment tribunals' below. Of course, the employer may agree to refund the fee as part of the settlement but is not obliged to do so.

19.19 Tribunal hearing fee

If the claim is to proceed to a final hearing, the claimant must pay a further fee, known as the 'hearing fee' – Article 4(1)(b) Fees Order. Note, as with all employment tribunal fees, that a hearing fee is only payable if the claim was submitted on or after 29 July 2013 – Article 15 Fees Order.

19.20 Amount of hearing fee
There are two levels of hearing fee in the employment tribunal, depending upon whether the claim is a Type A or Type B claim – see 'Types of tribunal claim subject to fees' above and the Appendix to this chapter. The hearing fee for:

- Type A claims is £230 – Article 6 Fees Order
- Type B claims is £950 – Article 7 Fees Order.

A claimant only has to pay a single hearing fee irrespective of the number of claims being brought. If all the claims are Type A, the standard Type A fee is payable – Article 9(b). Where at least one of the claims is Type B, the hearing fee is charged at the standard Type B rate – Article 9(a). For example, a claim containing a complaint of unpaid wages (a Type A claim) and unfair dismissal (a Type B claim) would attract a single hearing fee at the Type B rate.

19.21
Unsurprisingly, the HMCTS fees guidance makes it clear that payment of the hearing fee does not guarantee that the hearing will go ahead on its listed date. The guidance states: 'If your hearing cannot go ahead on a particular date and you have paid a hearing fee, we will not ask you to pay a separate fee for the new hearing.'

19.22 Final hearing
A hearing fee is only payable in respect of the 'final hearing'. This is defined by Article 2 of the Fees Order 2013 as 'the first hearing at which an employment tribunal will determine liability, remedy or costs'. This differs from the definition of a final hearing set out in rule 57 of the Tribunal Rules; namely, 'a hearing at which the tribunal determines the claim or such parts as remain outstanding following the initial consideration (under rule 26) or any preliminary hearing'. Rule 57 goes on to state that 'there may be different final hearings for different

issues (for example, liability, remedy or costs)'. The definition of final hearing under the Order – i.e. the *first* hearing on liability, remedy or costs – ensures that the claimant only has to pay one hearing fee, no matter how many further hearings there may be on those issues. Final hearings are dealt with in Chapter 12, 'The hearing'.

What if a preliminary hearing is converted to a final hearing? Under rule 48 **19.23** of the Tribunal Rules (one of the rules common to all kinds of hearing), a tribunal conducting a preliminary hearing may order that it should be treated as a final hearing – for further details, see Chapter 11, 'Case management', under 'Preliminary hearings – conversion from preliminary hearing to final hearing'. However, it is unclear how the requirement to pay a final hearing fee impacts on the application of rule 48 in those cases where the fee has not yet been paid by the date of the preliminary hearing. It may be that the claimant would have to commit to paying the fee (or seeking remission) after the hearing in order for the final hearing to go ahead. Some support for this approach comes from the only EAT decision on the impact of the fees regime to date – Dozie v Addison Lee plc 2013 ICR D38, EAT. There, D brought her appeals at short notice without paying the requisite appeal fee (as to which, see 'EAT fees – appeal fee' below) and AL plc argued that they should therefore be struck out. The EAT acknowledged that changes to the Employment Appeal Tribunal Rules 1993 SI 1993/2854 meant that, where an appeal had been properly instituted (as in the instant case), it was liable to be struck out if an issue fee had not been paid or remission applied for. However, the EAT noted that a properly instituted appeal will remain extant until such a strike-out is effected and while, in the vast majority of cases, the EAT is unlikely to take action until the question of fees is resolved, in an urgent case such as this it was entitled to proceed and the appellant would be expected to pay the fee or apply for remission in due course. Whether or not tribunals adopt a similar tactic when converting a preliminary hearing to a final hearing under rule 48 remains to be seen. However, it should be noted that the fee in question in Dozie was an issue fee, not a final hearing fee, and that the EAT proceeded on the ground that the matter was urgent. The element of urgency is unlikely to arise in many tribunal cases.

Note that under rule 4(1)(b) of the Fees Order the obligation to pay a final hearing fee only arises 'on the date specified in a notice accompanying the notification of the listing of a final hearing of the claim' – see 'Timing of payment' below. It could therefore be argued that, as the claimant in a case where a preliminary hearing has been converted to a final hearing under rule 48 has not received a notice under rule 4, he or she is not required to pay a final hearing fee at all. However, this argument is unlikely to find favour with HMCTS.

Timing of payment of hearing fee **19.24**
Article 4(1)(b) states that the hearing fee is payable 'on a date specified in a notice accompanying the notification of the listing of a final hearing of the

985

claim'. The Order does not specify how far before the hearing the fee is payable. Indeed, it does not specify that the fee must be payable before the hearing at all (although in the vast majority of cases the payment date is likely to precede the hearing). The Government's response to its consultation on the introduction of fees is instructive in this regard. It indicated that it was its intention to require the hearing fee to be paid around four to six weeks before the hearing as 'that offers the best balance for allowing sufficient time for parties to engage in successful settlement negotiations whilst reducing the likelihood that unnecessary resource is consumed by the employment tribunals in terms of court, judicial and member time due to cancelled hearings'. However, it also acknowledged the point made in consultation responses that the hearing fee should only be charged once witness statements have been exchanged in order to ensure that both sides can assess the weight of the evidence, since it is only at that stage that detailed discussions on settlement can take place. The Government said that it would 'take this into consideration when a final decision is made on this issue' and expressed the view that 'by seeking the hearing fee near to the hearing date, as far as possible after disclosure and the exchange of witness statements, this will offer ample opportunity for parties to settle'.

In the end, the Order did not specify that the fee should be paid a prescribed number of weeks prior to the hearing or after exchange of witness statements. It merely states that the hearing fee is payable 'on a date specified in a notice accompanying the notification of the listing of a final hearing of the claim' – Article 4(1)(b). This appears to give tribunals a great deal of discretion as to when the hearing fee should be paid and may lead to a diversity of approaches in practice. As yet there has been no guidance issued by HMCTS on this issue, although such guidance might be useful in helping to ensure a consistent approach.

19.25 Method of payment of hearing fee
The HMCTS fees guidance states that the fee can either be paid online with a debit or credit card or by post in the form of a cheque or postal order. According to the guidance, full details of how to pay will be sent with the hearing notice.

19.26 Consequence of non-payment of hearing fee
Rule 40(1) of the Tribunal Rules states that where a party has not paid a 'relevant tribunal fee' (which includes the fee payable for a tribunal hearing), or presented a remission application in respect of that fee (see 'Remission' below), the employment tribunal will send the party a notice specifying a date for payment (or presentation of a remission application). Since rule 40 is expressed to be 'subject to rule 11', it applies to all fees except issue fees. (Rule 11 provides that a claim that is presented without an issue fee or a remission application will be rejected – see 'Issue fee – consequence of non-payment of issue fee' above.)

986

Rule 40(2)(a) provides that 'where the tribunal fee is payable in relation to a claim', the claim will be dismissed 'without further order' if, by the specified date, the party has not paid the fee (or presented a remission application). Since the issue fee is excluded from the remit of rule 40, this provision applies exclusively to the hearing fee, which is the only other tribunal fee 'payable in relation to a claim'. Rule 40(2)(a) does not specifically state what happens if the claimant pays only part of the hearing fee by the date in question. It is, however, implicit from the wording of this provision that the whole fee must be payable by that date, failing which the claim will be dismissed.

19.27 A party may apply for a dismissed claim or response, or part of it, to be reinstated under rule 40(5), following which the tribunal 'may order reinstatement'. The tribunal's power to do so is, however, discretionary and it is, as yet, unclear the extent to which this power will be exercised. We suggest that, all things being equal, the discretion should be exercised in a claimant's favour unless there are countervailing reasons not to do so. Note that the reinstatement order will only be effective if the fee is paid (or a remission application is presented and accepted) by the date specified in the order – rule 40(5). Again, it appears that the claimant must pay exactly the right fee for rule 40(5) to come into play. Strictly speaking, therefore, the claim of a claimant who pays slightly less (or indeed slightly more) than the correct fee payable will not be reinstated.

Application-specific tribunal fees

19.28 As well as the issue and hearing fee, there are also 'application-specific fees' in the employment tribunal, payable by the party who makes the application. These are dealt with by Article 11 of the Fees Order and listed in Schedule 1 to that Order. They are as follows:

Type of application	Type A claim	Type B claim
Reconsideration of a default judgment	£100	£100
Reconsideration of a judgment following a final hearing	£100	£350
Dismissal following withdrawal	£60	£60
An employer's contract claim by way of application as part of the response to the employee's contract claim	£160	–

Note that only one fee is charged per application 'irrespective of the number of claims or of claimants named in the application' – Article 11(1). As with all employment tribunal fees, the fees are only payable if the claim was submitted on or after 29 July 2013 – Article 15.

19.29 As can be seen, the first two applications for which fees are payable are for reconsideration – of 'default judgments' and of judgments following a final hearing. Rules 70–73 of the Tribunal Rules set out the procedure for tribunals to 'reconsider' judgments. It is similar to the 'review' procedure that existed under old rules 33–36 of the Tribunal Rules 2004 and is dealt with in Chapter 15, 'Reconsideration of tribunal judgments and decisions'. The third type of application is for dismissal of a claim following withdrawal. Such applications will ordinarily be made by the respondent employer to ensure that the claimant cannot bring a further claim against it raising the same complaint. Occasionally, however, a claimant employee may wish to apply to dismiss an employer's counterclaim if it is later withdrawn.

Interestingly, the submission of an 'employer's contract claim' – the equivalent to a 'counterclaim' under the Tribunal Rules 2004 – is also treated as an 'application' for the purpose of fees. However, this seems a slightly artificial label. Indeed, the Tribunal Rules 2013 do not treat this type of claim as an application – see rules 23–25 and 40(2) – and in reality it has more in common with a claimant's employment tribunal claim in that it may be rejected on the same basis under rule 12 (which deals with rejection for substantive defects), in which case rule 13 (which deals with reconsideration of rejected claims) applies – rule 23. For this reason the fee for an employer's contract claim is discussed in a separate section – see 'Fee for employer's contract claim' below.

We now turn to discuss the three other application-specific employment tribunal fees in more detail.

19.30 **Reconsideration of 'default' judgments**
Schedule 1 of the Fees Order stipulates that a fee of £100 must be paid in order to apply for reconsideration of a 'default judgment'. Interestingly, the term 'default judgment' is no longer used in the Tribunal Rules but the Fees Order is almost certainly referring to judgments under rule 21 of the Tribunal Rules 2013, which deals with judgments following the non-presentation or rejection of a response. On a literal reading, therefore, there is no requirement to pay a fee for reconsideration of a judgment made under rule 21 as this is not specifically referred to in the Fees Order. However, it is clear from the Order that it is intended that a fee should be payable in the circumstances covered by rule 21 and it would be unsafe for parties to rely on this technicality as a basis for not paying the appropriate fee when applying for a reconsideration of a judgment made under that provision.

Judgments under rule 21 are dealt with in Chapter 6, 'Defending a claim', under 'Rule 21: "default judgments"'. Reconsideration of such judgments is dealt with in Chapter 15, 'Reconsideration of tribunal judgments and decisions', under 'Reconsideration of a tribunal judgment – reconsideration of a default judgment'.

Reconsideration of 'final hearing' judgments
19.31

A fee is also charged when applying for 'reconsideration of a judgment following a final hearing' (see Schedule 1 to the Fees Order). Here the fee differs depending on the type of claim being reconsidered. If the reconsideration involves one or more Type B claims, the fee is £350. Otherwise (i.e. if the reconsideration involves only a Type A claim (or claims)), the fee is £100.

In order to understand the circumstances in which this type of fee is payable, it is necessary to examine the meaning of the terms 'judgment' and 'final hearing'.

Meaning of 'judgment'. A 'judgment' is defined in rule 1(3)(b) of the Tribunal **19.32** Rules as 'a decision, made at any stage of the proceedings (but not including a decision under rule 13 or 19), which finally determines –

- a claim, or part of a claim, as regards liability, remedy or costs (including preparation time and wasted costs);

- any issue which is capable of finally disposing of any claim, or part of a claim, even if it does not necessarily do so (for example, an issue whether a claim should be struck out or a jurisdictional issue); or

- the imposition of a financial penalty under S.12A of the Employment Tribunals Act 1996'.

Note that it is only a decision which finally determines a *claim* or any issue in a *claim* that can constitute a judgment for the purposes of reconsideration under rule 70. A 'claim' is defined in rule 1(1) as 'any proceedings before an employment tribunal making a complaint'. In turn, a 'complaint' means anything that is referred to as a 'claim, complaint, reference, application or appeal in any enactment which confers jurisdiction on the Tribunal'.

Further discussion of the meaning of 'judgment' (in the context of **19.33** reconsideration) can be found in Chapter 15, 'Reconsideration of tribunal judgments and decisions', under 'Reconsideration of a tribunal judgment – what decisions constitute a "judgment"?'.

Meaning of 'final hearing'. As noted under 'Tribunal hearing fee – final hearing' **19.34** above, a 'final hearing' is defined in Article 2 of the Fees Order as 'the first hearing at which an employment tribunal will determine liability, remedy or costs'. This differs from the definition of a final hearing set out in rule 57 of the Tribunal Rules; namely, 'a hearing at which the employment tribunal determines the claim or such parts as remain outstanding following the initial consideration (under rule 26) or any preliminary hearing'. Rule 57 goes on to state that 'there may be different final hearings for different issues (for example, liability, remedy or costs)'. The definition under the Order – i.e. the *first* hearing on liability, remedy or costs – ensures that there is only one hearing fee, no matter how many further hearings there may be under the Rules on those issues.

989

Arguably, this means that a fee for *reconsideration* of a final hearing judgment also only applies to the *first* hearing on liability, remedy or costs. If an application for reconsideration is made in respect of a judgment that follows a second or third hearing on liability, remedy or costs, no fee would be payable. Whether such an interpretation would find favour with HMCTS remains to be seen. It may well take the view that reconsideration of 'a judgment following a final hearing' is wide enough to cover *any* judgment that is made after the first hearing on liability, even if there are further hearings in between.

19.35 **Dismissal following withdrawal**
A £60 fee is charged for making an application to dismiss a claim that has been withdrawn (see Schedule 1 to the Fees Order). The advantage to the respondent of making such an application is that this ensures that the claimant may not commence a further claim against the respondent raising the same complaint. However, a respondent will seldom need to *apply* to have the claim dismissed since under rule 52 the tribunal will automatically issue a judgment dismissing a claim following its withdrawal unless:

- the claimant has expressed at the time of withdrawal a wish to reserve the right to bring such a further claim and the tribunal is satisfied that there would be legitimate reason for doing so, or

- the tribunal believes that to issue such a judgment would be contrary to the interests of justice.

But the Rules are silent as to when withdrawal takes effect. Nor is there any timeframe within which the employment tribunal must issue its judgment dismissing the claim. Furthermore, the Rules do not explain the process where a claim is settled via Acas. Where there is a delay in the tribunal dismissing a claim following withdrawal, the respondent may be minded to apply for the claim to be dismissed, in which case the £60 fee would be incurred. It is also worth noting that even if the tribunal makes a decision under rule 52 not to dismiss the claim, the respondent may still apply to the tribunal for dismissal following withdrawal (provided it pays the £60 fee). Withdrawal (and dismissal) of claims is considered further in Chapter 4, 'Starting tribunal proceedings', under 'Withdrawals'.

19.36 **Timing of payment of application fee**
The relevant fee does not need to be paid when the application is made to the employment tribunal. Rather, it is payable on a date specified by the Lord Chancellor in a notice following the making of the application – Article 4(2). According to the HMCTS fees guidance, the tribunal will write to the applicant after receipt of the application explaining what he or she needs to pay.

Consequence of non-payment of application fee
19.37

Rule 40(1) of the Tribunal Rules states that where a party has not paid a 'relevant Tribunal fee' (which includes all fees other than the issue fee), or presented a remission application in respect of that fee (see 'Remission' below), the employment tribunal will send the party a notice specifying a date for payment (or presentation of a remission application).

Rule 40(2)(c) goes on to provide that 'where the tribunal fee is payable in relation to an application, the application shall be dismissed without further order' if, by the specified date, the party has not paid the fee (or presented a remission application). Rule 40(2)(c) does not specifically state what happens if the applicant pays only part of the fee by the due date but it is implicit from the wording of the provision that the exact fee is payable and failure to pay the full amount will lead to the application being dismissed.

Application for claim/response to be reinstated. A party may apply for a **19.38** dismissed claim or response (or part of it) to be reinstated under rule 40(5), following which the employment tribunal '*may* order reinstatement' (our stress). It is, as yet, unclear as to the extent to which this discretionary power will be exercised. We suggest that, all things being equal, the discretion should be exercised in a claimant's favour unless there are countervailing reasons not to do so. Note that the reinstatement order will only be effective 'if the tribunal fee is paid' (or a remission application is presented and accepted) by the date specified in the order – rule 40(5). Again, it appears from the wording that the applicant must pay exactly the right fee for rule 40(5) to come into play.

Fee for employer's contract claim
19.39

As noted under 'Application-specific tribunal fees' above, the submission of an 'employer's contract claim' – the equivalent to a 'counterclaim' under the Tribunal Rules 2004 – is (somewhat artificially) treated as an 'application' for the purposes of tribunal fees. Therefore, unlike employment tribunal claims submitted by employees, there is no 'issue fee' to be paid at the time the employer's contract claim is made (and no automatic rejection if the fee is not paid). Instead, a fee is payable 'on a date specified by the Lord Chancellor in a notice following the making of the application' – Article 4(2). The £160 fee payable for what is effectively a counterclaim reflects the fact that a breach of contract claim is a Type A claim, for which the issue fee is £160.

The Government's decision to charge a fee for counterclaims was relatively uncontentious. According to the Government's response to its consultation on the introduction of employment tribunal and EAT fees, the majority of business respondents seemed to recognise that to charge for a claim but not a counterclaim would be unfair. The Government also said that it would consider whether it would be appropriate to seek a hearing fee from the employer where the

991

employee's breach of contract claim was withdrawn but the counterclaim proceeded to a hearing. However, although the introduction of a fee in these circumstances would seem to make sense, it was not included in the Order. Employers' contract claims are discussed in Chapter 6, 'Defending a claim', under 'Employer's contract claim'.

19.40 Timing of payment of employer's contract claim fee

As noted above, the fee for an employer's contract claim does not need to be paid when the 'application' is made to the employment tribunal. Rather, it is payable on a date specified by the Lord Chancellor in a notice following the making of the application – Article 4(2). However, the HMCTS guidance, 'Responding to a claim to an employment tribunal' (T422), intimates that the fee *can* be paid with the response and counterclaim if the respondent so wishes. It states: 'You do not *have* to pay the fee with your response, but *if you do not* the tribunal will write to you and explain how much you have to pay and how to pay it' (our stress).

19.41 Consequence of non-payment of employer's contract claim fee

Rule 40(1) of the Tribunal Rules 2013 states that where a party has not paid a 'relevant Tribunal fee' (which includes all fees other than the issue fee), or presented a remission application in respect of that fee (see 'Remission' below), the employment tribunal will send the party a notice specifying a date for payment (or presentation of a remission application). Rule 40(2)(c) provides that 'where the tribunal fee is payable in relation to an employer's contract claim, the employer's contract claim shall be dismissed without further order' if, by the specified date, the party has not paid the fee (or presented a remission application). Rule 40(1) does not specifically state what happens if the employer pays only part of the fee by the due date but it is implicit from the wording of this provision that the exact fee must be paid by the specified date to avoid the counterclaim being dismissed.

A decision to reject a respondent's counterclaim is treated in the same way as a decision to reject a claimant's claim for the purpose of reconsideration – rules 12 and 13. (The definition of a 'claim' in rule 1(1) can include an 'employer's contract claim'.) And, as with a claimant's claim, there is no provision for the respondent to apply for a 'reconsideration' (i.e. a review) of an employment tribunal's decision to dismiss a counterclaim on the basis of non-payment of fees (or failure to present a remission application) – see 'Tribunal issue fee – consequence of non-payment of issue fee' above for further details.

19.42 As with a claimant's claim, it may nonetheless be arguable that the rejection of a contract claim is open to reconsideration under the general power in rule 70. However, there appears to be an easier route for respondents in this regard. Rule 40(5) provides that in the event of a dismissal under rule 40(2) – which includes dismissal of an employer's contract claim (rule 40(2)(b)) – a party may apply for the claim or response to be reinstated and the tribunal 'may' order a reinstatement if the tribunal fee is paid by the date specified in the order. Therefore, it seems that a respondent whose counterclaim has been dismissed for non-payment of a fee can simply apply for it to be reinstated upon payment of the correct fee at a later date. Contrast this with claims rejected for non-payment under rule 11, which are expressly excluded from the remit of rule 40 – see 'Tribunal issue fee – consequence of non-payment of issue fee'.

Judicial mediation fee

19.43

A fee of £600 will be charged for 'judicial mediation' – Article 4(3) Fees Order. The fee is payable by the respondent employer 'on a date specified in a notice accompanying a notification of listing for judicial mediation'. As with all employment tribunal fees, a judicial mediation fee is only payable if the claim was submitted on or after 29 July 2013 – Article 15 Fees Order.

The requirement that the judicial mediation fee be paid by the respondent employer is the exception to the general principle that the party who seeks the order pays the fee. The Government's rationale for this is that in employment disputes the cost of mediation, if provided externally, is borne by the respondent.

It is perhaps worth noting that, according to the Government's response to its **19.44** consultation on the introduction of employment tribunal and EAT fees, employment tribunal judges were 'strongly opposed' to this fee, on the basis that it would act as a barrier to judicial mediation going ahead. In their view, mediation should be encouraged as it reduces the costs of running the system and improves or at least maintains the employment relationship.

What is judicial mediation?

19.45

The term 'judicial mediation' is not defined. However, it is understood that the 'judicial mediation' fee is intended to apply to the mediation scheme currently offered by the Employment Tribunals Service. 'Judicial mediation' is a relatively new and novel concept in the context of employment law. Following a 12-month pilot scheme launched by the Employment Tribunals Service in 2006, S.7B was inserted into the Employment Tribunals Act 1996 by the Tribunals, Courts and Enforcement Act 2007. The section envisages a role for 'judicial mediation' in employment tribunal proceedings (although it does not specifically use that terminology) and allows for regulations to be made which would enable practice directions to provide for tribunal panel members and employment tribunal staff to act as mediators 'in relation to disputed matters in a case that is subject to proceedings'.

Regulation 11 of the Employment Tribunals (Constitution and Rules of Procedure) Regulations 2013 SI 2013/1237 ('the Tribunal Regulations') duly

993

enables the President of the Employment Tribunals to make practice directions about 'the provision by employment judges of mediation, in relation to disputed matters in a case that is the subject of proceedings, and may permit an employment judge to act as mediator in a case even though they have been selected to decide matters in that case'. No practice direction on 'judicial mediation' has yet been issued, although this has not prevented the introduction of the judicial mediation fee.

19.46 Consequence of non-payment of judicial mediation fee

The ultimate consequence of non-payment of this fee is simply that judicial mediation will not go ahead – rule 40(2)(d) Tribunal Rules.

19.47 Reimbursement

In this section, we consider the scope for an employment tribunal fee to be reimbursed – either by the tribunal itself or by the other side.

19.48 Reimbursement by employment tribunal

There is little scope for the employment tribunal to refund a fee once it has been paid as neither the Fees Order nor the Tribunal Rules make any provision for this. As the Law Society pointed out in its response to the Government's fees consultation, this may have the effect of discouraging settlement of the dispute: 'If a fee is non-refundable, a party may take the view that they have made the investment and, therefore, may as well proceed. This is counter to the objective of encouraging settlement where possible.'

19.49 Mistake made by employment tribunal.

The Government did concede in its consultation response that if there was an administrative error and two fees were taken by mistake, one would be refunded. However, this is not specifically stated in either the Rules or the Order. Rule 69 – which deals with correction of clerical mistakes and accidental slips – provides that an employment judge may at any time 'correct any clerical mistake or other accidental slip or omission in any *order, judgment or other document* produced by a tribunal' (our stress), but this does not appear to apply to mistakes made in respect of fees. Nevertheless, natural justice clearly requires an employment tribunal that mistakenly processes more than the legally required fee to reimburse the surplus.

19.50 Mistake made by claimant/applicant.

The HMCTS fees guidance only makes one reference to reimbursement of fees by the employment tribunal. It provides that if the tribunal realises that a claimant has paid a Type B fee but has only made a Type A claim, it will refund the difference. Interestingly, it does not state what would happen if the claimant (or applicant) mistakenly pays an amount that does not reflect a recognised tribunal fee, e.g. pays an issue fee of £180 for a Type A claim instead of £160 (which does not equate to the issue fee of £250 for a Type B claim). A strict reading of the Tribunal Rules suggests that such an overpayment would mean that the claimant (or applicant) has failed to pay a 'tribunal fee' as defined. The ramifications of this are discussed under 'Tribunal issue fee (payable by claimant) – consequence of non-payment of issue fee' above. Basically, if the claimant pays an amount that is more than the prescribed issue fee (and which is not a recognised tribunal fee) when submitting the claim form, then strictly speaking the claim form is not accompanied by a 'tribunal fee' as defined and should be rejected. Whether or not tribunals in practice simply accept the claim and reimburse the surplus remains to be seen.

Rejection of claim. An employment tribunal is not required to reimburse an **19.51** issue fee if it does not accept the claim – i.e. if the claim is rejected for a technical defect under rule 10 or a substantive defect under rule 12 (and the decision to reject is not overturned following reconsideration). Rejection of claims for technical or substantive defects is dealt with in Chapter 4, 'Starting tribunal proceedings', under 'Processing the claim form – rejection of claim'. Reconsideration of a decision to reject a claim is discussed in the same chapter under 'Processing the claim form – reconsideration of rejection'.

Withdrawal of claim shortly after submission. An employment tribunal is **19.52** not required to reimburse an issue fee if the claim is withdrawn shortly after it has been submitted. It is not uncommon for claimants to issue tactical claims to protect their position. For example, if employer and employee are still negotiating the terms of a settlement agreement on the day of limitation, it is generally considered advisable for the claimant to submit a 'holding' claim pending the anticipated conclusion of the agreement. Now the claimant will have to pay an issue fee in order to do so with no hope of the employment tribunal reimbursing the fee if the claim is subsequently withdrawn. Of course, the employer may agree to refund the fee as part of the settlement but is not obliged to do so.

Tribunal hearing does not take place. Once a hearing fee is paid, there is no **19.53** provision for it to be refunded if the case does not in fact go to a hearing. The Government's justification for this, as set out in its consultation response, is that the hearing fee secures the 'opportunity to have a hearing', not the hearing itself. Some respondents to the Government consultation argued that not refunding a hearing fee where the claim is settled was unfair. Moreover, it was argued that the lack of a refund would discourage settlement because either the respondent would wait to see if the claimant paid the hearing fee or the claimant would refuse to settle because he or she wanted the hearing he or she had paid for. The HMCTS fees guidance states that fees should be discussed as part of any agreement reached. In some cases, for example, the respondent may agree to reimburse any fees paid as part of the settlement.

It seems that the Government adopted the approach it did in order to tackle the 'culture of waiting until near to or the day of the hearing to settle or withdraw the case'. Now parties are more likely to settle or withdraw the case a day or two before the hearing fee is due, although the incentive for the respondent to do so is less acute, given that it does not have to pay a hearing fee. In this regard, the Government noted in its consultation response that by waiting until after a hearing fee has been paid before engaging in settlement negotiations, respondents increase their own potential financial liability as employment tribunals have the power to order them to pay the claimant's fees if he or she is successful at the hearing (see 'Reimbursement by other side' below). Furthermore, an employment judge can make an order for costs (if the party is represented) or for preparation time (if the party is unrepresented or represented by a lay person) if it is clear that unnecessary delaying tactics have resulted in increased costs. Costs and preparation time orders are dealt with in Chapter 20, 'Costs and penalties'.

19.54 **Reimbursement by other side**

As discussed under 'Reimbursement by employment tribunal' above, the scope for reimbursement by an employment tribunal is extremely limited. The main way in which a claimant (or respondent, as the case may be) can get a fee reimbursed is by applying for a costs order against the other side. A costs order for these purposes is an order requiring one party ('the paying party') to make a payment to another party ('the receiving party') in respect of a tribunal fee paid by the receiving party – rule 75(1)(b). The deadline for making the application is 28 days after the date on which the judgment finally determining the proceedings was sent to the parties – rule 77.

Rule 76(4) gives tribunals the power to award costs of the kind described in rule 75(1)(b) where the receiving party has paid a tribunal fee in respect of a 'claim, employer's contract claim or application'. It therefore covers the issue fee, the hearing fee (payable by the employee), the fee for submitting a counterclaim (payable by the employer) and the 'application-specific fees' for reconsideration or for dismissal following withdrawal (payable by the party who makes the application). However, it does not cover the fee for judicial mediation (payable by the employer).

19.55 Rule 76(4) only applies where the claim, counterclaim or application is decided, in whole or in part, in favour of the receiving party. In other words, it can only be made in favour of a successful (or partially successful) party who has paid a fee. Therefore a party cannot seek an order for reimbursement if he or she has lost the case (or the particular point at issue).

19.56 **Power to order reimbursement is discretionary.** A tribunal's power to order reimbursement is discretionary; i.e. reimbursement does not automatically follow if a fee-paying party is successful. Nevertheless, the discretion is likely to be exercised in the majority of cases to reimburse successful claimants for sums paid in respect of the issue and hearing fees. As noted in the HMCTS fees guidance, 'the general position is that, if you are successful, the respondent will be ordered to reimburse you'. It does, however, go on to state that 'ultimately it is for the tribunal to decide whether it is appropriate that the respondent should reimburse you some or all of the fees you have paid, if you are successful'.

In UNISON's recent judicial review of the introduction of employment tribunal and EAT fees – R (on the application of UNISON) v Lord Chancellor (Equality and Human Rights Commission intervening) 2014 IRLR 266, QBD – the High Court noted that the Lord Chancellor is to place on the Ministry of Justice website, as soon as possible, updated guidance stating that the general position is that a successful employee should expect to recover from the employer the fees he or she has incurred. Consideration is also being given to amending rule 76(4) of the Tribunal Rules and rule 34 of the Employment Appeal Tribunal Rules 1993 SI 1993/2854 ('the EAT Rules') so as to make this expectation clear. (This case is discussed in greater detail in the introduction to this chapter under 'Legal challenge to fees regime'.)

19.57 In the only reported case to date on question of fee reimbursement – Portnykh v Nomura International plc 2014 IRLR 251, EAT (which involved reimbursement of the appeal hearing fee) – the EAT made a conditional costs order under rule 34A(2A) of the EAT Rules requiring a respondent to repay the appellant's £1,600 fees in respect of his successful appeal against an employment tribunal's case management decisions. However, by the time his appeal succeeded, his remission application had yet to be decided and the EAT therefore made the order conditional on the appellant's pending application for a fee remission being rejected. This case is discussed in greater detail under 'EAT fees – reimbursement' below.

19.58 **Amount of the order.** Rule 78(1)(c) stipulates that the employment tribunal may order reimbursement of all or part of the tribunal fee. If the party is wholly successful in his or her application or claim, it appears likely that a tribunal will order reimbursement of the whole fee. However, as noted above, an order can also be made where a fee-paying party's claim or application is successful *in part*. In such circumstances, the tribunal may have to decide what amount of the tribunal fee it is appropriate to award.

'Fee group' claims

19.59

Articles 8–10 of the Fees Order deal with the issue and hearing fees for 'fee group' claims, i.e. claims involving more than one claimant. Group issue and hearing fees are higher than their 'single claimant' fee counterparts – the idea being that the respective fee will be divided between each member of the group.

As with single claimant fees, the group fee is payable:

- in the case of the issue fee, when the claim form is presented to an employment tribunal

- in the case of the hearing fee, on a date specified in a notice accompanying the notification of the listing of the final hearing of the claim – Article 4(1) Fees Order.

19.60 Definition of 'fee group'

'Fee group' is defined by Article 2 as 'the group of persons named as claimants in the claim form *at the time the claim was presented*' (our stress) – Article 2. It therefore does not include claimants who are joined to proceedings later on and are therefore not named in the original claim. It appears that such claimants will be treated as single claimants for the purpose of both the issue fee *and* the hearing fee. This is confirmed by the HMCTS guidance, 'Employment tribunal fees for groups and multiples' (T436), which states that 'if you start your claim as an individual you will pay the single hearing fee. Any decision an employment judge makes on the best way to decide your claim does not affect the fee you must pay.' In other words, a claimant can be joined to other tribunal proceedings for the purposes of his or her claim but will still be treated as a 'single claimant' for the purposes of any hearing fee. This represents something of a windfall for the HMCTS, as it will receive one or more additional hearing fees for the same hearing.

19.61 Amount of fee

The issue fee and hearing fee payable by a 'fee group' are higher than those payable by an individual claimant. The application-specific tribunal fees, on the other hand, remain fixed no matter how many claimants there are. The level of the group issue/hearing fee differs depending on how many people are in the group. The relevant group fee levels are set out in Table 4 of Schedule 2 to the Fees Order and are as follows:

Type A claim(s) Number of claimants	Issue fee	Hearing fee
2–10	£320	£460
11–200	£640	£920
Over 200	£960	£1,380
Type B claim(s)* Number of claimants	Issue fee	Hearing fee
2–10	£500	£1,900
11–200	£1,000	£3,800
Over 200	£1,500	£5,700

or a mixture of Type A and Type B claims

998

As can be seen, where there are between two and ten claimants, the total issue/ **19.62** hearing fee payable per group is twice the amount of the 'single claimant' fee; for between 11 and 200 claimants, it is four times as much; and where there are over 200 claimants, six times as much. As the Impact Assessment on the introduction of fees in the employment jurisdiction explained, this will mean that in a case where seven claims have been made against the same employer, the seven claimants collectively will pay twice the relevant single claim fee between them. Similarly, if there are 30 claims made against an employer, then all 30 claimants collectively will be liable to pay four times the single claim fee. Therefore, in general, the average fee paid by a claimant in a given multiple will fall as the total number of claims increases. For completeness, however, Article 10(a) states that 'any fee payable by a fee group... must not exceed an amount equal to the sum of the fees which the members of the fee group would have been liable to pay as single claimants'.

The rationale behind group fees is that the respective fee will be divided between each member of the group. However, since the claim form must be 'accompanied by the fee', it is not possible for each claimant to send their part of the fee separately. The HMCTS guidance, 'Employment tribunal fees for groups and multiples' (T436), states that both the group issue fee and the group hearing fee must be submitted as a single payment. Indeed, when submitting a group claim online, it is *only* possible to make a single online payment (by credit or debit card). Strictly speaking, it may be possible for a posted claim form to be accompanied by several cheques, representing each claimant's share of the group fee (provided that they add up to the total group fee due). However, to be on the safe side, a single cheque for the total amount should be sent. Indeed, the HMCTS guidance states that if several cheques are sent by post (in respect of either the issue fee or the hearing fee), it 'might' return them. In addition, in respect of the hearing fee, the guidance states that if payment is not made *in the right way* and on time, the hearing could be delayed or struck out.

Failure to pay the whole group fee   19.63
The *whole* group issue fee must be paid if the claim is to be accepted. There is no scope for the tribunal to accept the claim in respect of those claimants who have paid their share of the issue fee and reject it in respect of those who have failed to do so. This is because rule 11(1) states that the claim must be accompanied by a recognised 'tribunal fee' in order for it to be accepted – see 'Tribunal issue fee – paying the wrong amount' above. So, for example, if there are 11 claimants bringing a Type A claim, the issue fee is £640, amounting to £58.18 each. If ten out of the 11 claimants pay their share it seems that the *whole* claim will be rejected since the total amount paid (£581.80) is not a recognised 'tribunal fee'. The full £640 would need to be paid in order for a group claim involving 11 claimants to be accepted.

999

In the case of the hearing fee, Rule 40(1) provides that where a party has not paid a 'relevant tribunal fee' (which includes a hearing fee, but not an issue fee), or presented a remission application in respect of that fee, the tribunal will send the party a notice specifying a date for payment or presentation of a remission application – see 'Hearing fee – consequence of non-payment' above. Again, the *whole* group fee must be paid if the claim is to proceed to a hearing. Failure to pay the amount outstanding will lead to the entire claim being dismissed (i.e. even in respect of those who have paid their share of the hearing fee) – rule 40(2)(a). A claimant who wishes to continue with the claim must – before the date on which the claim is liable to be dismissed for non-payment – notify the Lord Chancellor under Article 12(1) of the Fees Order of his or her decision to no longer be part of the group. This is discussed under 'Electing to become a single claimant' below.

19.64 Electing to become a single claimant

If a claim has been rejected for non-payment of the group issue fee (in whole or in part) – and the time limit for presentation of the claim has yet to expire – a claimant can submit a claim on his or her own behalf and pay the 'single claimant' issue fee. If the time limit has expired, he or she would need to convince the employment tribunal to extend the deadline on the basis either that it was not reasonably practicable to submit the claim in time or that it is just and equitable to do so, depending upon the type of claim at issue. Where a claimant has run out of time because his or her original group claim was rejected on the ground that one or more of the other claimants failed to pay their share of the group issue fee, an employment tribunal may be willing to extend the limitation period, provided the claimant has not waited too long to resubmit his or her claim. Time limits for presenting tribunal claims are discussed in Chapter 5, 'Time limits'.

If a group claim has successfully been submitted but the group hearing fee remains unpaid (in whole or in part) after the due date specified in the notice issued by the tribunal under Article 4(1)(b), a member of the fee group can elect to become a 'single claimant'. Article 12(1) of the Fees Order provides that 'where a fee payable by a fee group remains unpaid after the date specified... a member of that fee group may, before the date on which the claim to which the fee relates is liable to be dismissed for non payment, notify the Lord Chancellor of that member's decision no longer to be part of the group'. Where such notice has been given, the claimant will be treated as a 'single claimant' for the purposes of the claim – Article 12(2). Thus a group claimant who receives a notice of non-payment of the group fee under rule 40(1) can write to the tribunal before the date on which the claim will be struck out expressing his or her wish to be separated from the fee group. Presumably, although this is not expressly stated, he or she will then be sent a separate notice specifying a date for payment of the 'single claimant' hearing fee.

Note that it does not appear to be possible for two or more members to 'break **19.65** away' from a fee group and be treated as a separate, smaller fee group. The only option for claimants wishing to leave a fee group is for them each to be treated as a 'single claimant' and each to pay the 'single claimant' fee.

EAT fees 19.66

Part 3 of the Fees Order deals with fees in the EAT. There are two different types of EAT fee:

- the appeal fee of £400 payable on submission of a notice of appeal (or cross-appeal), and
- the hearing fee of £1,200.

These amounts are set and do not vary according to the number of appellants or the nature of the claim or claims under appeal.

Appeal fee 19.67

A fee of £400 is payable by a party who submits a notice of appeal against an employment tribunal decision – Article 13 Fees Order. This could be either the employee or the employer, depending upon who is appealing. The fee is described as a 'logement fee' in the HMCTS guidance, 'Employment Appeal Tribunal fees' (T437).

Para 4.3 of the current EAT Practice Direction (which came into force on 29 July 2013) states that a fee is payable in respect of each separate decision appealed against. It also stipulates that if separate heads of claim are decided on separate occasions and separate judgments given – or if there are separate judgments or orders as to case management, or on preliminary issues, liability or compensation – they will be treated as separate decisions and a fee will be payable in respect of each of them in the event of an appeal. The fee is fixed at £400, irrespective of the number of appellants and the nature of the claim (or claims) being appealed, and is payable 'on the date specified in a notice issued by the Lord Chancellor' following receipt by the EAT of the notice of appeal. It does not, therefore, have to be paid when the notice of appeal is presented to the EAT.

Note that an appeal fee is only payable where the notice of appeal was received by the EAT on or after 29 July 2013 – Article 16 Fees Order.

Cross-appeal. According to para 12.2 of the Practice Direction, if a respondent's **19.68** answer to an appeal contains a cross-appeal, the respondent must pay a fee in respect of the cross-appeal in the same way that an appellant pays a fee in respect of the appeal. However, this does not accord with Article 13 of the Fees Order, which states that a 'fee... is payable by an appellant on the date specified in a notice issued by the Lord Chancellor, following the receipt by the EAT of a *notice of appeal*' (our stress). 'Notice of appeal' is defined in the Order as a

1001

notice referred to in rule 3(1)(a) of the Employment Appeal Tribunal Rules 1993 SI 1993/2854 ('the EAT Rules'), which does not include a cross-appeal contained within an answer under rule 6 of the EAT Rules. Moreover, the HMCTS guidance states that no fees are payable by a respondent who cross-appeals. As para 4.1 of the Practice Direction makes it clear that the Practice Direction is subject to the Order, we would respectfully suggest that a respondent is *not* liable to pay any form of fee in respect of a cross-appeal contained within an answer to an appeal.

19.69 Hearing fee

A hearing fee of £1,200 (regardless of the number of appellants and the nature of the claim or claims under appeal) is payable by the appellant(s) following a direction by the EAT that a matter proceed to a hearing at which the appeal is to be finally disposed of – Article 14 Fees Order. The hearing fee will become due on a date specified in a notice issued by the Lord Chancellor. Para 12.1 of the Practice Direction states that, until the hearing fee is paid (or a remission granted), the appeal will not be listed for hearing and the non-payment may result in the appeal being struck out at this stage.

Note that a hearing fee is only payable where the notice of appeal was received by the EAT on or after 29 July 2013 – Article 16 Fees Order.

19.70 Consequence of non-payment

Where, on receipt of a notice of appeal or after a direction by the EAT that a matter proceed to an oral hearing, the Lord Chancellor has issued a notice to the appellant specifying that a fee is payable and the appellant has not paid the fee (or presented a remission application – see 'Remission' below), on or before the date specified in that notice, the Registrar must strike out an appeal – rule 17A(1) EAT Rules.

Where an appeal has been struck out under rule 17A(1) the appellant may apply to have it reinstated by the Registrar if the fee specified in the Lord Chancellor's notice has been paid or where a remission application has been presented and accepted – rule 17A(4). Para 4.5 of the EAT Practice Direction explains that 'if an appeal is struck out for non-payment of fee/failure to apply for remission it is open to the intending appellant to seek reinstatement, provided the application is made promptly. Any such application will be treated as an interim application under Rules 19 and 20 [of the EAT Rules] and be considered by the Registrar. The grant of relief is entirely discretionary, and applicants have no right to demand it. They are unlikely to succeed unless there is clear evidence that the fee has been paid beforehand, or that an application for remission has been made, together in either case with a good explanation why the fee was not paid within the time prescribed.'

In Dozie v Addison Lee plc 2013 ICR D38, EAT, the EAT held that a properly **19.71** instituted appeal would remain extant until a strike out is effected. Furthermore, while in the vast majority of cases the EAT is unlikely to take action until the question of fees is resolved, in an urgent case (such as an appeal against a refusal by the tribunal to postpone a hearing) the Appeal Tribunal would be entitled to proceed with the appeal. In such a case, the appellant would be expected to pay the fee or apply for a remission in due course, and if a fee is payable, would be entitled to apply to the EAT for an order that the respondent reimburse it under rule 34A(2A) of the EAT Rules – see 'Reimbursement' below.

The approach taken by the EAT in Dozie appears to have been open to it given that, unlike the issue fee that must accompany claims to the employment tribunal, the EAT fee is only payable when, upon receipt of the appeal by the EAT, the Lord Chancellor issues a notice specifying that a fee is payable, not when the appeal is presented. This is confirmed in para 4.2 of the Practice Direction.

Reimbursement 19.72
Rule 34A(2A) of the EAT Rules allows for the reimbursement of 'any fee paid by the appellant under a notice issued by the Lord Chancellor' via a costs order against the respondent. Para 22.1 of the Practice Direction confirms that this can include employment tribunal, as well as EAT, fees paid by appellants.

The EAT can award costs of any amount no greater than any fee paid by the appellant where the appeal has been allowed, in full or in part. However, this power is discretionary and an order will not automatically be made if a fee-paying party is successful upon appeal. If, for example, the appellant succeeds on a technicality the EAT may decide that it is not appropriate to order the respondent to reimburse any fee paid. And if an appeal is only partially successful, the EAT may also decide that reimbursement is not appropriate. Alternatively, it may decide to award a proportion of any fee paid to reflect the proportion of the appeal that was successful.

It is of interest in this regard that in UNISON's recent application for judicial **19.73** review of the introduction of employment tribunal and EAT fees – R (on the application of UNISON) v Lord Chancellor (Equality and Human Rights Commission intervening) 2014 IRLR 266, QBD – the High Court noted that the Lord Chancellor is to place on the Ministry of Justice website, as soon as possible, updated guidance stating that the general position is that a successful employee should expect to recover from the employer the fees he or she has incurred. Consideration is also being given to amending rule 76(4) of the Tribunal Rules and rule 34 of the EAT Rules so as to make this expectation clear. (This case is discussed in greater detail in the introduction to this chapter under 'Legal challenge to fees regime'.)

In Portnykh v Nomura International plc 2014 IRLR 251, EAT, P appealed against an employment tribunal's case management decisions in his claim of

1003

unfair dismissal. He paid a hearing fee in relation to the appeal and applied for fee remission. However, by the time his appeal succeeded, his remission application had yet to be decided. The EAT considered whether it should order NI plc to repay all or part of the fee P had paid via a costs order under rule 34A(2A). It thought it doubtful that it would be able to make an order requiring the fees to be repaid in the event that the remission was successful, as neither the EAT Rules nor the Practice Direction make express or even implied provision for this situation. However, the EAT did not see any reason why it should not make a contingent order postponing payment until the outcome of the fee remission application is known and making payment conditional upon the application being rejected.

In considering whether to make such an order in the instant case, the EAT did not think that there should be any distinction between somebody who has paid a fee in order to get a case put back onto the right track in an interlocutory appeal and somebody who appeals against the outcome of a merits hearing. Nor did it take into account the fact that P had conducted the litigation in an unhelpful and uncooperative way, as this had made no significant difference to the conduct of the appeal. The EAT therefore concluded that NI plc should reimburse P's fee of £1,600. NI plc had the means to pay and, looking at the matter broadly, had substantially lost on the appeal. However, the EAT ordered that the sum should only be payable if P's application for fee remission is refused, in which case it had to be paid within 14 days of that refusal.

19.74 Fee remission

A system of fee waivers and reductions, known as the remission scheme, is in place for those who may have difficulty paying employment tribunal and EAT fees. The scheme – governed by Articles 17 and 18 of and Schedule 3 to the Fees Order – allows access to employment tribunals and the EAT either free of charge (a full remission) or at a reduced rate (a partial remission). When the Order originally came into force on 29 July 2013, the remission scheme was based on the one that applied in the civil courts at the time. However, a new remission scheme was brought into force on 7 October 2013 by the Courts and Tribunals Fee Remissions Order 2013 SI 2013/2302 ('the Remissions Order') for all courts and tribunals administered by HMCTS (including employment tribunals and the EAT), as well as the Supreme Court. A new Schedule 3 was duly inserted into the Fees Order 2013 to reflect this change. Guidance on the new scheme, entitled 'Court and Tribunal Fees – do I have to pay them?' (EX160A), has been produced by HMCTS. It is referred to throughout this section as 'the HMCTS remission guidance'.

In order to qualify for remission under the new scheme, an applicant must satisfy two tests. The first assesses disposable capital – see 'Disposable capital test' below. If the applicant satisfies this test, his or her gross monthly income

(GMI) will then be calculated in order to decide whether or not he or she is entitled to full (or partial) remission – see 'Gross monthly income test' below. In other words, both tests must be met in order for the applicant to be successful. If a party 'fails' either test, he or she will not be entitled to remission unless there are 'exceptional circumstances' which justify it – see 'Exceptional circumstances' below.

The guidance describes what appears to be a separate basis for full remission **19.75** – receipt of certain means-tested benefits, such as income-based jobseeker's allowance. This is described as 'Remission 1' both in the guidance and on the remission application form found at the back of the guidance. Remission based upon GMI is described as 'Remission 2'. However, Schedule 3 makes no mention of remission based upon a means-tested benefit and it seems that rather than a separate type of remission, 'Remission 1' is actually a subset of remission based upon GMI; i.e. evidence of certain means-tested benefits will be accepted as proof that the GMI test is satisfied. This is discussed further under 'Gross monthly income test – full remission based upon receipt of a specified benefit' below.

Who can apply for remission?   19.76
Entitlement to remission under Schedule 3 of the Fees Order is accorded to a 'party', defined as 'the individual who would, but for this Schedule, be liable to pay the fee required under this Order' – para 1(1). Therefore, only *individual* parties can apply for remission. This is confirmed by the HMCTS remission guidance, which explains that companies, charities or other organisations cannot apply for a fee remission. However, the guidance confirms that sole traders – meaning those who are responsible for running their own business as an individual and who are directly and solely responsible for the losses the business makes – are eligible to apply for a fee remission. It goes on: 'You are not a sole trader if your business is a limited company, an "ordinary" business partnership, a limited partnership, or a limited liability partnership; if your business pays corporation tax, or if your business is registered with Companies House'.

The guidance also states that prisoners can apply for remission, as can individuals who live outside the UK or are foreign nationals (although it points out that the means-tested benefits that qualify for full remission are only available to people who live in the UK, Republic of Ireland, Channel Islands or Isle of Man – see further 'Gross monthly income test – full remission based upon receipt of a specified benefit' below).

Paragraph 18 of Schedule 3 provides that a party is not entitled to fee remission **19.77** if he or she is in receipt of legal aid – in the form of legal representation – under Part 1 of the Legal Aid, Sentencing and Punishment of Offenders Act 2012 (which only applies to England and Wales, subject to minor exceptions that are not relevant for the purposes of this discussion) – S.152. By way of background, this Act drastically narrowed the scope for claiming legal assistance as from April 2013. Part 1 of Schedule 1 to the Act sets out the types of claim for which 'civil legal services' (legal aid) is still available, the most important for employment law purposes being claims for contravention of the Equality Act 2010 (or a previous discrimination enactment). Few of the other claims listed have any relevance to employment law. Furthermore, legal aid is not available for advocacy in employment tribunals and is only available for advocacy in the EAT in relation to discrimination claims. Therefore, the scope of para 18 is, in essence, restricted to discrimination appeals.

19.78 Disposable capital test
The disposable capital test is set out in paras 3–10 of Schedule 3. In order for applicants to satisfy the test, their disposable capital must not exceed prescribed thresholds – see 'Disposable capital thresholds' below. It is important to understand that satisfaction of this test does not mean that the applicant qualifies for remission. It merely allows his or her gross monthly income (GMI) to be assessed, which will ultimately decide the issue. If the applicant does not satisfy the disposable capital test, he or she will not qualify for remission and the GMI test becomes redundant.

19.79 Disposable capital thresholds. For applicants aged 61 or over there is a single disposable capital threshold (DCT) of £16,000, irrespective of the level of fee to be paid. The same single threshold applies for younger applicants whose partners are 61 or over. For all other applicants the DCT varies depending upon the level of fee being charged. The thresholds are set out in Table 1 of Schedule 3 as follows:

Fee charged	Disposable capital threshold
Up to £1,000	£3,000
£1,001 to £1,335	£4,000
£1,336 to £1,665	£5,000
£1,666 to £2,000	£6,000
£2,001 to £2,330	£7,000
£2,331 to £4,000	£8,000
£4,001 to £5,000	£10,000
£5,001 to £6,000	£12,000
£6,001 to £7,000	£14,000
£7,001 or more	£16,000

As can be seen from the above table, the DCT is £3,000 where the fee charged is £1,000 or less and since no employment tribunal fee currently exceeds

£1,000, the DCT will be £3,000 whatever type of fee is at issue. For EAT fees the DCT will be £3,000 for the (£400) appeal fee but £4,000 for the (£1,200) hearing fee. Note that the fee bands set out in Table 1 are not based upon the cumulative value of the fees (or prospective fees) throughout the proceedings. If an individual submits a Type B claim – which would incur a £250 issue fee and potentially a £950 hearing fee – the DCT is £3,000 in respect of each fee, not £4,000 in respect of the combined (£1,200) total.

What is disposable capital? Disposable capital is defined in para 5 as 'the **19.80** value of every resource of a capital nature belonging to the party on the date on which the application for remission is made, unless it is treated as income by this Order, or it is disregarded as excluded disposable capital'. Capital resources held abroad count towards disposable capital – para 7(1).

The HMCTS remission guidance gives the following examples of disposable capital:

- all capital held in any type of saving account; for example, ISAs, fixed rate bonds and market linked investment bonds
- redundancy capital payments
- stocks or shares
- any jointly held capital (where one or more parties have a financial interest in a disposable capital source). The parties will be treated as owning equal shares unless evidence to the contrary is produced – para 9
- second homes
- trust funds (where accessible), or any other fund available to the applicant
- any type of capital financial product (for example, unit trusts, Open-Ended Investment Company products, or derivatives).

Excluded disposable capital. Paragraph 10 sets out the following list of **19.81** excluded disposable capital (i.e. disposable capital that is not taken into account for the purpose of calculating DCTs):

- a property which is the main or only dwelling occupied by the party
- the household furniture and effects of the main or only dwelling occupied by the party
- articles of personal clothing
- any vehicle, the sale of which would leave the party, or their partner, without motor transport
- tools and implements of trade, including vehicles used for business purposes

1007

- the capital value of the party's or their partner's business, where the party or their partner is self-employed

- the capital value of any funds or other assets held in trust, where the party or their partner is a beneficiary without entitlement to advances of any trust capital

- a jobseeker's back-to-work bonus

- a payment made as a result of a determination of unfair dismissal by a court or tribunal, or by way of settlement of a claim for unfair dismissal

- any compensation paid as a result of a determination of medical negligence or in respect of any personal injury by a court, or by way of settlement of a claim for medical negligence or personal injury

- the capital held in any personal or occupational pension scheme

- any cash value payable on surrender of a contract of insurance

- any capital payment made out of the Independent Living Funds

- any bereavement payment

- any capital insurance or endowment lump sum payments that have been paid as a result of illness, disability or death

- any student loan or student grant

- any payments under the criminal injuries compensation scheme.

19.82 **Partner's capital.** Paragraph 14 of Schedule 3 stipulates that the disposable capital of an applicant's partner is to be treated as the applicant's disposable capital *unless* the partner has a 'contrary interest... in the matter to which the fee relates'. 'Partner' means 'a person with whom the party lives as a couple and includes a person with whom the party is not currently living but from whom the party is not living separate and apart' – para 1(1). 'Couple' is defined as:

- a man and woman who are married to each other and are neither (i) separated under a court order, nor (ii) separated in circumstances in which the separation is likely to be permanent

- a man and woman who are not married to each other but are living together as husband and wife

- two people of the same sex who are civil partners and are neither (i) separated under a court order, nor (ii) separated in circumstances in which the separation is likely to be permanent, or

- two people of the same sex who are not civil partners but are living together as if they were civil partners – para 1(1), Sch 3.

The HMCTS remission guidance states that a couple who are both parties in a multiple fee group can be considered as having a 'contrary interest'.

Assessing the value of non-monetary capital. Where disposable capital is in **19.83** non-monetary form (for example, a second home), its value is calculated based on the amount it would realise if sold, less:

- 10 per cent of the sale value, and

- any debt secured against it (for example, a mortgage) – para 6.

Assessing the value of capital resources held abroad. As noted above, capital **19.84** resources held abroad count towards disposable capital – para 7(1). If there is no prohibition in the foreign country against transferring the resource into the UK, its value is the amount it would realise if sold in that country, in accordance with para 6 (see 'Assessing the value of non-monetary capital' above) – para 7(2). If there is a prohibition in that country against transferring the resource into the UK, its value is the amount it would realise if sold to a buyer in the UK (in which case para 6 does not apply) – para 7(3).

Where disposable capital is held in currency other than sterling, the cost of any banking charge or commission that would be payable if that amount were converted into sterling is deducted from its value – para 8.

Depriving oneself of capital. The Government response to its consultation on **19.85** 'Fee remissions for the courts and tribunals' envisaged that the Fees Order would contain a provision stipulating that if an applicant has deliberately deprived him or herself of capital for the purpose of securing entitlement to remission or part-remission of fees, the applicant would be treated as possessing the deprived capital. Such a provision has not, however, found its way into the Order. Nevertheless, the HMCTS remission guidance warns that applicants or their partners must not deliberately deprive themselves of capital so that they are eligible for a fee remission. It provides the example of an individual temporarily giving a large portion of his or her savings to a friend or relative before making a fee remission application and goes on to state that if a court or tribunal believes an applicant has deliberately deprived him or herself of capital, it may request extra evidence to support the application. If the applicant refuses, the application will be rejected and the appropriate court or tribunal fee will have to be paid.

The guidance confirms that paying a debt or bill, or purchasing everyday goods or services (for example, food or transport), will not be considered as depriving oneself of capital.

Evidence of disposable capital not required. Unlike gross monthly income (as **19.86** to which, see 'Gross monthly income test – evidentiary requirements' below), applicants are not required to provide documentary evidence of their disposable capital. They are merely required to declare the amount of their disposable

1009

capital (see section 4 of the application form) – para 15(2)(b). However, the application form requires them to sign a declaration and statement of truth and sets out the consequences of failing to tell the truth. These are that:

- the application may be refused and the full fee will become payable

- any order or process obtained as a result of the application may be revoked

- criminal proceedings may be brought for fraud (if the untruthfulness is found to be deliberate).

19.87 Gross monthly income test
If a party satisfies the disposable capital test, a second test, based upon gross monthly income (GMI), will determine whether or not he or she is entitled to remission, either in full or in part. The GMI test is set out in paras 11–13 of Schedule 3. (Note that receipt of certain means-tested benefits will be accepted as evidence of entitlement for full remission, even though this is not prescribed by the Order itself – see 'Full remission based upon receipt of a specified benefit' below.)

19.88 Full remission under GMI test. To be entitled to *full* remission under the statutory GMI test, an applicant's gross monthly income must not exceed certain prescribed limits, as set out in para 11 and Table 2 of Schedule 3. These limits vary depending on whether the applicant is single or part of a couple and how many children the applicant or (where applicable) his or her partner has.

If the applicant is *single*, his or her gross monthly income must not exceed the following limits:

Number of children	Gross monthly income
None	£1,085
One	£1,330
Two	£1,575
More than two	£1,575 plus £245 for each additional child

19.89 If the applicant is part of a *couple*, the couple's gross monthly income must not exceed the following limits:

Number of children	Gross monthly income
None	£1,245
One	£1,490
Two	£1,735
More than two	£1,735 plus £245 for each additional child

'Child' is defined as a child or young person in respect of whom a party is entitled to receive child benefit in accordance with S.141 – and regulations made under S.142 – of the Social Security Contributions and Benefits Act 1992. The meaning of 'couple' is discussed under 'Disposable capital test – partner's capital' above. The meaning of 'gross monthly income' is discussed below.

Full remission based upon receipt of a specified benefit. The HMCTS **19.90** remission guidance suggests that an applicant who has passed the disposable capital test (see 'Disposable Capital Test' above) can bypass the GMI test by showing that he or she is receiving one of the means-tested benefits listed below, in which case full remission will automatically be granted:

Benefit	Evidence required
Income-based Jobseeker's Allowance	Letter (no more than one month old) from Jobcentre Plus/Department for Work and Pensions (DWP)
Income-related Employment and Support Allowance	Letter (no more than one month old) from Jobcentre Plus/DWP
Income support	Letter (no more than one month old) from Jobcentre Plus/DWP
Universal Credit – with gross annual earnings of less than £6,000	Letter (no more than one month old) from Jobcentre Plus/DWP
State Pension guarantee credit	Letter from the Pension Service/DWP (assessed income period should cover the current financial year)
Scottish Civil Legal Aid	Recent letter from the Scottish Legal Aid Board clearly showing a grant of support for the claim brought (or being brought)

Interestingly, receipt of *Scottish* legal aid entitles an individual to full remission, whereas receipt of legal aid in *England and Wales* is a bar to remission – see 'Who can apply for remission?' above.

Remission based upon means-tested benefits is described as 'Remission 1' both in **19.91** the guidance and on the remission application form itself (see section 5 of the form). Remission based upon GMI is described as 'Remission 2' (see section 6). The legal basis for this distinction is unclear as there is no mention in the Fees Order of remission based upon means-tested benefits. However, in its consultation response the Government stated that it 'propose[d] to accept that recipients of [certain means-tested benefits] would be automatically deemed to fall below [the gross monthly] income threshold. They will therefore receive a full remission if they also pass the household disposable capital test.' In other words, rather than being a separate type of remission, the Government is simply accepting evidence of receipt of the listed benefits as automatic proof that the gross monthly income test for full remission is satisfied. This is presumably because, due to the rigorous means testing that applies to these benefits, the disposable monthly incomes of individuals in receipt of them will never exceed the GMI thresholds for full remission. For convenience, it appears that the Government has decided to describe this as a separate type of remission ('Remission 1'), even though, legally speaking, this is not the case.

19.92 **Partial remission under GMI test.** As noted under 'Full remission under GMI test' above, a party whose GMI is lower than the relevant figure set out in Table 2 of Schedule 3 is entitled to full remission. And as explained under 'No entitlement to remission under GMI test' below, a party whose GMI is higher than the relevant figure set out in Table 3 of Schedule 3 is not entitled to any remission and must pay the full fee. That leaves those individuals whose GMI falls somewhere between the figures set out in the two tables and who are entitled to *partial remission* calculated in accordance with para 11(3) of Schedule 3. This states that for every £10 of GMI that exceeds the Table 2 limits (i.e. the limits for full remission), the party must pay £5 towards the relevant fee (up to the maximum amount of the fee payable). In essence, the more a party's GMI exceeds the limits prescribed for full remission, the more he or she will have to pay towards the fee in question.

19.93 **No entitlement to remission under GMI test.** An applicant will *not* be entitled to remission if his or her gross monthly income exceeds the prescribed limits set out in Table 3 of Schedule 3, which again vary depending upon relationship status and number of children – para 12.

An applicant who is single is not entitled to remission if his or her GMI exceeds the following limits:

Number of children	Gross monthly income
None	£5,085
One	£5,330
Two	£5,575
More than two	£5,575 plus £245 for each additional child

An applicant who is part of a couple is not entitled to remission if the couple's gross monthly income exceeds the following limits:

Number of children	Gross monthly income
None	£5,245
One	£5,490
Two	£5,735
More than two	£5,735 plus £245 for each additional child

What is gross monthly income? Paragraph 13 provides that gross monthly **19.94** income means 'the total monthly income, for the month preceding that in which the application for remission is made, from all sources, other than receipt of any of the excluded benefits'. As with disposable capital (see 'Disposable capital test – partner's capital' above), the GMI of a partner is to be treated as the GMI of the party *unless* the partner has a contrary interest – para 14.

Where a person's income derives from a 'trade, business or gainful occupation other than an occupation at a wage or salary' – in other words, income from a party's own business – it is calculated as:

- profits that have accrued or will accrue to the party (less any sums necessarily expended to earn those profits), and

- drawings of that party

in the month preceding that in which the application for remission is made – para 13(2) and (3).

Excluded benefits. Excluded benefits (i.e. benefits that are not taken into **19.95** account for the purpose of calculating GMI) are set out in para 1. They include the following:

- certain benefits payable under the Social Security Contributions and Benefits Act 1992, such as severe disablement allowance, carer's allowance, disability living allowance, any payment made out of the social fund and housing benefit

- any direct payment made under the Community Care, Services for Carers and Children's Services (Direct Payments) (England) Regulations 2009 SI 2009/1887, the Community Care, Services for Carers and Children's Services (Direct Payments) (Wales) Regulations 2011 SI 2011/831, or S.12B(1) of the Social Work (Scotland) Act 1968

- a back-to-work bonus payable under S.26 of the Jobseekers Act 1995

- any exceptionally severe disablement allowance paid under the Personal Injuries (Civilians) Scheme 1983 SI 1983/686

- any pension paid under the Naval, Military and Air Forces etc (Disablement and Death) Service Pension Order 2006 SI 2006/606

- any payment made from the Independent Living Funds listed at Reg 20(2)(b) of the Criminal Legal Aid (Financial Resources) Regulations 2013 SI 2013/471

- any financial support paid under an agreement for the care of a foster child, and

1013

- certain elements that make up an award of universal credit, including a housing costs element, a childcare costs element and a carer element.

This list is not exhaustive and reference should be made to Schedule 3 to the Fees Order, as amended by the Courts and Tribunals Fees (Miscellaneous Amendments) Order 2014 SI 2014/590 for a full list.

19.96 **Evidentiary requirements.** Unlike disposable capital (see 'Disposable capital test – evidence of disposable capital not required' above), applicants are required to provide documentary evidence of their GMI and the number of children they have – para 15(2)(c). The HMCTS remission guidance sets out the types of evidence of income that will be required, depending upon the circumstances of the case. These include:

- the applicants' last three months' bank statements (and those of his or her partner if applicable)

- original wage slips (not more than six weeks old)

- recent tax returns

- letters from any paying tenants confirming the tenancy arrangement, how much they pay and how often they pay, dated within the last month.

The guidance states that applications for fee remission will not be approved without the evidence it lists, unless the application is an emergency – see 'Procedural issues – applying for fee remission' below.

19.97 **Exceptional circumstances justifying remission**
It is important to note that even if a party fails to satisfy the disposable capital test and/or the gross monthly income test, a fee may nevertheless be remitted where the Lord Chancellor is satisfied that there are 'exceptional circumstances' which justify doing so – para 16, Sch 3. The Fees Order does not elaborate on the meaning of 'exceptional circumstances', although the HMCTS remission guidance states that the applicant must have suffered 'an unexpected event, that has seriously affected [his or her] ability to pay a court or tribunal fee'. It goes on to provide the following examples:

- the payment of a fee would mean non-payment of an essential service or utility bill (for example, water or gas) that is likely to lead to the service being cut off

- the payment of a fee would mean non-payment of rent or mortgage amounts that are overdue, which could lead to the applicant being made homeless

- the applicant has personal responsibility for caring for a dependent adult and that care can only be paid for from the applicant's own resources

1014

- the applicant has suffered unexpected and sudden personal and financial loss or expense due to the death of a close family member or dependent relative

- the applicant cannot pay the fee due to uninsured loss or damage to personal belongings as a result of fire, flood, theft or criminal damage.

The guidance states that the decision will be made by the Delivery Manager, whose decision in this regard cannot be appealed.

Procedural issues   19.98
In this section, we consider various procedural matters relating to remission, including the application process and what happens if the application is rejected.

Applying for remission. An application for remission of a fee must be made at   19.99
the time when the fee would otherwise be payable – para 15(1), Sch 3 Fees Order (but see 'Applying for remission when issuing a claim' below). Para 15(2) states that the party must:

- indicate the fee to which the application relates

- declare the amount of disposable capital, and

- provide documentary evidence of gross monthly income and number of children. As noted above, documentary evidence of a specified means-tested benefit is sufficient evidence of GMI.

The prescribed application form is two pages long and can be found at the back of the HMCTS remission guidance. The form does not contain a section for remission in 'exceptional circumstances' – see 'Exceptional circumstances justifying remission' above. An applicant who believes that such circumstances exist (and who does not qualify for remission under the usual tests) would therefore need to attach a document explaining what the exceptional circumstances are and providing accompanying evidence in support. The guidance gives the example of letters or notices threatening legal action due to non-payment of bills.

The guidance explains that if applying for remission of an employment tribunal   19.100
or EAT fee in England and Wales, the completed remission form (together with the application or claim to which the fee relates) must be sent to the Employment Tribunal Central Office or the Employment Appeal Tribunal Central Office in Leicester. Applications in Scotland must be sent to the respective employment tribunal and EAT central offices in Scotland.

Where an application for remission of a fee is made on or before the date on which a fee is payable, the date for payment of the fee is disapplied – para 15(3).

Emergency applications. Although this is not provided for in the Fees Order,   19.101
the guidance states that in a case of emergency, where an urgent decision of the

1015

court or tribunal is needed, the Delivery Manager can grant a fee remission without supporting evidence. His or her decision will be based upon:

- why evidence to support the remission application is not available at the time the application is made

- the applicant's ability to pay the court or tribunal fee, and

- whether the interests of justice will be compromised if there is a delay.

The Delivery Manager's decision is final and cannot be appealed.

19.102 Matters which could be considered an emergency can include applications involving:

- children or vulnerable adults

- domestic violence

- injunctions.

The element of urgency is unlikely to arise in many employment tribunal cases. However, if the Delivery Manager accepts that there is a genuine emergency, the applicant will be asked to give an undertaking that he or she will bring evidence in support of the remission application within five working days. The guidance notes that failure to comply with the undertaking carries serious sanctions which can result in:

- having the case stopped

- having the claim (or response) struck out, and

- having any order obtained on the back of the undertaking revoked.

19.103 *Retrospective application.* An applicant can also apply for a refund (known as a 'retrospective application') where, having paid a fee within the last three months, the applicant believes that he or she would have been granted a remission at the time that the fee was paid. In order to apply for the refund the application must provide evidence that the fee was paid in the last three months, and evidence that would have warranted remission being granted on the date on which the fee was paid.

19.104 **Remission refused (in full or in part).** If a remission application is refused, the applicant will have to pay the relevant fee and will be informed in writing of the date by which he or she must do so – para 15(4), Sch 3. Similarly, if only partial remission is granted, the claimant must pay the remainder of the fee within a period stipulated to him or her in writing.

Rule 11(3) of the Tribunal Rules states that if a remission application relating to the *issue fee* is refused (in part or in full), the tribunal shall send the claimant a notice specifying a date for payment of the fee and the claim will be rejected if the fee is not paid by the date specified. If the rejected remission application relates to a *hearing fee*, the claim will be dismissed 'without order' if the fee (or the remainder) is not paid by the specified date – rule 40(4) and 40(2)(a). Applications and counterclaims will be similarly dismissed if the appropriate fee is not paid on the date stipulated following a rejected remission application – rule 40(4), 40(2)(b) and 40(2)(c). In the EAT, non-payment of the fee could lead to the appeal being struck out – rule 17A Employment Appeal Tribunal Rules 1993 SI 1993/2854.

Appeals. According to the HMCTS remission guidance, if an application for **19.105** remission is refused then the applicant is entitled to appeal. This must be done in writing to the Delivery Manager at the Employment Tribunal Central Office/ Employment Appeal Tribunal Central Office in Leicester (where all remission applications are processed) by the date set out in the refusal letter (which will generally be 14 days from when the refusal letter is received). For appeals in Scotland the relevant EAT Central Office is located in Glasgow. The appeal should state why the applicant is not happy with the decision made and include any evidence that was supplied with the original remission application, as well as any extra evidence in support of the appeal. The Delivery Manager will then consider the appeal and communicate his or her decision to the applicant within ten working days. If the appeal is allowed and a full remission granted, a tribunal officer will process the papers to which the remission application relates. If the appeal is allowed for part-remission then the applicant will be told how much of the fee he or she must pay and the papers will not be processed until that amount is received. If the appeal is refused, the Delivery Manager will write to the applicant explaining the reasons for this. The applicant can then appeal one more time to the Operational Manager, whose name and address will be set out in the refusal letter. The appeal to the Operational Manager must follow the same process as that to the Delivery Manager. The Operational Manager's decision is final and cannot be appealed.

Applying for remission when issuing a claim   **19.106**
Rule 11 of the Tribunal Rules states that 'the tribunal shall reject a claim if it is not *accompanied* by a tribunal fee *or a remission application*' (our stress). Thus, if the claim form is being sent by post, the remission application must also be sent by post at the same time if the claim is to be accepted. However, where the claim is being submitted online, the position is complicated by the fact that it is not possible to make an online application for remission. This is presumably because the claimant needs to include original documentary evidence with the application. It would therefore appear to be impossible for an online claim form to be 'accompanied' by a remission application. If this literal interpretation is correct, it means that the online claims system cannot be used by claimants applying for remission.

There is nothing in the guidance issued by HMCTS addressing this issue. The guidance, 'Employment tribunal fees for individuals' (T435), simply says: 'It is very important that you send the correct fee or application to the remission scheme with your ET1 (the claim form). If you do not, we will reject your claim and return your claim form to you.' However, an individual who is going through the online process of submitting a claim is taken to a page that suggests that any 'accompanying' remission application can be sent by post. Specifically, it states 'if we do not receive the signed remission form and evidence in the post as soon as possible and within seven calendar days of submitting your ET1, your [remission] application will be refused and you will be required to pay the full fee for your claim'. It therefore appears that, for the purpose of the online system, a claim form will be 'accompanied by a remission application' if the claimant clicks 'yes' to the question, 'Do you intend to submit an application for remission?', and sends a remission application (with accompanying evidence) in the post to arrive at the Employment Tribunal Central Office in Leicester no later than seven calendar days after the online submission of the claim. This should mean that a claim submitted online at the very last moment should be accepted, even though the remission application does not arrive until after the time limit for presenting a claim has expired (provided, of course, that the application is received within seven days). Furthermore, it appears from what is stated online that if a remission application is not received within seven days (or at all), the claim will not be rejected outright. Instead, the claimant will be given an opportunity to pay the employment tribunal fee. It is doubtful whether this accords with rule 11 of the Tribunal Rules.

19.107 It is important to note that the question of whether or not an employee is entitled to remission does not have to be resolved at the time the claim is presented. Rule 11(1) of the Tribunal Rules merely requires the claim form to be accompanied by an *application* for remission. There appears to be nothing to stop claimants putting in a remission application, even if they know or suspect they are not entitled to remission. If the remission application is rejected, the claimant would then be given an opportunity to pay the fee, non-payment of which would lead to the claim form being rejected.

However, although a claim form will not be rejected under rule 11 if it is accompanied only by a remission application, it appears that the claim will only be officially accepted once the application is resolved one way or the other. The HMCTS remission guidance confirms that a claim will only be processed once the application for a full remission is approved. If the application is not approved (or only partial remission is granted), the claim would not be processed until the fee is paid.

19.108 **Impact of remission on 'fee group' claims**
Article 17(2) of the Fees Order provides that where an application for remission is made by a member of a fee group, 'Schedule 3 is to have effect for the

purposes of determining whether or not the member of the group would be entitled to remission (whether wholly or in part) if that person was a single claimant'. Note that each member of the group applying for remission needs to fill out individual application forms.

If one or more claimants are granted a remission, the remaining claimants will become responsible for the fee. However, Article 10(b) of the Order provides that the relevant group fee 'must not exceed an amount equal to the sum of the fees which the members of the fee group would be liable to pay as single claimants, taking into account any remission which would have been granted to individual members of the group if they were single claimants'. In other words, no claimant will be required to pay more than if they had been a single applicant. The effect of this provision can be illustrated as follows: 11 claimants are bringing a Type A claim, for which the group issue fee is £640, i.e. £58.18 each. If two of the 11 claimants are entitled to remission, the £640 issue fee divided between the nine remaining claimants is £71.11 each. This is well below the £160 single fee that would have been payable by each claimant. Therefore, the group fee remains £640. If, however, eight of the 11 claimants are entitled to remission, the £640 fee divided between the three fee-paying claimants would be £213.33 each. In these circumstances the amount payable by each claimant will be the lower 'single claimant' fee, i.e. £160 (meaning the total group fee will be reduced to £480).

19.109 The Lord Chancellor has the power to disregard an application for remission by a member of a fee group 'if the amount of the fee payable by the fee group would not be altered in consequence of the application being granted' – Article 18 Fees Order. On the face of it, this could neutralise the effect of para 15(3) of Schedule 3 to the Order, which states that where an application for remission is made on or before the date on which a fee is payable, the date for payment of the fee is disapplied. Returning to our 11 claimants, we saw that if only two of the claimants are entitled to remission, the group fee remains unchanged. By virtue of Article 18, it seems the Lord Chancellor is entitled to disregard the remission applications for the purpose of the claim, meaning that the £640 fee will need to accompany the claim form, failing which the claim will be rejected. Certainly, the online system requires payment of the fee upfront if it calculates, upon the information provided, that the remission application has no impact upon the group fee payable. However, according to the HMCTS remission guidance, if there are insufficient remission applications made to reduce the fee, the applications will not be processed and the tribunal will write to the fee group asking it to provide additional applications for claimants within the group, or to pay the fee.

19.110

Appendix – Type A claims

As noted under 'Types of tribunal claim subject to fees' above, employment tribunal claims are divided into two categories – 'Type A' and 'Type B' – for the purpose of assessing the level of fee payable. A full list of Type A claims (which attract the lower fee) can be found below. This replicates the list of Type A claims set out in Table 2 of Schedule 2 to the Employment Tribunals and the Employment Appeal Tribunal Fees Order 2013 SI 2013/1893 (as amended by the Courts and Tribunals Fees (Miscellaneous Amendments) Order 2014 SI 2014/590). Any claims not listed as Type A claims in Table 2 are Type B claims.

19.111 **Employment Agencies Act 1973**

Description of claim	Provision identifying the rights of the claimant	Provision conferring jurisdiction on tribunal
Application by the Secretary of State to prohibit a person from running an Employment Agency	S.3A	S.3A
Application by a person subject to a prohibition order to vary or set it aside	S.3C	S.3C

19.112 **Health and Safety at Work etc Act 1974**

Description of claim	Provision identifying the rights of the claimant	Provision conferring jurisdiction on tribunal
Appeal against improvement or prohibition notice	S.24	S.24

19.113 **Industrial Training Act 1982**

Description of claim	Provision identifying the rights of the claimant	Provision conferring jurisdiction on tribunal
Appeal against assessment of training levy	S.12	S.12

Trade Union and Labour Relations (Consolidation) Act 1992   19.114

Description of claim	Provision identifying the rights of the claimant	Provision conferring jurisdiction on tribunal
Complaint of deduction of unauthorised subscriptions	S.68	S.68A
Complaint relating to failure to deduct or refusal to deduct an amount to a political fund	S.86	S.87
Complaint that employer has failed to permit time off for carrying out trade union duties	S.168	S.168
Complaint that employer has failed to permit time off for union learning representatives	S.168A	S.168A
Complaint that employer has failed to pay for time off for union learning representatives	S.169	S.169
Complaint that employer has failed to permit time off for trade union activities	S.170	S.170
Complaint that employer has failed, wholly or in part, to pay remuneration under a protective award	S.190	S.192

Pension Schemes Act 1993   19.115

Description of claim	Provision identifying the rights of the claimant	Provision conferring jurisdiction on tribunal
Complaint that the Secretary of State has not paid, or has paid less than, the amount of relevant contributions which should have been paid into a pension scheme	S.124	S.126

1021

19.116 Employment Tribunals Act 1996

Description of claim	Provision identifying the rights of the claimant	Provision conferring jurisdiction on tribunal
Breach of contract (except where the employer's contract claim is made by way of application as part of the employer's response to the employee's contract claim*)	N/A	S.3 Articles 3 and 4 of the Employment Tribunals Extension of Jurisdiction (England and Wales) Order 1994 Articles 3 and 4 of the Employment Tribunals Extension of Jurisdiction (Scotland) Order 1994

* This makes it clear that an *employer's* contract claim is not a Type A claim that attracts a (Type A) issue fee and hearing fee. As noted under 'Application-specific tribunal fees' above, the submission of an 'employer's contract claim' is treated as an 'application' for the purposes of tribunal fees – see Article 4(2) of and Schedule 1 to the Fees Order. Therefore, unlike contract claims submitted by employees, there is no 'issue fee' to be paid at the time the employer's contract claim is made, no automatic rejection of the claim if the (application) fee is not paid, and no hearing fee payable in order for the application to be heard.

19.117 Employment Rights Act 1996

Description of claim	Provision identifying the rights of the claimant	Provision conferring jurisdiction on tribunal
Reference to determine what particulars ought to be included in a statement of employment particulars or changes to particulars	Ss.1 and 4	S.11
Reference to determine what particulars ought to be included in an itemised pay statement	S.8	S.11

Description of claim	Provision identifying the rights of the claimant	Provision conferring jurisdiction on tribunal
Complaint of unauthorised deductions from wages	S.13	S.23
Complaint that employer has received unauthorised payments	S.15	S.23
Complaint that employer has failed to pay guarantee payment	S.28	S.34
Complaint that employer has failed to permit time off for public duties	S.50	S.51
Complaint that employer has refused to permit, or has failed to pay for, time off to look for work or arrange training	Ss.52 and 53	S.54
Complaint that employer has refused to allow, or has failed to pay for, time off for ante-natal care	Ss.55, 56, 57ZA and 57ZB	Ss.57 and 57ZC
Complaint that employer has refused to allow time off for dependants	S.57A	S.57B
Complaint that employer has failed to allow, or to pay for, time off for trustee of pension scheme	Ss.58 and 59	S.60
Complaint that employer has failed to allow, or to pay for, time off for employee representative	Ss.61 and 62	S.63
Complaint that employer has failed to allow, or to pay for, time off for young people in Wales and Scotland	Ss.63A and 63B ERA	S.63C ERA

Description of claim	Provision identifying the rights of the claimant	Provision conferring jurisdiction on tribunal
Complaint that employer has failed to pay for time off on medical or maternity grounds	Ss.64, 68 and 68C	Ss.70 and 70A
Complaint that employer has failed to deal with an application in relation to study or training in accordance with regulations or refused the application on the basis of incorrect facts	Ss.63D–63H	S.63I
Complaint that employer has unreasonably failed to provide a written statement of reasons for dismissal or the particulars are inadequate or untrue	S.92	S.93
Reference in respect of a right to redundancy payment	S.135	Ss.163 and 177
Reference related to payment out of National Insurance Fund	S.166	S.170
References related to payments equivalent to redundancy payments	Ss.167, 168 and 177	S.177
Complaint that the Secretary of State has failed to make any, or insufficient, payment out of National Insurance Fund	S.182	S.188

19.118 National Minimum Wage Act 1998

Description of claim	Provision identifying the rights of the claimant	Provision conferring jurisdiction on tribunal
Appeal against a notice of underpayment	S.19C	S.19C

Equality Act 2006 19.119

Description of claim	Provision identifying the rights of the claimant	Provision conferring jurisdiction on tribunal
Appeal against a notice issued by the Commission for Equality and Human Rights where the notice relates to an unlawful act	S.21	S.21

Equality Act 2010 19.120

Description of claim	Provision identifying the rights of the claimant	Provision conferring jurisdiction on tribunal
Complaint that prospective employer made enquiries about disability or health	S.60	S.120
Application in relation to the effect of a non-discrimination rule in an occupational pension scheme	S.61	S.120
Complaint in relation to a breach of a maternity equality clause	S.73	S.127
Complaint in relation to a breach of, or application in relation to the effect of, a maternity equality rule in an occupational pension scheme	S.75	S.127
Complaint in relation to terms prohibiting discussions about pay	S.77	S.120
Complaint that a term in a collective agreement is void or unenforceable	S.145	S.146

19.121 Colleges of Education (Compensation) Regulations 1975

Description of claim	Provision identifying the rights of the claimant	Provision conferring jurisdiction on tribunal
Appeal of decision of compensating authority	Reg 42	Reg 42

19.122 Safety Representatives and Safety Committees Regulations 1977

Description of claim	Provision identifying the rights of the claimant	Provision conferring jurisdiction on tribunal
Complaint that employer has failed to pay for remunerated time off for safety representative	Reg 4(2) and Schedule 2	Reg 11

19.123 Occupational Pension Schemes (Contracting-Out) Regulations 1996

Description of claim	Provision identifying the rights of the claimant	Provision conferring jurisdiction on tribunal
Reference that there has been a failure to consult with employee representatives about contracting out of pension scheme	Reg 4 OPS(CO)R and Reg 9 of the Occupational Pensions Schemes (Disclosure of Information) Regulations 1996 (OPS(DI)R)	Reg 4 OPS(CO)R and Reg 9 OPS(DI)R

19.124 Health and Safety (Consultation with Employees) Regulations 1996

Description of claim	Provision identifying the rights of the claimant	Provision conferring jurisdiction on tribunal
Complaint that employer has failed to pay for time off to carry out safety representative duties or undertake training	Reg 7 and Schedule 1	Schedule 2

Working Time Regulations 1998

19.125

Description of claim	Provision identifying the rights of the claimant	Provision conferring jurisdiction on tribunal
Complaint that employer has refused to allow annual leave or make payment in respect of annual leave	Regs 13, 13A, 14 and 16	Reg 30
Appeal against improvement or prohibition notice	Para 6, Schedule 3	Para 6, Schedule 3

Control of Major Accident Hazards Regulations 1999

19.126

Description of claim	Provision identifying the rights of the claimant	Provision conferring jurisdiction on tribunal
Appeal against improvement or prohibition notice	Reg 18	Reg 18

Merchant Shipping (Working Time: Inland Waterways) Regulations 2003

19.127

Description of claim	Provision identifying the rights of the claimant	Provision conferring jurisdiction on tribunal
Complaint in relation to refusal of annual leave or to make payment in respect of such leave	Reg 11	Reg 18

Civil Aviation (Working Time) Regulations 2004

19.128

Description of claim	Provision identifying the rights of the claimant	Provision conferring jurisdiction on tribunal
Complaint in relation to refusal to provide paid annual leave	Reg 4	Reg 18
Complaint in relation to failure to provide free health assessments	Reg 5	Reg 18

19.129 **Fishing Vessels (Working Time: Sea-fishermen) Regulations 2004**

Description of claim	Provision identifying the rights of the claimant	Provision conferring jurisdiction on tribunal
Complaint in relation to refusal of annual leave or to make payment in respect of such leave	Reg 11	Reg 19

19.130 **Information and Consultation of Employees Regulations 2004**

Description of claim	Provision identifying the rights of the claimant	Provision conferring jurisdiction on tribunal
Complaint that employer has refused to allow or failed to pay for time off for information and consultation or negotiating representatives	Regs 27 and 28	Reg 29

19.131 **Road Transport (Working Time) Regulations 2005**

Description of claim	Provision identifying the rights of the claimant	Provision conferring jurisdiction on tribunal
Appeal against improvement notice	Para 6(2), Schedule 2	Para 6(2), Schedule 2

19.132 **Transfer of Undertakings (Protection of Employment) Regulations 2006**

Description of claim	Provision identifying the rights of the claimant	Provision conferring jurisdiction on tribunal
Complaint in relation to failure to pay compensation in pursuance of tribunal order	Reg 15(7) and 15(8)	Reg 15(10)

Occupational and Personal Pension Schemes (Consultation by Employers and Miscellaneous Amendment) Regulations 2006

19.133

Description of claim	Provision identifying the rights of the claimant	Provision conferring jurisdiction on tribunal
Complaint that employer has failed to allow, or pay for, time off for functions as employee representative	Paras 2 and 3, Schedule 1	Para 4, Schedule 1

European Cooperative Society (Involvement of Employees) Regulations 2006

19.134

Description of claim	Provision identifying the rights of the claimant	Provision conferring jurisdiction on tribunal
Complaint that employer has failed to allow, or pay for, time off for members of special negotiating body	Regs 28 and 29	Reg 30

Companies (Cross-Border Mergers) Regulations 2007

19.135

Description of claim	Provision identifying the rights of the claimant	Provision conferring jurisdiction on tribunal
Complaint that employer has failed to allow, or pay for, time off for members of special negotiating body	Regs 43 and 44	Reg 45

REACH Enforcement Regulations 2008

19.136

Description of claim	Provision identifying the rights of the claimant	Provision conferring jurisdiction on tribunal
Appeal against notice from Health and Safety Executive or a local authority	Reg 21 and Part 2, Schedule 8	Reg 21 and Part 2, Schedule 8

19.137 Ecclesiastical Offices (Terms of Service) Regulations 2009

Description of claim	Provision identifying the rights of the claimant	Provision conferring jurisdiction on tribunal
Reference to determine what particulars ought to be included in an itemised statement of stipend	Reg 6	Reg 9
Reference to determine what particulars ought to be included in a statement of particulars or changes to particulars	Regs 3 and 6	Reg 9

19.138 European Public Limited-Liability Company (Employee Involvement) (Great Britain) Regulations 2009

Description of claim	Provision identifying the rights of the claimant	Provision conferring jurisdiction on tribunal
Complaint that employer has failed to allow, or pay for, time off for members of special negotiating body	Regs 26 and 27	Reg 28

19.139 Energy Act 2013

Description of claim	Provision identifying the rights of the claimant	Provision conferring jurisdiction on tribunal
Appeal against improvement notice or prohibition notice	Para 6, Schedule 8	Para 6, Schedule 8

20 Costs and penalties

Historically, employment tribunals have been hesitant to make costs orders – **20.1** one of the traditional underpinnings of the tribunal system has been the ability of an employee to challenge the fairness of a dismissal, or to seek unpaid wages, without the lingering threat of having to pay the employer's costs in the event of defeat. The Annual Report of the Employment Tribunals Service 2000/01 revealed that, in that year, costs were awarded in only 247 cases, with the maximum award being £1,500. Most awards were of £500 or less, with costs in excess of that sum being awarded in only six cases.

Developments and changes. Sensitive to the need to release pressure on the **20.2** employment tribunal service by deterring those with unmeritorious claims from initiating proceedings, the Government introduced a number of changes to the costs regime in the Tribunal Rules 2001 – contained in the Employment Tribunals (Constitution and Rules of Procedure) Regulations 2001 SI 2001/1171. These included increasing the maximum sum of unassessed costs that employment tribunals have the power to award from £500 to £10,000, and providing tribunals with a power to award costs where the bringing or conducting of proceedings has been 'misconceived'. The maximum sum of unassessed costs that can be awarded was increased further still – to £20,000 – by the Employment Tribunals (Constitution and Rules of Procedure) (Amendment) Regulations 2012 SI 2012/468.

Additional changes were made by the Tribunal Rules 2004 – contained in the Employment Tribunals (Constitution and Rules of Procedure) Regulations

2004 SI 2004/1861 – which replaced the Tribunal Rules 2001. Of particular note was the new power for tribunals to make 'preparation time' orders in favour of unrepresented parties and 'wasted costs' orders directly against representatives. These changes have been consolidated into the Tribunal Rules 2013 set out in Schedule 1 to the Employment Tribunals (Constitution and Rules of Procedure) Regulations 2013 SI 2013/1237, along with some additional changes such as giving employment tribunal judges the power to carry out detailed assessment of costs over £20,000 without the need for referral to the county court.

20.3 **Increase in size and frequency of awards.** Partly owing to these changes, recent years have seen an increase in the size and frequency of costs awards. The Employment Tribunals and EAT statistics for April 2011 to March 2012 – produced by the Ministry of Justice – reveal that, in that year, 651 costs orders were made in employment tribunals (522 against claimants and 129 against respondents), the maximum award made being £54,740 and the average (mean) award being £3,141. This compares with 1,410 costs orders the previous year (1,294 against claimants and 116 against respondents), the maximum award being £36,466 and the mean award £1,292. Furthermore, these statistics only cover costs orders (in favour of parties who are represented). They do not include 'preparation time' orders (in favour of non-represented parties) or 'wasted costs' orders (against representatives, as opposed to parties). Nevertheless, the fundamental principle remains that costs orders are the exception rather than the rule – see the recent statement to that effect in Yerrakalva v Barnsley Metropolitan Borough Council 2012 ICR 420, CA. In addition, the range of circumstances in which costs are awarded in employment (and appeal) tribunals is much narrower than in the civil courts, where costs are said to 'follow the event'.

20.4 **Scope and layout of chapter.** In this chapter, we examine the costs regime in both the employment tribunal and the EAT, referring where appropriate to the Presidential Guidance on 'General Case Management' for England and Wales, which contains a short section on 'Costs'. First, we consider the types of order an employment tribunal is empowered to make relating to 'costs', 'preparation time', 'wasted costs' and the like. Next, we examine the grounds upon which the various types of order can be made. After that, we look at various factors that may be relevant when an employment tribunal is considering whether or not to exercise its discretion to order costs, etc. Then we discuss some general principles and factors that may be relevant to an employment tribunal's assessment of costs (and the like), and the various methods of assessment. We go on to consider the procedural requirements relating to these types of employment tribunal order. Following our consideration of the costs regime in the employment tribunal, we move on to consider the costs regime in the Employment Appeal Tribunal. Finally we consider costs beyond the EAT; specifically, the issues of costs protection and referrals to the ECJ.

What orders can employment tribunal make? 20.5

In this section we examine the various types of order that can be made under the employment tribunals' costs regime, including 'costs', 'preparation time' and 'wasted costs' orders. The term 'costs order' tends to be used – at least by lay people – to describe all the various orders that a tribunal can make. Strictly speaking, however, its traditional legal meaning is an order against one party to pay the 'costs' incurred by a represented party. This definition of 'costs order' is retained by rule 75(1)(a) of the Tribunal Rules 2013 – see 'Order to pay represented party's costs' below. Nevertheless, there has been some dilution of the traditional meaning in that orders to reimburse a tribunal fee and orders to reimburse witness expenses are now also described as 'costs orders' – see rule 75(1)(b) and 75(1)(c). Unlike 'costs orders' under rule 75(1)(a), these are not orders for 'costs' in the traditional (more general) sense. Rather, they are specific to a certain type of cost; namely, tribunal fees and witness expenses. We therefore deal with these orders separately – see 'Order to reimburse employment tribunal fee' and 'Order to reimburse witness expenses' below.

Order to pay represented party's costs 20.6
Rule 75(1)(a) of the Tribunal Rules – coupled with rule 76 – gives employment tribunals the power to make a costs order against one party to proceedings ('the paying party') to pay the costs incurred by another party ('the receiving party') on a number of different grounds – see 'Grounds for awarding costs' below. This general power used to be set out in rule 38(3) of the Tribunal Rules 2004. Under that previous set of rules the receiving party could only recover costs incurred while legally represented. Now the costs of a lay representative can also be recovered – see 'Costs incurred while represented' below.

It is worth noting that an employment tribunal can only order a party to pay the costs incurred by *another party*. It cannot order a party to contribute to the expenses incurred by the tribunal itself – Ashmead v Avon County Council EAT 332/89. It is also important to note that a tribunal cannot make a costs order *and* a preparation time order (as to which see 'Party must pay for unrepresented party's preparation time' below) in favour of the same party in the same proceedings – rule 75(3). The implications of this are discussed further under 'Costs incurred while represented' below. A tribunal may, however, decide in the course of the proceedings that a party is entitled to one order or the other and leave it until later to decide which kind of order to make – rule 75(3).

20.7 **Grounds for awarding costs.** The grounds for making a costs order are fully discussed under 'Grounds for making orders against a party' below. In brief, they are as follows:

- a party (or that party's representative) has acted vexatiously, abusively, disruptively or otherwise unreasonably in the bringing or conducting of proceedings (or part thereof) – rule 76(1)(a) (see 'Grounds for making orders against a party – conduct')

- a claim or response had no reasonable prospect of success – rule 76(1)(b) (see 'Grounds for making orders against a party – prospects of success')

- a party has breached an order or Practice Direction – rule 76(1)(2) (see 'Grounds for making orders against a party – breach of an order or Practice Direction')

- a hearing has been postponed or adjourned on the application of a party – rule 76(1)(2) (see 'Grounds for making orders against a party – postponements and adjournments')

- the employment tribunal decides an allegation or argument for substantially the reasons given in an earlier deposit order – rule 39(5) (see 'Grounds for making orders against a party – costs following the payment of a deposit' below).

20.8 **Meaning of 'costs'.** 'Costs' for these purposes means 'fees, charges, disbursements or expenses incurred by or on behalf of the receiving party (including expenses that witnesses incur for the purpose of, or in connection with, attendance at a tribunal hearing)' – rule 74(1) Tribunal Rules 2013. This is substantively the same definition as appeared in rule 38(3) of the Tribunal Rules 2004. As before, rule 74(1) goes on to clarify that in Scotland references to 'costs' should be read as references to expenses – i.e. the term used for 'costs' in Scotland.

20.9 **The 'paying party'.** Costs can only be awarded against a party to the proceedings. Rule 38(6) of the Tribunal Rules 2004 expressly stated that 'any costs order... shall be payable by the paying party and not his representative'. There is no equivalent provision in the Tribunal Rules 2013, not because this is no longer the case but because it was, presumably, considered to be superfluous. Who the paying party should be, however, is not always clear cut, as can be seen from the case of (1) Russia House Ltd (2) The Barry Martin Group (3) Martin v (1) Skerry (2) Lynchehaun EAT 859/93. There, S issued tribunal proceedings against the first respondent, RH Ltd, and the third respondent, M, while L issued proceedings against the second respondent, BMG. The identity of the two claimants' true employer was unclear, as a result of which the tribunal ordered that an interlocutory hearing be held to establish this. At the first preliminary hearing the solicitor appearing for all three respondents failed to produce any documentation to throw light on the matter. The hearing was adjourned and L, who was represented by a solicitor, sought costs. The tribunal awarded costs against M, which were subsequently paid. When the adjourned hearing was reconvened, the respondents' representative again failed to produce any documents as to the true identity of the claimants' employer. The tribunal made a further order for costs in favour of L against M. M appealed, arguing that since he was not a party to the action commenced by L, costs could not be awarded against him. The EAT noted that L's action was against BMG, but that it was unclear what this entity was because of the respondents' failure to produce evidence. The only information available indicated that BMG was actually M himself. In these circumstances the tribunal was entitled to conclude that BMG was in fact M and that the tribunal had, therefore, made a costs order against a party to the proceedings. For the avoidance of doubt, the EAT amended the order to state that it was made against both M and BMG.

Costs incurred while represented. A costs order under rule 75(1)(a) of the **20.10** Tribunal Rules 2013 can only be made in respect of the costs that a party to proceedings has incurred while represented, meaning either 'legally represented' or – in a departure from the old Tribunal Rules – 'represented by a lay representative'.

Legally represented. Being legally represented is defined by rule 74(2) as having **20.11** the assistance of a person who:

* has a right of audience in relation to any class of proceedings in any part of the Senior Courts of England and Wales, or all proceedings in county courts or magistrates' courts. In other words, the person has a general qualification within the meaning of S.71 of the Courts and Legal Services Act 1990 (i.e. a barrister, solicitor or legal executive)

* is an advocate or solicitor in Scotland, or

* is a barrister or solicitor in Northern Ireland.

Legal representation is dependent on the qualification of the individual concerned, irrespective of payment. A costs order can therefore be made in respect of costs incurred while represented by an in-house lawyer or by a lawyer acting pro bono. Rule 74(2) makes it clear that the legally qualified person may be the employee of the receiving party (i.e. an in-house lawyer).

The representative in question must have a current general qualification within **20.12** the meaning of the 1990 Act in order to constitute a legal representative. An example:

* **Ramsay and ors v Bowercross Construction Ltd and ors** EAT 0534/07: the claimants were ordered to pay BC Ltd's legal costs from the date on which they were served the company's response. The claimants argued that BC Ltd's solicitor, D, was not a legal representative for the purpose of what

is now rule 74(2) because she did not possess a current practising certificate and therefore her costs were not recoverable by way of a costs order. The employment judge, however, held that D's costs could be included within the costs order. She noted that, although D did not have a current practising certificate, she was a qualified solicitor, on the solicitors' roll, and had been authorised by the Bar Council to instruct counsel. In the judge's view, since BC Ltd was legally represented at the hearing by counsel, D's fees – which fell within the definition of 'costs' and related to the same proceedings – could also be claimed. The EAT – His Honour Judge Peter Clark sitting alone – overturned this upon appeal. While the barrister had a general qualification under S.71 of the Courts and Legal Services Act 1990 (and therefore his costs, which totalled £10,547.98, could be recovered under a costs order), D – for want of a practising certificate – had not. Therefore, her costs (of £2,062) could not be recovered under a costs order.

While the costs of lay representatives *can* now be recovered by way of a costs order, the distinction between 'legal' and 'lay' representatives is still important because the hourly rate of the latter is capped under rule 78(2) for the purpose of assessing costs (see below). There is no such cap for the fees of legal representatives.

20.13 Where a party has been represented by both a barrister *and* a solicitor, the question arises as to whether both sets of fees should be included in any costs award. The position appears to be that, while an order may cover just the solicitors' fees, the converse (i.e. an order covering just barristers' fees) will not generally be possible. In Verma v Harrogate and District NHS Foundation Trust EAT 0155/09 HHJ Peter Clark held that it was illogical for an employment judge to order the respondent Trust to pay V his barrister's costs but not his solicitor's costs incurred in respect of the Trust's 'hopeless' application to strike out his claims. He therefore ordered the Trust to pay V's solicitors' costs of over £6,000 plus VAT in addition to the counsel's fees already ordered. In doing so, HHJ Clark commented that he had seen occasions when counsel's fees have been disallowed and solicitors' costs ordered but never the other way around.

20.14 *Lay representative.* Previously, the costs of instructing a lay representative, as opposed to a legal representative, were not recoverable as part of a costs award – see rule 38 of the 2004 Tribunal Rules. During his review of the employment tribunal rules, Mr Justice Underhill (as he then was) took the view that those who choose to be represented by a non-lawyer, and who have paid for that service and advice, should not be put at a disadvantage when an employment tribunal concludes that the other party's conduct warrants a costs order. The Government agreed with this view and, as a result, rule 75(1)(a) expressly provides that a costs order can be made in favour of a party who is 'represented by a lay representative'. Such representation is defined by rule 74(3) as 'having the assistance of a person who does not satisfy any of the criteria in [rule 74(2)] and who charges for representation in the proceedings' – in other words, anyone charging for their services who is not a legally qualified and practising representative, as defined by rule 74(2).

In order to bring about this change, the Government considered it necessary to amend the Employment Tribunals Act 1996 (ETA), S.13(1)(a) of which sets out the power that enables the Secretary of State to make regulations permitting tribunal costs orders. The amendment – made by S.21(4) of the Enterprise and Regulatory Reform Act 2013 (ERRA) – introduced a definition of the term 'representative' into S.42(1) ETA, which extends to any person whom the party in question desires to represent him or her. This was intended to make it clear that S.13(1)(a) ETA covers orders in respect of the costs of representation by non-lawyers, thus paving the way for this to be prescribed under the new Tribunal Rules. Note, however, that while the costs of lay representatives are now recoverable, the hourly rate of such representatives is capped for the purpose of assessing costs: rule 78(2) provides that the applicable hourly rate should be no higher than the hourly rate used when calculating preparation time orders – currently (as from 6 April 2014) £34.

Overlap with 'preparation time' orders. As we shall see below (under 'Order **20.15** to pay for unrepresented party's preparation time') it is also possible for a tribunal to make a so-called 'preparation time order' (PTO) (which compensates for a party's preparation time, as opposed to costs) in favour of a party who has been represented by a lay representative. Nevertheless, rule 75(3) makes it clear that a costs order and a PTO may not be made in favour of the same party in the same proceedings. Therefore, a party who has been represented by a lay representative will need to make a choice as to which type of order to go for. In addition, a party who has been legally represented for only part of the proceedings but has represented him or herself for the remainder will also need to decide whether to apply for a costs order in respect of his or her legal representatives' costs or a PTO in respect of his or her own 'preparation time'. Ordinarily, it will probably be more lucrative to opt for a costs order since, as we shall see, the amount of preparation time a party can claim is capped at an hourly rate (akin to the cap on lay representatives' costs for the purpose of costs orders), whereas legal costs are not capped under the rules.

Amount of costs. Rule 78(1) of the Tribunal Rules sets out how the amount of **20.16** costs will be determined. As under the previous version of the Rules, there is provision for:

- 'unassessed costs' (which cannot exceed £20,000)

- a detailed assessment of costs (to be determined in accordance with the Civil Procedure Rules or, in Scotland, to be taxed according to the rules applicable in the sheriff court); or

- for the amount of costs to be agreed between the parties.

1037

All of the above are discussed in more detail under 'Methods of assessment and applicable statutory limits' below.

20.17 ## Order to pay for unrepresented party's preparation time
Before the Tribunal Rules 2004 came into force, an employment tribunal had no jurisdiction to make an order in favour of a litigant in person who may well have spent a great deal of time in preparing for his or her case – Kingston upon Hull City Council v Dunnachie (No.3) 2004 ICR 227, EAT. Rule 42 of the 2004 Rules changed that: for the first time a tribunal could make an order – known as a 'preparation time order' (PTO) – in favour of an unrepresented party to compensate him or her for time spent working on the case. The power to make PTOs has been carried forward into the Tribunal Rules 2013 and is now contained in rule 76 (coupled with rule 75(2)). Note that as well as being ordered in favour of an unrepresented party, it is also possible for a PTO to be awarded in favour of a party who is instructing a *lay* representative. This is discussed further below. As with costs orders, PTOs can only be made against (and in favour of) parties to proceedings.

20.18 **Grounds for making a PTO.** The grounds for making a PTO are fully discussed under 'Grounds for making orders against a party' below. In brief, they are as follows:

- a party (or that party's representative) has acted vexatiously, abusively, disruptively or otherwise unreasonably in the bringing or conducting of proceedings (or part thereof) – rule 76(1)(a)

- a claim or response had no reasonable prospect of success – rule 76(1)(b)

- a party has breached an order or practice direction – rule 76(1)(2)

- a hearing has been postponed or adjourned on the application of a party – rule 76(1)(2)

- the employment tribunal decides an allegation or argument for substantially the reasons given in an earlier deposit order – rule 39(5).

These are identical to the grounds for making a general costs order against a party under rule 75(1)(a) – see 'Order to pay represented party's costs' above. It is important, however, to note that a tribunal cannot make a PTO *and* a costs order in favour of the same party in the same proceedings – rule 75(3). This has implications for parties who are represented by a lay representative, since they can, in theory, apply for either a PTO or a costs order if one (or more) of the above grounds is met. (This point is discussed further under 'Preparation time while not legally represented' below.) A tribunal may, however, decide in the course of the proceedings that a party is entitled to one order or the other and leave it until later to decide which kind of order to make – rule 75(3).

1038

Definition of preparation time. 'Preparation time' means 'time spent by the **20.19** receiving party (including by any employees or advisers) in working on the case, except for time spent at the final hearing' – rule 75(2). It is interesting that time spent at the hearing is excluded, since often unreasonable conduct in the preparation for or conduct at the hearing will result in the hearing being extended. In such circumstances, the preferred route for a party who is paying for lay representation may be to apply for a costs order (instead of a PTO) since this would enable him or her to recover the cost of the additional time in the tribunal – see 'Order to pay represented party's costs' above). However, a party who is representing him or herself, or is represented by a voluntary adviser, does not have this option since costs orders can only be sought in respect of *paid* lay representatives.

Preparation time 'while not legally represented'. A PTO can only be made in **20.20** favour of a party who has not been legally represented. Specifically, it is defined by rule 75(2) as 'an order that a party… make a payment to another party… in respect of [that other] party's preparation time while not legally represented'. The definition of 'legally represented' for these purposes is found in rule 74(2) – see 'Order to pay represented party's costs – costs incurred while represented' above. As noted above, legal representation is dependent on the qualification of the individual concerned, irrespective of payment. It follows that a PTO cannot be made in respect of a party's preparation time if he or she is being represented by an in-house lawyer or by a lawyer acting pro bono. In such a case, the only option for the party in question would be to apply for a costs order.

There is nothing to stop a PTO being made in favour of a party who is represented by a *lay* representative. However, as we saw under 'Party must pay other side's costs – costs incurred while represented' above, the fees of a lay representative are now recoverable by way of a *costs order* under rule 75(1)(a). Since, as noted above, a PTO and costs order cannot be made in favour of the same party in the same proceedings, a party who is represented by – and paying for – a lay representative is likely to apply for a costs order (which can cover all the costs he or she has incurred while represented including during the hearing) rather than a PTO (which can only cover time spent working on the case, not including the hearing). The hourly rate of a lay representative is capped at £34 for the purpose of assessing costs under a costs order. This is the same hourly rate that applies for the purpose of assessing preparation time. Of course, if a party has spent more time working on the case than his or her lay representative, it may then be more advantageous for him or her to apply for a PTO.

The fact that a PTO and a costs order cannot be made against the same party **20.21** in the same proceedings can work against a party who is partially represented by someone meeting the rule 74(2) definition of 'legally qualified', and partially by someone not meeting that definition. An example:

- **Ramsay and ors v Bowercross Construction Ltd and ors** EAT 0534/07: the employer was represented by a barrister and a solicitor during the employment tribunal proceedings. On appeal from an employment judge's order that the employee pay the full extent of the employer's costs, the EAT pointed out that the solicitor did not satisfy the definition of 'legally qualified' (under then rule 38(5) of the Tribunal Rules 2004) as she did not hold a practising certificate and therefore did not fall within the scope of S.71 of the Courts and Legal Services Act 1990. It followed that her fees could not be recovered by way of a costs order and, since such an order had already been made in respect of counsel's fees, nor could they be recovered by way of a PTO.

20.22 **Assessment of preparation time.** Rule 79 requires a tribunal to decide the number of hours in respect of which a PTO should be made. This assessment must be based upon:

- information provided by the receiving party in respect of his or her preparation time – rule 79(1)(a), and

- its own assessment of what is a reasonable and proportionate amount of time for the party to have spent on preparatory work, with reference to such matters as the complexity of the proceedings, the number of witnesses and the documentation required – rule 79(1)(b).

The assessment of preparation time is discussed in more detail under 'Methods of assessment and applicable statutory limit – assessment of preparation time' below.

20.23 **Order to reimburse employment tribunal fee**

Rule 75(1)(b) of the Tribunal Rules 2013 introduces a new type of costs order requiring one party to pay another party in respect of a tribunal fee that has been paid in full. This obviously reflects the recent introduction of fees in the employment tribunal – see Chapter 19, 'Fees', for full details. Unlike a costs order under rule 75(1)(a) (as to which see 'Order to pay represented party's costs' above), such an order can be made in favour of *any* party who has paid a tribunal fee, whether represented or unrepresented. In addition, there is nothing to prevent a tribunal making this type of order as well as a PTO in favour of the same party in the same proceedings: although it is described as a 'costs order' by rule 75(1)(b), the rule prohibiting a costs order and PTO from being made in favour of the same party only applies to a costs order made under rule 75(1)(a) (see 'Order to pay represented party's costs – costs incurred while represented' above).

Rule 76(4) provides that a reimbursement of a fee costs order under rule 75(1)(b) can be made where a party has paid a tribunal fee in full in respect of a claim, employer's contract claim or application in circumstances where that claim, counterclaim or application has been decided, in whole or in part, in favour of that party. Rule 76(4) is apt to cover the issue fee, the hearing fee (payable by the employee), the fee for submitting a counterclaim (payable by the employer) and/or the 'application-specific fees' for reconsideration or for dismissal following withdrawal (payable by the party who makes the application). It does not, however, include the fee for judicial mediation (payable by the employer), which cannot therefore be recovered by way of a costs order under rule 76(4). For full details of these different types of fees, see Chapter 19, 'Fees'.

Ground for making the order. Rule 76(4) goes on to provide that an order can **20.24** be made where the claim, counterclaim or application is decided, in whole or in part, in favour of that party. In other words, it can be made in favour of a successful (or partially successful) party who has paid a fee. Note that the employment tribunal's power to order reimbursement is discretionary and does not automatically follow if a fee-paying party is successful. Nevertheless, the discretion is likely to be exercised in the majority of cases in order to reimburse successful claimants for sums paid in respect of the issue and hearing fees.

Amount of order. Rule 78(1)(c) provides that the employment tribunal may **20.25** order reimbursement of all or part of the tribunal fee. Such orders are not subject to the £20,000 limit that applies in respect of ordinary unassessed cost orders made where the receiving party is legally represented – see rule 78(3). If the party is wholly successful in his or her application or claim, it appears likely that a tribunal will order reimbursement of the whole fee. But where a fee-paying party's claim or application is only successful *in part*, the tribunal may have to decide what amount by way of reimbursement of the relevant tribunal fees it is appropriate to award.

Order to reimburse witness expenses
20.26

Where a witness has attended, or been ordered to attend, to give oral evidence at a hearing on behalf of a party to proceedings, an employment tribunal may order the other party to pay that party (or the witness) a specified amount in respect of 'necessary and reasonable' expenses – rules 75(1)(c), 76(5) and 78(1)(d) Tribunal Rules 2013. As rule 75(1)(c) makes clear, these must be expenses 'incurred, or to be incurred, for the purpose of, or in connection with, an individual's attendance as a witness at the tribunal'. There is no limit to the amount that can be awarded – rule 78(3). An order can be made in favour of a party where he or she has reimbursed the witness in question or in favour of the witness him or herself, if not.

Note that, unlike a costs order under rule 75(1)(a) (as to which see 'Order to pay represented party's costs' above), an order reimbursing witness expenses can be made in favour of *any party*, whether represented or not. In addition, there is nothing to prevent a tribunal making this type of order as well as a PTO

1041

in favour of the same party in the same proceedings: although it is described as a 'costs order' by rule 75(1)(c), the rule prohibiting a costs order and PTO from being made in favour of the same party (i.e. rule 75(3)) only applies to a costs order under rule 75(1)(a).

20.27 **'Necessary and reasonable' expenses.** It remains to be seen what tribunals will consider to be 'necessary and reasonable' expenses in the context of witness expenses orders. No guidance has been issued on this. The type and amount of expenses that could previously be claimed from the state (and which can still be claimed for claims brought on or before 5 April 2012) may perhaps provide some indication – see below. However, it would be wrong to set too much store by this, particularly since some of the limits on expenses that could be claimed from the state were relatively low.

20.28 **Claiming witness expenses via a 'costs order' under rule 75(1)(a).** The definition of 'costs' under rule 74(1) comprises expenses incurred by or on behalf of the receiving party, including expenses that witnesses incur for the purpose of, or in connection with, attendance at an employment tribunal hearing. Thus a party who is represented could potentially claim witness expenses by way of an ordinary order for 'costs' under rule 75(1)(a) – discussed under 'Order to pay represented party's costs' above. The stipulation that witness expenses must be 'reasonable and necessary' in respect of a witness expenses order under rule 75(1)(c) does not expressly apply if a party is claiming them by way of a costs order under rule 75(1)(a). Potentially, then, a (represented) party wishing to recover witness expenses could claim for a wider range of expenses under rule 75(1)(a) than he or she could in respect of an order under rule 75(1)(c). However, he or she would, of course, need to show that one of the grounds for making a 'costs' order is made out, as to which see 'Order to pay represented party's costs – grounds for awarding costs' above.

In addition, an order for 'costs' cannot be made as well as a PTO in favour of the same party – rule 75(3). This factor may be a particularly important consideration if the party in question is represented by a lay representative, since such a party is entitled to apply for either a PTO or a costs order. As noted under 'Order to pay for unrepresented party's preparation time – preparation time "while not legally represented"' above, if a party has spent more time working on the case than his or her lay representative, it may be more lucrative for him or her to apply for a PTO, as opposed to a costs order. Witness expenses would then need to be claimed by way of an order under rule 75(1)(c).

20.29 **Replacement of state-funded witness expenses.** Previously, parties and witnesses at employment tribunal hearings were entitled to claim certain expenses from the state – see below. However, this state-run system was removed for employment claims brought after 5 April 2012 by virtue of an amendment made to the previous Tribunal Rules 2004 by the Employment Tribunals (Constitution and Rules of Procedure) (Amendment) Regulations

2012 SI 2012/468. According to HM Courts and Tribunals Service (HMCTS), where an employment tribunal claim is made on or after 6 April 2012 expenses and allowances will only be paid to witnesses called to give medical evidence or to medical professionals asked to provide medical reports. Any other witnesses called by either party should be paid by that party, unless the tribunal makes a specific order for the payment of witness expenses – see www.justice.gov.uk/tribunals/employment/hearings.

The reason behind the change can be found in the 'Resolving Workplace Disputes' Consultation, in which the Government stated that it wished to shift the burden of paying for witness attendance from the state onto the party calling the witness. The consultation response envisaged employment tribunals having the power to direct parties to bear the costs of witness attendance 'where a witness has attended pursuant to a witness order'. This is reflected in rules 75(1)(c), 76(5) and 78(1)(d) of the Tribunal Rules 2013, except that – as with previous rule 38(1)(c) of the 2004 Tribunal Rules – there is no requirement that the witness must have attended pursuant to a witness order before a tribunal can order his or her expenses to be paid. In addition, given that the scope of a 'witness expenses' order is not limited to witnesses of the party who called them, a party could potentially find that he or she is ordered to pay the expenses of a witness called by another party to the claim.

20.30 The consultation response further envisaged that the party ultimately losing a case would reimburse the successful party for any witness expenses already paid out. Although the term 'reimbursement' is not used, this appears to be catered for by rule 78(1)(d), given that the order may be made in favour of a witness *or another party*.

20.31 *Position in respect of claims brought before 5 April 2012.* For claims brought on or before 5 April 2012, the old system of claiming expenses from the state continues to apply. Note that it is immaterial for these purposes when the hearing takes place. The system was put in place pursuant to S.5(3) ETA, which provided that 'the Secretary of State may pay to any other persons such allowances as he may with the consent of the Treasury determine for the purposes of, or in connection with, their attendance at employment tribunals'. Given the entirely discretionary nature of this provision, the Secretary of State was perfectly entitled to withdraw the system for claims brought after 5 April. It is important to note that a limited form of witness state funding will continue to apply for claims brought after that date: according to HMCTS, allowances will continue to be paid to witnesses called to give medical evidence or to medical professionals asked to provide medical reports (see www.justice.gov.uk/tribunals/employment/hearings).

As for claims brought on or before 5 April, a leaflet produced by the Employment Tribunals Service (ETS) dated October 2006 and entitled 'Expenses and allowances payable to parties and witnesses attending an Employment Tribunal' makes it clear that professional representatives – for example, full-time officials of unions or employers' organisations, paid consultants or lawyers – are not entitled to claim. The leaflet expressly states that this exclusion does not apply to Citizens Advice Bureau staff or to representatives acting for the Free Representation Unit or Pro Bono Unit, all of whom will, of course, generally be acting pro bono. In addition, other unpaid representatives, such as friends and relatives, will be able to claim their expenses.

20.32 As at the date of publication, the following expenses and allowances apply to claims brought on or before 5 April 2012:

- *travel costs* in excess of £5 will be paid. The first £5 of travel expenses will, however, be reimbursed where the employment tribunal has issued a witness order. In respect of travel by car or motorcycle, a mileage rate of 15p per mile will be paid. However, car park fees, toll fees or congestion charges will not be reimbursed. Taxi fares, even for short distances, will be paid only in exceptional circumstances, which must be stated with the claim and on provision of a receipt. Where long taxi journeys and substitutes for public transport options are proposed, prior written approval must be obtained from the Regional Secretary of the tribunal office where the case is to be heard. A copy of the approval letter along with a valid receipt must accompany the expenses claim. Necessary air travel may also be reimbursed but reimbursement will be limited to tourist or standard class fares and the approval of the tribunal office must be sought before travelling. Note that reimbursement of travel expenses is normally limited to travel within the UK and the Republic of Ireland. Only in exceptional cases will travel from overseas be paid and then only with the tribunal's prior approval

- *overnight expenses (covering dinner, bed and breakfast)* of up to £81 per night (inner London) or £71 per night (elsewhere) may be paid where an overnight stay is essential. In such circumstances, relevant receipts must be provided. An allowance of £21 per night can be claimed when staying with friends or relatives. The leaflet goes on to state that the tribunal office should be contacted in order to get its approval in writing

- payment may be made to cover *loss of earnings* up to a limit of £45 per day. The leaflet states that if the person claiming loss of earnings is employed, the employer must certify that he or she was not paid on the day(s) in question. If the person claiming is self-employed, he or she must provide a written declaration showing that work could not be deferred or advanced; the amount of income lost; the work which could not be carried out; and for whom the work was to be carried out. The employment tribunal office can provide a declaration form. There is no entitlement to loss of earnings allowance if the party or witness in question took paid holiday or special leave with pay to attend the hearing

- *child or adult care expenses* are payable if a registered child carer or adult carer is required in order to attend the hearing at a rate of up to £5.35 per hour (per child or adult). The employment tribunal will require an invoice or receipt as proof of expenditure. Such expenses will not be paid for any period covered by a claim for loss of earnings

- if someone attending the tribunal needs to be accompanied because of a *medical condition*, a friend or relative may claim the same travel and other expenses as the party needing such assistance. Where professional assistance is needed, reasonable costs are paid upon production of a receipt

- *language interpreters' costs* are payable if an attendee at the employment tribunal needs a professional interpreter. Once notified, the employment tribunal office will make arrangements for an interpreter to be engaged. If a friend or relative is desired, the employment judge's permission must be sought in advance of the hearing. If permission is granted, the friend or relative may claim the same travel and other expenses as the person needing an interpreter. They are not, however, eligible to claim for their interpreting service

- if the employment judge orders the production of *essential medical reports or evidence*, the payment for the costs incurred will be made 'in line with indicative ETS rates'. The leaflet states that tribunal staff will give these rates upon request. It also emphasises that a person so ordered should check the rates before any costs are incurred 'as a guide to what is reasonable'. (As noted above, according to HMCTS, allowances will still be paid to witnesses called to give medical evidence or to medical professionals asked to provide medical reports where an employment tribunal claim is made after 5 April 2012.)

20.33 The ETS has produced separate guidance for tribunal users who are deaf or hard of hearing – 'Guidance for tribunal users who are deaf or hard of hearing' (October 2004). It states that employment tribunals will meet reasonable costs of interpreting, lip-speaking and deaf-blind interpreting. Since this is an expense claimed from the tribunal, as opposed to the state – and in keeping with an employment tribunal's duty to make reasonable efforts to accommodate a service/tribunal user's disability – this should continue to apply for claims brought after 5 April 2012.

In so far as the previous regime for reimbursement of expenses out of state funds continues to apply, rule 83 of the Tribunal Rules 2013 allows a tribunal to make an order requiring a party or a representative to reimburse the Secretary of State (in whole or in part) for any allowances paid to any person for the purposes of, or in connection with, that person's attendance at the tribunal (other than allowances paid to tribunal members). However, such an order can only be made on the back of a costs order, PTO or – in the case of a representative

1045

– a wasted costs order. The rule states that where the tribunal makes a costs order or PTO against a party or a wasted costs order against a representative, it may also make an order that the party/representative reimburse the Secretary of State. In other words, it is not a free-standing order in its own right and is dependent upon one of those three orders being made against the party or representative in question.

20.34 Furthermore, even if one of those three orders has been made, it does not follow that an order under rule 83 will also be made. The tribunal's power under rule 83 is discretionary. Nevertheless, it is likely to be exercised in the majority of cases where the Secretary of State has paid an allowance and the tribunal has made a costs, preparation time or wasted costs order.

It is worth emphasising that rule 83 only applies to payments made by the Secretary of State. In other words, an employment tribunal cannot order a party or representative to reimburse payments the tribunal has made in respect of interpreters for those who are deaf or hard of hearing.

20.35 Finally, it should be noted that there is nothing to stop a person who has claimed expenses from the state also applying for a 'witness expenses' order under rule 75(1)(c). The advantage of doing so is that, as noted above, some of the limits on expenses that can be claimed from the state are relatively low. The person in question may perhaps be able to claim additional expenses by way of an order under rule 75(2)(c), applying the 'necessary and reasonable expenses' test.

20.36 **Order against respondent when unfair dismissal hearing postponed**

Rule 76(3) of the Tribunal Rules 2013 is specific to unfair dismissal proceedings. It provides that where, in proceedings for unfair dismissal, a final hearing is postponed or adjourned, the employment tribunal *shall* order the respondent to pay the costs incurred as a result of the postponement or adjournment if:

• the claimant has requested reinstatement or re-engagement at least seven days before the hearing

• the respondent has failed, without a special reason, to adduce reasonable evidence as to the availability of the job from which the claimant was dismissed or of comparable or suitable employment, and

• this failure has caused the postponement or adjournment.

Note that, unlike all the other types of employment tribunal orders discussed in this chapter, this one is not discretionary. The tribunal must make the order if the grounds for doing so are made out. In addition, the order can only be made against the respondent. Although not specifically stated in rule 76(3), it would seem that, as under the old rules, the costs are payable to the claimant.

As noted above, a 'costs order', as defined by rule 75(1)(a), cannot be made in **20.37** conjunction with a PTO in favour of the same party in the same proceedings – see 'Order to pay represented party's costs – costs incurred while represented'. However, an order in unfair dismissal proceedings against the respondent in respect of costs caused by an adjournment or postponement does not appear to be a costs order for this purpose – indeed, the term 'costs order' does not appear in rule 76(3) at all. This implies that such an order *can* be made in conjunction with a PTO and irrespective of whether or not the claimant is represented. (A costs order under rule 75(1)(a) can only be made in favour of a party who is represented.) The old rules, by contrast, expressly classified this type of order as a 'costs order' when it was made in favour of a claimant who was legally represented. As such, it could not be made in conjunction with a PTO in favour of the same party in the same proceedings – see rule 46(1) of the Tribunal Rules 2004.

Order against representative to pay 'wasted costs'   **20.38**
The Tribunal Rules 2004 introduced the power for employment tribunals to make an order against a party's representative – known as a 'wasted costs' order – as a result of the representative's conduct (old rule 48). This has been carried forward into the Tribunal Rules 2013, rule 80 of which provides that a tribunal may make a wasted costs order against a representative in favour of any party where that party has incurred 'wasted costs'.

Guidance from the civil courts. Rule 80 is based on the wasted costs provisions **20.39** that apply in the civil courts, with the definition of 'wasted costs' being identical to that contained in S.51(7) of the Senior Courts Act 1981 – see 'Meaning of "wasted costs"' below. Accordingly, the authorities applicable to wasted costs in the civil law generally are equally applicable in the employment tribunals – Ratcliffe Duce and Gammer v L Binns (t/a Parc Ferme) EAT 0100/08 and Mitchells Solicitors v Funkwerk Information Technologies York Ltd EAT 0541/07. The two leading authorities analysing the scope of S.51 and the circumstances in which such orders can be made are Ridehalgh v Horsefield 1994 3 All ER 848, CA, and Medcalf v Mardell and ors 2002 3 All ER 721, HL. In the Mitchells solicitors case, the EAT confirmed that these cases are 'sources of essential assistance' for employment tribunals in the matter of wasted costs.

Meaning of 'wasted costs'. 'Wasted costs' means costs incurred: **20.40**

- as a result of any improper, unreasonable or negligent act or omission on the part of the representative – rule 80(1)(a), or

- which, in the light of any such act or omission occurring after they were incurred, the employment tribunal considers it unreasonable to expect the party to pay – rule 80(1)(b).

1047

The meaning of 'wasted costs' therefore reflects the grounds for making such orders. These grounds are considered in more detail under 'Grounds for making orders against representatives' below.

20.41 Meaning of 'representative'. Wasted costs orders can only be made against a 'representative'. This is defined by rule 80(2) as 'a party's legal or other representative or any employee of such representative, but it does not include a representative who is not acting in pursuit of profit with regard to the proceedings'. So the term 'representative' is not limited to legally qualified representatives. However, persons such as trade union representatives, Citizens Advice Bureau advisers, and representatives of other voluntary bodies will not generally be at risk of wasted costs orders in that they will not be acting in pursuit of profit.

A legally qualified representative will not constitute a representative if he or she is not acting in pursuit of profit. An example:

- **Jackson v Cambridgeshire County Council and ors** EAT 0402/09: the EAT overturned a wasted costs order made by an employment tribunal against a solicitor, J. Although in no doubt that J's 'reprehensible' behaviour fell short of what was expected from a solicitor conducting himself in a professional manner, there were no grounds for concluding that J – who was representing a family member – was acting in pursuit of profit. He had denied as much when the wasted costs application was heard and this was exactly the type of case in which, because of the family element, he might be expected to be acting pro bono. In these circumstances, the employment tribunal needed solid grounds for reaching the opposite conclusion, which, in the EAT's view, it did not have. The tribunal had found that J's behaviour was designed to induce a financial settlement, which led it to 'suspect very strongly' that he was the beneficiary of a conditional fee agreement. However, the EAT considered that this was equally consistent with a representative acting on a pro bono basis and that there was no reason to assume that J might have agreed to take part of any ultimate settlement or award.

20.42 Rule 80(2) expressly provides that a representative acting on a contingency or conditional fee arrangement is considered to be acting in pursuit of profit. Thus, a wasted costs order can be made against such a person. Note, however, that a wasted costs order cannot be made against a representative where he or she is an employee of the party and is representing the party in his or her capacity as an employee – rule 80(3). An example could be an in-house lawyer.

20.43 In favour of any party. Rule 80(1) provides that a tribunal may make a wasted costs order in favour of any party – i.e. whether represented or unrepresented – where that party has incurred wasted costs. As emphasised by rule 80(3), this is irrespective of whether or not the party in question is legally represented. In addition, it clarifies that such an order can be made in favour of a representative's own client. In Medcalf v Mardell and ors (above) the House of Lords stated that it is possible to visualise situations where the negligence of an advocate might justify the making of a wasted costs order in favour of both parties, such as where an advocate fails to turn up at court so that a hearing date is lost.

Amount of wasted costs. Rule 81 provides that a wasted costs order may **20.44** require the representative to pay the whole or part of any wasted costs of the relevant party. It may also disallow any wasted costs otherwise payable to the representative and order the representative to repay his or her client any costs which have already been paid. The amount to be paid, disallowed or repaid must in each case be specified in the order. Note that there is no limit to the amount of wasted costs that can be ordered by an employment tribunal. The assessment of wasted costs is considered further under 'Methods of assessment and applicable statutory limits – assessment of wasted costs' below.

Practical difficulties. There are some potential practical difficulties arising out **20.45** of the application of the wasted costs rules. Most obviously, they may create a conflict of interest between a representative and his or her client if an employment tribunal is considering disallowing the representative's fees. For that reason the Court of Appeal in Ridehalgh v Horsefield (above) emphasised that a legal representative should not be held to have acted improperly, unreasonably or negligently simply because he or she acts on behalf of a party whose claim or defence is doomed to fail. Similarly, the House of Lords in Medcalf v Mardell and ors (above) commented that it is the duty of the advocate to present his or her client's case even though he or she may think that it is hopeless and even though he or she may have advised the client that it is. The willingness of professional advocates to represent litigants should not be undermined either by creating conflicts of interest or by exposing the advocates to pressures that will deter them from representing certain clients or from doing so effectively.

Another difficulty relates to the principle of legal professional privilege (see Chapter 9, 'Responding to opponent's case', under 'Disclosure and inspection of documents – privilege'). The question as to whether a legal representative was negligent may turn on what instructions were provided by the client and what advice was given by the representative, both of which are matters covered by legal professional privilege that can only be waived by the client. In cases where privilege is not waived, a representative may be prevented from advancing a full answer to the complaint made against him or her. The Court of Appeal in the Ridehalgh case provided some useful guidance in this regard. It recognised the difficulties that privilege might cause lawyers in these circumstances, and stated that judges who are invited to make a wasted costs order must make full allowance for the fact that legal representatives may be prevented from telling the full story. Where there is room for doubt in these circumstances, said the Court, the lawyers are entitled to the benefit of that doubt, and it is 'only when, with all allowances made, a lawyer's conduct of proceedings is quite plainly unjustifiable that it can be appropriate to make a wasted costs order'.

1049

20.46 This aspect of the Ridehalgh decision was approved by the House of Lords in the Medcalf case. Lord Bingham stated that the relevant passage in Ridehalgh 'read literally and applied with extreme care... ought to offer appropriate protection to a practitioner against whom a wasted costs order is sought in these circumstances'. He emphasised, however, that only exceptionally could the exacting conditions set out in Ridehalgh be satisfied, stating that 'where a wasted costs order is sought against a practitioner precluded by legal professional privilege from giving his full answer to the application, the court should not make an order unless, proceeding with extreme care, it is (a) satisfied that there is nothing the practitioner could say, if unconstrained, to resist the order and (b) that it is in all the circumstances fair to make the order'.

Both Ridehalgh and Medcalf were cited by Mr Justice Elias (as he then was) when President of the EAT in Ratcliffe Duce and Gammer v L Binns (t/a Parc Ferme) EAT 0100/08. He observed that where the privilege of the client is not waived, it will be a very exceptional case indeed where a court will be entitled to infer that a party is abusing the process of the court by pursuing a hopeless case – see further 'Grounds for making orders against representatives – improper, unreasonable or negligent' below.

20.47 **Order against employer to pay penalty**

By virtue of S.12A ETA employment tribunals have a discretionary power to impose a financial penalty on an employer found to have breached a claimant's employment rights if the tribunal considers that the breach had 'one or more aggravating features'. It provides that in a claim involving an employer and a worker the tribunal may order the employer to pay a penalty *to the Secretary of State* (whether or not the tribunal also makes a financial award against the employer on the claim itself) if it:

- 'concludes that the employer has breached any of the worker's rights to which the claim relates', and

- is of the opinion that the breach has 'one or more aggravating features'.

The power to impose a penalty applies in respect of cases decided on or after 6 April 2014. This type of order is discussed further under 'Penalties against employers' below.

20.48 ## Grounds for making orders against a party

In this section we consider in more detail when costs and preparation time orders will be made against a party in the employment tribunal. The grounds for making a costs order under rule 75(1)(a) of the Tribunal Rules 2013 and a preparation time order (PTO) under rule 75(2) are the same, namely:

- a party (or that party's representative) has acted vexatiously, abusively, disruptively or otherwise unreasonably in the bringing or conducting of proceedings (or part thereof) – rule 76(1)(a)

- the claim or response has no reasonable prospect of success – rule 76(1)(b)

- breach of an order or practice direction – rule 76(1)(2)

- postponement or adjournment of the hearing on the application of a party – rule 76(1)(2)

- the employment tribunal has decided an allegation or argument for substantially the reasons given in an earlier deposit order – rule 39(5).

All the above grounds are discretionary – i.e. the employment tribunal may make a costs (or preparation time) order if the ground is made out but is not obliged to do so. Note, however, that although the first two grounds are also discretionary, the tribunal is under a duty to consider making an order when they are made out – rule 76(1). It is worth re-emphasising that a costs order under rule 75(1)(a) can only be made in favour of a represented party and a PTO can only be made in favour of a party who has not been legally represented. In addition, it is not possible to make both types of order in favour of the same party in the same proceedings – rule 76(3).

Other grounds for making orders are as follows: **20.49**

- to reimburse an employment tribunal fee to a successful party, a costs order under rule 75(1)(b) can be made (see 'What orders can employment tribunal make? – order to reimburse employment tribunal fee' above)

- to reimburse witness expenses, a costs order under rule 75(1)(c) can be made (see 'What orders can employment tribunal make? – order to reimburse witness expenses' above)

- in proceedings for unfair dismissal, costs incurred as a result of the postponement or adjournment of a final hearing must be awarded against the respondent under rule 76(3), where this is caused by its failure to provide evidence about job availability when warned – at least seven days before the hearing – that the employee wishes to be reinstated or re-engaged (see 'What orders can employment tribunal make? – order against respondent when unfair dismissal hearing postponed' above)

- where an employer's breach of a claimant's employment rights has 'one or more aggravating features', employment tribunals will shortly be empowered to order the employer to pay a penalty to the Secretary of State under S.12A of the Employment Tribunals Act 1996 (see 'Penalties against employers' below).

1051

20.50 It can be seen that each of these grounds is specific to the type of order at issue. For example, a costs order under rule 75(1)(b) can only be made in respect of employment tribunal fees and a costs order under rule 75(1)(c) can only be made in respect of witness expenses. These more specific grounds are considered further under 'What orders can employment tribunal make?' above and (in the case of penalties) 'Penalties against employers' below. Note that if the ground set out in rule 76(3) (i.e. relating to unfair dismissal proceedings) is made out, the tribunal *must* make an order against the respondent in respect of costs incurred as a result. All the other grounds are discretionary – i.e. the tribunal may make an order if the ground is made out but is not obliged to do so.

We now consider the grounds for making costs orders under rule 75(1)(a) and PTOs under rule 75(2) in more detail.

20.51 Conduct

An employment tribunal has a discretionary power to make a costs order or PTO under rule 76(1)(a) of the Tribunal Rules 2013 where it considers that a party (or that party's representative) has acted 'vexatiously, abusively, disruptively or otherwise unreasonably' in either the bringing of the proceedings (or part) or the way that the proceedings (or part) have been conducted. As can be seen, a tribunal can make an order against a party, not only based upon the party's conduct, but also based upon his or her *representative's* conduct. This is briefly discussed under 'Representative's conduct' below.

The fact that a claimant or respondent may ultimately be successful does not necessarily prevent the tribunal from making an order of costs against him or her based on unreasonable conduct. An example:

• **Kotecha v Insurety plc (t/a Capital Healthcare) and ors** EAT 0461/07: K's claim for race discrimination was unsuccessful before the employment tribunal. After awarding judgment against him, the tribunal ordered him to pay I plc's costs of £10,000 on the ground that he had acted vexatiously in the conduct of proceedings and had not been honest with the tribunal. K successfully appealed against the tribunal's judgment in respect of his race discrimination claim and it was set aside on the ground that the tribunal had misdirected itself in relation to the burden of proof. K argued that the tribunal's costs order should also be set aside. The EAT held that there was no connection between the error of law made by the tribunal in the substantive case, which related to the burden of proof, and the conduct that gave rise to the costs order. The tribunal's perception of K's conduct was not affected by its misapplication of the burden of proof. It was therefore not realistic to suggest that the tribunal might have exercised its discretion differently in the matter of costs.

20.52 Duty to consider making an order. Where the conduct of a party (or of his or her representative) is 'vexatious, abusive, disruptive or otherwise unreasonable', rule 76(1) provides that the tribunal *shall consider* whether to make a costs order or PTO. Therefore, it has a duty to consider making an order but has the discretion whether to actually make the award. In other words, rule 76(1) imposes a two-stage test: first, a tribunal must ask itself whether a party's conduct falls within rule 76(1)(a); if so, it *must* go on to ask itself whether it is appropriate to exercise its discretion in favour of awarding costs against that party (perhaps taking into account some of the factors considered under 'Factors relevant to tribunal's discretion' below). This two-stage test is illustrated by the following cases:

- **Monaghan v Close Thornton Solicitors** EAT 0003/01: an employment tribunal stated that 'by making the respondents come to the tribunal today we consider that the applicant has acted unreasonably and therefore we make an award of costs of £500'. On appeal, the EAT set this costs order aside. In making the award, the tribunal did not seem to have in mind that it was not enough merely to point to the claimant having acted unreasonably to justify the exercise of the discretion to award costs. The EAT pointed out that the fact that the claimant had acted unreasonably justified only the existence or availability of that discretion. The tribunal had erred in moving directly from the existence of the discretion to making the award without any intervening pause to consider whether this step was appropriate

- **Beat v Devon County Council and anor** EAT 0534/05: the EAT held that an employment tribunal had erred in jumping from its finding that the bringing of proceedings had been unreasonable and misconceived to awarding costs of £10,000 against the claimant, without going through the process of exercising its discretion as to whether that order was appropriate. Having identified the aspects of the claimant's conduct that were unreasonable and misconceived, the tribunal should have stood back and looked at all the factors that have to be taken into account when assessing the appropriate level of costs. That involved the balancing of the amount of costs incurred by the unreasonableness of the conduct or the misconceived part of the claim against the other parts of the claim, and by taking account of the need – if the tribunal considered there was a need – for the respondent to be compensated by way of a costs order. The EAT decided to carry out this balancing exercise itself, as a result of which it reduced the costs order to £5,000

- **Lewald-Jezierska v Solicitors in Law Ltd and ors** EAT 0165/06: an employment tribunal decided that L-J had acted unreasonably and 'accordingly' awarded costs against her. The EAT overturned the award because the tribunal had not considered whether, in the circumstances, a costs award was appropriate. In particular, the tribunal made no reference to L-J's significant mental difficulties. These difficulties must have been apparent to the tribunal. Among other things, it had found her behaviour

1053

erratic and agitated, and it had access to contemporaneous evidence of her 'stress and mental exhaustion'.

20.53 Litigants in person. It is appropriate for a litigant in person to be judged less harshly in terms of his or her conduct than a litigant who is professionally represented. According to the EAT in AQ Ltd v Holden 2012 IRLR 648, EAT, an employment tribunal cannot, and should not, judge a litigant in person by the standards of a professional representative. Justice requires that tribunals do not apply professional standards to lay people, who may well be embroiled in legal proceedings for the only time in their life. Lay people are likely to lack the objectivity and knowledge of law and practice brought to bear by a professional legal adviser. The EAT stressed that tribunals must bear this in mind when assessing the threshold tests in the then equivalent to rule 76(1) of the Tribunal Rules 2013. It went on to state that, even if the threshold tests for an order for costs are met, the tribunal still has discretion whether to make an order. That discretion should be exercised having regard to all the circumstances. In this respect, it was not irrelevant that a lay person may have brought proceedings with little or no access to specialist help and advice. This was not to say that lay people are immune from orders for costs: far from it, as the cases make clear. Some litigants in person are found to have behaved vexatiously or unreasonably even when proper allowance is made for their inexperience and lack of objectivity. However, the EAT concluded that, in the instant case, the employment tribunal had been entitled to take into account the fact that H represented himself when refusing AQ Ltd its costs.

20.54 Representative's conduct. Rule 76(1)(a) provides that where a party's *representative* has acted vexatiously, abusively, disruptively or otherwise unreasonably in the bringing or conducting of the proceedings, an employment tribunal may make a costs order or PTO against the party in question. Note that rule 80 authorises tribunals to make awards of 'wasted costs' directly against representatives – see 'What orders can an employment tribunal make? – order against representative to pay "wasted costs"' above. In light of this power, some have suggested that the principle that a party can be liable to pay costs because of the way his or her representative has behaved is perhaps less significant. Nevertheless, as we shall see under 'Grounds for making orders against representatives – improper, unreasonable or negligent' below, the test for establishing wasted costs against a representative is much more stringent given that it is necessary to establish an abuse of process. Therefore, where a representative's conduct falls short of this (or where this is difficult to prove), an aggrieved party may still be able to get a costs order or PTO against the representative's client.

Note, however, that where the representative in question is inexperienced, an employment tribunal may be less likely to award costs against the party he or she is representing. In Francois v Castle Rock Properties Ltd (trading as Electric

Ballroom) EAT 0260/10 the EAT held that a tribunal had erred in making a costs order against a claimant, following a finding of unfair dismissal, for unreasonable conduct by his representative, who was not an experienced employment law advocate. It commented that it is inevitable that less experienced representatives may sometimes be slow in their presentation, or may slow the case down by taking points which might not be taken by a fully experienced representative. It does not follow that they have acted unreasonably; and it certainly does not follow that they should be expected to adhere to the standards expected of specialist advocates. It went on to state that careful findings are therefore required if it is to be said that the representative acted unreasonably merely by being slow in the presentation of a case. The tribunal should identify the delay and the cause of the delay and say why the conduct of the representative was unreasonable. If a representative had disobeyed a case management order (for example, a time limit on cross-examination or closing submissions) or ignored proper guidance or a warning from the tribunal, this may support a finding that the representative acted unreasonably. The EAT concluded that no such findings, however, had been made by the tribunal in the instant case.

Vexatious conduct. The term 'vexatious' was defined by the National Industrial **20.55** Relations Court in ET Marler Ltd v Robertson 1974 ICR 72, NIRC. The Court stated that: 'If an employee brings a hopeless claim not with any expectation of recovering compensation but out of spite to harass his employers or for some other improper motive, he acts vexatiously.' Of course, what applies to an employee bringing a claim applies equally to an employer or other respondent resisting a claim. So, it would appear that for conduct to be vexatious there must be evidence of some spite or desire to harass the other side, or the existence of some other improper motive. Simply being 'misguided' is not sufficient to establish vexatious conduct – AQ Ltd v Holden 2012 IRLR 648, EAT.

More recently, however, the Court of Appeal in Scott v Russell 2013 EWCA Civ 1432, CA (a case concerning costs awarded by an employment tribunal), cited with approval the definition of 'vexatious' given by Lord Bingham in Attorney General v Barker 2000 1 FLR 759, QBD (Civ Div). According to His Lordship, 'the hallmark of a vexatious proceeding is... that it has little or no basis in law (or at least no discernible basis); *that whatever the intention of the proceedings may be*, its effect is to subject the defendant to inconvenience, harassment and expense out of all proportion to any gain likely to accrue to the claimant, and that it involves an abuse of the process of the court, meaning by that a use of the court process for a purpose or in a way which is significantly different from the ordinary and proper use of the court process'. This suggests that where the *effect* of the conduct falls within Lord Bingham's stringent definition, this can amount to vexatious conduct, irrespective of the motive behind it.

1055

20.56 Some illustrations of conduct found to be vexatious in employment cases:

- **Wrenhurst v Catholic Herald Ltd** EAT 312/81: W pursued unsuccessful race discrimination and equal pay claims through a seven-day hearing. An employment tribunal found evidence that 'his purpose [was] to disrupt the business and other aspects of the respondents as much as possible' and awarded £1,000 costs. The EAT saw no ground in law to upset this decision, although it found it regrettable that the tribunal had not given W a formal warning about his conduct

- **French v Brent Walker Ltd** EAT 746/86: F, a director of a large public company, claimed unfair dismissal but the employment tribunal found that he had simply resigned in order to set up his own business and it awarded £1,000 costs. The EAT upheld this decision because, on the tribunal's findings of fact, F must have known that his claim was groundless and his intention was simply to harass the employer

- **Phillips v Whale Tankers Ltd** ET Case No.34762/84: P withdrew his tribunal application at 3.45 pm on the second day of the hearing. The employment tribunal found that the application had been bound to fail and was brought only out of spite to harass the employer. It awarded £500 costs

- **Sawers v British Railways Board** ET Case No.S/2648/88: S contended that she had been forced to resign from her job as a result of sexual harassment by a colleague and as a result claimed unfair dismissal and sex discrimination. An employment tribunal rejected both claims and awarded £100 costs against her. It felt that costs were appropriate because the allegations made against S's colleague were of a highly personal and damaging nature and entirely without substance. Furthermore, S's demeanour before the tribunal gave the impression that she had no belief in the genuineness of her case.

20.57 *Serial litigants.* It is worth noting that the ultimate sanction against 'serial' vexatious litigants is for the EAT – upon the application of the Attorney General or (in Scotland) the Lord Advocate – to make a restriction of proceedings order under S.33 ETA. S.33(1) provides that if, on an application made by the Attorney General or the Lord Advocate, the Appeal Tribunal is satisfied that a person has habitually and persistently and without any reasonable ground:

- instituted vexatious proceedings in an employment tribunal or before the Appeal Tribunal (whether against the same person or against different persons), or

- made vexatious applications in any proceedings in an employment tribunal or before the Appeal Tribunal,

the Appeal Tribunal may, after hearing the person or giving him or her an opportunity of being heard, make a restriction of proceedings order so that he or she cannot institute further proceedings without the leave of the EAT. For

1056

full details of the EAT's powers in respect of restriction of proceedings orders, see Chapter 17, 'Processing an appeal', under 'Vexatious proceedings'.

Abusive or disruptive conduct. A tribunal may also make a costs order or **20.58** PTO against a party who has acted abusively or disruptively in bringing or conducting proceedings (or his or her representative has done so). For example, in Garnes v London Borough of Lambeth and anor EAT 1237/97, a case which concerned a complaint of race discrimination, the tribunal office had made four attempts to fix a hearing, but had adjourned on the first three occasions at G's request. In addition, G had failed to attend two interlocutory hearings as he objected to their being held. At the fourth hearing, which was fixed for 15 days, G again said he could not proceed. The tribunal offered to adjourn for five days but G said he would not attend at any time during the 15-day period. The tribunal then adjourned for an hour to allow G to consider his position. The tribunal warned G that if he did not attend after the hour the case might be struck out and costs awarded against him. When G did not attend the tribunal struck out the case and awarded the respondent the costs of attending the tribunal hearing. The tribunal held that G had conducted the proceedings 'unreasonably, vexatiously and disruptively' and this was upheld by the EAT on appeal.

Unreasonable conduct. A costs order or PTO may also be awarded against a **20.59** party under rule 76(1)(a) where the party (or his or her representative) has acted unreasonably in bringing or conducting proceedings. 'Unreasonable' has its ordinary English meaning and is not to be interpreted as if it meant something similar to 'vexatious' – Dyer v Secretary of State for Employment EAT 183/83. It will often be the case, however, that a tribunal will find a party's conduct to be both vexatious and unreasonable.

In determining whether to make an order under this ground, an employment tribunal should take into account the 'nature, gravity and effect' of a party's unreasonable conduct – McPherson v BNP Paribas (London Branch) 2004 ICR 1398, CA (discussed in more detail below). However, a tribunal should not misunderstand that to mean that the circumstances of a case have to be separated into sections such as 'nature', 'gravity' and 'effect', with each section being analysed separately – Yerrakalva v Barnsley Metropolitan Borough Council 2012 ICR 420, CA (also discussed below). The Court of Appeal in Yerrakalva commented that it was important not to lose sight of the totality of the circumstances. The vital point in exercising the discretion to order costs (or a PTO) is to look at the whole picture. The tribunal has to ask whether there has been unreasonable conduct by the paying party in bringing, defending or conducting the case and, in doing so, identify the conduct, what was unreasonable about it, and what effect it had.

Reasonableness is a matter of fact for the employment tribunal, and it will be **20.60** difficult to argue that the tribunal has made an error of law unless it can be

1057

shown that it has neglected relevant considerations or taken into account irrelevant ones. In Khan v Heywood and Middleton Primary Care Trust 2006 ICR 543, CA, for example, the Court of Appeal stated that whether conduct could be characterised as unreasonable required an exercise of judgment about which there could be reasonable scope for disagreement among tribunals, properly directing themselves. It went on to uphold an employment tribunal's decision to award costs against K. While accepting that not all employment tribunals would characterise K's conduct as unreasonable, the Court of Appeal noted that there had been nothing wrong with the way in which the tribunal had exercised its discretion to order costs. This case is discussed further under 'Change of mind' below.

Employment tribunals must be careful not to penalise parties unnecessarily by labelling conduct 'unreasonable' when it may, in fact, be perfectly legitimate in the circumstances. An example:

- **Mackinnon v Bromley Appointments.com Ltd and ors** EAT 0639/04: an employment tribunal, having upheld M's sex discrimination complaints, considered the issue of compensation at a remedies hearing. However, the employer objected to the tribunal chairman sitting at the remedies hearing, arguing that the chairman had disclosed information described as commercially sensitive by the employer to M. Consequently, the chairman stood down. The day before the remedies hearing resumed, M's solicitors discovered that the matter was listed before both a new chairman and two new lay members. In view of their objection to the new lay membership, they asked for an adjournment. The tribunal held that this request was unreasonable, and went on to order the claimant to pay the employer's costs of £2,240. The EAT, however, disagreed, finding that the claimant's representatives had not acted unreasonably in making an application for an adjournment at this late stage. In the EAT's view, they had been entitled to assume, unless and until they had a clear and reasoned decision to the contrary, that the matter would be listed before the original lay members. In such circumstances, the order for costs had been wholly inappropriate and was therefore set aside.

20.61 *Persistent failure to provide information.* A persistent failure to provide information may be held to be unreasonable. In Kaur v John L Brierley Ltd EAT 783/00, for example, K and her advisers persistently failed to identify the unlawful deduction they were alleging had been made from her wages. This was despite repeated and reasonable requests from the employer's solicitors. Although she was not able to provide any explanation for this failure, K pursued the proceedings, causing the employer to incur additional and wholly unnecessary costs. When the final hearing was imminent K withdrew. The employment tribunal hearing the employer's application for costs ordered K to pay costs to be assessed in the county court. This decision was upheld by the EAT.

Lies and false evidence. Another relevant factor is the extent to which the **20.62** tribunal considers that a party was truthful in evidence. In Daleside Nursing Home Ltd v Mathew EAT 0519/08 the Appeal Tribunal held that an employment tribunal had reached a perverse decision when concluding that the making of a false allegation, which lay at the heart of a race discrimination claim, did not constitute unreasonable action in bringing the claim. However, the EAT was at pains to stress that this decision did not create a general principle. In the subsequent case of HCA International Ltd v May-Bheemul EAT 0477/10 the EAT noted the rejection in Daleside of any general principle and added: 'A lie on its own will not necessarily be sufficient to found an award of costs. It will always be necessary for the tribunal to examine the context and to look at the nature, gravity and effect of the lie in determining the unreasonableness of the alleged conduct.' This statement was subsequently endorsed by the Court of Appeal in Arrowsmith v Nottingham Trent University 2012 ICR 159, CA. In that case, the Court upheld the award of costs against a claimant whose complaint of sex discrimination relied on untrue assertions that job interviewers knew about her pregnancy when deciding not to offer her the job. Similarly, in Ghosh v Nokia Siemens Networks UK Ltd EAT 0125/12 the EAT upheld an employment tribunal's costs order against a claimant who had made a number of 'wholly unsubstantiated allegations' of discrimination. Making such serious and unsustained allegations was, in the EAT's view, 'undoubtedly' capable of amounting to unreasonable conduct.

More recently, the EAT confirmed that costs should not automatically be awarded simply because a party has knowingly given false evidence. In Kapoor v Governing Body of Barnhill Community High School EAT 0352/13 the Appeal Tribunal held that an employment tribunal erred when it stated that 'without more, to conduct a case by not telling the truth is to conduct a case unreasonably' and that costs in the sum of £8,900 should therefore be awarded against the claimant. Although in that case there were powerful factors that the tribunal could properly take into account – e.g. its view that the claimant had falsified documents and that her evidence was not worthy of belief – these were only relevant if the tribunal approached the exercise of its discretion on the matter of costs correctly, which, by virtue of its presumption that false evidence was synonymous with unreasonable conduct, it did not do in this case.

However, in Topic v Hollyland Pitta Bakery and ors EAT 0523/11 the EAT made **20.63** it clear that the question of whether or not a party lied should not be mistaken as a minimum threshold for determining that there has been unreasonable conduct such as to justify a costs order. In that case the EAT upheld the decision of an employment tribunal to award costs on the basis that T's allegations of direct sex discrimination and victimisation were misconceived and unreasonable. The tribunal had concluded that, although T did not lie, she had an unreliable and damaged perception of reality. On appeal, the Appeal Tribunal confirmed that the fact that T had not lied did not prevent the tribunal from finding that the

1059

claim had been misconceived and unreasonable. It also held that it was not a breach of T's right to a private and family life under Article 8 of the European Convention on Human Rights for the employment tribunal to take into account the state of her mental health and her refusal to seek treatment, in circumstances where that material had been put before the tribunal by T.

20.64 *Course of conduct.* It may be that a party's conduct, taken as a whole, amounts to unreasonable conduct. In Sahota v Dudley Metropolitan Borough Council EAT 0821/03, for example, S lied in his evidence, introduced new matters at a whim and, when faced with a cause or a point which was lost, would not concede it, meaning that the length of the hearing was unnecessarily prolonged. An employment tribunal concluded he had behaved unreasonably and awarded a costs order of £9,000 against him. This decision was upheld by the EAT, which also ordered him to pay an additional £1,000 towards the cost of the appeal.

20.65 *Change of mind.* A dramatic change of mind relating to the bringing or conducting of proceedings could amount to unreasonable conduct. This is illustrated by the case of Khan v Heywood and Middleton Primary Care Trust 2006 ICR 543, CA. Following an unsuccessful job application, K presented a tribunal claim alleging race discrimination against the Trust. He subsequently notified the tribunal that he wished to withdraw his claim and, accordingly, the tribunal notified both parties that the file had been closed. K then instructed new representatives, who made an application to the tribunal for an order setting aside his notice of withdrawal. The tribunal refused K's application and made a costs order against him on the basis that his conduct had been unreasonable. While acknowledging that not all employment tribunals would characterise K's change of mind as unreasonable, the Court of Appeal upheld the tribunal's decision, noting that there had been nothing wrong with the way in which the tribunal had exercised its discretion to order costs.

20.66 *Being 'overly legalistic' or technical.* Adopting an overly legalistic approach can, in certain circumstances, amount to unreasonable conduct of the proceedings. In Godfrey Morgan Solicitors Ltd v Marzan EAT 0465/11 the claimant, M, had brought an employment tribunal claim in respect of unpaid wages against 'Godfrey Morgan Solicitors t/a GMS Law'. There were, in fact, two legal entities with similar, but not matching names: 'Godfrey Morgan Solicitors' (a firm) and 'Godfrey Morgan Solicitors Limited t/a GMS Law' (a company). GM was both a partner in the firm and a director of the company. The firm's response to the claim was to argue that the tribunal had no jurisdiction to hear the claim as M had never been its employee. This was supported by a witness statement from GM in which he neglected to mention that he knew M personally, or that he was in possession of her contract of employment with the company. Upon ordering that the company be joined as a second respondent, the employment judge made a PTO against the firm on the basis that its conduct of the defence had been 'appalling' and unreasonable.

Upholding the decision to make a PTO, Mr Justice Langstaff (President of the EAT) stressed that since solicitors are officers of the court, they have a duty to facilitate the administration of justice and not to frustrate that process: where a respondent has been misidentified by a claimant (as in this case), the usual position would be that it puts the claimant on notice and gives him or her an opportunity to correct the error, since it is plain in most cases that it is an inadvertent error of no materiality to the issues in the case. It was contrary to the whole purpose of the employment tribunal system for the firm to take such a technical point, and it was fully within the employment judge's discretion to regard the defence as unreasonable. According to Langstaff P, 'tribunals must be alert to ensure that the party with the big bucks does not put the other party to such expense or trouble as to make it difficult for them to continue to litigate the real issues'.

Failure to instruct solicitors earlier. There is no obligation on a party to instruct **20.67** solicitors when bringing or pursuing proceedings. Therefore, the failure to instruct solicitors until late in proceedings will not constitute unreasonable conduct, even if time would have been saved had solicitors been instructed earlier. An example:

• **Larwood v Earth Tronics Inc Ltd** EAT 0558/03: L commenced proceedings in an employment tribunal alleging unfair dismissal. At that time he was representing himself, but subsequently discovered that he had insurance cover for the litigation, and instructed solicitors. The solicitors sought to amend his complaint to add a claim of constructive dismissal but the employer opposed that application. A hearing was subsequently held at which the amendment was allowed. However, the tribunal ordered L to pay the employer's costs with regard to the application, on the basis that his failure to instruct solicitors earlier resulted in the late application to amend the complaint and was unreasonable. This order was quashed by the EAT. Given that there was no obligation upon a party to instruct a solicitor, it could not, in the EAT's view, be unreasonable conduct, of itself, to instruct solicitors after proceedings had been instituted. Moreover, the hearing was only necessary because the application, which in the event substantially succeeded, was opposed by the employer.

Prolonging proceedings. A party who unduly protracts tribunal proceedings **20.68** may be acting unreasonably. Two contrasting examples:

• **South Eastern Electricity Board v McNeillis** EAT 353/81: the employer spent seven days (not the anticipated three) in presenting its case with a great deal of irrelevant detail. An employment tribunal, whose decision to award costs was upheld by the EAT, characterised this as 'using a sledgehammer to crack a nut'

- **Raveneau v London Borough of Brent** EAT 1175/96: the hearing of R's race discrimination complaint took over nine days. R adduced a lot of supporting evidence and conducted a wide-ranging investigation into her employment by the respondent. The employment tribunal felt that the hearing should have taken no more than three or four days and awarded costs of £500 against R. This order was quashed by the EAT. Another tribunal had earlier set a time estimate of ten days for the case, and it had therefore been completed within the allotted time span. The EAT stated that claims of discrimination require full and proper consideration and that, in the circumstances, the costs order was unfair.

20.69 *Withdrawal of claim.* It is not unreasonable conduct *per se* for a claimant to withdraw a claim – McPherson v BNP Paribas (London Branch) 2004 ICR 1398, CA. As the Court of Appeal in McPherson observed, it would be unfortunate if claimants were deterred from dropping claims by the prospect of an order for costs on withdrawal in circumstances where such an order might well not be made against them if they fought on to a full hearing and failed. It further commented that withdrawal could lead to a saving of costs and that tribunals should not adopt a practice on costs that would deter claimants from making 'sensible litigation decisions'. On the other hand, the Court was also clear that tribunals should not follow a practice on costs that might encourage speculative claims, allowing claimants to start cases and to pursue them down to the last week or two before the hearing in the hope of receiving an offer to settle, and then, failing an offer, dropping the case without any risk of a costs sanction. The critical question in this regard was whether the claimant withdrawing the claim has conducted the proceedings unreasonably, not whether the withdrawal of the claim is in itself unreasonable. Although the case related to the withdrawal of a claim, the same would, presumably, apply to the withdrawal of a response by a respondent. This scenario is considered further under 'Factors relevant to tribunal's discretion – late withdrawals' below.

20.70 *Use of expert evidence.* Guidance as to the standards to be expected from parties in cases involving expert evidence was provided by the EAT in De Keyser Ltd v Wilson 2001 IRLR 324, EAT. In that case the Appeal Tribunal stated that if a party fails, without good reason, to follow these guidelines and if, in consequence, another party suffers delay or is put to expense which a due performance of the guidelines would have been likely to avoid, then the tribunal may wish to consider whether there has been unreasonable conduct for the purpose of what is now rule 76(1)(a) of the Tribunal Rules 2013. The guidelines include the following points:

- joint instruction of experts is preferred

- a letter of instruction should specify in detail any particular questions that the expert is to answer and any general subjects which he or she is to address

- instructions are to avoid partisanship. It is important not to beg the very questions that are raised. The letter should emphasise the expert's duty to the tribunal

- separately instructed experts should attend a without prejudice meeting in an attempt to resolve conflict.

Bringing or conducting proceedings. A tribunal's discretion to make a costs **20.71** order or PTO under rule 76(1)(a) arises where a party has acted unreasonably in either the bringing or conducting of proceedings. This means that a party's conduct *prior* to proceedings cannot found a costs order or PTO. In **Health Development Agency v Parish** 2004 IRLR 550, EAT, for example, the Agency refused to provide P with a written statement giving the reasons for his dismissal and he brought a tribunal claim. The tribunal found that the Agency had acted vexatiously and unreasonably in the conduct of the proceedings, and ordered it to pay costs of £8,519. On appeal, the EAT held that the tribunal's finding that the Agency had acted unreasonably between the time it submitted its response to P's claim and the time reasons for dismissal were finally given was 'plainly and unarguably right'. However, it stressed that the respondent's conduct *prior* to proceedings could not found an award of costs. The tribunal did not have the power to award costs against the Agency in respect of the period before it filed its response.

Failure to accept an offer. In Lake v Arco Grating (UK) Ltd EAT 0511/04 the **20.72** respondent, prior to a tribunal hearing, offered not to pursue costs against L if he withdrew his unfair and wrongful dismissal claims within 24 hours. L did not do so and, in the event, his claims were unsuccessful. The employment tribunal awarded costs against L for having acted unreasonably in pursuing the proceedings after receiving the respondent's offer. On appeal, the EAT set aside that costs order, noting that a failure to accept the offer could not, in itself, constitute action in bringing or conducting the proceedings.

The practice of setting out a financial offer of settlement in writing accompanied by a warning as to costs – often referred to as a 'Calderbank letter' – is sometimes followed in the course of tribunal litigation. The strategy behind this is that if the offer is not accepted and the case proceeds to a final hearing, culminating in the rejecting party either losing the case or failing to recover compensation at least equivalent to the amount previously offered by way of settlement, then costs should be ordered against that party. For full details of this strategy and how it plays out in the context of tribunal litigation, see 'Factors relevant to tribunal's discretion – rejection of settlement offer' below.

Respondent who has not had a response accepted. Rule 38(4) of the Tribunal **20.73** Rules 2004 used to provide that 'a costs order may be made against or in favour of a respondent who has not had a response accepted in the proceedings in relation to the conduct of any part which he has taken in the proceedings'. This

1063

provision has not been replicated in the new rules. To understand the implications of this, it is worth turning to an EAT case that examined old rule 38(4) (and its relationship with other provisions in the Tribunal Rules 2004) in some detail – Sutton v The Ranch Ltd EAT 0072/06. There, the EAT considered whether this rule permitted costs to be awarded against a respondent who had failed to submit a response form. The facts were that, following R Ltd's failure to put in a response to S's various claims, a tribunal ruled in S's favour, awarded her compensation, and also made an order for costs against R Ltd in the sum of £5,500 on the basis that the company had conducted the proceedings unreasonably. At a review hearing, the tribunal chairman noted that rule 9 of the Tribunal Rules 2004 made it clear that a respondent was not entitled to take part in the proceedings if he or she has not presented a response, except in certain defined circumstances (which included making an application for a review of certain decisions). Since R Ltd had not presented a response, the company had not taken any part in the proceedings, save in respect of its review applications. Thus, the tribunal did not have the power to make a costs order against R Ltd under rule 38(4) for costs incurred up to and including the remedies hearing. The chairman revoked the order for costs, and this decision was upheld by the EAT. In the EAT's view, rule 38(4) allowed a tribunal to make an order for costs against or in favour of a respondent who had not put in a response, but only in relation to the limited scope for conducting proceedings permitted by rule 9.

It can be seen then that old rule 38(4) had a narrow ambit in that costs could only be awarded against (or in favour) of a respondent who had failed to put in a response in relation to the limited conduct of proceedings that was permitted by old rule 9. That rule allowed the respondent to take part in proceedings to make a request for written reasons; make an application to review a default judgment; make an application to have a decision reviewed; be called as a witness by another party; and be sent a copy of a document or corrected entry.

20.74 New rule 21 of the Tribunal Rules 2013 now provides that where no response has been presented (or any response received has been rejected) the respondent shall be entitled to notice of any hearings and decisions of the employment tribunal but – unless and until an extension of time is granted – shall only be entitled to participate in any hearing to the extent permitted by an employment judge. Thus the respondent's participation becomes a matter for the judge's discretion. To the extent that the judge does allow the respondent to participate in proceedings, we would suggest that – despite the absence of an equivalent to rule 38(4) in the new rules – a costs order or PTO could be made in the event that the respondent's participation in the proceedings is found to be unreasonable.

20.75 **Are costs limited to those attributable to the offending conduct?** In Health Development Agency v Parish 2004 IRLR 550, EAT, the EAT stated that where a tribunal has found that a party has conducted proceedings unreasonably, it must examine carefully what costs are *attributable* to that unreasonable conduct. This suggests that there must be a causal link between the conduct of the paying party and the costs that are awarded – and if there is no causal link, no costs order (or PTO) can be made. However, in McPherson v BNP Paribas (London Branch) 2004 ICR 1398, CA, Lord Justice Mummery stated that the Parish case is not authority for the proposition that what is now rule 76(1)(a) limits costs to those that are caused by or attributable to *specific instances* of unreasonable conduct on the part of the offending party. Mummery LJ, with whom the other members of the Court essentially agreed, stated that the Tribunal Rules do not impose any requirement that the costs must be caused by, or at least be proportionate to, the particular conduct that has been identified as unreasonable. In his view, it is not punitive and impermissible for a tribunal to order costs without confining them to those attributable to that conduct. He observed that the tribunal must have regard to the nature, gravity and effect of the unreasonable conduct as factors relevant to the exercise of the discretion, but that was not the same as requiring the costs-seeking party to prove that specific unreasonable conduct by the other party caused particular costs to be incurred.

Mummery LJ was nevertheless persuaded that the employment tribunal in this particular case had erred in law in ordering the claimant to pay the costs of the entirety of the proceedings on the basis that his conduct of 'the whole of this case' had been unreasonable. On the tribunal's own findings, M's unreasonable conduct began with his unjustified application for a postponement on medical grounds and 'continued as a history of procrastination, delay and lack of cooperation down to the notice of withdrawal'. There was, however, no evidence of any unreasonable conduct during the first 11 months of the proceedings. In the circumstances, the Court varied the costs order to make the claimant liable to pay the costs incurred by the respondent after the date of the postponement application.

20.76 The comments of Mummery LJ in McPherson caused a fair amount of confusion in employment tribunals as to the precise link (if any) that must be established between the unreasonable conduct and the actual costs incurred. In D'Silva v NATFHE (now known as University and College Union) EAT 0126/09 the EAT brought clarity to the situation by confirming that it was not, in the light of McPherson, necessary to establish a direct causal link between particular examples of unreasonable conduct and the costs incurred by the respondent. Once a finding of unreasonable conduct is made, the question of costs is then very much within the discretion of the tribunal. Similarly, in Salinas v Bear Stearns International Holdings Inc and anor 2005 ICR 1117, EAT, the EAT held that there was no requirement to identify with any particularity a causal link between the unreasonable conduct and the amount of costs ordered.

In Yerrakalva v Barnsley Metropolitan Borough Council (above) Mummery LJ himself had the opportunity to clarify what he had meant in the McPherson case. The tribunal below had ordered Y to pay all the Council's costs and, in doing so, had relied upon McPherson for the proposition that 'the exercise of the tribunal's discretion is not dependent upon the existence of any causal nexus between the conduct relied upon and the costs incurred'. When the case reached the Court of Appeal Mummery LJ acknowledged the confusion that his judgment in McPherson had created, and clarified that the main thrust of his judgment had been to reject the erroneous submission that, in deciding whether to make a costs order, the employment tribunal had to determine whether or not there was a precise causal link between the unreasonable conduct in question and the specific costs being claimed. It was never his intention to suggest that causation was irrelevant when deciding the amount of costs. Nor was he setting down a requirement that tribunals should dissect a case in detail and compartmentalise the relevant conduct under separate headings, such as 'nature', 'gravity' and 'effect'. His Lordship emphasised that the tribunal has a broad discretion and should avoid adopting an over-analytical approach. The vital point in exercising the discretion to order costs is to look at the whole picture of what happened in the case and to ask whether there has been unreasonable conduct by the claimant in bringing and conducting the case and, in doing so, to identify the conduct, what was unreasonable about it and what effects it had.

20.77 Mummery LJ further commented in Yerrakalva that it is not the function of an appeal court to 'tinker' with costs orders, which are by their nature 'based on and reflect broad brush first instance assessments'. However, in the instant case he considered it was appropriate to vary the tribunal's 100 per cent costs order, reducing it to 50 per cent. The claimant was guilty of unreasonable conduct in the proceedings, which gave the employment tribunal jurisdiction to order costs. It did not, however, follow that the claimant should pay all the Council's costs of the entire proceedings. The tribunal had rejected some of the Council's criticisms of the claimant. It had also criticised the Council for making more of a meal than was necessary when criticising the claimant's case at a pre-hearing review. Those factors were relevant as to how the tribunal's costs discretion should have been exercised and operated against a 100 per cent order in the Council's favour. In addition, costs should have been limited to those incurred by the Council in respect of the PHR and subsequent costs hearings: Y's unreasonable conduct and the 'overdone' defence of the Council were mainly material only to that phase of the proceedings.

The Yerrakalva case was endorsed by the Court of Appeal in Sud v Ealing London Borough Council 2013 ICR D39, CA, which held that when making a decision as to costs, an employment tribunal needed to consider whether the claimant's conduct of the proceedings was unreasonable and, if so, it was necessary to identify the particular unreasonable conduct, along with its effect. This process did not entail a detailed or minute assessment. Instead the tribunal should adopt a broad brush approach, against the background of all the relevant circumstances. In the particular case, the tribunal had identified several reasons to justify awarding 50 per cent costs against S. First, it had found that the manner in which one claim was brought was 'unfocused and extensive'. Secondly, she had obtained a medical report without seeking the tribunal's leave and had served it extremely late. This resulted in the medical expert having to be called to give evidence. Thirdly, S served a witness statement containing inadmissible material, which she declined to remove. The tribunal therefore had to give a ruling on admissibility, despite the fact that the witness was not, in the event, called by S to give evidence. Fourthly, it was clear that S had not been prepared to accept any reasonable and appropriate sum in settlement of her claims, focusing instead upon an 'exorbitant' sum by way of suggested compensation.

In the Court's judgment, all of these separate heads of unreasonable conduct **20.78** were precisely identified. The tribunal had sufficiently explained why, on each occasion, the behaviour was to be criticised. It was self-evident that, in each instance, the consequence was either to cause additional discrete costs or simply to extend the proceedings. It followed that the reasons for, and the bases of, the costs order were clearly specified, without the tribunal attempting to identity a precise causal link between the unreasonable conduct and the specific costs that were awarded. The tribunal was exercising its broad discretion, sufficiently identifying the relevant unreasonable conduct and its effect, without seeking to go beyond an appropriate 'broad brush first instance assessment' (to adopt the words of Mummery LJ in Yerrakalva). In the event, it had correctly avoided an over-analytical approach and the 50 per cent award could not properly be criticised as falling outside the parameters of a legitimate decision.

No reasonable prospects of success **20.79**
An employment tribunal has a discretion to make a costs (or preparation time) order where it considers that a claim or response has no reasonable prospect of success – rule 76(1)(b) Tribunal Rules 2013. As with rule 76(1)(a), a two-stage test applies: the tribunal has a *duty to consider* making an order where this ground is made out but a discretion whether to actually award costs. For further details of this two-stage test, see 'Conduct' above. Note that when exercising its discretion some of the factors discussed under 'Factors relevant to tribunal's discretion' below may be relevant. Again, as with rule 76(1)(a), whether or not the party has received legal advice or is acting completely alone may be an important consideration when deciding whether or not to make a costs order or PTO against him or her – see further the section 'Factors relevant to tribunal's discretion' below, under 'Has the party taken legal advice? – is the party represented?'.

Rule 76(1)(b) differs slightly from the old Tribunal Rules, rules 40(3) and 44(3) of which provided that a costs order or PTO could be made against a party where the bringing or conducting of the proceedings was misconceived. 'Misconceived', however, was defined by Reg 2(2) of the Tribunal Regulations

1067

2004 as including 'having no reasonable prospect of success'. Therefore, much of the old case law will still be relevant, particularly since it tended to treat the term 'misconceived' as synonymous with having no reasonable prospect of success.

20.80 **Genuine belief in wrongdoing no excuse.** It was well established under the old rules that the term 'misconceived' could cover unmeritorious claims brought by employees who, possibly because they are unrepresented, are unaware of the legal position and genuinely believe that their employers have committed illegal acts against them. This will continue to be the case under the Tribunal Rules 2013 – and of course the same will apply to unmeritorious responses put in by unrepresented employers – since now a tribunal merely has to decide whether or not a claim had reasonable prospects of success. Two examples under the old rules:

- **Scott v Inland Revenue Commissioners Development Agency** 2004 ICR 1410, CA: Lord Justice Sedley observed that 'misconceived' for the purposes of costs under the Tribunal Rules 2004 included 'having no reasonable prospect of success' and clarified that the key question in this regard is not whether a party *thought* he or she was in the right, but whether he or she had *reasonable grounds* for doing so. The Court of Appeal held that the tribunal's decision in this particular case not to award costs against S should be reconsidered, as it was not clear that the tribunal had directed its attention to the questions of whether S's case was doomed to failure or, if it was, from what point

- **Hamilton-Jones v Black** EAT 0047/04: B instituted tribunal proceedings against a number of parties, including H-J. In due course, the tribunal determined that H-J had never been B's employer and, accordingly, that he should not have been a party to the proceedings. Despite this, it refused H-J's application for a costs order to be made against B on the basis that B had a genuine belief that H-J was his employer. On appeal, the EAT held that the tribunal's decision could not stand. It understood why B, a layman without any legal experience, might not understand the true employment situation. His decision to issue proceedings against H-J was not therefore 'vexatious' (a word that connoted a degree of malice or ulterior motive). However, for the purposes of the 'misconceived' rule, that was not the point: the tribunal was simply required to assess *objectively* whether the claim had any prospect of success at any time of its existence. This it had not done. There had been no rational basis for B's belief (even if genuinely held) that H-J had been his employer, meaning that the claim against that respondent had been misconceived from the outset. The EAT remitted the matter to a different tribunal to decide whether costs should be awarded on this basis.

20.81 Nevertheless, as noted above, when exercising its discretion whether to award costs, the fact that the party in question is a litigant in person may well be a factor that is taken into account by a tribunal. In AQ Ltd v Holden 2012 IRLR 648, EAT, for example, the employer had made a number of attempts to settle the claim but H persisted and lost at the tribunal. Although the tribunal found his evidence to be inconsistent and lacking credibility, it declined to make a costs order against him, finding that the claim had not been misconceived and that it would be inappropriate to award costs as H had not been legally represented. Upholding that decision on appeal, the EAT stressed that, while the test under rule 40(2) and (3) (now rule 76(1)) is the same whether or not a litigant was professionally represented, a tribunal applying that test had to take the fact of representation into account. Although lay people are by no means immune from orders for costs, the tribunal had been entitled to take the paying party's lack of representation into account and could not be criticised for doing so.

Costs against respondents. Costs can, of course, be awarded against **20.82** respondents as well as claimants on the 'no prospects of success' ground. Some examples:

- **Morse v Tunstall Telecom Ltd** ET Case No.11512/84: a tribunal found that 'the respondent's decision to dismiss was based on an unholy mixture of vivid imagination, over-active suspicion and totally inadequate investigation', and that the company should have known that it had no defence to the ensuing unfair dismissal claim. Costs (to be assessed in the county court) were awarded

- **Levett v Merstan Holdings Ltd** COET 1613/222: L, an accountant, was unfairly dismissed for refusing to carry out highly irregular and probably illegal transactions on the employer's orders. A tribunal held that the employer should have known that there was no reasonable defence to the claim and awarded costs of £500

- **Meadowstone (Derbyshire) Ltd v Kirk and anor** EAT 0529/05: a tribunal found that the employer had unfairly and wrongfully dismissed the claimants and went on to say that the employer's defence had been misconceived. It ordered the employer to pay the claimants' costs, to be assessed by the county court. On appeal, the EAT upheld the tribunal's costs order. Not only was this a case where the employer knew that its defence was unmeritorious, it was also a case in which the employer knew that its defence was untrue.

Focus on the claim/response itself. Under rule 76(1)(b), the focus is simply **20.83** on the claim or response itself. By contrast, under the previous rule 40(3) of the Tribunal Rules 2004, the focus was on whether *the party's bringing or conducting of proceedings* had been misconceived. Case law had established that the misconceived bringing or conducting of proceedings must have been carried out by the potential paying party him or herself, and not by his or her representative. This point is illustrated by Hosie and ors v North Ayrshire

1069

Leisure Ltd EAT 0013/03, a case in which an employment tribunal ordered the claimants to pay costs following their unsuccessful sex discrimination claims. In the tribunal's view, the failure of the claimants' representative, UNISON, to give proper consideration to the relevant issues prior to the hearing of the claims meant that the claims were misconceived for the purposes of rule 40(3). The EAT, however, disagreed, holding that the tribunal had erred in taking into account the conduct of the claimants' representative – as opposed to the conduct of the claimants themselves – when determining whether the proceedings were misconceived. In the EAT's view, it was relevant for a tribunal to consider how a party's representative had conducted the proceedings only where it was considering whether the 'vexatiously, abusively, disruptively or otherwise unreasonably' tests in rule 40(3) (now rule 76(1)(a) of the Tribunal Rules 2013) had been met. A representative's conduct was not relevant to the question of whether proceedings were misconceived. The EAT went on to state that the tribunal had not addressed the proper test in this regard, which was whether the claimants' cases had any reasonable prospects of success either at the time of conception or during the course of their currency. In these circumstances, the tribunal's decision could not stand and the EAT quashed the order for costs. (It is perhaps worth noting that at the time the Hosie case was heard, tribunals did not have the power to make wasted costs orders against representatives, although they do now – see 'What orders can employment tribunal make? – order against representative to pay "wasted costs"' above).

Under the new rules, by contrast, the focus is simply on whether the claim (or response) had reasonable prospects of success. It would appear therefore that the issue of whether it was the claimant or his or her representative who is responsible for the claim being brought or pursued is now irrelevant. In other words, a party cannot hide behind the conduct of his or her representative for the purpose of deciding whether or not the 'prospects of success' ground is made out. Nevertheless, this will undoubtedly still be relevant when the tribunal is considering whether or not to exercise its discretion to order costs against the party in question.

20.84 Breach of an order or practice direction
Under rule 76(2) of the Tribunal Rules 2013 an employment tribunal has the discretionary power to make a costs order or PTO against a party who has breached an order or Practice Direction. There is currently one Practice Direction governing employment tribunal procedure in England and Wales (once the claim has been submitted). This was issued on 18 December 2013 and relates to the 'Address for serving documentation in special cases'. An identical Practice Direction was issued on 17 December for Scotland. For details, see Chapter 10, 'Service of notice and documents', under 'Delivery to non-parties – "special cases"'. In addition, the President of the Employment

Tribunals in Scotland has made Practice Directions relating to 'Intimation of list of documents 14 days before a hearing' and 'Sist for mediation'. For a general discussion of Practice Directions, see Chapter 1, 'Employment tribunals', under 'What are employment tribunals? – employment tribunal rules'.

Note that when costs are awarded under rule 76(2) – as distinct from rule 76(1)(a), for which see 'Conduct' above – there is no need to find that a party has acted 'vexatiously, abusively, disruptively or otherwise unreasonably'. It is sufficient that he or she is clearly responsible for the breach.

Postponements and adjournments
20.85

Under rule 76(2) of the Tribunal Rules 2013 (rule 40(1) of the Tribunal Rules 2004) an employment tribunal has the discretionary power to make a costs order or PTO where a hearing has been postponed or adjourned on the application of a party. Note that this is distinct from a mandatory order for costs against a respondent under rule 76(3) as a result of the postponement or adjournment of a final hearing in unfair dismissal proceedings – see 'What orders can employment tribunal make? – order against respondent when unfair dismissal hearing postponed' above. Old rule 40(1) used to provide that the order may be either against the party requesting the postponement or adjournment or in that party's favour, depending on the circumstances giving rise to the request. Although this is no longer specifically stated in the new rules, there is no reason why this should not still be the case.

The power to award costs under rule 76(2) is entirely discretionary, although the EAT has held (in the context of old rule 40(1)) that costs should only be awarded against a party if he or she is at fault in applying for a postponement or adjournment. In Rajguru v Top Order Ltd 1978 ICR 565, EAT, the employer raised new allegations against the claimant at the hearing resulting in his representative applying for an adjournment because of language problems in taking further instructions. The tribunal granted the adjournment but awarded costs against the claimant. The EAT overruled the award – the claimant was not at fault and it was neither reasonable nor proper to award costs against him.

Nevertheless, when costs are awarded under rule 76(2) – as distinct from rule 76(1)(a) (for which see 'Conduct' above) – there is no need to find that a party has acted 'vexatiously, abusively, disruptively or otherwise unreasonably' – Ladbroke Racing Ltd v Hickey 1979 ICR 525, EAT. It is sufficient that he or she is clearly responsible for the delay. Certainly, awards of costs need not reflect the overall merits of the case, and may be awarded against an ultimately successful party if he or she has caused unnecessary delays along the way.
20.86

Unlike old rule 40(1), rule 76(2) does not specifically provide that the tribunal may award only those costs incurred as a result of the postponement or adjournment. Under the old rule, costs that related to the general conduct and preparation of the case could not be awarded because they were attributable to the hearing itself (when it eventually took place) – Cooper and anor v Weatherwise (Roofing and Walling) Ltd 1993 ICR 81, EAT. It remains to be seen whether this will continue to be the case under the new rules.

20.87 ## Costs following the payment of a deposit

Rule 39 of the Tribunal Rules 2013 deals with deposit orders (for full details, see Chapter 11, 'Case management', under 'Deposit orders'). If, following a preliminary hearing, an employment tribunal decides that any specific allegation or argument in a claim or response has little reasonable prospect of success, it may make an order requiring a party to pay a deposit not exceeding £1,000 as a condition of continuing to advance that allegation or argument – rule 39(1). The tribunal must make reasonable enquiries into the party's ability to pay the deposit and have regard to any such information when deciding the amount of the deposit – rule 39(2). The tribunal's reasons for making the deposit order must be provided with the order and the party must be notified about the potential consequences of the order – rule 39(3).

Rule 39(5) provides that if the tribunal at any stage following the making of a deposit order decides the specific allegation or argument against the party in question for substantially the reasons given in the deposit order:

- that party shall be treated as having acted unreasonably in pursuing that specific allegation or argument for the purpose of rule 76, unless the contrary is shown – rule 39(5)(a), and

- the deposit shall be paid to the other party (or, if there is more than one, to such other party or parties as the tribunal orders) – rule 39(5)(b).

The rule goes on to provide that if the party is ultimately successful, the deposit will be refunded.

20.88 In Dorney and ors v Chippenham College EAT 10/97 the EAT said that there should not be a 'fine-tooth comb' approach to a comparison between the reasons for making the order at a pre-hearing review (PHR) and the reasons leading to a finding against the claimant. In that case the employment tribunal's subsequent reasons for finding that the respondent had established a potentially fair reason for dismissal were substantially the same as those given at the PHR stage. It was therefore open to the tribunal to make a costs award where the tribunal considered that the claimant was unreasonable in persisting in having the matter determined at a full hearing.

20.89 **'Treated as having acted unreasonably'.** Under rule 39(5)(a) the relevant party will be presumed to have acted unreasonably in pursuing the specific allegation or argument for the purpose of a costs or PTO. In other words, unless the party in question can prove the contrary, unreasonable conduct will be made out under rule 76(1)(a) and the employment tribunal *must consider* whether to make a costs order or PTO – see 'Conduct' above. There was no such presumption of unreasonableness under the previous rules – see old rule 47(1) and Gardiner and ors v VAW Motorcast EAT 262/00. Note, however, that the presumption of unreasonableness does not mean that the tribunal will automatically make an order: under rule 76(1) it must still ask itself whether it is appropriate to exercise its discretion in favour of awarding costs against that party.

Amount of costs or preparation time order. Rule 39(6) provides that if a **20.90** deposit has been paid to a party under rule 39(5)(b), the amount of the deposit shall count towards the settlement of any preparation time or costs order made in favour of the same party. It is important to note that, regardless of whether the tribunal decides to make a costs order or PTO, the deposit will still be paid to the other party under rule 39(5)(b). The old rules used to provide that if the amount of the deposit exceeded the amount of the costs order or PTO, the balance of the deposit had to be refunded – old rule 47(2). This does not appear to be the case under the Tribunal Rules 2013.

Grounds for making orders against representatives

20.91

Employment tribunals have the power to make a 'wasted costs' order against a representative in favour of any party where that party has incurred 'wasted costs' – rule 80 Tribunal Rules 2013. Such an order can be made against a representative to recover costs incurred:

- as a result of any improper, unreasonable or negligent act or omission on the part of any representative, or

- which, in the light of any such act or omission occurring after costs were incurred, the tribunal considers it unreasonable to expect that party to pay.

Rule 80 is based on the wasted costs provisions that apply in the civil courts, with the above definition of 'wasted costs' being identical to that contained in S.51(7) of the Senior Courts Act 1981. Accordingly, the authorities applicable to wasted costs in the civil law generally are equally applicable in the employment tribunals – Ratcliffe Duce and Gammer v L Binns (t/a Parc Ferme) EAT 0100/08 and Mitchells Solicitors v Funkwerk Information Technologies York Ltd EAT 0541/07. The two leading authorities analysing the scope of S.51 and the circumstances in which such orders can be made are Ridehalgh v Horsefield 1994 3 All ER 848, CA, and Medcalf v Mardell and ors 2002 3 All ER 721, HL. In the Mitchells solicitors case, the EAT confirmed that these cases are 'sources of essential assistance' for employment tribunals in the matter of wasted costs.

1073

20.92 Three-stage test

In Ratcliffe Duce and Gammer v L Binns (t/a Parc Ferme) EAT 0100/08 the EAT observed that the Court of Appeal in Ridehalgh had advocated a three-stage test for courts (and, by extension, employment tribunals) to adopt in respect of wasted costs orders:

- first, has the legal representative acted improperly, unreasonably, or negligently?

- secondly, if so, did such conduct cause the applicant to incur unnecessary costs?

- thirdly, if so, is it in the circumstances just to order the legal representative to compensate the applicant for the whole or any part of the relevant costs?

The Court of Appeal in Ridehalgh v Horsefield (above) emphasised that even where a court – and, by extension, an employment tribunal – is satisfied that the first two stages of the test are satisfied (i.e. conduct and causation) it must nevertheless consider again whether to exercise the discretion to make the order and to what extent. It still has a discretion at stage 3 to dismiss an application for wasted costs where it considers it appropriate to do so – for example, if the costs of the applicant would be disproportionate to the amount to be recovered, issues would need to be relitigated or questions of privilege would arise.

20.93 Improper, unreasonable or negligent

The Court of Appeal in Ridehalgh v Horsefield (above) examined the meaning of 'improper', 'unreasonable' and 'negligent' – subsequently approved by the House of Lords in Medcalf v Mardell and ors (above) – as follows:

- 'improper' covers, but is not confined to, conduct which would ordinarily be held to justify disbarment, striking off, suspension from practice or other serious professional penalty

- 'unreasonable' describes conduct that is vexatious, designed to harass the other side rather than advance the resolution of the case

- 'negligent' should be understood in a non-technical way to denote failure to act with the competence reasonably to be expected of ordinary members of the profession.

A legal representative should not be held to have acted improperly, unreasonably or negligently simply because he or she acts on behalf of a party whose claim or defence is doomed to fail – Ridehalgh v Horsefield (above). The House of Lords in Medcalf commented that it is the duty of advocates to present their client's case even though they may think that it is hopeless and even though they may have advised their client that it is. In Ratcliffe Duce and Gammer v L Binns (t/a Parc Ferme) EAT 0100/08 Mr Justice Elias (then President of the EAT) stated that the notion that a wasted costs order can be made against a

1074

lawyer simply because his client is pursuing a hopeless case is entirely erroneous. Such conduct does not of itself demonstrate that their representative has acted improperly or unreasonably. Clients frequently insist on pursuing a case against the best advice of their lawyers.

There must be an abuse of process. In Mitchells Solicitors v Funkwerk **20.94** Information Technologies York Ltd EAT 0541/07 the EAT considered that it was clear from the civil law authorities, in particular Ridehalgh and Medcalf, that a legal representative does not behave improperly, unreasonably or negligently simply by acting for a party who pursues a claim or defence which is plainly doomed to fail. Furthermore, even if a legal representative can be shown to have acted improperly, unreasonably or negligently in presenting a hopeless case, it remains vital to establish that the representative thereby assisted proceedings amounting to an abuse of the court's process (thus breaching his or her duty to the court) and that his or her conduct actually caused costs to be wasted. It therefore overturned a wasted costs order made against the claimant's solicitors, which had been based upon the employment tribunal's finding that any competent adviser would have told the claimant that her claim was highly unlikely to succeed.

Mr Justice Elias confirmed these principles in the Ratcliffe Duce and Gammer case (above), in which judgment was handed down shortly after that in Mitchells. He observed that, where a wasted costs order is concerned, the question is not whether the party has acted unreasonably. The test is a more rigorous one, as the leading authorities make plain. They demonstrate that a wasted costs order should not be made merely because a claimant pursues a hopeless case and his or her representative does not dissuade him or her from so doing. The distinction therefore is between conduct that is an abuse of process and conduct falling short of that. In this particular case there had been no attempt by the employment tribunal to determine whether there was an abuse of process, and there was no basis for supposing that there was. It had not been suggested that the case was being pursued for any improper purpose or anything of that nature. This was a case where the representative did not prevent a party pursuing what turned out to be a hopeless case. Even if it was fair to infer that the solicitor should have appreciated that it was hopeless – and it had to be remembered that the claimant was maintaining that he had relevant evidence to support his case until the last minute – it did not follow that the representative could have influenced his client to drop the case in any event. Since there was no evidence that the claimant would have withdrawn even if advised to do so, there was no basis for inferring that any costs had been incurred as a consequence of any misconduct. Elias P therefore set aside the tribunal's wasted costs order.

Both the Ratcliffe Duce and Mitchells cases will doubtless serve to reassure **20.95** advisers acting in litigation that has a slim chance of success. It was previously

1075

unclear how tribunals would approach the new wasted costs regime, despite its civil law origins, and so practitioners might have been wary of acting in litigation with poor prospects for fear of being penalised by the tribunal. These cases now establish that a wasted costs order requires a high standard of misconduct on a representative's part. Accordingly, acting on a client's instructions, even in a hopeless case, will not incur liability for costs in the absence of an abuse of process. These rulings confirm that it will be very difficult to succeed in a wasted costs application against a representative as a number of stringent conditions must be satisfied, including showing an abuse of the court. An abuse of the court includes such matters as issuing or pursuing proceedings for reasons unconnected with success in the litigation; pursuing a case known to be dishonest; and knowingly making incomplete disclosure of documents.

20.96 'Costs' or 'wasted costs'?

If a hopeless claim or defence is being pursued because of the representative's negligence or misconduct, the remedy to opt for would be a wasted costs order against the representative. Conversely, if the client insists upon pursuing the claim or defence despite advice to the contrary, the appropriate remedy would be a costs order against the client. However, given that client instructions and advice are covered by legal professional privilege, it will rarely be clear where the fault lies. In this situation, it is likely that applications will be brought against both the client and his or her representative. Note also that rule 76(1)(a) of the Tribunal Rules 2013 allows an employment tribunal to make a costs order or preparation time order *against the representative's client* where the representative has acted vexatiously, abusively, disruptively or otherwise unreasonably in the bringing or conducting of the proceedings. In practice, it will usually be easier to get an order against the representative's client (i.e. the party to proceedings) rather than the representative him or herself.

20.97 Factors relevant to tribunal's discretion

In the sections above – 'Grounds for making orders against a party' and 'Grounds for making orders against representatives' – we examined the various grounds upon which an employment tribunal may make an order for costs, etc, both against parties and against representatives. It is important to recognise that even if one (or more) of the grounds is made out, the tribunal is not *obliged* to make an order. Rather, it has a discretion whether or not to do so. The one exception to this is the ground set out in rule 76(3) of the Tribunal Rules providing that, where in unfair dismissal proceedings a final hearing is postponed or adjourned as a result of the respondent's failure to adduce reasonable evidence as to job availability, the tribunal *shall* order the respondent to pay the costs incurred as a result of the postponement or adjournment if the claimant has expressed a wish to be reinstated or re-engaged that has been communicated to the respondent not less than seven days before the hearing

1076

(see 'What orders can employment tribunal make? – order against respondent when unfair dismissal hearing postponed' above for further details).

Below, we examine some factors that may be relevant when a tribunal is considering whether or not to exercise its discretion to make an order. Some of the factors will have greater or lesser weight, depending upon the type of order at issue and the particular circumstances of the case. For example, different considerations will apply when a tribunal is considering making a wasted costs order against a representative, as opposed to a costs order against a party. It is also essential to bear in mind that, since a tribunal's power to award costs is discretionary, it cannot be fettered by case law. In Beynon and ors v Scadden and ors 1999 IRLR 700, EAT, the then President of the EAT emphasised that it is the relevant rules that must be construed and not the cases. Thus, the factors discussed below are just that; they are factors that may or may not be given weight by a tribunal.

Exception rather than the rule   20.98
As the Court of Appeal reiterated in Yerrakalva v Barnsley Metropolitan Borough Council 2012 ICR 420, CA, costs in the employment tribunal are still the exception rather than the rule. It commented that the tribunal's power to order costs is more sparingly exercised and is more circumscribed than that of the ordinary courts, where the general rule is that costs follow the event and the unsuccessful litigant normally has to foot the legal bill for the litigation. In the employment tribunal, by contrast, costs orders are the exception rather than the rule. In most cases the employment tribunal does not make any order for costs. If it does, it must act within rules that expressly confine the tribunal's power to specified circumstances, notably unreasonableness in the bringing or conduct of the proceedings. The tribunal manages, hears and decides the case and is normally the best judge of how to exercise its discretion.

In Salinas v Bear Stearns International Holdings Inc and anor 2005 ICR 1117, EAT, Mr Justice Burton, then President of the EAT, expressed the view that the reason why costs orders are not made in the substantial majority of tribunal cases is that the Tribunal Rules contain a high hurdle to be surmounted before such an order can be considered. In that particular case, however, the EAT rejected the claimant's appeal against a costs award that had been made against her. Burton P stated that 'even if the employment tribunal had not used words which had the effect of showing that they appreciated that the costs order was exceptional or rare, provided that they had applied the correct test, no error of law would have arisen'.

Costs are compensatory, not punitive   20.99
It remains a fundamental principle that the purpose of an award of costs is to compensate the party in whose favour the order is made, and not to punish the paying party. Questions of punishment are irrelevant both to the exercise of a

1077

tribunal's discretion as to whether to make an award and to the nature of the order that is made – Lodwick v Southwark London Borough Council 2004 ICR 884, CA.

It follows that a failure to consider what costs are involved may mean that an employment tribunal's order is set aside by the EAT. In Martinel v Walton Menswear Ltd EAT 886/83 M and another employee claimed unfair dismissal. The other employee won his case, but M lost and the tribunal awarded £300 against him for acting unreasonably. The EAT said that whether or not M had been unreasonable was a question of fact for the tribunal and that the size of the award was a matter for its discretion. However, the employer had incurred costs in resisting two claims – not just M's – and had been unsuccessful in one of them. The tribunal should have considered what additional expense was incurred by reason of M's claim: since it had not done this, the order would be set aside.

20.100 Given that costs are compensatory, it is necessary to examine what loss has been caused to the receiving party. In this regard the Court of Appeal in Yerrakalva v Barnsley Metropolitan Borough Council and anor 2012 ICR 420, CA, held that costs should be limited to those 'reasonably and necessarily incurred'. Furthermore, the amount of loss will not necessarily be determinative since a tribunal may take into account other factors, such as the means and the conduct of the parties (see below). As noted by the EAT in Howman v Queen Elizabeth Hospital Kings Lynn EAT 0509/12, any tribunal when having regard to a party's ability to pay needs to balance that factor against the need to compensate the other party who has unreasonably been put to expense. The former does not necessarily trump the latter, but it may do so.

20.101 Ability to pay

In deciding whether to make a costs, preparation time or wasted costs order (and if so in what amount) an employment tribunal *may* have regard to the paying party's (or, in the case of a wasted costs order, the representative's) ability to pay – rule 84 Tribunal Rules 2013. As can be seen, ability to pay can also be taken into account when assessing the amount to be awarded. This is considered further under 'Assessing amount: general considerations – ability to pay' below.

20.102 **No obligation to take account of means.** An employment tribunal is not obliged by rule 84 to have regard to ability to pay – it is merely permitted to do so. Although not obliged to take ability to pay into account, the EAT in Benjamin v Interlacing Ribbon Ltd EAT 0363/05 held that where a tribunal has been asked to consider a party's means, it should state in its reasons whether it has in fact done so and, if it has, how this has been done. This issue was further considered by the EAT in Jilley v Birmingham and Solihull Mental Health NHS Trust EAT 0584/06 where it was held that, if a tribunal decides *not* to take into account a party's ability to pay after having been asked to do so, it should say why. If it does decide to take into account ability to pay, it should set out its findings on the matter, say what impact these have had on its decision whether to award costs or on the amount of costs, and explain why. While lengthy reasons are not required, a succinct statement of how the tribunal has dealt with the matter and why it has done so is generally essential.

It seems clear from cases such as Benjamin v Interlacing Ribbon Ltd and Jilley **20.103** v Birmingham and Solihull Mental Health NHS Trust (above) that an employment tribunal must enquire as to a party's ability to pay when the issue has been raised by the party's representative (even if it ultimately decides not to take this into account when deciding to make an award). However, some case law suggests that the tribunal's duty of enquiry goes further than this. Two contrasting examples:

- **D'Silva v NATFHE (now known as University and College Union)** EAT 0126/09: the EAT considered that an employment tribunal had not fallen into error by failing to consider the claimant's means in circumstances where counsel had not made any submissions on the matter. In its view, it was not for the tribunal to take the initiative if the matter was not raised before it. It therefore upheld the tribunal's decision to order D'S to pay 50 per cent of NATFHE's costs for detailed assessment (estimated to be in the region of £37,000), despite the fact that upon appeal it was revealed that her means were limited. The EAT distinguished the Jilley decision (above) by pointing out that the tribunal there had heard extensive submissions as to the paying party's means

- **Doyle v North West London Hospitals NHS Trust** 2012 ICR D21, EAT: the EAT – relying in part upon the Jilley decision – held that, although an employment tribunal was not obliged to take into account ability to pay in deciding the amount of costs, it obviously had to act 'judicially' when deciding not to do so. In the instant case, the tribunal was being asked to make an order for costs in a very large amount against the claimant. The EAT observed that such an order would often be well beyond the means of the paying party and have very serious potential consequences and might act as a disincentive to other claimants bringing legitimate claims. For those reasons a tribunal should always be cautious before making such an order. It went on to hold that the tribunal had erred when ordering a detailed assessment of costs – estimated to be in the region of almost £100,000 – without giving consideration to the claimant's means, even though the claimant had been represented by experienced counsel who had not raised the question of her ability to pay. In reaching this decision, the EAT took into account a number of factors, including that there was nothing to indicate that the claimant was going to be able to pay such an amount and there was a risk that counsel had overlooked the point.

1079

It is worth noting that the EAT in Oni v NHS Leicester City 2013 ICR 91, EAT, observed in passing that – whether or not it is obligatory to do so as a matter of law – the decision in Doyle (above) shows the wisdom of the tribunal raising, at the very least in a case where costs are substantial, the question of means.

20.104 **Assessing means.** Any assessment of a party's means must be based upon the evidence before the employment tribunal. An example:

- **Oni v NHS Leicester City** (above): the EAT held that an employment tribunal had been wrong to hold that the claimant had the means to pay an award of costs (to be assessed in the county court). The tribunal had noted that neither the claimant nor her representative had chosen to disclose details of her financial means, although the representative had mentioned in passing that her only income was a state pension. Nevertheless, it had 'no doubt' that the claimant had the means to pay costs. Upon the claimant's appeal, the employer submitted that the tribunal was entitled to hold that the question of the claimant's means had not been properly raised and therefore to refuse to deal with it. The EAT, however, held that even if the tribunal could permissibly have declined to take means into account (for lack of sufficient evidence) it was not entitled to make a finding that the claimant had the means to pay costs: it had material before it to the effect that her only income was a state pension.

20.105 **Outside support.** It is possible that, where a claimant is supported by a trade union or another body, a tribunal may have regard to this fact when deciding whether to make a costs order against him or her. In Beynon and ors v Scadden and ors 1999 IRLR 700, EAT, the tribunal took into account the means of the claimants' trade union, UNISON, when deciding to order costs against them. Their claim, which was supported by UNISON, concerned a failure to consult under the then Transfer of Undertakings (Protection of Employment) Regulations 1981 SI 1981/1794 (TUPE). The tribunal held that the claim failed as the case concerned a share transfer and as such could not come within the scope of TUPE. In the tribunal's view, the claim had no reasonable prospect of success, as should have been clear to the union from an early stage. The tribunal also found that the union was pursuing the claim with a collateral purpose in mind – namely, to seek union recognition by the employer. The tribunal ordered the claimants to pay the respondent's costs on an indemnity basis. In making the costs order the tribunal said that 'this award has been made having taken into account, both the involvement of and the means of, the claimants' union, UNISON'. The award was upheld by the EAT, despite the fact that UNISON had given no express indemnity to the claimants in respect of costs.

20.106 **Costs warnings, deposit orders and preliminary hearings**
In order to deter an unmeritorious claim, an employment tribunal might issue a 'costs warning', expressing the view that if the claimant continues with the

claim and subsequently loses, he or she will face paying a proportion or the whole of the winning side's costs. Alternatively, the respondent might write to the claimant warning him or her that it will apply for costs if he or she persists with the claim or it could apply to the tribunal for a preliminary hearing if it considers that the claim has no prospects of success. Rule 39(1) of the Tribunal Rules 2013 provides that, where at a preliminary hearing a tribunal considers that any specific allegation or argument in a claim or response has little reasonable prospect of success, 'it may make an order requiring a party ("the paying party") to pay a deposit not exceeding £1,000 as a condition of continuing to advance that allegation or argument'. If he or she persists with the claim or response and subsequently loses, the employment tribunal may be entitled to make a costs (or preparation time) order against him or her – see 'Grounds for making orders against a party – costs following the payment of a deposit' above.

Tribunals must, however, be careful not to put undue pressure on a claimant, a **20.107** point illustrated by the two cases below with their contrasting outcomes:

- **Gee v Shell UK Ltd** 2003 IRLR 82, CA: an employment tribunal formed the view at a preliminary hearing that there was considerable doubt as to whether G had attained the requisite length of service required to pursue an unfair dismissal claim. It warned G that if she continued her claim and lost on the length of service issue at the full hearing, she was at risk of having to pay a substantial sum towards the respondent's costs. G, who was concerned that her house would be at risk if she continued with the proceedings, withdrew her claim. On appeal, however, the EAT found that the tribunal had acted unfairly and oppressively and had left G with no alternative but to withdraw. The Court of Appeal upheld the EAT's decision, finding that G had withdrawn her claim following unfair pressure from the tribunal and had thus been denied her right to a fair hearing. In the Court's view, tribunals must be careful not to put pressure on claimants disproportionate to the risk of a costs order being made against them, and should only issue a costs warning where there is a real risk that an order for costs will be made. In this case G's claim was arguable, and the prospect of any award of costs against her was remote

- **Adese v Coral Racing Ltd** EAT 0760/04: A was given a warning by an employment tribunal chairman that there was a risk that the respondent would apply for a costs order against him on the ground that his race discrimination claim was misconceived. A's claim form was insufficiently particularised and no supporting evidence had been presented. In response to the chairman's costs warning, A withdrew his claim. However, he subsequently appealed to the EAT, arguing that he had not received a fair hearing as the warning given by the tribunal had put undue pressure on him to withdraw. Having taken into account the Court of Appeal's decision in

Gee v Shell UK Ltd (above), the EAT concluded that there was no question that the tribunal had applied improper pressure in this case. Nor could it fairly be said that no reasonable tribunal could have given a costs warning in the circumstances. The warning, which was mild in tone, was delivered after it became clear that A's race discrimination claim was bound to fail, and where there was a real risk that an order for costs would be sought and made against him.

Equally, respondent employers should be cautious about issuing costs warnings. They should not do so as a matter of course but only if the circumstances truly warrant it. Otherwise they could be accused of unreasonable conduct, which could itself justify the imposition of a costs order against them.

20.108 **Relevance of costs warnings.** The fact that a costs warning has been given is a factor that may be taken into account by an employment tribunal when considering whether to exercise its discretion to make a costs order – see, for example, Oko-Jaja v London Borough of Lewisham EAT 417/00, where the EAT confirmed that a tribunal was entitled to take into account the fact that in a previous, similar claim made by O against the same respondent the tribunal had given a costs warning. Note that the fact that a party to proceedings has issued a costs warning does not mean that costs will follow. As noted by the EAT in Lake v Arco Grating (UK) Ltd EAT 0511/04, parties frequently make threats of costs applications prior to hearings.

The absence of a warning may be a relevant factor in deciding that costs should not be awarded. In Rogers v Dorothy Barley School EAT 0013/12, the EAT had 'no doubt' that it had jurisdiction to make an order for costs against R, a litigant in person, on the basis that his appeal was misconceived. The employment tribunal had correctly rejected his breach of contract claim on the basis that, as R was still employed by the school, it had no jurisdiction to hear it. However, in the circumstances of the case, the EAT concluded that it would not be right to order R to pay costs. The school had known for many months that R was acting in person and was simply not grasping the jurisdictional question that his appeal raised, yet it had not warned him that if he proceeded, an application for costs would be made.

20.109 Furthermore, in AQ Ltd v Holden 2012 IRLR 648, EAT, the EAT considered that an employment tribunal, when deciding not to award costs against H, a litigant in person, was entitled to take into account the fact that no application had been made on behalf of AQ for a pre-hearing review (now referred to collectively as a 'preliminary hearing' in the Tribunal Rules 2013) to determine the prospects of success of the claim. If the claim had truly been misconceived or vexatious there could have been an application to strike out or for a deposit order to be made. The matter was not in any sense decisive of the application for costs, but it was not irrelevant.

Costs warning not a precondition. A costs warning is not, however, a 20.110
precondition to the making of an order – Raveneau v London Borough of Brent
EAT 1175/96. This is illustrated by the case of Towu v Lewisham Hospital
NHS Trust EAT 0314/05. There, an employment tribunal made a costs order
of £10,000 against T, following an unsuccessful sex discrimination claim in
which he had represented himself. On appeal, T argued that, given that tribunals
are intended to be accessible to lay-people who bring their own claims, he
should have been given a warning that legal advice was required and that there
would be a likelihood of a costs award if he continued. His argument was
rejected by the EAT, which held that the issues he raised did not, in themselves,
amount to a point of law or suggest an error of law in the tribunal's reasons.
The EAT observed that T was himself a professional man. He had already
brought one employment tribunal claim. The desirability of obtaining
independent advice before pursuing claims of this kind, which are inevitably
expensive and time-consuming for all concerned, should have been apparent to
him; all the more so when the allegations that he was making were of some
seriousness – including allegations of discriminatory conduct by fellow
professionals and people in senior positions within the Trust.

Another stark illustration is provided by the case of Vaughan v London Borough
of Lewisham and ors 2013 IRLR 713, EAT, where the EAT upheld an employment
tribunal's order that an unrepresented claimant pay several respondents one
third of their costs (estimated to total around £260,000) on the basis that the
claims never had any reasonable prospects of success. This was despite the
respondents' failure to seek a deposit order or otherwise issue a costs warning.
The EAT thought it significant that at no stage had V indicated that if she had
been given such a warning she would have discontinued her claim. Indeed, in its
view, such an assertion would not, in any event have been credible. As the
tribunal found, she was convinced, albeit without any rational or evidential
basis, that she was the victim of a conspiracy and of a serious injustice. The EAT
considered it highly unlikely that a letter from the respondents, however well
crafted, would have caused 'the scales to fall from her eyes'.

The EAT also pointed out that respondents faced with what they believe to be 20.111
weak claims do not always seek deposit orders because, for example, they do
not wish to incur further expense or delay. The same could be said of the
tribunal's omission to make any observations at the case management
discussions or pre-hearing reviews (now referred to collectively as 'preliminary
hearings' under the Tribunal Rules 2013) to the effect that the claims appeared
weak. Whether to comment on the strength of a claim was often not a
straightforward question, so no conclusion could be drawn from the tribunal's
omission to do so.

The EAT did, however, comment that although, as a matter of law, notice or
warning was not required before a costs order could be made, the absence of

1083

such notice or warning could in some circumstances be relevant. Indeed, the absence of a warning was one of the reasons for the EAT not awarding costs under its cognate jurisdiction in Rogers v Dorothy Barley School (above). What – if any – weight this factor should be given in any particular case must be judged in the circumstances of that case. It was 'regrettable' that the employment tribunal did not expressly address the question, but in the circumstances of the particular case that did not undermine its decision to order costs.

20.112 Has the party taken legal advice?

The extent to which a party acts under legal advice might be a relevant factor for an employment tribunal considering making a costs (or preparation time) award against that party. Two contrasting examples:

- **Abrahams v Royal National Throat, Nose and Ear Hospital** EAT 183/82: A made a late withdrawal of his race discrimination claim and the employment tribunal ordered him to pay £500 costs for acting vexatiously and unreasonably. In setting aside this decision, the EAT held that there was no evidence that A had acted other than in good faith, so the tribunal must have been wrong to find his conduct 'vexatious'. Furthermore, he had originally been supported by the Commission for Racial Equality, had then waited for Acas to try to conciliate, and had eventually taken advice from a CAB before withdrawing his complaint. In the circumstances, the EAT did not think he had acted 'unreasonably'

- **Clarke t/a Marine Chart Services v Davenport and Bull** EAT 1120/96: the claimants were supported in their cases by a local Racial Equality Council. Although their claims failed, the employment tribunal refused to award costs as the claimants had been acting on the advice of the Council. The tribunal went on to say that the Council should have been aware of a previous case that rendered the claimants' cases hopeless and, had it had the power to do so, the tribunal would have awarded costs against the Council. The EAT, however, allowed the employer's appeal, stating that the fact that legal advice has been obtained is not a complete answer to an argument that the bringing of a case amounted to unreasonable conduct.

20.113 Is the party represented?

The fact that a party is unrepresented can also be a relevant consideration in deciding whether to award costs against him or her. In AQ Ltd v Holden 2012 IRLR 648, EAT, the EAT stated that the threshold tests governing the award of costs or a preparation time order in what is now rule 76(1) of the Tribunal Rules 2013 (previously rule 40(3) of the Tribunal Rules 2004) are the same whether a litigant is or is not professionally represented but that the application of those tests should take this factor into account. An employment tribunal cannot and should not judge a litigant in person by the standards of a professional representative. Lay people are entitled to represent themselves in

1084

tribunals and, since legal aid is not available and they will not usually recover costs if they are successful, it is inevitable that many lay people will represent themselves. Justice requires that tribunals do not apply professional standards to lay people, who may be involved in legal proceedings for the only time in their life. Lay people are likely to lack the objectivity and knowledge of law and practice brought by a professional legal adviser. Furthermore, the EAT observed, even if the threshold tests for an order for costs are met, the tribunal has discretion whether to make an order, which will be exercised having regard to all the circumstances. In its view, 'it is not irrelevant that a lay person may have brought proceedings with little or no access to specialist help and advice'.

It is important to emphasise, however, that the fact that a party is unrepresented is no barrier to an award of costs being awarded against him or her, should an employment tribunal think it appropriate to do so. The EAT in Holden went on to say: 'This is [not] to say that lay people are immune from orders for costs: far from it, as the cases make clear. Some litigants in person are found to have behaved vexatiously or unreasonably even when proper allowance is made for their inexperience and lack of objectivity.'

20.114 This point is amply demonstrated by the case of Vaughan v London Borough of Lewisham and ors 2013 IRLR 713, EAT, where the EAT, quoting from Holden, upheld an employment tribunal's order that an unrepresented claimant pay several respondents one third of their costs (estimated to total around £260,000). The costs order related to three sets of proceedings, culminating in a 20-day hearing, after which all of the claims were dismissed. The claims were complicated, involving allegations of discrimination, harassment and whistleblowing. The EAT, however, held that the tribunal's finding that the claims were misconceived from the start was 'unimpeachable'. It observed that the employment tribunal was well aware that V had been unrepresented throughout and there was no reason to suppose that it did not take that fact into account. Furthermore, the basis on which the costs threshold was crossed was not any conduct which could readily be attributed to the claimant's lack of experience as a litigant: it was her fundamentally unreasonable appreciation of the behaviour of her employer and colleagues.

It is, perhaps, worth noting in this regard that the Tribunal Rules 2013 do not oblige tribunals explicitly to remind claimants (or, indeed, respondents) that they are at risk of costs, especially where, as in the Vaughan case, a lengthy hearing has been scheduled. The consequences for claimants of a tribunal failing to do so may be dramatic, even more so now that fees for pursuing tribunal claims and appeals have come into effect – see Chapter 19, 'Fees'. The EAT in Vaughan was of the view that the claimant would have pressed on regardless, but, leaving her particular personality aside, litigants in person are potentially very vulnerable to making costly mistakes that impact not only on them but also on the other party, which may never recover its costs. The

Tribunal Rules 2013 have introduced a new procedure whereby employment judges will consider all the documents held by the tribunal to confirm whether there are arguable complaints and defences – see Chapter 7, 'Judicial sift', for further details. However, this sifting process will probably only weed out the most obviously unmeritorious claims, and is unlikely to protect claimants from running up huge costs for themselves and others further down the track.

20.115 Rejection of settlement offer

With regard to litigation in the civil courts, the rule in Calderbank v Calderbank 1975 3 All ER 333, CA, applies where a claimant, having succeeded on the issue of liability, obtains an award of damages equivalent to or less than an earlier settlement offer. The rule states that, in such circumstances, the claimant will bear the costs incurred by the respondent from the date on which the offer was rejected. In Kopel v Safeway Stores plc 2003 IRLR 753, EAT, however, the EAT held that the rule in Calderbank v Calderbank has no place in employment tribunal jurisdiction. In that case, a tribunal's decision to award costs of £5,000 against the claimant had been influenced by the fact that she had earlier rejected a settlement offer made 'without prejudice save as to costs' (known as a 'Calderbank offer') during the proceedings. On appeal, the EAT clarified that a tribunal claimant will not necessarily be liable for costs where he or she rejects a Calderbank offer and is eventually awarded less than that offer, or even nothing at all. However, a claimant's refusal of such an offer was a factor that a tribunal could take into account in deciding whether to award costs. In this particular case, not only had the tribunal found that the claimant had unreasonably rejected a generous offer but had also concluded that her claims were 'frankly ludicrous' and 'seriously misconceived', and that the documentary evidence did not support her case. In the circumstances, the tribunal had made no material error of law in finding that she had acted unreasonably in conducting proceedings. Nor had it made an error of law in awarding costs against her.

The approach advocated in Kopel was adopted by the EAT in Power v Panasonic (UK) Ltd EAT 0439/04. There, P's complaints of disability discrimination, unfair dismissal and breach of contract were upheld by a tribunal and she was awarded compensation of £5,855. Even so, P was ordered to pay £10,000 towards the respondent's costs on the basis that the respondent had made an offer to settle for £10,000 before the tribunal hearing. On appeal, P argued that the tribunal had, contrary to the Kopel decision, looked at the offer of £10,000 in isolation as if applying the 'Calderbank' principle. The EAT, however, upheld the tribunal's award. It noted that the tribunal had found the schedule of loss put forward by P to be 'unrealistically optimistic', and her approach to negotiations to have been 'intransigent'. In the circumstances, the tribunal had been entitled to find that P had conducted the proceedings unreasonably and therefore to exercise its discretion to award costs against her.

In Anderson v Cheltenham and Gloucester plc EAT 0221/13 the EAT reiterated **20.116**
that the Calderbank principle does not apply in full to employment tribunal
litigation but that the failure to accept a prior offer may have a bearing on
whether the claimant has conducted proceedings unreasonably or pursued a
claim that has no reasonable prospect of success. In that particular case,
although the EAT accepted that, when ordering costs of £10,000, the
employment tribunal had not specifically erred by applying the Calderbank
principle in undiluted form, it nevertheless held that the tribunal had erred in
concluding that the claimant had proceeded unreasonably by rejecting an offer
of £25,000 against the background of a discrimination claim for £1.2 million.
The size of the claim was explicable by the fact that, had she succeeded in that
claim, the claimant had an expectation of securing career-long loss. Given that
she had succeeded in an accompanying unfair dismissal claim and that there
had been no suggestion by the respondent that her discrimination claim was
misconceived, the EAT held that the tribunal's award of costs was unwarranted.

One other consideration is that the mere fact that the respondent has made an
offer to settle should not necessarily be taken as an indicator that it considers
that the claim in question has reasonable prospects of success. In Vaughan v
London Borough of Lewisham and ors 2013 IRLR 713, EAT, the EAT held that
nothing could be read into the respondents' offers to settle – culminating in an
offer of £95,000 – as these had been made on a purely 'commercial basis' to
avoid a 20-day hearing.

Nature of evidence/claim   **20.117**
The nature of the evidence available to the claimant and the nature of the claim
may be relevant to the exercise of discretion as to whether to make an order for
costs or preparation time. In Oko-Jaja v London Borough of Lewisham EAT
417/00 the claimant claimed that he had been victimised contrary to the then
Disability Discrimination Act 1995 when he was not appointed to a post as a
housing adviser. He had previously made a disability discrimination claim in
relation to another unsuccessful application for a job as a tenancy relations
officer with the same respondent, and argued that he failed to secure the second
post because of his claim of discrimination in relation to the first post. Both sets
of claims were unsuccessful, and in the second claim the tribunal made an
award of £250 costs against him. One of the factors that influenced the tribunal
was that it felt that 'all material potential evidence' had been available to him
at an early stage. The EAT held that the tribunal had erred in taking this into
account when concluding that the claimant had acted unreasonably. The EAT
pointed out that it is well recognised that direct evidence of victimisation is
often difficult to prove. A claimant will often rely on being able to show,
through cross-examination of witnesses, that the employer's stated reasons for
the treatment complained of were not in fact the true reasons. In this case, it
had been reasonable for the claimant to test the state of knowledge of the

1087

members of the interviewing panel at a tribunal hearing. Accordingly, the EAT quashed the costs order.

The difficulty of obtaining evidence of discrimination was also mentioned by the EAT in Saka v Fitzroy Robinson Ltd EAT 0241/00. In that case the EAT stated that there is very rarely overt evidence of discrimination and it may be difficult for a claimant to know whether or not he or she has any prospect of success until the explanation of the employer's conduct is heard, seen and tested. It followed from this, the EAT said, that a costs order against a claimant in a discrimination case was likely to be very rare, even exceptional. Costs were, however, ordered against the claimant in Vaughan v London Borough of Lewisham and ors (above), despite the fact that the claims were complicated in that they involved allegations of discrimination, harassment and whistleblowing. According to the EAT, the basis on which the costs threshold was crossed was not any conduct that could readily be attributed to the claimant's lack of experience or knowledge as a litigant, but rather her fundamentally unreasonable appreciation of the behaviour of her employer and colleagues.

20.118 Late withdrawals

A party might think that he or she can avoid a possible costs penalty if his or her claim (or response) is withdrawn before the hearing. But this is not necessarily so because costs may be incurred well in advance of the hearing proper. If a party allows preparations for the hearing to go on too long before abandoning an untenable case that party may be liable for costs on account of his or her conduct. Thus, where a case is settled – even if this is as late as at the door of the tribunal – the settlement itself should, if possible, deal with the question of costs.

In awarding costs against a claimant who has withdrawn a claim, an employment tribunal must consider whether the claimant has conducted the proceedings unreasonably in all the circumstances, and not whether the late withdrawal of the claim was in itself unreasonable – McPherson v BNP Paribas (London Branch) 2004 ICR 1398, CA. The same would presumably apply in respect of a respondent who withdraws its response. In the McPherson case, M withdrew an unfair dismissal claim just over two weeks before the postponed hearing of the claim was due to take place, and some 19 months after the claim was presented. The original hearing had been postponed at the claimant's request on medical grounds. Upon withdrawal, the respondent claimed costs, arguing that M's conduct of the claim in general had been unreasonable. The employment tribunal found that there had been unreasonable conduct and ordered M to pay the employer's costs in relation to the whole claim, which totalled more than £90,000. The EAT upheld the tribunal's decision and M appealed to the Court of Appeal, which warned that it would be wrong if, acting on a misconceived analogy with the Civil Procedure Rules, tribunals took the line that it was unreasonable conduct for tribunal claimants to withdraw claims, and that if they did so, they should be made liable to pay all the costs of the proceedings. The Court pointed out that, in fact, withdrawals could lead to a saving of costs, and that it would therefore be unfortunate if claimants were deterred from dropping claims by the prospect of an order for costs upon withdrawal that might well not be made against them if they fought on to a full hearing and failed. Therefore, before an order for costs can be made, it must be shown that the claimant's conduct of the proceedings has been unreasonable. This is determined by looking at the conduct overall. With these principles in mind, the Court found that in this particular case there was ample evidence to justify the tribunal's overall conclusion that there was unreasonable behaviour by M in the way in which the proceedings had been conducted. Consequently, the tribunal's ruling that it had jurisdiction to make a costs order against M was not perverse or otherwise wrong in law.

Previous or multiple tribunal claims 20.119

The fact that a claimant has brought and lost previous tribunal cases – or is bringing claims against a number of different respondents – may be a relevant factor when determining whether to make orders for costs or preparation time. Some examples:

- **Fitzroy Robinson Ltd v Saka** EAT 0241/00: S had made a complaint of race discrimination against a previous employer. That complaint failed and, in giving judgment, the employment tribunal set out in some detail the legal framework of a discrimination claim. In relation to S's subsequent complaint of discrimination against his next employer, the EAT held that the second tribunal was entitled to take into account the previous failed claim when ordering costs against him. The second tribunal had been aware that S was an intelligent man who was capable of reading the previous decision and understanding from it what a discrimination claim involved

- **Keane v Investigo and ors** EAT 0389/09: K, an accountant in her late forties, made around 20 applications for jobs for which she was overqualified. The job advertisements had been placed online by various employment agencies. All of the vacancies were clearly aimed at recently qualified accountants, involving responsibilities for someone of comparatively limited experience. When she was not offered an interview, she lodged tribunal claims of age discrimination against 11 agencies. Six of these settled while five proceeded to a hearing. The EAT considered it self-evident that an applicant who is not considered for a job in which he or she has no interest cannot be said to have suffered less favourable treatment or to have been put at a disadvantage as a result, even if the recruitment process potentially gave rise to discrimination on the ground of age. As a result, K was precluded from pursuing her claims for age discrimination. The EAT upheld the employment tribunal's order that she should pay costs to be assessed in the county court on the basis that her claims were misconceived and an abuse of process

- **Berry v Recruitment Revolution and ors** EAT 0190/10: B's claims for age discrimination against a number of recruitment agencies and employers were similarly rejected by an employment tribunal. Upholding this decision upon appeal, the EAT noted in passing that B had apparently contacted numerous employers about alleged age-discriminatory job advertisements, reaching out-of-court settlements with some of them. While not expressing a view on B's motivation, the EAT emphasised that the age discrimination legislation was not intended to provide a source of income for people who complain about discriminatory job advertisements but who have no desire to fill the vacancies in question. It added that those who try to exploit the legislation for financial gain were liable to have costs awarded against them, as indeed had happened to the claimant in the Keane case (above).

Note that ultimately, it may be possible for the Attorney General to apply for a restriction of proceedings order under S.33 ETA against a 'serial' litigant – Attorney General v Deman EAT 0113/06 (see Chapter 17, 'Processing an appeal', under 'Vexatious proceedings').

20.120 Assessing amount: general considerations

Once an employment tribunal has decided to make a costs order, it must then go on to decide how much to award. Some considerations – particularly in terms of the method of assessment and applicable statutory limits – are specific to the type of order at issue and we discuss these separately below (see 'Methods of assessment and applicable statutory limits'). Before doing so, we consider the general principles and factors that may be relevant to the tribunal's assessment – namely, the compensatory nature of costs, a party's ability to pay and the conduct of the parties.

20.121 Costs are compensatory, not punitive

The purpose of an award of costs is to compensate the party in whose favour the order is made, and not to punish the paying party – Lodwick v Southwark London Borough Council 2004 ICR 884, CA. Questions of punishment are irrelevant both to the exercise of a tribunal's discretion as to whether to make an award and to the amount of the order that is made.

20.122 Amount of loss.
Given that costs are compensatory, it is necessary to examine what loss has been caused to the receiving party. In this regard the Court of Appeal in Yerrakalva v Barnsley Metropolitan Borough Council and anor 2012 ICR 420, CA, held that costs should be limited to those 'reasonably and necessarily incurred'. Furthermore, the amount of loss will not necessarily be determinative since a tribunal may take into account other factors, such as the means and the conduct of the parties (see below). As noted by the EAT in Howman v Queen Elizabeth Hospital Kings Lynn EAT 0509/12, a tribunal having regard to a party's ability to pay needs to balance that factor against the

need to compensate the other party, who has unreasonably been put to expense. The former does not necessarily trump the latter, but it may do so.

Proportionate and reasonable. When exercising its discretion, the employment **20.123** tribunal is likely to look at both the proportionality and reasonableness of the costs incurred. In Yerrakalva (above), for example, the Court of Appeal held that costs should be limited to those 'reasonably and necessarily incurred'. Note that when calculating the amount of a preparation time order, an employment tribunal is expressly required by rule 79(1)(b) to assess what is a reasonable and proportionate amount of time for the party to have spent (see 'Methods of assessment and applicable statutory limits – assessment of preparation time' below).

Ability to pay   **20.124**

The issue of a party's ability to pay pursuant to a costs, preparation time or wasted costs order has already been considered in the context of whether or not to make any such order in the first place – see 'Factors relevant to tribunal's discretion – ability to pay' above. There is a lengthy discussion there as to the extent to which an employment tribunal should actively enquire into a party's ability to pay, a somewhat thorny issue. Here we look at relevance of a party's means to the tribunal's assessment of the amount to be awarded.

In deciding whether to make any of the above-mentioned orders and, if appropriate, the amount to be awarded, a tribunal may have regard to the paying party's (or, in the case of a wasted costs order, the representative's) ability to pay – rule 84 Tribunal Rules 2013. A tribunal is not obliged by rule 84 to have regard to this – it is merely permitted to do so. However, if a tribunal decides *not* to take into account a party's ability to pay, having been asked to do so, it should say why. If it does decide to take into account ability to pay, it should set out its findings about ability to pay, say what impact that had on its decision whether to award costs or on the amount of costs, and explain why – Jilley v Birmingham and Solihull Mental Health NHS Trust EAT 0584/06.

Assessing means. Once a tribunal has decided to have regard to the paying **20.125** party's ability to pay, it must take into account his or her capital, as well as income and expenditure. In Shields Automotive Ltd v Greig EATS 0024/10 the EAT stated that 'assessing a person's ability to pay involves considering their whole means. Capital is a highly relevant aspect of anyone's means. To look only at income where a person also has capital is to ignore a relevant factor.' The EAT also rejected the claimant's submission that capital is not relevant if it is not in immediately accessible form, observing that 'a person's capital will often be represented by property or other investments which are not as accessible as cash but that is not to say that it should be ignored.'

1091

In Howman v Queen Elizabeth Hospital Kings Lynn (above) the EAT held that, in deciding that it would have regard to the claimant's ability to pay costs, the tribunal should have taken account of the fact that he would have to sell the house that he shared with his wife and two dependent children and should, in view of this, have considered whether it ought to cap the amount the county court could order him to pay. The EAT did not accept that the potential effect of the order was mitigated by the fact that the county court could take into account H's ability to pay when seeking to enforce the order in accordance with S.71(2) of the County Courts Act 1984, which allows it to suspend or stay an order 'at any time' if the paying party is unable to pay. It observed that when assessing costs, the county court does not take into account the paying party's ability to pay. Furthermore, in the EAT's view, the court was likely to exercise its discretion under S.71(2) in a limited way, particularly since the court would give great weight to the employment tribunal's opinion at the time the order was made.

20.126   It is interesting to note that the EAT in Vaughan v London Borough of Lewisham and ors 2013 IRLR 713, EAT (which upheld a costs order estimated to be in the region of £60,000) was more inclined than the EAT in Howman to take account of the county court's role when enforcing the order. It commented that the county court could assess the claimant's financial position 'from time to time' and require payment by instalments. This case is further discussed immediately below.

20.127   **What the payer can afford to pay.** A tribunal is not required to limit costs to an amount that the paying party can afford to pay – Arrowsmith v Nottingham Trent University 2012 ICR 159, CA. Indeed, the Presidential Guidance on 'General Case Management' for England and Wales states that a tribunal may make a substantial order 'even where a person has no means of payment'. The Court of Appeal in the Arrowsmith case noted that the claimant's circumstances 'may well improve and no doubt she hopes that they will'. Although these comments were obiter, they suggest that the likelihood of a party's circumstances improving is a relevant factor when assessing the amount of costs in view of a party's means.

This was confirmed by the EAT in Vaughan v London Borough of Lewisham and ors (above), which upheld a tribunal's decision to order the claimant to pay a third of the respondent's costs even though her share was estimated to be around £60,000 and she could not at the time afford to pay it. The tribunal – referring to the judgment of Lord Justice Rimer in Arrowsmith – accepted that the claimant was not at present in a position to make any substantial payment but took the view that there was a realistic prospect that she might be able to do so in due course when her health improved and she was able to resume employment. The claimant's objection was not that this approach was wrong but that its application in the circumstances of the particular case was perverse. She submitted that there was no realistic chance that she would ever be in a position to pay anything like the £60,000 that the tribunal had in effect ordered her to pay and referred to the following factors in mitigation: her continuing mental ill-health; the obstacle which the stigma of dismissal presented to her finding other employment; her inevitable de-skilling the longer she was away from work; and the present climate of cuts in the public sector. Furthermore, even if she were eventually to get back into employment she could not expect to earn at the level that she was at the time of her dismissal, i.e. around £30,000 p.a.

Mr Justice Underhill conceded that this part of the claimant's submissions had **20.128** given the EAT some pause for thought. It was not hard to accept that V might face real difficulties getting back into employment in the foreseeable future, let alone at her pre-dismissal salary levels. And even if she were in fact able to do so, a liability of this size – representing, on the assumed figures, twice her pre-tax earnings at the date of her dismissal – would take very many years to pay off. It was a serious matter to saddle an unsuccessful claimant with a liability of this kind. Ultimately, however, he could see no error of law in the employment tribunal's decision. In Underhill P's view, the fact that the tribunal thought it right to have regard to the claimant's ability to pay (which was a matter for its discretion) did not mean that it was required to make a firm finding as to the maximum it believed she could pay, either right away or within some specified timescale, and to limit the award to that amount. There was no requirement in the Tribunal Rules to do so (and it would be particularly surprising if there were, given that there is no absolute obligation to have regard to means at all). If there were a realistic prospect that the claimant might at some point in the future be able to afford to pay a substantial amount, it was legitimate to make a costs order in that amount so that the respondent would be able to make some recovery when and if that occurred. In principle, the EAT considered, there is no reason why the question of affordability has to be decided once and for all by reference to the party's means as at the moment the order falls to be made. Indeed, that was the basis upon which the Court of Appeal proceeded in Arrowsmith, albeit that the relevant reasoning in that case was extremely briefly expressed. It had to be remembered that whatever order was made would have to be enforced through the county court, which would itself take into account the individual's means from time to time in deciding whether to require payment by instalments, and if so in what amount.

The EAT in the Vaughan case summarised the questions for the employment tribunal to ask on the basis that it was right to have regard to the claimant's means as follows:

- was there a reasonable prospect of V being able, in due course, to return to well-paid employment and thus to be in a position to make a payment of cost?

- if so, what limit ought nevertheless be placed on her liability to take account of her means and of proportionality?

20.129 As to the former question, views might legitimately differ as to the probabilities, but the employment tribunal was well placed – better than the EAT – to form a view that there was indeed a realistic prospect. As to the latter, the EAT could see the force of the argument that it would be pointless, and therefore not a proper exercise of discretion, to require the claimant to pay more (even in the optimistic scenario envisaged by the tribunal) than she could realistically pay over a reasonable period. Indeed, the EAT had been concerned whether the cap was simply set too high. However, questions of what is realistic or reasonable are very open-ended, and it saw nothing wrong, in principle, in the employment tribunal setting the cap at a level which gives the respondent the benefit of any doubt, even to a generous extent.

The EAT commented that since affordability is not, as such, the sole criterion for the exercise of the discretion, a 'nice estimate of what can be afforded is not essential'. Approached in that way, it was not ultimately possible to say that the limit of one third of the respondent's costs – whether that came to £60,000 or some other figure in the range – was perverse. It was of course 'rough-and-ready', but there was in truth no means of arriving at a more precise figure. The EAT could not say that a proportion of, say, a quarter would have been right while a third was wrong. It also had to be borne in mind that the respondent was the injured party and, even if the order did turn out to be recoverable in full at some point in the future, it would be out-of-pocket to the tune of two thirds of its assessed costs. It would be difficult to say in those circumstances that the award was disproportionate.

20.130 **Can costs be offset against compensation?** The EAT in Vaughan v London Borough of Lewisham and ors (above) thought it worth mentioning for completeness that it had raised in the course of argument the question of whether the employment tribunal could – or should – have taken into account the possibility that V might recover substantial compensation in her remaining claims (i.e. the ones that were not found to be misconceived). It might seem unjust if in that eventuality the respondents could not recover out of any such compensation their costs incurred as a result of the present claims being misconceived. Of course, it would have been wrong for the employment tribunal to attempt any kind of evaluation of the prospects of success in the outstanding claims; but the mere fact that they were outstanding might have been a relevant factor in the exercise of its discretion. However, since the point was not taken before the employment tribunal, the EAT did not think that it should attach any weight to it in the instant case.

The issue of whether costs can be offset against compensation is, however, at best unclear. In Anderson v Cheltenham and Gloucester plc EAT 0221/13 the EAT was 'not persuaded' that the power to set off costs against damages, which exists in ordinary civil litigation, can be transposed into the employment tribunal jurisdiction. In that case, there was a suggestion that the way in which the claimant could in effect be required to pay a costs award in respect of her failed discrimination claims was for the sum of costs awarded to be deducted from the compensation she was awarded as a result of her successful unfair dismissal claim. In the end, the EAT was not required to reach a conclusion on the matter because it overturned the costs order. However, His Honour Judge Peter Clark doubted that this option was available to the employment tribunal.

Conduct of the parties   20.131

As seen under 'Grounds for making orders against a party – conduct' above, an employment tribunal has the power to make a costs order based upon a party's conduct during the proceedings. The conduct of the parties – both the paying party and the receiving party – may also be relevant to the assessment of the amount of costs to be awarded, as the following case demonstrates:

- **Yerrakalva v Barnsley Metropolitan Borough Council and anor** 2012 ICR 420, CA: an employment tribunal made an order for costs against Y based upon her conduct during a pre-hearing review (PHR), which had been held to determine various issues relating to her disability discrimination claim. The tribunal found that Y had said things at the PHR about the state of her health, about her personal injury claims and about her financial means that were untrue. It regarded this conduct as an abuse of process and concluded that this made it appropriate to make a costs order against her. The tribunal rejected the employer's suggestions that Y's claim had had no merit from the outset and that she should bear all the blame for protracting and delaying the proceedings. On the contrary, it found that the employer had made more of a meal of the proceedings than had been necessary. Later in its judgment, the tribunal voiced further criticism, saying that the employer's costs were 'highly exorbitant' and that it had acted 'over-vigorously' in defence of the allegations and had run up costs that were disproportionate. Nevertheless, it ordered Y to pay all of the employer's costs. When the case reached the Court of Appeal, it held that this was an error of law. Y's conduct and its effect on costs should not have been considered in isolation from the rest of the case, including the employer's own conduct and its likely effect on the length and costs of the PHR. The Court therefore varied the employment tribunal's order so that Y had to pay just 50 per cent of the costs reasonably and necessarily incurred by the employer in relation to the PHR and the subsequent costs hearings. The criticisms of the employer, as well as the rejection of some of its criticisms of Y, were relevant to the exercise of the discretion.

Causal link between offending conduct and costs. In Yerrakalva v Barnsley   20.132
Metropolitan Borough Council (above) the Court of Appeal confirmed that, in deciding whether to make a costs order, a tribunal does not have to determine

whether or not there is a precise causal link between the unreasonable conduct in question and the specific costs being claimed. Nevertheless, that was not to say that causation was irrelevant when deciding the amount of costs. The vital point in exercising the discretion to order costs is to look at the whole picture of what happened in the case and to ask whether there has been unreasonable conduct by the claimant in bringing and conducting the case and, in doing so, to identify the conduct, what was unreasonable about it and what effects it had. This is further discussed under 'Grounds for making orders against a party – conduct' above.

20.133 Methods of assessment and applicable limits

In the previous section, 'Assessing amount: general considerations', we discussed some general principles and factors that may be relevant to an employment tribunal's assessment of costs. In this section we discuss methods of assessment and applicable limits – issues that are specific to the particular type of order under consideration. As under the previous Rules, there is provision in the Tribunal Rules 2013 for 'unassessed costs' (which cannot exceed £20,000), detailed assessment of costs (for which there is no upper limit but which must be determined in accordance with the Civil Procedure Rules or, in Scotland, the rules applicable in the sheriff court) and for the amount of costs to be agreed between the parties (again, with no upper limit) – rules 78(1)(a), 78(1)(b) and 78(1)(e). These different methods – which are discussed below under '"Unassessed costs" (capped at £20,000)', 'Detailed assessment of costs' and 'Agreed costs' respectively – apply to costs orders between parties (i.e. an order that one party pay the costs of another party – see 'What orders can employment tribunal make? – order to pay represented party's costs' above). After examining each of the above-mentioned methods of assessment of costs, we shall examine the ways in which preparation time and wasted costs orders are calculated – see 'Assessment of preparation time' and 'Assessment of wasted costs' respectively.

20.134 'Unassessed costs' (capped at £20,000)
The term 'unassessed costs' is commonly used to refer to general costs (which must not exceed an upper limit, currently £20,000) that can be awarded by an employment tribunal without the need for the precise amount to be determined separately by means of a 'detailed assessment' in accordance with the Civil Procedure Rules 1998 SI 1998/3132 (CPR) (or, in Scotland, in accordance with the rules applicable in the sheriff court). The majority of costs claimed in tribunals are 'unassessed', being for an amount far less than £20,000. This type of costs is now dealt with by rule 78(1)(a) of the Tribunal Rules 2013, which provides that a tribunal may 'order the paying party to pay the receiving party a specified amount, not exceeding £20,000, in respect of the costs of the receiving party'. Note that this only applies to costs orders between parties –

in other words, an order that one party pay the costs of another party (see 'What orders can employment tribunal make? – order to pay represented party's costs' above).

It is important to reiterate that the amount of unassessed costs that a tribunal can award outright (i.e. without a detailed assessment) is capped at £20,000. This statutory cap was increased from £10,000 in April 2012 by the Employment Tribunals (Constitution and Rules of Procedure) (Amendment) Regulations 2012 SI 2012/468. If a party wishes to recover costs that are likely to exceed £20,000, he or she will need to do so by way of an order for detailed assessment – see 'Detailed assessment of costs' below. Note that if a party is claiming the costs of a *lay* representative, there is an additional hourly cap, currently set at £34. In view of the double cap, it is hard to conceive that the total claimed costs of a lay representative could exceed £20,000.

The fact that such costs are commonly described as being 'unassessed' does not, **20.135** of course, mean that the tribunal may award an arbitrary figure without reference to any guiding principles or to the actual sum of costs incurred. Rule 75(1)(a) makes it clear that the order is in respect of costs incurred by a represented party – meaning fees, charges, disbursements and expenses incurred by or on behalf of that party (rule 74(1)) – and the amount of the order must obviously reflect that. In addition, as noted by the EAT in Sumukan (UK) Ltd and anor v Raghavan EAT 0087/09, the tribunal must state:

• on what basis – and in accordance with what established principles – it is awarding any sum of costs

• on what basis it arrives at the sum; and

• why costs are being awarded against the party in question.

In Richmond v Devon Doctors On Call EAT 0314/06 an employment tribunal was found to have failed to set out its reasoning on the above matters and the EAT therefore remitted the question of costs to the tribunal, commenting that 'it look[ed] as if [it had] simply plucked the figure of £4,000 out of the air without giving any adequate explanation as to why [it had] chosen this figure'.

Fixed sum preferable. In Lothian Health Board v Johnstone 1981 IRLR 321, **20.136** EAT, the EAT observed that it is preferable for a tribunal, when making a costs order, to award a fixed sum. For example, in Dixon v Hylton Typeset EAT 470/92 the tribunal had ordered D to pay 50 per cent of his employer's costs. On appeal, the EAT substituted an order that D should pay a nominal amount of £25 to reflect the fact that his case had in part been unreasonably conducted. It accepted D's argument that in general fixed sums are preferable to percentage awards and that 50 per cent was in any event excessive having regard to the circumstances of the case.

20.137 **Series of costs orders.** Although a £20,000 limit applies to unassessed costs, it is open to a tribunal to make a series of unassessed costs awards – each of up to £20,000 but which together may amount to more than the statutory limit – in respect of a single case. This was confirmed by the EAT in James v Blockbuster Entertainment Ltd EAT 0601/05 in respect of the then upper limit, which was £10,000. In the EAT's view, although it is normally only at the conclusion of a case that a tribunal focuses on the costs issue, there may be situations where, owing to the serious conduct of a party, the tribunal is invited to make an order for costs at an interim stage. In such circumstances, the EAT continued, 'we see no reason at all why similar to all other civil proceedings, a whole series of costs orders should not be made'. The EAT commented that each costs order would have to relate to separate and sequential stages of the proceedings to avoid duplication. However, it saw nothing wrong in a tribunal making one or more costs orders within proceedings if it was appropriate to do so.

In the circumstances of that particular case, the EAT's comments in James v Blockbuster were obiter. It ended up setting aside one of the two costs orders made by the tribunal (amounting to an award of £10,000), because it related to the striking out of two claims that were subsequently reinstated by the EAT. This left only a costs order of £1,000 in place based on the claimant's unreasonable conduct immediately after the tribunal had announced its decision to strike out the two claims. In principle, however, there was nothing wrong with the two separate orders being made, which together exceeded the then statutory limit of £10,000.

20.138 Potentially, therefore, an employment tribunal could order far in excess of the £20,000 limit by making a series of costs orders. Nevertheless, the prospects of this occurring are lessened somewhat by the necessity for the orders to relate to separate and sequential stages of the proceedings and each sequential cost order satisfying the requirements sets out in Sumukan (UK) Ltd and anor v Raghavan (above). In general, costs claimed in excess of £20,000 will need to be subjected to a detailed assessment (as explained below).

20.139 **Detailed assessment of costs**
An alternative method for determining the amount of costs between parties is for an employment tribunal to make an order for 'detailed assessment' – rule 78(1)(b) Tribunal Rules 2013. There is no limit to the amount of costs that can be claimed under such an order, unlike 'unassessed costs', which are capped at £20,000 – see '"Unassessed costs" (capped at £20,000)' above. While it is possible for the parties to *agree* a higher amount under rule 78(1)(e), this is unlikely to happen very often – see 'Agreed costs' below. Therefore, if a party wishes to recover costs in excess of £20,000, he or she will generally need to do so by way of an order for detailed assessment.

Rule 78(1)(b) provides that a tribunal may order one party to pay to pay the whole or a specified part of a (represented) party's costs with the amount to be paid being determined:

- in England and Wales by way of a 'detailed assessment' in accordance with the Civil Procedure Rules 1998 (CPR)

- in Scotland by way of taxation in accordance with the Act of Sederunt (Fees of Solicitors in the Sheriff Court) (Amendment and Further Provisions) 1993.

As is the case with unassessed costs, this provision only applies to costs orders **20.140** between parties – in other words, an order that one party pay the costs of a represented party's costs (see 'What orders can employment tribunal make? – order to pay represented party's costs' above). Indeed, it was judged to be an error of law for a tribunal to refer a wasted costs order for detailed assessment – see Casqueiro v Barclays Bank plc 2012 ICR D37, EAT (discussed in detail under 'Assessment of wasted costs' below). It is important to note that, unlike rule 78(1)(a) (which governs unassessed costs), there is no cap on the amount of costs that can be awarded under this provision. This is explicitly stated to be the case in rule 78(3).

There is, in essence, a two-stage procedure to assessing the amount of costs under rule 78(1)(b). First, the tribunal makes a costs order setting out what proportion of the receiving party's costs are to be paid – and thus referred for detailed assessment. Secondly, a detailed assessment takes place to assess the precise amount of those costs. Note that, in a change from the old rules, the detailed assessment may now take place under the jurisdiction of the tribunal itself, as opposed to being referred to the county court (or, in Scotland, the sheriff court). The two stages are discussed in more detail below.

Ordering detailed assessment. The first stage in the detailed assessment **20.141** process almost always involves the tribunal determining what percentage of the aggrieved party's costs should be paid and ordering the other party to pay that proportion. In Vaughan v London Borough of Lewisham and ors 2013 IRLR 713, EAT, the EAT stated that it had considered whether it might not have been preferable for the tribunal to express its cap as a *specific sum* rather than as a proportion of the costs. However, the point was not argued before it and it could, in any event, see nothing wrong in principle in the tribunal awarding one third of the respondents' costs even if the alternative of identifying a specific sum might have had advantages. The Vaughan case is considered in detail under 'Assessing amount: general considerations – ability to pay' above.

Some evidence as to the likely amount of the aggrieved party's costs may be required when considering what proportion to award. However, in Sharma v Ealing London Borough Council EAT 0399/05 the EAT held that it is not a prerequisite at the first stage that a tribunal should have a clear idea of the

1099

eventual sum. It was sufficient that it had broad knowledge of the likely effect of making a costs order for detailed assessment and that it had taken this into account when ordering the claimant to pay the whole of the employer's costs of the proceedings, as yet uncalculated. In that particular case the tribunal had stated that the costs were going to be 'very substantial'. It must have known from the nature and length of the proceedings – which involved a 13-day hearing with between 20 and 30 witnesses – that the costs would inevitably amount to many tens of thousands of pounds.

20.142 It is unusual for tribunals to make 100 per cent costs orders. Nevertheless, there is nothing to stop them from doing so where they consider that the circumstances warrant it. In Deer v Walford and anor EAT 0283/10, for example, the EAT held that, exceptional as the award of a full costs order may be, it agreed with the tribunal that in this case such an order was justified. The claimant had brought an expensive and damaging discrimination claim against the employer based on nothing more than 'implausible speculation' and had persisted in it after a clear warning from the tribunal.

20.143 *Terms of the order.* As noted above, a tribunal can specify what percentage of costs will be the subject of the detailed assessment. In Howman v Queen Elizabeth Hospital Kings Lynn EAT 0509/12 the EAT held that a tribunal, when making an order for detailed assessment of costs in the county court, was also entitled to specify that costs be assessed on an indemnity basis, as opposed to the standard basis (see 'The detailed assessment itself' below for a brief explanation of the distinction between the 'standard' and the 'indemnity' bases for assessing costs). The tribunal ordered H to pay the Trust's costs of defending his claim on the basis that it had no reasonable prospect of success and was therefore misconceived. In the tribunal's view, H must have known that his claim for unfair dismissal never had any chance of success, given the damning evidence against him and the fact that he had been advised by an employment judge to 'carefully consider his position' in the light of that evidence. In addition, the Trust's solicitors had put him on notice that it was likely to apply for costs if his claim was unsuccessful. The tribunal considered that, in view of this, the employee should be held responsible for the employer's entire costs (assessed to be in the region of £43,000) on an indemnity basis. On appeal, the EAT held that the tribunal had been entitled to treat this case as one of those rare instances in which an order for costs to be assessed on an indemnity basis was appropriate.

It is unclear whether, under the Tribunal Rules 2013, an employment tribunal may specify the way in which the detailed assessment is to be carried out. In Howman the EAT relied upon the fact that the previous rule (rule 41(1)(c) of the Tribunal Rules 2004) stated that 'the tribunal may order the paying party to pay the receiving party the whole or a specified part of the costs of the receiving party with the amount to be paid being determined by way of a detailed assessment in accordance with the Civil Procedure Rules 1999 or, in

Scotland, as taxed according to such part of the table of fees prescribed for proceedings in the sheriff court *as shall be directed by the order'* (our stress). In the EAT's view, the words 'as shall be directed by the order' gave the tribunal the power to direct the basis on which the county court should assess the costs. It is perhaps arguable that, upon a strict interpretation of the provision, those words only applied to proceedings in Scotland. In any event, they do not appear in rule 78(1)(b) of the Tribunal Rules 2013. This may indicate that the tribunal no longer has the power to stipulate the basis upon which costs will be assessed when making an order for detailed assessment (although, as noted above, under the current rules it can now carry out the detailed assessment itself).

Ability to pay. As noted under 'Assessing the amount: general considerations 20.144 – ability to pay' above, in deciding the amount to be awarded under a costs order, the tribunal may have regard to the paying party's ability to pay – rule 84. In Jilley v Birmingham and Solihull Mental Health NHS Trust EAT 0584/06 the EAT confirmed that this also applies when a tribunal is ordering a detailed assessment of costs – i.e. even when the tribunal is not assessing the precise amount of costs itself, it is still entitled to take into account a party's ability to pay. Having done so, it could, for example, order as part of its discretion that only a specified part of the payee's costs should be payable or it could place a cap on an award for costs. In the EAT's view, where the party has been frank as to his or her means, it is desirable to limit costs orders in this way as they could render the expense of a detailed assessment unnecessary or assist the parties to agree terms of payment. In the particular case, J had submitted evidence in respect of her limited means and yet the tribunal had made an order for detailed assessment, knowing that even if the costs were substantially reduced at the detailed assessment they were still likely to be beyond J's ability to pay. That did not mean that the tribunal was not entitled to take such a course but clear reasoning was required if it was to be taken. The EAT therefore remitted the matter to the tribunal to decide whether to take into account the claimant's means and, if so, how.

For a more detailed discussion of the relevance of a party's ability to pay in the context of the tribunal's assessment of the amount to be awarded, see 'Assessing amount: general considerations – ability to pay' above.

The detailed assessment itself. The second stage of the detailed assessment 20.145 process involves calculating the precise amount of costs to award under the order. Obviously this stage will not always take place since the parties may decide to settle in order to save time and further expense.

Who carries out the detailed assessment? Under rule 41(1)(c) of the Tribunal 20.146 Rules 2004 (the equivalent to rule 78(1)(b) of the Tribunal Rules 2013) employment judges *had* to refer the detailed assessment of costs to the county court (a similar procedure operated in Scotland, with assessments of costs taking place in the sheriff court). Therefore, where the costs being claimed exceeded the statutory cap, the matter had to be referred to the county court (or sheriff court). Conversely, costs for a lesser amount could be (and were) assessed by the tribunals.

The review of the Tribunal Rules carried out by Mr Justice Underhill (as he then was) concluded that in some instances referring costs for assessment to the county court or sheriff court caused undue delay, and the assessment of costs could properly be dealt with by an employment tribunal. During the consultation stage of the new rules, there was concern over whether employment judges were equal to carrying out detailed costs assessments, bearing in mind that county court judges performing this role are very experienced. However, Underhill J was of the opinion that 'many employment judges, at least in England, are qualified to perform a costs assessment, and retaining the process in the tribunal (where appropriate) may make the process simpler for beneficiaries of such awards'.

20.147 The Government agreed with Underhill J and rule 78(1)(b) now duly provides that the assessment may be carried out either by a county court in accordance with the CPR (as before) *or by an employment judge* applying the same principles. Similarly, in Scotland the assessment may be carried out by an employment judge applying the same principles as would be applied by the sheriff court auditor. In other words, employment judges are no longer required to refer the detailed assessment of costs exceeding £20,000 to the county court (or, in Scotland, the sheriff court).

20.148 *Procedure to be followed.* The procedure to be followed when carrying out a detailed assessment in England or Wales is set out in Part 47 CPR. The CPR's general rules about costs, which are contained in Part 44, are relevant for the determination of the amount to be awarded under the detailed assessment. Rule 44.3 CPR sets out two alternative methods by which the assessment of costs may be carried out in England and Wales: the standard basis and the indemnity basis. Both methods involve deciding whether costs were reasonably incurred and reasonable in amount. However, the standard basis also involves deciding whether claimed costs are proportionate. The question of what is reasonable, if in doubt, is resolved in favour of the paying party in a standard case and in favour of the receiving party under the indemnity principles. The default position is that costs are assessed on the standard basis (rule 44.4(4)) and, indeed, this is by far the most common method of assessment in practice. Costs will only be assessed on an indemnity basis (which is less favourable to the receiving party) if there are aggravating factors that justify this – see further under 'Terms of the order' below.

In Scotland, costs under rule 78(1)(b) are assessed in accordance with a table of prescribed fees set out in Schedule 1 to the Act of Sederunt (Fees of Solicitors in the Sheriff Court) (Amendment and Further Provisions) 1993.

Agreed costs

20.149

Aside from an order for 'unassessed costs' under rule 78(1)(a) of the Tribunal Rules 2013 or for 'detailed assessment' under rule 78(1)(b), there is an alternative method for determining the amount of costs, which is dependent upon the agreement of the parties concerned. Rule 78(1)(e) provides that a costs order may specify an amount agreed between the parties. Again, this applies only to costs orders against parties.

Under rule 41(1)(b) of the Tribunal Rules 2004, if the parties agreed a sum, the costs order *had* to be for that amount. The new rule provides that the costs order *may* reflect the amount agreed, suggesting that tribunals now have a discretion as to whether or not it will do so. Nevertheless, it is hard to see a tribunal departing from an amount that has been agreed.

As with detailed assessment, there is no limit on the amount that can be 20.150 awarded under this provision, which means that there is nothing to prevent parties asking the tribunal to make an order for costs over £20,000 (i.e. the statutory cap for unassessed costs), in the unlikely event that a higher amount is agreed.

Assessment of preparation time

20.151

The assessment of preparation time orders (PTOs) is dealt with by rule 79 of the Tribunal Rules 2013. To recap, a PTO is an order that a party make a payment to another party in respect of that party's preparation time while not legally represented – see 'What orders can employment tribunal make? – order to pay for unrepresented party's preparation time' above. In essence, such orders are made in favour of parties who are not represented, whereas general costs orders are made in favour of parties who are represented. The grounds for making preparation time orders are, however, the same as the grounds for making costs orders – see 'Grounds for making orders against a party' above.

However, in contrast to the assessment of costs orders, there is no provision for 'unassessed preparation time' or 'detailed assessment of preparation time'. Indeed, there is no provision for alternative methods of assessing preparation time at all – not even by agreement between the parties. Instead, rule 79 sets out a simple and universal formula for assessing preparation time, based upon the number of hours spent and a fixed hourly rate (currently £34, with a £1 increase per annum).

The previous Employment Tribunal Rules expressly stated that a PTO could 20.152 not exceed the sum of £20,000 – see rule 45(2) Tribunal Rules 2004. This does not appear in the Tribunal Rules 2013, presumably because – given the modest hourly rate – there is no realistic possibility of a PTO exceeding this sum.

1103

20.153 **Number of hours.** The assessment of the number of hours for the purposes of an order must be based upon:

- information provided by the receiving party in respect of his or her preparation time – rule 79(1)(a), and

- the employment tribunal's own assessment of what is a reasonable and proportionate amount of time for the party to have spent on preparatory work, with reference to such matters as the complexity of the proceedings, the number of witnesses and the documentation required – rule 79(1)(b).

As can be seen, the assessment is not simply based upon actual time spent – although this is one of the criteria – but also upon the tribunal's own assessment of what is proportionate and reasonable.

20.154 **Hourly rate.** For the purposes of calculating preparation time, the hourly rate is fixed, currently, at £34. This increases on 6 April each year by £1 – rule 79(2).

It is important to emphasise that under rule 79(1)(a) a PTO does not seek to reimburse a party for *money* spent on the preparation of a case, but for the *time* spent at the applicable fixed hourly rate. Thus, for example, a party who is paying an unqualified representative more than £34 per hour (being the rate applicable from 6 April 2014) will recover less than he or she has paid, whereas a party who is represented for free by an unqualified adviser might effectively receive a windfall of £34 per hour for his or her adviser's preparation time.

20.155 In addition, the formula is based, in part, upon what a tribunal considers to be proportionate and reasonable. Thus if a tribunal considers that a party's lay representative has spent longer than is reasonable on preparing for the case, it may limit the number of hours accordingly. Again, this means that a party could end up recovering less than he or she has paid in terms of the number of hours actually spent. In view of this, now that a costs order can cover a lay representative's fees, it would seem advisable for the party to go down that route instead: although the hourly rate of lay representatives is also capped at £34 (currently) for the purposes of assessing costs, there is no express requirement for the tribunal to take into account what is reasonable and proportionate, which therefore gives tribunals slightly more leeway. Nevertheless, these factors are likely to be taken into account when assessing the amount of costs – see 'Assessing amount: general considerations – costs are compensatory, not punitive'.

20.156 **Assessment of wasted costs**

The assessment of 'wasted costs' is dealt with by rule 81 of the Tribunal Rules 2013. To recap, rule 80 provides that a 'wasted costs order' may be made against a representative in favour of any party where that party has incurred costs as a result of any improper, unreasonable or negligent act or omission on the part of the representative, or which, in light of any such act or omission occurring after the costs were incurred, the tribunal considers it unreasonable to expect the receiving party to pay – see 'What orders can employment tribunal make? – order against representative to pay "wasted costs"' above.

In contrast to the assessment of costs orders (see 'Unassessed costs' and 'Detailed assessment of costs' above), there is no provision for alternative methods of assessing wasted costs, such as 'unassessed wasted costs' or 'detailed assessment of wasted costs'. Nor is there express provision for a wasted costs order to reflect an amount agreed between the parties.

Instead, rule 81 provides that a wasted costs order may: **20.157**

- require the representative to pay the whole or part of any wasted costs of the relevant party, or

- disallow any wasted costs otherwise payable to the representative (including ordering the representative to repay his or her client any costs which have already been paid).

The amount to be paid, disallowed or repaid must in each case be specified in the order. Note that there is no limit to the amount of wasted costs that can be ordered by a tribunal.

No detailed assessment. Unlike an order against a party to pay 'costs', there is **20.158** no requirement for amounts over £20,000 to be subjected to a detailed assessment. Since there is no cap on wasted costs orders, a tribunal can award any amount it chooses without troubling with a detailed assessment. Indeed, a tribunal which refers wasted costs for detailed assessment commits an error of law. An example:

- **Casqueiro v Barclays Bank plc** 2012 ICR D37, EAT: the EAT held that an employment judge had erred by referring the assessment of the amount of a wasted costs order to the county court. Although an employment tribunal could refer the amount of an 'ordinary' costs award to the county court for assessment under then rule 41(1)(c) of the Tribunal Rules 2004, no equivalent power of referral existed in respect of a wasted costs order under then rule 48 (now rule 81 of the Tribunal Rules 2013). While that may have been an oversight on the legislature's part, the Rules nevertheless required that an employment judge make his or her own assessment of the wasted costs incurred by the party in favour of whom the order is made, and specify that amount in the order.

It is interesting to note the EAT's speculation that the lack of a provision for detailed assessment of wasted costs may have been an oversight on the part of the legislature. However, given that the position remains the same under the Tribunal Rules 2013, this seems less likely. At first glance, it seems hard to see why a party's costs may need assessment in the context of a costs order but not in the context of a wasted costs order. Of course, as noted under

1105

'Detailed assessment of costs' above, the current Rules do contain provisions that will reduce the need for assessment of costs against parties to be referred to the county court. Under the old rules, an employment tribunal or judge could only assess costs up to a value of £20,000 – assessment of a larger amount could only be done by way of referral to the county court. Under the new rules, employment judges can make such assessments themselves, applying the relevant provisions of the Civil Procedure Rules 1998 (or, in Scotland, the rules applicable in the sheriff court). Nevertheless, even under the new rules, a tribunal may still refer assessment of costs against parties to the county or sheriff court. And even if it decides to carry out the assessment itself, it must still do so in accordance with the rules applicable in the county or sheriff court. No such requirement applies to tribunals assessing wasted costs over £20,000.

20.159 The fact that there is no need to refer wasted costs for detailed assessment, even where very large amounts are at stake, is mitigated – and perhaps even explained – by the fact that this type of order is very rare indeed. The grounds upon which such orders are made are very stringent (see 'Grounds for making orders against representatives' above) and there are also fairly stringent procedural requirements – see 'Procedural requirements – orders against representatives (wasted costs)' below.

20.160 **How will wasted costs be assessed?** Although a tribunal may order any amount in wasted costs without the need for a 'detailed assessment', this does not, of course, mean that it can do so with impunity and without regard to any established principles or to the actual costs incurred. Some of the principles discussed under 'Assessing amount: general considerations' above will be relevant – in particular, ability to pay. Indeed, rule 84 expressly states that in deciding whether to make a wasted costs order, and if so in what amount, a tribunal may have regard to the representative's ability to pay. It is likely that where the representative is a company or firm, it is the means of that entity rather than those of the individual representative that the tribunal might take into account, although this is not made clear by the Tribunal Rules.

20.161 *Causative link between conduct and wasted costs must be established.* As noted above, the wasted costs that are the subject of an order will be those incurred by a party *as a result of* any improper, unreasonable or negligent act or omission on the part of any representative, or which, in the light of any such act or omission occurring after costs were incurred, the tribunal considers it unreasonable to expect that party to pay – rule 80(1). In other words, there must be a causative link between the conduct in question and the amount of wasted costs. In Casqueiro v Barclays Bank plc (above) the EAT held that the employment judge had erred by failing to consider which specific costs were incurred as a result of the representative's conduct.

Procedural requirements

In this section we discuss various procedural requirements relating to costs and preparation time orders against parties and wasted costs orders against representatives.

Orders against parties (costs and preparation time)

The procedural requirements relating to costs and preparation time orders (PTOs) against parties are identical. Rule 77 of the Tribunal Rules 2013 provides that a party may apply for either type of order at any stage, although no later than 28 days after the date on which the judgment finally determining the proceedings was sent to the parties. Note that this also applies to costs orders to reimburse employment tribunal fees and witness expenses under rules 75(1)(b) and (c) (see 'What orders can employment tribunal make?' under 'Order to reimburse employment tribunal fee' and 'Order to reimburse witness expenses' above).

Under the previous rule 38(7) of the Tribunal Rules 2004, any application received by a tribunal more than 28 days after the date on which the judgment was sent would not be accepted or considered unless the tribunal or employment judge considered that it was in the interests of justice to do so. Rule 77 now makes no provision for any extension of time in the interests of justice. However, under rule 5 the tribunal may, on its own initiative or on the application of a party, extend or shorten any time limit specified in the rules. Under old rule 38(7) an application that was made after the hearing had to be in writing. There is no such express requirement under rule 77, although it would of course be advisable for any application to be in writing, setting out the reasons why it is being made.

Deciding which order to apply for. As previously noted, applications for **20.164** PTOs pursuant to rule 75(2) will generally be made by unrepresented parties, whereas applications for costs under rule 75(1)(a) will generally be made by represented parties. Note, however, that there is some overlap between the two since a party can recover the *costs* of lay representatives under rule 75(1)(a) (capped at a current hourly rate of £34) or the *preparation time* of lay representatives under rule 75(2) (also capped at an hourly rate of £34). The party in question may need to decide which type of order to apply for, since it is not possible for both to be made against the same party in the same proceedings – rule 75(3). However, rule 75(3) goes on to provide that a tribunal may, if it wishes, decide in the course of the proceedings that a party is entitled to one order or the other but defer until a later stage deciding which kind of order to make. This suggests that a party could apply for both types of order in the alternative if he or she is unable to decide which one would be more favourable to him or her.

1107

While it is not possible for the same party to be awarded a PTO and a general costs order simultaneously, it is perfectly possible for costs orders under rules 75(1)(b) and (c) in respect of reimbursement of tribunal fees and witness expenses to be awarded in conjunction with a PTO. As noted in the section on 'What orders can employment tribunal make?' under 'Order to reimburse employment tribunal fee – order to reimburse witness expenses' above, this type of order can be made in favour of any party to proceedings irrespective of whether or not he or she is unrepresented.

20.165 **On the employment tribunal's own initiative.** Strangely, rule 77 does not expressly state that a tribunal may make a costs or preparation time order on its own initiative. Contrast this with rule 82, which specifically provides that a wasted costs order against a representative may be made by the tribunal on the application of a party *or on its own initiative* – see further 'Procedural requirements: orders against representatives' below. Nevertheless, it is well established that a tribunal may make a costs order – and by the same token a PTO – on its own initiative and this is confirmed in the Presidential Guidance on 'General Case Management' for England and Wales. Indeed, as noted by the EAT in Deman v Victoria University of Manchester EAT 0211/06, a tribunal has a *mandatory* duty under what is now S.76(1)(a) to consider making an order for costs (or a PTO) where it is of the opinion that one of the following grounds has been made out:

- a party (or that party's representative) has acted vexatiously, abusively, disruptively or otherwise unreasonably in the bringing or conducting of proceedings, or

- any claim had no reasonable prospect of success.

(The above grounds for making costs and preparation time orders are considered in the section on 'Grounds for making orders against a party' above, under 'Conduct – prospects of success'.)

20.166 In the Deman case the EAT held that a tribunal had the power to make a costs award that extended beyond the terms of the respondent's written application. The fact that the University had made an application for costs based upon certain specific incidents did not prevent the tribunal from approaching the matter on a somewhat different basis and reaching the conclusion based upon its own findings – in this case, that the claimant had acted vexatiously, abusively and disruptively during the proceedings.

20.167 **Reasonable opportunity to make representations.** Old rule 38(9) used to provide that before any order for costs could be made, the Tribunal Secretary had to send notice to the proposed paying party giving it the opportunity to give reasons as to why the order should not be made. There is no such requirement to provide notice under the Tribunal Rules 2013. However, rule 77 provides that no costs or preparation time order may be made unless the proposed paying party has had a reasonable opportunity to make representations – in writing or at a hearing, as the tribunal may order – in response to the costs application. Case law under old rule 38(9) established that the claimant must be given a reasonable opportunity to make representations and this principle will therefore still be relevant. An example:

- **Gwara v Mid Essex Primary Care Trust** EAT 0074/13: G was represented by the Royal College of Nursing in respect of her tribunal claims of unfair dismissal and disability discrimination. However, the RCN withdrew from representation at the end of the first day of the hearing. The following day, G requested an adjournment to seek alternative representation, which the Trust opposed. The tribunal warned G that her case was not strong and that, if she lost, she might face a costs order. It then asked what the cost of an adjournment would be for the Trust and how G might pay for this. When the tribunal reconvened at noon the following day it agreed to the adjournment but made an award of costs against G, noting that the trigger for the delay in proceedings was her 'very unimpressive' evidence on the first day of the hearing. On appeal, the EAT overturned the costs order, holding that it was not sufficient that the tribunal had briefly discussed the question of costs during the application for an adjournment in the context of the prejudice that the Trust might suffer. Both natural justice and rule 38(9) required the tribunal to ensure that the paying party had a 'fair and reasonable' opportunity to give reasons why the order should not be made. Although advance written notice was not necessarily required, in the present circumstances, where no formal application for costs was made, the tribunal had been required to inform G in plain terms that it was minded to make an order, and on what basis and in what amount. It should then have given her an opportunity to make submissions, allowing her a reasonable time to do so.

Employment tribunal must provide reasons. Rule 62 provides that an **20.168** employment tribunal must give reasons for its decision on any disputed issue, including any decision on an application for orders for costs, preparation time or wasted costs. A tribunal's duty to give reasons is considered further in Chapter 14, 'Tribunal judgments', under 'Reasons for judgments – oral and written reasons'.

Orders against representatives (wasted costs) 20.169

Rule 82 of the Tribunal Rules provides that a wasted costs order may be made by an employment tribunal on its own initiative or on the application of any party. A party may apply for a wasted costs order at any stage up to 28 days after the date on which the judgment finally determining the proceedings as against that party was sent to the parties. Before such an order can be made the representative must have had a reasonable opportunity to make representations – in writing or at a hearing, as the employment tribunal may order – in response

1109

to the application or proposal. Where proceedings for wasted costs are being brought against a representative, the tribunal must inform his or her client in writing. It must also inform the client in writing if an order is made.

Although an employment tribunal is entitled to make a wasted costs order on its own initiative, the Court of Appeal in Ridehalgh v Horsefield 1994 3 All ER 848, CA, commented (in the context of the wasted costs provisions that apply in the civil courts) that save in the most obvious cases – such as failure to appear, lateness, negligence leading to an otherwise avoidable adjournment, gross repetition or extreme slowness – courts should be slow to initiate an inquiry into wasted costs since in complex cases this could lead to 'difficult and embarrassing issues'.

20.170 **Timing of the application.** As noted above, a party may apply for a wasted costs order at any stage up to 28 days after the date on which the judgment finally determining the proceedings as against that party was sent. In Filmlab Systems International Ltd v Pennington 1994 4 All ER 673, ChD, Mr Justice Aldous expressed the opinion that wasted costs orders should not, save in exceptional circumstances, be sought until after trial. He highlighted a number of dangers if applications were made at an interlocutory stage, among them the risk that a party's advisers might feel they could no longer act, so that the party would in effect be deprived of the advisers of his or her choice. In Ridehalgh v Horsefield (above) the Court of Appeal stated that it is impossible to lay down rules of universal application, and sometimes an 'interlocutory battle' is appropriate to resolve the dispute between the parties. However, it agreed with Aldous J that applications for wasted costs are generally best left until after the end of the trial.

20.171 **Reasonable opportunity to make representations.** Before a wasted costs order can be made, the representative must have had a reasonable opportunity to make representations in response to the application or proposal – rule 82. In Ridehalgh v Horsefield (above) the Court of Appeal commented that the procedure adopted in this regard should be as summary as is consistent with fairness. Fairness requires that the representative should be very clearly told what he or she is said to have done wrong and what is being claimed. However, the requirement of simplicity means that elaborate pleadings should in general be avoided. The Court could not, for example, imagine circumstances in which the person seeking wasted costs should be permitted to interrogate the representative, or vice versa. Hearings should be measured in hours, not in days or weeks.

20.172 *Cross-examination.* As previously noted, the Court of Appeal in Ridehalgh commented that it could not imagine circumstances in which the applicant should be permitted to interrogate the representative, or vice versa. The EAT went further in Ratcliffe Duce and Gammer v L Binns (t/a Parc Ferme) EAT 0100/08, stating that 'it will never be appropriate for the receiving party to cross-examine the representative against whom the order is being considered'. In Wilsons Solicitors v Johnson and ors 2011 ICR D21, EAT, the then President of the EAT, Mr Justice Underhill, doubted whether that was an absolute rule. And in Godfrey Morgan Solicitors Ltd v Cobalt Systems Ltd 2012 ICR 305, EAT, he stated that he could see no principled basis for a general rule that a respondent cannot make submissions or cross-examine the representative. In that case, the claimant's representative sought to overturn a wasted costs order on the ground that the employment judge had erred by allowing the person seeking the order to make submissions on the wasted costs issue and to cross-examine the representative. Rejecting the appeal, Underhill P held that the observation in Ratcliffe was obiter (i.e. non-binding) and in any event was made in the very different situation where the solicitor against whom the order was made had not been present at the final hearing and had not been invited to make representations as to why a wasted costs order should not be made. The EAT could see why, in those circumstances, it would not be appropriate to invite the other party to make further representations and have 'the last word', but did not see any principled basis for a general rule that the person seeking the order cannot make submissions or cross-examine the representative. In the instant case, the parties had agreed to deal with the issue of wasted costs at an oral hearing. That being so, the EAT saw nothing wrong with the evidence being tested in cross-examination.

Sufficient notice. The Presidential Guidance on 'General Case Management' **20.173** for England and Wales makes it clear that the representative from whom payment is sought is entitled to notice, as is the party he or she has been representing, as they may need separate representation at any costs hearing. In Jackson v Cambridgeshire County Council and ors EAT 0402/09 the EAT expressed 'some sympathy' with the appellant solicitor's contention that he had been given inadequate notice of the wasted costs application (and thus was not given a reasonable opportunity to make representations). The respondent Council had applied to strike out the claims that the appellant was pursuing on behalf of a family member and had simply given a one-line warning that it would apply for a wasted costs order if its strike-out application were successful. The employment tribunal upheld the strike-out application and proceeded to make a wasted costs order against the solicitor, having given him only half an hour to prepare. On appeal, the EAT did not have to make a final decision as to whether or not the solicitor had been given sufficient notice, having already upheld the appeal on the basis that a wasted costs order was not in any case appropriate because he was not acting in pursuit of profit – see 'What orders can employment tribunal make? – order against representative to pay "wasted costs"'. Nevertheless, it did make some general observations on the issue, noting that there is a real tension between the two conflicting aims identified by the Court of Appeal in Ridehalgh v Horsefield (above) in the context of wasted costs. On the one hand, the process is intended to be a summary one: the Court of Appeal in Ridehalgh made it clear that elaborate satellite litigation about wasted costs was strongly to be deprecated. On the other hand, the process must be fair. A finding that a solicitor or other professional representative has been negligent is a serious matter for the person affected, and fairness must come first. In the context of tribunal proceedings, this tension – said the EAT – quite commonly emerges, as here, in relation to the question of the stage at which a wasted costs application should be heard: should it be at the conclusion of the hearing which provides the basis for it or should it be adjourned to a later date?

The EAT emphasised that there is no general rule about the correct time to hear an application for a wasted costs order. The starting point is that it is better, for reasons of efficiency, to deal with the application at the same hearing. In many cases, no objection will be made to this, as the representative will have received prior notification of the grounds for the application or the matter will be sufficiently straightforward to be dealt with without prior notice – for example, where costs have been wasted because through carelessness the representative has appeared late. In other cases it will be unfair to proceed in this way, typically because the issues are not straightforward or perhaps simply because time is too short. In many such cases, where the hearing is an interim one it will not be difficult to postpone the application to a later stage in the proceedings, although if it is important that the same employment judge or tribunal hear it, that may sometimes create a problem. If, however, there would have to be a special hearing to determine the application, the tribunal will need to consider whether that is a proportionate course to take. If it is not, the application may simply be refused because 'the game is not worth the candle'.

20.174 **Employment tribunal must provide reasons.** Rule 62 of the Tribunal Rules 2013 provides that a tribunal must give reasons for its decision on any disputed issue, including any decision on an application for orders for costs, preparation time or wasted costs. A tribunal's duty to give reasons is considered further in Chapter 14, 'Tribunal judgments', under 'Reasons for judgments – oral and written reasons'.

20.175 # Penalties against employers

By virtue of S.16 of the Enterprise and Regulatory Reform Act 2013, the Employment Tribunals Act 1996 has been amended to confer upon employment tribunals a discretionary power to impose a financial penalty on an employer found to have breached a claimant's employment rights where the tribunal considers that the breach had 'one or more aggravating features'. S.12A ETA provides that in a claim involving an employer and a worker the tribunal may order the employer to pay a penalty to the Secretary of State (whether or not it also makes a financial award against the employer on the claim itself) if it:

- concludes that the employer has breached 'any of the worker's rights to which the claim relates', and

- is of the opinion that the breach has 'one or more aggravating features'.

The power to impose a penalty in accordance with the above applies in respect of cases decided on or after 6 April 2014.

Note that even if a tribunal finds 'aggravating features', it still has discretion to **20.176** decide whether or not to impose a penalty under S.12A. In deciding whether or not to do so, and when determining the appropriate amount of any such fine, a tribunal *must* have regard to an employer's ability to pay – S.12A(2). (This contrasts with costs, preparation time and wasted costs orders where the tribunal *may* – but does not have to – take ability to pay into account – see 'Factors relevant to tribunal's discretion – ability to pay' and 'Assessing amount: general considerations – ability to pay' above.)

Aggravating features   **20.177**
'Aggravating features' is not defined and is left to the discretion of the tribunal. According to the Government's Explanatory Notes to S.16 ERRA, however, 'an employment tribunal may be more likely to find that the employer's behaviour in breaching the law had aggravating factors where the action was deliberate or committed with malice, the employer was an organisation with a dedicated human resources team or where the employer had repeatedly breached the employment right concerned'. Conversely, 'the employment tribunal may be less likely to find that the employer's behaviour in breaching the law had aggravating factors where an employer has been in operation for only a short period of time, is a micro business, has only a limited human resources function, or the breach was a genuine mistake'.

Amount   **20.178**
The amount of the financial penalty that a tribunal may award ranges from a minimum of £100 and a maximum of £5,000 – S.12A(3) ETA. However, where the claimant has also been awarded compensation by the tribunal, any penalty must be half the amount of the sum awarded to the employee (subject to the minimum and maximum levels prescribed by S.12A(3)) – S.12A(5). Importantly, if the employer pays 50 per cent of the penalty within 21 days of the penalty notice being sent, its liability for the full amount is discharged – S.12A(10). This is intended to incentivise prompt payment.

Multiple claims   **20.179**
Section 12A(6) and (7) apply to penalties made in multiple claims cases – i.e. claims brought by different workers against the same employer. Where a financial award is made in such cases, the tribunal will have a discretion as to

1113

the amount of the financial penalty that it can impose in each claim, subject to a total minimum payment of £100 and to a maximum of £5,000, and, in a case where the tribunal also makes a financial award against the employer on the claim, no more than 50 per cent of the amount of the award.

Note that where a single act by an employer leads to multiple claims by a worker (for example, where a dismissal leads to claims for unfair dismissal and holiday pay), S.12A(8) provides that only one financial penalty can be imposed by the tribunal.

20.180 Reconsideration and appeal

Any 'judgment' of an employment tribunal may either be appealed to the EAT or be the subject of an application for reconsideration by the tribunal itself (formerly known as a 'review') provided that undertaking such a reconsideration is in the interests of justice. Following an amendment to the Tribunal Rules 2013 effected by para 6 of the Employment Tribunals (Constitution and Rules of Procedure) (Amendment) Regulations 2014 SI 2014/271, the definition of a 'judgment' for the purposes of the Rules has been extended to include 'the imposition of a financial penalty under S.12A ETA' – rule 1(3)(b) (as amended). It follows that an employer may apply for reconsideration of a decision to impose a financial penalty or otherwise seek to appeal against such a decision to the EAT. For full details regarding the reconsideration process, see Chapter 16, 'Reconsideration of judgments and decisions'; and for details of appealing to the EAT, see Chapter 17, 'The Employment Appeal Tribunal'.

20.181 Costs in the EAT

Whereas in the ordinary civil courts costs are routinely awarded against the losing party, costs in the EAT are the exception rather than the rule. Indeed, costs are ordered much less frequently even than in employment tribunals. In International Flavours and Fragrances (GB) Ltd v Lawrence EAT 742/97 the EAT noted in this regard that 'the making of an order for costs upon an appeal is an unusual course'.

Having said that, a new and more detailed costs regime in the EAT was introduced by the Employment Appeal Tribunal Rules (Amendment) Rules 2004 SI 2004/2526 in October 2004, which amended the Employment Appeal Tribunal Rules 1993 SI 1993/2854 ('the EAT Rules') to bring them more in line with the costs regime in employment tribunals. In particular, the circumstances in which a costs order can be made by the EAT were widened, and new powers were introduced enabling the EAT to award costs in favour of litigants in person and to make wasted costs orders against representatives. The relevant provisions are found in rules 34–34D of the EAT Rules. These are supplemented by para 22 of the Practice Direction (Employment Appeal Tribunal – Procedure) 2013.

1114

Costs orders against parties in the EAT   20.182
Rule 34(1) of the EAT Rules sets out the EAT's general power to make a costs order against one party to proceedings ('the paying party') in favour of another party to proceedings ('the receiving party'). The grounds for doing so are set out in rule 34A and are discussed under 'Grounds for making costs orders against a party in the EAT' below. Such an order will require the paying party to make a payment in respect of the costs incurred by the receiving party. It is worth noting that a costs order under rule 34(1) can also be made against – and in favour of – a 'special advocate', meaning a person appointed pursuant to rule 30A(4) (i.e. the rule relating to proceedings in cases concerning national security) – rule 2(1). In summary, 'special advocates' can be appointed (both in the employment tribunal and the EAT) to represent parties who have been excluded from proceedings in the interest of national security. 'National security proceedings' and the use of special advocates are outside the scope of this Handbook.

Meaning of 'costs'. 'Costs', for the purposes of rule 34(1), are defined as   20.183
including 'fees, charges, disbursements and expenses incurred by or on behalf of a party… in relation to the proceedings, including the reimbursement allowed to a litigant in person' – rule 34(2). Para 22.1 of the Practice Direction states that 'costs' also includes 'allowances paid by the Secretary of State and payment in respect of time spent in preparing a case'.

Costs awardable only in respect of parties to proceedings. 'Special   20.184
advocates' aside, costs under rule 34 can only be awarded against – and, indeed, in favour of – parties to the proceedings. Therefore, an employer was prevented from recovering costs against the employment tribunal itself in G Baxter Ltd v Quinn EAT 1043/93. The tribunal had refused to adjourn a hearing and the EAT overturned that ruling. The employer then argued that since the appeal was necessitated by the tribunal's unreasonable refusal to grant an adjournment, he should have the costs of the appeal paid by the Secretary of State or an officer of the tribunal. The EAT rejected this novel proposition, holding to the traditional view that costs could only be awarded against a party to the proceedings.

Furthermore, a party can only be made to pay costs if he or she was a party to the proceedings at the time that the costs were incurred. In Lowbey v Lindo 1981 ICR 216 (Note), EAT, an employee complained to an employment tribunal of unfair dismissal, but the employer did not enter a response or appear at the hearing of the complaint. The tribunal found the dismissal unfair and awarded the employee compensation. The employer then applied for a review of that decision, which was refused. Solicitors acting for the employer then signed and submitted notices of appeal against the tribunal's unfair dismissal finding and its refusal of the review. Subsequently, the solicitors notified the EAT that they had ceased to act for the employer. The appeals were dismissed.

The employee's counsel then applied for an order for the solicitors who had previously acted for the employer to be joined as a party to the proceedings, with a view to applying for a costs order against them. The EAT, however, refused the application on the ground that the EAT Rules only permitted costs to be awarded against a person who was a party at the time the costs were incurred.

20.185 Equally, in order for costs to be awardable, they must be incurred by a party to the proceedings. In Wilson v Metropolitan Borough of Knowsley EAT 430/88 the respondent to the appeal needlessly required the production of 100 pages of the employment tribunal chairman's notes of evidence. Although the EAT was minded to make the respondent pay for the costs of compiling the notes, it concluded that it had no power to do so since the chairman was not a party to the proceedings.

Unlike general orders for costs in the employment tribunal (see 'What orders can employment tribunal make? – order to pay represented party's costs' above), the EAT Rules do not stipulate that a costs order can only be made in respect of costs incurred by a *represented* party. Therefore, costs orders in the EAT can be made against *any* party to proceedings, whether they are legally represented, instructing a lay representative or litigants in person. Note, however, that the EAT Rules contain additional provisions regarding the assessment of costs orders in favour of litigants in person. These are discussed under 'Deciding how much to award in the EAT – costs orders in favour of litigants in person' below.

20.186 **Order against respondent to reimburse ET and EAT fees**
To reflect the introduction of commencement and hearing fees in the EAT and in employment tribunals (see Chapter 19, 'Fees'), rule 34A(2A) of the EAT Rules introduces a new type of costs order – solely to be made against respondents (which of course, could be the employer or the employee) – allowing for the reimbursement of 'any fee paid by the appellant under a notice issued by the Lord Chancellor'. Para 22.1 of the Practice Direction confirms that this can include employment tribunal, as well as EAT, fees paid by appellants. The EAT can make this type of 'fee-specific' costs order in favour of an appellant if it allows his or her appeal in full or in part.

As for the amount to be ordered, rule 34A(2) provides that it must be no greater than the amount of any fee paid. Note that the EAT's power to order reimbursement is discretionary and does not automatically follow if a fee-paying party is successful upon appeal. If, for example, the appellant succeeds upon a technicality the EAT may decide that it is not appropriate to order the respondent to reimburse any fee paid. Where a fee-paying appellant's appeal is only *partially* successful, the EAT may also decide that reimbursement is not appropriate. Alternatively, it may decide to award a proportion of any fee paid to reflect the proportion of the appeal that was successful.

The case outlined below provides an early example of the EAT making an order **20.187** requiring the respondent to pay the appellant's fees in respect of a successful appeal. Interestingly, the order made was conditional on the appellant's pending application for a fee remission being rejected:

- **Portnykh v Nomura International plc** 2014 IRLR 251, EAT: P sought to appeal against an employment tribunal's case management decisions in his claim of unfair dismissal. He paid a hearing fee in relation to the appeal and applied for fee remission. However, by the time the EAT upheld his appeal, his remission application had still to be decided. The Appeal Tribunal considered whether it should order NI plc to repay all or part of the fee P had paid under rule 34A(2A) of the EAT Rules. The EAT considered it doubtful that it would be able to make an order requiring the fees to be repaid in the event that the remission was successful, as neither the Rules nor the EAT Practice Direction make express or even implied provision for this situation. However, the EAT saw no reason why it should not make a contingent order postponing payment until the outcome of the fee remission application was known and making payment conditional upon the application being rejected. In considering whether to make such an order, the EAT did not consider that a distinction should be drawn between somebody who has paid a fee in order to get a case put back onto the right track in an interlocutory appeal and somebody who appeals against the outcome of a merits hearing. Nor did it think it right to take into account the fact that P, while conducting the case himself, had not conducted the litigation in a helpful or cooperative way. The EAT therefore concluded that NI plc should reimburse P's fee of £1,600 given that it had the means to pay and, looking at the matter broadly, had substantially lost on the appeal. However, the EAT ordered that the sum would only be payable if P's application for fee remission was refused, in which case it must be paid within 14 days of that refusal.

Grounds for making costs orders against a party in the EAT **20.188**
Under rule 34A(1) of the EAT Rules, a costs order may be made against a party to proceedings where it appears to the EAT that:

- the proceedings were unnecessary, improper or vexatious
- the proceedings were misconceived
- there has been unreasonable delay in the bringing or conducting of proceedings, or
- there has been other unreasonable conduct in the bringing or conducting of proceedings.

Rule 34A(2) goes on to provide that the EAT may 'in particular' make a costs order against a party when he or she has:

- not complied with a direction of the EAT
- amended a notice of appeal, answer or cross-appeal, or
- caused an adjournment of proceedings.

20.189 Note that the above grounds apply only to costs orders against parties to proceedings. The grounds for making a wasted costs order against a representative are set out separately in rule 34C – see '"Wasted costs"' orders against representatives' below.

The vast majority of costs cases in the EAT concern rule 34A(1) – i.e. the first four grounds set out above. We consider these four grounds in more detail below. Note that in examining whether an appeal falls within one of these categories, it is necessary to look only at the proceedings before the EAT. It is not appropriate to look at the history of the matter in the employment tribunal – Somjee v North West Regional Health Authority and anor EAT 87–88/90.

20.190 **Unnecessary, improper or vexatious proceedings.** The meaning of the words 'unnecessary', 'improper' and 'vexatious' has been considered in a number of cases.

20.191 *Unnecessary.* In Rima Electric Ltd v Taylor EAT 553/79 the EAT stated that appeals were 'unnecessary' if 'there is some other alternative procedure available, such as an application for a review [now termed reconsideration], to provide an inexpensive and expeditious remedy'. Thus, costs were awarded by the EAT in the case of William P Harrower Ltd v Hogg EAT 215/78 after it had held that the appellant's application to admit new evidence should have been dealt with by way of review rather than appeal.

In Charalambous and anor t/a Posidonia Wine Bar v Hercules EAT 302/88 the employer's appeal succeeded only on the point that the employment tribunal had awarded compensation in excess of the statutory maximum. The EAT pointed out, however, that tribunals have the power to recall their decisions to correct minor discrepancies (see Chapter 15, 'Reconsideration of tribunal judgments and decisions', under 'Correcting mistakes') and said that the employer should simply have notified the tribunal of the error rather than brought an appeal. The EAT went on to make an award of £750 costs against him.

20.192 The EAT has also held that an appeal may be unnecessary if its outcome can make no or very little difference to the situation of the parties – CW Coates and Sons Ltd v Kendrick EAT 178/79. In Chard Toys Ltd v Rowe EAT 360/76 there was an appeal against an award of a redundancy payment of £39. The EAT considered this unnecessary and awarded £100 costs against the employer.

The case of **British School of Motoring v Fowler** EAT 0059/06 was another in which the EAT awarded costs against a successful appellant on the ground that an appeal was unnecessary. There, F presented unfair and wrongful dismissal claims against his former employer, BSM. Owing to BSM's failure to file a response, the tribunal issued a direction that the company take no further part in proceedings. BSM subsequently wrote to the tribunal informing it that it had been subject to a takeover and that it could not trace receipt of the original tribunal papers, and asked for them to be re-sent. The tribunal treated this letter as an application for review and refused it without a hearing. BSM appealed to the EAT. While critical of BSM's conduct, the EAT nevertheless held that the tribunal had erred in its approach. In the EAT's view, having properly obtained F's comments, the tribunal chairman should have gone back to BSM for a reply. At the very least, given that the tribunal was effectively rejecting BSM's account of why it had not responded to the claim, BSM should, as a matter of simple fairness, have been given an opportunity to respond before the tribunal reached its conclusion. The tribunal had erred in law by dealing with the matter without recourse to the employer and in not directing a review hearing under what was then rule 36 of the Tribunal Rules 2004. The EAT allowed BSM's appeal and ordered that a full review hearing take place before a different tribunal. It went on to hold, however, that the appeal proceedings were 'unnecessarily caused by errors on the part of [BSM] or its advisers. Had this case been dealt with properly in the first instance... none of this would have happened.' It therefore awarded F the full costs of his appeal, assessed at over £5,500.

Improper or vexatious. If an appeal is found to be 'improper', it will almost **20.193** certainly be held to be 'vexatious' as well (and vice versa). According to the EAT in Rima Electric Ltd v Taylor (above), 'improper' denotes 'some degree of impropriety on the part of the appellant'. In CW Coates and Sons Ltd v Kendrick (above) the EAT thought that 'improper or vexatious' must probably 'connote something to do with motive for bringing the appeal'. A mere error of judgment in challenging the tribunal's decision did not make the appeal improper or vexatious.

At employment tribunal level, costs can be awarded where a party to the proceedings, or a party's representative, has acted vexatiously – see 'Grounds for making orders against a party – conduct' above. It is therefore useful to consider the meaning that the term has been given at that level. The definition that is generally followed was given by the National Industrial Relations Court in ET Marler Ltd v Robertson 1974 ICR 72, NIRC, which stated that 'if an employee brings a hopeless claim not with any expectation of recovering compensation but out of spite to harass his employers or for some other improper motive, he acts vexatiously'. Two examples of vexatious appeals to the EAT:

- **Mach v British Telecommunications** EAT 847/83: the EAT found that M had carried out a 'deliberate campaign calculated to cause the maximum of distress and inconvenience to the respondents'. There was a clear pattern of last-minute applications for adjournments and for leave to alter his position which could only be described as 'irresponsible and capricious'

- **Meghani v Clark Pixley** EAT 1120/96: the employment tribunal awarded £1,250 costs against M, who it found had lied in material respects and made false allegations in support of his race discrimination claim. A vexatious complaint was then compounded by a vexatious appeal at which the EAT found that M made further false allegations, which were contradicted by notes of evidence at the tribunal. The EAT awarded a further £1,000 in costs.

20.194 **Misconceived proceedings.** Since 2004 the EAT has had the power to make costs awards where appeal proceedings were 'misconceived'. The term 'misconceived' is not defined in the EAT Rules, but in Vernon v Loks Plasma Services Ltd EAT 0018/05 the EAT confirmed that its essential sense is defined by (the now repealed) Reg 2 of the Tribunal Regulations 2004. Thus, misconceived proceedings for the purposes of rule 34A include those 'having no reasonable prospect of success'. Note that the term 'misconceived' is no longer used in the Tribunal Rules 2013, which simply refer to a claim or response having 'no reasonable prospect of success' – see 'Grounds for making orders against a party – prospects of success' above. This does not, however, mean that the old definition of 'misconceived' is no longer applicable under the EAT Rules.

The EAT's decision with regard to costs in Iron and Steel Trades Confederation v ASW Ltd (in liquidation) 2004 IRLR 926, EAT (which was made pursuant to the EAT Rules prior to the amendments made in 2004), might have been different under the amended EAT Rules. In that case an employment tribunal decided that it had no jurisdiction to hear a union's claim for a protective award, since the claim had been brought four months out of time. The union appealed and the EAT, while noting that the appeal had been brought with little prospect of success, nonetheless held that the union had not acted unreasonably in the bringing or conducting of proceedings. Consequently, it declined to make a costs order. In reaching this decision the EAT was influenced by the fact that, under the EAT Rules applicable at the time, there was no provision whereby costs could be awarded if proceedings were 'misconceived'.

20.195 Two examples of costs being awarded by the EAT based upon the ground that the appeal was misconceived:

- **BMB Recruitment v Hunter** EAT 0056/05: the EAT concluded that an employer's appeal against an employment tribunal's findings of unfair dismissal and sex discrimination was wholly misconceived where the tribunal had clearly made no error of law. The appellant had argued that the tribunal should have found differently without pointing to any good reason in support of that assertion. Accordingly, a costs order of £1,500 was appropriate

- **Royal Mail Group Ltd v Lall** EAT 0228/12: the EAT ordered RMG Ltd to pay L's costs amounting to £4,000 on the basis that its appeal against an employment tribunal's finding of unfair dismissal (for misconduct) was misconceived. There was a 'towering body' of Court of Appeal authority against the proposition RMG Ltd was advancing by way of appeal. The parties had put before the EAT 19 authorities in total. Most of these cases were against RMG Ltd's proposition and should have indicated to it how difficult it is to overturn a tribunal's finding of unfair dismissal for misconduct. In any event, RMG Ltd could not hope to overturn the tribunal's judgment without a detailed examination of many of the relevant authorities (which it had not undertaken). Furthermore, the EAT observed that the company had adopted a 'pernickety and hypercritical' analysis of the language used by the tribunal in its judgment. As noted by the Court of Appeal in Brent London Borough Council v Fuller 2011 ICR 806, CA, 'the reading of an employment tribunal decision must not... be so fussy that it produces pernickety critiques. Over-analysis of the reasoning process; being hypercritical of the way in which the decision is written; focusing too much on particular passages or turns of phrase to the neglect of the decision read in the round: those are all appellate weaknesses to avoid.'

Unreasonable delay. Delay in the context of costs generally refers to matters **20.196** other than the lodging of an actual notice of appeal. As explained in Chapter 17, 'Processing an appeal', under 'Time limit for lodging an appeal', a strict time limit is in place to ensure that an appeal is lodged promptly.

An example of unreasonable delay can be found in Collier v AKC Catering BV EAT 19/81. In that case the appellant was advised by his solicitor that there was a prospect of a successful appeal against an employment tribunal's decision, and he was granted legal aid to obtain a counsel's opinion. However, he failed to do this in time for the hearing and sought an adjournment – albeit too late to allow the respondent's operations manager and personnel officer to alter their arrangements to travel from Aberdeen to appear at the hearing of the appeal. The EAT adjourned the appeal to a date convenient to the respondent but ordered the appellant to pay £100 towards the respondent's costs.

Unreasonable conduct. Costs were awarded by the EAT on the ground of **20.197** unreasonable conduct in the following cases:

- **Mahlangu v London Borough of Hackney Construction Services** EAT 598/95: the EAT had no hesitation in finding that M had acted unreasonably. M had sought advice from an employment tribunal as to the availability of injunctive relief in a race discrimination claim, and the tribunal had advised that such relief was not available. Nevertheless, M persisted in applying to

1121

the employment tribunal for an injunction. This case failed and M appealed. The EAT held that M had acted unreasonably in bringing a hopeless appeal and awarded costs of £250

- **Charalambous v Patel Dodhia and Co** EAT 160/95: C brought an employment tribunal claim against PD and Co, asserting entitlement to a redundancy payment. The issue arose as to whether he was in fact self-employed, meaning that he was not entitled to a redundancy payment, and the tribunal ordered discovery of various documents relating to his tax and national insurance position. C's appeal against the order for discovery was based on the fact that he was self-employed. The EAT held that C had acted unreasonably in pursuing the appeal. The appeal stood no chance of succeeding and C's position as to his employment status had been ambiguous throughout. The EAT ordered C to pay costs of £500

- **Monfort International plc v McKenzie** EAT 0155/06: the EAT held that it was unreasonable of MI plc not to make a counter-offer or even respond to an offer of settlement made by M. The EAT ordered it to pay M's costs to the tune of £2,631.70

- **G4S Security Services (UK) v Rondeau** EAT 0207/09: the EAT held that R's previous refusal to accept offers by G4SS(UK) in the same terms as were accepted at the door of the Appeal Tribunal amounted to unreasonable conduct. It therefore ordered R to pay G4SS(UK)'s costs in the sum of £3,420.

20.198 *Representative's conduct.* The EAT has occasionally been prepared to make an award of costs against a party based upon the unreasonable behaviour of that party's representative. In Wright t/a Merseyside and North Wales Fencing v Davies EAT 836/93, for example, the employer's solicitors misled the employee into thinking that an EAT hearing had been cancelled. The EAT thought that an award for costs against the employer was appropriate.

Similarly, the unreasonable conduct of an adviser was taken into account in Minehead Royal British Legion Club Ltd v Gunter EAT 84–85/94. In that case the EAT ordered the employer to pay 25 per cent of the assessed costs of the appeal as the conduct of the appeal by the employer's advisers had fallen outside the 'reasonable way in which these matters should be conducted'. In particular, the EAT took into account the 'voluminous nature of both the Notice of Appeal and the Skeleton Argument'. The EAT remarked that the skeleton argument was 'not a Skeleton Argument at all, it [was] more of a short story and not very short at that'.

20.199 Note that, following the amendments to the EAT Rules in 2004, the EAT can now make awards of wasted costs directly against a party's representative, albeit the grounds for doing so are stringent – see '"Wasted costs" orders against representatives' below.

Factors relevant to the EAT's discretion to award costs

20.200

The decision as to whether or not to award costs in a case where the conditions of rule 34A of the EAT Rules are met is a matter for the Appeal Tribunal's discretion. We consider below a number of factors that may influence the EAT in the exercise of that discretion.

Withdrawing appeals. If a hopeless appeal is withdrawn *promptly*, this may **20.201** make it less likely that costs will be ordered. In Jolliff v Bayley Bartlett EAT 253/77 the appellant withdrew an interlocutory appeal three weeks after serving notice of it. The EAT refused to award costs, stating: 'It seems to us that the appellant should not be penalized because... he saw the light, changed his mind and decided to abandon the appeal... We certainly do not want to discourage parties who may have taken a wrong or unwise step from changing their minds and abandoning the appeal.' This sentiment was echoed by another division of the EAT in Neckles v Yorkshire Rider t/a First Huddersfield and ors EAT 1509/98, which held that parties should not be discouraged from either settling their disputes or from withdrawing their appeals 'if on mature reflection they think that it would be better not to pursue them'.

On the other hand, preparing for an appeal can be an expensive business, especially when professional legal advisers are involved. It can be very frustrating, therefore, when a party who has instituted an appeal subsequently withdraws it after time and money have been spent in preparation for the hearing. In approaching applications for costs in cases where an appeal has been withdrawn somewhat less promptly, the EAT has paid particular attention to factors such as the reasons for the withdrawal, whether the institution of the appeal was itself unreasonable and the timing of the withdrawal. Some examples:

- **Rocha v Commonwealth Holiday Inns of Canada Ltd** EAT 13/80: the appellant's solicitors withdrew the appeal just two days before the hearing. In fact, the other side learned of this only on the day of the hearing itself. The EAT held that it was appropriate to hear the respondent's application for costs even though neither the appellant nor his representatives were present. As the respondent had incurred costs and expenses in the preparation of the case and in making arrangements for appearing, and as there was no explanation for the lateness of the withdrawal, the EAT made an order for £50 by way of expenses to be paid by the appellant to the respondent

- **Stevenage Borough Council v Hensby** EAT 57/80: an appeal was withdrawn 18 days before the hearing date. The withdrawal was prompted by the legal advice that the appellant sought almost six months after lodging the appeal. The EAT held that as there was no explanation for the delay in taking advice, the appellant was guilty of unreasonable delay and unreasonable conduct. An order for costs was made against him

1123

- **Snowflake Insulations Ltd v Kennedy and ors** EAT 32/91: the respondent was not told that an appeal was being abandoned until four months after the appellant had been advised by his lawyer that the appeal could not succeed. The EAT, which held that even apart from this delay the appeal should never have been brought in the first place, awarded costs of £4,000.

20.202   Although there is no general rule that an early withdrawal will never attract an order for costs, the scale of costs incurred by the other side is likely to be considerably smaller than in the case of a late withdrawal. Therefore a party who has instituted an appeal which, as it appears later, is without merit, would be well advised to withdraw it as soon as possible.

20.203   **Failing to turn up at the hearing.** In Croydon v Greenham (Plant Hire) Ltd 1978 ICR 415, EAT, the Appeal Tribunal held that the failure of the appellant to appear at the hearing and argue his appeal made it difficult for the EAT to do its job properly and amounted to unreasonable conduct. Since that case, however, the EAT's attitude has shifted somewhat. Chronic delays in the disposal of appeals have meant that the EAT is no longer so averse to dealing with an appeal on the basis of the papers in front of it. If one party has attended the hearing and the other has chosen not to, then there is nothing to stop the EAT from hearing the party who has attended and considering the written submissions of the absent party. This, of course, may operate to the disadvantage of the absent party, but there are unlikely to be any major costs implications simply with regard to the failure of a party to attend the hearing.

20.204   **The effect of legal advice.** In Rima Electric Ltd v Taylor EAT 553/79 the EAT made it clear that where an appeal discloses no possible error of law on the part of the employment tribunal, the fact that grounds of appeal were prepared by a barrister will not necessarily protect the appellant from an order for costs – although costs were not actually awarded on the facts of that case. This demonstrates that acting upon legal advice when prosecuting an appeal will not necessarily prevent the EAT from finding that a party's actions constitute, for example, unreasonable conduct.

Where, however, an appeal is actively supported by a statutory body such as the Equality and Human Rights Commission, the EAT may be reluctant to made a costs award. In Chaplin v Re-Mark (Agricultural) Ltd EAT 434/82 the claimant alleged that, as one of the employer's area sales managers, she should have been paid at the same rate as one of the other (male) area sales managers under the then Equal Pay Act 1970 (now subsumed into the Equality Act 2010). The employer successfully defended the claim before the employment tribunal on the ground that the variation in the employees' rates of pay was genuinely due to a material difference between the complainant's case and her comparator's. The claimant appealed, with the support of what was then the Equal Opportunities Commission (EOC), but the EAT dismissed the appeal, holding that it was wholly misconceived in that it was an attempt to obtain before the

Appeal Tribunal a review of the employment tribunal's findings of fact. The employer applied for costs and the EAT held that had the appellant pursued the appeal without the support of an outside body and without legal advice, her conduct would have been adjudged to be unreasonable. As, however, she had been supported by the EOC in bringing the appeal, her conduct could not be so characterised. The EAT expressed regret that it had no power to award costs against the EOC. (Note that a similar case might be decided differently under the amended EAT Rules, since the EAT now has the power to award costs where an appeal is 'misconceived' – see 'Grounds for making costs orders against a party in the EAT – misconceived proceedings' above.)

Failing to realise that an appeal is hopeless may lead to a costs order if the EAT **20.205** feels that the unsuccessful party should have taken legal advice. This is most likely when the appellant is the employer. Two examples:

- **Redland Roof Tiles Ltd v Eveleigh** 1979 IRLR 11, EAT: the EAT found that had the company taken counsel's opinion before launching the appeal, it would have been advised that the appeal would be a non-starter because no point of law could be raised that would have the remotest chance of success. The employer's conduct in bringing the appeal was unreasonable and the appeal was dismissed with costs

- **Highland Meats Ltd v Corbett** EAT 730/87: the employer – without taking legal advice – mistakenly pursued what the EAT considered to be a quite untenable point to an appeal. The EAT noted that the employer was a substantial company which could reasonably have been expected to take legal advice and awarded £100 costs against that company for unreasonable conduct of the appeal.

Litigants in person. The fact that the appellant is a litigant in person may be a **20.206** relevant factor in the exercise of its discretion by the EAT whether to award costs. In Rogers v Dorothy Barley School EAT 0013/12 the Appeal Tribunal had 'no doubt' that it had jurisdiction to make an order for costs against R, a litigant in person, on the basis that his appeal was misconceived. The employment tribunal had correctly rejected his breach of contract claim on the basis that, as R was still employed by the school, it had no jurisdiction to hear it. However, in the circumstances of the case, the EAT concluded that it would not be right to order R to pay costs. The respondent school had known for many months that R was acting in person and was simply not grasping the jurisdictional question that his appeal raised, yet it had not warned him that if he proceeded, an application for costs would be made.

Surviving the initial sift. The EAT's practice of listing all appeals for a **20.207** preliminary hearing was abandoned in 2002. The Registrar now carries out an initial sift of all notices of appeal and, where it appears to the Registrar or a judge from the papers that the stated grounds of appeal do not give the EAT jurisdiction, the appeal will not be registered (see Chapter 17, 'Processing an appeal', under 'The sift', for details). Nevertheless, one possible result of the sifting process is that a preliminary hearing will take place to determine whether the grounds in the notice of appeal raise a point of law that gives the appeal a reasonable prospect of success at a full hearing.

It seems that costs may be awarded when a case is dismissed at a preliminary hearing on the ground that the appeal does not disclose any arguable point of law. In Ravelin v Bournemouth Borough Council EAT 284/86 Mr Justice Popplewell said that 'the preliminary hearing is part of the appeal procedure and if, at the end of a preliminary hearing, a claimant has not disclosed a reasonably arguable point of law, this Tribunal has no jurisdiction to entertain it and, in those circumstances, Rule [34] seems to us to apply absolutely'. In practice, however, the fact that an appeal is dismissed at a preliminary stage does not, without more, tend to result in an order for costs. It should also be borne in mind that it is not necessary for the respondent to an appeal to appear at the preliminary hearing, so the costs should not have substantially accumulated at this early stage of an appeal.

20.208 The fact that an appeal has been allowed to proceed to a full hearing either at the initial sifting stage or after a preliminary hearing is not necessarily a safeguard against costs being awarded if the case is ultimately held to lack merit. In Iron and Steel Trades Confederation v ASW Ltd (in liquidation) 2004 IRLR 926, EAT, the EAT did not believe that there ought to be a practice that, where a case has gone through the sift, or indeed a preliminary hearing, costs would only be awarded in exceptional circumstances, or in circumstances in which the EAT has been misled. Any such practice, the EAT felt, might be an 'impermissible trammel' of its power under rule 34 to award costs. Nevertheless, it went on to say that the fact that a case has been sifted to a full hearing, or progressed past a preliminary hearing, will be taken into account when considering whether the appeal was brought unreasonably and whether costs should be awarded.

A similar approach was taken by the EAT in JO Sims Ltd v McKee EAT 0518/05. In that case, the claimant brought an unfair dismissal claim against his employer which was out of time. In defending the claim, the employer argued that the proceedings were misconceived and threatened to make an application for costs. The employment tribunal, however, took the view that it had not been reasonably practicable for the claim to be brought within the three-month period and allowed the employee's claim to proceed. The employer appealed to the EAT. Having considered the evidence, it held that the tribunal's conclusion was unimpeachable and dismissed the appeal. It went on to award costs against the employer on the basis that the appeal was misconceived within the meaning of rule 34A. In reaching that decision, the EAT emphasised that

1126

the fact that the appeal had been allowed to proceed following the preliminary hearing was not a talisman against a costs order ultimately being made.

Ability to pay. Unlike the Tribunal Rules 2013, the EAT Rules do not expressly **20.209** state that, in deciding whether or not to make a costs order, the EAT may have regard to the paying party's ability to pay, although rule 34B does state that this may be taken into account when considering the *amount* of a costs order (see 'Deciding how much to award in the EAT' below). Nevertheless, the fact that this is not expressly stated does not mean that the EAT cannot take this factor into account when deciding whether or not to make an order, although examples of this are rare. Ability to pay, in the context of whether or not to make an order under the Tribunal Rules 2013, is considered further under 'Assessing amount: general considerations – ability to pay' above.

Methods of assessing costs in the EAT **20.210**
Rule 34B of the EAT Rules states that the amount of a costs order can be determined in the following ways:

- the EAT may specify a sum to be paid – rule 34B(1)(a)

- the parties may agree on a sum to be paid and the costs order will be for that agreed sum – rule 34B(1)b), or

- the EAT may order the sum payable to be determined by way of detailed assessment in the High Court in accordance with the Civil Procedure Rules 1998 (or, in Scotland, the EAT may direct the sum to be taxed by the Auditor of the Court of Session) – rule 34B(1)(c).

These are similar to the methods of assessing costs orders against parties in the employment tribunal, i.e. unassessed costs, agreed costs and detailed assessment of costs – see 'Methods of assessment and applicable statutory limits' above. There are, however, some differences, which we discuss below. Note also that additional rules relating to the assessment of costs apply where the EAT makes an order in favour of a litigant in person. This point is discussed under 'Costs orders in favour of litigants in person' below.

'Unassessed costs'. Similar to costs in the employment tribunal, the term **20.211** 'unassessed costs' is commonly used to refer to general costs that are awarded by the EAT without the need for the precise amount to be determined separately in the High Court by way of 'detailed assessment' (or, in Scotland, to be taxed in the Court of Session). There is an important distinction, however: unlike unassessed costs in employment tribunals (which are capped at £20,000 – see 'Methods of assessment and applicable statutory limits – "Unassessed costs" (capped at £20,000)' above), there is no limit on the amount of unassessed costs that the EAT can order.

1127

20.212 **Agreed costs.** Rule 34B(1)(b) of the EAT Rules deals with agreed costs in the EAT and provides that if the parties agree the amount of costs to be paid, the order will be in that amount. Note that, unlike agreed costs in employment tribunals, the order *must* be for the amount agreed. As noted under 'Methods of assessment and applicable statutory limits – agreed costs' above, rule 78(1)(a) of the Tribunal Rules 2013 provides that the costs order *may* reflect the amount agreed, suggesting that employment tribunals now have a discretion as to whether or not it will do so.

20.213 **Ordering detailed assessment.** Rule 34B(1)(c) of the EAT Rules provides that the Appeal Tribunal may order the sum payable to be determined by way of detailed assessment in the High Court in accordance with the Civil Procedure Rules 1998 (or, in Scotland, the EAT may direct the sum to be taxed by the Auditor of the Court of Session). Unlike costs in the employment tribunals, the detailed assessment/taxation *must* be carried out in the High Court/Sheriff Court. As noted under 'Methods of assessment and applicable statutory limits – detailed assessment of costs' above, judges in employment tribunals may, in contrast, now carry out the detailed assessment/taxation themselves.

Rule 34B(3) provides that the costs of an 'assisted person' in England and Wales *must* be determined by detailed assessment in accordance with the CPR. The phrase 'assisted person' is not defined by the EAT Rules. Nevertheless, it seems clear that it bears the same definition as set out in the Civil Legal Aid (General) Regulations 1989 SI 1989/339 – i.e. a person in respect of whom a 'legal aid certificate' has been issued, certifying eligibility for legal aid assistance. Note that the scope for providing such assistance for the purposes of pursuing or defending employment tribunal proceedings has been drastically narrowed since April 2013 as a result of the reform of legal aid introduced by the Legal Aid, Sentencing and Punishment of Offenders Act 2012. Part 1 of Schedule 1 to the Act sets out the types of claim for which 'civil legal services' (legal aid) is still available, the most important for employment law purposes being claims for contravention of the Equality Act 2010 (or a previous discrimination enactment) – para 43. Few of the other claims listed have any relevance to employment law. Part 3 of Schedule 1 then goes on to state that the services described in Part 1 do not include advocacy except as provided for in Part 3. There is an exception in Part 3 for advocacy in the EAT, but only in relation to discrimination claims. Therefore the scope of rule 34B(3) is, in essence, restricted to discrimination appeals.

20.214 Rule 34B does not appear to require the detailed assessment of an assisted person's costs to be referred to the High Court. Therefore it seems that this can be carried out by the EAT itself, although it must do so in accordance with the CPR. The procedure to be followed when carrying out a detailed assessment in England or Wales is set out in Part 47 CPR. The CPR's general rules about costs, which are contained in Part 44, are relevant for the determination of the amount to be awarded under the detailed assessment. Note that Rule 34B only applies to assessing the costs of assisted persons in England and Wales. There is no equivalent provision that the costs of persons receiving legal assistance in Scotland must be taxed according to the rules applicable in the Sheriff Court.

Deciding how much to award in the EAT
20.215

When deciding how much to award by way of costs under rule 34B(1)(a) of the EAT Rules (or what proportion of costs should be subjected to a detailed assessment under rule 34B(1)(c)), the EAT will look at the costs claimed by the receiving party with a view to ascertaining whether they are reasonable. It may also have regard to the paying party's ability to pay. Note that the EAT Rules contain additional provisions regarding the assessment of costs orders in favour of litigants in person. These are discussed under 'Costs orders in favour of litigants in person' below.

Are the costs claimed reasonable? In Vernon v Loks Plasma Services Ltd EAT   20.216
0018/05 the EAT held that the total costs of £4,380.50 claimed by the employer in respect of solicitors' fees were not reasonable and accordingly revised the schedule of solicitors' costs to £2,797. In that case there was found to be no explanation as to why five individuals were needed to work on the case, and the EAT therefore considered that it was impossible not to conclude that there had been an element of overlap between what they were doing, which the paying party could not reasonably be expected to pay for.

Ability to pay. As with costs in employment tribunals, when considering the   20.217
amount of a costs order, the EAT *may* have regard to the paying party's ability to pay – rule 34B(2) EAT Rules. So the EAT may wish to consider specific evidence of an individual's means where it is satisfied that some form of costs order should be made. This happened in Ahmed v Kentucky Fried Chicken (GB) Ltd EAT 197/93, where the Appeal Tribunal ruled that its order for costs could not be enforced until the employer applied to have it enforced – at which time it would hear evidence regarding the appellant's means and ability to pay. Ability to pay – in the context of assessing the amount of an employment tribunal order – is considered in detail under 'Assessing amount: general considerations – ability to pay' above.

Costs orders in favour of litigants in person
20.218

The EAT Rules (as amended in 2004) contain additional provisions regarding the assessment of costs orders in favour of litigants in person.

Definition of 'litigant in person'. Rule 34D(7) defines 'litigant in person'   20.219
as including:

- a company or corporation which is acting without a legal representative

1129

- a barrister, solicitor, solicitor's employee or other authorised litigator who is acting for him or herself (or, in Scotland, an advocate or solicitor who is acting for him or herself).

This definition of 'litigant in person' would appear to cover a company represented by an in-house lawyer or an individual represented by a non-legal representative, such as a family member or friend.

20.220 **Limits on what a litigant in person can claim.** Rule 34D(2) provides that costs awarded in favour of litigants in person must not exceed – except in the case of disbursement – two thirds of the amount that would have been allowed if the litigant in person had been legally represented.

20.221 **Costs recoverable by a litigant in person.** Subject to the 'two thirds' restriction set out in rule 34D(2), the particular costs recoverable are stipulated in rule 34D(3) to be as follows:

- costs for the same categories of work and disbursements that would have been allowed if the relevant party had been represented by a legal representative

- payments reasonably made for legal services relating to the conduct of the proceedings

- costs of obtaining expert assistance in assessing the costs claim, and

- other expenses incurred by the party in relation to the proceedings.

Rule 34D(6) provides that a litigant in person who is allowed costs for attending a hearing to conduct his or her case will not be entitled to a witness allowance in respect of the same attendance.

20.222 **Can the litigant in person prove financial loss?** Under rule 34D(4) of the EAT Rules, the amount that a litigant in person will be allowed in respect of any item of work differs according to whether or not he or she can prove financial loss. If such loss can be proved, the amount will be that which he or she can prove was lost for the time reasonably spent doing the work. A party unable to prove financial loss will be entitled to be recompensed for the time the tribunal considers was reasonably spent on doing the work at a flat rate of £35 an hour (with effect from 6 April 2014). This rate is increased by £1 on 6 April every year – rule 34D(5).

20.223 **Procedural requirements for costs orders in the EAT**
The procedural requirements relating to costs orders are set out in rule 34 of the EAT Rules and para 22 of the EAT Practice Direction.

20.224 **Application for costs.** An application for costs must be made either during or at the end of a relevant hearing, or in writing to the Registrar within 14 days of the seal date on which the order of the EAT disposing of proceedings is sent to the parties – para 22.4 EAT Practice Direction.

The party seeking the order must state the legal ground on which the application is based and the facts on which it is based and, by a schedule or otherwise, show how the costs have been incurred. If the party against whom the order is sought wishes the EAT to have regard to means and/or an alleged inability to pay, a witness statement giving particulars and exhibiting any documents must be served on the other party and presented to the EAT – para 22.3 EAT Practice Direction.

Notice to the paying party. Under rule 34(5) of the EAT Rules, no costs order **20.225** shall be made unless the Registrar has sent notice to the paying party giving him or her the opportunity to give reasons why the order should not be made. Such notice is not required, however, where the party in question has had the opportunity to give such reasons to the EAT orally.

Hearing the parties. The question of whether the parties should have an oral **20.226** hearing of costs applications was considered by the EAT in McDonald v London Borough of Ealing EAT 406/99. In that case the Appeal Tribunal accepted that Article 6 of the European Convention on Human Rights (the right to a fair trial), which is annexed to the Human Rights Act 1998, may mean that in future it should convene an oral hearing on the issue of costs. However, it went on to state that there were powerful arguments against such a conclusion, particularly where the claimant does not expressly ask for an oral hearing.

Note that the Practice Direction 2013, which was introduced well after the Human Rights Act 1998 came into effect, states that a costs application 'may be resolved by the EAT on the papers, provided that the opportunity has been given for representations in writing by all relevant parties, or the EAT may refer the matter for an oral hearing, and may assess the costs either on the papers or at an oral hearing, or refer the matter for detailed assessment' – para 22.4 EAT Practice Direction.

Written reasons for costs order. Where a costs order is made, reasons for it **20.227** must be given in writing if such a request is made within 21 days of the date of the costs order – rule 34(6) EAT Rules. Para 22.6 of the EAT Practice Direction adds that where the EAT decides on the papers (rather than at a hearing) to order costs, it shall provide written reasons to the parties in any event.

'Wasted costs' orders against representatives   **20.228**

The EAT has the power to make a wasted costs order against a party's representative under rule 34C of the EAT Rules. For all practical purposes, this rule is very similar to rule 80 of the Tribunal Rules 2013, discussed under 'What orders can employment tribunal make? – order against representative to pay "wasted costs"' above. As with a wasted costs order in the employment tribunal, the EAT may disallow, or order the representative of a party to meet, the whole or part of any wasted costs of any party – rule 34C(2).

'Wasted costs' are defined by rule 34C(3) as any costs incurred by a party:

- as a result of any improper, unreasonable or negligent act or omission on the part of any representative, or

- which, in the light of any act or omission occurring after they were incurred, the EAT considers it unreasonable to expect that party to pay.

20.229 A 'representative' is defined in rule 34C(4) as a party's legal or other representative or any employee of such representative. Rule 34C(4) used to provide that 'representative' does not include a representative who is not acting in pursuit of profit. However, these words were repealed by the Employment Appeal Tribunal (Amendment) Rules 2013 SI 2013/1693.

An application for wasted costs *must* be made in writing, setting out the nature of the case upon which it is based and the best particulars of the costs sought to be recovered – para 22.5 EAT Practice Direction. This application must be lodged with the EAT and served upon the party against whom an order is being sought. Unusually, there is no stated time limit for making a wasted costs application in either the EAT Rules or the Practice Direction. It is likely, however, that the EAT will only consider applications made within a reasonable time.

20.230 Rule 34C(5) states that before a wasted costs order is made, the representative in question must be given reasonable opportunity to make oral or written representations as to why an order should not be made. This rule goes on to provide that the EAT may have regard to the representative's ability to pay when considering whether to make a wasted costs order or how much that order should be.

The Registrar must inform the client of the representative in question of any proceedings under rule 34(C) or of any order made under this rule against that party's representative – rule 34(C)(7). Finally, having made a wasted costs order, the EAT must, by virtue of rule 34C(8), provide written reasons for doing so where the representative against whom the order has been made requests such reasons within 21 days of the date of the order.

20.231 **Guidance from the civil courts.** As with wasted costs orders in employment tribunals, the authorities applicable to wasted costs in the civil law generally are equally applicable in the EAT. The two leading authorities analysing the scope of such orders and the circumstances in which they can be made are Ridehalgh v Horsefield 1994 3 All ER 848, CA, and Medcalf v Mardell and ors 2002 3 All ER 721, HL. These are fully discussed under 'What orders can employment tribunal make? – order against representative to pay "wasted costs"'; 'Grounds for making orders against representatives', and 'Procedural requirements – orders against representatives (wasted costs)' above.

Costs beyond the EAT

20.232

If a case progresses beyond the EAT, costs will be dealt with under the Civil Procedure Rules 1998 SI 1998/3132 (CPR), and this will generally mean that the successful party will recover costs. However, the Court of Appeal may be willing to grant 'costs protection' to a party when a case is being appealed from the EAT. This is discussed under 'Costs protection' below.

An anomaly arises when the EAT refers a case to the European Court of Justice (ECJ). In such cases, the hearing before the ECJ is treated, for costs purposes, as part of the hearing before the national court that referred the matter. If the Court of Appeal refers the case, for instance, then costs will be dealt with under the CPR, and this will generally mean that the successful party will recover costs. If, however, it is the EAT that refers the matter to the ECJ, then costs can only be awarded in the limited circumstances allowed under the EAT Rules. This matter is further discussed under 'References to the ECJ' below.

Costs protection

20.233

If a case progresses beyond the EAT, then costs will be dealt with under the CPR, and this will generally mean that the unsuccessful party will have to pay the other side's costs. However, when a case is being appealed from the EAT the Court of Appeal may be willing to grant 'costs protection' to a party under rule 52.9A CPR. This rule, which came into force on 1 April 2013, provides that 'in any proceedings in which costs recovery is normally limited or excluded at first instance, an appeal court may make an order that the recoverable costs of an appeal will be limited to the extent which the court specifies'.

Rule 52.9A was introduced to address the 'mischief' that had emerged in cases such as Eweida v British Airways plc 2009 EWCA Civ 1025, CA, where the claimant, who was appealing from the EAT to the Court of Appeal, applied for costs protection on the basis that she was moving from a 'no costs' jurisdiction to a 'costs shifting' jurisdiction. The Court dismissed the application on the ground that it did not have the power to make a protective costs order. In Manchester College v Hazel and anor 2013 IRLR 563, CA (discussed further below), Lord Justice Jackson observed that, while that was the correct decision on the law as it then stood, it was unsatisfactory for a number of reasons. In particular, individuals of modest means who litigate in a 'no costs' jurisdiction are often without legal representation and it is usually unjust to subject such litigants to the risk of costs when they proceed to a higher level – especially where a claimant wins in the employment tribunal and is then 'dragged unwillingly' into an appeal. It might also be unjust to impose a costs risk on a litigant who loses at first instance but has proper grounds for bringing an appeal, as in Eweida.

1133

20.234 With the coming into force of rule 52.9A CPR, the injustice highlighted by Jackson LJ has been mitigated, but it is still not the case that the Court of Appeal will automatically award costs protection in employment cases. In exercising its discretion under rule 52.9A, the Court is likely to take into account factors similar to those taken into account in Manchester College v Hazel (above), a case in which the Court of Appeal did grant costs protection to the claimants. The application for costs protection in that case preceded the coming into force of rule 52.9A and therefore the Court of Appeal applied the general powers contained in rule 52.9 permitting an appeal court to impose conditions upon which an appeal may be brought where there is a 'compelling reason' for doing so. Nevertheless, the Court of Appeal's judgment provides a useful indication as to how the new provision will operate.

The facts of the Hazel case were as follows. CH and NH were employed by A4E Ltd to teach prison inmates taking adult education courses. Their employment was transferred to the College via the Transfer of Undertakings (Protection of Employment) Regulations 2006 SI 2006/246 (TUPE). When the College moved them onto new, less favourable contracts, they successfully claimed automatic unfair dismissal under Reg 7(1) TUPE. The College unsuccessfully appealed to the EAT and it was granted permission to appeal further by the Court of Appeal. Upon learning that, under rule 52.10 CPR, they could be liable to pay costs if unsuccessful in the Court of Appeal, the claimants applied to the Court for a costs protection order preventing the College from applying for its appeal costs if it were to win. The claimants also undertook that, if they were successful in the Court of Appeal, they would not apply for their costs against the College. Lord Justice Elias granted the order. Unhappy with this decision, the College applied to the Court of Appeal to reconsider the order and have it set aside.

20.235 Lord Justice Jackson, who sat alone in the Court of Appeal, noted that rule 52.9(1)(c) CPR allows the appeal court to impose conditions upon which an appeal may be brought, but only if there is a 'compelling reason for doing so' – rule 52.9(2). Jackson LJ noted a number of points supporting such a reason in the instant case. First, the claimants' claim had been vindicated at two tribunal hearings and might prevail in the Court of Appeal. He also accepted that the claimants would not pursue their claim any further unless they were protected against the risk of costs. Furthermore, it was not reasonable to expect the claimants to incur the risk of costs up to £20,000. Given the general approach taken by the Court of Appeal in relation to costs orders, Jackson LJ did not think that the claimants could count upon a 'merciful approach' being adopted should the College win its appeal and, if they were ordered to pay costs, this would be a 'disaster' for the claimants, bearing in mind that they were earning 'normal salaries'. For the College, in contrast, the cost of a few sets of employment tribunal proceedings was a foreseeable cost of restructuring.

Since the claimants had undertaken not to apply for their costs if successful, Elias LJ's order achieved a 'level playing field'.

Finally, Jackson LJ considered that it would in any event serve no useful purpose to set aside Elias LJ's order because the claimants would be able to make a fresh application under new rule 52.9A – which, as noted above, specifically deals with costs protection orders – once it came into force in two weeks' time. In his view, such an application was bound to succeed. In his Lordship's view, the present appeal was a 'classic case' in which it would be appropriate to make an order under rule 52.9A. Jackson LJ accordingly refused the College's application to have Elias LJ's order set aside, emphasising that he was not relying upon any one of the above factors in isolation, but that, cumulatively, he was quite satisfied that they constituted a 'compelling reason' under rule 52.9(2).

20.236 Although Jackson LJ granted costs protection in this case, he did go on to make the point that it is not always desirable to suspend the 'costs shifting' rule when a case comes up from a 'no costs' jurisdiction. For example, in a case involving issues of principle or practice on which substantial sums turn, there may be no compelling reason to disapply the normal 'costs shifting' rules where one party is a well-resourced employer and the other is an employee or a group of employees backed, say, by their trade union.

Another case in which costs protection was granted by the Court of Appeal (again under rule 52.9A CPR) is UNISON v Kelly 2012 IRLR 951, CA. As in Manchester College v Hazel (above), rule 52.9A (the new costs protection rule) was not yet in force when the Court heard the appellant union's application. Nevertheless, it also provides a useful indication of factors that will be taken into account under rule 52.9A. Four UNISON members had brought a successful claim against the union under provisions in the Trade Union and Labour Relations (Consolidation) Act 1992 prohibiting 'unjustifiable discipline' of union members. The Court of Appeal subsequently granted UNISON permission to appeal, but acceded to the members' application to attach the condition that UNISON would not seek to recover any of its costs against them in the event that it won the appeal. Since rule 52.9A was not yet in force, the Court dealt with the application under rule 52.9(1)(c) and (2), which, as noted above, allow an appeal court to impose conditions upon which an appeal may be brought where there is a 'compelling reason' for doing so.

20.237 In deciding to exercise its discretion to permit the appeal to proceed on condition that the union members were protected from costs, the Court took into account the fact that the appeal raised an issue of wider public interest – namely, the compatibility of the 'unjustifiable discipline' provision in the 1992 Act with a union's right to administer its own affairs under Article 11 of the European Convention on Human Rights – and that it was necessary to hear both sides of the argument. It was also relevant that denial of the grant of costs protection would mean that the union members would not run the risk of appearing before the Court on the appeal. In return for cost protection, they were prepared to give an undertaking that they would not seek costs from UNISON if successful, given that they were represented by counsel acting pro bono. And the Court also took into account that the appeal was from a cost-free jurisdiction, at least in the typical case. In its view, Parliament recognised the importance of enabling employees and other workers to pursue their claims (in the employment tribunal and the EAT) without risking heavy cost burdens if a reasonably pursued claim failed. That public policy objective could be undermined if the union members, who had already succeeded twice below, were liable for costs before the Court of Appeal. Furthermore, it was a relevant factor that the members were simply defending the litigation; the case was not analogous to one in which a party was seeking protection from costs in order to advance a claim.

20.238 References to the ECJ

So far as matters of employment law are concerned, a reference can be made to the European Court of Justice (ECJ) by an employment tribunal, the EAT, the Court of Appeal and the Supreme Court. When such a reference is made, the hearing before the ECJ is treated, for costs purposes, as part of the hearing before the national court (or tribunal) that referred the matter. In Burton v British Railways Board 1983 ICR 544 (Note), ECJ, Mr Justice Browne-Wilkinson (as he then was) highlighted the possible anomaly that arises when the EAT (as opposed to a higher court) refers a case to the ECJ. In that situation costs can only be awarded in the limited circumstances allowed under the EAT Rules. Conversely, if the Court of Appeal refers a case, then costs will be dealt with under the CPR, in which case the successful party will, more often than not, recover the costs incurred as a result of the reference made.

Browne-Wilkinson J observed that costs incurred at the ECJ are very much larger than costs at the EAT and it may be unfair that merely because a reference is being made by the EAT, as opposed to the Court of Appeal, the successful party would be unable to recover the costs of that reference (except to the limited extent allowed by the EAT Rules). In Browne-Wilkinson J's view, it seemed unfortunate that if the circumstances before the EAT suggested a reference to be desirable, the case had to be 'forced up' to the Court of Appeal before any court could have effective jurisdiction in respect of the costs that would be incurred as a result. Browne-Wilkinson J went so far as to suggest that the EAT Rules might be modified to rectify this anomalous position.

20.239

There is, however, no sign of such an amendment being made. In the interim, Browne-Wilkinson J suggested that the EAT should consider making any reference to the ECJ conditional upon the parties' coming to an agreement as to how the question of costs should be dealt with. Whether it is right to require an undertaking as to the costs of a reference would, said Browne-Wilkinson J, depend on the circumstances of each particular case. He observed that if no such agreement can be reached and the case is decided by the EAT without a reference to Europe, there would have to be an appeal to the Court of Appeal, which would then refer the matter to Europe (if it agreed that this was a desirable course of action). When the matter came back to the Court of Appeal, costs would then follow the event in the ordinary way. However, the exact basis for requiring the parties to make such an undertaking before a reference is made by the EAT is unclear. There is nothing to the point in the EAT Rules themselves, unless one relies, somewhat tenuously, upon the overriding objective set out in rule 2A to ensure that the parties are on an equal footing and to ensure that a case is dealt with expeditiously and fairly.

21 Enforcement of tribunal awards

Overview
Obtaining information from debtors
Taking control of goods
Third party debt orders
Statutory demands
Enforcement of Acas-conciliated settlements

Most employers who are found liable to pay compensation or costs by an **21.1** employment tribunal pay the awarded sum without undue delay. Unfortunately, that is not invariably the case and sometimes it will be necessary for an employee to take further steps to make the employer pay up. The position may be reversed in cases where a tribunal has awarded costs against the employee.

Employment tribunals are not themselves responsible for the enforcement of their own awards. Once a tribunal has reached a decision on compensation, an employee who wishes to force a reluctant employer to pay the amount due must do so via the civil courts. This chapter aims to give an overview of the procedures that must be gone through in seeking to enforce a tribunal's award of compensation. It gives a brief outline of the main methods of enforcement available in respect of awards made by county courts and deals in some detail with the methods of enforcement most appropriate to orders for compensation made by employment tribunals. The standard forms and leaflets referred to in this chapter are available from HM Courts and Tribunals Service (hmctsformfinder.justice.gov.uk).

The key provision governing the legal framework for enforcement of **21.2** employment tribunal awards is S.15(1) of the Employment Tribunals Act 1996 (ETA) (as amended with effect from 6 April 2014 by the Tribunals, Courts and Enforcement Act 2007). S.15(1) provides: 'Any sum payable in pursuance of a decision of an employment tribunal in England and Wales which has been registered [on the Register of judgments] shall be recoverable under S.85 of the County Courts Act 1984 or otherwise as if it were payable under an order of the county court.' This means that it is to the county court enforcement procedures that claimants must look to enforce payments of compensation awarded by a tribunal if the respondent fails to pay up voluntarily.

---**1139**

With regard to the position in Scotland, S.15(2) of the 1996 Act goes on to provide: 'Any order for the payment of any sum made by an employment tribunal in Scotland (or any copy of such an order certified by the Secretary of the Tribunals) may be enforced as if it were an extract registered decree arbitral bearing a warrant for execution issued by the sheriff court of any sheriffdom in Scotland.' The very different language of S.15(2) compared with S.15(1) reflects the fact that the procedures for enforcement in Scotland are quite distinct from those in England and Wales. Scottish enforcement procedures are not dealt with in this Handbook.

21.3 Overview

The rules governing enforcement in the civil courts have undergone a number of changes over the years. In 1999 the rules relating to civil procedure were completely overhauled in view of recommendations made by Lord Woolf in his Report, 'Access to Justice' (July 1996). These were codified as the Civil Procedure Rules 1998 SI 1998/3132 (CPR) and came into force on 26 April 1999. Although, at that time, the existing provisions for enforcement of court orders were left untouched, some important changes were eventually brought into effect by the Civil Procedure (Amendment No.4) Rules 2001 SI 2001/2792, which came into force on 25 March 2002. The primary effect of these was to introduce a modified regime for enforcement by inserting new Parts 70–73 into the CPR. Part 70 contains the general rules dealing with enforcement and Parts 71–73 provide for specific enforcement procedures governing, respectively, orders to obtain information from debtors (formerly known as oral examinations); third party debt orders (known as garnishee orders under earlier rules); and charging orders, stop orders and stop notices.

There is also a procedure for the seizure and sale of goods by bailiffs (formerly known as execution against goods) – this is one of the more common methods of enforcing unpaid tribunal awards. Until recently, this procedure was initiated by applying for a warrant of execution in the county court (Order 26 of the County Court Rules, set out in Schedule 2 to the CPR) or a writ of fieri facias ('fi fa') in the High Court (Orders 46 and 47 of the Rules of the Supreme Court, set out in Schedule 1 to the CPR). As of 6 April 2014, it was replaced by a new procedure, 'taking control of goods', set out in Schedule 12 to the Tribunals, Courts and Enforcement Act 2007 (TCEA). For further details, see 'Taking control of goods' below. As a result of these changes, the Civil Procedure (Amendment) Rules 2014 SI 2014/407 inserted into the CPR a new Part 83, 'Writs and warrants – general provisions', and Part 84, 'Enforcement by taking control of goods' (with effect from 6 April 2014).

21.4 Prior to April 2009, a claimant had to register an employment tribunal's award of compensation or order for payment in the county court before applying to use one of the court's enforcement mechanisms. The county court would then issue an order requiring the employer to pay by a specified date, and the claimant was entitled to commence one of the prescribed methods of enforcement only if the employer failed to comply. S.15(1) ETA was amended with effect from 1 April 2009 by the TCEA so that unpaid employment tribunal awards no longer need to be registered before enforcement action can be initiated. Instead, they can be enforced through the civil courts as soon as the time limit for payment has passed. In this regard, it should be noted that a sum ordered to be paid by a tribunal is normally due within 14 days of the date of the judgment or order unless otherwise specified – rule 66 Tribunal Rules 2013 (see Chapter 14, 'Tribunal judgments', under 'Promulgating judgments – when a judgment takes effect'). If the tribunal's award is not honoured within the 14-day period, it becomes enforceable as a debt through one of the six methods described under 'Outline of enforcement methods' below. This is subject, however, to the tribunal's decision being filed with the county court together with certain prescribed information (see 'Filing the decision' below).

The general procedure for enforcing tribunal awards is set out in rule 70.5 CPR, as supplemented by Practice Direction 70, 'Enforcement of judgments and orders'. This procedure is available in respect of the award of *any sum payable in pursuance of a tribunal decision* unless the judgment or order has been set aside (see rule 70.6). The enforcement procedures in the CPR do not apply to awards following Acas arbitration (as distinct from Acas conciliation) – rule 70.5(2)(b) – but they do apply to orders for the payment of costs – rule 70.1(2)(d). Under S.19A of the ETA, sums payable under Acas-conciliated settlements are enforceable in England and Wales as if they were sums payable under a county court order – see 'Enforcement of Acas-conciliated settlements' below.

Filing the decision   21.5

Although it is no longer necessary to obtain an order enabling the employment tribunal's decision to be enforced as if it were a county court judgment, the employee still needs to file a copy of the tribunal's decision (or Acas settlement) at the appropriate county court before pursuing the chosen method of enforcement – rule 70.5(2A)(a) CPR. The claimant must also provide the court with the information required by Practice Direction 70 – rule 70.5(2A)(b). Once the decision has been filed and the relevant information provided, the employee may, for the purpose of enforcement, treat the tribunal's decision as a county court judgment. No fee is payable for filing the decision (except in the case of an Acas conditional settlement, which requires the court's permission to proceed – see 'Enforcement of Acas-conciliated settlements' below). However, the employee will have to pay a fee to start enforcement proceedings.

In most cases, the appropriate form for filing the decision or Acas settlement and providing the required information is N322B (or N322A for Acas conditional settlements) – see para 4.1 Practice Direction 70. Form N322B requires the claimant to certify the amount of the original award, the calculation

1141

of interest thereon, the amount of any sum paid and the balance of the amount owing, together with any costs claimed. It also requires the claimant (or his or her solicitor) to sign a 'Statement of Truth' confirming his or her belief that the facts stated in the application are true. The claimant must attach a copy of the tribunal's decision or Acas settlement to the form, which should then be sent to the appropriate county court office. This is the court for the district in which the debtor (i.e. the employer) resides or carries on business, unless the court orders otherwise – rule 70.5(4)(b) CPR.

21.6 Where the employee wishes to enforce a decision of an employment tribunal or Acas settlement by way of a writ of control in the High Court (previously known as a writ of fieri facias ('fi fa')), the appropriate form is N471 (tribunal decisions) or N471A (Acas settlements) – para 4.1A Practice Direction 70. This form is used to file the award with the county court and, at the same time, request a High Court writ. An employee who wishes to proceed by this route can use the Acas and Employment Tribunal Fast Track, in which case a High Court Enforcement Officer will complete the relevant form on his or her behalf before taking steps to recover the debt – see 'Taking control of goods – Acas and Employment Tribunal Fast Track' below.

Once a copy of the tribunal's decision has been filed with the county court, the employer will, as of 1 April 2009, have its name entered in the Register of Judgments, Orders and Fines – Regs 8(1)(d) and 9A(b) Register of Judgments, Orders and Fines Regulations 2005 SI 2005/3595. The Register is available for inspection by members of the public. It is often consulted by banks, building societies and credit reference agencies in connection with applications for loans, overdrafts or other credit. This may make it more difficult for employers in default to obtain credit, thereby providing an incentive to pay the sum due.

21.7 Outline of enforcement methods

There are basically six ways of enforcing a county court judgment debt:

- *seizure and sale of goods*. This procedure authorises bailiffs or enforcement officers to seize goods belonging to the debtor and sell them in order to raise money to repay the debt. Since April 2010, employees have been able to invoke the Acas and Employment Tribunal Fast Track scheme, whereby a High Court Enforcement Officer is assigned to the case and pursues the unpaid tribunal award on the employee's behalf. With effect from 6 April 2014, the old rules on execution against goods were replaced by a new procedure referred to as 'taking control of goods'

- *an attachment of earnings order*. This is an order to the debtor's employer to make deductions from his or her pay until such time as the debt is paid. Obviously it is only of practical use if the debtor is an employee, rather than a company or an unemployed person

- *a third party debt order.* Such an order is directed not to the debtor but to someone who owes money to the debtor, and is often used to freeze a bank or building society account. It instructs the third party to pay the money he or she owes directly to the creditor

- *a charging order.* This is an order preventing the debtor from selling land, bonds, stocks or shares without settling the debt. The court may also order the debtor to sell land or securities in order to pay off the debt. The procedures involved in obtaining this kind of order are complex and it is strongly advisable to obtain professional legal advice if this method of enforcement is to be used

- *the appointment of a receiver by way of equitable execution.* Under this method of enforcement, the court appoints a receiver to collect monies, such as rent, which are payable to the debtor. The costs involved in appointing a receiver are substantial, and once again the procedures that must be gone through are rather involved

- *the issue of a judgment summons.* In practice this method is only used in enforcing maintenance orders or debts owed to Her Majesty's Revenue and Customs. It allows the court to commit a debtor to prison if the debt is not paid in the manner prescribed by the court.

21.8 A creditor may (unless a statutory provision, rule or Practice Direction stipulates otherwise) use any method of enforcement that is available and use more than one method either at the same time or one after another – rule 70.2 CPR. So far as the enforcement of tribunal awards is concerned, the most appropriate methods of enforcement are likely to be either the seizure and sale of goods or third party debt proceedings. Both of these are dealt with in detail under 'Taking control of goods' and 'Third party debt orders' below.

Enforcing against partnerships and firms

21.9 Special rules governing the enforcement of awards against a partnership or firm are now found in para 6A of Practice Direction 70, 'Enforcement of judgments and orders'. Para 6A.1 provides that a judgment or order against a partnership may be enforced against any property of the partnership within England and Wales. Enforcement action can be directed against any person who is not a limited partner and who:

- acknowledged service of the claim form as a partner

- having been served as a partner with the claim form, failed to acknowledge service of it

- admitted in his or her statement of case that he or she is or was a partner at the material time, or

1143

- was found by the court to have been a partner at the material time – para 6A.2 Practice Direction 70.

21.10 A judgment or order made against a partnership cannot be enforced against a limited partner or a member of the partnership who was ordinarily resident outside the jurisdiction when the claim form was issued *unless* he or she acknowledged service of the claim as a partner, was served within England and Wales with the claim form as a partner, or was served with a claim form outside England and Wales with the permission of the court – para 6A.3.

Where a creditor wishes to enforce a judgment against a partner in any other circumstances, he or she must apply to the court for permission to enforce the judgment or order – para 6A.4.

21.11 Effectiveness of the enforcement regime

Difficulties in enforcing awards of compensation were highlighted by the National Association of Citizens Advice Bureaux (NACAB) as long ago as 2004. In its report, 'Empty Justice' (September 2004), NACAB set out its concerns in relation to the seemingly widespread non-payment of employment tribunal awards and Acas-conciliated settlements by employers, and the legal and financial obstacles to enforcement in the civil courts. This was followed by another NACAB report, 'Hollow Victories' (March 2005), indicating that each year, the CAB service in England and Wales deals with 650–700 cases of non-payment of tribunal awards, amounting to one in 20 of all awards made by the tribunals. Given that only a 'small proportion' of tribunal claims involve a CAB, the charity concluded that the overall rate of non-payment may be considerably higher.

A further report by NACAB, 'Justice Denied' (October 2008), suggested that employers fail to pay up in as many as one in ten cases and set out recommendations for reform of the existing system. NACAB recommended that, where an employer fails to pay a tribunal award within a reasonable period, the state should pay the award to the claimant and then pursue the employer for the relevant sum and the costs of enforcement. While such state-sponsored enforcement could be conducted through the civil courts, in NACAB's view it might be better pursued through more direct action, such as adding the amount of the award (plus enforcement costs) to the employer's owed tax. NACAB considers that the mere existence of a state-led enforcement regime would be capable of discouraging non-payment by 'rogue employers', who might otherwise drag out and obstruct enforcement action, causing many claimants to give up in frustration. To date, however, this suggestion has not been implemented.

21.12 Research conducted on behalf of the Government confirms a pattern of employers defaulting on employment tribunal awards and Acas settlements. In 2009, the Ministry of Justice (MoJ) commissioned its own research into the non-payment of tribunal awards. The study revealed that, while 61 per cent of claimants had received full or part-payment of their tribunal award, only 51 per cent had achieved this without enforcement action – 'Research into enforcement of employment tribunal awards in England and Wales', Research Series 9/09 (May 2009). In April 2010, the then Labour Government introduced the Acas and Employment Tribunal Fast Track scheme, which was intended to simplify and speed up the process of enforcing tribunal awards and Acas settlements through the civil courts. Under this scheme, workers can pay a fee of £60 to have their unpaid award or Acas settlement enforced by a High Court Enforcement Officer. Despite its relatively low cost and apparent simplicity, the Fast Track scheme appears so far to have a low take-up and success rate – see 'Taking control of goods – Acas and Employment Tribunal Fast Track' below.

More recently, Government research has confirmed that claimants continue to fare badly when it comes to enforcing unpaid tribunal awards. The Payment of Tribunal Awards 2013 Study (November 2013), carried out on behalf of the Department for Business, Innovation and Skills (BIS), revealed that, even after enforcement, only 49 per cent of claimants were paid their tribunal award in full. A further 16 per cent were paid in part, meaning that 35 per cent received nothing at all. The most common reason for non-payment was that the employer had become insolvent, but many claimants citing this reason believed that the company they had worked for was now trading again under a different name. Worryingly, the proportion of unpaid claimants who resorted to an enforcement procedure remained at the same level as in 2008, when the 2009 MoJ research was conducted. This suggests that the Fast Track procedure has not led to an overall increase in the number of claimants taking enforcement action. Of those claimants who had pursued enforcement action to recover their award, only around half were successful in receiving all or some of it.

21.13 The Government responded to the study by announcing plans to deal with 'rogue employers' who fail to pay. It stated that it was considering a number of measures, including fixed-penalty notices for late payment, naming and shaming employers, and giving employment judges the power to demand deposits from employers who it is thought might not pay up. The Government was also looking at ways of increasing claimant awareness of enforcement mechanisms. Overall, only 41 per cent of claimants in the 2013 study said that they were aware of the options open to them if their employer did not pay, falling to only 28 per cent of those who had had no recourse to any of the enforcement measures.

The 2013 BIS study acknowledges that the issue of non-payment of tribunal awards is 'perhaps a particular concern' in light of the introduction of fees from 29 July 2013 for bringing claims in the employment tribunal (for further details, see Chapter 19, 'Fees'). In response to the study, NACAB published a further

1145

report, 'The Cost of a Hollow Victory' (November 2013), which points out that, since fees were introduced, 'claimants are effectively being asked to gamble their money on a system with very poor odds, in order to try and obtain their rights', and that claims for lower amounts, such as unpaid wages or notice pay, are often 'simply not viable'. In NACAB's view, 'there can be no justification for [tribunal fees] if ultimately the service charged for does not deliver results'.

21.14 The public services union UNISON recently brought a judicial review action challenging the fees regime for employment tribunal and EAT cases – R (on the application of UNISON) v Lord Chancellor (Equality and Human Rights Commission intervening) 2014 IRLR 266, QBD. UNISON argued that the introduction of fees, viewed in the context of widespread non-payment of tribunal awards, means that many claimants will be deterred from bringing claims because the likely cost of proceedings outweighs the benefits. In particular, evidence of non-payment was cited in support of the argument that the requirement to pay fees breaches the EU principle of effectiveness, whereby domestic procedural rules must not render practically impossible or excessively difficult the exercise of rights conferred by EU law. In February 2014, the Administrative Court rejected UNISON's claim, stating that it was unconvinced at present by the hypothetical evidence regarding the impact of tribunal fees and preferred to adopt a 'wait and see' approach. In the course of his judgment, however, Lord Justice Moses referred to the 2013 BIS study and acknowledged 'the inadequacies of the system for enforcement'.

21.15 Obtaining information from debtors

One thing that all methods of enforcement have in common is that they will be of no use at all if the debtor (i.e. the employer) has no money or assets to meet the debt. Furthermore, the choice of method of enforcement lies with the creditor (i.e. the employee) and not the court. If an employer is insolvent, there are special procedures providing for the recovery of judgment debts. Furthermore, a former employee may be able to recover some of the outstanding sum from the National Insurance Fund.

Part 71 of the CPR (accompanied by Practice Direction 71, 'Orders to obtain information from judgment debtors') provides a useful mechanism whereby the financial means of a debtor can be ascertained. It allows the employee to apply for an order requiring the employer to attend court to provide information for the purpose of enabling the enforcement of a tribunal's judgment or order. The employee may apply for such an order either against an individual or, if the employer is a company or other corporation, against an officer of the company or corporation. Details are set out in leaflet EX324, 'How do I apply for an order? Order to obtain information from a person who owes you money'.

1146

Applying for an order to attend court   21.16

Application is made by completing a standard form N316 (in the case of an individual debtor) or form N316A (in the case of a company). Payment of a fixed fee of (currently) £50 must normally accompany the application, although remission may be available depending on the claimant's financial situation. The claimant has to state the name and address of the debtor, the sum outstanding, any specific questions which are required to be asked of the debtor and any specific documents that the claimant wishes the debtor to be ordered to produce. Where the debtor is a company or corporation, the claimant must also specify the name and position of the officer of the company whom he or she is seeking to have questioned. If the debtor is a limited company – as will be the case in most instances where enforcement of a tribunal award is necessary – then the creditor may apply for the examination of a director, the company secretary or any officer of the company. And if the debtor is a partnership, such as a solicitors' firm, then the application may, in some circumstances, be made against any one of the partners of the firm – see 'Overview – enforcing against partnerships and firms' above.

If the application is granted, the court will issue an order to the named debtor or company official requiring that he or she attend the court at the time and place specified, produce at court the documents in his or her control as specified in the order and answer on oath such questions as the court may require. Ordinarily, the debtor or other person to be questioned will be required to attend the county court for the district in which he or she resides or carries on business, unless a judge decides otherwise – para 2.1 Practice Direction 71. The order must contain a warning to the individual in the following terms: 'If you the within-named [ ] do not comply with this order you may be held to be in contempt of court and imprisoned or fined, or your assets may be seized' – rule 71.2(7) CPR.

Service of court's order   21.17

Prior to the amendments to the CPR, the power to issue a warrant for committal for failing to attend was given to the court only once it had followed up a notice served by post with a further notice served by a bailiff or other court official demanding attendance at a rescheduled hearing. However, in order to streamline the procedure, this two-stage notice provision was abandoned in favour of a single notice that must be served personally on the person required to attend and which warns of the possible draconian consequences of default (see 'Applying for an order to attend court' above).

Unless the court directs otherwise, service of the order has to be effected by serving it personally on the person required to attend not less than 14 days before the scheduled hearing – rule 71.3(1) CPR. The order may be served by a county court bailiff, a High Court Enforcement Officer or the creditor him or herself (or a person acting on his or her behalf). In that case, the creditor must

1147

inform the court not less than seven days before the scheduled hearing if he or she has been unable to serve it – rule 71.3(2). The creditor must also file an affidavit (i.e. a sworn statement) by the person who served the order giving details of how and when the order was served and how much of the debt remains outstanding – rule 71.5(1)(a) and (c). The affidavit must either be filed not less than two days before the hearing or, if the creditor decides to attend in person, produced at the hearing itself – rule 71.5(2).

21.18 The person whose attendance is required may, within seven days of service of the order, ask the creditor to pay a sum reasonably sufficient to cover his or her travelling expenses to and from court – rule 71.4(1) CPR. If so requested, the creditor must pay that sum. He or she must also file an affidavit stating either that no request has been made for travelling expenses or that a request, having been made, has been complied with – rule 71.5(1)(b). Where the creditor him or herself effected service of the court order on the person whose attendance at court is required, then a single affidavit covering both confirmation of service and the issue of travelling expenses will suffice.

21.19 Documentation to be produced by debtor

The order to attend court will inform the person required to attend that he or she must produce certain standard documentation in addition to specific documents that, following the claimant's request, the court has ordered to be disclosed. In the case of an officer of a debtor company, these include bank statements, share certificates, hire purchase and similar agreements, outstanding bills owed to and by the company, two years' accounts, current management accounts and any court orders on which money is still owed. It is important to note that the purpose of these will be to assist in the examination of the means of the debtor company rather than those of the individual officer answering the questions.

21.20 The examination hearing

Unless the court so orders, the questioning at the hearing will be conducted by a court officer – rule 71.6(2) CPR. Compelling reasons have to be shown by the applicant if he or she wishes the questioning to be conducted by a judge. If such reasons exist, they must be asserted on the application form. In terms of the questions that will be asked, forms EX140 and EX141 are used by the court to record answers given in a standard questioning procedure by, respectively, an individual debtor or an officer of a company or corporation.

In respect of an individual debtor, he or she will be required to provide personal information (including details of any dependants, employment status, earnings from employment or, if self-employed, annual turnover and amount drawn from the business). Form EX140 also enquires into any property owned by the debtor, the amount of Council Tax paid, any income derived from lettings or rentals, savings, investments and assets and details of other debts or court orders.

In respect of a company officer, he or she will be asked to provide general **21.21** information about the company or corporation, its current operational and financial status, its assets and property, any liabilities it has and other information such as its place of business, other trading addresses and whether any of the company's assets have been transferred to the officer being questioned or to any other director or person associated with the company.

In either case, the debtor or, as the case may be, company officer will be asked whether the debtor or company is prepared to make an offer of payment, and, if so, how much, or if not, why not. A list of the documents produced by the debtor or company officer has also to be supplied. And finally, the debtor or officer will be asked to certify that the record of the answers he or she has given to the questions is correct. If the person in question refuses to sign, that fact will be recorded by the court official.

Sanctions for default by debtor
21.22

If a person against whom an order is made fails to attend court, or refuses at the hearing to take the oath or to answer any question, or otherwise fails to comply with any requirement specified in the order, then the court will refer the matter to a circuit judge or High Court judge. So long as the judge is satisfied that the creditor has complied with the rules relating to payment of travelling expenses and filing of affidavits (see 'Service of the court's order' above), he or she may make a committal order against the person for contempt of court – rules 71.8(2) and (3) CPR. If such an order is made, the judge will direct that it will be suspended provided that the person attends court at a rescheduled hearing and complies with all the terms not only of the original order but of the committal order – rule 71.8(4)(a). If the person fails to attend court for a second time, he or she may be arrested and brought before a judge to consider whether committal for contempt should take place – rule 71.8(4)(b).

Tribunals, Courts and Enforcement Act 2007
21.23

Part 4 of the Tribunals, Courts and Enforcement Act 2007 (TCEA) contains new court-based measures designed to help creditors gain access to information about the debtor. These provisions have not yet been brought into force. In a written ministerial statement issued on 17 March 2009, the then Labour Government stated that, following a comprehensive review of the enforcement provisions, it had decided not to implement Part 4 of the 2007 Act. (Nevertheless, it subsequently implemented Ss.93 and 94, which appear in Part 4 and which made changes to the charging orders regime.) However, in March 2011 the Ministry of Justice published a consultation paper on reforming civil justice in England and Wales, 'Solving disputes in the county courts: creating a simpler, quicker and more proportionate system' (CP6/2011). On 9 February 2012, the Coalition Government published its response to that consultation (Cm 8274), indicating (among other things) that the new measures concerning access to

1149

information would be 'an important progressive step towards improving the effectiveness of enforcement options' and would be implemented when resources were available.

The unimplemented measures concerning information requests and orders in Part 4 of the TCEA (Ss.95–105) include a power for both the High Court and county courts, on application by a creditor, to make a 'departmental information request' seeking information from government departments such as the Department for Work and Pensions or HM Revenue and Customs in relation to a debtor who has failed to respond to the judgment or comply with court-based methods of enforcement – Ss.96(2)(a) and 97. The kind of information contemplated by these provisions includes the debtor's name, address, date of birth, national insurance number, whether he or she is employed and, if so, the name and address of his or her employer. In addition, the new measures would give the relevant court the power to make an 'information order' against a prescribed person (including a bank or credit reference agency) requiring that person to disclose the information about the debtor requested by the court – Ss.96(2)(b) and 98. Such an order would have to be complied with unless that person did not hold the requested information or was unable to establish whether the information was held, or obtaining the requested information would involve unreasonable effort or expense.

21.24 Under S.101 TCEA, the relevant court (i.e. the court that made the departmental information request or information order) would be permitted to use any information disclosed pursuant to the request or order as a means of providing the creditor with information about what kind of action (if any) it would be appropriate to take to recover the debt. If such recovery action were taken, the relevant court could use the debtor information in the course of carrying out its functions in relation to that action or pass the information to any other court in respect of which the enforcement action was being pursued. If and when these new procedures are brought into effect, regulations will flesh out the details of how they will operate in practice.

21.25 Taking control of goods

Of all the methods of enforcement, the procedure for the seizure and sale of goods is the most frequently used. This involves obtaining an order instructing a county court bailiff or a High Court Enforcement Officer (HCEO) to seize goods belonging to the debtor, which are then sold (usually by public auction) in order to satisfy the debt plus the costs of removing the goods and conducting the sale. Until recently, this method involved applying for a warrant of execution in the county court or a writ of fieri facias ('fi fa') in the High Court. With effect from 6 April 2014, the TCEA replaced the old procedure (known as 'execution against goods') with a new procedure, 'taking control of goods'. 'Warrants of execution' have been renamed 'warrants of control', and 'writs of fieri facias' are now known as 'writs of control'. As a result of these changes, the Civil Procedure (Amendment) Rules 2014 SI 2014/407 inserted into the CPR a new Part 83, 'Writs and warrants – general provisions', and Part 84, 'Enforcement by taking control of goods' (with effect from 6 April 2014).

An employee wishing to enforce an award of less than £600 by seizure and sale of goods must proceed in the county court. If the sum owed is between £600 and £5,000, the employee has the choice of enforcing the award in the county court or in the High Court. The High Court has exclusive jurisdiction where the unpaid sum is £5,000 or more – Article 8(1) High Court and County Courts Jurisdiction Order 1991 SI 1991/724.

21.26 Since April 2010, employees seeking to enforce payment of a tribunal award by the seizure and sale of goods have been able to invoke the Acas and Employment Tribunal Fast Track scheme, whereby an HCEO is assigned to the case and pursues the unpaid tribunal award on the employee's behalf. HCEOs can recover amounts of more than £600 and this will often be the cheapest and most convenient means of enforcement. Alternatively, the employee may register the tribunal's judgment in the county court him or herself and apply for a warrant of control. In this section we outline the main elements of the Fast Track scheme and the alternative route of applying directly to the county court for a warrant of control. We then discuss the 'taking control of goods' procedure introduced by the TCEA.

Acas and Employment Tribunal Fast Track

21.27 An employee seeking to enforce an employment tribunal award of more than £600 by means of seizure and sale of goods can use the Acas and Employment Tribunal Fast Track scheme, which allows a High Court Enforcement Officer (HCEO) to be assigned to the case as soon as the respondent has failed to pay the relevant sum and pursue the award on the employee's behalf. The scheme was introduced in April 2010 to simplify and speed up the process of enforcing employment tribunal awards. It is run by Registry Trust Ltd, a not-for-profit company which operates the Register of Judgments, Orders and Fines for England and Wales on behalf of the Ministry of Justice.

Details of the Fast Track scheme are set out in leaflet EX727. To use the scheme, the employee must complete form EX727 (which appears at the end of the leaflet) and pay a fee (currently £60). The form invites the employee to provide relevant information that may be useful to the HCEO, e.g. details of the employer's trading stock, vehicles and last known trading address. The employee should send the completed form to Registry Trust Ltd together with the employment tribunal decision (or a certified copy), and either a cheque for £60 or an application for remission of the fee. Leaflet EX160A, 'Court fees – Do I have to pay them?', includes a fee exemption application form (form EX160) for those on low incomes.

21.28 Once Registry Trust Ltd receives the form, an HCEO is allocated to the case. Under the supervision of a solicitor, he or she will file the unpaid tribunal award with the county court using form N471 and, at the same time, request a writ of control from the High Court (see 'Overview – filing the decision' above). The HCEO will then attempt to recover the unpaid award on the employee's behalf, together with interest at the appropriate rate, enforcement costs and the £60 court fee. If the HCEO is unsuccessful, the employee loses the court fee but there is nothing more to pay. If the HCEO recovers only part of the amount owed, his or her fees are deducted first but are reduced in proportion to the amount recovered. The Fast Track scheme is also available for the enforcement of unpaid Acas settlements – for further details, see leaflet EX728.

Despite its relatively low cost and apparent simplicity, the Fast Track scheme appears so far to have a low take-up and success rate. In its first year of operation (2010/11), there were only 1,499 referrals, and in response to a question in the House of Commons in March 2012, Jonathan Djanogly MP indicated that only 37 per cent of completed cases had resulted in fully recovered awards (Hansard, House of Commons, 27 March 2012, column 1074W). In June 2012, the response to a written Parliamentary Question indicated that, of the 1,052 completed cases referred to HCEOs under the Fast Track scheme in its second year of operation (2011/12), the award was fully enforced in 515 cases (49 per cent). The two most common reasons for non-enforcement were that the employer had become insolvent or the HCEOs were unable to make contact with the employer (Hansard, House of Commons, 11 June 2013, column 349W).

21.29 The National Association of Citizens Advice Bureaux referred to the low take-up rate for the Fast Track scheme in its November 2013 report, 'The Cost of a Hollow Victory'. It made various recommendations, including the abolition of the £60 fee for accessing the Fast Track scheme; the provision to claimants of appropriate and consistent information on enforcement; and the establishment of a specialist enforcement team within the employment tribunal administration to take responsibility for appointing HCEOs to enforce awards. To date, those recommendations have not been implemented.

21.30 **Warrants of control**
As an alternative to pursuing an unpaid employment tribunal award through the Acas and Employment Tribunal Fast Track scheme, an employee may apply him or herself to the county court for a warrant of control (previously called a warrant of execution). The county court currently has jurisdiction to enforce seizure and sale of goods for sums up to £5,000 – Article 8(1) High Court and County Courts Jurisdiction Order 1991 SI 1991/724.

The procedure for obtaining warrants of execution was previously set out in Order 26 of the County Court Rules (in Schedule 2 to the CPR), together with

1152

an accompanying Practice Direction entitled 'Execution'. The relevant provisions are now contained in Parts 83 and 84 of the CPR (inserted from 6 April 2014), introduced as a result of the new 'taking control of goods' procedure introduced by the TCEA. At the time of writing, however, details of the amendments were not available. Accordingly, this section refers to the CPR provisions *as they stood prior to 6 April 2014* and it is important to bear in mind that the unamended provisions use the old terminology, e.g. 'warrant of execution' as opposed to 'warrant of control'.

At the time of writing, it was necessary for an employee seeking to obtain a **21.31** warrant of execution in the county court to complete form N323 (request for warrant of execution). An explanatory leaflet, 'How do I ask for a warrant of execution?' (EX322), is available on the HM Courts and Tribunals Service website. A £100 fee is immediately payable, but this cost is added to the amount to be recovered (although it cannot be refunded if the warrant does not succeed in securing sufficient funds to meet the debt in full). The completed form and the fee must then be given or sent to the appropriate county court office, together with a stamped addressed envelope if the creditor wishes to receive written confirmation that the warrant has been issued. The warrant will usually be issued by the court within ten working days. Where the request for a warrant has been made by a solicitor acting for the creditor, the sum due on the warrant will include a sum for the solicitor's fixed costs.

Rule 5, Order 26 of the County Court Rules currently provides that in certain circumstances, the leave of the court is needed before a warrant of execution can be issued. These are where:

- six years or more have elapsed since the date of the judgment
- any change has taken place in the identity of the parties entitled to enforce the debt or liable to have it enforced against them (e.g. the death of one of the parties)
- the judgment is against the assets of a deceased person and the assets came into the hands of the executors after the date of the judgment
- any goods to be seized under the warrant are in the hands of a receiver appointed by a court.

In these circumstances, an application for leave should be accompanied by a **21.32** witness statement or affidavit (i.e. a sworn statement) establishing the creditor's right to obtain relief.

Where the debtor is in breach of a previous order establishing payment by instalments, a warrant may be issued either for the whole of the debt and costs remaining unpaid or part of the total sum remaining unpaid, so long as that is not less than £50, the amount of one month's instalment or four weekly instalments (whichever is the greater) – rule 1(2), Order 26 County Court Rules.

21.33 **Suspension of warrant.** At the time of writing, the debtor may apply to the court (using form N245) to have the warrant suspended, i.e. not enforced – rule 8, Order 25 County Court Rules. To do so, the debtor has to inform the court of the proposed terms upon which the suspension should take place and include a signed statement of means. One sensible course at this stage is for the debtor to pay such proportion of the debt as he or she can afford. The court will then send a copy of the application to suspend, together with a copy of the signed statement of the debtor's means, to the creditor. The latter must reply within 14 days indicating whether or not the debtor's proposals are acceptable. If the creditor fails to do this, the court officer has power to make an order suspending the warrant on terms of payment – rule 8(1)–(4), Order 25.

If the creditor objects to the debtor's proposals as to the terms offered, the court can determine the rate and schedule for payment and make an order suspending the warrant of execution on condition that payment is received on these terms – rule 8(5), Order 25 County Court Rules. Once an order of suspension has been made, either party has 14 days to apply for the order to be reconsidered. A hearing will be fixed before a district judge at which both parties may make their representations, following which the judge may confirm, set aside or vary the terms of the order as he or she thinks fit – rule 8(6) and (7), Order 25.

21.34 The effect of having a warrant of execution suspended is to give the debtor more time to pay the balance of the debt. If the conditions to which the order of suspension are subject are not complied with by the debtor, the creditor may apply to have the warrant of execution reissued – rule 8(9), Order 25.

If the creditor objects to the debtor's proposals and wishes the bailiff to proceed to execute the warrant, the court will fix a date for a hearing before a district judge. The court must give the parties not less than two days' notice of the hearing – rule 8(8), Order 25.

21.35 *Editor's note:* Order 25 was repealed on 6 April 2014 and the regime outlined above has been replaced by new rules that are not available at the time of writing.

21.36 **Tribunals, Courts and Enforcement Act 2007**
The Tribunals, Courts and Enforcement Act 2007 (TCEA), which received Royal Assent on 19 July 2007, introduced wide-ranging reforms to debt recovery, particularly as regards the law on seizure of goods. Prior to the changes, the relevant law was spread across various statutes, pieces of secondary legislation and provisions of the common law, and much of the language was archaic. There were many different types of bailiff and enforcement officer, depending on the type of debt. Seizure and sale was effected by High Court Enforcement Officers in respect of High Court writs of fieri facias ('fi fa'), and bailiffs employed by HM Courts and Tribunals Service in respect of county

court warrants of execution. The regulatory structure for these officers was fragmented and the fees and costs regime was complex. Furthermore, some bailiffs resorted to unacceptable methods – for example, misrepresenting their legal authority, charging excessive fees and using threatening behaviour.

The TCEA was designed to address these concerns. Part 3 (Ss.62–70), together with Schedules 12 and 13, introduced a new procedure – 'taking control of goods' – which replaced the old common law and statutory rules with effect from 6 April 2014. The 2007 Act unified the law in this area and modernised the relevant terminology. In particular, 'warrants of execution' were renamed 'warrants of control' and 'writs of fieri facias' became 'writs of control' – S.62(4). Under the new provisions, all types of bailiff are referred to as 'enforcement agents', and are required (subject to certain exceptions) to hold a valid certificate issued by a county court or district judge – Ss.63 and 64. Schedule 12 to the TCEA sets out a detailed new procedure governing enforcement agents' powers of entry to premises, the goods they can seize, the sale of the goods and the distribution of the proceeds; while Schedule 13 has made consequential amendments to existing primary legislation. S.70 gives the High Court the power to stay execution of a writ of control for such period of time and on such conditions as the court determines in line with the county court's power to stay execution – see 'Warrants of control – suspension of warrant' above.

21.37 The new regime, which came into effect on 6 April 2014, is of general application but extends to the situation in which an employee seeks to exercise the power conferred by a writ or warrant of control to recover an unpaid tribunal award.

21.38 **Legislative background.** The relevant provisions of the TCEA have a complicated legislative history, reflected in the long delay in their implementation. As originally drafted, Schedule 12 gave enforcement agents significantly wider powers than those that they had previously enjoyed. However, in a written ministerial statement issued on 17 March 2009, the Government stated that, following a comprehensive review of the enforcement provisions, it had decided not to extend powers of entry and the use of force by enforcement agents. It added: 'We will produce a consultation paper which will set out the Government's intentions for a package of measures which will address concerns that have been raised about the behaviour of bailiffs, the fees charged and proposals for the regulation of the bailiff industry. It will also set out draft regulations on seizure of goods, and allow for detailed consideration of a standardised fee structure.'

Meanwhile, in advance of full independent regulation of enforcement agents, the Government implemented certain measures – namely, an online register allowing debtors to check bailiffs' certification status; an extension to the certification process to ensure that all bailiffs provided a Criminal Records Bureau (CRB) check with their application (note that the CRB has since been replaced by the Disclosure and Barring Service); and minimum training and skills requirements. In January 2012, the Government also updated the voluntary 'National Standards for Enforcement Agents' to tackle intimidating and threatening behaviour, prevent bailiffs from misrepresenting their powers, and reinforce rules about how firms should resolve complaints about rogue agents.

21.39 On 17 February 2012 the Ministry of Justice published a consultation paper, 'Transforming bailiff action: How we will provide more protection against aggressive bailiffs and encourage more flexibility in bailiff collections' (CP 5/2012). The consultation closed on 14 May 2012 and the Government published its response (CP(R)12/2013) on 25 January 2013. The response set out 19 recommendations, many of which were designed to address the misrepresentation of legal authority, use of threatening behaviour and charging of excessive fees by enforcement agents. The Government took the view that Part 3 of the TCEA (including Schedules 12 and 13) should be amended in various respects before being brought into force. It also proposed a transparent fee structure and greater controls on enforcement agents, including a competence criterion for entry to the profession and a mandatory training regime.

The amendments to Schedule 12 TCEA were given effect by S.25 of the Crime and Courts Act 2013 (with effect from 6 April 2014). S.25 amends Schedule 12 in three key respects. First, it removes the power to make regulations allowing enforcement agents to use reasonable force against the person. That amendment came into effect on 15 July 2013 – see the Crime and Courts Act 2013 (Commencement No.3) Order SI 2013/1725. Secondly, S.25 creates an express statutory power for enforcement agents to use reasonable force to secure entry to commercial premises. Thirdly, S.25 amends Schedule 12 so as to allow enforcement agents to re-enter any premises – domestic or commercial – where the debtor is in breach of a controlled goods agreement. These amendments are designed to codify in statute existing common law powers.

21.40 Three sets of regulations, all of which came into force on 6 April 2014, supplement Schedule 12 and form part of the package of measures adopted in response to the Government's consultation. The Taking Control of Goods Regulations 2013 SI 2013/1894 set out further details of the procedure that enforcement agents must follow when taking control of, and selling, goods to recover a debt. The Taking Control of Goods (Fees) Regulations 2014 SI 2014/1 govern the recovery of agents' fees and disbursements in Schedule 12 proceedings and the calculation of those fees. The third and final set of Regulations, the Certification of Enforcement Agents Regulations 2014 SI 2014/421, deals with the new training and certification requirements applicable to enforcement agents.

21.41 **Procedure for taking control of goods.** Once the employee (or the High Court Enforcement Officer if the Fast Track scheme is used) has obtained a warrant or writ of control, the 'taking control of goods' procedure in Schedule 12 to the TCEA will apply. A detailed discussion of the new regime is outside the scope of this Handbook but an overview of the key provisions is set out below. It should be noted that the new procedure is likely to necessitate changes to the provisions discussed in 'Acas and Employment Tribunal Fast Track' and 'Warrants of control' above. At the time of writing, however, details of those changes were not available.

Notice to the debtor. Under the Schedule 12 procedure, the debtor must be **21.42** given written notice before the enforcement agent takes control of his or her goods – para 7, Sch 12. The detailed notice requirements are set out in Regs 6–8 of the Taking Control of Goods Regulations 2013. The notice must contain the information prescribed by Reg 7 and must be delivered by one of the methods detailed in Reg 8. Notice must generally be given to the debtor not less than seven clear days before enforcement action is taken. (Sundays, bank holidays, Good Friday and Christmas Day do not count in calculating this period.) However, where the court considers it likely that the goods will be moved to other premises or otherwise disposed of in an attempt to avoid enforcement action, it can specify a shorter period of notice – Reg 6.

The enforcement agent must generally take control of goods within 12 months beginning with the date of the notice of enforcement – Reg 9. This is subject to an exception where the debtor enters into a repayment arrangement after the notice is given and then breaches the terms of that arrangement; in that case, the 12-month period begins with the date of the breach. On application by the enforcement agent or creditor, the court may extend the 12-month period by a further 12 months if there are reasonable grounds for not taking enforcement action within the original period.

Relevant goods. Once notice has been given, the enforcement agent may take **21.43** control of goods belonging to the debtor with a view to selling them. An agent is entitled to take control of goods only if they are:

- on premises that the agent has power to enter, or on a highway (para 9, Sch 12)

- goods of the debtor (para 10, Sch 12), and

- not exempt (para 11, Sch 12).

'Goods of the debtor' means goods in which the debtor has a beneficial interest, but does not include trust property unless the whole beneficial interest in the goods is vested in the debtor – para 3(2), Sch 12.

Certain categories of goods are exempt from enforcement. These are defined in Reg 4 of the Taking Control of Goods Regulations 2013, and include items or equipment (for example, tools, books, telephones, computer equipment and vehicles) which are necessary for use personally by the debtor in his or her employment, business, trade, profession, study or education and which have an aggregate value of no more than £1,350; and such clothing, bedding,

1157

furniture, household equipment, items and provisions as are reasonably required to satisfy the basic domestic needs of the debtor and every member of the debtor's household.

21.44 *Taking control.* Taking control of the goods may involve physically removing them – but not necessarily. There are four ways in which an agent may take control:

- by securing the goods on the premises where they are found

- by securing the goods on the highway, either where they are found or within a reasonable distance

- by removing the goods and securing them elsewhere, or

- by entering into a controlled goods agreement with the debtor – para 13(1), Sch 12 TCEA.

Regulations 9–15 of the Taking Control of Goods Regulations deal with the actual taking of control, both regarding goods on premises and goods on a highway, including the time limit for taking control, the circumstances in which control must not be taken, and the days and hours during which control may be taken. The permitted methods of securing goods (e.g. by fitting an immobilisation device) are set out in Regs 16–19.

21.45 If the parties enter into a controlled goods agreement (previously known as a 'walking possession' agreement), the debtor is permitted to retain custody of the goods. However, he or she acknowledges that the enforcement agent is taking control of the goods and agrees not to remove or dispose of them, nor to permit anyone else to, before the debt is paid – para 13(4), Sch 12. Where such an agreement is in place, the agent may enter the premises repeatedly to inspect the goods or to remove them for storage or sale – para 16, Sch 12. Detailed requirements concerning controlled goods agreements are set out in Regs 14 and 15 of the Taking Control of Goods Regulations.

21.46 *Powers of entry.* An enforcement agent will often need to enter premises to search for and take control of goods. He or she may enter 'relevant premises' without a warrant authorising entry – para 14(1), Sch 12. For present purposes, premises are 'relevant premises' if the agent reasonably believes that they are the place, or one of the places, where the debtor usually lives or carries on a trade or business – para 14(6), Sch 12.

In specified circumstances, the agent has a general power to use reasonable force to enter premises or to do anything for which entry is authorised – para 17, Sch 12. The power to use reasonable force extends to the situation in which the debtor is in breach of a controlled goods agreement and has been given notice of the agent's intention to re-enter the premises to inspect the goods or remove them for storage or sale – para 19A, Sch 12 (inserted by S.25

of the Crime and Courts Act 2013). However, it does not include the power to use force against persons – para 24(2), Sch 12 (as amended by S.25 of the Crime and Courts Act 2013).

The rules governing the times of day when entry to premises is permitted are set **21.47** out in Regs 21 and 22 of the Taking Control of Goods Regulations. Subject to certain exceptions, the agent may enter premises on any day of the week between 6 am and 9 pm. Normally, the agent must give at least two clear days' notice of his or her intention to re-enter premises (Reg 25), and there are restrictions on repeated entry to premises where the agent has already determined that there are insufficient goods to pay the outstanding sum (Reg 24).

The enforcement agent must, on request, show the debtor and any person who appears to be in charge of the premises evidence of his or her identity and authority to enter – para 26, Sch 12. After entering the premises, the agent must provide the debtor with a notice giving information about what the agent is doing – para 28, Sch 12. The detailed notice requirements are set out in Regs 30–32 of the Taking Control of Goods Regulations. The agent must, as soon as reasonably practicable, provide the debtor with an inventory of the goods taken control of – para 34, Sch 12 and Reg 33, and is under a duty to take reasonable care of the controlled goods – para 35, Sch 12 and Reg 34.

Sale of goods. Prior to sale, the enforcement agent must make or obtain a **21.48** valuation of the controlled goods and give the debtor (and any co-owner) an opportunity to obtain an independent valuation – para 36(1), Sch 12 and Reg 35. The agent is under a duty to sell the goods for the best price that can reasonably be obtained – para 37(1), Sch 12. The sale must not normally take place before the end of the 'minimum period', i.e. seven clear days from the removal of the goods, except with the agreement of the debtor and any co-owner – para 39, Sch 12 and Reg 37. The debtor (and any co-owner) must be given seven clear days' notice of the date, time and place of sale – para 40, Sch 12 and Regs 38–40. The sale will take place by way of a public auction unless, following an application by the agent, the court orders otherwise – para 41, Sch 12 and Reg 41. Further provisions concerning the place and conduct of the sale are set out in Regs 42–43.

Fees and disbursements. The Taking Control of Goods (Fees) Regulations **21.49** 2014 govern the recovery of enforcement agents' fees and disbursements from the debtor in Schedule 12 proceedings and the calculation of those fees. In summary, Regs 4–7 provide that fees are recoverable at a fixed rate, based on the stage of the enforcement procedure (as specified in the Schedule to the Regulations). In certain situations, additional fees can be recovered as a percentage of the value of the goods over which control is taken. Regs 8–10 deal with the recovery of enforcement costs out of the proceeds of sale. Such disbursements can be considerable and may include the cost of storing goods, the hire of locksmiths to enter and to secure premises, court fees for various

1159

applications relating to the Schedule 12 process, and the costs of sale. Regs 11 and 12 make specific provision aimed at protecting vulnerable debtors and minimising fees and disbursements.

It should be noted that goods disposed of at auction will not usually fetch their full market value. This is particularly so for electronic items such as computers. Reg 13 of the Fees Regulations provides for the order of application of the proceeds where the amount recovered is less than the amount outstanding. Priority is given to any fees and expenses owed to an auctioneer and the compliance stage fee for the enforcement agent, with the remaining proceeds being divided pro rata between payment of the debt and payment of the agent's remaining fees and disbursements.

21.50 Third party debt orders

If the taking control of goods procedure seems inappropriate or if enforcement by that method has not succeeded, then an order can be obtained requiring an individual, business or bank owing the debtor money to pay that money to the creditor rather than to the debtor. This procedure – previously known as a 'garnishee order' but now renamed a 'third party debt order' – is governed by Part 72 of the CPR and supplemented by Practice Direction 72, 'Third party debt orders'. In practice, this sort of order is most often made against the debtor's bank or building society – money held by such institutions in current and savings accounts being regarded as a debt owed to the customer. Further details are set out in leaflet EX325, 'Third party debt orders and charging orders'.

21.51 Advantages and drawbacks of third party debt orders

Although in their former guise third party debt orders were the least used of all enforcement procedures, they are, in fact, a powerful and direct way of obtaining satisfaction of debts owed by debtors. The order achieves this by freezing and seizing money owed to the debtor and redirecting that money directly to the creditor. The one major drawback, even in the more streamlined procedure introduced under the CPR, is that the creditor does have to discover and provide basic information regarding the banking details of the debtor in order to persuade the court to issue an order. The courts will be careful to ensure that this particular method of enforcement is not used as a 'fishing expedition' or based on the flimsiest of evidence that a third party owes money to the debtor. Obtaining this information would be made significantly easier by the proposed introduction of 'information orders', whereby the court can require third parties such as banks to supply information about a debtor. The power to make such an order is included in Part 4 of the TCEA but the relevant provisions have not yet been brought into force – see 'Obtaining information from debtors – Tribunals, Courts and Enforcement Act 2007' above.

To ensure that he or she has substantive grounds for applying for a third party debt order, a creditor would be well advised to use the procedure for obtaining information from the debtor in conjunction with, or as a prelude to, an application for the third party debt order. The creditor can also request – in advance of applying for a third party order – that his or her own bank manager discover from the debtor's bank manager whether the debtor is creditworthy. Although the actual amount held in the debtor's account(s) will not currently be disclosed, basic information as to creditworthiness will be provided and this will at least avoid the creditor launching fruitless enforcement proceedings against what transpires to be a 'man of straw'.

It is important to note that the debt owed by the third party to the debtor must **21.52** be in existence at the time the third party debt order is made. Accordingly, no order can be made against a bank, for example, if the debtor's account is overdrawn. It is not possible to issue the order and then wait for the debtor to come into funds. Another difficulty relates to joint accounts: case law applicable to garnishee orders makes it clear that such orders cannot target an account held in joint names even if each individual account holder has authority to draw on the account – Hirschhorn v Evans 1938 2 KB 801, CA. All of these 'drawbacks' were considered as part of a review of enforcement procedures conducted by the Government. However, there currently appear to be no specific proposals to remedy these difficulties – see 'Proposals for reform' below.

Applying for an order
21.53

As with the former garnishee order, a third party debt order will not be issued in final form unless and until an interim procedure has been completed. The first step is for the claimant to apply to the county court for an order on a standard form N349. The application can be lodged without giving prior notice to the debtor or to the third party against whom the creditor wishes the order to be made.

Form N349 invites the claimant to give specific details about the third party whom it is alleged owes money to, or holds money to the credit of, the debtor. If the third party is a bank or building society, the information sought includes the address of the head office, the particular branch at which the creditor's account is held, the account number, the sort code, the name and address of any person (apart from the debtor) who has a claim to the money owed by the third party and the grounds of that belief or knowledge. Except for the head office details of the particular bank or building society, the form anticipates that some or all of the above details may not be known. For this reason, a 'not known' box is provided against each of the above items. The claimant must provide a short statement setting out the basis upon which the information provided is known or believed to be correct, which will entail explaining the sources of that information. The form also requires the claimant to provide details of any other applications for third party debt orders made by the

1161

claimant in respect of the same debt. Finally, the claimant (or his or her solicitor) must sign a 'Statement of Truth' to the effect that the facts stated in the application are believed to be true.

21.54 A fee of (currently) £100 is chargeable for an application for a third party debt order and that fee must be paid in respect of each party against whom an order is sought. This means that if there are two or more banks or building societies which the claimant wishes to be subject to an order, the application fee has to be paid separately in respect of each.

21.55 **Grant and service of interim order**

On receiving the application, a district judge will initially consider whether to make an interim order without a hearing – rule 72.4(1) CPR. If made, the order will specify the amount of the money that the third party must retain. This comprises the balance outstanding under the judgment or order and the fixed costs (including the application fee) recoverable by the creditor in respect of his or her application – rule 72.4(3). The order will inform the third party of the date fixed by the judge for a hearing to consider whether to make the third party debt order final and will direct that until that hearing the third party may not make any payment that reduces the amount owed to the debtor to less than the amount specified in the order – rule 72.4(2). The date of the hearing to consider the application for a final third party order must not be less than 28 days after the interim order is made – rule 72.4(5).

The interim order becomes binding on the third party as soon as it is served – rule 72.4(4) CPR. Copies of the order and supporting documentation must be served on the third party at least 21 days before the date of the fixed hearing and on the debtor at least seven days after service on the third party but not less than seven days before the hearing – rule 72.5(1). This tight and specific schedule ensures that the debtor, though given sufficient notice of the hearing, is not given wind of the third party order before the third party, so enabling him or her to take steps to drain his or her bank accounts of funds and thus avoid the efficacy of the enforcement mechanism. Copies of the order and accompanying documents are served personally on the relevant parties either by the court bailiff service or by the creditor him or herself. If the latter is responsible for the service, then he or she must either file a certificate of service not less than two days before the hearing or, if attending in person, produce such a certificate at the hearing – rule 72.5(2).

21.56 A bank or building society served with a third party debt order must carry out a search of all accounts held by it in the debtor's name and disclose to both the court and the creditor within seven days certain details in respect of each of those accounts – rule 72.6(1) and (2) CPR. The details in question are: the number of the account, whether the account is in credit, and, if so, whether the balance of the account is sufficient to cover the amount specified in the order.

If the amount of the balance is less than the amount specified in the order, the bank or building society has to disclose the precise amount of the balance as at the date the order was served. This duty to search for all connected accounts is an important feature of third party debt orders compared to the old garnishee orders, which targeted only accounts specifically named in the order. This development could help a creditor in a situation in which a debtor holds several accounts with the same bank or building society.

If the debtor does not hold an account with the bank or building society or if the bank or building society is unable to comply with the order for any other reason (e.g. because it has more than one account holder whose details match the information contained in the order and cannot identify which account the order applies to), then the court and creditor have to be informed of this fact in writing within seven days of service of the order – rule 72.6(3) CPR.

21.57 Where a debt is due from a partnership, an interim third party debt order must be served on a member of the partnership within England and Wales, a person authorised by a partner or some other person having the control or management of the partnership business – para 3A.2 Practice Direction 72.

If the debtor is an individual (as opposed to a company), the effect of freezing funds in his or her bank accounts pending the hearing may cause hardship. Rule 72.7 CPR provides for a procedure whereby the court is given discretion, on the application of the debtor, to make a 'hardship payment order'. Essentially, if the court is satisfied that hardship will be suffered on the basis of detailed evidence adduced by the debtor, a hardship payment order permits the third party to make one or more payments out of the otherwise frozen funds to any person specified under the terms of the order.

Hearing and final order
21.58
If the debtor or the third party objects to the court making a final third party debt order, he or she must file and serve written evidence stating the grounds of objection as soon as possible and in any case not less than three days before the date fixed for the hearing of the third party debt order application – rule 72.8(1) and (4) CPR. If the creditor wishes to dispute any assertion made by the third party that no money is owed by it to the debtor or that the sum which is owed is less than the amount specified in the interim order, then the creditor must, not less than three days before the hearing, file and serve a notice setting out the grounds on which the third party's case is disputed – rule 72.8(3) and (4). If the court is notified by the debtor or third party that some person other than the debtor him or herself may have a claim to the money specified in the interim order, that person will be served with notice of the application for the third party debt order together with the notice of hearing – rule 72.8(5).

At the hearing, the court may do any of the following:

- make a final third party debt order

- discharge the interim order and dismiss the application

- decide any issues in dispute between the parties or between any of the parties and any other person who has a claim to the money specified in the interim order, or direct a trial of such issues and, if necessary, give directions – rule 72.8(6).

21.59 If a final third party order is issued, it will be enforceable just as if it were an order for the payment of money. The third party's own debt to the debtor is offset by paying monies to the creditor in compliance with the order. In particular, the third party stands discharged of the debt owed to the debtor to the extent of the amount paid under the order – rule 72.9(2). This applies even if at a later date the original judgment or order against the debtor is set aside – rule 72.9(3).

21.60 Proposals for reform
In March 2011, the Ministry of Justice published a consultation paper on reforming civil justice in England and Wales, 'Solving disputes in the county courts: creating a simpler, quicker and more proportionate system' (CP6/2011). On 9 February 2012, the Government published its response to that consultation (Cm 8274), indicating (among other things) its intention to streamline the procedure for obtaining third party debt orders. The Government's objectives are to reduce duplication in court processes, improve the efficiency of those processes, extend the range of bank accounts to which third party debt orders apply, and permit the courts to trace accounts that are moved. At the time of going to press, however, detailed proposals for legislation were still awaited.

21.61 Statutory demands

If the debtor is a company, then one way of encouraging the satisfaction of an unpaid employment tribunal award may be to issue a statutory demand for the amount due. Essentially, a statutory demand is a method of establishing that a company is insolvent, i.e. unable to pay its debts as they fall due. S.123(1)(a) of the Insolvency Act 1986 states that a company will be deemed to be unable to pay its debts if a creditor to whom the company owes more than (currently) £750 has served a written demand requiring the company to pay the sum due and the company has for three weeks thereafter neglected to pay the sum. The demand must be served by leaving it at the company's registered office. Although this is not a method of recovering the debt as such, a company that fails to meet a statutory demand may be declared insolvent and subjected to a winding-up order. There is, therefore, a considerable incentive for a company served with a statutory demand to meet the debt – if that is at all possible.

The demand must be issued in the form prescribed by rule 4.5 and 4.6 of the Insolvency Rules 1986 SI 1986/1925. Essentially, the notice must set out the amount of the debt and the circumstances in which it arises (including the rate of interest chargeable where such an element is included in the sum claimed). Furthermore, the statutory demand must state expressly that if it is not complied with, proceedings may be instituted for the winding up of the company, and it must give a date by which compliance must have occurred and the methods of compliance that are acceptable. The company has the right to apply to the court for an injunction restraining the creditor from presenting or advertising a winding-up petition – rule 4.6A.

21.62 If the terms of the demand are not met within 21 days of its service, the creditor is entitled to present a petition to the High Court for winding up. Although the county courts have concurrent jurisdiction with the High Court in this regard, their jurisdiction is limited to cases where the share capital of a company registered in England and Wales does not exceed £120,000 – S.117 Insolvency Act 1986. A winding-up order will generally be granted as a matter of right – Re James Millward and Co Ltd 1940 Ch 333, CA – although whether or not to issue the order remains a matter within the court's discretion. This means that if a claim is disputed by a company on genuine and substantial grounds, an order may be refused. If the debtor makes payments within the 21-day period that reduce the debt owed to or below the £750 threshold for issuing a statutory demand, then the creditor cannot pursue insolvency proceedings. However, if no grounds for non-payment can be proved and the sum of more than £750 remains outstanding, the company's failure to pay will, in itself, be regarded as sufficient evidence of its inability to pay its debts and an order will usually be granted – Taylor's Industrial Flooring Ltd v M and H Plant Hire (Manchester) Ltd 1990 British Company Cases (BCC) 44, CA.

Enforcement of Acas-conciliated settlements

21.63 The position regarding binding conciliated settlements of employment tribunal proceedings has been fully discussed in Chapter 3, 'Conciliation, settlements and ADR'. Sums payable under Acas-conciliated settlements are enforceable in England and Wales as if they were sums payable under a county court order.

It used to be the case that there were no special statutory provisions dealing with the enforcement of Acas-conciliated settlements in the event of a party failing to honour the financial terms of such a settlement. However, S.142 TCEA introduced specific new provisions regarding recovery of sums payable under Acas-conciliated settlements by inserting a new S.19A into the Employment Tribunals Act 1996 with effect from 1 April 2009. This provides that any sum payable under the terms of a settlement that has been certified by an Acas conciliation officer (CO) will be enforceable by execution issued from the county court or otherwise as if the sum were payable under an order of that court (or, in Scotland, the equivalent order or decree of a sheriff court). This does not, however, apply if the person who is required to pay the sum under the

1165

agreement obtains a declaration from the employment tribunal or county/ sheriff court that the sum would not be recoverable from him or her under the general law of contract. S.19A ETA envisages that rules may be enacted detailing matters such as applicable time limits, and also providing for a period to be specified – starting from the date of the issue of the CO's certificate – during which steps towards the execution of the conciliated settlement should not be taken.

21.64 An order from the county court is required to enforce an Acas *conditional* settlement, i.e. a settlement that requires the employee to undertake certain actions in addition to discontinuing or not starting proceedings – S.19A(6) ETA and rule 70.5(3)–(7A) CPR. It should be noted that an Acas conditional settlement cannot be enforced through the Fast Track scheme – see 'Taking control of goods – Acas and Employment Tribunal Fast Track' above.

Case list

(Note that employment tribunal cases are not included in this list.)

A

J Sainsbury Ltd v Savage 1981 ICR 1, CA — 5.78
J Sainsbury plc v Moger 1994 ICR 800, EAT — 16.33, 17.79
Jackson v Cambridgeshire County Council and ors EAT 0402/09 — 20.41, 20.173
Jackson v Ghost Ltd and anor 2003 IRLR 824, EAT — 2.52, 13.13
James v Blockbuster Entertainment Ltd EAT 0601/05 — 20.137
James W Cook and Co (Wivenhoe) Ltd (in liquidation) v Tipper and ors
  1990 ICR 716, CA — 5.53, 5.93
Jamieson v Nationwide Building Society EATS 0028/13 — 18.78
Jananyagam v Commonwealth Secretariat EAT 0443/06 — 2.145
Jansen Van Rensburg v Royal Borough of Kingston-upon-Thames and ors
  EAT 0096/07 — 11.163
Jilley v Birmingham and Solihull Mental Health NHS Trust
  EAT 0584/06 — 20.102, 20.103, 20.124, 20.144
Joao v Mesh Computers plc EAT 0529/08 — 8.49
Jocic v Hammersmith and Fulham LBC EAT 0194/07 — 16.43
John Lewis Partnership v Charman EAT 0079/11 — 5.48, 5.81
Johnson v Chief Adjudication Officer 1995 ICR 375, ECJ — 5.16
Johnson v Edwardian International Hotels Ltd EAT 0588/07 — 11.173
Johnson v Gore Wood and Co 2002 2 AC 1, HL — 2.105, 2.120, 2.122
Johnson v Oldham Metropolitan Borough Council EAT 0095/13 — 11.156
Jolliff v Bayley Bartlett EAT 253/77 — 20.201
Jones v Corbin t/a Boo EAT 0504/10 — 12.57
Jones v DAS Legal Expenses Insurance Co Ltd and ors 2004 IRLR 218, CA — 12.177
Jones v Governing Body of Burdett Coutts School 1999 ICR 38, CA — 18.18, 18.44, 18.47,
  18.48, 18.50, 18.52
Jones v London Borough of Havering and anor EAT 1099/01 — 12.120, 12.160
Jones v Secretary of State for Employment 1982 ICR 389, EAT — 11.78
Jones v Secretary of State for Wales and ors 1995 70 P and CR 211, CA — 12.185
Jones v Standard Life Employee Services Ltd EATS 0023/13 — 9.56
Jones v Standard Life Employee Services Ltd EATS 0034/13 — 12.33
Jones v University of Warwick 2003 3 All ER 760, CA — 13.57
Judge v Crown Leisure 2005 IRLR 823, CA — 12.157
Jurkowska v Hlmad Ltd 2008 ICR 841, CA — 17.45, 17.47, 17.50, 17.54, 18.18

K

Kammack 1988 Ltd v Ellison EAT 844/93 — 8.61
Kanapathiar v London Borough of Harrow 2003 IRLR 571, EAT — 17.18
Kapoor v Governing Body of Barnhill Community High School EAT 0352/13 — 20.62
Kapur v Shields 1976 ICR 26, QBD — 8.61
Kaur v John L Brierley Ltd EAT 783/00 — 20.61
Keane v Investigo and ors EAT 0389/09 — 20.119
Kennaugh v Lloyd-Jones t/a Cheshire Tree Surgeons EAT 0710/07;
  2013 EWCA Civ 1, CA — 12.162, 17.12, 17.37
Kennedy t/a Snappy Snaps v Warwick EAT 0118/04 — 12.159
Khan v Golechha International Ltd 1980 1 WLR 1482, CA — 2.119
Khan v Heywood and Middleton Primary Care Trust
  2006 ICR 543, CA; 2007 ICR 24, CA — 2.108, 2.110, 4.92, 20.60, 20.65
Khan v Trident Safeguards Ltd and ors 2004 ICR 1591, CA — 4.16
Khan v Vignette Europe Ltd EAT 0134/09 — 12.69

M

1184

Palmer and anor v Southend-on-Sea Borough Council 1984
  ICR 372, CA   5.43, 5.79, 5.81, 5.96
Panama v London Borough of Hackney 2003 IRLR 278, CA   12.158
Parekh v London Borough of Brent EAT 0097/11; 2012
  EWCA Civ 1630, CA   8.13, 11.13
Parker v Northumbrian Water Ltd 2011 ICR 1172, EAT   2.121, 2.122
Parry Bros (Builders) Co Ltd v Brown EAT 714/84   8.76
Partners of Haxby Practice v Collen EAT 0120/12   14.18
Parums v West Dorset General Hospital NHS Trust EAT 0288/04   11.110
Parveen v International Dance Shoes Ltd and anor EAT 0447/10   8.71
Pasha v DHSS EAT 556/80   11.54
Patel v Babcock Airports Ltd EAT 0037/12   15.63
Patel v Nagesan 1995 ICR 988, CA   5.11
Patel v RCMS Ltd 1999 IRLR 161, EAT   2.16
Patel v South Tyneside Council EAT 0917/11   17.44
Peach Grey and Co v Sommers 1995 ICR 549, QBD   11.182, 11.183
Pearson v British Airports Authority EAT 324/84   11.102
Peart v Dixons Store Group Retail Ltd EAT 0630/04   13.22, 13.33, 16.43
Peixoto v British Telecommunications plc EAT 0222/07   11.144, 11.145
Peninsula Business Services Ltd and anor v Rees and ors EAT 0333/08   12.171
Peninsula Business Services Ltd v Sweeney 2004 IRLR 49, EAT   2.12
Pepper (Inspector of Taxes) v Hart 1993 ICR 291, HL   13.48
Perry v Imperial College Healthcare NHS Trust EAT 0473/10   16.56
Persson v Matra Marconi Space UK Ltd EATRF 95/1565–66/B, CA   18.79
Perth and Kinross Council v Townsley EAT 0010/10   5.109
Pervez v Macquarie Bank Ltd (London Branch) and anor 2011 ICR 266, EAT   2.49
Peter Simper and Co Ltd v Cooke 1986 IRLR 19, EAT   12.180, 12.182
Peters v Sat Katar Co Ltd (in liquidation) 2003 ICR 1574, CA   17.56
Peters v Science Museum, unreported 29.11.79, CA   12.142, 18.63
Photostatic Copiers (Southern) Ltd v Okuda and Japan Office Equipment Ltd
  (in liquidation) 1995 IRLR 11, EAT   18.39
Piggott Brothers and Co Ltd v Jackson and ors 1992 ICR 85, CA   16.54
Pinnock v Birmingham City Council and anor EAT 0185/13   9.56
Plymouth City Council v White EAT 0333/13   9.66
Polkey v AE Dayton Services Ltd 1988 ICR 142, HL   18.18, 18.45
Pomphrey of Sittingbourne Ltd v Reed EAT 457/94   3.45
Porter v Bandridge Ltd 1978 ICR 943, CA   5.41, 5.44
Porter v Magill 2002 2 AC 357, HL   12.161, 18.18
Portnykh v Nomura International plc 2014 IRLR 251, EAT   13.62, 13.70, 13.73,
                                                                  19.57, 19.73, 20.187
Post Office v Moore 1981 ICR 623, EAT   4.43, 5.30
Post Office v Sanhotra 2000 ICR 866, EAT   5.52
Potter and ors v North Cumbria Acute Hospitals NHS Trust 2009 IRLR 900, EAT   1.36
Powdrill and anor v Watson and anor and other cases 1995 ICR 1100, HL   4.14
Powell v OMV Exploration and Production Ltd EAT 0131/13   2.40, 2.43, 2.44, 2.74
Power v Panasonic (UK) Ltd EAT 0439/04   20.115
Prakash v Wolverhampton City Council EAT 0140/06   8.47
Preedy v HMO Giddy t/a Easterhill Furniture EAT 0287/03   12.18
Prescription Pricing Authority v Ferguson 2005 IRLR 464, Ct Sess (Inner House)   2.54

Savings and Investment Bank Ltd (in liquidation) v Fincken 2004 1
  WLR 667, CA   13.71, 13.73
Scanfuture UK Ltd v Secretary of State for Trade and Industry 2001 ICR 1096, EAT   1.59
Schlecker (t/a Firma Anton Schlecker) v Boedeker 2013 ICR 1274, ECJ   2.62
Schultz v Esso Petroleum Co Ltd 1999 ICR 1202, CA   5.74
Science Research Council v Nassé 1979 ICR 921, HL   9.63, 9.65, 9.72
Scotford and anor v Smithkline Beecham 2002 ICR 264, EAT   17.35
Scotthorne v Four Seasons Conservatories (UK) Ltd EAT 0178/10   9.80
Scottish Ambulance Service v Laing EATS 0038/12   11.134, 11.155
Scottish Opera Ltd v Winning EATS 0047/09   8.7
Scottish Shellfish Marketing Group Ltd v Connelly EATS 0008/06   13.35
Scott v Commissioners of Inland Revenue 2004 ICR 1410, CA   9.62
Scott v Inland Revenue Commissioners Development Agency 2004 ICR 1410, CA   20.80
Scott v Russell 2013 EWCA Civ 1432, CA   20.55
Secretary of State for Business, Innovation and Skills v McDonagh and ors
  2013 ICR 1177, EAT   13.49
Secretary of State for Children, Schools and Families v Fletcher and another
  case 2010 ICR 815, CA; 2011 ICR 495, SC   2.91, 2.93
Secretary of State for Employment v Banks and ors 1983 ICR 48, EAT   5.114, 5.116
Secretary of State for Health and anor v Rance and ors 2007 IRLR 665, EAT 18.18, 18.52
Secretary of State for Trade and Industry v Cook 1997 ICR 288, EAT   16.5, 16.29
Secretary of State for Work and Pensions (Jobcentre Plus) v Constable EAT 0156/10   9.13
Sefton Metropolitan Borough Council and anor v Hincks and ors 2011
  ICR 1357, EAT   8.19
Selkent Bus Co Ltd v Moore 1996 ICR 836, EAT   8.4, 8.6, 8.17, 8.18, 8.23, 8.31, 8.32,
                                                  8.34, 8.36, 8.38, 8.43, 8.48, 8.50,
                                                  8.54, 8.61, 8.62, 8.65, 8.68

Senator Hotels Ltd v Ratkowski EAT 0318/12   12.111, 12.135
Senyonjo v Trident Safeguards Ltd and anor EAT 0316/04   1.14
Setiya v East Yorkshire Health Authority 1995 ICR 799, EAT   17.61
Sharma v Ealing London Borough Council EAT 0399/05   20.141
Sharma v New College Nottingham EAT 0287/11   11.164
Sharpe v Worcester Diocesan Board of Finance Ltd EAT 0243/12   13.53
Sheibani v Elan and Co LLP 2012 ICR D38, EAT   12.158
Sheringham Development Co Ltd v Browne 1977 ICR 20, EAT   4.90, 10.27
Shestak v Royal College of Nursing and ors EAT 0270/08   11.123
Shields Automotive Ltd v Greig EATS 0024/10   20.125
Shortall t/a Auction Centres v Carey EAT 351/93   15.29
Short v Birmingham City Council and ors EAT 0038/13   7.10, 11.122
Siebe plc v Baker EAT 505/92   11.50
Simpson v Intralinks Ltd 2012 ICR 1343, EAT   2.35, 2.46, 2.50, 2.63, 2.99
Simpson v Merrick (formerly t/a WA Merrick and Co Solicitors) EAT 0490/09   2.6, 2.16
Sinclair Roche and Temperley and ors v Heard and anor EAT 0637/05;
  2004 IRLR 763, EAT   12.143, 18.18, 18.68, 18.69
Singh v London Country Bus Services Ltd 1976 IRLR 176, EAT   12.18
Siraj-Eldin v Campbell Middleton Burness and Dickson 1989 IRLR 208,
  Ct Sess (Inner House)   5.59
Slack and ors v Cumbria County Council 2009 ICR 1217, CA   18.44
Slack v Greenham (Plant Hire) Ltd and anor 1983 ICR 617, EAT   3.60, 3.120

1193

T

W

Index

1213

1217

Living accommodation
jurisdiction, 2.8

M
Mediation
cross-border disputes, 2.20, 5.7
fees, 19.2
judicial mediation
background, 3.143
fees, 3.143
operation of scheme, 3.143
practice directions, 3.144
purpose, 3.143
suitable cases, 3.143
Medical evidence
ill health
absence of evidence, 12.54
assessment of evidence, 12.51–12.53
time limits, 5.74, 5.75
Medical reports
confidentiality, 9.69
privilege, 9.69
Mental capacity
Acas conciliation, 3.129
case management, 11.173–11.174
invalid agreements, 3.129
Minors
case management, 11.172, 11.173
time limits, 5.89
Misrepresentation
opt-out agreements, 3.127, 3.128
settlement agreements, 3.127, 3.128
time limits, 5.50
Mistake
Acas-conciliated agreements, 3.124
correction
generally, 15.76
recalling parties, 15.77–15.78
slip rule, 15.79–15.80
opt-out agreements, 3.124
reimbursement of fee, 19.49, 19.50
slip rule, 15.79–15.80
Mistakes
settlement agreements, 3.124
Mutual trust and confidence
jurisdiction, 2.9

N
National security
appeals, 17.4
constitution of tribunals, 1.58
Employment Tribunal Rules of
Procedure, 1.7
hearings, 12.82–12.86
private hearings, 12.74, 12.82–12.86
privilege, 9.74–9.76
proceedings, 1.58
public interest, 9.74–9.76
Natural justice
cross-examination, 12.159–12.160
equality of arms, 12.151
hearing both sides, 12.149–12.151
knowing case that has to be met,
12.155–12.158
overriding objective, 12.148
preliminary view given by tribunal,
12.152–12.154
principles, 12.147
private hearings, 12.70
requirements, 12.147
Negligence
advisers, 5.59
Negotiations
pre-termination negotiations
Acas Code of Practice, 13.77
confidentiality, 13.77–13.88
costs, 13.88
improper behaviour, 13.84–13.86
meaning, 13.81–13.82
procedural steps, 13.83
without prejudice communications,
13.87
settlement
costs, 13.88
exceptions, 13.69–13.70
generally, 3.4
pre-termination negotiations,
13.77–13.88
unambiguous impropriety,
13.71–13.75
waiver of privilege, 13.67–13.68
settlement agreements
generally, 3.96
risk to employer, 3.97
subject to contract, 3.98, 3.99

1244